INTERACTIVE CASEBOOK SERIES^{SM}

BUSINESS ORGANIZATIONS

A Contemporary Approach

THIRD EDITION

Alan Palmiter

WILLIAM T. WILSON, III, PRESIDENTIAL CHAIR FOR BUSINESS LAW
WAKE FOREST UNIVERSITY SCHOOL OF LAW

Frank Partnoy

ADRIAN A. KRAGEN PROFESSOR OF LAW
UC BERKELEY SCHOOL OF LAW

Elizabeth Pollman

PROFESSOR OF LAW
LOYOLA LAW SCHOOL, LOS ANGELES
UNIVERSITY OF PENNSYLVANIA LAW SCHOOL

WEST
ACADEMIC
PUBLISHING

Interactive Casebook Series is a servicemark registered in the U.S. Patent and Trademark Office.

© 2010 Thomson Reuters
© 2014 LEG, Inc. d/b/a West Academic
© 2019 LEG, Inc. d/b/a West Academic
    444 Cedar Street, Suite 700
    St. Paul, MN 55101
    1-877-888-1330

Printed in the United States of America

ISBN: 978-1-64020-268-9

Overview

This is an interactive casebook about business organizations.

As you'll discover, it has many of the elements of a traditional casebook: it lays out the rules and principles of business law and uses court decisions and statutes to identify key issues. But, as you'll also discover, this casebook has a modern feel: it uses interactive elements, such as examples, hypos, statutory excerpts, real-life documents, and sidebar boxes. It covers novel and complex areas of law and legal practice with more narrative description than you would find in a traditional casebook. And the online version of this casebook allows you to search the book for particular terms and to easily access a wealth of additional hyperlinked material.

Who is this book for? We designed the book for anyone taking a course on Business Associations or Corporations. Whether you're taking the course because you know the topic will be on the bar exam, you're curious to understand corporations and their impact on society, or because you've dreamed of being a business lawyer since you were young, we've tried to make this book relevant to you. You'll find lots of useful new vocabulary and black-letter rules, a good dose of novel concepts and policy analysis, and the tools to become a top-notch business lawyer.

Before you dig in, we wanted to give you an overview of how we've organized the vast subject of business law and show you some of the features of the book.

A. Organization of this Casebook

The law of business organizations is a sprawling, even daunting topic. The business firm, especially the corporation, reaches into every aspect of our social, economic, and political lives. How is it possible to understand it?

We believe that a business firm can be understood by focusing on the questions that you would ask if you were thinking of investing. You would want to know how long your commitment will last, who is liable if something goes wrong, how much control you will have, how accountable those running the business will be, whether you can get out, and what happens if the business is ever sold. Answering these questions will help you master the law of business organizations.

To help you keep things straight, we've organized the book into modules that reflect the essential questions you would ask before investing in a business firm, particularly a corporation. Here are the ten modules of the book, with the specific questions addressed in each module. (Each of the 32 questions represents one chapter.) Don't worry right now if some of the words in this outline are unfamiliar. We just want you to have a sense of what we'll be covering. You might want to return to this outline periodically, to remind yourself where you are in the "big picture" of this course.

(1) Fundamentals
- What is a business firm?
- What are the basic rules that govern the principal-agent relationship?
- What are the basic principles of partnership law?
- What are the basic attributes of the corporation?

(2) Corporation in society
- What law governs the corporation?
- What is the purpose of the corporation?
- What role does (and can) the corporation play in politics?

(3) Choice of entity and the corporate form
- What business firm choices are available in organizing a business?
- How is a corporation formed?
- Where is the locus of decision making in a corporation?

(4) Corporate finance
- What basic accounting and finance should corporate lawyers know?
- How does money come into and go out of the corporation?

(5) Corporate externalities
- What is corporate limited liability and when can it be disregarded?
- When can the corporation and its insiders be criminally liable?
- When can corporate actors be liable for environmental harm?

No doubt you probably have some questions about all of this: What are corporate externalities? What does it mean that shareholders are active? What are corporate groups? What is the difference between publicly-traded and closely-held corporations? How do corporate mergers and acquisitions happen?

We will answer these and many other questions. But we want to emphasize that the questions and answers will be much clearer if you keep in mind how they fit into the bigger picture.

B. Features of this Casebook

Our purpose in this book is to engage (and even entertain) you in your study of the law of business organizations. We have tried to do this in a number of ways. First, you'll notice that we've streamlined the case decisions to cut out extraneous material such as unrelated discussion, citations to other cases, and even pin cites. Second, we follow up the cases and other primary materials with "Points for Discussion." We've kept these brief and to the point by using straightforward comments and questions to focus your attention on the important concepts from the cases. Third, we've included important statutes and rules, and even actual corporate documents, in special text boxes. Sometimes the most important thing for you to know is the actual legal language, so we've put it right in the book.

At various points you also will see examples and hypos, set apart in their own separate boxes. They are meant to give you a specific idea to think about, and to help you better understand the broader concepts of the main readings. The examples, often drawn from actual cases, fill in the details and thus complement the main cases and statutes. The hypos are there to animate your thinking about the material you're reading and to provoke discussion, not to quiz you for a particular "right" answer.

Perhaps the most unusual feature of this book (and the other interactive casebooks in this West series) are the breakout boxes, which we see as a kind of seasoning that gives flavor to the main ingredients of the book. The boxes draw your attention to noteworthy matters or to issues that deserve deeper reflection. Here are descriptions of the eight different kinds of breakout boxes that we've included:

FYI. These boxes are self-explanatory bits of useful or interesting information relevant to material in the text.

 Take Note! These boxes prompt you to take special notice of something in the case or text that deserves your attention.

 Business Lingo. These boxes explain special business terms that arise in corporations and stock markets.

 Practice Pointer. These boxes give you advice on lawyering and legal practice related to the material covered in the text.

 What's That? These boxes explain the meaning of special legal terms that appear in the text. You can access *Black's Law Dictionary*® definitions by clicking on the hyperlinked term.

 Make the Connection. These boxes refer to places elsewhere in the book, sometimes earlier and sometimes later, where you can find related information.

 Go Online. These boxes allow you to access relevant online resources with hyperlinks or web search suggestions.

 Food for Thought. These boxes pose questions that ask you to think about deeper issues raised in the readings.

In addition to the breakout boxes, another special feature of this interactive casebook is that it is also available online. In the electronic version, the cases, statutes and other materials—as well as internal references—are hyperlinked. (The hyperlinks are a light blue type in the printed text, and for some of the hyperlinked material you'll need a Westlaw® account to get access.) The electronic version also allows you to highlight and take notes, and to search the book with ease.

Go Online

Check out the inside front cover for instructions on how to access the online version of this Interactive Casebook.

There you have it. Now you're ready to begin your study of business organizations.

Editor's Note

We have written this book to be a teaching resource, not a research tool. Toward this end, we have edited the cases heavily, generally without adding ellipses or brackets to signal our edits. This means we have omitted citations and footnotes, even whole paragraphs and sections, without any identifying notations. Likewise, to aid readability, we have removed words, phrases, and sections from statutes, official comments, and regulations, again without signaling these edits.

In short, as with many secondary references, you should use caution when quoting primary materials from this book. The full text of the cases and other primary materials are readily available by using the online version of the book, which has hyperlinks to the original sources.

In addition, the book does not have a suggested printed statutory supplement. Instead, we expect that students will rely on the statutory excerpts in the text, as well as the online statutory materials (including the Delaware General Corporation Law and the Model Business Corporation Act, both of which are linked here).

Acknowledgements

We are grateful to our students for their comments and enthusiasm. In particular, we thank Mike Garrison and Camryn Keeter (Wake Forest 2019) for their superb research and editorial help. We appreciated help from our assistants, Arlene Penticoff and Cynthia Ring. We also benefited greatly from conversations and correspondence with Professors Jayne Barnard, Lynne Dallas, Steve Diamond, Sarah Duggins, Jared Ellias, George Georgiev, Sarah Haan, Michael Halberstam, Cathy Hwang, Daniel Kleinberger, Jennifer Kreder, Justin Levitt, Jeffrey Lipshaw, Lynn LoPucki, Mohsen Manesh, Seth Oranburg, Maggie Sachs, Steven Solomon, Lynn Stout, Geiza Vargas-Vargas, Andrew Verstein, and Amy Westbrook.

Table of Contents

Table of Cases

The principal cases are in bold type. Cases cited or discussed in the text are in roman type. References are to pages. Cases cited in principal cases and within other quoted materials are not included.

BUSINESS ORGANIZATIONS

A Contemporary Approach

THIRD EDITION

Module I – Business Organizations Fundamentals

CHAPTER 1

Introduction to the Firm

This chapter introduces you to the roles played by the key actors in a business organization. And we examine the essential function of law in business firms.

We start with perhaps the most famous case of U.S. business organization law. It arose from a dispute between two co-venturers in a commercial real estate project. The case raises fundamental questions about the legal relationship between investors and managers.

As you'll notice, the two people who joined together in this business had different interests and skills. One had more money to invest, the other greater expertise. Both wanted to make money from the business, but each anticipated a different role—with different prerogatives and different protections. That is not unusual. Specialization is at the core of business law.

Their venture, like any other, involved taking on risks. Their initial relationship allocated the risks to best serve their individual interests—and to promote their mutual interests in minimizing conflicts (selfishness) and maximizing profits. The issue before the court was whether their relationship extended to new business opportunities that arose from the initial project.

We use the case for two purposes. First, we introduce you to how risks can be allocated in a business organization. Second, we provide you an overview of one of the core concepts in agency, partnership, LLC, and corporate law—fiduciary duties. You will notice that both topics reappear throughout this book.

Take Note!

As you will see, even a business with just two people raises a lot of questions:

- Who should bear the key risks?
- How should they divide profits and losses?
- How should they allocate authority and responsibilities?
- How long should their business and their responsibilities last?
- How should they be able to change or end their relationship?

These questions permeate business law, and they form the building blocks of this book.

Meinhard v. Salmon

164 N.E. 545 (N.Y. 1928)

CARDOZO, C. J.

On April 10, 1902, Louisa M. Gerry leased to the defendant Walter J. Salmon the premises known as the Hotel Bristol at the northwest corner of Forty-Second Street and Fifth Avenue in the city of New York. The lease was for a term of 20 years, commencing May 1, 1902, and ending April 30, 1922. The lessee undertook to change the hotel building for use as shops and offices at a cost of $200,000. Alterations and additions were to be accretions to the land.

Salmon, while in course of treaty with the lessor as to the execution of the lease, was in course of treaty with Meinhard, the plaintiff, for the necessary funds. The result was a joint venture with terms embodied in a writing. Meinhard was to pay to Salmon half of the moneys requisite to reconstruct, alter, manage, and operate the property. Salmon was to pay to Meinhard 40 percent of the net profits for the first five years of the lease and 50 percent for the years thereafter. If there were losses, each party was to bear them equally. Salmon, however, was to have sole power to 'manage, lease, underlet and operate' the building. There were to be certain preemptive rights for each in the contingency of death.

The two were coadventurers, subject to fiduciary duties akin to those of partners. As to this we are all agreed. The heavier weight of duty rested, however, upon Salmon. He was a coadventurer with Meinhard, but he was manager as well. During the early years of the enterprise, the building, reconstructed, was operated at a loss. If the relation had then ended, Meinhard as well as Salmon would have carried a heavy burden. Later the profits became large with the result that for each of the investors there came a rich return. For each the venture had its phases of fair weather and of foul. The two were in it jointly, for better or for worse.

When the lease was near its end, Elbridge T. Gerry had become the owner of the reversion. He owned much other property in the neighborhood, one lot adjoining the Bristol building on Fifth Avenue and four lots on Forty-Second Street. He had a plan to lease the entire tract for a long term to some one who would destroy the buildings then existing and put up another in their place. In the latter part of 1921, he submitted such a project to several capitalists and dealers. He was unable to carry it through with any of them. Then, in January, 1922, with less than four months of the lease to run, he approached the defendant Salmon. The result was a new lease to the Midpoint Realty Company, which is owned and controlled by Salmon, a lease covering the whole tract, and involving a huge outlay. The term is to be 20 years, but successive covenants for renewal will extend it to a maximum of 80 years at the will of either party. A new building to cost

$3,000,000 is to be placed upon the site. The rental, which under the Bristol lease was only $55,000, is to be from $350,000 to $475,000 for the properties so combined. Salmon personally guaranteed the performance by the lessee of the covenants of the new lease until such time as the new building had been completed and fully paid for.

The lease between Gerry and the Midpoint Realty Company was signed and delivered on January 25, 1922. Salmon had not told Meinhard anything about it. Whatever his motive may have been, he had kept the negotiations to himself. Meinhard was not informed even of the bare existence of a project. The first that he knew of it was in February, when the lease was an accomplished fact. He then made demand on the defendants that the lease be held in trust as an asset of the venture, making offer upon the trial to share the personal obligations incidental to the guaranty. The demand was followed by refusal, and later by this suit. The case is now here on an appeal by the defendants.

Go Online

The building project undertaken by Salmon, one of the most important in New York City in the 1920s, resulted in the "Salmon Tower." The 60-story building at 42nd Street and Fifth Avenue, across from the New York City Public Library, was for a time the second tallest building in the city. Designed by the architectural firm Shreve Lamb & Harmon (the same firm that designed the Empire State Building), it remains a landmark of the New York skyline. You can go online to see a <u>city map</u> showing the building's location, as well as pictures of Hotel Bristol (the <u>original building</u> on the site).

Joint adventurers, like copartners, owe to one another, while the enterprise continues, the duty of the finest loyalty. Many forms of conduct permissible in a workaday world for those acting at arm's length, are forbidden to those bound by fiduciary ties. A trustee is held to something stricter than the morals of the market place. Not honesty alone, but the punctilio of an honor the most sensitive, is then the standard of behavior. As to this there has developed a tradition that is unbending and inveterate. Uncompromising rigidity has been the attitude of courts of equity when petitioned to undermine the rule of undivided loyalty by the 'disintegrating erosion' of particular exceptions. Only thus has the level of conduct for fiduciaries been kept at a level higher than that trodden by the crowd. It will not consciously be lowered by any judgment of this court.

The owner of the reversion, Mr. Gerry, had vainly striven to find a tenant who would favor his ambitious scheme of demolition and construction. Baffled in the search, he turned to the defendant Salmon in possession of the Bristol, the keystone of the project. He figured to himself beyond a doubt that the man in possession would prove a likely customer. To the eye of an observer, Salmon held the lease as owner in his own right, for himself and no one else. In fact he held it as a fiduciary, for himself and another, sharers in a common venture. The trouble about his conduct is that he excluded his coadventurer from any chance to compete, from any chance to enjoy the opportunity for benefit that had come to him alone by virtue of his agency. This chance, if nothing more, he was under a duty to concede. The price of its denial is an extension of the trust at the option and for the benefit of the one whom he excluded.

No answer is it to say that the chance would have been of little value even if seasonably offered. Such a calculus of probabilities is beyond the science of the chancery. Salmon, the real estate operator, might have been preferred to Meinhard, the woolen merchant. On the other hand, Meinhard might have offered better terms, or reinforced his offer by alliance with the wealth of others. All these opportunities were cut away from him through another's intervention. He knew that Salmon was the manager. As the time drew near for the expiration of the lease, he would naturally assume from silence, if from nothing else, that the lessor was willing to extend it for a term of years, or at least to let it stand as a lease from year to year. At least, there was nothing in the situation to give warning to any one that while the lease was still in being, there had come to the manager an offer of extension which he had locked within his breast to be utilized by himself alone. The very fact that Salmon was in control with exclusive powers of direction charged him the more obviously with the duty of disclosure, since only through disclosure could opportunity be equalized. If he might cut off renewal by a purchase for his own benefit when four months were to pass before the lease would have an end, he might do so with equal right while there remained as many years. He might steal a march on his comrade under cover of the darkness, and then hold the captured ground. Loyalty and comradeship are not so easily abjured.

Little profit will come from a dissection of the precedents. Authority is, of course, abundant that one partner may not appropriate to his own use a renewal of a lease, though its term is to begin at the expiration of the partnership. The lease at hand with its many changes is not strictly a renewal. Even so, the standard of loyalty for those in trust relations is without the fixed divisions of a graduated scale. To say that a partner is free without restriction to buy in the reversion of the property where the business is conducted is to say in effect that he may strip the good will of its chief element of value, since good will is largely dependent upon continuity of possession. Equity refuses to confine within the bounds of classified transactions its precept of a loyalty that is undivided and unselfish. Certain it is also that there may be no abuse of special opportunities growing out of a special trust as manager or agent. A constructive trust is, then, the remedial device through which preference of self is made subordinate to loyalty to others.

We have no thought to hold that Salmon was guilty of a conscious purpose to defraud. Very likely he assumed in all good faith that with the approaching end of the venture he might ignore his coadventurer and take the extension for himself. He had given to the enterprise time and labor as well as money. He had made it a success. Meinhard, who had given money, but neither time nor labor, had alread been richly paid. There might seem to be something grasping in his insistence upon more. Such recriminations are not unusual when coadventurers fall out. They are not without their force if conduct is to be judged by the common standards of competitors. That is not to say that they have pertinency here. Salmon had put himself in a position in which thought of self was to be renounced, however hard the abnegation. He was much more than a coadventurer. He was a managing coadventurer. For him and for those like him the rule of undivided loyalty is relentless and supreme. A different question would be here if there were lacking any nexus of relation between the business conducted by the manager and the opportunity brought to him as an incident of management. For this problem, as for most, there are distinctions of degree. If Salmon had received from Gerry a proposition to lease a building at a location far removed, he might have held for himself the privilege thus acquired, or so we shall assume. Here the subject-matter of the new lease was an extension and enlargement of the subject-matter of the old one.

Food for Thought

Notice that the rule (or duty) applied by Judge Cardozo is contextual. If Salmon had received information about a real estate opportunity far removed geographically or involving a non-real estate investment opportunity, Judge Cardozo suggests the result would have been different. Does it make sense for the application of fiduciary duties to vary depending on the parties' specific relationship?

A question remains as to the form and extent of the equitable interest to be allotted to the plaintiff. The trust as declared has been held to attach to the lease which was in the name of the defendant corporation. We think it ought to attach at the option of the defendant Salmon to the shares of stock which were owned by him or were under his control. The difference may be important if the lessee shall wish to execute an assignment of the lease, as it ought to be free to do with the consent of the lessor. On the other hand, an equal division of the shares might lead to other hardships. It might take away from Salmon the power of control and management which under the plan of the joint venture he was to have from first to last. The number of shares to be allotted to the plaintiff should, therefore, be reduced to such an extent as may be necessary to preserve to the defendant Salmon the expected measure of dominion. To that end an extra share should be added to his half.

ANDREWS, J. (dissenting)

I am of the opinion that the issue here is simple. Was the transaction, in view of all the circumstances surrounding it, unfair and inequitable? I reach this conclusion for two reasons. There was no general partnership, merely a joint venture for a limited object, to end at a fixed time. The new lease, covering additional property, containing many new and unusual terms and conditions, with a possible duration of 80 years, was more nearly the purchase of the reversion than the ordinary renewal with which the authorities are concerned.

Were this a general partnership between Mr. Salmon and Mr. Meinhard, I should have little doubt as to the correctness of this result, assuming the new lease to be an offshoot of the old. Such a situation involves questions of trust and confidence to a high degree; it involves questions of good, will; many other considerations. As has been said, rarely if ever may one partner without the knowledge of the other acquire for himself the renewal of a lease held by the firm, even if the new lease is to begin after the firm is dissolved. Warning of such an intent, if he is managing partner, may not be sufficient to prevent the application of this rule. . . .

What then was the scope of the adventure into which the two men entered? It is to be remembered that before their contract was signed Mr. Salmon had obtained the lease of the Bristol property. Very likely the matter had been earlier discussed between them. But it has been held that the written contract defines their rights and duties. Having the lease, Mr. Salmon assigns no interest in it to Mr. Meinhard. He is to manage the property. It is for him to decide what alterations shall be made and to fix the rents. But for 20 years from May 1, 1902, Salmon is to make all advances from his own funds and Meinhard is to pay him personally on demand one-half of all expenses incurred and all losses sustained 'during the full term of said lease,' and during the same period Salmon is to pay him a part of the net profits. There was no joint capital provided.

It seems to me that the venture so inaugurated had in view a limited object and was to end at a limited time. There was no intent to expand it into a far greater undertaking lasting for many years. The design was to exploit a particular lease. Doubtless in it Mr. Meinhard had an equitable interest, but in it alone. This interest terminated when the joint adventure terminated. There was no intent that for the benefit of both any advantage should be taken of the chance of renewal—that the adventure should be continued beyond that date. Mr. Salmon has done all he promised to do in return for Mr. Meinhard's undertaking when he distributed profits up to May 1, 1922.

———————

Points for Discussion

1. What roles?

What roles do you think Meinhard and Salmon expected that each would play? How might their expectations have affected the judges' views of their business relationship? Should their expectations matter?

2. What risks?

How did Meinhard and Salmon divide the risks of their business relationship? How would you have advised them to do so? Could they have allocated the risks in advance, so that they could have avoided this dispute?

A. Risk Allocation in the Firm

Before turning to the court's decision on fiduciary duties, it is useful to first consider how Meinhard and Salmon allocated (and might have allocated) the business risks in their venture. You can think of Meinhard and Salmon as having a kind of "business firm." To be successful, business firms must identify and manage risk. There are different ways to manage business risk, sometimes by externalizing it and sometimes by allocating it within the firm to the parties who are willing and able to assume it. Legal rules also play a role in allocating risks.

1. Nature of Risk

Risk comes in different forms. And different people, or the same people in different contexts, have different attitudes about risk. How each person in a business firm views and handles risk often affects how well the venture manages risk—and thus whether it is a success or a failure.

What's That?

"Business firms"—sometimes called "business organizations" or "business enterprises"—are formed according to the interests of the parties. When many investors come together and seek common management, the usual choice is a "corporation" (with its attributes of perpetual life, centralized management, free transferability of shares, and limited liability). When the parties seek to have equal financial and management rights, a "partnership" is a common choice.

Business parties can craft their firm to have the attributes that suit them best. A hybrid "limited liability company" provides the flexibility to create a firm with both corporate attributes (such as limited liability) and partnership attributes (such as non-transferable shares). The parties' agreement fixes the terms.

By the way, a "joint venture" is a "partnership" with a limited duration or scope, unless it has been organized in a different form.

Two types of risk. Like all business people, Meinhard and Salmon faced two categories of business risk: non-controllable risks and controllable risks. "Non-controllable risks" are risks the parties in a business firm cannot control—like the U.S. economy, bank interest rates, and the New York City commercial leasing market. Although non-controllable risks affect different businesses differently, they cannot be completely eliminated.

Parties in a business firm also face "controllable risks," which they can control. For example, Meinhard and Salmon could decide on the kinds of tenants they would have, the quality and safety of the building materials they would use to refurbish the building, and how the project would be advertised to potential tenants. These risks also are important to the business, but unlike the non-controllable risk that the stock market might crash (or boom), the parties can control how they structure their rental agreements.

Expected returns. Some risks cannot be quantified. It would be difficult to quantify the risks of climate change or a financial meltdown. But it often is possible to determine or estimate the probabilities of uncertain events. Business firms frequently try to quantify their risks, even when they know their estimates might not be precise. By quantifying the risks associated with a particular decision, the firm can determine the "expected return," or average return, of that decision.

For example, when Meinhard originally decided to invest $100,000 in the venture with Salmon, he had a sense for what the returns might be. We might imagine there was a chance (slim perhaps) that the project would lose money—let's assume under this scenario that losses would be $12,000 a year for the full twenty years. We might estimate that the probability of this "worst-case" scenario would be 20%. There was also a more "likely" scenario (say, half of the time) that the project would produce steady profits of $20,000 a year. There was also a possible "best-case" scenario that the project would succeed beyond expectations with profits of $30,000 a year. We might assess the chances of this "best-case" scenario as 30%.

What would be Meinhard's expected return—assuming the following probabilities for the different scenarios and a 50-50 sharing of profits and losses? Meinhard would envision a 20% probability of losing $6,000, a 50% probability of earning profits of $10,000, and a 30% probability of earning profits of $15,000. Here's a simple chart to show how Meinhard might assess his expected return. Note that the expected return column reflects a weighted average of the three scenarios.

	Meinhard's share	Probability	Expected return
Worst-case scenario	($6,000)	20%	($1,200)
Likely scenario	$10,000	50%	$5,000
Best-case scenario	$15,000	30%	$4,500
		Total	**$8,300**

Now, of course, we could play with the probabilities of each of the different scenarios, or even add additional scenarios. You might try doing so in a spreadsheet, to see what effect changing different numbers has on the expected return. Overall, using the assumptions of our simplified example, Meinhard could expect a return of $8,300 per year—not bad, an 8.3% return on his investment (assuming he gets back the $100,000 initial investment at the end of the 20 years).

Risk tolerance. Notice Meinhard was willing to risk losing not only his investment, but shouldering his share of business losses. How did he view risk? We know from experience that people think differently about risk. Some people are "risk averse": they prefer avoiding risk. To persuade a risk averse person to invest, you would have to offer sizeable potential returns or federally-insured deposit insurance.

Take Note!

The math in this book won't get more complicated than basic arithmetic. And mathematical tools are important. For example, the concepts reflected here are useful in illustrating how investors think about risk and return. If you browse forward in this book, you'll notice that the text is not heavy on numbers or math. In fact, we use numbers only occasionally. But this simple tabular calculation anticipates Chapter 11, Numeracy for Corporate Lawyers, which introduces you to basic accounting and business valuation.

Other people, perhaps Meinhard, are "risk seekers": they love to bet on investments even when safer returns are available (like a bank CD paying guaranteed interest). Remember that Meinhard was a wool merchant—in fact, a very successful one. His investment in Salmon's initial project was unlikely to have ruined him, though his later multi-million dollar exposure in the expanded project actually did!

In between risk aversion and risk seeking is "risk neutrality." A risk neutral person coolly calculates probabilities and returns, and makes decisions based solely on expected returns. Such a person would be happy to take on risk anytime it will generate a benefit on average. For example, if Meinhard were risk neutral and had also been offered another investment (such as 20-year bonds offered by General Electric) with an expected return of 7.9%, he would have chosen the higher "expected return" project with Salmon, even though the GE bonds carried less risk.

This discussion about risk is not merely theoretical. Appetite for risk can dramatically affect decision making, particularly when the structure the parties choose for their business relationship creates incentives to take on or avoid risk. For example, will Salmon manage the venture to attract high-rent tenants (and risk low occupancy) or low-rent tenants (and risk low, but assured returns)? The answer depends on how willing Salmon is to assume risk, which in turn depends on his risk tolerance and the incentives in the business relationship. If he is not risk averse and his compensation is in the form of profits, as it was in the case, he might go for the high-rent option. But if he is risk averse and his compensation was a fixed salary, he might prefer the safe low-rent option to make sure the project does not fail and he gets paid.

Business Lingo

In addition to some math, we also will be introducing many business and finance concepts. Some of this lingo will be new to many of you. If you have no experience with these concepts, this might seem like a vocabulary course more than a law course, at least at first. Don't worry— we'll explain these concepts as they arise. Anyway, now is a good time to start. Most of you will confront these terms—in life if not in practice. And you can always go to a dictionary or online to find a definition.

2. Methods to Manage Risk

The success of a business depends on how well it manages risk. Successful firms exploit favorable developments and minimize the effects of unfavorable ones. How well a business manages risk depends on how the parties allocate different risks, which in turn determines the incentives of the firm's participants. It is impossible for a business to avoid dealing with risk.

Insurance. One way for people to manage risk is "insurance." In purchasing insurance, a person or business pays a fee upfront, sometimes called an insurance premium, in exchange for the right to payment if a specified event occurs. Many people insure against risks in their private lives by purchasing car, fire, health, or life insurance. The same type of insurance is available for many business risks. Insurance offers private parties the ability to pool risks. When you buy car insurance, you and many other people each pay an insurance premium, and if you are involved in a car accident, you receive a payment that is drawn from the pool of insurance premiums (less the sometimes very substantial cost—and haggling— associated with the insurance company).

By using insurance to pool risks, each member of the pool bears a pro rata share of the pool's total loss, which is easier to predict than the loss to any particular member. For example, Meinhard and Salmon could have purchased insurance against declines in the stock market (tied to the commercial leasing market in New York City). Business insurance is available from private insurance companies and also can be purchased in the financial markets. Today they could have bought futures contracts on an exchange in Chicago that permits parties to bet on the direction of the stock markets or even real estate markets.

Business Lingo

A "futures contract" is a standardized contract, traded on a futures exchange (like the Chicago Board of Trade, CBOT) in which parties agree to buy or sell an underlying instrument (like a pool of corporate stocks) at a certain date in the future—at a fixed price. For example, one could buy a futures contract on the Dow Jones Industrial Average (DJIA), which is an "index" (or the weighted average) of the stock prices of the 30 largest publicly-traded corporations in the United States. You also could buy a futures contract based on the price of real estate in a particular region or city.

Diversification. A second way to manage risk is through "diversification." A person or business can diversify by participating in numerous ventures, each of which involves different risks. For example, an investor in the stock market might guard against the risk of armed hostilities (or peace) by investing in both weapons suppliers and cruise ships. Although diversification will not completely eliminate the risk of loss in any given stock, it will reduce the total risk because the performance of the entire portfolio is more likely to be balanced between gains and losses. Thus the diversified portfolio will offer a more certain return than can be obtained from any particular stock.

Diversification can take many forms. For example, if the main variable affecting commercial real estate in New York City is the investment climate in the United States, a real estate investor might diversify his risk by investing in real estate ventures in other countries. In this way, if the U.S. economy falters, real estate in other economies may prosper. Likewise, such an investor could also diversify by buying commodities (like oil or timber land), foreign stocks and bonds, or Impressionist paintings, each of which involves risks that are different from, and somewhat independent of, the risks associated with the New York City commercial real estate market.

Internal risk allocation. The third way to manage risk is to "allocate" the risk. Parties in a business firm might allocate risks to the person who is most willing or best able to bear them, perhaps because he is in a better position to insure or diversify. Alternatively, a more sophisticated party with superior information might allocate risks to the person who is least likely to understand the risks.

For example, Meinhard (the capitalist) would seem to have been in a better position than Salmon (the manager) to bear the risk associated with a real estate downturn. Meinhard might have been wealthier or more sophisticated, and therefore better able to buy insurance or diversify. As it turned out, Salmon was willing to compensate Meinhard for taking on the project's risks by letting him share in profits. On the other hand, Salmon might have shifted the risk to Meinhard, because he believed Meinhard did not understand risk very well, and therefore agreed to bear it cheaply.

Risk externalization. Another (sometimes controversial) way for business firms to manage risk is to "externalize" it—that is, to move the risk to other people outside the firm. (Notice that insurance is a form of risk externalization, where insiders pay outsiders to bear firm risks.) One significant way that modern business firms externalize risk is through limited liability, which applies to corporations and other limited liability entities. The effect of limited liability is to make participants liable only up to the amount they invest in the business. Thus, outside parties that deal with the corporation must bear any loss should the corporation be unable to fulfill its obligations.

For example, if Salmon and Meinhard had incorporated their venture and their corporation had contracted to buy building supplies, the outside supplier would have had no recourse against them individually if the corporation became insolvent and was unable to pay for the supplies. For this reason, when Gerry leased the expanded property to Midpoint Realty Corporation (the corporation created and owned by Salmon), he obtained personal guarantees from Salmon to assume the obligations under the lease if the corporation failed to pay.

Not all outside parties, however, are able to obtain personal guarantees from those who own and operate business firms. In particular, people who are injured by business activities (such as tort victims) often have to bear the loss themselves— or obtain their own insurance—in the event the business lacks the resources to compensate them. This problem is aggravated when businesses externalize risks on society—such as through activities that threaten the environment—where there is no mechanism to have the business or its participants take responsibility for the losses borne by everyone else. The externalization of risk is the hallmark of the modern business firm—and one of its most controversial characteristics.

3. Business Firm as Risk Allocation

Let's return to risk allocation within the firm. How might parties allocate business risks between themselves? For the sake of simplicity, let's assume there are two distinct roles the parties might play: principal and agent. We use "principal" to refer to the role of investor/owner and "agent" to refer to the role of manager/employee. After assigning each party a role, we can consider the incentives of each party. Next we can see how different organizational choices—or allocations of risk—affect outcomes in their business venture. Then we can consider what happens if business risks are allocated to the principal, and then what happens if they are allocated to the agent. Which is preferable? Or does it depend?

Incentives of principal and agent. When a principal and agent join in a for-profit business venture, the tensions between them are inevitable. The principal will want to maximize the expected return on his investment. He will want the agent to use as much effort as possible to make the venture a success. Predictably, he will want for himself the bulk of the venture's profits. He will want the agent to put the principal's interests above the interests of others—even above the agent's own interests. He will want to know that the agent is working for him and to have the means to impose his will, if necessary.

The agent, on the other hand, will also have an interest in maximizing the expected return on his efforts, given the alternative uses of his time. He will want to be compensated munificently for his effort, even if the business does not succeed. Given human nature, he will want to expend as little effort as necessary to make the venture a success. He will want the discretion to accomplish the goals of the venture, without interference from the principal or blame should the venture fail.

Given the divergence in their interests, the principal will understandably want to "monitor" the agent to ensure he does as expected. If he does not do as expected, the principal will want to "discipline" the agent by imposing appropriate sanctions. Even then, the agent will probably get away with some shirking or laziness. For the principal, these monitoring and disciplining efforts—and the agent's inevitable shirking—are the "agency costs" of working through a principal-agent arrangement. Despite these costs, however, both parties see potential gains from entering into the venture together. Business firms are built on the premise that participants must specialize and cooperate to accomplish their individual interests.

Matters addressed by business organization. We must remember that the parties cannot know with certainty what the future holds. The principal cannot know whether the agent will be honest, hard-working, and obedient. The agent cannot know whether the principal will be steady and wise. Neither can be sure that the venture will succeed in a real world of uncertainty.

To do this, their agreement (or the rules under which they implicitly choose to operate) must address:

- the term of their relationship

- the sharing of financial rights and obligations, including profits and losses

- the discretion and responsibilities of the agent

- the supervisory powers of the principal, including access to information

- the ability of either participant to terminate their relationship

- the means by which they can change their relationship.

Make the Connection

The basic issues that Salmon and Meinhard had to address arise in all business organizations. As you'll notice, they reflect the main topics (or modules) of this casebook: the basics of business organizations, corporate formation, corporate finance, corporate externalities, corporate governance, fiduciary duties, stock trading, and corporate acquisitions.

Much of their relationship will be decided *before* the venture begins—from an *ex ante* perspective. But some terms of their relationship will be resolved only *after* the venture has begun or problems arise—from an *ex post* perspective. As we will see, business organization law (which includes corporate law) offers rules that resolve many of these issues, sometimes by mandating particular results and more often by providing standardized default terms that the parties can rewrite if they want.

Participants in a business have many choices about how to structure their relationship and allocate their risks. Contracting for the optimal structure, however, will not be costless. They will have to identify their own individual interests, as well as the interests of the other party. Among other things, they will have to decide on the term of their relationship, the allocation of gains and losses of the venture, the decision-making authority and discretion of each participant, and the circumstances in which they can exit from their relationship.

Contract or law. There are two sources of rules for parties to use in structuring their business relationship: contract and law. First, in allocating risks by contract, the parties are forced in their private agreement to address the allocation of non-controllable and controllable risks. Second, by choosing a particular legal regime, the parties accept the "off the shelf" allocation of the regime they choose. In some cases, the law will mandate the allocation of risks between the parties. But in other cases, the legal rules will permit the parties to choose among different ways to allocate risks.

Before looking at how legal rules serve to allocate risks, consider how principals and agents might allocate risks through contract. We already have discussed the allocation of non-controllable risks, such as the risk of a financial downturn on Wall Street. The allocation of controllable risks is different, because principals and agents can affect controllable risks, by acting or not acting. For example, if the venture's success depends on Salmon actively seeking high-rent tenants, a risk to the venture is that Salmon will not make the effort. Controllable risks can be reduced by monitoring and disciplining devices that align the agent's incentives with the interests of the principal.

The difficulty in allocating risk among the parties is that the party who bears the consequences of the risk will have a greater incentive to control the risk, but the other party will not. For example, if Salmon receives a fixed salary no matter how many high-rent tenants he develops, he will have little incentive to promote the venture. This neglect or failure is called "shirking." (More generally, the danger that a person who does not bear a risk will not take steps to control that risk is referred to as "moral hazard." In general, moral hazard refers to an increase in risk when some activity is insured—the increased risk of arson when a person buys fire insurance is a common example.) To avoid the agent's self-interested shirking, the principal, who *does* bear the risk, must monitor the agent to ensure that he takes risk reducing precautions. Often it will be more efficient to place the risk on the agent and thus avoid the monitoring costs.

At the same time, however, the party who is in the best position to control risks might not be the best person to bear them. For example, if Salmon is less wealthy, more risk averse, and less able to insure or diversify, he might not want to assume the risk of low occupancy rates in the building. Who should bear the risk? Each party, perhaps justifiably, would want the other to bear it. There is a clear tension between controlling risk and bearing risk. Is there a compromise?

Allocating risks to the principal. First, let's explore the allocation of risks to the principal. Some risks are most efficiently borne by the principal—that is, the person who assumes the attributes of owner or holder of the firm's residual profits. If the principal is less risk averse than the agent, the principal will be more willing to bear the non-controllable risk of business success or failure. The agent, on the other hand, will prefer a fixed compensation. In this way, the principal accepts the uncertainty of business success or failure, and receives as compensation for this risk-taking the bulk of the returns if the business succeeds. This makes sense particularly if the principal is wealthier and has the opportunity to insure or diversify, a strategy less available to the agent.

If the agent does not bear the risks of the business, but receives a fixed compensation, there arises the controllable risk that the agent will be lazy or even corrupt. This risk of agent shirking will predictably lead the principal to want to monitor and discipline the agent. First, the principal must decide what constitutes optimal performance by the agent—an *ex ante* task. Second, having decided this, the principal must determine whether the desired level of performance is occurring or has occurred—from an *ex post* perspective. The principal will want to minimize these agency costs.

How might the principal monitor the agent? One solution would be direct supervision where the principal both prescribes optimal standards, observes whether they are being met, and punishes the agent if not. This approach has obvious drawbacks. Deciding what the agent should do, obtaining information about whether he did it, and then disciplining wayward behavior would be time-consuming and costly. It would undermine the very reason that the principal hired an agent, namely to delegate decision-making authority to another. Of course, the principal could hire a supervisor. Doing that, however, would create an additional problem: Who supervises the supervisor? Maybe another supervisor, like a board of directors. But in a small business, the principal might search for another less cumbersome solution.

An alternative monitoring device might be an employment contract between the principal and agent. Such a contract could both specify the agent's duties and decision-making discretion, and prescribe sanctions (including dismissal) if the agent failed to perform those duties. It would also specify the principal's oversight and decision-making powers, and the sanctions should the agent fail to comply with his duties.

Is such a contract desirable? Although some aspects of the agent's work can be satisfactorily defined in a contract, others are more problematic. For example, in their joint venture agreement, Meinhard and Salmon specified that Salmon would be the "manager," but apparently without specifying all his tasks. This left open the question whether Salmon was obligated to bring to Meinhard's attention post-venture investment opportunities.

Because of the *ex ante* drafting difficulty, shirking might continue even with a contract. Nonetheless, a contract might still be useful if it takes an *ex post* perspective. For example, Meinhard might have insisted on the following:

> Salmon will use his best efforts as manager. Any dispute over whether Salmon has used his best efforts will be resolved by an independent arbitrator of Meinhard's choosing.

This "best efforts" clause prescribes Salmon's efforts *ex ante*. Meinhard's hope is that the clause will lead Salmon to expend the effort he would if he were the owner—that is, if he bore the controllable risks of the business. Consistent with this view of Salmon's role, the clause delegates discretion to Salmon to perform his tasks according to the actual circumstances as they arise in the building. The clause, however, makes the heroic assumption that the diligence and loyalty implicit in "best efforts" will be clear to Salmon, and that Meinhard will be able to monitor his efforts.

To deal with the difficulties of *ex ante* specification, the clause's enforcement mechanism addresses agency costs from an *ex post* perspective. In deciding whether to enforce the clause, Meinhard might find it easier to determine whether Salmon was shirking by looking at the results of his efforts. For example, he could compare the rentals received in previous years or the occupancy rate in other office buildings. After this comparison, if the current rentals or occupancy rates were high, Meinhard could infer that Salmon used his best efforts. If low, Meinhard could then invoke his arbitration rights. Notice that this *ex post* mechanism will also have *ex ante* effects. Since Salmon cannot be sure whether Meinhard will enforce his contract rights, he has an incentive not to shirk.

Contracting, however, has its limits. For example, in their long-term venture, it was hard for Meinhard and Salmon to imagine and foresee all contingencies, such as the possibility that the Gerry estate might make adjacent properties available for an expanded building project. When such contingencies arise, should the parties be able to amend their contract, under what procedures? Or should the parties be able to withdraw from the contract, on what terms? Which course will be optimal? Although contracting offers advantages in reducing controllable risks, it has its limits.

Remember also that contracting is costly. Information, negotiation, and drafting costs all must be incurred—and lawyers' time is not cheap. The potential cost of enforcing contracts is high and cannot be disregarded, even if the need never actually materializes. And a contract inevitably shifts the ultimate resolution of a dispute to a third party—often a court—thereby adding new uncertainty and risk.

Allocating risks to the agent. Now let's assume the agent bears the risks. For example, Meinhard could have lent money to the project with fixed interest and allow Salmon to retain all the project profits. Such an arrangement would allow Meinhard to reduce his monitoring costs (though he would still want to make sure Salmon set aside enough money to repay the loan). The bulk of the monitoring would be Salmon's self-monitoring. If he works less hard, it will be because he values his non-work activities more than the fruits of his work; his reduced business profits will be counterbalanced by the value he places on those activities.

Or only some of the risk might be allocated to the agent, such as by basing the agent's compensation in part on the success (or failure) of the business. For example, Meinhard and Salmon might have agreed as follows:

> Salmon is to be paid an annual salary of $5,000. But if the project's annual net income is less than $10,000, his annual salary shall be reduced by 50 percent.

Is such a provision desirable? The project's profitability probably depends on numerous factors. Some are beyond the control of either party; and some are within their control, but unrelated to the specific problem of shirking. If shirking is Meinhard's main concern, he can tie Salmon's salary to net rentals. So if profitability depends on Salmon's efforts, the clause would create incentives for Salmon and reduces the need to monitor and discipline his performance. As a partial claimant to residual profits, Salmon would see the project from Meinhard's perspective.

Another option for the principal is to hire the agent to a long-term contract. This would then more closely align the agent's incentives with the principal's long-term interests. But this might also work against the principal. In our example, if Salmon becomes a malingerer and Meinhard cannot fire him, he will have created new agency costs. A year-to-year arrangement then would have the advantage that Salmon must prove himself with each rental cycle. A shorter term would also allow Meinhard to adapt to changing circumstances, such as unforeseen competitive pressures or the availability of MBA-trained building managers. A short-term contract puts Salmon at risk by effectively giving Meinhard the ability unilaterally to exit their arrangement, perhaps in ways that frustrate Salmon's expectations.

Finally, consider what happens if Salmon stops working for Meinhard. If he shirked for Meinhard, he might damage his reputation, reducing his value to other capitalists. Instead, Salmon will want Meinhard and others to conclude that he worked diligently for him, a signal to future owners to increase his pay and reduce their monitoring of him. Thus, reputation serves as a self-effectuating monitoring device. It is particularly useful since it does not involve any reallocation of the risks or returns of the venture.

Which allocation of risks is better? If risk is the main concern, the principal might be the better risk-bearer because of his ability to diversify and insure, or simply because he prefers risk. But under this model the principal must incur monitoring/disciplining costs to reduce the costs of agent shirking. If shirking is the main concern, the agent might be the better risk-bearer since entitlement to profits will give him incentives to maximize the venture's success. But the agent might not be willing or able to bear all the risks.

Perhaps there is a satisfactory middle ground. Suppose (as happened in the case) Meinhard and Salmon agree to divide the venture's profits 50-50, or some other mutually agreeable ratio. Even if Salmon received a fixed salary (which was not clear from the facts of the case), he had a residual claim to project profits. Although Salmon would have some incentive to shirk, it would be minimized since any shirking would decrease his share of the profits. Meinhard would still need to monitor, but not as much. This solution, however, means that Meinhard sacrificed some of his returns from the project in the hope of reducing agency costs. It also means that some risks were allocated to Salmon, who may have been less able to bear them.

In searching for this middle ground, one dynamic affecting the parties' allocation of risk will be the specialized knowledge that the agent acquires over time while working for the principal—or in the situation of Salmon and Meinhard, it was the specialized knowledge developed by the partner who provided managerial services to the venture compared with the partner who acted as a passive investor. This was the linchpin in the case. As Salmon became more familiar with commercial real estate management and with the 42nd Street and Fifth Avenue location, he became more valuable to Meinhard. Over time, he could have opportunistically demanded greater independence or a larger share of profits. But Salmon's greater specialization would have been a two-edged sword. His acquired skills and knowledge could have been primarily valuable only to Meinhard, on whom Salmon could become dependent. How should the parties allocate risk (such as the possibility of an expanded building project) as their symbiotic relationship matures? Since their contract did not resolve it, it was left to the law.

4. Role of Law in Business Firms

Thus far, our discussion of risk allocation and firm design has assumed a simplified two-person business firm. Similar allocations of risk among creditors, suppliers, employees, and owners occur in more complex business firms. The business firm can be understood as a complex network of arrangements between various participants, each adding specialized inputs. Within this network, some risk allocations happen by means of contracting, but legal rules also define the relationship among the parties.

To save firm participants the costs of contracting, the law of business relationships (including agency law, partnership law, LLC law, and corporate law) provides the parties a set of "off the rack" rules by which they can define their relationship. These laws specify the allocation of risks, by specifying various roles and rights for the firm participants. In most situations the parties can change the rules to suit their circumstances—that is, the rules are the default unless the parties agree otherwise. Sometimes the rules are mandatory, and the parties cannot agree otherwise.

What's That?

The law provides mandatory and default rules that apply to businesses. An example of a "mandatory" rule is the minimum wage: parties cannot agree to a lower wage than set by law. An example of a "default" rule is the "at will" employment doctrine: either party can terminate employment unless the parties specify limits.

There are various kinds of default rules. A default rule is "majoritarian" if most parties would bargain for it. Is "at will" employment a majoritarian default?

A default rule is "tailored" if it tries to fit a relationship. For example, employees might have a duty to inform employers of "material" information—a duty that varies according to their situation.

A default rule is a "penalty" default if it encourages parties to bargain and specify their relationship. For example, a rule that permits employees to compete with employers after employment ends imposes a "penalty" unless the parties agree to a non-compete clause.

Mandatory rules assume that private bargaining won't adequately protect weaker parties or might cause social harm. Default rules recognize the value of party autonomy, an underlying thesis of much of business law which is largely enabling to allow parties to privately order their affairs.

B. Fiduciary Duties

We now return to the central issue in *Meinhard v. Salmon*—what are the implicit duties of firm participants to each other? The law of business firms generally assumes that when management authority is delegated in the firm, those who run the firm have "fiduciary duties" to those who entrusted them with this authority. But to say that fiduciary duties exist only begins to frame the issue.

1. Theory of Fiduciary Duties

In a broad sense, fiduciary duties seek to protect those who delegate authority against the negligence, disloyalty, or worse of those who exercise this authority on their behalf. It is inevitable that when people take on different roles in a business firm there will be conflict—one will want things done her way, the other his way. It's just human nature. But just because "friction" is inevitable does not mean the "engine" of working together should be discarded.

So how do we know specifically what are the fiduciary duties in a business firm? One answer might be that such duties exist only to the extent the parties have specified them. That is, the parties would have to negotiate and contract for their own rules. But this would be nearly impossible. It would be costly and difficult to foresee and negotiate an agreement that covered all possible scenarios.

There would inevitably be gaps. Any contract would be incomplete. Instead, the law steps in with its own (often vague) rules that state broadly that the fiduciary must exercise care, diligence, honesty, and loyalty with respect to the firm and its participants.

As you can see, fiduciary duties constitute the "golden rule" in business firms. Without them, people might be less inclined to join together in a business for profit. Sometimes, though, departures from the ideal will be hard to detect. And sometimes the law—and judges—may not be the best arbiters of what constitutes faithful or unfaithful conduct. Fiduciary duties, enforced through legal processes, cannot be the balm for everything that ails a business firm.

Not surprisingly, discussion of fiduciary duties (nebulous as they are) often evokes poetry—that is, judges just have a feeling for what's fair and good, but have trouble expressing it with clarity and specificity. Judge Cardozo's opinion in *Meinhard v. Salmon* is illustrative. It is widely recognized as a stylistic masterpiece, and many lawyers and judges recall the poetic "punctilio of an honor the most sensitive."

2. Meaning of *Meinhard v. Salmon*

Many lessons are embedded in the case. One way to view *Meinhard v. Salmon* is as a classic statement of the fidicuary duties in a partnership. A partnership exists when two or more persons agree to carry on as co-owners a business for profit. Both Judge Cardozo and Judge Andrews agreed that when a partnership exists, the partners owe each other the fiduciary duty of loyalty. But they disagreed about how to apply the law to the facts of the case, which presented a close call. Did the opportunity belong to the existing venture, or was the scope of their original venture narrower and limited only to the first original lease?

Meinhard v. Salmon was no ordinary business dispute. It was well known in New York social circles that Meinhard and Salmon were very close. Their business fallout was part of a personal fallout. (Maybe Cardozo was thinking in these terms when he described the devotion that business partners owe each other.) After the court decision, Meinhard (and then his estate when he died in 1931) became responsible for his half stake in the Salmon Tower, whose losses during the Depression were borne equally by Salmon and Meinhard. According to some accounts, Salmon sent Judge Cardozo a bouquet of flowers every anniversary of the court decision—in appreciation for Cardozo having reduced by half the losses Salmon had to bear.

Another way to view the case is through the lens of our free-market capitalist system. What protections are capitalists (Meinhard) entitled to when they delegate operational discretion to a manager (Salmon)? Judge Andrews, in dissent, takes the view that the capitalist was entitled to protections only within the context of their original agreement, which did not include any right in the capitalist to participate in post-venture business opportunities undertaken by the manager. Judge Cardozo, for the majority, takes the view that the parties' relationship existed beyond the "morals of the marketplace" and compelled the manager to make any related opportunities available to the capitalist.

Points for Discussion

1. Beyond contract.

Fiduciary duties exist beyond contractual agreements. Even Andrews agrees the result in *Meinhard v. Salmon* would have been different if the parties had agreed to an indefinite partnership, as opposed to a 20-year joint venture. But could Salmon have included a clause in their original agreement that he retained the option to enter into other projects involving the same real estate, without notifying or otherwise including Meinhard? That is, are fiduciary duties default terms, subject to the parties' agreement otherwise? As we will see, the law is still struggling on with this question and it varies by form of business organization.

2. Judge-made law.

The law in the case is judge-made. No one mentions any statutes. This seems quite odd given that your professor may have asked you to buy a thick statutory supplement for this course. What is the purpose of extensive statutes if the most important aspects of business organization law are decided by judges without reference to those statutes? As we will see, business law is a mix of statutes and case law—a dialogue between legislatures and courts.

3. Gap-filling function.

Would the parties have negotiated for the right of first refusal that Cardozo gave Meinhard? Was it really implicit in their relationship that Salmon would give Meinhard a chance to share in any post-venture opportunities related to their business? Meinhard contributed capital, for which he received promises of profit sharing. But did Meinhard also pay for the option to extend their business venture if a good opportunity arose? If we decided that his initial $100,000 contribution only covered his sharing of net profits, it would seem the court enforced more than the parties' expectations.

4. Utility of fiduciary duties.

If you were inventing a capitalist system, would you impose extra-contractual fiduciary duties on managers that, as happened in this case, require sharing of outside business opportunities? Would such duties of loyalty lead to more efficient and productive business firms?

———————

CHAPTER 2

Agency Basics

In Chapter 1, we discussed a classic case involving co-venturers who were different in many ways, but were useful archetypes for considering how two people might go into business. We introduced the concepts of principal and agent, and we described various ways a principal and agent might allocate a range of risks. Now we turn to questions about the legal rules that govern participants in a business, beginning with how the law addresses principal-agent relationships, and then turning to the law of partnerships and corporations. We start here with the law of agency.

The law has long had rules concerning when an agency relationship is formed, the duties and obligations between a principal and agent, and legal consequences with third parties that flow from the agency relationship. These are the basic principles of agency law that we will study in this chapter.

At the outset, you might take a moment to notice that agency relationships are ubiquitous. You interact with agents in your everyday life, from a store clerk who assists you with a purchase to the professor who acts on behalf of the university in teaching a course. An agency relationship exists between employer and employee, corporation and officer, client and lawyer, and partnership and general partner. People often retain agents to perform specific services such as in real estate transactions and in the sports and entertainment industry where, for example, authors, performers, and athletes often retain agents to represent their interests in dealing with third parties. In short, agency is a building

Take Note!

Each state has its own agency law that has been enacted as a statute by the state legislature or judicially created over time through case law. In addition, the general principles of agency law are captured in the Restatement (Third) of the Law of Agency. The Restatement is an influential secondary source of law drafted by the American Law Institute. Originally published in 1933 (First), the Restatement was updated in 1958 (Second), and again in 2006 (Third). Thus, if you were to deal with a real-world agency law issue in practice you would consider what is the relevant jurisdiction and then research the state agency law applicable to your matter at hand. Here, the focus is on understanding general principles, and we refer to the Restatement (Third) of Agency.

block concept that has relevance for many types of business relationships and organizations, including sole proprietorships, partnerships, corporations, and limited liability companies (LLCs). That's why we start with it.

A. Formation of the Agency Relationship

The Restatement (Third) of Agency § 1.01 provides the definition of the agency relationship:

> Agency is the fiduciary relationship that arises when one person (a "principal") manifests assent to another person (an "agent") that the agent shall act on the principal's behalf and subject to the principal's control, and the agent manifests assent or otherwise consents so to act.

Thus, the agency relationship is created between two parties—an agent and a principal—and includes three basic elements: (1) mutual assent, (2) control, and (3) acting on behalf of a principal.

The facts are important for each of these three elements. First, the parties must assent that the agent will act on behalf, and subject to the control, of the principal. However, it is not required that the parties intend to enter into something called an agency relationship or that they are aware of the legal consequences. Generally, no writing is required. In addition, how the parties characterize the relationship or popular usage is not dispositive in determining whether an agency relationship exists. This means, for example, that a contract provision disclaiming an agency relationship could be relevant, but not dispositive, in determining whether an agency relationship exists.

To determine whether the agent and principal have assented to their relationship with each other, courts look to the parties' outward manifestations from the viewpoint of a reasonable person rather than to their inner, subjective thoughts. Each party must have objectively manifested assent to the agency relationship, whether by words or conduct. Notably, the consensual aspect of agency does not mean that agency is limited to commercial settings or that an enforceable contract with consideration necessarily underlies the relationship. Many agents act or promise to act gratuitously, without compensation or bargained-for exchange, and this assent still suffices for purposes of creating an agency relationship. You might be surprised to learn that just agreeing to do a requested favor for a friend could create an agency relationship.

Second, control is evidenced in agency by a consensual relationship in which the principal has the power and right to direct the agent as to the goal of the relationship. We might colloquially refer to this as whether the principal is "in charge" or able to instruct the agent.

Finally, in an agency relationship, the agent is acting on behalf of the principal. From the principal's perspective, this is indeed the point of creating the agency relationship—the principal wants someone else to take some action on their behalf. For example, a sole proprietor who wants to grow her business might hire an agent so that someone else can act on her behalf in carrying out business matters. This element gets at the idea that the agent is acting in a representative capacity or to further the interests of the principal.

B. Rights and Duties Between Principal and Agent

Why does it matter that an agency relationship exists? One reason is because once this relationship is created the principal and agent owe each other certain obligations and duties under the law.

1. Principal's Obligations to Agent

The obligations owed by the principal to the agent are relatively straightforward. Restatement (Third) of Agency § 8.14 provides that the principal has a duty to reimburse or indemnify the agent for any promised payments, any payments the agent makes within the scope of actual authority, and when the agent "suffers a loss that fairly should be borne by the principal in light of their relationship." In addition, under § 8.15, a principal has an obligation to deal with the agent fairly and in good faith. The principal should also generally cooperate with the agent and not unreasonably interfere with the agent's performance of his or her duties.

2. Agent's Fiduciary Duties to Principal

More notably, the duties that are owed by the agent to the principal are not just obligations, but are *fiduciary duties*. This is an important topic that we saw in the previous chapter and we will see throughout the course, as fiduciary duties arise or can arise in agency, partnership, corporations, and LLCs.

A fiduciary is someone, such as an agent or a partner or a corporate director, who stands in a special relation of trust, confidence, or responsibility in certain obligations to others. A fiduciary relationship requires one party to put the other party's interests ahead of her own. An agent is a fiduciary with respect to matters within the scope of the agency relationship. Fiduciary duties are well established and deeply ingrained in the law, though as we have already seen, the rationales have been stated in various ways ranging from moralistic terms to efficiency rationales, such as reducing transaction and monitoring costs.

The Restatement (Third) of Agency §§ 8.01–8.11 explain that the agent owes the principal the duties of care and loyalty, and certain duties related to information and confidentiality. The duty of care refers to the level of care, competence, and diligence that an agent exercises. If an agent claims to have special skills or knowledge, then the agent has a duty to act with the care normally exercised by agents with such skills or knowledge. Otherwise, the standard is simply the ordinary care that an agent would use in similar circumstances, if the agent is paid, or gross negligence for unpaid agents.

The duty of loyalty refers to the idea that the agent must not put his or her own interests ahead of those of the principal when the agent is acting within the agency relationship. The agent should act for the benefit of the principal in all matters connected with the agency. For example, the agent must not compete with the principal, act adversely to the principal, take a business opportunity that belongs to the principal, or abuse the agent position to earn unauthorized side profits, bribes, or tips.

Finally, the agent has duties related to information. An agent has a duty to provide information to the principal that the agent knows or has reason to know that the principal would wish to have, as well as to provide the facts that are material to the agent's duties to the principal. Further, the duty of confidentiality means that the agent must not disclose or misuse confidential information. Unlike the other duties, the duty of confidentiality notably remains in force even after the agency relationship has terminated.

If an agent breaches any of these duties without the consent of the fully informed principal, the agent could be liable to the principal for any resulting damages. The agent could also be liable to disgorge to the principal any profit made by the agent in breach of a duty.

The following case involves a lawsuit brought by a small machine shop business, General Automotive Manufacturing Company ("Automotive"), against John Singer, a former employee. Singer was a well-regarded expert at machine work, known for being able to use special techniques and qualified in estimating the costs and competitive prices of machine-shop products.

Automotive hired Singer as the general manager of its business pursuant to a written contract which set out his compensation as a fixed monthly salary and a commission of 3% of the gross sales. In exchange, the contract provided that Singer promised "to devote his entire time, skill, labor and attention to said employment, during the term of this employment, and not to engage in any other business or vocation of a permanent nature during the term of this employment." He was not to disclose any information concerning the business or affairs that he acquired in the course of his employment for his own benefit or to the detriment of his employer. It also provided that, as a manager, Singer was a fiduciary agent with respect to solicitation of business and was bound to exercise the utmost good faith and loyalty to his employer.

A dispute later arose when it came to Automotive's attention that Singer was secretly profiting while in its employ. The trial court found in favor of Automotive. Singer appealed.

General Automotive Mfg. v. Singer

120 N.W.2d 659 (Wis. 1963)

BROWN, CHIEF JUSTICE.

Study of the record discloses that Singer was engaged as general manager of Automotive's operations. Among his duties was solicitation and procurement of machine shop work for Automotive. Because of Singer's high reputation in the trade he was highly successful in attracting orders.

Automotive is a small concern and has a low credit rating. Singer was invaluable in bolstering Automotive's credit. For instance, when collections were slow for work done by Automotive Singer paid the customer's bill to Automotive and waited for his own reimbursement until the customer remitted. Also, when work was slack, Singer set Automotive's shop to make parts for which there were no present orders and himself financed the cost of materials for such parts, waiting for recoupment until such stock-piled parts could be sold. Some parts were never sold and Singer personally absorbed the loss upon them.

As time went on a large volume of business attracted by Singer was offered to Automotive but which Singer decided could not be done by Automotive at all, for lack of suitable equipment, or which Automotive could not do at a competitive price. When Singer determined that such orders were unsuitable for Automotive he neither informed Automotive of these facts nor sent the orders back to the customer. Instead, he made the customer a price, then dealt with another machine shop to do the work at a less price, and retained the difference between the price quoted to the customer and the price for which the work was done. Singer was actually behaving as a broker for his own profit in a field where by contract he had engaged to work only for Automotive. We concur in the decision of the trial court that this was inconsistent with the obligations of a faithful agent or employee.

Singer finally set up a business of his own, calling himself a manufacturer's agent and consultant, in which he brokered orders for products of the sort manufactured by automotive—this while he was still Automotive's employee and without informing Automotive of it. Singer had broad powers of management and conducted the business activities of Automotive. In this capacity he was Automotive's agent and owed a fiduciary duty to it. Under his fiduciary duty to Automotive Singer was bound to the exercise of the utmost good faith and loyalty so that he did not act adversely to the interests of Automotive by serving or acquiring any private interest of his own. He was also bound to act for the furtherance and advancement of the interest of Automotive.

If Singer violated his duty to Automotive by engaging in certain business activities in which he received a secret profit he must account to Automotive for the amounts he illegally received.

The present controversy centers around the question whether the operation of Singer's side line business was a violation of his fiduciary duty to Automotive. The trial court found this business was conducted in secret and without the knowledge of Automotive. There is conflicting evidence regarding this finding but it is not against the great weight and clear preponderance of the evidence and, therefore, cannot be disturbed.

The trial court found that Singer's side line business, the profits of which were $64,088.08, was in direct competition with Automotive. However, Singer argues that in this business he was a manufacturer's agent or consultant, whereas Automotive was a small manufacturer of automotive parts. The title of an activity does not determine the question whether it was competitive but an examination of the nature of the business must be made. In the present case the conflict of interest between Singer's business and his position with Automotive arises from the fact that Singer received orders, principally from a third-party called Husco, for the manufacture of parts. As a manufacturer's consultant he had to see that these orders were filled as inexpensively as possible, but as Automotive's general manager he could not act adversely to the corporation and serve his own interests. On this issue Singer argues that when Automotive had the shop capacity to fill an order he would award Automotive the job, but he contends that it was in the exercise of his duty as general manager of Automotive to refuse orders which in his opinion Automotive could not or should not fill and in that case he was free to treat the order as his own property. However, this argument ignores, as the trial court said, "defendant's agency with plaintiff and the fiduciary duties of good faith and loyalty arising therefrom."

Rather than to resolve the conflict of interest between his side line business and Automotive's business in favor of serving and advancing his own personal interests, Singer had the duty to exercise good faith by disclosing to Automotive all the facts regarding this matter. Upon disclosure to Automotive it was in the latter's discretion to refuse to accept the orders from Husco or to fill them if possible or to sub-job them to other concerns with the consent of Husco if necessary, and the profit, if any, would belong to Automotive. Automotive would then be able also to decide whether to expand its operations, install suitable equipment, or to make further arrangements with Singer or Husco. By failing to disclose all the facts relating to the orders from Husco and by receiving secret profits from these orders, Singer violated his fiduciary duty to act solely for the benefit of Automotive. Therefore he is liable for the amount of the profits he earned in his side line business.

We conclude that Singer's independent activities were in competition with Automotive and were in violation of his obligation of fidelity to that corporation, as stated in Finding of Fact No. 10 and Singer must account for his profits so obtained. Judgment affirmed.

Points for Discussion

1.   Did it matter that the parties had a contract that specified that Singer was an agent who owed the fiduciary duty of loyalty? Or would the court have applied agency and fiduciary law principles anyway based on the facts?

2.   What remedy does Automotive get from Singer? How is this different from what the remedy would have been had the court's ruling been based on breach of contract?

3.   How could Singer have avoided liability in these circumstances? Would it have been enough to avoid liability if Singer had told General Automotive what he was doing?

We have so far examined the inward-looking consequences of the agency relationship—the rights and duties between the principal and agent. The next section examines the outward-looking consequences of the agency relationship— the contract and tort liability that the principal can incur based on the agent's actions, and related topics.

C. Contract Liability: Principals

When can a third party hold a principal liable in contract for the actions of the agent? There are five bases by which a principal (or purported principal) can incur contract liability: actual authority, apparent authority, undisclosed principal liability, ratification, and estoppel.

It is possible for more than one of these bases to be present in a particular factual circumstance, but any one of these would be sufficient for holding a principal (or purported principal) liable. We will give special attention to the first two—actual authority and apparent authority—which are the most common.

1. Actual Authority

Actual authority is authority that the agent reasonably believes she has based on the principal's manifestations, expressed through words or other conduct. Restatement (Third) of Agency § 2.01 tells us:

> An agent acts with actual authority when, at the time of taking action that has legal consequences for the principal, the agent reasonably believes, in accordance with the principal's manifestations to the agent, that the principal wishes the agent so to act.

For example, a principal tells an agent: "Do X." Upon hearing this, the agent reasonably believes that the principal wants her to do X and she has actual authority to do so. If the agent carries out the instruction by entering into a contract on behalf of the principal, the principal is bound to the contract.

How do you know if the agent's understanding of the principal's manifestations are reasonable? An agent's belief is reasonable if it reflects any meaning that the agent knows from the principal is to be ascribed or if it accords with the inferences that a reasonable person in the agent's position would draw in light of the context.

Actual authority may be express or implied. That is, actual authority encompasses both the authority to do what the principal explicitly instructs (i.e. express) as well as what a reasonable person in the agent's position would understand to be reasonably included (i.e. implied) in those instructions in order to accomplish the objective. Implied authority can be inferred from the words the principal used, from custom, or from the relations between the parties. It includes the notion that the agent can do incidental acts that are related to a transaction that is authorized.

Mill St. Church of Christ v. Hogan

785 S.W.2d 263 (Ky. Ct. App. 1990)

HOWARD, JUDGE.

Samuel Hogan filed a claim for workers' compensation benefits for an injury he received while painting the interior of the Mill Street Church of Christ on December 15, 1986. In 1986, the Elders of the Mill Street Church of Christ decided to hire church member, Bill Hogan, to paint the church building. The Elders decided that another church member, Gary Petty, would be hired to assist if any assistance was needed. In the past, the church had hired Bill Hogan for similar jobs, and he had been allowed to hire his brother, Sam Hogan, the respondent, as a helper. Sam Hogan had earlier been a member of the church but was no longer a member.

Dr. David Waggoner, an Elder of the church, soon contacted Bill Hogan, and he accepted the job and began work. Apparently Waggoner made no mention to Bill Hogan of hiring a helper at that time. Bill Hogan painted the church by himself until he reached the baptistry portion of the church. This was a very high, difficult portion of the church to paint, and he decided that he needed help. After Bill Hogan had reached this point in his work, he discussed the matter of a helper with Dr. Waggoner at his office. According to both Dr. Waggoner and Hogan, they discussed the possibility of hiring Gary Petty to help Hogan. None of the evidence indicates that Hogan was told that he had to hire Petty. In fact, Dr. Waggoner apparently told Hogan that Petty was difficult to reach. That was basically all the discussion that these two individuals had concerning hiring a helper. None of the other Elders discussed the matter with Bill Hogan.

On December 14, 1986, Bill Hogan approached his brother, Sam, about helping him complete the job. Bill Hogan told Sam the details of the job, including the pay, and Sam accepted the job. On December 15, 1986, Sam began working. A half hour after he began, he climbed the ladder to paint a ceiling corner, and a leg of the ladder broke. Sam fell to the floor and broke his left arm. The church Elders did not know that Bill Hogan had approached Sam Hogan to work as a helper until after the accident occurred.

After the accident, Bill Hogan reported the accident and resulting injury to Charles Payne, a church Elder and treasurer. Payne stated in a deposition that he told Bill Hogan that the church had insurance. At this time, Bill Hogan told Payne the total number of hours worked which included a half hour that Sam Hogan had worked prior to the accident. Payne issued Bill Hogan a check for all of these hours.

It is undisputed in this case that Mill Street Church of Christ is an insured employer under the Workers' Compensation Act. Sam Hogan filed a claim under the Workers' Compensation Act. As part of their argument, petitioners argue the Workers' Compensation Board erred in finding that Bill Hogan possessed implied authority as an agent to hire Sam Hogan. Petitioners contend there was neither implied nor apparent authority in the case at bar.

It is important to distinguish implied and apparent authority before proceeding further. Implied authority is actual authority circumstantially proven which the principal actually intended the agent to possess and includes such powers as are practically necessary to carry out the duties actually delegated. Apparent authority on the other hand is not actual authority but is the authority the agent is held out by the principal as possessing. It is a matter of appearances on which third parties come to rely.

Petitioners attack the Workers' Compensation Board's findings concerning implied authority. In examining whether implied authority exists, it is important to focus upon the agent's understanding of his authority. It must be determined whether the agent reasonably believes because of present or past conduct of the principal that the principal wishes him to act in a certain way or to have certain authority. The nature of the task or job may be another factor to consider. Implied authority may be necessary in order to implement the express authority. The existence of prior similar practices is one of the most important factors. Specific conduct by the principal in the past permitting the agent to exercise similar powers is crucial.

The person alleging agency and resulting authority has the burden of proving that it exists. Agency cannot be proven by a mere statement, but it can be established by circumstantial evidence including the acts and conduct of the parties such as the continuous course of conduct of the parties covering a number of successive transactions. Specifically one must look at what had gone on before to determine if the agent had certain authority. If considering past similar acts done in a similar manner, it is found that the present action was taken within the scope of the agent's authority, the act is binding upon the principal.

In considering the above factors in the case at bar, Bill Hogan had implied authority to hire Sam Hogan as his helper. First, in the past the church had allowed Bill Hogan to hire his brother or other persons whenever he needed assistance on a project. Even though the Board of Elders discussed a different arrangement this time, no mention of this discussion was ever made to Bill or Sam Hogan. In fact, the discussion between Bill Hogan and Church Elder Dr. Waggoner, indicated that Gary Petty would be difficult to reach and Bill Hogan could hire whomever he pleased. Further, Bill Hogan needed to hire an assistant to complete the job for which he had been hired. The interior of the church simply could not be painted by one person. Maintaining a safe and attractive place of worship clearly is part of the church's function, and one for which it would designate an agent to ensure that the building is properly painted and maintained.

Finally, in this case, Sam Hogan believed that Bill Hogan had the authority to hire him as had been the practice in the past. To now claim that Bill Hogan could not hire Sam Hogan as an assistant, especially when Bill Hogan had never been told this fact, would be very unfair to Sam Hogan. Sam Hogan relied on Bill Hogan's representation. The church treasurer in this case even paid Bill Hogan for the half hour of work that Sam Hogan had completed prior to the accident. Considering the above facts, we find that Sam Hogan was within the employment of the Mill Street Church of Christ at the time he was injured. The decision of the Workers' Compensation Board is affirmed. All concur.

---

2. Apparent Authority

Apparent authority arises, according to Restatement (Third) of Agency § 2.03, "when a third party reasonably believes the actor has authority to act on behalf of the principal and that belief is traceable to the principal's manifestations." Claims of apparent authority commonly arise when a third party seeks to bind a principal who created the impression that an agent had authority for a particular action when in fact he or she did not. It is a doctrine that protects the reasonable beliefs of third parties.

Apparent authority may be the basis for contract liability where an agent acts beyond the scope of their actual authority or even where there is not a true agency relationship. This is because the focus of apparent authority is on what a third party reasonably believes one person has authorized another to do. When we think about apparent authority, there might not be an "actual" principal arising from the principal-agent relationship; instead, there might only be an "apparent" principal, from the third party's perspective.

Thus, whereas *actual authority* depends on the *agent's* reasonable beliefs, *apparent authority* depends on the *third party's* reasonable beliefs. For apparent authority, it is critical to determine whether a principal or purported principal has made a manifestation that led a third party to reasonably believe that the agent or actor had authority to act on behalf of the principal or purported principal. A manifestation could be words or conduct, and for apparent authority it must be traceable to the principal, for example, through an intermediary or by the principal giving an agent a certain title or position.

Comment c to § 2.03 explains:

[Manifestations] include explicit statements that a principal makes directly to a third party, as well as statements made by others concerning an actor's authority that reach the third party and are traceable to the principal. For example, a principal may make a manifestation about an agent's authority by directing that the agent's name and affiliation with the principal be included in a listing of representatives that is provided to a third party. The principal may make a manifestation by directing an agent to make statements to third parties or directing or designating an agent to perform acts or conduct negotiations, placing an agent in a position within an organization, or placing the agent in charge of a transaction or situation.

The following case illustrates how apparent authority can bind a principal to contract liability. The case involved OSL, an ophthalmology medical practice, owned by Dr. William J. Andreoni, that entered into a contract with Paychex for payroll processing services. Paychex's office handled payroll services for about 7,000 clients based on the information provided by the clients. Paychex would ask each new client for a designated payroll contact who would provide Paychex with the relevant employee information including names, addresses, social security numbers and salary information so that it could process the client's payroll. Paychex provides reports on a regular basis to clients, including information about checks before they are paid to employees, and invoices indicating how many paychecks were issued per pay period because Paychex charges its clients per check processed.

For over ten years, OSL's office manager Carleen Connor was the designated payroll contact. For several of those years, Connor told Paychex to direct deposit into her bank account more money than she was supposed to receive—indeed, she was paid $233,159 more than her authorized salary during that time. Paychex sent to OSL reports confirming all payments made. These reports were sent to Connor's attention and OSL's owner, Dr. Andreoni, said that he saw none of these reports because they were not sent directly to his attention. When another employee took over Connor's duties, OSL discovered the unauthorized payments. OSL then tried to get out of the responsibility for the extra money that had been paid to Connor by filing a breach of contract action against Paychex. The district court issued summary judgment in favor of Paychex. OSL appealed.

Ophthalmic Surgeons, Ltd. v. Paychex, Inc.

632 F.3d 31 (1st Cir. 2011)

TORRUELLA, CIRCUIT JUDGE.

Although we have found that the contract creates no obligation for Paychex to verify the information that the payroll contact provides, we must now examine whether agency law creates such an obligation. OSL argues that the district court erred by ignoring a disputed issue of material fact regarding Connor's lack of apparent authority to "specify" the withdrawal of payments adding up to more than her authorized weekly salary. We find that OSL's argument is without merit.

A corporation must, by necessity, act through its agents. It is undisputed that Connor was in fact authorized to handle payroll and was the designated payroll contact assigned to communicate with Paychex. Connor's actual authority, however, did not extend to embezzling funds by authorizing the issuance of paychecks in amounts in excess of her salary as this is not what OSL, the principal, instructed her to do. The question remains, however, as to whether Connor was cloaked with apparent authority such that Paychex could have reasonably relied upon her authority to issue additional paychecks in her name. Restatement (Third) of Agency § 2.03 cmt. a ("Apparent authority may survive the termination of actual authority or of an agency relationship."). OSL argues that Connor had no apparent authority where OSL, as principal, did not act in a way that gave the appearance that Connor had the authority to order the paychecks at issue here and that Paychex is therefore liable for making the unauthorized payments.

We recognize that "[t]he mere creation of an agency for some purpose does not automatically invest the agent with 'apparent authority' to bind the principal without limitation." Under New York law, apparent authority can only be created through *"words or conduct of the principal*, communicated to a third party" such that a third party can reasonably rely on the "appearance and belief that the agent possesses authority to enter into a transaction."

We find that Paychex's reliance was reasonable and that Connor had apparent authority because OSL put Connor in a position where it appeared that she had the power to authorize additional paychecks. *Telenor Mobile Commc'ns AS v. Storm LLC*, 584 F.3d 396, 411 (2d Cir. 2009) ("Under New York law, an agent has apparent authority if 'a principal places [the] agent in a position where it appears that the agent has certain powers which he may or may not possess.'"). In her position as the designated payroll contact, Connor often called in more than one week's worth of payroll at a time without objection from OSL. Further, Dr. Andreoni admits that, after 1989, he had no further contact with Paychex. Even if we assume that, in 1989, the purported conversation between Dr. Andreoni, as agent of OSL, and a representative of Paychex occurred and that during that conversation, Dr. Andreoni informed Paychex that he wanted OSL employees to be paid weekly for fifty-two weeks each year, OSL's argument fails. This conversation does not expressly convey a limitation on Connor's authority, especially where the conversation did not occur in connection with the formation of the 1994 Agreement. Further, it was reasonable for Paychex to assume its clients' needs might change and that the payroll contact would be authorized to convey such a change.

Paychex's reliance was also reasonable because of OSL's failure to object to the transactions that Connor authorized.

> A principal's inaction creates apparent authority when it provides a basis for a third party reasonably to believe the principal intentionally acquiesces in the agent's representations or actions. . . . If the third party has observed prior interactions between the agent and the principal, the third party may reasonably believe that a subsequent act or representation by the agent is authorized because it conforms to the prior pattern observed by the third party. The belief is thus traceable to the principal's participation in the pattern and failure to inform the third party that no inferences about the agent's authority should be based upon it.

Restatement (Third) of Agency § 3.03 cmt. b (internal citation omitted). In *Minskoff v. American Express Travel Related Services. Co., Inc.*, 98 F.3d 703 (2d Cir. 1996), the Second Circuit found such inaction or omission sufficient to create apparent authority in an agent who was fraudulently using her employer's credit card.

We find the Second Circuit's reasoning in *Minskoff* persuasive. *Minskoff* involved an office assistant, Susan Schrader Blumenfeld, who was explicitly responsible for the personal and business affairs of a company's president and CEO. Her duties included screening her employer's mail, reviewing credit card statements, and forwarding these statements to the company's bookkeepers for payment. Less than a year after she began working for the company, Blumenfeld fraudulently requested that American Express issue an additional credit card in her name for the company's corporate account. After discovering the fraud over one year later, the company filed a suit to recover the money the company had paid in connection with the unauthorized charges and sought a declaration that it was not liable for the outstanding balances. The court held that, pursuant to the Truth in Lending Act, Blumenfeld acted without actual, implied, or apparent authority when she forged the credit card applications. However, the court held that there was apparent authority for Blumenfeld's subsequent use of the fraudulently obtained credit card where the company failed to examine credit card and bank statements documenting the fraudulent charges. *Id.* at 709–10 ("A cardholder's failure to examine credit card statements that would reveal fraudulent use of the card constitutes a negligent omission that creates apparent authority for charges that would otherwise be considered unauthorized under the [Truth in Lending Act].").

We find *Minskoff* directly applicable to these circumstances. Like the company in *Minskoff*, OSL failed to examine the payroll reports that Paychex sent. That these reports were sent to Connor's attention is not dispositive where OSL, as principal, did not convey any instructions to Paychex that it should do otherwise. Further, OSL's failure to object to the "extraordinary" transactions would reasonably convey to a third party that it acquiesced in its agent's acts. *Cf. id.* at 710 (noting that the company's omissions created a continuing impression that nothing was wrong with the accounts); *Bus. Integration Servs., Inc. v. AT & T Corp.*, 251 F.R.D. 121, 128 (S.D.N.Y. 2008) ("Applying the general principles of agency, we find that [the principal's] failure to respond in any way to the allegedly unauthorized disclosure [of its agent], . . . of which it obviously has been aware for a long time, justifies the 'reasonable assumption' [of assent]. . . . Silence may constitute a manifestation when . . . a reasonable person would express dissent to the inference that other persons will draw from silence.").

We find that by placing Connor in a position where it appeared that she had authority to order additional checks and by acquiescing to Connor's acts through its failure to examine the payroll reports, OSL created apparent authority in Connor such that Paychex reasonably relied on her authority to issue the additional paychecks.

Points for Discussion

1. Was OSL or Paychex in a better position to avoid paying Connor an extra $233,159? Does the apparent authority rule put the burden on the party better able to avoid the loss?

2. *Paychex* illustrates how a principal can be held liable on a contract with a third party on the basis of apparent authority even when the agent acted beyond the scope of actual authority. In a situation like this, what were the principal's options? Who did it have a claim against?

------

3. Undisclosed Principal Liability

Most of the time when a third party is dealing with an agent, the third party knows the identity of the principal on whose behalf the agent is acting. But sometimes situations arise in which a third party does not have notice that the person they are dealing with is an agent acting on behalf of someone else—we refer to the principal in this situation as "undisclosed." If the agent was acting within the scope of authority when dealing with the third party, the undisclosed principal can be held liable on the basis of actual authority. But even if the agent was not acting within the scope of actual authority, the undisclosed principal could still be held liable.

The Restatement acknowledges that there are only a "small universe of cases" applying the undisclosed principal doctrine and it previously used a vague broader category called "inherent authority" for these cases.

Among the few undisclosed principal cases, the best known remains an old English case, *Watteau v. Fenwick*, 1 Q.B. 346 (Queen's Bench 1893), which involved a beerhouse named the Victoria Hotel. The business was originally owned by Humble, who sold it to the defendants, Fenwick et al. After the sale

> **Restatement (Third) of Agency § 2.06**
>
> **Liability of Undisclosed Principal**
>
> (1) An undisclosed principal is subject to liability to a third party who is justifiably induced to make a detrimental change in position by an agent acting on the principal's behalf and without actual authority if the principal, having notice of the agent's conduct and that it might induce others to change their positions, did not take reasonable steps to notify them of the facts.
>
> (2) An undisclosed principal may not rely on instructions given an agent that qualify or reduce the agent's authority to less than the authority a third party would reasonably believe the agent to have under the same circumstances if the principal had been disclosed.

of the business, Humble stayed on as manager, the license remained in his name, and his name was still painted over the door. Fenwick told Humble that he had no authority to buy any goods for the business except bottled ales and minerals; all other goods would be supplied by Fenwick. Despite this limitation of authority, Humble had bought for the business other items such as cigars and bovril (a popular wintertime drink) from a third party supplier, Watteau.

At the time of entering into these transactions, Watteau did not know that Humble was an agent. Thus, Watteau could not invoke the doctrine of apparent authority, since he did not even know of the existence of the principal. But when Watteau later learned of Fenwick, the court allowed Watteau to hold Fenwick to the contract, noting, "otherwise, in every case of undisclosed principal, or at least in every case where the fact of there being a principal was undisclosed, the secret limitation of authority would prevail and defeat the action of the person dealing with the agent and then discovering that he was an agent and had a principal." The court reasoned that if it did not uphold liability in these circumstances "very mischievous consequences would often result."

4. Ratification

Ratification is a doctrine that allows a person to retroactively bind herself to a contract entered into purportedly on her behalf, even though the agent or purported agent was not acting with authority at the time he entered into the contract. In the words of § 4.01 of the Restatement (Third) of Agency, it is "the affirmance of a prior act done by another, whereby the act is given effect as if done by an agent acting with actual authority." The effect of ratification is to validate the contract as if the principal or purported principal had originally authorized it. Upon ratification, the agent or purported agent is relieved of liability for breach of her duty to her principal. Both parties to the contract are bound following a valid ratification.

Ratification can be express or implied. Express ratification refers to when a person objectively manifests acceptance of the transaction, such as through oral or written statements. Implied ratification occurs when the person engages in conduct that justifies a reasonable assumption that the person consents to the transaction. For example, implied ratification commonly occurs when a principal accepts the benefits of an unauthorized transaction entered into purportedly on her behalf, such as by accepting payment.

There are a number of additional rules about ratification, captured in the Restatement (Third) of Agency §§ 4.02–4.07, including that valid ratification requires that the principal or purported principal is fully aware of all material facts involved in the transaction. Further, ratification is all or nothing—there is no partial ratification or cherry picking parts of an act or contract that a principal wants to ratify. Ratification operates through equitable principles so the ratification is ineffective if it would be inequitable to the third party as a result of a material change in circumstances or if a third party has already manifested an intention to withdraw from the transaction.

5. Estoppel

Estoppel is an equitable doctrine. In the context of agency, the idea is that the principal or purported principal is "estopped" from disclaiming contractual liability. Estoppel does not create a binding contract between the parties, it is simply a doctrine that can prevent a principal or purported principal from avoiding an obligation by arguing that no authority existed at the time the agent or actor entered into a contract.

The estoppel doctrine can apply regardless of whether an agency relationship actually existed—it is typically raised where a purported agent did not have actual or apparent authority, but the plaintiff asks the court to hold the defendant liable due to some fault.

Notice that estoppel is similar to apparent authority in that both apply where a principal or purported principal leads a third party to believe that an agent or actor is authorized to act on the principal's behalf, even though no actual authority exists. However, there are two ways in which estoppel is different from apparent authority. First, estoppel requires a showing that the third party detrimentally changed position in reliance on the principal or purported principal, whereas apparent authority does not require a showing of detrimental reliance. Second, estoppel is a one-way street: it allows the third party to hold the principal liable, but does not give the principal any rights against the third party (unless the principal were to ratify the transaction). The remedy is generally for damages rather than making the defendant a party to the contract.

> **Restatement (Third) of Agency § 2.05**
>
> **Estoppel to Deny Existence of Agency Relationship**
>
> A person who has not made a manifestation that an actor has authority as an agent and who is not otherwise liable as a party to a transaction purportedly done by the actor on that person's account is subject to liability to a third party who justifiably is induced to make a detrimental change in position because the transaction is believed to be on the person's account, if
>
> (1) the person intentionally or carelessly caused such belief, or
>
> (2) having notice of such belief and that it might induce others to change their positions, the person did not take reasonable steps to notify them of the facts.

D. Contract Liability: Agents

We started by studying the five different bases by which a principal (or purported principal) may be bound to contract liability. But what about *the agent's* liability?

The answer depends on whether the agent has entered into the contractual obligation with the third party on behalf of a disclosed, unidentified, or undisclosed principal.

When an agent acting with actual or apparent authority makes a contract on behalf of a disclosed principal, it is only the principal and the third party who are parties to the contract. The agent is not a party to the contract unless the agent and third party agree otherwise. This rule conforms to common sense—the third party knows that the agent is acting on behalf of a principal and the third party knows who that principal is, and so the third party's expectation is that she is contracting with that principal and not the agent. When you go to a store and make a purchase, you understand your transaction is between you and the store owner and not the clerk who might have assisted you.

When an agent acting with actual or apparent authority makes a contract on behalf of an unidentified principal, all three—the principal, agent, and third party—are all parties to the contract unless the agent and the third party agree otherwise regarding the agent's liability. A principal is "unidentified" if, when an agent and a third party interact, the third party has notice that the agent is acting for a principal but does not have notice of the principal's identity.

Similarly, when an agent acting with actual authority makes a contract on behalf of an undisclosed principal, the agent and third party are parties to the contract; and unless excluded, the principal is also a party to the contract.

The lesson for the agent is clear: if the agent does not want to be liable on the contract, then she must disclose that she is acting on behalf of a principal and provide the identity of that principal.

E. Tort Liability

As you probably learned in your Torts class, a person is liable for a tort that he or she commits. When can a *principal* also be held liable in tort? That is what agency law adds to the equation.

There are a few instances in which a third party can hold a principal directly liable. Most notably, a principal can be held directly liable when an agent acts with actual authority to commit a tort or when the principal ratifies the agent's conduct. In addition, the law has established special circumstances for direct liability such as if the activity engaged in by the agent is "inherently dangerous"—demolition, blasting, or any activity which is likely to cause harm or damage unless precautions are taken.

FYI

If the third party succeeds in holding the principal vicariously liable for the agent's tort, the principal is usually separately entitled to indemnification from the agent. As a practical matter, however, the principal may have deeper pockets than the agent and may not be able to actually obtain the indemnification.

More commonly, third parties attempt to hold a principal liable for the tort of an agent through the doctrine of vicarious liability. The Restatement (Third) of Agency § 7.07 explains that vicarious liability (also known as "respondeat superior") requires a showing that the agent was an "employee" who committed a tort while acting "within the scope of employment."

1. Employee Status

Agency law distinguishes between types of agents—some are "employees" and some are "independent contractors" (also referred to as "non-employee agents"). The Restatement (Third) of Agency § 7.07(3) provides that an agent is an "employee" for purposes of vicarious liability if the principal controls or has the right to control the manner and means by which the agent performs his or her duties. Both the right to exercise control and the actual exercise of control are typically evaluated.

There are at least a couple of main policy justifications for distinguishing between the two types of agents and holding the principal vicariously liable for the torts of agents over which it holds a higher level of control. One is that where a principal gets the benefits of control of an agent, the principal should also have the corresponding obligation of liability for the agent's actions. This rationale is rooted in a fairness principle that holds accountable the person or enterprise that stands to benefit from the risk-creating activities rather than the innocent injured plaintiff.

The other main policy rationale is economic—the concept often referred to as placing the loss on the "lowest cost avoider." The party with control over the agent is in the best position to prevent the agent from engaging in careless or improper conduct and has the greatest incentive to take cost-effective precautions or get insurance. Creating a legal rule that holds the principal liable encourages efficient precautions to be taken and spreads the risk. The employer can anticipate the risks inherent in the enterprise, spread the risk through insurance, take into account the cost of insurance in setting the price for its goods and services, and spread the risk among those who benefit from the goods and services. By definition, the principal does not supervise the details of the independent contractor's work and therefore is not in as good a position to monitor the work and prevent negligent performance.

2. Scope of Employment

A principal's vicarious liability only results if the employee's tort occurred within the scope of employment. The same rationales of fairness and economic policy apply to this second element.

What counts as "within the scope of employment"? This is a question that many courts have addressed, but not always consistently.

Courts have used two main approaches to determining whether a tort occurred within the scope of employment. The first is referred to as the "motive" or "purpose" test and it is reflected in the Restatement (Third) of Agency § 7.07(2), which provides:

> An employee acts within the scope of employment when performing work assigned by the employer or engaging in a course of conduct subject to the employer's control. An employee's act is not within the scope of employment when it occurs within an independent course of conduct not intended by the employee to serve any purpose of the employer.

An example would be when a bouncer in a bar is aggressive and commits a tort such as assault or battery while doing his or her job. Notice that "within the scope of employment" is not strictly limited to the employee's proper or authorized conduct. There is some wiggle room around the concept such that an employee might be taking an action incidental to that instructed by the employer and still be held to have acted within the scope of employment. This line is sometimes described as the difference between "frolic and detour." A "frolic" is when an employee substantially deviates from or abandons the scope of employment. By contrast, if an employee is still engaged in the scope of employment but strays slightly from the assignment, this is a mere "detour."

> **FYI**
>
> Can an employee's intentional tort be within the scope of employment? Yes. Although most vicarious liability cases involve torts of negligence, the intentional nature of the tort does not preclude vicarious liability. As a general matter, it is just less likely that an intentional tort would be held to have occurred within the scope of employment.

Some courts have criticized the purpose test and have instead used a "foreseeability" test, asking whether the employee's conduct should fairly have been foreseen from the nature of the employment or whether the risk of such conduct was typical or incidental to the employer's enterprise.

A famous case using this approach is *Ira S. Bushey & Sons, Inc. v. United States*, 398 F.2d 167 (2d Cir. 1968), a Second Circuit opinion written by Judge Friendly. The case involved a sailor who, after a night of drinking, came back to the ship where he was supposed to sleep and damaged the dock. The court held the employer, the United States government, liable for the damage to the dock owner. Although the court acknowledged that the sailor was not motivated by the purpose of serving his employer, the court held the conduct was nonetheless within the scope of employment because it was foreseeable activity: "[T]he proclivity of seamen to find solace for solitude by copious resort to the bottle while ashore has been noted in opinions too numerous to warrant citation." The court explained the underlying rationale, "that a business enterprise cannot justly disclaim responsibility for accidents which may fairly be said to be characteristic of its activities."

In contrast, the following case gives a colorful example of vicarious liability that uses an approach like that summarized by the Restatement (Third) of Agency. The plaintiff, Margaret Clover, sued the Snowbird Ski Resort for injuries she sustained from a ski accident in which one of the resort's employees collided with her. The employee, Chris Zulliger, worked as a chef at the Plaza Restaurant, which was located at the base of the resort. Zulliger was also instructed by his supervisor to make periodic trips to monitor the operations at the Mid-Gad, a restaurant halfway to the top of the mountain. Snowbird gave employees ski passes as part of their compensation and preferred that their employees know how to ski because it made it easier for them to get to and from work.

On the day of the accident, Zulliger was asked to inspect the operation of the Mid-Gad before starting work at the Plaza Restaurant at 3 p.m. Zulliger went skiing with another employee-friend and they stopped at the Mid-Gad in the middle of their first run. Zulliger and his employee-friend then skied four runs before heading down the mountain to begin work. On their final run, they took a route that was often taken by Snowbird employees to travel from the top of the mountain to the Plaza. About mid-way down the mountain, at a point above the Mid-Gad, Zulliger decided to take a jump off a crest. There was a sign instructing skiers to ski slowly at this point in the run. The ski patrol often instructed people at this location not to become airborne because of the steep drop off, which also impaired visibility of skiers below. Zulliger, however, ignored the sign and skied over the crest at a significant speed. When Zulliger went over the jump, he collided with Clover, who was injured.

Clover brought claims against Zulliger and Snowbird. Zulliger settled separately with Clover. On a motion for summary judgment, the trial judge dismissed Clover's claims against Snowbird on the basis that Zulliger was not acting within the scope of his employment at the time of the collision. Clover appealed.

Clover v. Snowbird Ski Resort

808 P.2d 1037 (Utah 1991)

Hall, Chief Justice.

Under the doctrine of respondeat superior, employers are held vicariously liable for the torts their employees commit when the employees are acting within the scope of their employment. Clover's respondeat superior claim was dismissed on the ground that as a matter of law, Zulliger's actions at the time of the accident were not within the scope of his employment. In a recent case, *Birkner v. Salt Lake County*, this court addressed the issue of what types of acts fall within the scope of employment. In *Birkner*, we stated that acts within the scope of employment are " 'those acts which are so closely connected with what the servant is employed to do, and so fairly and reasonably incidental to it, that they may be regarded as methods, even though quite improper ones, of carrying out the objectives of the employment.' " The question of whether an employee is acting within the scope of employment is a question of fact that must be submitted to a jury "whenever reasonable minds may differ as to whether the [employee] was at a certain time involved wholly or partly in the performance of his [employer's] business or within the scope of employment."

In *Birkner*, we observed that the Utah cases that have addressed the issue of whether an employee's actions, as a matter of law, are within or without the scope of employment have focused on three criteria. "First, an employee's conduct must be of the general kind the employee is employed to perform. . . . In other words, the employee must be about the employer's business and the duties assigned by the employer, as opposed to being wholly involved in a personal endeavor." Second, the employee's conduct must occur substantially within the hours and ordinary spatial boundaries of the employment. "Third, the employee's conduct must be motivated at least in part, by the purpose of serving the employer's interest."

In applying the *Birkner* criteria to the facts in the instant case, it is important to note that if Zulliger had returned to the Plaza Restaurant immediately after he inspected the operations at the Mid-Gad Restaurant, there would be ample evidence to support the conclusion that on his return trip Zulliger's actions were within the scope of his employment. There is evidence that it was part of Zulliger's job to monitor the operations at the Mid-Gad and that he was directed to monitor the operations on the day of the accident. There is also evidence that Snowbird intended Zulliger to use the ski lifts and the ski runs on his trips to the Mid-Gad. It is clear, therefore, that Zulliger's actions could be considered to "be of the general kind that the employee is employed to perform." It is also clear that there would be evidence that Zulliger's actions occurred within the hours and normal spatial boundaries of his employment. Zulliger was expected to monitor the operations at the Mid-Gad during the time the lifts were operating and when he was not working as a chef at the Plaza. Furthermore, throughout the trip he would have been on his employer's premises. Finally, it is clear that Zulliger's actions in monitoring the operations at the Mid-Gad, per his employer's instructions, could be considered "motivated, at least in part, by the purpose of serving the employer's interest."

The difficulty, of course, arises from the fact that Zulliger did not return to the Plaza after he finished inspecting the facilities at the Mid-Gad. Rather, he skied four more runs and rode the lift to the top of the mountain before he began his return to the base. Snowbird claims that this fact shows that Zulliger's primary purpose for skiing on the day of the accident was for his own pleasure and that therefore, as a matter of law, he was not acting within the scope of his employment.

There is ample evidence that there was a predominant business purpose for Zulliger's trip to the Mid-Gad. Therefore, this case is better analyzed under our decisions dealing with situations where an employee has taken a personal detour in the process of carrying out his duties.

Under the circumstances of the instant case, it is entirely possible for a jury to reasonably believe that at the time of the accident, Zulliger had resumed his employment and that Zulliger's deviation was not substantial enough to constitute a total abandonment of employment. First, a jury could reasonably believe that by beginning his return to the base of the mountain to begin his duties as a chef and to report concerning his observations at the Mid-Gad, Zulliger had resumed his employment. In past cases, in holding that the actions of an employee were within the scope of employment, we have relied on the fact that the employee had resumed the duties of employment prior to the time of the accident. This is an important factor because if the employee has resumed the duties of employment, the employee is then "about the employer's business" and the employee's actions will be "motivated, at least in part, by the purpose of serving the employer's interest." The fact that due to Zulliger's deviation, the accident occurred at a spot above the Mid-Gad does not disturb this analysis. In situations where accidents have occurred substantially within the normal spatial boundaries of employment, we have held that employees may be within the scope of employment if, after a personal detour, they return to their duties and an accident occurs.

Second, a jury could reasonably believe that Zulliger's actions in taking four ski runs and returning to the top of the mountain do not constitute a complete abandonment of employment. It is important to note that by taking these ski runs, Zulliger was not disregarding his employer's directions. In *Cannon v. Goodyear Tire & Rubber Co.*, wherein we held that the employee's actions were a substantial departure from the course of employment, we focused on the fact that the employee's actions were in direct conflict with the employer's directions and policy. In the instant case, far from directing its employees not to ski at the resort, Snowbird issued its employees season ski passes as part of their compensation.

These two factors, along with other circumstances—such as, throughout the day Zulliger was on Snowbird's property, there was no specific time set for inspecting the restaurant, and the act of skiing was the method used by Snowbird employees to travel among the different locations of the resort—constitute sufficient evidence for a jury to conclude that Zulliger, at the time of the accident, was acting within the scope of his employment. In light of the genuine issues of material fact in regard to each of Clover's claims, summary judgment was inappropriate. Reversed and remanded for further proceedings.

Points for Discussion

1. Why did the *Clover* court conclude that it would be possible for a jury to reasonably believe that at the time of the accident, Zulliger had resumed his employment and that Zulliger's deviation was not substantial enough to constitute a total abandonment of employment?

2. Is the foreseeability or purpose test a better test for determining activity "within the scope of employment"? Why?

F. Termination of the Agency Relationship

We have now studied formation of the agency relationship, the duties and obligations of the agent and principal to each other, and the liability in contract and tort of the principal and agent to third parties. What is left is to learn about how the agency relationship comes to an end.

Recall that agency is a relationship that requires mutual assent to exist. Consequently, either the principal or the agent can terminate the agency relationship at any time and for any reason by communicating to the other that the relationship is at an end. The terminology is "renunciation" by the agent and "revocation" by the principal. A renunciation or revocation is effective when the other party has notice of it. If the parties have a contractual relationship as well as agency it is possible that one of the parties could be in breach, but that does not impinge upon each party's unilateral power to terminate the agency relationship.

Take Note!

There is one other type of vicarious liability: apparent agency. This doctrine was developed by courts willing to extend the contract concept of apparent authority to the area of torts. The Restatement (Third) of Agency § 7.08 provides: "A principal is subject to vicarious liability for a tort committed by an agent in dealing or communicating with a third party on or purportedly on behalf of the principal when actions taken by the agent with apparent authority constitute the tort or enable the agent to conceal its commission." The comment to § 7.08 explains that apparent agency applies in situations in which an agent appears to deal or communicate on behalf of a principal and the agent's appearance of authority enables the agent to commit a tort or conceal its commission. Examples of such torts include defamation and fraudulent or negligent misrepresentations.

The Restatement (Third) of Agency §§ 3.06–3.10 also provides several other ways that an agency relationship can end, including by:

- Death of the agent or principal (when the agent or third party has notice)

- Loss of capacity of the principal (when the agent or third party has notice)

- The expiration of a specified term, if there was one, for the agency relationship

- The occurrence of circumstances on the basis of which the agent should reasonably conclude that the principal no longer would assent to the agent's taking action on the principal's behalf (i.e., accomplishment of a specified purpose of the agency relationship, facts constituting a supervening frustration in the agent's ability to accomplish the principal's objectives)

If the original manifestations of agency set no specific time or purpose, the agency continues until a reasonable time has passed. Determining whether the agency is at end would then require a reasonable, objective appraisal of the parties' conduct, which would be highly fact-specific.

What are the consequences of terminating the agency relationship? Under traditional common law principles, the agent's actual authority to bind the principal ends when the agency ends. The agent may compete with her former principal after the agency relationship is terminated, but some duties continue such as the duty to not disclose confidential or proprietary information learned during the agency relationship.

Because apparent authority arises because of the reasonable beliefs of a third party, the termination of actual authority does not by itself end any apparent authority held by an agent. Section 3.11 provides: "Apparent authority ends when it is no longer reasonable for the third party with whom an agent deals to believe that the agent continues to act with actual authority." Thus to avoid lingering apparent authority, the principal may need to give notice of the termination to third parties.

CHAPTER 3

Partnership Basics

The partnership is one the oldest forms of business organization. It is "an association of two or more persons to carry on as co-owners a business for profit." Uniform Partnership Act (1997) § 202(a). Similar to agency, the formation of a general partnership requires no written agreement or governmental action. The association must be voluntary, but it does not need to be with the partners' knowledge or intent to form a partnership as such. It is known as a "residual form" of business organization, existing if some other form such as a corporation or LLC has not been formed.

A few key features of the general partnership are worth noting at the outset. Perhaps of greatest note, general partnerships do not have limited liability. That is, each partner is jointly and severally liable for the debts of the partnership—unlimited personal liability. Unless otherwise agreed, each partner has the ability to participate in the control and management of the partnership. Also, unless otherwise agreed, partners share profits equally (and allocate losses in the same proportion). As far as tax treatment, partnerships have "flow-through" taxation, which means that the partnership itself is not taxed on income and instead the profits or losses of the partnership flow through to the partners to include on their personal tax returns.

Partnerships are generally governed by state law. A majority of states have adopted a uniform partnership statute that is known as "RUPA"—short for the Revised Uniform Partnership Act (cited as Uniform Partnership Act (1997) and harmonized and renumbered in 2013). Several states continue to operate under the predecessor, Uniform Partnership Act (1914), also known as "UPA." The codified versions of RUPA or UPA (together with state case law) are understood as the "default rules" of partnership law because they are the rules that typically apply if the partners have not agreed otherwise. Unless otherwise noted, we refer to the 1997 version of RUPA here.

RUPA § 103 sets forth a list of the relatively few rights and duties that are nonwaivable, or in other words, cannot be contracted around by the partners. The partnership agreement may not, for example, unreasonably restrict a partner's right of access to partnership books and records, eliminate the duty of care or loyalty, or restrict the rights of third parties. With few mandatory rules, partnership is a highly flexible form of business organization. We will study the basic rules for general partnerships and then the variety of limited liability forms of partnership that have developed in the law.

A. Partnership Formation

Because certain legal consequences follow from the partnership relationship, such as fiduciary duties owed between the partners and the personal liability of partners for the partnership debts to third parties, many cases have involved a determination of whether a particular relationship constitutes a partnership or something else (e.g., borrower-lender, employer-employee). The starting point of analysis is the statute, section 202 below, and then courts have reasoned based on

---

Uniform Partnership Act (1997)
§ 202. Formation of Partnership

(a) Except as otherwise provided in subsection (b), the association of two or more persons to carry on as co-owners a business for profit forms a partnership, whether or not the persons intend to form a partnership.

(b) An association formed under a statute other than this [Act], a predecessor statute, or a comparable statute of another jurisdiction is not a partnership under this [Act].

(c) In determining whether a partnership is formed, the following rules apply:

(1) Joint tenancy, tenancy in common, tenancy by the entireties, joint property, common property, or part ownership does not by itself establish a partnership, even if the co-owners share profits made by the use of the property.

(2) The sharing of gross returns does not by itself establish a partnership, even if the persons sharing them have a joint or common right or interest in property from which the returns are derived.

(3) A person who receives a share of the profits of a business is presumed to be a partner in the business, unless the profits were received in payment:

    (i)   of a debt by installments or otherwise;
    (ii) for services as an independent contractor or of wages or other compensation to an employee;
    (iii) of rent;
    (iv) of an annuity or other retirement or health benefit to a beneficiary, representative, or designee of a deceased or retired partner;
    (v) of interest or other charge on a loan, even if the amount of payment varies with the profits of the business, including a direct or indirect present or future ownership of the collateral, or rights to income, proceeds, or increase in value derived from the collateral; or
    (vi) for the sale of the goodwill of a business or other property by installments or otherwise.

whether the relationship has characteristics of a typical partnership, such as profit sharing, participation in management, and risk of loss.

The statute provides the definition of a partnership and establishes a presumption of partnership if there is profit sharing unless it is of a listed type that does not connote co-ownership of a business.

Now we turn to a classic case on the issue of partnership formation. It involved a story of friendship and financial disaster that put at risk the fortunes of the wealthy defendants who had helped out a friend by investing in his partnership. It all started in the spring of 1921 when the partnership of Knauth, Nachod, & Kuhne (K. N. & K.) found itself in serious financial difficulties after having engaged in unwise speculations. The partnership had securities, but of a quality too risky to be able to use as collateral to get a bank loan. One of the partners, John Hall, had friends who were anxious to help him—the defendants, William Peyton, George W. Perkins, Jr., and Edward W. Freeman.

Peyton, Perkins, and Freeman entered into an agreement in which they would loan to K. N. & K. $2.5 million worth of securities, which were to be returned to them on or before April 1923. During the loan period, the partnership could use these securities as collateral to secure business loans for the partnership up to $2 million. In order to protect the defendants against loss, K. N. & K. would meanwhile turn over to them a large number of speculative securities to hold. In compensation for this loan, the defendants were to receive 40% of the partnership profits until the return was made, but in any event not less than $100,000 and not more than $500,000. The defendants were also given an option to join the partnership if any of them expressed a desire to do so before June 1923. The court examined the other terms of the agreement in determining whether a partnership was formed. A great deal was at stake as other creditors to K. N. & K. later sued Peyton, Perkins, and Freeman, claiming they were partners of K. N. & K. who could be held personally responsible for the debts of the firm. No good deed goes unpunished!

Martin v. Peyton

158 N.E. 77 (N.Y. 1927)

ANDREWS, JUDGE.

Partnership results from contract, express or implied. If denied it may be proved by the production of some written instrument; by testimony as to some conversation; by circumstantial evidence. If nothing else appears the receipt by the defendant of a share of the profits of the business is enough.

Assuming some written contract between the parties the question may arise whether it creates a partnership. If it be complete; if it expresses in good faith the full understanding and obligation of the parties, then it is for the court to say whether a partnership exists. It may, however, be a mere sham intended to hide the real relationship. Then other results follow. In passing upon it, effect is to be given to each provision. Mere words will not blind us to realities. Statements that no partnership is intended are not conclusive. If as a whole a contract contemplates an association of two or more persons to carry on as co-owners a business for profit a partnership there is. On the other hand, if it be less than this no partnership exists. Passing on the contract as a whole, an arrangement for sharing profits is to be considered. It is to be given its due weight. But it is to be weighed in connection with all the rest. It is not decisive. It may be merely the method adopted to pay a debt or wages, as interest on a loan or for other reasons.

In the case before us the claim that the defendants became partners in the firm of Knauth, Nachod & Kuhne, doing business as bankers and brokers, depends upon the interpretation of certain instruments. We refer to circumstances surrounding their execution only so far as is necessary to make them intelligible. And we are to remember that although the intention of the parties to avoid liability as partners is clear, although in language precise and definite they deny any design to then join the firm of K. N. & K.; although they say their interests in profits should be construed merely as a measure of compensation for loans, not an interest in profits as such; although they provide that they shall not be liable for any losses or treated as partners, the question still remains whether in fact they agree to so associate themselves with the firm as to "carry on as co-owners a business for profit."

The answer depends upon an analysis of various provisions. As representing the lenders, Mr. Peyton and Mr. Freeman are called "trustees." The loaned securities when used as collateral are not to be mingled with other securities of K. N. & K., and the trustees at all times are to be kept informed of all transactions affecting them. To them shall be paid all dividends and income accruing therefrom. They may also substitute for any of the securities loaned securities of equal value. With their consent the firm may sell any of its securities held by the respondents, the proceeds to go, however, to the trustees. In other similar ways the trustees may deal with these same securities, but the securities loaned shall always be sufficient in value to permit of their hypothecation for $2,000,000. If they rise in price the excess may be withdrawn by the defendants. If they fall they shall make good the deficiency.

So far there is no hint that the transaction is not a loan of securities with a provision for compensation. Later a somewhat closer connection with the firm appears. Until the securities are returned the directing management of the firm is to be in the hands of John R. Hall, and his life is to be insured for $1,000,000, and the policies are to be assigned as further collateral security to the trustees. These requirements are not unnatural. Hall was the one known and trusted by the defendants. Their acquaintance with the other members of the firm was of the slightest. These others had brought an old and established business to the verge of bankruptcy. As the respondents knew, they also had engaged in unsafe speculation. The respondents were about to loan $2,500,000 of good securities. As collateral they were to receive others of problematical value. What they required seems but ordinary caution. Nor does it imply an association in the business.

The trustees are to be kept advised as to the conduct of the business and consulted as to important matters. They may inspect the firm books and are entitled to any information they think important. Finally they may veto any business they think highly speculative or injurious. Again we hold this but a proper precaution to safeguard the loan. The trustees may not initiate any transaction as a partner may do. They may not bind the firm by any action of their own. Under the circumstances the safety of the loan depended upon the business success of K. N. & K. This success was likely to be compromised by the inclination of its members to engage in speculation. No longer, if the respondents were to be protected, should it be allowed. The trustees, therefore, might prohibit it, and that their prohibition might be effective, information was to be furnished them. Not dissimilar agreements have been held proper to guard the interests of the lender.

As further security each member of K. N. & K. is to assign to the trustees their interest in the firm. No loan by the firm to any member is permitted and the amount each may draw is fixed. No other distribution of profits is to be made. So that realized profits may be calculated the existing capital is stated to be $700,000, and profits are to be realized as promptly as good business practice will permit. In case the trustees think this is not done, the question is left to them and to Mr. Hall, and if they differ then to an arbitrator. There is no obligation that the firm shall continue the business. It may dissolve at any time. Again we conclude there is nothing here not properly adapted to secure the interest of the respondents as lenders. If their compensation is dependent on a percentage of the profits still provision must be made to define what these profits shall be.

The "indenture" is substantially a mortgage of the collateral delivered by K. N. & K. to the trustees to secure the performance of the "agreement." It certainly does not strengthen the claim that the respondents were partners.

Finally we have the "option." It permits the respondents or any of them or their assignees or nominees to enter the firm at a later date if they desire to do so by buying 50 per cent or less of the interests therein of all or any of the members at a stated price. Or a corporation may, if the respondents and the members agree, be formed in place of the firm. Meanwhile, apparently with the design of protecting the firm business against improper or ill-judged action which might render the option valueless, each member of the firm is to place his resignation in the hands of Mr. Hall. If at any time he and the trustees agree that such resignation should be accepted, that member shall then retire, receiving the value of his interest calculated as of the date of such retirement.

This last provision is somewhat unusual, yet it is not enough in itself to show that on June 4, 1921, a present partnership was created nor taking these various papers as a whole do we reach such a result. It is quite true that even if one or two or three like provisions contained in such a contract do not require this conclusion, yet it is also true that when taken together a point may come where stipulations immaterial separately cover so wide a field that we should hold a partnership exists. As in other branches of the law a question of degree is often the determining factor. Here that point has not been reached. The judgment appealed from should be affirmed, with costs.

Take Note!

So far we have focused on the notion of true general partnerships, in which the issue is whether there is an "association of two or more persons to carry on as co-owners a business for profit." A doctrine also exists to protect creditors in situations where there is reliance on a purported partner. A claim of "partnership by estoppel" does not allege a real partnership existed, but instead that a person becomes subject to partnership liability if that person purported to be a partner or consented to being represented as such, and a third party relied on that representation in entering into the transaction. RUPA § 308.

B. Partnership Fiduciary Duties and Information Rights

Each partner owes fiduciary duties to the other partners and to the partnership itself. We have already seen in Chapter 1 the most famous case involving partnership fiduciary duties: *Meinhard v. Salmon*. Here, we examine how the modern RUPA approaches fiduciary duties as a statutory matter. Section 404 sets out the standards of conduct, providing that a partner owes to the partnership and the other partners the duties of care and loyalty.

The duty of care of a partner "is to refrain from engaging in grossly negligent or reckless conduct, willful or intentional misconduct, or a knowing violation of law."

The fiduciary duty of loyalty includes the duties: to account to the partnership for any property, profit, or benefit derived by the partner from using or appropriating partnership property; to refrain from dealing with the partnership on behalf of a person having an interest adverse to the partnership; and to refrain from competing with the partnership in the conduct of the partnership's business. All partners may authorize or ratify, after full disclosure of all material facts, a specific act or transaction by a partner that otherwise would violate the duty of loyalty. Thus, recalling *Meinhard v. Salmon* and applying RUPA, if Salmon had told his partner Meinhard all of the material facts about the lease opportunity and Meinhard had consented to Salmon taking it, then Salmon would not have breached his fiduciary duty of loyalty by taking the opportunity for himself.

Because partners owe fiduciary duties, generally participate in management, and are exposed to liability for partnership debts, it is important that they have access to information about the partnership. RUPA § 403 sets out the relevant rules. It requires a partnership to keep its books and records at its principal office. Further, it provides that the partnership shall furnish to each partner any information concerning the partnership's business and other circumstances which the partnership knows and is material to the proper exercise of the partner's rights and duties. Upon a partner's request, the partnership must also provide any other information except to the extent the request is unreasonable or otherwise improper under the circumstances.

C. Partnership Management

One of the distinctive characteristics of a general partnership is its default structure of decentralized management: each partner is an agent of the partnership for conducting the partnership's business. This means that unless the partnership agreement says otherwise, each partner has actual authority to bind the partnership in the ordinary course of business. RUPA § 301 provides this rule and also the rule that a partner has apparent authority that can bind the partnership to a contract in the ordinary course of the partnership business or business of the kind carried on by the partnership, unless the third party knew or had notice that the partner lacked actual authority. RUPA § 305 provides that a partnership is liable for a partner's tort when the partner was acting in the ordinary course of partnership business when the tort occurred or with authority of the partnership.

In addition to making each partner a managerial agent by default, partnership rules also provide each partner with equal voting rights in management. For example, imagine a three-person partnership of A, B, and C. A contributes 70% of the partnership capital, B contributes 20%, and C contributes 10%. By default, the amounts of capital contribution make no difference to their voting power in management—A, B, and C each have one equal vote.

What happens when the partners disagree about how to manage the partnership? RUPA § 401 provides: "A difference arising as to a matter in the ordinary course of business may be decided by a majority of the partners. An act outside the ordinary course of business of a partnership and an amendment to the partnership agreement may be undertaken only with the affirmative vote or consent of all of the partners." This is a default rule that can be altered by agreement, such as often happens in large law firms where it may be unworkable for decisions to be made by majority rule or unanimity. Large partnerships will often have executive committees with delegated authority because of the high costs of communication and negotiation between all partners, collective action problems, and the risk of hold-outs.

Notably, the default rules of management can lead to potential deadlock problems in partnerships with an even number of partners, especially those with just two partners. The following case applies the basic partnership management rules to a deadlock.

National Biscuit Company, Inc. v. Stroud

106 S.E.2d 692 (N.C. 1959)

PARKER, JUSTICE.

C. N. Stroud and Earl Freeman entered into a general partnership to sell groceries under the firm name of Stroud's Food Center. There is nothing in the agreed statement of facts to indicate or suggest that Freeman's power and authority as a general partner were in any way restricted or limited in respect to the ordinary and legitimate business of the partnership. Certainly, the purchase and sale of bread were ordinary and legitimate business of Stroud's Food Center during its continuance as a going concern.

Several months prior to February 1956 Stroud advised plaintiff that he personally would not be responsible for any additional bread sold by plaintiff to Stroud's Food Center. After such notice to plaintiff, it from 6 February 1956 to 25 February 1956, at the request of Freeman, sold and delivered bread in the amount of $171.04 to Stroud's Food Center.

The General Assembly of North Carolina in 1941 enacted a Uniform Partnership Act, which became effective 15 March 1941. G.S. § 59–39 is entitled "Partner Agent of Partnership as to Partnership Business," and subsection (1) reads: "Every partner is an agent of the partnership for the purpose of its business, and the act of every partner, including the execution in the partnership name of any instrument, for apparently carrying on in the usual way the business of the partnership of which he is a member binds the partnership, unless the partner so acting has in fact no authority to act for the partnership in the particular matter, and the person with whom he is dealing has knowledge of the fact that he has no such authority." G.S. § 59–39(4) states: "No act of a partner in contravention of a restriction on authority shall bind the partnership to persons having knowledge of the restriction." G.S. § 59–45 provides that "all partners are jointly and severally liable for the acts and obligations of the partnership."

G.S. § 59–48 is captioned "Rules Determining Rights and Duties of Partners." Subsection (e) thereof reads: "All partners have equal rights in the management and conduct of the partnership business." Subsection (h) hereof is as follows: "Any difference arising as to ordinary matters connected with the partnership business may be decided by a majority of the partners; but no act in contravention of any agreement between the partners may be done rightfully without the consent of all the partners."

Freeman as a general partner with Stroud, with no restrictions on his authority to act within the scope of the partnership business so far as the agreed statement of facts shows, had under the Uniform Partnership Act "equal rights in the management and conduct of the partnership business." Under G.S. § 59–48(h) Stroud, his co-partner, could not restrict the power and authority of Freeman to buy bread for the partnership as a going concern, for such a purchase was an "ordinary matter connected with the partnership business," for the purpose of its business and within its scope, because in the very nature of things Stroud was not, and could not be, a majority of the partners. Therefore, Freeman's purchases of bread from plaintiff for Stroud's Food Center as a going concern bound the partnership and his co-partner Stroud.

In *Crane on Partnership*, 2d Ed., p. 277, it is said: "In cases of an even division of the partners as to whether or not an act within the scope of the business should be done, of which disagreement a third person has knowledge, it seems that logically no restriction can be placed upon the power to act. The partnership being a going concern, activities within the scope of the business should not be limited, save by the expressed will of the majority deciding a disputed question; half of the members are not a majority." *Sladen, Fakes & Co. v. Lance*, 151 N.C. 492, 66 S.E. 449, is distinguishable. That was a case where the terms of the partnership imposed special restrictions on the power of the partner who made the contract.

At the close of business on 25 February 1956 Stroud and Freeman by agreement dissolved the partnership. By their dissolution agreement all of the partnership assets, including cash on hand, bank deposits and all accounts receivable, with a few exceptions, were assigned to Stroud, who bound himself by such written dissolution agreement to liquidate the firm's assets and discharge its liabilities. It would seem a fair inference from the agreed statement of facts that the partnership got the benefit of the bread sold and delivered by plaintiff to Stroud's Food Center, at Freeman's request, from 6 February 1956 to 25 February 1956. *See Blackstone Guano Co. v. Ball*, 201 N.C. 534, 160 S.E. 769. But whether it did or not, Freeman's acts, as stated above, bound the partnership and Stroud. The judgment of the court below is affirmed.

Points for Discussion

1.   Explain the court's basis for deciding in favor of National Biscuit.

2.   Why wasn't Stroud's notification to National Biscuit enough for him to restrict Freeman's ability to bind the partnership?

3.   What kinds of problems might arise in partnerships that have two partners with equal management rights? How might you have drafted the partnership agreement to avert or mitigate the problem that gave rise to the litigation in this case? In a "deadlock" situation where there is one partner "for" a proposed action and one partner "against," how do you know which partner wins?

———————————

D. Partnership Property, Liability, and Finances

Now that we have examined how a partnership is formed, the fiduciary duties of partners, and the basic rules of management, let's turn to the financial aspects of this form of business organization.

1. Property

Partnerships are businesses and businesses typically need money or other property in order to carry out their operations, and if things go well, then they are making profits. "Partnership property" refers to everything the partnership owns, including both capital and property that is subsequently acquired in partnership transactions and operations. Partnership "capital," by the way, is the property or money contributed by each partner for the partnership's business.

A partner has a certain financial interest as a co-owner of the business, but she does not directly own or control the property of the partnership. Under default rules, a partner may use or possess partnership property only on behalf of the partnership, not for her personal purposes.

Does a partner have any interest in the partnership that she can transfer? The answer is yes, but it is a limited economic right or asset. The partner's "transferable interest" is treated as "personal property" that can be transferred without dissociating the partner or dissolving the partnership and it is attachable by personal creditors of the partner. Transfer of the partner's transferable interest gives the transferee no rights of management of the partnership or access to partnership records. It merely entitles the transferee to receive distributions to which the transferring partner would otherwise be entitled (and a right to an accounting in a dissolution of the partnership). This is because, under RUPA § 401, a partner may not transfer her status as partner or unilaterally make someone else a partner without the unanimous consent of the other partners.

Regarding the point that the partner's transferable interest is attachable by creditors as it is personal property, RUPA § 504 provides that a judgment creditor of a partner or transferee may apply to a court for a "charging order" against the transferable interest for the unsatisfied amount of the judgment. A charging order is a lien on a judgment debtor's transferable interest. It requires the partnership to pay over to the person with the charging order any distribution that would otherwise be paid to the judgment debtor.

2. Liability

Under general partnership law, all partners are jointly and severally liable to outside creditors for the partnership's obligations. Creditors must first seek to recover from partnership assets before proceeding against an individual partner's assets, but the rule of joint and several liability ultimately means that partners have personal, unlimited liability for the entire amount of partnership liabilities. This is one of the major consequences of operating as a general partnership and one of the key reasons for choosing to operate instead as a limited liability entity such as an LLP, corporation, or LLC.

Although each partner is subject to joint and several liability from outside creditors, as between the partners, each partner is only responsible for his share of the partnership obligation. If one partner pays off a partnership obligation, he is entitled to indemnification from the partnership. If the partnership lacks the funds to indemnify the partner, the partners are required to contribute according to their loss shares.

3. Finances

How do the finances—that is, the accounting and profit-sharing—in a partnership work? Under RUPA (1997), each partner has an account that is credited (increased) with the amount equal to the value of the partner's contribution (the "capital" the partner puts in), plus her share of the profits. The account is debited (decreased) when there are distributions to the partner, as well as for her share of any losses and partnership liabilities. The account is a book-keeping tally that tracks each partner's financial position in the partnership.

Capital contributions are not required from partners. If a partner does make a contribution, it becomes partnership property, and she gets credit for the value of it in the partnership accounting. But, unless otherwise agreed, a partner generally has no right to be compensated for services rendered to the partnership.

By default under RUPA (1997), profit sharing is done on an equal basis and losses are allocated in the same proportion as profits. This default rule applies regardless of how much capital a partner has contributed or how much a partner has worked for the partnership. So, for example, if the partners did not make an agreement on this topic, then their sharing would be equal as to both profits and losses (i.e., if there were two partners, then 50/50 profits and losses). This default rule also means that if a partnership agreement established a profit-sharing percentage but neglected to specify an allocation for loss sharing, the loss sharing percentage would mirror the profit-sharing percentage. For example, if the partners agreed to share profits 60/40 but did not specify the loss allocation, then losses would also be shared 60/40.

Note that loss sharing agreements among partners do not affect the personal liability of each partner to third party creditors for the debts of the partnership. That is, partners in a general partnership remain jointly and severally liable for all of the partnership debts. But they can agree how to allocate losses among themselves.

When do partners get to take profits out of the partnership for their own personal use? RUPA is silent on when such distributions occur. A well-drafted partnership agreement will address this. If not, a comment to § 401 provides the following guidance: "Absent an agreement to the contrary . . . the interim distribution of profits [is] a matter arising in the ordinary course of business to be decided by majority vote of the partners."

E. Partnership Dissociation and Dissolution

Our last topic on the general partnership form is a challenging one. For a full picture of this topic, you can read Articles 6, 7, and 8 of RUPA. By way of overview, RUPA provides rules concerning two different concepts:

- *Partner dissociation* refers to a change in the relationship of the partners caused by any partner ceasing to be associated in the carrying on of the business. In other words, this happens when a partner leaves the partnership.

- *Partnership dissolution* is the first of three phases (dissolution, winding up, termination) by which a partnership can come to an end.

The UPA used to provide only for the concept of "dissolution," and thus when a partner left a partnership it was automatically deemed a dissolution. This made the general partnership form unstable since it would be dissolved anytime a partner died or left the partnership. RUPA establishes the new concept of "dissociation" to refer to when a partner leaves (voluntarily or involuntarily), and RUPA sets out default rules providing that a dissociation leads to dissolution in some but not all circumstances.

We will study both scenarios—dissociation with and without dissolution. These two scenarios lead to very different outcomes. When dissolution is triggered, unless it is rescinded, the partnership needs to begin winding up its affairs, pay off its debts, and settle the partners' accounts in accordance with RUPA § 807. After this process is completed, the partnership ends. By contrast, when there is a dissociation without triggering dissolution, then a partner leaves the partnership and the partnership continues to operate so long as there are still two or more partners. The dissociated partner is entitled to a buyout of his or her interest.

Take Note!

A partnership is either "term" or "at will." A "term" partnership refers to where the partners have agreed to carry on the partnership for a particular term of time or for the accomplishment of a particular undertaking. If the partners have not so agreed, the partnership is "at will."

In a term partnership, when a partner withdraws before the end of the term, that partner "wrongfully dissociates." The partner is still entitled to a buyout, but it is minus any damages from the wrongful dissociation and the partner does not have to be paid the buyout amount until the end of the term, unless she goes to court and proves it would not be an undue hardship for the partnership to pay it out earlier.

Under the 1997 version of RUPA, in an at-will partnership, any partner may dissociate and thereby trigger dissolution by simply giving notice to the partnership of his will to cease association with the partnership. At-will partnerships can be tenuous or unstable because any partner at any time can force dissolution, and this will lead to winding up the partnership business unless the dissolution is rescinded.

1. Dissociation Followed by Dissolution

If any of these circumstances listed in RUPA § 801 occur, then dissolution is triggered:

- In an at-will partnership, any partner who gives notice of his express will to withdraw;

- In a term partnership, if all agree to dissolve or if the term expires;

- In a term partnership if one partner dissociates wrongfully, dissolution occurs if, within 90 days after the dissociation, one-half of the remaining partners agree to wind up the partnership;

- Upon an event agreed to in the partnership agreement resulting in the dissolution and winding up of the partnership business;

- Upon an event that makes it unlawful for all or substantially all of the business of the partnership to be continued;

- Upon application by a partner to a court for an order of judicial dissolution on the grounds that the economic purpose of the partnership is likely to be unreasonably frustrated, another partner has engaged in conduct that makes it not reasonably practicable to carry on business with that partner, or it is otherwise not reasonably practicable to carry on the partnership business in conformity with the partnership agreement;

- Upon the passage of 90 consecutive days during which the partnership does not have at least two partners.

Remember these are default rules and it is possible for partners to agree otherwise. It is indeed common for partnership agreements to provide for buyout and continuation agreements to avoid dissolution in the circumstances listed above. RUPA also includes a provision that enables a partnership to rescind its dissolution.

2. Dissociation Without Dissolution

Not all circumstances in which a partner withdraws from a partnership leads to dissolution. If the event of dissociation is not listed in RUPA § 801, then the partner leaves the partnership and the partnership continues as the same entity. Some examples include when a partner dies, leaves a term partnership before the end of the term, or is expelled pursuant to a partnership agreement, judicial determination, or an unanimous vote of the other partners in certain circumstances.

The "buyout price" to which the dissociated partner is entitled is defined in § 701(b) as the amount distributable to the partner if, on the date of dissociation, the assets of the partnership were sold using the greater of either the "going concern" value or the "liquidation value" of the partnership. "Going concern" value refers to the value of the business as an operating entity. "Liquidation value" refers to the price one could get by selling all of the assets of the business. The value is therefore determined by imagining hypothetically that the partnership is being sold or liquidated—it is not actually, this is simply a default way of determining a valuation for the partner's buyout price. Interest accrues on the buyout price from the date of dissociation to the date of payment. If no agreement for the buyout has been reached by 120 days after a written demand for the payment, then the partnership must pay the default buyout amount.

If it was a "wrongful dissociation," however, then the damages for that action get taken out of that buyout amount and the payment may be deferred. A wrongful dissociation occurs when a partner leaves a term partnership in breach of a provision of the partnership agreement or before the end of the term or completion of the undertaking that was agreed upon.

F. Other Partnership Forms (LPs, LLPs, LLLPs)

A key characteristic of the general partnership is that the partners are subject to personal liability for the debts and obligations of the partnership. Other partnership forms have developed to provide a form of limited liability for some or all of the partners. Each of these partnership forms requires filing a certificate with the secretary of state in the jurisdiction chosen by the parties in order to accomplish formation (and if this is not done or not done correctly, the parties may have inadvertently formed a general partnership). To understand these other partnership forms, it is helpful to know about their history and typical uses, as well as their defining characteristics.

1. Limited Partnerships (LPs)

A limited partnership is a partnership composed of one or more general partners and one or more limited partners. You can think of the limited partners as silent partners who do not participate in the management of the business—they invest money in return for transferable interests in the partnership. Because the limited partners do not control how the business is run, the law provides that their liability is limited to the amount of their investment. As noted above, forming a limited partnership requires filing a certificate of limited partnership with the secretary of state in the jurisdiction chosen by the parties.

The defining characteristics are:

- Separation of ownership and management functions. Under statutory default norms, the limited partners are passive investors with essentially no day-to-day management power and no authority to act as agents for the business. General partners are the active managers, empowered to carry out the limited partnership's business. Because of their management role, only the general partners owe fiduciary duties of care and loyalty to the partnership.

- Limited liability. The limited partners are not personally liable for the obligations of the limited partnership. General partners are jointly and severally liable for the limited partnership's obligations.

The LP form of business organization developed in part as a matter of historical circumstance. Before the mid-nineteenth century, states required a special act of the legislature in order to get a charter for a corporation (and in turn, at least a measure of limited liability for shareholders). As a result, before the mid-nineteenth century corporate charters were often difficult or expensive to obtain. In 1822, New York became the first state to enact a limited partnership act, which served some of the same purposes as incorporation—allowing for a form of passive investment to be done in the business organization and to provide limited liability for that role. Put differently, the LP form was desirable because it helped solve the economic problem of how to finance a business that required significant capital from a large number of individuals. Giving management rights to a large number of partners could be unwieldy for running the business and investors worried about putting all of their personal assets at risk, as they would have to do as a general partner in a partnership. The LP solved the problem by allowing for one or a small group of general partners to manage the enterprise and for a large number of limited partners to invest without risking more than the amount invested.

The LP form spread across states and the Uniform Limited Partnership Act (ULPA) was first adopted in 1916. The Revised Uniform Limited Partnership Act (RULPA) was updated in 2001.

RULPA differs in some ways from RUPA, the uniform partnership act. For example, RULPA §§ 503 and 504 provide that absent a partnership agreement otherwise, profits and losses in a limited partnership are allocated and distributed in proportion to "the value . . . of contributions made by each partner and to the extent they have been received by the partnership and have not been returned."

A frequently litigated question regarding LPs, at least historically, was whether a limited partner had exercised control in the business, thereby subjecting herself to liability as a general partner (i.e., unlimited personal liability for partnership debts). Amendments to ULPA have liberalized the "control" rule, broadening the ability of limited partners to engage in voting oversight and some management of the business, thus narrowing the instances in which limited partners can be held personally liable.

Another development regarding LP law has been to allow the general partner to be a corporation. This allows the "general partner" to enjoy limited liability.

At this point, you might wonder why anyone would use the LP form anymore, since other forms like the corporation and LLC have become readily available. Indeed, the LP is used in somewhat limited settings in current times.

First, it is used in certain sophisticated business settings in which the parties want a customizable form for limited investments. A key example is in the venture capital setting in which a firm seeks to raise a large amount of money to invest in start-up companies, and the investment capital typically comes as investment opportunities arise. The LP form allows for making the investors' ownership interests "assessable," so that they can be made to forfeit their ownership interest if they do not contribute on demand to cover the need for additional investment capital.

Second, the LP form is sometimes used as an estate planning device. For example, parents might form a LP with the family business and serve as general partners. Over time, they might give portions of their limited partnership interests to their children. Because of the restrictions on transfer and management power that might come with those limited partnership interests, the value is often discounted and the parents can transfer family wealth to future generations while maintaining control of the business and reducing tax costs.

2. Limited Liability Partnerships (LLPs) and Limited Liability Limited Partnerships (LLLPs)

LLPs are general partnerships that have made an election to be treated as limited liability partnerships (LLPs) and file a form with the secretary of state. The effect is to shield the partners from personal liability for all partnership debts. Partners remain liable for their own actions as partners, but when they are part of a LLP they are shielded from being held personally liable for their partners' actions. For example, a partner in a law firm structured as a LLP remains liable for her own malpractice, and the partnership itself can be held liable for such malpractice, but the other partners cannot be held personally liable for any short-fall. The same liability shield is provided to general partners in a LP that elects to become a limited liability limited partnership (LLLP).

The partnership forms developed in the law before the limited liability company (LLC), which we will study in Chapter 8, Organizational Choices. LLPs and LLLPs are somewhat less commonly used now that the LLC form has become available, but some states have limitations on certain professional business firms (such as law firms and accounting firms) using the LLC form and so if they still want limited liability they turn to the LLP form.

Chapter 4

Corporation Basics

Corporations are the dominant structure through which joint business enterprise is conducted in the United States and throughout the world. Corporate law is central to economics and business. Most of you deal with numerous corporations every day, when you buy your morning coffee, fill your car with gas or electricity, withdraw money from the bank, or see a movie. For better or worse, you cannot avoid corporations. Corporations range from multinational, publicly-owned firms, such as ExxonMobil and Facebook, to local family-owned businesses.

Corporations also have a dramatic effect on society. They are important in economic and financial terms: they hire employees and provide investments for people to save for retirement. But they also are important in social and political terms: they affect the environment, contribute to charities, and influence government.

This chapter gives you an overview of several important topics we return to throughout this book. First, we describe some fundamental notions about corporations—what corporations are, the role of corporate shareholders, and the protections available to shareholders. Next we cover some basic vocabulary. For many of you, this course will be like learning a foreign language, so we offer definitions of relevant terms upfront. Finally, we apply some of this vocabulary by looking at one basic corporate fact pattern: the board's decision on the timing and location of the shareholders' annual meeting. This application illustrates an important and recurring concept: even when corporate law rules appear to be clear, their boundaries often are hazy and can depend on equitable principles, which shape corporate fiduciary law.

> **FYI**
>
> There are more than 13 million business firms registered in the 50 U.S. states. Of these, most are closely-held by private owners, and their shares do not trade on public stock markets. Only about 3,600 operating corporations have their shares traded on public stock markets like the New York Stock Exchange and NASDAQ.

A. Fundamental Aspects of the Corporation

There is no universally-agreed upon definition of a corporation. It is a legal entity that can own property, enter into contracts, sue—and be sued. It is a team of people, including suppliers of money and labor, who work together to earn a return on their investments. It is a web of contracts among investors, employees, customers, and community. It is an investment vehicle that can be used for good or for ill. In many ways, the corporation is a drama: over time, the corporate actors—shareholders, directors, officers, and other employees—work through the conflicts that arise from their different investments, incentives, and goals.

Public and private ordering. Corporations can be seen as an amalgam of statutory, judicial, and private rules. To create a corporation, one must file the articles or certificate of incorporation with a designated state office and pay required fees. The governing documents for corporations (the articles or certificate of incorporation and the bylaws) allocate rights and responsibilities among the shareholders and directors. Shareholders elect directors to a corporate board with authority to manage the business and affairs of the corporation, including by delegating responsibilities to the corporation's officers and employees.

Fundamental shareholder rights. The corporation's board of directors, not shareholders, makes or delegates most business decisions. This a basic principle of corporate law. Corporate law limits the role of shareholders to a handful of fundamental rights, which we label generally as the rights (1) to voice views on various issues, primarily by voting, (2) to litigate claims against the corporation and its directors, officers and controlling shareholders, (3) to exit the corporation, by selling shares. In shorthand, so they are easy for you to remember, we refer to these rights as the rights to vote, sue, and sell.

All of these rights can be limited in various ways, as we will see throughout this book. For example, some shareholders receive only limited voting rights. Corporations can specify the forum in which shareholders may sue the corporation and its directors and officers. And some shareholders face restrictions on their ability to sell shares without approval of the board of directors.

One central question of corporate law is how shareholders can maintain an appropriate amount of power, while ceding responsibility for most corporate decisions to directors and officers, sometimes referred to collectively as managers. Put another way, how can shareholders ensure that corporate managers will be accountable? Imagine that you own shares in a corporation, but you don't like how the managers are running the business. You might believe the directors have paid the officers too much money. Or perhaps you believe it is socially irresponsible for the corporation to be engaged in a particular activity. What can you do?

One strategy is simply to sell your shares. By selling, you exit the corporation, effectively severing your connection. Another strategy is to try to influence directors and officers by speaking out, submitting shareholder proposals to change their approach, attending the annual shareholders meeting, or even mounting a voting contest to replace the directors.

Which would you choose? Exit through selling is typically the cheaper option, particularly for investors who own a relatively small number of shares that are tradeable on public markets. For many shareholders, the cost of trying to influence directors and officers is greater than the potential benefit. In theory, shareholders can exert pressure or influence directors and officers by threatening to sell their shares, or by actually selling. However, if selling is the favored option, the most quality-conscious participants in the corporation are likely to exit first, leaving shareholders who are less able to help the corporation overcome its problems. Further, the stock price at which a shareholder sells will typically reflect the mismanagement or other problems that may be creating the shareholder's dissatisfaction.

Make the Connection

We have used the three fundamental shareholder rights to vote, sue, and sell as organizing principles for this book:

- Vote (Module VI—Corporate Governance, Chapters 16–18): Shareholders elect directors, vote on specified transactions and voice concerns at shareholder meetings
- Sue (Module VII—Fiduciary Duties, Chapters 19–24): Shareholders file litigation claiming the corporation's directors, officers, or controlling shareholders breached their duties
- Sell (Modules IX and X—Stock Trading and M&A, Chapters 27–32): Shareholders sell shares in the market or to an acquiror in a corporate takeover

Some shareholders and directors have recognized the limits of exit, and recent structural changes in markets have promoted the role of voice. Technological advances have made voice less costly. Increasingly, institutional investors such as mutual funds and pension funds hold shares in large blocks, and therefore would capture a larger portion of any gains to the corporation from the exercise of voice. Moreover, because many such institutional investors must maintain a diversified portfolio of investments in different companies, exit has become a less viable option and exercising voice is a more important avenue.

Finally, there is the possibility of shareholders bringing what is known as a derivative suit on behalf of the corporation against its directors in situations where the directors have harmed the corporation, such as by breaching their fiduciary duties of care or loyalty. As we will learn, the law has established obstacles to bringing these suits and a judicial presumption that directors exercise their business judgment properly. The law has also created ways for directors to be exculpated, indemnified, or insured for settlements and damages, such that directors rarely pay out of pocket. Accountability through litigation can be elusive except in egregious circumstances.

These concepts illustrate some of the central themes in this book. At their core, corporate law and policy are about the dramatic tensions among the participants in the corporation. The overarching legal question we will address is: how do law, markets, and contract enable each of these participants to protect themselves? And the overarching policy question we will address is: for whose benefit should the corporation be run?

B. Basic Corporate Vocabulary

1. The Corporation

A corporation is a legal entity. Like human beings, corporations can enter into contracts, commit torts, sue and be sued. They are creatures of state law, which permits the formation of corporations as separate legal entities. When lawyers think about or deal with a corporation, they often start by drawing a diagram. When you read cases that involve many corporations, you might find it useful to draw boxes, with each representing a corporation, particularly if there are complex relationships among them.

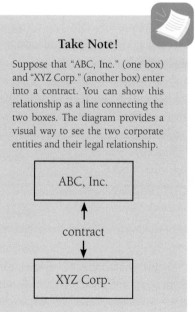

Take Note!

Suppose that "ABC, Inc." (one box) and "XYZ Corp." (another box) enter into a contract. You can show this relationship as a line connecting the two boxes. The diagram provides a visual way to see the two corporate entities and their legal relationship.

Corporate categories. There are numerous categories of corporations, and several important distinctions among types of corporations:

> *"For-profit" vs. "nonprofit."* Although the typical corporations we discuss in this book are "for-profit" corporations, many corporations are not-for-profit or "nonprofit" corporations. In general, a "for-profit" corporation is established to generate financial wealth which it can distribute to shareholders, whereas a "nonprofit" corporation may be established for a range of purposes and does not have shareholders. Charities, and most hospitals and private universities, are examples of nonprofit corporations.

"Public" vs. "close." Corporations whose shares are publicly traded on stock exchanges are known as "public" corporations, whereas corporations without publicly traded stock are called "close," "closely held," or "private" corporations. ExxonMobil is a publicly traded corporation, but many individual Exxon gas stations are franchisees, organized as close corporations with privately held stock.

This distinction between "public" and "close" corporations is particularly important. In a close corporation, there is no ready market for the corporation's securities and there is usually a substantial overlap among some or all of the participants in how they govern the corporation's business. For example, directors and officers of close corporations often have substantial ownership stakes, and shareholders of close corporations often are involved in management. In contrast, the shares of public corporations are freely traded: shareholders of public corporations typically can sell their shares easily on stock markets, and people without any relationship to the corporation can become shareholders by buying shares in the market. Shareholders of public corporations typically do not play a management role; although directors and officers of public corporations often own shares of their corporations, their ownership percentage typically is much smaller than the ownership stakes of owners of close corporations.

There is a curious ambiguity in corporate nomenclature. The terms "private" and "public" corporation mean different things in different contexts. Sometimes people refer to close corporations as "private" corporations since their shares are not traded on a public stock exchange. But sometimes people refer to "private" corporations as those that are *not owned* by the government. In this sense Bank of America is a "private" corporation since its shares (as of this writing) are not owned by the government, but instead by shareholders who acquired their shares on stock markets open to the public. In this sense, the Federal Deposit Insurance Corporation (a corporation owned by the government) is a "public" corporation since it is not "private." Got it?

In this book, when we refer to "public" corporations we are talking about non-governmental, for-profit corporations whose shares are traded on public stock markets. And when we refer to "private" corporations, we are referring to "close" or "closely held" corporations that are non-governmental, for-profit corporations whose shares are not traded on public stock markets.

Tax status. Although corporations are creatures of state law, the decision about what type of corporation to form often is driven by federal income tax treatment. Most public corporations also are known as "C Corporations," based on the subchapter of the Internal Revenue Code that applies to them. Many close corporations are formed as "S Corporations," based on a different

Internal Revenue Code subchapter. We will discuss basic income tax issues in Chapter 8, Organizational Choices.

Other statutory corporate forms. Most state statutes permit the formation of other types of corporations. For example, some states permit certain professionals to form "professional corporations," which have many of the attributes of normal corporations, though with ownership limits and sometimes special liability rules. In addition, entrepreneurs who seek to blend profits and social good can form a "benefit corporation," which requires that managers consider the impact of their decisions not only on shareholders, but also society and the environment. We will discuss the differences among corporations and other unincorporated forms of doing business, including partnerships and limited liability companies, in detail in Chapter 8, Organizational Choices.

Corporate characteristics. We will discuss various conceptions of the corporation in this book, but it is worth noting upfront that there are certain key characteristics of the basic business corporation. These characteristics illustrate not only the advantages of the corporate form, but also some of the reasons why tensions arise among the main actors in the corporate drama.

Separate entity. Every corporation is a legal entity that is separate from the investors who provide it with money and the people who manage its business. Investors who buy ownership interests in a corporation are known as shareholders or stockholders. The

Go Online

You can also see the essential structure of the corporation by looking at a corporate statute. Browsing the table of contents will tell you a lot. For example, here are the main topics of the Delaware General Corporation Law (DGCL), the country's leading state for incorporation of public corporations:

- (§§ 101–111) the incorporation process
- (§§ 121–124) the powers of the corporation
- (§§ 131–136) the corporation's registered agent and office for service of process
- (§§ 141–146) the powers of the corporation's board of directors and officers
- (§§ 151–169) the corporation's issuance of shares
- (§§ 170–174) the corporation's payment of profits to shareholders
- (§§ 201–203) the transfers of shares
- (§§ 211–233) the voting of shares at shareholder meetings
- (§§ 251–264) the merger or other combination of corporations
- (§§ 271–285) the sale of corporate assets and dissolution of the corporation
- (§§ 291–296) the treatment of insolvent corporations
- (§§ 341–356) the special rules that govern close corporations

Notice that the statute describes key events for corporations—how they are created, what they can do, how they make decisions, how they conduct their affairs, how they can merge, and how they are dissolved.

people who manage the corporation's business are known as directors and officers. The corporation is a separate legal entity from all of these people

Perpetual existence. As a general rule, corporations have an unlimited existence. The individual corporate actors inevitably will change over time. Shareholders sell their shares. Corporate directors come and go. Employees retire, quit, are fired, or die. But the corporation remains intact and can exist forever.

Limited liability. A corporation's shareholders cannot lose more money than they invested. In other words, a shareholder's liability is limited to the amount of money she paid for her shares. It is the corporation, not the shareholders, that owns the assets of the business and is liable for business debts.

Centralized management. Shareholders elect a corporation's directors, who have the power to manage and oversee the corporation's business. Shareholders agree to play only a limited governance role, in part because the directors have fiduciary duties to act in the best interests of the corporation. The directors typically delegate responsibility for daily decisions to corporate officers. The separation between shareholder ownership and managerial control is one of the distinctive features of modern public corporations.

Transferability of ownership interests. Shareholders can transfer to others their ownership interests in a corporation. In publicly-owned corporations, this is accomplished on stock exchanges and similar stock trading markets.

These are the basic characteristics of corporations, but there are many exceptions. Indeed, corporate law essentially is a set of enabling "default rules" setting forth the relationship among corporate actors unless they agree otherwise. Particularly for small firms, the law governing the participants in a corporation is largely contractual, and the parties can and do alter or amend many of the basic corporate terms. Large firms, in contrast, are increasingly governed by government regulation, which they often cannot avoid by contract.

2. Articles of Incorporation and Bylaws

Articles of incorporation. Just about anyone can create a corporation by filing "articles of incorporation" with the relevant state officials and paying the required (often modest) fees. Remember that corporations are creatures of state law. The people who form a corporation will file the articles in one particular state. The basic structure and most rules for the corporation will be set forth in that state's corporation statute and judicial interpretation.

The "articles of incorporation" are like the "constitution" of the corporation. Although the term "articles" is plural, the "articles" of incorporation are really just one legal document, with a number of provisions or articles. The document typically is brief, sometimes just one page, though in public corporations they can be much longer. The articles establish the corporation and contain basic provisions required by the state, such as the precise name of the corporation, its agent and address for service of process, and the number of authorized shares. The articles must be filed and accepted for filing by the relevant state officials, typically the Secretary of State, Corporations Division. The articles are sometimes called the "certificate of incorporation," depending on the state, or colloquially referred to as the "corporate charter."

Go Online

Besides browsing corporate statutes, you will find it useful to browse some typical articles and bylaws.

For corporations subject to disclosure requirements under the federal securities laws, these organic documents can often be found as attachments to disclosure documents filed with the Securities and Exchange Commission at https://www.sec.gov/edgar/searchedgar/companysearch.html.

In addition, most public corporations provide links to these documents on their websites—usually under "investor relations."

Bylaws. In addition to the articles of incorporation, a corporation's founders also will draft and adopt "bylaws." The bylaws, which are not filed with the state, set out the governing details of the corporation. Bylaws typically are lengthier than the articles of incorporation. Bylaws vary widely, but frequently include items such as: the powers of directors and officers, procedures for electing directors and filling director vacancies, required notice periods and details for calling and holding meetings of shareholders and directors, and similar internal governance issues.

Organic documents. The articles of incorporation and bylaws are sometimes referred to as the "organic documents" or "constitutive documents" of the corporation. They set out the essential information about the corporation and its internal governance, but most of the rules that govern the corporation are those of the applicable corporate statute and the judge-made law that fills the statutory gaps.

In this course, we will see numerous planning challenges and conflicts among the various corporate participants. In theory, the organic documents are supposed to work together to assist these participants in achieving their objectives. In practice, shareholders, directors, and officers can disagree about how these documents can or should be changed during the life of a corporation. In general, corporate law creates a simple and powerful legal hierarchy: the corporation's articles cannot conflict with the statute under which the corporation is organized, and the corporation's bylaws cannot conflict with the statute or the articles.

3. Corporate Actors

The corporation can be thought of as a drama, with several actors. Within the governance of the corporation, there are three categories of actors: shareholders, directors, and officers. There also are numerous categories of corporate stakeholders. Each of these actors can play an important role in corporate decision making.

Moreover, some individuals can play more than one of these roles simultaneously. For example, a person might be a shareholder, a director, and an officer. Corporate actors can wear more than one hat.

Shareholders. "Shareholders"—sometimes called "stockholders"—are often described as the "owners" of the corporation, but more precisely they are owners of stock. In the simplest case, shareholders contribute capital to the corporation in exchange for "common shares" of the corporation. These common shares represent a divided economic stake in the equity of the corporation. Although corporate law often seems to envision this simplest case, and some corporations raise capital exclusively through common shares, many corporations also use other forms to raise capital, including other corporate "securities," which are described below.

Take Note!

The relationships of corporate actors are also the subject of other courses in a typical law school curriculum. Here are a few:

Corporate Finance covers the corporation's capital structure, the valuation of corporate securities, and the issuance of corporate debt.

Debtor-Creditor Law and Bankruptcy cover the rights of creditors when a debtor, including a corporate debtor, is unwilling or unable to pay its debts.

Labor and Employment Law covers the rights of employees under the many laws (federal and state) that regulate the employment relationship.

Securities Regulation covers the federal registration and public disclosure regime and exemptions for private placements of securities.

Like participants in a representative democracy, shareholders do not control the corporation directly. Instead, shareholders generally play a mostly passive role and their voting rights are limited. Shareholders elect directors and must approve (after board initiation) certain fundamental transactions, such as amendments to the articles or a merger with another corporation. Shareholders also can amend the bylaws, although the extent to which shareholders can do so unilaterally, when the directors oppose the amendment, is controversial.

Directors. "Directors" are individuals who are elected by the shareholders to be responsible for managing or supervising the corporation's business. The directors act on behalf of the corporation only collectively as the "board" or "board of directors." Directors owe duties to act on behalf of the corporation, and directors are supposed to represent the interests of the corporation. Given the potentially competing interests among the various corporate actors, it can be difficult for directors to determine when a particular decision will be in the corporation's interests, as opposed to the narrow interest of one of the corporate actors. They must inform themselves and use their good faith business judgment.

Directors are not considered employees or agents of the corporation, although corporate employees can serve as directors. An "outside" director is a person who generally does not have any affiliation with the corporation, other than his or her role as a director. An "inside" director is a person who is both a director and a corporate employee—such as when the company's CEO (an employee) also serves as a director on the board. The question of whether a director is "disinterested" (not financially interested in a particular corporate decision) or "independent" (not beholden to an interested party) will recur throughout this course.

Practice Pointer

In practice, the roles of these three categories of corporate actors can be complex and overlapping, particularly in close corporations. When you consider a problem, or read a case, first consider whether the corporation at issue is public or close. In a public corporation, the roles of the parties often are cleanly divided, with shareholders playing a limited role in the business. In contrast, the shareholders of a close corporation typically are more active, and often wear several hats. The directors and officers of a close corporation frequently will be substantial shareholders. In a close corporation, personal and family relationships can matter more than title or position.

Officers. "Officers" are corporate employees. Corporate statutes and bylaws give broad discretion to directors to delegate responsibility to officers, and describe the duties of officers in only general terms. Typically, the board delegates the responsibility for running the corporation's day-to-day business to the Chief Executive Officer (CEO) and other officers such as the Chief Financial Officer (CFO) and Chief Operating Officer (COO). The board selects the most senior officers, and one of the important responsibilities of the board is the hiring, and potential firing, of the CEO.

Stakeholders. Other corporate actors are known as "stakeholders." They include creditors, employees, customers, and the community, people and institutions who are involved with and depend on the corporation but do not fit the legal categories of shareholders, directors, or officers. Creditors are people and entities that lend money to a corporation in exchange for the corporation's promise to make periodic interest payments and to return the principal of the loan after a specified time or maturity. Although corporate directors and officers generally owe fiduciary duties to the corporation and its shareholders, they typically do not owe such duties to creditors. Instead, creditors typically protect themselves by contract, including covenants in bond or loan documents that restrict certain corporate actions. Bankruptcy law also protects creditors. They are entitled to payment first, before shareholders.

Employees obviously have a stake in the corporation, too. However, their protections derive primarily from sources other than corporate law. Employees can be protected by employment contracts, common law, and regulatory statutes, which govern workplace safety, discrimination, and various labor issues. Likewise, suppliers and customers enter into contractual relationships with the corporation or are covered by common and statutory law.

Finally, the community can be an important corporate stakeholder, because it depends on the corporation to employ its citizens, pay taxes, and contribute to various cultural and community affairs. When a major corporation leaves a community, its departure can be a serious blow to the community's health or even survival.

Who does the corporation serve? One question that will resurface throughout this course, and in corporate law, is this: for whose benefit

Take Note!

It is useful to diagram the relationships in the corporation. The following schematic represents one way to do so:

Influenced by the law and economics movement, some scholars argue that shareholders occupy the role of "owners" or "principals." The board of directors acts as "agent" for the shareholders, with delegated power to manage and supervise the business and affairs of the corporation. The board selects the officers, who along with employees, represent the corporate "bureaucracy" and carry out the day-to-day business of the corporation. The stakeholders reside "outside" the corporation and have contractual, tort, regulatory, and social claims on the corporation. There are other ways of thinking about the corporation, which we explore in Chapter 6.

should the corporation be run? There are no easy answers to this question. Probably, each of you already has some notion of the kinds of roles you ideally would want the for-profit corporation to play in society. Should it be managed for the exclusive benefit of shareholders? Should it be managed for the benefit of society overall? Or is it possible to describe how the corporate objective might occupy some middle ground between these seemingly polar goals? We will return to this question at several points, especially in Chapter 6, Corporation in Society.

4. Corporate Securities

Corporations raise money by issuing shares or other securities to their investors. Securities used to be issued as hard copy certificates that the corporation gave to investors in exchange for cash. Today, there are no pieces of paper for most securities. Instead, ownership of securities is documented through computer records.

There are three basic categories of securities: common shares, preferred shares, and debt. These categories vary in terms of risk and expected return.

Debt securities. Debt is the least risky security and has the lowest expected return. A holder of debt typically expects to receive only fixed payments of interest over time. Even if the corporation does well, debt securities will receive only fixed payments—debtholders are creditors. If the corporation becomes insolvent, and its assets must be sold for cash (liquidated), debt securities will have priority.

Equity securities. Common shares take on greater risk, and also have greater expected return. Common shares have a claim to the residual financial rights to the corporation's income and assets. Once the corporation has paid everyone it owes, the common shares are entitled (at the discretion of the board of directors) to whatever is left. Common shares can receive payment through "dividends," which are cash payments the corporation can make, upon approval by the board. If the corporation becomes insolvent and cannot pay its debts, common shares—as the residual claim—are the last to receive any proceeds. This last-in-line position (sometimes referred to as being the "residual claimant") is often said to be the rationale for giving the common shareholders the right to vote in the corporation.

Take Note!

As securities become riskier, investors typically demand greater expected returns in exchange for their investment. Thus, while investors may be satisfied with 4.1% interest on short-term corporate debt, they may demand a 10.0% dividend rate on preferred shares of the same corporation, and 25.4% returns on common shares of the corporation. In fact, these are the expected returns as of 2009 on the securities of General Electric Co.

Increasing Risk and Increasing Expected Return

| Common shares |
| Preferred shares |
| Debt |

Preferred shares are "equity," like common shares, but preferred shares have certain priorities over the common stock. For example, preferred shares often carry the right to receive dividends before common shares receive a dividend. Likewise, preferred shares typically have priority over common shares if the corporation becomes insolvent. Thus, preferred shares typically have less risk than common shares, but more risk than debt. The exact "preferences" that the preferred stock is entitled to is a matter of contract.

Business Lingo

The term "stock" is often used interchangeably with the term "shares" to refer to ownership units of "equity" securities. Likewise, the terms "bonds," "debentures," and "notes" often are used to describe different classes of "debt" securities. Ultimately, the claims of securities are generally governed by their terms, not their labels.

Authorized, issued and outstanding shares. There are three terms to describe the three stages that shares can occupy. First is "authorized." The corporation's articles of incorporation specify how many shares of common and preferred stock the corporation is "authorized" to issue. Additional shares can be issued only if the articles are amended to increase the number of authorized shares.

Second is "issued." Of the corporation's authorized shares, the corporation might issue all, or just a portion, of those shares to its shareholders. Frequently, a corporation will not issue all of its authorized shares. One reason for this practice is that a corporation's board of directors generally is free to sell authorized but unissued shares on whatever terms it decides are reasonable—without shareholder approval. In contrast, if the board wants to raise capital by issuing more shares than the number of authorized shares, the corporation will need to amend its articles of incorporation, which requires shareholder approval.

Third is "outstanding." The portion of the authorized stock that has been sold and remains in the hands of stockholders is the stock "outstanding." Because the corporation can repurchase issued shares (which are called "treasury shares" and are held by the corporation, and this practice is referred to as "stock buybacks"), some of the issued shares might not be outstanding.

Example 4.1

The articles of XYZ, Inc. authorize 100 common shares. The board approves the issuance of 80 shares, which are sold to investors. At that point 80 shares are outstanding. The board can issue 20 more shares, but if it wants to issue more than that, the articles would have to be amended.

The corporation then repurchases 10 of the 80 shares that are issued and outstanding. This means that of the 100 shares authorized, there are now 70 shares outstanding. There are also 10 treasury shares (repurchased and unissued) and 20 authorized, but unissued shares—all of them capable of being issued.

5. Corporate Fiduciary Duties

Duties of care and loyalty. We have seen fiduciary duties in agency and partnership law, in Chapters 2 and 3, and we will also study the specific law on fiduciary duties in the corporate context in several chapters of this book. The relationships among the various corporate actors are governed in part by express legal rules and in part by fiduciary principles created mostly by the courts. The basic fiduciary duties that directors and officers owe to the corporation are the duty of care and the duty of loyalty.

The duty of care requires managers to be attentive and prudent in making decisions. The duty of loyalty requires managers to put the corporation's interests ahead of their own. The duties of care and loyalty are embodied in numerous statutes and cases, and arise in a wide range of contexts. For now, we simply want to highlight the general nature of these twin duties.

Business judgment rule. Notwithstanding these duties, a central thesis of corporate law is that courts defer to the board of directors, who have significant discretion in making corporate decisions, even when their well-meaning decisions result in failure. Courts have developed a rule of abstention or standard of review—known as the "business judgment rule" (BJR)—under which courts defer to the judgment of the board of directors absent a conflict of interest, bad faith, or gross inattention.

In general, the BJR presumes that director decisions (1) are informed, (2) made in good faith, and (3) in the honest belief that the action taken is in the best interests of the corporation. As a procedural matter, this judicial presumption is important. In order for a plaintiff to shift the burden to the directors (which typically means that the directors must establish that a decision was fair to the corporation), the plaintiff must show that a decision: (1) was grossly uninformed (2) did not have a rational business purpose (i.e., constituted waste), (3) was made by directors with a personal or financial interest in the decision, or (4) was made by directors who were not independent (i.e., were beholden to someone who had an interest in the decision).

We will cover the details of the BJR later in the course. For now, it is enough to recognize that the BJR plays a central role in the American system of corporate law. The BJR creates a presumption that, absent evidence of self dealing, illegality or the directors not being reasonably informed, all board decisions are intended to advance the interests of the corporation and its shareholders. Consequently, courts will not entertain shareholder suits that challenge the wisdom of such decisions. Structurally, the BJR implements the basic corporate attribute of centralized management by insulating the board's decision-making prerogatives from shareholder, and judicial, second guessing.

> **Example 4.2**
> <u>*Bayer v. Beran*, 49 N.Y.S.2d 2 (Sup. Ct. 1944)</u>
>
> The board of directors of Celanese Corporation approved a $1 million advertising budget to sponsor a radio variety show during World War II when the company was running at full capacity. The show hired, among other entertainers, the spouse of the company president as a singer.
>
> Issue #1: Was the ad expenditure exorbitant and thus a violation of the directors' duty of care? No, because the BJR protects rational business decisions, even if questionable.
>
> Issue #2: Was sponsorship of the show, which indirectly benefitted the company president, a conflict of interest that violated the directors' duty of loyalty? Different question. Here no, because the court scrutinized the transaction and determined the wife's singing and pay were "at market" and the result of a fair corporate decision-making process.

Liability to corporation and shareholders. Corporate managers who breach their fiduciary duties can be held liable for any losses they cause the corporation. Fashioning procedures to enforce managers' fiduciary duties raises difficult issues about who can enforce corporate interests. More often than not, the managers whose conduct is at issue control the corporate decision-making apparatus and are not likely to sue themselves. Moreover, shareholders are not authorized to act directly for the corporation, and thus cannot enforce a corporate claim against the managers.

The "derivative suit" was developed to solve this problem. The derivative suit is an action in equity brought by a shareholder on behalf of the corporation. The action is brought against the corporation as a nominal defendant, and the plaintiff-shareholder (and his lawyer) controls prosecution of the suit against other defendants such as directors and officers. Any recovery belongs to the corporation for whose benefit the suit has been brought.

In addition, shareholder plaintiffs (and their lawyers) also file federal, and less frequently state, class action lawsuits against corporations and their managers alleging various violations of law, in particular federal securities fraud. At any point in time, hundreds of public corporations face the threat of civil liability in both derivative and class action lawsuits brought by shareholders. However, most of these corporations have agreed to indemnify or insure their managers against liability in many instances, and nearly all the suits (even when meritorious) are settled without going to trial. As a result, it is rare for a non-interested director personally to pay money damages in a lawsuit brought by shareholders.

Duties of shareholders. Although directors owe fiduciary duties, shareholders generally do not. Of course, a person might be a shareholder and a director, and therefore owe duties because of her director role. But simply being a shareholder generally will not subject a shareholder to any fiduciary duties. There is, however, one major exception. If shareholders exercise control through their share ownership (as opposed to any other role they might play within the corporation), courts often will hold that such controlling shareholders owe fiduciary duties to other shareholders. This issue arises in corporate groups, where parent corporations have controlling interests in partially-owned subsidiary corporations and exercise their power to the disadvantage of other shareholders in the subsidiary. The issue also commonly arises in close corporations, where a shareholder has a substantial ownership stake and acts in a way that is oppressive to other shareholders.

6. Corporate Law vs. Other Areas of Law

Sources of corporate law. The legal rules governing the corporation's actors are an amalgam of state statutes, judicial decisions, and privately created default rules. State corporation statutes are not all-encompassing, and court decisions fill many of the gaps. In fact, a central aspect of corporate law—corporate fiduciary duties—is largely judge-made. Although each state's corporate case law is based on that state's corporate statute, many court decisions refer to corporate law principles that are generally accepted throughout the country.

Make the Connection

Unlike other areas of law where Restatements collect and synthesize judge-made rules, there is no restatement for U.S. corporate law. Instead, in 1994, the American Law Institute produced a set of statements and suggested rules on corporate law, the "ALI Principles of Corporate Governance: Analysis and Recommendations." These "ALI Principles" have been controversial and only somewhat influential. We will refer to them at various points, but bear in mind that they often differ from prevailing corporate law practices.

No two state statutes are identical, yet there has been a trend toward uniformity in many areas. Many states rely on the "model" corporate law rules in the Model Business Corporation Act (MBCA), which was drafted and continues to be revised by the Corporate Laws Committee of the Business Law Section of the American Bar Association. However, many state statutes—importantly, California and New York—differ from the MBCA in certain areas, either because the legislators have adopted different policies or because the MBCA has changed and states have not yet updated their statutes to reflect these revisions. We will point out many of these differences in various chapters.

We frequently will cite to the law of one state: Delaware. Delaware is the leading corporate law state. A majority of publicly-traded corporations, and many close corporations, are incorporated there. Delaware's corporate law statute, the Delaware General Corporation Law (DGCL) is unique and differs in many areas from the MBCA. Delaware's courts have provided significant guidance in interpreting the DGCL and in understanding corporate law more generally. Courts of other states often refer to court decisions from Delaware, whose case law is the most comprehensive and highly regarded among the states. This book contains many Delaware court decisions.

In your study of corporate law, you will find it invaluable to understand the text and meaning of these and other state corporate statutes. We will refer to various statutory provisions in this book and will quote from some of them. Links to these statutes are available in the online version of this book. The statutes are also available from numerous sources online (including through Westlaw).

Take Note!

Our citations to the Delaware corporate statute are linked to the state's online statutory code. *See* Delaware Code, Title 8, Chapter 1 (General Corporation Law). Our citations to the MBCA are linked to the 2016 revision, available from the American Bar Association.

Internal affairs doctrine. U.S. corporate law also is distinctive in its important choice of law rule, known as the "internal affairs doctrine," a topic we cover in detail in the next chapter on Corporate Federalism. The rule is this: in general, the law of the state of incorporation governs the "internal affairs" of the corporation. This rule means that the relationships between shareholders and managers (directors and officers) are governed by the corporate statutes and case law of the state where the corporation is incorporated. If a suit raising corporate law issues is brought in a state other than the state of incorporation, the incorporating state's rules apply and determine the outcome.

The internal affairs doctrine has significant implications for the operation and development of U.S. corporate law. For one, it means that corporate planners can be reasonably confident about the rules that apply to corporate decisions and actions. For another, states can compete for incorporations since the corporate participants choose where the corporation is incorporated or re-incorporated. Does this competition lead to corporate law that systematically favors management—a "race to the bottom"? Or does the competition lead to corporate law that reflects the optimal bargain between shareholders and managers—a "race to the top"? These questions also will resurface throughout the course.

Corporate planning. Corporate law differs from other courses in another important way. Whereas other courses focus on after-the-fact litigation and dispute
resolution, the study and practice of corporate law includes a major component of
before-the-fact planning. Business people, and their lawyers, typically spend more
of their time planning than litigating, or at least that is the way they hope to spend
their time. Lawyers who deal with corporations, even if they are not specialists in
corporate law, often are asked to play the role of planner or counselor. Although
much of the law school curriculum introduces students to these roles only casu-
ally, we want to expose you to these roles in a deeper way.

Remember that business people want to succeed. They want to make money
by investing or working (or both), and typically do not want to end up embroiled
in litigation if they can avoid it. The open-ended nature of corporate law, and
particularly corporate statutes, leaves lawyers the ability to help the parties choose
the state in which the business will be incorporated, as well as create the documents and "private law" that govern their relationships. Because corporate statutes
are essentially "enabling" statutes, they often leave private parties to arrange their
affairs as they would like. That is, many provisions are default rules that can
be contracted around in the corporate bylaws or other corporate documents.
Although law school emphasizes litigation, many lawyers—particularly corporate
lawyers—more frequently play the role of advisor than litigator. The materials in
this book emphasize the use of corporate law to plan transactions.

At first, you might find the role of planner somewhat uncomfortable. A real
client expects her lawyer to structure corporate transactions so as to maximize
benefits and minimize legal and business costs. These transactions must be
accomplished in a world fraught with uncertainty, often raising novel and difficult
legal questions. Just as often there will be scant statutory and case law directly on
point. The client, however, is interested in more than the arguments that can be
made on either side. She is paying high rates for the benefits of her lawyer's legal
expertise, experience, and, most of all, judgment.

In this book, we occasionally will ask you to recommend a course of action
to a client. Making such recommendations should help you develop the sound
judgment prized in business lawyers. You will also have the chance to be creative
by suggesting alternative approaches to surmount legal or business obstacles, and
achieve your client's objectives. Clients rarely want to hear "You can't do it." They
are paying their lawyers to figure out, within the constraints of ethics and law,
how to do something. The experienced, creative lawyer provides value by chart-
ing a lawful strategy that allows the client to accomplish her objectives.

C. Basic Corporate Law Question: Changing the Annual Meeting

This chapter introduces you to the basics of corporate law, so we will start by analyzing some Delaware statutory provisions (DGCL) and case law on a basic question: under what circumstances may the board change the timing or location of the annual shareholders' meeting? In assessing this basic question, we will refer to many of the basic vocabulary terms and concepts covered in the previous section of this chapter.

The annual meeting can be important, in part because it is the opportunity for shareholders to exercise one of their basic rights: the right to vote for election of directors. Although the directors generally manage the business of the corporation, if a shareholder is unhappy with the board's approach, and wants the corporation to change direction, the shareholder can attempt to persuade other shareholders to vote to elect new directors at the annual meeting.

Annual meetings frequently are routine: the incumbent board proposes a slate of directors for election, and the shareholders approve the slate. But when there is tension between a dissident shareholder and the board, the annual meeting can become a dramatic contest. If a shareholder has persuaded other shareholders to vote to replace the board, the directors might find it to their advantage to change the date of the annual meeting. Their reasons might be legitimate, or not. Directors might want to give shareholders an opportunity to consider carefully the best interests of the corporation. Alternatively, they might want to move the meeting forward or backward to an inconvenient date or location to make it more difficult for a dissident shareholder to mount a campaign against them.

As with other corporate law rules, the rules governing annual meetings are specified in various sources: statutes, case law, and corporate documents. The DGCL contains the following provisions regarding the corporation's annual meeting. Imagine that you are a lawyer advising a corporation's board. How does each of these provisions empower or limit the board's ability to change the timing or location of the annual meeting? Alternatively, imagine that you are a dissident shareholder challenging the board. What protections do the DGCL provisions give you?

DGCL § 211
Meetings of Stockholders.

(a)(1) Meetings of stockholders may be held at such place, either within or without this State as may be designated by or in the manner provided in the certificate of incorporation or bylaws, or if not so designated, as determined by the board of directors.

(b) Unless directors are elected by written consent in lieu of an annual meeting as permitted by this subsection, an annual meeting of stockholders shall be held for the election of directors on a date and at a time designated by or in the manner provided in the bylaws.

(c) . . . If there be a failure to hold the annual meeting . . . for a period of 13 months after . . . [the corporation's] last annual meeting . . ., the Court of Chancery may summarily order a meeting to be held upon the application of any stockholder or director.

DGCL § 222
Notice of Meetings and Adjourned Meetings.

(a) Whenever stockholders are required or permitted to take any action at a meeting, a written notice of the meeting shall be given which shall state the place, if any, date and hour of the meeting.

(b) Unless otherwise provided in this chapter, the written notice of any meeting shall be given not less than 10 nor more than 60 days before the date of the meeting to each stockholder entitled to vote at such meeting.

A fundamental issue that arises throughout this course is the tension between the text of corporate statutes and principles of fairness. Just as fiduciary duties serve as a backdrop rule governing the relationships of shareholders and managers, so too does the potential for judicial intervention serve as a backdrop principle of fairness. The issue often arises when one or more corporate law statutory provisions are in conflict, or when directors have interpreted a statutory provision in a way that shareholders believe is unfair. In some cases, the plaintiff shareholders have challenged the actions of managers by arguing that the directors were improperly motivated.

The two cases that follow are classic examples of how the Delaware courts have dealt with these kinds of conflicts. The specific language of the relevant statutory provisions differed somewhat for *Schnell*, which was decided several decades earlier than *Stahl*, but the essential substance of the statute was the same. In keeping with the "basics" theme of this chapter, these two cases also will give you an opportunity to become familiar with much of the vocabulary of corporations.

As you will see, the cases present complex fact patterns in battles for corporate control. The cases are important, not only for the substantive law they address, but also for the vocabulary and tactics that are the backdrop to the litigation. In both cases, imagine yourself advising the various parties in their battle for control.

The Delaware judiciary, at least in corporate law cases, is a model of efficiency. Cases are filed in the Court of Chancery, which has five chancellors, who sit alone and decide corporate law cases without a jury. Appeals from the Court of Chancery go directly to the Supreme Court of Delaware, which has five justices. Most decisions by the Court of Chancery are affirmed; most decisions by the Supreme Court are unanimous. Delaware regularly is voted by business people as one of the "most business friendly states" in the country.

Schnell v. Chris-Craft Industries, Inc.

285 A.2d 437 (Del. 1971)

[Plaintiffs, a group of Chris-Craft shareholders, were dissatisfied with the company's economic performance. They resolved to seek control by electing a new board of directors at Chris-Craft's next annual shareholders' meeting. On October 16, 1971, as required by federal law, they filed documents announcing their intentions with the Securities and Exchange Commission.

On October 18, Chris-Craft's board met and amended the corporation's bylaws, which had previously fixed January 11, 1972, as the date of the annual meeting. The new bylaws read as follows:

1. Annual Meeting. The annual meeting of stockholders of Chris-Craft Industries, Inc. shall be held for the election of the directors in the two month period commencing December 1 and ending on January 31 and at such time as shall be designated by the Board.

At this same October 18 meeting, the directors fixed December 8, 1971, at 9:30 a.m. as the date and time for the annual meeting, and named the Holiday Inn at Cortland, New York, where Chris-Craft operated a plant, as the place.

Cortland is a small town far from any transportation hubs. The board said it changed the meeting date because weather conditions made it difficult to get to Cortland in January and because holding the meeting well before Christmas would reduce problems with the mail. A notice with this information was mailed to shareholders on November 8, 1971, more than 60 days before January 11, 1972.

The trial court found that the defendants' actions, including the change in the date of the annual meeting, were designed to obstruct the plaintiffs' efforts to gain control. But the court declined to reschedule the meeting on its original date, holding that the plaintiffs had delayed too long in seeking judicial relief. On appeal, the Supreme Court reversed.]

HERRMANN, JUSTICE for the majority of the Court:

It will be seen that the Chancery Court considered all of the reasons stated by management as business reasons for changing the date of the meeting; but that those reasons were rejected by the Court below in making the following findings:

"I am satisfied, however, in a situation in which present management has disingenuously resisted the production of a list of its stockholders to plaintiffs or their confederates and has otherwise turned a deaf ear to plaintiffs' demands about a change in management designed to lift defendant from its present business doldrums, management has seized on Delaware Corporation Law for the purpose of cutting down on the amount of time which would otherwise have been available to plaintiffs and others for the waging of a proxy battle. Management thus enlarged the scope of its scheduled

Make the Connection

The case involves a "proxy contest" in which a group of shareholders dissatisfied with current management sought to replace the incumbent directors with their own slate of directors. The new board, they hoped, would steer the corporation in a new and more profitable direction. The insurgent group sought voting authority—or "proxies"—from other shareholders to vote their shares for the new board slate.

Proxy contests are rare. As we will see in Chapter 16, Shareholder Voting, the insurgent must bear the expenses of the contest (such as hiring lawyers, obtaining a shareholders' list to solicit proxies, and mailing disclosure documents to all shareholders) and can hope for reimbursement from the corporation for its election expenses only if successful.

More frequently, shareholders or other outsiders who think the corporation will be more profitable under new management will seek to buy sufficient shares to have a controlling interest—a takeover! We will see takeover fights throughout this book, including in the next case and particularly in Chapters 31 and 32, Antitakeover Devices and Deal Protection Devices.

October 18 directors' meeting to include the bylaw amendment in controversy after the stockholders committee had filed with the S.E.C. its intention to wage a proxy fight on October 16.

> "Thus plaintiffs reasonably contend that because of the tactics employed by management (which involve the hiring of two established proxy solicitors as well as a refusal to produce a list of its stockholders, coupled with its use of Delaware Corporation Law to limit the time for contest), they are given little chance, because of the exigencies of time, including that required to clear material at the S.E.C., to wage a successful proxy fight between now and December 8."

In our view, those conclusions amount to a finding that management has attempted to utilize the corporate machinery and the Delaware Law for the purpose of perpetuating itself in office; and, to that end, for the purpose of obstructing the legitimate efforts of dissident stockholders in the exercise of their rights to undertake a proxy contest against management. These are inequitable purposes, contrary to established principles of corporate democracy. The advancement by directors of the bylaw date of a stockholders' meeting, for such purposes, may not be permitted to stand.

When the bylaws of a corporation designate the date of the annual meeting of stockholders, it is to be expected that those who intend to contest the reelection of incumbent management will gear their campaign to the bylaw date. It is not to be expected that management will attempt to advance that date in order to obtain an inequitable advantage in the contest.

Management contends that it has complied strictly with the provisions of the new Delaware Corporation Law in changing the bylaw date. The answer to that contention, of course, is that inequitable action does not become permissible simply because it is legally possible.

Accordingly, the judgment below must be reversed and the cause remanded, with instructions to nullify the December 8 date as a meeting date for stockholders; to reinstate January 11, 1972 as the sole date of the next annual meeting of the stockholders of the corporation; and to take such other proceedings and action as may be consistent herewith regarding the stock record closing date and any other related matters.

Stahl v. Apple Bancorp, Inc.

579 A.2d 1115 (Del. Ch. 1990)

ALLEN, CHANCELLOR.

On March 28, 1990 Stanley Stahl, who is the holder of 30% of the outstanding common stock of Apple Bancorp, Inc. ("Bancorp"), announced a public tender offer for all of the remaining shares of Bancorp's stock. Mr. Stahl had earlier informed Bancorp's board of an intention to conduct a proxy contest for the election of directors to the company's board.

On April 10 Bancorp's board of directors elected to defer the company's annual meeting, which it had intended to call for mid-May, and announced it would explore the advisability of pursuing an extraordinary transaction, including the possible sale of the company. Mr. Stahl filed this action on April 12.

The complaint seeks an order requiring the directors of Bancorp to convene the annual meeting of the stockholders on or before June 16, 1990. The suit is not brought under Section 211 of the Delaware General Corporation Law which creates a right in shareholders to compel the holding of an annual meeting under certain circumstances. Rather, the theory of the complaint is that the directors of Bancorp had intended to convene an annual meeting in May or June—and had gone so far as to fix April 17 as the record date for the meeting—but dropped that plan when it appeared that a proxy contest by plaintiff was likely to succeed. This change in plans

William T. Allen was Chancellor of the Delaware Court of Chancery from 1985–1997, perhaps the most tumultuous period of U.S. corporate law. As the chief trial judge of Delaware, Allen authored some of the most far-reaching decisions in corporate law—many of them in this casebook—on such topics as the role of the board in defending against takeover bids, responding to voting insurgencies, and overseeing illegal corporate behavior. Many of his important decisions were not appealed, but became the law of Delaware by virtue of his judicial reputation. Symposia and conferences have been held to analyze (and celebrate) Allen's impact on corporate law. Today Allen is director of a law and business center at New York University.

What's That?

A "tender offer" is a publicized offer to purchase shares held by a corporation's shareholders—typically so the offeror can acquire a majority of voting shares. The offeror agrees to purchase the shares at a specified price and commits to leave the offer open for a specified period of time. The specified price usually is at a significant premium to the market price of the target corporation's shares—reflecting the value to the offeror of obtaining control.

The "record date" is a date fixed by the board of directors that identifies which shareholders will vote at an upcoming shareholders meeting. Thus, when the board in this case fixed April 17 as the record date, any person who held shares on that date would be entitled to vote them. If the shares were sold before the shareholders meeting, the buyer would have to make arrangements to get the seller's proxy to vote the shares.

is said, in the circumstances, to constitute inequitable conduct because it seeks to protect no legitimate interest of the corporation but is designed principally to entrench defendants in office.

Defendants are the members of the board of directors of Bancorp. They answer the complaint by saying that in not scheduling the 1990 annual meeting in the Spring of the year as has been the practice, they are behaving responsibly in the best interests of the corporation and its shareholders. They claim that their decision to delay the annual meeting was not a response to a proxy contest by plaintiff but was a response to the announcement of plaintiff's tender offer which they conclude is coercive and at an inadequate price.

Each director of the company is named as a defendant. Mr. McDougal is chairman of the board and chief executive officer of the company. Mr. Brown is the company's president and its chief operating officer. All other directors of the company appear to be outside directors.

Mr. Stahl, who is Bancorp's largest shareholder, began acquiring shares of Apple Bank in 1986. Gradually he increased his holdings through open market purchases and privately negotiated transactions. By November 7, 1989, he owned approximately 30.3% of the outstanding Bancorp shares. As Stahl's proportionate share of Bancorp stock rose above 20%, Bancorp's financial advisor, and a large stockholder, each expressed concern to Mr. McDougal that Stahl might obtain control of the company without paying a control premium.

Why does a bidder buy shares in the market before making a tender offer? Shares acquired in the market give the bidder some advantages. First, shares typically are cheaper on the market, compared to shares bought in a tender offer that usually reflects a control premium. Second, shares bought at market reduce the number of shares that must be acquired in the tender offer. Third, a bidder with a large shareholding is often more persuasive before a judge in seeking to strike down defensive barriers.

On November 15, 1989, the company's board of directors met to consider what action, if any, should be taken with respect to Stahl's stock accumulation. On November 22, 1989, Stahl delivered to the company a proposal to be submitted to a vote at the next annual meeting of stockholders, calling for an amendment to the company's bylaws increasing the number of directors of the company from 12 to 21. In the proposal Stahl nominated 13 individuals (including himself) to be named to the board if his bylaw proposal were approved.[3] He nominated four individuals to be elected if his bylaw proposal were defeated.

---

[3] Apple has a staggered board. Under the company's certificate of incorporation and bylaws, only 4 seats are open for election this year. Thus, in order for Stahl to gain majority control of the board, the bylaw proposal must be approved.

On March 19, 1990 the board fixed April 17, 1990 as the record date for determining the shareholders entitled to vote at the company's 1990 annual meeting. While no date for the annual meeting was fixed, it was anticipated that the meeting would be held in May 1990. Section 213 of the Delaware General Corporation Law provides that the record date for an annual meeting shall not be less than 10 or more than 60 days before the date the meeting is held. Thus, the latest date at which an annual meeting could be held with an April 17 record date would be June 16.

On March 28, 1990, Stahl commenced a tender offer to purchase any and all outstanding shares of common stock of the company at $38 cash per share.[4] The offer is conditioned upon the expansion of the company's board of directors to 21 members and the election of Stahl's 13 nominees to serve on the board. In his tender offer documents, Stahl reiterated his intent to solicit proxies in support of his proposal to expand the company's board and to elect his nominees as directors.

On April 9 and 10, the company's board of directors held a special meeting. The company's proxy solicitor informed the board that it was likely if the board did not present the stockholders with an economic alternative to Stahl's offer that Stahl would prevail in a proxy fight by a significant margin. The company received from its financial advisors a written opinion that Stahl's offer, which represented a 17% premium over the prior market price, was inadequate and unfair to the stockholders from a financial point of view. The financial advisors advised the board that greater value for the stockholders could be obtained through certain alternative strategies. They further advised the board that adequate exploration of those alternatives would require more time than was available before the meeting, if the record date stood at April 17.

The board resolved to recommend to Bancorp's stockholders that they reject Stahl's offer. It further resolved to withdraw the April 17 record date in order to allow itself more time to pursue alternatives to the Stahl offer. The directors decided that "it is not in the best interest of the company and its stockholders to hold the annual meeting until the company has had a fair opportunity to explore and pursue alternatives to the Stahl offer which would enable the company to maximize stockholder value." These alternatives included the sale of the company or the merger of the company with another financial institution.

On May 9 Mr. Stahl sent out proxy solicitation materials to Bancorp's stockholders even though no meeting was at that time scheduled. The pending motion was presented on May 14. Stahl asserts and it is not denied that defendants intended to hold Bancorp's 1990 annual meeting in May 1990. He claims that by requiring shareholders to submit matters to be voted upon at the annual meet-

---

[4] The closing market price of Bancorp stock on March 27, 1990 was $32 1/4 (per share). On May 8, 1990, the shares closed at $43 1/8.

ing by November 1989 (which the board interpreted Bancorp's bylaws to do) and by fixing an April 17 record date, the defendants have initiated the proxy contest process. It is argued that the withdrawal of the record date is essentially a postponement of Bancorp's 1990 annual meeting, and that the postponement was effected in order to avoid the defeat the incumbent directors anticipated that they would suffer if the election of directors were held in May. Stahl argues that the board's action constitutes an impermissible manipulation of the corporate machinery having the effect of disenfranchising the company's stockholders and entrenching the incumbent directors.

Defendants do not dispute that the board originally intended to hold the 1990 annual meeting in late May. They point out, however, that no meeting date had been set, and under neither 8 Del. C. § 211 nor Bancorp's bylaws, was one required until September of 1990. Thus, it is said, the board's withdrawal of the April 17 record date was not an action that impeded a shareholder vote. Defendants assert that the withdrawal of the April 17 record date did not render a shareholder vote ineffective, but simply delayed it.

It is an elementary proposition of corporation law that, where they exist, fiduciary duties constitute a network of responsibilities that overlay the exercise of even undoubted legal power. Thus it is well established, for example, that where corporate directors exercise their legal powers for an inequitable purpose their action may be rescinded or nullified by a court at the instance of an aggrieved shareholder. The leading Delaware case of *Schnell v. Chris-Craft Industries, Inc.* announced this principle and applied it in a setting in which directors advanced the date of an annual meeting in order to impede an announced proxy contest.

Under this test the court asks the question whether the directors' purpose is "inequitable." An inequitable purpose is not necessarily synonymous with a dishonest motive. Fiduciaries who are subjectively operating selflessly might be pursuing a purpose that a court will rule is inequitable.

Prior cases dealt with board action with a principal purpose of impeding the exercise of stockholder power through the vote. They could be read as approximating a per se rule that board action taken for the principal purpose of impeding the effective exercise of the stockholder franchise is inequitable and will be restrained or set aside in proper circumstances.

Action designed principally to interfere with the effectiveness of a vote inevitably involves a conflict between the board and a shareholder majority. Judicial review of such action involves a determination of the legal and equitable obligations of an agent towards his principal. This is not, in my opinion, a question that a court may leave to the agent finally to decide so long as he does so honestly and competently; that is, it may not be left to the agent's business judgment.

These statements are simply restatements of the principle applied in *Schnell*. The fundamental question when the motion is evaluated under these cases may be expressed as whether the defendants have exercised corporate power inequitably. In answering that question, it is necessary to ask, in the context of this case, whether they have taken action for the purpose of impairing or impeding the effective exercise of the corporate franchise and, if they have, whether the special circumstances are present (compelling justification) warranting such an unusual step.

In my opinion one employing this method of analysis need not inquire into the question of compelling justification in this instance, for I cannot conclude that defendants have taken action for the primary purpose of impairing or impeding the effective exercise of the corporate franchise.

For these purposes I do not rest my opinion on the ground that a board may always postpone a meeting for a substantial period on the eve of an annual meeting if it concludes that it will lose a proxy contest and thus decides to authorize a significant new development, such as the sale of the company.[8]

Rather, I place my opinion on the narrow ground that the action of deferring this company's annual meeting where no meeting date has yet been set and no proxies even solicited does not impair or impede the effective exercise of the franchise to any extent. To speak of the effective exercise of the franchise is to imply certain assumptions concerning the structure and mechanism that define the vote and govern its exercise. Shares are voted at meetings; meetings are generally called as fixed in bylaws. While the refusal to call a shareholder meeting when the board is not obligated to do so might under some imaginable circumstance breach a fiduciary duty, such a decision does not itself constitute an impairment of the exercise of the franchise that sparked the close judicial scrutiny of *Schnell*.

In no sense can the decision not to call a meeting be likened to kinds of board action found to have constituted inequitable conduct relating to the vote. In each of these franchise cases the effect of the board action-to advance (Schnell) or defer (Aprahamian) a meeting; to adopt a bylaw (Lerman); or to fill board vacancies (Blasius)—was practically to preclude effective stockholder action (Schnell, Blasius, Lerman) or to snatch victory from an insurgent slate on the eve of the noticed meeting (Aprahamian). Here the election process will go forward at a time consistent with the company's bylaws and with Section 211 of our corporation law. Defendant's decision does not preclude plaintiff or any other Bancorp share-

---

[8] *See Gintel v. Xtra Corp.*, Del. Ch., C.A. No. 11422, Allen, C. (February 27, 1990) (oral ruling) (board required to hold annual meeting close to the time set where, on the eve of the meeting, the board—upon receiving advice that it would lose the election—declared that the meeting would be postponed in order that it might find a buyer for and negotiate a sale of the company).

holder from effectively exercising his vote, nor have proxies been collected that only await imminent counting. Plaintiff has no legal right to compel the holding of the company's annual meeting under Section 211(c) of the Delaware General Corporation Law, nor does he, in my opinion, have a right in equity to require the board to call a meeting now.

This view may be criticized as placing undue emphasis on the formal act of fixing the date of the annual meeting. However, that is an act of some dignity and significance. Once fixed that date may be postponed at least in some circumstances. But, while postponement of a noticed meeting will in some circumstances constitute an inequitable manipulation, I can in no event see that the franchise process can be said to be sufficiently engaged before the fixing of this meeting date to give rise to that possibility.

As indicated above, inquiries concerning fiduciary duties are inherently particularized and contextual. It is probably not possible to work out rules that will be perfectly predictive of future cases involving claimed impediments to the shareholder vote. It is sufficient to express a reasoned judgment on the facts presented. This I have now tried to do. The application for a preliminary injunction will be denied.

Points for Discussion

1. Source of law.

There is no doubt that the bylaw change in *Schnell* was authorized by the applicable statute. Indeed, although the trial court's opinion, quoted by the Supreme Court, stated that "management has seized on a relatively new section of the Delaware Corporation Law," the change would also have complied with the old provision. What, then, is the law that the Supreme Court found defendants to have violated?

2. Reconcile these two cases.

Schnell and *Stahl*, though separated by two decades, presented the Delaware courts with a similar dispute related to setting the date of an annual meeting. In both cases, plaintiffs argued that the board's decision to change the meeting date, though it complied with the statute, should be enjoined because the transaction was improperly motivated. In *Schnell* the court sided with the insurgent shareholders; in *Stahl* the court sided with the incumbent board of directors. Can the cases be reconciled?

3. Relevance of pending insurgency.

Would the *Schnell* court have reached the same result had management changed the challenged bylaw before learning of the insurgents' plans? Conversely, would the *Stahl* court have reached the same result if the evidence showed the primary reason the directors delayed the annual meeting date was to thwart Stahl? In other words, is a detrimental effect on plaintiffs sufficient to justify judicial relief, or is an improper purpose during a pending insurgency required as well?

———————

Test Your Knowledge

To assess your understanding of the Chapter 1, 2, 3, and 4 material in this module, click here to take a quiz.

MODULE II – CORPORATIONS AND POLICY

CHAPTER 5

Corporate Federalism

This module includes three chapters meant to give you a sense of some of the fundamental policy issues involving the corporation. In this chapter, we identify where the corporation fits in our federal-state legal system. The next chapter considers the duality of the corporation as a private economic framework and as a social institution. The last chapter looks at how the corporation is viewed and regulated as a "political person."

One of the most important issues in corporate law, as in constitutional law, is federalism. Although there are federal statutes that govern a good deal of corporate activity, there is no federal corporation law (although some legislators have proposed that). Instead, corporations are largely creatures of state law, specifically the law of the state in which they are incorporated.

A corporation can be incorporated (or "chartered") in any state, even if it does not do business in that state. Moreover, it is relatively easy for a corporation to reincorporate in another state if the corporate law of the other state better serves its needs. Many people view the development of U.S. corporate law as a story about competition among the various states, with Delaware firmly established as the leading state of incorporation for public corporations.

> **Practice Pointer**
>
> Reincorporation usually happens by means of a merger where the corporation seeking a new corporate home forms a shell corporation in the "destination state." The corporation then merges into this shell and, in the process, disappears. The result is a new corporation with all the business, assets and liabilities of the original corporation, but now with a new state of incorporation. The merger requires the approval of the corporation's board of directors and its shareholders.

Of course, the federal government regulates corporations in many ways, under antitrust, banking, civil rights, environmental, labor and product safety laws. In addition, corporations whose securities are traded on public securities markets are subject to extensive disclosure obligations under federal securities laws, first passed in response to the

Stock Market Crash of 1929. Indeed, federal regulation of public corporations has increased in recent years, as Congress has reacted to corporate and financial scandals and the Financial Crisis of 2008 by federalizing many areas that traditionally were covered by state law.

This chapter looks at the role of federalism in corporate law. First, we give a brief history of corporate law in the United States, tracing state and federal law over time. Next, we turn to the "internal affairs" doctrine, a key concept in U.S. corporate law. This doctrine holds that the law of the state in which a business is incorporated governs the legal relationships of the corporation's shareholders and managers, even if that law conflicts with the law of a state where the business is headquartered or does substantial business. Then, we look at how the U.S. Supreme Court has viewed state law efforts to regulate corporate takeovers, transactions that occur on national stock trading markets. Finally, we conclude by addressing the policy implications of a market for state corporate charters.

A. Brief History of U.S. Corporate Law

To understand corporate federalism in the United States, it's helpful to understand the basic history of U.S. corporations. The attributes of corporations have evolved over time.

1. Early Antecedents

The concept of a corporation is not new. In ancient Rome, the government created business entities that had mixed private-state ownership. In the Middle Ages, governments in Continental Europe (particularly Italy) created corporations to undertake state functions, such as the monopoly to trade in a particular commodity.

In sixteenth-century England, ecclesiastical, municipal, and charitable corporations emerged as devices to hold property and to ensure continuity. In addition, borrowing from their Italian counterparts, English business corporations (known as joint stock companies) obtained concessions from the state and typically were granted monopoly rights in trade.

Joint stock companies, such as the East India Company, took on many of the characteristics of modern corporations. They were separate legal entities that took stock subscriptions from many investors, who then could transfer their interests in the enterprise to others. A joint stock company's trading business was ongoing and perpetual, and the investors' liability was limited to the cost of their stock.

Some English joint stock companies were not created by state concession, but instead obtained their corporate attributes through complex deeds of settlement that provided for transferability of shares, continuity of life, and central management. The incorporated and unincorporated joint stock companies were the forerunners of the U.S. business corporation.

During the early 1700s, England experienced a speculative boom in joint stock companies, stimulated by the scheme of the South Sea Company to acquire almost the entire English national debt by buying out existing debt holders, often with South Sea Company shares. In response, Parliament in 1720 enacted the "Bubble Act" (not very subtly subtitled "An Act to Restrain the Extravagant and Unwarranted Practice of Raising Money by Voluntary Subscriptions for Carrying on Projects Dangerous to the Trade and Subjects of this Kingdom"). But by prohibiting unincorporated companies with transferable shares, the Bubble Act actually protected the incorporated South Sea Company's access to investors' capital.

2. Early Development of U.S. Corporate Law

State chartering. In the American colonies, the Bubble Act prohibited the formation of unincorporated joint stock companies. Although duly chartered corporations were permitted, the colonists generally resisted such entities as instruments of royal prerogative and antithetical to economic equality. After independence, however, corporate chartering became more accepted. The earliest U.S. corporations were non-business entities such as charities, churches, and municipalities. Soon after, state legislatures granted charters by special acts to banks, insurance, and infrastructure companies building turnpikes and canals—businesses with large capital needs and often special monopoly privileges.

By 1800 there were about 335 incorporated businesses in the United States, all created by such acts. Corporate law and policy during this period was shaped primarily by legislative practice. A corporate charter was considered a valuable privilege, and the legislative monopoly conferring this privilege created obvious temptations, to which many legislators and entrepreneurs inevitably yielded—to their mutual profit.

The resulting corruption led the business community to argue that incorporation should be a right, not a privilege. For many businesses, incorporation had become a matter of economic necessity. As industrial and manufacturing concerns grew, individuals and partnerships no longer had enough capital to finance such enterprises. In response, states enacted general corporation laws that allowed any group of persons to organize a corporation by complying with prescribed statutory conditions. New York was the pioneer. In 1811, it permitted self-incorporation to the organizers of certain manufacturing companies, limiting their capital to $100,000 and their existence to 20 years.

Corporate personhood. From the beginning, a corporation was considered a "person" for many purposes. Although not a natural person, it had many legal attributes of a natural person that flowed from state law. A corporation could own property, enter into contracts, sue and be sued in its own name, and be held liable for its debts. In other words, a corporation was understood to be an artificial being that was given legal personality by a state's corporation statute.

In the early nineteenth century, the Supreme Court began to address questions concerning the treatment of corporations under the U.S. Constitution. One of the most notable early decisions involving the issue of corporate personhood is *Trustees of Dartmouth College v. Woodward*, 17 U.S. 518 (1819). In 1769, the British Crown had granted articles of incorporation to the trustees of Dartmouth College. After the American Revolution, New Hampshire, as successor to the Crown, enacted laws amending Dartmouth's charter so as to give state officials a major role in the governance of the college. Dartmouth sued, claiming the amendments violated the contract clause of the Constitution.

The Court invalidated New Hampshire's action on the ground the charter constituted a contract between the state and the college that was "within the letter of the Constitution and within its spirit also." In an oft-quoted opinion, Chief Justice Marshall described a corporation's basic attributes—suggesting that a corporation is both a fictional state-created entity and the product of a contract among private parties:

> A corporation is an artificial being, invisible, intangible, and existing only in contemplation of law. Being the mere creature of law, it possesses only those properties which the charter of its creation confers upon it, either expressly, or as incidental to its very existence. These are such as are supposed best calculated to effect the object for which it was created. Among the most important are immortality, and, if the expression may be allowed, individuality; properties, by which a perpetual succession of many persons are considered as the same, and may act as a single individual. They enable a corporation to manage its own affairs, and to hold property, without the perplexing intricacies, the hazardous and endless necessity, of perpetual conveyances for the purpose of transmitting it from hand to hand. It is chiefly for the purpose of clothing bodies of men, in succession, with these qualities and capacities, that corporations were invented, and are in use. By these means, a perpetual succession

of individuals are capable of acting for the promotion of the particular object, like one immortal being. But this being does not share in the civil government of the country, unless that be the purpose for which it was created. Its immortality no more confers on it political power, or a political character, than immortality would confer such power or character on a natural person. It is no more a state instrument, than a natural person exercising the same powers would be.

Although the Court held that a state could not unilaterally amend the provisions of the state-granted charter, Justice Story (in a concurring opinion) suggested states could avoid this restriction by granting future charters subject to a reserved right to amend them. States seized upon this suggestion and began to include in all corporate charters a clause reserving the state's power to amend or repeal any authority granted to the corporation. When general corporation laws came into vogue, states added similar reserved powers clauses to their constitutions, their general corporation laws, or both. Currently, all states reserve the power to amend the statutes that govern corporations. *See* MBCA § 1.02; DGCL § 394.

The liberalization of the U.S. corporation continued into the second half of the 1800s. Unfettered from the constraints of special charters and shaped by the burgeoning railroad industry, corporations continued to flourish. Railway companies, which required a larger central organization and significant capital inputs, used a variety of financial instruments, for which the corporate form proved convenient. In addition, railway companies generally became more dependent on the availability of an open market for their securities to raise necessary capital.

Checks on corporate power. This rapid growth of corporations in size and number did not occur without opposition. Throughout its history, some in America have feared the aggregations of capital and the power in American society that corporations represent. But this opposition did little to stem the tide of corporate growth; other states soon followed New York's lead from the early 1800s and enacted general corporation laws. Many of the restrictions on size and duration were lifted.

The growth of corporate power and unchecked abuses disturbed many Americans. Pressure grew to reform internal corporate governance and to impose limits on corporations' power. By the 1860s, the device of the shareholder "derivative" suit (in which individual shareholders can sue on behalf of the corporation to enforce corporate duties) had been developed to deal with managers' corruption and fraud, and other doctrines were emerging aimed at imposing greater control over corporate management. (Remember the shareholder derivative suit: it will play an important role in various chapters.)

Railway regulation was a leading public issue in the 1870s, and in the 1880s the Interstate Commerce Commission was created, primarily for the purpose of controlling the railroads. In 1890 the Sherman Act was passed to combat "trusts" that dominated major industries. Thus, while businesses were free to adapt the corporate instrument to their will, regulatory efforts also were initiated to circumscribe some of the power and impact of large corporations and their managers.

New Jersey was the first state to depart from the philosophy of strict limitations on corporations, beginning with its 1888 incorporation statute, which it revised in 1896. Delaware, a small state, passed a statute in 1899 modeled on New Jersey's statute with a view to attracting incorporations and thereby generating franchise tax revenues. When New Jersey amended its corporation law in 1913 to reimpose a number of restrictive provisions, Delaware kept the "enabling" nature of its statute, and emerged as the venue of choice, at least for publicly-traded corporations.

3. The Modern Corporation

Property or institution? The nature of the modern corporation—especially the large, publicly traded corporation—continues to be debated. For many, the corporation is private property, owned by and operated exclusively for the benefit of its shareholders. For others, the corporation is a creation of the state, an institution formed to advance the broader interests of the public, whose interests include both increasing shareholders' wealth *and* taking into account others affected by corporate activities. Many prominent shareholders argue that the corporation should take into account the broader interests of society, including employees and members of the community.

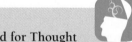

Food for Thought

In the mid-twentieth century, the prevalence and increasing uniformity of state enabling laws led some to conclude that all interesting questions of corporation law had been answered. In 1962 <u>Bayless Manning</u>, a leading corporate law professor, wrote, "corporation law, as a field of intellectual endeavor, is dead in the United States. We have nothing left but our great empty corporation statutes—towering skyscrapers of rusty girders, internally welded together and containing nothing but wind."

One way to finesse the debate is with the notion of long-run profit maximization. Thus, while accepting that corporations exist exclusively for shareholders' benefit, managers can advance the interests of non-shareholder groups on the claim it will benefit shareholders in the long run. The concept of "sustainability" suggests that the corporation should be managed in a way that can be sustained throughout future generations.

Corporate takeovers. The 1980s had a profound effect on the property-institution debate. During the decade, a handful of corporate "raiders" borrowed huge amounts of money to make uninvited bids for the shares of public corporations. The media labeled these bids "hostile," because they were unsolicited. But while the bids indeed were hostile to managers, and frequently the bidders explicitly sought to replace incumbent directors and officers, they were attractive to most shareholders, because they offered to buy shares for a substantial premium above the market price.

Remarkably, during the 1980s, nearly half of all major U.S. corporations received an unsolicited takeover offer. Although not all the firms were taken over, many restructured on their own in response to hostile threats. This wave of merger, takeover, and financial restructuring activity in the 1980s transformed the relationship between public shareholders and corporate management. Takeovers gave passive shareholders a chance to exercise their "exit" rights and obtain a higher price for their shares. Even in those companies that were not targets of a takeover offer, management was forced to become responsive to shareholder demands for higher share values.

Behind the 1980s takeover movement were new communication and information technologies that made fast-moving leveraged bids possible, and ongoing deregulation that invited new industry alignments. Coupled with these external changes were internal changes in the ownership of U.S. corporations, which were increasingly owned by institutional investors, such as pension funds, mutual funds, insurance companies, and endowments. As capital markets discovered the inefficiency of conglomeration in the 1960s and 1970s, in which companies from different industries were brought together in large holding companies, capital markets reversed this strategy by breaking up the conglomerates through takeovers and leveraged buyouts.

For managers, this new era of corporate governance contrasted starkly with the prevailing managerial climate before 1980, when managers were loyal to the corporation, not necessarily shareholders. At first, corporate managers fought the new takeover wave with legal tactics and by enlisting political and popular support. By the late 1980s, hostile takeovers declined significantly. Some attributed this decline to lobbying by managers in

Business Lingo

A "leveraged buyout" (or LBO) occurs when an outside acquiror buys a controlling interest in a corporation's equity, where the bulk of the purchase price comes from borrowed money (leverage). The assets of the acquired corporation are used as collateral for the borrowed money. The bonds or other debt issued to finance the acquisition carry higher risk and higher returns than most corporate debt—thus earning the name "junk bonds." When the corporation's own managers carry out the transaction as acquirors, it is known as a "management buyout" (or MBO).

state legislatures that passed special antitakeover laws and to state judges who endorsed company-specific antitakeover measures. Others viewed hostile take-overs as having run their course as the pool of attractive targets was depleted.

After a brief decline in takeover activity around 1990, takeovers rebounded to even higher levels in the 1990s. This time the pattern was not one of leverage and hostility. Instead, active boards and institutional investors took the lead. With stock options that created incentives to drive up their company's stock price, corporate managers came to realize that they could share in the enhanced value of a restructured company. During the 1990s mergers and restructurings were negotiated and friendly. Instead of leverage, most deals were paid for with stock of the acquiring company.

Business Lingo

A "hedge fund" is an investment fund open to a limited group of investors, such as wealthy individuals and large institutional investors (like pension plans and university endowments). Hedge funds, unlike mutual funds sold to the public, are not heavily regulated and can undertake a wide range of investments and trading activities. Although hedge funds (as the name implies) originally were designed for investors that wanted to offset potential losses in capital markets, many hedge funds do not hedge their investments, but engage in high-risk strategies with the hope of high returns. Hedge fund managers typically earn performance fees that can run in the billions of dollars if their fund is successful.

Shareholder activism. In the 2000s, "hostility" returned, this time in a new guise. Activist investors known as "hedge funds" began pressuring managers to generate greater returns for shareholders, and they threatened some of the same takeover tactics that had become popular during the 1980s.

While other institutional investors, such as pension funds and mutual funds, typically held diversified portfolios, with relatively small stakes in each of hundreds of companies, activist hedge funds focused on just a few target companies. When hedge fund managers found a company they believed should restructure, sell assets, or merge, they bought a stake of typically 5–10% of that company's shares and then began urging its managers to change. The number of hedge funds acquiring substantial stakes and using their "voice" in individual companies increased during the 2000s and shareholder activism continued to be a dominant and prominent force during the 2010s.

In addition, institutional shareholders, including broadly diversified index funds, which passively owned stakes in most companies, flexed their voting and governance muscles, both by frequently siding with shareholder activists and by proposing their own reforms. Institutional investors sought a greater say in director elections and corporate governance, with increasing success. Shareholders also became more activist in their support of environmental, social, and governance goals, collectively known as "ESG."

Sarbanes-Oxley Act. Besides changes in the shareholder-management relationship, modern corporations have also experienced a shift in corporate law from the state to federal level. The Sarbanes-Oxley Act of 2002 imposed federal standards in areas previously subject to state corporate law. For example, the Act specified the functions and membership of the audit committees of public corporation boards, required senior corporate executives to personally certify the company's financial statements, banned public corporations from making loans to their directors and executives, and told the SEC to require lawyers who represent public corporations to become "whistle blowers" when there is evidence of corporate corruption or fraud.

One provision of the Act, Section 404, was particularly controversial. It required public corporations to undertake the costly process of assessing their internal controls over financial reporting and possible corporate wrongdoing. Over time, the application of Section 404 has been limited, but internal controls and compliance remain important, particularly at large public companies.

> An important aspect of the federal regulation of public corporations has been the "securities fraud class action." This is a private lawsuit brought under federal securities law on behalf of many investors who have suffered losses because of fraud by the corporation or its auditors. Typically, the lawsuit is brought when securities have fallen in value because of false or misleading statements by corporate executives intended to artificially inflate stock prices in the market. Federal law requires that such lawsuits be brought in federal court. We will study these lawsuits in Chapter 19, Shareholder Litigation, and Chapter 28, Securities Fraud.

Dodd-Frank Act. In 2010, Congress passed the Dodd-Frank Wall Street Reform and Consumer Protection Act. Although the legislation was a response to the Financial Crisis of 2008, and the increase in risk-taking by banks in particular, the 2,319-page statute reached well beyond banks. For example, it required new rules regarding "say-on-pay," a required advisory vote by shareholders on the compensation practices of public companies. Many provisions were controversial, such as a requirement that companies disclose sourcing details about products that contain "conflict minerals," which are mined in the Democratic Republic of Congo. After the D.C. Circuit held that some disclosure aspects of the rule were unconstitutional, the rule was suspended in 2017. Overall, these new rules raise questions about the traditional role of the states in regulating corporate governance.

B. Horizontal Federalism: State View of Corporate Law

Corporate federalism—the relationship between federal and state law on corporations—operates on two planes. The first plane is the horizontal competition among the states to obtain incorporations by offering an attractive set of corporate law rules and procedures. This competition is made possible by the prevailing choice of law rule that the state of incorporation, not the forum state or the state where the corporation does business, supplies the rules governing the corporation's internal affairs—a remarkable state abstention.

1. Internal Affairs Doctrine

The internal affairs doctrine is a widely accepted choice of law rule. It provides that the law of the state of incorporation should govern any disputes regarding that corporation's "internal affairs." Thus, a business with shareholders in Florida, headquartered in California, doing business throughout the South, and incorporated in Delaware would be subject to the corporate law rules of—Delaware! And this would be the result wherever litigation involving the corporation's shareholders and managers might arise.

A strong argument for the internal affairs doctrine is that any other choice of law rule would be extremely difficult to administer when the corporation conducts a multi-state business. For example, how could one decide which shareholders were entitled to vote at an annual meeting if it were necessary to follow each potentially conflicting law of every state in which the corporation did business? Obviously, a choice must be made and the internal affairs doctrine tells courts to make this choice by deciding questions of internal corporate affairs according to the law of the state of incorporation.

What are internal affairs? Courts have said they are the matters peculiar to the relationships among the corporation and its officers, directors, and shareholders. For example, internal affairs typically include the right of shareholders to vote, to receive distributions of corporate property (including dividends), to receive information from the management about corporate affairs, to limit the powers of the corporation to specified activities, and to bring suit on behalf of the corporation when the managers refuse to do so. Internal affairs include the duties that managers owe to shareholders, as well as certain actions by the board of directors, such as decisions to indemnify officers, issue stock, or merge with other corporations.

In contrast, a corporation's external affairs are generally governed by the law where the activities occur and by federal and state regulatory statutes—not by the state of incorporation. For example, a state's employment laws govern conditions of employment of all business operations within the state, wherever the business might be incorporated. State tax laws generally apply to activities of any corporation within the state, especially taxes on corporate real estate and income. When corporations enter into contracts, commit torts, and deal in property, the internal affairs doctrine does not apply.

Sometimes corporate activities can be governed by both internal and external rules. For example, state corporation law controls the right to merge and the procedure to be followed, but mergers are also independently subject to federal antitrust laws and securities laws (federal securities laws specify the disclosure that shareholders must receive when they vote on a merger).

What happens when a court in one state is asked to resolve a corporate dispute involving a corporation incorporated in a state whose corporate law is at odds with that state's corporate law? The following is a leading case from Delaware that addresses this situation. You will notice that the corporate law of Panama, where the corporation at issue was incorporated, conflicted with the corporate law of Delaware and, in fact, that of all U.S. states. The result in the case may surprise you.

McDermott Inc. v. Lewis

531 A.2d 206 (Del. 1987)

We confront an important issue of first impression whether a Delaware subsidiary of a Panamanian corporation may vote the shares it holds in its parent company under circumstances which are prohibited by Delaware law, but not the law of Panama. Necessarily, this involves questions of foreign law, and applicability of the internal affairs doctrine under Delaware law.

[Plaintiffs sued in the Court of Chancery to enjoin the 1982 Reorgani-

What's That?

A "subsidiary" is a corporation that is controlled by another corporation, often referred to as the "parent." The subsidiary can be "wholly-owned" when the parent holds 100% of the subsidiary's voting shares, or "partially-owned" when the parent holds less than all of the subsidiary's shares, but effectively controls the subsidiary's board of directors.

zation under which McDermott Incorporated, a Delaware corporation ("McDermott Delaware"), became a 92%-owned subsidiary of McDermott International, Inc., a Panamanian corporation ("International"). Plaintiffs are stockholders of McDermott Delaware, which emerged from the Reorganization owning approximately 10% of International's common stock. Plaintiffs challenged this aspect of the Reorganization, and the Court of Chancery granted partial summary judgment in their favor, holding that McDermott Delaware could not vote its stock in International.]

We conclude that the trial court erred in refusing to apply the law of Panama to the internal affairs of International. Accordingly, we reverse. In so doing, we reaffirm the principle that the internal affairs doctrine is a major tenet of Delaware corporation law having important federal constitutional underpinnings.

I.

International was incorporated in Panama on August 11, 1959, and is principally engaged in providing worldwide marine construction services to the oil and gas industry. Its executive offices are in New Orleans, Louisiana, and there are no operations in Delaware.

McDermott Delaware and its subsidiaries operate throughout the United States in three principal industry segments: marine construction services, power generation systems and equipment, and engineered materials. McDermott Delaware's principal offices are in New Orleans.

Following the 1982 Reorganization, McDermott Delaware became a 92%-owned subsidiary of International. The public stockholders of International hold approximately 90% of the voting power of International, while McDermott Delaware holds about 10%.

At the time of the reorganization, International's prospectus admitted the 10% voting interest given to McDermott Delaware would be voted by International, "and such voting power could be used to oppose an attempt by a third party to acquire control of International if the management of International believes such use of the voting power would be in the best interests of the stockholders of International."

What's That?

A "prospectus" is a disclosure document that a company provides investors to inform them about the securities being offered. The document includes material information about the company, its risks, its financial condition, its management, and the securities being offered. Federal securities laws specify the contents of the prospectus and how it is distributed to investors.

The applicable Panamanian law is set forth in the record by affidavits and opinion letters of Ricardo A. Durling, Esquire [a practicing Panamanian lawyer who wrote the first treatise on Panama corporate law], and the deans of two Panamanian law schools, to support the claim that McDermott Delaware's retention of a 10% interest in International, and its right to vote those shares, is permitted by the laws of Panama. Significantly, the plaintiffs have not offered any contrary evidence.

II.

We note at the outset that if International were incorporated either in Delaware or Louisiana, its stock could not be voted by a majority-owned subsidiary. 8 Del.C. § 160(c); La. Rev. Stat. Ann. § 12:75(G). No United States jurisdiction of which we are aware permits that practice.

The trial court concluded that since both Delaware and Louisiana law prohibit a majority-owned subsidiary from voting its parent's stock, the device was improper. We consider this an erroneous application of both Delaware and Panamanian law.

It is apparent that under limited circumstances the laws of Panama permit a subsidiary to vote the shares of its parent. All three legal experts agreed that McDermott Delaware could vote the shares it held in International. Further, Dean Fernandez specifically stated that it "is a principle of law that in matters of public law one can only do what is expressly allowed by the law; while in private law all acts not prohibited by law can be performed." This fully accords with basic principles of Delaware corporate law.

Given the uncontroverted evidence of Panamanian law, establishing that a Panamanian corporation may place voting shares in a majority-owned subsidiary of a publicly-traded corporation registered with the National Securities Commission of Panama, we turn to the fundamental issues presented by application of the internal affairs doctrine.

III.

Internal corporate affairs involve those matters which are peculiar to the relationships among or between the corporation and its current officers, directors, and shareholders. The internal affairs doctrine requires that the law of the state of incorporation should determine issues relating to internal corporate affairs. Under Delaware conflict of laws principles and the United States Constitution, there are appropriate circumstances which mandate application of this doctrine.

Delaware's well established conflict of laws principles require that the laws of the jurisdiction of incorporation—here the Republic of Panama—govern this dispute involving McDermott International's voting rights.

The traditional conflicts rule developed by courts has been that internal corporate relationships are governed by the laws of the forum of incorporation. As early as 1933, the Supreme Court of the United States noted:

> It has long been settled doctrine that a court, state or federal, sitting in one state will, as a general rule, decline to interfere with, or control

by injunction or otherwise, the management of the internal affairs of a corporation organized under the laws of another state but will leave controversies as to such matters to the courts of the state of the domicile.

Rogers v. Guaranty Trust Co. of New York, 288 U.S. 123, 130 (1933) (citations omitted).

A review of cases over the last twenty-six years finds that in all but a few, the law of the state of incorporation was applied without any discussion.

The policy underlying the internal affairs doctrine is an important one, and we decline to erode the principle:

> Under the prevailing conflicts practice, neither courts nor legislatures have maximized the imposition of local corporate policy on foreign corporations but have consistently applied the law of the state of incorporation to the entire gamut of internal corporate affairs. In many cases, this is a wise, practical, and equitable choice. It serves the vital need for a single, constant and equal law to avoid the fragmentation of continuing, interdependent internal relationships. The *lex incorporationis* validates the autonomy of the parties in a subject where the underlying policy of the law is enabling. It facilitates planning and enhances predictability. In fields like torts, where the typical dispute involves two persons and a single or simple one-shot issue and where the common substantive policy is to spread the loss through compensation and insurance, the preference for forum law and the emphasis on the state interest in forum residents which are the common denominators of the new conflicts methodologies do not necessarily lead to unacceptable choices. By contrast, applying local internal affairs law to a foreign corporation just because it is amenable to process

What's That?

A "foreign corporation" is one incorporated in a jurisdiction other than the one where it is doing business or involved in litigation. To "do business" in a state where it is not incorporated, the foreign corporation must register. ("Doing business" involves a minimum contacts analysis, similar to that for personal jurisdiction under the Fourteenth Amendment.) All state corporate statutes permit foreign corporations to register, which typically involves a simple informational filing and small filing fee. MBCA § 15.03; DGCL § 371. A foreign corporation that does business in a state, but fails to register, will not be recognized in that state as a corporation. This prevents the corporation from suing in the state and exposes its participants to individual liability for any corporate contracts or torts.

in the forum or because it has some local shareholders or some other local contact is apt to produce inequalities, intolerable confusion, and uncertainty, and intrude into the domain of other states that have a superior claim to regulate the same subject matter.

Kozyris, *Corporate Wars and Choice of Law*, 1985 Duke L.J. 1, 98.

Given the significance of these considerations, application of the internal affairs doctrine is not merely a principle of conflicts law. It is also one of serious constitutional proportions—under due process, the commerce clause and the full faith and credit clause—so that the law of one state governs the relationships of a corporation to its stockholders, directors and officers in matters of internal corporate governance. The alternatives present almost intolerable consequences to the corporate enterprise and its managers. With the existence of multistate and multinational organizations, directors and officers have a significant right, under the fourteenth amendment's due process clause, to know what law will be applied to their actions. Stockholders also have a right to know by what standards of accountability they may hold those managing the corporation's business and affairs. That is particularly so here, given the significant fact that in the McDermott Group reorganization, and after full disclosure, 89.59% of the total outstanding common shares of McDermott Delaware were tendered in the exchange offer.

Addressing the facts originally presented to the trial court and to us, we must conclude that due process and the commerce clause, in addition to principles of Delaware conflicts law, mandate reversal. Due process requires that directors, officers and shareholders be given adequate notice of the jurisdiction whose laws will ultimately govern the corporation's internal affairs. Under such circumstances, application of 8 Del.C. § 160(c) to International would unfairly and, in our opinion, unconstitutionally, subject those intimately involved with the management of the corporation to the laws of Delaware.

Moreover, application of Section 160(c) to International would violate the commerce clause. Delaware and Panama law clearly differ in their treatment of a subsidiary's voting rights under the facts originally presented here. For Delaware now to interfere in the internal affairs of a foreign corporation having no relationship whatever to this State clearly implies that International can be subjected to the differing laws of all fifty states on various matters respecting its internal affairs. Such a prohibitive burden has obvious commerce clause implications, and could not pass constitutional muster.

Points for Discussion

1. Corporation voting of its own shares.

The plaintiffs complained that, after the recapitalization, McDermott International was able to vote its own shares held by its subsidiary McDermott Delaware. What is wrong with this? Why is this practice prohibited in Delaware and all other 50 states?

2. Why the internal affairs doctrine?

Notice that the effect of the recapitalization and the allocation of McDermott International's voting shares to its Delaware subsidiary diminished the ability of International's shareholders to sell in a takeover. Why? How did the reduction of these rights promote the "autonomy of the parties"? What protections do shareholders have if management chooses to incorporate in a jurisdiction that disfavors shareholder interests?

3. Importance of internal affairs doctrine to Delaware.

Notice the effort that the Delaware court made to justify the application of Panamanian law. At one level, it would seem the court should have wanted to uphold the corporate rule in Delaware (and every other U.S. jurisdiction) that parent companies cannot place their voting shares in a controlled subsidiary. Yet the court went out of its way to apply "rogue" Panamanian law. Why?

Perhaps the answer is that Delaware is the home to roughly half of all public corporations. As such, it has an interest in the uniform and unswerving application of the internal affairs doctrine. Under this choice of law rule, any business that chooses to incorporate in Delaware will be assured—wherever corporate litigation might arise—that Delaware corporate law will apply to the internal disputes between shareholders and managers, and among shareholders.

————

2. State Regulation of Pseudo-Foreign Corporations

Despite the internal affairs doctrine, a few states have chosen by statute to impose their own corporate rules on the internal affairs of "pseudo-foreign corporations"—that is, corporations that are incorporated outside the state, but conduct most of their business and have most of their shareholders in the state.

> ### Cal. Corp. Code
> ### § 2115
>
> (a) A foreign corporation is subject to the requirements of subdivision (b) if:
>
> (1) the average of the property factor, the payroll factor, and the sales factor with respect to it is more than 50 percent during its latest full income year and
>
> (2) more than one-half of its outstanding voting securities are held of record by persons having addresses in this state appearing on the books of the corporation.
>
> (c) This section does not apply to any corporation (1) with outstanding securities listed on the New York Stock Exchange, the NYSE Amex, the NASDAQ Global Market, or the NASDAQ Capital Market, or (2) if all of its voting shares (other than directors' qualifying shares) are owned directly or indirectly by a corporation or corporations not subject to this section.

The California "pseudo-foreign corporation" statute is both broad and narrow. On one hand, § 2115(b) covers a wide range of corporate "internal affairs," such as the annual election of directors, removal of directors, filling of director vacancies, directors' standard of care, indemnification of directors and officers, limitations on corporate distributions of cash or property, annual shareholders' meeting, shareholder's right to cumulative voting, limitations on sale of assets or mergers, dissenters' rights, and rights of inspection. On the other hand, § 2115 does not apply to public corporations whose shares are traded on a national exchange.

Two cases illustrate the different approaches taken by courts faced with "pseudo-foreign corporations" operating in California, but incorporated in another state (in one case Utah and the other case Delaware). Both cases raised the question of which law applied to shareholder voting rights. The first case—decided by a California appellate court—chose California law. The second case—decided by the Delaware Supreme Court—chose Delaware law. Why the inconsistency?

California approach. The California court framed the issue as being whether California could "constitutionally impose its law requiring cumulative voting by shareholders upon a corporation which is domiciled elsewhere, but whose contacts with California are greater than those with any other jurisdiction." *Wilson v. Louisiana-Pacific Resources, Inc.*, 187 Cal. Rptr. 852 (Cal. Ct. App. 1982).

Since Congress had not exercised its Commerce Clause powers to regulate the corporate internal affairs at issue, the decision turned on "the negative implications of dormant congressional authority." The court pointed out that California's corporate law was even-handed and applied cumulative voting equally to foreign corporations and domestic corporations. The corporation argued that the California statute might lead some foreign corporations "already operating in California to reduce their property, payroll, and sales in this state below the statutory 50 percent level, and could deter foreign corporations contemplating the transaction of business in this state from increasing their business activities above that level." But the court was not persuaded that cumulative voting interfered with interstate commerce, since the corporation's president said "he knew of no adverse effect on the corporation's business which would be caused by cumulative voting."

Finally, the California court pointed out:

> The potential for conflict and resulting uncertainty from California's statute is substantially minimized by the nature of the criteria specified in section 2115. A corporation can do a majority of its business in only one state at a time; and it can have a majority of its shareholders resident in only one state at a time. If a corporation meets those requirements in this state, no other state is in a position to regulate the method of voting by shareholders on the basis of the same or similar criteria. It might also be said that no other state could claim as great an interest in doing so. In any event, it does not appear that any other state has attempted to do so. If California's statute were replicated in all states, no conflict would result. We conclude that the potential for conflict is, on this record, speculative and without substance.

What's That?

"Straight voting" is the dominant form for electing corporate directors. Each voting share receives one vote per open board seat, and the top vote-getters are elected to the board. Thus, if AB Corporation has 100 voting shares outstanding and five open board positions, Shareholder A with 80 shares can vote all 80 shares for each of five different candidates— winning each seat. Shareholder B with 20 shares is outvoted 80–20 each time.

"Cumulative voting" allows shareholders to cumulate their votes and allocate them to one or more candidates as they choose. Thus, Shareholder B could decide to cast 100 votes (20 times 5 open board seats) for one candidate, thus ensuring that her candidate will be one of the top five vote-getters. Shareholder A, with only 400 votes (80 times 5), cannot cast more than 100 votes for each of his five candidates. As you can see, cumulative voting facilitates minority representation on the board.

Delaware approach. In a similar case, but in Delaware, the Delaware Supreme Court addressed the applicability of Delaware law (the state of incorporation) or California law (the state where the business had most of its operations and shareholders) as both a matter of choice of law and constitutional law. *VantagePoint Venture Partners 1996 v. Examen, Inc.,* 871 A.2d 1108 (Del. 2005).

The Delaware court showed little concern that the complaining shareholder, which controlled a majority of the corporation's preferred shares, could have vetoed the merger if California law applied. Nor was the court impressed with the argument that California had significant interests in regulating corporations doing the bulk of their business in the state.

The Delaware court stated it is "an accepted part of the business landscape in this country for States to create corporations, to prescribe their powers, and to define the rights that are acquired by purchasing their shares. A State has an interest in promoting stable relationships among parties involved in the corporations it charters, as well as in ensuring that investors in such corporations have an effective voice in corporate affairs." The Delaware court explained that the internal affairs doctrine reflects "a long-standing choice of law principle" that only one state—the state of incorporation—should regulate a corporation's internal affairs.

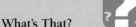

What's That?

"Class voting," which is the default rule under the MBCA, provides for separate voting by each class (or separate category) of voting shares on important corporate transactions, like mergers. Thus, if a corporation has common shares and preferred shares (each with different rights to be paid dividends), a merger would have to be approved by a majority of the common AND a majority of the preferred.

Under Delaware's corporate statute, *all* voting shares vote together on a merger, unless class voting is specified in the articles or by special board resolution. Thus, for a merger to be approved in Delaware, it is sufficient for a majority of all shares (common and preferred) to approve the transaction. This helps facilitate corporate transactions by preventing a veto by any one class of shares.

Finally, the Delaware court then turned to the U.S. Constitution:

The internal affairs doctrine is not, however, only a conflicts of law principle. Pursuant to the Fourteenth Amendment Due Process Clause, directors and officers of corporations "have a significant right to know what law will be applied to their actions" and "stockholders have a right to know by what standards of accountability they may hold those managing the corporation's business and affairs." Under the Commerce Clause, a state "has no interest in regulating the internal affairs of foreign corporations." Therefore, this Court has held that an "application of the internal affairs doctrine is mandated by constitutional principles, except in the 'rarest situations,'" e.g., when "the law of the state of incorporation is inconsistent with a national policy on foreign or interstate commerce."

Accordingly, we hold Delaware's well-established choice of law rules and the federal constitution mandated that the corporation's internal affairs, and in particular, the complaining shareholder's voting rights, be adjudicated exclusively in accordance with the law of its state of incorporation, in this case, the law of Delaware.

Points for Discussion

1. Nature of shareholder voting.

Why does California law require cumulative voting and class voting for shareholders of pseudo-foreign corporations operating primarily in California? Is it legitimate for California to seek to protect investors in the state from unfair business practices? Is shareholder voting really an internal affair of the corporation?

2. Reconciling the cases.

The California and Delaware courts don't leave much room for doubt. Is there any way the two cases can be reconciled? Both involved closely-held corporations with most of their operations and shareholders in California. And both involved voting rights that, if California law had applied, would have given minority shareholders important governance prerogatives. In the first case the complaining shareholder got voting rights different from those implicit in the corporation's Utah charter. In the second case, the complaining shareholder got only the votes implicit in the Delaware charter. That is, we might say the first shareholder got voting rights he had not negotiated for; and the second shareholder got exactly what he negotiated for.

3. Gender diversity and boards.

In late 2018, California enacted a statute that required public corporations with their "principal executive office" in California to have a specified number of women on their boards. Many commentators suggested that the statute would be vulnerable on internal affairs grounds. Public corporations disclose one "principal executive office" in their securities filings. Does the use of "principal executive office" change how a court should analyze a state law that regulates corporations that are incorporated out of state?

C. Vertical Federalism: Federal View of Corporate Law

The second plane on which corporate federalism operates is the vertical relationship between federal law and state corporate law. The U.S. Constitution supplies the simple choice of law rule that federal law is supreme and can pre-empt state law. Thus, the federal securities laws apply to disclosure by public corporations wherever incorporated, and any class action alleging securities fraud must be brought in federal court. Nonetheless, federal courts have assumed that corporate law (absent a clear federal statutory intervention) is essentially a matter of state law—an important federal abstention.

Corporate takeovers have tested the limits of federal abstention to state corporate law. When the sale of corporate shares changes the control of a corporation—and thus affects the people and communities where the corporation operates—states have sought to regulate the changes in control. Normally, such regulation would seem to fall within the state's police powers to regulate behavior affecting the state and its citizens. But interference in commercial transactions occurring outside the state, such as sales of shares on national stock exchanges, can violate the implicit (dormant) limitations of the federal Commerce Clause.

1. State Antitakeover Regulation

What are the federal limits on state corporate law? In two cases from the 1980s, the Supreme Court defined the powers of states to regulate the internal affairs of multi-state corporations. Without explicitly resolving whether the internal affairs doctrine is constitutionally mandated, the Court nonetheless made clear the doctrine's vaunted place in U.S. corporate law. States have broad authority to choose the corporate rules that apply to corporations incorporated in the state.

The two Supreme Court cases involved challenges to state statutes that sought to regulate corporate takeovers. Beginning in the 1960s, and intensifying during the 1980s, many companies became the objects of "hostile" takeover bids. Acquirers bypassed incumbent managers and made "tender offers" to the shareholders, usually at a substantial premium to the current share price. After buying voting control, the acquirers would then acquire the remaining shares in a back-end merger.

First-generation antitakeover laws. Corporate managers argued that tender offers posed a threat to the long-term interests of the corporation. They claimed that hostile bidders would restructure the business, lay off employees, and abandon communities where the corporation operated—not to mention move the corporation's tax base elsewhere. In the 1960s and 1970s, several states responded by adopting "first generation" antitakeover laws designed to protect corporations conducting business in the state from takeover bids opposed by the corporation's management. In particular, these laws gave state regulators the power to decide if tender offers could be made to residents in their states.

For example, an Illinois statute required offerors to give the Secretary of State twenty days advance notice of any bid and authorized the Secretary to hold a hearing to determine the fairness of the offer. In a splintered opinion, the Supreme Court held in *Edgar v. MITE Corp.*, 457 U.S. 624 (1982), that such a statute was unconstitutional on one or more grounds. The Court rejected Illinois's claim that the internal affairs doctrine protected the law from constitutional attack, noting that the law was not limited to Illinois corporations but also covered foreign corporations that had the requisite proportion of Illinois shareholders and either their principal office or 10% of their assets in Illinois.

What's That?

A "tender offer"—the offer by a bidder to buy shares during a specified period subject to certain conditions—permits a bidder to acquire control of the corporation without dealing with the incumbent board of directors. Rather than approach the board to negotiate a merger, the bidder makes a tender offer directly to the shareholders and thus sidesteps the board.

After acquiring enough voting shares, the bidder can then replace the board with its own nominees and negotiate a "back-end merger." Such a merger does not require the vote of the (now minority) shareholders who did not sell their shares in the tender offer. For this reason, shareholders who are confronted with a tender offer may feel coerced to tender their shares at the offered (premium) price—rather than face an uncertain fate in the back-end merger.

Second-generation antitakeover laws. Following *Edgar v. MITE*, many states (often at the behest of corporate managers) began adopting "second generation" antitakeover statutes. Rather than regulate the sale of shares, which had been the approach of the "first generation" statutes, the states focused on the internal affairs of domestic corporations. Among the first of these "second generation" antitakeover laws was the Indiana Control Shares Acquisition Chapter, which differed from the Illinois law in *MITE* by revising the state's corporation statute. The law applied only to Indiana-incorporated corporations, provided they had (1) at least 100 shareholders, (2) their principal place of business or substantial assets in Indiana, and (3) a significant portion of Indiana shareholders.

The Indiana "control share" law provided that any person who acquired a control block of shares would not be entitled to vote those shares in favor of a merger unless a majority of that corporation's disinterested shareholders voted to approve the acquisition. The Indiana law called for a special shareholders' meeting within 50 days after a control-share acquisition began, thus giving the target corporation's managers almost two months to attempt to defeat the hostile bid, and providing the target shareholders some protection against coercive takeover bids.

Dynamics, the owner of 9.6% of CTS, an Indiana corporation covered by the Indiana "control share" law, announced a tender offer for sufficient shares to increase its ownership interest to 27.5%, thus triggering the law. Dynamics simultaneously sued to enjoin enforcement of the law, claiming it was preempted by the Williams Act (a federal statute that specifies disclosure and time frames for tender offers in public corporations) and violated the Commerce Clause. The Seventh Circuit, relying on *MITE*, agreed that the Indiana law was unconstitutional on both grounds.

The Supreme Court was confronted with some important choices. On one hand, it could decide the Indiana law conflicted with the time deadlines imposed by the Williams Act and was thus preempted. But this would have made federal law the primary regulator of hostile tender offers. On the other hand, the Court could decide the Indiana law interfered with interstate commerce under the Commerce Clause. But this would open the way for federal judge-made guidelines on state corporate rules that interfered with corporate takeovers.

The Court noted that the Indiana statute did not adversely affect interstate commerce by subjecting activities to inconsistent regulations. The Court recognized that, so long as each state regulated voting rights only in the corporations it created, each corporation would be subject to the law of only one state. To the limited extent the Indiana statute affected interstate commerce, that effect was justified in defining the attributes of shares in its corporations and in protecting its shareholders. Deterring takeovers might, or might not, have been a good idea; the Supreme Court wasn't going to opine either way. As Justice Powell wrote, "The Constitution does not require the States to subscribe to any particular economic theory." The key point was that federal courts should abstain from regulating the internal affairs of U.S. corporations unless a federal statute applied and required a different result.

Third-Generation Antitakeover Laws. After *CTS*, a number of states (reassured by the Supreme Court that their efforts would not be in vain) adopted laws that provided even more protection against takeovers than the Indiana law. Some of these new "third generation" statutes used the Indiana law as a model to strengthen the less restrictive "second generation" statutes, and others tested the *CTS* limits by mandating constraints on bidders that went further than the Indiana law.

Lower courts have uniformly read *CTS* to create a blueprint for antitakeover laws. While uniformly upholding all "third generation" laws that regulate the internal affairs of "domestic corporations," the courts have struck down under the Commerce Clause all "third generation" laws that regulate takeover bids directed at "foreign corporations." The courts have reasoned that antitakeover laws aimed at foreign corporations create the risk of inconsistent state regulation.

In addition, courts have not required that the state antitakeover law require additional business or shareholder connections to the state. These conditions were generally dropped from the "third generation" statutes—without any constitutional effect.

2. Delaware's Antitakeover Law

Perhaps the most important reaction to *CTS* happened in Delaware, the leading state for public corporations, which enacted a relatively mild "third generation" statute. DGCL § 203. Delaware seemed to have been motivated, at least in part, by the fear that some Delaware corporations would reincorporate in states with antitakeover laws if Delaware did not act. Delaware feared, rightly or wrongly, that inaction would hurt its preeminence in the incorporation business.

The Delaware antitakeover law imposed a three-year moratorium on any merger by the target corporation after a hostile takeover, unless the bidder acquired 85% control in the initial tender offer. The effect of the Delaware law was to force bidders to offer significant premiums for shares in a tender offer—to reach the 85% threshold. Or bidders that did not borrow money to make their takeover bid (and thus did not need to engage in a back-end merger to repay debt) could simply wait the three years before consolidating control in a merger.

Relying on *CTS*, courts have upheld Delaware's antitakeover law, which applies to Delaware corporations without regard to where they do business or where their shareholders reside.

D. Market in State Charters

In both its horizontal and vertical aspects, U.S. corporate law is essentially a matter of incorporation-based private choice. The choice of the parties to incorporate the business in a particular state is respected both at the state level under the internal affairs doctrine and at the federal level under the assumption that states operate as adaptive laboratories and efficient producers of corporate law. As a result, U.S. corporate law can be seen as a product that states offer to persons interested in joining together in business firms.

This leads to a couple questions. First, how is state corporate law actually produced—particularly in Delaware, the leading producer of corporate law for public corporations? Second, has the state competition to produce corporate law led to efficient results? Or is corporate law the result of a "race to bottom" as states (especially Delaware) seek to attract self-serving managers? Or perhaps is corporate law the result of a "race to the top" as states (especially Delaware) seek to balance the interests of managers and shareholders?

1. Production of Corporate Law

State corporate law is a combination of statutory law and judge-made law. Most of statutory corporate law, as we have seen, is a set of default rules. The statutes establish the basic rules on corporate formation, financial rights and duties, governance structure, procedures for structural changes, transfer of corporate interests, and access to judicial protection.

Judges are critical in interpreting the corporate law statutes and filling in the gaps, particularly by defining and shaping corporate fiduciary duties. As you will see in this book, most of the important corporate law cases are resolved not by turning to statutory rules, but by deciding on the existence and reach of corporate fiduciary duties. And corporate innovations often arise when corporate lawyers dream up new financing and other corporate mechanisms, later approved by judges.

We focus on the production of corporate law in Delaware—both by its legislature and its judiciary—since the state is the dominant producer of U.S. corporate law, particularly for public corporations. Other states produce statutory corporate law in much the same way as Delaware—through bar association drafting committees. But Delaware is unique among the states in the way it produces judge-made law—through its expert, independent judges.

Delaware's corporate statute. Delaware's corporate statute is the most far-reaching and innovative of any U.S. corporate statute—even though its dense wording is also sometimes the hardest to decipher. Its legislature is usually the first mover on corporate law reforms, such as simplified merger procedures, teleconferencing at board meetings, hybrid financing techniques, and electronic shareholder voting. Once Delaware acts, other states tend to mimic the leader.

Delaware's corporate statute, however, is not really the product of the state's legislature. Instead, virtually all reforms to the corporate statute are drafted by a special committee of the Delaware bar association—the Council of the Corporate Law Section—and then passed by the state legislature. The Council is composed mostly of private corporate lawyers who represent corporate management, but also includes shareholder plaintiffs' lawyers and representatives of the Delaware's secretary of state's office.

To ensure that corporate law reforms come only from the Council and not special-interest groups, the Delaware constitution requires that all amendments to the state's corporate statute be passed by two-thirds of each legislative chamber. And to seal the deal, the Delaware constitution cannot be amended through the legislative process. Thus, no single corporation or corporate interest group can wield control over Delaware's corporate statute.

Although some have asserted that the Delaware statute balances the interests of the modern corporation's multiple constituencies (managers, shareholders, creditors, employees, suppliers, consumers, communities), the reality is that the statutory drafters focus almost exclusively on management prerogatives and shareholder rights—with management prerogatives their main drafting imperative. That is, the production of Delaware corporate law has favored ever more enabling state corporate statutes.

Other states, most of which have adopted some variant of the MBCA, produce corporate statutory law in similar ways. The MBCA—drafted by a special ABA subcommittee composed of by-invitation-only corporate lawyers, law professors and in-house counsel—generally mirrors the Delaware corporate statute. Although most states have revised and adapted the MBCA provisions to meet their state's special needs, the redrafting has been done not by legislative committee, but instead by each state's bar association and its corporate law committee. This is also true for states, such as California and New York, that have not followed the MBCA but have their own special corporate statute.

Nonetheless, the corporate statutes in states other than Delaware often reflect input by a powerful corporation in the state—particularly with respect to antitakeover provisions. But otherwise there is no corporate or other special-interest lobby behind corporate statutory revisions. As in Delaware, corporate law is generally the product of a private group of corporate law practitioners, law professors and state bureaucrats. State legislatures are usually happy that somebody else has done the specialized work of creating and updating the state's corporate statute.

Delaware's corporate judiciary. In Delaware, all cases involving corporate law issues go to the Delaware Court of Chancery, whose judges are appointed on the basis of their corporate law expertise. The chancery court sits in equity without a jury, and has a docket with large numbers of corporate law cases. This means that chancery court judges both ascertain the facts and decide how the law applies to them, thus resolving corporate law cases with remarkable speed. Delaware judges are the rock stars of corporate law. Their opinions, speeches and law review articles are widely followed and discussed by corporate lawyers.

Delaware seeks to ensure that its judges are independent of the political process in a number of ways. Delaware judges are nominated by a bipartisan nominating committee charged with selecting the best-qualified candidates. Delaware judges are then appointed by the governor to 12-year terms, among the longest in the country. Delaware law requires that judicial appointments maintain an equal balance between the two political parties.

Delaware's judiciary is especially known for its large, well-developed body of case law on corporate law. On many corporate law topics, Delaware decisions outnumber those of all other U.S. courts combined. Delaware's large body of case law is seen as providing predictability on a wide range of corporate law issues. Furthermore, with a large number of cases involving Delaware corporations and knowledgeable and sophisticated jurists, the law continually evolves in response to a changing business environment.

A number of states have sought to replicate Delaware's judicial advantage in corporate law by creating special business courts. These state courts have special jurisdiction to hear business cases, especially those arising under the state's corporate statutes. But these special courts suffer from a number of disadvantages in competing for incorporation business. In many, the facts are determined by juries, not judges; the judges are appointed through a political process and serve relatively short terms; and decisions by trial judges do not have precedential value. In addition, no state has a body of case law that compares with Delaware's.

Take Note!

Many Delaware judges have become important figures in corporate law. Leo E. Strine, the current Chief Justice of the Delaware Supreme Court, and previously the Chancellor of the Delaware Court of Chancery, is widely recognized as a leading scholar. The current Chancellor, Andre G. Bouchard, was a prominent Delaware lawyer and has authored several significant opinions. Chief Justice Strine's predecessor in the role of Chancellor, William Chandler, wrote, among many others, the decisions involving The Walt Disney Company and Citigroup, which we will read later in this book. His predecessor, William Allen, decided many of the important takeover cases of the 1980s and 1990s.

2. Race to the Bottom or to the Top?

The crucial policy question that arises from Delaware's dominance in the market for corporate chartering of public corporations is the quality of the Delaware product. Although there is no doubt that Delaware has led the "race of laxity"—one of increasing flexibility in U.S. corporate law—the question is whether Delaware has sold out to corporate managers, at the expense of corporate shareholders and other constituencies.

The early debate. Beginning in the 1960s many academics concluded that Delaware was in the for-profit business of selling its corporation law in exchange for filing fees. The prevailing assumption was that corporate managers, who controlled the decision of where to incorporate or reincorporate the business, pressed for incorporation in Delaware to increase their power (and compensation) as managers.

William Cary (a law school professor and former SEC chair) was the main spokesman for the thesis that Delaware was engaged in a "race to the bottom." He contended that Delaware systematically had eliminated or reduced shareholder protections. As evidence, he pointed to statutory provisions that had reduced the shareholder vote to approve mergers from two-thirds to a majority, as well as numerous court decisions that he interpreted as liberally applying the business judgment rule and permitting corporate managers to resist hostile tender offers.

Central to Cary's argument was that horizontal corporate federalism allowed managers to choose among fifty states. If one state imposed policies that managers didn't like, they could simply reincorporate the business in a different, more management-friendly state. Cary proposed minimum federal standards to prevent this managerial opportunism.

In response to Cary's argument, Ralph Winter (a federal appeals court judge and former law school professor) argued that market forces resulted in a "race to the top" that Delaware was winning. Winter argued that it did not make sense that Delaware was engaged in a race to the bottom, since doing so would disadvantage Delaware corporations in attracting capital. In particular, Winter explained that if Delaware actually permitted managers to profit at the expense of its shareholders, shareholders would discover this and not invest in Delaware corporations. This would cause share prices to decline and create incentives for hostile bidders to buy the cheap shares and reincorporate in a more shareholder-friendly state.

Winter noted that although Cary's argument enjoyed almost universal academic support, it was implausible on its face. Why would shareholders voluntarily invest in corporations permitted to steal from them? Winter argued that competition for corporate charters led states to create corporate law that provided the greatest benefit to shareholders. He opposed interference in this market, particularly at the federal level. According to Winter, the greater danger was not that states would compete for charters but that they would not.

Recent questions. Since Cary and Winter, much ink has been spilled on this debate. There have been numerous *event studies* of whether reincorporation in Delaware affects share prices. Some studies find moving to Delaware increases share prices, though it is unclear whether this is due to Delaware law or an increased chance the corporation will be sold.

Other studies have tried to measure whether Delaware corporations are more financially successful. Results are mixed: one study found a "Delaware effect" during the 1990s, when by one measure Delaware firms were more valuable, but more recent studies have questioned those results and show that the effect disappeared in later years. The debate continues.

What's That?

An "event study" is a statistical assessment of how an event (such as a merger or the passage of a new law) affects the share prices of a firm. The fluctuation in the firm's shares prices around the event date are compared to fluctuations in share prices of comparable firms or even the market as a whole. The idea is to find abnormal returns (positive or negative) that would indicate the event created or destroyed firm value.

Whether or not Delaware offers a superior product, its corporate law is likely to remain on top. Corporate managers are lured to Delaware by flexible laws regarding executive compensation, self-dealing, and indemnification. Corporate counsel often prefer the Delaware brand. And investment bankers (who help companies sell shares to the public) prefer Delaware's certainty (and its case law encouraging the use of investment bankers).

FYI

In 2007 North Dakota entered the market for chartering public corporations by enacting its Publicly Traded Corporations Act. Meant to provide an alternative to the "cozy relationship" between Delaware and corporate America, the Act has been described as the most shareholder friendly corporation law in the country. The Act, which was drafted by corporate law scholars, seeks to increase board independence, management accountability, and shareholder involvement. Among its provisions, it grants shareholders an advisory vote on executive compensation, allows 5% shareholders to nominate directors using the company's proxy statement, mandates corporate reimbursement to shareholders for successful proxy contests, separates the role of CEO and board chair, and restricts antitakeover devices used to entrench incumbent management.

A good portion of Delaware's state budget is funded by corporate franchise taxes and incorporation fees, not to mention revenues from litigation. The state bar, legislature, administrative agencies, and judiciary understand the importance of maintaining Delaware's dominance and don't want to jeopardize the goose that lays the golden eggs—an attitude that reassures the U.S. business community, which regularly chooses Delaware as one of the most business-friendly states in the nation.

Given Delaware's dominance, you might wonder whether there really is vigorous competition among the states for corporate charters. After all, the vast majority of companies that incorporate out of their home state do so in Delaware—no other state is even close. Maybe the "race to the top or bottom" debate is misconceived, and Delaware's <u>primary competition</u> comes not from other states but from the federal government. Delaware authorities are always aware that if they misstep, the federal authorities may step in—as has happened after recent financial scandals and crises.

Points for Discussion

1. Corporate law as product.

Is it appropriate to describe state corporate law (statutes, court system, lawyers) as a "product"? If so, is corporate law unique, or do states sell other law products? Isn't this unseemly?

2. Delaware's partial dominance.

Although Delaware is the legal home of about half of public corporations in the United States, it is far less dominant with respect to close corporations. If Delaware corporate law offers so many advantages to public corporations, why don't close corporations also flock to Delaware? (Delaware offers special statutory provisions, DGCL §§ 341–356, just for close corporations.)

3. Assessing Delaware's corporate law.

The Cary-Winter debate, which still persists, is ultimately based on two testable views of Delaware corporate law. Cary sought to prove that Delaware law was deficient since it had abandoned two-thirds voting for mergers and adopted a majority-voting requirement in its place. Winter pointed to the willingness of investors to invest in Delaware companies as proof that Delaware's corporate law is no worse, and perhaps better, than any other. How would you assess whether Delaware corporate law is, indeed, a superior product?

CHAPTER 6

Corporation in Society

One of the central questions in corporate law is the purpose of the corporation. For whose benefit should the corporation be run—for the primary benefit of its shareholders or to benefit society overall, or some combination of both? The answer to this question can lead to different conclusions about whether particular corporate decisions are proper.

This chapter introduces you to the debate over the corporation's place in society. First, we lay out the debate, which basically pits those who see the corporation as a set of contractual/property rights against those who see the corporation as a social institution with responsibilities to its many constituents. Then, we look at how the debate has played out in two specific contexts—the distribution of firm profits and charitable giving by modern corporations. Finally, we consider the role of directors and corporate lawyers faced with issues of social responsibility and corporate purpose—specifically, when a multinational corporation considers moving operations overseas.

A. Whom Does the Corporation Serve?

The debate over the purpose of the corporation has dominated corporate law since the aftermath of the "Great Crash" of 1929 and the economic depression that followed. During the early 1930s, Congress held a series of hearings about the role of the modern corporation. Testimony focused on the major scandals of that era and leading scholars debated the appropriate role of corporate law, policy, and power. Historically, the debate was framed by two polar views, generally labeled as "shareholder primacy" and "corporate social responsibility." More recently, CSR questions have been reframed as related to environmental, social, and governance (ESG) questions, as well as corporate sustainability.

1. Corporation as Private Property

Adolf Berle, a Wall Street lawyer and law professor, developed an early version of the shareholder primacy view during the early 1930s. He argued in an influential law review article that corporate powers were held in trust "at all times exercisable only for the ratable benefit of all the shareholders." During the following three decades, as Berle modified some of his views, economist Milton Friedman emerged as the leading proponent of shareholder primacy.

Friedman argued that the only social responsibility of a corporation is to maximize profits for its shareholders within the confines of the law. According to Friedman, private for-profit corporations had developed a proven ability to maximize shareholder wealth, and he argued that they should pursue this goal. In his view, "there is one and only one social responsibility of business: to use its resources and engage in activities designed to increase its profits so long as it stays within the rules of the game, which is to say, engages in open and free competition, without deception or fraud."

Friedman was not opposed to social responsibility. But he argued that social responsibility was for individuals and government, not corporations. If individual shareholders wanted to

Adolf Berle was a Wall Street lawyer and law professor whose book *The Modern Corporation and Private Property* is among the most (if not, the most) influential books on corporate law. In the early 1930s, Berle (along with his co-author economist Gardiner Means) studied 200 of the largest U.S. public corporations and concluded that executives effectively controlled nearly all decision making in the firms, with shareholders playing a mostly perfunctory role. The book's conclusion that "ownership is separated from control" in public corporations remains a guiding thesis of corporate law scholarship and legal reform. Berle's calls for greater disclosure by public companies and a greater role for shareholders served as the underpinnings for the federal securities laws. Ultimately, Berle argued for government regulation that promoted the corporation's responsibilities toward society, beyond maximizing shareholder financial profits.

Take Note!

In this debate, it is important to recognize that some employees do better than others—in some situations, much better! We devote an entire chapter to the issue of executive pay and the huge gap between the pay of senior officers and lower-level employees: Chapter 22, Executive Compensation. Ironically, the issue has brought together those who argue for shareholder primacy (seeing big paychecks for non-performing executives as a failure of the corporation to serve shareholder interests) and those who argue for the corporation as social institution (seeing the same paychecks as a failure of the corporation to value workers).

be socially responsible by contributing their own money to social causes, that was fine. And Friedman favored government intervention to correct market failures, to provide important public services, and to protect and enforce contract and property rights. But those responsibilities were not the job of business corporations.

Over time, many "law and economics" academics and financial leaders have come to share Friedman's view that the corporation exists primarily to generate shareholder wealth. They have explained that other corporate constituencies, such as employees and creditors, are protected by contracts with the corporation. They have seen other constituencies' interests as incidental and subordinate to the goal of maximizing shareholder wealth. Delaware Chancellor William Allen labeled this view the "property" model, because it envisions the corporation as a form of privately held property.

Notice that the property model explicitly assumes the corporation is run for the benefit of shareholders rather than employees. In fact, U.S. corporate law focuses on contributors of capital (shareholders) instead of contributors of other inputs (employees, suppliers, communities). Why should corporate law favor capital over these other inputs, which often may be as or more important to the success of the corporation? The answer by those who advocate for shareholder primacy has been that these other inputs are protected by free markets, contractual negotiations, and government regulation—not corporate law.

2. Corporation as Social Institution

The leading 1930s proponent of the contrary view, which later became known as corporate social responsibility, was law professor E. Merrick Dodd. A year after Berle published his influential pro-shareholder article, Dodd countered that the business corporation should be viewed as something far more significant than merely a shareholder profit maximizing machine. Dodd contended that the business corporation was properly seen "as an economic institution which has a social service as well as a profit making function."

Dodd's view spread widely. It appealed to people who found the notion of corporate citizenship and responsibility attractive, and the business community endorsed the economic case for corporate social responsibility. Many corporate executives complained that shareholders were too short-sighted, with no real stake in the long-term health of the corporation. They asserted that shareholders wrongly viewed the corporation as their private property, when the superior view was that

Take Note!

The social responsibility/sustainability movement in the United States has mostly been voluntary. Companies have adopted standards and programs on environmental stewardship, workplace standards, and sustainability initiatives in response to consumer and investor pressures—and sometimes to stave off government regulation. One of the leading groups in the CSR movement, Ceres, was formed in 1989 in response to the Exxon-Valdez oil spill. The non-profit promotes social well-being and environmental protection by bringing together institutional shareholders, corporate management, and "thought leaders" to encourage companies to adopt social responsibility-focused governance structures, stakeholder engagement, public disclosures, and operational performance. *See* http://www.ceres.org.

directors should focus on the corporation's long-term interests as an economic entity, including attention to non-shareholder constituencies. In this view, the directors owed duties to the corporation itself as an entity, not merely to the corporation's shareholders. Chancellor Allen labeled this competing view the "entity" model.

More recently, consumers and other corporate stakeholders have pressed corporations to consider issues of business ethics and sustainability. Social awareness initiatives and socially responsible investing have led to increased pressure on corporations to behave responsibly. Some prominent corporate leaders, including Warren Buffett, have asserted that corporations must focus on "people, communities, and the environment"—the keys to profitability and thus shareholder value. And some leading academics have argued that the theory of shareholder primacy is actually inconsistent with traditional rules of corporate law, the actual economic structure of business corporations, and the empirical evidence on what makes corporations work. They point out that corporate law actually gives directors broad discretion to consider non-shareholder constituents, corporate boards are not bound to allocate residual profits only to shareholders, and long-term corporate returns are not necessarily linked to shareholder empowerment. Instead, these academics point out that the most successful corporations often focus on maximizing "firm value," which includes the value to all corporate constituents, not just shareholders.

Other commentators have argued that CSR and ESG initiatives have spread, not because managers naturally want to pursue a social responsibility agenda, but instead because such an agenda is good public relations. Cynics argue that some corporations implement socially responsible policies and produce glossy sustainability reports to distract the public from ethical questions posed by their core operations. Most large public corporations have social responsibility-related links on their home pages, which often include ESG and sustainability reports and presentations. In part, this is because many institutional shareholders are now insisting that the corporations in which they invest have a clearly articulated "social purpose," with specific environmental, social and governance targets. You might want to take a few minutes now to pick a public corporation you find interesting, and check its website to see what sustainability initiatives and ESG metrics the company has highlighted.

Go Online

Many students find the 2003 documentary "The Corporation" entertaining and thought provoking. The film portrays the modern corporation as often dysfunctional, even sociopathic. Featuring several prominent commentators, including Milton Friedman and Bob Monks, it describes the shareholder primacy and CSR arguments. "The Corporation" is available on YouTube and will soon have a sequel. *See* http://www.thecorporation.com.

3. Implications of Board Discretion

A central tenet of modern U.S. corporate law is that the board of directors supervises and manages the business and affairs of the corporation. Does the board have the discretion to decide that the corporation pursue an agenda other than exclusively maximizing shareholder value? Many modern corporate statutes, though interestingly not Delaware's, specifically recognize the discretion of the board to make decisions that take into account non-shareholder constituents.

Ohio Revised Code § 1701.59
Authority of Directors

(A) All of the authority of a corporation shall be exercised by or under the direction of its directors.

(E) For purposes of this section, a director, in determining what the director reasonably believes to be in the best interests of the corporation, shall consider the interests of the corporation's shareholders and, in the director's discretion, may consider any of the following:

(1) The interests of the corporation's employees, suppliers, creditors, and customers;

(2) The economy of the state and nation;

(3) Community and societal considerations;

(4) The long-term as well as short-term interests of the corporation and its shareholders, including the possibility that these interests may be best served by the continued independence of the corporation.

The discretion and responsibilities of the board are particularly tested in corporations that operate globally. Multinational corporations must account for the different legal, regulatory, and business risks they face in the many countries where they operate. Simply complying with national laws and regulations often might not be enough. In many countries, particularly in continental Europe, non-shareholder stakeholders wield greater power, and the social responsibility movement is widely accepted. Multinational corporations must decide whether to treat workers better than local workplace rules may require, or whether to implement environmentally friendlier policies than otherwise would apply. These decisions depend not only on the legal rules of the countries where the corporation operates, but also on the perceptions and preferences of the corporation's shareholders and stakeholders throughout the world.

Boards also have discretion to make charitable contributions on behalf of the corporation. Naturally, there is a concern that corporate directors might prefer their own pet charities and causes. They might make contributions for which they receive personal benefits, such as a seat on the board of trustees of a prestigious university. Given these concerns, should shareholders have a greater voice in how the corporation spends money on ESG and sustainability?

Practice Pointer

The tension between the corporation as profit maximizer and social institution, though it arises regularly in business practice, does not come up that often in court cases. When it does, courts have been ambivalent. Some courts have accepted that corporate boards can make choices that protect "corporate culture" at the expense of immediate shareholder gains. See *Paramount Communications, Inc. v. Time, Inc.*, 571 A.2d 1140 (Del. 1989).

Other courts have taken the view that corporate boards must make choices that maximize shareholder value. For example, the Eleventh Circuit interpreted Florida's corporations statute to require that a newspaper company be valued according to how it "should have been run" to maximize short-term shareholder value, rather than how it "actually was run" to support local news reporting, employee benefits, and the local arts community—sometimes at the expense of short-term shareholder returns. *Cox Enterprises, Inc. v. Davidson*, 510 F.3d 1350 (11th Cir. 2007).

And, more recently, the Delaware Chancery decided that the board of Craigslist, Inc. could not protect its "online community" from profit-maximizing shareholders that might seek to change the company's user-friendly pricing structure. The court said, "Directors of a for-profit Delaware corporation cannot [consistent with their fiduciary duties] defend a business strategy that openly eschews stockholder wealth maximization." *eBay Domestic Holdings, Inc. v. Newmark*, 16 A.3d 1 (Del. Ch. 2010).

The case, needless to say, has been controversial. It was one of the reasons Delaware in 2013 adopted a "public benefit corporation" statute that explicitly permits corporations that choose the status of a benefit corporation to balance a stated public-benefit purpose (which can be "artistic, charitable cultural, economic, educational environmental literary, medical, religious, scientific or technological") and "stockholders' pecuniary interests." DGCL §§ 361–368 (new Subchapter XV). In addition to Delaware, over thirty states have adopted benefit corporation legislation that provides an option for stakeholder-oriented governance. To learn more about this new form of corporation and follow the status of legislation in various states, see https://benefitcorp.net/.

The materials that follow raise some of the fundamental questions about corporate law and policy. What is the corporation? Is it essentially the private property of the shareholders, or is it an entity (a social institution) that should serve public ends? Is it contractual in nature or is it a creature of the state that created it and to which it is responsible? To whom are the corporation and its directors and officers accountable? What interests must or may the board consider? Under what circumstances may the directors favor interests other than those of shareholders?

B. Social Responsibility in Context

We now turn to two business contexts that raise many of the challenging questions related to the social responsibility of corporations. First, we look at the dispute between the Dodge brothers and Henry Ford—a classic, one hundred-year-old case in corporate law. *Dodge v. Ford Motor Co.* illustrates the polar views of the purpose of the modern for-profit corporation, and also shows how some people (including judges) might try to use the rhetoric of shareholder primacy or social responsibility to further their own objectives. Second, we look at how corporate law treats corporate charitable giving and then consider some suggestions for reform.

1. The "Classic" Case

Although the principal issue in *Dodge v. Ford Motor* was whether the corporation could be compelled to pay dividends to shareholders, the case is best remembered for its discussion of the role of the corporation in society, given Henry Ford's insistence on stating his motives for business decisions in terms of social rather than economic values.

This action was brought by the Dodge brothers, two minority shareholders, against the Ford Motor Company, Henry Ford, and other members of the board of directors. The plaintiffs sought (1) to compel the payment of a special dividend and (2) to enjoin Ford's plan to vertically integrate by purchasing iron ore mines in the Northern Peninsula of Michigan, then transporting the ore to smelters to be erected in the company's River Rouge property, and finally constructing steel manufacturing plants to produce steel for the manufacture of cars in the company's factories. The lower court granted all relief requested by plaintiffs.

Ford Motor Company was organized in 1903 with an initial capitalization of $150,000. At the time the suit was brought, the company's paid-in capital was $2,000,000, with the plaintiffs owning 10% of the outstanding shares and Ford owning 58% and completely dominating the company.

Originally, Ford cars had sold for more than $900. But over time, the selling price was lowered and the car itself was improved. In 1916, the car's sales price was reduced from $440 to $360. As the company lowered the price of its cars, sales soared. The following chart shows the company's remarkable success:

Fiscal Year	Cars sold	Profits	Special dividends
1910	18,664	$4,521,509	
1911	34,466	$6,275,031	
1912	68,544	$13,057,312	$3,000,000
1913	168,304	$25,046,767	$12,000,000
1914	248,307	$30,338,454	$11,000,000
1915 (10 mos.)	264,351	$24,641,423	$14,000,000
1916	472,350	$59,994,918	$5,000,000

Besides the regular quarterly dividends amounting to $1,200,000 per year, the company also paid special dividends totaling $45 million from 1911 through 1916. Then, in 1916, Ford "declared it to be the settled policy of the company not to pay in the future any special dividends, but to put back into the business for the future all of the earnings of the company other than the regular dividend."

The defendants appealed from the lower court order directing the corporation to pay a special dividend of $19 million, enjoining it from building the smelter and steel furnaces at the River Rouge facilities, and restraining it from "increasing the fixed capital assets" or "holding liquid assets in excess of such as may be reasonably required in the proper conduct and carrying on of the business and operations" of the corporation.

Dodge v. Ford Motor Co.

170 N.W. 668 (Mich. 1919)

OSTRANDER, C.J.

When plaintiffs made their complaint and demand for further dividends, the Ford Motor Company had concluded its most prosperous year of business. The demand for its cars at the price of the preceding year continued. It could make and could market in the year beginning August 1, 1916, more than 500,000 cars. The cost of materials was likely to advance, and perhaps the price of labor; but it reasonably might have expected a profit for the year of upwards of $60,000,000. In justification of their dividend policy and business plan, the defendants proved the following facts: It had been the policy of the corporation for a considerable time to annually reduce the selling price of cars, while keeping up, or improving, their quality. As early as in June, 1915, a general plan for the expansion of the productive capacity of the concern by a practical duplication of its plant had been talked over by the executive officers and directors and agreed upon. It is hoped, by Mr. Ford, that eventually 1,000,000 cars will be annually produced. The contemplated changes will permit the increased output.

The plan, as affecting the profits of the business for the year beginning August 1, 1916, and thereafter, calls for a reduction in the selling price of the cars. It is true that this price might be at any time increased, but the plan called for the reduction in price of $80 a car. The capacity of the plant, without the additions thereto voted to be made, would produce more than 600,000 cars annually. This number, and more, could have been sold for $440 instead of $360, a difference in the return for capital, labor, and materials employed of at least $48,000,000. In short, the plan does not call for and is not intended to produce immediately a more profitable business, but a less profitable one; not only less profitable than formerly, but less profitable than it is admitted it might be made. The apparent immediate effect will be to diminish the value of shares and the returns to shareholders.

It is the contention of plaintiffs that the apparent effect of the plan is intended to be the continued and continuing effect of it, and that it is deliberately proposed to continue the corporation henceforth as a semi-eleemosynary institution and not as a business institution. In support of this contention, they point to the attitude and to the expressions of Mr. Henry Ford.

Mr. Henry Ford is the dominant force in the business of the Ford Motor Company. No plan of operations could be adopted unless he consented, and no board of directors can be elected whom he does not favor. A business, one of the largest in the world, and one of the most profitable, has been built up. It employs many men, at good pay.

"My ambition," said Mr. Ford, "is to employ still more men, to spread the benefits of this industrial system to the greatest possible number, to help them build up their lives and their homes. To do this we are putting the greatest share of our profits back in the business."

"With regard to dividends, the company paid sixty per cent on its capitalization of two million dollars, or $1,200,000, leaving $58,000,000 to reinvest for the growth of the company. This is Mr. Ford's policy at present, and it is understood that the other stockholders cheerfully accede to this plan."

He had made up his mind in the summer of 1916 that no dividends other than the regular dividends should be paid, "for the present."

"Q. For how long? Had you fixed in your mind any time in the future, when you were going to pay? A. No.

"Q. That was indefinite in the future? A. That was indefinite; yes, sir."

The record, and especially the testimony of Mr. Ford, convinces that he has to some extent the attitude towards shareholders of one who has dispensed and distributed to them large gains and that they should be content to take what he chooses to give. His testimony creates the impression, also, that he thinks the Ford Motor Company has made too much money, has had too large profits, and that, although large profits might be still earned, a sharing of them with the public, by reducing the price of the output of the company, ought to be undertaken. We have no doubt that certain sentiments, philanthropic and altruistic, creditable to Mr. Ford, had large influence in determining the policy to be pursued by the Ford Motor Company—the policy which has been herein referred to.

It is said by his counsel that—

Although a manufacturing corporation cannot engage in humanitarian works as its principal business, the fact that it is organized for profit does not prevent the existence of implied powers to carry on with humanitarian motives such charitable works as are incidental to the main business of the corporation.

The cases referred to by counsel, like all others in which the subject is treated, turn finally upon the question whether it appears that the directors were not acting for the best interests of the corporation. The case presented here is not like any of them. The difference between an incidental humanitarian expenditure of corporate funds for the benefit of the employees, like the building of a hospital for their use and the employment of agencies for the betterment of their condition, and a general purpose and plan to benefit mankind at the expense of others, is obvious. There should be no confusion (of which there is evidence) of the duties which Mr. Ford conceives that he and the stockholders owe to the general public and the duties which in law he and his codirectors owe to protesting, minority stockholders. A business corporation is organized and carried on primarily for the profit of the stockholders. The powers of the directors are to be employed for that end. The discretion of directors is to be exercised in the choice of means to attain that end, and does not extend to a change in the end itself, to the reduction of profits, or to the nondistribution of profits among stockholders in order to devote them to other purposes.

There is committed to the discretion of directors, a discretion to be exercised in good faith, the infinite details of business, including the wages which shall be paid to employees, the number of hours they shall work, the conditions under which labor shall be carried on, and the price for which products shall be offered to the public.

As we have pointed out, and the proposition does not require argument to sustain it, it is not within the lawful powers of a board of directors to shape and conduct the affairs of a corporation for the merely incidental benefit of shareholders and for the primary purpose of benefiting others, and no one will contend that, if the avowed purpose of the defendant directors was to sacrifice the interests of shareholders, it would not be the duty of the courts to interfere.

We are not, however, persuaded that we should interfere with the proposed expansion of the business of the Ford Motor Company. In view of the fact that the selling price of products may be increased at any time, the ultimate results of the larger business cannot be certainly estimated. The judges are not business experts. It is recognized that plans must often be made for a long future, for expected competition, for a continuing as well as an immediately profitable venture. The experience of the Ford Motor Company is evidence of capable management of its affairs. It may be noticed, incidentally, that it took from the public the money required for the execution of its plan, and that the very considerable salaries paid to Mr. Ford and to certain executive officers and employees were not diminished. We are not satisfied that the alleged motives of the directors, in so far as they are reflected in the conduct of the business, menace the interests of shareholders. It is enough to say, perhaps, that the court of equity is at all times open to complaining shareholders having a just grievance.

The decree of the court below fixing and determining the specific amount to be distributed to stockholders is affirmed. In other respect, the said decree is reversed.

Points for Discussion

1. Shareholder wealth maximization.

Dodge v. *Ford Motor* is often cited by academic writers as support for the shareholder primacy view: "A business corporation is organized and carried on primarily for the profit of the stockholders." Does it support that view? Notice the court used the word "primarily," not "exclusively," suggesting that "an incidental humanitarian expenditure for the benefit of the employees" would be permissible. Thus, the decision seems to leave room for activities that are not profit maximizing if they are "incidental" to the "primary" purpose of the corporation.

In addition, it is worth noting that the court refused to question the business judgment of management and enjoin the proposed vertical expansion of the company even though that expansion would reduce short-term profits. As the court said, "The judges are not business experts."

2. Precedential value.

In assessing the precedential force of *Dodge v. Ford Motor*, keep in mind the underlying business struggle. At the time of the case, Ford's business principally involved assembling cars using parts supplied by others. The Dodge brothers, who owned 10% of Ford Motor's shares, were among Ford's largest suppliers. In addition, the Dodges had begun assembling cars in competition with Ford.

The Dodge brothers were mostly concerned about Ford's plans to develop the River Rouge factories and to vertically integrate the company (from ore mining to smelting to manufacturing to car assembly). Access to capital was not a problem for them, and before the case Ford had offered them $30 million for their interest in the company. Why didn't they accept?

In ruling (in part) for the Dodges, the Michigan court may have been more concerned about the state of competition in the state's burgeoning auto industry, as well as the economic and political implications of a one-company industry, than it was about shareholder rights. That is, the court's decision may have been as much about social responsibility as the stated views of Henry Ford!

3. Long-term vs. short-term?

Was Henry Ford really sacrificing corporate profits for the welfare of non-shareholder constituents? Ford had asserted on numerous occasions that he wanted only a small profit from his venture:

> I hold this view because it enables a large number of people to buy and enjoy the use of a car and because it gives a larger number of men employment at good wages. Those are the two aims I have in life. But I would not be counted a success if I could not accomplish that and at the same time make a fair amount of profit for myself and the men associated with me in the business.

> And let me say right here, that I do not believe that we should make such an awful profit on our cars. A reasonable profit is right, but not too much. So it has been my policy to force the price of the car down as fast as production would permit, and give the benefits to users and laborers, with resulting surprisingly enormous benefits to ourselves.

Does Ford's refusal to "make such an awful profit" actually make good business sense and contain the seeds of substantial future profits (and dividends) for the shareholders? Was Ford thinking about sustainability?

2. Corporate Charitable Giving

In the early twentieth century, many courts held that corporate charitable contributions were *ultra vires*, or beyond the powers granted by the articles of incorporation with respect to the corporation's business. In response to these decisions, nearly all states amended their corporate statutes to authorize corporate charitable giving. These statutes, like the statute in the case that follows, gave corporations the power to make charitable gifts, but did not specify whether such gifts had to be aimed at advancing the corporation's business interests.

The following case raises the question whether corporate charitable giving is appropriate and how courts should evaluate a shareholder's challenge to such giving. The case arose out of the ill will from a family divorce in which the wife (and her daughter) challenged the husband's decision to have the corporation he dominated donate company stock to fund a camp for "underprivileged boys."

Girard Henderson had dominated the affairs of Alexander Dawson, Inc. for many years, through his controlling interest in that corporation. In 1955, as part of a separation agreement, he transferred 11,000 shares of common stock to his wife, Theodora Henderson, who also owned in her own name 37,000 shares of Alexander Dawson preferred stock. In 1967, Mrs. Henderson formed the Theodora Holding Corp. (plaintiff in the case) and transferred to the holding company her 11,000 shares of Alexander Dawson common stock, which at the time had a market value of $15,675,000. During the year of the disputed corporate charitable donation, the corporation paid dividends on the preferred and common stock held by Mrs. Henderson and her holding company totaling $286,240.

From 1960 to 1966, Girard Henderson had caused Alexander Dawson to make annual corporate contributions ranging from $60,000 to more than $70,000 to the Alexander Dawson Foundation (the Foundation), which Henderson had formed in 1957. All contributions were unanimously approved by the shareholders. In 1966, Alexander Dawson donated to the Foundation a large tract of land valued at $467,750 for the purpose of establishing a camp for under-privileged boys. In April 1967, Mr. Henderson proposed that the board approve a $528,000 gift of company stock to the Foundation to finance the camp. One director, Theodora Ives (the daughter of Mrs. Henderson), objected and suggested that the gift be made instead to a charitable corporation supported by her mother and herself. Girard Henderson responded by causing a reduction in the Alexander Dawson board of directors from eight members to three. The newly-composed board, which did not include Theodora Ives, thereafter approved the gift of stock to the Foundation.

Theodora Holding Corp. then brought suit against certain individuals, including Girard Henderson, challenging the stock gift and seeking an accounting and the appointment of a liquidating receiver for Alexander Dawson.

Theodora Holding Corp. v. Henderson

257 A.2d 398 (Del. Ch. 1969)

MARVEL, VICE CHANCELLOR.

Title 8 Del.C. § 122 provides as follows:

Every corporation created under this chapter shall have power to—

(9) Make donations for the public welfare or for charitable, scientific or educational purposes, and in time of war or other national emergency in aid thereof.

There is no doubt but that the Alexander Dawson Foundation is recognized as a legitimate charitable trust by the Department of Internal Revenue. It is also clear that it is authorized to operate exclusively in the fields of "religious, charitable, scientific, literary, or educational purposes, or for the prevention of cruelty to children or animals". Furthermore, contemporary courts recognize that unless corporations carry an increasing share of the burden of supporting charitable and educational causes that the business advantages now reposed in corporations by law may well prove to be unacceptable to the representatives of an aroused public. The recognized obligation of corporations towards philanthropic, educational and artistic causes is reflected in the statutory law of all of the states, other than the states of Arizona and Idaho.

In *A.P. Smith Mfg. Co. v. Barlow*, 13 N.J. 145, 98 A.2d 581 (1953), a case in which the corporate donor had been organized long before the adoption of a statute authorizing corporate gifts to charitable or educational institutions, the Supreme Court of New Jersey upheld a gift of $1500 by the plaintiff corporation to Princeton University, being of the opinion that the trend towards the transfer of wealth from private industrial entrepreneurs to corporate institutions, the increase of

Make the Connection

The study of corporate law frequently requires knowledge of the tax code and regulations. For example, corporate directors and officers typically are more likely to approve, and shareholders are less likely to contest, charitable contributions if they are tax deductible by the corporation, so that the charitable contribution reduces the amount of corporate income subject to tax. Internal Revenue Code § 170(a) generally allows tax deductions for charitable contributions. Today, § 170(b)(2)(A) provides that, with certain limited exceptions: "The total deductions under subsection (a) for any taxable year . . . shall not exceed 10 percent of the taxpayer's taxable income." When *Henderson* was decided, the limitation on charitable deductions was only 5 percent.

taxes on individual income, coupled with steadily increasing philanthropic needs, necessitate corporate giving for educational needs even were there no statute permitting such gifts. The court also noted that the gift tended to bolster the free enterprise system and the general social climate in which plaintiff was nurtured. And while the court pointed out that there was no showing that the gift in question was made indiscriminately or to a pet charity in furtherance of personal rather than corporate ends, the actual holding of the opinion appears to be that a corporate charitable or educational gift to be valid must merely be within reasonable limits both as to amount and purpose.

I conclude that the test to be applied in passing on the validity of a gift such as the one here in issue is that of reasonableness, a test in which the provisions of the Internal Revenue Code pertaining to charitable gifts by corporations furnish a helpful guide. The gift here under attack was made from gross income and had a value as of the time of giving of $528,000 in a year in which Alexander Dawson's total income was $19,144,229.06, or well within the federal tax deduction limitation of 5% of such income.

The contribution under attack can be said to have "cost" all of the stockholders of Alexander Dawson including plaintiff, less than $80,000, or some fifteen cents per dollar of contribution, taking into consideration the federal tax provisions applicable to holding companies as well as the provisions for compulsory distribution of dividends received by such a corporation. It is accordingly obvious, in my opinion, that the relatively small loss of immediate income otherwise payable to plaintiff and the corporate defendant's other stockholders had it not been for the gift in question, is far out-weighed by the overall benefits flowing from the placing of such gift in channels where it serves to benefit those in need of philanthropic or educational support, thus providing justification for large private holdings, thereby benefiting plaintiff in the long run. Finally, the fact that the interests of the Alexander Dawson Foundation appear to be increasingly directed towards the rehabilitation and education of deprived but deserving young people is peculiarly appropriate in an age when a large segment of youth is alienated even from parents who are not entirely satisfied with our present social and economic system.

On notice, an order in conformity with the holdings of this opinion may be presented.

Points for Discussion

1. Relevance of statute.

Notice that the court, while initially reciting the Delaware statute that authorizes corporate charitable giving, does not mention it again. Instead, the court adopted a rule of "reasonableness" for reviewing corporate giving, even though the statute states no such limitation. Where does the "reasonableness" standard come from?

2. Corporate gifts as profit maximizers.

Corporations frequently cite their own economic interests in justifying corporate gifts. The New Jersey Supreme Court, in *A.P. Smith Manufacturing Co. v. Barlow*, cited by the *Henderson* court, upheld the corporate gift to Princeton University, citing the company's argument that the gift arguably advanced its long-run business interests. Would you advise a corporation to make only those gifts that managers believe further the corporation's long-run business interests? Must the managers quantify how much the charitable contributions will enhance the corporation's business interests or its reputation for social responsibility? Should corporations be permitted to make contributions that do not generate demonstrable benefits for the corporation? Put another way, must the corporation limit its activities solely to maximizing profits?

Take Note!

How much do corporations give to charities? In its annual report for 2017, the Giving USA Foundation found that total corporate charitable giving (including by corporate foundations) amounted to $20.8 billion. This represented only 5.1% of all charitable giving in the country, and only 0.9% of corporate pretax profits.

By comparison, charitable giving by non-corporate foundations totaled $66.9 billion, or 16.3% of all charitable giving. And giving by individuals, mostly to churches, amounted to $286.7 billion, representing 69.9% of all charitable contributions and 2.0% of disposable personal income.

3. Corporate gifts as social function.

As Professor Berle observed, *Barlow* recognized that "modern directors are not limited to running business enterprise for maximum profit, but are in fact and recognized in law as administrators of a community system." Is *Henderson* also consistent with this view? Does the corporation owe something to society in exchange for the privileges that society bestows on corporations, including limited liability for shareholders? Can corporate philanthropy be seen a kind of repayment? If so, should it be required?

4. Corporate gifts as self dealing.

Does the calculus change when corporate charity is tinged with conflicts of interest? For example, suppose a major oil company agrees to donate $50 million to help build an art museum that will house the art collection of the company's founder and CEO. Is the fairness of the gift subject to searching judicial review? That is, given the apparent conflict of interest, should a court scrutinize whether the corporation will actually realize $50 million worth of advertising and reputational benefits? Or will it be enough that the gift was considered by a group of independent directors (not financially beholden to the CEO) who concluded the donation was reasonable in light of the company's revenues and earnings? For Delaware's answer, see *Kahn v. Sullivan*, 594 A.2d 48 (Del. 1991) (upholding chancery court's conclusion that charitable donations approved by independent directors are subject to review under business judgment rule).

5. Should shareholders decide?

Shareholders generally cannot challenge corporate gifts, given the discretion afforded corporate directors under the business judgment rule, and shareholders have no formal voice in how and in what amounts corporations engage in charitable giving. Some commentators have argued that, after directors decide how much money a corporation will give to charities, shareholders should then be able to select the beneficiaries. Does this seem like a useful solution to the problem of directors giving away "other people's money"?

6. Disclosure of corporate gifts?

Managers also have broad discretion over charitable contributions because corporations generally are not required to disclose such contributions to shareholders. Securities regulators are reluctant to require such disclosure. As former SEC Chairman, Richard Breeden, once said, "If I were still in government, I would not want to touch the issue of 'regulating' corporate philanthropy with a 500 foot pole." If disclosure rules are unlikely, should corporate law play a more prominent role in making corporate charitable contributions more transparent?

C. Role of Corporate Lawyers

Now that we have seen how malleable corporate law is toward matters of social responsibility, we consider the roles assumed by corporate lawyers in advising corporations on such matters. We start by considering the appropriate role of lawyers in advising corporate clients on moral and ethical matters, beyond questions of legality. Then we consider the hypothetical case of Exogen, which puts you (as corporate counsel) in the position of advising the board of a multinational corporation that is considering moving some of its operations overseas—to engage in legal arbitrage.

1. Roles of Corporate Lawyers

Corporate lawyers are frequently called on to advise boards of directors and other corporate decision makers on matters beyond the legality and legal consequences of particular corporate actions. What is the role of the corporate lawyer in such situations? The ABA Model Rules of Professional Conduct answer the question first by making clear that the corporate lawyer represents "the corporation," not any particular constituent, and second by identifying an independent role that may extend beyond legal matters to encompass "moral, economic, social and political factors."

ABA Model Rules of Professional Conduct
Rule 1.13 Organization as Client

A lawyer employed or retained by an organization represents the organization acting through its duly authorized constituents.

* * *

Rule 2.1 Advisor

In representing a client, a lawyer shall exercise independent professional judgment and render candid advice. In rendering advice, a lawyer may refer not only to law but to other considerations such as moral, economic, social and political factors, that may be relevant to the client's situation.

So, what does "independent professional judgment" entail? That is, what kind of advisor should a corporate lawyer be? Some commentators take the view that a lawyer should not attempt to interject her personal moral or ethical views, but should instead simply advise corporate decision makers about the law and the consequences of complying or not complying with legal standards. To do otherwise, Justice Potter Stewart asserted in an influential law review article, might lead the corporate client to look for another lawyer who would not overstep his limited (professional) role as legal advisor. That is, corporate lawyers should observe the "morals of the marketplace."

During the heyday of corporate takeovers in the 1980s, Chancellor William Allen took the view that corporate lawyers had a special responsibility to be the conscience for their corporate clients, particularly when the interests of various corporate constituents in a takeover were in conflict. In fact, asserted Allen, outside lawyers should be prepared to resign from a corporate representation if corporate managers took a decision that the lawyer found at odds with his moral or ethical compass. That is, corporate lawyers—like outside directors on the board—should maintain their personal and professional "independence."

Recognizing that corporate lawyers (both outside lawyers and in-house counsel) often have a relational position with the corporation, Professor Richard Painter has argued that corporate lawyers should not wash their hands when the corporate decision makers face difficult moral or ethical issues. Instead, corporate lawyer should help corporate directors and officers understand the full implications of their decisions and steer them in the right direction. That is, the lawyer should seek to remain relevant and develop an "interdependent" relationship in which corporate decision makers turn to the lawyer, and the lawyer recognizes the tension in this sometimes difficult role.

2. Legal Arbitrage in Multinational Corporations

Assume that you are the outside corporate counsel of (fictitious) Exogen, a company that manufactures components for electric cars. One of the solvents used in the manufacturing process, Durasol, has been implicated as a potential carcinogen in recent medical studies. The data from this research is consistent with internal reports by Exogen scientists about the dangers of Durasol. The Occupational Health and Safety Administration (OSHA) has begun to consider banning the use of Durasol because of its effect on workers who breathe its fumes. OSHA has asked the company voluntarily to discontinue the use of the solvent.

At a meeting of the Exogen board of directors, corporate officials have sought guidance on discontinuing the use of Durasol. The officials are concerned, however, that doing so will increase the costs of manufacturing, since the chemical that would replace it is much more expensive. The company is in the process of moving its major manufacturing operations to Ruranesia

FYI

"Arbitrage" is the financial practice of taking advantage of a price differential in two markets. By entering into matching buy and sell transactions, an arbitrageur can make a profit equal to the difference in market prices.

"Legal arbitrage" (also known as "regulatory arbitrage") occurs when a person or business takes advantage of a difference in legal treatment in two jurisdictions or a gap in the law. For example, a company that operates in a country with high minimum wages can move its production to a low-wage country, while selling the goods in the high-wage country.

(a fictitious developing country that has become a manufacturing center for many multinational corporations). The officials expect these operations will be up and running within two years, or perhaps faster. Occupational health regulation in Ruranesia is lax, and government regulators are poorly paid and often corrupt. The Exogen officials believe that the company could use Durasol in its operations there.

Company officials suggest to the Exogen board that the company should not voluntarily cease using Durasol, but instead insist that OSHA institute formal proceedings to prohibit its use. This would require hearings, the opportunity for Exogen to question whether Durasol is actually harmful, and other elaborate procedural measures. At the same time, Exogen would continue with the plans to move the company's manufacturing operations to Ruranesia—as quickly as possible.

The directors turn to you for advice.

Points for Discussion

1. Ethics vs. legality.

How would you advise the board proceed? What are the pros and cons to what the company officials are proposing? What are the legal risks—under U.S. law or Ruranesia law? Should you advise the board only about legalities or also about ethics?

2. Foreign Corrupt Practices Act.

Dealings by U.S. public corporations with foreign government officials and regulators are subject to the Foreign Corrupt Practices Act. Under the FCPA, public companies must be transparent and keep books and records that "accurately and fairly reflect the transactions and dispositions of the assets of the issuer." In addition, public companies cannot engage in bribery of foreign officials. Specifically, the Act prohibits payments to foreign government officials to induce action or non-action in their official capacity for the purpose of obtaining or retaining business (with an exception for bribes to "expedite or secure performance of routine government action." Violations can result in civil penalties and criminal prosecution—both of companies and individuals. Does this affect your advice to the Exogen board, given the "legal arbitrage" that the company seems to be considering?

In addition, recent Delaware cases have emphasized the duties of directors of multinational corporations to be informed about the company's legal compliance with both domestic and foreign legal requirements—including by personally visiting foreign operations. Directors who fail to properly oversee the company's legal compliance (including the anti-bribery norms of the FCPA) face the possibility of personal liability in a shareholders' derivative suit.

3. Duties of corporate directors.

You may have noticed that how a corporate lawyer should advise a board of directors on a matter involving social responsibility, ESG, or sustainability raises an obvious question: What are the legal constraints that the board faces in such situations? This question has been the subject of considerable debate in corporate law. Do cases such as *Dodge v. Ford* suggest that the board must focus only on maximizing shareholder profits? Can broader considerations about society fit into such an analysis? Is there room to argue that corporate directors are not only able but obligated to consider the interests of stakeholders?

There is no shortage of legal sources that purport to guide directors regarding questions of shareholders versus employees, short-term versus long-term, and legality versus morality. Consider the ALI Principles of Corporate Governance. Do they provide any guidance for lawyers seeking to advise corporate clients on decisions that raise social responsibility issues?

ALI Principles of Corporate Governance

§ 2.01 The Objective and Conduct of the Corporation

(a) Subject to the provisions of Subsection (b), a corporation should have as its objective the conduct of business activities with a view to enhancing corporate profit and shareholder gain.

(b) Even if corporate profit and shareholder gain are not thereby enhanced, the corporation, in the conduct of its business:

(1) Is obliged, to the same extent as a natural person, to act within the boundaries set by law;

(2) May take into account ethical considerations that are reasonably regarded as appropriate to the responsible conduct of business; and

(3) May devote a reasonable amount of resources to public welfare, humanitarian, educational, and philanthropic purposes.

4. A new era in social responsibility?

Lately, institutional shareholders have become more interested in the environmental/social/governance (ESG) focus of the companies held in their investment portfolios. For example, in a widely-circulated letter the CEO of Blackrock (the world's largest investment firm) announced that the firm would not invest its discretionary funds in companies that did not articulate a strategy for long-term growth that included how structural trends "from slow wage growth to rising automation to climate change" could impact the company's strategy. Essential to sustainable growth, the letter pointed out, is how companies are managing ESG matters, which "we are increasingly integrating into our investment processes." *See* Larry Fink, "Letter to CEOs—A Sense of Purpose" (Jan. 2018).

In response to this pressure from institutional shareholders, public corporations in the United States and throughout the world have sought to show their new-found sensitivity to "social purpose" and ESG issues. Many companies now include on their websites, often with prominent mention on their home pages, their attention to ESG and their goals to reduce their carbon footprint, manage water usage, create a more diverse workforce, and ensure their adherence to global fair labor standards. In fact, you might find it interesting to browse the home page of a company that interests you and see how the company explains its ESG efforts.

As a result of this new attention by the investment community on ESG, a number of organizations—including the largest proxy advisory firm, Institutional Shareholder Services—have begun rating how well companies are addressing ESG matters. ISS, for example, now ranks companies into deciles based on their disclosures (and omissions) on ESG matters. In particular, these ranking look at eight broad categories (using 380 different factors) that measure companies' disclosures of how they are managing environment risk, dealing with climate change, protecting natural resources, avoiding waste, protecting human rights, ensuring compliance with fair labor standards, engaging with non-shareholder stakeholders, and ensuring product safety. *See* ISS, "Launch of E&S QualityScore Corporate Profiling" (Feb. 5, 2018).

How does this affect your advice to the Exogen directors on management's proposal to move Durosal manufacturing to Ruranesia?

CHAPTER 7

Corporation as Political Actor

A corporation is a "person" for many, but not all, purposes. It can own property, enter into contracts, and sue and be sued. Furthermore, under the Supreme Court's interpretations of the U.S. Constitution, a corporation is entitled to equal protection and due process under the law, can seek fair compensation when the government takes its property, and even has speech rights. But a corporation cannot vote, claim the privilege against self-incrimination, or expect the same privacy interests as individuals. That is, although corporations have some rights similar to those of individuals, their rights are not entirely the same.

This chapter looks at corporations as political actors. Other law school courses cover the "ins and outs" of election law and campaign finance. Here, we are focused on one important Supreme Court decision, *Citizens United v. Federal Election Commission*, which found unconstitutional a legislative ban on corporate spending in federal elections. The various opinions of the justices reflect a long-standing dialogue on the Court about the corporation in society and politics. Is the corporation an artificial being as to which the state can "giveth and taketh"? Is the corporation a real entity, greater than the sum of its parts, with its own separate existence and interests? Is the corporation a voluntary association with rights similar to those of the individuals who constitute it?

We begin with a thumbnail sketch of corporations under the Constitution, first as economic actors in our multistate economy and then as political actors in federal and state elections. We then lay out the Court's decision in *Citizens United*, along with excerpts from the concurring and dissenting opinions. Although some political repercussions of the decision have already been felt, our concluding thoughts focus on *Citizens United* and modern corporate governance.

A. The World Before *Citizens United*

1. Corporations Under the Constitution

At the founding of the United States in 1787, most corporations were municipal, religious or charitable institutions, and very few business corporations existed. The Constitution does not expressly refer to corporations. In 1819, when the Supreme Court decided one of the earliest cases on corporate rights, the corporation at issue was Dartmouth College and it claimed protection under the Contracts Clause of the Constitution. Chief Justice Marshall's opinion described the corporation as an "artificial being" and explained that it "possesses only those properties which the charter of its creation confers upon it either expressly or as incidental to its very existence." But, the Court also recognized that a corporate charter is a contract between the state and the private individuals forming the corporation, and once granted it cannot be impaired by the state absent a reservation of authority giving the state the power to do so.

Early decisions such as *Dartmouth College* granting contracts clause protection were narrow in scope and the Court also established limitations to corporate rights. For example, in a pre-Civil War decision, the Court held that out-of-state corporations were not "citizens" under the Privileges and Immunities Clause of Article IV of the Constitution. As a result, states could regulate, or even keep out, corporations that were chartered in other states.

In the late 1800s, as the size and number of business corporations increased in the United States, the Supreme Court expanded the rights of corporations. In a series of headnotes and dicta, the Court stated that a corporation is included in the designation of "person" under the Fourteenth Amendment and has the right to equal protection and due process. By the turn of the century, there was little doubt that corporations could claim constitutional protections related to contract and property interests.

The Court, however, did not extend the same constitutional protections to corporations' non-commercial activities. In the early twentieth century, the Court stated that the liberty protected by the Fourteenth Amendment is "the liberty of natural, not artificial persons." Further, in *Hale v. Henkel*, the Court held that a corporation is not a "person" for purpose of the privilege against self-incrimination because that right "is purely a personal privilege of the witness." But a corporation could claim Fourth Amendment protections against unreasonable searches and seizures because it "is, after all, but an association of individuals under an assumed name and with a distinct legal entity," And, as the twentieth century continued, the Court displayed a willingness to grant expressive and associational protections to media corporations and nonprofits.

2. Regulation of Corporations as "Political Actors"

The early case law left open the question of how corporations could be regulated as political actors. Before the "progressive era," corporate political contributions, and even bribes, were at the center of allegations of political corruption. Congress responded to these scandals by prohibiting corporations from contributing to or supporting the campaign of any candidate or party in connection with any federal election. President Theodore Roosevelt heralded this legislation as necessary to instill the confidence of "the plain people of small means" in the electoral process and eradicate perceived political corruption. The legislation also prevented corporate managers from using "other people's money" to advance their own political agendas.

Specifically, the Tillman Act of 1907 prohibited corporations from spending "treasury funds" (general corporate assets) on campaign contributions or independent expenditures "advocating the election or defeat of a clearly identified candidate." 2 U.S.C. § 441.

Despite these limits, corporations found other ways to be politically involved. In 1971, Congress passed the Federal Elections Campaign Act (FECA), which allowed corporations and unions to establish "separate segregated funds," popularly called political action committees (PACs). PACs receive voluntary contributions from people with ties to the corporation, not from the corporation's treasury funds. In other words, PAC money comes directly from shareholders, executives, and employees with their consent, instead of coming from the corporation's general funds as determined by the managers who control the corporation.

In addition to using PACs, corporations can pay for communications to their employees and shareholders that expressly support or oppose candidates and pay for "issue ads." Corporations also can donate to charitable and educational organizations, including "think tanks" that advocate political views.

FYI

Regulation of the financing of federal elections arises under the Federal Election Campaign Act (FECA), passed by Congress in 1971.

In 1976, Congress amended FECA to establish the Federal Election Commission (FEC) to ensure compliance with federal election law and to further regulate federal campaign finance.

In 2002 Congress amended FECA in the McCain-Feingold Bipartisan Campaign Reform Act (BCRA) to regulate certain types of "electioneering" activities on the eve of a federal election. Among other things, BCRA prohibits political ads immediately before an election made in a broadcast communication (though not print media) that clearly identifies a candidate for office and is distributed within 30 days of a primary election or within 60 days of a general election.

Corporations also can, and do, lobby. Corporate lobbyists must register and disclose any payments they receive if they engage in "direct communications with members of Congress on pending or proposed federal legislation." But many activities that might pass as lobbying—such as TV ads and appearances, congressional testimony, letter-writing campaigns, and comments on government regulations—are not subject to lobbyist disclosure rules.

3. Pre-*Citizens United* Case Law

Citizens United was not written on a blank slate. In several key cases starting in the 1970s, the Supreme Court recognized commercial speech protection, and most importantly for our focus here, addressed whether corporations could spend money from their general treasury funds on politics.

FYI

Justice Lewis Powell wrote the majority opinion in *Bellotti*, which later served as the basis for the majority opinion in *Citizens United*. The justices' deference to Powell's views on corporate law matters is not surprising.

Over the last half century, Powell (who served on the Court from 1972–1987) has been the only corporate lawyer on the Court. He is responsible for writing many of the most important Supreme Court securities and corporate law decisions during this period. You may remember that *CTS v. Dynamics* (Chapter 5, Corporate Federalism) was written by Powell, and we will later see that he wrote the foundational opinions on insider trading in *United States v. Chiarella* and *SEC v. Dirks* (Chapter 29, Insider Trading).

As a former securities/corporate lawyer, Powell influenced the other justices on the Court to narrow the reach of federal and state regulation into corporate affairs.

First, in 1978, the Court held that the First Amendment limited the ability of states to regulate corporate speech in connection with a referendum. *First National Bank of Boston v. Bellotti*, 435 U.S. 765 (1978) (Powell, J.) The case involved a Massachusetts law that banned corporations from placing political ads for or against pending referenda. A bank that sought to oppose a referendum introducing an individual graduated income tax in the state claimed the legislative ban violated its rights under the First Amendment. The Court agreed and concluded the state had no compelling justifications for targeting the corporate speech at issue in the case. The Court pointed out that if the concern was the use of corporate resources in the political process, the state should also have banned lobbying by corporations. According to the Court, there was no showing "that the relative voice of corporations has been overwhelming or even significant in influencing referenda in Massachusetts." Further, the Court reasoned that referenda are ballot initiatives held on issues rather than candidates for public office and thus do not pose the same type of risk of corruption or perception of corruption. And the concern about dissenting shareholders being compelled to fund corporate political speech did not constitute a compelling governmental interest because the "procedures of corporate democracy" already provide sufficient protection and ultimately allow shareholders to decide "whether their corporation should engage in debate on public issues."

Then, in 1986, the Court recognized that not all corporations are the same and held that states could not ban political advocacy by nonprofit corporations. *Federal Election Comm'n v. Massachusetts Citizens for Life, Inc. (MCFL)*, 479 U.S. 238 (1986) (Brennan, J.). The case again arose in Massachusetts where a membership nonprofit corporation that opposed abortion rights sent out a newsletter urging voters to support certain pro-life candidates. The nonprofit used its own funds, not those of a corporate PAC, to finance this voting advocacy. The Court held that the federal ban against independent expenditures by an advocacy nonprofit was unconstitutional, given that such nonprofits are "formed for the express purpose of promoting political ideas" and supported entirely by individuals.

Just a few years later, the Court reversed direction and upheld the power of states to ban for-profit corporations from spending their general funds for or against political candidates. *Austin v. Michigan Chamber of Commerce*, 494 U.S. 652 (1990) (Marshall, J.). The case involved a Michigan law that banned for-profit corporations from making campaign contributions or expenditures in support or opposition of state candidates. The Michigan Chamber of Commerce, funded in part by for-profit corporations, sought to make expenditures supporting certain candidates in state elections. The Court held that the state law was constitutional. The Court pointed out that corporations are creatures of state law and, given their "unique legal and economic characteristics," regulation was needed to avoid the "the corrosive and distorting effect of immense aggregations of wealth" accumulated through the corporate form. In addition, the Court pointed out that corporate expenditures might not reflect the views of the corporations' shareholders and customers.

Tensions in the Court's jurisprudence on corporate political spending had grown. *MCFL* made sense as an extension of the First Amendment's protection of associational rights. But it was difficult to reconcile *Bellotti* and *Austin*. *Austin* was not a "change in personnel" story: both Justices Blackmun and Stevens were in the majority in each case, though neither wrote an opinion explaining their seemingly inconsistent support for *both* results. Some argued that *Bellotti's* specific regulation of corporate spending in political referenda was more suspect than *Austin's* generalized regulation of all corporate spending in state elections. Others said *Bellotti* reflected a belief that the Massachusetts banks may have had a direct interest in maintaining a favorable tax climate so as to attract bank executives, while the Michigan ban on spending by for-profit corporations reflected a concern about the ineluctable "quid pro quo" motives of such spending.

In any event, the two cases stood in stark contrast, until . . .

B. The Court's Decision in *Citizens United*

The Court's various opinions in *Citizens United* span more than 100 pages. Justice Kennedy wrote the majority opinion, which concluded that the federal statute banning corporations from using their general treasury funds to make independent expenditures that expressly advocate for or against a candidate in connection with federal elections, 2 U.S.C. § 441b, could not be read narrowly to avoid constitutional infirmity and held that *Austin* had to be overruled. Nonetheless, the Court opinion upheld certain disclosure and disclaimer requirements of FECA.

Justices Stevens, Ginsburg, Breyer, and Sotomayor dissented from the Court's decision, except the part upholding the disclosure and disclaimer requirements. Justice Thomas joined as to all of Justice Kennedy's opinion, except on upholding the disclosure and disclaimer requirements. Chief Justice Roberts wrote separately to express his view on *stare decisis*, and Justice Scalia wrote in response to the Stevens dissent and articulated the importance of corporate speech at the founding. Justice Alito joined in the Roberts and Scalia opinions.

As you go through the various opinions, ask yourself how the justices seem to view the modern corporation.

(1) Creature of state law: The corporation is an artificial entity created by the state, which can regulate its creations when there are "compelling justifications" or simply "reasonable" concerns about corporate participation in political speech.

(2) Real entity: The corporation itself is a speaker and the state must provide "compelling reasons" to silence its speech. The corporate person has autonomy and appropriately speaks through management, subject to oversight by shareholders who can replace misguided managers.

(3) Private voluntary association: The corporation is an aggre-

Take Note!

One of the issues in *Citizens United*, though not included in our excerpts of the justices' opinions, was the constitutionality of the "electioneering" provisions of the Bipartisan Campaign Reform Act of 2002, which in § 203 prohibited "any broadcast, cable, or satellite communication" that "refers to a clearly identified candidate for Federal office" and is made within 30 days of a primary or 60 days of a general election.

The electioneering ban, which had earlier been upheld in *McConnell v. Federal Election Comm'n*, 540 U.S. 93 (2003), was found unconstitutional in *Citizens United*. In overruling *McConnell*, the Court concluded as a matter of statutory interpretation that the § 203 prohibition of electioneering communications covered "Hillary" and that it was a "classic example of censorship."

After the Court's decision, corporations are allowed to broadcast electioneering communications, even if they fall just before a primary or general election.

gate of its participants who understand that management will speak and act on behalf of their collective interests. Shareholders who don't like this can invest elsewhere or use their corporate governance tools to change corporate decision making.

In January 2008, Citizens United, a political advocacy nonprofit corporation, released a video documentary critical of then-Senator Hillary Clinton, who at the time was the leading candidate for the Democratic nomination for President. Citizens United planned to run TV ads announcing that "Hillary" would be available before the primary elections on cable television through video-on-demand. Citizens United was mostly funded by donations from individuals, but also accepted a small portion of funds from for-profit corporations. Concerned about possible civil and criminal penalties for violating § 441b, it sued the Federal Election Commission (FEC) seeking declaratory and injunctive relief.

Citizens United argued that § 441b was unconstitutional as applied to "Hillary" and that BCRA's disclaimer, disclosure, and reporting requirements were also unconstitutional as applied to "Hillary" and its proposed TV ads. The District Court granted summary judgment to the FEC.

Citizens United v. Federal Election Commission

558 U.S. 310 (2010)

JUSTICE KENNEDY delivered the opinion of the Court.

Federal law prohibits corporations and unions from using general treasury funds to make independent expenditures for speech expressly advocating the election or defeat of a candidate. *Austin v. Michigan Chamber of Commerce* had held that political speech may be banned based on the speaker's corporate identity.

In this case, we are asked to reconsider *Austin*. We hold that *stare decisis* does not compel the continued acceptance of *Austin*. The Government may regulate corporate political speech through disclaimer and disclosure requirements, but it may not suppress that speech altogether.

Federal law prohibits corporations and unions from using general treasury funds to make *direct contributions* to candidates or independent expenditures that expressly advocate the election or defeat of a candidate, through any form of media, in connection with certain qualified federal elections.

Citizens United asks us to carve out an exception to § 441b's expenditure ban for nonprofit corporate political speech funded overwhelmingly by individuals. In *MCFL*, the Court found unconstitutional § 441b's restrictions on corporate expenditures as applied to nonprofit corporations that were formed for the sole purpose of promoting political ideas, did not engage in business activities, and did not accept contributions from for-profit corporations or labor unions. Citizens United does not qualify for the *MCFL* exemption, however, since some funds used to make the movie were donations from for-profit corporations.

We decline to adopt an interpretation that requires intricate (and chilling) case-by-case determinations to verify whether political speech is banned, especially if we are convinced that this corporation has a constitutional right to speak on this subject.

III

The law before us is an outright ban, backed by criminal sanctions. Section 441b makes it a felony for all corporations—including nonprofit advocacy corporations—either to expressly advocate the election or defeat of candidates. These prohibitions are classic examples of censorship.

Section 441b is a ban on corporate speech notwithstanding the fact that a PAC created by a corporation can still speak. A PAC is a separate association from the corporation. So the PAC exemption from § 441b's expenditure ban, § 441(b)(2), does not allow corporations to speak. Even if a PAC could somehow allow a corporation to speak—and it does not—the option to form PACs does not alleviate the First Amendment problems with § 441b. PACs are burdensome alternatives; they are expensive to administer and subject to extensive regulations.

PACs have to comply with these regulations just to speak. This might explain why fewer than 2,000 of the millions of corporations in this country have PACs. Given the onerous restrictions, a corporation may not be able to establish a PAC in time to make its views known regarding candidates and issues in a current campaign.

Section 441b's prohibition on corporate independent expenditures is thus a ban on speech. As a "restriction on the amount of money a person or group can spend on political communication during a campaign," that statute "necessarily reduces the quantity of expression by restricting the number of issues discussed, the depth of their exploration, and the size of the audience reached." *Buckley v. Valeo*, 424 US. 1 (1976). If § 441b applied to individuals, no one would believe that it is merely a time, place, or manner restriction on speech. Its purpose and effect are to silence entities whose voices the Government deems to be suspect.

Speech is an essential mechanism of democracy, for it is the means to hold officials accountable to the people. The right of citizens to inquire, to hear, to speak, and to use information to reach consensus is a precondition to enlightened self-government and a necessary means to protect it. The First Amendment "has its fullest and most urgent application to speech uttered during a campaign for political office."

Premised on mistrust of governmental power, the First Amendment stands against attempts to disfavor certain subjects or viewpoints. Prohibited, too, are restrictions distinguishing among different speakers, allowing speech by some but not others. As instruments to censor, these categories are interrelated: Speech restrictions based on the identity of the speaker are all too often simply a means to control content.

Quite apart from the purpose or effect of regulating content, moreover, the Government may commit a constitutional wrong when by law it identifies certain preferred speakers. By taking the right to speak from some and giving it to others, the Government deprives the disadvantaged person or class of the right to use speech to strive to establish worth, standing, and respect for the speaker's voice. The Government may not by these means deprive the public of the right and privilege to determine for itself what speech and speakers are worthy of consideration. The First Amendment protects speech and speaker, and the ideas that flow from each.

Food for Thought

Was Justice Kennedy right that PACs are not a viable option for corporate speech? Consider the rules that apply to corporate PACs.

PACs may contribute to federal election campaigns, up to $5,000 per candidate per election. (By comparison, individual contributions are limited to $2,600 per candidate per election.) PACs, like individuals, can also make unlimited independent expenditures for or against a clearly identified candidate at any time. (But if the PAC coordinates its message with a candidate or campaign, any expenditure is limited as an in-kind campaign contribution.)

PACs are subject to guidelines in soliciting contributions from corporate constituents, with contributions to the PAC limited to $5,000 per person per calendar year.

PACs are also subject to detailed record-keeping and disclosure requirements. In election years, PACs must submit monthly reports to the FEC that disclose, among other things, their total assets, itemized receipts by individual contributors, total contributions itemized by recipient, and operating costs.

Further, for each public communication, whether or not it expressly advocates for or against a candidate, the PAC must include a disclaimer ("I am Citibank PAC and I paid for this message").

It is inherent in the nature of the political process that voters must be free to obtain information from diverse sources in order to determine how to cast their votes. At least before *Austin*, the Court had not allowed the exclusion of a class of speakers from the general public dialogue.

We find no basis for the proposition that, in the context of political speech, the Government may impose restrictions on certain disfavored speakers. Both history and logic lead us to this conclusion.

The Court has recognized that First Amendment protection extends to corporations. This protection has been extended by explicit holdings to the context of political speech. Under the rationale of these precedents, political speech does not lose First Amendment protection "simply because its source is a corporation." *Bellotti* at 784; *Pacific Gas & Elec. Co. v. Public Util. Comm'n of Cal.*, 475 U.S. 1, 8 (1986) (plurality opinion) ("The identity of the speaker is not decisive in determining whether speech is protected. Corporations and other associations, like individuals, contribute to the 'discussion, debate, and the dissemination of information and ideas' that the First Amendment seeks to foster").

Bellotti struck down a state-law prohibition on corporate independent expenditures related to referenda issues. Thus the law stood until *Austin*, which "upheld a direct restriction on the independent expenditure of funds for political speech for the first time in [this Court's] history." There, the Michigan Chamber of Commerce sought to use general treasury funds to run a newspaper ad supporting a specific candidate. Michigan law, however, prohibited corporate independent expenditures that supported or opposed any candidate for state office. A violation of the law was punishable as a felony. The Court sustained the speech prohibition.

To bypass *Bellotti*, the *Austin* Court identified a new governmental interest in limiting political speech: an antidistortion interest. *Austin* found a compelling governmental interest in preventing "the corrosive and distorting effects of immense aggregations of wealth that are accumulated with the help of the corporate form and that have little or no correlation to the public's support for the corporation's political ideas.

The Court is thus confronted with conflicting lines of precedent: a pre-*Austin* line that forbids restrictions on political speech based on the speaker's corporate identity and a post-*Austin* line that permits them.

In its defense of the corporate-speech restrictions in § 441b, the Government notes the antidistortion rationale on which *Austin* and its progeny rest in part, yet it all but abandons reliance upon it. It argues instead that two other compelling interests support *Austin*'s holding that corporate expenditure restrictions are constitutional: an anticorruption interest, and a shareholder protection interest.

1

As for *Austin*'s antidistortion rationale, the Government does little to defend it. And with good reason, for the rationale cannot support § 441b.

If the First Amendment has any force, it prohibits Congress from fining or jailing citizens, or associations of citizens, for simply engaging in political speech. If the antidistortion rationale were to be accepted, however, it would permit Government to ban political speech simply because the speaker is an association that has taken on the corporation form. The Government contends that *Austin* permits it to ban corporate expenditures for almost all forms of communication stemming from a corporation.

Political speech is "indispensible to decision making in a democracy, and this is no less true because the speech comes from a corporation rather than an individual." *Bellotti* (the worth of speech "does not depend upon the identity of its source, whether corporation, association, union, or individual"). This protection of speech is inconsistent with *Austin's* anti-distortion rationale. *Austin* sought to defend the antidistortion rationale as a means to prevent corporations from obtaining 'an unfair advantage in the market place' by using 'resources amassed in the economic marketplace.' But *Buckley* rejected the premise that the Government has an interest "in equalizing the relative ability of individuals and groups to influence the outcome of elections." *Buckley* was specific in stating that "the skyrocketing cost of political campaigns could not sustain the governmental prohibition. The First Amendment's protections do not depend on the speaker's financial ability to engage in public discussion."

The *Austin* majority undertook to distinguish wealthy individuals from corporations on the ground that "state law grants corporations special advantages such as limited liability, perpetual life, and favorable treatment of the accumulation and distribution of assets." This does not suffice, however, to allow laws prohibiting speech. "It is rudimentary that the State cannot exact as the price of those special advantages the forfeiture of First Amendment rights."

All speakers, including individuals and the media, use money amassed from the economic marketplace to fund their speech. The First Amendment protects the resulting speech, even if it was enabled by economic transactions with persons or entities who disagree with the speaker's ideas. "Many persons can trace their funds to corporations, if not in the form of donations, then in the form of dividends, interest, or salary."

Austin's antidistortion rationale would produce the dangerous, and unacceptable, consequence that Congress could ban political speech of media corporations. Media corporations are now exempt from § 441b's ban on corporate expenditures. Yet media corporations accumulate wealth with the help of the corporate form, the largest media corporations have "immense aggregations of wealth," and the views expressed by media corporations often "have little or no correlation to the public's support" for those vies. Thus, under the Government's reasoning, wealthy media corporations could have their voices diminished to put them on part with other media entities. There is no precedent for permitting this under the First Amendment.

The law's exception for media corporations is, on its own terms, all but an admission of the invalidity of the antidistortion rationale. And the exemption results in a further, separate reason for finding this law invalid: Again by its own terms, the law exempts some corporations but covers others, even though both have the need or the motive to communicate their views. The exemption applies to media corporations owned or controlled by corporations that have diverse and substantial investments and participate in endeavors other than news. So even assuming the most doubtful proposition that a news organization has a right to speak when others do not, the exemption would allow a conglomerate that owns both a media business and an unrelated business to influence or control the media in order to advance its overall business interest. At the same time, some other corporation, with an identical business interest but no media outlet in its owner-ship structure, would be forbidden to speak or inform the public about the same issue. This differential treatment cannot be squared with the <u>First Amendment</u>.

Austin interferes with the "open marketplace" of ideas protected by the First Amendment. It permits the Government to ban the political speech of millions of associations of citizens. Most of these are small corporations without large amounts of wealth.

When Government seeks to use its full power, including the criminal law, to command where a person may get his or her information or what distrusted source he or she may not hear, it uses censorship to control thought. This is unlawful. The First Amendment confirms the freedom to think for ourselves.

2

The Government falls back on the argument that corporate political speech can be banned in order to prevent corruption or its appearance. In *Buckley*, the Court found this interest "sufficiently important" to allow limits on contributions but did not extend that reasoning to expenditure limits. When *Buckley* examined an expenditure ban, it found "that the governmental interest in preventing cor-ruption and the appearance of corruption [was] inadequate to justify [the ban] on independent expenditures."

With regard to large direct contributions, *Buckley* reasoned that they could be given "to secure a political *quid pro quo*." The Court, in consequence, has noted that restrictions on direct contributions are preventative, because few if any contributions to candidates will involve *quid pro quo* arrangements. The *Buckley* Court, nevertheless, sustained limits on direct contributions in order to ensure against the reality or appearance of corruption. That case did not extend this rationale to independent expenditures, and the Court does not do so here.

The absence of prearrangement and coordination of an expenditure with the candidate or his agent not only undermines the value of the expenditure to the candidate, but also alleviates the danger that expenditures will be given as a *quid pro quo* for improper commitments from the candidate. Limits on independent expenditures, such as § 441b, have a chilling effect extending well beyond the Government's interest in preventing *quid pro quo* corruption. The anticorruption interest is not sufficient to displace the speech here in question.

Independent expenditures do not lead to, or create the appearance of *quid pro quo* corruption. In fact, there is only scant evidence that independent expenditures even ingratiate. Ingratiation and access, in any event, are not corruption. When Congress finds that a problem exists, we must give that finding due deference; but Congress may not choose an unconstitutional remedy. If elected officials succumb to improper influences from independent expenditures; if they surrender their best judgment; and if they put expediency before principle, then surely there is cause for concern. However, an outright ban on corporate political speech during the critical preelection period is not a permissible remedy. Here Congress has created categorical bans on speech that are asymmetrical to preventing *quid pro quo* corruption.

3

The Government contends further that corporate independent expenditures can be limited because of its interest in protecting dissenting shareholders from being compelled to fund corporate political speech. This asserted interest, like *Austin*'s antidistortion rationale, would allow the Government to ban the political speech even of media corporations. Assume, for example that a shareholder of a corporation that owns a newspaper disagrees with the political views the newspaper expresses. Under the Government's view, that potential disagreement could give the Government the authority to restrict the media corporation's political speech. The First Amendment does not allow that power. There is, furthermore, little evidence of abuse that cannot be corrected by shareholders "through the procedures of corporate democracy."

Our precedent is to be respected unless the most convincing of reasons demonstrates that adherence to it puts us on a course that is sure error. These considerations counsel in favor of rejecting *Austin*, which itself contravened this Court's earlier precedents in *Buckley* and *Bellotti*. "This Court has no hesitated to overrule decisions offensive to the First Amendment." "*Stare decisis* is a principle of policy and not a mechanical formula of adherence to the latest decision."

Our Nation's speech dynamic is changing, and informative voices should not have to circumvent onerous restrictions to exercise their First Amendment rights. Speakers have become adept at presenting citizens with sound bites, talking points, and scripted messages that dominate the 24-hour news cycle. Corporations, like individuals, do not have monolithic views. On certain topics corporations may possess valuable expertise, leaving them the best equipped to point out errors or fallacies in speech of all sorts, including the speech of candidates and elected officials.

Rapid changes in technology-and the creative dynamic inherent in the concept of free expression-counsel against upholding a law that restricts political speech in certain media or by certain speakers. Today, 30-second television ads may be the most effective way to convey a political message. Soon, however, it may be that Internet sources such as blogs and social networking Web sites, will provide citizens with significant information about political candidates and issues. Yet, § 441b would seem to ban a blog post expressly advocating the election or defeat of a candidate if that blog were created with corporate funds. The First Amendment does not permit Congress to make these categorical distinctions based on the corporate identity of the speaker and the content of the political speech.

Due consideration leads to this conclusion: *Austin* should be and now is overruled. We return to the principle established in *Buckley* and *Bellotti* that the Government may not suppress political speech on the basis of the speaker's corporate identity. No sufficient governmental interest justifies limits on the political speech of nonprofit or for-profit corporations.

IV.

Citizens United next challenges BCRA's disclaimer and disclosure provisions as applied to *Hillary* and the three advertisements for the movie. Under BCRA § 311, televised electioneering communications funded by anyone other than a candidate must include a disclaimer that " _____ is responsible for the content of this advertising." Under BCRA § 201, any person who spends more than $10,000 on electioneering communications within a calendar year must file a disclosure statement with the FEC. That statement must identify the person making the expenditure, the amount of the expenditure, the election to which the communication was directed, and the names of certain contributors.

Disclaimer and disclosure requirements may burden the ability to speak, but they impose no ceiling on campaign-related activities," and "do not prevent anyone from speaking."

In *Buckley*, the Court explained that disclosure could be justified based on a governmental interest in "providing the electorate with information" about the sources of election-related spending that would help citizens "make informed choices in the political marketplace."

Citizens United argues that the disclaimer requirements in § 311 are unconstitutional as applied to its ads. It contends that the governmental interest in providing information to the electorate does not justify requiring disclaimers for any commercial advertisements, including the ones at issue here. We disagree. The disclaimers required by § 311 "provide the electorate with information," and "insure that the voters are fully informed" about the person or group who is speaking. At the very least, the disclaimers avoid confusion by making clear that the ads are not funded by a candidate or political party.

The Court has explained that disclosure is a less restrictive alternative to more comprehensive regulations of speech. In *Buckley*, the Court upheld a disclosure requirement for independent expenditures even though it invalidated a provision that imposed a ceiling on those expenditures. And the Court has upheld registration and disclosure requirements on lobbyists, even though Congress has no power to ban lobbying itself.

Citizens United also disputes that an information interest justifies the application of § 201 to its ads. Even if the ads only disclose the funding sources for the ads, the public has an interest in knowing who is speaking about a candidate shortly before an election.

Last, Citizens United argues that disclosure requirements can chill donations to an organization by exposing donors to retaliation. Some *amici* point to recent events in which donors to certain causes were blacklisted, threatened, or otherwise targeted for retaliation. In *McConnell*, the Court recognized that § 201 would be unconstitutional as applied to an organization if there were a reasonable probability that the group's members would face threats, harassment, or reprisals if their names were disclosed. The examples cited by *amici* are cause for concern. Citizens United, however, has offered no evidence that its members may face similar threats or reprisals. To the contrary, Citizens United has been disclosing its donors for years and has identified no instance of harassment or retaliation.

Shareholder objections raised through the procedures of corporate democracy can be more effective today because modern technology makes disclosures rapid and informative. A campaign finance system that pairs corporate independent expenditures with effective disclosure has no existed before today. It must be noted, furthermore, that many of Congress' findings in passing BCRA were premised on a system without adequate disclosure. With the advent of the Internet, prompt disclosure of expenditures can provide shareholders and citizens with the information needed to hold corporations and elected officials accountable for their positions and supporters. Shareholders can determine whether their corporation's political speech advances the corporation's interest in making profits, and citizens can see whether elected officials are " 'in the pocket' of so-called moneyed interests." The First Amendment protects political speech; and disclosure permits citizens and shareholders to react to the speech of corporate entities in a proper way. This transparency enables the electorate to make informed decisions and give proper weight to different speakers and messages.

Some members of the public might consider *Hillary* to be insightful and instructive; some might find it to be neither high art nor a fair discussion on how to set the Nation's course; still others simply might suspend judgment on these points but decide to think more about issues and candidates. Those choices and assessments, however, are not for the Government to make. "The First Amendment underwrites the freedom to experiment and to create in the realm of thought and speech. Citizens must be free to use new forms, and new forums, for the expression of ideas. The civic discourse belongs to the people, and the Government may not prescribe the means used to conduct it."

The judgment of the District Court is reversed with respect to the constitutionality of 2 U.S.C. § 441b's restrictions on corporate independent expenditures. The judgment is affirmed with respect to BCRA's disclaimer and disclosure requirements. The case is remanded for further proceedings consistent with this opinion.

CHIEF JUSTICE ROBERTS, with whom JUSTICE ALITO joins, concurring.

[Justice ROBERTS explained the Court's decision to overrule *Austin*. He pointed out that the Government's arguments in the case would authorize the Government "to prohibit newspapers from running editorials or opinion pieces supporting or opposing candidates for office, so long as the newspapers were owned by corporations—as the major ones are. First Amendment rights could be confined to individuals, subverting the vibrant public discourse that is at the foundation of our democracy."

Justice ROBERTS further points out that "*Austin* nowhere relied upon the only arguments the Government now raises to support that decision. In fact, the only opinion in *Austin* endorsing the Government's argument based on the threat of *quid pro quo* corruption was Justice STEVEN's concurrence. Moreover, the Court's only discussion of shareholder protection in *Austin* appeared in a section that sought merely to distinguish *MCFL*. Nowhere did *Austin* suggest that the goal of protecting shareholders is itself a compelling interest authorizing restrictions on First Amendment rights."

Justice ROBERTS concluded: "Because continued adherence to *Austin* threatens to subvert the "principled and intelligible" development of our First Amendment jurisprudence, I support the Court's determination to overrule that decision."]

JUSTICE SCALIA, concurring.

I write separately to address Justice STEVENS' discussion of the original understanding of the First Amendment. The dissent embarks on a detailed exploration of the Framers' views about the "role of corporations in society." The Framers didn't like corporations, the dissent concludes, and therefore it follows (as night the day) that corporations had no rights of free speech.

To the contrary, colleges, towns, and cities, religious institutions, and guilds had long been organized as corporations at common law and under the King's charter, and the practice of incorporation only expanded in the United States. Both corporations and voluntary associations actively petitioned the Government and expressed their views in newspapers and pamphlets. For example: An anti-slavery Quaker corporation petitioned the First Congress, distributed pamphlets, and communicated through the press in 1790. The New York Sons of Liberty sent a circular to colonies farther south in 1766. And the Society for the Relief and Instruction of Poor Germans circulated a biweekly paper from 1755 to 1757. The dissent offers no evidence—none whatever—that the First Amendment's unqualified text was originally understood to exclude such associational speech from its protection.

The dissent says that "speech" refers to oral communications of human beings, and since corporations are not human beings they cannot speak. This is sophistry. The authorized spokesman of a corporation is a human being, who speaks on behalf of the human beings who have formed that association—just as the spokesman of an unincorporated association speaks on behalf of its members.

The Amendment is written in terms of "speech," not speakers. Its text offers no foothold for excluding any category of speaker, from single individuals to partnerships of individuals, to unincorporated associations of individuals, to incorporated associations of individuals—and the dissent offers no evidence about the original meaning of the text to support any such exclusion. A documentary film critical of a potential Presidential candidate is core political speech, and its nature as such does not change simply because it was funded by a corporation. Nor does the character of that funding produce any reduction whatever in the "inherent worth of the speech" and "its capacity for informing the public." Indeed, to exclude or impede corporate speech is to muzzle the principal agents of the modern free economy. We should celebrate rather than condemn the addition of this speech to the public debate.

Justice Stevens, with whom Justice Ginsburg, Justice Breyer, and Justice Sotomayor join, concurring in part and dissenting in part.

The real issue in this case concerns how, not if, the appellant may finance its electioneering. Citizens United is a wealthy nonprofit corporation that runs a political action committee (PAC) with millions of dollars in assets. Under the Bipartisan Campaign Reform Act of 2002 (BCRA), it could have used those assets to televise and promote *Hillary: The Movie* wherever and whenever it wanted to. Neither Citizens United's nor any other corporation's speech has been "banned." All that the parties dispute is whether Citizens United had a right to use the funds in its general treasury to pay for broadcasts. The notion that the First Amendment dictates an affirmative answer to that question is, in my judgment, profoundly misguided. Even more misguided is the notion that the Court must rewrite the law relating to campaign expenditures by *for-profit* corporations and unions to decide this case.

In the context of elections to public office, the distinction between corporate and human speakers is significant. Although they make enormous contributions to our society, corporations are not actually members of it. They cannot vote or run for office. Because they may be managed and controlled by nonresidents, their interests may conflict in fundamental respects with the interests of eligible voters. The financial resources, legal structure, and instrumental orientation of corporations raise legitimate concerns about their role in the electoral process. Our lawmakers have a compelling constitutional basis, if not also a democratic duty, to take measures designed to guard against the potentially deleterious effects of corporate spending in local and national races.

Thomas Jefferson famously fretted that corporations would subvert the Republic. General incorporation statutes, and widespread acceptance of business corporations as socially useful actors, did not emerge until the 1800's.

The Framers thus took it as a given that corporations could be comprehensively regulated in the service of the public welfare. Unlike our colleagues, they had little trouble distinguishing corporations from human beings, and when they constitutionalized the right to free speech in the First Amendment, it was the free speech of individual Americans that they had in mind. While individuals might join together to exercise their speech rights, business corporations, at least, were plainly not seen as facilitating such associational or expressive ends. Even "the notion that business corporations could invoke the First Amendment would probably have been quite a novelty," given that "at the time, the legitimacy of every corporate activity was thought to rest entirely in a concession of the sovereign." In light of these background practices and understandings, it seems to me implausible that the Framers believed "the freedom of speech" would extend equally to all corporate speakers, much less than it would preclude legislatures from taking limited measures to guard against corporate capture of elections.

These basic points help explain why corporate electioneering is not only more likely to impair compelling governmental interests, but also why restrictions on that electioneering are less likely to encroach upon First Amendment freedoms. One fundamental concern of the First Amendment is to "protect the individual's interest in self-expression." Freedom of speech helps "make men free to develop their faculties," it respects their "dignity and choice," and it facilitates the value of "individual self-realization." Corporate speech, however, is derivative speech, speech by proxy. A regulation such as the one challenged here may affect the way in which individuals disseminate certain messages through the corporate form, but it does not prevent anyone from speaking in his or her own voice.

It is an interesting question "who" is even speaking when a business corporation places an advertisement that endorses or attacks a particular candidate. Presumably it is not the customers or employees, who typically have no say in such matters. It cannot realistically be said to be the shareholders, who tend to be far removed from the day-to-day decisions of the firm and whose political preferences may be opaque to management. Perhaps the officers or directors of the corporation have the best claim to be the ones speaking, except their fiduciary duties generally prohibit them from using corporate funds for personal ends. Some individuals associated with the corporation must make the decision to place the ad, but the idea that these individuals are thereby fostering their self-expression or cultivating their critical faculties is fanciful. It is entirely possible that the corporation's electoral message will conflict with their personal convictions. Take away the ability to use general treasury funds for some of those ads, and no one's autonomy, dignity, or political equality has been impinged upon in the least.

The majority's unwillingness to distinguish between corporations and humans similarly blinds it to the possibility that corporations' "war chests" and their special "advantages" in the legal realm may translate into special advantages in the market for legislation. Corporations, that is, are uniquely equipped to seek laws that favor their owners, not simply because they have a lot of money but because of their legal and organizational structure. Remove all restrictions on their electioneering, and the door may be opened to a type of rent seeking that is "far more destructive" than what noncorporations are capable of.

The PAC mechanism, by contrast, helps assure that those who pay for an electioneering communication actually support its content and that managers do not use general treasuries to advance personal agendas. It "allows corporate political participation without the temptation to use corporate funds for political influence, quite possibly at odds with the sentiments of some shareholders or members." A rule that privileges the use of PACs thus does more than facilitate the political speech of like-minded shareholders; it also curbs the rent seeking behavior of executives and respects the views of dissenters. *Austin's* acceptance of restrictions on general treasury spending "simply allows people who have invested in the business corporation for purely economic reasons"—the vast majority of investors, one assumes—"to avoid being taken advantage of, without sacrificing their economic objectives."

Justice Thomas, concurring in part and dissenting in part.

I join all but Part IV of the Court's opinion.

Congress may not abridge the "right to anonymous speech" based on the "simple interest in providing voters with additional relevant information." In continuing to hold otherwise, the Court misapprehends the import of "recent events" that some *amici* describe "in which donors to certain causes were blacklisted, threatened, or otherwise targeted for retaliation." The Court properly recognizes these events as "cause for concern," but fails to acknowledge their constitutional significance. *Amici's* examples relate principally to Proposition 8, a state ballot proposition [defining marriage as only "between a man and a woman"] that California voters narrowly passed in the 2008 general election. Some opponents of Proposition 8 compiled donor information and created Web sites with maps showing the locations of homes or businesses of Proposition 8 supporters. Many supporters (or their customers) suffered property damage, or threats of physical violence or death, as a result.

The success of such intimidation tactics has apparently spawned a cottage industry that uses forcibly disclosed donor information to preempt citizens' exercise of their First Amendment rights. These instances of retaliation sufficiently demonstrate why this Court should invalidate mandatory disclosure and reporting requirements. But amici present evidence of yet another reason to do so—the threat of retaliation from elected officials. My point is not to express any view on the merits of the political controversies I describe. Rather, it is to demonstrate—using real-world, recent examples—the fallacy in the Court's conclusion that "disclaimer and disclosure requirements . . . impose no ceiling on campaign-related activities, and do not prevent anyone from speaking." Of course they do. Disclaimer and disclosure requirements enable private citizens and elected officials to implement political strategies specifically calculated to curtail campaign-related activity and prevent the lawful, peaceful exercise of First Amendment rights.

——

Points for Discussion

1. Expenditures vs. Contributions

In summary, the Court in *Citizens United* decided:

(1) the government may not, under the First Amendment, suppress political speech on the basis of the speaker's corporate identity, overruling *Austin v. Michigan Chamber of Commerce*, 494 U.S. 652 (1990).

(2) the disclaimer and disclosure provisions of Bipartisan Campaign Reform Act of 2002 did not violate the First Amendment, as applied to a nonprofit corporation's documentary and advertisements for the documentary.

Citizens United allows corporations to spend unlimited amounts from their general treasury on independent expenditures supporting or opposing candidates to federal office. In overruling *Austin* on this point, the Court stated that independent expenditures, uncoordinated with the candidate, do not give rise to corruption or the appearance of corruption. The Court identified the governmental interest in preventing corruption or the appearance of corruption as limited to *quid pro quo* corruption, noting that "appearance of influence or access, furthermore, will not cause the electorate to lose faith in our democracy."

Nonetheless, the Court left standing FECA's *direct contribution* prohibition to prevent the appearance of *quid pro quo* corruption. Also, *Citizens United* did not overturn the BCRA's disclosure and disclaimer requirements. What is the basis for distinguishing so sharply between expenditures and contributions? Do you agree that independent expenditures from corporations do not give rise to compelling concerns about corruption?

2. What kind of person is the corporation?

The Supreme Court (and different justices) have variously viewed the corporation (1) as a creature of state law (a "concession" theory), (2) as a distinct legal entity separate from the incorporating state and its shareholders (a "real entity" theory), and (3) as a voluntary association of participants (an "aggregate" theory).

The "concession" theory is reflected in the <u>Dartmouth College</u> case, in which the Supreme Court disallowed states from unilaterally changing the corporate charter, viewing the corporation as an "artificial being" created by the law and a binding contract between two parties—the state and the private individuals who formed the corporation. The "real entity" theory has also appeared in Court decisions, such as when the Court denied "citizen" status to corporations under the Privileges and Immunities Clause, and when it has referred to corporations as having dignity or autonomy interests. In *Citizens United* and other cases granting protections to corporations, the Court has often used the language of the "aggregate" theory, characterizing the corporation as a group of individuals from whom rights can be derived.

Which view best describes the corporation? Does it make sense to determine corporate rights based on these theories of the corporation?

3. Do shareholders have a voice in corporate political activities?

Justice Kennedy pointed out that dissenting shareholders can protect themselves "through the procedures of corporate democracy." How might this happen? The Court did not explain. In the earlier *Bellotti* opinion, the Court referenced state corporate law:

> Acting through their power to elect the board of directors or to insist upon protective provisions in the corporation's charter, shareholders normally are presumed competent to protect their own interests. In addition to intracorporate remedies, minority shareholders generally have access to the judicial remedy of a derivative suit to challenge corporate disbursements alleged to have been made for improper corporate purposes or merely to further the personal interests of management.

Further, the *Bellotti* opinion noted that "the shareholder invests in a corporation of his own volition and is free to withdraw his investment at any time and for any reason."

However, in pointing to the "procedures of corporate democracy" in *Bellotti* and *Citizens United*, the Court did not acknowledge that shareholders often have incomplete information about a corporation's political spending. In addition, many Americans invest indirectly through pension funds and mutual funds, and lack a ready means of exit. And, in any case, selling stock provides a solution only prospectively and does nothing to address the political spending that already occurred.

As a matter of state corporate law, while shareholders elect the board of directors, they generally do not have proxy access to nominate directors. Waging a proxy fight is expensive and it's unclear shareholders would vote to oust directors for approving political spending the directors believed was in the corporation's best interests. Shareholders can also sue the directors for violating their fiduciary duties, but absent fraud or self-dealing, the business judgment rule protects political spending decisions if the board had plausible reasons for its decision.

Shareholders have another avenue for voice—they can propose and vote on precatory (non-binding) resolutions. But many proposals get settled before going to a shareholder vote and even if the proposal receives majority support, the board is not required to follow the shareholders' recommendations. Nonetheless, since *Citizens United*, shareholder proposals concerning corporate political spending have dramatically increased and resulted in some corporations making voluntary reports about their spending.

Are the "procedures of corporate democracy" sufficient to protect shareholders? Should political expenditures be considered ordinary business decisions subject to business judgment rule protection? Are corporate directors best equipped to make political decisions for the corporation?

4. What must corporations disclose about political spending?

Corporations have only limited duties under federal law to disclose their political spending. For example, corporations that engage in express advocacy to the public, for the election or defeat of a particular federal candidate, must report to the FEC on a quarterly basis spending of more than $250 per year. Corporations are subject to 48-hour reporting requirements for spending of more than $10,000 in a calendar year on electioneering communications that clearly refer to a federal candidate within a certain period before an election. In addition, disclosure of express advocacy to internal corporate constituencies (employees, shareholders, or management) is required for expenditures above $2,000 per election.

Corporations are also subject to a patchwork of disclosure laws regarding state and local elections. Of particular note, in some states, corporations are allowed to contribute directly to state candidates, and the campaigns will generally disclose the contributions.

Some additional information about corporate political spending is available because some corporations make voluntary disclosures, and some groups such as PACs and Super PACs are required to make disclosures about contributors, including corporations. However, corporations can fund other groups that do not disclose their donors, such as "social welfare" organizations and trade associations that are organized under sections 501(c)(4) and (c)(6) of the tax code. For example, the U.S. Chamber of Commerce, a 501(c)(6) trade association funded by corporations, is one of the top spenders in lobbying for business interests and is not required to disclose its contributors. The lack of transparency of 501(c)(4) and (c)(6) organizations and "dark money" more generally has attracted significant concern and ongoing litigation about disclosure obligations when organizations reach a threshold of election-related activity.

Finally, in the aftermath of *Citizens United*, the Securities and Exchange Commission considered specifically mandating disclosure of corporate political spending, but did not take action.

Test Your Knowledge

To assess your understanding of the Chapter 5, 6, and 7 material in this module, click here to take a quiz.

Module III – Choice of Entity and the Corporate Form

CHAPTER 8

Organizational Choices

The chapters in this module introduce you to topics that are familiar to business lawyers—choice of business entity and the preliminaries of the corporation. In this chapter, we identify the menu of options available to those who want to organize a business firm. We take a comparative approach to partnerships and corporations, which we have already seen, and we introduce the basics of limited liability companies (LLCs). The next chapter begins our deeper study of corporations by examining how a corporation is incorporated and the issues that arise in the incorporation process. The last chapter of the module looks at how authority to act on behalf of the corporation is allocated—and ascertained.

All around us, businesses carry suffixes: Inc., Corp., Co., LLP, LLC, PC. What do these mean? And why would business owners choose one form over another?

Since the 1990s, there has been an explosion of business forms in this country as state legislatures (at the behest of the business community) have expanded the options available to business people beyond the corporation and the partnership—the two stalwarts of U.S. business organization. Today it is possible to customize a business to achieve the precise mix of characteristics desired by the parties: duration, allocation of liability, control rights, management authority, financial rights, withdrawal rights, change options, and even tax attributes.

This chapter introduces you to the organizational choices for modern business. We identify the principal business forms available today (a veritable "alphabet soup") and the basic rules that apply to each. We then identify how the right organizational choice depends on the economics of the venture and the preferences of the organizers and participants. Finally, we look at the basic tax implications of the choice.

Make the Connection

This book has introduced agency, partnership, and corporation basics in Chapters 2–4. This chapter introduces limited liability companies (LLCs), a form of business organization that has some partnership-like characteristics and some corporate-like characteristics. Further, it offers a comparative perspective on choosing a form of business organization.

A. Alphabet Soup

Today there is a wide range of business organization options. We start with a description of the main features of the primary organizational choices—the partnership, the corporation, and the limited liability company. We then turn to specific rules on formation, liability, control, management, financial rights, withdrawal, transferability of interests, and fundamental changes to allow you to compare and contrast the different forms.

In their default form—that is, the rules that exist by operation of law absent an agreement to the contrary—the general partnership and the corporation are polar opposites. In a general partnership the default rule is equality: each participant has an equal voice in partnership management, each has the authority as agent to bind the partnership, and each has unlimited personal liability for partnership obligations. In contrast, a corporation is based upon principles of centralized management and limited liability for the participants.

Hypo 8.1

Two entrepreneur-capitalists plan to start a new business that will design and install energy-saving systems in existing homes. The business, which they will call "Your Green Home," will hire a staff of "green" designers, along with a work force of skilled installers of solar panels, heat collectors, insulation systems, and high-efficiency heat pumps and electric generators.

Anita is an MBA business journalist, with spare cash. Brandon is an experienced mechanical engineer, without much savings. Anita will put in the bulk of the capital and oversee the firm's finances; Brandon will manage the business. What organizational form should they choose?

Today, between the general partnership and the corporation, there lies a dizzying range of options. In the 1990s the limited liability company (LLC) became generally available, offering a hybrid combination of flow-through taxation and limited liability. Other organizational choices, each with their own abbreviations and statutory regimes, allow business planners to custom-fit the business form according to client needs and preferences.

Partnership. As we have seen, the most basic business organization is a general partnership (GP). But not every partnership is a GP. A partnership can also be a limited partnership (LP), a limited liability partnership (LLP), or a limited liability limited partnership (LLLP). In virtually all states, the GP and the LP are governed by uniform statutes—for a GP the Uniform Partnership Act (UPA) or the Revised Uniform Partnership Act (RUPA), and for an LP the Uniform Limited Partnership Act (ULPA) or the Revised Uniform Limited Partnership Act (RULPA). All these statutes allow considerable flexibility in the organization and operation of partnerships.

A GP is defined as an "association of two or more persons to carry on as co-owners a business for profit." RUPA § 202(a). Each partner possesses an equal voice in management and the authority to act as agent for the partnership. RUPA §§ 301, 401. Each partner can be held personally liable for all debts of the partnership, as well as for torts committed by other partners within the course of the partnership's business. RUPA § 306.

An LP is defined as a "partnership formed by two or more persons and having one or more general partners and one or more limited partners." RULPA § 101(7). In a limited partnership, a limited partner is a passive investor who has no voice in the active management of the LP, which is conducted by the general partner. RULPA § 303. In an LP, every general partner is personally liable for business obligations, but every limited partner's liability is limited to the capital he has contributed to the partnership. RULPA §§ 404(a), 303.

> **FYI**
>
> In order to promote uniform rules for unincorporated business forms, the Uniform Law Commission (also known as the National Conference of Commissioners on Uniform State Laws) has promulgated a series of uniform laws.
>
> - Partnership: Uniform Partnership Act (1914); Revised Uniform Partnership Act (1997)
> - Limited Partnership: Uniform Limited Partnership Act (1916); Revised Uniform Limited Partnership Act (1976, amended 1985), Uniform Limited Partnership Act (revised 2001)
> - LLC: Uniform Limited Liability Company Act (1996, revised 2006)
>
> Only the ULLCA and the recent revisions to ULPA have not been widely adopted. Notably, in recent years, the Uniform Law Commission has engaged in a project to harmonize the language of all of the uniform unincorporated entity acts.

Recently, many states have adopted statutes providing for the creation of LLPs and LLLPs. By electing (through a filing with the state) to operate as an LLP or LLLP, the partners in a GP or the general partners in an LP can limit their liability to whatever amount they have invested, though they remain personally liable for tortious conduct for which they are responsible or (under some statutes) employees operating under their supervision are responsible.

Here are the basic partnership forms and their rules on management and liability:

Partnership Forms			
GP	*LLP*	*LP*	*LLLP*
Each partner has equal management rights and is an agent for the business.		The general partner has management rights; limited partners have restricted governance rights. Only the general partner is an agent for the business.	
Each partner is liable for business obligations.	Only the LLP (the entity) is liable for business obligations (partners personally liable for own tortious conduct or of those they supervise).	The general partner is liable for business obligations; limited partners have limited liability.	All partners have limited liability.

Make the Connection

Notice that uniformity has been sought for unincorporated businesses, but not corporations. There is no uniform corporation statute. Instead, each state chooses the statute most suited to its business climate. Delaware has enacted a corporation statute aimed at public corporations; other states, following the Model Business Corporation Act, generally have aimed their statutes at locally-operated close corporations. Some states, like New York and California, have their own idiosyncratic corporate statutes.

LLC statutes have also followed this path. Most states have chosen not to adopt the ULLCA, but instead have copied the statutes of other states or gone their own way. The issue in most states has been whether to have default terms that position the LLC closer to a partnership or a corporation. Delaware's LLC statute, for example, is more corporate like—with provisions that provide for the continuity of a LLC.

Corporation. At the opposite end of the continuum, a corporation is a legal entity distinct from its owners. The principal differences between a corporation and a GP lie in the management structure, liability provisions, and withdrawal rights. In contrast to the GP, the management of the corporation is centralized in a board of directors. MBCA § 8.01. Shareholders' liability is limited to whatever amounts they have agreed to contribute to the corporation and does not extend to any debts of or liabilities incurred by the corporation. MBCA § 6.22. Shareholders cannot force the corporation to buy back their shares, though they have broad rights to sell to other investors. MBCA § 6.27.

Limited liability company. The LLC is a form of business entity that combines certain aspects of partnership and corporation law. Like the corporation, it is a legal entity distinct from its investors, who are called "members." Members, like shareholders in a corporation, have limited liability. But like a partnership, management in an LLC generally is specified in an *operating agreement* and can involve either decentralized *member management* or centralized *manager management*. In either event, an LLC can elect to be taxed as a partnership—making the LLC an attractive choice in a variety of business settings.

In addition to its combination of limited liability and flow-through taxation, another defining characteristic of LLC law is its strong focus on contractual freedom to flexibly structure the company's internal governance by agreement. Although it is often referred to as a hybrid, an LLC is its own form of business entity and is not a species of corporation. The "C" in "LLC" stands for company, not corporation.

State LLC statutes, which were first introduced in the United States in 1979, vary much more than do state corporation and partnership statutes. In 1996 the Commissioners of Uniform State Laws promulgated a Uniform Limited Liability Company Act that, while not widely adopted, led to greater uniformity among state LLC statutes.

Nomenclature			
	Partnership	*Corporation*	*LLC*
Required document for formation	None	Articles of incorporation (aka certificate of incorporation or charter)	Articles of organization (aka certificate of organization or formation)
Other key organizational documents	Partnership agreement	Bylaws	Operating agreement (aka LLC agreement)
Participants holding a financial interest	Partners	Shareholders (aka stockholders)	Members

B. Default Structures

As you can see, business organizations are mostly sets of default rules that apply absent an agreement otherwise. Thus, the differences between a corporation and a partnership (after some tinkering by a business planner) can be less in practice than theory. LLCs and partnerships can be tailored to meet parties' precise needs.

Next we describe the default rules that govern partnerships, corporations and LLCs. We've interlaced our description with examples, many drawn from court cases, to give you a sense for how the rules operate in practice.

1. Formation

Forming a general partnership (GP) requires no filing with the state. Most partnerships are formed by consent—when two or more persons enter into a contract (usually called a partnership agreement) that will govern the relationship of the partners, including such matters as managerial rights, distribution rights, interests in profits and losses, and rights upon dissolution of the enterprise. A GP can arise inadvertently, however, without the parties being aware they have formed a partnership. A GP is formed by operation of law if two or more persons associate to carry on as co-owners a business for profit. Inadvertent partnerships can have unforeseen consequences, such a partner's liability for business debts incurred by another partner.

> ### Example 8.1
>
> A operates a beauty shop and hires B as a receptionist. When B asks for a raise, they agree in writing that B will share in profits. Their agreement states they are a "partnership."
>
> Under RUPA, they are not co-owners and thus not partners. A contributed everything to the shop and controls the business. B's sharing in profits is only a wage increase. Labels that parties use are not dispositive. Their relationship is that of employer-employee, not partners.
>
> *See* RUPA § 202, *Comment 1.*

The formation of a corporation requires formal action with the state. To incorporate, the persons creating the corporation (called "incorporators") must file articles of incorporation that contain required information about the company and its incorporators, such as the corporate name, the number of authorized shares, and the name and address of each incorporator. *See* MBCA § 2.02; DGCL § 102. The articles may also contain other information, such as the corporate purpose, provisions regulating the management of the corporation, and limitations on the powers of the corporation and its shareholders, officers or directors. The corporation's existence begins when its articles of incorporation are properly filed.

Other entities having limited liability—LLP, LP, LLLP or LLC—must also file with the state. For a limited partnership (LP), a *certificate* is filed naming the LP, designating its office and agent for service of process, and identifying the general partners. *See* RULPA § 201. If new general partners are added, amended filings are necessary. For a limited liability company (LLC), *articles of organization* are filed naming the LLC, as well as designating its office and agent for service of process. ULLCA § 201. The members then enter into an *operating agreement* (which some statutes call the "regulations" of the LLC) that sets forth the members' rights and duties. Some statutes require that the operating agreement be written; others allow oral operating agreements.

2. Liability

Limited liability is a key feature of the corporation, which is a separate legal entity responsible for its own debts and other liabilities. The most a shareholder can lose is generally limited to his original investment in the corporation. Limited liability is a default rule. Shareholders can contractually waive limited liability by giving personal guarantees as to particular loans or other credit extended to the business—a common stipulation when banks lend to small corporations.

Make the Connection

There are four main exceptions to the rule of limited liability. First, promoters can be liable when the corporation is not properly formed (Chapter 9, Incorporation). Second, shareholders can commit to make additional capital contributions to the corporation (Chapter 12, Capital Structure). Third, to achieve equity or prevent fraud, the veil of limited liability can be pierced, thus exposing shareholders to personal liability, in order to achieve equity or prevent fraud (Chapter 13, Piercing the Corporate Veil). Fourth, shareholders and other corporate participants can be liable under other regulatory regimes, such as securities regulation or environmental law (Chapter 14, Corporate Criminality, and Chapter 15, Corporate Environmental Liability).

A GP differs from a corporation in that the partners, as individuals, can be held jointly and severally liable for partnership obligations—whether in contract or in tort. Each partner also has the power to bind the GP, and thus the other partners, provided that the partner acted in the ordinary course of the partnership's business. *See* RUPA § 301.

Example 8.2

A provides capital and controls day-to-day operations in B's custom auto-making business. B agrees to build a car for X, but fails to perform and disappears. X seeks to hold A liable on the contract on the theory A was B's partner, not his "banker."

Under RUPA, even though A and B did not intend to create a partnership, they became partners as a matter of law. By sharing profits and control, A is a partner of B and became liable to X on the contract.

See RUPA § 202, §301; *see also Lupien v. Malsbenden*, 477 A.2d 746 (Me. 1984).

In an LP the general partners face the same unlimited liability as partners in a GP. The financial exposure of limited partners, on the other hand, depends on the rule adopted by the state governing the LP. In a pre-2001 ULPA jurisdiction, limited partners have limited liability, so long as they do not participate in the management of the LP. Courts have struggled to determine what constitutes "participation in management," but the cases paint no bright lines. "Participation" is defined to exclude certain activities, such as advising the general partner with respect to the business and voting on critical transactions. *See* RULPA (1985) § 303. Thus, the statute allows some participation without withdrawing from limited partners the protection of limited liability. The most recent version of RULPA provides that a limited partner's limited liability is not affected by participating in LP management. *See* RULPA (2001) § 303.

An LP can be structured in an innovative way so all participants have limited liability. To do this the general partner is structured as a corporation. The corporation is then liable for all unpaid obligations of the LP, but the individual directors, officers, and shareholders of the corporate general partner are shielded from liability.

The liability rules for the limited liability partnership (LLP) vary from state to state. Like a GP, the LLP (an entity) is liable for all tort and contract obligations that arise in the ordinary course of its business. Under most state statutes, though, a general partner in an LLP can be held personally liable only for partnership obligations that arise as a consequence of the wrongful or negligent acts committed by that partner or an employee under his supervision. This limitation on personal liability makes the LLP form of organization particularly attractive to professionals such as attorneys, accountants and physicians, especially since some state laws only allow individuals or partnerships to engage in these professions.

Example 8.3

A and B agree to form a law partnership, which they constitute as an LLP by filing the appropriate papers. B litigates a products liability case; one of the firm's associates (an employee) misses a filing deadline, and the case is dismissed. The client brings a malpractice action against the LLP, and against A and B.

Generally, only the LLP would be liable, not A or B. But this is a professional LLP, and in many states, B might be liable since he supervised the errant associate who committed malpractice.

See RUPA § 1001.

The LLC limits the liability of its members and managers for all of its obligations. LLCs are usually more attractive than LPs because they allow their members to participate fully in management and still receive limited liability. But, as is the case with shareholders of a corporation, LLC members may be liable when the entity is not properly formed, for unpaid capital contributions, and when the veil of limited liability is pierced.

> **Example 8.4**
>
> A and B are members of Preferred Income Investors, LLC. They hire C to build a new restaurant. During negotiations, A gives C a business card with his name, business address and the initials "P.I.I." C renders services and sends a bill, which goes unpaid.
>
> Because A and B failed to fully identify their LLC as principal in the transaction, they are individually liable for the bill.
>
> See *Water, Waste & Land, Inc. DEBA Westec v. Lanham*, 955 P.2d 997 (Colo. 1998).

3. Management and Control

The management of a corporation is centralized in its board of directors. Under the statutory default model, shareholders elect the board of directors. The board is charged with managing or overseeing the corporation's day-to-day management, which the board delegates to corporate officers appointed by the board. MBCA § 8.01; DGCL § 141. As we have seen, once shareholders have elected the board, the business judgment rule bars courts from second-guessing or overruling good faith decisions the board makes with respect to the corporation's business.

Corporate statutes generally provide that, unless the articles otherwise provide, directors are elected by a plurality of shares entitled to vote, MBCA § 7.28, and that each share is entitled to one vote. MBCA § 7.21. In close corporations, the owners often provide otherwise—by including provisions in the articles, bylaws or a shareholders' agreement that guarantee shareholder representation on the board or specify shareholder governance powers.

In a GP, absent contrary provisions in the partnership agreement, management authority is vested in all the partners. Each partner has an equal voice, regardless of the amount of his capital contribution. RUPA § 401. Decisions generally are made by majority vote of the partners, but major changes (like modification of a partner's decision-making authority) require the consent of all partners. RUPA § 401. Partners are agents of the GP and can bind the GP when apparently carrying on in the ordinary course of GP business. RUPA § 301.

> **Example 8.5**
>
> A and B form a GP that rents properties. They do not specify who has authority if there is a disagreement. A wants to increase rents, while B does not. A sues B for lost profits they could have made if rents had been increased.
>
> Under UPA, the decision of the majority governs. If the partners are equally divided, and without an agreement for breaking their impasse, the remedy is dissolution. A's suit fails.
>
> See *Covalt v. High*, 675 P.2d 999 (N.M. Ct. App. 1983).

Like corporate shareholders, partners often include provisions in their partnership agreement that modify these default rules. For example, many partnership agreements provide that a partner's voice in management will be in proportion to his capital contribution. Thus, a partner who contributes 60% of a partnership's capital would be entitled to 60% of the voting power. Some partnership agreements, including those of most large law firms, assign exclusive responsibility for managing various aspects of the partnership's business to one partner or a committee of partners.

In an LP, under older versions of the ULPA, limited partners could not participate in the management of the business without losing the protection of limited liability. Thus, under these older statutes, the general partners had responsibility for most management decisions. Over time ULPA has been modernized. More recent versions of ULPA specify that limited partners do not lose limited liability if they vote on certain major decisions, including dissolution, changing the nature of the business, the removal of a general partner and certain other extraordinary events. ULPA (1985) §§ 302, 303. The most recent version of ULPA states that limited partners do not become liable for LP obligations, even if they participate in control and management. RULPA (2001) § 303. In an LP, the limited partners have voting rights as specified by agreement; the general partner is an agent of the LP and can bind the LP when apparently carrying on in the ordinary course of LP business. RULPA § 402.

> ### Example 8.6
>
> A and B form a limited partnership to hold real estate (a shopping center). A is the limited partner and provides the capital; B is the general partner and manages the business. But their agreement specifies that A must sign all checks drafted by B, and outside parties believe A to be a general partner.
>
> Under older versions of ULPA, A may have crossed the line and be treated as a general partner, exposing her to general partner liability. But under ULPA § 303 (2001), A would not be liable for LP debts because limited partners are not liable "even if the limited partner . . . participates" in management.
>
> *See* ULPA (1985) § 303; ULPA (2001) § 303.

An LLC can be either *member-managed* or *manager-managed*; it is a flexible form that allows for significant choice in the mode of management. In a member-managed LLC, members can be given the authority to make management decisions and generally to act as agents for the LLC. In a manager-managed LLC, members are not agents of the entity and typically make only major decisions. The managers, who do not have to be members, usually make most ordinary business decisions and can be given the authority to act as agents of the LLC.

Practice Pointer

Fiduciary duties are the glue in all U.S. business organizations. Typically, they run from those with control (management) to those who invest (risk capital). The duties are often articulated as duties of care and loyalty, as well as good faith. There is significant (and ongoing) debate on whether these duties are default terms that the parties can vary or waive by agreement, or whether they are mandatory features of the "organization."

In fact, many business planners will choose more contractual business forms (partnerships and LLCs) on the assumption they permit modification of fiduciary duties by agreement. The statutory corporation is generally viewed as having inherent, non-waivable fiduciary protections.

4. Financial Rights

Financial rights in a corporation are allocated according to shares. Corporate shareholders have no right to share in business profits, unless the board of directors declares a dividend based on profits or other distribution of corporate assets. MBCA § 6.40; DGCL § 141. This assures the business a source of capital that can be put to long-term uses. Directors and officers have no right to compensation, except by contract.

Partners in a GP, unless agreed otherwise, have a right to share equally in business profits and are obligated to share in business losses in proportion to their share in profits. RUPA § 401(b). Each partner can enforce the right to profits or the sharing of losses through a judicial accounting proceeding. RUPA § 405(b). Partners have no right to compensation for their services, unless otherwise agreed.

Example 8.7

A and B form a logging GP—A contributes capital and B the equipment. They do not specify in their agreement how losses will be shared. The business does not generate enough profits to cover A's capital contribution, and A asks B to share in the net losses.

Under the UPA, the general rule is that partners share jointly in both profits and losses, unless otherwise agreed. Thus, B must contribute toward the loss (including the capital loss) according to his share in the profits. [Some courts, however, give B credit for his labor—see next example.]

See Richert v. Handly, 330 P.2d 1079 (Wash. 1958).

> **Example 8.8**
>
> A and B form a remodeling GP in which A contributes all the capital while B contributes only his skill and labor. The GP generates a loss, and A seeks contribution from B, for a share of A's capital losses. B refuses.
>
> Although under the UPA partners generally share in both profits and losses, when one partner only contributes capital, he cannot recover his capital losses from the other partner who only contributed services. Thus, A (the capital partner) cannot force B (the service partner) to share in capital losses. (This result is controversial and a minority approach).
>
> *See Kovacik v. Reed*, 315 P.2d 314 (Cal. 1957).

Financial sharing in LPs is not equal by default. Instead, profit sharing and distributions in an LP occur according to the capital contributions of the limited and general partners. RULPA (2001) §§ 503, 504. Only general partners in an LP must share in losses, again according to their capital contributions. (General partners in an LLLP have limited liability and do not bear business losses.)

LLC statutes vary on the allocation of financial rights. Some specify sharing of profits according to member contributions; others provide for equal sharing. ULLCA § 405(a) (equal shares). Statutes generally require that distributions be approved by all the members, absent an agreement otherwise. ULLCA § 404(c). And, absent an agreement, members generally have no right to remuneration. ULLCA § 403(d).

5. Continuity of Existence (and Withdrawal)

A corporation has perpetual existence, though the articles of incorporation may provide for a shorter term. The parties also may agree in advance that the corporation will be dissolved in specified circumstances, such as the death or disability of one of the key participants. Otherwise, voluntary dissolution of the corporation (that is, liquidation of its assets, payment of creditors, and distribution of the net proceeds to shareholders) can only happen when the board recommends dissolution and a majority of voting shares approve. Shareholders have no right to withdraw and demand payment for their shares from the corporation.

A GP can be either for a term or at will. Absent contrary provisions in the partnership agreement, an at-will GP (not for a definite term or particular undertaking) is dissolved on the withdrawal of any partner. *See* RUPA §§ 601, 801. The withdrawing partner can demand that the business be liquidated and the net proceeds distributed to the partners in cash. When a partner dies, the surviving partners can choose to continue the GP and pay the estate of the deceased partner the buyout value of his partnership interest, without having to liquidate the business.

> ### Example 8.9
>
> A and B are partners in a family GP. They have no written agreement about dissolution. A wants to end the partnership, sell (liquidate) the business assets, and then split the cash proceeds. B wants to divide the assets in-kind between them, but not sell.
>
> Under the UPA, a partner in an at-will GP can withdraw (causing dissolution) and share in a forced liquidation of partnership assets, provided creditors are first fully paid.
>
> *See Dreifuerst v. Dreifuerst*, 280 N.W. 2d 335 (Wis. Ct. App. 1979)

In an LP, the business generally continues upon the death, bankruptcy or voluntary withdrawal of a limited partner, but the LP agreement must specify the latest date upon which the partnership must be dissolved. *See* RULPA § 201(a)(4). Most LP agreements restrict a limited partner's right to withdraw his capital. Absent a provision to the contrary in the LP agreement, an LP is dissolved only when a general partner withdraws. *See* RULPA § 801.

LLC statutes generally provide that an LLC exists in perpetuity, unless its operating agreement or articles of organization otherwise provide. States have widely different approaches, however, to the question of how a member may leave an LLC.

Some states follow a partnership model for withdrawing LLC members, but often with important differences. Under RULLCA, the unilateral withdrawal of a member by express will does not result in a dissolution. This makes the LLC a more stable form of entity than an at-will GP. Another difference is that, unlike its predecessor uniform statute, RULLCA does not provide for default buyout rights for members.

Other states follow a corporate model, preventing a member from withdrawing or resigning unless permitted in the LLC agreement. For example, the Delaware LLC statute provides simple default rules for dissolution, but does not mention dissociation. Unless otherwise provided in the operating agreement, a member cannot unilaterally resign or withdraw until the LLC has been dissolved and wound up. Members of a Delaware LLC should therefore carefully consider whether to include a term in the operating agreement providing for an exit mechanism besides dissolution. Otherwise, a member that wants to exit the LLC will have limited options: she could try to negotiate with other members for a buyout or to dissolve the LLC, or petition the Court of Chancery for judicial dissolution.

6. Transferability of Interests

Corporate shareholders are free to transfer their stock without obtaining the consent of the corporation or other shareholders. In close corporations, however, the owners often agree to restrictions on the transferability of stock to restrict who can participate and vote in the corporation.

Since partners can bind the GP and thus subject other partners to personal liability, the default rule is that all current partners must consent to the transfer of a GP interest and the admission of a new partner. RUPA § 401. But a partner is allowed to transfer his financial (as opposed to governance) interest in the GP (the "transferable interest"), and the transferee can share in the partnership's profits but without a voice in management. RUPA § 502. For example, a partner can pledge his transferable interest to obtain personal loans, without having to obtain the consent of the other partners.

The default rule is similar in an LP. Limited partners can transfer their financial interests, but the assignee may only exercise governance rights of a limited partner with the consent of all the remaining partners. RULPA § 702. Transfers of limited partner interests do not create risks of personal liability, and LP agreements often allow the limited partners to transfer their financial and governance interests without the consent of the other partners.

LLC statutes generally permit transferability only of the member's financial interest, but not his governance interest. *See* RULLCA § 502. A member can, however, withdraw (dissociate) and avoid any continuing voting/management responsibilities or fiduciary duties. RULLCA § 603.

7. Mergers and Consolidations

Corporations can combine through a technique called a merger. The assets and liabilities of both corporations in the merger are automatically combined in a surviving corporation. The consideration paid to shareholders in the merger— whether shares, cash or other financial instruments—is determined in a merger plan. The merger plan must typically be approved by the boards of directors of both corporations, as well as the shareholders of both corporations. After approval, articles of merger are filed with state authorities.

The merger or consolidation of general partnerships remains true to the simplicity of the GP form. Generally, merging GPs do not have to file articles of merger to be considered a single taxable entity. The partnerships simply combine assets by agreement. In a limited partnership, mergers are possible if agreed to by all the partners, both the limited and general partners.

Most states permit the merger of LLCs. A plan of merger must be adopted by each LLC; the merger plan must be approved by all the members; and merger documentation must be filed with the state. One LLC survives the merger and the other ceases to exist.

C. Balancing Ownership Interests

People who join together in a business generally do so with mutual trust and shared commitment to a shared vision. They may be reluctant to contemplate that, at some point, somebody may behave opportunistically—that is, promote his interests at the expense of the other participants. The prudent planner should consider how the organizational form deals with opportunistic behavior.

In a GP, the default rule allowing at-will dissolution is critical. Minority partners who disagree with decisions by the majority can withdraw and dissolve the partnership. The firm's assets are then liquidated at a judicial sale (typically purchased by the majority partners), and the withdrawing partner then receives his share of the net proceeds.

Minority partners can also use at-will dissolution opportunistically. For example, suppose a minority partner develops special business skills that would be hard to replace. The minority partner can bargain for undeserved concessions from the majority by threatening to withdraw. Even if the majority could show the minority partner's withdrawal was wrongful, the cost of litigation and the available remedies might not fully compensate the majority.

To deal with problems like this, those planning a partnership should consider drafting provisions that reduce the risk of opportunism. The partnership agreement might call for a specified undertaking or term, with any withdrawal before the agreed undertaking or term constituting a wrongful dissolution. Or if the concern is potential shirking by minority partners, the partnership agreement could permit the expulsion of a partner under specified conditions and for a specified payment.

Food for Thought

Fiduciary duties in LLCs, and the extent to which they can be contracted around or eliminated, have been a subject of considerable controversy. RULLCA provides for fiduciary duties of care and loyalty owed by members (in a member-managed LLC) and managers (in a manager-managed LLC) and sets limitations on modifications to such duties. Some states such as Delaware allow even broader flexibility. Delaware's LLC statute provides that default fiduciary duties exist unless the operating agreement provides otherwise—and it allows fiduciary duties to be "expanded or restricted or eliminated" in the operating agreement. An LLC might, therefore, choose to completely eliminate the protections of fiduciary duties.

By contrast, corporate law favors the prerogatives of the majority. Decision-making authority is centralized in the board of directors, all of whom can be elected by the majority shareholder, if there is one. Board decisions that advance the interests of the majority, unless they involve self dealing or bad faith, are insulated by the business judgment rule from challenge by minority shareholders. A minority shareholder unhappy with the direction of the business may want to sell his shares. But the majority shareholder is likely to be the only person interested in buying—potentially at a price less than the minority shareholder would consider fair. Some states allow a minority shareholder to seek a judicially-ordered involuntary dissolution if the majority's actions are oppressive. But this is far less certain than the option of unilateral withdrawal and cash payment in an at-will partnership.

D. Tax Consequences (Brief Overview)

Often the choice of business organization turns on the federal income tax consequences of the choice. (State income tax tends to follow the federal lead.) Even if you have not studied tax, you will see that the choice comes down to whether the business is taxed as a corporation or as a partnership.

1. Corporation vs. Partnership

The Internal Revenue Code classifies every business organization as either a corporation or a partnership—with very different tax treatment for each. A corporation is treated as a taxpaying entity separate from its shareholders. The corporation itself pays taxes on business income and the shareholders are also taxed on any dividends they receive—what is known as "double taxation."

A partnership, by contrast, is treated as an aggregate of individuals rather than a separate entity. The partnership is not a taxpayer, though partnerships must file an information return so the partners (and the IRS) know how much business income or loss to include on the partners' personal income tax returns. Partnership income and expenses "flow through" to the partners in proportion to their ownership interests. This applies to partners who participate materially in the partnership's business. An individual partner who does not participate materially in the business can only use partnership losses to offset ordinary income from other sources *after* the partner disposes of his entire interest in the partnership.

So, what counts as a corporation or a partnership for tax purposes? The answer may surprise you. Under so-called "check the box" regulations adopted by the IRS in 1997, every unincorporated entity can choose to be taxed as a partnership, regardless of whether it has corporate attributes such as centralized management, limited liability, free transferability of shares, and perpetual life. *See* Treas. Reg. § 301.7701. This means that every GP, LLP, LP, LLLP, and LLC is taxed as a partnership, unless its owners elect for the entity to be taxed as a corporation by checking a box. *See* I.R.S. Form 8832.

Corporations are generally subject to business-level tax under IRC Subchapter C (and are commonly referred to as "C Corporations"). There is an exception for certain corporations that elect to be taxed on a flow-through basis under IRC Subchapter S (so-called "S corporations," which we describe below).

Why do corporate planners seek to avoid being taxed as a corporation? The answer: corporations are subject to "double taxation." The corporation pays tax on income it earns. When the corporation distributes a portion of that income to its shareholders as dividends, the shareholders pay income tax on the dividends, with no deduction or other allowance for the tax the corporation has paid. In contrast, a partnership pays no tax. The income from the business is taxed only once—to the partners— whether or not the income is actually distributed.

Consider an example. Suppose Anita and Brandon come to own Your Green Home as a partnership (or other unincorporated entity, like an LLC). At the end of each year, the partnership will compute its net income and file an information return. The partnership pays "salaries" to Anita and Brandon and distributes to them some or all of the business net income. The partnership pays no tax on its net income. Anita and Brandon pay taxes, at their respective individual tax rates, on the

Take Note!

Until 1997, Treasury regulations known as the "Kintner" regulations provided that an unincorporated business organization would be classified as an "association taxable as a corporation" if it had two or more of the following characteristics: (1) limited liability of owners; (2) centralized management; (3) free transferability of interests; and (4) continuity of life. If it had only one of these characteristics, it would be taxed as a partnership.

To make sure LLCs were taxed as partnerships, statutory drafters and business planners sought to eliminate at least two of the corporate attributes. Thus, LLC statutes initially provided for dissolution upon withdrawal (no continuity), restricted free transferability of interests, and specified manager-managed structures (no centralized management)—while providing for limited liability. Business planners then drafted complex LLC agreements to avoid the impact of these restrictions. The U.S. Treasury responded to this complexity in a surprising fashion. Rather than "fine tune" the Kintner regulations, the Treasury adopted a radically simple "check the box" approach. This allowed LLCs to simply choose flow-through taxation and it allowed LLC statutes across the country to evolve in ways not tied to partnership-law characteristics.

"salaries" they received plus the net business income, whether or not distributed to them. To determine how much of the business income profit is attributed to each partner, reference is made initially to the partnership agreement. If there is no agreement on this point, the tax rules assume equal partners. And if the partnership operates at a loss, each partner can use his proportionate share of that loss to offset income received from other sources.

Now suppose that Anita and Brandon own the business as a corporation that pays them the same salaries and retains the same amount of net business income. Unlike a partnership, the corporation pays taxes on its net income, after deducting the owners' salaries as a business expense. The owners pay taxes on their salaries but, unlike partners in a partnership, they will *not* pay taxes on any business income, unless the corporation distributes profits as dividends. Nor can they claim a personal income deduction if the corporation operates at a loss.

Two examples illustrate the costs of corporate "double taxation" compared to a "flow-through" partnership, whether the business is profitable or operates at a loss (both examples use 2019 tax rates for individuals and corporations).

Example 8.10
(business is profitable)

Assume a business with *net income* of $80,000, after Owners pay themselves salaries totaling $70,000. If the business is taxed as a flow-through partnership (no business level tax), Owners must include distributions from the business in their personal income taxes and thus are taxed on $150,000 in total income. If the business is taxed as a corporation, the corporation will incur income tax. If the corporation distributes its profits as dividends, Owners are taxed on their combined salaries and dividends.

	Partnership (000)	Corporation (000)
Business		
Income (loss)	$80	$80
Business tax	$0	$16.8
Distribution to Owners	$80	$62.2
Personal		
Salaries	$70	$70
Distributions from business	$80	$62.2
Taxable income	$150	$132.2
Personal tax*	$11.4	$9.2
TOTAL TAX	**$11.4**	**$26.0**

* assumes Owners received equal salaries and are married, filing jointly.

Thus, owners can reduce their overall tax bill by about $14,600 by using the flow-through partnership as opposed to the double-taxed corporation.

Example 8.11
(business operates at a loss)

Assume a business with *net losses* of $20,000, after Owners pay themselves salaries totaling $70,000. If the business is taxed as a flow-through partnership (no business level tax), Owners deduct the business losses in their individual tax returns and are taxed on $50,000 in income. If the business is taxed as a corporation, the corporation will not incur income tax, but can carry forward its tax losses to offset income in future years (if there is any), but Owners cannot reduce their individual taxable income using the corporate business losses.

	Partnership (000)	Corporation (000)
Business		
Income (loss)	($20)	($20)
Business tax	$0	$0
Personal		
Salaries	$70	$70
Distributions	($20)	$0
Taxable income	$50	$70
Personal tax*	$0.1	$2.1
TOTAL TAX	**$0.1**	**$2.1**

* assumes Owners received equal salaries and are married, filing jointly.

Thus, owners can reduce overall taxes by about $2,000 by using the flow-through partnership. The corporation's carry-forward losses may (or may not) be usable in future years, and are unlikely to have a present value of more than $2,000.

2. Avoiding Corporate Double Tax

As you can see, doing business in the corporate form creates a separate tax-paying entity that is both subject to an additional layer of taxes (if there are business profits) and that prevents the owners from individually deducting any business losses.

But there are ways to reduce the impact of corporate-level tax. Even before the IRS "check the box" regulations, business planners used various techniques to avoid corporate-level tax, while keeping the advantages of corporate limited liability and continuity. These techniques remain relevant for businesses organized as corporations.

Subchapter S. The Internal Revenue Code (Subchapter S) permits a corporation to elect flow-through tax treatment that is similar to that of a partnership.

To qualify as an "S corporation," the corporation must be a domestic corporation or LLC with no more than 100 shareholders. The shareholders themselves must be individuals, estates or qualified trusts, or tax-exempt entities (such as employee stock ownership plans, pension plans, and charities). No shareholder can be a nonresident alien. The corporation can have only one class of stock, although shares with different voting rights are treated as part of the same class if they are otherwise alike. All the shareholders must consent to election of Subchapter S treatment.

Once an election is made, corporate income, losses, and credits are attributed to shareholders according to the number of shares they hold. (But shareholders of an S Corporation can only write off losses up to the amount of capital they invested, with losses above capital investment carried forward and recognized in future years.) The Subchapter S election terminates if over any three-year period more than 25% of the corporation's gross receipts constitute passive investment income. The election also terminates if the number of shareholders exceeds 100 or any shareholder is not qualified. Thus, a transfer by an existing qualified shareholder to an unqualified entity or individual will automatically terminate the Subchapter S election.

Zeroing Out Income. Another way to flow business income to corporate shareholders, and thus avoid tax at the corporate level, is to "zero out" corporate income by having the corporation pay shareholders *deductible* salaries, bonuses, rental payments, or interest. By deducting these items from income at the corporate level and thus reducing the corporation's taxable income to zero, the effect is to have taxes paid only at the shareholder level.

Example 8.12

A and B form a "C corporation" and decide to treat their capital contributions as loans to the corporation. While dividends are not deductible, interest on corporate debts is—even when paid to a shareholder. If interest on their loans matches the corporation's income, the use of debt can eliminate income tax at the corporate level. (A and B will, of course, have to pay individual taxes on their interest income.)

There may, however, be too much of a good thing. The IRS may scrutinize debt held by insiders or rental payments paid to the owners, particularly if the terms are different from those that would be found in an arm's-length transaction. Likewise, if the salaries or bonuses paid to the owner-employees are not reasonable (the tax code requires that they be "ordinary and necessary"), the extra compensation may be treated as disguised and thus non-deductible dividends.

CHAPTER 9

Incorporation

Forming a corporation is simple. But choosing the internal structure can be a complex art.

This chapter focuses on the steps involved in forming a corporation. First, we look at the formal requirements, the factors involved in the choice of the state of incorporation, and the role of the lawyer when there are multiple parties in a new corporation. Next, we consider the powers the corporation can exercise and the effect of limitations in the corporate articles. Finally, we review the legal rules that apply if there are incorporation defects.

Make the Connection

We leave to later chapters the many specific provisions that might go into the corporation's constitutive documents. For example, shark repellents (that discourage shareholder insurgents) such as staggered boards or advance notice provisions for director nominations are covered in Chapter 16, Shareholder Voting. Waivers of directors' fiduciary duties through exculpation clauses are covered in Chapter 20, Board Decision Making. Modifications to the general principle of majority rule are covered in Chapter 25, Planning in the Close Corporation.

A. Process of Incorporation

1. Formal Requirements

The filing requirements and procedures for forming a corporation are simple and quick. Although the procedures vary slightly from state to state, the MBCA is typical. Incorporation is formally accomplished by an "incorporator"—a capacity that has no further significance once the corporation is organized. The incorporator signs and files the articles of incorporation (a public document) with the Secretary of State or another designated official. There is a filing fee, which is usually a flat rate (such as $100) or in some states, notably Delaware, calculated on the basis of the number of authorized shares. Under most statutes, formal corporate existence commences with the filing of the articles of incorporation.

MBCA § 2.01
Incorporators

One or more persons may act as the incorporator or incorporators of a corporation by delivering articles of incorporation to the secretary of state for filing.

What goes into the articles? Very little is required, though much can be included. Under most statutes the articles *must* include only (1) the name of the corporation, (2) the number of shares it is authorized to issue, (3) the name and address of each incorporator, and (4) the name and address of the corporation's registered office and registered agent (the person and place to receive service of process or other official notices). There is no need to identify the directors, the officers, or the shareholders—the internal functioning and ownership of the corporation is mostly a private matter, at least under state law. Nor is there a need to disclose the corporation's specific purposes, powers, and responsibilities—these are typically described only in general terms as engaging in any lawful business.

Under the MBCA (and most state statutes), the articles can include provisions that insulate directors from liability, or "exculpate" them. An exculpation clause limits the personal liability of directors to the corporation or its shareholders, subject to some exemptions. Indemnification provisions also can obligate the corporation to reimburse directors for personal liability, again with exceptions.

MBCA § 2.02
Articles of Incorporation

(a) The articles of incorporation must set forth:

    (1) a corporate name for the corporation that satisfies the requirements of section 4.01 [which requires the name include "corporation" or "corp." or other specified indication it is incorporated, and the name must be "distinguishable" from other existing corporations in the state];

    (2) the number of shares the corporation is authorized to issue;

    (3) the street address of the corporation's initial registered office and the name of its initial registered agent at that office; and

    (4) the name and address of each incorporator.

(b) The articles of incorporation may set forth:

(1) the names and addresses of the individuals who are to serve as the initial directors;

(2) provisions not inconsistent with law regarding:

(i) the purpose or purposes for which the corporation is organized;

(ii) managing the business and regulating the affairs of the corporation;

(iii) defining, limiting, and regulating the powers of the corporation, its board of directors, and shareholders;

(iv) a par value for authorized shares or classes of shares;

(v) the imposition of personal liability on shareholders for the debts of the corporation to a specified extent and upon specified conditions;

(3) any provision that under this Act is required or permitted to be set forth in the bylaws;

(4) a provision eliminating or limiting the liability of a director to the corporation or its shareholders for money damages for any action taken, or any failure to take any action, as a director, except liability for (A) the amount of a financial benefit received by a director to which he is not entitled; (B) an intentional infliction of harm on the corporation or the shareholders; (C) a violation of section 8.33 [which creates liability for directors who approve unlawful distributions to shareholders]; or (D) an intentional violation of criminal law; and

(5) a provision permitting or making obligatory indemnification of a director for liability (as defined in section 8.50(5)) to any person for any action taken, or any failure to take any action, as a director except liability for (A) receipt of a financial benefit to which he is not entitled, (B) an intentional infliction of harm on the corporation or its shareholders, (C) a violation of section 8.33, or (D) an intentional violation of criminal law.

(c) The articles of incorporation need not set forth any of the corporate powers enumerated in this Act.

(d) Provisions of the articles of incorporation may be made dependent upon facts objectively ascertainable outside the articles of incorporation in accordance with section 1.20(k).

After the corporation comes into legal existence, an organizational meeting must be held. This is done either by the incorporator or by the initial board. At this first meeting (or when the incorporator simply signs a consent form), a number of standard tasks happen: (1) the election of directors (or of additional directors if directors were named in the articles); (2) the adoption of bylaws; (3) the appointment of officers; (4) the designation of a bank as depository for corporate funds; and (5) approval of the sale of stock to the initial shareholders.

<u>**MBCA § 2.05**</u>
<u>**Organization of Corporation**</u>

(a) After incorporation:

(1) if initial directors are named in the articles of incorporation, the initial directors shall hold an organizational meeting, at the call of a majority of the directors, to complete the organization of the corporation by appointing officers, adopting bylaws, and carrying on any other business brought before the meeting;

(2) if initial directors are not named in the articles, the incorporator or incorporators shall hold an organizational meeting at the call of a majority of the incorporators:

(i) to elect directors and complete the organization of the corporation; or

(ii) to elect a board of directors who shall complete the organization of the corporation.

(b) Action required or permitted by this Act to be taken by incorporators at an organizational meeting may be taken without a meeting if the action taken is evidenced by one or more written consents describing the action taken and signed by each incorporator.

(c) An organizational meeting may be held in or out of this state.

As you can see, it is not necessary to have a lawyer to incorporate a business. In fact, many people incorporate without a lawyer, either on their own or by using a corporation service company or online provider. Service companies can provide standard articles of incorporation, bylaws, and forms of stock certificate. They also file the necessary documents with the state, act as registered agent for the corporation, qualify the corporation to do business in other jurisdictions, and assist in the filing of annual and other reports required by the state of incorporation and other states where the corporation is registered as a foreign corporation. In many cases, the service companies charge less than lawyers for comparable work. Lawyers offer planning counsel regarding governance and other considerations that can provide value beyond the task of incorporation.

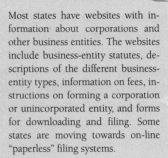

Go Online

Most states have websites with information about corporations and other business entities. The websites include business-entity statutes, descriptions of the different business-entity types, information on fees, instructions on forming a corporation or unincorporated entity, and forms for downloading and filing. Some states are moving towards on-line "paperless" filing systems.

2. Choice of the State of Incorporation

The choice of the state of incorporation typically follows a rule of thumb: firms that expect to operate locally incorporate locally; businesses that expect to have national operations or sell stock to public investors incorporate in Delaware.

As the dominant producer of U.S. corporate law, Delaware offers certain advantages, as discussed in Chapter 5, Corporate Federalism. Delaware's corporate case law is extensive, the statute is kept up to date, and the corporate judiciary is world renowned for its expertise and efficiency.

For firms with a local reach, incorporation in the state where the firm actually operates reduces filing, reporting, and tax burdens. If the firm does not operate in more than one state, local incorporation avoids the bother and costs of incorporating in another state and then qualifying to do business as a foreign corporation in the local state. Foreign incorporation makes sense if the local state has particular provisions of its corporation law that are burdensome to the investors or managers of the firm, or if the local state's administrative or court system is especially weak. This is unusual for most small businesses. Moreover, local law firms often prefer local incorporation: they know the law and courts, and Delaware litigation can be costly and involve fee-sharing with Delaware counsel. In fact, some public corporations choose to incorporate (or stay incorporated) in the state of their headquarters because they expect their state's courts and legislature to be more sympathetic and responsive.

3. Representing Multiple Parties in a Business Formation

What should be the role of the lawyer who assists in the formation of a multi-party business? Often a standard form will not suffice. Instead, the lawyer will want to help the parties address fundamental issues of organization, control, governance, finance, and allocation of profit and risk. And in a business with multiple parties there will be inevitable tensions and sometimes conflicts between the parties' respective interests.

Attorney-client relationship. If you are a lawyer for multiple parties who want to incorporate a business, who is the client? The question is important because the lawyer has duties to clients that he does not have to non-clients.

Here's a quick primer on the professional rules that apply to lawyers. A lawyer must promptly inform a client of any situation requiring the client's informed consent. The lawyer must consult with the client about objectives and how they will be accomplished. The lawyer must keep the client reasonably informed and promptly comply with the client's information requests. The lawyer cannot disclose information about a client without the client's informed consent. The lawyer must obtain informed consent before representing one or more clients who may have a conflict of interest, or must decline the representation altogether.

FYI

The basic rules on lawyer professional duties can be found in the ABA Model Rules of Professional Conduct. The Model Rules were created (and are regularly revised) by the American Bar Association (ABA) to prescribe the standards of legal ethics and professional responsibilities for U.S. lawyers. The Model Rules are not binding, but constitute recommendations on what states should adopt. Nearly all states (except California) have adopted the rules in whole or in part.

Normally, the attorney-client relationship is created either by agreement or by the client requesting, and the attorney performing, legal services for the client. But when there are multiple parties to a corporate formation, it may be unclear whether the client is (or will be) the corporation or is also the individual parties, particularly when one of them may be a previous or existing client.

Multiple representation, of course, has its advantages. Having one lawyer for the transaction is less expensive than each party retaining his own lawyer. Justice Louis Brandeis, when a private practitioner in Boston, envisioned a role for transactional lawyers to mediate and resolve the parties' varying objectives. He referred to the role as "lawyer for the situation."

ABA Model Rules of Professional Conduct
Rule 1.13 Organization as Client

(a) A lawyer employed or retained by an organization represents the organization acting through its duly authorized constituents.

(f) In dealing with an organization's directors, officers, employees, members, shareholders or other constituents, a lawyer shall explain the identity of the client when the lawyer knows or reasonably should know that the organization's interests are adverse to those of the constituents with whom the lawyer is dealing.

COMMENT

[1] An organizational client is a legal entity, but it cannot act except through its officers, directors, employees, shareholders and other constituents. Officers, directors, employees and shareholders are the constituents of the corporate organizational client. The duties defined in this Comment apply equally to unincorporated associations.

[2] When one of the constituents of an organizational client communicates with the organization's lawyer in that person's organizational capacity, the communication is protected by Rule 1.6 [attorney-client privileged communications]. Thus, by way of example, if an organizational client requests its lawyer to investigate allegations of wrongdoing, interviews made in the course of that investigation between the lawyer and the client's employees or other constituents are covered by Rule 1.6. This does not mean, however, that constituents of an organizational client are the clients of the lawyer.

[10] There are times when the organization's interest may be or become adverse to those of one or more of its constituents. In such circumstances the lawyer should advise any constituent, whose interest the lawyer finds adverse to that of the organization of the conflict or potential conflict of interest, that the lawyer cannot represent such constituent, and that such person may wish to obtain independent representation. Care must be taken to assure that the individual understands that, when there is such adversity of interest, the lawyer for the organization cannot provide legal representation for that constituent individual, and that discussions between the lawyer for the organization and the individual may not be privileged.

"Entity" vs. "Aggregate." Courts and professional ethics rules generally follow one of two approaches when considering who lawyers, and their law firms, are deemed to represent. Under the "entity theory," the lawyer represents only the corporation, not the individuals involved in the business. Thus, there is no disabling conflict if a lawyer's law firm later sues any of the individuals on an unrelated matter, even if the law firm obtained personal information from the individuals while forming and representing the corporation. If individuals present information to a lawyer about themselves before the corporation has been formed, courts and bar rules applying the "entity theory" wave a magic wand: they deem the lawyer's pre-incorporation involvement to be a retroactive representation of the entity-to-be-formed, not of the individuals (assuming incorporation eventually happens).

In contrast, courts and bar rules sometimes apply the "aggregate theory," and assume that lawyer represents both the participants and the corporation. The "aggregate theory" is more likely to apply when the business involves only a few participants, particularly when the participants (such as members of a partnership) believed that the lawyer was representing them in their individual capacities. For example, if a lawyer helps three people form a corporation, and then buys shares from two of them that the third shareholder claimed he wanted to buy, the "aggregate theory" would suggest that the lawyer breached a duty to the third shareholder, who justifiably understood that the lawyer had acted as personal counselor for all three of them.

Reasonable expectations. As you can see, the question of who the lawyer represents boils down to what the participants had been led to expect. For this reason, a corporate lawyer from the start should explain to the participants who he is representing, which communications between them will be privileged and which not, and what action the lawyer may take if conflicts arise between the participants. Who pays the lawyer is not dispositive, though courts have viewed payments to the lawyer from the corporation as evidence that the lawyer was counsel to the entity.

A lawyer who plans to be counsel only to the entity should make clear (usually in an engagement letter) that the lawyer does *not* represent the participants collectively. However, if an engagement letter or oral representation by the lawyer suggests that he is representing the participants as an aggregate, the lawyer assumes ethical obligations to *each* participant. Such aggregate representation is proper if the lawyer explains to each client that the lawyer may have to withdraw from representing *each* client if a conflict arises *among* them.

> ### Hypo 9.1
>
> You are approached by Basil, Sybil, and Gowan to help form a business. Who do you represent?
>
> Assume you had represented Basil in his divorce. You know that he is strapped for cash, given his spousal maintenance obligations. If the parties tell you that they expect that Basil will run the new business, and make decisions about whether to re-invest or pay out earnings, should you (can you) tell the others about Basil's personal financial situation?

B. Corporate Powers (and the *Ultra Vires* Doctrine)

In early U.S. corporations one of the most important features of the statutory charter was a statement of corporate purposes. Under the common law doctrine of *ultra vires* ("beyond the power"), a corporation could not engage in activities outside the scope of its defined purposes. The doctrine reflected both the public suspicion of concentrations of private economic power and the desire of corporate investors to limit their financial exposure to specified business risks.

In the nineteenth century, the law of corporations was mainly devoted to the resolution of disputes arising under the *ultra vires* doctrine. Today the issue rarely arises. Clearly, the original purpose of the doctrine to curb the powers of large corporations has failed, largely replaced by expanded fiduciary duties.

Once states began in the mid-1800s to enact general incorporation statutes, corporate lawyers circumvented the limitations of the *ultra vires* doctrine simply by drafting the articles of incorporation in broad terms. "Purpose clauses" often went on for pages, listing every conceivable activity in which a corporation might engage, even if the promoters intended only to undertake limited activities.

Today, such drafting is unnecessary. Modern statutes typically include broad provisions such as the one in the MBCA that "Every corporation incorporated under this Act has the purpose of engaging in any lawful business unless a more limited purpose is set forth in the articles of incorporation." MBCA § 3.01(a). A similar breadth is found with respect to corporate powers. MBCA § 3.02.

So does the *ultra vires* doctrine have any continuing relevance? In close corporations, where investors may want to limit the scope of the corporation's business and thus limit management discretion, it is possible to place limits on the corporation's purpose and powers in the articles. Then, if the corporate managers exceed what the articles permit (such as when a photocopy shop begins to sell lawn furniture), the corporation or shareholders acting on its behalf can disavow transactions that exceed the corporate powers. MBCA § 3.04. Similarly, benefit corporations that specify in their articles of incorporation particular social or environmental purposes may be limited in the scope of their corporate activities. Otherwise, the doctrine of *ultra vires* cannot be used as a defense to an otherwise valid obligation.

Take Note!

As noted in our earlier discussion of corporate social responsibility, entrepreneurs increasingly are forming corporations with a stated social purpose or purposes, and states have adopted various statutory provisions that govern these new categories of entities. For example, "benefit corporations" often include a specified social purpose in their articles or a "general social benefit" statement (for example, "a material positive impact on society and the environment, taken as a whole"). States take varying approaches to benefit corporations, and the types of descriptions of corporate powers and purposes in benefit corporations' articles is evolving: some descriptions are specific and narrow, while others are general and broad.

C. Defective Incorporation

When does the corporation come to life? The question is important for those who want the advantage of corporate limited liability, so business liabilities do not create personal liability. Modern corporate statutes (the MBCA is typical) identify a precise moment when the corporation comes into existence: the filing of the articles.

MBCA § 2.03
Incorporation

(a) Unless a delayed effective date is specified, the corporate existence begins when the articles of incorporation are filed.

(b) The secretary of state's filing of the articles of incorporation is conclusive proof that the incorporators satisfied all conditions precedent to incorporation except in a proceeding by the state to cancel or revoke the incorporation or involuntarily dissolve the corporation.

What happens if a "corporation" enters into a business transaction—but before the corporation exists? This problem used to be common, when the incorporation process took longer than a simple filing, and required approval by a state official and formalities such as multiple signatures, notarization, and local county filings. Given these difficulties, third parties sometimes would do deals with a "corporation to be formed." Other times, parties thought the corporation existed, unaware of some incorporation delay or defect.

The heavily-litigated question that arose was whether third parties could sue *personally* those individuals who purported to act for the corporation. When both parties knew that the corporation had not yet been formed, the question was whether the "promoter" was liable. When one or both of the parties was unaware that there was a defect in incorporation, the question was whether the court should infer limited liability on equity grounds.

Today, with incorporation so simple, these cases do not arise as often. It is now possible to incorporate a business in a matter of hours. Third parties can go online and check the secretary of state's records to see if a business is incorporated. But there is still a possibility that business transactions will happen with a "corporation" that does not yet exist.

Hypo 9.2

Manuel and Polly go into business together. They read a "do it yourself" website that says business people wanting a corporation need not go through the trouble (or expense) of incorporation. They can, according to the website, simply act as a corporation. Believing everything they read on the web, the two entrepreneurs act as a corporation. First, Manuel orders new office furniture from a local merchant for the account of "M&P Corporation." Second, the furniture delivery person slips and is injured on a slick sidewalk at the "M&P" offices. They have no insurance.

The business assets are insufficient to pay for the furniture or the injury. Are Manuel and Polly personally liable?

---

1. Both Parties Know There Is No Corporation

Suppose two parties enter into a contract, and one acts on behalf of a corporation to be formed. If both parties know that there has been no incorporation, traditional principles of contract and agency law present some conceptual questions: Can the corporation, once formed, become bound by the contract and, if so, under what theory? Is the "promoter" who executes the contract liable on the contract if the corporation never comes into existence? If the corporation comes into existence and

What's That?

A "novation" is a three-party arrangement in which a new party replaces an existing party to a contract. In a pre-incorporation contract, the newly-formed corporation assumes all of the rights and liabilities of the promoter under the contract, thus discharging the promoter.

adopts the contract as its own, is the promoter off the hook? And can the corporation now sue on the contract?

Here's the general rule: when a promoter contracts for the benefit of a corporation that is contemplated but not yet organized, the promoter is personally liable on the contract in the absence of an agreement otherwise. Furthermore, the promoter is not discharged from liability simply because the corporation is later organized and receives the benefits of the contract, even where the corporation adopts the contract. The parties may agree to discharge the promoter's liability—but to do so they must agree there will be a novation once the corporation is formed and formally accepts the contract.

The question becomes one of intent. When the parties' contract does not directly address the issue, courts have discerned the parties' intent from their contract and their dealings. Factors include:

- the form of signature—did the promoter sign as an agent of the corporation?

- actions of the third party—did the third party plan to look only to the corporation for performance?

- partial performance—did the promoter's partial performance of the contract indicate an intent to be held personally liable?

- novation—did later actions taken by the parties discharge the promoter's liability?

Consider the following signature line: "D.J. Geary, for a bridge company to be organized and incorporated." What did the parties intend? Perhaps Geary would use his best efforts to bring a corporation into existence and to have it adopt the contract as its own; thus Geary would not be bound personally. Perhaps Geary would be liable on the contract until such time as he has successfully incorporated the corporation and it has adopted the contract. Perhaps Geary would be bound on the contract and would remain bound even if the corporation came into existence and adopted the contract.

Which of these interpretations is most logical? The RESTATEMENT (SECOND) OF AGENCY § 326 (1958) provides: "Unless otherwise agreed, a person who, in dealing with another, purports to act as agent for a principal whom both know to be non-existent or wholly incompetent, becomes a party to such contract." Under this default rule, Geary would be bound on the contract and would remain bound even if the corporation were ultimately to adopt it.

2. Both Parties Mistakenly Believe Corporation Exists

When contracting parties *mistakenly* assume a corporation exists, courts have developed equitable doctrines that give limited liability to the party purporting to act for the (nonexistent) corporation.

Judicial doctrines. Under the doctrine of *de facto* corporation, courts infer limited liability if (1) the promoters in the would-be corporation had made a good faith effort to incorporate; (2) the promoters were unaware that the incorporation had not happened; and (3) the promoters used the corporate form in a transaction with a third party.

Under the doctrine of *corporation by estoppel*, courts prevent a contracting party from asserting the promoter's personal liability when the contracting party assumed the only recourse would be against the business assets.

Statutory approach. Some modern statutes have viewed these two doctrines as relics of an era when incorporation was formalistic and uncertain. To avoid the doctrines' supposed uncertainties, MBCA § 2.04 (laid out below) creates what its drafters viewed as a bright-line rule. As you'll notice, the statute seems to preserve a version of the *de facto* doctrine, focusing on the lack of knowledge (and thus "good faith") of the person purporting to act for the corporation.

MBCA § 2.04
Liability for Preincorporation Transactions

All persons purporting to act as or on behalf of a corporation, knowing there was no incorporation under this Act, are jointly and severally liable for all liabilities created while so acting.

OFFICIAL COMMENT

Incorporation under modern statutes is so simple and inexpensive that a strong argument may be made that nothing short of filing articles of incorporation should create the privilege of limited liability. A number of situations have arisen, however, in which the protection of limited liability arguably should be recognized even though the simple incorporation process established by modern statutes has not been completed.

(1) The strongest factual pattern for immunizing participants from personal liability occurs in cases in which the participant honestly and reasonably but erroneously believed the articles had been filed. In *Cranson v. International Business Machines Corp.*, 234 Md. 477, 200 A.2d 33 (1964),

for example, the defendant had been shown executed articles of incorporation some months earlier before he invested in the corporation and became an officer and director. He was also told by the corporation's attorney that the articles had been filed, but in fact they had not been filed because of a mix-up in the attorney's office. The defendant was held not liable on the "corporate" obligation.

(2) Another class of cases, which is less compelling but in which the participants sometimes have escaped personal liability, involves the defendant who mails in articles of incorporation and then enters into a transaction in the corporate name; the letter is either delayed or the secretary of state's office refuses to file the articles after receiving them or returns them for correction. E.g., *Cantor v. Sunshine Greenery, Inc.*, 165 N.J.Super. 411, 398 A.2d 571 (1979).

After a review of these situations, it seemed appropriate to impose liability only on persons who act as or on behalf of corporations "knowing" that no corporation exists.

While no special provision is made in section 2.04, the section does not foreclose the possibility that persons who urge defendants to execute contracts in the corporate name knowing that no steps to incorporate have been taken may be estopped to impose personal liability on individual defendants. This estoppel may be based on the inequity perceived when persons, unwilling or reluctant to enter into a commitment under their own name, are persuaded to use the name of a nonexistent corporation, and then are sought to be held personally liable under section 2.04 by the party advocating that form of execution.

Academic studies. Academic studies have sought to find consistency in the disarray of judicial doctrines. One early study, looking at cases through 1952, concluded that courts rarely provided "either real reasons or good reasons" when deciding defective incorporation cases. Based on this study, the MBCA drafters sought to eliminate the *de facto* and *estoppel* doctrines.

Subsequent studies have found that courts generally uphold the understandings and expectations of the parties, and infer limited liability if there is a good faith attempt to incorporate and both parties believe the transaction was with a corporation. Other research shows that courts continue to apply the *de facto* and *estoppel* doctrines, and that the doctrines are largely indistinguishable and depend on whether the person acting on behalf of the defectively incorporated entity was found to have acted in good faith. In sum, even though the MBCA sought to abolish these judicial doctrines, courts have continued to infer limited liability when parties assume in good faith that a corporation exists.

3. Reinstatement After Administrative Dissolution

Contracting with a non-existent corporation can also happen when a corporation, though properly formed, has been dissolved by administrative order for failure to pay franchise taxes, to report a change in registered agent, or to file annual reports. Many state statutes address these situations by allowing the corporation to pay the back taxes or make the required filings, and then apply for reinstatement. For example, MBCA § 14.22 provides for reinstatement within two years of administrative dissolution. The effect of reinstatement is the retroactive recognition of the corporation, along with all corporate attributes including limited liability.

CHAPTER 10

Actions Binding the Corporation

> **MBCA § 8.01**
>
> <u>Requirements for and Functions of Board of Directors</u>
>
> (b) All corporate powers shall be exercised by or under authority of the board of directors of the corporation, and the business and affairs of the corporation shall be managed by or under the direction, and subject to the oversight, of its board of directors.

Who acts for the corporation? In the standard governance model, the board of directors has the central role. The board need not manage the corporation's day-to-day business, but may (and often does) delegate responsibility to the corporation's officers and employees. Thus, whenever an officer or employee enters into a transaction in the corporate name, the corporate official is doing so under delegated authority.

Shareholders do not act for the corporation. Even though they are often described as the "owners" of the corporation, shareholders cannot bind the corporation. Rather, they exercise their governance rights primarily by electing the board and approving fundamental transactions.

In sum, corporate statutes establish a basic governance structure in which shareholders elect the corporation's directors, the board of directors is charged with managing the corporation's business, and officers and employees carry on day-to-day operations under power delegated by the board of directors.

Take Note!

You will notice two "protection" themes running through this chapter. The first is the protection of reasonable expectations of outside parties who deal with the corporation, thus to promote easy transacting with the corporation. The second theme is the protection of the corporation from unauthorized or faithless agents whose actions usurp the corporation's centralized decision maker—the board of directors.

This chapter focuses on how the corporation "acts" with outside parties. First, we review how authority is delegated to officers and employees, a delegation that turns largely on agency principles that we saw in Chapter 2. Next, we describe the formalities of board action. Finally, we consider the legal opinions that lawyers are called on to give regarding corporate authority and board action.

A. Board Delegation of Authority

1. Reviewing Basic Agency Concepts

The corporation, a legal construct, can act only through the agency of human beings. An understanding of authority within the corporation, therefore, requires some knowledge of the law of agency, which we first introduced in Chapter 2.

Agency is a consensual relationship between two parties, the "principal" and the "agent." The principal selects the agent, who agrees to act on the principal's behalf and subject to the principal's control. The principal has the power to terminate the agency relationship unilaterally and can dictate to the agent how the agent will perform his duties.

The agent is a "fiduciary" of the principal, which means the agent owes to the principal duties of care and loyalty. Within the relationship, the agent must always put the interests of the principal above the agent's own interests. In addition, the agent has "a duty to obey all reasonable directions" of the principal given within the scope of the agent's service.

An agent has the "legal authority" to bind the principal in legal relationships with third parties. Authority comes in different forms. First, the principal may have granted the agent "actual authority" to bind the principal. Under actual authority, the principal manifests consent to the agent to bind the principal (such as by telling the agent to sign a contact on the principal's behalf).

Actual authority may be "express," growing out of explicit words or conduct granting the agent power to bind the principal, or may be "implied" from words or conduct taken in the context of the relations between the principal and the agent. In either case, the principal causes the agent to reasonably believe that the principal desires the agent to act on the principal's behalf. In assessing actual authority, the focus is on the reasonable belief of the agent.

> ### Example 10.1
>
> Priscilla Principal, a horse breeder, says to her agent Andrew, "Andy, please go down to the stables, put up a sign, 'HORSES FOR SALE,' and sell all of my horses for $500 apiece." Andrew has "express authority" to sell the horses.
>
> Andrew accepts a $500 check from a customer for one of Priscilla's horses. He probably has "implied authority" to accept an apparently valid check in payment. As long as Priscilla had not previously demanded cash in such transactions, it is reasonable for Andrew to assume that she intended he could accept checks.
>
> Andrew accepts a used car worth $500 as trade for another of Pricilla's horses. He probably lacks authority depending on what would be reasonably understood from the circumstances (such as the normal practices in the trade or in the locality) and from the prior dealings between him and Priscilla.

Second, an agent also may bind a principal even though the principal lacks actual authority. A principal may create "apparent authority" by written or spoken words or any other conduct that, reasonably interpreted, causes a third person to believe that the principal has consented to the agent acting for the principal. While "actual" authority turns on manifestations by the principal to the agent, "apparent" authority depends on communications by the principal to the third party. In other words, to create apparent authority the principal must do or say something that induces the third party to believe that the principal has given authority to the agent. Whereas actual authority focused on the agent and principal, in assessing apparent authority, the focus is on the perspective of the third party.

> ### Example 10.2
>
> Priscilla gives Andrew the same instructions, but adds, "But don't sell Secretariat." She sends letters to prospective buyers saying, "I am selling off my horses. If you are interested, please see Andrew at the stables. He is authorized to act for me."
>
> Andrew sells Secretariat to a recipient of the letter. Priscilla is bound on the contract. By communicating what a reasonable person would understand to be an intention to give Andrew the authority to sell Secretariat, she has cloaked him with "apparent authority." She is bound by his act, even though Andrew lacked actual authority (because his act was contrary to her actual instructions).

As we saw in Chapter 2, it is also possible for a principal or purported principal to be held liable on the basis of undisclosed principal liability, ratification, and estoppel.

2. Authority of Corporate Directors and Officers

What is the authority of corporate directors and officers? There is no simple answer, since corporate authority can arise from different agency theories. Corporate law vests authority in the board of directors as a collective body. Individual directors are not agents by virtue of their role as directors. They have authority to act as a board of directors through the means specified by corporate law, such as through meetings and written consents. As for officers, in some cases, courts find that officers have authority by being appointed to their office by the board of directors. In other cases, courts find that the officer has apparent authority because a person dealing with the corporation reasonably believes the officer has authority. Or, sometimes courts find ratification has occurred because of prior dealings between the officer and a third party that the board never challenged.

The key corporate officers, along with their functions and general authority, are usually specified in the corporation's bylaws. Below we lay out the provisions of the Google bylaws, to give you a sense for the role of officers in a large corporation. Notice that except for the chief executive officer (CEO) and secretary, the Google bylaws give broad latitude to the board to specify the officers and their functions.

Example 10.3

Bylaws of Google, Inc.
(as adopted on October 22, 2002)

ARTICLE V—OFFICERS [excerpted]

5.1 OFFICERS. The officers of the corporation shall be a Chief Executive Officer [CEO] and a secretary. The corporation may also have, at the discretion of the Board, one or more presidents, a chief financial officer, a treasurer, one or more vice presidents, one or more assistant vice presidents, one or more assistant treasurers, one or more assistant secretaries, and any such other officers as may be appointed in accordance with the provisions of these bylaws. Any number of offices may be held by the same person.

5.2 APPOINTMENT OF OFFICERS. The Board shall appoint the officers of the corporation, subject to the rights, if any, of an officer under any contract of employment.

5.4 REMOVAL AND RESIGNATION OF OFFICERS. Subject to the rights, if any, of an officer under any contract of employment, any officer may be removed, either with or without cause, by an affirmative vote of the majority of the Board at any regular or special meeting of the Board.

5.7 CHIEF EXECUTIVE OFFICER. The chief executive officer shall, subject to the control of the Board, have general supervision, direction, and control of the business and affairs of the corporation and shall report directly to the Board. All other officers, officials, employees and agents shall report directly or indirectly to the chief executive officer.

5.8 PRESIDENT. In the absence or disability of the chief executive officer, a president shall perform all the duties of the chief executive officer. A president shall have such other powers and perform such other duties as from time to time may be prescribed for him by the Board, these bylaws, the chief executive officer or the chairperson of the Board.

5.9 VICE PRESIDENTS. In the absence or disability of any president, the vice presidents, if any, in order of their rank as fixed by the Board or, if not ranked, a vice president designated by the Board, shall perform all the duties of a president.

5.10 SECRETARY. The secretary shall keep or cause to be kept, at the principal executive office of the corporation or such other place as the Board may direct, a book of minutes of all meetings and actions of directors, committees of directors, and stockholders.

5.11 CHIEF FINANCIAL OFFICER. The chief financial officer shall keep and maintain, or cause to be kept and maintained, adequate and correct books and records of accounts of the properties and business transactions of the corporation, including accounts of its assets, liabilities, receipts, disbursements, gains, losses, capital retained earnings, and shares. The books of account shall at all reasonable times be open to inspection by any director.

The chief financial officer shall deposit all moneys and other valuables in the name and to the credit of the corporation with such depositories as the Board may designate. The chief financial officer shall disburse the funds of the corporation as may be ordered by the Board.

5.16 AUTHORITY AND DUTIES OF OFFICERS. In addition to the foregoing authority and duties, all officers of the corporation shall respectively have such authority and perform such duties in the management of the business of the corporation as may be designated from time to time by the Board or the stockholders.

One practical concern is the extent to which the third party must investigate the authority of the officer. Given that actual authority is within the knowledge of the corporation, not the third party, courts have developed rules of thumb to facilitate dealings between the corporation and third parties. One such rule of thumb is the distinction between "ordinary" and "extraordinary" transactions.

Courts generally assume that the CEO, whether known as the president or by some other title, has authority to bind the corporation in transactions entered into in the "ordinary course of business." In contrast, such a corporate officer would not have authority to enter into contracts of an "extraordinary" nature. The distinction between "ordinary" and "extraordinary" is often unclear, and is subject to a broad range of interpretation.

FYI

The role of "corporate secretary" is not clerical or administrative in the typical sense of the word "secretary." Instead, a corporate secretary is a senior, managerial position, and he or she has a high-level of responsibility, including corporate governance and compliance matters.

The growth and development of the "ordinary" vs. "extraordinary" distinction occurred during the late nineteenth and early twentieth centuries, when the corporate form was new and not well understood. Over time, as corporations grew, courts realized that, although boards of directors still nominally controlled corporate affairs, in fact officers and managers frequently ran the business with little, if any, board supervision. As a result, third parties often came to rely on the authority of such officials. Even by the mid-twentieth century, courts regarded the pace of modern business life as too swift to insist on board approval of any transaction that might be "unusual" in some way.

For example, in *Lee v. Jenkins Brothers*, 268 F.2d 357 (2d Cir. 1959), *cert. denied*, 361 U.S. 913 (1959), the court held that a life pension offered by the company's president to attract a new executive could be found to be within the president's apparent authority.

But whether a promise of a life pension might seem "ordinary" likely would depend on the facts. What if the life pension was set to be ten times the employee's salary? What if the company had never previously offered a life pension to its employees? What if the practice in the industry was that life pensions were rare, and were only given with board approval? The facts could well show that the life pension was "extraordinary."

FYI

What is the difference between the CEO and the chair of the board of directors? The CEO is the corporation's highest-level officer, in charge of the corporation's day-to-day business. The chair is the leader of the board, setting the agenda and presiding at board meetings. In many corporations, the same person is both CEO and chair. This is changing, particularly in public corporations, where it is thought that the person in charge of the business should not be the one who guides the corporation's supervisory body.

Moreover, it is hard to generalize about the authority of officers subordinate to the president or chief executive officer. Their authority depends on how a board has delegated responsibility within the particular corporation's management structure. As with more senior officers, any given case will turn on a court's assessment of the facts and circumstances of the transaction at issue. But a third party who deals with a corporation's subordinate officers generally bears the burden of demonstrating that an act was within the officer's authority.

Issues of authority can often be quite complex. In the following case, a group of shareholders collectively called Sarissa Capital had purchased shares of Innoviva, Inc., a Delaware public corporation, and were upset with Innoviva's poor performance. Sarissa Capital said the Innoviva directors were grossly overpaid and had failed to fulfill their fiduciary duties, and they sought to replace the directors through a "proxy contest," in which they would advocate for a new slate of Sarissa Capital's nominees in Innoviva's next election.

In April 2017, the parties began to negotiate a settlement. The two main negotiators were Alexander Denner, Sarissa Capital's founder, and James Tyree, the vice chairman of Innoviva's board. Two days before the annual meeting, Denner and Tyree spoke on the phone. Denner said Sarissa Capital would end its proxy fight if Innoviva would expand its board from seven to nine directors, appoint two of Sarissa Capital's directors to fill the two new spots, and forgo a "standstill." Standstills are important: the agreement would require Sarissa Capital to "stand still" temporarily, and not buy more stock or pursue its proxy fight. Tyree responded that Innoviva would agree to expand its board and appoint Sarissa Capital's two directors, but it insisted on a standstill.

The next day, with less than twenty-four hours before a vote, the Innoviva directors learned that some of its largest shareholders were leaning in Sarissa Capital's favor. Shortly after noon, they learned that Vanguard, a large mutual fund group planned to vote for Sarissa Capital's nominees. The board expected that it also would lose the support of BlackRock, another large shareholder. It appeared that the board would lose the proxy fight, so that afternoon they decided to capitulate.

That afternoon the board met and agreed that Innoviva would expand the board and support Sarissa Capital's two nominees, and would not require a standstill. The board authorized Tyree to tell Denner that Innoviva would settle on these terms. Tyree immediately called Denner, and Denner accepted orally.

While the lawyers were drafting the settlement documents, the Innoviva directors learned that BlackRock had just voted in favor of them, not Sarissa Capital's nominees. The directors decided to go ahead with the election the next day. Tyree contacted Denver and told him the "deal" that they had struck on the phone a few hours earlier was now "no deal." Sarissa Capital sued seeking a declaration that Tyree orally bound Innoviva during the earlier call. Innoviva argued that the parties never entered into a binding agreement, because Tyree lacked authority to bind Innoviva to the alleged oral contract.

Sarissa Capital Domestic Fund LP v. Innoviva, Inc.

No. 2017–0309–JRS (Del. Ch. Dec. 8, 2017)

SLIGHTS, VICE CHANCELLOR

1. Tyree Had Actual Authority

Actual authority requires an extant agency relationship. An agency relationship "arises when one person [or entity] (a 'principal') manifests assent to another person [or entity] (an 'agent') that the agent shall act on the principal's behalf and subject to the principal's control, and the agent manifests assent or otherwise consents so to act." Actual authority, then, "is created by a principal's manifestation to an agent that, as reasonably understood by the agent, expresses the principal's assent that the agent take action on the principal's behalf."

Where the principal is a corporation, such assent may be manifested in provisions of the corporation's certificate of incorporation or bylaws, or otherwise through board action. Thus, a corporation's governance documents may grant actual authority to certain of its directors and officers to bind the corporation in contract—whether to a particular contract or type of contract, or more generally. Alternatively, a corporation's board of directors, as such, may cause the corporation to manifest assent that a particular director or officer shall have the power to bind the corporation in contract, provided the corporation's certificate and bylaws do not prohibit such action by the board.

The scope of an agent's actual authority is determined by the agent's reasonable understanding of the principal's manifestations and objectives. Accordingly, "[a]n agent has actual authority to take action designated or implied in the principal's manifestations to the agent and [to take] acts necessary or incidental to achieving the principal's objectives, as the agent reasonably understands the principal's manifestations and objectives when the agent determines how to act."

In this case, Tyree had actual authority to bind Innoviva to an oral settlement agreement with Sarissa within certain parameters. This authority can be traced to the express manifestations of Innoviva's Board (and thus, Innoviva) prior to and during the Board's April 19 afternoon meeting (from 1:30 to 1:47 PM), and Tyree's reasonable understanding of those manifestations. Before that meeting, Innoviva's Board had appointed Tyree to act as Innoviva's "lead negotiator" in settlement discussions with Sarissa, and Tyree had accepted that appointment, thus creating a specific agency relationship between Tyree and Innoviva. And during that meeting, Innoviva's Board manifested assent that Tyree contact Denner "to negotiate to see if a settlement agreement including a press release between Sarissa and

[Innoviva] could be reached." In that regard, the Board also manifested assent that Tyree convey to Denner the following:

- that Innoviva was willing to settle with Sarissa without a standstill;

- that, as part of that settlement, Innoviva would expand its Board from seven to nine members and appoint any two of Sarissa's nominees to the Board to fill the resulting vacancies; *and*

- that Sarissa would be required to include a conciliatory quote about Innoviva in the joint press release announcing the settlement.

The Board's authorization of Tyree to offer these terms on the afternoon of April 19, came in the midst of the Board's expectation that BlackRock would vote for "at least two" of Sarissa's director nominees, meaning (1) that "at least two" of Sarissa's three nominees would be elected to the seven-member Board; *and* (2) that "at least two" of Innoviva's existing directors would be replaced. The Board also expected that the final vote tally—including BlackRock's vote—would be published between 4:00 PM and 5:00 PM that day. And with the revelation of BlackRock's (expected) vote for Sarissa's nominees, Sarissa would no longer have an incentive to settle its proxy contest. Thus, for Innoviva's Board, the "clock was ticking down" for Innoviva to reach a binding settlement with Sarissa—and thereby avert an (expected) electoral rout.

Under these circumstances, Tyree reasonably understood the Board's (and thus Innoviva's) manifestations to him during the Board's April 19 afternoon meeting to express Innoviva's assent that (1) within the Settlement Agreement Parameters, Tyree was authorized to make an oral settlement offer on Innoviva's behalf; *and* (2) Denner's oral acceptance of that offer (on Sarissa's behalf) would bind Innoviva to the settlement. And the record reflects that this was, in fact, Tyree's understanding. Accordingly, Tyree had actual authority to convey to Denner an oral settlement offer on behalf of Innoviva (on the terms approved by the Board) and to bind Innoviva to a settlement with Sarissa on those terms.

2. Tyree Had Apparent Authority

Unlike actual authority, apparent authority does not depend on the existence of an underlying agency relationship, and may arise even where no such relationship exists. Apparent authority "is the power held by an agent or other actor to affect a principal's legal relations with third parties when a third party reasonably believes the actor has authority to act on behalf of the principal and that belief is traceable to the principal's manifestations." Thus, even if a person lacks actual authority to bind an entity to a contract with a third party, the person still may have *apparent* authority to do so. For instance, a non-agent director has apparent authority to bind the corporation to a contract with a third party if (1) the third party reasonably believes that the director has such authority; and (2) that belief is traceable to the corporation's manifestations.

A corporate principal may make a manifestation to a third party concerning an agent's authority "by placing [the] agent in charge of a transaction or situation." In particular, where a corporate principal has designated an agent as its "exclusive channel of communication" with a third party, that designation can "constitute a manifestation of [the corporation's] assent to be bound in accordance with . . . communication[s]" made through that channel.[208]

Here, the evidence clearly reveals that Tyree had apparent authority to bind Innoviva to a settlement agreement with Sarissa. *First*, Denner, Sarissa's principal, believed that Tyree spoke on behalf of Innoviva's Board (and so Innoviva), and thus was authorized to enter into a settlement agreement on Innoviva's behalf. *Second*, it was reasonable for Denner to believe this. Tyree was Innoviva's "lead negotiator" in settlement discussions with Sarissa and the only Innoviva Board member with whom Denner negotiated during the critical April 18–19 time period. In addition, there is no evidence that Innoviva then communicated (or otherwise indicated) to Denner that Tyree was not authorized to enter into a settlement agreement on Innoviva's behalf. *Finally*, Denner's reasonable belief that Tyree was authorized to take such action on Innoviva's behalf is traceable to Innoviva's manifestations, namely, (1) Innoviva's having appointed Tyree as Innoviva's "lead negotiator" in settlement discussions with Sarissa; *and* (2) Innoviva's having permitted Tyree to serve as Innoviva's exclusive channel of settlement-related communications with Denner during the critical April 18–19 time period. For these reasons, I find that Tyree had apparent authority to bind Innoviva to a settlement agreement with Sarissa.

3. There Was No Improper Delegation of the Board's Duties

Innoviva contends that Tyree "did not have authority . . . to enter into the alleged oral agreement because this would involve an improper delegation of the Board's fiduciary and statutory duties." Specifically, Innoviva argues that, under 8 *Del. C.* §§ 141(b), 223(a)(1) and Section 3.9 of Innoviva's Bylaws, "decisions regarding who should fill Board vacancies cannot be delegated to an individual director or a third person, but must be decided by the entire Board acting by majority vote." Innoviva's argument, however, misapprehends the facts proven at trial and the statutory and bylaw provisions upon which it relies.

Section 3.9 of Innoviva's Bylaws is complementary to Section 3.2 of Innoviva's Bylaws, which provides that Board approval (by majority resolution) is required to expand the size of the Board, consistent with 8 *Del. C.* § 141(b). Section 3.9, in turn, provides that newly created Innoviva directorships may only be filled by a "majority vote of directors then in office," consistent with 8 *Del. C.* § 223(a)(1). Nothing in this section prohibits a majority of Innoviva's Board from deciding (without a formal vote) who should fill "to-be-created" directorships and, upon reaching a decision in that regard, authorizing an individual director to bind the Board to that decision via contract. In other words, Section 3.9 does not prohibit what happened here.

During the Board's April 19 afternoon meeting, the Board conditionally resolved to expand the size of the Board from seven to nine members, consistent with Section 3.2 of Innoviva's Bylaws. This was done in anticipation of Innoviva's entry into a settlement with Sarissa. The Board also authorized Tyree to represent (or offer) to Denner that the Board would appoint (presumably by later vote) any two of Sarissa's three nominees to the Board if the proxy contest was settled. That is to say, if Sarissa accepted Innoviva's settlement proposal, then Innoviva's Board would be expanded from seven to nine members, and "a majority . . . of [the seven] directors then in office" would vote to appoint any two of Sarissa's three nominees to fill the resulting Board vacancies—consistent with Section 3.9 of Innoviva's Bylaws.

Here, it was Innoviva's Board that made the foregoing determinations, not Tyree. Indeed, the settlement terms that Tyree was authorized to convey to Denner were *Innoviva's* settlement terms, *i.e.*, the settlement terms approved by Innoviva's Board. Under these circumstances, as proven by Sarissa at trial, I am satisfied that Tyree's authority to bind Innoviva to an oral settlement agreement with Sarissa on terms approved by Innoviva's Board was entirely consistent with Section 141(b)'s and 223(a)(1)'s requirements that the creation and filling of new directorships be properly authorized by the board of directors in accordance with the corporation's governing documents.

Points for Discussion

1. Analysis of decision.

Do you think the Innoviva directors believed they had given Tyree actual authority to call Denner to enter into the settlement, and Tyree understood this? Would the directors have been better off telling Tyree he was not authorized to finalize an agreement until they had more information about the likely outcome of the vote? How would you advise directors involved in settlement talks about authorizing one of their members to deal with the other party?

2. Third-party expectations.

Suppose that Denner had real doubts about whether the board had authorized Tyree to agree to a settlement without a standstill. Would that have changed things? What more, if anything, should Denner have done to ascertain whether Tyree had actual authority to agree to the settlement? How would you advise a shareholder negotiating a deal with an individual director who purports to have authority to be sure the director actually has authority?

> ### Hypo 10.1
>
> You are outside counsel to Home Supplies, Inc. Your client is planning to build a new warehouse and is negotiating with Construx Corp. to be the general contractor. But Home Supplies is worried about Construx's financial condition. Construx presents Home Supplies with a "guarantee" for the construction project signed by the Treasurer of Big Machines, Inc., a large construction equipment manufacturer.
>
> You are skeptical about this guarantee. How do you ensure that Big Machines is actually bound on the guarantee? What documents will you want to see?

---

3. Ascertaining Corporate Authority

Lawyers for parties who deal with a corporation are often called on to advise their third-party clients on the existence of corporate authority—to ensure that the corporation will be bound in the transaction. Counsel representing a party involved in a major transaction with a corporation usually will insist on receiving evidence that the individuals who purport to act for the corporation have authority. The evidence can come from a number of sources: (1) a provision of statutory law, (2) the articles of incorporation, (3) a bylaw of the company, (4) a resolution of the board of directors, or (5) evidence that the corporation had allowed the officer to act in similar matters and has recognized, approved, or ratified those actions.

Courts vary on how much they require that third parties investigate corporate authority. One important factor is whether the transaction at issue involved a conflict of interest. Courts are more likely to require third parties to investigate corporate authority when they are aware that the transaction involves a conflict of interest. For example, when the third party knows a corporate officer stands to benefit personally from the transaction, the third party must treat the transactions as "extraordinary" and inquire into whether the officer has valid authority to enter into the transaction. But other courts are more lenient about conflicts of interest and uphold transactions even when the parties have not engaged in much investigation. Because the law in this area is rarely clear, lawyers are well advised to investigate the sources of authority clearly, particularly when they are aware of conflicts of interest.

Another factor is whether the corporation acquiesced to the transaction. Even when authority appears not to exist, the corporation's inaction following a transaction with a third party can nevertheless be binding. For example, in *Scientific Holding Co., Ltd. v. Plessey Inc.*, 510 F.2d 15 (2d Cir. 1974), during the negotiations for the sale of a business, the president and chief operating officer of the selling corporation expressed doubts about his authority to sign an amendment to the purchase agreement. Despite the officer's lack of authority, he nonetheless signed. Several months later when the purchaser sought to enforce the amended agreement, the corporation repudiated it. The court agreed that the officer's authority to sign to the amendment was unclear. But even if he lacked authority, the corporation's "failure to repudiate the amendment for lack of authorization [from March] until mid-July estopped it from doing so later." The amended agreement stood.

Usually, the best evidence of delegated authority will be a copy of the minutes of the board of directors meeting at which the board adopted a resolution formalizing its grant of authority. The resolution, in addition to stating the board's approval of the transaction in question, should designate the CEO or some other officer to execute the documents and do the other acts necessary to consummate the transaction. For significant transactions, the minutes should attach a copy of the contract that the board has authorized the officer to sign.

Less important transactions may be covered by more general delegations of authority. For example, the bylaws might state the officer's general authority or a board might generally authorize the CEO or other officer to enter into contracts of a certain type or up to a certain value. If a party to a transaction with the corporation has doubts about the authority of an executive with whom he is dealing, he can request a copy of the resolution delegating the authority and the minutes of the board meeting at which the resolution was adopted.

But a question remains: how can a third party be sure the minutes and resolution are genuine? Customary practice is to have the secretary of the corporation (or other officer charged with maintaining the corporation's books and records) certify the minutes and resolution. The secretary generally is held to have apparent authority to certify such documents, so that a corporation is bound by the secretary's certification. This means that a third party seeking to confirm an officer's authority can proceed with confidence once the secretary has certified the minutes and resolution, and need not ask the directors to personally swear that the board voted to authorize the officer to act.

> ### Example 10.4
> #### Certificate of Corporate Authority
>
> At a special meeting of the Board of Directors of the Corporation, held upon due notice at the offices of the Corporation located at 123 Main St., Our Town, New Columbia, on September 30, 2019, at 4:00 PM, all the Directors being present and voting, the Board unanimously voted to approve the following resolution:
>
> > BE IT RESOLVED, that the President Smith or Vice-President Jones or either of them acting individually, be hereby authorized (1) to market, list, offer for sale, and sell the plot of land known as Blackacre in the name of this Corporation, and (2) to sign all documents related to said transaction.
>
> * * *
>
> I, William Black, Secretary of ABC Corporation, incorporated under the laws of New Columbia, do hereby certify that the foregoing is a true copy of a resolution duly adopted by the Board of Directors of said Corporation at a meeting duly held on September 30, 2019, at which a quorum was present and voting, and that the same has not been repealed or amended and remains in full force and effect and does not conflict with the bylaws of said Corporation.
>
> _____   _____
> Secretary   Date

B. Formalities of Board Action

1. Board Action at a Meeting

The board of directors acts as a collective body and traditionally takes formal action by vote at a meeting. Each director has one vote and may not vote by proxy. (Recall that shareholders can vote by giving a written authorization, or proxy, indicating how their votes should be cast. Directors cannot do that.) Unless the articles or bylaws provide otherwise, the vote of a majority of the directors present at a board meeting at which there is a quorum is necessary to pass a resolution.

Why must the board come together at a meeting to act? The board is a collegial and deliberative body. By consulting together, board members may draw on each other's knowledge and experience. More ideas and points of view are likely to be considered in the formulation of decisions, which may produce better results than if the directors act without meeting.

An illustration of the wisdom of the "meeting rule" can be found in *Baldwin v. Canfield,* 1 N.W. 261 (Minn. 1879), where all the directors had separately signed a real estate deed, but the board had never approved the transfer at a meeting. The court stated:

As we have already seen, the court below finds that, by its articles of incorporation, the government of the corporation, and the management of its affairs, was vested in the board of directors. The legal effect of this was to invest the directors with such government and management *as a board,* and not otherwise. This is in accordance with the general rule that the governing body of a corporation, as such, are agents of the corporation only as a board, and not individually. Hence it follows that they have no authority to act, save when assembled at a board meeting. The separate action, individually, of the persons comprising such governing body, is not the action of the constituted body of men clothed with the corporate powers.

Had the board met, they might have discovered that the corporation's sole shareholder planned to give the deed to a third-party purchaser, even though the shareholder had before pledged his stock in the corporation for a bank loan. At a meeting, the directors might have been more disposed to question the transaction and ascertain whether the company's real estate was indirectly encumbered by the stock pledge.

Courts have refused to uphold informal action by directors without a meeting when the board's alleged authority to bind the corporation was challenged by the corporation, the directors of the corporation, the corporation's trustee in bankruptcy, or pledgees of the corporation's stock. Although courts frequently fail to articulate their reasons for requiring formal board action, many courts rely on the policy of protecting shareholders and their investment from arbitrary or irresponsible decisions by directors.

Courts nonetheless recognize that informal board action, particularly in close corporations, is common. This reality has led courts to seek to protect innocent third parties from the strict application of the traditional meeting rule. Courts have relied on different justifications to bind corporations on agreements not approved at formal board meetings.

Unanimous director approval. When all the directors separately approve a transaction, a meeting will usually not serve any purpose. In such circumstances, even if a meeting had been held, the directors would probably not have discussed the matter or come to a different result, but would simply have approved the action.

Emergency. Situations arise where the board must make very quick decisions to prevent great harm or to take advantage of great opportunity. In such situations, it may be impossible to assemble the board at a meeting. The corporation must proceed on the opinions of those directors who can be contacted in whatever manner contact may be made.

Unanimous shareholder approval. If all the shareholders in a close corporation meet, the conclusion they reach will likely bind the corporation. The board meeting rule, which is meant to protect shareholders from unconsidered board action, would work a hardship against third parties when shareholders approved the transaction.

Majority shareholder-director approval. If the directors who participate in the informal action constitute a majority of the board and own a majority of the corporation's issued and outstanding shares, the corporation is bound.

To buttress these common law exceptions to the general rule, most states have enacted statutory provisions allowing informal director action under some conditions. MBCA § 8.21, for example, allows board action to be taken without a meeting on the unanimous written consent of the directors. By signing a unanimous written consent, the directors can ratify a previous action where there is concern the action was not properly authorized, such as when the original authorization came at a meeting that did not meet the formal meeting requirements. The Official Comment notes: "Under section 8.21 the requirement of unanimous consent precludes the possibility of stifling or ignoring opposing argument. A director opposed to an action that is proposed to be taken by unanimous consent, or uncertain about the desirability of that action, may compel the holding of a directors' meeting to discuss the matter simply by withholding his consent."

> **FYI**
>
> State corporate law rules vary regarding the ability of a board of directors to take action by written consent without a board meeting. Delaware's statute, like the MBCA, authorizes a board to act without a meeting by means of unanimous written consent. DGCL § 141(f).

In addition, board meetings need not be conducted in person. MBCA § 8.20(b) permits the board to conduct a meeting by "any means of communication by which all directors participating may simultaneously hear each other during the meeting"—such as a telephone conference call. The Official Comment to MBCA § 8.20 states: "The advantage of the traditional meeting is the opportunity for interchange that is permitted by a meeting in a single room at which members are physically present. If this opportunity for interchange is thought to be unavailable by the board of directors, a meeting may be conducted by electronic means although no two directors are physically present at the same place."

2. Notice and Quorum

Notice and quorum requirements apply to board meetings. Notice facilitates personal attendance by directors. For special meetings, MBCA § 8.22(b) requires that two days' notice be given of the date, time and place of meeting, unless the articles of incorporation or bylaws impose different requirements. For regular meetings, directors are assumed to know the schedule, and MBCA § 8.22(a) does not require notice. Nonetheless, many companies provide directors with notice of the purpose of all meetings, to better prepare directors to discuss the matters on the agenda. Action taken at a board meeting held without the required notice is invalid.

Any director who does not receive proper notice may waive notice by signing a waiver before or after the meeting, MBCA § 8.23(a), or by attending or participating in the meeting and not protesting the absence of notice. MBCA § 8.23(b). A director who attends a meeting solely to protest the manner in which it was convened is not deemed to have waived notice. MBCA § 8.23(b).

The quorum requirement precludes action by a minority of the directors. The statutory norm for a quorum is a majority of the total number of directors, although the articles of incorporation or bylaws may increase the quorum requirement or reduce it to no less than one-third of the board. MBCA § 8.24. Action taken in the absence of a quorum is invalid.

Hypo 10.2

The bylaws of Widget Corporation, incorporated in an MBCA jurisdiction, provide for an eight-person board of directors. Wanda, Widget's CEO, has just negotiated a sale of a company factory. The sale agreement requires board authorization. Four Widget directors are in town available to meet; another is in a local hospital for minor surgery; and the other three are sailing in the Caribbean.

(1) Wanda e-mails all the directors giving notice of a special meeting in two days. Would a unanimous vote by the four available directors at a special meeting of the board be effective?

> No. Four is not enough. A quorum constituting a majority of the board must be at the meeting. *See* MBCA §§ 8.20, 8.22, 8.23, 8.24.

(2) Wanda visits the ailing board member in the hospital, explains the sale fully, and has her execute a proxy authorizing Wanda to cast the director's vote in favor of the sale at the board meeting. Will this work?

> No. Directors cannot vote by proxy. *See* MBCA §§ 8.20, 8.22.

(3) Can the director in the hospital call into the meeting by phone?

> Yes, so long as the director can be heard by, and herself hear, all present. *See* MBCA §§ 8.20, 8.21.

(4) By the way, was the email notice sufficient for the three directors sailing the Caribbean? Or is it enough that five directors were at the meeting?

> Notice is required. It must be sent in a way calculated for directors to receive it. For a special meeting two-days notice is required, unless a different period is specified in the articles or bylaws. MBCA § 8.22(b).

(5) Suppose the hospitalized director, who called into the meeting by phone, had never received the email notice. Does the board's action at the meeting fail?

> No. The director's attendance and participation waives any notice defects. Federal law and exchange rules set committee standards for public company boards of directors. MBCA § 8.23.

3. Committees of the Board

Boards with many members, such as the boards of publicly-held corporations, can be unwieldy and often find it difficult to discharge all of their responsibilities acting through the full board. The trend in recent years toward increasing the proportion of outside directors has exacerbated this problem. Many companies have responded by delegating responsibility for many board functions to committees empowered to exercise, in defined areas, the authority of the board. Corporate statutes authorize this practice.

The executive committee is a common board committee because it can have the full authority of the board in all but a few essential transactions such as the declaration of a dividend or approval of a merger. MBCA § 8.25(e). Thus the executive committee often is the vehicle through which the board acts between meetings on less important matters of corporate housekeeping which, for technical reasons, require board approval.

The audit committee is another common board committee, particularly in publicly-held corporations. Its functions usually include selection of the company's auditors, specification of the scope of the audit, review of audit results, and oversight of internal accounting procedures. Both the New York Stock Exchange and the National Association of Securities Dealers now require publicly-held companies to have audit committees.

Other relatively common committees include finance (usually responsible for giving advice on financial structure, the issuance of new securities, and the management of the corporation's investments), nomination (responsible for nominating new directors and officers), compensation (responsible for fixing the salaries and other compensation of executives), and risk management (responsible for managing risks, oversight, and compliance). Boards often create specialized committees to deal with specific problems. For example, in Chapter 19 we discuss the use of special litigation committees in connection with derivative suits.

A board committee can be permanent or temporary. Its functions can be active—making decisions on behalf of the board. Or the committee can be passive—doing research and presenting information so the full board can make more informed decisions. Case law and statutes increasingly reflect the view that committees are desirable because directors who are committee members have more incentive to develop expertise in the area of the committee's responsibility. MBCA § 8.30(b) recognizes the expanding use of committees and permits a director to rely on the reports or actions of a committee on which she does not serve, so long as the committee reasonably merits her confidence.

C. Legal Opinions

An important part of being a transactional lawyer is giving opinions as to the legality of proposed or completed transactions. "Opinion" in the corporate setting is a term of art. It does not have its usual colloquial meaning, like "in my opinion, chocolate ice cream is better than strawberry." Rather it expresses a lawyer's conclusion as to how the relevant law applies to a given state of facts.

Parties entering into a transaction with a corporation often will require the corporation's outside lawyer to provide an opinion on legal matters affecting the transaction. This opinion will typically address such matters as the corporation's existence, its good standing under state corporate law, its power to enter into the transaction, and a corporate official's authority to act on behalf of the corporation. Similarly, the opinion may state that an agreement to which the corporation is a party is legal, valid, binding, and enforceable against the corporation in accordance with its terms.

Legal opinions are highly stylized documents. Bar associations have developed guidelines for the methodology and language employed in giving legal opinions, together with standards for interpreting them. These guidelines describe how an opinion should be dated, to whom it should be addressed, how its scope can and should be limited, the documents that should be examined, and whether the lawyer may rely on facts supplied by third parties or opinions of other counsel.

Legal opinions serve as a hedge against business risks. If the transaction fails, the disappointed party can look to the lawyer on whose assurances the party relied. Whether the party can recover, however, is far from clear. A lawyer is not

Take Note!

Legal opinions come in different flavors.

"Unqualified" opinions (sometimes called flat or clean) apply the law to the facts and reach a clear legal conclusion free from doubt. For example: "The Shares have been duly authorized and validly issued and are fully paid and nonassessable." Such an opinion may be limited by customary assumptions or exceptions for that type of opinion, such as the assumption that the articles of incorporation on file with the State were validly filed.

"Qualified" opinions contain exceptions or limitations that are not customary for the particular type of opinion. For example: "Based on my review of [the relevant documents], the President has authority to enter into the Transaction on behalf of the Corporation."

"Reasoned" (or explained) opinions include the lawyer's reasoning, along with stating legal conclusions. Such explanations are advisable when the law or facts are unclear, or reasonable arguments might lead to different legal interpretations. The reasoned opinion may often take the form of a memorandum of law.

liable simply because the opinion was mistaken. Instead, it must be shown that the opinion was negligently rendered and that any losses were proximately caused by the lawyer's failure to meet the relevant professional standards. Although there is little case law, lawyers are most likely to face liability where the opinion assists a client in a fraud or the commission of a crime.

Example 10.5

Third Party Opinion

[Firm letterhead]
[Date]

Ladies and Gentlemen:

We have acted as counsel to ABC Corporation (the "Company") in connection with the transaction (the "Transaction") contemplated by the Sales Agreement dated July 1, 2019 (the "Agreement") between the Company and XYZ Ltd. (the "Other Party").

We have reviewed such documents and considered such matters of law and fact as we, in our professional judgment, have deemed appropriate to render the opinions contained herein. With respect to certain facts, we have considered it appropriate to rely upon certificates or other comparable documents of public officials and officers or other appropriate representatives of the Company, without investigation or analysis of any underlying data contained therein.

The opinions set forth herein are limited to matters governed by the laws of the State of New Columbia, and no opinion is expressed herein as to the laws of any other jurisdiction.

Based upon and subject to the foregoing and the further assumptions, limitations and qualifications hereinafter expressed, it is our opinion that:

1. The Company is duly incorporated, validly existing and in good standing under the laws of the State of New Columbia.

2. Company is authorized to transact business in the State of New Columbia.

3. The authorized capital stock of the Company consists of 1,000,000 common shares, of which 750,000 shares are outstanding. The Shares have been duly authorized and validly issued, and are fully paid and nonassessable.

4. The Company has the corporate power to execute, deliver and perform its obligations under the Transaction Documents.

5. The Company has authorized the execution, delivery and performance of the Transaction Documents by all necessary corporate action and has duly executed and delivered the Transaction Documents.

6. The Agreement constitutes the legal, valid and binding obligation of the Company, enforceable against the Company in accordance with its terms.

7. The execution and delivery by the Company of the Agreement and the performance by the Company of its obligations therein (a) do not violate the articles of incorporation or bylaws of the Company, (b) do not breach or result in a default under any Other Agreement, and (c) do not violate the terms of any Court Order. For purposes hereof, (I) the term "Other Agreement" means any of those agreements listed on the officer's certificate rendered to us in connection with this opinion and (II) the term "Court Order" means any judicial or administrative judgment, order, decree or arbitral decision that names the Company and is specifically directed to it or its properties and that is listed on the officer's certificate rendered to us in connection with this opinion or that is known to us.

8. The execution and delivery by the Company of the Agreement, and performance by the Company of its obligations therein, do not violate applicable provisions of statutory laws or regulations.

9. No consent, approval, authorization or other action by, or filing with, any governmental authority of the United States or the State of New Columbia is required for the Company's execution and delivery of the Transaction Documents and consummation of the Transaction.

The opinions expressed above are subject to the following assumptions, qualifications and limitations:

(a) This opinion is subject to the effect of applicable bankruptcy, insolvency, reorganization, fraudulent conveyance, moratorium and similar laws affecting the enforcement of creditors' rights generally.

(b) This opinion is subject to the effect of general principles of equity (regardless of whether considered in a proceeding in equity or at law), which may, among other things, deny rights of specific performance.

(c) We do not express any opinion as to the enforceability of provisions of the Agreement purporting to require a party thereto to pay or reimburse attorneys' fees incurred by another party, or to indemnify another party therefore, which provisions may be limited by applicable statutes and decisions relating to the collection and award of attorneys' fees.

(d) We do not express any opinion as to the enforceability of provisions of the Agreement providing for arbitration.

In addition, we advise you that to our knowledge, there is no action, suit or proceeding at law or in equity, or by or before any governmental instrumentality or agency or arbitral body, now pending or overtly threatened against the Company, except as listed on the officer's certificate rendered to us in connection with this opinion.

This opinion letter is delivered solely for your benefit in connection with the Transaction and may not be used or relied upon by any other person or for any other purpose without our prior written consent in each instance. Our opinions expressed herein are as of the date hereof, and we undertake no obligation to advise you of any changes in applicable law or any other matters that may come to our attention after the date hereof that may affect our opinions expressed herein.

Very truly yours,

Signature of Opining Lawyer or Firm

Points for Discussion

1. Scope of opinion.

Notice the organization of the sample legal opinion. It begins by identifying its subject matter and what materials were consulted. In what ways is the opinion limited or qualified? Why so narrow?

2. "Best of our knowledge."

Notice that the sample opinion does not include, as many legal opinions do, the phrase "to the best of our knowledge." This qualification makes clear that the opining law firm is not omniscient and that there may be relevant facts the firm does not know. Does the sample opinion, by failing to include this magic phrase, mean that the law firm is assuring its awareness of all relevant facts? How does the sample letter deal with the question of the firm's knowledge or awareness?

In addition, what knowledge is properly imputed to the opining law firm? The knowledge of the signing partner, all the partners, all the firm's lawyers, all the personnel in the firm? And whose files should be considered to be part of this "knowledge base"? To clarify these matters, the trend is toward defining "knowledge" in the opinion letter itself.

3. Materials consulted.

Consider the statement in the sample opinion above: "1. The Company is duly incorporated, validly existing and in good standing under the laws of the State of New Columbia." What documents did the opining lawyers likely consult to make this statement?

Consider also the statement: "5. The Company has authorized the execution, delivery and performance of the Transaction Documents by all necessary corporate action and has duly executed and delivered the Transaction Documents." How would the lawyers giving the opinion reach this conclusion? What documents should they have consulted?

4. Who speaks for the firm?

A law firm's legal opinion raises questions of authority within the firm. Who has authority to speak for the firm and give a binding legal opinion—only "partners" or similar principals of the firm? Or does it depend on how important the opinion is?

Many law firms, particularly the larger ones, have procedures for issuing opinions. Often, a firm's opinion policy will require that only certain persons may sign opinion letters and only after a specified review process, such as by the firm's "opinion committee." To ensure that the firm's opinions are consistent and do not conflict with the positions of actual or potential clients, many firms catalogue the opinion letters issued by the firm.

Test Your Knowledge

To assess your understanding of the Chapter 8, 9, and 10 material in this module, click here to take a quiz.

MODULE IV – CORPORATE FINANCE

Chapter 11

Numeracy for Corporate Lawyers

This module introduces you to the important financial concepts arising in the corporation. In this chapter, we offer you a primer on financial accounting and business valuation. The next chapter describes the capital structure of the corporation—how money moves in and out of the corporation.

The next pages contain a set of financial statements—really just a bunch of numbers. You might think of skipping these pages, at least at first, but we urge you not to. Hidden in these numbers is an interesting story about a business, which we have not very creatively called "Widget, Inc." Spend a few minutes now looking at these numbers. Pause at each one and ask yourself, "What does this number tell me about this corporation?" Can you tell a story about Widget, Inc. based on these financial statements?

Our goal in this chapter is to help you understand a business story by looking at financial statements and to give you a sense of how financial figures can be used to estimate firm value. First, we explain why corporate lawyers should understand financial accounting when they represent business clients, as well as the limitations of accounting. Next, we introduce you to the "fundamental equation" that underlies all financial accounting and the three basic financial statements—the balance sheet, the income statement, and the statement of cash flows—using the Widget, Inc. financials. Finally, we tell a parable to illustrate how productive assets (a business) might be valued using inputs from financial statements, and we apply these lessons to valuing Widget, Inc.

WIDGET, INC. BALANCE SHEET (As of December 31)		
Assets	**Year 2**	**Year 1**
Current Assets		
Cash	100,000	275,000
Accounts Receivable	1,380,000	1,145,000
Inventories	1,310,000	1,105,000
Prepaid expenses	40,000	35,000
Total Current Assets	2,830,000	2,560,000
Property, Plant, and Equipment		
Land*	775,000	775,000
Buildings**	2,000,000	2,000,000
Machinery**	1,000,000	935,000
Office Equipment**	225,000	205,000
Total PP&E	4,000,000	3,915,000
Accumulated Depreciation***	(1,620,000)	(1,370,000)
Intangible Assets****	50,000	0
Total Long-term Assets	2,430,000	2,545,000
Total Assets	5,260,000	5,105,000
Liabilities and Equity		
Current Liabilities		
Accounts payable	900,000	825,000
Notes payable, 11% due next July 1	0	355,000
Accrued expenses payable	250,000	235,000
Other liabilities	600,000	570,000
Total Current Liabilities	1,750,000	1,985,000
Long-term Notes payable, 12.5% due in ten years	2,000,000	2,000,000
Total Liabilities	3,750,000	3,985,000
Stockholders' Equity		
Common stock (1,000 shares authorized and outstanding)		
Paid-in capital	200,000	200,000
Retained earnings	1,310,000	920,000
Total Equity	1,510,000	1,120,000
Total Liabilities and Equity	5,260,000	5,105,000

* The land was purchased 15 years ago for $775,000, the price shown on the balance sheet. A comparable property nearby recently sold for $975,000.

** The machinery and equipment are in good repair. The fair market value of the building and equipment are about $200,000 more than historical cost.

*** Depreciation is on a level (straight line) basis over the estimated useful life.

**** Intangible assets include patent acquired for $50,000 during Year 2.

STATEMENT OF INCOME
(Year Ended December 31)

	Year 2	Year 1	Year 0
Net sales	7,500,000	7,000,000	6,800,000
Operating Expenses			
Cost of goods sold	4,980,000	4,650,000	4,607,000
Depreciation	250,000	240,000	200,000
Selling and admin expense*	1,300,000	1,220,000	1,150,000
R&D	50,000	125,000	120,000
Operating Income	920,000	765,000	723,000
Interest expense	320,000	375,000	375,000
Income before taxes	600,000	390,000	348,000
Income taxes	210,000	136,000	122,000
Net Income	**390,000**	**254,000**	**226,000**

* Includes $130,000 salaries paid to the owners in Year 2; $100,000 in Year 1; and $100,000 in Year 0, and bonuses totaling $120,000 in Year 2; $100,000 in Year 1; and $80,000 in Year 0.

STATEMENT OF CASH FLOWS
(Year Ended December 31)

	Year 2	Year 1	Year 0
From Operating Activities			
Net Income	390,000	254,000	226,000
Decrease (Increase) in accts receivable	(235,000)	(34,000)	(32,000)
Decrease (Increase) in inventories	(205,000)	(28,000)	(33,000)
Decrease (Increase) in prepaid expenses	(5,000)	(3,000)	(3,000)
Increase (Decrease) in accounts payable	75,000	25,000	20,000
Increase (Decrease) in accr exp payable	15,000	7,000	5,000
Depreciation	250,000	240,000	200,000
Total from Operating Activities	285,000	461,000	383,000
From Investing Activities			
Sales (Purchases) of machinery	(65,000)	(378,000)	(263,000)
Sales (Purchases) of office equipment	(20,000)	(27,000)	(25,000)
Sales (Purchases) of patents	(50,000)	0	0
Total from Investing Activities	(135,000)	(405,000)	(288,000)
From Financing Activities			
Increase (Decrease) in short-term debt	30,000	(40,000)	(35,000)
Increase (Decrease) in long-term debt	(355,000)	0	0
Total from Financing Activities	(325,000)	(40,000)	(35,000)
Increase (Decrease) in Cash Position	**(175,000)**	**16,000**	**60,000**

A. Financial Accounting for Lawyers

If you are a typical law student, you probably ignored our pleas to spend some time with these financial statements, and you skipped to this sentence. Or perhaps you diligently read through them and tried to figure out the story of Widget, Inc., only to find it dull and uneventful. Either way, at this point, you might be a little disappointed. We started with several chapters chock full of colorful cases, discussion of policy, and even some nuts and bolts of corporate law practice. And then, this. Pages filled with numbers? Accounting? You are in *law school*, after all. If you were good with numbers, wouldn't you be doing something else with your life?

We have included this chapter, and believe it is important, because the reality is that you cannot escape accounting and numbers, even in law school, and especially in law practice. Whether you practice corporate law or litigation, whether you work in the private sector or in government, you inevitably will confront financial accounting. You will find basic accounting and financial numeracy to be useful, whatever you decide to do with your life. So if you don't have it yet, you might as well learn it now, in the relative comfort of a law school course. It will be easier than picking it up on the job. And for those of you who have taken accounting courses, have experience with financial statements, or for other reasons believe you already understand the intricacies of financial accounting, our advice is to approach this chapter with an open mind. We are going to cover accounting from a different perspective than you may have encountered before—that of law and policy.

Hypo 11.1

You represent an investor group interested in buying Widget, Inc. Looking at the financial statements, what aspects of the business appear to be attractive? What aspects appear to be worrisome? What accounting items should lead the buyers to make further inquiries?

How might the buyers value the business of Widget, Inc.? What should they focus on—the accounting value of the business assets? The extent that assets exceed liabilities? The annual revenues of the business? The net profits of the business? The cash flow generated by the business? And should they be looking at these items for the past year or over time?

Purposes for accounting. This chapter is designed to introduce basic accounting and valuation concepts to law students who have *no* training in accounting or finance. It also introduces an approach to accounting that students with training in accounting or finance might find unfamiliar. Most accounting and finance courses are oriented to the perspective of idealized business owners and managers, who use financial information to keep track of, and exercise control over, the businesses they own or operate. From the perspective of such idealized owner/managers, the most useful financial statements are those that come as close as possible to presenting the objective truth about the firm's financial status and the results of its operations.

In contrast, lawyers frequently must deal with financial statements in adversarial or quasi-adversarial settings. When a financial statement has been prepared by or on behalf of an opposing party, the lawyer must appreciate the possibility that this statement—even if it has been prepared by a Certified Public Accountant (CPA) who has opined that it presents financial information "fairly" and "in accordance with generally accepted accounting principles" (GAAP)—will in fact represent a subjective and self-serving picture of the opposing party's financial situation. Lawyers know that the idealized business person does not exist.

But lawyers also deal with financial statements when advising parties in a non-adversarial manner. For example, the seller and buyer of a business ideally will agree to a deal that is a "win-win" for both of them. Transactional lawyers often act as dealmakers or advisers in situations different from the adversarial role assumed in the litigation-focused world of many law school courses. For lawyers to play such a role effectively, so that they add value to their clients' transactions, they must understand business, including financial and accounting issues.

State law typically requires corporations to furnish their shareholders with annual balance sheets and income statements, but allows corporations to decide what accounting principles to use when preparing those statements. Most firms, and all public corporations, use GAAP, but recognize that the rules do not embody immutable scientific or mathematical truths. Instead, GAAP represent the often-controversial judgments and policy preferences of a group of highly-qualified accounting professionals from the Financial Accounting Standards Board (FASB). As the perceptions, judgments and preferences of FASB change over time, so do the GAAP on how various transactions must be presented.

GAAP generally assume that a business enterprise is an accounting unit separate and distinct from its owners, whether or not it has a separate legal existence.

They also assume that a business is a "going concern" that will continue in operation for the foreseeable future. In general, the business must apply the same accounting concepts, standards, and procedures from one period to the next. Finally, the business is supposed to disclose all material information and follow a *Conservatism Principle* that profits not be anticipated and that probable losses be recognized as soon as possible.

Accounting is subjective. Although financial statements appear precise, those numbers often reflect highly subjective judgments. Many transactions can be conceptualized in different ways, all of them consistent with GAAP. People naturally will want to use the flexibility inherent in GAAP to present financial information in a way that best serves their interests. A manager will want the business to appear as profitable as possible. A divorcing spouse may try to minimize her business's asset values. A person selling a business will attempt to make the business appear free of risks. An accountant will want to keep her clients happy, by painting the picture of their business that they want to see. We are all human.

It is important to note that the choices people make regarding GAAP might be entirely legitimate without being manipulative. Simply put, there are different ways to account for different items. If your company buys a building, you should list that building as an asset. But how much should you record its worth? The amount you paid? What if you got a really good deal and bought it for half of its market value—should you then record this amount rather than its cost? Should you record changes in the value of the building over time? And how much? These are difficult questions, and there are different legitimate answers.

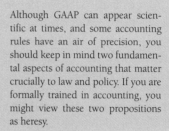

Food for Thought

Although GAAP can appear scientific at times, and some accounting rules have an air of precision, you should keep in mind two fundamental aspects of accounting that matter crucially to law and policy. If you are formally trained in accounting, you might view these two propositions as heresy.

There is no such thing as objective truth in accounting.

People naturally will present financial information that suits their interests.

For example, some business people are tempted to manipulate accounting to make the company look better than it is. Corporate officers, and their accountants, are frequently accused of "managing earnings"—that is, manipulating the corporation's financial statements to make it appear that the corporation is earning consistent and increasing profits. The extent of earnings management can vary, from merely smoothing quarterly or annual income over time to outright fraud.

Lawyers in both the deal-making and litigation settings frequently bring a healthy skepticism to their assessment of financial statements.

There is an old joke about a client conducting interviews in search of a new CPA. The client asks each candidate several detailed accounting questions. One candidate answers all of the questions correctly. Then, the client asks one final "killer" question, the answer to which clinches the job:

Client: OK, and finally, how much is two plus two?
    (Previous candidates had answered "four.")

CPA: How much do you want it to be?

The joke illustrates not only the willingness of accountants to stretch the rules, but also the pressure applied by managers who often view GAAP not as a standard to be met, but as an obstacle to be overcome. Of course, many—perhaps most—managers and accountants are honest and do their best to follow the rules. But it is important to note that the two fundamental aspects of accounting we have mentioned—the lack of objective truth and the incentives for people to present favorable information—can be a dangerous combination.

Stages of accounting. Financial statements are produced through a three-stage process. First is the "recording and controls" stage, in which a company records in its books information concerning every transaction in which it is involved. Second is the "audit" stage, in which the company, sometimes with the assistance of independent accountants, verifies the accuracy of the information it has recorded. Third is the "accounting" stage, in which the company classifies and analyzes the audited information and presents it in a set of financial statements. At each stage, there are opportunities for managers and accountants to be truthful and forthcoming, or not.

Although public companies always go through these three stages, private companies often do not. The audit and accounting process is expensive, and many small companies are not in a position to pay to have their financial statements audited by an outside, independent accounting firm. As you might suspect, the managers of private companies might not produce entirely accurate financial statements, either because they don't have the time and resources to do so or they don't care enough. Someone considering buying a private business would want to know who prepared the financial statements, how they were prepared, and whether any third party reviewed them. In our example, the buyers of Widget, Inc. certainly would want answers to these questions, particularly because the company's financial statements are not audited. (If they had been audited, a signed audit opinion would have accompanied the financial statements—there is no such opinion here.)

The fall of companies such as Enron, WorldCom, Bear Stearns, and Lehman Brothers sharpened the focus of lawyers on financial accounting issues. One major accounting firm, Arthur Andersen, collapsed under the pressure of the Enron scandal, and numerous firms, including many law firms, were sued because of accounting improprieties. The Financial Crisis of 2008 generated claims that many companies, including American International Group, the world's largest insurance company, did not accurately account for its assets and liabilities. Lawyers involved in planning and disclosing the affairs of corporations frequently deal with complex accounting issues.

Accounting as art, not science. The materials that follow will help you to understand the basics of financial accounting. We want to emphasize that these are just the basics, though. Public companies' financial statements stretch to dozens of pages, with detailed footnotes describing contingent liabilities, stock option grants, and complex financial instruments.

Inevitably, preparing and reading financial statements is an art, not a science. Even though numbers are involved, this is not mathematics. It is more like a forensic investigation, an attempt to construct a plausible story about what has happened in a business, thus to evaluate its risks and its value. The goal of financial statements is to convey information, but financial statements alone rarely tell the entire story. As you read the materials that follow, ask yourself what additional information a prospective buyer would want to understand the real story of Widget, Inc. With these inquiries, you will begin to perform one of a lawyer's most important functions in a business transaction: helping her client ask the right questions.

In the remainder of this chapter, we will cover a detailed analysis of the three basic financial statements: the balance sheet, the income statement, and the cash flow statement. We will give you several examples based on Widget, Inc., so that you can discern a more detailed story of that company. We then will spend some time on valuation, again using the story of Widget, Inc., to give you a sense of how business people value a corporation. In other chapters, we offer "Points for Discussion" after various sections of materials; here, there are so many points for discussion that we raise them as questions throughout the materials.

B. The Fundamental Equation

We begin our analysis of financial statements with the balance sheet. You can think of the balance sheet as a "snapshot"—it is a picture of the business at a particular moment. In the case of Widget, Inc., we have given you a picture of the corporation as of two moments. The first column is a snapshot of its assets and liabilities as of December 31 of Year 2, and the second column is a snapshot as of December 31 of Year 1.

Note that the balance sheet is in "balance"—total assets are equal to total liabilities plus total equity. For Year 2, Total Assets is $5,260,000, and Total

Liabilities and Equity is also $5,260,000. This also holds true for Year 1. This equating of assets to liabilities plus equity is known as the "fundamental equation" of financial accounting:

ASSETS = LIABILITIES + EQUITY

"Assets" refers to the property, both tangible and intangible, owned by the firm. "Liabilities" refers to the amount that the firm owes to others, whether pursuant to written evidence of indebtedness or otherwise. "Equity" represents the accounting value of the interest of the firm's owners. Equity initially includes the value of the property (including money) the owners contribute when they organize the firm.

Assets are sometimes referred to as the "left side" of the balance sheet, and liabilities and equity the "right side." (Imagine that the balance sheet was presented with assets on the left, and liabilities and equity on the right, rather than assets on top, and liabilities and equity on the bottom). In simple terms, the right side of the balance sheet shows where the firm's money came from, and the left side of the balance sheet shows where it went. How did Widget, Inc. obtain money? It issued common stock to its owners and it also borrowed money from outside parties. It then used this money to buy assets.

Cookie jar accounting. Before we go through the balance sheet in detail, we want to work through an example to show how the fundamental equation works. Imagine that our corporation is an empty jar. It has no assets, no liabilities, and no equity. At the start, the fundamental equation looks like this:

Step One: Suppose the owner of the firm invests $12. You might imagine that the owner actually puts $12 in the jar. Now, the firm's balance sheet is:

Note that the balance sheet is in balance. The $12 of assets recorded on the left balances the $12 of equity recorded to the right.

Step Two: Next assume the firm borrows an additional $10. You might imagine that a lender puts $10 in the jar and records an "IOU" for $10. Now, the balance sheet is:

The balance sheet is still in balance, but this time the increased assets were matched with an increase in liabilities. The same will be true every time the firm obtains money from the outside, whether in the form of equity or debt. Every such transaction will increase assets and increase either liabilities or equity, depending on the source of the money. Each transaction will affect both the left and right side of the balance sheet, which will always remain in balance.

Step Three: Next the firm buys two felt-tip pens for $2 each. You might imagine that the firm takes $4 of cash out of the jar and puts $4 of pens into the jar. Because one asset is exchanged for another, the balance sheet remains unchanged.

Note that in recording the value of the pens as an asset, we follow the *Cost Principle*, which holds that historic cost provides the best basis for recording a transaction, because it can be determined objectively and is verifiable. If you wanted to be more precise, you could break the assets into two groups: $18 of cash and $4 of pens. Either way, the total assets are $22.

<u>Step Four</u>: Then the firm buys scissors on credit for $5. It puts scissors worth $5 in the jar and incurs a liability of $5, which can be envisioned as a bill for $5 also placed in the jar.

<u>Step Five</u>: Then the firm sells one of the felt-tip pens for $3. It exchanges a pen that cost $2 for $3 in cash. The $1 profit results in an increase in Assets of $1.

Note that the cookie jar is now weighted more heavily on the left side than on the right, because the assets are greater than the sum of liabilities plus equity. We have a problem now, because we know that the balance sheet must balance. How can we get it to balance? Recall that the right side of the balance sheet represents where the firm's money came from. We know that the value of the equity entry on the balance sheet increased when the owner put money into the firm. In addition, the equity entry will change to reflect the firm's profits and losses. When the firm makes money, equity will increase; when it loses money, equity will decline.

Because the firm has made $1, the equity entry also should increase by $1. The actual increase appears in "Retained Earnings," which is a component of equity. Once we reflect the increased value of equity, the fundamental equation again holds.

See if you can provide the explanation for why the firm would account for the following three transactions:

<u>Step Six</u>: The firm pays the bill for the scissors.

<u>Step Seven</u>: The firm pays $2 in rent for the use of the jar.

<u>Step Eight</u>: Finally, the owner takes $5 out of the jar so she can get herself a treat.

C. Balance Sheet

Now that we understand the basics of the balance sheet, we will work through each of the most important balance sheet accounts. As you read this section, you should look at each individual entry on Widget, Inc.'s balance sheet to be sure you understand what the entry means and why it might have changed over time.

1. Balance Sheet Assets

Assets are listed in the balance sheet in the order of their liquidity, beginning with cash, followed by assets that the firm expects to convert to cash in the reasonably near future, and continuing to other assets, such as plant and equipment, that the firm uses in its business over the longer term.

Current assets. We will begin with the four items of current assets on Widget, Inc.'s balance sheet. Current assets include cash and other assets that in the normal course of business will be converted into cash in the reasonably near future, generally within one year of the date of the balance sheet. Note that Widget, Inc.'s cash declined from Year 1 to Year 2, while its other current assets increased.

Current Assets	Year 2	Year 1
Cash	100,000	275,000
Accounts Receivable	1,380,000	1,145,000
Inventories	1,310,000	1,105,000
Prepaid expenses	40,000	35,000
Total Current Assets	2,830,000	2,560,000

Cash. Cash, the first current asset, represents money actually in hand and deposited in the bank. Because it includes bank deposits, the balance sheet concept of cash is broader than the physical bills and coins held by a corporation. Widget, Inc. had $275,000 of cash at the end of Year 1, and $100,000 of cash at the end of Year 2. What could account for such a significant decline in Widget, Inc.'s cash position? Is that decline a concern? It might be a sign that Widget, Inc. is financially weak. Or perhaps it is a sign that Widget, Inc. found some attractive business opportunities this year, and decided to use more of its cash to pay for them.

You might imagine that accounting for cash is a straightforward exercise, and for many businesses, including Widget, Inc., it probably is. Many firms use their surplus cash to purchase liquid securities, such as commercial paper and treasury bills, with a view to generating interest income. Some firms also purchase publicly-traded debt and equity securities. Many small

What's That?

Commercial paper is short-term highly-rated debt issued by public corporations, typically with a maturity of less than 270 days. Treasury bills are obligations of the U.S. government with a maturity of less than one year. You should be wary of descriptions of short-term investments. What some companies describe as "cash" or "marketable securities" might actually consist of riskier investments. For example, during the Financial Crisis of 2008, investors learned that many corporations, most notably American International Group (AIG), had exposure to the risks of subprime mortgages through their short-term highly-rated investments.

businesses, such as Widget, Inc., keep their short-term investments exclusively in cash, and do not own marketable securities. Larger public corporations typically separate a balance sheet item reflecting "cash and cash equivalents" from "short term investments." Some of the investments in these categories will be securities and investments that are not really equivalent to "cash."

Because the value of marketable securities typically can readily be determined, GAAP generally provide that such securities shall be reported at their fair market value, rather than at their cost. Fluctuations in the value of marketable securities are recorded as income or loss on the reporting firm's income statement. This principle of accounting is known as "mark to market," because the securities are "marked" on the balance sheet to their market price.

In recent years, it has become common for firms to buy and sell large amounts of a variety of financial instruments, either to hedge against fluctuations in interest rates, exchange rates, commodity prices, or other values or to seek trading gains. In general, such instruments also must be "marked to market" as of the date of the balance sheet, and the difference between their cost and market value must be recorded as a gain or loss. Where market prices cannot readily be determined, management is required to make a good faith estimate of market value.

As you might imagine, this is an area where managers and accountants might try to be aggressive. For example, Enron and several financial institutions in the early 2000s were accused of assigning unrealistic values to some of the financial instruments they held. During the Financial Crisis of 2008, there was extensive debate about whether financial assets with exposure to subprime mortgages should be "marked to market" or recorded at a higher value given the belief that market prices were artificially depressed due to mistaken market pessimism. Many banks recorded financial assets—especially assets backed by home mortgages—at values that were much greater than the prices they would have fetched in the market.

Accounts receivable. The second current asset is accounts receivable, sometimes simply called "receivables" or "A/R." These are amounts not yet collected from customers to whom goods have been shipped or services delivered. Widget, Inc. had $1,145,000 of receivables at the end of Year 1, and $1,380,000 of receivables at the end of Year 2. What might have caused this increase?

Accounts receivable can increase for two reasons. First, the corporation's sales might have increased. The additional receivables might simply reflect that more customers have purchased goods or services. Second, receivables might have increased because customers were paying more slowly, or not at all. That is, an increase in accounts receivable might be a positive sign or a negative sign.

When a firm sells to customers on credit and the customers don't pay their bills on time, GAAP require that the firm reduce its accounts receivable by deducting an allowance (or "reserve") for bad debts. Firms usually calculate bad debt allowances based on past customer behavior. However, when a firm's customer base or business conditions change, those calculations might not prove accurate. Likewise, some firms sell goods subject to a right of return. They record sales based on assumptions about returns, but those assumptions also might change.

How much of Widget, Inc.'s accounts receivable reflect a reduction for "doubtful accounts"? Who do you think determined that amount, and how did they arrive at the number?

Corporations often record other kinds of receivables on their balance sheets. For example, notes or loans receivable represent money owed to the corporation. Widget, Inc. did not record any of these receivables, but they can be significant for firms engaged in businesses that involve customer financing. For these firms, the allowance for bad debts can have a major impact on results. Financial institutions frequently are forced to "write off" payments they expect to receive from customers and counterparties.

Inventory. Inventory, the third current asset, represents goods held for use in production or for sale to customers. For Widget, Inc., its inventory consists of the widgets it hopes to sell. Widget's inventories increased from $1,105,000 at the end of Year 1 to $1,310,000 at the end of Year 2. Is this increase in inventory good or bad?

As with receivables, the increase might be positive if it reflects increasing sales. On the other hand, increasing inventories might reflect declining customer purchases. At this point, you probably are beginning to see that, although the numbers in the financial statements appear to be precise, behind those numbers there is a more complex, real-life story about what has happened to the corporation.

Firms that want to play games to maximize the value of their reported assets might "cherry pick" their inventories by assuming that only the least expensive items are the ones sold. If costs were increasing, they might assume that the first (and cheapest) items on the shelf were sold. In contrast, if costs were declining, they might assume that the most recent (and cheapest) items on the shelf were sold. If the inventories are fungible—as they would be with widgets or many products—firms might manipulate their decisions about which items in their inventories were sold during a given period.

GAAP establish a uniform set of rules for inventory reporting, in part to prevent such gaming. Firms can opt to use one of three methods to value their closing inventory: (1) average cost; (2) first in, first out (FIFO); and (3) last in, first out (LIFO). Each of these methods is an assumption about which items in inventory actually are sold to customers. Most firms will find it more practical to use one of these assumptions than to try to keep track of the actual cost of each item sold from inventory.

Here are some ways to visualize each of the three assumptions about how firms sell inventory:

- Average cost: inventory is sold at random from a bin
- FIFO: inventory is pushed through a pipeline
- LIFO: inventory is added and sold from the top of a stack

Example 11.1
LIFO/FIFO

Imagine that Widget, Inc. produced three widgets over time, at costs that increased from $10 to $20 to $30. The total value of its inventory, as listed in its balance sheet, would be $60. Next, imagine that Widget, Inc. sold two of the three widgets in its inventory. The inventory that Widget, Inc. would assume was sold would depend on its assumptions, as follows:

- Average cost: each widget sold cost $20
- FIFO: the first widget sold cost $10; the second widget sold cost $20
- LIFO: the first widget sold cost $30; the second widget sold cost $20

The value of Widget, Inc.'s remaining inventory then depends on the valuation method it chose. The balance sheet value of the one remaining widget in inventory under each method would be:

- Average cost: $20 ($60 minus the assumed cost of the two sold widgets of $40)
- FIFO: $30 ($60 minus the assumed cost of the two sold widgets of $30)
- LIFO: $10 ($60 minus the assumed cost of the two sold widgets of $50)

As you might have noticed, the inventory valuation method will also have an effect on stated income and income taxes that are owed. If the cost of inventory is increasing, a firm using LIFO will record a lower inventory value, lower income, and lower taxes—this is because it will assume that it was selling from the more expensive "last in" inventory. In contrast, a firm using FIFO will record a higher inventory value, higher income and higher taxes. Higher costs reduce income and therefore reduce taxes, whereas lower costs have the opposite effect. The opposite conclusions will hold if the cost of inventory is decreasing. The average cost method will generate values in between FIFO and LIFO.

Which method is most realistic? The answer depends on how the costs of inventory actually change over time. GAAP recognize that, in many lines of business, inventory values can decline sharply: technologies improve; clothing goes out of style. If the value of items in inventory drops below their cost, GAAP require that the balance sheet "book" value of the inventory be reduced. (This decline also is recorded on the income statement, as a charge against earnings of an equivalent amount—we will get to the income statement soon.)

A corporation's managers usually are in the best position to decide on an appropriate inventory method, or to determine when an inventory charge is necessary. On the other hand, managers might make such decisions to maximize reported income and to avoid charges. These determinations inevitably involve value judgments.

Prepaid expenses. Balance sheets often contain other current assets. We have included one, prepaid expenses, which are payments the corporation has made in advance for services it will receive in the coming year. Widget, Inc. had relatively small prepaid expenses, which increased only slightly during Year 2.

Remember that this category is part of current assets, which means that the corporation has prepaid expenses during the upcoming year. For example, prepaid expenses might include the value of ten months of payments on a one-year insurance policy that a firm purchased and paid for in full two months before the end of the year.

Prepaid expenses are an example of a "deferred charge," an asset that reflects payments made in the current period for goods or services that will generate income in subsequent periods. A typical example of a deferred charge is advertising to introduce a new product. Firms sometimes inflate their reported profits by recording as deferred charges payments that should be charged against current income because they are unlikely to produce future benefits. You should be wary of a large deferred charge account, and especially a large and growing deferred charge account. Fortunately, Widget, Inc. has not recorded such an asset.

Fixed assets. Next, we cover the fixed assets on Widget, Inc.'s balance sheet. Fixed assets are longer-term assets, which, unlike current assets, are not expected to be converted into cash within a year. Notice that Widget's fixed assets are accompanied by notes, which sometimes tell more of a story than the numbers themselves.

Property, Plant, and Equipment	Year 2	Year 1
Land*	775,000	775,000
Buildings**	2,000,000	2,000,000
Machinery**	1,000,000	935,000
Office Equipment**	225,000	205,000
Total PP&E	4,000,000	3,915,000
Accumulated Depreciation***	(1,620,000)	(1,370,000)
Intangible Assets****	50,000	0
Total Long-term Assets	2,480,000	2,545,000

* The land was purchased 15 years ago for $775,000, the price shown on the balance sheet. A comparable property nearby recently sold for $975,000.

** The machinery and equipment are in good repair. The fair market value of the building and equipment are about $200,000 more than historical cost.

*** Depreciation is on a level (straight line) basis over the estimated useful life.

**** Intangible assets include patent acquired for $50,000 during Year 2.

PP&E and depreciation. Most fixed assets typically are grouped under the label "Property, Plant, and Equipment," or PP&E. PP&E represent assets the firm uses to conduct its operations, as opposed to assets it holds for sale. Under GAAP, when a firm acquires a fixed asset, it records the asset on its balance sheet at cost. This policy reflects a compromise between the goals of presenting accurate and reliable information and the fact that it is easier to record the cost of an asset than to investigate and assess its market value.

Note that Widget, Inc. has recorded several types of fixed assets—land, buildings, machinery, and office equipment—all at cost. In other words, the balance sheet value of the fixed asset remains constant over time, set at the historic cost of the asset. Given that the balance sheet records the cost of fixed assets, why would the entries for Widget, Inc.'s machinery and office equipment increase in value during Year 2?

The footnotes to Widget, Inc.'s balance sheet contain additional information about the fixed assets. For example, although Widget, Inc. reports the value of its land as $775,000, its original cost, one might argue that the corporation's assets actually are more valuable: a comparable nearby property recently sold for $975,000, and probably represents a more accurate valuation of Widget, Inc.'s land. However, a more precise conclusion about the market value of the land would require Widget, Inc. to consider the degree of similarity of the comparable property, the changes in price of land over time, and any unique characteristics of the land. For some assets, such as marketable securities, the answers to these questions are relatively straightforward, and GAAP require that they be "marked to market." But that is not true for many fixed assets.

Instead, GAAP recognize that the value of fixed assets might decline over time, and provide a mechanism for attempting to reflect more accurately the value of fixed assets on the balance sheet. For example, it doesn't necessarily make sense to require firms to keep the value of their fixed assets at cost over time. Everyone knows the office equipment Widget, Inc. owns will deteriorate in value. A computer Widget, Inc. purchased today will not be worth its cost in one year, and will be worth considerably less as time goes on.

Because the firm uses fixed assets to generate revenue, GAAP require that the firm charge a portion of the fixed assets' costs against the revenues received during the period the fixed assets are in use. These charges, known as a "depreciation expense," can be calculated using any of several formulas and is reflected in regular and periodic charges during the useful life of the asset in question. Depreciation is an accounting fiction that reduces a corporation's reported income even though it does not reflect any current cash expense; the cash was spent when the asset was acquired.

Under GAAP, all depreciation expenses accrued with respect to a firm's fixed assets must be added up and recorded, on the asset side of the balance sheet, in an account called "allowance for depreciation" or "accumulated depreciation," which is then subtracted from the cost of the firm's fixed assets. Widget, Inc. has included entries for accumulated depreciation. These entries are adjustments to the historic cost of Widget, Inc.'s assets, to account for the fact that the value of these assets has declined as the company continues to use them to generate revenue. In its footnotes, Widget, Inc. has indicated that its depreciation is on a "straight line" basis. In other words, if Widget, Inc. purchased a machine for $10,000, and estimated the useful life of the machine as 10 years, it would record depreciation of $1,000 per year, the same "straight line" amount per year.

Once an asset has been fully depreciated, it will have a balance sheet value of zero, even if it is still a valuable asset. This somewhat odd result occurs because the accounting concept of the useful life of an asset does not necessarily correspond to the asset's actual useful life.

The balance sheet "book" value of a firm's fixed assets—cost less the allowance for depreciation—is not intended to reflect, and usually does not reflect, either the current market value of those assets or what the firm would have to pay to replace them. In times of inflation, the book value of fixed assets often is much lower than either their current value or their replacement value. The book value of fixed assets also can exceed those assets' market value if the assets have become obsolete. In that event, as with inventory, the carrying value of those assets must be written down and earnings must be reduced by an equivalent amount.

Intangible assets. Intangible assets, the other main category of fixed assets, have no physical existence, but often have substantial value—a cable TV franchise granting a company the exclusive right to service certain areas, for example, or a patent or trademark. GAAP require firms to carry intangible assets at cost, less an allowance for "amortization" (the equivalent of depreciation, applied to intangibles). However, GAAP do not allow a firm to record as an asset the value of an intangible asset that the firm has developed or promoted on its own, rather than purchased. Consequently, the values of many extremely well-known and valuable intangible assets, such as the brand names "Coke" and "Windows," are not reflected on the balance sheets of the firms that own them.

How might you assess the value of Widget, Inc.'s intangible assets? The only intangible asset listed on Widget, Inc.'s balance sheet is a patent it acquired during Year 2 for $50,000. Why should this intangible asset be listed on the balance sheet, while others are not? How might you tell whether the cost of this patent is a reliable measure of its value?

As with intangible assets, when a firm incurs expenditures for research and development (R&D), GAAP require the firm to treat those expenditures as current expenses and charge them against current revenues. A firm is not allowed to record R&D expenditures as intangible assets or deferred charges even where they have produced discoveries or led to development of products that will generate substantial revenues in future years. In this respect, the accounting system's conservative bias produces balance sheets that understate the value of firm assets. There is also some evidence that this bias leads those managers who are preoccupied with short term earnings to underinvest in R&D.

Financial statements sometimes include an intangible asset called "goodwill," which is wholly the product of accounting conventions. Assume one firm acquires another for a price that exceeds the fair market value of the acquired firm's identifiable assets. How should the acquiring firm account for that difference? Under GAAP, it must record the difference as "goodwill." Goodwill is particularly important for companies that have undertaken significant acquisitions. That said, it is important to distinguish between this accounting notion of "goodwill" and "goodwill" in the way people normally use the term, as in a favorable business reputation. A business might be particularly valuable if it has a good location or enjoys a positive reputation with its clients, employees, and other stakeholders, but that kind of economic goodwill will not appear on the balance sheet.

2. Balance Sheet Liabilities

Liabilities usually are divided into current liabilities and long-term liabilities. Reproduced below is the liability section of Widget, Inc.'s balance sheet. Traditionally, assets appeared on the left-hand side of the balance sheet, while liabilities appeared on the right. Today, it is common for corporations to record their assets first, and then their liabilities below the assets.

Current Liabilities	Year 2	Year 1
Accounts payable	900,000	825,000
Notes payable, 11% due next July 1	0	355,000
Accrued expenses payable	250,000	235,000
Other liabilities	600,000	570,000
Total Current Liabilities	1,750,000	1,985,000
Long-term Notes payable, 12.5% due in ten years	2,000,000	2,000,000

Current liabilities. Current liabilities are the debts a firm owes that must be paid within one year of the balance sheet date. Current liabilities often are evaluated in relation to current assets, which in a sense are the source from which current liabilities must be paid. Hopefully, at this point, you are getting a better sense of how accounting conventions work, so we won't belabor each entry with a lengthy description.

Widget, Inc.'s current liabilities include accounts payable, which represents short-term obligations of Widget, Inc. to suppliers. Some of Widget, Inc.'s notes are due within one year as well. Widget, Inc. also has accrued expenses payable, which represents short-term debts it has incurred but not yet paid, as well as a category of "other liabilities." How do Widget, Inc.'s total current liabilities of $1,750,000 affect your assessment of the firm?

Long-term liabilities. Long-term liabilities, the other main category of liabilities, are debts due more than one year from the balance sheet date. Balance sheets usually list fixed liabilities, such as mortgages and bonds, by their maturities and the interest rates they bear. Some long-term liabilities must be estimated. An insurance company, for example, can only estimate the amounts it will have to pay out on the policies it has written. Those estimates usually have a material impact on both the company's balance sheet and its income statement.

Widget, Inc. lists just one long-term liability, $2,000,000 of "Notes payable, 12.5% due in ten years." If these Notes required an annual payment, Widget, Inc. would be obligated to pay $250,000 of interest every year for ten years and then at the end of the ten-year period to repay the principal amount of $2,000,000.

Off balance sheet liabilities. In recent years, business firms have developed a variety of techniques for engaging in "off balance sheet financing"—transactions that involve long-term financial obligations, but which, because of their form, are not recorded as liabilities on the balance sheet. GAAP generally require that firms discuss such off balance sheet financing in footnotes to their financial statements. These footnotes can be extraordinarily complex. GAAP also are complex with respect to how "contingent liabilities"—such as loan guarantees, warranty obligations, and potential claims by plaintiffs in civil suits—are to be calculated and when they must be disclosed. These items might not appear as liabilities on the balance sheet, even though they would matter to someone assessing the business.

3. Balance Sheet Equity

Equity represents the owners' interest in a firm. The terminology used for equity accounting will vary, depending on whether the firm is a sole proprietorship, a partnership, an LLC or a corporation. Whatever the form, the amount of a firm's equity—also often referred to as its "net worth"—will equal the difference between the book values of the firm's assets and liabilities. Recall the fundamental equation:

$$ASSETS = LIABILITIES + EQUITY$$

The balance sheet value of equity typically does not represent the actual market value of a firm's equity. For many firms, the "book" value of equity, from the balance sheet, will be well below the market value of equity. (For some firms, the opposite will be true.) It is possible for balance sheet equity to be a negative number, if the firm has recorded liabilities that exceed its assets, and yet the market value of the equity (ownership interest) of the firm still might be positive. This is because the balance sheet does not include many of a corporation's assets, such as intangibles, and because it does not record every entry at market value.

Corporations' balance sheets generally include two or three equity accounts. State laws once required, and now permit, corporations to issue stock with "par value" or "stated value." As explained in more detail in the next chapter, par or stated value can be established arbitrarily, but once established, it has legal and accounting significance. When a corporation issues stock with a "par value" or "stated value," its balance sheet must include a "stated capital" or "legal capital" account for each class of such stock. The amount in each of those accounts is calculated by multiplying the par value of that class of stock by the number of shares issued and outstanding.

In economic terms, a corporation's equity has two components. The first, often recorded as "paid-in capital," reflects the total amount the corporation has received from those who have purchased its stock. (A corporation with par value stock often will divide paid-in capital between two accounts entitled "stated capital" and "capital surplus." Terminology varies though, and other account titles sometimes are used.) The second, called "retained earnings" or "earned surplus," reflects the cumulative results of the corporation's operations since it was formed. Each year, this account increases or decreases in an amount equal to the corporation's net income or net loss. This account also is reduced by an amount equal to any distributions the corporation has made to its shareholders in the form of "dividends" or any amounts the corporation has paid to repurchase its shares.

Now consider Widget, Inc.'s equity. The details are reproduced below.

Stockholders' Equity	Year 2	Year 1
Common stock (1,000 shares authorized and outstanding)		
Paid-in capital	200,000	200,000
Retained earnings	1,310,000	920,000
Total Equity	1,510,000	1,120,000

Widget, Inc.'s paid-in capital did not change, because the corporation did not issue any new shares. If it had issued new shares, it's paid-in capital would have increased. However, Widget, Inc.'s total equity did increase, by $390,000. Why did the book value of the equity increase by this amount? The answer to this question comes from the income statement, which we will discuss in a moment. You will notice that this change is equal to the net income Widget, Inc. generated during Year 2.

4. Balance Sheet Analysis

The balance sheet provides useful information about the ability of a company to meet its obligations. For example, do you think Widget, Inc. has sufficient "liquidity" from cash, or assets it is likely to convert into cash, to meet its financial obligations as they come due? One commonly used indicator of a firm's liquidity is its *current ratio*, which is computed by dividing current assets by current liabilities.

As a rule of thumb, analysts often prefer a current ratio of at least 2:1—current assets at least twice as large as current liabilities. But this is a generalization. Some firms can operate safely with a lower current ratio, while other firms, such as firms with a large amount of inventory (which can be converted into cash only by first selling the goods in inventory and then collecting the resulting accounts receivable) might need a higher current ratio.

A gradual increase in a firm's current ratio, based on a comparison of successive balance sheets, is a sign of financial strength. But too large a current ratio might signal that the firm is not managing current assets efficiently.

Creditors also are interested in the right-hand side of the balance sheet, because it gives them information about whether a firm will be able to pay its debts on time. They frequently will compute a firm's *debt-equity ratio*, dividing a firm's long-term debt by the book value of its equity. A ratio of more than 1:1 may indicate the firm is relying principally on borrowed capital. This poses some danger for debtholders, especially where the ratio is much higher than 1:1, because if the firm's business falters, the firm may be unable to generate sufficient revenues to pay the interest due on its debt. In effect, the firm's debtholders may be bearing risks similar to those customarily borne by equity investors. When deciding whether to extend credit to the firm, creditors will want to be compensated for bearing those risks.

Additional insight into the risk a firm will be unable to service its debts ccomes from computing the *interest coverage ratio*—dividing the firm's annual earnings by the annual interest payments due on its long-term debt. Most analysts consider debt a safe investment if a firm's interest coverage ratio is at least 3:1. What do you think of Widget, Inc.'s ability to meet its obligations, based on the right side of its balance sheet?

D. Income Statement

Managers, investors, and creditors are not interested only in a snapshot of the firm's assets and liabilities. They also want to know about the firm's operations over time. The balance sheet provides only limited information about how much money the firm made during a particular period of time. By examining the change in retained earnings on the balance sheet over time, we can get some sense of how much money the firm made or lost during a particular period. For example, we can tell that Widget, Inc. had retained earnings of $920,000 at the end of Year 1 and $1,310,000 at the end of Year 2. We have a sense that this increase in retained earnings occurred because the firm made money during Year 2, just as the jar made money by selling the pen.

In other words, we know that assets increased, and that the retained earnings portion of equity also increased to keep the balance sheet in balance. But we don't have any of the details about the firm's accounting income. The statement of income provides this information. It is the "bridge" between successive balance sheets, in that it records whether the firm realized a profit or loss during the period between successive balance sheets. That profit or loss then is reflected on the firm's balance sheet as of the end of that period by increasing or decreasing the owners' equity account by the amount of that profit or loss. For example, Widget, Inc.'s Net Income during Year 2 was $390,000, and the increase in the balance sheet value of Widget, Inc.'s equity from the end of Year 1 to the end of Year 2 also was $390,000 ($390,000 equals $1,510,000 minus $1,120,000).

Whereas the balance sheet was a "snapshot," the income statement is a "motion picture." The income statement—sometimes called a statement of income or profit and loss statement—provides a view of how the firm has performed *during* a period of time. Widget, Inc.'s balance sheet is just one frame of the motion picture—it shows the value of Widget, Inc.'s assets, liabilities, and equity as of December 31. In contrast, Widget, Inc.'s statement of income includes every frame, from the beginning to the end of the year—it shows how much accounting income Widget, Inc. had during the year ended December 31.

The fundamental equation, and thus the balance sheet, represents the conceptual core of a firm's financial statements. Investors and creditors, however, often are more interested in a firm's income statement. They view information about the results of past operations as the best available indicator of a firm's ability to generate profits in the future. Moreover, investors seem to place a very high value on firms whose profits rise steadily. Most people are risk averse and pay more attention to potential losses than potential gains. Thus, the more volatile a firm's income, the less they will be prepared to pay for any given level of anticipated earnings. This gives managers an economic incentive to "manage" the earnings their firm reports to eliminate volatility.

Not surprisingly, managers are sensitive to how investors evaluate income statements. Because of the flexibility inherent in GAAP, it is not uncommon for a firm's managers to "massage" their firm's income statement so as to report steady profits or, better yet, steadily rising profits. In the discussion of financial statement terms and concepts in this and the following section, we note several areas in which GAAP provide opportunities for such "massaging" of financial statement numbers. As you read these sections, consider whether there is anything in Widget, Inc.'s financial statements that suggests the owners were "massaging" the company's income.

The GAAP requirement that most firms use *accrual accounting* to prepare their financial statements is central here. Under the *Realization Principle*, a firm must recognize revenue in the period that services are rendered or goods are shipped, even if payment is not received in that period (and cannot recognize revenue until services are rendered or goods are shipped). Under the *Matching Principle*, a firm must allocate the expenses it incurred to generate certain revenues to the period in which those revenues are recognized. Consider how these requirements would affect a lawyer who provided $1,000 in services in Year 1, who paid $250 for secretarial support in that year, and whose bill for $1,000 was not paid until Year 2. If the lawyer used *cash accounting*, she would report the $1,000 as earned in Year 2, when payment was received, but deduct the charge for secretarial support in Year 1, when it was paid. Using accrual accounting, which focuses not on cash movements but on the performance of services and on matching income to expenses, the lawyer would recognize the $1,000 in income in Year 1 and would also record the $250 secretarial expense in Year 1.

Taken together, the Realization and Matching Principles go a long way toward ensuring that an income statement prepared using accrual accounting presents a conceptually sound picture of the economic results of a firm's operations for a given period. Those principles also limit substantially a firm's ability to manipulate its payment and receipt of cash so as to "manage" the earnings it reports. But because recognition of revenues and recording of expenses are tied to events more difficult to measure than the movement of cash, the Realization and Matching Principles also increase substantially the subjectivity of the information included in accrual basis financial statements. How, for example, should a lawyer record the cost, paid in Year 1, of a party to publicize the opening of her office? Is it all an expense incurred in Year 1, since the lawyer paid it all in Year 1, or should only a portion of the publicity expense be allocated to Year 1 and the remainder be deducted in future years so long as the lawyer believes that the publicity will continue to produce benefits for several years?

1. Income Statement Items

Next, we will go through the details of the statement of income, in the same way we did with the balance sheet. For each entry, you should look at Widget, Inc.'s numbers, and the changes from year to year. What "story" can you tell about how these numbers changed over time?

	Year 2	Year 1	Year 0
Net sales	7,500,000	7,000,000	6,800,000
Operating Expenses			
Cost of goods sold	4,980,000	4,650,000	4,607,000
Depreciation	250,000	240,000	200,000
Selling and admin expense*	1,300,000	1,220,000	1,150,000
R&D	50,000	125,000	120,000
Operating Income	920,000	765,000	723,000
Interest expense	320,000	375,000	375,000
Income before taxes	600,000	390,000	348,000
Income taxes	210,000	136,000	122,000
Net Income	390,000	254,000	226,000

* Includes $130,000 salaries paid to the owners in Year 2; $100,000 in Year 1; and $100,000 in Year 0, and bonuses totaling $120,000 in Year 2; $100,000 in Year 1; and $80,000 in Year 0.

Net sales. The statement of income begins with Net Sales, sometimes listed as "Revenue" and referred to colloquially as "Top Line Revenue" (because it is on the top line). This number represents the total value of Widget, Inc.'s revenue during the relevant year. Notice that Widget, Inc.'s net sales increased steadily during the three years.

Operating expenses. Once we know the total revenues, we can deduct expenses. We start with Cost of Goods Sold, or COGS. COGS generally represents the cost of items sold from inventory. You'll notice that for Widget, Inc., as for many corporations, the COGS entry represents the largest expense, and that this expense increases along with the increase in net sales.

Next we deduct *depreciation*, which also was discussed above when we covered balance sheet details. Depreciation is a non-cash expense that represents the decline in the value of fixed assets that we "match," following GAAP, with each particular year. Widget, Inc.'s depreciation expense increased somewhat over time, because the total amount of the fixed assets it was depreciating increased over time.

Remember that depreciation is fiction, not fact. Depreciation is not an actual, cash expense. Therefore, although depreciation expenses will reduce accounting income, they will not reduce the amount of operating cash a corporation generates. Indeed, many managers prefer to maximize depreciation expenses—even though these expenses reduce net income—for one simple reason: depreciation is a tax-deductible expense. A depreciation expense might not matter directly to how much money the corporation actually is making, but it matters indirectly because depreciation reduces tax payments, which are based on income.

Selling and administrative expense is the general catch-all category for expenses, sometimes referred to as "overhead." These expenses have different names. You might see them referred to as selling, general, and administrative expenses. Widget, Inc. included salaries in this category. Other firms will include a separate line in the statement of income for salary or compensation expenses.

Research and development also is an expense, often called "R&D." Note that Widget, Inc.'s declining R&D expenses are both positive and negative for the firm. On one hand, the decline in expenses increased Widget, Inc.'s income. On the other hand, if Widget, Inc. is not spending enough money on R&D, its future income might suffer. Whether a firm is balancing these effects properly, such as by buying third-party patents, is a difficult question: too little spending on R&D might be a bad sign, but so might too much R&D spending.

> ### Food for Thought
>
> As you might imagine, the assessment of the value of COGS could be quite subjective. GAAP generally require inventory to be valued at the lower of cost or market value. The value a firm reports for its inventory will affect both the firm's balance sheet and its income statement. Firms that hold a relatively small number of identifiable items in inventory often use the "specific identification method." They value each inventory item at cost, unless its market value is lower than cost, and compute COGS by adding up the actual cost of all inventory items sold during the relevant period.
>
> In addition, GAAP require that firms apply uniform assumptions about which items are sold to customers. To compute COGS, these firms add their *purchases* during a reporting period to the value of their inventory at the start of the period (called *opening inventory*) and then subtract the value of their *closing inventory*. By conducting a physical count at the end of an accounting period, a firm can determine the number of items in its closing inventory. Thus, GAAP attempt to require a process that will produce relatively uniform assessments of COGS.

All of the above expenses are *operating expenses*, because they are costs associated with the operation of a business. To obtain *operating income*, we subtract all of these expenses from net sales. Operating income is sometimes referred to as *EBIT*, for Earnings Before Interest and Taxes.

EBITDA. In assessing firms, many investors like to examine EBITDA, initials that stand for a firm's Earnings Before Interest, Taxes, Depreciation, and Amortization. In other words, EBITDA represents net sales minus all operating expenses except depreciation. To calculate EBITDA, you would simply add depreciation to EBIT. For example, in Year 2 Widget, Inc. had operating income, or EBIT, of $920,000. It had depreciation expenses during that period of $250,000. Accordingly, its EBITDA would be the sum of these two numbers, or $1,170,000.

The rationale for examining EBITDA is that it gives an investor a clearer sense of how much money the firm generated from its "core" business, just taking into account operations, and not accounting for non-cash items such as depreciation and amortization or non-core items such as taxes and interest. Although the "ITDA" part affects the company's net income, some investors believe that they can get a better sense of what a firm actually is worth by looking at earnings before the "ITDA" factors are taken into account.

Interest expense and taxes. Finally, the statement of income also accounts for interest payments and taxes. *Interest expense* represents the amount of interest the firm paid on its debt during the year. Note that Widget, Inc.'s interest expense declined during Year 2. Why?

Income before taxes is obtained by subtracting interest expense from operating income. Income before taxes is sometimes called "taxable income." This is the number the Internal Revenue Service cares about. Note that Widget, Inc.'s *income taxes* track its income before taxes. This is because Widget, Inc.'s tax rate is roughly the same over time. Income taxes are not necessarily constant, and can vary based on changes in tax regulations and legislation, or changes in a firm's approach to its taxes during a particular year. Again, depreciation is important, in part, because it reduces a corporation's taxable income.

Net income. We have reached net income, an important number in the financial statements. It is often referred to as the "bottom line," because it typically is just that: the bottom line of the

You'll notice that the Widget, Inc. financials reflect a corporate tax rate of approximately 35%, which was the federal tax rate before the Tax Cuts and Jobs Act of 2017. The TCJA eliminated the graduated corporate tax schedule and set the federal corporate tax rate at 21% beginning with tax year 2018. Given that our stylized financials are assumed to be historic and that the TCJA's viability is uncertain, we have stayed with a 35% tax rate.

Later in the chapter when we look at how the Widget, Inc. financials might be used to value the company, it's conceivable that the company's valuation might increase if future earnings and cash flows were expected to rise—on the assumption of a smaller tax bill. But it's also conceivable the company's valuation might not change or even fall if the 21% tax rate and the current tax code's various tax write-offs were not expected to be permanent. How do you think things will go?

income statement. Many investors look simply at net income, or net income per share, in assessing investments. Moreover, net income is the link to both the balance sheet and the cash flow statements. Whatever is left from net income, after a firm pays dividends, goes to Retained Earnings in the firm's balance sheet. If net income after dividends is positive, retained earnings increases by the same amount. Can you see that link for Widget, Inc.?

Note that Widget, Inc.'s net sales increased by about 3% from Year 0 to Year 1 and by about 7% from Year 1 to Year 2, while net income increased by more than 12% in Year 1 and by more than 53% in Year 2. What might explain these disproportionate increases in Widget, Inc.'s profitability?

Two possibilities are that Widget, Inc. was able to increase its *profit margin* on the products it produced and sold or that it was able to generate increased sales without increasing, or even reducing, its fixed costs and overhead. It also is possible, though less likely, that profits increased because Widget, Inc. was able to reduce significantly either its interest expense or the percentage of income it was paying as taxes. To determine which of these factors explains the increases in Widget, Inc.'s profitability, an analyst would calculate the ratio of the expense items in Widget, Inc.'s income statement to its net sales.

Which of Widget, Inc.'s expenses increased as a percentage of its net sales in each of the three years for which information is provided? Which decreased? Would doing these calculations provide you with a better idea now of how the managers were able to increase Widget's profits so dramatically? Was it due to an increase in efficiency or a reduction in discretionary expenses? What do you think of the change in R&D expenses? Does it seem likely that any new owners or managers of Widget, Inc. would be able to sustain similar profits?

One could obtain added insight into the potential value of Widget, Inc.'s business by comparing its profit margin to those of other firms in the same line of business. If Widget, Inc.'s profit margin is comparatively low, the potential may exist to improve profits by improving management. If Widget, Inc.'s profit margin is comparatively high, the potential for such improvement is less likely to exist. If profit margins of all firms in Widget, Inc.'s line of business are relatively low, then competition probably is intense and increasing its profit margin is likely to be difficult.

2. Comparison of Income Statement to Balance Sheet Items

Inferences also can be drawn by comparing certain balance sheet data to income statement data. In the ordinary course, for example, one would expect a firm's accounts receivable and inventory to change at about the same rate as its sales. For example, if sales increased by 15%, accounts receivable and inventory both could be expected to increase by roughly 15% to reflect a higher level of sales on credit and the higher level of inventory needed to support a higher level of sales. Changes in these accounts that are not proportionate are not necessarily a sign of problems—for example, an unanticipated increase in sales might lead to a short term decline in a firm's inventory—but they often are a signal that further inquiry is required. Calculate the relative change in these accounts at Widget, Inc. and consider what additional questions, if any, you would ask.

Finally, a key indicator of a firm's value often is its *return on equity*, which one can compute by dividing equity at the end of the previous year (*not* the current year) into the net income reported for the current year. That percentage return then can be compared to the returns available on alternative investments. For example, if return on a firm's equity is less than the return available on a risk-free investment such as U.S. Treasury notes (and if reported income accurately reflects the results of the firm's operations), an analyst is likely to conclude that the firm is worth considerably less than its net book value. After all, why bear the risk of buying a business for its book value if one could earn a larger return on a risk-free investment of the same amount?

Similarly, if a firm's return on equity greatly exceeds the returns available from risk-free investments, an analyst might conclude (subject to the *caveat* noted above and the risks associated with the firm's business) that the firm is worth considerably more than its book value. In essence, the analyst would infer that a significant portion of the firm's earning power is attributable to the existence of intangible assets, the value of which, due to GAAP, is not reflected on the firm's balance sheet.

Net income is not only important for analyzing accounting income or calculating return on equity. It also is the starting point for the statement of cash flows, the third financial statement we have provided.

E. Statement of Cash Flows

The use of GAAP addresses some of the problems of subjectivity in accounting by requiring firms to prepare a *statement of cash flows*. Cash is important—some even say it is king. A firm must use cash, not income, to pay its bills, repay its debts, and make distributions to its owners. Over a period of many years, a firm's total income and cash flow usually will approximate each other. But over a shorter period of time, income and cash flow may differ substantially. As one accounting adage goes, "income is a fiction, but cash is a fact."

The statement of cash flows, as its name suggests, reports on the movement of cash into and out of a firm. The statement reflects all transactions that involve the receipt or disbursement of cash, whether they relate to operations or involve only balance sheet accounts such as purchases of plant and equipment, new borrowings, repayment of loans, equity investments, or distributions to equity holders. The statement of cash flows is split into three parts, based on whether the cash flow is from *operating activities*, *investing activities*, or *financing activities*.

Most investors focus on cash flow from operating activities as of primary importance, because operating cash flow is the best indicator of how much cash the firm is generating from its core operations. In contrast, cash flow from investing activities merely reflects how much cash was invested in the firm, and cash flow from financing activities merely reflects how much cash the firm borrowed. Of course, investing and borrowing matter to a firm's bottom line—cash is cash, after all—but operating cash flows provide a better gauge of how much cash the firm's true operations are generating, and hopefully will generate in the future.

Structurally, the statement of cash flows starts with net income and then "corrects" for each of the non-cash changes reflected in the balance sheet and income statement. For example, if the firm reported an increase in non-cash assets, such as accounts receivable, inventories, or prepaid expenses, it would need to correct for that increase by reducing its net income. In other words, the firm, in calculating net income, assumed that it got the benefit of income from the increase in these non-cash items. However, that increase was an accounting increase only—it wasn't cash. In order to get back to cash, the statement of cash flows reduces net income for the increase in non-cash assets. Conversely, it increases net income for any decrease in non-cash assets.

The cash flow statement follows the opposite approach for liabilities. For example, if the firm reported an increase in non-cash liabilities, such as accounts payable or accrued expenses payable, it would need to correct for that increase by increasing its net income. Remember that any increase in liabilities was an accounting increase only—it wasn't cash. In order to get back to cash, the statement of cash flows increases net income for the increase in non-cash liabilities. Conversely, it reduces net income for any decrease in non-cash items.

Boy, that sounds confusing! To clarify, we will go through an example from Widget, Inc.'s statement of cash flows.

	Year 2	Year 1	Year 0
From Operating Activities			
Net Income	390,000	254,000	226,000
Decrease (Increase) in accts receivable	(235,000)	(34,000)	(32,000)
Decrease (Increase) in inventories	(205,000)	(28,000)	(33,000)
Decrease (Increase) in prepaid expenses	(5,000)	(3,000)	(3,000)
Increase (Decrease) in accounts payable	75,000	25,000	20,000
Increase (Decrease) in accr exp payable	15,000	7,000	5,000
Depreciation	250,000	240,000	200,000
Total from Operating Activities	285,000	461,000	383,000
From Investing Activities			
Sales (Purchases) of machinery	(65,000)	(378,000)	(263,000)
Sales (Purchases) of office equipment	(20,000)	(27,000)	(25,000)
Sales (Purchases) of patents	(50,000)	0	0
Total from Investing Activities	(135,000)	(405,000)	(288,000)
From Financing Activities			
Increase (Decrease) in short-term debt	30,000	(40,000)	(35,000)
Increase (Decrease) in long-term debt	(355,000)	0	0
Total from Financing Activities	(325,000)	(40,000)	(35,000)
Increase (Decrease) in Cash Position	**(175,000)**	**16,000**	**60,000**

Note that Widget, Inc.'s net income for Year 2 was $390,000. This is our starting point for analyzing cash flows. Recall that in calculating Widget, Inc.'s net income, the income statement included numerous non-cash items. These items have to be corrected in the cash flow statement. The first such item is accounts receivable, an asset. According to the balance sheet, Widget, Inc.'s accounts receivable increased in Year 2 from $1,145,000 to $1,380,000, an increase of $235,000. That means that, as a result of Widget, Inc.'s sales during the year, it was owed an additional $235,000. This amount is an asset, but it is a non-cash asset. It is a valuable asset for Widget, Inc. to be owed an extra $235,000—it hopes it will collect that full amount in cash someday. But it hasn't done that yet, and so if we assumed that $235,000 was received in cash, we made a mistake.

Where did we make this mistake? In the statement of income, Widget, Inc.'s net sales included both sales for cash and sales on credit. However, the sales on credit increased during Year 2. By how much? $235,000. If we had been focused on the "fact" of cash, rather than the accounting "fiction" of income, when we prepared the statement of income, we wouldn't have included that $235,000.

We correct this mistake in the statement of cash flows. Specifically, we reduce Widget, Inc.'s net income by $235,000 to account for the fact that net income reflected increased sales on credit, for which the company has not yet collected cash. The second line of the statement of cash flows contains this correction for Year 2.

The same analysis applies to the other entries on the cash flow statement. If net income assumed Widget, Inc. received cash, but it did not, we subtract. If net income assumed Widget, Inc. paid cash, but it did not, we add. For example, the amount Widget, Inc. charges as a depreciation expense each year shows up as a positive entry in the statement of cash flows, while Widget, Inc.'s purchases of machinery reduces cash flows.

Many students find it difficult to "translate" income into cash flows by making these corrections. We suggest that you try picking a few of the numbers in the statement of cash flows and tell the story of what these numbers mean. Why are they positive or negative? What correction are they making to the income statement? If you can tell these stories, you can be reasonably confident that you understand financial statement analysis.

What does Widget, Inc.'s statement of cash flows tell you about the firm that its balance sheet and statement of income did not? Are you worried about the $175,000 overall decrease in Widget, Inc.'s cash position during Year 2? Why or why not? What about the difference between Widget, Inc.'s statement of cash flow for Year 2, which shows a decrease in cash position, and its statement of income for the same year, which shows an increase in net income?

As should be clear by now, income is a concept, and computation of a firm's income generally depends on numerous subjective judgments and is heavily influenced by the assumptions underlying GAAP. Cash, on the other hand, is tangible; one can touch, smell, and even taste it. More importantly, a company needs cash to pay its bills, repay its debts, and make distributions to its owners.

Firms frequently report significantly different amounts of income and cash flow for any given year. The disparity most often is attributable, at least in part, to GAAP requirements relating to accounting for fixed assets. Recall that when a firm acquires a fixed asset, it records that asset at cost on its balance sheet and then, over the useful life of that asset, records a portion of its cost as a charge against income—a depreciation expense—on its income statement. That "expense" does not reflect a current disbursement of cash; the cash was spent when the asset was acquired. As a result, cash flow will be lower than reported income in years in which large amounts of fixed assets are purchased and will be higher than reported income in years in which (non-cash) depreciation expenses are greater than the amounts spent to purchase fixed assets.

Comparison of a firm's income and cash flow statements often will provide insights into the direction of its business or suggest further inquiries that one might make. Consider, for example, the implications when cash flow from operations lags income. Is the shortfall due to rapid growth in the firm's business? If so, is substantial additional financing necessary to sustain that growth? Do increases in inventory and accounts receivable reflect long-term growth in the firm's business, or a short-term effort to pump up reported earnings? If accounts receivable and inventory decreased, does that suggest the firm is managing its current assets more efficiently or that its business is declining? By asking these and similar questions, one can obtain a better understanding of a firm's business than would be the case if one analyzed that firm's balance sheet and income statement alone. Note again that while the financial statements provide a good deal of useful data, it is the user's task to recognize and ask the additional questions that arise from that data.

F. The Basics of Business Valuation

Now that we've covered the basics of financial statements, we can use them to value the business of Widget, Inc. Ultimately, the motivating question in the valuation of Widget, Inc. (or any business) will be how much cash is the business likely to produce each year for its owners? Then, we will want to consider how much that cash in the future is worth in today's dollars? Thus, the real question in the valuation will be how much might someone be willing to pay today for the future returns promised by Widget, Inc.?

1. The Old Man and the Tree: A Parable of Valuation

Before we turn to answering these questions, you might want to jettison your intuitions about what something is worth. Here's a classic parable that describes different ways a business might be valued.

* * *

Once there was a wise old man who owned an apple tree. With a little care, the tree produced each year a crop of apples that the man sold for $100. When the man decided to retire, he placed a "for sale" in front of the tree. He wanted to sell for the right price and was curious to see how people would value his tree.

Asset value. The first person to respond, a logger, offered $50. The old man asked how he had arrived at that amount, and the logger said that was how much he could get by chopping down the tree and selling it for firewood. The old man said, "You are offering only the salvage value of this tree. But my tree produces apples and is worth much more than $50."

Next arrived an accountant, who asked to see the old man's books. The accountant saw the recorded value for the tree of $75, based on its purchase price ten years ago. When he offered this amount, the old man said, "You fail to see that this tree is worth more than book value—in fact, you could sell this year's apple crop for more than that!"

Earnings methods. The next person to come to see the old man, a retired sales executive, offered to pay $100 for the tree. She said that $100 was what she expected to earn for selling this year's crop of apples. "You are not quite as foolish as the logger," responded the old man. "At least you see this tree has value as a producer of apples. But $100 is not the right price. You are not considering the value of next year's crop of apples, nor those of the years after."

Then came a marketing whiz, "I'll offer you $3,000 for the tree. I figure it will live another thirty years. I'm sure I can sell $100 worth of apples a year, that totals $3,000." The old man answered, "I should accept your offer because you've over-valued the tree. You fail to understand the time value of money. Sure, the $100 you'll make selling the apples this year might be worth about $100 today. But what about $100 you will make selling the apples thirty years from now? Those $100 in the future are not worth $100 today. In fact, they're worth far less. Suppose you put just $25 in an investment that pays 10% per year, you'll end up with more than $100 in thirty years—in fact, you would have $436! So you can't just add up $100 a year for thirty years because you've failed to take into account the time value of money."

Take Note!

As the parable makes clear, when valuing any money-making enterprise or investment, it is extremely important to keep in mind the *time value of money*. Simply put, a dollar today is worth more than a dollar tomorrow, and a dollar tomorrow is worth less than a dollar today. Why? You could put a dollar in the bank today and end up with more than a dollar tomorrow. Conversely, that larger amount that the bank will pay tomorrow is only worth one dollar today.

The "time value of money" is one of the most important concepts in business. The process of figuring out how much future cash flows are worth today is called *discounting*, and the value of future cash flows in today's terms is called *present value*. The interest rate used to convert future cash into present cash (the "discount rate") will depend on inflation and the risks of the investment.

Thus, you should notice that money has three dimensions: its nominal amount (how much), its time dimension (when), and its risk (whether).

Market comparables. A wealthy man, who overheard the previous offer, stepped forward and offered $2,900 for the tree on the spot. "I don't know much about apple trees, but I know the last person was willing to pay you $3,000, so that's the market price. I'll buy it for a bit less." The old man sighed, "If there were an active market in apple trees like this one, the market prices might be a good indication of value. But there is no such market. The isolated offer I just got tells very little about how much my tree is worth."

Capitalization of earnings. Then an MBA student arrived. After looking at the old man's books, the student noted there were expenses (fertilizer, pruning, tools, and carting the apples to town) that should be subtracted from the $100 in apple sales. And there was also depreciation and taxes, as well. She concluded that the net income from the tree was $50 last year. "In addition, she went on, "future net income from this tree is unlikely to be as high as last year. My judgment based on likely changes in the market is that net earnings of $45 per year from this tree is more realistic."

"OK," said the old man. "So to value the tree, I would need to compute the present value of a perpetual stream of $45 per year. I remember from high school that the present value of a perpetuity can be computed by dividing each future payment by an assumed interest rate. That is, I can divide $45 by, let's say, 5%. That would give me a value of $900, if my math is right. Another way to look at this is that if you put $900 in a bank account that paid interest of 5% per year, your bank account would produce interest payments of $45 every year—in perpetuity."

"Not so fast, old man," the MBA student replied. "If this tree produced steady and predictable earnings each year, it might warrant using a low interest rate, like 5%. But its earnings are not guaranteed. We have to think about risk. There could be an apple glut, and I'd have to cut the price. Or a medical study might come out that eating apples is not actually healthy. Or my costs might skyrocket. Or a drought might hurt the crop. Or the tree could become diseased and die."

The MBA student continued, "To take account for risk, I should look at the rate of return offered by investment opportunities comparable to your apple tree in the agribusiness industry. I have concluded that 20% is the rate of return I should expect for a tree like yours. If you disagree, I can always buy a strawberry patch instead. That is, your apple tree is worth the amount of money that would generate $45 per year where we assume a rate of return of 20%. Using your math, the tree is worth $45 divided by 20% (or 0.2)—which happens to be the same as $45 multiplied by 5, the capitalization rate. I think the tree is worth $225."

"In fact," continued the MBA student, "strawberry patches have been selling for five times earnings. That is, for every $1 of strawberry earnings, strawberry patches sell for $5. Using a price-earnings (or P-E) ratio or multiple of 5, we get to the same result. The P-E multiple tells you what number you should multiply times the expected annual earnings from an investment to determine what that investment is worth. So multiplying the tree's estimated annual earnings of $45 by a P-E ratio of 5, I get a value of $225. That's my offer." The old man, impressed by the MBA's student's calculations and fancy MBA lingo, said he would think about it.

Discounted cash flow. The next day when the MBA student returned, the old man was tapping away at a laptop. "I think my tree is worth more than you figured. The 'earnings' you derived from my books may not be what really matters. The tree won't produce earnings for you, it will produce cash. Your calculations, which included things like depreciation, did not look at the 'cash flow' that the tree will likely produce. These are the dollars you can spend or give to your grandchildren."

"My estimate is that the apple tree, after expenses, will produce cash of $50 for the next five years. After that, according to the tree doctor who I consulted, production will fall off and the tree after expenses will only produce $40 a year for the next ten years. Then, after its productive life, we can throw in $50 after 15 years when the tree is sold for firewood. Finally, we can calculate what those future cash flows are worth today—that is, we can discount to present value those future cash flows."

"I've thought about the discount rate we should use," continued the old man. "You could buy five-year government notes that pay 3% interest. Assuming the government will be good on it promise to pay, we can assume 3% as the risk-free rate. But I accept, as you pointed out, that the apple tree's returns are not riskless. A higher discount rate will compensate you for the risk in your investment. Let's agree that we should discount each of the future cash flows by 15% per year. This is about the rate applied to investments with a similar magnitude of risk. You can check that out with my nephew who used this discount rate when he recently sold his strawberry patch. According to my calculations using this discount rate, the present value of the anticipated annual net cash flows is $267.57, and the present value of the tree being sold as firewood in 15 years is $6.14, making a grand total of $273.71."

The old man showed the MBA student his spreadsheet and announced, "I'll take $270 even. Notice that the discount rate of 15% allows for the apple tree's risk. If you discounted the cash flow stream at 5%, the discounted cash flow would come to $482.58."

The MBA student looked at the old man's spreadsheet:

		Present Value of Apple Tree	
		Discount rate	
Year	Cash flow	5%	15%
1	$50.00	$47.62	$43.48
2	$50.00	$45.35	$37.81
3	$50.00	$43.19	$32.88
4	$50.00	$41.14	$28.59
5	$50.00	$39.18	$24.86
6	$40.00	$29.85	$17.29
7	$40.00	$28.43	$15.04
8	$40.00	$27.07	$13.08
9	$40.00	$25.78	$11.37
10	$40.00	$24.56	$9.89
11	$40.00	$23.39	$8.60
12	$40.00	$22.27	$7.48
13	$40.00	$21.21	$6.50
14	$40.00	$20.20	$5.65
15	$40.00	$19.24	$4.92
Salvage	$50.00	$24.05	$6.14
	Total	$482.58	**$273.71**

After a few minutes reflection, the MBA student said to the old man, "I have enjoyed this little exercise. But whether we figure value using the discounted cash flow method or the capitalization of earnings, so long as we apply both methods consistently we should come out at the same point. You increased the valuation by assuming that the annual cash flows would be higher and that the discount rate would be lower. And you picked an arbitrary terminal time and value. We could argue about these assumptions forever. Tell you what, I'll offer you $250. My cold analysis tells me I'm overpaying, but I really like that tree. Sitting in its shade will be worth something to me."

"It's a deal," said the old man. "I never said I was looking for the highest offer, but only the *best* offer."

2. Valuing Widget, Inc. Based on Financials

We hope you enjoyed the parable and got something from it. But you might be wondering how these business valuation concepts are actually applied in the real world—let's say to Widget, Inc. That is, can we undertake a valuation for

Widget, Inc. using the information we have about the company? That's what we'll do next. Using some assumptions about the company and its financial statements, we will suggest how the basic valuation methods—the asset methods, the market comparables/earnings method, and the DCF method—might be used to come up with a "fair market value" for Widget, Inc.

Asset methods. Remember that one of the offers the old man received for his apple tree was based on the accounting value of the tree. This will often be the starting place for valuing a business. So let's look at the "book value"—accounting assets minus liabilities—of Widget, Inc. In the most recent fiscal year, the book value was $1,510,000 (Assets of $5,260,000 minus Liabilities of $3,750,000)—or Total Equity. This represents what Widget, Inc. would fetch assuming its balance sheet actually reflected all of its assets and liabilities, all of its assets were sold at the value carried on its books, and all of its liabilities were paid at stated value.

But as we pointed out in discussing financial statements, these assumptions will rarely hold true. That is, book value will generally not reflect intrinsic value. Assets are generally carried at historic cost, but may have far different market values; accounting depreciation (and other markdowns) may not reflect market realities; and accounting book value will typically not include intangible assets, like intellectual property and economic goodwill, which may be the driving factors in a business valuation. That is, book value reflects a static picture of asset acquisition price, without considering the value of the assets in a going concern.

Food for Thought

For many people, buying a business is a life-long dream. Some prospective purchasers, however, become captured by their dreams. They then ignore important facts relating to the business they have become interested in purchasing. They fail to ask the seller: How did you start the business? What have been your most difficult hurdles? Why do people buy your product? How have you kept your customers happy? What production problems have you had? How did you find and keep your sales and production staff? What has been your biggest success, your biggest failure? How do you see the future?

It should not surprise you that this over-optimism in buying a business also affects executives in public corporations. It is widely-documented that public corporations regularly overpay for the businesses they buy. In fact, stock markets seem to know this, and the share prices of acquiring firms generally fall on the announcement of an acquisition!

But sometimes a business may be worth more being liquidated (its assets sold for cash) than continuing as a going concern. To make this determination, the "market value" of the assets and liabilities (including those not on the balance sheet) can be determined, by making appropriate adjustments to the balance sheet. For example, it is possible—given some of Widget, Inc.'s apparent trouble in moving inventory and collecting from customers—that a liquidation of the company might be a viable option and thus a useful way to value the business.

What's That?

Fair market value (FMV) is a concept well-known in the law. It is the price at which property (here a business) would change hands between a willing buyer and a willing seller, neither being under any compulsion to buy or sell and both having reasonable knowledge of the relevant facts. For example, it's the price at which corporate securities are traded in a stock market with many buyers and sellers and with widely-available information about the corporation and its securities. Sometimes FMV is referred to as "intrinsic value."

But FMV is not the same as fair value (FV), a legal term that we will encounter with some regularity in this course. In corporate law, FV is generally the pro rata value of corporate shares based on the value of the overall business. In most contexts, FV is not equal to FMV. In computing FV of shares, unlike their FMV, the shares' value is not reduced to reflect the shares' lack of control ("control discount") or the difficulty in selling them ("illiquidity discount"). Corporate law calls for a valuation based on FV (not FMV) when minority shareholders seek judicial dissolution in the case of majority oppression (Chapter 26, Oppression in the Close Corporation) or seek a judicial appraisal after dissenting from a corporate merger (Chapter 31, Antitakeover Devices).

The valuation of corporations and their shares comes up repeatedly in this book. For example, when a board of directors decides whether to make a distribution to shareholders (Chapter 12, Capital Structure), the question of how the distribution affects the corporation's value will often turn on the valuation methods we consider here. In voting contests (Chapter 18, Public Shareholder Activism), the voting insurgent and incumbent management will often take different views on the value of competing business plans, with shareholders left to value each one again using the methods we describe. Likewise, in takeover contests (see Chapter 31, Antitakeover Devices), the "fairness" of an outside bidder's offer—that is, whether the offer reflects the FMV of the shares being sought—will determine whether the target's board of directors can interpose takeover defenses.

Consider what the "adjusted book value" of Widget, Inc. might be if we adjusted the value of certain of its assets:

Assets	Year 2	Adjusted
Current Assets		
Cash	100,000	100,000
Accounts Receivable *	1,380,000	690,000
Inventories **	1,310,000	655,000
Prepaid expenses	40,000	40,000
Total Current Assets	2,830,000	1,485,000
Property, Plant, and Equipment		
Land***	775,000	1,200,000
Buildings****	2,000,000	2,000,000
Machinery****	1,000,000	1,000,000
Office Equipment****	225,000	225,000
Total PP&E	4,000,000	4,425,000
Accumulated Depreciation****	(1,620,000)	(620,000)
Intangible Assets		
Patent	50,000	50,000
Trademarks*****		400,000
Total Intangible Assets	50,000	450,000
Total Long-term Assets	2,430,000	4,255,000
Total Assets	5,260,000	5,740,000

* Assuming only half of accounts receivable will be paid
** Assuming only half of inventory will be sold
*** Assuming FMV of land is $1,200,000
**** Assuming Accumulated Depreciation is $1,000,000 more than actual loss in FMV of Buildings, Machinery and Office Equipment
***** Assuming Trademarks (brand and customer loyalty) is $400,000

Based on these assumptions, we can calculate Widget, Inc.'s adjusted book value to be $1,990,000 (Total Assets of $5,740,000 minus Total Liabilities of $3,750,000). But there other ways to calculate its value.

Market-comparable/earnings methods. Another way to value a going-concern business is to look at what comparable businesses have sold for—remember the strawberry patch. It's a little like using somebody else's homework, it will be important to make sure their homework was based on the same questions and assumptions you are making.

So to value Widget, Inc. in this way, we'll have to make some assumptions about how similar businesses have been valued. A frequent valuation method—which the MBA student used in the valuation of the apple tree—is to use a price-earnings ratio (or P/E ratio). Suppose that a basket of companies similar to Widget, Inc. have recently been purchased on average at 6.3 times "trailing earnings," That is, the P/E ratio in these transactions has been 6.3—meaning that the purchase price paid for these companies has been 6.3 times recent annual net earnings as stated in the companies' financial statements. (This information, as you might guess, is collected and carefully guarded by business valuators.)

If Widget, Inc. were to be valued on this basis, a prospective purchaser might be willing to pay $2,457,000 based on the company's most recent earnings of $390,000 (where 6.3 times $390,000 is equal to $2,457,000). Or, the purchaser might look at an average of Widget Inc.'s earnings over the past several years and apply the P/E ratio to this average. Given that Widget Inc.'s net earnings averaged $290,000 for the three most recent years, the purchaser might be willing to pay instead only $1,827,000 (where $290,000 times 6.3 equals $1,827,000).

Another indication of the market value of a company might be found in the price at which shares of the company have been trading. For publicly-traded companies, this is one of the most frequent methods for company valuation. For example, we know that buyers are typically willing to purchase control of publicly-traded companies for more than the total market price of their issued shares (their "market capitalization"). Thus, suppose the "control premium" in a particular industry is 30% and that a company has 10,000,000 common shares outstanding (and no other equity shares) and the shares trade at $25/share, we can make a rough guess of the company's market value. The market capitalization would be $250 million, and applying the control premium of 30% (or $75 million), we can estimate a purchaser might pay $325 million for the company.

Let's suppose Widget, Inc. has 500,000 shares outstanding and that recently some of the shares sold in a

Food for Thought

The comparables method of valuation ultimately depends on prices paid for the companies in market transactions and the assumption that these *other* companies were valued accurately. That might or might not be true. For example, "comps" of publicly-held companies with multiple lines of business may not be accurate when valuing a closely-held company that operates only in one line of business. And valuations of publicly-traded companies fluctuate with values in financial markets, which have a propensity to cycle through periods of mania, panic, and crash. For example, the Dow Jones Industrial Average tripled in value from 1994 through spring 2000. Yet during the same period, basic economic indicators did not come close to tripling. Then, during 2000, the markets fell precipitously and remained below pre-2000 levels for several years. Their recovery was rudely interrupted by the Financial Crisis of 2008, when the values of public corporations were nearly sliced in half. If you value a company based on "comps," the valuation will gyrate along with the markets.

thinly-traded market for between $2.00 and $2.50. Given that Widget, Inc. is a closely-held corporation, we know that a purchaser of these minority shares will have discounted the shares' value both because they lack control and because they lack a ready market. These discounts vary from company to company, but often combine to be more than 50%. In the case of Widget, Inc., let's suppose that the minority shares carry a total discount of 60%. That is, full value (no discounts) for these shares would have been $3.33 and $4.17 (discounting each of these amounts by 60% is . . . yep, $2.00 and $2.50). Thus, the overall value of the company (full value of shares times the number of outstanding shares) ends up being between $1,666,667 and $2,083,333—averaged to $1,875,000.

DCF methods. The "gold standard" among business valuators—and, as we saw, the old man selling his apple tree—is the *discounted cash flow* (DCF) method. The method assumes that the value of a business is the sum of all of its future cash returns, each discounted to present value. Under this method, the first step is to calculate the company's expected stream of cash flows. This is often accomplished by normalizing and adjusting accounting earnings, and then making assumptions about their upward and downward swings in the future. In the case of Widget, Inc., the cash flow statement shows adjusted earnings from operations ($285,000 in the most recent year), which can then be "normalized" to reflect that bonuses paid to the owners ($120,000 in the most recent year) were de facto dividends—thus increasing expected cash flow. Based on these calculations, this means Widget, Inc.'s adjusted/normalized cash flow from operations for the most recent year would be $405,000 (that is, $285,000 from the cash flow statement plus the $120,000 in bonuses). This then becomes the baseline for future cash flow estimates.

Assume that the expected future cash flows for Widget, Inc. are:

Year 1	$440,000 (an increase from the most recent year)
Year 2	$410,000 (a tough year)
Year 3	$520,000 (a good year)
Year 4	$480,000 (old equipment must be replaced)
Year 5	$550,000 (new equipment pays off)
Year 6 and beyond	$560,000 (a guess into the indefinite future)

Next we discount these future cash flows to determine their present value.

Let's assume a discount rate of 25%, given the various risks of firms in the widget market. Here are the spreadsheet computations:

Year	FV	PV
1	$440,000	$352,000
2	$410,000	$262,400
3	$520,000	$266,240
4	$480,000	$196,608
5	$550,000	$180,224
Terminal value	$2,240,000	$734,003
	Total PV	$1,991,475

Notice that to compute present value of the "terminal value," we first computed the value of a $560,000 perpetuity (cash flows in Year 6 and beyond) as of the beginning of Year 5. This terminal value (as of Year 5) is then discounted to present value. All the years' present values—discounted cash flows—are then summed. The value of Widget, Inc. under these assumptions is about $1,990,000.

That was a lot of math! We hope that you followed it (if not the first time through, perhaps the second time) and that you noticed how our many calculations made assumptions about market valuations and transactions, prevailing discount rates, and assessment of future business conditions. That is, each of the methods that we used in valuing Widget, Inc. was really a style of art.

3. Some Final Thoughts on Valuing Businesses

So how much should Widget, Inc. sell for? Notice that our three valuation methods—based on assets, comps/earnings, and DCF—came to similar results, ranging between $1.8 million and $2.0 million. That's not bad,

Take Note!

However one values a business, the company's financial statements will be a source of important information. But the financial statements should not be accepted at face value. Prospective purchasers will want to perform their "due diligence" and look behind the financial statement numbers. For example, a purchaser should inquire what is behind the cost of goods sold, investigate overhead charges, understand the selling and marketing expenses, determine whether receivables really are collectible, and ascertain whether inventory is obsolete. In addition, an important part of "due diligence" is to inquire into contingent liabilities, such as possibly costly environmental claims or potential liability to customers.

though perhaps a bit suspicious. When valuation experts testify about business value in court cases, it's not unusual for their expert opinions to vary by more than a factor of ten. For example, it's not unusual for one expert to make some reasonable assumptions and value a business at $500,000, while another expert makes equally reasonable different assumptions and values the business at $5,000,000. Our tight range of valuations reflected—as you might have noticed—some convenient assumptions that we made about asset market values, normalized earnings, market comparables, and discount rates.

Ultimately, valuation is similar to financial analysis and accounting more generally. We are studying art, not science.

————————

Chapter 12

Capital Structure

In the previous chapter, we focused on the details of financial statements, including the assets on the left-hand side of the balance sheet. Now we take a more detailed look at the right-hand side of the balance sheet. These entries—including debt and equity—are a window into the key attributes and tensions of many corporations. They show how the corporation raised its funds and who have claims on the corporation's income. They also reveal the potential for dramatic conflict.

When we say "capital structure," we refer to the "structure" of the right-hand side of the balance sheet. How did the corporation raise its capital? Did it simply issue shares of stock? Or did it also borrow money? What are the relative portions of equity and debt? Did the corporation raise money by issuing more complex financial instruments? Did it grant stock options to employees? These are questions of capital structure, which essentially ask how the corporation has been financed and whether money has been (and can be) paid to those who hold the corporation's debt and equity.

Food for Thought

In theory, capital structure should not matter much to corporate decision making. Instead, at least theoretically, the value of the corporation should depend on the return of the assets represented by the left-hand side of the balance sheet. Two financial economists, Franco Modigliani and Merton Miller, won Nobel Prizes in Economics partly for their suggestion that in an efficient market with perfect information (and no taxes or bankruptcy costs) the value of a corporation would not be affected by how it was financed. The simple metaphor for their theorem is a pizza: the value of the pizza depends on the ingredients, not on how it is sliced. Likewise, the value of a corporation depends on its income-producing assets, not whether it obtained financing by issuing equity or debt, or some portion of each.

In reality, the Modigliani-Miller assumptions rarely hold, and capital structure matters greatly to corporations. Managers of a corporation with no debt obviously worry less about bankruptcy than managers of a corporation with massive obligations. Corporations can deduct interest payments on debt for tax purposes (recall that taxes were calculated based on income after interest payments). However, dividend payments on equity are not tax deductible.

As this chapter illustrates, corporations with different capital structures—that is, different ratios of debt and equity—face different challenges. Remember the central question of this course: for whose benefit should the corporation be run? Should corporate managers run the corporation for the exclusive benefit of equity? Or for some combination or equity and debt? And, if so, how should managers take debt into account in making decisions?

These are just a few questions we will pose about capital structure in this chapter. We begin by describing different possible capital structures depending on the mix of debt, equity, preferred, and options. Then we turn to how inevitable conflicts arise when there are different claimants to the corporation's assets and cash flow, as reflected on the right-hand side of the balance sheet. Finally, we analyze two legal and policy issues that arise from the capital structure: the treatment of so-called "legal capital" and the corporation's payment of dividends to equity.

A. Slicing up the Corporation: Some Details on Capital Structure

Recall that corporations can raise money by issuing securities to investors. The investors are willing to give money to the corporation, in exchange for securities, because they expect a return on their investment. Corporations have considerable flexibility in tailoring the terms of their securities to allocate control, profit, and risk among the various investors.

Corporate securities can be divided into two broad categories: equity and debt. In general, equity securities represent permanent commitments of capital to a corporation, while debt securities represent capital invested for a limited period of time. Returns on equity securities generally depend on the corporation earning a profit. Although equity securities might share in the corporation's assets in the event of liquidation, the rights of equity securities are subordinated to the claims of creditors, including those who hold the corporation's debt securities. On the other hand, holders of equity securities typically elect the corporation's board of directors and thus exert more control over the conduct of the corporation's business and the risks it incurs.

In contrast, debt securities typically represent temporary contributions of capital (for example, until the maturity date of a loan). Debt securities are more likely to have priority in terms of payment if the firm becomes insolvent or liquidates voluntarily. Because debt securities are less risky, they typically are entitled only to a fixed return. Holders of debt securities can secure their rights by placing liens on some or all of a corporation's assets or by negotiating contractual covenants restricting the corporation's operations. Apart from such covenants, however, debtholders ordinarily play no role in the management of the firm.

Although the distinction between equity and debt is not always sharp or well defined, it is a standard distinction and most people use it. In the remainder of this section, we will describe more details about the differences between equity and debt. But before we do so, let's start with an example, so you can see that the tensions inherent in the capital structure are not merely abstractions, but actually arise in real life and are often part of real human drama. Some of the terms in the example might not be entirely clear—we will go through everything in detail in a moment. Later, once we have covered the detailed capital structure descriptions, we will return to this example, to be sure you have a sense of how capital structure matters.

1. The Drama of Widget, Inc.

Three of our former students—Justin, Kathy, and Lorenzo—have read through the financial statements of Widget, Inc. from the previous chapter. After much debate, they agree that an appropriate valuation of Widget, Inc. is in the range of $2 million. They form JKL Corporation and offer to pay $2 million to acquire all of Widget's assets, tangible and intangible, and to assume all of the liabilities listed on Widget's balance sheet. In addition to financing the purchase of Widget's business, Justin, Kathy, and Lorenzo want to provide JKL Corporation with an additional $150,000 to finance an expansion of the business. Thus, they need to raise a total of $2,150,000.

Justin and Kathy each are prepared to commit $200,000 to JKL Corporation. Kathy can provide that amount in cash, but Justin cannot provide more than $100,000, though he is prepared to sign a note obligating him to pay JKL Corporation the additional $100,000 in the future. In exchange for their investments, Justin and Kathy each expect to receive 40% of JKL's common shares.

Lorenzo is prepared to invest $600,000 of cash in JKL. In exchange for $100,000 of his investment, he will receive 20% of JKL's common shares. Lorenzo is willing to invest the remaining $500,000 either by purchasing preferred shares or making a long-term loan to JKL. Whatever the form of that investment, Lorenzo wants to be assured that he will receive at least $50,000 in income from JKL every year before any payments (other than salary) are made to Justin and Kathy. In addition, if JKL is liquidated, the $500,000 will be repaid to him before any payments are made with respect to JKL's common shares.

In addition to the $900,000 of cash that Justin, Kathy, and Lorenzo are prepared to invest, JKL has arranged to borrow $500,000 from First National Bank

("Bank"). JKL has agreed to repay that principal amount in five annual install-
ments of $100,000 each, the first of which will be due in five years, and to pay
interest at 10% per annum on the unpaid principal. The bank will not have any
right to participate in the management of JKL or any right to receive payments
other than those just described. However, the bank has required JKL and Lorenzo
to agree that, whatever form Lorenzo's $500,000 investment takes, Lorenzo's
funds will remain committed to JKL until the bank's loan has been repaid in full
and, in the event JKL is liquidated, Lorenzo's claims will be subordinated to those
of the bank.

Even with the $500,000 loan from Bank, Justin, Kathy, and Lorenzo would
be $750,000 short of the total they need. However, the Widget brothers, who
founded Widget, Inc. and are eager to retire, have agreed to offer "seller financing"
to cover this shortfall and take a note for $750,000 of the $2 million purchase
price. The note will require JKL to make annual interest payments of $75,000
(equal to 10% of the face value of the note) and to repay the principal of $750,000
to the Widget brothers in 10 years. If JKL fails to make any interest payment when
due, the $750,000 in principal will become due immediately. The Widget broth-
ers will not have any right to participate in the management of JKL or any right to
receive payments, except as just described.

The capital structure that will result from these different sources of financing
is fairly typical for a corporation such as JKL. Justin, Kathy, and Lorenzo will own
40%, 40% and 20% of JKL's common shares, respectively. Lorenzo also will own
preferred shares or a debt security. First National Bank and the Widget brothers will hold debt securities that provide no right to participate in the general
management of JKL.

2. Equity Securities

We use the terms *common shares* and *preferred shares* to describe the two basic
kinds of equity securities. Corporate statutes require that at least one class of
equity security have voting rights and the right to receive the net assets of the
corporation in dissolution or liquidation. These rights usually are assigned to
common shares, although they also can be assigned to preferred shares. We begin
by describing some basic terms that apply to all equity securities and then some
differences between common and preferred shares.

Basic terms of equity securities. When a corporation is formed, its articles of
incorporation create *authorized* shares. Until shares are first sold to shareholders, they are *authorized but unissued*. When sold, they are *authorized and issued*
or *authorized and outstanding*. If repurchased by the corporation, they become
authorized and issued, but not outstanding—commonly referred to as *treasury shares*.

Corporation statutes do not dictate how many or what kind of shares must be authorized. But the statutes do require that the articles specify the number of shares that a corporation is authorized to issue and, unless they are common shares, describe the characteristics of those shares. If a corporation has issued all the shares authorized in its articles, it cannot issue more shares unless the articles are amended to authorize additional shares. For this to happen, the board of directors must recommend the amendment, which must then be approved by holders of at least a majority of its outstanding voting shares. However, if a corporation has not issued all the shares authorized in its articles, then the board can decide on what terms to issue these authorized but unissued shares. Consequently, if a corporation's shareholders authorize more shares than the corporation currently plans to issue, they also delegate authority to the board to decide if, when and on what terms additional shares should be issued.

You might be wondering: should the organizers of a corporation authorize more shares than they initially plan to issue? They might want to issue additional shares at a later date to raise new money, to use for employee benefit plans, or to acquire other companies. As a practical matter, it may seem tempting to authorize a large number of shares at first so the corporation has the flexibility to issue additional shares in the future without the bother of amending the articles.

However, convenience might not be the only issue, especially in a close corporation. Shareholders might wish to keep control over the issuance of new shares by authorizing only the number of shares the company will issue immediately. For example, the articles might authorize 100 shares. For the company to issue more shares in the future, there would have to be another shareholder vote to amend the articles (to increase the number of authorized shares above 100). The need for an additional vote can protect minority shareholders and preserve existing control relationships. However, such a limitation might enable one or more shareholders to prevent the company from raising additional capital by blocking the vote to authorize additional shares.

In large corporations, shareholders usually exert relatively little influence over day-to-day management, and allowing the board to issue additional common shares may not constitute the surrender of much real power. Convenience usually decides the question in favor of an initial (and subsequent) authorization of many more shares than the corporation has current plans to issue. Under the MBCA, shareholders nonetheless retain some power over the issuance of additional shares of authorized stock, in that shareholder approval is required if the corporation issues, for consideration other than cash or a cash equivalent, shares with voting power equal to more than 20% of the voting power outstanding immediately before the issuance.

The precise number of shares that a shareholder owns in a corporation at a particular time determines her position relative to other shareholders. What is important, however, is not the absolute *number* of shares owned, but the *percentage* of the corporation's outstanding stock those shares represent (or more specifically, the voting power). Assume that two corporations are identical except that Corp. A has two shares of common shares outstanding and Corp. B has 1,000 shares outstanding. One share of Corp. A, representing 50% of its outstanding shares, clearly would have more value and greater proportionate voting power than 100 shares of Corp. B, representing 10% of its outstanding shares.

Practice Pointer

When additional shares are sold to other investors, the voting power of existing shareholders is diminished in relative terms—or "diluted." This is a problem for shareholders who want to maintain their proportionate voting interest to exercise a degree of control.

The common law doctrine of "preemptive rights" addressed concerns about dilution. Courts held a shareholder had an inherent right to maintain her proportionate interest in a corporation by purchasing a proportionate number of any new shares issued for cash. For example, a shareholder who owned 100 shares in a corporation with 1,000 shares issued and outstanding would be entitled to purchase 10% of any new issue. Although the preemption rights worked in closely-held corporations with simple capital structures, it became problematic in corporations with several classes of shares or those that issued shares in exchange for property to be used in the business. Preemptive rights also were of questionable value in publicly-held corporations: a typical public shareholder, owning far less than 1% of the outstanding shares, presumably would care little about being diluted, so long as the overall value of her shares were not affected. Moreover, if she believed the firm was selling new shares at too low a price, she could protect herself simply by purchasing additional shares on the open market.

Over time, courts and legislatures addressed the problems posed by preemptive rights. First, courts developed several exceptions to the rule that shareholders always had preemptive rights. Later legislatures modified state corporate laws to allow corporations to avoid preemptive rights and almost all public corporations exercised this option.

Today, many states have adopted an "opt-in" approach to preemptive rights. MBCA § 6.30(a) provides that "The shareholders of a corporation do not have a preemptive right to acquire the corporation's unissued shares except to the extent the articles of incorporation so provide." To provide shareholders with such rights, the articles must include an appropriate provision. A simple declaration, such as "The corporation elects to have preemptive rights," will do. Absent such a declaration in the articles, no preemptive rights exist.

Delaware's corporate statute no longer explicitly addresses preemptive rights. Nonetheless, DGCL § 157 authorizes a corporation to issue rights to purchase its shares, which can include preemptive rights. In addition, a Delaware corporation can include a provision in its articles creating preemptive rights.

Common shares. Common shares are the most basic of all corporate securities. All corporations have common shares, and many small corporations issue no other kind of equity security. Holders of common shares usually have the exclusive power to elect a corporation's board of directors, although in some corporations one or more classes of common shares are non-voting and in many corporations preferred shares have limited voting rights.

Common shares represent a "residual claim" on both the current income and the assets of a corporation. All income that remains after a corporation has satisfied the claims of creditors and holders of its more senior securities—preferred shares and debt—"belongs" in a conceptual sense to the holders of common shares. If no income remains, shareholders receive nothing. If some income remains, the board of directors can distribute it to shareholders in the form of a "dividend" or can choose to have it reinvested in the business. At least in theory, the board should choose to reinvest income only if it believes that the future returns from that investment will be greater than those that shareholders could generate by investing that income on their own elsewhere.

If the corporation is liquidated, common shares also represents a residual claim on the corporation's assets. This means that in liquidation the corporation must first pay the claims of creditors and holders of preferred shares. Common shareholders receive whatever "residual" remains. As a consequence, common shareholders are the first to lose their investment if the corporation experiences economic difficulties and have the greatest potential for gain if the corporation is successful.

Common shares generally represent a permanent commitment of capital to a corporation. Holders of common shares, if they wish to get out of their investment, generally do so by "exit"—selling their shares to other investors, who buy at a price that reflects the firm's current value. Generally, common shares are not redeemable, and the corporation has no obligation to repurchase them from shareholders. If a corporation is paying large current dividends or is reinvesting its income successfully, shareholders often will be able to realize substantial gains by selling their common shares to other investors. However, as we've noted earlier, shareholders of close corporations might not be able to find a ready market for their shares.

Although common shareholders are last in line when it comes to distributions of income and in liquidation, they generally are first in line with respect to control. They often have the exclusive right to elect the board of directors and to vote on other matters that require shareholders' approval. This combination of voting rights and a residual claim on profits and assets gives shareholders a strong incentive to ensure that the corporation is operated efficiently. If shareholders elect competent directors and monitor their performance effectively, they will realize the benefits of those directors' sound business decisions. If shareholders elect incompetent directors or fail to monitor their performance effectively, they will bear the loss if the directors mismanage the corporation's business or misappropriate its assets.

Common shareholders also are seen as the primary beneficiaries of the fiduciary duties that corporate law imposes on the board of directors. As we have seen, courts defer to a considerable degree to directors' business judgments, but they do so on the assumption that directors have exercised reasonable diligence and acted in the corporation's and thus the shareholders' best interests. These obligations extend to decisions concerning whether a corporation should reinvest its profits or distribute them as dividends. In addition, directors have a duty to refrain from engaging in transactions that will provide them with unfair profits at the corporation's expense. In short, directors have broad discretion to manage, but must bear in mind that they are managing other people's money and that they have obligations to do so with care, loyalty, and good faith.

Preferred shares. Preferred shares have economic rights senior to those customarily assigned to common shares. Preferred shares vary widely, depending on the attributes assigned to them in the articles of incorporation. If no attribute is assigned to a class of shares with respect to its voting rights, right to dividends, or rights to redemption or in liquidation, courts generally will presume that "stock is stock"—that stock with certain preferences otherwise have the same rights as does common stock. Thus, although the rights attached to preferred shares are set forth in or pursuant to the articles authorizing such shares, the rights of preferred shares are viewed as part of a contract between the preferred shareholders and the corporation.

Preferred shares almost always have dividend rights senior to those of common shares. This means that payment of dividends on common shares cannot happen until dividends due on preferred shares have been paid. A preferred share's dividend preference usually will be stated as a fixed amount that must be paid annually or quarterly. The preference may expire if a dividend due for a given period is not paid or it may be "cumulative"—meaning that if a dividend is not paid when due, the right to receive that dividend accumulates and all accrued dividend arrearages must be paid before any dividends can be paid on common shares.

Preferred shares also may be "participating." This means preferred shares will receive dividends whenever they are paid on common shares, either in the same amount as or as a multiple of the amount paid on common shares.

In addition to a dividend preference, preferred shares often have a preference in liquidation, generally stated as a right to receive a specified amount before any amounts are distributed with respect to common shares. The amount of this preference most often is the amount that the corporation received when it sold the preferred shares plus, in the case of cumulative preferred, any accumulated unpaid dividends. In some instances, there may also be a specified "liquidation premium" that must be paid. However, as with common shares, the liquidation rights of preferred shares are subordinate to the claims of creditors. Consequently, when a corporation does not have assets sufficient to pay its debts, the preferred shareholders receive nothing in the event of liquidation.

Preferred shares sometimes represent a permanent commitment of capital to a corporation and sometimes do not. In the latter event, the shares are "redeemable" for some specified amount—that is, the corporation will repurchase the shares from the preferred shareholders. The right to require redemption may be held by the shareholder, by the corporation, or by both. The amount for which shares are to be redeemed generally is equal to the preference to which they are entitled in the event of liquidation, although it is not unusual to provide that, when shares are redeemable by the corporation, some premium above that amount must be paid by the corporation.

Preferred shares can have voting rights, and will be deemed to have voting rights equal to those of common shares, unless the articles of incorporation provide otherwise. Sometimes the preferred have voting rights on an "as-converted" basis with the common shares, but often the voting rights of preferred shares are limited to specified issues and circumstances. Preferred shares usually have a statutory right to vote on changes in the corporate structure that affect adversely their rights and preferences. In addition, preferred shares are often given the right to elect some or all of a corporation's directors if dividends due on the preferred shares are not paid for some designated period. Such provisions reflect the nature of the contract between holders of preferred shares and the corporation. In short, the preferred shareholders may relinquish their right to participate in control in exchange for a priority claim to periodic dividends, but if the corporation fails to pay those dividends preferred shareholders then become entitled to exert control.

The standard features of preferred shares may be supplemented by a variety of other features, including the right to convert preferred shares into common shares at some specified ratio, the right to vote on certain transactions, or the right to require the corporation to redeem preferred shares if and when specified events should occur. As noted, these rights are essentially contractual in nature and must be spelled out in the articles. Moreover, most courts have taken the position that the preferred shareholders are owed fiduciary duties only when they rely on a right shared equally with the common stock and not when they invoke their special contractual rights.

Corporations often raise money by selling preferred shares in lieu of taking on debt. The two have obvious similarities. The price at which a company can sell preferred shares is influenced by factors similar to those that determine the price at which it can borrow—the dividend rate, the redemption features, whether the preferred can be converted into common shares and, if so, at what price. Consequently, the requirement that the terms of preferred shares be spelled out in the articles can pose real timing problems, especially in the case of a publicly-held company. It usually takes a minimum of 30 days to obtain shareholder approval of an amendment to the articles of incorporation authorizing new preferred shares. By the end of that period, market conditions are likely to have changed enough so that whatever terms were specified at the beginning of the period must again be modified.

> **FYI**
>
> Preferred shares are a favorite way for "venture capital" (VC) firms to finance "start-up" or "early-stage" businesses, particularly in areas of new technology. After such companies have raised their initial capital and need more money to expand or survive, they often will raise money from VC firms, which manage investment pools comprised of wealthy individuals and large institutional investors, like pension plans and university endowments.
>
> Why do VC firms prefer preferred? The hybrid nature of preferred, where dividends are promised though not required, gives the VC firms some assurance of a return on investment. At the same time, the company is not obligated to make dividend payments, as happens with interest on debt. VC firms can negotiate specific protections in their preferred, including a liquidation preference, the right to elect a certain number of directors to the board, and the ability to convert their preferred shares into common shares if the company goes public.

Most corporation statutes address this timing problem by permitting the articles to authorize "blank check preferred shares," the essential characteristics of which—rights to dividends, liquidation preferences, redemption rights, voting rights, and conversion rights—can be set by the board of directors at the time the shares are sold. Such an authorization may facilitate the sale of preferred shares, but it also enhances substantially the power of a corporation's board of directors by allowing it to issue preferred shares with rights that may materially impinge on those of common shares without first obtaining explicit shareholder approval. For example, many corporate boards use blank check preferred shares as part of "poison pill" rights plans, because the issuance does not require shareholder approval.

Make the Connection

A "poison pill" is an antitakeover device that dilutes the financial position of an acquiror that buys an interest exceeding a specified threshold in a corporation without first obtaining the permission of the corporation's board of directors. The device thus compels would-be acquirors to negotiate with the board. Poison pills come up with regularity in the book: Chapter 16, Shareholder Voting Rights; Chapter 18, Public Shareholder Activism; and Chapter 31, Antitakeover Devices.

3. Debt Securities

Debt securities represent a corporation's liabilities to lenders. They can be labeled *notes*, *debentures*, or *bonds*—and sometimes these terms are used interchangeably. Typically, notes and debentures have shorter maturities than bonds, and debentures are usually not secured by corporate assets. Some short-term debt securities resemble accounts payable or the debts of trade creditors. But typically, debt securities are part of a company's long-term capital structure, and reflect long-term interests in a corporation's financial fortunes.

The terms of a bond typically are fixed by a complex contract known as an *indenture* that specifies the rights and obligations of the bondholders and the corporation. Whether or not an indenture is used, certain fundamental terms are set forth in every debt contract. For example, the corporate borrower is obliged to repay a fixed amount of *principal* on a particular date. Typically, *interest* must be paid at periodic intervals, whether the interest is a floating rate that varies over time or is fixed throughout the term of the contract. Importantly, the interest obligation does not depend on whether the corporation earns a profit. If the corporation fails to pay interest on a bond when interest is due, it will be deemed in default. Typically, an event of default will cause the entire principal amount of the bond to become due immediately, and this "acceleration" entitles the bondholders to pursue all legal remedies for which they have bargained, including the right to initiate bankruptcy proceedings.

The indenture can require that the corporation repay the entire principal amount all at once at maturity, or it can specify that the corporation make periodic principal payments, so that the principal amount is "amortized" over time. Some indentures require that borrowers make payments into a "sinking fund" that will be used to repay part of the principal prior to the bond's maturity date.

If a bond is secured, the debt contract also must specify the terms of the security arrangement and the collateral that secures the bond. The debt contract also may include provisions, known as *covenants* or *negative covenants*, requiring the borrower to refrain from taking certain actions that might jeopardize the position of the bondholders. A corporation may agree, for example, not to pay any dividends or repurchase any of its own shares unless it meets certain financial conditions.

Bonds may be made redeemable or "callable" at a fixed price at the option of the corporation. This right can be valuable to a corporation; if interest rates decline, it can redeem outstanding high-interest bonds by issuing lower-interest bonds or otherwise borrowing at a lower interest rate. To compensate bondholders for their loss of income, a bond's redemption price usually is set at something above the principal that the bondholders would be entitled to receive when the bonds mature.

Because the terms and conditions of debt securities are fixed entirely by contract and often are the result of extensive negotiations, many other provisions may be included in a debt contract. For example, the corporation might give the bondholder the right to convert bonds into common shares. So-called *convertible debentures* are hybrid securities that closely resemble convertible preferred shares—indeed, two such instruments might have all of the same substantive terms so that the only real difference is the label.

FYI

Bonds usually do not carry the right to vote (although corporate statutes, such as DGCL § 221, authorize voting debt). Moreover, a borrower corporation's directors owe bondholders only such obligations as are spelled out in the debt contract, or are otherwise part of contract law. Directors generally are not fiduciaries for bondholders. Consequently, bondholders' interests generally are protected only to the extent that they have negotiated appropriate covenants as part of their debt contracts.

Unless the articles of incorporation provide to the contrary, a corporation's board of directors has the authority to issue debt securities without shareholder approval. The board decides whether the corporation should incur new debt, in what amount, and on what terms and conditions. The board must involve shareholders only if it decides to issue bonds that will be convertible into shares and the corporation does not have enough authorized shares to satisfy the bonds' conversion rights. In such a case, the board must seek shareholder approval of an amendment to the articles increasing the number of authorized shares. However, shareholders need not approve the issuance of the convertible debt securities.

The use of long-term debt as part of a corporation's capital structure creates a tension between debt and equity investors. Both have stakes in the long-term health of the corporation, and both benefit if the corporation accumulates funds in excess of the amount it needs for current operations. But holders of debt and equity have agreed to different trade-offs between risk and reward, and each thus has a different perspective on how much risk that a corporation should assume.

Unless she has bargained for a right to convert her debt into equity, a bond-holder has accepted rights to fixed payments of interest and repayment of her capital in lieu of the possibly higher, but uncertain, returns available to holders of equity securities, especially common shares. Common shareholders have assumed more risk, but also can exercise more control over the conduct of the corporation's business. A debtholder is viewed as an outsider entitled only to the protection specified in her contract. In contrast, common shareholders are protected by directors' fiduciary duties, including the duty to advance the interests of the common shareholders even if at the expense of the interests of non-shareholders.

4. Options

In addition to debt and equity, companies often issue *options*, which are the right to buy securities, typically common shares, at a specified time and price. Stock options are important pieces of the financial accounting and valuation puzzle. Corporate lawyers frequently deal with options, in part because most publicly traded companies and many private companies award stock options to managers and employees.

The definition of an option is simple: it is the right to buy or sell something in the future. Options are everywhere. A tenant with the right to renew a lease at a particular monthly rate owns an option. A car rental company that permits a client to purchase the car's tank of gasoline in advance is selling an option. Any corporation that gives its employees the right to buy its shares at a set time and price also has issued an option.

Options generally are known as *contingent claims*, because they are assets whose value and future payoff depend on the outcome of some uncertain contingent event, such as fluctuations in rental markets, gasoline use on a trip, or changes in the corporation's stock price. Remember: a party who owns an option has a contractual *right* (to buy or sell), but not a contractual *obligation* to do so. A tenant with a right to renew the lease need not renew; a car renter who prepurchases a tank of gas need not use all of it; and an employee with stock options is not obligated to buy corporate stock. Simply stated, option holders have rights, not obligations.

The most familiar type of option is the stock option. Corporations frequently grant stock options to their employees, particularly senior managers, as compensation. Again, the option holder has the right—but not the obligation—to buy shares of the company.

Make the Connection

In 1995 The Walt Disney Company hired Michael Ovitz, a Hollywood talent broker. Besides agreeing to pay Ovitz a base salary of $1 million and a discretionary bonus, Disney issued stock options that entitled Ovitz to purchase five million shares of Disney stock. When Disney's stock price went up, the right to buy five million shares of Disney stock proved to be highly valuable. Fourteen months after being hired, Disney terminated Ovitz, who exercised his stock options and made $130 million. Disney shareholders claimed this was excessive—particularly for someone who had done a poor job. In Chapter 22, Executive Compensation, we take up the Delaware judicial response to this famous shareholder suit.

Options have a special terminology:

- The right to buy shares is known as a *call option*, whereas the right to sell is known as a *put option*.

- The price specified in an option contract is known as the *strike price* or *exercise price*.

- The date specified in an option contract is known as the *maturity date* or *expiration date*.

Corporations typically issue only call options. When issued to the public, call options are sometimes known as *warrants*. Stock options awarded to managers typically are call options with a ten-year maturity date and an exercise price equal to the market price when the options were awarded. As incentive compensation, the options may be subject to a vesting period over which time the rights become exercisable.

Points for Discussion

1. Allocating risk and return.

Return to the capital structure of our JKL Corporation. What are the rights of each of the parties with regard to (1) participating in the management of JKL, (2) receiving current income with respect to their investments, and (3) recovering the capital they are committing to JKL? How are the parties' attitudes toward risk likely to differ? How does JKL's capital structure allocate risk—assume, for example, that the corporation becomes insolvent or that it becomes a huge financial success? How does the way they have elected to slice JKL's capital structure affect the expected returns of each party?

2. Debt vs. equity.

How can the Widget brothers protect their interests as creditors of JKL? How does their approach differ from the approach Justin, Kathy or Lorenzo might use to protect their interests as shareholders?

3. Debt vs. preferred.

Would it be better for Lorenzo to receive preferred shares or a debt security for the $500,000 he proposes to invest beyond what will be allocated to common shares? What business and legal risks does the choice entail for JKL and the three shareholders? What risks and benefits does the choice entail for Lorenzo? If Lorenzo elects to purchase preferred shares, how should the terms be structured to protect Lorenzo's interest in receiving income of $50,000 a year with respect to this portion of his investment?

4. Options?

How might you advise the parties to use options, if at all? For example, would you advise the Widget brothers to ask for options in lieu of other protections? How should JKL respond if the Widget brothers request that the corporation issue stock options to them?

B. Capital Structure in the Real World: Taxes, Bankruptcy, and Conflicts

As noted above, the term "capital structure" describes how a company has raised funds using corporate securities. Some corporations have an all-equity capital structure consisting only of common shares. Other corporations have small amounts of equity and large amounts of debt. Some corporations have complicated capital structures, with numerous slices, each with different claims on the corporation.

Investing is a voluntary act. People with funds to invest will buy a security only if they perceive it to be more attractive than other available investments. Consequently, those who organize a corporation cannot simply select a capital structure and impose it on potential investors. They must design a capital structure for the firm in general, and specify the terms of the securities it will issue in particular, so that investors find the rights embodied in those securities—relating to participation in management, claims on the firm's income, rights in the event of liquidation and potential financial rewards—sufficiently attractive to justify investing in one or more of them.

Within the limits imposed by market forces, however, persons organizing a corporation generally have the ability to select among different capital structures that reflect differing allocations of control, risk, and claims on the corporation's income and assets. As is the case when choosing an organizational form, federal income tax considerations often will influence the organizers' choice. Likewise, the costs of bankruptcy will constrain a corporation's ability to issue increasing amounts of debt. Finally, capital structure choices inevitably create conflict among parties with potentially competing claims to a corporation's income, and frequently different agendas and risk preferences. We next address each of these issues: taxes, bankruptcy, and conflicts.

1. Taxes

The Internal Revenue Code gives corporations a powerful incentive to favor debt in their capital structure. Specifically, it allows corporations to deduct from their taxable income all interest paid on bonds they have issued. The code does not allow corporations to deduct dividends paid on preferred or common shares. Repayment of the principal of a bond also typically is treated as a tax-free return of capital.

Recall the capital structure of Widget, Inc., from the financial statements at the beginning of the previous chapter. The Balance Sheet showed that Widget, Inc. had issued $2 million of Notes payable, 12.5%. The annual interest payment on that debt was $250,000 ($2 million times 12.5%). Widget, Inc. was entitled to deduct this amount from its income to calculate its "Income before taxes."

What if Widget, Inc. had decided that instead of issuing debt it would raise the $2 million by issuing preferred shares with a 12.5% dividend? If Widget, Inc. paid a dividend of $250,000 in its most recent year, it would *not* have been entitled to deduct that payment, because it was a "dividend" not "interest." Accordingly, the company's "Income before taxes" for the most recent year would have been $850,000, not $600,000, and it would have paid tax on this higher amount.

So why don't corporations always issue bonds rather than preferred shares? And why don't corporations raise as much of their capital as possible by selling debt to persons who might otherwise purchase common shares? One answer is that preferred stock has other advantages. For example, preferred stock is more flexible than debt. The corporation must make interest payments to debtholders, but can choose to forego dividend payments on preferred stock when the corporation has a bad year. Because debtholders have the ability to accelerate debt and force bankruptcy proceedings if the company fails to make payments, many equity investors prefer that companies not have too much debt. For most companies, there is some optimal mix of capital structure that includes both debt and equity, notwithstanding the tax advantages of debt.

Thus, because of taxes, capital structure matters. For tax purposes, corporations have an incentive to issue debt instead of equity. On the other hand, corporations that issue too much debt might lose the tax advantage if challenged. On balance, taxes are a "thumb" on the capital structure scale that favors debt over equity.

2. Bankruptcy and Leverage

In contrast to taxes, the specter of bankruptcy is a disincentive for corporations to issue debt. At the extreme, an equity-only corporation will never have to worry about bankruptcy. If business goes poorly, the equity investors lose their money; but if there are no debts to repay, there are no potential bankruptcy costs.

Financing a corporation with debt has advantages. A corporation will find it profitable to finance business activities with borrowed money whenever it can earn more income from those activities than it will pay in interest on the borrowed money. This concept is known as *leverage*. Whatever the corporation earns in excess of its interest costs will increase the corporation's income and benefit its shareholders. In effect, the corporation is using the borrowed money as a lever to increase its shareholders' income.

Practice Pointer

Given the tax advantages of characterizing corporate payments as payments on debt and not on equity, the IRS will not simply accept the label used by the corporation. Instead, the IRS and the courts consider numerous factors in assessing whether debt really is debt. The court in *Slappey Drive Industrial Park v. United States*, 561 F.2d 572 (5th Cir. 1977), provided a useful list, although not exhaustive:

(1) the names given to the certificates evidencing the indebtedness;

(2) the presence or absence of a fixed maturity date;

(3) the source of payments;

(4) the right to enforce payment of principal and interest;

(5) participation in management flowing as a result;

(6) the status of the contribution in relation to regular corporate creditors;

(7) the intent of the parties;

(8) "thin" or adequate capitalization;

(9)   identity of interest between creditor and stockholder;

(10) source of interest payments;

(11) the ability of the corporation to obtain loans from outside lenders;

(12) the extent to which the advance was used to acquire capital assets;

(13) the failure of the debtor to repay or seek to postpone on the due date.

But leverage also increases shareholders' risk. If a corporation earns less from the activities being financed than the interest on the borrowed money, the corporation's income will decline because the corporation must pay interest on the borrowed funds whether or not the investment financed proves to be profitable. Consequently, if a corporation is not confident that leverage will work to its advantage, it often will choose to issue new equity rather than rely on borrowed money to finance its activities.

For example, suppose that you have $1 million and want to start a corporation. You have determined that your corporation needs $2 million of initial capital. Therefore, you must raise an additional $1 million by issuing corporate securities. Assuming debt is available at an interest rate of 10%, so that annual interest payments are $100,000, should the corporation issue equity or debt to raise the additional $1 million?

The answer depends on how much money you expect the corporation to make. (For this analysis, we are isolating the effects of leverage, and therefore we will ignore the effect of taxes, which as we know would make debt relatively more attractive.) If the corporation earns $200,000 of income before interest, you will earn $100,000 in both scenarios. If you borrow, you will pay $100,000 of interest, leaving $100,000 of income for the equity, all of which you own. If you issue equity,

Make the Connection

The story of Toys "R" Us illustrates the dangers of too much debt. Founded in 1948, the company had great success in the toy retail business in the 1980s and 1990s. But then in the 2000s, the company began to lose business to mass merchants like Walmart and online sellers like Amazon. In 2005, a consortium of three private equity firms purchased the ailing company for $6.6 billion in a leveraged buyout that resulted in the company holding $5.3 billion in debt. After the buyout, Toys "R" Us was unable to expand its businesses or reduce its debts. In September 2016, to get ready for the holiday season, the company sought to increase its inventory, but product vendors refused to ship without being paid up-front. Unable to obtain new financing for the $1.0 billion that the company needed in new liquidity, Toys "R" Us filed that month for bankruptcy. In January 2018, unable to obtain new debt financing and no longer able to service its $5 billion debt, the company announced it would liquidate and close up to 182 of its stores.

you will not owe any interest, so you will split 50-50 the corporation earnings of $200,000 with the other equity holder, leaving you with $100,000 of income. The results of this break-even scenario are depicted below.

Break-Even Scenario *+1 stock*

	Issue debt	Issue equity
Income Before Interest	$200,000	$200,000
(Interest)	($100,000)	$0
Net Income	$100,000	$200,000
Return on equity	10%	10%

← b/c you split 50%. w/ new equity holder

If the corporation earns less than $200,000, the negative effects will be magnified if you borrow. For example, if the corporation earned just $50,000, you would lose $50,000 if you borrowed, whereas you would earn $25,000 if you sold shares. This Negative Scenario is depicted below.

Negative Scenario

	Issue debt	Issue equity
Income Before Interest	$50,000	$50,000
(Interest)	($100,000)	$0
Net Income	($50,000)	$50,000
Return on equity	(minus 5%)	2.5%

If the corporation earns more than $200,000, the positive effects will be magnified if you borrow. For example, if the corporation earned $500,000, you would earn $400,000 if you borrowed, but just $250,000 if you sold shares.

Positive Scenario

	Issue debt	Issue equity
Income Before Interest	$500,000	$500,000
(Interest)	($100,000)	$0
Net Income	$400,000	$500,000
Return on equity	40%	25%

Thus, leverage increases risk—both on the upside and downside. Shareholders who are risk seekers might prefer debt, while shareholders that are risk averse might prefer more equity. There is no "rule of thumb" describing the optimal share of equity and debt.

What about debt taken by insiders? If a corporation has too much inside debt—that is, debt taken by shareholders of the corporation—a bankruptcy court might re-characterize this debt as equity, pushing it further down in the capital structure, and making it less likely that the inside debtholders will receive anything in the bankruptcy process. Under the "Deep Rock Doctrine," named for a bankrupt company involved in the leading case of *Taylor v. Standard Gas & Electric Co.*, 306 U.S. 307 (1939), bankruptcy courts have exercised their equity jurisdiction to subordinate the claims of inside creditors to those of outside creditors when they conclude the insiders have not invested adequate equity capital in a corporation. When this "equitable subordination" doctrine is invoked, inside creditors usually receive no repayment with respect to the "debt" they hold.

3. Tension in the Capital Structure

Capital structure also matters to corporations because slicing the capital structure creates tensions among the parties who contribute money to the corporation. Consider the inevitable tensions between managers and shareholders of a corporation. Capital structure can minimize these agency costs. For example, a corporation might use debt as a disciplining device to constrain managers, who might be less likely to slack if they must be sure the corporation repays its debts.

Some of these tensions arise because of "optionality" in capital structure. Remember that an option is a right. For example, the holder of a call option has the right to buy some asset at a specified price—such as if Widget, Inc. were to issue options to employees giving them the right to buy 100 shares for $100 per share anytime during the next four years.

There is a separate, different way to think about options in the context of capital structure. Some people find this concept difficult, but it illustrates the inevitable tensions among different parts of the capital structure. Here is the basic idea: equity is an option. Can you see how?

Imagine a company with $100 of debt. You can think of equity as having the right to buy the company's assets for $100 from the debt holder. If the equity doesn't pay the $100 debt, the corporation goes into bankruptcy and the equity receives little or nothing of the remaining assets. But if the equity repays the $100 debt, then equity keeps all of the upside from the assets. This is why equity is sometimes called the "residual" claim. Equity gets to keep what is left after repaying the debt—that potential for upside is option-like.

Thus, options are more than merely types of corporate securities. They also are conceptual tools that help illuminate the roles of various participants in a corporation. For example, in the JKL problem at the beginning of this chapter, the relative positions of Justin, Kathy, and Lorenzo, on one hand, and First National Bank, on the other hand, can be described using options.

One way of thinking about the shareholder-bank relationship is that the shareholders have bought a call option from the Bank. The shareholders have the right to receive the residual profits of the corporation after it repays the Bank's loan. The exercise price of this option is the amount of the loan, and the expiration dates are the dates that payments are due under the loan. Like any call option, the shareholders' position increases in value as the underlying assets increase in value. And like any call option, the shareholders' position has a limited downside. Shareholders have the right, but not the obligation, to the upside associated with JKL's assets. If those assets are worth less than the loan amount, the shareholders simply decline to exercise their call option, which becomes worthless (along with their initial investment). The Bank, which takes on the risk associated with JKL's assets as they decline in value, suffers the losses.

Make the Connection

Another way of thinking about the relationship between the shareholders and the bank is that the shareholders own the assets of JKL and have purchased a "put option" from the bank. This put option gives the shareholders the right to "sell" the corporate assets to the bank in the event of bankruptcy. In other words, the put option is an insurance policy that protects the shareholders from losing more than their initial investment—the bank bears any additional declines in value. This insurance protection is another way of thinking about limited liability, one of the central concepts of corporate law.

Thinking about the shareholders and Bank from the perspective of options theory helps illuminate the principle of leverage. A person who owns assets and buys a put option is limiting her downside, just as a person who borrows money to invest in a business is limiting her downside. Likewise, a person who buys a call option is magnifying her exposure to the underlying assets: she has the potential to increase the profit associated with an investment, with limited downside risk.

Leverage and the limited liability of shareholders are also related in an important way. As a company's leverage increases, so does the chance that the shareholders lose all of their initial investment. Because limited liability means that shareholders cannot lose more than their initial investment, higher leverage increases the risks of other corporate creditors, including holders of debt and preferred stock.

As you read the next case, which highlights the tension that arises from the capital structure, consider how corporate law allocates rights to the various participants in the corporation. The case highlights the tension between common shareholders and preferred shareholders in a startup corporation, where the preferred shareholders (venture capital firms) wanted to cut their losses and have the corporation dissolve and liquidate its assets, repaying them at least some of their investment. Meanwhile, the common shareholders didn't anticipate they would get much of anything in liquidation and instead wanted to take on new financing (here, debt financing) and hope that the corporation could recover and become profitable. The case presents a quite common scenario in VC-financed startups.

Equity-Linked Investors, L.P. v. Adams

705 A.2d 1040 (Del. Ch. 1997)

Allen, Chancellor.

This case involves a conflict between the financial interests of the holders of a convertible preferred stock with a liquidation preference, and the interests of the common stock. The conflict arises because the company, Genta Incorporated, is on the lip of insolvency and in liquidation it would probably be worth substantially less than the $30 million liquidation preference of the preferred stock. Thus, if the liquidation preference of the preferred were treated as a liability of Genta, the firm would certainly be insolvent now.

Yet Genta, a bio-pharmaceutical company that has never made a profit, does have several promising technologies in research and there is some ground to think that the value of products that might be developed from those technologies could be very great. Were that to occur, naturally, a large part of the "upside" gain would accrue to the benefit of the common stock, in equity the residual owners of the firm's net cash flows. (Of course, whatever the source of funds that would enable a nearly insolvent company to achieve that result would also negotiate for a share of those future gains—which is what this case is about). But since the current net worth of the company would be put at risk in such an effort—or more accurately would continue at risk—if Genta continues to try to develop these opportunities, any loss that may eventuate will in effect fall, not on the common stock, but on the preferred stock.

The Genta board sought actively to find a means to continue the firm in operation so that some chance to develop commercial products from its promising technologies could be achieved. It publicly announced its interest in finding new sources of capital. Contemporaneously, the holders of the preferred stock, relatively few institutional investors, were seeking a means to cut their losses, which meant, in effect, liquidating Genta and distributing most or all of its assets to the preferred. The contractual rights of the preferred stock did not, however, give the holders the necessary legal power to force this course of action on the corporation. Negotiations held between Genta's management and representatives of the preferred stock with respect to the rights of the preferred came to an unproductive and somewhat unpleasant end in January 1997.

Shortly thereafter, Genta announced that a third party source of additional capital had been located and that an agreement had been reached that would enable the corporation to pursue its business plan for a further period. The evidence indicates that at the time set for the closing of that transaction, Genta had available sufficient cash to cover its operations for only one additional week. A Petition in Bankruptcy had been prepared by counsel.

This suit by a lead holder of the preferred stock followed the announcement of the loan transaction. Plaintiff is Equity-Linked Investors, one of the institutional investors that holds Genta's Series A preferred stock. The suit challenges the transaction in which Genta borrowed on a secured basis some $3,000,000 from Paramount Capital Asset Management, Inc. in exchange for a note, warrants exercisable into half of Genta's outstanding stock, and other consideration.

From a realistic or finance perspective, the heart of the matter is the conflict between the interests of the preferred stock and the economic interests of the common stock.

While the facts indisputably entail the imposition by the board of (or continuation of) economic risks upon the preferred stock which the holders of the preferred did not want, and while this board action was taken for the benefit largely of the common stock, those facts do not constitute a breach of duty. While the board in these circumstances could have made a different business judgment, in my opinion, it violated no duty owed to the preferred in not doing so. The special protections offered to the preferred are contractual in nature. The corporation is, of course, required to respect those legal rights. But, aside from the insolvency point, generally it will be the duty of the board, where discretionary judgment is to be exercised, to prefer the interests of common stock—as the good faith judgment of the board sees them to be—to the interests created by the special rights, preferences, etc., of preferred stock, where there is a conflict. The facts of this case do not involve any violation by the board of any special right or privilege of the Series A preferred stock.

I conclude that the directors of Genta were independent with respect to the loan transaction, acted in good faith in arranging and committing the company to that transaction, and, in the circumstances faced by them and the company were well informed of the available alternatives to try to bring about the long-term business plan of the company. In my opinion, they breached no duty owed to the company or any of the holders of its equity securities. While certainly some corporations at some points ought to be liquidated, when that point occurs is a question of business judgment ordinarily and in this instance.

Points for Discussion

1. Resolving tensions.

Where are the tensions? If you could have anticipated the problems at Genta Incorporated, could you have set up a different structure to avoid the conflict that arose in the case? For example, what do you think would have happened if the preferred shareholders had sought to obtain greater governance rights to influence corporate action? Would the parties likely have agreed to different terms?

2. Fiduciary duties in startups.

Startup companies that take venture capital financing typically have a capital structure with common and preferred stock as we saw in *Equity-Linked Investors*. The composition of the board of directors is usually negotiated and includes designated seats for venture capital investors who hold preferred stock. Designated members of the board are known as "constituency directors."

In carrying out their fiduciary duties, can such constituency directors favor the interests of the preferred shareholders over those of the common shareholders? Delaware courts have answered no. In a notable decision, the Court of Chancery explained: "[T]he standard of conduct for directors requires that they strive in good faith and on an informed basis to maximize the value of the corporation for the benefit of its residual claimants, the ultimate beneficiaries of the firm's value, not for the benefit of its contractual claimants." *In re Trados, Inc. Sh. Litig.*, 73 A.3d 17, 40-41 (Del. Ch. 2013). The court criticized the directors who "did not understand their job was to maximize the value of the corporation for the benefit of the common shareholders." *Id.* at 62. How are constituency directors to navigate dual obligations they have to the company on whose board they sit and to the investment funds which they represent?

3. Do labels matter?

Options offer new ways of thinking about the economic positions of equity and debt. But they also present challenging questions. What if JKL had issued $1,500,000 of call options to Justin, Kathy, and Lorenzo, and issued $500,000 of equity to the Bank? JKL still would have raised the same amount of equity and capital, and the parties still would have the same priority in JKL's capital structure. But now the labels have changed. Should those labels matter? Should you think about the corporation any differently if its capital structure is composed of "options" instead of "equity" and "equity" instead of "debt"? Does *Equity-Linked Investors* depend on labels?

4. Corporate insolvency.

Note that Chancellor Allen intimates that "at the point of insolvency" the duties of the board may shift from maximizing the interests of the common stock to protecting the interests of the corporation's creditors. But what if the corporation has not yet reached the point of insolvency? Delaware courts have rejected an approach that would shift fiduciary duties when the corporation is merely in the "zone of insolvency." *See N. Am. Catholic Educ. Programming Found. v. Gheewalla*, 930 A.2d 92 (Del. 2007). Furthermore, insolvency is now best understood as giving the board a choice in discharging its fiduciary duty. The board can decide whether to maximize the interests of creditors or shareholders within the purview of its business judgment. *See Quadrant Structured Products Co. v. Vertin*, 102 A.3d 155 (Del. Ch. 2014).

C. Capital Structure Law and Policy

Next we turn to three legal and policy issues related to capital structure. First, we describe the legal capital regime, which is antiquated and often makes little sense, yet still affects the behavior of corporations and their lawyers. Second, we cover some related—and sometimes counterintuitive—rules governing distributions to shareholders. Finally, we address some law and policy questions surrounding two judicial decisions on the payment of dividends, which highlight the challenges boards face related to capital structure.

1. Legal Capital

Historically, state corporation laws purported to protect debtholders by regulating "legal capital," sometimes called "stated capital." You can think of legal capital as a "cushion" of capital designed to ensure there is enough money to protect the interests of debtholders. The law generally provided that the corporation could not "eat into" this cushion of legal capital by paying out too much money to shareholders.

a. The Basic Concept

If you imagine the right-hand side of the balance sheet, legal capital represents a portion of the equity that is off limits to shareholders. The idea is that this should give the debtholders some confidence that this cushion amount will be available to repay the money they are owed.

Legal capital is a counterintuitive concept. It is easy to calculate the amount of legal capital, but hard—if not impossible—to understand how and why legal capital might actually protect debtholders. Let's get the easy part out of the way first. The formula for calculating legal capital is simple. It is the product of the number of shares outstanding and the "par value" of those shares. For now, just think of par value as an arbitrary number set by the corporation. All you have to do to compute legal capital is multiply those two numbers.

Legal capital = outstanding shares x par value

The number of outstanding shares is straightforward: you simply add up the number of issued shares held by the corporation's shareholders. Although we will discuss par value in greater detail in a moment, for now all you need to know is that par value is set forth in the articles of incorporation. If the corporation has set a par value of $1 per share, and there are 100 shares outstanding, that corporation's legal capital is $100. That's it.

b. Some Context and History

The more difficult part is to understand how and why legal capital and par value came to be an important part of corporate law. This story begins with a vivid metaphor: stock watering. Imagine a rancher from the nineteenth century filling his livestock with water before selling them. This process of "aquatizing" the herd made them appear larger and heavier than they really were, which—the rancher hoped—would yield a higher price for them at market.

As the story goes, Daniel Drew, a cattle-driver-turned-financier, brought this practice to Wall Street—but with shares instead of cows. Corporations would issue shares for more than the corporation's assets were worth. These overvalued shares became known as "watered stock," after their livestock counterparts, referring to the fact that the value of the stock was artificially inflated.

As sharp promoters prowled the countryside, selling shares of dubious corporations for progressively higher prices, the concept of "par value" developed. Equity investors began to expect, or at least hope, that every subscriber would pay the same amount and receive the same value. Ideally, the stock they bought would have some benchmark value reflecting that equal amounts of cash had been contributed for each share and that none of the shares would have been watered. This benchmark amount came to be known "par value," or just "par" for short. Investors imagined that it reflected both the amount paid for the stock and its value.

Concepts of legal capital arose from the concept of par value. Judges and legislators were concerned about the potential inequities of watered stock. For example, suppose a promoter had contributed land worth $20,000 to a corporation, and drafted articles of incorporation that authorized 1,000 shares of common stock at $100 par value. Then, the promoter (after taking 500 shares for contributing the land, which he over-valued at $50,000) would try to sell the remaining shares for $100 each, even though their value had been watered. Such abuses led some to believe that strong legal capital rules would protect outside shareholders and creditors. Such rules would ensure that all investors (both insiders and outsiders) paid the same amount for their shares, and would assure lenders and other creditors that the amounts invested in the business by shareholders actually existed.

Over time, the received wisdom became that legal capital, based on par value, was a proxy for the value of a corporation's assets. Judges and legislators began to accept the notion that creditors were willing to lend on the basis of "par value," because that amount represented the contributions of shareholders, and was a rough approximation of the value of the firm's assets. That value, the story went, gave lenders confidence that they would be repaid.

In fact, this received wisdom was a ruse far from reality. Several scholars, led by Bayless Manning, demonstrated that the idealized world of legal capital was a fiction. Manning argued that par value was an arbitrary number that persisted only because corporate statutes required that it be used and stated in the corporate charter. Creditors didn't actually rely on par value for protection, and par value usually didn't reflect economic value. By the 1970s, few people believed that par value reflected actual value or that legal capital actually protected anyone.

Food for Thought

From an investor's perspective, holding debt is typically less risky than holding equity. Why is this? One reason is that the claims of debtholders (often called creditors) have priority over the claims of equity holders in bankruptcy. When a corporation goes under, debt is paid first, before equity. Another reason debt is less risky is that debtholders typically bargain for contractual protections in their agreements with the corporation. Thus, debtholders are protected by covenants, written provisions that limit the corporation's ability to put them at risk. In addition, some debts are secured by the corporation's assets. In practice, these factors matter more than legal capital in reducing the risk of debt.

Nevertheless, corporate statutes continued to require that corporations state a par value for their shares, and corporations were prohibited from distributing more than their legal capital to shareholders. Over time, rules were liberalized, and states permitted corporations to issue low-par or no-par stock. In the modern context, par value, when used, is understood as the minimum price at which the stock can be issued and it can be set at a tiny number such as a fraction of a cent. In 1984, the MBCA did away with the concept of par value. But other states, including Delaware, maintain traditional legal capital rules. Thus, legal capital statutes govern a majority of public corporations today, and remain as potential traps for the unwary lawyer.

Lawyers need to understand legal capital rules, old or new, for at least three reasons. First, one condition of many financing transactions is that the corporation's lawyer opine that all of the corporation's stock is "validly issued, fully paid and nonassessable." To render such an opinion, a lawyer must review all transactions in which the corporation has issued stock to see whether they were effectuated in compliance with the governing statutory provisions, including legal capital provisions.

Second, although many states once limited the consideration the corporation could accept for the issuance of shares—for example, not permitting future services or unsecured promissory notes as consideration—those limits have been supplanted. Today, the only requirement (in Delaware and the MBCA) is that the board determine the consideration is adequate, and this determination is conclusive. Thus, the corporate lawyer must also ensure that the board has properly determined that the consideration for the issued shares is adequate.

Third, most corporate statutes explicitly provide that directors can be held personally liable if they approve the issuance of shares or other distributions to shareholders in violation of applicable statutory provisions. Understandably, directors often seek the advice of counsel before making what might otherwise seem to be no more than a garden variety business judgment.

c. Delaware Example

To help you see legal capital in action, we set forth below some relevant portions of Delaware's corporate statute. These provisions contain the legal capital rules that should help you advise Justin, Kathy, and Lorenzo about being sure their new corporation complies with Delaware's legal capital regime.

DGCL § 151
Classes and Series of Stock

(a) Every corporation may issue 1 or more classes of stock or 1 or more series of stock within any class thereof, any or all of which classes may be of stock with par value or stock without par value.

DGCL § 152

Issuance of Stock

The consideration [for] the capital stock to be issued by a corporation shall be paid in such form and in such manner as the board of directors shall determine. The board of directors may authorize capital stock to be issued for consideration consisting of cash, any tangible or intangible property or any benefit to the corporation, or any combination thereof. In the absence of actual fraud in the transaction, the judgment of the directors as to the value of such consideration shall be conclusive.

DGCL § 153

Consideration for Stock

(a) Shares of stock with par value may be issued for such consideration, having a value not less than the par value thereof, as determined from time to time by the board of directors, or by the stockholders if the certificate of incorporation so provides.

(b) Shares of stock without par value may be issued for such consideration as is determined from time to time by the board of directors, or by the stockholders if the certificate of incorporation so provides.

Recall from our example that Justin, Kathy, and Lorenzo have agreed to pay a total of $500,000 for the common shares of JKL. Suppose that they also have agreed that JKL initially will issue 5,000 shares of common shares. Kathy will pay $200,000 in cash for 2,000 shares ($100 per share). Justin will pay $100,000 in cash and give JKL a note for $100,000 in exchange for another 2,000 shares. Lorenzo will pay $100,000 in cash for the remaining 1,000 shares. Lorenzo also will invest an additional $500,000 in 20-year subordinated notes.

Assume that JKL is incorporated in Delaware. Justin, Kathy, and Lorenzo have asked the following questions:

- Will the corporation need to set a par value for its common shares?

- What would be the consequence of setting the par value of JKL's shares at $100 per share—the price for which the shares will be sold—or at some lower value, such as $1 per share?

- Does the Delaware legal capital regime limit JKL's choice in setting par value?

- How would JKL reflect the transaction on its balance sheet if it sets the par value at $100 per share? At $1 per share?

- If JKL decides to issue no-par stock, is its board of directors required to take any further action? Would any such action be desirable?

- Can JKL accept Justin's personal note as partial payment for the 2,000 shares he will receive?

d. Reality of Legal Capital Rules

Although you might imagine some interesting interpretive questions under these statutory provisions, in practice they virtually never arise. Corporate lawyers avoid problems by setting par value far below the price at which the corporation plans to sell its shares. One choice is whether to use low-par or no-par stock. The choice usually depends on the manner in which the relevant jurisdiction calculates the tax or "franchise fee" payable on incorporation. That fee frequently is calculated on the basis of the aggregate authorized capital of the corporation, with no-par stock "deemed" to have some arbitrary par value for this purpose.

States that follow the MBCA have jettisoned the traditional approach to legal capital. They abandon the concept of par value as a rule (although they permit corporations to use par value in their articles). Instead, corporations may issue shares for whatever consideration the board authorizes, based on a variety of factors. The crucial determination for the board is based on business conditions, not the artificial notion of par value. According to the Official Comment to MBCA § 6.21, "there is no minimum price at which specific shares must be issued and therefore there can be no 'watered stock' liability for issuing shares below an arbitrarily fixed price." This reflects the drafters' belief that the old system of legal capital did not protect creditors' interests.

2. Distributions to Shareholders

A second capital structure issue—when a corporation may pay money to shareholders—is related to the concept of legal capital. The conflict between equity and debt is particularly acute when it comes to such distributions. If a corporation pays a dividend to shareholders or uses cash to repurchase shares, that money is no longer available to repay holders of debt.

The traditional approach to regulating distributions to shareholders looked back to the concept of legal capital. Recall that legal capital was a kind of "cushion" that corporations were required to maintain for the protection of creditors. The law provided that corporations could not make distributions that eroded this cushion.

However, corporations could make distributions out of "surplus" that left the cushion intact. Let's return to the right-hand side of the balance sheet. Recall that the equity portion of the balance sheet consists of both legal capital or stated capital (sometimes referred to as paid-in capital) as well as additional equity (sometimes referred to as retained earnings or earned surplus). Traditional statutes provided that corporations could make distributions out of this surplus as long as it did not impair their legal capital.

Today, states vary in their approach to distributions, but generally prohibit corporations from making distributions that will render them unable to pay debts or make them essentially insolvent. Some states, such as California, go further and also require that the corporation's balance sheet assets equal a specified percentage of its balance sheet liabilities. Any distribution that reduces assets below this level is not permitted.

The consequences of violating a state's unlawful distribution rules can be serious. When an unlawful distribution leads to creditor losses, the directors who authorized the distribution can be held personally liable. For example, in Delaware, directors remain liable for unlawful distributions even if they acted in good faith. (Later in this book, we will see that Delaware and other states permit corporations to "exculpate" directors from liability for breaches of the duty of care if they satisfied a good faith requirement; however, exculpation is not permitted for directors' liability for unlawful distributions.)

In reality, the strict rules and harsh penalties for unlawful distributions are rarely a serious concern, and restrictions on distributions based on the concept of legal capital are largely ineffective. For example, corporations can avoid the applicable statutes by amending their articles of incorporation to reduce the par value of its outstanding stock, thus expanding the available "surplus" and minimizing the "cushion" designed to protect creditors.

Courts also have permitted directors to justify distributions by "revaluing" their assets. In basic terms, the "revaluation" of the corporation's assets (on the left-hand side of the balance sheet) increases the available "surplus" for distributions (on the right-hand side of the balance sheet). For example, if a corporation held property carried at a cost of $1 million, but the board determined the fair market value of that property was $2 million, the board could justify a larger distribution to shareholders, without putting creditors at risk.

Take Note!

Not all dividends involve the distribution of cash to stockholders. Corporations occasionally declare "stock dividends" and distribute additional shares of stock to their shareholders. In economic terms, such dividends result in no meaningful change in the financial status of the corporation or its shareholders. They merely divide shareholders' ownership interests in the corporation into a greater number of pieces while leaving each shareholder's proportionate interest unchanged. Indeed, such "dividends" may be declared to produce the appearance that shareholders are receiving something of value with respect to their stock when the corporation is not in a position to pay a dividend in cash.

Since stock dividends do not result in the distribution of any real assets, there is no need to limit them for the protection of creditors. Indeed, because the par value (if any) of the shares distributed must be added to stated capital, a stock dividend can actually benefit creditors. The MBCA recognizes that a stock dividend involves the issuance of shares "without consideration" and thus stock dividends are excluded from the definition of "distribution."

The following case relies on similar reasoning to allow a Delaware corporation to repurchase a substantial portion of its outstanding stock—an action that has the same impact on creditors as the payment of a dividend. Under the DGCL and other corporate statutes, a repurchase of shares by the corporation is treated as a "distribution" subject to essentially the same restrictions applicable to payment of a dividend.

Klang v. Smith's Food & Drug Centers, Inc.

702 A.2d 150 (Del.1997)

Veasey, Chief Justice.

Smith's Food & Drug Centers, Inc. ("SFD") is a Delaware corporation that owns and operates a chain of supermarkets in the Southwestern United States. Slightly more than three years ago, Jeffrey P. Smith, SFD's Chief Executive Officer, began to entertain suitors with an interest in acquiring SFD.

On January 29, 1996, SFD entered into an agreement with The Yucaipa Companies ("Yucaipa"), a California partnership also active in the supermarket industry. Under the agreement, the following would take place:

(1) Smitty's Supermarkets, Inc. ("Smitty's"), a wholly-owned subsidiary of Yucaipa that operated a supermarket chain in Arizona, was to merge into Cactus Acquisition, Inc. ("Cactus"), a subsidiary of SFD, in exchange for which SFD would deliver to Yucaipa slightly over 3 million newly-issued shares of SFD common stock; and

(2) SFD was to undertake a recapitalization, in the course of which SFD would assume a sizable amount of new debt, retire old debt, and offer to repurchase up to fifty percent of its outstanding shares (other than those issued to Yucaipa) for $36 per share.

SFD hired the investment firm of Houlihan Lokey Howard & Zukin ("Houlihan") to examine the transactions and render a solvency opinion. Houlihan eventually issued a report to the SFD Board replete with assurances that the transactions would not endanger SFD's solvency, and would not impair SFD's capital in violation of 8 Del.C. § 160. On May 17, 1996, in reliance on the Houlihan opinion, SFD's Board determined that there existed sufficient surplus to consummate the transactions, and enacted a resolution proclaiming as much. On May 23, 1996, SFD's stockholders voted to approve the transactions, which closed on that day. The self-tender offer was over-subscribed, so SFD repurchased fully fifty percent of its shares at the offering price of $36 per share.

A corporation may not repurchase its shares if, in so doing, it would cause an impairment of capital under 8 Del.C. § 160. A repurchase impairs capital if the funds used in the repurchase exceed the amount of the corporation's "surplus," defined by 8 Del.C. § 154 to mean the excess of net assets over the par value of the corporation's issued stock.

During the 1990s and 2000s, many of the most important decisions on corporate law were authored by E. Norman Veasey, who served as Chief Justice of the Delaware Supreme Court from 1992 to 2004. Besides solidifying Delaware's reputation for "fair, reasonable and efficient" litigation (according to the U.S. Chamber of Commerce), Veasey has been a national leader on professionalism reform. He chaired a special ABA committee that proposed ethics rules for lawyers (Ethics 2000) that, among other things, permitted lawyers to violate attorney-client confidences to prevent financial crimes. Since leaving the bench, Veasey has been a practicing corporate lawyer in Delaware, a frequent lecturer and writer on corporate law, and an adjunct professor at two law schools.

Plaintiff asked the Court of Chancery to rescind the transactions in question as violative of Section 160.

Plaintiff relies on an April 25, 1996 proxy statement in which the SFD Board released a pro forma balance sheet showing that the merger and self-tender offer would result in a deficit to surplus on SFD's books of more than $100 million. Plaintiff asks us to adopt an interpretation of 8 Del.C. § 160 whereby balance-sheet net worth is controlling for purposes of determining compliance with the statute. In response, defendants do not dispute that SFD's books showed a negative net worth in the wake of its transactions with Yucaipa, but argue that corporations should have the presumptive right to revalue assets and liabilities to comply with Section 160.

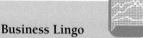

Business Lingo

"Pro forma" is from Latin meaning "as a matter of form." Pro forma financial statements are produced only as a matter of form, or—more precisely—in a way that does not conform to GAAP. Typically, a pro forma financial statement will look better than a financial statement that conforms to GAAP. Regulators have been concerned about companies using pro forma figures to mislead investors, and require that they be clearly disclosed. The rationale for preparing a pro forma balance sheet is that there are unusual or nonrecurring transactions that distort the GAAP picture of a company's financial position. But notice that even the pro forma balance sheet for SFD, which reflected the effects of the merger and self-tender offer, showed that SFD had a negative net worth. Do you think anyone believed that this result was accurate?

Plaintiff advances an erroneous interpretation of Section 160. We understand that the books of a corporation do not necessarily reflect the current values of its assets and liabilities. Among other factors, unrealized appreciation or depreciation can render book numbers inaccurate. It is unrealistic to hold that a corporation is bound by its balance sheets for purposes of determining compliance with Section 160. Accordingly, we adhere to the principles of *Morris v. Standard Gas & Electric Co.*, 63 A.2d 577 (Del. Ch. 1949), allowing a corporation to revalue properly its assets and liabilities to show a surplus and thus conform to the statute.

Plaintiff further contends that SFD's repurchase of shares violated Section 160 even without regard to the corporation's balance sheets. Plaintiff claims that the SFD Board was not entitled to rely on the solvency opinion of Houlihan, which showed that the transactions would not impair SFD's capital given a revaluation of corporate assets.

On May 17, 1996, Houlihan released its solvency opinion to the SFD Board, expressing its judgment that the merger and self-tender offer would not impair

SFD's capital. Houlihan reached this conclusion by comparing SFD's "Total Invested Capital" of $1.8 billion—a figure Houlihan arrived at by valuing SFD's assets under the "market multiple" approach—with SFD's long-term debt of $1.46 billion. This comparison yielded an approximation of SFD's "concluded equity value" equal to $346 million, a figure clearly in excess of the outstanding par value of SFD's stock. Thus, Houlihan concluded, the transactions would not violate 8 Del.C. § 160.

Plaintiff contends that Houlihan's analysis relied on inappropriate methods to mask a violation of Section 160. Noting that 8 Del.C. § 154 defines "net assets" as "the amount by which total assets exceeds total liabilities," plaintiff argues that Houlihan's analysis is erroneous as a matter of law because of its failure to calculate "total assets" and "total liabilities" as separate variables.

We believe that plaintiff reads too much into Section 154. The statute simply defines "net assets" in the course of defining "surplus." It does not mandate a "facts and figures balancing of assets and liabilities" to determine by what amount, if any, total assets exceeds total liabilities. The statute is merely definitional. It does not require any particular method of calculating surplus, but simply prescribes factors that any such calculation must include. Although courts may not determine compliance with Section 160 except by methods that fully take into account the assets and liabilities of the corporation, Houlihan's methods were not erroneous as a matter of law simply because they used Total Invested Capital and long-term debt as analytical categories rather than "total assets" and "total liabilities."

We are satisfied that the Houlihan opinion adequately took into account all of SFD's assets and liabilities. In cases alleging impairment of capital under Section 160, the trial court may defer to the board's measurement of surplus unless a plaintiff can show that the directors failed to fulfill their duty to evaluate the assets on the basis of acceptable data and by standards which they are entitled to believe reasonably reflect present values. In the absence of bad faith or fraud on the part of the board, courts will not substitute our concepts of wisdom for that of the directors. Therefore, we defer to the board's determination of surplus, and hold that SFD's self-tender offer did not violate 8 Del.C. § 160.

Points for Discussion

1. The balance sheet?

If the Court's description of the balance sheet is correct, what good is the balance sheet? Why did SFD's pro forma books show a negative net worth?

2. Valuation.

Looking back to the previous chapter, what valuation method does it appear that Houlihan used in rendering its solvency opinion? What is the "market multiple" approach that Houlihan used to calculate the value of SFD's assets? Do you agree that Houlihan had adequately taken into account SFD's assets and liabilities, even though the investment firm did not calculate "net assets" and "total liabilities"?

———————

3. Corporate Law on Dividend Policy

Decisions as to whether distributions lawfully can be made arise mostly when corporations are in financial difficulty. In solvent corporations, decisions relating to whether and in what amounts to make distributions involve a basic financial policy issue: should cash not needed for current operations be reinvested in the business or distributed to shareholders? Statutory constraints are a legal formality, not an impediment, in these circumstances and the decision usually turns on business strategy.

Decisions about payment of dividends generally are governed by the business judgment rule. Thus, generally, only if it can be shown that the decision was tainted by fraud, illegality, or a conflict of interest can the presumption be overcome that the directors acted on an informed basis, with good faith and in the best interests of the corporation. Of all business decisions, the decision whether to distribute profits to shareholders or to re-invest them in the business is one of the most important, and courts are loathe to intervene.

We include as an example below a New York case that involved a dividend decision by the board of a public corporation that ended up favoring "accounting fiction" over "tax reality." In 1972, American Express purchased almost two million shares of stock in Donaldson, Lufkin & Jenrette, Inc. (DLJ), for $29.9 million. By 1975, the stock had declined in value to approximately $4 million. American Express announced that it would distribute the DLJ stock as a dividend. Two shareholders sued to enjoin the distribution. They argued that American Express would be better off selling the DLJ stock.

The shareholders pointed out that a distribution of the DLJ stock would not have any impact on American Express's liability for income taxes. On the other hand, if American Express sold the DLJ stock, it could reduce otherwise taxable capital gains by an amount equal to its roughly $26 million loss on the DLJ stock and thus save approximately $8 million in taxes. In effect, the shareholders' argument was that rather than distribute $4 million in DLJ stock as a dividend, American Express could sell the stock, save $8 million in taxes, and then (if it wished) distribute $12 million (the sale price plus the tax savings) as a dividend. This was the "tax reality."

The American Express board of directors considered the shareholders' argument at a meeting on October 17, 1975, and decided to proceed with the dividend. The board had previously been advised by its accountants that if the DLJ stock was distributed as a dividend, rather than sold, American Express would not have to reduce its reported income for 1975 to reflect its loss on its investment. Rather, it could bypass its income statement and simply reduce retained earnings by $29.9 million—the book value of the stock it would be distributing. This was the "accounting fiction."

Kamin v. American Express Co.

383 N.Y.S.2d 807 (Sup. Ct. 1976)

EDWARD J. GREENFIELD, JUSTICE.

Examination of the complaint reveals that there is no claim of fraud or self-dealing, and no contention that there was any bad faith or oppressive conduct. The law is quite clear as to what is necessary to ground a claim for actionable wrongdoing.

More specifically, the question of whether or not a dividend is to be declared or a distribution of some kind should be made is exclusively a matter of business judgment for the Board of Directors.

Courts will not interfere with such discretion unless it be first made to appear that the directors have acted or are about to act in bad faith and for a dishonest purpose. It is for the directors to say, acting in good faith of course, when and to what extent dividends shall be declared.

Food for Thought

Recall that the business judgment rule is a presumption protecting board decision making. The BJR is analogous to rational basis review for legislative actions: the courts give deference with the understanding they lack the expertise to sustain a more intense level of review. In some BJR cases, the courts focus on whether the decision was rational from a business perspective. In other cases, the courts focus on whether the board engaged in a satisfactory process.

In *Kamin*, the court determined that the board's decision had a business justification and was the product of a satisfactory process. It applied the business judgment rule and dismissed the complaint. Does that mean that the court is condoning the board's decision to avoid showing a loss on the DLJ stock in its financial statements?

Thus, a complaint must be dismissed if all that is presented is a decision to pay dividends rather than pursuing some other course of conduct. The directors' room rather than the courtroom is the appropriate forum for thrashing out purely business questions which will have an impact on profits, market prices, competitive situations, or tax advantages.

The affidavits of the defendants and the exhibits annexed thereto demonstrate that the objections raised by the plaintiffs to the proposed dividend action were carefully considered and unanimously rejected by the Board at a special meeting called precisely for that purpose at the plaintiffs' request. The minutes of the special meeting indicate that the defendants were fully aware that a sale rather than a distribution of the DLJ shares might result in the realization of a substantial income tax saving. Nevertheless, they concluded that there were countervailing considerations primarily with respect to the adverse effect such a sale, realizing a loss of $25 million, would have on the net income figures in the American Express financial statement. Such a reduction of net income would have a serious effect on the market value of the publicly traded American Express stock. This was not a situation in which the defendant directors totally overlooked facts called to their attention. They gave them consideration, and attempted to view the total picture in arriving at their decision.

The only hint of self-interest which is raised, not in the complaint but in the papers on the motion, is that four of the twenty directors were officers and employees of American Express and members of its Executive Incentive Compensation Plan. Hence, it is suggested, by virtue of the action taken earnings may have been overstated and their compensation affected thereby. Such a claim is highly speculative and standing alone can hardly be regarded as sufficient to support an inference of self-dealing. There is no claim or showing that the four company directors dominated and controlled the sixteen outside members of the Board.

Points for Discussion

1. Accounting vs. markets.

Do you think the American Express board was correct in its belief that stock market investors are more interested in the accounting treatment of a dividend payment, here American Express's divestiture of its interest in DLJ, than in that transaction's actual financial impact on American Express? Even if the board's assessment was correct, should the court have allowed the board to seek to increase the market price of American Express stock by rejecting a transaction (selling the DLJ stock and recording the loss) that would have produced a real economic benefit worth $8 million to the company? Would it matter if the compensation of the inside directors was based on accounting performance rather than the corporation's share price?

2. Public vs. close corporations and dividend policy.

Judges are reluctant to interfere with dividend policies in public corporations. By contrast, as we will see in Module VIII when we cover close corporations, courts in many states are willing to rigorously review these decisions in close corporations.

Why is this? Basically, in the public corporation a poorly-conceived dividend policy will be subject to market discipline, including even a takeover. But in the close corporation there is no market for corporate shares and thus the discipline for misguided dividend policies has come from the courts. Under the "oppression" doctrine, covered in Chapter 26, courts have protected the reasonable expectations of minority shareholders, including to be paid dividends or to have their shares bought out by the majority.

For example, in *Bonavita v. Corbo*, 692 A.2d 119 (N.J. Ch. Div. 1996), a longtime family business came to be held 50-50 by the sister of one of the co-founders and her nephew, who ran the business. The court found that the sister had "reasonable expectations" of having money for retirement from the business, and ordered the corporation to repurchase her shares - in effect, a lump-sum payment of her dividend rights.

Test Your Knowledge

To assess your understanding of the Chapter 11 and 12 material in this module, click here to take a quiz.

MODULE V – CORPORATE EXTERNALITIES

CHAPTER 13

Piercing the Corporate Veil

This module introduces you to "corporate externalities"—that is, the shifting of costs created by the corporation to persons outside the corporation. In this chapter, we describe limited liability and when limited liability is disregarded to make corporate insiders personally liable to corporate outsiders. The next chapter describes when a corporation and its insiders can become criminally liable for corporate actions. The last chapter in this module looks at how environmental law imposes liability on the corporation and its actors.

Recall that the corporate capital structure is split between shareholders and creditors. This split creates tension, but it also illuminates one major attraction of the corporate form for shareholders: limited liability. In general, a shareholder's liability is limited to the amount she invests in the business. After that money is gone, creditors bear any additional losses. With limited liability, the corporation is like a sealed box, a no-recourse structure in which creditors can look only to corporate assets for payment of their claims (unless shareholders personally guarantee the corporate obligation).

But sometimes courts disregard the corporate entity and allow creditors to recover directly from shareholders—that is, they "pierce the corporate veil" (or PCV). Many states have established the PCV doctrine through case law, rather than statute. Piercing the corporate veil can be thought of as an exception to the general rule of limited liability and it arises when the corporation lacks sufficient assets to satisfy a plaintiff's claim, and the plaintiff seeks to hold shareholders personally liable. Plaintiffs could be tort victims or contract claimants against the corporation. And the concept of piercing can apply within corporate groups, such as when a plaintiff seeks to hold a parent corporation liable for the debt of a subsidiary. PCV is the most litigated issue in corporate law, and the one most often confronted by attorneys who specialize in areas outside corporate law.

Let us warn you in advance: if you are like most other law students—or lawyers—you will find piercing cases confusing. The courts use metaphors, templates, and multi-pronged tests to disguise doctrinal uncertainty. The case law is sprinkled with colorful terms such as "alias," "alter ego," "corporate double," "dummy," and "instrumentality."

We will try to help you understand piercing, first by providing a "scorecard" of the key factors that courts often discuss in deciding whether to pierce the corporate veil, and second by examining the policy issues related to limited liability. But this assistance will be brief and fleeting, and will last just a few pages. It is no substitute for carefully reading cases in the area, to get a better sense of relevant arguments and issues. Accordingly, the bulk of this chapter is a set of representative cases. The devil will be in the details, and lawyers who confront piercing—either in advising corporate clients about how to avoid it, or in advising litigants after the fact—spend most of their time dealing with the unique facts of particular cases.

A. Piercing Scorecard

Piercing the corporate veil is an equitable doctrine created by the courts to "prevent fraud and achieve justice." There is no one PCV test or rule that governs the cases. States generally have adopted some version of a test that looks at whether (1) there is a "unity of interest and ownership" between the corporation and the shareholder being sued (sometimes phrased as an "alter ego relationship" or one of "domination and control"), and (2) whether there was deceit or wrongdoing, or some element of unfairness or wrong that goes beyond the mere fact of the creditor's inability to collect. But courts have stated the legal test in many different ways and the cases often seem to turn on whether the court sees the defendants as "good" or "bad." The fact-dependent question is often: did the defendants abuse the "privilege" of corporate limited liability?

Although piercing factors vary depending on the facts, as a general matter courts are more likely to pierce in the following situations—a sort of scorecard, or checklist, for assessing the likelihood of piercing in a particular case.

Corporation is closely-held. Nearly all piercing cases involve closely-held corporations. Close corporation shareholder-managers typically have more to gain personally by taking risks that shift losses to creditors than do the managers of public companies. An individual is more likely to be able to dominate and control a close corporation than a public corporation.

The defendant actively participated in the business. Courts are more likely to disregard limited liability when a shareholder actively participated in the business. The reason is simple: passive shareholders are less likely to have acted to disadvantage creditors. As with other factors such as deception, much of piercing doctrine is about fairness.

Insiders failed to observe corporate formalities. Judges perceive a sense of injustice in permitting someone who has not respected the corporate form (such as by failing to hold regular corporate meetings, obtain board authorizations, or keep proper minutes) to seek insulation through the corporate form. The lack of corporate formalities also may indicate that the insiders were indifferent about the corporation's obligations to outsiders.

Insiders commingled business and personal assets. Commingling is another sign that insiders did not respect the corporate form and that creditors might have been confused. Judges want insiders to respect the separateness of the corporation and to make sure the corporation takes its obligations seriously.

Insiders did not adequately capitalize the business. Courts are reluctant to permit insiders to "externalize" the risks of the business and place them on outsiders, particularly in tort cases. (Externalization happens when business losses are borne by outsiders, such as contract creditors or tort victims, rather than insiders protected by limited liability.) Courts will look to whether the business was adequately capitalized when formed and whether it then continued to maintain adequate capital or carried insurance to cover the risks of its activities.

Insiders deceived creditors. Deception is an important factor in piercing cases, in part because courts perceive inequities in protecting individuals who engage in deceptive conduct from personal liability, but also because—at least in contract cases—deception prevents injured parties from protecting themselves in advance.

> To give you a sense of history, in a landmark study on PCV, Professor Robert Thompson looked at all the reported piercing cases on Westlaw through 1985. *Piercing the Corporate Veil: An Empirical Study*, 76 CORNELL L. REV. 1036 (1991). The study found that piercing rarely happens in public companies (in fact, it was attempted in only 9 of the some 1600 cases in the study).
>
> The Thompson study also found that the most predictive factor in PCV was misrepresentation by corporate insiders. When a court found such misrepresentation, piercing happened 91.6% of the time.
>
> Other PCV factors were also predictive of when courts pierce. When courts found the commingling of personal and business assets, piercing happened 85.3% of the time. For a finding of inadequate capitalization, the piercing rate was 73.3%. And for a finding of failure to observe corporate formalities, the piercing rate was 66.9%.
>
> In addition, piercing happened more frequently in one-person corporations (49.6%) than in those with more than three shareholders (35.0%). And piercing also happened more often against individual shareholders (43.1%) than against corporate shareholders (37.2%).

* * *

The above checklist is not foolproof, and it does not always capture the important facts in particular cases. But it is a good starting point in your analysis of why and when a court might pierce the corporate veil.

B. Piercing Policy

To understand piercing cases, it helps to understand a bit about the policy implications of piercing. Limited liability can result in creditors, rather than shareholders, bearing much of the costs of business failure. Piercing shifts those costs back to shareholders. So a preliminary question is this: why do states allow shareholders to limit their liability? Why give shareholders this "gift"?

1. Rationales for Limited Liability

The concept of limited liability spread in the nineteenth century to encourage capital formation from many small investors. Early incorporation statutes authorized manufacturing firms to incorporate without the risks of operating in the partnership form—thus permitting the firm to be centrally managed and relieving investors of any responsibility beyond their initial subscription or a specified limit. This policy allowed people to feel comfortable investing in companies without putting their personal assets at risk and it enabled companies to pool large amounts of investment for large-scale ventures. For example, New York's legislative policy in the nineteenth century to promote incorporation through limited liability fostered the growth of an urban society whose members could participate broadly in business firms organized as corporations.

Limited liability continues to promote these social and democratic goals. In recent years state legislatures have authorized new forms of limited liability business organizations, such as LLCs and LLPs—forms widely used by small-scale entrepreneurs who often invest much of their personal wealth in their businesses.

Limited liability also promotes the organization of large, publicly-held corporations. It helps reduce costs that shareholders might otherwise feel obligated to bear, such as closely monitoring managers or even other shareholders. Further, limited liability allows shareholders to diversify their investments without exposing their personal assets to additional liability

Practice Pointer

Limited liability is a default rule. Parties can (and frequently do) contract around the rule and create personal liability for corporate insiders. For example, banks lending to small close corporations will often demand personal guarantees from the owners of the business.

with each investment. In turn, diversified shareholders are willing to let managers take on valuable, but risky projects they might otherwise avoid. And, to the extent limited liability makes shares fungible, it creates the potential for additional monitoring by shareholders who can buy large blocks of shares and pressure directors and officers.

Many of the economic arguments in favor of limited liability do not apply to close corporations, where ownership and management are often not separated. Monitoring costs don't matter if the owners and managers are the same people. The effects on share trading don't matter if shares don't trade. These are some reasons why piercing happens only in close corporations.

A separate set of issues arises when dealing with corporate groups (companies that operate through subsidiary corporations), our third category of piercing cases in the next section. The central question here is whether disregarding separate incorporation should be easier in a holding company structure. That is, should corporate (compared to individual) shareholders have more responsibility for the debts of their subsidiaries?

As originally conceived, the corporation was an "enterprise" to carry on the operations of a given business. Early corporate statutes prohibited one corporation from holding the stock of another. But these prohibitions disappeared and many corporations began to operate through subsidiaries that were more or less indistinguishable parts of a larger enterprise. At first, courts responded by employing "enterprise liability" theories to hold parent corporations responsible for the liabilities of their subsidiaries. But over time, the courts accepted the separate legal personality, so long as the subsidiary was funded with assets sufficient to give it a reasonable chance of business success.

More recently, courts have tended to apply the same rule of limited liability to individual and corporate shareholders. Does it make sense that corporate investment should be encouraged as much as individual investment? Although it might seem unjust to hold individual public shareholders liable for the actions of corporate managers, this argument seems less persuasive when applied to a parent corporation that controls a subsidiary. Do any of the advantages of limited liability—such as encouraging investment—apply when one corporation capitalizes another corporation? Some argue that reinvigorating the doctrine of enterprise liability for corporate groups would make it difficult for corporations to externalize risk by using thinly-capitalized subsidiaries.

On the other hand, a rule of enterprise liability would discourage some worthwhile investments. Why penalize a corporation that has integrated some of its economic functions into a corporate group? If Widget, Inc. purchased Raw Materials, Inc. and held it as a subsidiary, should a court be more likely to pierce in a suit against the integrated corporate group than when the two companies remained separate? One key issue in such cases is whether a person dealing with separate companies is led to believe the companies are operating as a group. In other words, deceit can be an especially important factor in corporate group cases.

2. Alternative Exceptions to Limited Liability

You should keep in mind that there are alternative exceptions to limited liability outside of the piercing context. Examples include the doctrines of fraudulent conveyance and equitable subordination.

Under the doctrines of fraudulent conveyance and equitable subordination, courts can set aside transactions that defraud creditors. The Uniform Fraudulent Conveyance Act (UFCA), codified in the U.S. Bankruptcy Code and many state statutes, protects creditors from two types of transfers: (1) transfers with the intent to defraud creditors, and (2) transfers that constructively defraud creditors. Showing intentional fraud requires that the court find an actual intent by the debtor to "hinder, delay or defraud." But constructive fraud can be shown if the debtor makes a transfer while insolvent or near insolvency—if the transfer lacks fair consideration.

In the bankruptcy context, the UFCA is used instead of veil piercing to set aside transfers by the corporation to its shareholders when the transfer undermines creditor claims. The courts set aside the transfer and apply it against the corporation's debts to its creditors. For example, the UFCA has been used to set aside "excess" salary payments from a corporation to its sole shareholder that far exceeded the value of the shareholder's services to the corporation.

The UFCA helps explain why courts consider corporate formalities and the intermingling of corporate and personal assets in veil piercing cases. The disregard of corporate formalities often provides indirect evidence of fraudulent conveyances; and the intermingling of corporate and personal assets often provides direct evidence of fraudulent conveyances.

But the UFCA has limitations—compared to veil piercing. First, the UFCA requires a specific finding of a fraudulent transaction, which may be difficult to establish, particularly when there is a lack of corporate formalities. Second, unlike veil piercing, which imposes unlimited liability on shareholders, the UFCA only allows a court to set aside specific fraudulent conveyances, which may not satisfy a creditor's entire claim.

In addition, the doctrine of equitable subordination is another method to protect creditors' interests. This doctrine, applicable only in federal bankruptcy proceedings, subordinates—or pushes to the back of the line—some creditors' claims (typically those of corporate insiders) to reach an equitable result. Subordination thus allows outside creditors to receive payment before insiders. The result is significant since priority in bankruptcy often determines which creditors will get paid.

Before courts invoke the equitable subordination doctrine, there must be a showing of fraudulent conduct, mismanagement, or inadequate capitalization. As a baseline, courts generally look to whether a claimant engaged in some form of "inequitable conduct" and whether the misconduct resulted in injury to the debtor's creditor or conferred an unfair advantage on the claimant.

Equitable subordination also has limitations—compared to veil piercing and fraudulent conveyance principles. Equitable subordination does not increase the overall size of the pie available to creditors. Nor does it hold shareholders personally liable for corporate obligations. It only alters the normal priority of insider claims against the available corporate resources.

However, these alternatives should give you a sense that piercing is not the only way for shareholders to be held liable for corporate actions. Still, piercing is an important part of corporate law, and given that it is litigated so frequently, it is worth studying it with some care. As you read through the following six cases, think about the PCV scorecard and policy arguments. Which factors were key to the decision to pierce, and which were not? And why?

C. Piercing in Tort Cases

Now we turn to an assortment of cases. First are tort cases, in which a plaintiff seeks to pierce the veil of the corporate tortfeasor and get to a shareholder who has sufficient assets. Second are contract cases, in which a plaintiff seeks to pierce the veil of the corporate counterparty and recover from a shareholder who is not a party to the agreement. Third are corporate group cases in which a plaintiff seeks to pierce the corporate veil of a wrongdoing subsidiary to recover from its parent, or to recover from some other entity or entities related to the wrongdoer. Courts sometimes apply the same test in all of these contexts and do not draw distinctions, but commentators have long debated whether they raise different policy concerns.

Tort creditors are involuntary. That means they have limited opportunities to protect themselves from a corporation that causes them a loss. A pedestrian does not have an opportunity to bargain with the corporation that owns a delivery van before the van hits them.

As a result, one might expect that courts would be much more willing to pierce the corporate veil in the tort context than in the contract context. Yet some studies suggest that the opposite is true: that courts are equally likely or even less likely to pierce in tort actions. Can you think of any reasons why courts might be reluctant to pierce in tort actions? Which factors are likely to be most important to piercing cases brought by tort victims? The following two cases are examples of numerous similar cases. Which factors were dispositive in these cases?

Walkovszky v. Carlton

223 N.E.2d 6 (N.Y. 1966)

Fuld, Judge.

This case involves what appears to be a rather common practice in the taxicab industry of vesting the ownership of a taxi fleet in many corporations, each owning only one or two cabs.

The complaint alleges that the plaintiff was severely injured four years ago in New York City when he was run down by a taxicab owned by the defendant Seon Cab Corporation and negligently operated at the time by the defendant Marchese. The individual defendant, Carlton, is claimed to be a stockholder of 10 corporations, including Seon, each of which has but two cabs registered in its name, and it is implied that only the minimum automobile liability insurance required by law (in the amount of $10,000) is carried on any one cab. Although seemingly independent of one another, these corporations (and the corporate owner of the garage) are alleged to be "operated as a single entity, unit and enterprise" with regard to financing, supplies, repairs, employees and garaging, and all are named as defendants. The plaintiff asserts that he is also entitled to hold their stockholders personally liable for the damages sought because the multiple corporate structure constitutes an unlawful attempt "to defraud members of the general public" who might be injured by the cabs.

The defendant Carlton has moved to dismiss the complaint on the ground that as to him it "fails to state a cause of action." The Appellate Division, by a divided vote, held that a valid cause of action was sufficiently stated.

The law permits the incorporation of a business for the very purpose of enabling its proprietors to escape personal liability but, manifestly, the privilege is not without its limits. Broadly speaking, the courts will disregard the corporate form, or, to use accepted terminology, "pierce the corporate veil," whenever necessary "to prevent fraud or to achieve equity." Such liability, moreover, extends not only to the corporation's commercial dealings but to its negligent acts as well.

In the case before us, the plaintiff has explicitly alleged that none of the corporations "had a separate existence of their own." However, it is one thing to assert that a corporation is a fragment of a larger corporate combine which actually conducts the business. It is quite another to claim that the corporation is a "dummy" for its individual stockholders who are in reality carrying on the business in their personal capacities for purely personal rather than corporate ends. Either circumstance would justify treating the corporation as an agent and piercing the corporate veil to reach the principal but a different result would follow in each case. In the first, only a larger corporate entity would be held financially responsible while, in the other, the stockholder would be personally liable.

The individual defendant is charged with having "organized, managed, dominated and controlled" a fragmented corporate entity but there are no allegations that he was conducting business in his individual capacity. The fact that the fleet ownership has been deliberately split up among many corporations does not ease the plaintiff's burden in that respect. The corporate form may not be disregarded merely because the assets of the corporation, together with the mandatory insurance coverage of the vehicle which struck the plaintiff, are insufficient to assure him the recovery sought. If Carlton were to be held individually liable on those facts alone, the decision would apply equally to the thousands of cabs which are owned by their individual drivers who conduct their businesses through corporations organized pursuant to the Business Corporation Law, and carry the minimum insurance required by the Vehicle and Traffic Law. These taxi owner-operators are entitled to form such corporations, and we agree with the court at Special Term that, if the insurance coverage required by statute "is inadequate for the protection of the public, the remedy lies not with the courts but with the Legislature." The responsibility for imposing conditions on the privilege of incorporation has been committed by the Constitution to the Legislature and it may not be fairly implied, from any statute, that the Legislature intended, without the slightest discussion or debate, to require of taxi corporations that they carry automobile liability insurance over and above that mandated by the Vehicle and Traffic Law.

This is not to say that it is impossible for the plaintiff to state a valid cause of action against the defendant Carlton. However, the simple fact is that the plaintiff has just not done so here. While the complaint alleges that the separate corporations were undercapitalized and that their assets have been intermingled, it is barren of any "sufficiently particular(ized) statements" that the defendant Carlton and his associates are actually doing business in their individual capacities, shuttling their personal funds in and out of the corporations "without regard to formality and to suit their immediate convenience." Such a "perversion of the privilege to do business in a corporate form" would justify imposing personal liability on the individual stockholders. Nothing of the sort has in fact been charged, and it cannot reasonably or logically be inferred from the happenstance that the business of Seon Cab Corporation may actually be carried on by a larger corporate entity composed of many corporations which, under general principles of agency, would be liable to each other's creditors in contract and in tort.[3]

In sum, then, the complaint falls short of adequately stating a cause of action against the defendant Carlton in his individual capacity.

The order of the Appellate Division should be reversed, with leave to serve an amended complaint.

KEATING, JUDGE dissenting:

The defendant Carlton, the shareholder here sought to be held for the negligence of the driver of a taxicab, was a principal shareholder and organizer of the defendant corporation which owned the taxicab. The sole assets of these taxicab corporations are the vehicles themselves and they are apparently subject to mortgages.

> **FYI**
>
> The medallions were considered judgment proof when the case was decided. Since the case, NYC taxicab medallions are no longer considered judgment proof. In fact, when a medallion is sold, the new owner must set up an escrow account to ensure compensation of tort victims by the previous owner. In many locations around the world, ride-hailing companies have disrupted the taxi industry and the value of medallions.

From their inception these corporations were intentionally undercapitalized for the purpose of avoiding responsibility for acts which were bound to arise as a result of the operation of a large taxi fleet having cars out on the street 24 hours a day and engaged in public transportation. And during the course of the corporations' existence all income was continually drained out of the corporations for the same purpose.

The issue presented by this action is whether the policy of this State, which affords those desiring to engage in a business enterprise the privilege of limited liability through the use of the corporate device, is so strong that it will permit that privilege to continue no matter how much it is abused, no matter how irre-

---

[3] In his affidavit in opposition to the motion to dismiss, the plaintiff's counsel claimed that corporate assets had been "milked out" of, and "siphoned off" from the enterprise. Quite apart from the fact that these allegations are far too vague and conclusory, the charge is premature. If the plaintiff succeeds in his action and becomes a judgment creditor of the corporation, he may then sue and attempt to hold the individual defendants accountable for any dividends and property that were wrongfully distributed.

sponsibly the corporation is operated, no matter what the cost to the public. I do not believe that it is.

Under the circumstances of this case the shareholders should all be held individually liable to this plaintiff for the injuries he suffered. At least, the matter should not be disposed of on the pleadings by a dismissal of the complaint. "If a corporation is organized and carries on business without substantial capital in such a way that the corporation is likely to have no sufficient assets available to meet its debts, it is inequitable that shareholders should set up such a flimsy organization to escape personal liability. The attempt to do corporate business without providing any sufficient basis of financial responsibility to creditors is an abuse of the separate entity and will be ineffectual to exempt the shareholders from corporate debts." (Ballantine, Corporations (rev.ed., 1946), § 129, pp. 302–303.)

The defendant Carlton claims that, because the minimum amount of insurance required by the statute was obtained, the corporate veil cannot and should not be pierced despite the fact that the assets of the corporation which owned the cab were "trifling compared with the business to be done and the risks of loss" which were certain to be encountered. I do not agree.

The Legislature in requiring minimum liability insurance of $10,000, no doubt, intended to provide at least some small fund for recovery against those individuals and corporations who just did not have and were not able to raise or accumulate assets sufficient to satisfy the claims of those who were injured as a result of their negligence. It certainly could not have intended to shield those individuals who organized corporations, with the specific intent of avoiding responsibility to the public, where the operation of the corporate enterprise yielded profits sufficient to purchase additional insurance. Moreover, it is reasonable to assume that the Legislature believed that those individuals and corporations having substantial assets would take out insurance far in excess of the minimum in order to protect those assets from depletion. Given the costs of hospital care and treatment and the nature of injuries sustained in auto collisions, it would be unreasonable to assume that the Legislature believed that the minimum provided in the statute would in and of itself be sufficient to recompense "innocent victims of motor vehicle accidents for the injury and financial loss inflicted upon them."

The defendant contends that the court will be encroaching upon the legislative domain by ignoring the corporate veil and holding the individual shareholder [liable]. This argument was answered by Mr. Justice Douglas: "In the field in which we are presently concerned, judicial power hardly oversteps the bounds when it refuses to lend its aid to a promotional project which would circumvent or undermine a legislative policy. To deny it that function would be to make it impotent in situations where historically it has made some of its most notable contributions. If the judicial power is helpless to protect a legislative program from schemes for easy avoidance, then indeed it has become a handy implement of high finance."

The defendant contends that a decision holding him personally liable would discourage people from engaging in corporate enterprise. What I would merely hold is that a participating shareholder of a corporation vested with a public interest, organized with capital insufficient to meet liabilities which are certain to arise in the ordinary course of the corporation's business, may be held personally responsible for such liabilities. Where corporate income is not sufficient to cover the cost of insurance premiums above the statutory minimum or where initially adequate finances dwindle under the pressure of competition, bad times or extraordinary and unexpected liability, obviously the shareholder will not be held liable. The only types of corporate enterprises that will be discouraged as a result of a decision allowing the individual shareholder to be sued will be those such as the one in question, designed solely to abuse the corporate privilege at the expense of the public interest.

For these reasons I would vote to affirm the order of the Appellate Division.

———————

Radaszewski v. Telecom Corp.

981 F.2d 305 (8th Cir. 1992)

RICHARD S. ARNOLD, CHIEF JUDGE.

This is an action for personal injuries filed on behalf of Konrad Radaszewski, who was seriously injured in an automobile accident on August 21, 1984. Radaszewski, who was on a motorcycle, was struck by a truck driven by an employee of Contrux, Inc. The question presented on this appeal is whether the District Court had jurisdiction over the person of Telecom Corporation, which is the corporate parent of Contrux. This question depends, in turn, on whether, under Missouri law, Radaszewski can "pierce the corporate veil," and hold Telecom liable for the conduct of its subsidiary, Contrux, and Contrux's driver.

I.

In general, someone injured by the conduct of a corporation or one of its employees can look only to the assets of the employee or of the employer corporation for recovery. The shareholders of the corporation, including, if there is one, its parent corporation, are not responsible. To the general rule, though, there are exceptions. There are instances in which an injured person may "pierce the corporate veil," that is, reach the assets of one or more of the shareholders of the corporation whose conduct has created liability.

Under Missouri law, a plaintiff in this position needs to show three things.

(1) Control, not mere majority or complete stock control, but complete domination, not only of finances, but of policy and business practice in respect to the transaction attacked so that the corporate entity as to this transaction had at the time no separate mind, will or existence of its own; and

(2) Such control must have been used by the defendant to commit fraud or wrong, to perpetrate the violation of a statutory or other positive legal duty, or dishonest and unjust act in contravention of plaintiff's legal rights; and

(3) The aforesaid control and breach of duty must proximately cause the injury or unjust loss complained of.

Collet v. American National Stores, Inc., 708 S.W.2d 273, 284 (Mo.App.1986).

Because Telecom, as such, has had no contact with Missouri, whether Missouri courts have jurisdiction over Telecom depends on whether the corporate veil of Contrux can be pierced. The parties have argued the case as one of jurisdiction, and so will we, but in fact the underlying issue is whether Telecom can be held liable for what Contrux did.

II.

To satisfy the second element of the *Collet* formulation, plaintiff cites no direct evidence of improper motivation or violation of law on Telecom's part. He argues, instead, that Contrux was undercapitalized.

Undercapitalizing a subsidiary, which we take to mean creating it and putting it in business without a reasonably sufficient supply of money, has become a sort of proxy under Missouri law for the second *Collet* element. The reason, we think, is not because undercapitalization, in and of itself, is unlawful (though it may be for some purposes), but rather because the creation of an undercapitalized subsidiary justifies an inference that the parent is either deliberately or recklessly creating a business that will not be able to pay its bills or satisfy judgments against it.

Here, the District Court held, and we assume, that Contrux was undercapitalized in the accounting sense. Most of the money contributed to its operation by

Telecom was in the form of loans, not equity, and, when Contrux first went into business, Telecom did not pay for all of the stock that was issued to it. Telecom says, however, that this doesn't matter, because Contrux had $11,000,000 worth of liability insurance available to pay judgments like the one that Radaszewski hopes to obtain. No one can say, therefore, the argument runs, that Telecom was improperly motivated in setting up Contrux, in the sense of either knowingly or recklessly establishing it without the ability to pay tort judgments.

In fact, Contrux did have $1,000,000 in basic liability coverage, plus $10,000,000 in excess coverage. This coverage was bound on March 1, 1984, about five and one-half months before the accident involving Radaszewski. Unhappily, Contrux's insurance carrier became insolvent two years after the accident and is now in receivership. But this insurance, Telecom points out, was sufficient to satisfy federal financial-responsibility requirements applicable to interstate carriers such as Contrux.

The District Court rejected this argument. Undercapitalization is undercapitalization, it reasoned, regardless of insurance. The Court said:

> The federal regulation does not speak to what constitutes a properly capitalized motor carrier company. Rather, the regulation speaks to what constitutes an appropriate level of *financial responsibility*.

This distinction escapes us. The whole purpose of asking whether a subsidiary is "properly capitalized," is precisely to determine its "financial responsibility." If the subsidiary is financially responsible, whether by means of insurance or otherwise, the policy behind the second part of the *Collet* test is met. Insurance meets this policy just as well, perhaps even better, than a healthy balance sheet.

At the oral argument, counsel for Radaszewski described the insurance company in question as "fly-by-night." He pointed out, and this is in the record, that the insurance agency that placed the coverage, Dixie Insurance Agency, Inc., was, like Contrux, a wholly owned subsidiary of Telecom. (Apparently the $1,000,000 primary policy is still in force. It is only the $10,000,000 excess policy that is inoperative on account of the insolvency of the excess carrier, Integrity Insurance Co.) Plaintiff argues that if the case went to trial he could show that the excess carrier "was an insurance company with wobbly knees for years before its receivership." He also says that the excess carrier was not strong enough even to receive a minimum rating in the Best Insurance Guide. Finally, plaintiff suggests that Contrux bought "its insurance from a financially unsound company which most certainly charged a significantly lower premium."

Here, it is beyond dispute that Contrux had insurance, and that it was considered financially responsible under the applicable federal regulations. We see nothing sinister in the fact that the insurance was purchased through an agency wholly owned by Telecom. This is a common business practice. The assertion that a reduced premium was paid is wholly without support in the record. It is based on speculation only. There is no evidence that Telecom or Contrux knew that the insurance company was going to become insolvent, and no reason, indeed, that we can think of why anyone would want to buy insurance from a company that he thought would become insolvent.

The doctrine of limited liability is intended precisely to protect a parent corporation whose subsidiary goes broke. That is the whole purpose of the doctrine, and those who have the right to decide such questions, that is, legislatures, believe that the doctrine, on the whole, is socially reasonable and useful. We think that the doctrine would largely be destroyed if a parent corporation could be held liable simply on the basis of errors in business judgment. Something more than that should be shown, and *Collet* requires something more than that. In our view, this record is devoid of facts to show that "something more."

HEANEY, SENIOR CIRCUIT JUDGE, dissenting:

I respectfully dissent. In every respect on the basis of the record now before us, Contrux was nothing but a shell corporation established by Telecom to permit it to operate as a nonunion carrier without regard to the consequences that might occur to those who did business with Contrux or those who might be affected by its actions.

The majority asks why anyone would want to buy insurance from an insolvent company. An answer readily comes to mind. The purchase was a cheap way of complying with federal regulations and furthered the illusion to all concerned that Contrux was a viable company able to meet its responsibilities.

As the matter now stands, the innocent victim may have to bear most of the costs of his disabling injuries without having the opportunity to prove that Contrux was intentionally undercapitalized. I believe this is wrong and inconsistent with Missouri law. I would thus remand for trial.

Points for Discussion

1. Enterprise liability.

The plaintiff in *Walkovszky* sought liability from two sources: (1) the ten taxicab corporations and corporate garage under common ownership, and (2) Carlton individually. The case was appealed only on the issue of whether the plaintiff sufficiently stated a valid cause of action against Carlton. The possibility of "enterprise liability" against corporations that are operated as a single economic unit expands the assets available to corporate creditors, without imposing liability on individual shareholders. In some instances, this may be enough to satisfy liabilities to creditors. But in *Walkovszky* the assets of the other corporations were heavily mortgaged or otherwise judgment-proof. (*Radaszewski* involved a parent-subsidiary corporate relationship and a tort claimant. We include it here as a tort case, but you can also think about it as an example of a corporate group case, which we'll study in more detail later in this chapter.)

2. Advising.

Following the decision in the *Walkovszky* case, the plaintiff amended his complaint to allege with more specificity that Carlton had conducted business in his individual capacity. Carlton again moved to dismiss but this time the trial court denied his motion, which was affirmed on appeal. The case then settled. Given this outcome, how would you advise an owner of a taxi fleet in New York City to organize and run their business?

3. Compare *Walkovszky* and *Radaszewski*.

Both cases involved involuntary tort claimants; both cases involved operating companies that had carried the minimum insurance required by law; and both cases (over a strong dissent) concluded that piercing was not appropriate. Do you think both courts got it right? Are the cases different in any way that should matter?

4. Formalities in the tort setting.

Many cases mention "disregard of corporate formalities" as a factor in PCV. But why should the internal operations of a corporation (regular meetings, minutes, resolutions, and so on) be relevant to liability for torts? More specifically, why would formalities matter to tort victims who never interacted with the corporation before the unfortunate event? Some argue that if corporate formalities are flouted, corporate owners should not be allowed to rely on limited liability. What is the justification for such a quid pro quo?

5. Undercapitalization.

Some courts also mention undercapitalization (the failure to maintain an adequate financial cushion) as a piercing factor, particularly if the business engages in potentially hazardous activities. Courts are more likely to pierce, especially in tort cases, when the decisions mention undercapitalization. Why? And, by the way, what is undercapitalization? Should it be measured when the business was organized or at the time of the corporate wrong? If a business begins operating with sufficient capital to cover its anticipated business losses, but then loses money over time, must shareholders invest additional capital on pain of losing their limited liability? What if the business enters a new, riskier line of business? Should buying the minimum-required insurance be enough to preserve the limited liability shield? What if the business operates in an industry without minimum insurance requirements?

D. Piercing in Contract Cases

Contract creditors are in a different position than tort creditors. Most important, they are voluntary. They know or can ascertain that they are dealing with a no-recourse corporation and have the opportunity to bargain for a risk premium, shareholder guarantees, or restrictions on distributions.

Yet the fact that a plaintiff had a contractual relationship with a corporation—and therefore had the opportunity to negotiate in advance—does not necessarily prevent the plaintiff from piercing the corporate veil. Indeed, many contract cases involve misrepresentations that undermine the expectation of a non-recourse relationship. That is one reason why courts pierce so frequently in contract cases. As with the tort cases, these two contract cases are representative. The relationships among the various parties are complex. What are the key factors in these cases?

Freeman v. Complex Computing Co.

119 F.3d 1044 (2d Cir. 1997)

MINER, CIRCUIT JUDGE.

While pursuing graduate studies under a fellowship at Columbia University in the early 1990s, defendant Jason Glazier co-developed computer software with potential commercial value and negotiated with Columbia to obtain a license for the software. Columbia apparently was unwilling to license software to a corporation of which Glazier was an officer, director, or shareholder. Nonetheless, Columbia was willing to license the software to a corporation that retained Glazier as an independent contractor.

Accordingly, in September of 1992, Complex Computing Co., Inc. ("C3") was incorporated, with an acquaintance of Glazier's as the sole shareholder and initial director, and Seth Akabas (a partner of Glazier's counsel in this action) as the president, treasurer and assistant secretary. In November of 1992, another corporation, Glazier, Inc., of which Glazier was the sole shareholder, entered into an agreement with C3 (the "consulting agreement").[1] Under the consulting agreement, Glazier, Inc. was retained as an independent contractor (titled as C3's "Scientific Advisor") to develop and market Glazier's software, which was licensed from Columbia, and to provide support services to C3's clients. Glazier was designated the sole signatory on C3's bank account, and was given a written option to purchase all of C3's stock for $2,000.

In September of 1993, C3 entered into an agreement with plaintiff Daniel Freeman (the "C3–Freeman Agreement"), under which Freeman agreed to sell and license C3's computer software products for a five-year term. In exchange, C3 agreed to pay Freeman commissions on the revenue received by C3 over a ten-year period from the client-base developed by Freeman, including the revenue received from sales and licensing, maintenance and support services. The C3–Freeman Agreement included provisions relating to Freeman's compensation if C3 terminated the agreement prior to its expiration, or if C3 made a sale that did not result in revenues because of a future merger, consolidation, or stock acquisition. The agreement included an arbitration clause.

Schedule 1 of the C3–Freeman Agreement listed the customers from whom Freeman would receive commissions. Although C3's president signed the C3–Freeman Agreement, Glazier personally signed the periodic amendments to Schedule 1. On March 24, 1994, Glazier signed an amended Schedule 1 that listed as customers, among numerous others, Thomson Financial, Banker's Trust and Chemical Bank. The amendment provided that "to date, Dan Freeman has performed—and will continue to perform—material marketing services" as regards these customers.

On August 22, 1994, C3 and Thomson Investment Software (Thomson) entered into a licensing agreement that granted Thomson exclusive worldwide sales and marketing rights of C3's products. Freeman contends that the licensing agreement resulted from efforts made by him over approximately nine months to bring the transaction to fruition.

In October of 1994, C3 gave Freeman the requisite 60-days notice of the termination of its agreement with him. The letter of termination, signed by Glazier, explained that C3's exercise of its option to terminate Freeman's employment was "an action to combat the overly generous termination clause we committed to, and to force a renegotiation of your sales contract."

---

[1] Although the consulting agreement was between C3 and Glazier, Inc., numerous provisions in the agreement made express reference to Glazier personally. For example, the consulting agreement provided that it was terminable if Glazier himself was unable to perform or supervise performance of Glazier, Inc.'s obligations.

Glazier was hired in January of 1995 as Thomson's Vice President and Director of Research and Development at a starting salary of $150,000 plus additional payments of "incentive compensation" based in part upon the revenues received by Thomson in connection with the sale or license of products developed by Glazier. On the same day, Thomson and C3 entered into an assets purchase agreement. As part of the transaction, Thomson assumed C3's intellectual products, trademarks and tradenames. The Thomson Agreement set forth a list of C3 agreements assumed by Thomson, but expressly excluded the C3–Freeman Agreement. Thomson paid a total of $750,000, from which Glazier was paid $450,000 as a "signing bonus" in connection with his new employment contract.

In May of 1995, Freeman commenced the action giving rise to this appeal. He estimated that he was due more than $100,000, and that the moneys due him in the future under the agreement would be in excess of $5 million.

The district court found that both C3 and Glazier should be compelled to arbitrate their disputes with Freeman in accordance with the C3–Freeman Agreement. The district court found that Glazier was subject to the arbitration clause of the C3–Freeman Agreement because he "did not merely dominate and control C3—to all intents and purposes, he was C3" and because he held the "sole economic interest of any significance" in the corporation.

II. Piercing the Corporate Veil

Neither party disputes that New York law applies to these issues. We review de novo the district court's legal conclusions.

A. Glazier's Equitable Ownership of C3

Glazier contends that he should not be held personally liable under a veil-piercing theory because he is not a shareholder, officer, director, or employee of C3. We reject this argument.

New York courts have recognized for veil-piercing purposes the doctrine of equitable ownership, under which an individual who exercises sufficient control over the corporation may be deemed an "equitable owner," notwithstanding the fact that the individual is not a shareholder of the corporation.

Because Glazier "exercised considerable authority over the corporation to the point of completely disregarding the corporate form and acting as though its assets were his alone to manage and distribute," he is appropriately viewed as C3's equitable owner for veil-piercing purposes. If there were board meetings, no minutes were kept from August 1994 through May 1995. Glazier agreed to personally indemnify C3's sole shareholder and director against any liability arising from the performance of his duties as C3's director. The president of C3 never attended a meeting of the Board of Directors. No shareholder received dividends or other distributions, despite the corporate income of $563,257 in 1994 and $200,000 from the assets sale to Thomson.

Glazier used C3 to sell his intellectual product and powers, including the software that he had co-developed at Columbia and which Columbia licensed to C3. Through payments from C3 to Glazier, Inc., he received the vast majority of the resulting revenues.[5] Both Glazier, Inc. and C3 were located at Glazier's apartment, and Glazier was the sole signatory on C3's bank account. Glazier, Inc.'s consulting agreement with C3 expressly provided that it was terminable if Glazier himself was unable to perform or supervise the performance of Glazier, Inc.'s obligations to C3, which were described as "marketing C3's software products, developing new software products, enhancing C3's existing software products, and providing support services to C3's clients." These obligations essentially described C3's entire business.

Glazier himself gave Thomson a resume stating that from 1992 to the present, Glazier was the principal, owner and manager of C3, and that Glazier, Inc. was the predecessor to C3. C3 paid over $8000 to the law firm that represented Glazier personally in his negotiations with Thomson. These negotiations resulted in Thomson employing Glazier and paying him a $450,000 signing bonus. C3 then paid Glazier, through Glazier, Inc., an additional $210,000 out of the proceeds of the assets and other funds that were in the C3 bank account following the assets purchase. After payment of taxes and other expenses, this left only $10,000 in C3's account. Freeman contends that this balance renders C3 unable to fulfill its alleged obligations to him. Additionally, Glazier had an option to purchase all the shares of C3 from its sole shareholder for $2000. Thus, at his discretion, he could have become the sole shareholder for a small payment.

The district court found that "to regard Glazier as anything but the sole stockholder and controlling person of C3 would be to exalt form over substance." Under the unique facts of the instant case, viewed in their totality, we agree that it is appropriate to treat Glazier as an "equitable owner" for veil-piercing purposes.

B. Piercing the C3 Veil

Glazier next argues that the district court's determination that he controlled C3 does not justify piercing the corporate veil in the absence of a factual finding

---

[5] The consulting agreement provided that C3 would not pay anyone compensation unless Glazier, Inc. had first received its share in full. The consulting agreement obligated C3 to pay Glazier, Inc. annual compensation of $150,000, with "cost-of-living" adjustments. In addition, it was to pay Glazier, Inc. a bonus for each calendar year equal to 60% of the first $200,000 in revenues received by C3, 70% of the next $200,000, 80% of the third $200,000, and 85% of all revenues received thereafter.

that he used his control over C3 to wrong Freeman. We agree that the district court erred in piercing the corporate veil before finding that Glazier used his domination of C3 to wrong Freeman.

The presumption of corporate independence and limited shareholder liability serves to encourage business development. Nevertheless, that presumption will be set aside, and courts will pierce the corporate veil under certain limited circumstances. To pierce the corporate veil under New York law, a plaintiff must prove that "(1) the owner has exercised such control that the corporation has become a mere instrumentality of the owner, which is the real actor; (2) such control has been used to commit a fraud or other wrong; and (3) the fraud or wrong results in an unjust loss or injury to plaintiff."

The element of domination and control never was considered to be sufficient of itself to justify the piercing of a corporate veil. Even if a plaintiff showed that the dominator of a corporation had complete control over the corporation so that the corporation "had no separate mind, will, or existence of its own," New York law will not allow the corporate veil to be pierced in the absence of a showing that this control "was used to commit wrong, fraud, or the breach of a legal duty, or a dishonest and unjust act in contravention of plaintiff's legal rights, and that the control and breach of duty proximately caused the injury complained of."

As discussed in the context of equitable ownership, the record is replete with examples of Glazier's control over C3. Therefore, the district court's finding of control was not erroneous. However, the district court erred in the decision to pierce C3's corporate veil solely on the basis of a finding of domination and control. Thus, while we accept the district court's factual finding that Glazier controlled C3, we remand to the district court the issue of whether Glazier used his control over C3 to commit a fraud or other wrong that resulted in unjust loss or injury to Freeman. Though there is substantial evidence of such wrongdoing, a finding on this issue must be made in the first instance by the district court before veil-piercing occurs.

GODBOLD, SENIOR CIRCUIT JUDGE, concurring in part, dissenting in part:

I concur in affirming the district court's holding that Glazier was in total control of C3. I see no need, however, to remand the case to the district court for it to determine whether "Glazier used his control over C3 to commit a fraud or other wrong that resulted in an unjust loss or injury to Freeman." The record before us discloses fraud or other wrong by Glazier, through C3, resulting in an unjust loss or injury to Freeman. Consequently C3's corporate veil is to be pierced, and, without more, arbitration should proceed against Glazier as well as C3.

C3 is Glazier's creature, subject to his "complete control" ("he was C3"). C3 agreed with Freeman for him to sell and license C3's software products for five years and to receive commissions for ten years on revenue received from Freeman's clients. Plus, if C3 merged or consolidated, Freeman was to receive an additional payment of 10 percent of the total consideration conveyed. The agreement contained a termination clause. C3 could terminate on sixty days notice, but Freeman was entitled to receive all compensation for services previously rendered as well as the commissions that accrued over a ten year period (presumably to include 10 percent of the consideration for a buy out or merger).

Approximately a year after the C3–Freeman agreement was made C3 entered into an agreement with Thomson Trading Services, Inc., an account developed by Freeman, to make Thomson its exclusive worldwide marketer. Thomson took over existing C3 agreements, but not C3's agreement with Freeman. That agreement remained C3's responsibility. But C3 has paid Freeman nothing.

It remained for C3 to get rid of Freeman. It did so by a purported termination of the C3–Freeman agreement. C3 recited that it was exercising its option to terminate as "an action to combat the overly generous termination clause we committed to, and to force a renegotiation of your sales contract." In short, Freeman was not to receive the benefits guaranteed him by the termination clause; the termination was to force him to give up the "overly generous" termination benefits he was entitled to receive. The asserted termination was not to implement the provision for termination but in derogation of it.

By this Tinker-to-Evers-to-Chance play:

• C3's business has gone to Thomson.

• Thomson has handsomely rewarded Glazier.

• Thomson, in acquiring C3, has not assumed responsibility for the Freeman agreement.

• Glazier is enjoying the generous fruits of the C3–Thomson deal while C3 has been reduced to a shell.

• Freeman has been stripped of his benefits, paid nothing, and hung out to dry, on the asserted ground that benefits (past and future) agreed to be paid to him by C3 were too generous.

This is fraud by Glazier—a fully revealed rip off. But if one shrinks from the word "fraud" it is at least a "wrongful injury."

The next case, *Theberge v. Darbro, Inc.*, also raises the issue of piercing in a contract case. The business is commercial real estate, with the selling and buying of real estate among various business groups—with first, second, and third mortgages, sometimes with personal guarantees and sometimes without. The case involves seller financing for which there were no written personal guarantees.

The story begins with Michael and Thomas Theberge, who owned seven rental properties, which in August 1986 they sold for $900,000 to the Worden Group for cash and a $180,000 promissory note secured by a second mortgage (the "Theberge mortgage"). Later that year, the Worden Group agreed to sell the seven properties for $970,000 to Darbro, Inc., which was owned by Albert and Mitchell Small. Prior to the closing, the Smalls informed the Worden Group and the Theberges that the purchaser would not be Darbro, but instead Horton Street Associates, Inc., a newly formed corporation owned by the Smalls.

To finance the purchase of the seven buildings, Horton Street borrowed a total of $840,000 from Casco Northern Bank and executed promissory notes secured by first and third mortgages on the premises. Horton Street also assumed the existing $180,000 Theberge mortgage note owed by the Worden Group to the Theberges. Finally, Horton Street executed a $20,000 note payable to the Worden Group.

The lenders to Horton Street received various guarantees and other financial protections. Darbro guaranteed $450,000—and Albert Small personally guaranteed $330,000—of the Casco Northern first mortgage. Albert co-signed the promissory note given to Casco Northern on the third mortgage, as well as the $20,000 note payable to the Worden Group.

Soon after the purchase, Horton Street began to lose money. There was a downturn in the real estate market, an increase in vacancy rates, a flood that damaged one of the buildings, and unexpected repairs that were required on the properties. To compensate for these losses, Albert loaned money to Darbro, which in turn loaned money to Horton Street.

In the spring of 1989, Horton Street sold two of the seven buildings. As a result of these sales, and pursuant to the terms of the Theberge mortgage, Horton Street paid the Theberges to partially discharge the second mortgage, retired the third mortgage to Casco Northern, and reduced the balance on the Casco Northern first mortgage.

By May 1989, Darbro had loaned to Horton Street approximately $225,000 and had received only "a couple small payments." Albert then decided that Darbro would not loan additional monies to Horton Street, and advised the Theberges that he could not make any further payments and that he wished to negotiate "a solution."

When these negotiations failed, the Theberges and the Worden Group brought an action against Horton Street to recover the outstanding balance on the $180,000 promissory note. The court issued a default judgment against Horton Street.

The Theberges and the Worden Group then instituted a second action against Darbro, Albert Small, and Mitchell Small, seeking a judgment on the unpaid balance of the note. The plaintiffs alleged (1) Horton Street was the alter ego of Darbro, Albert and Mitchell; (2) the sale to Horton Street was based on representations that Albert would "stand behind" the Theberge mortgage.

The trial court made factual findings, some of which favored the Smalls. The court specifically found that the defendants had not acted illegally or fraudulently and that they had not guaranteed the payment of the Theberge promissory note. The court further found that the Theberges were sophisticated real estate investors and understood the formalities, and the effect, of a personal guarantee in a real estate transaction.

But the court also found that Horton Street had no separate offices, utilities, or employees; maintained no corporate records or books; commingled its business with that of the other defendants; and failed to conduct formal corporate meetings. According to the court, both Horton Street and Darbro were, in essence, Albert—as evidenced by the fact that, when in a financial crisis, Albert "unilaterally assumed full control of Horton Street on his own initiative" and acted to the defendants' own benefit and to the detriment of the plaintiffs.

The trial court concluded that "notions of equitable estoppel ought to preclude" the defendants from asserting Horton Street's corporate status and that the defendants were liable to the plaintiffs for the outstanding balance on the Theberge mortgage.

Theberge v. Darbro, Inc.

684 A.2d 1298 (Me. 1996)

GLASSMAN, JUSTICE.

On appeal, the defendants contend that the trial court erred by determining that their conduct justified piercing the corporate veil of Horton Street. We agree. It is well established that "corporations are separate legal entities with limited liability." Although the corporate entity may be pierced if it is merely the alter ego of an individual or other corporation, we will "disregard the legal entity of a corporation with caution and only when necessary in the interest of Justice." When the plaintiff attempts, in the context of a contractual dispute, to pierce the corporate veil, courts generally apply "more stringent standards because the party seeking relief in a contract case is presumed to have voluntarily and knowingly entered into an agreement with a corporate entity, and is expected to suffer the consequences of the limited liability associated with the corporate business form."

The plaintiffs contend, and the trial court determined, that the oral representations that Albert was a person of financial substance who would stand behind the obligations of Horton Street, and the financial arrangement between Albert and Casco Northern, effectively extinguishing the Theberge mortgage, justifies piercing the corporate veil. We disagree. The court found, and the record supports, that the defendants did not act illegally or fraudulently, but, rather conducted themselves "shrewdly" and employed "sharp business practices." The court determined that the defendants did not formally, personally guarantee the transaction and that the plaintiffs were sophisticated real estate professionals who understood the significance of a personal guarantee. Indeed, the success of the Worden Group in securing Albert's personal liability on the $20,000 note to them belies the contention of a reasonable expectation that Albert would "stand behind" the Theberge mortgage in the absence of a formal guarantee.

When the Theberges permitted the assumption by Horton Street of their mortgage, they protected themselves by refusing to release the Worden Group from liability. Casco Northern also protected its interest in the loans to Horton Street by obtaining guarantees from Darbro and Albert in amounts sufficient to cover the loan amounts. The plaintiffs, by contrast, failed to obtain any such guarantee from any of the defendants and instead opted to proceed with the transaction. We decline to reconstruct the agreement negotiated between the parties to effect a result beyond the plain meaning of that bargain.

Considering all the evidence in the instant case, we determine that it is insufficient to justify piercing the corporate veil of Horton Street.

Points for Discussion

1. Advising.

On remand, the district court in *Freeman* found that Glazier's actions constituted fraudulent or other wrongful behavior because they left Freeman as "a general creditor of an essentially defunct corporation with virtually no assets." The court entered an order compelling Glazier to arbitrate plaintiff's claim. How does this resolution affect how you might advise parties contemplating negotiations after *Freeman*?

2. Formalities.

Compare the observance of corporate formalities in *Freeman* and *Theberge*. Who seemed to have followed corporate formalities more rigorously—Jason Glazier or the Smalls? The court pierces in *Freeman*, not in *Theberge*. Isn't this the opposite of what you would expect?

3. Deceit.

Compare the level of deceit in the two cases. Was Freeman led to believe that C3 was well-capitalized or falsely told that Glazier would stand behind the corporation? And why didn't the court in *Theberge* find it relevant that Albert Small had said he would stand behind the corporation's obligations or that the Smalls had engaged in "sharp business practices"?

E. Piercing in Corporate Groups

Which entity or entities should be liable when there is a group of corporations? For example, what if one corporation owns the stock of another, but only the subsidiary damaged the plaintiff? The plaintiff might seek damages against the parent corporation as well the subsidiary. Or what if the parent corporation owns the stock of many subsidiaries, which are affiliates of each other? The plaintiff might seek damages against all of the corporations, on a theory of "enterprise liability." There are legitimate reasons to divide a business into multiple corporations, including convenience and profit maximization. Sometimes courts will respect the limited liability of each corporation, but other times they will pierce one or more of the veils in a corporate group. Here are two examples.

Food for Thought

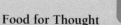

The Thompson study, which looked at all PCV cases through 1985, found that piercing is more frequent in contract cases (42.0% of the time) compared to tort cases (31.0% of the time). This is contrary to the assumption that courts in piercing cases are more sympathetic to tort victims, who cannot protect themselves by contract. In fact, some commentators have argued that contract creditors should not be able to pierce the corporate veil at all, on the theory they can always obtain personal guarantees. For some contract creditors, PCV is arguably a financial windfall.

In a follow-up study of piercing cases through 2006, Professor Peter Oh found a similar rate of piercing in contract cases (46.2% of the time) as in tort cases (47.8% of the time), after excluding cases involving fraud claims. *Veil-Piercing*, 89 Tex. L. Rev. 81 (2010). Although less dramatic than the Thompson study, the Oh study raises the question why piercing happens as often in contract cases as tort cases. Perhaps contract PCV cases are brought by commercial litigators, who recognize that sometimes businesses fail and don't bring borderline claims, while tort PCV are brought by personal-injury lawyers, who are always looking for a deep pocket, even when the odds are against them?

Gardemal v. Westin Hotel Co.

186 F.3d 588 (5th Cir. 1999)

DeMoss, Circuit Judge.

Lisa Cerza Gardemal sued Westin Hotel Company (Westin) and Westin Mexico, S.A. de C.V. (Westin Mexico), under Texas law, alleging that the defendants were liable for the drowning death of her husband in Cabo San Lucas, Mexico. The district court granted Westin's motion for summary judgment, and Westin Mexico's motion to dismiss for lack of personal jurisdiction. We affirm the district court's rulings.

In June 1995, Gardemal and her husband John W. Gardemal, a physician, traveled to Cabo San Lucas, Baja California Sur, Mexico, to attend a medical seminar held at the Westin Regina Resort Los Cabos (Westin Regina). The Westin Regina is owned by Desarollos Turisticos Integrales Cabo San Lucas, S.A. de C.V. (DTI), and managed by Westin Mexico. Westin Mexico is a subsidiary of Westin, and is incorporated in Mexico. During their stay at the hotel, the Gardemals decided to go snorkeling with a group of guests. According to Gardemal, the concierge at the Westin Regina directed the group to "Lovers Beach" which, unbeknownst to the group, was notorious for its rough surf and strong undercurrents. While climbing the beach's rocky shore, five men in the group were swept into the Pacific Ocean by a rogue wave and thrown against the rocks. Two of the men, including John Gardemal, drowned.

Gardemal, as administrator of her husband's estate, brought wrongful death and survival actions under Texas law against Westin and Westin Mexico, alleging that her husband drowned because Westin Regina's concierge negligently directed the group to Lovers Beach and failed to warn her husband of its dangerous condition. Westin then moved for summary judgment, alleging that although it is the parent company of Westin Mexico, it is a separate corporate entity and thus could not be held liable for acts committed by its subsidiary. [The magistrate judge recommended that Westin be dismissed from the action, accepting Westin's separate corporate identity. The magistrate also recommended granting Westin Mexico's motion to dismiss on the ground that it had insufficient minimum contacts to bring it within the personal jurisdiction of the court.] The district court then accepted the magistrate judge's recommendations and dismissed Gardemal's suit. We affirm.

In this action Gardemal seeks to hold Westin liable for the acts of Westin Mexico by invoking two separate, but related, state-law doctrines. Gardemal first argues that liability may be imputed to Westin because Westin Mexico functioned as the alter ego of Westin. Gardemal next contends that Westin may be held liable on the theory that Westin Mexico operated a single business enterprise.

Under Texas law the alter ego doctrine allows the imposition of liability on a corporation for the acts of another corporation when the subject corporation is organized or operated as a mere tool or business conduit. Alter ego is demonstrated "by evidence showing a blending of identities, or a blurring of lines of distinction, both formal and substantive, between two corporations." An important consideration is whether a corporation is underfunded or undercapitalized, which is an indication that the company is a mere conduit or business tool.

On appeal Gardemal points to several factors which, in her opinion, show that Westin is operating as the alter ego of Westin Mexico. She claims, for example, that Westin owns most of Westin Mexico's stock; that the two companies share common corporate officers; that Westin maintains quality control at Westin Mexico by requiring Westin Mexico to use certain operations manuals; that Westin oversees advertising and marketing operations at Westin Mexico through two separate contracts; and that Westin Mexico is grossly undercapitalized. We are not convinced.

The record, even when viewed in a light most favorable to Gardemal, reveals nothing more than a typical corporate relationship between a parent and subsidiary. It is true, as Gardemal points out, that Westin and Westin Mexico are closely tied through stock ownership, shared officers, financing arrangements, and the like. But this alone does not establish an alter-ego relationship.

In this case, there is insufficient record evidence that Westin dominates Westin Mexico to the extent that Westin Mexico has, for practical purposes, surrendered its corporate identity. In fact, the evidence suggests just the opposite, that Westin Mexico functions as an autonomous business entity. There is evidence, for example, that Westin Mexico banks in Mexico and deposits all of the revenue from its six hotels into that account. The facts also show that while Westin is incorporated in Delaware, Westin Mexico is incorporated in Mexico and faithfully adheres to the required corporate formalities. Finally, Westin Mexico has its own staff, its own assets, and even maintains its own insurance policies.

Gardemal is correct in pointing out that undercapitalization is a critical factor in our alter-ego analysis, especially in a tort case like the present one. But as noted by the district court, there is scant evidence that Westin Mexico is in fact undercapitalized and unable to pay a judgment, if necessary. This fact weighs heavily against Gardemal because the alter ego doctrine is an equitable remedy which prevents a company from avoiding liability by abusing the corporate form. In this case, there is insufficient evidence that Westin Mexico is undercapitalized or uninsured. Moreover, there is no indication that Gardemal could not recover by suing Westin Mexico directly.

Likewise, we reject Gardemal's attempt to impute liability to Westin based on the single business enterprise doctrine. Under that doctrine, when corporations are not operated as separate entities, but integrate their resources to achieve a common business purpose, each constituent corporation may be held liable for the debts incurred in pursuit of that business purpose. Like the alter-ego doctrine, the single business enterprise doctrine is an equitable remedy which applies when the corporate form is "used as part of an unfair device to achieve an inequitable result."

On appeal, Gardemal attempts to prove a single business enterprise by calling our attention to the fact that Westin Mexico uses the trademark "Westin Hotels and Resorts." She also emphasizes that Westin Regina uses Westin's operations manuals. Gardemal also observes that Westin allows Westin Mexico to use its reservation system. Again, these facts merely demonstrate what we would describe as a typical, working relationship between a parent and subsidiary. Gardemal has pointed to no evidence in the record demonstrating that the operations of the two corporations were so integrated as to result in a blending of the two corporate identities. Moreover, Gardemal has come forward with no evidence that she has suffered some harm, or injustice, because Westin and Westin Mexico maintain separate corporate identities.

Reviewing the record in the light most favorable to Gardemal, we conclude that there is insufficient evidence that Westin Mexico was Westin's alter ego. Similarly, there is insufficient evidence that the resources of Westin and Westin Mexico are so integrated as to constitute a single business enterprise.

[The court also affirmed the district court's decision granting Westin Mexico's motion to dismiss for lack of personal jurisdiction.]

OTR Associates v. IBC Services, Inc.

801 A.2d 407 (N.J. Super. Ct. App. Div. 2002)

PRESSLER, P.J.A.D.

The single dispositive issue raised by this appeal is whether the trial court, based on its findings of fact following a bench trial, was justified, as a matter of law, in piercing the corporate veil and thus holding a parent corporation liable for the debt incurred by its wholly owned subsidiary. We are satisfied that the facts, both undisputed and as found, present a textbook illustration of circumstances mandating corporate-veil piercing.

Plaintiff OTR Associates, a limited partnership, owns a shopping mall in Edison, New Jersey, in which it leased space in 1985 for use by a Blimpie franchisee, Samyrna, Inc., a corporation owned by Sam Iskander and his wife. The franchise agreement, styled as a licensing agreement, had been entered into in 1984 between Samyrna and the parent company, International Blimpie Corporation (Blimpie). Blimpie was the sole owner of a subsidiary named IBC Services, Inc. (IBC), created for the single purpose of holding the lease on premises occupied by a Blimpie franchisee. Accordingly, it was IBC that entered into the lease with OTR in July 1985 and, on the same day and apparently with OTR's consent, subleased the space to the franchisee. The history of the tenancy was marked by regular and increasingly substantial rent arrearages, and it was terminated by a dispossess judgment and warrant for removal in 1996. In 1998 OTR commenced this action for unpaid rent, then in the amount of close to $150,000, against Blimpie. The action was tried in December 2000, and judgment was entered in favor of OTR against Blimpie in the full amount of the rent arrearages plus interest thereon, then some $208,000. Blimpie appeals, and we affirm.

We consider the facts in the context of the well-settled principles respecting corporate-veil piercing. Nearly three-quarters of a century ago, the Court of Errors and Appeals made clear that while "ownership alone of capital stock in one corporation by another, does not create any relationship that by reason of which the stockholding company would be liable for torts of the other," nevertheless "where a corporation holds stock of another, not for the purpose of participating in the affairs of the other corporation, in the normal and usual manner, but for the purpose of control, so that the subsidiary company may be used as a mere agency or instrumentality for the stockholding company, such company will be liable for injuries due to the negligence of the subsidiary." The conceptual basis of the rule, which is equally applicable to contractual obligations, is simply that "it is where the corporate form is used as a shield behind which injustice is sought to be done by those who have control of it that equity penetrates the corporate veil."

Thus, the basic finding that must be made to enable the court to pierce the corporate veil is "that the parent so dominated the subsidiary that it had no separate existence but was merely a conduit for the parent." But beyond domination, the court must also find that the "parent has abused the privilege of incorporation by using the subsidiary to perpetrate a fraud or injustice, or otherwise to circumvent the law." And the hallmarks of that abuse are typically the engagement of the subsidiary in no independent business of its own but exclusively the performance of a service for the parent and, even more importantly, the undercapitalization of the subsidiary rendering it judgment-proof.

Blimpie concedes that it formed IBC for the sole purpose of holding the lease on the premises of a Blimpie franchisee. It is also clear that IBC had virtually no assets other than the lease itself, which, in the circumstances, was not an asset at all but only a liability since IBC had no independent right to alienate its interest therein but was subject to Blimpie's exclusive control. It had no business premises of its own, sharing the New York address of Blimpie. It had no income other than the rent payments by the franchisee, which appear to have been made directly to OTR. It does not appear that it had its own employees or office staff. We further note that Blimpie not only retained the right to approve the premises to be occupied by the franchisee and leased by IBC, but itself, in its Georgia headquarters, managed all the leases held by its subsidiaries on franchisee premises. As explained by Charles G. Leaness, presently Executive Vice President of Blimpie and formerly corporate counsel as well as vice-president and secretary of IBC, in 1996, the year of IBC's eviction for non-payment of rent, he was Blimpie's Corporate Counsel Compliance Officer. Blimpie, he testified, is exclusively a franchising corporation with "hundreds and hundreds" of leases held by its wholly-owned leasehold companies, which are, however, overseen by Blimpie's administrative assistants, that is "people in our organization that do this communicate with landlords as their everyday job. Because we have—you know—there are various leases, various assignments." Leaness also made clear that the leasing companies, whose function he explained as assisting franchisees in negotiating leases, "don't make a profit. There's no profit made in a leasehold."

Domination and control by Blimpie of IBC is patent and was not, nor could have been, reasonably disputed. The question then is whether Blimpie abused the privilege of incorporation by using IBC to commit a fraud or injustice or other improper purpose. We agree with the trial judge that the evidence overwhelmingly requires an affirmative answer. The *leit motif* of the testimony of plaintiff's partners who were involved in the dealings with IBC was that they believed that they were dealing with Blimpie, the national and financially responsible franchising company, and never discovered the fact of separate corporate entities until after the eviction. While it is true that IBC never apparently expressly claimed to be Blimpie, it not only failed to explain its relationship to Blimpie as a purported independent company but it affirmatively, intentionally, and calculatedly led OTR to believe it was Blimpie. Illustratively, when OTR was pre-leasing space in the mall, the first approach to it was the appearance at its on-site office of two men in Blimpie uniforms who announced that they wanted to open a Blimpie sandwich shop. One of the men was the franchisee, Iskander. The other was never identified but presumably was someone with a connection to Blimpie. It is also true that the named tenant in the lease was IBC Services, Inc., but the tenant was actually identified in the first paragraph of the lease as "IBC Services, Inc. having an address at c/o International Blimpie Corporation, 1414 Avenue of the Americas, New York, New York." It hardly required a cryptographer to draw the entirely reasonable inference that IBC stood for International Blimpie Corporation. The suggestion, unmistakably, was that IBC was either the corporate name or a trading-as name and that International Blimpie Corporation was the other of these two possibilities.

Beyond the circumstances surrounding the commencement of the tenancy relationship, the correspondence through the years between plaintiff and the entity it believed to be its tenant confirmed plaintiff's belief that Blimpie was its tenant. Blimpie's letters to OTR were on stationary headed only by the Blimpie logo. There is nothing in any of that correspondence that would have suggested the existence of an independent company standing between the franchisor and the franchisee, and, indeed, the correspondence received by OTR from its lessee typically referred to the sub-tenant, Samyrna, as "our franchisee."

As we understand Blimpie's defense and its argument on this appeal, it asserts that it is entitled to the benefit of the separate corporate identities merely because IBC observed all the corporate proprieties—it had its own officers and directors albeit interlocking with Blimpie's, it filed annual reports, kept minutes, held meetings, and had a bank account. But that argument begs the question. The separate corporate shell created by Blimpie to avoid liability may have been mechanistically impeccable, but in every functional and operational sense, the subsidiary had no separate identity. It was moreover not intended to shield the parent from responsibility for its subsidiary's obligations but rather to shield the parent from its own obligations. And that is an evasion and an improper purpose, fraudulently conceived and executed. The corporate veil was properly pierced.

———————————

Points for Discussion

1. Do the rules matter?

Both Westin and Blimpie observed corporate formalities. Why in *Gardemal* is it a "typical corporate relationship between a parent and subsidiary" and in *OTR Associates* "a textbook illustration of circumstances mandating corporate-veil piercing"? Do the results in the cases vary because of the different PCV rules used by the courts?

2. Distinguish the cases.

The *Gardemal* case involved a tort claimant, but the court did not pierce. The *OTR Associates* case involved a contract claimant, and the court did pierce. Does this make sense? Arguably, the Gardemals justifiably assumed that the Westin logo on the hotel in Mexico assured quality and responsibility. And, arguably, the mall lessor (of all people) should have known to ask what entity was signing the lease and to demand a guarantee from the parent corporation.

3. Contract vs. tort.

Would the results have been the same if Westin Mexico had been sued in contract, and Blimpie had been sued in tort?

CHAPTER 14

Corporate Criminality

When a corporate agent commits a crime in his corporate capacity, who is criminally liable—the agent alone, the agent's supervisor, the corporate managers who could have prevented the crime, the corporation, or no one?

This chapter considers corporate criminality and how criminal law has been used as a tool to internalize corporate social harms. First, we look at the prosecution of the corporation for the bad acts of its agents. This raises questions about why the corporation (not just its human agents or their supervisors) should be punished, how the corporation can have criminal intent, and why the corporation and ultimately its shareholders should be subject to fines and other monetary punishment for the actions of rogue agents.

Second, we consider the criminal liability of corporate directors and executives charged with overseeing the corporation's business. This raises questions about whether failures to supervise can create strict liability, what responsibilities corporate managers have to implement legal compliance programs, how the Federal Sentencing Guidelines encourage such compliance programs, and whether too much corporate conduct has been criminalized.

As you consider the question of corporate criminality, you will notice the animating question of the chapter is whether corporate criminality is a useful way to induce the corporation to consider and respond to its natural tendency to externalize costs and risks. Perhaps making the corporation civilly liable for failures to protect consumers, provide a safe workplace, or comply with environmental regulation is enough. And, perhaps, the piercing doctrine compels shareholders to ensure that their corporation complies with external legal norms. In the end,

Food for Thought

The first state to enact a general statute on corporate criminality was Delaware in 1972. 11 Del. Code Ann. § 281. Why would "corporation friendly" Delaware turn on the state's most important patron? Some have suggested that corporate criminality serves as a foil to protect corporate executives. By diverting the attention of the prosecutor, and the wrath of the public, away from individuals in the corporation, corporate criminality can be seen as pro-management.

you will want to ask whether criminal liability (where fines imposed on the corporation are the usual sanction) accomplishes the purposes of criminal law: retribution, deterrence, incapacitation, rehabilitation, and restoration.

A. Corporation as Criminal Actor

Although the corporation by its nature is a "person" for purposes of owning property, contracting, and being a party to civil litigation, the early common law treated criminal conduct by corporate agents as *ultra vires* and thus beyond corporate capacity. Since the twentieth century, criminal statutes, and cases interpreting them, have come to define the corporation as a person for purposes of criminal liability.

Corporate criminality is a messy concept. What is accomplished by holding the corporation criminally responsible for the bad acts (almost always unauthorized) of corporate agents? Why isn't individual criminality enough? How can the corporation, itself a legal fiction, harbor criminal intent? Since the corporation cannot be flogged or imprisoned, what punishment is appropriate? Why should shareholders (and sometimes other corporate constituents) pay for the misdeeds of corporate agents? What does criminal liability accomplish that civil liability doesn't?

The following case addresses many of these questions.

State v. Christy Pontiac-GMC, Inc.

354 N.W.2d 17 (Minn. 1984)

SIMONETT, JUSTICE.

We hold that a corporation may be convicted of theft and forgery, which are crimes requiring specific intent, and that the evidence sustains defendant corporation's guilt.

In a bench trial, defendant-appellant Christy Pontiac-GMC, Inc., was found guilty of two counts of theft by swindle and two counts of aggravated forgery, and was sentenced to a $1,000 fine on each of the two forgery convictions. Defendant argues that as a corporation it cannot, under our state

FYI

Pontiac was one of the divisions of General Motors Corporation, before the company went bankrupt in 2009. The Pontiac brand, which began in 1928 and came to be known for its sporty "muscle" cars, was discontinued as part of the company's restructuring.

statutes, be prosecuted or convicted for theft or forgery and that, in any event, the evidence fails to establish that the acts complained of were the acts of the defendant corporation.

Christy Pontiac is a Minnesota corporation, doing business as a car dealership. It is owned by James Christy, a sole stockholder, who serves also as president and as director. In the spring of 1981, General Motors offered a cash rebate program for its dealers. A customer who purchased a new car delivered during the rebate period was entitled to a cash rebate, part paid by GM and part paid by the dealership. GM would pay the entire rebate initially and later charge back, against the dealer, the dealer's portion of the rebate. Apparently it was not uncommon for the dealer to give the customer the dealer's portion of the rebate in the form of a discount on the purchase price.

At this time Phil Hesli was employed by Christy Pontiac as a salesman and fleet manager. On March 27, 1981, James Linden took delivery of a new Grand Prix. Although the rebate period on this car had expired on March 19, the salesman told Linden that he would still try to get the $700 rebate for Linden. Later, Linden was told by a Christy Pontiac employee that GM had denied the rebate. Subsequently, it was discovered that Hesli had forged Linden's signature twice on the rebate application form submitted by Christy Pontiac to GM, and that the transaction date had been altered and backdated to March 19 on the buyer's order form. Hesli signed the order form as "Sales Manager or Officer of the Company."

On April 6, 1981, Ronald Gores purchased a new Le Mans, taking delivery the next day. The rebate period for this model car had expired on April 4, and apparently Gores was told he would not be eligible for a rebate. Subsequently, it was discovered that Christy Pontiac had submitted a $500 cash rebate application to GM and that Gores' signature had been forged twice by Hesli on the application. It was also discovered that the purchase order form had been backdated to April 3. This order form was signed by Gary Swandy, an officer of Christy Pontiac.

Both purchasers learned of the forged rebate applications when they received a copy of the application in the mail from Christy Pontiac. Both purchasers complained to James Christy, and in both instances the conversations ended in angry mutual recriminations. Christy did tell Gores that the rebate on his car was "a mistake" and offered half the rebate to "call it even." After the Attorney General's office made an inquiry, Christy Pontiac contacted GM and arranged for cancellation of the Gores rebate that had been allowed to Christy Pontiac. Subsequent investigation disclosed that of 50 rebate transactions, only the Linden and Gores sales involved irregularities.

In a separate trial, Phil Hesli was acquitted of three felony charges but found guilty on the count of theft for the Gores transaction and was given a misdemeanor disposition. An indictment against James Christy for theft by swindle was dismissed, as was a subsequent complaint for the same charge, for lack of probable cause. Christy Pontiac, the corporation, was also indicted, and the appeal here is from the four convictions on those indictments. Before trial, Mr. Christy was granted immunity and was then called as a prosecution witness. Phil Hesli did not testify at the corporation's trial.

Christy Pontiac argues on several grounds that a corporation cannot be held criminally liable for a specific intent crime. Minn.Stat. § 609.52, subd. 2 (1982), says "whoever" swindles by artifice, trick or other means commits theft. Minn. Stat. § 609.625, subd. 1 (1982), says "whoever" falsely makes or alters a writing with intent to defraud, commits aggravated forgery. Christy Pontiac agrees that the term "whoever" refers to persons, and it agrees that the term "persons" *may* include corporations, but it argues that when the word "persons" is used here, it should be construed to mean only natural persons. This should be so, argues defendant, because the legislature has defined a crime as "conduct which is prohibited by statute and for which the actor may be sentenced to imprisonment, with or without a fine," Minn. Stat. § 609.02, subd. 1 (1982), and a corporation cannot be imprisoned. Neither, argues defendant, can an artificial person entertain a mental state, let alone have the specific intent required for theft or forgery.

What's That?

Specific intent is "the intent to accomplish the precise criminal act that one is later charged with."

We are not persuaded by these arguments. The Criminal Code is to "be construed according to the fair import of its terms, to promote justice, and to effect its purposes." The legislature has not expressly excluded corporations from criminal liability and, therefore, we take its intent to be that corporations are to be considered persons within the meaning of the Code in the absence of any clear indication to the contrary. We do not think the statutory definition of a crime was meant to exclude corporate criminal liability; rather, we construe that definition to mean conduct which is prohibited and, if committed, *may* result in imprisonment. Interestingly, the specific statutes under which the defendant corporation was convicted, sections 609.52 (theft) and 609.625 (aggravated forgery), expressly state that the sentence may be either imprisonment *or* a fine.

Nor are we troubled by any anthropomorphic implications in assigning specific intent to a corporation for theft or forgery. There was a time when the law, in its logic, declared that a legal fiction could not be a person for purposes of criminal liability, at least with respect to offenses involving specific intent, but that time is gone. If a corporation can be liable in civil tort for both actual and punitive damages for libel, assault and battery, or fraud, it would seem it may also be criminally liable for conduct requiring specific intent. Most courts today recognize that corporations may be guilty of specific intent crimes. Particularly apt candidates for corporate criminality are types of crime, like theft by swindle and forgery, which often occur in a business setting.

We hold, therefore, that a corporation may be prosecuted and convicted for the crimes of theft and forgery.

There remains, however, the evidentiary basis on which criminal responsibility of a corporation is to be determined. Criminal liability, especially for more serious crimes, is thought of as a matter of personal, not vicarious, guilt. One should not be convicted for something one does not do. In what sense, then, does a corporation "do" something for which it can be convicted of a crime? The case law, as illustrated by the authorities above cited, takes differing approaches. If a corporation is to be criminally liable, it is clear that the crime must not be a personal aberration of an employee acting on his own; the criminal activity must, in some sense, reflect corporate policy so that it is fair to say that the activity was the activity of the corporation. There must be, as Judge Learned Hand put it, a "kinship of the act to the powers of the officials, who commit it." *United States v. Nearing*, 252 F. 223, 231 (S.D.N.Y. 1918).

We believe, first of all, the jury should be told that it must be satisfied beyond a reasonable doubt that the acts of the individual agent constitute the acts of the corporation. Secondly, as to the kind of proof required, we hold that a corporation may be guilty of a specific intent crime committed by its agent if: (1) the agent was acting within the course and scope of his or her employment, having the authority to act for the corporation with respect to the particular corporate business which was conducted criminally; (2) the agent was acting, at least in part, in furtherance of the corporation's business interests; and (3) the criminal acts were authorized, tolerated, or ratified by corporate management.

> ### Make the Connection
>
> In agency law, an employer's liability for negligence committed by employees depends on whether the employee acted within the scope of employment, while employer liability for fraud is based on whether the employee had authority to act. Which standard does *Christy Pontiac* use?

This test is not quite the same as the test for corporate vicarious liability for a civil tort of an agent. The burden of proof is different, and, unlike civil liability, criminal guilt requires that the agent be acting at least in part in furtherance of the corporation's business interests. Moreover, it must be shown that corporate management authorized, tolerated, or ratified the criminal activity. Ordinarily, this will be shown by circumstantial evidence, for it is not to be expected that management authorization of illegality would be expressly or openly stated. Indeed, there may be instances where the corporation is criminally liable even though the criminal activity has been expressly forbidden. What must be shown is that from all the facts and circumstances, those in positions of managerial authority or responsibility acted or failed to act in such a manner that the criminal activity reflects corporate policy, and it can be said, therefore, that the criminal act was authorized or tolerated or ratified by the corporation.

> **FYI**
>
> Most criminal prosecutions of corporations arise under federal law, where federal courts have adopted a *respondeat superior* standard that is less demanding than that articulated in *Christy Pontiac*. Under the federal standard, which borrows from tort law, a corporation can be criminally liable if corporate employees were acting within the "scope of their employment," without the government having to prove that the corporation itself was somehow culpable for authorizing the employees' criminal actions or not having compliance measures to prevent such actions. *See* Sara Sun Beale, *The Development and Evolution of the U.S. Law of Corporate Criminal Liability* (2013).

This brings us, then, to the third issue, namely, whether under the proof requirements mentioned above, the evidence is sufficient to sustain the convictions. We hold that it is.

The evidence shows that Hesli, the forger, had authority and responsibility to handle new car sales and to process and sign cash rebate applications. Christy Pontiac, not Hesli, got the GM rebate money, so that Hesli was acting in furtherance of the corporation's business interests. Moreover, there was sufficient evidence of management authorization, toleration, and ratification. Hesli himself, though not an officer, had middle management responsibilities for cash rebate applications. When the customer Gores asked Mr. Benedict, a salesman, about the then discontinued rebate, Benedict referred Gores to Phil Hesli. Gary Swandy, a corporate officer, signed the backdated retail buyer's order form for the Linden sale. James Christy, the president, attempted to negotiate a settlement with Gores after Gores complained. Not until after the Attorney General's inquiry did Christy contact divisional GM headquarters. As the trial judge noted, the rebate money "was so obtained and accepted by Christy Pontiac and kept by Christy Pontiac until somebody blew the whistle. We conclude the evidence establishes that the theft by swindle and the forgeries constituted the acts of the corporation.

We wish to comment further on two aspects of the proof. First, it seems that the state attempted to prosecute both Christy Pontiac and James Christy, but its prosecution of Mr. Christy failed for lack of evidence. We can imagine a different situation where the corporation is the alter ego of its owner and it is the owner who alone commits the crime, where a double prosecution might be deemed fundamentally unfair. Secondly, it may seem incongruous that Hesli, the forger, was acquitted of three of the four criminal counts for which the corporation was convicted. Still, this is not the first time different trials have had different results. We are reviewing this record, and it sustains the convictions.

Points for Discussion

1. Statutory construction.

The *Christy Pontiac* decision reflects the willingness of modern courts to extend criminal statutes to corporate defendants, even though the legislature enacting the statute may not have contemplated the possibility. For example, courts recognize that corporations can be prosecuted for violations of the federal antitrust laws, even though when Congress passed the Sherman Act in 1890 the doctrine of corporate criminality was still a twinkle in prosecutors' eyes. *See United States v. Hilton Hotels Corp.*, 467 F.2d 1000 (9th Cir. 1972) ("The text of the Sherman Act does not expressly resolve the issue. It is reasonable to assume that Congress intended to impose liability upon business entities for the acts of those to whom they choose to delegate the conduct of their affairs, thus stimulating a maximum effort by owners and managers to assure adherence by such agents to the requirements of the Act.").

2. Vicarious specific intent.

As *Christy Pontiac* makes clear, a corporation can harbor criminal intent vicariously. But not every individual in the corporation—or his state of mind—can bind the corporation in a criminal case. Instead, the question is whether the individual was in some sense acting on behalf of the corporation. Courts have taken different approaches to discerning a corporation's intent.

Some courts, including the federal courts, accept the same *respondeat superior* standard that applies for civil liability—namely that the agents' acts fall "within the scope of their employment." Thus, criminal liability extends to actions taken within the employee's general line of work where outsiders would assume the employee had the authority to act.

Many state courts (including *Christy Pontiac*), however, require more to prove vicarious corporate liability. The jury must find beyond a reasonable doubt (1) the agent was acting within the course and scope of employment; (2) the agent was furthering the corporation's business interests; and (3) corporate management authorized, tolerated, or ratified the conduct.

A few courts go further and apply the higher standard of the Model Penal Code, which requires that criminal conduct be "authorized, requested, commanded, performed or recklessly tolerated by the board of directors or by a high managerial agent acting in behalf of the corporation within the scope of his office or employment." MODEL PENAL CODE § 2.07(1)(c) (Proposed Official Draft 1962).

What if an employee engages in illegal conduct contrary to specific instructions or stated corporate policies—thus belying any actual corporate authority? At one level, prosecuting the corporation would seem to miss the mark. But without the threat of corporate criminality, there would be fewer incentives for corporate shareholders and boards of directors to institute safeguards against illegal conduct by corporate employees. As the Supreme Court explained in

Food for Thought

Older cases took the view that the corporation could not be guilty of crimes involving specific intent. The reasoning was that acts of malfeasance were not authorized and thus *ultra vires*. Over time, as corporate civil liability expanded, so did corporate criminal liability. The state of mind of corporate agents was imputed to the corporation.

upholding corporate criminal liability for the first time, adhering to "the old and exploded doctrine that a corporation cannot commit a crime would virtually take away the only means of effectually controlling the subject-matter and correcting the abuses aimed at." *New York Cent. & Hudson River R.R. Co. v. United States*, 212 U.S. 481 (1909). And allowing the corporation to disown the crimes of its employees carried out in the corporate name would raise serious questions about the corporation as a legitimate member of society.

3. Organizational crime.

Corporate criminality also recognizes that prosecuting individuals for the crimes of the organization is sometimes difficult. When there is illegal conduct that benefits a company, such as in *Christy Pontiac* where the car dealership stood to gain from customers receiving the GM rebates, the individual agents might understandably assert, "I was just doing what the boss expected me to do." Exposing the corporation to the threat of conviction may spur corporate decision makers to prevent violations by employees.

Limiting prosecutions to responsible individuals might also leave many commercial crimes unpunished. Juries and judges may be sympathetic with corporate agents who are just doing their job (as may have happened in *Christy Pontiac*, where Hesli was mostly exonerated). Further, it may be hard to identify responsible individuals in complex and decentralized business structures. Given that many corporate crimes are profitable for the business, corporate criminality serves to induce corporate decision makers to have the corporation internalize the costs of illegal conduct within the organization.

An interesting question that arises when the corporation is charged with a crime is how to determine whether the entity had the requisite criminal intent. Federal courts have looked at the corporation's "collective" knowledge and action, even when no one individual committed the offense. Thus, the state of mind and conduct of multiple employees are aggregated and imputed to the corporation. For example, in *U.S. v. Bank of New England*, 821 F.2d 844 (1st Cir. 1987), the court deemed a corporation to have full knowledge if "one part of the corporation has half the information making up the item, and another part of the entity has the other half." This aggregation can lead to corporate criminal liability even when no individual in the corporation had the necessary *mens rea*.

4. Monetary penalties.

Does punishment of the corporation serve the general criminal justice goals of retribution, deterrence, incapacitation, rehabilitation, and restoration? Although it is easy to make the case for locking up white-collar criminals, it is harder to justify corporate criminality. The corporation cannot be jailed or physically punished, so incapacitation has to happen through other means. Instead, the corporation can be fined—with the financial burden falling on investors who often had nothing to do with the crime. And a fine, particularly if corporate management simply sees it as a cost of doing business, does not necessarily keep the corporation from committing the same crimes again.

> **FYI**
>
> Under the Federal Sentencing Guidelines, if the court finds that an organization "operated primarily for a criminal purpose or primarily by criminal means," the appropriate punishment is a fine sufficient to divest the organization of all net assets. U.S. Sentencing Guidelines Manual § 8C1.1 (2018).

> **FYI**
>
> The question whether a corporation, and therefore its shareholders, can be subject to criminal fines under the Due Process Clause was first addressed by the U.S. Supreme Court in *New York Central & Hudson River R.R. Co. v. United States*, 212 U.S. 481 (1909). The case arose under a provision of the Interstate Commerce Commission Act of 1887, which prohibited railroads from discriminating against smaller shippers, such as farmers, by giving price discounts to large shippers. When New York Central engaged in this price discrimination, federal prosecutors charged the railroad under the Elkins Act of 1903, which had created corporate criminal liability when railroad employees acted in violation of the statute within the scope of their employment. The Court acknowledged that under the common law a corporation could not commit a crime, but that Congress had concluded that corporate immunity would "take away the only means of effectively controlling" corporations engaged in interstate commerce. Further, punishing only individuals within the corporation, who the Court saw as merely "instruments" of the corporation, would not get the attention of the corporation's officers and directors. Although the Court recognized that the financial burden of criminal fines would fall on shareholders, the Court upheld the statutory scheme as critical to the success of rate regulation.

Do fines and other monetary punishment imposed against the corporation actually lead to changes in corporate behavior? Or are fines paid by the corporation simply a way for corporate executives to shift the blame and the liability on someone else? There is evidence that when executives who commit the actions that lead to corporate convictions are fired, they have difficulty finding similar work. That is, there is some evidence that corporate governance mechanisms may work to discipline employees who engage in criminal conduct.

So if monetary sanctions work, why not use civil penalties? For example, in cases of securities fraud, the SEC can collect substantial civil fines (through both enforcement and administrative proceedings), issue cease and desist orders, obtain injunctions, and even force corporations to operate under court-appointed monitors. These options would seem a better fit to rectify and deter corporate misconduct than complicated criminal proceedings and monetary sanctions.

5. Corporate "death penalty."

A corporate conviction can trigger a variety of sanctions whose purpose (or collateral effect) is to put the company out of business. Is this fair? A firm's demise can impose significant hardship on innocent corporate constituents, like employees, suppliers, creditors, and even entire communities.

Of course, the threat of putting the firm out of business can create powerful compliance incentives. But harsh entity-level penalties, which are not necessarily borne by those charged with implementing and monitoring internal compliance programs, may not adequately deter criminal conduct. And given the potential for severe collateral consequences, some have argued that corporate sanctions should be limited to monetary fines that do not trigger the firm's demise.

A "corporate death penalty" can happen in different ways: (1) the judge imposes fines that force the firm to divest itself of all its assets or that render it insolvent; (2) the criminal conviction, as happened to Arthur Andersen (see box on next page), prevents the firm from continuing business in certain regulated fields; and (3) the criminal conviction, compared to civil liability, triggers defaults under loan covenants or irreparably damages the firm's reputation in stock, bond, or customer markets. Should judges, through sentencing, be able effectively to put firms out of business?

Some commentators have argued that banks in particular have become "too big to jail," the idea being that a criminal prosecution of a large bank would lead not only to that bank's collapse but potentially would endanger the global economy. Should prosecutors consider the macroeconomic implications of the corporate death penalty when they decide whether to bring a case against banks or other systemically important institutions?

6. Deferred prosecution agreements.

Since Arthur Andersen's demise, other firms facing potential criminal liability have taken notice. And prosecutors have used this heightened concern to extract cooperation and concessions from targeted corporations—without ever indicting the corporation.

The primary method of avoiding indictment is through deferred prosecution agreements. For example, when the government found that KPMG, another accounting firm, had been helping clients evade more than $2.5 billion in taxes, the firm entered into an agreement with the government that it would turn over documents, pay fines of $450 million, and stop the practice—on the promise the government would not indict. KPMG thus avoided being branded a criminal or even an accused criminal.

But deferred prosecution agreements may come at the price of civil liberties. Corporate executives, when they learn of government concerns, are compelled to cooperate fully by assembling and turning over documents, identifying culpable individuals in the firm, waiving attorney-client privilege, and accepting whatever plea bargain the government offers. Prosecutors claim that their tactics are no different from those used in drug conspiracy cases. But corporate executives (and their lawyers) have cried foul.

7. Punishing shareholders.

When the corporation is punished, shareholders inevitably bear the

The most famous instance of a firm conviction leading to the firm's demise is Arthur Andersen LLP. The once "Big Five" accounting firm had been the auditor for Enron Corporation. When Enron experienced financial difficulties in 2001 and its accounting practices came into question, some executives and employees of Arthur Andersen destroyed documents related to prior Enron audits. A jury found Arthur Andersen guilty of "knowingly . . . corruptly persuading" another person to "alter documents" for use in an "official proceeding."

As a result of the conviction, Arthur Andersen could no longer serve as a public accounting firm because of rules that prohibit convicted criminals from being CPAs, and the firm went out of business. The conviction was later reversed by the Supreme Court, *Arthur Andersen LLP v. United States*, 544 U.S. 696 (2005), on the grounds the jury instructions failed to convey that the firm's document shredding had to be consciously wrong. Arthur Andersen executives had urged employees to observe "document retention policies," which the prosecution argued was code for employees to shred documents related to a brewing SEC investigation. The jury instructions, the Court held, incorrectly created the impression Arthur Andersen could be convicted even if its executives believed their conduct was lawful and their document retention policies (and shredding) were innocent.

But the Supreme Court reversal came too late. The damage had been done. Arthur Andersen had already been dissolved, and its clients had moved on. The lesson of the case is that being convicted, or simply being indicted, can have dire consequences to a firm's business—tantamount to a death sentence.

brunt of the monetary punishment. Should shareholders be punished for the bad acts of corporate employees and managers?

One argument is that shareholders bear responsibility for these bad acts, since they can monitor corporate agents and they benefit from the crime. But the average investor in a public corporation is arguably too removed to be an effective monitor. At most, shareholders elect the directors whose responsibility is to monitor corporate agents.

Business Lingo

An indexed mutual fund is one that attempts to mirror the returns of a particular financial index, such as the S&P 500 or the Dow Jones Industrial Average, by maintaining a portfolio of all companies in the index.

Do shareholders benefit from corporate crimes? Long-term shareholders (such as indexed mutual funds that invest retirement savings) are more likely to be around when the corporation is caught and pays a penalty. But short-term investors, who are in and out of the company's stock, may benefit from the corporate crime, without later bearing the costs of the penalty. Thus, for some investors crime pays!

B. Corporate Executives and Directors as Criminals

Corporate statutes specify that the board of directors manages and supervises the corporation's business and affairs. Given their oversight role, can directors be subject to individual criminal liability for failing to adequately supervise subordinates' activities? What about executives who manage the day-to-day business? If the animating purpose of corporate criminality is deterrence, wouldn't criminal liability for corporate directors and high-level executives be a better (and more certain) way to ensure legal compliance by the corporation?

The answer is that the law is ambivalent. Although corporate managers can be held liable for failing to prevent criminal conduct in the corporation, judges have shown some reluctance to punish individuals for organizational misdeeds. Nonetheless, the legislative trend has been to "throw the book" at the corporate scoundrels,

Take Note!

Corporate crime is not limited to fraud and business cover-ups, but also includes violations of environmental regulations, employment law, and other areas of law in which corporate activities may create externalities.

and corporate managers live under a real threat of individual prosecution if the corporation spirals into criminality.

Points for Discussion

1. Strict liability regimes.

Like criminal liability for corporations, criminal liability for corporate managers is relatively recent. Early prosecutions of managers often arose under strict liability statutes, where a failure to supervise can create liability. In 1943 the U.S. Supreme Court held corporate managers could be liable for criminal acts committed by their subordinates. In *United States v. Dotterweich*, 320 U.S. 277 (1943), the Court found that the president of a food company was subject to criminal prosecution for "introducing or delivering adulterated or misbranded drugs into interstate commerce" in violation of the Food and Drug Act. The Court held that because the Food and Drug Act contained no criminal *mens rea* (or guilty mind) requirement, the prosecution did not have to prove the president had criminal knowledge. This "puts the burden of acting at hazard upon a person otherwise innocent but standing in a responsible relation to a public danger."

Strict liability statutes put great pressure on corporate managers to institute legal compliance programs. In *United States v. Park*, 421 U.S. 658 (1975), the president of a food distributor was charged, along with his company, with five violations of the Federal Food, Drug, and Cosmetics Act for allowing food to be held in a company warehouse where it was contaminated by rodents. Park was convicted by a jury and fined $50 on each of the five counts. The Supreme Court affirmed his conviction:

> In providing sanctions which reach and touch the individuals who execute the corporate mission—and this is by no means necessarily confined to a single corporate agent or employee—the Act imposes not only a positive duty to seek out and remedy violations when they occur but also, and primarily, a duty to implement measures that will insure that violations will not occur. The requirements of foresight and vigilance imposed on responsible corporate agents are beyond question demanding, and perhaps onerous, but they are not more stringent than the positions of authority in business enterprises whose services and products affect the health and well-being of the public that supports them.

The Court interpreted "responsible corporate agent" to preclude a conviction on the basis of an officer's corporate position alone. Rather, the Court explained that criminal liability attached only if the jury could find Park "had a responsible relation to the situation, and by virtue of his position had authority and responsibility to deal with the situation." The Court found significant Park's awareness that the company's internal system for ensuring its sanitary conditions in its warehouses was not working and his failure to restructure that system once he was on notice of sanitary problems at company warehouses.

The Court recognized internal compliance systems are not infallible. The Court indicated that Park could have raised an affirmative defense that he was powerless to prevent the violation and have sought a jury instruction that the government was required to prove beyond a reasonable doubt that he could have prevented the violation.

2. Wrongful failure to supervise.

Criminal liability of managers is trickier when the regulatory regime, such as environmental protection, does not impose strict liability. Criminal liability is readily established when a director knew of the environmental violation, either instructing subordinates to perform the illegal acts or simply acquiescing in their performance. But when the director did not participate in the illegal acts, prosecution under statutes requiring proof of criminal knowledge is more difficult.

Prosecutions of senior officials for wrongful failure to supervise are especially difficult in cases involving securities or bank fraud. In fact, no senior managers of major banks were prosecuted for crimes related to the Financial Crisis of 2008. The reasons for the lack of prosecutions were complicated, but they illustrate the difficulties associated with holding senior executives responsible for acts committed by their subordinates (or their subordinates' subordinates).

Take Note!

Under the Resource Conservation and Recovery Act, "responsible corporate officers" may be held liable for violations of the statute, which makes it a crime to "knowingly transport or cause to be transported any hazardous waste." Courts differ on the requisite knowledge for criminal liability under the state. Some courts require proof the officer knew the waste was hazardous. *United States v. MacDonald & Watson Waste Oil Co.*, 933 F.2d 35 (1st Cir. 1991). Others accept proof that the officer knew the waste had the potential to be hazardous. *United States v. Kelly*, 167 F.3d 1176 (7th Cir. 1999).

3. Failure to institute legal compliance programs.

Are there criminal consequences for directors who fail to institute legal compliance programs? The Federal Sentencing Guidelines for Organizations, adopted in 1991, call for substantial fines for any corporation convicted of a federal crime.

But the Guidelines reduce a corporation's monetary sanctions if the corporation "maintains internal mechanisms for deterring, detecting, and reporting criminal conduct."

Interestingly, the Sentecing Guidelines do not address the question of *individual* criminal liability for directors when the corporation has committed a crime. The Guidelines assume that corporate-level sanctions will motivate directors and officers to implement legal compliance programs in the best interests of the corporation. Given that legal compliance programs are effectively required as a matter of corporate fiduciary duties (as we will see in Chapter 23, Board Oversight), corporate directors have strong reasons to avoid the risk of personal civil liability in a derivative suit for not implementing a legal compliance program that would satisfy the Sentencing Guidelines.

To take advantage of the sentencing reductions offered by the Guidelines' safe harbor, the corporation's compliance program must be detailed and must comply with all industry standards and government regulations, and any offense charged to the corporation must be committed by low-level, non-supervisory personnel. An ineffective compliance program does not mitigate corporate liability any more than no program at all.

Make the Connection

A derivative suit is one brought by a shareholder on behalf of the corporation to recover losses caused by a breach of a director's fiduciary duty. *See* Chapter 4, Corporation Basics; Chapter 19, Shareholder Litigation.

4. Sentencing of white-collar criminals.

The Federal Sentencing Guidelines, in addition to specifying sanctions for corporate criminality, address the disparity in the sentencing of similarly situated offenders, particularly in white-collar cases. The Guidelines initially established *mandatory* ranges of maximum and minimum sentences for specified offenses based on the characteristics of the crime.

The Sentencing Guidelines, which included stiff sentences for white-collar criminals, had the effect of reducing the disparity in sentencing. But in 2005, the Supreme Court held in *United States v. Booker*, 543 U.S. 220 (2005), that the mandated use of enhancing factors not found by a jury was unconstitutional, thus rendering the Guidelines advisory only.

After *Booker*, judges began to deviate from the sentencing ranges, often with downward-departure sentences for white-collar offenders. Some argued that the intention of Congress in the Guidelines to have judges impose sentences in white-collar cases that correspond to the impact of the offender's crime on society had been frustrated.

But when Enron and other frauds were revealed in the early 2000s, Congress responded in 2002 with the Sarbanes-Oxley Act and the White Collar Crime Penalty Enhancement Act. Maximum sentences for mail and wire fraud (the most common form of fraud) were quadrupled, and many frauds previously subject to regulatory civil enforcement were criminalized. Although the new laws increased sentencing ranges, they did not provide much guidance to judges on using the higher range to punish and deter white-collar crime. Judges imposing sentences under the new law have been inconsistent in imposing higher sentences on white-collar defendants, often showing leniency to high-profile corporate offenders compared to low-value economic offenders (such as check forgers).

Food for Thought

After the collapse of Enron, the company's former CEO Jeff Skilling was originally sentenced to 24 years in prison, slightly above the minimum sentence called for by the Federal Sentencing Guidelines. Was the sentencing judge lenient? Consider that under Texas law, the minimum sentence for first-degree murder is five years. Was orchestrating one of the largest accounting frauds in U.S. corporate history, which resulted in billions in losses to investors and left thousands unemployed, the equivalent of a murder spree?

Ultimately, after appealing his sentence to the U.S. Supreme Court, Skilling was able to reach a deal with federal prosecutors to reduce his sentence to 14 years. He completed his sentence in February 2019.

5. Over-criminalization of corporate law.

Whether talking about individual or entity liability in the corporation, many scholars have criticized the "over-criminalization" of corporate law. They point to a tendency to regulate what before had been non-criminal behavior through criminal prosecutions. Is it fair, for example, that a bank official who participates in illegal money transfers should be charged criminally under a statute without *mens rea* (strict liability)?

Making corporate executives criminally liable reflects a sense of social condemnation of corporate executives who in the name of increasing corporate profits disregard how corporate activities affect others. Perhaps individual punishment satisfies the longing for retribution, even though judges show less blood-thirst than the public and press. But if the goal is primarily deterrence and rehabilitation, isn't corporate-level punishment more effective and thus preferable for inducing attitudes of corporate responsibility?

CHAPTER 15

Corporate Environmental Liability

Much of modern regulation seeks to correct failures in private markets. One such market failure arises from "externalities," costs that corporations impose on third parties who are not paid and do not agree to bear those costs. A classic example of an externality is environmental pollution that corporations "externalize" to the rest of society. In other words, corporations can benefit from activities that generate pollution, but not bear the full cost of those activities—instead, society bears those costs.

This chapter identifies how federal environmental law seeks to shift these externalized costs back on the corporation and corporate insiders. Essentially, there are two approaches. First, regulation can hold *corporations* responsible for externalizing costs. A corporation might be found directly liable for its own actions or indirectly liable for actions taken by one of its subsidiaries. The federal environmental statutes uniformly define regulated "persons" to include corporations.

Second, regulation can hold *individuals* responsible for externalizing costs. As with corporate liability, there is a direct-indirect distinction: individuals might be directly liable for violating environmental standards, or they might be indirectly liable if they supervised others who violated the law. Indirect liability can implicate officers and directors.

Both corporations and individuals can be found civilly or criminally liable for violating environmental laws. Corporate civil liability is the norm and often arises without need to show fault. Individual civil liability typically arises when high-level employees or employees charged with environmen-

Make the Connection

Regulatory recognition of the corporation is sometimes confused with piercing the corporate veil (see Chapter 13, Piercing the Corporate Veil). In piercing cases, courts decide in a fact-specific setting whether to disregard corporate limited liability to protect outsiders' expectations under state contract and tort law. In regulatory cases, courts and administrative agencies ask whether the statutory scheme (federal or state) recognizes corporate attributes arising from state corporate law, such as corporate personality or limited liability.

tal compliance fail to supervise other employees or fail to adopt remedial measures. Criminal liability is less common, but typically arises under similar circumstances, when one or more corporate actors knowingly violate an environmental standard—whether government prosecutors have targeted the corporation or individuals, or both simultaneously. Note that when the corporation is found civilly or criminally liable, any uninsured payments are borne by shareholders.

Although state law generally governs issues of liability within the corporation, federal law trumps state law. As the Supreme Court has said, a state may not endow its "corporate creatures with the power to place themselves above the Congress of the United States and defeat the federal policy which Congress has announced." *Anderson v. Abbott,* 321 U.S. 349 (1944). Although both state and federal law regulate corporate environmental practices, here our focus is on federal environmental law, which has created regulatory schemes applicable to corporations in every state.

Environmental law casebooks typically examine a broad range of federal statutes, but here our goal is more modest. We focus on one statute, the Comprehensive Environmental Response, Compensation and Liability Act (the Superfund statute), which was passed by Congress in 1980 to remedy toxic waste sites around the country and to create a liability scheme in which responsible parties pay for the costs of remediation. The Superfund statute raises questions that also arise more generally in environmental law: Do corporate agency and limited liability principles apply in the context of environmental regulation? When can corporations be held civilly or criminally liable under federal environmental laws? What is the liability of corporate parents whose subsidiaries have engaged in harmful environmental practices? We focus on the Superfund statute, because the leading Supreme Court case of *United States v. Bestfoods,* addresses many of these questions.

At the end of the chapter, we briefly consider the potential liability of corporate directors and officers for corporate violations of environmental law. Reflecting a desire to create individual incentives for environmental compliance, environmental regulation sometimes disregards the usual rules of limited liability and imposes individual liability on corporate executives who supervised employees who engaged in environmental misdeeds.

A. Corporate Environmental Liability

Comprehensive Environmental Response, Compensation and Liability Act (CERCLA) § 107 (42 U.S.C. § 9607)

(a) (2) Covered persons; scope; recoverable costs and damages

Any person who at the time of disposal of any hazardous substance owned or operated any facility at which such hazardous substances were disposed of . . . shall be liable for . . . all costs of removal or remedial action incurred by the United States Government or a State.

CERCLA imposes liability for the costs of cleaning up toxic waste sites on the "owners" and "operators" of facilities where hazardous chemicals have been dumped. It was adopted in 1980 in response to the serious environmental and health risks posed by industrial pollution.

CERCLA defines the term "person" to include corporations and other business organizations. But the phrase "owner or operator" is defined only by tautology as "any person owning or operating" a facility. This circular definition generates more questions than it answers. For example, a significant question under the statute, given that many companies that actually owned and operated these facilities have gone bankrupt or were sold before Superfund claims were made, has been whether parent corporations can be liable for the clean-up costs.

Food for Thought

Does a company's market reputation suffer when it becomes liable for environmental violations? A comprehensive study of corporate environmental liability found declines in share prices of companies held liable, but the declines did not exceed the amount paid in fines and compliance costs. Of the 478 cases studied, only 28 involved criminal claims, compared to 197 civil suits and 146 regulatory actions.

Of the 148 firms for which information about legal penalties was available, the study found average (median) fines of $13.2 million ($1.52 million) and average (median) compliance costs of $93.6 million ($13.5 million). Average costs were higher given the handful of companies that incurred extraordinarily high penalties (such as the $5.3 billion *Exxon Valdez* settlement).

Normal rules of limited liability—which allow the separation of assets and risks within corporate groups—would say no. That is, corporate parents can place risks in separately-incorporated subsidiaries without incurring liability, except when exceptional circumstances call for piercing the corporate veil. But over the first two decades of Superfund enforcement, federal courts often interpreted the "owner" and "operator" categories expansively to impose liability on parent corporations for the dumping activities of their subsidiaries.

United States v. Bestfoods involved a suit brought by the federal government for the costs of cleaning up industrial waste generated by a chemical plant in Muskegon, Michigan. The plant had begun dumping hazardous chemicals in 1957. The company that owned the plant then was sold in 1965 to CPC International, Inc., the original defendant in the case. CPC operated the business as a wholly-owned subsidiary, keeping many of the original managers who performed duties for both corporations. The dumping continued under CPC's ownership until 1972, when the subsidiary was sold to another company, which eventually went bankrupt.

In 1981, the Environmental Protection Agency began to clean up the site, with a remedial plan costing tens of millions of dollars. To recover some of that money, the United States filed an action under § 107 against CPC and others. The District Court held a trial on liability and found that CPC, as the parent corporation of the subsidiary engaged in the hazardous dumping, had "owned or operated" the facility under the statute.

A divided panel of the Sixth Circuit reversed, concluding that a parent corporation can be held liable as an operator "only when the requirements necessary to pierce the corporate veil under state law are met." Applying Michigan veil-piercing law, the Court of Appeals decided that CPC was not liable for the actions of its subsidiary, since the parent and subsidiary maintained separate personalities and the parent did not use the corporate form to perpetrate fraud or subvert justice.

The issue before the Supreme Court was whether under CERCLA a parent corporation that actively participated in, and exercised control over, the operations of a subsidiary may, without more, be held liable as an "owner" or "operator" of a polluting facility owned or operated by its subsidiary. The Supreme Court answered that the corporate parent could not be held *indirectly* (or *derivatively*) liable, unless the corporate veil could be pierced. But the Court also held that a corporate parent that actively participated in, and exercised control over, the operations of the facility itself could be held *directly* liable in its own right as an "operator" of the facility.

In other words, in *United States v. Bestfoods,* the Supreme Court rejected the more expansive approaches to defining "owner" and "operator" used by some lower courts. It held that "owner" or "operator" liability under CERCLA should conform to corporate law norms of limited liability. As you read the case, notice the pervasive presence of state corporate law in this area of federal environmental regulation.

United States v. Bestfoods

524 U.S. 51 (1998)

Justice Souter delivered the opinion of the Court.

It is a general principle of corporate law deeply "ingrained in our economic and legal systems" that a parent corporation (so-called because of control through ownership of another corporation's stock) is not liable for the acts of its subsidiaries. Thus it is hornbook law that "the exercise of the 'control' which stock ownership gives to the stockholders will not create liability beyond the assets of the subsidiary. That 'control' includes the election of directors, the making of bylaws and the doing of all other acts incident to the legal status of stockholders. Nor will a duplication of some or all of the directors or executive officers be fatal." Although this respect for corporate distinctions when the subsidiary is a polluter has been severely criticized in the literature, nothing in CERCLA purports to reject this bedrock principle, and against this venerable common-law backdrop, the congressional silence is audible.

But there is an equally fundamental principle of corporate law, applicable to the parent-subsidiary relationship as well as generally, that the corporate veil may be pierced and the shareholder held liable for the corporation's conduct when, inter alia, the corporate form would otherwise be misused to accomplish certain wrongful purposes, most notably fraud, on the shareholder's behalf. Nothing in CERCLA purports to rewrite this well-settled rule, either. CERCLA is thus like many another congressional enactment in giving no indication that "the entire corpus of state corporation law is to be replaced simply because a plaintiff's cause of action is based upon a federal statute," and the failure of the statute to speak to a matter as fundamental as the liability implications of corporate ownership demands application of the rule that "in order to abrogate a common-law principle, the statute must speak directly to the question addressed by the common law." The Court of Appeals was accordingly correct in holding that when (but only when) the corporate veil may be pierced, may a parent corporation be charged with derivative CERCLA liability for its subsidiary's actions.[10]

If the Act rested liability entirely on ownership of a polluting facility, this opinion might end here; but CERCLA liability may turn on operation as well as ownership, and nothing in the statute's terms bars a parent corporation from direct liability for its own actions in operating a facility owned by its subsidiary.

---

[10] Some courts and commentators have suggested that this indirect, veil-piercing approach can subject a parent corporation to liability only as an owner, and not as an operator. We think it is otherwise, however. If a subsidiary that operates, but does not own, a facility is so pervasively controlled by its parent for a sufficiently improper purpose to warrant veil piercing, the parent may be held derivatively liable for the subsidiary's acts as an operator.

The fact that a corporate subsidiary happens to own a polluting facility operated by its parent does nothing to displace the rule that the parent "corporation is itself responsible for the wrongs committed by its agents in the course of its business," and whereas the rules of veil piercing limit derivative liability for the actions of another corporation, CERCLA's "operator" provision is concerned primarily with direct liability for one's own actions. It is this direct liability that is properly seen as being at issue here.

Under the plain language of the statute, any person who operates a polluting facility is directly liable for the costs of cleaning up the pollution. This is so regardless of whether that person is the facility's owner, the owner's parent corporation, or even a saboteur who sneaks into the facility at night to discharge its poisons out of malice. If any such act of operating a corporate subsidiary's facility is done on behalf of a parent corporation, the existence of the parent-subsidiary relationship under state corporate law is simply irrelevant to the issue of direct liability.

This much is easy to say: the difficulty comes in defining actions sufficient to constitute direct parental "operation." Here, of course, we may again rue the uselessness of CERCLA's definition of a facility's "operator" as "any person operating" the facility. In the organizational sense, the word ordinarily means "to conduct the affairs of; manage: operate a business." So, under CERCLA, an operator must manage, direct, or conduct operations specifically related to pollution, that is, operations having to do with the leakage or disposal of hazardous waste, or decisions about compliance with environmental regulations.

With this understanding, we think that the appeals court erred in limiting direct liability under the statute to a parent's sole operation, so as to eliminate any possible finding that CPC is liable as an operator on the facts of this case.

By emphasizing that "CPC is directly liable under section 107(a)(2) as an operator because CPC actively participated in and exerted significant control over the subsidiary's business and decision-making," the District Court applied the "actual control" test of whether the parent "actually operated the business of its subsidiary," as several Circuits have employed it.

The well-taken objection to the actual control test, however, is its fusion of direct and indirect liability; the test is administered by asking a question about the relationship between the two corporations (an issue going to indirect liability) instead of a question about the parent's interaction with the subsidiary's facility (the source of any direct liability). If, however, direct liability for the parent's operation of the facility is to be kept distinct from derivative liability for the subsidiary's own operation, the focus of the enquiry must necessarily be different under the two tests. "The question is not whether the parent operates the subsidiary, but rather whether it operates the facility, and that operation is evidenced by participation in the activities of the facility, not the subsidiary." The analysis should rest on the relationship between CPC and the Muskegon facility itself.

In addition to (and perhaps as a reflection of) the erroneous focus on the relationship between CPC and the subsidiary, even those findings of the District Court that might be taken to speak to the extent of CPC's activity at the facility itself are flawed, for the District Court wrongly assumed that the actions of the joint officers and directors are necessarily attributable to CPC.

In imposing direct liability, the District Court failed to recognize that "it is entirely appropriate for directors of a parent corporation to serve as directors of its subsidiary, and that fact alone may not serve to expose the parent corporation to liability for its subsidiary's acts."

This recognition that the corporate personalities remain distinct has its corollary in the "well established principle [of corporate law] that directors and officers holding positions with a parent and its subsidiary can and do 'change hats' to represent the two corporations separately, despite their common ownership." It cannot be enough to establish liability here that dual officers and directors made policy decisions and supervised activities at the facility. The Government would have to show that, despite the general presumption to the contrary, the officers and directors were acting in their capacities as CPC officers and directors, and not as subsidiary officers and directors, when they committed those acts.

In sum, the District Court's focus on the relationship between parent and subsidiary (rather than parent and facility) treated CERCLA as though it displaced or fundamentally altered common-law standards of limited liability. Indeed, if common corporate personnel acting at management and directorial levels were enough to support a finding of a parent corporation's direct operator liability under CERCLA, then the resort to veil piercing to establish indirect, derivative liability for the subsidiary's violations would be academic. There would in essence be a relaxed, CERCLA-specific rule of derivative liability that would banish traditional standards and expectations from the law of CERCLA liability. But, such a rule does not arise from congressional silence, and CERCLA's silence is dispositive.

In our enquiry into the meaning Congress presumably had in mind when it used the verb "to operate," we recognized that the statute obviously meant something more than mere mechanical activation of pumps and valves, and must be read to contemplate "operation" as including the exercise of direction over the facility's activities. The Court of Appeals recognized this by indicating that a parent can be held directly liable when the parent operates the facility in the stead of its subsidiary or alongside the subsidiary in some sort of a joint venture.

We anticipated a further possibility above, however, when we observed that a dual officer or director might depart so far from the norms of parental influence exercised through dual officeholding as to serve the parent, even when ostensibly acting on behalf of the subsidiary in operating the facility. Yet another possibility, suggested by the facts of this case, is that an agent of the parent with no hat to wear but the parent's hat might manage or direct activities at the facility.

Identifying such an occurrence calls for line-drawing yet again, since the acts of direct operation that give rise to parental liability must necessarily be distinguished from the interference that stems from the normal relationship between parent and subsidiary. Again norms of corporate behavior (undisturbed by any CERCLA provision) are crucial reference points. "Activities that involve the facility but which are consistent with the parent's investor status, such as monitoring of the subsidiary's performance, supervision of the subsidiary's finance and capital budget decisions, and articulation of general policies and procedures, should not give rise to direct liability." The critical question is whether, in degree and detail, actions directed to the facility by an agent of the parent alone are eccentric under accepted norms of parental oversight of a subsidiary's facility.

There is, in fact, some evidence that CPC engaged in just this type and degree of activity at the Muskegon plant. The District Court's opinion speaks of an agent of CPC alone who played a conspicuous part in dealing with the toxic risks emanating from the operation of the plant. Williams worked only for CPC; he was not an employee, officer, or director of Ott II, and thus, his actions were of necessity taken only on behalf of CPC. The District Court found that "CPC became directly involved in environmental and regulatory matters through the work of Williams, CPC's governmental and environmental affairs director. Williams became heavily involved in environmental issues at Ott II." He "actively participated in and exerted control over a variety of Ott II environmental matters," and he "issued directives regarding Ott II's responses to regulatory inquiries."

We think that these findings are enough to raise an issue of CPC's operation of the facility through Williams's actions, though we would draw no ultimate conclusion from these findings at this point.

Points for Discussion

1. "Owner" or "operator" liability.

As *Bestfoods* makes clear, CERCLA liability turns on whether a corporation is the "owner" or "operator" of a polluting facility. Because the purpose of the statute is to identify responsible persons so they can pay for remediation, doesn't it make sense to interpret these words so that any corporation that conducts its for-profit operations through a subsidiary, and controls the subsidiary's board and its operations, should be deemed both the owner and operator of the subsidiary's facilities? If the purpose of the statute is remediation, why should taxpayers foot the bill to clean up toxic waste sites, rather than the business entities that profited from and had the power to prevent the pollution?

Why did the Supreme Court decide that in the normal parent-subsidiary situation, the parent corporation was neither the owner nor the operator of the polluting facilities?

2. Derivative vs. direct liability.

The Supreme Court identified two types of CERCLA liability for parent corporations whose subsidiaries owned or operated a polluting facility. The Court held that *derivative* (or *indirect*) liability could arise only under traditional veil-piercing standards—that is, the parent would assume the liability of the subsidiary when the corporate form had been "misused to accomplish certain wrongful purposes." The Court held that *direct* liability could arise when the parent "operates the facility, evidenced by participation in the activities of the facility"—noting that "norms of corporate behavior are crucial reference points."

Food for Thought

Following the Supreme Court's decision in *Bestfoods*, did environmental operations by subsidiaries change in jurisdictions where the courts had previously adopted veil-piercing standards that created parent liability more readily than allowed by the Court? A study found that the increased liability protection for corporate parents led to a 10% increase in toxic emissions by subsidiaries, an increase not linked to increased production. In fact, after the Court's decision, subsidiaries were 12–25% less likely to engage in pollution abatement activities related to production. The study found—consistent with the view that limited liability induces risk-shifting behavior—that these effects were more pronounced in less-solvent subsidiaries, as well as parents closer to financial distress. Does the study support the view that limited liability creates a "moral hazard" that encourages economic actors to be less responsible?

Given that both derivative and direct liability require a showing of abnormal corporate behavior, what's the difference between the two standards?

3. Deference to corporate norms.

In articulating the standards for parent liability under CERCLA, the Court refers to corporate limited liability as a "bedrock principle," though without mentioning that it arises under state law. Why this oversight? Why should *state* limited liability norms govern a *federal* regulatory regime, whose purpose is to have parties pay for clean-up costs of toxic waste sites for which they were responsible? Isn't federal law supreme?

In short, aren't national environmental policies <u>more important</u> than state-based policies favoring capital formation?

Make the Connection

As you will discover when we look at corporate fiduciary duties, corporate directors have oversight responsibilities—and what's sometimes described as a "duty of obedience"—that requires that they ensure the corporation complies with internal and external norms. This means, among other things, that directors must implement legal compliance programs that ensure the corporation abides by relevant legal requirements, such as money-laundering rules for banks and pollution-abatement requirements for industrial companies. Further, corporate directors and officers cannot choose to disregard external norms on a cost-benefit analysis based on a calculation of the expected profitability versus the likelihood of detection and costs of getting caught. As legal scholars have pointed out, knowing non-compliance with legal norms is not only a breach of fiduciary duty, but also unprotected by the business judgment rule and director-exculpation charter provisions. Thus, directors can be held personally liable for illegal acts committed by the corporation "even though committed to benefit the corporation." *Miller v. Am. Tel. & Telegraph Co.*, 507 F.2d, 759, 761 (3d Cir. 1974). Isn't it curious that even though *environmental law* may not require parent corporations to ensure environmental compliance by their subsidiaries, *corporate law* may compel corporate directors and officers to ensure such compliance?

---

4. Rewarding laxity?

Notice that the Court's standards for parent liability under CERCLA are more lenient for corporations that put their environmentally-sensitive operations in a wholly-owned subsidiary and then make no effort to oversee the subsidiary's environmental compliance or handling of toxic chemicals, compared to corporations that seek to direct and manage the subsidiary's environmental practices. Does this make sense?

Food for Thought

Does corporate environmental friendliness pay? One <u>study</u> looked at whether companies reaped financial benefits by engaging in positive, voluntary environmental action. The study found that some environmental initiatives, such as philanthropic gifts, resulted in higher share value, but others, such as voluntary emissions reductions, resulted in lower share value. Sometimes it seems no good deed goes unpunished.

5. Whose corporate norms?

The Court left open whether "norms of corporate behavior" would be borrowed from state law or would be a matter of federal common law. If a matter of state law, should they come from the state of incorporation? Does it make sense for a state (or even a foreign country) with stringent piercing norms to set the standards for environmental liability that apply to another state where the toxic dumping occurred?

B. Environmental Liability of Directors and Officers

Parent corporations are often the only deep pockets in cases of environmental liability. But deterrence and punishment may be more effective when liability is aimed at individuals in the polluting corporation. Generally, environmental statutes contemplate civil and criminal liability for individuals who *directly* violate environmental law. In fact, courts have imposed criminal liability on low-level employees under statutes aimed at persons "in charge" of a polluting facility.

But what about *indirect* violations of law? Can corporate directors and officers be held responsible for misdeeds by others in the corporation, even when they did not engage in the illegal conduct? Normally, regulatory schemes impose liability on corporate managers only if their actions constituted an independent wrong. Thus, for example, a manager who engages in sexual harassment in the workplace may be personally liable, in addition to making the corporation liable. However, managers who supervise others generally can avoid personal liability by asserting that they did not order or condone the wrongful conduct, which they will invariably cast as being against "corporate policy."

> **FYI**
>
> Courts in cases involving statutory liability have been less willing to use traditional piercing factors. In fact, according to the Thompson study (which was described in Chapter 13, Piercing the Corporate Veil), courts in these cases refer to such traditional piercing factors as undercapitalization, failure to follow formalities, and misrepresentation only half as often as they do in contract cases.

Environmental laws, however, are different. Federal environmental laws create an exception to the norms of corporate limited liability and impose personal liability on corporate executives responsible for environmental compliance. For example, prosecutors have used the Resource Conservation and Recovery Act to prosecute individual corporate officers for their supervisory role. Not only does the statute explicitly refer to "responsible corporate officer" liability, but prosecutors often assert that officers have the authority to prevent hazardous environmental practices.

Likewise, both the Clean Air Act and Clean Water Act specifically include "any responsible corporate officer" in the definition of "person" for criminal violations. 42 U.S.C. § 7413(c)(6) (2000) (CAA); 33 U.S.C. § 1319(c)(6) (2000) (CWA). Prosecutors have brought cases against individuals, including officers and directors, under these statutes as well.

Despite these prosecutions, some courts have been hesitant to accept the imposition of federal environmental liability on officers and directors. Following the philosophy articulated in *Bestfoods*, some judges have been reluctant to find a director's or officer's corporate position and power alone to be enough to create individual liability. Although prosecutors continue to target both corporations and individuals, their efforts clearly are not sufficient to have corporations or individuals internalize the full cost of environment-related externalities. Total civil enforcement case initiations and conclusions at the Environmental Protection Agency declined from nearly 4,000 in 2008 to fewer than 2,000 in 2018. The number of criminal cases opened annually by the EPA has declined from more than 300 in 2008 to just over 100 in 2018. Although there were several large criminal settlements during the 2010s, against British Petroleum in 2013, Duke Energy in 2015, and Volkswagen in 2017, the total amount of EPA criminal fines, restitution, and court ordered projects in 2018 was just $88 million.

Food for Thought

Despite evidence that limited liability encourages externalization of environmental costs, a growing body of academic literature suggests that corporations often comply with environmental regulations and even *voluntary* environmental standards. For example, a recent large-sample study that surveyed managers at industrial companies throughout the United States found high levels of compliance with *voluntary* environmental programs and the institution of corporate environmental stewardship practices beyond what regulation requires. Sometimes looming regulation explained these beyond-compliance actions, but so too did such factors as support from top-level management and companies that sought community support. In short, "tone at the top" seems to matter, and individual liability for violations of environmental regulation may serve as a useful subliminal "nudge."

Interestingly, it has been easier to impose civil liability rather than criminal liability on individual managers, particularly under CERCLA. In Superfund cases courts have regularly sidestepped the traditional veil-piercing criteria—such as active participation and lack of corporate formalities—to impose direct "operator" liability on individual officers who "could have prevented" the hazardous dumping. In addition, some lower courts have used traditional piercing analysis to impose *derivative* CERCLA liability on individuals for an insolvent corporation's CERCLA obligations.

In other words, in the non-criminal context, environmental policies seem to matter more than corporate law notions of limited liability for corporate executives.

Test Your Knowledge

To assess your understanding of the Chapter 13, 14, and 15 material in this module, click here to take a quiz.

MODULE VI – CORPORATE GOVERNANCE

CHAPTER 16

Shareholder Voting Rights

The three chapters in this module of the book introduce you to the role of shareholders in corporate governance, with a focus on shareholder voting rights. Voting is one of the central issues in corporate governance, and is the first of the shareholder rights—vote, sue, and sell—that we mentioned early in the book.

In this chapter, we lay out the basics of shareholder voting rights and how corporate law protects them. The next chapter describes how shareholders obtain information in exercising their voting rights and how the law attempts to ensure honest and complete disclosure to shareholders. The last chapter in this module looks at shareholder activism in the public corporation.

Shareholders are often called the "owners" of the corporation. But their governance role is limited by corporate law's tenet of centralized management. The board of directors, not the shareholders, has the authority to manage and direct the business and affairs of the corporation.

Shareholders exercise their limited corporate governance role mostly by voting. Shareholders annually elect the corporation's directors, and they can remove and replace directors in some circumstances. Shareholders frequently decide whether to approve certain *fundamental transactions*—such as mergers, sale of the corporation's significant business assets, voluntary dissolution of the corporation, and amendments to the articles of incorporation. Shareholders also can make recommendations to the board concerning matters within the board's sphere of responsibility, and they have the power to amend the bylaws.

This chapter has three parts. First, we outline the basics of shareholder voting, including the annual election of directors to the board. Second, we consider the power of shareholders to initiate changes by making recommendations to the board, by altering the board's composition, and by amending the corporation's bylaws. Finally, we consider how courts respond when the board seeks to interfere with shareholder initiatives.

A. Basics of Shareholder Voting

1. Shareholder Meetings

Shareholders act at regularly scheduled annual meetings and at special meetings convened for particular purposes. At the annual meeting the only matter required of shareholders is to elect directors. Nonetheless, boards of directors often seek shareholder approval of other matters, such as the appointment of auditors, the adoption of management compensation plans, or the ratification of some decisions the board has made during the past year.

If an annual meeting has not been held in the previous 15 months (13 months under Delaware's statute), any holder of voting stock can require the corporation to convene an annual meeting, at which new directors can be elected. Special meetings may be called by the board or by a person authorized in the articles or bylaws, or under some statutes (but not in Delaware) by any 10% shareholder.

Shareholders can also act by means of written consent instead of a meeting. Some statutes require action by written consent to be unanimous, effectively limiting the procedure to closely-held corporations. Under Delaware's statute, action by written consent can be taken by a majority of a corporation's voting shares. This gives shareholders of Delaware corporations the power—often useful in battles for corporate control—to act without waiting for a meeting and without having to provide advance notice to the company's management or to other shareholders. The consent procedure can be eliminated or restricted in the articles. The Delaware statute also contains a separate provision that requires unanimous written consent when shareholders elect directors by written consent in lieu of holding an annual meeting.

2. Shareholder Voting Procedures

Shareholders entitled to vote must receive written notice of the shareholder meeting. The notice, which typically must be sent at least 10 days, but no more than 60 days, before the meeting, describes the time and location of the meeting. The notice for special meetings must also describe the purpose of the meeting.

The shares entitled to be voted at the meeting are fixed on the "record date," a date set by the board before notice is sent to shareholders. Only those shareholders whose ownership is reflected on the corporation's books as of the record date are entitled to notice and to vote. In other words, shareholders who *sell* between the record date and the meeting date are entitled to vote, but shareholder who *buy* between the record date and the meeting date are not.

Most statutes require that shareholder meetings have a quorum equal to a majority of shares entitled to vote. The quorum may be increased or reduced in the articles or bylaws, though some statutes (including in Delaware) require a quorum of at least one-third. Quorum requirements protect against a minority faction calling a meeting and taking action without the presence of a majority.

Shareholders can vote in person at a meeting. Alternatively, unlike directors, shareholders can choose not to attend a meeting and instead vote by proxy. A proxy is simply the signed appointment in writing of an agent to appear and vote on behalf of the shareholder. The proxy may give the proxy holder discretion to vote as he pleases or may direct a particular vote. Unless made irrevocable, the proxy can be revoked by the shareholder at any time by submitting a notice of revocation, signing a later-dated proxy, or appearing in person at the meeting. Many statutes limit proxies to 11 months, unless a longer term is specified.

Once proxy holders present their proxies at the meeting and establish they are the agent for the shares represented, they cast their ballot (which may have been decided by the shareholder). When questions arise about the validity of proxies, the board typically designates an election inspector—a professional hired to verify signatures, ensure proper voting by fiduciaries, confirm the dating of proxies, count ballots, and certify the result. Delaware's statute requires that public corporations appoint one or more inspectors in advance of any shareholder meeting.

3. Shareholder Voting Rights

The general corporate law rule is one-share/one-vote, unless the articles specify otherwise. Supermajority voting or voting caps on any shareholder who owns more than a specified percentage of shares are permissible, but mostly used in closely-held corporations. Non-voting shares are also permissible, as are classes of shares that have greater or lesser votes. For example, Google's Class A shares have one vote each, but its Class B shares, which are controlled by the company's founders, have ten votes each. Snap issued public shares that have no vote.

Shareholders must approve certain fundamental transactions as specified in the relevant corporate statute. Some statutes specify a *simple majority* for shareholder approval of fundamental transactions: "the votes cast favoring the action exceed the votes cast opposing the action." Other statutes, including in Delaware, specify an *absolute majority*: "a majority of the outstanding stock of the corporation entitled to vote thereon." Shareholder voting on fundamental transactions is mandatory. Shareholder approval cannot be waived or be based on less than the specified majority.

> ### Example 16.1
>
> ABC Corporation has 100 shares outstanding, with 60 shares present or represented at a shareholders' meeting. If a simple majority is required for shareholder approval, the vote of 31 shares entitled to vote is sufficient. If an absolute majority is required, 51 of the 100 shares entitled to vote is required.

All directors are up for election at the annual meeting, unless the articles of incorporation provide for *staggered* terms, in which event shareholders elect directors for terms of two or three years. The power of shareholders to elect directors is exclusive, except when a board seat is vacant. In that case, the vacancy can be filled either by shareholders or by the remaining directors, unless the articles provide otherwise.

Directors can be elected either by *plurality voting*, which means that the top vote-getters for open directorships win those seats, or by *majority voting*, which means that each elected director must obtain a majority. Thus, under plurality voting, if a corporation has 9 open seats and the board nominates 9 directors and there are no other nominees, all of the board's nominees are elected so long as a quorum is present and each nominee receives at least one vote. Recently, in response to shareholder pressure, many public corporations—and most large public corporations—now provide for majority voting in director elections. To be seated, each nominee must receive a majority of votes cast. Any nominee who does not receive a majority must resign (or act consistently with the majority voting bylaw provision). That seat is then filled by the board or left open until a future election.

What's That?

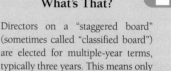

Directors on a "staggered board" (sometimes called "classified board") are elected for multiple-year terms, typically three years. This means only part of the board (one-third) is up for election each year, making a takeover or voting insurgency more difficult.

"Cumulative voting" allows shareholders to concentrate their votes for particular candidates, thus increasing the likelihood of minority representation on the board. Cumulative voting, once required in corporations, is now optional under most state corporate laws.

Food for Thought

Generally, the incumbent board uses corporate funds to call and conduct shareholder meetings. This includes soliciting proxies, the principal means by which shareholders in public corporations exercise their voting rights. Financial control by incumbent directors over the voting mechanism has substantial, long-standing support in the cases. Incumbents thus have a tremendous advantage in voting contests. Insurgents seeking to displace the incumbent board must use their own funds to finance a proxy solicitation, and can recover their costs only if they prevail and receive shareholder ratification. Is this one-sided corporate voting democratic?

Shareholders typically can remove directors with or without cause, unless the articles provide that directors can be removed only for cause. The power of shareholders to remove directors for cause is mandatory, and it cannot be restricted.

B. Shareholder Power to Initiate Action

Shareholder rights to approve or veto fundamental transactions are passive. The board initiates the decision to merge or engage in a similar transaction. Shareholders react to that decision.

In contrast, in this section, we consider three "active" shareholder powers: to make recommendations, to remove and/or replace directors, and to amend bylaws. Unlike in the previous section, here the shareholders (not the board) are the ones who initiate action.

Although corporate statutes give the board the power to "manage and direct" the business and affairs of the corporation, they do not specify when shareholders can direct or advise the board. Instead, the statutes leave open a broad continuum of possible roles for shareholders. At one extreme, shareholders might have the power to command the board to consider a specific decision. At the other extreme, shareholders might have no voice at all. Or shareholders might have some intermediate role: to suggest that the board take certain actions or report to them on particular matters, but not to require board action. Given the lack of specificity in corporate statutes, the challenge for judges over the years has been to determine where shareholder powers to initiate action should fall along this continuum.

Questions about what powers shareholders can initiate in a corporation resemble questions about what powers the electorate can initiate in a political democracy. Even in a representative government, voters can do more than vote: there are propositions, referenda, petitions, lobbying, and opinion polls. This section is about similar initiatives in the context of the corporation.

1. Shareholder Recommendations and Removal/Replacement of Directors

Shareholder recommendations are an important part of the shareholders' power to initiate action. For example, the SEC's shareholder proposal rule allows shareholders in public corporations to propose resolutions for the adoption by fellow shareholders through the corporate-financed proxy mechanism, provided the proposal is *proper under state law.* Accordingly, one important question is: what matters are proper?

The leading case establishing the ground rules for shareholder resolutions under state corporate law is *Auer v. Dressel*. The plaintiffs in that case owned a majority of the Class A stock of R. Hoe & Co., Inc. They brought an action for an order to compel the president of the corporation to call a special shareholders' meeting pursuant to a bylaw provision requiring such a meeting when requested by holders of a majority of the stock. The articles of incorporation provided for an eleven-member board, nine of whom were to be elected by the Class A stockholders and two of whom were to be elected by the Common stockholders.

The stated purposes of the special meeting were:

A. To vote on a resolution endorsing the administration of Joseph L. Auer, the former President and demanding his reinstatement;

B. To amend the articles of incorporation and bylaws to provide that vacancies on the board of directors arising from the removal of a director by the shareholders be filled only by the shareholders; and

C. To consider and vote on charges to remove four Class A directors for cause and to elect their successors.

The president refused to call the meeting on the grounds, among others, that the foregoing purposes were not proper subjects for a Class A shareholder meeting.

Auer v. Dressel

118 N.E.2d 590 (N.Y. 1954)

DESMOND, JUDGE.

The obvious purpose of the meeting here sought to be called (aside from the endorsement and reinstatement of former president Auer) is to hear charges against four of the class A directors, to remove them if the charges be proven, to amend the bylaws so that the successor directors be elected by the class A stockholders, and further to amend the bylaws so that an effective quorum of directors will be made up of no fewer than half of the directors in office and no fewer than one third of the whole authorized number of directors. No reason appears why the class A stockholders should not be allowed to vote on any or all of those proposals.

The stockholders, by expressing their approval of Mr. Auer's conduct as president and their demand that he be put back in that office [purpose (A)], will not be able, directly, to effect that change in officers, but there is nothing invalid in their so expressing themselves and thus putting on notice the directors who will stand for election at the annual meeting.

As to purpose (B), that is, amending the charter and bylaws to authorize the stockholders to fill vacancies as to class A directors who have been removed on charges or who have resigned, it seems to be settled law that the stockholders who are empowered to elect directors have the inherent power to remove them for cause [purpose (C)]. Of course, there must be the service of specific charges, adequate notice and full opportunity of meeting the accusations, but there is no present showing of any lack of any of those in this instance.

Since these particular stockholders have the right to elect nine directors and to remove them on proven charges, it is not inappropriate that they should use their further power to amend the bylaws to elect the successors of such directors as shall be removed after hearing, or who shall resign pending hearing. Such a change in the bylaws, dealing with the class A directors only, has no effect on the voting rights of the common stockholders, which rights have to do with the selection of the remaining two directors only. True, the certificate of incorporation authorizes the board of directors to remove any director on charges, but we do not consider that provision as an abdication by the stockholders of their own traditional, inherent power to remove their own directors. Rather, it provides an additional method. Were that not so, the stockholders might find themselves without effective remedy in a case where a majority of the directors were accused of wrongdoing and, obviously, would be unwilling to remove themselves from office.

We fail to see, in the proposal to allow class A stockholders to fill vacancies as to class A directors, any impairment or any violation of paragraph (h) of article Third of the certificate of incorporation, which says that class A stock has exclusive voting rights with respect to all matters "other than the election of directors." That negative language should not be taken to mean that class A stockholders, who have an absolute right to elect nine of these eleven directors, cannot amend their bylaws to guarantee a similar right, in the class A stockholders and to the exclusion of common stockholders, to fill vacancies in the class A group of directors.

Points for Discussion

1. Court's holdings and dissent.

Judge Van Voorhis dissented in *Auer v. Dressel* on the ground that the cited purposes were not appropriate subjects for action by shareholders at the requested meeting. Proposal A, the endorsement of Auer's tenure as president, was only "an idle gesture." Proposal B was improper because the articles of incorporation authorized the directors to fill vacancies on the board, and the change sought would have denied the common stockholders their rights to a voice in the replacement of directors through their two representatives on the board. Proposal C, the removal of directors, was improper because a shareholders meeting was "altogether unsuited to the performance of duties which partake of the nature of the judicial function." Since most shareholders would vote by proxy, their decision would have to be made before the meeting at which the charges against the directors would be made and discussed.

Why should shareholders be allowed to state their non-binding preference and thus engage in "an idle gesture"? Why should shareholders be entitled to state their views on a matter entrusted to the board's discretion—namely, the selection of the corporate president? The shareholders cannot mandate whom the board selects as president.

2. Power over board composition.

The case also reflects a judicial attitude that voting by different shareholder classes should be separate and distinct. The Court upheld the power of Class A shareholders to remove and replace Class A directors, effectively sidestepping the directors elected by the common shareholders. Could the articles have specified that only the board could replace directors removed from office? Or is replacement of directors an inherent shareholder prerogative?

3. Power over articles and bylaws.

Notice that under Proposal B, the shareholders sought to amend the articles and the bylaws so that only shareholders would fill vacancies arising from the removal of directors. The court finessed the issue, by holding that shareholders could amend the bylaws, without mentioning whether they could also amend the articles in this regard. Why not? Remember that amendment of the articles, including in New York, must be initiated by the board and then approved by the shareholders.

———————————

The power of shareholders to elect directors would seem to imply a power to remove directors and to fill the resulting vacancies. But the power to remove and replace directors at any time could undermine board continuity and director independence, potentially leading to corporate instability.

Just as removing public officials in mid-term is generally more difficult than electing them, removal of corporate directors faces a number of obstacles under corporate law. A meeting must be called; notices must be sent; and proxies must be solicited. And, as the following case makes clear, when shareholders seek to remove a director *for cause*, sufficient charges must be proffered and a defense allowed.

The next case involved a battle for control of Loew's Inc. (a public corporation) by two factions, one headed by its President, Vogel, and the other by Tomlinson. At the February shareholders' meeting the two factions effected a compromise; each faction was to have six directors and a neutral director would complete the 13-member board. The peace was a short one. In July, two of the Vogel directors, one Tomlinson director and the neutral director resigned. On July 30, there was a board meeting attended only by the five Tomlinson directors, who attempted to fill two vacancies. The Delaware Chancery Court ruled the filling of the vacancies to be invalid for lack of a quorum. Meanwhile, on July 29, Vogel, as president, sent out a notice calling a special shareholders' meeting for September 12 for the following purposes:

1. to fill director vacancies;

2. to amend the bylaws to increase the number of board members from 13 to 19; to increase the quorum from 7 to 10; and to elect six additional directors;

3. to remove Tomlinson and Stanley Meyer as directors and to fill the vacancies thus created.

The plaintiff sued to enjoin this special shareholder's meeting. The court first considered plaintiff's claim that Vogel, as president, lacked the power to call a stockholders' meeting to amend the bylaws and fill vacancies on the board. Relying on a bylaw explicitly granting the president power to call special meetings of stockholders "for any purpose," the court rejected this claim. Then the court considered the plaintiff's various arguments that the shareholders' powers to initiate action should be limited.

Campbell v. Loew's, Inc.

134 A.2d 852 (Del. Ch. 1957)

SEITZ, CHANCELLOR.

Plaintiff next argues that the stockholders have no power between annual meetings to elect directors to fill newly created directorships.

Plaintiff argues in effect that since the Loew's bylaws provide that the stockholders may fill "vacancies," and since our Courts have construed "vacancy" not to embrace "newly created directorships," the attempted call by the president for the purpose of filling newly created directorships was invalid.

Conceding that "vacancy" as used in the bylaws does not embrace "newly created directorships" does not resolve this problem. I say this because the stockholders have the inherent right between annual meetings to fill newly created directorships. The statute has since been amended to provide that not only vacancies but newly created directorships "may be filled by a majority of the directors then in office." 8 Del.C. § 223. Obviously, the amendment to include new directors is not worded so as to make the statute exclusive. It does not prevent the stockholders from filling the new directorships.

Plaintiff next argues that the shareholders of a Delaware corporation have no power to remove directors from office even for cause and thus the call for that purpose is invalid. The defendant naturally takes a contrary position.

While there are some cases suggesting the contrary, I believe that the stockholders have the power to remove a director for cause. This power must be implied when we consider that otherwise a director who is guilty of the worst sort of violation of his duty could nevertheless remain on the board. It is hardly to be believed that a director who is disclosing the corporation's trade secrets to a competitor would be immune from removal by the stockholders. Other examples, such as embezzlement of corporate funds, etc., come readily to mind.

But plaintiff correctly states that there is no provision in our statutory law providing for the removal of directors by stockholder action. In contrast he calls attention to § 142 of 8 Del.C., dealing with officers, which specifically refers to the possibility of a vacancy in an office by removal. He also notes that the Loew's bylaws provide for the removal of officers and employees but not directors. From these facts he argues that it was intended that directors not be removed even for cause. I believe the statute and bylaw are of course some evidence to support plaintiff's contention. But when we seek to exclude the existence of a power by implication, I think it is pertinent to consider whether the absence of the power can be said to subject the corporation to the possibility of real damage. I say this because we seek intention and such a factor would be relevant to that issue. Considering the damage a director might be able to inflict upon his corporation, I believe the doubt must be resolved by construing the statutes and bylaws as leaving untouched the question of director removal for cause. This being so, the Court is free to conclude on reason that the stockholders have such inherent power.

I therefore conclude that as a matter of Delaware corporation law the stockholders do have the power to remove directors for cause. I need not and do not decide whether the stockholders can by appropriate charter or bylaw provision deprive themselves of this right.

I turn next to plaintiff's charges relating to procedural defects and to irregularities in proxy solicitation by the Vogel group.

Plaintiff's first point is that the stockholders can vote to remove a director for cause only after such director has been given adequate notice of charges of grave impropriety and afforded an opportunity to be heard.

I am inclined to agree that if the proceedings preliminary to submitting the matter of removal for cause to the stockholders appear to be legal and if the charges are legally sufficient on their face, the Court should ordinarily not intervene. The sufficiency of the evidence would be a matter for evaluation in later proceedings. But where the procedure adopted to remove a director for cause is invalid on its face, a stockholder can attack such matters before the meeting. This conclusion is dictated both by the desirability of avoiding unnecessary and expensive action and by the importance of settling internal disputes, where reasonably possible, at the earliest moment. Otherwise a director could be removed and his successor could be appointed and participate in important board action before the illegality of the removal was judicially established. This seems undesirable where the illegality is clear on the face of the proceedings.

Turning now to plaintiff's contentions, it is certainly true that when the shareholders attempt to remove a director for cause," there must be the service of specific charges, adequate notice and full opportunity of meeting the accusation." *See Auer v. Dressel*. While it involved an invalid attempt by directors to remove a fellow director for cause, nevertheless, this same general standard was recognized in [an earlier decision by the Delaware Chancery Court]. The Chancellor said that the power of removal could not "be exercised in an arbitrary manner. The accused director would be entitled to be heard in his own defense."

Plaintiff asserts that no specific charges have been served upon the two directors sought to be ousted; that the notice of the special meeting fails to contain a specific statement of the charges; that the proxy statement which accompanied the notice also failed to notify the stockholders of the specific charges; and that it does not inform the stockholders that the accused must be afforded an opportunity to meet the accusations before a vote is taken.

Matters for stockholder consideration need not be conducted with the same formality as judicial proceedings. The proxy statement specifically recites that the two directors are sought to be removed for the reasons stated in the president's accompanying letter. Both directors involved received copies of the letter. Under the circumstances I think it must be said that the two directors involved were served with notice of the charges against them.

I next consider plaintiff's contention that the charges against the two directors do not constitute "cause" as a matter of law. It would take too much space to narrate in detail the contents of the president's letter. I must therefore give my summary of its charges. First of all, it charges that the two directors (Tomlinson and Meyer) failed to cooperate with Vogel in his announced program for rebuilding the company; that their purpose has been to put themselves in control; that they made baseless accusations against him and other management personnel and attempted to divert him from his normal duties as president by bombarding him with correspondence containing unfounded charges and other similar acts; that they moved into the company's building, accompanied by lawyers and accountants, and immediately proceeded upon a planned scheme of harassment. They called for many records, some going back twenty years, and were rude to the personnel. Tomlinson sent daily letters to the directors making serious charges directly and by means of innuendos and misinterpretations.

Are the foregoing charges, if proved, legally sufficient to justify the ouster of the two directors by the stockholders? I am satisfied that a charge that the directors desired to take over control of the corporation is not a reason for their ouster. Standing alone, it is a perfectly legitimate objective which is a part of the very fabric of corporate existence. Nor is a charge of lack of cooperation a legally sufficient basis for removal for cause.

The next charge is that these directors, in effect, engaged in a calculated plan of harassment to the detriment of the corporation. Certainly a director may examine books, ask questions, etc., in the discharge of his duty, but a point can be reached when his actions exceed the call of duty and become deliberately obstructive. In such a situation, if his actions constitute a real burden on the corporation then the stockholders are entitled to relief. The charges in this area made by the Vogel letter are legally sufficient to justify the stockholders in voting to remove such directors. In so concluding I of course express no opinion as to the truth of the charges.

I therefore conclude that the charge of "a planned scheme of harassment" as detailed in the letter constitutes a justifiable legal basis for removing a director.

I next consider whether the directors sought to be removed have been given a reasonable opportunity to be heard by the stockholders on the charges made.

There seems to be an absence of cases detailing the appropriate procedure for submitting a question of director removal for cause for stockholder consideration. I am satisfied, however, that to the extent the matter is to be voted upon by the use of proxies, such proxies may be solicited only after the accused directors are afforded an opportunity to present their case to the stockholders. This means, in my opinion, that an opportunity must be provided such directors to present their defense to the stockholders by a statement which must accompany or precede the initial solicitation of proxies seeking authority to vote for the removal of such director for cause. If not provided then such proxies may not be voted for removal. And the corporation has a duty to see that this opportunity is given the directors at its expense. Admittedly, no such opportunity was given the two directors involved.

I therefore conclude that the procedural sequence here adopted for soliciting proxies seeking authority to vote on the removal of the two directors is contrary to law. The result is that the proxy solicited by the Vogel group, which is based upon unilateral presentation of the facts by those in control of the corporate facilities, must be declared invalid insofar as they purport to give authority to vote for the removal of the directors for cause.

Points for Discussion

1. What constitutes "cause"?

The *Campbell v. Loew's* case arose before Delaware had enacted its statute (DGCL § 141(k) reproduced below) on director removal. The case's principal holding that shareholders have an inherent power to remove directors is now codified. In some instances, director removal requires "cause" and the case is useful in understanding how courts approach that issue. Notice that the court concludes that merely disagreeing with management or seeking to take control is not "cause" for removal, but "a planned scheme of harassment" is. When shareholders elect directors they face no constraints on whom they choose. Why should they be constrained when they seek to remove a director?

2. Removal procedures.

The case also lays out the procedures by which directors in a public corporation may be removed for cause. Given that shareholder voting in a public corporation happens through proxies, those seeking removal must proffer charges in a document, known as a proxy statement, distributed to all shareholders. The targeted director, according to the court, must be given a chance to respond to the charges. But notice how the court handles the question of timing. Rather than have the director respond to the charges *after* they have been distributed to

Make the Connection

The SEC has promulgated a comprehensive set of rules that regulate the proxy process for public corporations. The SEC proxy rules specify the disclosure that shareholders must receive in "proxy statements" whenever their votes are solicited, whether by the company or by an insurgent. We take up the SEC proxy regime in Chapter 17, Shareholder Information Rights, and Chapter 18, Public Shareholder Activism.

the shareholders, the court requires that the director be permitted, at corporate expense, to respond *before* or *at the same time* as the charges are presented to the shareholders. Why is this? Remember that the rule in proxy voting is the proxy submitted "last in time" is the one that counts. Couldn't shareholders who receive the proxy statement making charges against the director and send in a proxy voting to remove that director always revoke and change their proxy?

3. Removal as impeachment.

The rules on director removal seek to ensure continuity and independence for elected directors, while still providing some measure of protection against renegade directors. Why are fiduciary duties not enough? That is, why not require that shareholders bring a claim to enjoin a director's behavior that violates fiduciary duties and then elect a replacement at the next election of directors?

4. Delaware Statute.

As noted above, Delaware's corporate statute now addresses the removal and replacement of directors.

> ### <u>DGCL § 141</u>
> ### <u>Board of Directors; Removal</u>
>
> (k) Any director or the entire board of directors may be removed, with or without cause, by the holders of a majority of the shares then entitled to vote at an election of directors, except as follows:
>
> > (1) Unless the certificate of incorporation otherwise provides, in the case of a corporation whose board is classified . . ., shareholders may effect such removal only for cause; or
> >
> > (2) In the case of a corporation having cumulative voting, if less than the entire board is to be removed, no director may be removed without cause if the votes cast against such director's removal would be sufficient to elect such director if then cumulatively voted at an election of the entire board of directors, or, if there be classes of directors, at an election of the class of directors of which such director is a part.

Does the language of Section 141(k) help describe the extent of shareholders' power to remove directors? What are the exceptions to the shareholders' power to remove directors without cause? Do they make sense? Who has the power to fill vacancies on the board?

§ 223 Vacancies and Newly Created Directorships

(a) Unless otherwise provided in the certificate of incorporation or bylaws:

(1) Vacancies and newly created directorships . . . may be filled by a majority of the directors then in office, although less than a quorum, or by a sole remaining director;

(2) Whenever the holders of any class or classes of stock or series thereof are entitled to elect 1 or more directors by the certificate of incorporation, vacancies and newly created directorships of such class or classes or series may be filled by a majority of the directors elected by such class or classes or series thereof then in office, or by a sole remaining director so elected.

If at any time, by reason of death or resignation or other cause, a corporation should have no directors in office, then any officer or any stockholder . . . may call a special meeting of stockholders in accordance with the certificate of incorporation or the bylaws, or may apply to the Court of Chancery for a decree summarily ordering an election.

(c) If, at the time of filling any vacancy or any newly created directorship, the directors then in office shall constitute less than a majority of the whole board (as constituted immediately prior to any such increase), the Court of Chancery may, upon application of any stockholder or stockholders holding at least 10 percent of the voting stock at the time outstanding having the right to vote for such directors, summarily order an election to be held to fill any such vacancies or newly created directorships, or to replace the directors chosen by the directors then in office as aforesaid.

2. Bylaw Amendments

The power of shareholders to amend the bylaws has, in recent years, become a critical issue in corporate governance. A proper bylaw is binding on the board of directors, unlike most shareholder resolutions. For this reason, activist shareholders have proposed bylaw amendments in public corporations, seeking to move the balance of power away from the board and toward shareholders.

Bylaw amendments pose difficult questions, since in most corporations the power to amend the bylaws is *shared* by the board and the shareholders. Moreover, the authority over the corporation's business and affairs resides with the board, thus arguably limiting the extent to which shareholders can compel corporate action in the bylaws.

Make the Connection

Under the SEC shareholder proposal rule, shareholders are able to place their proposals for corporate reform on the company-funded proxy ballot. Shareholders that meet the ownership qualifications ($2,000 in company stock for at least one year) and other submission requirements (one proposal per year) may make "proper" proposals. We take up the shareholder proposal rule in Chapter 18, Public Shareholder Activism.

To illustrate some of the difficulties, consider a few passages of the Delaware General Corporation Law, which empowers the shareholders to adopt, amend, or repeal the corporation's bylaws and allows for the company's articles of incorporation to also give the board this power. However, there are tensions in various parts of the statute.

For example, Delaware's Section 109(a) provides:

After a corporation has received any payment for any of its stock, the power to adopt, amend or repeal bylaws shall be in the stockholders entitled to vote; provided, however, any corporation may, in its certificate of incorporation, confer the power to adopt, amend or repeal bylaws upon the directors. The fact that such power has been so conferred upon the directors shall not divest the stockholders of the power, nor limit their power to adopt, amend or repeal bylaws.

The language "shall not divest" suggests that both the board and the shareholders can have the power with respect to the bylaws. This language suggests that only the Delaware legislature, not a company's board, can take away this shareholder power.

Then Section 109(b) provides:

The bylaws may contain any provision, not inconsistent with law or with the certificate of incorporation, relating to the business of the corporation, the conduct of its affairs, and its rights or powers or the rights or powers of its stockholders, directors, officers or employees.

The language is broad: it suggests that the bylaws "may" contain "any" provision "relating to" shareholders' rights. Given that shareholders clearly have the right to vote, this language seems to suggest that the bylaws can include broad shareholder powers. But what if the board and shareholders disagree? Could the board amend the bylaws, and the shareholders change them, and so on? That back-and-forth obviously would be inefficient and indeterminate.

One might look to the articles of incorporation to address this puzzle. Section 102(b)(1) states that the articles "may" contain the following:

Any provision for the management of the business and for the conduct of the affairs of the corporation, and any provision creating, defining, limiting and regulating the powers of the corporation, the directors and the stockholders, or any class of the stockholders; if such provisions are not contrary to the laws of this State. Any provision which is required or permitted by any section of this chapter to be stated in the bylaws may instead be stated in the certificate of incorporation.

This language suggests that articles may contain any provision limiting either the directors' or the shareholders' powers, and that the articles may contain anything that could be stated in the bylaws. Is that language helpful? Or does it simply permit the corporation to allocate power either in the articles (which require both shareholder and board approval) or the bylaws (which, once shareholders have delegated power, require only board approval)?

And then there is Delaware's Section 141(a):

The business and affairs of every corporation organized under this chapter shall be managed by or under the direction of a board of directors, except as may be otherwise provided in this chapter or in its certificate of incorporation.

Delaware law explicitly states that the directors have the power to manage the business and affairs of the corporation. As we have seen, the shareholders lack such powers and instead play a more passive role, only voting on major questions such as the election of directors or fundamental corporate changes, when either the articles or the statute specifically authorizes a vote. Does this language give the directors the primary power to amend the bylaws as part of running the corporation, provided they do not violate their fiduciary duties in doing so? How much power can this language give the directors, without stripping away the express shareholder power to amend the bylaws in Section 109(a)?

The Delaware Supreme Court addressed this thorny question in *CA, Inc. v. AFSCME Employees Pension Plan*, 953 A.2d 227 (Del. 2008), a case involving a bylaw amendment proposed by shareholders that would require the board to reimburse shareholders' proxy expenses. The court analyzed the various statutory provisions above and concluded:

> It is at this juncture that the statutory language becomes only marginally helpful in determining what the Delaware legislature intended to be the lawful scope of the shareholders' power to adopt, amend and repeal bylaws. To resolve that issue, the Court must resort to different tools, namely, decisions of this Court and of the Court of Chancery that bear on this question.

> It is well-established Delaware law that a proper function of bylaws is not to mandate how the board should decide specific substantive business decisions, but rather, to define the process and procedures by which those decisions are made. As the Court of Chancery has noted: "Traditionally, the bylaws have been the corporate instrument used to set forth the rules by which the corporate board conducts its business. To this end, the DGCL is replete with specific provisions authorizing the bylaws to establish the procedures through which board and committee action is taken. There is a general consensus that bylaws that regulate the process by which the board acts are statutorily authorized."

The court cited several process-oriented bylaws that had been held appropriate, such as fixing number of directors on the board, some quorum and vote requirements, and even a few bylaws requiring unanimous board action. These were sufficiently procedural in nature that they did not improperly encroach upon the board's managerial authority under Section 141(a).

The court found that, in theory, a bylaw amendment requiring reimbursement of shareholder proxy expenses could be similarly process focused, and therefore would not violate any provision of Delaware law. However, the court also found that there was a risk that mandatory reimbursement could force the board to violate its fiduciary duties. What if the insurgent shareholder was a competitor? Or was motivated by "personal or petty concerns" or interests adverse to the corporations' interests? The court held that the particular bylaw at issue was problematic because it contained no language permitting the directors to deny reimbursement to shareholders when it would require the directors to breach their fiduciary duties.

Essentially, the court interpreted Section 109 as secondary to Section 141, which the court described as a "cardinal precept" of corporate law. Therefore, the power of shareholders to amend the bylaws must be consistent with the power of the board to manage the affairs and business of the corporation. Nonetheless, shareholders still have some room to operate. For example, the bylaws might provide for a "fiduciary out" so that the board could exercise discretionary power when fiduciary duties require that they do so? Could the bylaw be redrafted to satisfy the court's objections?

Another important type of bylaw is the "advance notice" bylaw, which requires that shareholders submit to the board any proposals they want to bring up at a meeting months in advance of the applicable meeting date. One rationale for advance notice bylaws is that they help companies conduct more orderly meetings by ensuring that a shareholder will not suddenly raise a last-minute issue. The Delaware courts have accepted this rationale and have permitted companies to implement such bylaws. However, the courts also have indicated that they will closely scrutinize advance notice bylaws if they intrude on shareholder rights. For example, if the bylaw mentions the nomination of directors but does not specifically cover shareholder proposals, then advance notice is not required for shareholder proposals.

Example 16.2

Shareholders of Flame Corp. (incorporated in an MBCA jurisdiction) propose a bylaw amendment that would require that any poison pill plan adopted by the board be submitted for shareholder approval at the next annual meeting. (A "poison pill" is a device that forces those seeking to acquire a corporation to seek permission from the board or suffer significant financial dilution of their shares.) Flame's articles do not specify that the board has the power to adopt poison pill plans.

Although the MBCA authorizes the "corporation" to issue rights (the essential financial instrument in a poison pill plan) and specifies that the terms of any such rights are to be determined by the board, it does not state that only the board can act for the corporation in issuing rights. Thus, the power to issue rights is not vested exclusively in the board. Shareholders can specify the procedures by which rights are issued, specifically under a poison pill plan. *See International Brotherhood of Teamsters General Fund v. Fleming Cos.*, 975 P.2d 907 (Okla. 1999) (interpreting Oklahoma statute, modeled on Delaware statute, which is similar to MBCA in this regard).

C. Board Responses to Shareholder Initiatives

What happens when the board interferes with the rights of shareholders to initiate action? The question is central to corporate law and we consider it in two contexts: board interference with shareholder voting, and board actions to preserve its future power.

1. Interference with Shareholder Voting

The following important case arose from a contest between a shareholder insurgent and an incumbent board about who would set the strategic direction of the corporation. To carry out its strategic plan, the insurgent proposed to obtain shareholder consents to increase the board size and pack the board with its nominees. But before the insurgent could solicit the consents, the board responded by engaging in its own board-packing—effectively undercutting the insurgent's plan. Both sides claimed they had a better vision for the corporation's future.

Below are the relevant provisions of the applicable Delaware statute:

DGCL § 228
Consent of Stockholders in Lieu of Meeting

(a) Unless otherwise provided in the certificate of incorporation, any action required by this chapter to be taken [or which may be taken] at any annual or special meeting of stockholders may be taken without a meeting, without prior notice and without a vote, if a consent or consents in writing, setting forth the action so taken, shall be signed by the holders of outstanding stock having not less than the minimum number of votes that would be necessary to authorize or take such action at a meeting at which all shares entitled to vote thereon were present and voted and shall be delivered to the corporation.

(c) Every written consent shall bear the date of signature of each stockholder, and no written consent shall be effective to take the corporate action referred to therein unless, within 60 days of the earliest dated consent delivered to the corporation, written consents signed by a sufficient number of holders or members to take action are delivered to the corporation.

The dispute occurred after Blasius Industries, Inc. began to accumulate shares of Atlas Corp. in July 1987. On October 29, Blasius disclosed that it owned 9.1% of Atlas' common stock and stated that it intended to encourage Atlas' management to consider a restructuring of the company. Blasius also disclosed that it was exploring the feasibility of obtaining control of Atlas.

Atlas' management did not welcome the prospect of Blasius' controlling shareholders involving themselves in Atlas' affairs. Atlas' new CEO, Weaver, had overseen a business restructuring of a sort and thought it should be given a chance to produce benefit before another restructuring was attempted.

Early in December, Blasius suggested that Atlas engage in a leveraged restructuring and distribute to its shareholders a one-time dividend of $35 million in cash and $125 million in subordinated debentures. Atlas' management responded coolly to this proposal. Mr. Weaver expressed surprise that Blasius would suggest using debt to accomplish a substantial liquidation of Atlas at a time when Atlas' future prospects were promising.

On December 30, Blasius delivered to Atlas a signed written consent (1) adopting a precatory resolution recommending that the board develop and implement a restructuring proposal, (2) amending the Atlas bylaws to, among other things, expand the size of the board from seven to fifteen members—the maximum number allowed by Atlas' articles of incorporation, and (3) electing eight named persons to fill the new directorships. Blasius also informed Atlas of its intent to solicit consents from other Atlas shareholders pursuant to DGCL § 228.

Mr. Weaver immediately conferred with Mr. Masinter, Atlas' outside counsel and a director, who viewed the consent as an attempt to take control of Atlas. They decided to call an emergency meeting of the board, even though a regularly scheduled meeting was to occur only one week hence, on January 6, 1988. In a telephone meeting held the next day, the board voted to amend Atlas' bylaws to increase the size of the board from seven to nine and then appointed John M. Devaney and Harry J. Winters, Jr. to fill the two newly created positions.

Blasius Industries, Inc. v. Atlas Corp.

564 A.2d 651 (Del. Ch. 1988)

ALLEN, CHANCELLOR.

Plaintiff attacks the December 31 board action as a selfishly motivated effort to protect the incumbent board from a perceived threat to its control of Atlas.

Defendants, of course, contest every aspect of plaintiffs' claims. They claim the formidable protections of the business judgment rule.

While I am satisfied that the evidence is powerful, indeed compelling, that the board was chiefly motivated on December 31 to forestall or preclude the possibility that a majority of shareholders might place on the Atlas board eight new members sympathetic to the Blasius proposal, it is less clear with respect to the more subtle motivational question: whether the existing members of the board did so because they held a good faith belief that such shareholder action would be self-injurious and shareholders needed to be protected from their own judgment.

On balance, I cannot conclude that the board was acting out of a self-interested motive in any important respect on December 31. I conclude rather that the board saw the "threat" of the Blasius recapitalization proposal as posing vital policy differences between itself and Blasius. It acted, I conclude, in a good faith effort to protect its incumbency, not selfishly, but in order to thwart implementation of the recapitalization that it feared, reasonably, would cause great injury to the Company.

The real question the case presents, to my mind, is whether, in these circumstances, the board, even if it is acting with subjective good faith, may validly act for the principal purpose of preventing the shareholders from electing a majority of new directors. The question thus posed is not one of intentional wrong (or even negligence), but one of authority *as between the fiduciary and the beneficiary*.

The shareholder franchise is the ideological underpinning upon which the legitimacy of directorial power rests. Generally, shareholders have only two protections against perceived inadequate business performance. They may sell their stock (which, if done in sufficient numbers, may so affect security prices as to create an incentive for altered managerial performance), or they may vote to replace incumbent board members.

It has, for a long time, been conventional to dismiss the stockholder vote as a vestige or ritual of little practical importance. It may be that we are now witnessing the emergence of new institutional voices and arrangements that will make the stockholder vote a less predictable affair than it has been. Be that as it may, however, whether the vote is seen functionally as an unimportant formalism, or as an important tool of discipline, it is clear that it is critical to the theory that legitimates the exercise of power by some (directors and officers) over vast aggregations of property that they do not own. Thus, when viewed from a broad, institutional perspective, it can be seen that matters involving the integrity of the shareholder voting process involve consideration not present in any other context in which directors exercise delegated power.

The distinctive nature of the shareholder franchise context also appears when the matter is viewed from a less generalized, doctrinal point of view. From this point of view, as well, it appears that the ordinary considerations to which the business judgment rule originally responded are simply not present in the shareholder voting context. That is, a decision by the board to act for the primary purpose of preventing the effectiveness of a shareholder vote inevitably involves the question who, as between the principal and the agent, has authority with respect to a matter of internal corporate governance. That, of course, is true in a very specific way in this case which deals with the question who should constitute the board of directors of the corporation, but it will be true in every instance in which an incumbent board seeks to thwart a shareholder majority. A board's decision to act to prevent the shareholders from creating a majority of new board positions and filling them does not involve the exercise of *the corporation's power* over its property, or with respect to *its* rights or obligations; rather, it involves allocation, between shareholders as a class and the board, of effective power with respect to governance of the corporation. Action designed principally to interfere with the effectiveness of a vote inevitably involves a conflict between the board and a shareholder majority. Judicial review of such action involves a determination of the legal and equitable obligations of an agent towards his principal. This is not, in my opinion, a question that a court may leave to the agent finally to decide so long as he does so honestly and competently; that is, it may not be left to the agent's business judgment.

Plaintiff argues for a rule of *per se* invalidity once a plaintiff has established that a board has acted for the primary purpose of thwarting the exercise of a shareholder vote.

A *per se* rule that would strike down, in equity, any board action taken for the primary purpose of interfering with the effectiveness of a corporate vote would have the advantage of relative clarity and predictability. It also has the advantage of most vigorously enforcing the concept of corporate democracy. The disadvantage it brings along is, of course, the disadvantage a *per se* rule always has: it may sweep too broadly.

In two recent cases dealing with shareholder votes, this court struck down board acts done for the primary purpose of impeding the exercise of stockholder voting power. In doing so, a *per se* rule was not applied. Rather, it was said that, in such a case, the board bears the heavy burden of demonstrating a compelling justification for such action.

In my view, our inability to foresee now all of the future settings in which a board might, in good faith, paternalistically seek to thwart a shareholder vote, counsels against the adoption of a *per se* rule invalidating, in equity, every board action taken for the sole or primary purpose of thwarting a shareholder vote, even though I recognize the transcending significance of the franchise to the claims to legitimacy of our scheme of corporate governance. It may be that some set of facts would justify such extreme action. This, however, is not such a case.

The board was not faced with a coercive action taken by a powerful share-holder against the interests of a distinct shareholder constituency (such as a public minority). It was presented with a consent solicitation by a 9% shareholder. More-over, here it had time (and understood that it had time) to inform the sharehold-ers of its views on the merits of the proposal subject to stockholder vote. The only justification that can, in such a situation, be offered for the action taken is that the board knows better than do the shareholders what is in the corpora-tion's best interest. While that premise is no doubt true for any number of mat-ters, it is irrelevant (except insofar as the shareholders wish to be guided by the board's recommendation) when the question is who should comprise the board of directors. The theory of our corporation law confers power upon directors as the agents of the shareholders; it does not create Platonic masters. It may be that the Blasius restructuring proposal was or is unrealistic and would lead to injury to the corporation and its shareholders if pursued. The board certainly viewed it that way, and that view, held in good faith, entitled the board to take certain steps to evade the risk it perceived. It could, for example, expend corporate funds to inform shareholders and seek to bring them to a similar point of view. But there is a vast difference between expending corporate funds to inform the electorate and exercising power for the primary purpose of foreclosing effective shareholder action. A majority of the shareholders, who were not dominated in any respect, could view the matter differently than did the board. If they do, or did, they are entitled to employ the mechanisms provided by the corporation law and the Atlas certificate of incorporation to advance that view. They are also entitled, in my opinion, to restrain their agents, the board, from acting for the principal purpose of thwarting that action.

I therefore conclude that, even finding the action taken was taken in good faith, it constituted an unintended violation of the duty of loyalty that the board owed to the shareholders. I note parenthetically that the concept of an unintended breach of the duty of loyalty is unusual but not novel. That action will, therefore, be set aside by order of this court.

————————

Points for Discussion

1. Platonic masters.

Why aren't directors Platonic masters? Haven't shareholders deferred to their authority—as reflected in DGCL § 141—when they invested in the corporation?

2. Power vs. duty.

Blasius is a pillar of Delaware corporate law. It applies the principle announced in *Schnell v. Chris-Craft Indus., Inc.*, a case we saw in Chapter 4, Corporation Basics, that involved an incumbent board's attempt to move forward the meeting date in a way that impeded an ongoing proxy contest. The Delaware Supreme Court said that "inequitable action does not become permissible simply because it is legally possible." Thus, even though there was no question that the Atlas board had the power to increase the board size and fill the resulting vacancies, the question was whether the power had been exercised consistently with the board's fiduciary duties. Why was it not enough that the board's motives were pure and the board was convinced in good faith that the recapitalization proposed by Blasius was a terrible idea?

3. Compelling circumstances.

Blasius rejects a *per se* rule of invalidity, contemplating the possibility of "compelling justifications" that would permit the board to interfere with shareholder voting in limited circumstances. When might interference be justified? Although the decision makes clear that the board's doubts about an insurgent's plans are not compelling, would it be justifiable for a board to impede a consent solicitation to replace the board on the eve of a shareholder vote to adopt a pending merger proposal?

4. Limiting the right to sue.

Some companies have added provisions to their charter or bylaws that limit shareholder litigation rights. For example, many boards added clauses requiring that securities claims be arbitrated in individual cases, not as class actions. However, in 2015, Delaware prohibited the use of arbitration clauses in corporate documents for "internal corporate claims." Should corporations nevertheless be permitted to limit shareholders' rights with respect to external claims, such as violations of federal securities law?

The extent to which companies can limit the right to sue is evolving. For example, some companies have gone public with provisions in their articles or bylaws that require that certain federal claims by shareholders under the Securities Act of 1933 be litigated in federal court, not state court. In *Sciabacucchi v. Salzberg*, 2018 WL 6719718 (Del. Ch. 2018), the Delaware Court of Chancery held that such provisions are improper both in the articles under Section 102(b)(1) and in the bylaws under Section 109(b). Prior to this decision, the Delaware courts had held that Delaware corporations are permitted to adopt forum-selection bylaws with respect to "internal affairs" claims, such as breach of fiduciary duty claims. *See Boilermakers Local 154 Ret. Fund. v. Chevron Corp.*, 73 A.3d 934 (Del. Ch. 2013). In other words, Delaware law appears to permit corporations to limit the rights of shareholders to sue with respect to internal relationships, but not external ones.

2. Preserving the Power of the Board

Another way that incumbent directors have sought to preserve their prerogatives is to diminish the power of *subsequent* boards. Although shareholder
voting rights are unaffected, the ability to seat a completely-empowered board is
diminished. Can the board do this?

In the case below, Mentor Graphics sought to acquire Quickturn Design
Systems. Mentor was in the business of electronic design automation software
and hardware, and Quickturn, a publicly traded Delaware corporation, was the
market leader in emulation technology used to verify the design of silicon chips
and electronics systems.

Although Quickturn had been a growth company with increasing earnings
and revenues, its fortunes turned in the spring of 1998 when its growth and stock
price declined because of the downturn in the semiconductor industry, especially
in Asia. Smelling a bargain, Mentor began to explore the possibility of acquiring
Quickturn. Mentor, which had been barred in patent litigation with Quickturn
from competing in the U.S. emulation market, would realize a special benefit
by acquiring Quickturn. If Mentor owned Quickturn, it could "unenforce" the
Quickturn patents and enter the U.S. emulation market.

When Quickturn's stock price began to decline in May 1998, Mentor moved to
acquire Quickturn for a cheap price. Mentor assembled financial and legal advisors,
as well as proxy solicitors. And on August 12, Mentor made a cash tender offer for
all outstanding common shares of Quickturn at $12.125 per share, representing a
nearly 50% premium over Quickturn's pre-offer price, but a 20% discount from
Quickturn's February 1998 stock price. Mentor announced that its tender offer,
once consummated, would be followed by a second step merger in which Quickturn's nontendering stockholders would receive the same $12.125 per share.

Mentor also announced its intent to solicit proxies to replace the board at
a special meeting. Using Quickturn's bylaw governing the call of special stockholders' meetings, Mentor began soliciting agent designations from Quickturn
stockholders to satisfy the bylaw's stock ownership requirements to call such a
meeting.

Under federal securities law, Quickturn was required to inform its shareholders of its response to Mentor's offer no later than ten business days after the
offer was commenced. During that ten-day period, the Quickturn board met three
times to consider Mentor's offer and ultimately to decide how to respond. Quickturn's board consisted of eight members, all but one of whom were outside, independent directors. All had distinguished careers and significant technological
experience. Collectively, the board had more than 30 years of experience in the

electronic design automation industry and held one million shares (about 5%) of Quickturn's common stock.

After hearing presentations from its financial advisers, the Quickturn board concluded that Mentor's offer was inadequate, and decided to recommend that Quickturn shareholders reject the offer. In addition, the Quickturn board adopted two defensive measures in response to Mentor's hostile takeover bid. First, the board amended Quickturn's bylaws, which permitted stockholders holding 10% or more of Quickturn's stock to call a special stockholders meeting. The amendment provided that if any special meeting is requested by shareholders, the board could determine the time and place of the meeting.

> **What's That?**
>
> What is a hostile bid? It is a tender offer made to shareholders, without the approval or support of the target board. It is not "hostile" as to the shareholders, who may well be thrilled to be offered a premium for their shares over the current market price. Instead, it is "hostile" as to the board of directors (and often incumbent executives), who understand that if the bid succeeds they may lose their positions.

Second, the board amended Quickturn's shareholder Rights Plan or "poison pill" to add a Deferred Redemption Provision or DRP, under which no newly elected board could redeem the Rights Plan for six months after taking office, if

> **What's That?**
>
> A poison pill (or Rights Plan) is designed to make a hostile acquisition financially prohibitive unless the target's board approves the deal. Essentially, the poison pill gives "rights" to shareholders (other than the acquirer) that dilute the acquirer's stake in the corporation's shares.
>
> How does a poison pill work? The typical pill begins with the distribution to each common shareholder of one Right to purchase company securities, often preferred stock. The Rights attach to the common stock, and each Right initially entitles the holder to purchase a given amount of preferred stock for a specified price, such as $100. This price is set unrealistically high, so the Rights when issued have no financial value.
>
> Instead, the Rights become valuable when an unwanted acquirer triggers the plan by making a tender offer (or buying) for more than a stated percentage (such as 15%) of the company's common stock. Once this happens, the Rights can be exercised to buy the company's common shares (or other specified securities) at half price. All Rights holders (except the acquirer) can "flip in" their Rights, producing massive dilution to the value of the unwanted acquirer's holdings. Or, a pill could be designed so that if the target company is merged into the acquirer, the Rights holders can "flip-over" their Rights and buy shares of the acquirer at half price, thus drastically impairing the acquirer's financial structure and diluting its other shareholders.
>
> The target board holds the "antidote" to this poison. It can redeem the Rights at any time before they expire, typically on such terms as the directors "in their sole discretion" choose.

the redemption would facilitate a transaction with an "Interested Person" (one who proposed, nominated or financially supported the election of the new directors to the board). Mentor would be an Interested Person.

The effect of the bylaw amendment would be to delay a shareholder-called special meeting for at least three months. The effect of the DRP would be to delay the ability of a newly-elected, Mentor-nominated board to redeem the Rights Plan for six months. Thus, their combined effect would be to delay any acquisition of Quickturn by Mentor for at least nine months.

Mentor challenged the legality of both defensive maneuvers in the Court of Chancery. After a trial on the merits, the Court of Chancery determined the bylaw amendment was valid, but the DRP was invalid on fiduciary grounds.

Quickturn appealed the DRP finding, but Mentor did not file a cross-appeal on the validity of the bylaw amendment. Consequently, the Delaware Supreme Court reviewed only the finding that Quickturn's directors breached their fiduciary duty by adopting the DRP.

Quickturn Design Systems, Inc. v. Shapiro

721 A.2d 1281 (Del. 1998)

HOLLAND, JUSTICE.

In this appeal, Mentor argues that the judgment of the Court of Chancery should be affirmed because the Delayed Redemption Provision (DRP) is invalid as a matter of Delaware law. According to Mentor, the DRP will impermissibly deprive any newly elected board of both its statutory authority to manage the corporation under 8 Del.C. § 141(a) and its concomitant fiduciary duty pursuant to that statutory mandate. We agree.

One of the most basic tenets of Delaware corporate law is that the board of directors has the ultimate responsibility for managing the business and affairs of a corporation. Section 141(a) requires that any limitation on the board's authority be set out in the certificate of incorporation. The Quickturn certificate of incorporation contains no provision purporting to limit the authority of the board in any way. The DRP, however, would prevent a newly elected board of directors from completely discharging its fundamental management duties to the corporation and its stockholders for six months. While the DRP limits the board of directors' authority in only one respect, the suspension of the Rights Plan, it nonetheless restricts the board's power in an area of fundamental importance to the shareholders—negotiating a possible sale of the corporation. Therefore, we hold that the DRP is invalid under Section 141(a), which confers upon any newly elected board of directors full power to manage and direct the business and affairs of a Delaware corporation.

In discharging the statutory mandate of Section 141(a), the directors have a fiduciary duty to the corporation and its shareholders. This unremitting obligation extends equally to board conduct in a contest for corporate control. The DRP prevents a newly elected board of directors from completely discharging its fiduciary duties to protect fully the interests of Quickturn and its stockholders.

This Court has recently observed that "although the fiduciary duty of a Delaware director is unremitting, the exact course of conduct that must be charted to properly discharge that responsibility will change in the specific context of the action the director is taking with regard to either the corporation or its shareholders." This Court has held "to the extent that a contract, or a provision thereof, purports to require a board to act or not act in such a fashion as to limit the exercise of fiduciary duties, it is invalid and unenforceable." The DRP "tends to limit in a substantial way the freedom of [newly elected] directors' decisions on matters of management policy." Therefore, "it violates the duty of each [newly elected] director to exercise his own best judgment on matters coming before the board."

In this case, the Quickturn board was confronted by a determined bidder that sought to acquire the company at a price the Quickturn board concluded was inadequate. Such situations are common in corporate takeover efforts. This Court has held that no defensive measure can be sustained when it represents a breach of the directors' fiduciary duty. *A fortiori*, no defensive measure can be sustained which would require a new board of directors to breach its fiduciary duty. In that regard, we note Mentor has properly acknowledged that in the event its slate of directors is elected, those newly elected directors will be required to discharge their unremitting fiduciary duty to manage the corporation for the benefit of Quickturn and its stockholders.

The DRP would prevent a new Quickturn board of directors from managing the corporation by redeeming the Rights Plan to facilitate a transaction that would serve the stockholders' best interests, even under circumstances where the board would be required to do so because of its fiduciary duty to the Quickturn stockholders. Because the DRP impermissibly circumscribes the board's statutory power under Section 141(a) and the directors' ability to fulfill their concomitant fiduciary duties, we hold that the DRP is invalid.

Points for Discussion

1. Beyond *Blasius*?

Notice that *Quickturn* does not say that the board violated its fiduciary duties by adopting a poison pill that tied the hands of future boards, but rather that limiting the board's future ability to exercise its fiduciary duties was beyond the board's power. In this sense, *Quickturn* goes beyond *Blasius* to declare some board actions as fundamentally inconsistent with shareholder voting rights—here the right to elect a fully-empowered board of directors. *Quickturn* does not mention a "compelling justifications" exception.

2. Dead hand pill.

Notice that to make the Rights Plan less susceptible to challenge, the Quickturn board eliminated a "dead hand" feature of the Rights Plan. This feature had provided that if an insurgent holding more than 15% of Quickturn's common stock successfully waged a proxy contest to replace a majority of the board, only "continuing directors" (those directors in office at the time the poison pill was adopted) could redeem the rights. In an earlier decision, not appealed to the Delaware Supreme Court, the Chancery Court had held that that such a "dead hand" poison pill was invalid both because it violated DGCL § 141 and because the directors had violated their fiduciary duties by adopting such a poison pill. *Carmody v. Toll Brothers, Inc.*, 723 A.2d 1180 (Del. Ch. 1998).

3. Consistency with *CA, Inc. v. AFSCME*?

The focus in *Quickturn* on the board's power in adopting the Rights Plan, rather than its fiduciary duties, suggests that any limits on the board's control of a poison pill must come (if at all) from the articles of incorporation. The decision suggests that a bylaw amendment initiated by shareholders to limit board prerogatives in creating or continuing a poison pill would face a statutory impediment. Some have <u>read</u> *Quickturn* merely to state that "the board's authority to manage the business and affairs of a corporation is inherently limited by the power of the stockholders to exercise decision-making authority for the voting and sale decisions assigned to them." Is this reading of *Quickturn* consistent with the more recent 2008 decision in *CA, Inc. v. AFSCME*, which holds that shareholders cannot impose procedures that limit the ability of directors to exercise their fiduciary duties?

4. Shareholder duties in amending bylaws.

The power of shareholders to amend the bylaws may also be constrained by fiduciary duties—that is, when a controlling shareholder seeks to amend the bylaws for its own selfish purposes. The Delaware courts have held that bylaw amendments initiated by a controlling shareholder are invalid if they have an inequitable purpose and effect. For example, bylaw amendments approved by a controlling shareholder to strip independent directors on the board of their power to consider a strategic direction that the controlling shareholder opposed have been held invalid. *Hollinger International, Inc. v. Black*, 844 A.2d 1022 (Del. Ch. 2004), *aff'd*, 872 A.2d 559 (Del. 2005).

CHAPTER 17

Shareholder Information Rights

To exercise fully their right to vote, and especially their right to initiate corporate reforms, shareholders must often obtain information from the corporation. State and federal law create a mosaic of informational rights to support the shareholder franchise. State law allows shareholders to inspect corporate books and records if they have a "proper purpose." Federal law requires that shareholders in public corporations receive a formal disclosure document called a "proxy statement" when their vote is solicited. And federal law, as well as state fiduciary law, requires that any communication soliciting shareholder votes be honest and complete.

This chapter begins with a look at shareholder inspection rights, which have assumed increased importance as a pre-litigation tool for shareholders to obtain information from their corporations. Next we summarize the *ex ante* rights of shareholders to information when they vote, both under state law and federal proxy rules. Finally, we

Make the Connection

Although the rights to voting-related information exist in both close and public corporations, they are much more significant in public corporations where shareholders would otherwise lack access to corporate information relevant to their voting decisions. In close corporations, the majority typically has full access to corporate information, and the minority lacks the votes to affect the outcome. *See* Chapter 25, Planning in the Close Corporation.

consider the *ex post* rights of shareholders to complain about misinformation during the voting process, particularly in an implied private cause of action fashioned by federal courts.

A. Shareholder Inspection Rights

Shareholders have long had equitable rights to inspect corporate books and records. State corporate statutes codify these rights, specifying when and how inspection can be had.

Here is the principal provision of the all-important inspection statute in Delaware:

DGCL § 220
Inspection of Books and Records

(b) Any stockholder shall, upon written demand under oath stating the purpose thereof, have the right during the usual hours for business to inspect for any proper purpose, and to make copies and extracts from:

(1) The corporation's stock ledger, a list of its stockholders, and its other books and records; and

(2) A subsidiary's books and records [subject to certain conditions].

A proper purpose shall mean a purpose reasonably related to such person's interest as a stockholder. The demand under oath shall be directed to the corporation at its registered office in this State or at its principal place of business.

Most statutes, including in Delaware and under the MBCA, permit inspection by both shareholders of record (whose names appears on the corporation's stock ledger) and beneficial shareholders (whose stock is held by another, such as a securities firm). Some states once limited inspection to shareholders owning a certain percentage of a corporation's shares or holding their shares for a minimum period. But over time the inspection right has been "democratized"—subject to the general requirement that the inspecting shareholder have a "proper purpose."

There is some variance in the statutes on what shareholders can inspect. As you can see, Delaware permits inspection of the stock ledger, the shareholder list, and other "books and records" upon the showing of a proper purpose. The burden for this showing depends on which item the shareholder seeks. The statute specifies that if the shareholder seeks books and records other than the stock ledger or list of shareholders, then such shareholder has the burden of show-

Take Note!

Directors also have inspection rights. In Delaware, for example, directors can seek inspection of "the corporation's stock ledger, a list of its stockholders and its other books and records for a purpose reasonably related to the director's position as a director." Whose inspection rights are broader—those of shareholders or those of directors?

ing a proper purpose as to each item sought. With regard to the stock ledger and list of shareholders, the burden is on the corporation to show that the shareholder seeks inspection for an improper purpose.

Under the MBCA, ready inspection is available for the articles of incorporation, bylaws, minutes of shareholder meetings, the names of directors and officers, and like documents. But inspection of board minutes, accounting records, and shareholder lists requires the showing of a proper purpose. Interestingly, the MBCA does not mention the availability of "books."

When shareholders ask for the good stuff, the MBCA requires that the shareholder describe "with reasonable particularity" the purpose and the records to be inspected. The purpose must be "proper," and the records must be "directly connected" with that purpose. As we will soon see, Delaware courts have imposed similar procedural hoops for shareholders seeking inspection.

The traditional remedy of a shareholder who is denied inspection is a judicial order compelling inspection. In fact, most statutes provide for a summary or expedited procedure. And to prevent obstruction of inspection rights, some statutes make the corporation pay the shareholder's costs, including reasonable attorneys' fees, unless the corporation can establish it acted reasonably in denying the shareholder's inspection request.

Lately, shareholder inspection has become an important pre-filing tactic by plaintiffs bringing lawsuits to vindicate shareholder rights. Interestingly, the Delaware Supreme Court has encouraged (even chastised) plaintiffs to seek inspection before bringing lawsuits. Inspection allows plaintiffs to obtain factual support for their allegations, thus avoiding dismissal of unsupported claims. (We look at the tough pleading standards for derivative suits, especially in Delaware, in Chapter 19, Shareholder Litigation.) In addition, shareholders making claims of corporate fraud under the federal securities laws have increasingly relied on state inspection rights to obtain documents to plead securities fraud in federal court. (We look at these pleading standards in our chapter on class actions brought in federal court alleging fraud in securities markets. *See* Chapter 28, Securities Fraud.)

1. Proper Purpose

The key to inspection is showing a proper purpose. Statutes usually do not define the term or define it vaguely as "a purpose reasonably related to such person's interest as a stockholder."

The following two cases illustrate how shareholders have used inspection— and how courts view the role of shareholders in the corporation. The first case,

Pillsbury v. Honeywell, takes a jaundiced view of shareholder activism, commenting that "the power to inspect may be the power to destroy." Meanwhile, the second case, *Saito v. McKesson*, describes inspection as a meaningful "statutory tool" that permits shareholders to protect their legitimate (financial) interests in the corporation.

In the first case, Charles A. Pillsbury, a scion of a prominent and wealthy Minneapolis family, wanted to stop production by Honeywell Inc. of anti-personnel fragmentation bombs used in Vietnam. He purchased 100 shares for the "sole purpose" of gaining a voice in Honeywell's affairs and then requested a shareholders' list to solicit proxies for the election of new directors. When Honeywell refused his request, he filed for a writ of mandamus. After discovery, the trial court denied him relief, holding that he had not stated a "proper purpose germane to his interest as a stockholder" under both Minnesota law and the law of Delaware, Honeywell's state of incorporation.

State ex rel. Pillsbury v. Honeywell, Inc.

191 N.W.2d 406 (Minn. 1971)

Kelly, Justice.

Petitioner contends that a stockholder who disagrees with management has an absolute right to inspect corporate records for purposes of soliciting proxies. He would have this court rule that such solicitation is per se a "proper purpose." Honeywell argues that a "proper purpose" contemplates concern with investment return. We agree with Honeywell.

This court has had several occasions to rule on the propriety of shareholders' demands for inspection of corporate books and records. Minn.St. 300.32, not applicable here, has been held to be declaratory of the common-law principle that a stockholder is entitled to inspection for a proper purpose germane to his business interests. While inspection will not be permitted for purposes of curiosity, speculation, or vexation, adverseness to management and a desire to gain control of the corporation for economic benefit does not indicate an improper purpose.

Several courts agree with petitioner's contention that a mere desire to communicate with other shareholders is, per se, a proper purpose. This would seem to confer an almost absolute right to inspection. We believe that a better rule would allow inspections only if the shareholder has a proper purpose for such communication.

The act of inspecting a corporation's shareholder ledger and business records must be viewed in its proper perspective. In terms of the corporate norm, inspection is merely the act of the concerned owner checking on what is in part his property. In the context of the large firm, inspection can be more akin to a weapon in corporate warfare. Because the power to inspect may be the power to destroy, it is important that only those with a bona fide interest in the corporation enjoy that power.

That one must have proper standing to demand inspection has been recognized by statutes in several jurisdictions. Courts have also balked at compelling inspection by a shareholder holding an insignificant amount of stock in the corporation.

Petitioner's standing as a shareholder is quite tenuous. He only owns one share in his own name, bought for the purposes of this suit. He had previously ordered his agent to buy 100 shares, but there is no showing of investment intent. While his agent had a cash balance in the $400,000 portfolio, petitioner made no attempt to determine whether Honeywell was a good investment or whether more profitable shares would have to be sold to finance the Honeywell purchase.

Petitioner had utterly no interest in the affairs of Honeywell before he learned of Honeywell's production of fragmentation bombs. Immediately after obtaining this knowledge, he purchased stock in Honeywell for the sole purpose of asserting ownership privileges in an effort to force Honeywell to cease such production. But for his opposition to Honeywell's policy, petitioner probably would not have bought Honeywell stock, would not be interested in Honeywell's profits and would not desire to communicate with Honeywell's shareholders. His avowed purpose in buying Honeywell stock was to place himself in a position to try to impress his opinions favoring a reordering of priorities upon Honeywell management and its other shareholders. Such a motivation can hardly be deemed a proper purpose germane to his economic interest as a shareholder.[5]

From the deposition, the trial court concluded that petitioner had already formed strong opinions on the immorality and the social and economic wastefulness of war long before he bought stock in Honeywell. His sole motivation was to change Honeywell's course of business because that course was incompatible with his political views. If unsuccessful, petitioner indicated that he would sell the Honeywell stock.

---

[5] We do not question petitioner's good faith incident to his political and social philosophy; nor did the trial court. In a well-prepared memorandum, the lower court stated: "This Court cannot but draw the conclusion that the Petitioner is sincere in his political and social philosophy, but this Court does not feel that this is a proper forum for the advancement of these political-social views by way of direct contact with the stockholders of Honeywell Company."

We do not mean to imply that a shareholder with a bona fide investment interest could not bring this suit if motivated by concern with the long-or short-term economic effects on Honeywell resulting from the production of war munitions. Similarly, this suit might be appropriate when a shareholder has a bona fide concern about the adverse effects of abstention from profitable war contracts on his investment in Honeywell.

In the instant case, however, the trial court, in effect, has found from all the facts that petitioner was not interested in even the long-term well-being of Honeywell or the enhancement of the value of his shares. His sole purpose was to persuade the company to adopt his social and political concerns, irrespective of any economic benefit to himself or Honeywell. This purpose on the part of one buying into the corporation does not entitle the petitioner to inspect Honeywell's books and records.

Petitioner argues that he wishes to inspect the stockholder ledger in order that he may correspond with other shareholders with the hope of electing to the board one or more directors who represent his particular viewpoint. While a plan to elect one or more directors is specific and the election of directors normally would be a proper purpose, here the purpose was not germane to petitioner's or Honeywell's economic interest. Instead, the plan was designed to further petitioner's political and social beliefs. Since the requisite propriety of purpose germane to his or Honeywell's economic interest is not present, the allegation that petitioner seeks to elect a new board of directors is insufficient to compel inspection.

The order of the trial court denying the writ of mandamus is affirmed.

———————————

Points for Discussion

1. Shareholder wealth maximization.

Would Pillsbury have been more successful if the request had been couched in terms of shareholder wealth maximization? For example, would the court have been more sympathetic if Pillsbury had sought to contact shareholders to urge them to demand that the company discontinue the production of anti-personnel fragmentation bombs on the grounds it could lead to legal liability, could result in consumer boycotts of the company's other products, or could damage the corporation's reputation? In short, was the problem one of poor lawyering?

2. Purpose of the corporation.

The case returns us to themes from Chapter 6 where we first encountered the question of the purpose of the corporation. Is the Minnesota Supreme Court correct in assuming that shareholders can only have an economic interest in the corporation and the corporation is only an economic institution? Is the result in the case consistent with non-shareholder constituency statutes that permit the board of directors to consider, among other things, "societal considerations"? If corporations can have purposes other than shareholder primacy, why shouldn't a shareholder be able to contact other shareholders to install a new board committed to corporate social responsibility?

Saito v. McKesson HBOC, Inc.

806 A.2d 113 (Del. 2002)

BERGER, JUSTICE.

In this appeal, we consider the limitations on a stockholder's statutory right to inspect corporate books and records. The statute, 8 Del.C. § 220, enables stockholders to investigate matters "reasonably related to [their] interest as [stockholders]" including, among other things, possible corporate wrongdoing. It does not open the door to the wide ranging discovery that would be available in support of litigation. For this statutory tool to be meaningful, however, it cannot be read narrowly to deprive a stockholder of necessary documents solely because the documents were prepared by third parties or because the documents predate the stockholder's first investment in the corporation. A stockholder who demands inspection for a proper purpose should be given access to all of the documents in the corporation's possession, custody or control, that are necessary to satisfy that proper purpose. Thus, where a § 220 claim is based on alleged corporate wrongdoing, and assuming the allegation is meritorious, the stockholder should be given enough information to effectively address the problem, either through derivative litigation or through direct contact with the corporation's directors and/ or stockholders.

Factual and Procedural Background

On October 17, 1998, McKesson Corporation entered into a stock-for-stock merger agreement with HBO & Company ("HBOC"). On October 20, 1998, appellant, Noel Saito, purchased McKesson stock. The merger was consummated in January 1999 and the combined company was renamed McKesson HBOC, Incorporated. HBOC continued its separate corporate existence as a wholly-owned subsidiary of McKesson HBOC.

Starting in April and continuing through July 1999, McKesson HBOC announced a series of financial restatements triggered by its year-end audit process. During that four month period, McKesson HBOC reduced its revenues by $327.4 million for the three prior fiscal years. The restatements all were attributed to HBOC accounting irregularities. The first announcement precipitated several lawsuits, including a derivative action pending in the Court of Chancery, captioned Ash v. McCall, Civil Action No. 17132. Saito was one of four plaintiffs in the Ash complaint, which alleged that: (i) McKesson's directors breached their duty of care by failing to discover the HBOC accounting irregularities before the merger; (ii) McKesson's directors committed corporate waste by entering into the merger with HBOC; (iii) HBOC's directors breached their fiduciary duties by failing to monitor the company's compliance with financial reporting requirements prior to the merger; and (iv) McKesson HBOC's directors failed in the same respect during the three months following the merger. Although the Court of Chancery granted defendants' motion to dismiss the complaint, the dismissal was without prejudice as to the pre-merger and post-merger oversight claims.

In its decision on the motion to dismiss, the Court of Chancery specifically suggested that Saito and the other plaintiffs "use the 'tools at hand,' most prominently § 220 books and records actions, to obtain information necessary to sue derivatively." Saito was the only Ash plaintiff to follow that advice. The stated purpose of Saito's demand was:

> (1) to further investigate breaches of fiduciary duties by the boards of directors of HBO & Co., Inc., McKesson, Inc., and/or McKesson HBOC, Inc. related to their oversight of their respective company's accounting procedures and financial reporting; (2) to investigate potential claims against advisors engaged by McKesson, Inc. and HBO & Co., Inc. to the acquisition of HBO & Co., Inc. by McKesson, Inc.; and (3) to gather information relating to the above in order to supplement the complaint in Ash v. McCall, et al., in accordance with the September 15, 2000 Opinion of the Court of Chancery. Saito demanded access to eleven categories of documents, including those relating to Arthur Andersen's pre-merger review and verification of HBOC's financial condition; communications between or among HBOC, McKesson, and their investment bankers and accountants concerning HBOC's accounting practices; and discussions among members of the Boards of Directors of HBOC, McKesson, and/or McKesson HBOC concerning reports published in April 1997 and thereafter about HBOC's accounting practices or financial condition.

After trial, the Court of Chancery found that Saito stated a proper purpose for the inspection of books and records—to ferret out possible wrongdoing in connection with the merger of HBOC and McKesson. But the court held that Saito's proper purpose only extended to potential wrongdoing after the date on which Saito acquired his McKesson stock. The court also held that Saito did not have a proper purpose to inspect documents relating to potential claims against third party advisors who counseled the boards in connection with the merger. Finally, the court held that Saito was not entitled to HBOC documents because Saito was not a stockholder of pre-merger HBOC, and, with respect to post-merger HBOC, he did not establish a basis on which to disregard the separate existence of the wholly-owned subsidiary.

DISCUSSION

Stockholders of Delaware corporations enjoy a qualified common law and statutory right to inspect the corporation's books and records. Inspection rights were recognized at common law because, "as a matter of self-protection, the stockholder was entitled to know how his agents were conducting the affairs of the corporation of which he or she was a part owner." The common law right is codified in 8 Del.C. § 220, which provides in relevant part:

> (b) Any stockholder shall, upon written demand under oath stating the purpose thereof, have the right to inspect for any proper purpose the corporation's stock ledger, a list of its stockholders, and its other books and records, and to make copies or extracts therefrom. A proper purpose shall mean a purpose reasonably related to such person's interest as a stockholder.

Once a stockholder establishes a proper purpose under § 220, the right to relief will not be defeated by the fact that the stockholder may have secondary purposes that are improper. The scope of a stockholder's inspection, however, is limited to those books and records that are necessary and essential to accomplish the stated, proper purpose.

After trial, the Court of Chancery found "credible evidence of possible wrongdoing," which satisfied Saito's burden of establishing a proper purpose for the inspection of corporate books and records. But the Court of Chancery limited Saito's access to relevant documents in three respects. First, it held that, since Saito would not have standing to bring an action challenging actions that occurred before he purchased McKesson stock, Saito could not obtain documents created before October 20, 1998. Second, the court concluded that Saito was not entitled to documents relating to possible wrongdoing by the financial advisors to the merging companies. Third, the court denied Saito access to any HBOC documents, since Saito never was a stockholder of HBOC. We will consider each of these rulings in turn.

A. The Standing Limitation

By statute, stockholders who bring derivative suits must allege that they were stockholders of the corporation "at the time of the transaction of which such stockholder complains." 8 Del. C. § 327. The Court of Chancery decided that this limitation on Saito's ability to maintain a derivative suit controlled the scope of his inspection rights. As a result, the court held that Saito was "effectively limited to examining conduct of McKesson and McKesson HBOC's boards following the negotiation and public announcement of the merger agreement."

Although we recognize that there may be some interplay between the two statutes, we do not read § 327 as defining the temporal scope of a stockholder's inspection rights under § 220. The books and records statute requires that a stockholder's purpose be one that is "reasonably related" to his or her interest as a stockholder. The standing statute, § 327, bars a stockholder from bringing a derivative action unless the stockholder owned the corporation's stock at the time of the alleged wrong. If a stockholder wanted to investigate alleged wrongdoing that substantially predated his or her stock ownership, there could be a question as to whether the stockholder's purpose was reasonably related to his or her interest as a stockholder, especially if the stockholder's only purpose was to institute derivative litigation. But stockholders may use information about corporate mismanagement in other ways, as well. They may seek an audience with the board to discuss proposed reforms or, failing in that, they may prepare a stockholder resolution for the next annual meeting, or mount a proxy fight to elect new directors. None of those activities would be prohibited by § 327.

Even where a stockholder's only purpose is to gather information for a derivative suit, the date of his or her stock purchase should not be used as an automatic "cut-off" date in a § 220 action. First, the potential derivative claim may involve a continuing wrong that both predates and postdates the stockholder's purchase date. In such a case, books and records from the inception of the alleged wrongdoing could be necessary and essential to the stockholder's purpose. Second, the alleged post-purchase date wrongs may have their foundation in events that transpired earlier. In this case, for example, Saito wants to investigate how McKesson's merger was consummated. Due diligence documents generated before the merger agreement was signed may be essential to that investigation. In sum, the date on which a stockholder first acquired the corporation's stock does not control the scope of records available under § 220.

B. The Financial Advisors' Documents

The Court of Chancery denied Saito access to documents in McKesson HBOC's possession that the corporation obtained from financial and accounting advisors, on the ground that Saito could not use § 220 to develop potential claims against third parties. On appeal, Saito argues that he is seeking third party documents for the same reason he is seeking McKesson HBOC documents—to investigate possible wrongdoing by McKesson and McKesson HBOC. Since the trial court found that to be a proper purpose, Saito argues that he should not be precluded from seeing documents that are necessary to his purpose, and in

McKesson HBOC's possession, simply because the documents were prepared by third party advisors.

We agree that, generally, the source of the documents in a corporation's possession should not control a stockholder's right to inspection under § 220. The issue is whether the documents are necessary and essential to satisfy the stockholder's proper purpose. In this case, Saito wants to investigate possible wrongdoing relating to McKesson and McKesson HBOC's failure to discover HBOC's accounting irregularities. Since McKesson and McKesson HBOC relied on financial and accounting advisors to evaluate HBOC's financial condition and reporting, those advisors' reports and correspondence would be critical to Saito's investigation.

C. HBOC Documents

Finally, the Court of Chancery held that Saito was not entitled to any HBOC documents because he was not a stockholder of HBOC before or after the merger. Although Saito is a stockholder of HBOC's parent, McKesson HBOC, stockholders of a parent corporation are not entitled to inspect a subsidiary's books and records, "absent a showing of a fraud or that a subsidiary is in fact the mere alter ego of the parent." The Court of Chancery found no basis to disregard HBOC's separate existence and, therefore, denied access to its records.

We reaffirm this settled principle, which applies to those HBOC books and records that were never provided to McKesson or McKesson HBOC. But it does not apply to relevant documents that HBOC gave to McKesson before the merger, or to McKesson HBOC after the merger. We assume that HBOC provided financial and accounting information to its proposed merger partner and, later, to its parent company. As with the third party advisors' documents, Saito would need access to relevant HBOC documents in order to understand what his company's directors knew and why they failed to recognize HBOC's accounting irregularities.

Points for Discussion

1. "Proper purpose."

The *Saito* decision identifies a number of proper purposes for shareholder inspection. Is there a unifying thread? For example, does the Delaware court address the question whether a shareholder could seek documents about the company's social or political activities?

By the way, who has the burden on the question of "proper purpose"? In Delaware, the statute splits the burden. With regard to the corporation's stock ledger or list of stockholders, the corporation must demonstrate the shareholder seeks inspection for an improper purpose. But the shareholder must establish a proper purpose for inspecting other books and records. *See* DGCL § 220(c). Does this make sense?

2. Nature of judicial review.

Notice that in *Saito* the Delaware Supreme Court, like the Court of Chancery, engages in a demand-by-demand review of the different categories of documents sought by the shareholder. Is this what the statute requires? Isn't this like judicial supervision of discovery during litigation? Why not simply make inspection a part of the litigation process, rather than its own separate procedure—and litigation? That is, wouldn't Delaware's stated purpose to provide a forum for corporate litigation be better served by not requiring (inspection) litigation prior to (derivative) litigation?

3. Fishing expeditions.

Like judges refereeing discovery disputes, Delaware judges in inspection cases frequently admonish shareholders that they will not permit "fishing expeditions." Why not? If, as the Delaware courts have required, shareholders seeking inspection must "present some credible basis from which the Court can infer that waste or mismanagement may have occurred," where does this pre-inspection information come from?

4. Inspection of Subsidiary's Documents.

Soon after the *Saito* decision, the Delaware legislature revised § 220 to allow for inspection of the "books and records" of a Delaware corporation's subsidiaries, provided the corporation could obtain such documents through the exercise of control over the subsidiary. Under the provision, such inspection can be denied if it would violate an agreement between the corporation and the subsidiary or if the subsidiary has a legal right under applicable law (such as that of the jurisdiction of its incorporation) to deny inspection. Would you advise a corporation to enter into agreements with its subsidiaries that block inspection rights of the subsidiary's documents?

5. Confidentiality conditions.

Not only does DGCL § 220 contemplate that the court may "prescribe conditions with reference to inspection," but Delaware courts have used "wide discretion" to decide the scope of inspection—including the execution of a confidentiality agreement as a condition for inspection. Just like discovery!

6. Publicly available information.

Should a shareholder be able to seek inspection of information or documents that are already publicly available? As we will see in the next section, the SEC requires the disclosure and filing of important documents in many transactions involving public corporations. The Delaware courts have carved out an exception to the statutory inspection rights when the "detailed information" available in SEC filings essentially discloses all facts material to the shareholder's purpose for inspection. Is this fair? For example, if SEC disclosures summarize opinion letters on company value in a going-private transaction (where the company buys its shares and as a result management acquires control), should shareholders seeking information about company value be denied inspection of the actual opinion letters and the documents on which they are based? Should the shareholder be forced to wait for discovery of this critical information in an appraisal lawsuit?

---

2. "Stockholder List"

In the United States, unlike many other parts of the world, shares of stock are not issued in "bearer form" so that whoever holds the stock certificate (or its electronic equivalent) owns the stock. Instead, U.S. corporations are required to maintain records that list the names of *stockholders of record*—persons holding legal title to outstanding shares of stock.

The "transfer agent," usually a bank or trust company, keeps the corporation's stock ledger. Among the services provided are issuing and canceling stock certificates to reflect changes in ownership, paying dividends or other distributions to shareholders, sending out proxy materials and other reports, exchanging a company's stock in a merger, or holding tendered shares in a tender offer.

A "stock ledger" records all stock transactions in the corporation, such as initial issuance and any subsequent transfer. The stock ledger shows for each stock transaction the stock certificate number that is affected and the name of the shareholder who owns the certificate.

The "list of stockholders" includes other lists of shareholders maintained by the corporation. For example, beneficial shareholders who agree (do not object) to having their names and addresses revealed to the company can be found on a Non-Objecting Beneficial Owner (NOBO) list.

Street name ownership. With the advent of electronic data storage and the disappearance of paper stock certificates, investors have changed how they own stock. Today, most investors in public corporations are not record holders, but instead hold their stock in nominee accounts in "*street name.*" Even though corporations (or their transfer agents) often keep electronic records of current shareholders, these lists do not show who really (or beneficially) owns the stock. Thus, the requirement under the Delaware inspection statute that the corporation produce its "stock ledger" (a list of stockholders of record) is of little practical use. Such data lists mostly nominee holders and does not give information for contacting other shareholders.

Most stock brokerage firms and financial institutions—"first tier" nominees—are members of Depository

Trust Company, which holds their customers' stock. Depository Trust registers all of its members' stock in one name, "CEDE & Co.," which allows it to simplify stock transfers among its members. As a result, most corporations' stockholder lists show only that CEDE & Co. owns a large portion of their stock—often more than 80%. The lists do not identify which brokerage firms and institutions hold their stock or who the beneficial owners are.

How can a corporation know who really owns its stock, for example to distribute disclosure documents? The corporation can ask Depository Trust to prepare a "CEDE breakdown"—a list of all brokerage firms and institutions holding stock in the name of CEDE & Co. Using this breakdown, the corporation then can contact the firms on the list to determine the number of beneficial owners each represents, so as to facilitate distribution of annual reports, notices of shareholder meetings, and other information. The brokerage firms and institutions generally will not volunteer the names of their customers since they consider that information confidential.

To get information on actual beneficial owners, corporations can ask brokerage firms for the names of those customers who do not object to having their identity revealed to the corporation. Brokerage firms are required by SEC rule to maintain a list of non-objecting beneficial owners ("NOBO list") and make it available to requesting corporations within seven days.

What can be inspected? Delaware courts have interpreted the "list of stockholders" mentioned in the Delaware inspection statute to include both CEDE breakdowns and NOBO lists within the corporation's possession. If the corporation does not already possess these lists, courts have required that the corporation request that the CEDE breakdown be produced, but have not required that the corporation request a NOBO list.

3. Shareholder Standing and "Encumbered Shares"

Which shareholders have inspection rights? Although most statutes permit both record and beneficial shareholders to seek inspection, the question is not as easy as it sounds. Given the proliferation of financial

FYI

Information on the shareholders in public companies is available from other sources, as well. The federal securities laws require institutional shareholders (with more than $100 million in assets) to file reports of their securities holdings. In addition, shareholders that hold more than 10% of the outstanding shares of public companies must file reports on their holdings and any trading. In addition, public companies must list holdings by (certain) shareholders in their prospectuses and annual reports, as well as holdings of corporate directors and officers.

hedging techniques, shareholders frequently hold offsetting positions that reduce or eliminate the financial incentives associated with share ownership.

Suppose you buy a share for $100. If the share price goes up, you have made money; if it declines, you have lost. Now suppose that you also have "shorted" the same share. In a "short" transaction, you borrow a share from a broker and then sell the share. You get the money from the sale upfront, but you have the obligation to return the borrowed share to the broker. If the share price goes up, you lose money, because you have to buy a more expensive share to return to the broker. If the share price goes down, you make money, because you can buy a less expensive share to return. Financially, a "short" is like the mirror opposite of a share purchase.

In this example, if you both purchased a share ("long position") and shorted a share ("short position"), your net financial position would be zero. Upfront, the $100 you received from shorting would offset the $100 you paid for the share. And when you satisfied your obligation to return a share to the broker, you would simply give the broker the share you own. There would be no need to buy a share in the marketplace, so your fortunes would not depend at all on the share price. If the price went up to $110, you would make $10 on the share you bought, but lose $10 on your short. If the price dropped to $90, you would lose $10 on your share, but make $10 on your short.

Some investors only own shares long without short positions ("pure" shareholders). But some investors have both long and short positions. You can think of a short position as financially "encumbering" the long position, weighing down the shares owned by the investor with opposite positions that take away the upside when share prices rise (and reduce the downside when prices fall). In the extreme, an investor might have more shorts than longs, so that she would make money if the share price declined. Such an investor would not have the economic incentives of a shareholder—in fact, the opposite would be true. Should a shareholder with a net short position be entitled to the same rights as pure shareholders? Should courts or legislatures take into account short positions?

Delaware courts have sidestepped the issue. The Court of Chancery has held that an investor that held both long and short positions was entitled to exercise inspection rights based on its long positions—that is, beneficial ownership determines shareholder rights, not the investor's net financial position. *Deephaven Risk Arb Trading Ltd. v. UnitedGlobalCom, Inc.*, 2005 WL 1713067 (Del. Ch. 2005). In the case, an arb (an investment firm that places bets on corporate transactions, like mergers) was betting against a merger happening and had taken a net short position in the corporation that was planning the merger. When the corporation decided to curtail a planned rights offering, suggesting that the merger would go through, the arb sought inspection of documents concerning the rights offering.

The Vice Chancellor allowed inspection by the arb, even though it was net short—even though its shares were "encumbered" by short positions:

> Practically, requiring an analysis of why and under what circumstances a § 220 plaintiff came to hold a company's shares could significantly complicate the nature of this summary and often expedited proceeding. It potentially would force courts to undertake a complex analysis to determine the plaintiff's financial position net of stock, options and other derivatives. One can imagine cases in which financial experts might be necessary to make such a determination. Moreover, the specter of being forced to disclose sophisticated and proprietary trading techniques could have a chilling effect on the use of § 220 by a substantial segment of stockholders. Finally, unlike in other situations such as voting, the § 220 analysis includes its own safeguard against plaintiffs with economic incentives that are not aligned with other stockholders: the proper purpose analysis.

The court then found a "credible basis" that the rights offering may have involved mismanagement and permitted the inspection.

Points for Discussion

1. Separation of ownership and control?

Does recognizing shareholder rights for investors who are betting against the corporation serve any corporate interest? Should short selling and use of other derivatives change the meaning of who is a "shareholder"?

2. Brave new world.

The *Deephaven* court understandably wanted to avoid the "complex analysis" of the true motivations of investors in the corporation. Can you suggest a way to deal with investors who hold "encumbered shares" and are "net short"—that is, investors who nominally own an interest in future corporate profitability, but whose true financial interests are aligned with corporate financial failure? Isn't this essentially the issue that the court faced in *Pillsbury v. Honeywell*?

B. Information Required for Shareholder Voting

1. State Law: Notice of Shareholder Meetings

As we saw when we looked at the basics of shareholder voting, state law requires only minimal information when shareholders vote. Shareholders receive notice of when and where the shareholder meeting will happen, but generally do not get information about the matters on which they will vote. Only if there is a special meeting (or a proposal to amend the articles) must shareholders be provided with notice of the matter to be voted on (or a copy or summary of the amendment).

2. SEC Rules: Disclosure in Proxy Statements

Disclosure under federal law is a different story. Shareholders in public corporations receive extensive information on all matters (such as board elections, amendments of articles, approval of mergers) on which they are asked to vote. A comprehensive regulatory regime created by SEC rules requires that any solicitation, whether by management or by another shareholder, seeking shareholder proxies be accompanied by a disclosure document called a "proxy statement."

Take Note!

Remember that state corporate statutes authorize shareholders to vote by proxy—that is, by giving an agent authority to vote in their place at a shareholder meeting. This is how most voting happens in public corporations—so it is no surprise that federal regulation of shareholder voting in public corporations is called "proxy regulation."

Make the Connection

As you can imagine, regulation of the method and information involved in soliciting shareholder votes can crimp shareholder activism. Generally, activists seeking shareholder support for their reforms are subject to the SEC proxy rules to the same extent as management. Over the past two decades, the SEC has undertaken some reforms to avoid over-regulating shareholder activism. We will return to the SEC proxy rules (and reforms) in the next chapter when we look at shareholder activism in public corporations.

The extensive disclosure required under the SEC proxy regime stands in marked contrast to the bare-bones notice required by state corporate statutes. The federal rules cover companies whose shares are traded on public stock markets. They regulate all "proxy solicitations," a term defined broadly by SEC rules and court decisions. In most proxy solicitations, not only must shareholders receive a proxy statement, but the statement must be filed with (and sometimes reviewed by) the SEC. If shareholders are asked to vote, they must receive a "proxy card" with a specified format and voting options.

In short, the federal proxy regime creates a system of prior restraints and content regulation of corporate speech that relates to shareholder voting. Promulgated pursuant to § 14(a) of the Securities Exchange Act of 1934, the purpose is to ensure informed and fair suffrage in public corporations.

Public companies. What are public companies? The SEC proxy rules generally apply to every company that has a class of securities (equity or debt) listed on a stock exchange or has a class of equity securities owned by 2,000 or more holders of record and assets of at least $10,000,000. Securities Exchange Act § 12(b), (g).

There are approximately 3,600 public companies subject to SEC regulation. Besides having to provide information to shareholders when they vote, public companies must file informational reports annually (10-K), quarterly (10-Q), and when there are special events (8-K). Their insiders (directors, officers, and more than 10% shareholders) are required to disclose any trading in the company's equity shares. We take up the questions of disclosure in public markets in Chapter 27, Securities Markets.

One important note: you should be aware that foreign companies whose securities are traded on U.S. public markets are only subject to the periodic disclosure requirements, but not the requirements applicable to proxy voting or disclosure of insider trading.

Management proxy solicitations. Before soliciting shareholder proxies, management must prepare a proxy statement (a detailed disclosure document describing board candidates and the matters on which shareholders will vote) and a form of proxy (the instructions that specify how shareholders want their shares to be voted).

Schedule 14A is the SEC form (really a set of instructions) that specifies what must be disclosed in the management proxy statement. For a usual annual meeting, the bulk of the proxy statement includes information about director nominees and management's compensation arrangements.

If there are any proposals requiring a shareholder vote (such as an amendment of the corporate articles or approval of an executive compensation plan), the proxy statement must describe the proposal fully—including both its negative and positive aspects. Thus, for example, if management asks shareholders to approve a charter amendment that will create a staggered board, the proxy statement might read as follows:

> **Example 17.1**
> **Proxy Statement**
>
> A classified Board of Directors with staggered terms would facilitate continuity and stability of leadership and policy by assuring that experienced personnel familiar with the Company and its business will be on the Board of Directors at all times. The Company believes that three-year terms for its directors will be more attractive to potential director candidates. A classified board with staggered terms would prevent precipitous changes in the composition of the Board of Directors and, thereby, would make it more difficult to effect changes in the Company's policies, business strategies and operations.
>
> However, a classified board with staggered terms will make it more difficult for stockholders to change the composition of the Board of Directors even if the stockholders believe such a change would be desirable. A staggered Board of Directors will require at least two Annual Meetings of stockholders, instead of one, for stockholders to effect a change in the majority of the Board of Directors. Although staggered board provisions are not designed to be, and are not, effective against an any-and-all cash tender offer, staggered board provisions have provided boards of directors with additional leverage to negotiate protections for corporate constituencies even after a takeover bidder has acquired a majority of their company's stock. Thus, a staggered board provision might tend to discourage certain types of tender offers, perhaps including some tender offers at a purchase price that is higher than the current market price.

Management must file preliminary copies of non-routine proxy statements and forms of proxy with the SEC at least 10 days before sending them to shareholders. The SEC staff endeavors to review and comment on preliminary proxy materials within this 10-day period. (The SEC permits limited confidential treatment for proxy filings related to business combinations or other extraordinary transactions.)

The SEC does not review routine proxy materials covering uncontested annual meetings (unopposed election of directors, ratification of company auditors, and voting on shareholder proposals). Instead, these materials are filed with the SEC when sent to shareholders.

Every "proxy solicitation" (basically, a request for the shareholder's proxy) by management must be accompanied or preceded by the *definitive* proxy statement, as filed with the SEC. In addition, if management is soliciting proxies for a meeting at which directors are to be elected, shareholders must also receive the company's annual report. Recent SEC rules permit these documents to be disseminated to shareholders, if they consent, by email or other electronic means.

Proxy card. The SEC proxy rules <u>also regulate</u> the "form of proxy"—that is, the voting ballot sent to shareholders. The proxy card must give shareholders an opportunity to vote either for or against each non-election matter. And if directors are to be elected, the proxy card must allow shareholders to withhold their votes on directors as a group or on individual candidates. (In companies that use "majority voting," shareholders must be able to vote for or against directors as a group or individually.)

> **Go Online**
>
> All proxy statements, once filed with the SEC, become publicly available on the SEC's website (www.sec.gov/edgar). You might be interested to see what a proxy statement looks like. For example, how did Oracle Corporation explain the $79.6 million in new stock options granted to its CEO Larry Ellison in 2013, even though the company's stock returns were only barely above the market? [Oracle, Schedule 14A-DEF (Sep. 20, 2013)]

The proxy holder (typically a member of the company's management) must vote according to the shareholder's instructions. A proxy may confer discretionary authority on matters where the shareholder does not specify a choice or if unforeseen matters come up at the meeting.

Example 17.2

Here is a typical proxy card, front and back:

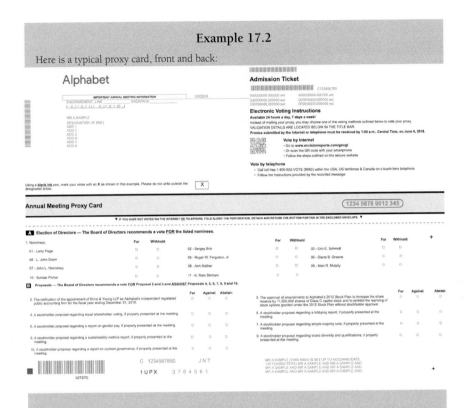

The proxy card offers a treasure trove of insights into the proxy machinery. It is divided into two separate voting categories—those matters supported by management and those opposed by management. It does not allow shareholders to vote for write-in or alternative candidates. It requires that the proxy be signed and dated, since the last-dated proxy is the one that counts. It tells shareholders they can give their proxy online.

C. Regulation of Proxy Fraud

Besides specifying the information that shareholders must receive in any proxy solicitation, the SEC rules under § 14(a) also require the information they receive to be full and complete. Under Rule 14a–9, false or misleading statements are prohibited:

> ### SEC Rule 14a–9
> ### Securities Exchange Act of 1934
>
> (a) No solicitation subject to this regulation shall be made by means of any proxy statement containing any statement which is false or misleading with respect to any material fact, or which omits to state any material fact necessary in order to make the statements therein not false or misleading.
>
> (b) The fact that a proxy statement has been filed with or examined by the Commission shall not be deemed a finding by the Commission that such material is accurate or complete or not false or misleading.

1. Implied Federal Cause of Action

Notice that Rule 14a–9 prohibits misrepresentations in proxy statements, but does not specify a remedy. Although the 1934 Act authorizes the SEC to sue to enforce provisions of the statute and its rules, there is no explicit private enforcement mechanism for the rule. To fill this gap, federal courts fashioned an implied private action for misrepresentations that violate Rule 14a–9 on the theory that the SEC cannot review and ensure the accuracy of every proxy statement. The private action tracks the elements of a typical fraud action. The plaintiff must show (1) a false or misleading statement (2) of material fact (3) upon which shareholder voters relied (4) causing them to suffer losses. (The Supreme Court has not yet decided the standard of culpability and whether the misrepresentations must have been intentional or negligent.)

The implied private action under § 14(a) and Rule 14a–9 offers an interesting window into corporate federalism. In the belief that state remedies against management abuse of the shareholder franchise were inadequate, the Supreme Court in the 1960s and 1970s inferred a new level of federal protection. But in the 1980s the Court lost some of its enthusiasm, perhaps as state corporate law and remedies expanded. Today private 14a–9 actions are unusual. Aggrieved shareholders typically turn to state fiduciary protection when their voting rights are disregarded.

But the federal proxy fraud cases still warrant your attention. The ways in which they resolve the critical elements of materiality, reliance, and causation inform state fiduciary law. They also illustrate the federal-state dynamic in corporate law in which federal authorities have stepped in to correct perceived deficiencies in state law and then back out as state law rises to the challenge.

Federal Proxy Fraud Action		
Issue	**Case**	**Holding**
Implied private action	J.I. Case Co. v. Borak (1964)	Private right of action exists under § 14(a) of the 1934 Act, subject to federal procedures and permitting both injunctive and monetary relief
Elements		
(1) false or misleading statement	Virginia Bankshares, Inc. v. Sandberg (1991)	A statement of belief or opinion by the board of directors can be actionable, since shareholders rely on the board
(2) material fact	TSC Industries, Inc. v. Northway, Inc. (1976)	"An omitted fact is material if there is a substantial likelihood that a reasonable shareholder would consider it important in deciding how to vote" or "the omitted fact would have been viewed by the reasonable investor as having significantly altered the 'total mix' of information made available"
	Virginia Bankshares, Inc. v. Sandberg (1991)	A statement of belief or opinion is "material" if the subject matter of the statement was false *and* the maker of the statement could not reasonably have believed it was true
(3) culpability	Virginia Bankshares, Inc. v. Sandberg (1991)	Question reserved. Lower courts are divided on whether those making misstatements in a proxy statement must have acted intentionally or only negligently
(4) reliance	Mills v. Electric Auto-Lite Co. (1970)	Given the impracticality of determining reliance by thousands of shareholders, if the alleged misstatement or omission is material, then reliance is presumed
(5) causation	Mills v. Electric Auto-Lite Co. (1970)	Causation can be established by showing the proxy statement was an "essential link" in the transaction
	Virginia Bankshares, Inc. v. Sandberg (1991)	If solicited shareholders did not own enough shares to block the transaction, a false proxy statement cannot be an "essential link" to the transaction
Attorneys' fees	Mills v. Electric Auto-Lite Co. (1970)	Court may compel corporation to pay class plaintiff's litigation expenses and reasonable attorneys' fees, upon showing corporation violated Rule 14a–9

In looking at this snapshot of the federal proxy fraud action, you should notice some things. First, the implication of a *federal* cause of action meant that shareholders unhappy about the results of a transaction approved by a shareholder majority could seek relief in federal court, and were not relegated to state law remedies and procedures. Second, all of the cases involved challenges to shareholder approval of *corporate mergers*, which traditionally received deferential review under state law and left dissenting shareholders with an uncertain appraisal remedy. Third, a federal proxy fraud action did not require a showing that the actual voting outcome would have been different if shareholders had been fully and honestly informed, only that reasonable shareholders would have considered the alleged misstatements to be "important." Fourth, showing materi-

Make the Connection

The elements of a "proxy fraud" action under Rule 14a–9 parallel those of a "securities fraud" action under Rule 10b–5. *See* Chapter 28, Securities Fraud. In fact, federal courts used the standard of materiality developed in proxy fraud cases in fashioning a materiality standard for securities fraud cases. The elements, however, are not all the same. Perhaps the most important difference between the two actions is that a proxy fraud action does not require the pleading or proof of actual intent, which imposes a significant hurdle in securities fraud cases.

ality under the "would consider it important" standard created a presumption that shareholders relied on the misstatements. Finally, if minority shareholders did not have enough votes to block a merger, any misstatements to them could not have caused their losses.

2. Duty of Disclosure Under State Law

At about the time that § 14(a) actions reached their apex in the 1970s, state courts began to show an interest in ensuring honesty in communications to shareholders. In an important 1977 case, Delaware articulated a duty of "complete candor" that borrowed the framework, sometimes verbatim, of the federal proxy fraud action. *See Lynch v. Vickers Energy Corp.*, 383 A.2d 278 (Del. 1977).

Shareholders in Delaware corporations have used the duty of candor (which the Delaware courts renamed "duty of disclosure") to successfully challenge mergers, reorganizations, and charter amendments accomplished through false or misleading proxy statements. Over time, for many shareholders and their lawyers, Delaware has proved to be preferable to federal court. Under Delaware's rescissory damages standard (what the shares would be worth absent the challenged transaction) rather than the federal out-of-pocket standard (what the shares should have fetched absent the misinformation), shareholders can recover the loss of synergy value in a completed merger. In addition, Delaware allows attorneys' fees to be computed on the basis of class action results, not the less generous federal "lodestar" method. *See* Chapter 19, Shareholder Litigation.

Why go to federal court when state (Delaware) courts are so inviting?

CHAPTER 18

Public Shareholder Activism

Public shareholder activism has become one of the most important topics in business law. Shareholder activism challenges the basic framework of the separation of ownership and control.

As we have already seen, corporate law establishes a hierarchical governance structure for the corporation in which shareholders elect a board of directors that directs and supervises the corporation's business and affairs. The board selects the officers who run the corporation's day-to-day business. Most decisions about corporate strategy and operation are removed from the shareholders. The model largely divorces ownership from control.

In practice, the separation of ownership and control in *public corporations* is even greater. Shareholders, to be sure, *elect* directors, but historically they have rarely played a meaningful role in *selecting* them. The state and federal rules on proxy voting make it difficult and expensive for shareholders in public corporations to nominate or solicit support for board candidates. The incumbent board controls access to the corporation's proxy mechanism and effectively determines who is nominated—and thus who is elected.

Hedge funds, and to some extent other institutional investors, have pressed against this governance structure. As institutional ownership of shares has increased during the previous couple of decades, voting power in public corporations has become more concentrated. Today, large index funds families such as BlackRock, State Street, and Vanguard often control 15–20% of the outstanding shares of public companies. They are vocal proponents of corporate governance reforms and often push for boards to consider sustainability and other long-run objectives, as opposed to short-term shareholder gain. Large hedge fund activists control billions of dollars and frequently challenge boards to change their strategies, often with the support of the index funds. Collectively, shareholder activists have exercised a newfound voice and have pushed for a variety of governance reforms, such as new methods for electing directors, shareholder access to the nomination process, and greater say in corporate operations.

This chapter looks at the governance role of activist shareholders in public corporations. We begin with a big picture overview of the "collective action" problem of shareholder voting and we describe various "theories of the firm." We then turn to a description of shareholder activism, and the role of institutional investors generally. Next, we describe the law affecting shareholder activism in public corporations, first under state corporate law and then under the federal proxy regime. Finally, we look at the SEC shareholder proposal rule, which creates (some) shareholder access to the company-funded proxy machinery.

A. The Big Picture: Collective Action and Theories of the Firm

We begin with some fundamental questions about the role of shareholders in public corporations. Should they be passive or active? Should they be given a strong voice or simply a tangential role? What should the relationship be between shareholders and the board of directors? Who should stand at the center of corporate governance?

In this section, we introduce you to the academic literature and the main commentators on the role of shareholders in the public corporation, in their own words. First is the collective action question. Why do shareholders of public corporations only rarely use their rights to oppose management? The following is a classic answer from Professor Robert Clark, former dean of Harvard Law School.

ROBERT CHARLES CLARK, CORPORATE LAW 389–94 (1986)

Whenever shareholders of a publicly held company vote upon matters affecting the corporation, they engage in collective action that suffers from many systemic difficulties. Such difficulties include "rational apathy" of shareholders, the temptation of individual shareholders to take a "free ride," and unfairness to certain shareholders even where collective action is successful.

Often the aggregate cost to shareholders of informing themselves of potential corporate actions, independently assessing the wisdom of such actions, and casting their votes will greatly exceed the expected or actual benefits garnered from informed voting. Recognition of this phenomenon accounts for the usual rules that entrust corporate management with all ordinary business decisions. But the same problem still exists with respect to the major subjects of shareholder voting: the election of directors and the approval or rejection of major organic changes such as mergers.

Consider a simplified case. Outta Control Corp., with 1 million voting common shares outstanding, has 10,000 shareholders, each of whom owns 1 block of 100 shares. The directors propose to merge Outta Control into Purchaser Corp., which would result in the acquisition by the former Outta Control shareholders, in exchange for their old shares, of voting common shares in Purchaser with a total market value of $50 million. In fact, Purchaser would have been willing to exchange $60 million worth of its shares if it had not agreed, under prodding by Outta Control's managers and in return for their cooperation in recommending the merger, to give extraordinary salary increases to those officers of Outta Control who would continue their employment after the merger.

Assume that all of this information is contained in a 240-page proxy statement that is sent to Outta Control's shareholders and that any rational shareholder who reads it would decide to vote against the merger. Assume further that if the merger proposal were disapproved, a new one would be adopted that would yield these shareholders the additional $10 million gain which Purchaser Corp. was prepared to pay. Thus, the actual benefit to be derived from collective shareholder action against the merger plan would be $1000 per shareholder.

Shareholders do not expect, however, to discover a reason for concluding that disapproval will avert a corporate harm or open the door to a larger corporate gain every time they read a proxy statement. To make our problem complete, assume that the shareholders in it make a rational assessment of the probabilities of such an occurrence. Because of their assessment, they assign an expected benefit of $50 per shareholder to collective action of the sort described, that is, action based on each shareholder's reading the proxy statement, making up his mind, and voting.

Now suppose the average cost of informed shareholder action is simply the opportunity cost (the cost of doing one thing to the exclusion of others) of reading the proxy statement before sending in the proxy card and that this amount is $120 per shareholder (three hours of reading at $40 per hour—a rather low estimate). Thus the total cost of collective action would be $1.2 million. This cost would still be less than the actual benefit to be gained in this case, from collective action by informed voters. But the cost of such collective action greatly exceeds the expected benefit—$120 versus $50 per shareholder—so sensible shareholders will not read the proxy statement. They will be rationally apathetic.

One legal approach toward improving the efficiency of collective action is to make it cheaper for each shareholder to act in an informed way. Suppose that in our example the opportunity cost of reading the proxy statement concerning the proposed merger were only $10 per shareholder, because the SEC had devised a system of proxy rules that produced extremely concise, quickly understandable proxy statements that emphasize crucial data. Suppose that the SEC also monitors the statement and requires that the crucial information appear in bold face type. The expected benefit of collective action by informed voting is still $50 per shareholder, but the cost of such action is now only $10 per shareholder. The net expected benefit is therefore $40 per shareholder.

Yet the desired collective action still may not occur. Any one shareholder may realize that only 50% of the shareholders are needed to block the merger. If the shareholder believes that enough other shareholders will respond to the incentive of the $40 net expected benefit and will act accordingly to produce the desirable collective result, he might decide to save himself the cost of reading the streamlined proxy statement. He can still participate in any benefits of collective action that arise through the work of the other shareholders. He will be a free rider on their efforts. The net expected benefit of his action as a free rider would be $50 rather than $40.

Of course, it may also occur to him that if all the other shareholders thought similarly, no collective action would be taken, and everyone would lose the chance of reaping the benefits. He might realize that giving in to the temptation to achieve an individual gain superior to everyone else's would jeopardize the attainment of collective benefits. Conceivably this realization might prompt him to read the proxy statement. But it is doubtful whether this would happen in practice and, as a matter of theory (game theory, that is), a rational, self-interested shareholder would not do so.

Why not? Because, whether he assumes the other shareholders will read or will not read, he will expect to be better off if he doesn't. Assume the others will read: His own expected benefit is $50 if he doesn't read, and $40 if he does. Assume the others will not read (so the original merger plan goes through): His own expected benefit is $0 if he doesn't read, but minus $10 if he does. The situation is like the prisoner's dilemma of game theory and may call for solutions similar in strategy to those that would solve that dilemma.

What's That?

The "prisoner's dilemma" is a classic in game theory. Suppose you and a companion have been arrested for bank robbery. The police interrogate both of you in separate rooms. You are told the following: if you alone confess (defect), you will go free; if your companion confesses (defects) while you remain silent, you will receive the full 10-year sentence. But you know that if you both are silent, you will both be sentenced to six months on a minor charge. You should remain silent, but you can't trust your companion. So you confess.

Let us again alter the hypothetical so that the free rider problem, like the rational apathy problem, effectively disappears. Suppose that one shareholder, Ajax, owns 200,000 shares, while every other shareholder owns only one block of 100 shares. The other facts remain the same. The expected benefit to Ajax is now $100,000, which is, let us assume, more than the expected cost of reading the proxy statement and convincing the holders of 300,100 other shares also to vote against the merger. (He would do this by waging a proxy contest.) Unless it deeply galls Ajax to think that he will be treated unfairly, he will take action to achieve the collective benefit even if he cannot be reimbursed for the costs and risks of such action.

Acting strictly for his own benefit, he will nevertheless have created a collective good for all the other shareholders in the company. The smaller shareholders will get the benefit of his concern without bearing a pro rata share of cost. This phenomenon is an example of what one economist calls the systematic exploitation of the large by the small. (We can assume that Ajax will not try to be a free rider because his particular expected benefit is so high that he would not risk depending on action by other shareholders.)

The obvious problem here is one of fairness to the guardian shareholder. The prospect of being taken advantage of by the smaller shareholders may deter investors from becoming dominant shareholders in the first place. The problem once again resembles the prisoner's dilemma, but in this situation the players are all investors as they contemplate buying into any publicly held corporation. But in the real world there are many factors that tempt investors to obtain large percentage interests in companies, not the least of which is the chance of acquiring the various special benefits of controlling the corporation on an ongoing basis. Any force toward misallocation created by the phenomenon of exploitation of the large by the small is likely to be more than offset by these factors. Thus, the only remaining problem will be unfair treatment of the large, but not controlling, shareholder who undertakes a proxy contest or similar action for the corporation's benefit.

***

We next turn to several theories of the firm, all of which take the collective action problem of the public corporation as a starting point, but then reach very different conclusions.

1. Berle-Means Corporation

The modern debate about the role of public shareholders in corporate governance dates from the 1932 publication of THE MODERN CORPORATION AND PRIVATE PROPERTY by two Columbia professors, Adolf Berle (law) and Gardiner Means (economics). The book, which studied the characteristics of the 200 largest corporations listed on the New York Stock Exchange, identified a separation between ownership and control. According to Berle and Means, the large body of shareholders in public corporations had no real control over the enterprise. Instead, control resided with the board of directors and the corporation's top executives—that is, with corporate management.

Berle and Means found that public shareholders had little say in the composition of the board:

> In the election of the board the stockholder ordinarily has three alternatives. He can refrain from voting, he can attend the annual meeting and personally vote his stock, or he can sign a proxy transferring his voting power to certain individuals selected by the management of the corporation, the proxy committee. As his personal vote will count for little or nothing at the meeting unless he has a very large block of stock, the stockholder is practically reduced to the alternative of not voting at all or else of *handing over his vote to individuals over whom he has no control and in whose selection he did not participate.* In neither case will he be able to exercise any measure of control. Rather, control will tend to be in the hands of those who select the proxy committee by whom, in turn, the election of directors for the ensuing period may be made. Since the proxy committee is appointed by the existing management, the latter can virtually dictate their own successors. Where ownership is sufficiently sub-divided, the management can thus become a self-perpetuating body even though its share in the ownership is negligible. This form of control can properly be called "management control."

For Berle and Means, the prescription to mitigate the separation of ownership from control was added legal protection for shareholders to protect them from unfettered management self-interest. This also would serve, they thought, to control the power of corporations in society. One solution was greater information to shareholders in the voting process; another was heightened fiduciary duties. The abuses exposed by the stock market crash of 1929 cast doubt on market forces as adequate protection against management overreaching.

The argument that shareholder owners were protected by market forces, however, did not die. In 1967, Henry Manne (a George Washington University law professor and later dean of George Mason University's law school) agreed that Berle and Means had correctly diagnosed the separation of ownership and control in the public corporation, but had written the wrong prescription. In an influential (and still controversial) article, Manne asserted that centralized management is essential for the public corporation to raise large amounts of capital:

> If the principal economic function of the corporate form was to amass the funds of investors *qua* investors, we should not anticipate their demanding or wanting a direct role in the management of the company. Management, and the selection of particular managers, is not, in

theory at least, a function of capital investors. Management is a discrete economic service of function, and the selection of individuals to perform that function, whether undertaken at the outset or during the later life of a company, is a part of the entrepreneurial job. Centralizing management serves simply to specialize these various economic functions and to allow the system to operate more efficiently.

While recognizing the problems of the separation of ownership and control identified by Berle and Means, Manne contended that the market for corporate control represented the most efficient solution to this separation:

> The market for corporate control serves an extraordinarily important purpose in the functioning of the corporate system. Unless a publicly traded company is efficiently managed, the price of its shares on the open market will decline, thus lowering the price at which an outsider can take over control of the corporation. The constant pressure provided by the threat of a takeover probably plays a larger role in the successful functioning of our corporate system than has been generally recognized. It conditions managers to a specific point of view perfectly consistent with the shareholders' interest, to wit, keeping the price of the company's shares as high as possible. Even this, of course, is no guarantee that an outsider will not feel that he can do better; but if the management group performs relatively efficiently, the dangers of losing control are not great.

2. "Nexus of Contracts" Corporation

In the late 1970s, a number of economists and law professors advanced a theory of the corporation as a "nexus of contracts" among the corporate participants. Under this theory, investment is voluntary and the relationships between shareholders and managers are essentially contractual. Freedom of contract dictates that the parties be permitted to structure their relations as they choose, and the role of the state is limited to identifying and enforcing their voluntary consensual arrangements. Because corporations must compete for investors' capital, they will design governance structures to reduce the risks of management overreaching—to attract investment.

The "nexus of contracts" corporation stands in stark contrast with the corporation as a "creature of law," which supports state intervention through direct regulation and shareholder litigation. The contractual theory views the corporation as a private contract, where the state's role is limited to enforcing the parties' understandings. The corporation, rather than a ward of the state, is the result of contracts among the owners and managers. In short, the role of shareholders is whatever they have voluntarily chosen.

The contractarians recognized, however, that market forces did not always protect against opportunistic managers. For example, in "final period" transactions (such as a merger) where there is no market after the transaction, managers may rationally seek to benefit themselves at the expense of shareholders. For the contractarians, the answer to such opportunism lay in corporate fiduciary duties that they viewed as filling the gaps in the corporation's contractual structure.

The contractarian theory—the first systematic effort to respond to Berle and Means—has influenced the intellectual development of corporate law. Drawing on economic rather than legal literature, it suggested a new way to view the corporate structure. Its leading proponents, Frank Easterbrook (a Chicago law professor and now Seventh Circuit judge) and Daniel Fischel (a Northwestern law professor), argued that corporate law rules, such as limited liability and board prerogatives, could be explained as a reflection of the bargains that corporate constituents would have agreed to on their own. That is, shareholders have the (limited) rights under corporate law because they agreed to this efficient outcome.

Although some writers continue to advocate a strict contractarian view that public shareholders have the rights that they have voluntarily accepted, many have come to recognize that the linchpin of the contractarian theory (the market for corporate control) has not operated as predicted. First, the stock market—upon which the market in corporate control depends—has not been as efficient as contractarians supposed. Second, takeovers are expensive, and not every badly managed company is subject to their discipline. Third, management has installed anti-takeover devices (sometimes with shareholder consent) even though contractarian theory predicts that the managers should have faced market discipline for installing such devices and shareholders should have rejected them as contrary to their best interests. Finally, state anti-takeover statutes passed at the behest of corporate managers, generally without shareholder participation, have undermined the effectiveness of the market for corporate control.

3. "Political Product" Corporation

If the contractarian model does not explain the Berle and Means separation of ownership and control in the modern U.S. public corporation, what does? Some scholars, most notably Mark Roe (a Penn, and now Harvard, law professor), have suggested the role of the public shareholder is the product of a combination of political and economic forces.

The prevailing paradigm is that the modern corporation survived because it was the fittest means of dealing with large-scale organization. But if politics cut off lines of development, then whether it is the inevitable form for large-scale firms becomes doubtful. Politics and the organization of financial intermediaries cannot be left out of the equation.

Professor Roe has <u>asserted</u> that corporate structures with strong managers and weak owners developed in the United States partly due to path dependence—that is, a path that "winds and goes here instead of there, when a straight road would be a much easier drive." The path taken by U.S. corporate law does not necessarily reflect the approach that would be chosen today. But, having invested in the original path and in the resources alongside the path, it is easier staying on the winding road than taking another.

The rules and practices that weakened financial intermediaries arose because the American public historically abhorred private concentrations of economic power—concentrations that more powerful financial institutions would create, concentrations that a more powerful central government would have made politically palatable, concentrations that would probably be regulated, not destroyed, were they first arising today.

As large-scale industry arose at the end of the nineteenth century, it faced two financing problems created by the absence of nationwide financial institutions: big industry needed to gather lots of capital nationally, and certain organizational forms that worked well with strong financial institutions were unavailable. We developed very good substitutes. We developed, for example, high-quality securities markets, which allowed firms to raise capital in a national market, to remedy the absence of truly national financial institutions. We developed antitrust rules that promoted competition and, because competition pushes even firms with substandard internal governance toward efficiency, the costs of internal governance problems were reduced.

In time, we adopted new legal and economic institutions that are still not as well developed in other advanced nations. Corporate boards now have well defined legal duties that partly constrain managers, and we have an active bar that pursues lawsuits, some of which are legitimate and functional. We have developed a professionalism that motivates some managers. We have had hostile takeovers, which constrained managers.

4. "Team Production" Corporation

Notice that these theories of the public corporation do not resolve whether the corporation should be run for the benefit of shareholders. Thus, the famous Berle-Dodd debate continues (recall that we first saw the debate in Chapter 6, Corporation in Society). Most contractarians assert that the corporation should be run for shareholders—a "shareholder primacy" norm. Contractarians justify this view by pointing out that shareholders are residual claimants in the corporation, entitled to whatever remains after payment is made to nonshareholders such as employees, managers, and creditors. This last-in-line position makes shareholders most sensitive to corporate performance, and thus most like "owners."

But as we have seen, shareholders do not "own" the corporation in the same way a proprietor owns her own business. The shareholders cannot determine what products the corporation will sell, who will run the day-to-day operations, whether profits will be paid to the owners, when the business will take on new debt, or even whether the business should be sold.

The shareholder primacy norm has therefore been the subject of significant debate. Must directors make every business decision solely on the basis of maximizing the financial wealth of current shareholders? Some commentators have argued that corporate law does not require this. Instead, corporate fiduciary duties are generally understood as running to the "corporation" itself or the "corporation and its shareholders" and are framed from a long-term perspective. And the business judgment rule gives directors broad latitude to make decisions that do not necessarily maximize shareholder value.

Furthermore, contemporary corporate statutes that authorize charitable contributions and, in some states, permit directors to consider nonshareholder constituencies seem inconsistent with shareholder wealth maximization. In fact, corporate directors often say they operate by considering the impact of their business decisions on all the corporation's constituencies, not just shareholders.

> **Make the Connection**
>
> We have seen these conceptions of the corporation before. Recall the distinction between the "property" theory of the corporation, with its emphasis on maximizing returns for shareholders, and the "entity" theory of the corporation, which recognizes the role of the corporation in society. *See* Chapter 6.

Seeking to bridge theory and reality, Professors Margaret Blair (an economist, who has taught at Georgetown and Vanderbilt law schools) and the late Lynn Stout (a law professor at Georgetown, UCLA, and Cornell) offer an alternative model that they describe as "team production." Drawing on work by financial economists, they <u>argue</u> that a business corporation "requires inputs from a large number of individuals, including shareholders, creditors, managers, and rank-and-file employees"—all of whom constitute a "team." Corporate law calls on team members to cede control of the enterprise to the board of directors. In so doing, "the team members have created a new and separate entity that takes on a life of its own and could, potentially, act against their interests, leading them to lose what they have invested in the enterprise."

Why would team members give up control to the board in this way? For Blair and Stout, the answer is that team members believe there will be more efficient team production and their share will reflect this if they and other corporate participants defer to the board. In this model, the board becomes the focal point for resolving the claims of all the team members—a "mediating hierarchy."

> Our argument suggests that it is misleading to view a public corporation as merely a bundle of assets under common ownership. Rather, a public corporation is a team of people who enter into a complex agreement to work together for their mutual gain. Participants—including shareholders, employees, and perhaps other stakeholders such as creditors or the local community—enter into a "pactum subjectionis" under which they yield control over outputs and key inputs (time, intellectual skills, or financial capital) to the hierarchy. They enter into this mutual agreement in an effort to reduce wasteful shirking and rent-seeking by relegating to the internal hierarchy the right to determine the division of duties and resources in the joint enterprise. They thus agree not to specific terms or outcomes (as in a traditional "contract"), but to participation in a process of internal goal setting and dispute resolution. . . .

> The mediating hierarchy model of the public corporation necessarily implies that authority for making some allocative decisions—those that take place "within" the firm—ultimately rests with the board of directors, whose decisions cannot be overturned by appealing to some outside authority, like a court. This claim should not be read too broadly. When members of the hierarchy behave in ways that threaten the hierarchy itself (as when corporate directors violate their duty of loyalty to the firm through self-dealing), courts will intervene. . . .

> We realize that this approach may seem odd—even counterintuitive— to corporate theorists accustomed to thinking of corporations in terms of a grand-design principal-agent model where shareholders are the principals and directors are their agents. Nevertheless, our claim that directors should be viewed as disinterested trustees charged with faithfully representing the interests not just of shareholders, but of all team members, is consistent with the way that many directors have historically described their own roles. Our claim also resonates with the views of legal scholars who argue that directors should view their jobs in these terms. Most importantly, our model of corporations is consistent with the law itself.

5. "Board-Centric" Corporation

Notice that the various theories of the public corporation assume that legal (if not actual) control of the corporation resides with the board of directors. Some (such as Berle and Means) see this as a problem and favor increased regulation to move control back to shareholders. Others (such as the contractarians) see board centrality as the result of implicit bargaining and would only seek to ensure that markets, particularly the market in corporate control, remain functional. Yet others see the powerful role of the board as the outcome of politics (the political realists) or the current state of the law (the team production theorists)—without coming to a view on the efficiency of the status quo.

Some corporate scholars have resolved these questions by asserting that the Berle-Means separation of ownership and control is not only real, but highly efficient. By placing control in the board of directors, these scholars—led by Professor Stephen Bainbridge (a UCLA law professor)—argue that the modern corporation, particularly in the United States, has succeeded in organizing social resources (labor, capital, goods) to produce enormous social wealth. Further empowering of shareholders, beyond minor modifications to existing rules, would be a mistake—for shareholders. Professor Bainbridge <u>argues</u>:

Any model of corporate governance must answer two basic sets of questions: (1) Who decides? In other words, which corporate constituency possesses ultimate decision-making power? (2) When the ultimate decisionmaker, whoever it may be, is presented with a zero sum game in which it must prefer the interests of one corporate constituency over those of all others, whose interests prevail?

On the means question, prior scholarship typically favored either shareholder primacy or managerialism. In contrast, . . . the power and right to exercise decision-making fiat is vested neither in the shareholders nor the managers, but in the board of directors. According to this director primacy model, the board of directors is not a mere agent of the shareholders, but rather is a sort of Platonic guardian serving as the nexus of the various contracts making up the corporation. As a positive theory of corporate governance, the director primacy model strongly emphasizes the role of fiat—i.e., the centralized decision-making authority possessed by the board of directors. As a normative theory of corporate governance, director primacy claims that resolving the resulting tension between authority and accountability is the central problem of corporate law.

The substantial virtues of fiat can be realized only by preserving the board's decision-making authority from being trumped by either shareholders or courts. . . . At some point, greater accountability necessarily makes the decision-making process less efficient, while highly efficient decision-making structures necessarily reduce accountability. In general, that tension is resolved in favor of authority.

Because only shareholders are entitled to elect directors, boards of public corporations are insulated from pressure by nonshareholder corporate constituencies, such as employees or creditors. At the same time, the diffuse nature of U.S. stock ownership and regulatory impediments to investor activism insulate directors from shareholder pressure. Accordingly, the board has virtually unconstrained freedom to exercise business judgment. . . . Ultimately, fiat is both the defining characteristic of corporate governance and its overarching value. . . .

As an account of the ends of corporate governance, prior scholarship has tended to favor either shareholder primacy or various forms of stakeholderism. Again, the director primacy model developed herein rejects both approaches. [D]irector decisionmaking primacy can be reconciled with a contractual obligation on the board's part to maximize the value of the shareholders' residual claim.

Points for Discussion

1. Shareholder incentives.

What is the "collective action" problem in shareholder voting and how might institutional ownership solve it?

2. Which theory?

The five theories articulate different roles for shareholders. Which anticipates the most shareholder activism? Which the least? Which theory best matches your views on what should be the role of public shareholders in corporate governance?

3. Role of law?

What might the role of law be under each of these theories? Which theories anticipate that the law should seek to "reform" the role of shareholders in the corporation? Which theories seek to maintain corporate law as it is—or as the theorists perceive it to be?

B. Institutional Shareholders and Shareholder Activism

We now consider some specific details about the role of institutional shareholders and shareholder activism. Shareholder activism is not a new phenomenon. Large block shareholders pressured the managers of corporations during late nineteenth and early twentieth centuries. During the 1980s, there was surge of takeover-driven shareholder activism, led by corporate "raiders" who bought large numbers of shares and then pushed for corporations to be sold or broken into pieces. Nevertheless, the recent increase in activism is noteworthy, if not unprecedented.

When we discuss shareholder activism, we generally are talking about activism by institutions, not individuals. In 1950, institutions held only 9% of U.S. stocks; in 1983 they crossed the 50% threshold; today, they hold the vast majority of shares. Equity ownership is also concentrated in the largest institutional shareholders. The top 25 institutional holders account for about one-third of all publicly-held stock, and the top 100 holders represent more than 50%. This means that the persons acting on behalf of the majority shareholders of corporate America could all fit into a large law school classroom. Professor John Coates predicts a future "Problem of 12," meaning that twelve institutions soon could collectively have a controlling stake in all public corporations.

The shift from individuals to institutions promised improvements in corporate governance. Hopes ran high during the 1990s that institutional investors could overcome the rational apathy and collective action problems faced by individual investors. In theory, increasing institutionalization narrows the separation of ownership from control highlighted by Berle and Means. Voting apathy is less rational as shareholdings grow, and economies of scale make monitoring easier. An institution that votes on the same proposals at a number of companies reduces its per-company monitoring costs.

But institutional shareholders, themselves agents for their beneficiaries, face their own conflicting interests that discourage them from activism. That is, the institutional agents may not have incentives to act as principals. These conflicts are different for each institution:

- *Mutual funds.* Mutual funds (which obtain much of their business from employer-based savings plans, such as 401(k) plans) view portfolio companies as customers. Thus, fund managers face pressure, often subtle, from corporate management to vote according to management's interests or risk that management will withdraw its savings plan and move it elsewhere. This threat is even greater for mutual funds that are part of financial conglomerates, which also offer investment banking and corporate lending services.

- *Corporate pension plans.* Corporate pension plans (which invest corporate money to provide retirement benefits to employees) are managed by in-house plan administrators, usually corporate executives. These administrators face conflicts between managing the pension fund for the benefit of plan participants, as required by the Employee Retirement Income Security Act (ERISA), and managing it for the benefit of corporate management.

- *State pension plans.* State pension plans (which invest their assets for state employee retirement) face an entirely different set of pressures. Unlike their private counterparts, which worry about offending corporate management, public pension managers often have political aspirations and seek to be a thorn in the side of corporate management—to advance particular economic, social, or political causes that may be at odds with maximizing fund performance.

- *Insurance companies.* Insurance companies (which invest their assets to cover their insurance liabilities and also manage insurance-based retirement plans) face similar pressures as mutual funds. Activism risks antagonizing corporate clients and, even worse, creating a climate that invites scrutiny of corporate management across the board, including at insurance companies.

Besides these conflicts, institutional investors that index their investments (tracking the performance of a particular stock index, such as the S&P 500) have little incentive to undertake the expense of shareholder activism, even if it might improve portfolio performance. Since such institutions compete on cost, they have an incentive not to engage in corporate governance activities that would increase costs more than those of competitors. For many institutional investors, indexing is a significant part of their investment strategy.

> **Business Lingo**
>
> The "turnover rate" of an investment portfolio is the frequency that securities in the portfolio are sold and then replaced with other securities. For example, if a mutual fund has 20 stocks in its portfolio, and 15 are sold in a particular year so the fund can buy 15 other stocks, the turnover rate would be 75% (15 / 20 = 0.75). Academic studies generally show that higher turnover rates, and thus higher trading costs, are related to lower portfolio returns.

Another explanation for institutional passivity is that institutions have a strong preference (sometimes mandated by law) for liquidity rather than control. Open-end mutual funds, for example, must stand ready to redeem their investors' shares. And many mutual funds and insurance companies see their business model as buying and selling stock in their portfolios, with annual turnover rates often exceeding 100%. They don't have time to treat portfolio companies as an owner. Only when an institution is constrained from selling the stock, because the size of its ownership will depress the market price, does an institution have the incentive to exercise voice in corporate affairs.

The institutional culture also is at odds with shareholder activism. Institutional managers often feel an "obedience to the mores of the financial community," which disdains shareholder activism. Institutional managers sometimes express their worry about developing a reputation as an activist, as though it were a communicable disease.

Marbled into these conflicts are various legal impediments to an institutional governance role—the result of a deep-seated American suspicion of concentrated financial power. As we will next see, the SEC proxy rules often discourage communications among shareholders seeking to make control changes. Federal law requires disgorgement of short-swing profits by 10% shareholders and federal securities disclosure rules applicable to 5% toehold positions impose additional costs on institutions seeking to take meaningful ownership positions. The possibility of disgorgement liability also discourages institutional investors from installing representatives on company boards. Regulation FD (the rule against selective corporate disclosures) raises questions about the legality of behind-the-scenes communications with corporate insiders on governance issues. And any legal liability that may arise from over-activism is borne by the institutional investor alone—another free-riding cost.

Despite these problems, there has been a steady increase over the past decade in institutional activism. Some institutions (primarily state pension plans and labor union pension funds) have become regular and effective users of the shareholder proposal rule. Their submissions on corporate governance reforms—such as majority voting in director elections, restrictions on poison pills, and redesigned executive compensation—have received regular majority support from fellow shareholders. And management implementation of some majority-supported proposals, particularly those dealing with majority voting for directors, has been widespread.

FYI Some institutions, particularly mutual funds and investment funds with social/political investment policies, invest only in companies that meet certain criteria. For example, Domini Social Investments, which manages more than $1.2 billion in assets for individual and institutional investors, invests only in firms that meet specified criteria for corporate citizenship, diversity in employment, employee relations, environment, overseas operations, and safe and useful products.

Other institutions, particularly the retirement fund for college professors (TIAA-CREF) and the largest state pension plan (CalPERS), have targeted under-performing companies and engaged in behind-the-scenes negotiations with corporate management to seek desired reforms. Studies indicate that some of these negotiations have produced positive effects on stock prices.

Institutional shareholders also have become subject to rules requiring that they vote the stock they hold. In carrying out these duties, institutional shareholders have often relied on the recommendations of proxy advisory firms, particularly the dominant Institutional Shareholder Services (ISS). Thus, for example, mutual funds often follow ISS recommendations on removing anti-takeover measures, even when opposed by management. By adhering to ISS recommendations, institutional investors assure themselves of being in the voting mainstream.

Over the past decade, shareholder proposals on topics of board structure and takeover defenses have regularly received majority support. This compares to the lukewarm reception that institutional shareholders have given proposals on social/political topics (such as child labor, global warming, political contributions, or environmental concerns).

Hedge funds are very different from the other types of institutional investors described above. Hedge funds are pooled, privately organized investment vehicles that are not widely available to the public and operate outside the securities regulation and registration requirements that apply to mutual funds and pension funds. Hedge funds are administered by professional investment managers with performance-based compensation and significant investments in the fund. Hedge funds typically charge their investors not only a fixed percentage fee based on the size of assets under management, but also a performance fee (often 20% of the profits). Thus, hedge fund managers typically have significantly greater financial incentives to achieve gains for shareholders than do the managers of other institutions.

The sharp financial incentives of hedge funds, and their size, have made them a more formidable threat to incumbent directors than other institutional investors. Recall that incumbent directors have significant advantages over insurgents in corporate elections: they control the distribution of proxy materials and can use corporate funds to pay for their reelection campaigns. It is difficult for shareholders to remove official director nominees.

Nevertheless, hedge fund activists have brought numerous campaigns against incumbent boards, and their proxy contests have succeeded more frequently than efforts by other institutions. The largest hedge funds, who have demonstrated the capacity to launch a proxy contest and oust one or more directors, have also been the most successful funds, and as a result are also among the largest.

Federal securities law provides that once a shareholder activist acquires 5% or more of the shares of a public corporation, it must disclose its ownership. The filing the shareholder must make is called a Schedule 13D: it must be filed with the Securities and Exchange Commission within 10 days by anyone who acquires beneficial ownership of a class of publicly traded securities of a public company. Studies of hedge fund activism consistently show that the announcement of activism, and the filing of a Schedule 13D, is associated with significant positive returns, in the range of 7% above other investments during the several days surrounding the announcement. There is a debate about whether those returns are sustained over the longer term, and whether the gains for shareholders come at the expense of other constituents.

Hedge fund activism has generated strong views and strident debate. Shareholder advocacy groups and institutional investors generally favor activism by hedge funds. Directors, officers, and lawyers who represent large public corporations frequently oppose it.

Points for Discussion

1. Possible reforms.

Given the emergence of institutional shareholders, can you think of any reforms to improve the mechanisms of "shareholder democracy"? Consider the following:

- Large shareholders or shareholder groups (with more than 5% of the shares) can use the company proxy statement to nominate directors and include information on their candidates.

- The board must nominate at least two candidates for each open directorship, thus giving shareholders some choice.

- Mutual funds and other institutional intermediaries must solicit views from their investors, perhaps through scientific polling, on particular issues.

2. Re-theorizing the corporation.

The theories of the corporation generally assume passive shareholders, who go along with management's slate of directors and their agenda. The "contract" theory assumes that markets (in which shareholders can sell their shares, and thus control, to an outside bidder) protect their interests. The "political product" theory assumes different institutions (such as securities markets and courts) serve this protective role. The "team production" theory assumes that mediator-directors balance the interests of shareholders with those of others. The "director primacy" theory assumes it is efficient for shareholders to have limited voting rights. Does the emergence of institutional investors affect the descriptive power of these theories?

3. Disclosure as tool of destruction.

The mutual fund proxy disclosure rules were controversial. The mutual fund industry argued that fund investors are not interested in how fund managers perform their voting function. The industry also predicted that disclosure would politicize proxy voting and expose mutual funds to pressure from "activist groups with a political or social ax to grind with corporate America." Do you agree? Has this happened?

C. Law on Shareholder Activism

One barrier to shareholder activism is the law on shareholder voting. State law on the reimbursement of election-related expenses of shareholder insurgents chills activism. Generally, only the incumbent board can use corporate funds to solicit proxies. Insurgents must use their own funds to finance a proxy contest and can recover their election-related costs only if they win. But this edifice has been shifting.

The federal proxy rules, which impose burdensome and expensive requirements on insurgents organizing a proxy contest, add another layer of discouragement. Reforms promulgated in 1992 tried to ease the burden on shareholder activists, without much effect. Further reforms after the Dodd-Frank Act of 2010 gave shareholders an advisory "say on pay," and an SEC "proxy access" rule (later overturned by the courts) sought to allow shareholders to nominate directors to the board. The full effect of these efforts to level the playing field for shareholder activists has yet to be seen.

1. State Reimbursement Rule

We begin our look at the law of shareholder activism by considering the state proxy reimbursement rule. The rule, described in the case below, essentially gives financial control over the voting mechanism to incumbent management. Is this good? On one hand, the rule limits wasteful spending by the corporation on shareholder initiatives supported by less than a shareholder majority. On the other hand, the rule discourages shareholder activism and helps entrench management.

Rosenfeld v. Fairchild Engine & Airplane Corp.

128 N.E.2d 291 (N.Y. 1955)

Froessel, Judge.

In a stockholder's derivative action brought by plaintiff, an attorney, who owns 25 out of the company's over 2,300,000 shares, he seeks to compel the return of $261,522, paid out of the corporate treasury to reimburse both sides in a proxy contest for their expenses. The Appellate Division has unanimously affirmed a judgment of an Official Referee dismissing plaintiff's complaint on the merits, and we agree.

Of the amount in controversy $106,000 were spent out of corporate funds by the old board of directors while still in office in defense of their position in said contest; $28,000 were paid to the old board by the new board after the change of management following the proxy contest, to compensate the former directors for such of the remaining expenses of their unsuccessful defense as the new board found was fair and reasonable; payment of $127,000, representing reimbursement of expenses to members of the prevailing group, was expressly ratified by a 16 to 1 majority vote of the stockholders.

The Appellate Division found that the difference between plaintiff's group and the old board 'went deep into the policies of the company,' and that among these [the former CEO's] contract was one of the 'main points of contention.'

Other jurisdictions and our own lower courts have held that management may look to the corporate treasury for the reasonable expenses of soliciting proxies to defend its position in a bona fide policy contest.

If directors of a corporation may not in good faith incur reasonable and proper expenses in soliciting proxies in these days of giant corporations with vast numbers of stockholders, the corporate business might be seriously interfered with because of stockholder indifference and the difficulty of procuring a quorum, where there is no contest. In the event of a proxy contest, if the directors may not freely answer the challenges of outside groups and in good faith defend their actions with respect to corporate policy for the information of the stockholders, they and the corporation may be at the mercy of persons seeking to wrest control for their own purposes, so long as such persons have ample funds to conduct a proxy contest. The test is clear. When the directors act in good faith in a contest over policy, they have the right to incur reasonable and proper expenses for solicitation of proxies and in defense of their corporate policies, and are not obliged to sit idly by.

It is also our view that the members of the so-called new group could be reimbursed by the corporation for their expenditures in this contest by affirmative vote of the stockholders. With regard to these ultimately successful contestants, as the Appellate Division below has noted, there was, of course, 'no duty of the corporation to pay for such expense'. However, where a majority of the stockholders chose in this case by a vote of 16 to 1 to reimburse the successful contestants for achieving the very end sought and voted for by them as owners of the corporation, we see no reason to deny the effect of their ratification nor to hold the corporate body powerless to determine how its own moneys shall be spent.

The rule then which we adopt is simply this: In a contest over policy, as compared to a purely personal power contest, corporate directors have the right to make reasonable and proper expenditures, subject to the scrutiny of the courts when duly challenged, from the corporate treasury for the purpose of persuading the stockholders of the correctness of their position and soliciting their support for policies which the directors believe, in all good faith, are in the best interests of the corporation. The stockholders, moreover, have the right to reimburse successful contestants for the reasonable and bona fide expenses incurred by them in any such policy contest, subject to like court scrutiny.

Points for Discussion

1. Actually, a close case.

At first glance, the *Rosenfeld* decision seems cut and dried. Incumbents (whether they win or lose) are paid their reasonable expenses in a proxy contest, so long as the contest is one of "policy." Insurgents can be reimbursed for their reasonable election expenses only if the shareholders vote for reimbursement—which as a practical matter means only when they win.

But three judges dissented, arguing that it should be illegal for incumbents (unless they receive the unanimous consent of shareholders) to use corporate funds in a proxy contest beyond that necessary to give notice of the meeting and the matters to be decided at the meeting. They argued against allowing corporate reimbursement of expenses incurred by incumbents on high-pressure election tactics (such as entertainment, limousines, public relations counsel, and proxy solicitors). In fact, prior cases had held that corporate payment of election expenses (to either side in a proxy contest) is *ultra vires*.

2. Policy vs. personal.

What are "policy" questions that warrant reimbursement, as opposed to "personal" questions that do not? For example, suppose that an insurgent thinks the corporation's CEO is "too high and mighty" and is paid more than he deserves. Is an election contest to remove the directors who hired the CEO a matter of policy or driven by personal motives?

3. Compare to political voting.

The government does not reimburse political candidates for their campaign expenditures, except for presidential candidates (whether or not incumbents) who qualify for matching funds. Although the government pays for the voting apparatus (polling places, voting machines, election officials), it leaves the candidates and their supporters to finance their own election campaigns. Why should the corporation be different? Why should corporate incumbents, but not insurgents, be allowed to use corporate funds as a matter of course to defray their election-related expenses?

4. Consider the alternative.

Consider the plight of insurgents in a corporate election contest. Their election-related expenses are reimbursable only if approved by shareholders. (Otherwise, reimbursement by the board would be self-dealing.) The practical effect is that insurgents are unlikely to seek to oust incumbents unless there is an excellent chance of winning. Thus, the reimbursement rule greatly reduces the chances that shareholders are offered an alternative slate of directors.

Would it be better if both sides were reimbursed their reasonable election expenses? Would that improve corporate governance? Or perhaps such an approach would be destabilizing. The reimbursement rule, which clearly favors incumbents, may simply reflect the assumption that shareholders are satisfied with current management. If not, they would not have elected them. There is no reason to promote dissension where none exists.

———

2. Federal Regulation of Shareholder Communications

The SEC proxy rules constitute the principal law of voting in public companies. The rules aim to ensure informed shareholder voting—whether proxies are solicited by incumbent management or outside insurgents. Although disclosure varies depending on who solicits proxies, the federal regime assumes that mandatory disclosure will best protect the shareholder franchise.

For shareholder voting in the public corporation, the basic disclosure document is the "proxy statement"—which must be filed with the SEC and disseminated to all shareholders whose votes are being solicited. Besides specifying its contents, SEC rules require that in voting contests the proxy statement be submitted to the SEC for pre-approval.

Make the Connection

As we saw in the last chapter, misinformation in the proxy statement (whether by management or the insurgent) can become the basis for a private lawsuit under the SEC rule prohibiting false or misleading proxy solicitations.

Any shareholder activity that qualifies as a "proxy solicitation" must comply with the filing and dissemination requirements of the SEC proxy rules. For example, sending a letter to fellow shareholders to organize a "shareholder revolt" or putting an ad in a newspaper to urge shareholders "to rise up" can violate the SEC rules—unless a proxy statement has been filed and disseminated to shareholders.

SEC Rule 14a–1
Securities Exchange Act of 1934

Proxy solicitation is defined:

> (i) any request for a proxy whether or not accompanied by or included in a form of proxy;

> (ii) any request to execute or not to execute, or to revoke, a proxy; or

> (iii) the furnishing of a form of proxy or other communication to security holders under circumstances *reasonably calculated* to result in the procurement, withholding or revocation of a proxy.

Notice that "proxy solicitation" is defined to cover not only the usual requests for a proxy, but also communications reasonably calculated to result in requesting proxies. What does "reasonably calculated" mean? Most lower courts have held that there can be civil liability for misstatements in a proxy statement made negligently.

Thus, a shareholder who sends a letter seeking shareholder support to inspect a shareholder list for the purpose of eventually asking shareholders to remove the incumbent board has been held to have engaged in a proxy solicitation. Before sending such a letter, the insurgent shareholders would have to file a proxy statement with the SEC and then disseminate it to all solicited shareholders. The theory has been that "one need only spread the misinformation adequately before beginning to solicit, and the Commission would be powerless to protect shareholders." In short, the SEC proxy rules assume shareholders in public corporations must be protected from ruthless, deceptive insurgents.

The rules governing "proxy solicitations" sometimes raise free speech implications. In one well-known case, *Long Island Lighting Co. v. Barbash*, 779 F.2d 793 (2d Cir. 1985), the court addressed whether a political advertisement accusing a utility of mismanagement was a "proxy solicitation." The ad claimed that managers were trying to have ratepayers pay needless costs relating to construction of a nuclear power plant, and urged that the utility be acquired by the public power authority. The managers complained that the ad was unlawful because no proxy statement had been filed and it was false and misleading.

Management sought to enjoin further ads by the group until their allegedly false statements were corrected and an appropriate SEC filing had been made. The district court declined to hold the ad constituted a "proxy solicitation" because it appeared in a general publication and could only indirectly affect the proxy contest at LILCO. The Second Circuit held that the ad was "reasonably calculated" to influence shareholder votes, even though it might not have been "targeted directly" at shareholders. Judge Ralph Winter dissented, arguing that when "advertisements are critical of corporate conduct but are facially directed solely to the public, in no way mention the exercise of proxies, and debate only matters of conceded public concern, I would construe federal proxy regulation as inapplicable, whatever the motive of those who purchase them."

In response to criticism that the proxy rules discouraged shareholder activism, the SEC responded with a set of "shareholder communications" rules to facilitate shareholder activism. But you'll notice it was a cautious reform. Here are the highlights:

- Solicitations by those who do not seek proxy authority and do not furnish shareholders with a form of proxy are exempted from the filing and dissemination requirements. Rule 14a–2.

- Shareholders generally can solicit other shareholders to vote in a particular way without filing notice with the SEC if the solicitation (1) is oral or (2) is by a shareholder who owns less than $5 million of the company's shares. But a shareholder who solicits in writing and owns more than $5 million in company shares must file a notice with the SEC within three days after sending the solicitation. The notice must state the solicitor's name and address, and attach the soliciting materials. The solicitation is subject only to the Rule 14a–9 prohibition against materially false and misleading statements in a proxy solicitation.

Take Note!

In 2009 the SEC took an important step to increase the voting power of institutional investors. By approving a NYSE rule that prevents brokers from voting their customers' shares for which instructions have not been given in director elections at public companies, the SEC effectively gave greater weight to votes actually cast by shareholders—mostly institutional investors. The prior practice, known as "broker voting," permitted brokers who held shares in "street name" to cast votes in director elections as they chose, unless actually directed by the beneficial owners of the shares. The rule change could affect director elections, particularly for companies that have adopted a majority-vote standard—a recent trend in corporate governance.

- Shareholders can announce how they intend to vote and explain their reasons. Such announcements can be published, broadcast, or disseminated to the media. And because they are not deemed a solicitation, the proxy rules do not apply.

D. Shareholder Proposals

Although shareholders can propose and adopt resolutions at shareholder meetings, shareholders of public corporations who do not have access to the proxy machinery, will find this approach difficult and expensive. Only in the most unusual circumstances would it be cost-justified to submit a proposal at the shareholder-proponent's expense.

The SEC shareholder proposal rule, adopted in 1942, attempted to solve the problem of shareholder access to the proxy machinery. Under Rule 14a–8, any shareholder who meets the ownership requirements of the rule and submits a proposal in a timely fashion and in proper form can have the proposal included in the company's proxy materials for a vote at the shareholders' annual meeting. That is, the rule compels the company to subsidize proper shareholder proposals.

1. Operation of Rule 14a–8

Rule 14a–8, amended in 1998 using a plain English "Q & A" format, sets forth procedural and substantive requirements that shareholder proponents must meet to have their proposals included in the company's proxy statement.

Eligibility and procedural hoops. To be eligible, the proponent must have continuously held at least 1% or $2,000 worth of the company voting shares for at least one year. (Shareholders holding their shares in street name can establish beneficial ownership with a copy of their brokerage statement.) The proponent must then continue to hold the shares and present the proposal at the meeting.

A proponent may submit no more than one proposal per company for a particular shareholders' meeting. The proposal, including any accompanying supporting statement, may not exceed 500 words. The proposal must be submitted to the company not less than 120 calendar days before the date of the company's last-year proxy statement—the deadline can be found in last year's proxy statement.

If the company includes the proposal in its proxy materials, it may (and usually does) recommend that shareholders vote against the proposal and give reasons for its opposition. The proponent has no chance for rebuttal, but can contact the SEC staff if she believes the company's opposition contains materially false or misleading statements.

SEC no-action review. If the company omits the proposal from its proxy materials, it must notify the SEC by filing the proposal and the company's reasons for exclusion. The SEC staff (in the Division of Corporate Finance) then advises the company whether or not it will recommend that the Commission take any enforcement action if the company omits the proposal. If the answer is no, the staff response is known as a "no-action" letter.

The no-action process resembles a ritual dance. The shareholder first sends the proposal to the company,

> **What's That?**
>
> A no-action letter by the SEC staff indicates that the staff will not recommend agency action should a company proceed as planned. A typical no-action letter involving a shareholder proposal reads: "There appears to be some basis for your view that the proposal may be excluded pursuant to Rule 14a–8." A refusal to state a no-action position reads: "The Division is unable to concur in your view that the proposal may be excluded."
>
> A no-action letter is not binding on the SEC, but allows staff to communicate its legal views to interested parties. The no-action process is used in many areas of securities regulation.

sometimes with a supporting legal opinion. The company then decides whether to include it in the proxy materials or exclude it. If included, the SEC is not involved. If excluded, the company must explain itself to the SEC, sometimes with an opinion of counsel that identifies the grounds for exclusion and analyzes past staff no-action letters—like a litigation brief. The proponent can submit a reply, sometimes with a contrary legal opinion.

Go Online

The 14a–8 no-action letters, which number about 300–400 per year, are available on the SEC website (www. sec.gov). They represent the common law of Rule 14a–8.

Shareholders have an implied right of action to seek injunctive relief against the company's omission of a proposal. In addition, the SEC can seek an injunction to compel inclusion of a proper proposal. Rarely does either happen: shareholders rarely undertake the expense to sue and companies uniformly acquiesce in the SEC staff's views. Thus, the 14a–8 no-action process constitutes an alternative dispute mechanism in which the SEC staff decides the proper role of public shareholders in corporate governance. It is also worth noting that in some instances when a company receives a shareholder proposal, it negotiates behind the scenes with the shareholder to reach an agreed-upon solution, without involving the SEC in the process.

Are no-action letters binding law? The SEC has taken the position that no-action letters are not agency "rulings" or "decisions" on the merits. Courts have agreed and held that the no-action letters do not constitute a final order under the Administrative Procedure Act. Thus, a shareholder disappointed by an SEC no-action letter cannot sue the SEC.

Food for Thought

Where does the SEC get authority to give shareholders access to the company-funded proxy mechanism? Recall that the SEC has authority under § 14(a) of the 1934 Act to ensure fair and full disclosure in proxy solicitations, but not to create new substantive rights.

Here's an <u>answer</u>. Rule 14a–8 can be seen as regulation of deception in the proxy solicitation process. Given that the company's proxy statement must reflect all the voting matters that management anticipates will come up at the shareholders meeting, it must disclose any *proper* shareholder proposals that will come up at the meeting. Failure to disclose (and describe) the proposal would be misleading.

2. Proper Proposals

Analytical framework. What shareholder proposals are proper? An early case provides an analytical framework. *SEC v. Transamerica Corp.*, 163 F.2d 511 (3d Cir. 1947). In the case a shareholder submitted several proposals (before the rule permitted only one proposal per shareholder) for inclusion in the corporation's proxy statement: (1) a proposal that shareholders elect the company's independent public auditors; (2) a proposal to amend the procedure for amending the company's bylaws; and (3) a request that the corporation send a report of the annual meeting to the shareholders. When management excluded all the proposals, the SEC sought to enjoin the company's proxy solicitation.

Make the Connection

What topics are proper subjects for shareholders under state law? The principal case is *Auer v. Dressel*, which we saw in Chapter 16 on Shareholder Voting Rights. There the New York Court of Appeals decided that a shareholder proposal *recommending* the re-hiring of the company president was proper. Although the recommendation did not bind the board, the directors were put on notice if they acted against shareholder wishes.

The court agreed with the SEC that a "proper subject" is one that a shareholder may properly bring to a vote under the law of the corporation's state of incorporation. It ruled that all three proposals were properly includable in the company's proxy materials: (1) the election of auditors was clearly of shareholder concern since the corporation is run for their benefit, and its financial condition (as shown in the financial statements) is critical to the corporation; (2) the amendment to the bylaws was proper because Delaware law specifically allows shareholders to amend the bylaws; and (3) the report of the meeting was proper because "we can perceive no logical basis for concluding that it is not a proper subject for action by the security holders."

In short, there is a federal-state symbiosis. The shareholder proposal rule is a federal mechanism to facilitate state-created shareholder voting rights.

Grounds for exclusion. The thirteen substantive grounds for the exclusion of shareholder proposals are the heart of the shareholder proposal rule.

SEC Rule 14a–8(i)
Securities Exchange Act of 1934

Question 9: If I have complied with the procedural requirements, on what other bases may a company rely to exclude my proposal?

(1) Improper under state law: If the proposal is not a proper subject for action by shareholders under the laws of the jurisdiction of the company's organization;

Note to paragraph (i)(1): Depending on the subject matter, some proposals are not considered proper under state law if they would be binding on the company if approved by shareholders. In our experience, most proposals that are cast as recommendations or requests that the board of directors take specified action are proper under state law. Accordingly, we will assume that a proposal drafted as a recommendation or suggestion is proper unless the company demonstrates otherwise.

(2) Violation of law: If the proposal would, if implemented, cause the company to violate any state, federal, or foreign law to which it is subject;

(3) Violation of proxy rules: If the proposal or supporting statement is contrary to any of the Commission's proxy rules, including Rule 14a–9, which prohibits materially false or misleading statements in proxy soliciting materials;

(4) Personal grievance; special interest: If the proposal relates to the redress of a personal claim or grievance against the company or any other person, or if it is designed to result in a benefit to you, or to further a personal interest, which is not shared by the other shareholders at large;

(5) Relevance: If the proposal relates to operations which account for less than 5 percent of the company's total assets at the end of its most recent fiscal year, and for less than 5 percent of its net earnings and gross sales for its most recent fiscal year, and is not otherwise significantly related to the company's business;

(6) Absence of power/authority: If the company would lack the power or authority to implement the proposal;

(7) Management functions: If the proposal deals with a matter relating to the company's ordinary business operations;

(8) Director elections: If the proposal: (i) would disqualify a nominee who is standing for election; (ii) would remove a director from office before his or her term expired; (iii) questions the competence, business judgment, or character of one or more nominees or directors; (iv) seeks to include a specific individual in the company's proxy materials for election to the board of directors; or (v) otherwise could affect the outcome of the upcoming election of directors [as amended in 2010];

(9) Conflicts with company's proposal: If the proposal directly conflicts with one of the company's own proposals to be submitted to shareholders at the same meeting;

(10) Substantially implemented: If the company has already substantially implemented the proposal;

> Note to paragraph (i)(10): A company may exclude a shareholder proposal that would provide an advisory vote or seek future advisory votes to approve the compensation of executives as disclosed pursuant to Item 402 of Regulation S–K (a "say-on-pay vote") . . . .
>
> (11) Duplication: If the proposal substantially duplicates another proposal previously submitted to the company by another proponent that will be included in the company's proxy materials for the same meeting;
>
> (12) Resubmissions: If the proposal deals with substantially the same subject matter as another proposal or proposals that has or have been previously included in the company's proxy materials within the preceding 5 calendar years, a company may exclude it from its proxy materials for any meeting held within 3 calendar years of the last time it was included if the proposal received [less than 3%, 6% or 10% depending on how many times the proposal has been submitted in the past 5 years];
>
> (13) Specific amount of dividends: If the proposal relates to specific amounts of cash or stock dividends.

Notice that some of the exclusions seek to protect centralized corporate management—(1), (5), (7), (13). Others seek to prevent interference with management's solicitation of proxies—(8), (9), (11), (12). And others seek to prevent misguided proposals that are illegal, deceptive, or abusive—(2), (3), (4), (6), (10).

Three exclusions get the most use: (1) for proposals that are not "proper subjects" under state law; (5) proposals that are not "significantly related to business"; and (7) proposals that deal with "ordinary business operations." Furthermore, in its note to exclusion (1), the SEC takes the view that resolutions *binding* the board (other than a bylaw amendment) are inconsistent with state law and thus not a "proper subject" for shareholder voting. In addition, the SEC deems resolutions dealing with "ordinary business" to be exclusively for the board. Thus, shareholders must fashion resolutions to be non-binding (precatory) and to address fundamental business strategies or matters of "public policy."

What about the "significantly related" exclusion (5)? Can a proposal be significant even though it fails to account for more than 5% of sales, assets, or earnings? The following case addresses the "otherwise significant" test.

Lovenheim v. Iroquois Brands, Ltd.

618 F. Supp. 554 (D.D.C. 1985)

GASCH, DISTRICT JUDGE.

Plaintiff Peter C. Lovenheim, owner of two hundred shares of common stock in Iroquois Brands, Ltd. (hereinafter "Iroquois/Delaware"), seeks to bar Iroquois/Delaware from excluding from the proxy materials being sent to all shareholders in preparation for an upcoming shareholder meeting information concerning a proposed resolution he intends to offer at the meeting. Mr. Lovenheim's proposed resolution relates to the procedure used to force-feed geese for production of paté de foie gras in France,[2] a type of paté imported by Iroquois/Delaware. Specifically, his resolution calls upon the Directors of Iroquois/Delaware to:

> form a committee to study the methods by which its French supplier produces paté de foie gras, and report to the shareholders its findings and opinions, based on expert consultation, on whether this production method causes undue distress, pain or suffering to the animals involved and, if so, whether further distribution of this product should be discontinued until a more humane production method is developed.

Iroquois/Delaware has refused to allow information concerning Mr. Lovenheim's proposal to be included in proxy materials being sent in connection with the next annual shareholders meeting. In doing so, Iroquois/Delaware relies on an exception to the general requirement of Rule 14a–8, Rule 14a–8(c)(5). [Before the 1998 amendments, the (i)(5) exclusion was numbered (c)(5).].

Iroquois/Delaware's reliance on the Rule 14a–8(c)(5) exception for proposals not "significantly related" to the company's business is based on the following information contained in the affidavit of its president: Iroquois/Delaware has annual revenues of $141 million with $6 million in annual profits and $78 million in assets. In contrast, its paté de foie gras sales were just $79,000 last year, representing a net loss on paté sales of $3,121. Iroquois/Delaware has only $34,000 in assets related to paté. Thus none of the company's net earnings and less than .05 percent of its assets are

---

[2] Paté de foie gras is made from the liver of geese. According to Mr. Lovenheim's affidavit, force-feeding is frequently used in order to expand the liver and thereby produce a larger quantity of paté. Mr. Lovenheim's affidavit also contains a description of the force-feeding process:

Force-feeding usually begins when the geese are four months old. On some farms where feeding is mechanized, the bird's body and wings are placed in a metal brace and its neck is stretched. Through a funnel inserted 10–12 inches down the throat of the goose, a machine pumps up to 400 grams of corn-based mash into its stomach. An elastic band around the goose's throat prevents regurgitation. When feeding is manual, a handler uses a funnel and stick to force the mash down.

Plaintiff contends that such force-feeding is a form of cruelty to animals. Plaintiff has offered no evidence that force-feeding is used by Iroquois/Delaware's supplier in producing the paté imported by Iroquois/Delaware. However his proposal calls upon the committee he seeks to create to investigate this question.

implicated by plaintiff's proposal. These levels are obviously far below the five percent threshold set forth in the first portion of the exception claimed by Iroquois/Delaware.

Plaintiff does not contest that his proposed resolution relates to a matter of little economic significance to Iroquois/Delaware. Nevertheless he contends that the Rule 14a–8(c)(5) exception is not applicable as it cannot be said that his proposal "is not otherwise significantly related to the issuer's business" as is required by the final portion of that exception. In other words, plaintiff's argument that Rule 14a–8 does not permit omission of his proposal rests on the assertion that the rule and statute on which it is based do not permit omission merely because a proposal is not economically significant where a proposal has "ethical or social significance."[8]

Iroquois/Delaware challenges plaintiff's view that ethical and social proposals cannot be excluded even if they do meet the economic or five percent test. Instead, Iroquois/Delaware views the exception solely in economic terms as permitting omission for any proposals relating to a de minimis share of assets and profits. Iroquois/Delaware asserts that since corporations are economic entities, only an economic test is appropriate.

The Court would note that the applicability of the Rule 14a–8(c)(5) exception to Mr. Lovenheim's proposal represents a close question given the lack of clarity in the exception itself. In effect, plaintiff relies on the word "otherwise," suggesting that it indicates the drafters of the rule intended that other noneconomic tests of significance be used. Iroquois/Delaware relies on the fact that the rule examines other significance in relation to the issuer's business. Because of the apparent ambiguity of the rule, the Court considers the history of the shareholder proposal rule in determining the proper interpretation of the most recent version of that rule.

Prior to 1983, paragraph 14a–8(c)(5) excluded proposals "not significantly related to the issuer's business" but did not contain an objective economic significance test such as the five percent of sales, assets, and earnings specified in the first part of the current version. Although a series of SEC decisions through 1976 allowing issuers to exclude proposals challenging compliance with the Arab economic boycott of Israel allowed exclusion if the issuer did less than one percent of their business with Arab countries or Israel, the Commission stated later in 1976 that it did "not believe that subparagraph (c)(5) should be hinged solely on the eco-

---

[8] The assertion that the proposal is significant in an ethical and social sense relies on plaintiff's argument that "the very availability of a market for products that may be obtained through the inhumane force-feeding of geese cannot help but contribute to the continuation of such treatment." Plaintiff's brief characterizes the humane treatment of animals as among the foundations of western culture and cites in support of this view the Seven Laws of Noah, an animal protection statute enacted by the Massachusetts Bay Colony in 1641, numerous federal statutes enacted since 1877, and animal protection laws existing in all fifty states and the District of Columbia. An additional indication of the significance of plaintiff's proposal is the support of such leading organizations in the field of animal care as the American Society for the Prevention of Cruelty to Animals and The Humane Society of the United States for measures aimed at discontinuing use of force-feeding.

nomic relativity of a proposal." Thus the Commission required inclusion "in many situations in which the related business comprised less than one percent" of the company's revenues, profits or assets "where the proposal has raised *policy questions* important" enough to be considered "significantly related' to the issuer's business."

As indicated above, the 1983 revision adopted the five percent test of economic significance in an effort to create a more objective standard. Nevertheless, in adopting this standard, the Commission stated that proposals will be includible notwithstanding their "failure to reach the specified economic thresholds if a significant relationship to the issuer's business is demonstrated on the face of the resolution or supporting statement." Thus it seems clear based on the history of the rule that "the meaning of" "significantly related' is not *limited* to economic significance."

The Court cannot ignore the history of the rule, which reveals no decision by the Commission to limit the determination to the economic criteria relied on by Iroquois/Delaware. The Court therefore holds that in light of the ethical and social significance of plaintiff's proposal and the fact that it implicates significant levels of sales, plaintiff has shown a likelihood of prevailing on the merits with regard to the issue of whether his proposal is "otherwise significantly related" to Iroquois/Delaware's business.

[The court then granted plaintiff's motion for a preliminary injunction.]

Points for Discussion

Food for Thought

A national electronics retailer, like Best Buy, receives a shareholder proposal from a religious group to keep minors from buying violent or sexually explicit video games. The group points out that some state legislatures are considering new laws that would fine store owners that sell such games to minors.

Company management responds by agreeing to be more vigilant about preventing such sales. Is it because of corporate social responsibility or straight shareholder-value concerns?

1. Amendments to Rule 14a–8.

The *Lovenheim* decision refers to a number of SEC amendments to Rule 14a–8. The SEC has actually amended the rule 17 times—apparently the record for any SEC rule. Why do you think the rule has been amended so often?

2. Ordinary business.

Could Mr. Lovenheim's proposal have been excluded as relating to "ordinary business decisions"—that is, the company's product line, its choice of suppliers, its public image? Doesn't the business judgment rule protect board decisions, and prevent shareholders from second-guessing the board's judgment, so long as there is a rational business purpose?

3. Limits on shareholder access.

The 14a–8 exclusions represent the SEC's views on the proper role of public shareholders in corporate governance and shareholder voting. Notice that Rule 14a–8 does not allow shareholders to nominate their own board candidates [exclusion (8)], to oppose management proposals [exclusion (9)], or to question specific dividend payments [exclusion (13)]. Does state law prevent input by shareholders on these matters? Has the SEC defined the scope of shareholder rights under state law correctly?

————————

3. Ordinary Business vs. Public Policy

When does corporate action go beyond "ordinary business" and become instead a matter of "public policy"? The boundary between these two concepts raises fundamental issues about corporate social responsibility. Both the courts and the SEC have long recognized this, as the following cases and line of SEC interpretations make clear.

The *Medical Committee (Napalm)* case. In 1970 during the height of the Vietnam War, a public interest group (Medical Committee for Human Rights) that opposed the War sought to end the manufacture of napalm for use in the War by Dow Chemical Company. (Napalm is an incendiary gel that was used by the U.S. military in the Vietnam War first to clear jungles, but later against people, producing terrible physical and psychological effects.) Although napalm constituted a small and not very profitable part of Dow's business, napalm was important to the government's war effort, and Dow management strongly defended its manufacture on patriotic grounds.

The Medical Committee submitted a shareholder proposal requesting that the Dow board amend Dow's certificate of incorporation to bar the sale of napalm unless the buyer gave assurances the napalm would not be used on human beings. Dow refused to include the proposal on the grounds that it promoted a political cause (which was then, but is no longer, a ground for exclusion under Rule 14a–8) and that it related to Dow's ordinary business.

The D.C. Circuit held that Dow could not omit the proposal. *Medical Committee for Human Rights v. SEC*, 432 F.2d 659 (D.C. Cir. 1970), *vacated as moot,* 404 U.S. 403 (1972). The "overriding purpose of Section 14(a) is to assure corporate shareholders the ability to exercise their right—some would say their duty—to control the important decisions which affect them as owners of the corporation." The court accepted that the shareholders could seek to have "their assets used in a manner which they believe to be more socially responsible but possibly less profitable than that which is dictated by present company policy." Moreover, since Dow management had proclaimed its support for making napalm "not *because* of business considerations, but *in spite of* them," management decisions involving "personal political or moral predilections" could not be insulated from shareholder oversight.

SEC interpretive release (1976). Does *Medical Committee* mean that any issue taken from the headlines (such as global warming, child labor, business outsourcing, and so on) becomes "significantly related" to a company's business and not "ordinary business"—thus a "proper subject" for shareholder consideration at company expense?

In 1976 the SEC attempted to draw the line in an <u>interpretive release</u> that continues to influence both the SEC and the courts.

> The term "ordinary business operations" has been deemed on occasion to include certain matters which have significant policy, economic or other implications inherent in them. For instance, a proposal that a utility company not construct a proposed nuclear power plant has in the past been considered excludable. In retrospect, however, it seems apparent that the economic and safety considerations attendant to nuclear power plants are of such magnitude that a determination whether to construct one is not an "ordinary" business matter.

> Where proposals involve business matters that are mundane in nature and do not involve any substantial policy or other considerations, the subparagraph may be relied upon to omit them.

The *Trinity Wall Street v. Wal-Mart* case. The issue of what constitutes an excludable ordinary business matter more recently arose in a shareholder proposal case concerning Wal-Mart's sale of high-capacity guns. The proposal was submitted by Trinity Church, an Episcopal parish in New York City with a long-held commitment to social justice. As a shareholder of Wal-Mart, it requested that the board develop and implement standards for management to use in deciding whether to sell a product that (1) "especially endangers public safety"; (2) "has the substantial potential to impair the reputation of Wal–Mart"; and/or (3) "would reasonably be considered by many offensive to the family and community values integral to the Company's promotion of its brand." *Trinity Wall Street v. Wal-Mart Stores, Inc.*, 792 F.3d 323, 327 (3d Cir. 2015). Wal-Mart sought to exclude the proposal from its proxy materials on the basis that it related to "ordinary business operations."

The district court ruled in favor of the church, viewing the proposal as one focused principally on board governance and raising a significant social policy issue—the sale of high-capacity guns by one of the world's largest retailers. The Third Circuit reversed, holding that the proposal was excludable: "Stripped to its essence, Trinity's proposal—although styled as promoting improved governance—goes to the heart of Wal–Mart's business: what it sells on its shelves." The court explained that when a proposal "targets day-to-day decision-making," the social policy issues do not "transcend a company's ordinary business" and the proposal is properly excluded.

The Third Circuit distinguished between "stop-selling" proposals aimed at "pure-play" manufacturers with a narrow product line, such as a tobacco or gun manufacturer, for which such proposals raise a transcendent issue that "relates to the seller's very existence," and retailers that sell thousands of products for which stop-selling proposals are enmeshed in management's daily business decisions. According to the court, Wal-Mart was in the latter category as a big-box retailer:

> Decisions relating to what products Wal–Mart sells in its rural locations versus its urban sites will vary considerably, and these are quintessentially calls made by management. Wal–Mart serves different Americas with different values. Its customers in rural America want different products than its customers in cities, and that management decides how to deal with these differing desires is not an issue typical for its Board of Directors. And whether to put emphasis on brand integrity and brand protection, or none at all, is naturally a decision shareholders as well as directors entrust management to make in the exercise of their experience and business judgment.

In concluding, the court noted the difficulty of its job interpreting "hard-to-define exclusions," and suggested that the SEC "consider revising its regulation of proxy contests and issue fresh interpretive guidance."

Example 18.1

Is discrimination in the workplace based on sexual orientation "ordinary business" or "public policy"? In 1992 the New York City Comptroller (manager of the city's employee retirement fund) submitted a proposal to Cracker Barrel Old Country Store to ends its practice of firing gay employees. The company excluded the proposal as an ordinary employment matter, and the SEC staff issued a "no-action" letter accepting the company's position. The full Commission later upheld the staff policy.

But the New York City Comptroller stuck with it, bringing an unsuccessful lawsuit and then urging the SEC to change its position. In 1998 the SEC changed its policy to allow proposals dealing with employment discrimination. Four annual meetings later, the Comptroller's proposal at Cracker Barrel received 58% shareholder support—the first ever CSR proposal to receive majority support. Soon after, the company's board announced it would accept the proposal as company policy.

4. Evaluating the Shareholder Proposal Rule

Over the past couple decades, the shareholder proposal rule has become an important tool for certain kinds of shareholder activism. Proposals brought by individual activists and a handful of activist pension funds, but supported by an awakened community of institutional investors, may be realizing the hope that large shareholders can overcome their collective action problems to be an effective voice in corporate governance.

Proposals have spanned the gamut. Some focus on governance issues (declassified boards, poison pills, shareholder ability to nominate directors); others deal with operational issues (pay for performance, shareholder approval of severance packages, longer vesting of stock options); and others present social/political issues (global warming, child labor, political contributions, equal employment, environment).

The mix of proposals has shifted over time, with more proposals recently dealing with governance issues. And the number of proposals that receive majority votes has increased steadily since the mid–1990s. (Before then, during the first 50 years of Rule 14a–8, only two shareholder proposals opposed by management received majority shareholder support.) In addition, many proposals are withdrawn or not even submitted after shareholder proponents enter into discussions with management and negotiate corporate changes that the proposal sought.

A growing number of precatory resolutions that receive majority support are soon implemented by management, despite initial objections. The broad adoption by companies of majority voting in director elections is a case in point. Although implementation rates were low at first, companies increased their adoption of majority voting. Today it is the prevalent method for electing directors in public corporations.

And even though CSR proposals rarely garner majority support, their proponents often find success by raising the issue with management. In fact, it is now common that CSR proponents withdraw their proposals after management agrees to undertake some or all of the proposed reforms. This avoids annoying a vocal shareholder minority and garners a public relations victory.

5. Proxy Access

Shareholders have tried various tactics to improve their access to the proxy machinery that is controlled by corporate directors and officers. Beginning in the early 2000s, some large institutions pressed for new rules that would permit shareholders who held a significant percentage of the companies' shares to nominate a few directors (though not a majority). Corporate managers opposed these rules. When the SEC proposed a new rule in 2003 that would give shareholders greater access to the director nomination process, management groups claimed the SEC was interfering with a matter of corporate governance beyond its authority and argued that shareholder-nominated board members would disrupt the collegial working relationships on corporate boards. At first the SEC dithered and then eventually decided not to pursue its rulemaking.

In response, several activist union and state pension funds began a company-by-company movement proposing amendments to company bylaws modeled on the abandoned SEC proxy access rule. The proponents sought to use the shareholder proposal rule to create a process for shareholders to nominate "short slates" to boards constituting fewer than a majority of directors. At first the SEC staff accepted such proposals as proper under the rule, but later reversed course and allowed their exclusion under the rule's then-existing exclusion (8): proposals that "relate to a nomination or an election for membership on the company's board of directors."

Disappointed by the SEC's flip-flop, one of the institutional proponents—the pension fund for the American Federation of State, County & Municipal Employees (AFSCME)—brought a lawsuit in federal district court against the American International Group to require that the Delaware-incorporated insurance company include a shareholder-submitted "proxy access" proposal in the company's proxy statement. The district court concluded that neither Rule 14a–8 nor state law required inclusion of the proposal, suggesting that the litigants (and the law professors who had filed an amicus brief in the case) look to the regulatory and legislative processes for their reform initiative.

To give you a sense for the details of "proxy access," here is the proposal submitted by AFSCME in the *AIG* case:

RESOLVED, pursuant to Section 6.9 of the By-laws (the "Bylaws") of American International Group Inc. ("AIG") and section 109(a) of the Delaware General Corporation Law, stockholders hereby amend the Bylaws to add section 6.10:

"The Corporation shall include in its proxy materials for a meeting of stockholders the name, together with the Disclosure and Statement (both defined below), of any person nominated for election to the Board of Directors by a stockholder or group thereof that satisfies the requirements of this section 6.10 (the "Nominator"), and allow stockholders to vote with respect to such nominee on the Corporation's proxy card. Each Nominator may nominate one candidate for election at a meeting. To be eligible to make a nomination, a Nominator must:

(a) have beneficially owned 3 or more of the Corporation's outstanding common stock (the "Required Shares") for at least one year;

(b) provide written notice received by the Corporation's Secretary within the time period specified in section 1.11 of the Bylaws containing (i) with respect to the nominee, (A) the information required by Items 7(a), (b) and (c) of SEC Schedule 14A (such information is referred to herein as the "Disclosure") and (B) such nominee's consent to being named in the proxy statement and to serving as a director if elected; and (ii) with respect to the Nominator, proof of ownership of the Required Shares; and

(c) execute an undertaking that it agrees (i) to assume all liability of any violation of law or regulation arising out of the Nominator's communications with stockholders, including the Disclosure (ii) to the extent it uses soliciting material other than the Corporation's proxy materials, comply with all laws and regulations relating thereto.

The Nominator shall have the option to furnish a statement, not to exceed 500 words, in support of the nominee's candidacy (the "Statement"), at the time the Disclosure is submitted to the Corporation's Secretary. The Board of Directors shall adopt a procedure for timely resolving disputes over whether notice of a nomination was timely given and whether the Disclosure and Statement comply with this section 6.10 and SEC Rules."

On appeal, the Second Circuit reversed and held that Rule 14a–8 (as then worded) permitted shareholders to propose bylaw amendments to create "proxy access." *See AFSCME v. AIG, Inc.*, 462 F.3d 121 (2d. Cir. 2006). The court concluded that such proposals "establish a procedure by which shareholder-nominated candidates may be included on the corporate ballot [and thus do] not relate to an election within the meaning of the Rule 14a–8." The case turned on the phrase "relates to an election," which the court interpreted (based on prior SEC interpretations) to mean that proposals were excludable when they related to a specific election for a particular director seat—but not to proposals creating general guidelines or procedures for director elections.

In response to the *AIG* decision, the SEC revised Rule 14a–8 to broaden the "election" exclusion to specifically cover proposals relating to procedures for nominating directors. The SEC said it saw the rule change as temporary while it sought a permanent resolution of the basic tension between board control of director nominations and shareholder voting rights.

In 2010 Congress put proxy access back on the corporate governance agenda in the Dodd-Frank Act, which specifically authorized the SEC to promulgate a proxy access rule. Within months of the law's enactment, the SEC accepted the Dodd-Frank invitation and repromulgated proxy access rules. The plot thickened when corporate managers, supported by the Business Roundtable and U.S. Chamber of Commerce, challenged the new rules, claiming the SEC failed to adequately consider the costs and benefits of the new governance rights. The D.C. Circuit agreed and held that the SEC had failed to consider the rule's effect on "efficiency, competition and capital formation." Even though Dodd-Frank seemed to have authorized the SEC to make this cost-benefit determination, the SEC decided not to appeal the decision to the Supreme Court and not to propose the rule again, apparently worried it could not meet the (unusually) high standard of review set by the D.C. Circuit.

In response, many shareholder activists adopted a company-by-company approach. The SEC has made it clear that shareholders can propose general procedures for nominating directors, and the Delaware legislature has provided that shareholders can amend company bylaws to provide for proxy access as well as mandatory reimbursement of proxy expenses incurred by shareholders in director elections. Under these revised corporate statutes, the bylaws can address such matters as ownership requirements for nominating shareholders, disclosure by the nominating shareholder, and caps on the number of shareholder-nominated directors. Hedge fund activists approach proxy access differently, by running either or "short slate" of directors to replace a portion of the board, or by mounting a proxy fight to replace the entire board. These activities are expensive, because the hedge fund does not have "proxy access," meaning it must pay for its own proxy materials and process. Proxy access remains a controversial issue.

Points for Discussion

1. Company-by-company access vs. SEC rule.

Shareholders have the power to submit proxy access bylaw amendments for shareholder approval—with the question of whether this is "proper" largely resolved under state law. Thus, proxy access can vary from company to company. What are the pros and cons of shareholder access varying in this way, compared to a single uniform standard set by the SEC?

2. Just restrict shareholder proposals?

If the SEC shareholder proposal rule depends on state-created shareholder rights, can corporations prevent nettlesome shareholders from interfering with board-centric corporate governance? Could shareholders amend the articles or the bylaws to prohibit any company-financed shareholder proposals at all—or to fully permit such proposals, or to permit certain proposals, but not others? Is Rule 14a–8 mandatory? That is, could corporations opt out of the rule—by establishing either more or less shareholder democracy?

3. The power struggle over proxy access.

You might wonder what all the fuss is about. At most, proxy access gives shareholders a chance to create proxy access and then to nominate and place a handful, but not a majority, of directors on the board in the following annual voting cycle. Why would shareholder activists be so anxious to be able to put minority directors on the board? Can't these activists simply approach the board with their thoughts or plans?

And why has corporate management fought this? Why would incumbent directors be so bothered about having co-directors on the board who were nominated by a sizeable group of shareholders and then elected by a majority of shareholders? What's the danger when minority directors can be outvoted and excluded from important committees?

In short, activist shareholders don't seem to have much to gain from proxy access, and corporate management doesn't seem to have much to lose.

Test Your Knowledge

To assess your understanding of the Chapter 16, 17, and 18 material in this module, click here to take a quiz.

MODULE VII – FIDUCIARY DUTIES

CHAPTER 19

Shareholder Litigation

Shareholders can vote, sue, and sell. In the previous module, we focused on the right of shareholders to vote and use their voice to influence corporate behavior. In this module we turn to the right to sue. We introduce you to fiduciary duties in the corporation and their enforcement in shareholder litigation.

In this chapter, we identify the different actions available to shareholders to enforce the duties of corporate fiduciaries and the special procedures that apply to shareholder litigation. The next chapters identify the fiduciary duties (and judicial review) that arise when the board makes poor business decisions, when directors enter into transactions at odds with corporate interests, when the board sets compensation for corporate executives, and when the board fails in its oversight function. In the final chapter of this module, we look at fiduciary duties within corporate groups, mostly when parent corporations deal with their subsidiaries.

Shareholder litigation is an important topic, and in this chapter we can only brush the surface. We won't get into the details of shareholder litigation that are covered in a securities course or an upper-level course in corporate governance or "mergers and acquisitions" law. Our primary ambition here is to give you a basic overview of how shareholder litigation matters to corporations, and to cover some of the key distinctions in the area.

Hundreds of securities class action lawsuits are filed every year, along with many more derivative lawsuits. In the 2000s, there was an increase in the number of "mega" settlements of shareholder litigation, with several multi-billion dollar settlements, including those based on scandals at Enron, WorldCom, AOL Time Warner, and other large public companies. The Financial Crisis of 2008 also generated a surge in shareholder lawsuits, such as those arising from the collapse of Lehman Brothers, the role of Citibank in the subprime mortgage market, and Bank of America's acquisition of Merrill Lynch. For many years, merger litigation focused on Delaware, but recent cases dismissing shareholder litigation have led many suits to migrate to federal court, where they are framed in terms of the violation of federal disclosure rules instead of the breach of state fiduciary duties.

Opinion about these lawsuits is sharply divided. Some argue that shareholder litigation benefits all shareholders because the threat of litigation polices the conduct of managers and private lawsuits fill gaps left by lapses in regulation and the weaknesses of market forces. Others argue that shareholder litigation is parasitic and imposes great costs on corporations with little benefit. Whatever one's view, it is clear that litigation plays an important role in the relationship between shareholders and directors.

Keep in mind that the central actor in shareholder litigation typically is not the shareholder. Instead, it is the plaintiffs' lawyer. The law provides plaintiffs' securities lawyers with strong financial incentives to monitor corporate behavior and to litigate when information about an alleged fraud is revealed and has a negative impact on the value of a corporation's securities. Whenever a plaintiffs' law firm detects apparent wrongdoing, litigates, and then settles a lawsuit that a court deems to be successful, the court will award the firm attorneys' fees that, in most cases, will compensate it relatively generously for the time devoted to bringing the action and the risk incurred by undertaking to represent shareholders' interests on a contingent fee basis. Of course, not every case settles or is successful.

In this chapter, we tackle several of the questions posed by shareholder litigation. First, we examine a choice many plaintiffs' attorneys—and therefore courts—must make in individual cases: is the case appropriately a derivative action or a direct action? Often, the distinction is not clear, and some cases may fit both categories. Second, we focus on one particularly important aspect of derivative actions, known as the demand requirement. In simple terms, courts (especially in Delaware) have developed tests to decide whether plaintiffs must first "demand" that a corporation's board take action before they are permitted to sustain their own lawsuit. In practice, the fate of a lawsuit depends on whether demand is required. Third, we ask who is an appropriate plaintiff, with a focus on the adequacy and standing of particular types of plaintiffs. Finally, we consider some of the policy implications of shareholder litigation.

A. Derivative vs. Direct

Many plaintiffs' securities firms view federal class actions and state derivative actions as alternatives: they might file one, or the other, depending on the relative costs and benefits. We begin by analyzing one crucial distinction between these two types of litigation: whether the nature of the injury to shareholders is direct or derivative.

1. Derivative

Recall that a derivative action is an unusual type of lawsuit. It typically is brought by a shareholder *on behalf of the corporation* in which they hold stock. The shareholder asserts rights belonging to the corporation because the board of directors has failed to do so. The corporation is named as a nominal defendant. Any amounts recovered belong to the corporation, not the shareholder-plaintiff. The incentive for bringing a derivative suit often lies in the rule that a successful plaintiff can recover attorneys' fees from the corporation.

In theory, a shareholder can bring a derivative action against any party who has harmed the corporation, whether an insider or outsider. In practice, nearly all derivative actions are brought against directors or controlling shareholders who have breached duties to the corporation. Suing an outside party—for example, claiming breach of a contract with the corporation—is more often seen as a business judgment reserved for the board of directors.

The shareholder-plaintiff who brings a derivative action represents the corporation to vindicate the interests of all shareholders. For example, Federal Rule of Civil Procedure 23.1 requires that the derivative suit "fairly and adequately represent the interests of the shareholders similarly situated in enforcing the rights of the corporation." The shareholder-plaintiff "is a self-chosen representative and a volunteer champion"—and thus assumes fiduciary responsibilities. For example, a plaintiff cannot later abandon a derivative action for personal gain.

Take Note!

The derivative action is a strange animal. Historically, it arose in America during the nineteenth century, as courts recognized the importance of permitting minority shareholders to sue when corporate directors breached their duties. Judges saw derivative actions as an equitable remedy designed to give shareholders the ability to enforce corporate rights against directors or other wrongdoers when the people who controlled the corporation refused to do so. You already have read several cases involving derivative actions. Take a few minutes to flip back through the earlier cases in this book. Which ones involve derivative actions? Why were they brought as derivative actions? Keep the derivative vs. direct distinction in mind as you read cases in future chapters.

2. Direct

Shareholders can also sue directly *on their own behalf* to vindicate individual rights, rather than corporate rights. In public corporations, direct actions are often brought as class actions, in which a shareholder-representative brings the

Make the Connection

Two important kinds of "direct" shareholder actions are covered elsewhere in the book. As we have seen, claims by shareholders that the corporation (or others) has deceived them in connection with the voting of their shares can be brought in federal and state court as direct actions. *See* Chapter 17, Shareholder Information Rights. And as we will see later, claims by investors involving deception in connection with the buying and selling of securities can be brought in federal court as direct class actions. *See* Chapter 28, Securities Fraud.

action on behalf of similarly situated shareholders. Direct actions, though they have their own procedural rules, are attractive because they avoid the procedural hurdles that apply to derivative actions—principally, the requirement of pre-suit demand on the board and the board's power to seek dismissal of the derivative suit before trial. (We will discuss this demand requirement in detail in the next section.) On the other hand, direct actions are subject to other limitations and restrictions, many arising under federal securities law. So the question of whether a direct action is superior to a derivative action can be a difficult one.

3. Direct vs. Derivative Distinction

As you can imagine, corporate actions often affect shareholders both directly and derivatively. When is an action direct and when is it derivative? The answers—to the extent there are any—are in a handful of judicial opinions, primarily in Delaware. As we learned during our discussion of corporate federalism, derivative actions typically are based on the law of the state of incorporation. Derivative actions are often filed in Delaware, where roughly half of all publicly-traded companies are incorporated. Accordingly, the Delaware courts are the most frequent arbiter of whether an injury is direct or derivative.

Although the case law is not a model of clarity, the following actions are generally treated as direct, thus not subject to derivative action procedures:

- **Protection of financial rights**—compel dividends or protect accrued dividend arrearages, compel dissolution, appoint a receiver, or obtain similar equitable relief

- **Protection of voting rights**—enforce the right to vote, prevent the improper dilution of voting rights, protect preemptive rights, or enjoin the improper voting of shares

- **Protection of governance rights**—enjoin an *ultra vires* or unauthorized act, challenge the use of corporate machinery or the issuance of stock for a wrongful purpose (such as to

perpetuate management in control), require notice or holding
of a shareholders' meeting

- **Protection of minority rights**—challenge the improper
  expulsion of shareholders through mergers, redemptions, or
  other means, prevent oppression of, or fraud against, minority
  shareholders, or hold controlling shareholders liable for their
  acts that depress minority share value

- **Protection of informational rights**—inspect corporate books
  and records

Historically, some courts sought to distinguish direct actions from derivative
actions by looking at whether the shareholder-plaintiff suffered a special injury
(direct) or whether all shareholders were affected equally (derivative). This "special injury" approach created confusion. In response, the Delaware Supreme Court
tried to simplify the task of distinguishing the two actions. Here is that attempt.

Tooley v. Donaldson, Lufkin, & Jenrette, Inc.

845 A.2d 1031 (Del. 2004)

VEASEY, CHIEF JUSTICE.

Plaintiff-stockholders brought a purported class action in the Court of
Chancery, alleging that the members of the board of directors of their corporation breached their fiduciary duties by agreeing to a 22-day delay in closing a
proposed merger. Plaintiffs contend that the delay harmed them due to the lost
time-value of the cash paid for their shares. The Court of Chancery granted the
defendants' motion to dismiss on the sole ground that the claims were, "at most,"
claims of the corporation being asserted derivatively. They were, thus, held not
to be direct claims of the stockholders, individually. Thereupon, the Court held
that the plaintiffs lost their standing to bring this action when they tendered their
shares in connection with the merger.

Although the trial court's legal analysis of whether the complaint alleges a
direct or derivative claim reflects some concepts in our prior jurisprudence, we
believe those concepts are not helpful and should be regarded as erroneous. We
set forth in this Opinion the law to be applied henceforth in determining whether
a stockholder's claim is derivative or direct. That issue must turn *solely* on the following questions: (1) who suffered the alleged harm (the corporation or the suing
stockholders, individually); and (2) who would receive the benefit of any recovery
or other remedy (the corporation or the stockholders, individually)?

Plaintiffs are former minority stockholders of Donaldson, Lufkin & Jenrette, Inc. (DLJ). DLJ was acquired by Credit Suisse Group (Credit Suisse) in the Fall of 2000. Before that acquisition, AXA Financial, Inc. (AXA), which owned 71% of DLJ stock, controlled DLJ. Pursuant to a stockholder agreement between AXA and Credit Suisse, AXA agreed to exchange with Credit Suisse its DLJ stockholdings for a mix of stock and cash.

The tender offer price was set at $90 per share in cash. The tender offer was to expire 20 days after its commencement. The merger agreement, however, authorized two types of extensions. First, Credit Suisse could unilaterally extend the tender offer if certain conditions were not met. Alternatively, DLJ and Credit Suisse could agree to postpone acceptance by Credit Suisse of DLJ stock tendered by the minority stockholders.

Credit Suisse availed itself of both types of extensions to postpone the closing of the tender offer. Plaintiffs challenge the second extension that resulted in a 22-day delay. They contend that this delay was not properly authorized and harmed minority stockholders while improperly benefiting AXA. They claim damages representing the time-value of money lost through the delay.

The order of the Court of Chancery dismissing the complaint is based on the plaintiffs' lack of standing to bring the claims asserted therein. Thus, when plaintiffs tendered their shares they lost standing under the contemporaneous holding rule. The ruling before us on appeal is that the plaintiffs' claim is derivative, purportedly brought on behalf of DLJ. The Court of Chancery, relying upon our confusing jurisprudence on the direct/derivative dichotomy, based its dismissal on the following ground: "Because this delay affected all DLJ shareholders equally, plaintiffs' injury was not a special injury, and this action is, thus, a derivative action, at most."

In our view, the concept of "special injury" that appears in some Supreme Court and Court of Chancery cases is not helpful to a proper analytical distinction between direct and derivative actions. We now disapprove the use of the concept of "special injury" as a tool in that analysis.

The analysis must be based solely on the following questions: Who suffered the alleged harm—the corporation or the suing stockholder individually—and who would receive the benefit of the recovery or other remedy? This simple analysis is well imbedded in our jurisprudence, but some cases have complicated it by injection of the amorphous and confusing concept of "special injury."

The Chancellor, in *Agostino v. Hicks,* 845 A.2d 1110 (Del. Ch. 2004), correctly points this out and strongly suggests that we should disavow the concept of "special injury." In a scholarly analysis of this area of the law, he also suggests that the inquiry should be whether the stockholder has demonstrated that he or she has suffered an injury that is not dependent on an injury to the corporation. In the context of a claim for breach of fiduciary duty, the Chancellor articulated the inquiry as follows: "Looking at the body of the complaint and considering the nature of the wrong alleged and the relief requested, has the plaintiff demonstrated that he or she can prevail without showing an injury to the corporation?"[9] We believe that this approach is helpful in analyzing the first prong of the analysis: what person or entity has suffered the alleged harm? The second prong of the analysis should logically follow.

Determining whether an action is derivative or direct is sometimes difficult and has many legal consequences, some of which may have an expensive impact on the parties to the action. For example, if an action is derivative, the plaintiffs are then required to comply with the requirements of Court of Chancery Rule 23.1, that the stockholder: (a) retain ownership of the shares throughout the litigation; (b) make presuit demand on the board; and (c) obtain court approval of any settlement. Further, the recovery, if any, flows only to the corporation. The decision whether a suit is direct or derivative may be outcome-determinative. Therefore, it is necessary that a standard to distinguish such actions be clear, simple and consistently articulated and applied by our courts.

A court should look to the nature of the wrong and to whom the relief should go. The stockholder's claimed direct injury must be independent of any alleged injury to the corporation. The stockholder must demonstrate that the duty breached was owed to the stockholder and that he or she can prevail without showing an injury to the corporation.

In this case it cannot be concluded that the complaint alleges a derivative claim. There is no derivative claim asserting injury to the corporate entity. There is no relief that would go the corporation. Accordingly, there is no basis to hold that the complaint states a derivative claim.

But, it does not necessarily follow that the complaint states a direct, individual claim. While the complaint purports to set forth a direct claim, in reality, it states no claim at all. The trial court analyzed the complaint and correctly concluded that it does not claim that the plaintiffs have any rights that have been injured. Their rights have not yet ripened. The contractual claim is nonexistent until it is ripe, and that claim will not be ripe until the terms of the merger are fulfilled, including the extensions of the closing at issue here. Therefore, there is no direct claim stated in the complaint before us.

---

[9] The Chancellor further explains that the focus should be on the person or entity to whom the relevant duty is owed. As noted in *Agostino*, this test is similar to that articulated by the American Law Institute (ALI), a test that we cited with approval in *Grimes v. Donald*, 673 A.2d 1207 (Del. 1996).

Due to the reliance on the concept of "special injury" by the Court of Chancery, the ground set forth for the dismissal is erroneous, there being no derivative claim. That error is harmless, however, because, in our view, there is no direct claim either.

Points for Discussion

1. ALI Principles.

The ALI Principles of Corporate Governance attempt to distinguish between direct and derivative actions. The following Comment to ALI Principles § 7.01 sets forth four policy considerations that the ALI Principles say "deserve to be given close attention by the court." Are these criteria helpful? Or are they merely conclusory results of the characterization?

ALI Principles § 7.01
Direct and Derivative Actions Distinguished

First, a derivative action distributes the recovery more broadly and evenly than a direct action. Because the recovery in a derivative action goes to the corporation, creditors and others having a stake in the corporation benefit financially from a derivative action and not from a direct one. Similarly, although all shareholders share equally, if indirectly, in the corporate recovery that follows a successful derivative action, the injured shareholders other than the plaintiff will share in the recovery from a direct action only if the action is a class action brought on behalf of all these shareholders.

Second, once finally concluded, a derivative action will have a preclusive effect that spares the corporation and the defendants from being exposed to a multiplicity of actions.

Third, a successful plaintiff is entitled to an award of attorneys' fees in a derivative action directly from the corporation, but in a direct action the plaintiff must generally look to the fund, if any, created by the action.

Finally, characterizing the action as derivative may entitle the board to take over the action or to seek dismissal of the action. Thus, in some circumstances the characterization of the action will determine the available defenses.

2. Applying the tests.

Are the *Tooley* and ALI approaches the same? Would they lead courts to reach different conclusions? For example, how would each test suggest a court should assess a shareholder claiming denial of preemptive rights, which ensure proportional voting and financial rights? Is such a claim direct or derivative? What about a suit challenging the board's decision to give a CEO guaranteed lifetime employment?

3. What about close corporations?

The policy reasons for requiring a shareholder to sue derivatively when her claim is based on an alleged injury to the corporation may not be present when the suit involves a close corporation in which there is a close identity between shareholders and managers. In addition, litigation-related agency costs are much less likely to arise in a suit involving a close corporation because the plaintiff generally will have substantial financial interests in the action and is more likely to monitor the attorneys. Nevertheless, there may be other reasons for requiring that such an action be maintained as a derivative suit; for example, having damages awarded to the corporation, rather than to an individual shareholder, may be necessary to protect creditors' interests. Should courts consider different factors in derivative suits involving close corporations?

B. Demand Requirement

Rule 23.1 of the Federal Rules of Civil Procedure provides that the complaint in a derivative suit shall "allege with particularity the efforts, if any, made by the plaintiff to obtain the action plaintiff desires from the directors and the reasons for the plaintiff's failure to obtain the action or for not making the effort." Delaware Chancery Court Rule 23.1 contains a similar provision. Although the demand requirement is framed as a pleading rule, courts treat it as a matter of substantive law governing the allocation of power within the corporation.

Practice Pointer

As a practical matter, it is rare for a shareholder to make a demand. The reason for this is that if a shareholder makes a demand, and the board refuses the demand, a court will apply the business judgment rule to the board's decision. The shareholder would only have a potential claim for wrongful refusal of demand—which would be an exceedingly difficult claim to win. Accordingly, the plaintiff typically just files a derivative action and includes in the complaint a claim that demand is excused, and an explanation as to why it is excused.

The demand requirement is a way for judges to filter those derivative suits that appear to have merit from those that do not. By deciding whether "demand" on the board is required, courts essentially decide whether the shareholder can proceed with a lawsuit on behalf of the corporation. If demand is required, the derivative suit ends—and the shareholder is left to intra-corporate remedies. If demand is excused, the suit proceeds. The demand requirement applies only to derivative actions, not to direct actions.

The premise of the demand requirement arises from the general rule that the board, not shareholders, manages the corporation. Accordingly, the board normally would have the power to decide whether the corporation should bring a lawsuit. Derivative actions are an exception to the general rule, because they permit shareholders—rather than the board—to act on behalf of the corporation in bringing, maintaining, and settling litigation. Thus, the demand requirement is a way for judges to balance the board's managerial prerogatives and the desirability, in certain circumstances, of allowing shareholders to litigate on behalf of the corporation.

1. Demand Futility

Early cases made it easy for shareholders to meet the demand requirement by making boilerplate allegations that demand would be futile because the corporation's directors either had benefitted improperly from the transaction at issue or were dominated or controlled by the people who had benefitted. Alternatively, courts allowed shareholder-plaintiffs to name all directors as defendants and then assert that the board could not be expected to sue because the directors were potentially liable for having approved the transaction at issue or for failing to seek to hold liable whoever was responsible for approving it.

Courts soon realized that permitting plaintiffs to make conclusory allegations begged the key question posed by the statutory demand requirement: when would demand be excused as futile? The following case—the leading case on "demand futility"—represents the Delaware Supreme Court's attempt to answer, or at least clarify, this question. This excerpt is lengthy, but it serves both as an application of demand futility to particular facts and a kind of treatise on the relationship between demand futility and the business judgment rule.

The test in *Aronson v. Lewis* can seem confusing at first. Keep in mind that there are two main inquiries to be made in considering demand futility. Although the *Aronson* decision suggests that the test is conjunctive, requiring both elements, later courts have made it clear that the test is disjunctive. In other words, the bottom line is that plaintiffs must allege particularized facts creating a reasonable doubt that the directors are distinterested and independent *or* that the underlying transaction was the product of a valid exercise of business judgment. The bar is high for plaintiffs under *Aronson*, but either of these showings is enough to establish demand futility and survive a motion to dismiss.

Aronson v. Lewis

473 A.2d 805 (Del. 1984)

MOORE, JUSTICE.

When is a stockholder's demand upon a board of directors, to redress an alleged wrong to the corporation, excused as futile prior to the filing of a derivative suit? We granted this interlocutory appeal to the defendants, Meyers Parking System, Inc. (Meyers), a Delaware corporation, and its directors, to review the Court of Chancery's denial of their motion to dismiss this action, pursuant to Chancery Rule 23.1, for the plaintiff's failure to make such a demand or otherwise demonstrate its futility. The Vice Chancellor ruled that plaintiff's allegations raised a "reasonable inference" that the directors' action was unprotected by the business judgment rule. Thus, the board could not have impartially considered and acted upon the demand.

We cannot agree with this formulation of the concept of demand futility. In our view demand can only be excused where facts are alleged with particularity which create a reasonable doubt that the directors' action was entitled to the protections of the business judgment rule. Because the plaintiff failed to make a demand, and to allege facts with particularity indicating that such demand would be futile, we reverse the Court of Chancery and remand with instructions that plaintiff be granted leave to amend the complaint.

I.

The issues of demand futility rest upon the allegations of the complaint. The plaintiff, Harry Lewis, is a stockholder of Meyers. The defendants are Meyers and its ten directors, some of whom are also company officers.

In 1979, Prudential Building Maintenance Corp. (Prudential) spun off its shares of Meyers to Prudential's stockholders. Prior thereto Meyers was a wholly owned subsidiary of Prudential. Meyers provides parking lot facilities and related services throughout the country. Its stock is actively traded over-the-counter.

This suit challenges certain transactions between Meyers and one of its directors, Leo Fink, who owns 47% of its outstanding stock. Plaintiff claims that these transactions were approved only because Fink personally selected each director and officer of Meyers.

Prior to January 1, 1981, Fink had an employment agreement with Prudential which provided that upon retirement he was to become a consultant to that company for ten years. This provision became operable when Fink retired in April 1980. Thereafter, Meyers agreed with Prudential to share Fink's consulting services and reimburse Prudential for 25% of the fees paid Fink. Under this arrangement Meyers paid Prudential $48,332 in 1980 and $45,832 in 1981.

On January 1, 1981, the defendants approved an employment agreement between Meyers and Fink for a five-year term with provision for automatic renewal each year thereafter, indefinitely. Meyers agreed to pay Fink $150,000 per year, plus a bonus of 5% of its pre-tax profits over $2,400,000. Fink could terminate the contract at any time, but Meyers could do so only upon six months' notice. At termination, Fink was to become a consultant to Meyers and be paid $150,000 per year for the first three years, $125,000 for the next three years, and $100,000 thereafter for life. Death benefits were also included. Fink agreed to devote his best efforts and substantially his entire business time to advancing Meyers' interests. The agreement also provided that Fink's compensation was not to be affected by any inability to perform services on Meyers' behalf. Fink was 75 years old when his employment agreement with Meyers was approved by the directors. There is no claim that he was, or is, in poor health.

Additionally, the Meyers board approved and made interest-free loans to Fink totaling $225,000. These loans were unpaid and outstanding as of August 1982 when the complaint was filed. At oral argument defendants' counsel represented that these loans had been repaid in full.

The complaint charges that these transactions had "no valid business purpose", and were a "waste of corporate assets" because the amounts to be paid are "grossly excessive", that Fink performs "no or little services", and because of his "advanced age" cannot be "expected to perform any such services". The plaintiff also charges that the existence of the Prudential consulting agreement with Fink prevents him from providing his "best efforts" on Meyers' behalf. Finally, it is alleged that the loans to Fink were in reality "additional compensation" without any "consideration" or "benefit" to Meyers.

The complaint alleged that no demand had been made on the Meyers board because:

13. Such attempt would be futile for the following reasons:

(a) All of the directors in office are named as defendants herein and they have participated in, expressly approved and/or acquiesced in, and are personally liable for, the wrongs complained of herein.

(b) Defendant Fink, having selected each director, controls and dominates every member of the Board and every officer of Meyers.

(c) Institution of this action by present directors would require the defendant-directors to sue themselves, thereby placing the conduct of this action in hostile hands and preventing its effective prosecution.

The relief sought included the cancellation of the Meyers-Fink employment contract and an accounting by the directors, including Fink, for all damage sustained by Meyers and for all profits derived by the directors and Fink.

IV

A.

A cardinal precept of the General Corporation Law of the State of Delaware is that directors, rather than shareholders, manage the business and affairs of the corporation. 8 Del.C. § 141(a). Section 141(a) states in pertinent part:

> "The *business and affairs* of a corporation organized under this chapter *shall be managed by or under the direction* of a board of directors except as may be otherwise provided in this chapter or in its certificate of incorporation."

8 Del.C. § 141(a) (Emphasis added). The existence and exercise of this power carries with it certain fundamental fiduciary obligations to the corporation and its shareholders. Moreover, a stockholder is not powerless to challenge director action which results in harm to the corporation. The machinery of corporate democracy and the derivative suit are potent tools to redress the conduct of a torpid or unfaithful management. The derivative action developed in equity to enable shareholders to sue in the corporation's name where those in control of the company refused to assert a claim belonging to it. The nature of the action is two-fold. First, it is the equivalent of a suit by the shareholders to compel the corporation to sue. Second, it is a suit by the corporation, asserted by the shareholders on its behalf, against those liable to it.

By its very nature the derivative action impinges on the managerial freedom of directors. Hence, the demand requirement of Chancery Rule 23.1 exists at the threshold, first to insure that a stockholder exhausts his intracorporate remedies, and then to provide a safeguard against strike suits. Thus, by promoting this form of alternate dispute resolution, rather than immediate recourse to litigation, the demand requirement is a recognition of the fundamental precept that directors manage the business and affairs of corporations.

In our view the entire question of demand futility is inextricably bound to issues of business judgment and the standards of that doctrine's applicability. The business judgment rule is an acknowledgment of the managerial prerogatives of Delaware directors under Section 141(a). It is a presumption that in making a business decision the directors of a corporation acted on an informed basis, in good faith and in the honest belief that the action taken was in the best interests of the company. Absent an abuse of discretion, that judgment will be respected by the courts. The burden is on the party challenging the decision to establish facts rebutting the presumption.

The function of the business judgment rule is of paramount significance in the context of a derivative action. It comes into play in several ways—in addressing a demand, in the determination of demand futility, in efforts by independent disinterested directors to dismiss the action as inimical to the corporation's best interests, and generally, as a defense to the merits of the suit. However, in each of these circumstances there are certain common principles governing the application and operation of the rule.

First, its protections can only be claimed by disinterested directors whose conduct otherwise meets the tests of business judgment. From the standpoint of interest, this means that directors can neither appear on both sides of a transaction nor expect to derive any personal financial benefit from it in the sense of self-dealing, as opposed to a benefit which devolves upon the corporation or all stockholders generally. Thus, if such director interest is present, and the transaction is not approved by a majority consisting of the disinterested directors, then the business judgment rule has no application whatever in determining demand futility.

Second, to invoke the rule's protection directors have a duty to inform themselves, prior to making a business decision, of all material information reasonably available to them. Having become so informed, they must then act with requisite care in the discharge of their duties. While the Delaware cases use a variety of terms to describe the applicable standard of care, our analysis satisfies us that under the business judgment rule director liability is predicated upon concepts of gross negligence.

However, it should be noted that the business judgment rule operates only in the context of director action. Technically speaking, it has no role where directors have either abdicated their functions, or absent a conscious decision, failed to act. But it also follows that under applicable principles, a conscious decision to refrain from acting may nonetheless be a valid exercise of business judgment and enjoy the protections of the rule.

Delaware courts have addressed the issue of demand futility on several earlier occasions. The rule emerging from these decisions is that where officers and directors are under an influence which sterilizes their discretion, they cannot be considered proper persons to conduct litigation on behalf of the corporation. Thus, demand would be futile.

However, those cases cannot be taken to mean that any board approval of a challenged transaction automatically connotes "hostile interest" and "guilty participation" by directors, or some other form of sterilizing influence upon them. Were that so, the demand requirements of our law would be meaningless, leaving the clear mandate of Chancery Rule 23.1 devoid of its purpose and substance.

The trial court correctly recognized that demand futility is inextricably bound to issues of business judgment, but stated the test to be based on allegations of fact, which, if true, "show that there is a reasonable inference" the business judgment rule is not applicable for purposes of a pre-suit demand.

The problem with this formulation is the concept of reasonable inferences to be drawn against a board of directors based on allegations in a complaint. As is clear from this case, and the conclusory allegations upon which the Vice Chancellor relied, demand futility becomes virtually automatic under such a test. Bearing in mind the presumptions with which director action is cloaked, we believe that the matter must be approached in a more balanced way.

Our view is that in determining demand futility the Court of Chancery in the proper exercise of its discretion must decide whether, under the particularized facts alleged, a reasonable doubt is created that: (1) the directors are disinterested and independent and (2) the challenged transaction was otherwise the product of a valid exercise of business judgment. Hence, the Court of Chancery must make two inquiries, one into the independence and disinterestedness of the directors and the other into the substantive nature of the challenged transaction and the board's approval thereof. As to the latter inquiry the court does not assume that the transaction is a wrong to the corporation requiring corrective steps by the board. Rather, the alleged wrong is substantively reviewed against the factual background alleged in the complaint. As to the former inquiry, directorial independence and disinterestedness, the court reviews the factual allegations to decide whether they raise a reasonable doubt, as a threshold matter, that the protections of the business judgment rule are available to the board. Certainly, if this is an "interested" director transaction, such that the business judgment rule is inapplicable to the board majority approving the transaction, then the inquiry ceases. In that event futility of demand has been established by any objective or subjective standard.[8]

However, the mere threat of personal liability for approving a questioned transaction, standing alone, is insufficient to challenge either the independence or disinterestedness of directors, although in rare cases a transaction may be so egregious on its face that board approval cannot meet the test of business judgment, and a substantial likelihood of director liability therefore exists. In sum the entire review is factual in nature. The Court of Chancery in the exercise of its sound discretion must be satisfied that a plaintiff has alleged facts with particularity which, taken as true, support a reasonable doubt that the challenged transaction was the product of a valid exercise of business judgment. Only in that context is demand excused.

B.

Having outlined the legal framework within which these issues are to be determined, we consider plaintiff's claims of futility here: Fink's domination and control of the directors, board approval of the Fink-Meyers employment agreement, and board hostility to the plaintiff's derivative action due to the directors' status as defendants.

Plaintiff's claim that Fink dominates and controls the Meyers board is based on: (1) Fink's 47% ownership of Meyers' outstanding stock, and (2) that he "personally selected" each Meyers director. Plaintiff also alleges that mere approval of the employment agreement illustrates Fink's domination and control of the board. In addition, plaintiff argued on appeal that 47% stock ownership, though less than a majority, constituted control given the large number of shares outstanding, 1,245,745.

Such contentions do not support any claim under Delaware law that these directors lack independence. In *Kaplan v. Centex Corp.*, 284 A.2d 119, 123 (Del. Ch. 1971), the Court of Chancery stated that "stock ownership alone, at least when it amounts to less than a majority, is not sufficient proof of domination or control." Moreover, in the demand context even proof of majority ownership of a company does not strip the directors of the presumptions of independence,

---

[8] We recognize that drawing the line at a majority of the board may be an arguably arbitrary dividing point. Critics will charge that we are ignoring the structural bias common to corporate boards throughout America, as well as the other unseen socialization processes cutting against independent discussion and decisionmaking in the boardroom. The difficulty with structural bias in a demand futile case is simply one of establishing it in the complaint for purposes of Rule 23.1. We are satisfied that discretionary review by the Court of Chancery of complaints alleging specific facts pointing to bias on a particular board will be sufficient for determining demand futility.

and that their acts have been taken in good faith and in the best interests of the corporation. There must be coupled with the allegation of control such facts as would demonstrate that through personal or other relationships the directors are beholden to the controlling person. To date the principal decisions dealing with the issue of control or domination arose only after a full trial on the merits. Thus, they are distinguishable in the demand context unless similar particularized facts are alleged to meet the test of Chancery Rule 23.1.

The requirement of director independence inheres in the conception and rationale of the business judgment rule. The presumption of propriety that flows from an exercise of business judgment is based in part on this unyielding precept. Independence means that a director's decision is based on the corporate merits of the subject before the board rather than extraneous considerations or influences. While directors may confer, debate, and resolve their differences through compromise, or by reasonable reliance upon the expertise of their colleagues and other qualified persons, the end result, nonetheless, must be that each director has brought his or her own informed business judgment to bear with specificity upon the corporate merits of the issues without regard for or succumbing to influences which convert an otherwise valid business decision into a faithless act.

Thus, it is not enough to charge that a director was nominated by or elected at the behest of those controlling the outcome of a corporate election. That is the usual way a person becomes a corporate director. It is the care, attention and sense of individual responsibility to the performance of one's duties, not the method of election, that generally touches on independence.

We conclude that in the demand-futile context a plaintiff charging domination and control of one or more directors must allege particularized facts manifesting "a direction of corporate conduct in such a way as to comport with the wishes or interests of the corporation (or persons) doing the controlling." The shorthand shibboleth of "dominated and controlled directors" is insufficient. In recognizing that *Kaplan* was decided after trial and full discovery, we stress that the plaintiff need only allege specific facts; he need not plead evidence. Otherwise, he would be forced to make allegations which may not comport with his duties under Chancery Rule 11.

Here, plaintiff has not alleged any facts sufficient to support a claim of control. The personal-selection-of-directors allegation stands alone, unsupported. At best it is a conclusion devoid of factual support. The causal link between Fink's control and approval of the employment agreement is alluded to, but nowhere specified. The director's approval, alone, does not establish control, even in the face of Fink's 47% stock ownership. The claim that Fink is unlikely to perform any services under the agreement, because of his age, and his conflicting consultant work with Prudential, adds nothing to the control claim. Therefore, we cannot conclude that the complaint factually particularizes any circumstances of control and domination to overcome the presumption of board independence, and thus render the demand futile.

C.

Turning to the board's approval of the Meyers-Fink employment agreement, plaintiff's argument is simple: all of the Meyers directors are named defendants, because they approved the wasteful agreement; if plaintiff prevails on the merits all the directors will be jointly and severally liable; therefore, the directors' interest in avoiding personal liability automatically and absolutely disqualifies them from passing on a shareholder's demand.

Such allegations are conclusory at best. In Delaware mere directorial approval of a transaction, absent particularized facts supporting a breach of fiduciary duty claim, or otherwise establishing the lack of independence or disinterestedness of a majority of the directors, is insufficient to excuse demand. Here, plaintiff's suit is premised on the notion that the Meyers-Fink employment agreement was a waste of corporate assets. So, the argument goes, by approving such waste the directors now face potential personal liability, thereby rendering futile any demand on them to bring suit. Unfortunately, plaintiff's claim fails in its initial premise. The complaint does not allege particularized facts indicating that the agreement is a waste of corporate assets. Indeed, the complaint as now drafted may not even state a cause of action, given the directors' broad corporate power to fix the compensation of officers.

In essence, the plaintiff alleged a lack of consideration flowing from Fink to Meyers, since the employment agreement provided that compensation was not contingent on Fink's ability to perform any services. The bare assertion that Fink performed "little or no services" was plaintiff's conclusion based solely on Fink's age and the *existence* of the Fink-Prudential employment agreement. As for Meyers' loans to Fink, beyond the bare allegation that they were made, the complaint does not allege facts indicating the wastefulness of such arrangements. Again, the mere existence of such loans, given the broad corporate powers conferred by Delaware law, does not even state a claim.

D.

Plaintiff's final argument is the incantation that demand is excused because the directors otherwise would have to sue themselves, thereby placing the conduct of the litigation in hostile hands and preventing its effective prosecution. This bootstrap argument has been made to and dismissed by other courts. Its acceptance would effectively abrogate Rule 23.1 and weaken the managerial power of directors. Unless facts are alleged with particularity to overcome the presumptions of independence and a proper exercise of business judgment, in which case the directors could not be expected to sue themselves, a bare claim of this sort raises no legally cognizable issue under Delaware corporate law.

VI.

In sum, we conclude that the plaintiff has failed to allege facts with particularity indicating that the Meyers directors were tainted by interest, lacked independence, or took action contrary to Meyers' best interests in order to create a reasonable doubt as to the applicability of the business judgment rule. Only in the presence of such a reasonable doubt may a demand be deemed futile, hence, we reverse the Court of Chancery's denial of the motion to dismiss, and remand with instructions that plaintiff be granted leave to amend his complaint to bring it into compliance with Rule 23.1 based on the principles we have announced today.

Reversed and remanded.

Points for Discussion

1. How high is the bar?

Aronson's holding that a plaintiff must demonstrate demand futility by setting forth "particularized facts," rather than "conclusory allegations," can put plaintiffs in a Catch-22. Without discovery, a plaintiff may not be able to learn the facts necessary to establish demand futility. Yet without those facts, a plaintiff will not be entitled to engage in discovery. How difficult do you think it would be for a plaintiff to satisfy *Aronson*? (In fact, when the plaintiff in *Aronson* filed an amended, more particularized complaint, the Court of Chancery held it satisfied the new, more stringent, pleading requirement.)

2. Why not the BJR?

The court in *Aronson* explained that the demand requirement ensures that intra-corporate remedies are exhausted and supports the mandate of DGCL § 141(a) that the board of directors shall manage or oversee the management of the corporation. The court notes that if plaintiffs are allowed to proceed on the basis of "conclusory allegations, demand futility becomes virtually automatic." Yet the court does not apply the business judgment rule to derivative suits. Why not? How do directors' decisions about litigation differ from other decisions? Is it just the threat of personal liability? Is the major distinction that courts are more qualified to weigh directors' decisions about potential corporate litigation than they are to make decisions about other commercial or financial issues (which are protected by the BJR)?

3. The MBCA approach: universal demand.

The MBCA does away with the demand excused/required distinction. To avoid two separate litigation phases (first to determine whether demand was required and then to decide the substance of the plaintiff's claim), the MBCA requires demand on the board in all derivative suits. After making the demand, the claimant-shareholder must then wait 90 days for the board to take corrective action, unless the board rejects the demand earlier or the corporation would suffer irreparable injury by waiting. MBCA § 7.42. Once the 90 days have expired, the shareholder may then bring a derivative claim in court. If the board has rejected the demand, the shareholder must plead with particularity that the board's rejection was flawed because it was either not informed, not disinterested, or not in good faith.

Even if the demand is not rejected, the board under the MBCA continues to have a voice after the derivative suit is filed. For example, the board can move for dismissal of the suit based on a showing that a majority of independent directors determined in good faith and after a "reasonable inquiry" that maintaining the suit is not in the corporation's best interests. MBCA § 7.44. As we'll see next, director "independence" under the MBCA has been interpreted much the same way as in Delaware. *See Einhorn v. Culea* below.

---

2. Special Litigation Committees

In response to a derivative action, a corporation often will form a "Special Litigation Committee," or SLC. The central premise of an SLC is that it will be independent: its members typically are independent directors, who are not defendants in the derivative action, and the SLC typically hires independent lawyers and advisors. The SLC investigates the claims in the complaint, and then acts for the corporation to recommend to the court whether to allow the litigation to proceed. SLCs frequently recommend against the litigation proceeding and move to dismiss.

Early cases held that the business judgment rule precluded judicial review of the substance of a recommendation by an SLC that a derivative suit be dismissed. More recent cases have scrutinized SLC recommendations more closely. One of the primary concerns about SLCs is the degree to which their members might be influenced by other non-SLC directors, including the defendants in the derivative action. The judicial focus on SLCs is often on the independence or interest of individual directors. Many cases address "structural bias," the notion that even members of independent committees can be subject to the influence of other directors.

SLC recommendations were being litigated before *Aronson*, and the case law on SLCs varies by jurisdiction. We will read more about SLCs in later chapters. For now, we just summarize two of the leading SLC cases. *Auerbach* applies a business judgment rule-style analysis to SLCs, and defers to their judgment. *Zapata* scrutinizes the SLC more carefully.

BJR deference. *Auerbach v. Bennett*, 393 N.E.2d 994 (N.Y. 1979), a leading early SLC decision, involved a derivative suit filed by shareholders of General Telephone and Electronics Corporation (GTE) to recover from the responsible GTE officials more than $11 million in bribes and kickbacks that GTE, in an SEC filing, acknowledged it had paid. An SLC, comprised of three directors who had joined the GTE board after the incidents in question, was appointed to consider the shareholders' claim. The SLC conducted an investigation and concluded that none of the defendants had breached his duty of care or profited personally from the challenged payments and that it was not in GTE's best interest for the suit to proceed. (Had the suit proceeded to trial, GTE no doubt would have been forced to disclose publicly the identities of those to whom it had paid bribes and kickbacks—information that it had not disclosed in its SEC filing.) Based on the findings of the SLC, the corporation then filed, and the trial court granted, a motion for summary judgment dismissing the shareholders' claim.

On appeal, the court held that the business judgment rule would not foreclose inquiry into either the disinterestedness and independence of the members of the SLC or the adequacy and appropriateness of the SLC's investigative procedures and methodologies. However, plaintiffs had not called either of these matters into question. As to plaintiffs' request that the court review the merits of the SLC's "ultimate substantive decision" that it was not in GTE's interests to pursue the claims advanced, the New York Court of Appeals took the position that such an inquiry would be inappropriate:

> [The committee's substantive decision] falls squarely within the embrace of the business judgment doctrine, involving as it did the weighing and balancing of legal, ethical, commercial, promotional, public relations, fiscal and other factors familiar to the resolution of many if not most corporate problems. To this extent the conclusion reached by the special litigation committee is outside the scope of our review. Thus, the courts cannot inquire as to which factors were considered by that committee or the relative weight accorded them in reaching that substantive decision. Inquiry into such matters would go to the very core of the business judgment made by the committee. To permit judicial probing of such

issues would be to emasculate the business judgment doctrine as applied to actions and determinations of the special litigation committee.

Two-tiered judicial scrutiny. In contrast, *Zapata Corp. v. Maldonado*, 430 A.2d 779 (Del. 1981), rejected *Auerbach's* deferential approach. The court concluded that empathy can make directors appointed to an SLC reluctant to support the continuance of claims against their fellow board members. In *Zapata*, the plaintiff alleged that certain actions constituted a breach of fiduciary duty and that demand was excused because a majority of the directors had benefited from the challenged decision. The corporation did not contest plaintiff's claim of demand futility. Instead, it created an "Independent Investigation Committee of Zapata Corporation," composed of two new directors. This Committee retained counsel, filed a report recommending that the suit be dismissed, and caused Zapata to move to have the suit dismissed. The Delaware Chancery Court denied Zapata's motion. The Delaware Supreme Court agreed, and proposed a two-part test for assessing an SLC's decision to dismiss a derivative suit:

> After an objective and thorough investigation of a derivative suit, an independent committee may cause its corporation to file a pretrial motion to dismiss in the Court of Chancery. The basis of the motion is the best interests of the corporation, as determined by the committee. The Court should apply a two-step test to the motion.

> First, the Court should inquire into the independence and good faith of the committee and the bases supporting its conclusions. Limited discovery may be ordered to facilitate such inquiries. The corporation should have the burden of proving independence, good faith and a reasonable investigation, rather than presuming independence, good faith and reasonableness. If the Court determines either that the committee is not independent or has not shown reasonable bases for its conclusions, or, if the Court is not satisfied for other reasons relating to the process, including but not limited to the good faith of the committee, the Court shall deny the corporation's motion. If, however, the Court is satisfied that the committee was independent and showed reasonable bases for good faith findings and recommendations, the Court may proceed, in its discretion, to the next step.

> The second step provides, we believe, the essential key in striking the balance between legitimate corporate claims as expressed in a derivative stockholder suit and a corporation's best interests as expressed by an independent investigating committee. The Court should determine,

applying its own independent business judgment, whether the motion should be granted.[18] This means, of course, that instances could arise where a committee can establish its independence and sound bases for its good faith decisions and still have the corporation's motion denied. The second step is intended to thwart instances where corporate actions meet the criteria of step one, but the result does not appear to satisfy its spirit, or where corporate actions would simply prematurely terminate a stockholder grievance deserving of further consideration in the corporation's interest. The Court of Chancery of course must carefully consider and weigh how compelling the corporate interest in dismissal is when faced with a non-frivolous lawsuit. The Court of Chancery should, when appropriate, give special consideration to matters of law and public policy in addition to the corporation's best interests.

Food for Thought

The opinion in *Zapata* was written by Delaware Supreme Court Justice William Quillen. Quillen retired from the court after *Zapata* and—just two years later—was the lead counsel for the defendants in *Aronson*, where he argued for narrowing the application of his decision in *Zapata*, to make it harder for plaintiffs to use. Interestingly, neither of the other two judges who decided *Zapata* were on the *Aronson* panel. What do you think about Quillen writing a decisive opinion, and then arguing about its meaning before his former court, though not his former colleagues?

Other courts have expressed concerns similar to those expressed in *Zapata*, primarily because of "structural bias" concerns that SLC members might be influenced by other directors, including defendants in the relevant derivative action. The following case illustrates the way courts approach the question whether SLC members are "independent."

Einhorn v. Culea

612 N.W.2d 78 (Wis. 2000)

ABRAHAMSON, CHIEF JUSTICE.

Under Wis. Stat. § 180.0744, the corporation may create a special litigation committee consisting of two or more independent directors appointed by a majority vote of independent directors present at a meeting of the board of directors. The independent special litigation committee determines whether the derivative action is in the best interests of the corporation. If the independent special litigation

---

[18] This step shares some of the same spirit and philosophy of the statement by the Vice Chancellor: "Under our system of law, courts and not litigants should decide the merits of litigation."

committee acts in good faith, conducts a reasonable inquiry upon which it bases its conclusions and concludes that the maintenance of the derivative action is not in the best interests of the corporation, the circuit court shall dismiss the derivative action. The statute thus requires the circuit court to defer to the business judgment of a properly composed and properly operating special litigation committee.

Given the finality of the ultimate decision of the committee to dismiss the action, judicial oversight is necessary to ensure that the special litigation committee is independent so that it acts in the corporation's best interest. At issue is whether the special litigation committee created in the present case under Wis. Stat. § 180.0744 was composed of independent directors as required by statute.

Although the plain language of Wis. Stat. § 180.0744 requires the directors who are members of the special litigation committee to be independent, the statute does not define the word "independent." Rather, § 180.0744(3) merely instructs that whether a director on the committee is independent should not be determined solely on the basis of any of the following three factors set forth in the statute: (1) whether the director is nominated to the special litigation committee or elected by persons who are defendants in the derivative action, (2) whether the director is a defendant in the action, or (3) whether the act being challenged in the derivative action was approved by the director if the act resulted in no personal benefit to the director.

The legislature allows the circuit court to give weight to these factors; but the presence of one or more of these factors is not solely determinative of the issue of whether a director is independent. The legislature recognized, for example, that a shareholder could prevent the entire board of directors from serving on the special litigation committee merely by naming all the directors as defendants in the derivative action.

We now discuss the appropriate test to be applied to determine whether directors who are members of a special litigation committee are independent under Wis. Stat. § 180.0744. This question is one of first impression in Wisconsin. Nothing in the statute expressly states the factors to be examined to determine whether directors who are members of a committee are independent.

The Model Business Corporation Act (upon which Wis. Stat. § 180.0744 is based) builds on the law relating to special litigation committees developed by a number of states. We are therefore informed by the case law of other states, and we derive from this case law the following test to determine whether a member of a special litigation committee is independent.

Whether members are independent is tested on an objective basis as of the time they are appointed to the special litigation committee. Considering the totality of the circumstances, a court shall determine whether a reasonable person in the position of a member of a special litigation committee can base his or her decision on the merits of the issue rather than on extraneous considerations or influences. In other words, the test is whether a member of a committee has a relationship with an individual defendant or the corporation that would reasonably be expected to affect the member's judgment with respect to the litigation in issue. The factors a court should examine to determine whether a committee member is independent include, but are not limited to, the following:

(1) *A committee member's status as a defendant and potential liability.* Optimally members of a special litigation committee should not be defendants in the derivative action and should not be exposed to personal liability as a result of the action.

(2) *A committee member's participation in or approval of the alleged wrongdoing or financial benefits from the challenged transaction.* Optimally members of a special litigation committee should not have been members of the board of directors when the transaction in question occurred or was approved. Nor should they have participated in the transaction or events underlying the derivative action. Innocent or *pro forma* involvement does not necessarily render a member not independent, but substantial participation or approval or personal financial benefit should.

(3) *A committee member's past or present business or economic dealings with an individual defendant.* Evidence of a committee member's employment and financial relations with an individual defendant should be considered in determining whether the member is independent.

(4) *A committee member's past or present personal, family, or social relations with individual defendants.* Evidence of a committee member's non-financial relations with an individual defendant should be considered in determining whether the member is independent. A determination of whether a member is independent is affected by the extent to which a member is directly or indirectly dominated by, controlled by or beholden to an individual defendant.

(5) *A committee member's past or present business or economic relations with the corporation.* For example, if a member of the special litigation committee was outside counsel or a consultant to the corporation, this factor should be considered in determining whether the member is independent.

(6) *The number of members on a special litigation committee.* The more members on a special litigation committee, the less weight a circuit court

may assign to a particular disabling interest affecting a single member of the committee.

(7) *The roles of corporate counsel and independent counsel.* Courts should be more likely to find a special litigation committee independent if the committee retains counsel who has not represented individual defendants or the corporation in the past.

Some courts and commentators have suggested that a "structural bias" exists in special litigation committees that taints their decisions. They argue that members of a committee, appointed by the directors of the corporation, are instinctively sympathetic and empathetic towards their colleagues on the board of directors and can be expected to vote for dismissal of any but the most egregious charges. They assert that the committees are inherently biased and untrustworthy. Wisconsin Stat. § 180.0744 and the Model Business Corporation Act are designed to combat this possibility.

A court should not presuppose that a special litigation committee is inherently biased. Although members of a special litigation committee may have experiences similar to those of the defendant directors and serve with them on the board of directors, the legislature has declared that independent members of a special litigation committee are capable of rendering an independent decision. The test we set forth today is designed, as is the statute, to overcome the effects of any "structural bias."

A circuit court is to look at the totality of the circumstances. A finding that a member of the special litigation committee is independent does not require the complete absence of any facts that might point to non-objectivity. A director may be independent even if he or she has had some personal or business relation with an individual director accused of wrongdoing.

It is vital for a circuit court to review whether each member of a special litigation committee is independent. The special litigation committee is, after all, the "only instance in American Jurisprudence where a defendant can free itself from a suit by merely appointing a committee to review the allegations of the complaint." We agree with the Delaware Court of Chancery that the trial court must be "certain that the SLC is truly independent." While ill suited to assessing business judgments, courts are well suited by experience to evaluate whether members of a special litigation committee are independent.

———

C. Who Qualifies as Plaintiff?

As noted above, shareholder litigation typically is driven by plaintiffs' law firms. But obviously, to file lawsuits those firms must have clients. Who are those clients? In federal securities class actions, the nature of the clients has changed dramatically since 1995, when the Private Securities Litigation Reform Act instructed federal courts to select as a lead plaintiff the one "most capable of adequately representing the interests of class members." In response, plaintiffs' law firms increasingly have courted clients who could satisfy this "most capable" requirement.

In general, courts have found that the "most capable" plaintiff is the one with the greatest financial stake in the outcome of the case, so long as the plaintiff satisfied the requirements of Rule 23 of the Federal Rules of Civil Procedure, which governs class actions. Indeed, the 1995 Act established a rebuttal presumption that the plaintiff with the greatest financial stake will be the lead plaintiff.

Derivative actions are not governed by the 1995 Act, but still are subject to the general requirement that a named plaintiff must be capable of adequately and fairly representing the interests of shareholders on whose behalf the suit has been brought. (These requirements are set forth in F.R.C.P. 23.1 and in various state statutes.)

We discuss two procedural issues that arise in the context of determining who qualifies as a plaintiff. First is the "adequacy" requirement, which is relatively easy to satisfy. Second is "standing," which can be more complicated. This is not a civil procedure class, so we will not delve into the nuances of the rules. But these two requirements are at the heart of shareholder litigation, particularly derivative actions, so they deserve some attention.

1. Adequacy

As noted above, F.R.C.P. 23 (which governs class actions) and F.R.C.P 23.1 (which governs derivative suits) both require that a named plaintiff be capable of adequately and fairly representing the interests of the shareholders (in a class action) and the corporation (in a derivative suit) on whose behalf the suit has been brought. Most states have similar requirements. In the vast majority of decisions by federal and state courts, so long as a plaintiff is represented by a qualified attorney and does not have interests antagonistic to the class or the corporation, they satisfy the adequacy requirement.

> ### Example 19.1
>
> *Surowitz v. Hilton Hotels Corp.*, 383 U.S. 363 (1966), involved a derivative claim filed by a Polish immigrant who had a very limited grasp of English and who, when deposed by defendants, had demonstrated almost no understanding of the charges in the complaint. The record, however, also contained evidence that Mrs. Surowitz, the named plaintiff, had filed suit only after her attorney in the case and her son-in-law—a prominent attorney and investment advisor—had investigated certain transactions involving the defendant corporation and found evidence that strongly suggested manipulation of the price of its stock and egregious self dealing.
>
> Reversing a lower court decision dismissing the suit, the Court noted that although one purpose of Rule 23.1 was to "discourage 'strike suits' by people who might be interested in getting quick dollars by making charges without regard to their truth so as to coerce corporate managers to settle worthless claims in order to get rid of them," it also was true that "derivative suits have played a rather important role in protecting shareholders of corporations from the designing schemes and wiles of insiders who are willing to betray their company's interests in order to enrich themselves." Noting that "it is not easy to conceive of anyone more in need of protection against such schemes than little investors like Mrs. Surowitz," the Court held that it was error to dismiss this apparently meritorious claim simply because Mrs. Surowitz had advanced it on the advice of others.

Courts analyzing the adequacy requirement often look to the role the plaintiffs' lawyer plays in the litigation. The following case is representative.

In re Fuqua Industries, Inc. Shareholder Litigation

752 A.2d 126 (Del. Ch. 1999)

CHANDLER, CHANCELLOR.

The question I must answer is whether I should disqualify a derivative plaintiff who is unfamiliar with the basic facts of his or her lawsuit and who exercises little, if any, control over the conduct of such suit?

The first derivative plaintiff Mrs. Abrams has held Fuqua shares for over thirty years. The quantity of her holdings has ranged from as much as 12,008 Fuqua shares to the current level of 8000 shares. The decision to purchase Fuqua shares, as most all of Abrams' investment decisions including the decision to file this suit, was made jointly with her husband, Burton Abrams, a retired trial attorney.

During the long pendency of this litigation Mrs. Abrams fell ill. As she concedes, her memory and faculties have suffered as a result. In a 1998 deposition, it was evident that Mrs. Abrams lacked a meaningful grasp of the facts and allegations of the case prosecuted in her name. While at times she appeared able to provide a general understanding of her claim, she was unable to articulate the understanding with any particularity and she was obviously confused about basic facts regarding her lawsuit.

Alan Freberg, the second derivative plaintiff in this action, purchased twenty-five Fuqua shares in 1989. In 1991, presumably upon concluding that Fuqua directors and Triton had engaged in self-dealing transactions, Freberg retained counsel and filed his first complaint.

Freberg's deposition testimony evidences that his knowledge of the case is at best elliptical. Defendants argue that before his "cram" session immediately before the deposition, Freberg knew absolutely nothing about this matter and had not even been privy to the third amended complaint. Defendants also point out (with much scorn) Freberg's general ignorance of the six or seven other lawsuits in which he was, or still is, the named representative plaintiff. The subtext of defendants' motion is that Freberg has no knowledge of this case because he has no real economic interest at stake. In defendants' view, Freberg is a puppet for his fee-hungry lawyers.

Court of Chancery decisions hold that a representative plaintiff will not be barred from the courthouse for lack of proficiency in matters of law and finance and poor health so long as he or she has competent support from advisors and attorneys and is free from disabling conflicts. This conclusion is both just and sensible.

Defendants' attack on Abrams' and Freberg's adequacy raises serious concerns. The allegation that attorneys bring actions through puppet plaintiffs while the real parties in interest are the attorneys themselves in search of fees is an oft-heard complaint from defendants in derivative suits. Sometimes, no doubt, the allegation rings true.

By the same token, however, the mere fact that lawyers pursue their own economic interest in bringing derivative litigation cannot be held as grounds to disqualify a derivative plaintiff. To do so is to impeach a cornerstone of sound corporate governance. Our legal system has privatized in part the enforcement mechanism for policing fiduciaries by allowing private attorneys to bring suits on behalf of nominal shareholder plaintiffs. In so doing, corporations are safeguarded from fiduciary breaches and shareholders thereby benefit. Through the use of cost and fee shifting mechanisms, private attorneys are economically incentivized to perform this service on behalf of shareholders.

To be sure, a real possibility exists that the economic motives of attorneys may influence the remedy sought or the conduct of the litigation. This influence, however, is inherent in private enforcement mechanisms and does not necessarily vitiate the substantial beneficial impact upon the conduct of fiduciaries.

Nonetheless, in some instances, the attorney in pursuit of his own economic interests may usurp the role of the plaintiff and exploit the judicial system entirely for his own private gain. Such extreme facts call for the court to exercise its discretion and to curb the agency costs inherent in private regulatory and enforcement mechanisms. These agency costs should not be borne by society, defendant corporations, directors or the courts.

I cannot say that either Abrams or Freberg is an inadequate plaintiff in this case. Contrary to defendants' assertions, Freberg does in fact understand the basic nature of the derivative claims brought in his name, even if barely so.

As defendants have adduced no evidence that Freberg has interests antagonistic to the interests he purports to represent, or that class counsel is incompetent or inexperienced, I conclude that Freberg meets Rule 23.1's minimum adequacy requirements. Interestingly, much of defendants' brief is devoted to demonstrating Freberg's surprising level of ignorance with respect to *other* lawsuits in which he is a representative plaintiff. For better or worse, however, no limit exists on the number of lawsuits one individual can bring in a lifetime. Thus, this fact alone is insufficient to disqualify Freberg.

Like Mrs. Surowitz with the aid of her son-in-law, Mrs. Abrams discovered her injury and filed this lawsuit with the aid of her husband. Even though the defendant in *Surowitz* demonstrated that Mrs. Surowitz did not "understand" her complaint and did not make any decisions with respect to the prosecution of the litigation, a unanimous Supreme Court did not dismiss her case; nor did it disqualify her as an inadequate plaintiff. I am reluctant to do differently here.

Abrams has been a substantial holder of Fuqua stock for thirty years. When she and her husband grew dissatisfied with Fuqua management, Mr. Abrams wrote letters to Fuqua's board demanding that certain measures be taken to improve the company's share price. His letters were disregarded. Determining that she had suffered legally cognizable harm, Mr. and Mrs. Abrams retained counsel in an effort to redress their grievances. They placed their trust and confidence in their lawyers as clients have always done.

Our legal system has long recognized that lawyers take a dominant role in prosecuting litigation on behalf of clients. A conscientious lawyer should indeed take a leadership role and thrust herself to the fore of a lawsuit. This maxim is particularly relevant in cases involving fairly abstruse issues of corporate governance and fiduciary duties.

I deny defendants' motions to disqualify Virginia Abrams and Alan Freberg as representative plaintiffs in this action.

---

2. Standing

Because a derivative suit seeks to enforce a right in the name of the corporation, standing generally has been limited to those with an equity interest in the corporation. But what does it mean to have an equity interest in the corporation? The question presents three issues: the nature of the plaintiff's holding, timing, and the plaintiff's countervailing interests.

Nature of the holding. First, consider the nature of the plaintiff's holding. In most jurisdictions, a derivative suit may be brought by either a shareholder of record or a beneficial owner of stock. A "shareholder" includes both a person whose shares are held in a voting trust as well as the more traditional "street name" owner of shares.

What about other participants in the corporation's capital structure, such as creditors? Remember the right-hand side of the balance sheet—can holders of debt also bring derivative actions?

In general, the answer is no. A creditor typically is not allowed to maintain a derivative suit, although, when a corporation becomes bankrupt, its receiver may assert its rights in a suit that primarily will benefit its creditors. One reason for this rule is that the interests of creditors often are adverse to those of shareholders; risky investments that have the potential to enrich shareholders often jeopardize creditors' interests. A second is that creditors can negotiate contractual provisions restricting managers' discretion and therefore do not need the added protection of the derivative suit.

> **What's That?**
>
> "Street name" refers to shares that are held electronically in the account of a stock broker. Historically, shareholders received physical share certificates, pieces of paper representing their ownership interest. The shareholder could either keep those pieces of paper at home, or "deposit" them—in the same way one might deposit money at a bank—with a Wall Street stock broker. Over time, corporations shifted to electronic ownership, with the actual shareholder holding a "beneficial ownership" interest. Today, shares typically are held in the name of the broker, or in "street" name.

Some commentators have argued for a more relaxed rule. Although large creditors might be able to protect themselves contractually against an increased risk of default arising after the loan has been made, smaller creditors often do not have the economic leverage to negotiate such protection. Some have argued that directors should owe fiduciary duties to creditors and that creditors should have standing to bring a derivative suit where stockholder action is unlikely to occur or it is necessary to provide adequate protection to creditors. Whatever the theoretical force of these arguments, courts have almost universally rejected them.

However, in some "mega" settlements, the recovery has gone primarily to holders of securities other than shares. In some cases, the company becomes insolvent after the alleged fraud is revealed, and holders of securities with claims more senior than shares assume priority. This was true in both the *Cendant* litigation, where the primary recovery was to holders of hybrid preferred securities, and the *WorldCom* litigation, where the primary recovery was to certain bondholders. In the *Enron* litigation, the plaintiffs included not only shareholders, but also holders of numerous other securities, including preferred stock and options. These three cases involved some of the largest settlements in history, yet the focus was on non-shareholder claimants.

Another question about the nature of the holding arises when the plaintiff is not and never was a shareholder of the corporation injured by the transaction of which she complains, but instead owns stock in a direct or indirect parent of that corporation. The action would then be a "double" derivative action (or possibly a "triple"). In other words, the plaintiff would bring a derivative action to force the parent to force the subsidiary to bring a suit. The rationale for such claims, which sometimes are allowed, is that the same wrongdoers controlled both the parent and the subsidiary.

Timing. In many jurisdictions, the plaintiff must have been a shareholder at the time of the wrongdoing and at the time suit is filed and must remain a shareholder throughout the litigation. The idea is that the plaintiff not only must have been injured by the wrongdoing, but also must fairly and adequately represent the interest of other shareholders. Put simply, the question is whether someone who is no longer a shareholder can enforce the rights of the corporation.

The issue often arises when shareholders assert a claim on behalf of a corporation that has been merged out of existence or on behalf of the surviving corporation in a merger. The general rule is that a shareholder of a corporation that did not survive a merger lacks standing to sue derivatively for misconduct that occurred before the merger because the claim now is an asset of the surviving corporation. Courts generally do not apply this rule where the merger itself is the subject of a claim or when the merger involved a reorganization that did not eliminate the plaintiff's economic interest in the enterprise. In addition, share-holders who claim they were defrauded in connection with a merger often will have standing to maintain a direct suit on their own behalf or a class action on behalf of all similarly situated former shareholders of the merged corporation.

Such contemporaneous ownership requirements often are justified on the grounds that they serve to assure that the corporation's rights will be prosecuted by a plaintiff who has incurred actual harm and who will benefit from a successful outcome. This justification assumes that the principal purpose of the derivative suit is compensation. Absent the contemporaneous ownership requirement, a person could purchase stock in a company at a price that reflected the harm already done, bring a derivative suit and, if the suit succeeded, realize a windfall equal to a pro rata share of whatever amount the company recovered.

> ### Example 19.2
>
> In *Bangor Punta Operations, Inc. v. Bangor & Aroostook Railroad Co.*, 417 U.S. 703 (1974), the Court dismissed a suit brought by a railroad corporation against its former owner for damages caused by its alleged breaches of fiduciary duty. The Court reasoned that because the shareholder currently in control of the railroad had acquired more than 99% of its stock from the former owner after the alleged wrongs occurred, equitable principles relating to unjust enrichment required it to dismiss the suit, even though it had been filed by the railroad itself, rather than derivatively by its new controlling shareholder. The Court acknowledged that, if the purpose of derivative suits was deterrence, a different result would follow. Then, "any plaintiff willing to file a complaint would suffice. No injury or violation of a legal duty to the particular plaintiff would have to be alleged."

When a derivative suit is filed on behalf of a typical public corporation, however, the rationale supporting the contemporaneous ownership requirement is less compelling. Some shareholders will have sold their stock at prices that reflect the harm the wrongdoers caused and will not share in any subsequent recovery, while other shareholders will have purchased their stock after the wrong occurred and will realize a windfall if the suit succeeds. This suggests that the main purpose of the contemporaneous ownership requirement, at least in public companies, may not be to prevent a windfall but to make it more difficult for a plaintiffs' attorney to "buy into a lawsuit." *Fuqua* makes clear that courts will allow a plaintiffs' attorney to file a derivative suit in the name of a "figurehead plaintiff," but the contemporary ownership requirement imposes on a plaintiffs' attorney the burden of locating a plaintiff who owned the subject corporation's stock at the time the alleged wrongdoing occurred.

Some jurisdictions, such as California, have relaxed the contemporaneous ownership requirement. California permits a suit if there is a strong *prima facie* case in favor of the claim asserted on behalf of the corporation and the plaintiff acquired the shares before there was disclosure to the public or to the plaintiff of the wrongdoing. A plaintiff who qualifies under this standard will not realize a windfall because, if the wrongdoing has not been disclosed, the price at which they purchased will not reflect that wrongdoing. But the requirement that the wrongdoing not yet be disclosed also largely eliminates the possibility that the plaintiff acquired stock so as to qualify to bring a derivative suit.

In a class action, the typicality requirement serves much the same function as does the contemporaneous ownership requirement in a derivative suit. If a plaintiff did not hold stock at the time of the alleged wrongful conduct, their injuries, if any, will differ from those of shareholders who did hold stock and their claims then will not be typical of those asserted on behalf of the purported class.

Countervailing Interests. Plaintiff shareholders also can face standing or other challenges based on their other interests. For example, suppose a shareholder who owns just one share of a corporation files a derivative action, and the court learns that the shareholder also holds a large "short" position. That shareholder's net position will benefit if the corporation loses money. Is that the kind of shareholder who should be permitted to bring a derivative action on behalf of the corporation?

What's That?

A "short seller" borrows shares they do not own and then sells the shares in the market. They remain obligated to deliver shares to the lender in the future. If the shares decline in value, they make money by repurchasing lower priced shares to return to the lender. If the shares increase in value, they lose money. Conceptually, selling short is the opposite of buying stock: short sellers make money when the share price declines and lose money when it rises.

Increasingly, shareholders hold such countervailing positions, and therefore are "economically encumbered." They are burdened by their other positions, and therefore face very different incentives, suffer different losses, and reap different gains than other shareholders. A person who owns shares of a company and who also has sold short shares is not injured by a corporate action that causes the value of shares to decline. Should such a person be permitted to double dip, by making money on their short position from the corporation's wrongdoing, and then suing to recover the losses on the shares they own based on the same wrongdoing?

Another problem associated with security ownership arises from share lending. Shares of public companies are held by brokers who can and do lend them to other shareholders. Brokerage agreements frequently provide that shareholders agree to such lending. Short sellers borrow shares from brokers, who obtain those shares from shareholders' accounts (in particular, from *margin accounts*, accounts in which shareholders are entitled to borrow money to buy shares "on margin").

Food for Thought

When Mylan Pharmaceuticals made a bid for King Pharmaceuticals, Carl Icahn—a major shareholder of Mylan—was not pleased. He thought the offering price for King was too high, and he wanted to block the deal and persuade other shareholders to vote against it. In contrast, shareholders of King Pharmaceuticals, including Perry Corporation, wanted Mylan to approve the deal. To help ensure that Mylan shareholders would vote yes, Perry Corporation bought 9.99% of the outstanding shares of Mylan—in addition to its stake in King. It then entered into a "swap" transaction with a bank, in which it offloaded the economic risk of its stake in Mylan. In other words, the sum of Perry's two positions—the 9.99% ownership in Mylan minus the swap—was zero. It had no financial stake in Mylan. However, Perry nevertheless owned the Mylan shares, and it voted those shares in favor of the deal. Icahn sued and the deal fell apart. But it raised an issue that continues to perplex courts and regulators: how should they treat someone like Perry, who owns shares but also has an offsetting financial interest? For example, what if Perry wanted to file a derivative suit to force Mylan's board to go through with the deal?

Whereas the shorting party can, and does, undertake to pay any dividend declared by the corporation, the shorting party cannot similarly undertake to transfer standing or other plaintiff's rights. Consequently, because there are only a finite number of shares, when a shareholder permits a share to be borrowed for shorting, they essentially create a new shareholder. Share lending thereby creates the illusion that there are more shares owned beneficially than are actually registered. The last buyer of shares in the chain of lending and shorting is the final shareholder of record. Should only that person have standing as a plaintiff?

In a shareholder class action, distributions (either in a settlement or judgment) are made to any shareholder who can demonstrate ownership of the stock during the class period. The settlement and judgment amount is based upon the number of record shares outstanding during the class period; however, due to lending and shorting, the actual number of shares is greater than this number. Moreover, economically encumbered shareholders are entitled to recover, even if they were not damaged (or even if, as a result of their net short position, they profited). Because encumbered shares are entitled to recover pro rata, unencumbered shares receive less than the compensation necessary to make them whole, and encumbered shares receive a windfall. Overall, countervailing interests can make shareholder litigation complex, and puzzling.

D. Some Policy Implications of Shareholder Litigation

We close this chapter by touching on several policy issues. Shareholder litigation is enormously controversial, and many of these thorny questions will not be resolved anytime soon.

Agency costs of litigation. Most shareholder lawsuits are brought in a representative capacity, as class actions or derivative suits. Collective action problems limit the ability of shareholders to police managers through litigation. A shareholder who chooses to devote resources to monitoring managers' performance must bear the costs of such efforts, as well as the risk that no wrongdoing will be found. Moreover, even if the shareholder succeeds in identifying a breach of fiduciary duty and remedying it through a class or derivative action, the only benefit will be a pro rata portion of whatever is recovered in a class action or whatever increase in the value of that shareholder's shares results from a successful derivative suit. Instead, it is the shareholder-plaintiffs' lawyer who stands to earn attorneys' fees and thus has a much greater incentive to bring litigation based on managerial misconduct.

Just as agency costs arise from the different incentives of principal and agent, or shareholder and manager, so do agency costs arise from the different incentives of shareholder and lawyer. The plaintiffs' attorney typically will have a much greater financial stake in shareholder litigation than an individual shareholder. Moreover, plaintiffs' attorneys can sometimes benefit from shortchanging or even injuring the interests of the shareholders whose interests they supposedly represent. For example, a plaintiffs' law firm might agree to a settlement that shareholders collectively would reject, rather than take a case to trial, so as to assure the firm will receive a fee for the work it has done. Alternatively, a firm might file a suit that has little merit from the standpoint of most shareholders, but substantial nuisance value, in the hope that a defendant corporation will agree to a settlement that includes substantial attorneys' fees.

Plaintiffs' attorneys are constantly on the watch for cases. They typically look for evidence of two factors in deciding whether to file a lawsuit on behalf of shareholders. First, is there sufficient evidence of liability so that they can survive the pleading stage? For this question, evidence can come from publicly filed restatements of a corporation's financial condition, whistleblowers who have evidence of wrongdoing, government investigations, or even the plaintiffs' lawyers' own investigation.

If there is evidence of liability, the second question is whether there is sufficient evidence of damages so that the plaintiffs' lawyers can obtain an attractive settlement. The primary source of evidence regarding damages is public information. Was news about the allegations revealed on a particular date or dates? If so, how much did the company's share price decline when news about the allegations was announced? If the news filtered out in stages, how much did each stage impact the share price? How many shares were outstanding and how actively traded were those shares? Are the plaintiffs' lawyers confident they can establish that the price declines were caused by the revelation of information about the allegations?

As discussed above, even if there is sufficient evidence of these factors, one important question remains: who will be the plaintiff? Before the enactment of the Private Securities Litigation Reform Act of 1995 (PSLRA), plaintiffs' lawyers would file cases immediately after a company's share price declined on behalf of one or more individual investors with relatively small shareholdings. Some "professional" plaintiffs held a few shares of many companies in anticipation of a lawsuit, and courts selected the "lead plaintiff" and his law firm based in part on who had been the first to file a complaint.

In 2006, one of the most prominent plaintiffs' law firms, Milberg Weiss Bershad & Schulman, and two of its name partners, were criminally indicted for allegedly participating in a scheme in which several individuals were paid millions of dollars in secret kickbacks in exchange for serving as named plaintiffs in more than 150 class-action and shareholder derivative-action lawsuits. The indictment alleged that the firm received more than $200 million in attorneys' fees from these lawsuits.

The PSLRA changed the landscape of federal securities litigation by shifting from a first-to-file presumption to a size-of-loss presumption. Congress mandated that in appointing a lead plaintiff, "the court shall adopt a presumption that the most adequate plaintiff . . . is the person or group of persons that . . . has the largest financial interest in the relief sought by the class." Securities Exchange Act § 27(a)(3)(B)(iii)(I). The PSLRA's Conference Report explained that "class members with large amounts at stake will represent the interests of the plaintiff class more effectively than class members with small amounts at stake." H.R. Conf. Rep. 104–369, at 34 (1995). Today, federal district courts compare the financial stakes of the various plaintiffs and determine which has the most to gain from the lawsuit. Essentially, the test is a mechanical one based on which shareholder has the "largest financial interest" in the litigation, and therefore which one has the greatest relative incentive to pursue the litigation effectively on behalf of all shareholders. That plaintiff's law firm then represents the class.

Challenges of settlements. The settlement of lawsuits also presents policy challenges. Settlements occur more frequently in shareholder litigation than in other cases. Suits often are initiated by plaintiffs' attorneys who represent "figurehead" clients. Many plaintiffs' attorneys are committed to protecting the interests of the shareholders they represent, but almost all such attorneys work on a contingent fee basis. Thus, their personal financial interests lie in maximizing the fees they will earn for any given amount of work and minimizing the risk that they will receive no fee for their efforts. This produces a bias in favor of smaller, speedier settlements over trials that, if unsuccessful, will leave attorneys without compensation after years of work. In addition, plaintiffs' attorneys may find it financially attractive to initiate "strike suits" that have little prospect of success on the merits but that impose litigation costs on the defendant corporation and thus have nuisance, and therefore settlement, value.

Shareholders' financial interest, in contrast, lies in realizing the largest recovery, adjusted for litigation risk, that a suit has the potential to generate. At times, shareholders also may benefit from changes in the governance practices of the defendant corporation or from enhanced or corrective disclosure of material information. Shareholders, however, realize no benefits from strike suits or from settlements that produce only symbolic governance changes or meaningless disclosures.

The key safeguard against opportunism in shareholder litigation is the requirement in F.R.C.P. 23 and 23.1, and the comparable requirement in most states' statutes or rules, that a court both approve any settlement, compromise, discontinuance, or dismissal of a derivative suit or shareholder class action and also determine what fee should be awarded to plaintiffs' attorneys.

It is up to the court to decide whether to approve a settlement that typically has been negotiated by plaintiffs' attorneys without input from many of the "clients" they represent. The courts attempt to ensure that settlements are fair to absent class members and other shareholders. The proponents of a settlement bear the burden of convincing the court that it is fair. In most cases, that determination will depend largely on the adequacy of the amount being recovered when compared to the potential recovery were plaintiff to succeed at trial. In making this evaluation, the court will discount the potential recovery at trial by the risk factors inherent in any litigation and the time value of money over the period during which recovery will be delayed.

Practice Pointer

Important questions in evaluating settlements include the following:
- How strong are the claims on the merits?
- How much delay and expense would be involved in continued litigation?
- Could any judgment actually be collected?
- How much of a compromise is the settlement?
- How do both parties view the settlement?

Evaluation of a settlement becomes more difficult when it involves non-pecuniary benefits to the corporation or the plaintiff class. For example, settlements of derivative suits may involve agreements to add outside directors to the board, to create more independent audit, compensation, or nominating committees, or to require managers to surrender stock options. Class action settlements may require additional disclosure before a planned transaction is consummated. Although settlements calling for improved governance mechanisms may reduce the prospect of future wrongdoing, they raise a separate problem (described by the ALI): "such therapeutic relief can sometimes represent a counterfeit currency by which the parties can increase the apparent value of the settlement and thereby justify higher attorney's fees for plaintiff's counsel, who is often the real party in interest." To deal with this problem, the ALI recommends that the court review the value of non-pecuniary relief both when evaluating the settlement and when computing plaintiff's counsel fees. ALI PRINCIPLES § 7.14, Comment c.

The integrity of the shareholder litigation process depends to a considerable degree on the rigor with which courts review proposed settlements and requests for attorneys' fees. However, a number of factors impair the effectiveness of courts' review. Perhaps the most important is that settlement hearings rarely are adversarial. As Judge Henry Friendly pointed out many years ago: "Once a settlement is agreed, the attorneys for the plaintiff stockholders link arms with their former adversaries to defend the joint handiwork." Absent a well prepared objector, courts thus must take the initiative in reviewing proposed settlements, yet courts often have an incentive to approve a proposed settlement, if for no other reason than to clear from their overcrowded dockets potentially complex cases that otherwise are likely to require a great deal of judicial attention.

Affected shareholders are made aware of proposed settlements through the notices required by F.R.C.P. 23 and 23.1 and comparable provisions of state law. Largely as a consequence of collective action problems, though, affected shareholders rarely object. They usually do not have detailed information about the merits of the action or the manner in which the settlement has been negotiated. To obtain this information, a shareholder has to challenge both the plaintiffs' attorneys, who nominally represent the shareholders' interests but who always have a strong interest in having the settlement approved, and the attorneys representing the defendants and the corporation. In addition, a shareholder often will have only a relatively brief period in which to object before the hearing on the settlement is scheduled to be held. Despite these problems, courts usually treat the absence of a large number of objections as a factor supporting approval of a proposed settlement. Even courts that are skeptical about the benefits of a proposed settlement often are reluctant to reject it.

Attorneys' fees. Under the "American" rule, which generally applies in litigation in the United States, the successful party is not entitled to recover attorneys' fees from the losing party. However, courts have created a partial exception to this rule for shareholder class and derivative litigation. If a defendant prevails, the American rule still applies. But if a plaintiff prevails on the merits or obtains a settlement, her attorneys can apply to the court for a fee award. In a class action, that fee will be payable out of whatever "common fund" the action creates. In a derivative suit, the corporation customarily is required to pay whatever fee is awarded on the grounds that it has derived a benefit, either monetary or non-monetary, from the successful prosecution or settlement of the suit.

Fees generally are calculated on either a "lodestar" or percentage of recovery basis. In 1985, a Third Circuit Task Force Report describes the "lodestar" method as follows:

> First, the court must determine the hours reasonably expended by counsel that created, protected, or preserved the fund. Second, the number of compensable hours is multiplied by a reasonable hourly rate for the attorney's services. Hourly rates may vary according to the status of the attorney who performed the work (that is, the attorney's experience, reputation, practice, qualifications, and similar factors) or the nature of the services provided. This multiplication of the number of compensable hours by the reasonable hourly rate [constitutes] the "lodestar" of the court's fee determination.

> The "lodestar" then could be increased or decreased based upon the contingent nature or risk in the particular case involved and the quality of the attorney's work. An increase or decrease of the lodestar amount is referred to as a "multiplier." In determining whether to increase the lodestar to reflect the contingent nature of the case, "the district court should consider any information that may help to establish the probability of success." However, "the court may find that the contingency was so slight or the amount found to constitute reasonable compensation for the hours worked was so large a proportion of the total recovery that an increased allowance for the contingent nature of the fee would be minimal." As to the quality multiplier, it was to be employed only for "an unusual degree of skill, superior or inferior, exhibited by counsel in the specific case before the court."

The percentage of recovery method, as its name implies, involves awarding a fee calculated as a percentage of the value of whatever the suit has produced. Fee awards generally range between 20–35% when the recovery is below $100 million and are lower percentages for higher amounts. Some retention agreements provide for a staggered schedule, so that the fee percentage declines as the settlement size increases.

Neither approach is entirely successful in resolving the structural conflicts inherent in shareholder litigation. If the lodestar formula is used, plaintiffs' attorneys have an interest in prolonging the litigation so as to maximize the amount of time for which they will be paid. Thus, counsel may reject an early settlement offer or engage in extended "confirmatory" discovery if a settlement has been negotiated. Defendants' counsel may tacitly acquiesce in such a scenario, as it also may benefit their interests. Such structural collusion may benefit all the attorneys involved, but it works against the plaintiff-shareholders and the corporation's interest in settling the case as favorably and quickly as possible. Moreover, because the fees to be awarded will not be directly linked to the amount of any settlement, counsel may be prepared to settle for less than the shareholders, if fully informed, would be prepared to accept.

The percentage of recovery method can be similarly problematic. Plaintiffs' attorneys may find it attractive to settle a case very early so as to avoid expending very much time. Their marginal return on their investment in a case generally will decline as the amount of time they invest in it increases. At some point, any increase in the amount recovered, even if it is attainable, will be unlikely to lead to any significant increase in their fee. Plaintiffs' attorneys also may be reluctant to include non-pecuniary terms in a settlement because no value may be attached to any benefits they provide when the attorneys' fees are calculated.

The percentage of recovery value method also tends to increase case splitting and fee splitting among different counsel. By diversifying the risks involved in any one case among a number of different lawyers, the lead counsel can reduce the effort put into the case and, hence, the costs that would be incurred if the case is not settled or litigated successfully. Such case splitting both decreases the incentive for plaintiff's counsel to settle early and reduces the effectiveness of counsel's work, thereby weakening the likelihood of a large recovery for the corporation.

CHAPTER 20

Board Decision Making

You learned from the last chapter that shareholder litigation drives the enforcement of directors' fiduciary duties. However, we didn't say much there about the substance of those fiduciary duties, which lie at the core of corporate law. In the next chapters of this module, we peel away at their substance.

Corporate fiduciary duties have a long and complex history. Traditionally, it has been common to regard fiduciary duties as being split between the duty of care and the duty of loyalty. Behind these twin fiduciary duties is the business judgment rule (BJR), the rebuttable presumption insulating directors' decisions from judicial scrutiny if they act in an honest, well-meaning, informed, and rational manner. In other words, the BJR presumes that directors don't breach their fiduciary duties.

In general, the duty of care has been described as a duty to act honestly, in good faith, and in an informed manner. Directors who behaved unreasonably, or in a grossly negligent manner, violated their duty of care. The idea was that directors should act with the care that an ordinarily prudent person would reasonably be expected to exercise in a like position and under similar circumstances.

In contrast, the duty of loyalty has been described as a duty to act in the best interests of the corporation and avoid self dealing. The duty of loyalty applied when a director wore "two hats"—because he or she had a personal stake (a conflict of interest) in a corporate decision. Applying the duty of loyalty, judges scrutinized director involvement in conflicted decisions, and applied various tests and remedies to ensure that those decisions were fair to the corporation and its shareholders.

Over time, the application of the legal doctrines surrounding the duties of care and loyalty has grown more complicated, primarily in response to two factors. First, courts (particularly in Delaware) have shifted their descriptions and categorization of the legal doctrines that govern director behavior. Second, legislatures (again, beginning in Delaware) have protected directors by statute from personal liability for certain actions. The result has been both to blur the lines of the duties of care and loyalty, and to focus more on the types of director conduct at issue than on jurisprudential categories.

This shift is one reason why we covered shareholder litigation first: one key to understanding corporate fiduciary duties is to see how judges and legislatures have responded to particular lawsuits, based on particular facts, framed in particular ways. In turn, it's useful to notice how plaintiffs' lawyers have responded to court decisions and statutes that insulate directors from liability with new litigation strategies. The development of fiduciary duties has been a kind of dance—with judges, legislators, and lawyers each taking a turn as the lead.

Make the Connection

Directors' fiduciary duties arise in all corporations, including those that are closely-held. But the fiduciary duties of majority shareholders to minority shareholders in the close corporation are more exacting than in the public corporation. *See* Chapter 26, Oppression in the Close Corporation. For example, majority shareholders face limits in paying salaries and declaring dividends if their actions undermine the "reasonable expectations" of minority shareholders.

Likewise, controlling shareholders of public corporations (such as parent corporations that hold partially-owned subsidiaries whose shares are publicly-traded) also have fiduciary duties to minority shareholders. But these duties are somewhat less exacting than those of directors. *See* Chapter 24, Duties in Corporate Groups. For example, parent corporations can exploit business opportunities for themselves with greater freedom than can directors.

In the next chapters, we will try to help you understand fiduciary duties by focusing on several different substantive categories of director action that can be subject to challenge. First, directors make decisions for the corporation. Second, directors face conflicts of interest (including when setting executive compensation, an important topic that we devote an entire chapter to). Third, directors oversee certain aspects of corporate activity. These three areas—board decision making, director conflicts, and board oversight—are analytically distinct.

Still, these three categories can overlap. Plaintiffs' lawyers often seek to characterize certain board decisions as conflicted or as involving a lapse in oversight. Likewise, judges have changed how they characterize fiduciary duty categories. At first, decision-making and oversight cases generally fell under the duty of care; more recently, judges have put oversight cases under the duty of loyalty, along with self dealing. For this reason, we look at director conflicts before turning to board oversight.

We begin this chapter with some more detail on the BJR, and a colorful case about the Chicago Cubs' decision to shun nighttime baseball. We then turn to a famous Delaware case that generated an equally famous statutory provision. The case, *Smith v. Van Gorkom*, held directors personally liable for their decisions in a merger and is one of the most widely criticized—and cited—corporate law cases.

The case led the Delaware legislature to adopt DGCL § 102(b)(7), which allows corporations to adopt charter provisions to insulate directors from personal liability for certain kinds of decisions. We conclude the chapter by discussing the various ways directors can avoid liability by having the corporation purchase insurance on their behalf, or by indemnifying them if they are held liable.

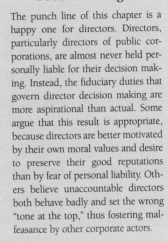

Food for Thought

The punch line of this chapter is a happy one for directors. Directors, particularly directors of public corporations, are almost never held personally liable for their decision making. Instead, the fiduciary duties that govern director decision making are more aspirational than actual. Some argue that this result is appropriate, because directors are better motivated by their own moral values and desire to preserve their good reputations than by fear of personal liability. Others believe unaccountable directors both behave badly and set the wrong "tone at the top," thus fostering malfeasance by other corporate actors.

A. Business Judgment Rule Revisited

The BJR protects directors from liability for business decisions, even those that were ill-chosen and resulted in losses to the corporation. The BJR has been part of the common law for at least one hundred fifty years. Traditionally, it has shielded directors from personal liability and their decisions from review. If the BJR applies, courts do not interfere with or second-guess directors' actions and board decisions—in essence, it's a doctrine of judicial abstention. If the BJR does not apply, courts may scrutinize the decision as to its fairness to the corporation and its shareholders.

The BJR is both procedural and substantive. As a procedural matter, the BJR creates a rebuttable presumption that the directors exercised reasonable diligence and acted in good faith. Therefore, a plaintiff challenging a board's decision bears the burden of rebutting this presumption, by showing that the directors engaged in self dealing or acted in bad faith, or that the decision was not a proper exercise of business judgment.

As a substantive matter, the BJR reflects the view that directors are better than courts at making business judgments. Thus, courts applying the BJR have adopted standards of review that assume courts should not second-guess directors, unless it is clear the court is in a better position to protect corporate interests. Although the basic idea behind the BJR seems simple, it is hard to express the boundaries of the rule using words. Many corporate statutes, including Delaware's, do not even try; instead, they leave it to courts to define the scope of the BJR and determine whether the basic concept applies in particular cases.

Even the MBCA's attempt to define the parameters related to business judgment can be maddeningly vague. For example, consider the meaning of one phrase, which appears in the Official Comment to MBCA § 8.30, stating that a director has the latitude to take action that he or she "reasonably believes to be in the best interests of the corporation."

First, the Comment states that "the phrase 'reasonably believes' is both subjective and objective in character. Its first level of analysis is geared to what the particular director, acting in good faith, actually believes. The second level of analysis is focused specifically on whether a director's belief is reasonable (i.e., could—not would—a reasonable person in a like position and acting in similar circumstances have arrived at that belief) and ultimately involves an overview that is objective in character."

Second, the Comment explains "best interests of the corporation" as key to an explication of a director's duties: "The term 'corporation' is a surrogate for the business enterprise as well as a frame of reference encompassing the shareholder body. In determining the corporation's 'best interests,' the director has wide discretion in deciding how to weigh near-term opportunities versus long-term benefits as well as in making judgments where the interests of various groups within the shareholder body or having other cognizable interests in the enterprise may differ."

Make the Connection

Recall the property/entity dichotomy we covered early in this book. Any discussion of the "best interests of the corporation" raises the recurring question whether the corporation is a device for the maximization of shareholder profits (a "property" perspective) or whether the corporation is a social institution with responsibilities to its many constituents (an "entity" perspective). Consider the two key parts of this phrase. What is the "corporation"? Whose interests does it include, and how much focus should there be on shareholders? And what are the corporation's "best interests"? How should directors decide what is "best"?

Again, the bottom line is that the BJR tells courts to abstain from interfering in corporate decisions and gives directors broad latitude in making these decisions. If the decision is within the "realm of reason," it generally will be protected—a sort of "rational basis" test.

Shlensky v. Wrigley

237 N.E.2d 776 (Ill. Ct. App. 1968)

SULLIVAN, JUSTICE.

This is an appeal from a dismissal of plaintiff's amended complaint on motion of the defendants. The action was a stockholders' derivative suit against the directors for negligence and mismanagement. The corporation was also made a defendant. Plaintiff sought damages and an order that defendants cause the installation of lights in Wrigley Field and the scheduling of night baseball games.

Plaintiff is a minority stockholder of defendant corporation, Chicago National League Ball Club (Inc.), a Delaware corporation with its principal place of business in Chicago, Illinois. Defendant corporation owns and operates the major league professional baseball team known as the Chicago Cubs. The corporation also engages in the operation of Wrigley Field, the Cubs' home park, the concessionaire sales during Cubs' home games, television and radio broadcasts of Cubs' home games, the leasing of the field for football games and other events and receives its share, as visiting team, of admission moneys from games played in other National League stadia. The individual defendants are directors of the Cubs and have served for varying periods of years. Defendant Philip K. Wrigley is also president of the corporation and owner of approximately 80% of the stock therein.

Plaintiff alleges that since night baseball was first played in 1935 nineteen of the twenty major league teams have scheduled night games. In 1966, out of a total of 1620 games in the major leagues, 932 were played at night. Plaintiff alleges that every member of the major leagues, other than the Cubs, scheduled substantially all of its home games in 1966 at night, exclusive of opening days, Saturdays, Sundays, holidays and days prohibited by league rules. Allegedly this has been done for the specific purpose of maximizing attendance and thereby maximizing revenue and income.

The Cubs, in the years 1961–65, sustained operating losses from its direct baseball operations. Plaintiff attributes those losses to inadequate attendance at Cubs' home games. He concludes that if the directors continue to refuse to install lights at Wrigley Field and schedule night baseball games, the Cubs will continue to sustain comparable losses and its financial condition will continue to deteriorate.

Plaintiff alleges that, except for the year 1963, attendance at Cubs' home games has been substantially below that at their road games, many of which were played at night. Plaintiff compares attendance at Cubs' games with that of the Chicago White Sox, an American League club, whose weekday games were generally played at night. The weekend attendance figures for the two teams was similar; however, the White Sox week-night games drew many more patrons than did the Cubs' weekday games.

Plaintiff alleges that the funds for the installation of lights can be readily obtained through financing and the cost of installation would be far more than offset and recaptured by increased revenues and incomes resulting from the increased attendance.

Plaintiff further alleges that defendant Wrigley has refused to install lights, not because of interest in the welfare of the corporation but because of his personal opinions "that baseball is a 'daytime sport' and that the installation of lights and night baseball games will have a deteriorating effect upon the surrounding neighborhood." It is alleged that he has admitted that he is not interested in whether the Cubs would benefit financially from such action because of his concern for the neighborhood, and that he would be willing for the team to play night games if a new stadium were built in Chicago.

Plaintiff alleges that the other defendant directors, with full knowledge of the foregoing matters, have acquiesced in the policy laid down by Wrigley and have permitted him to dominate the board of directors in matters involving the installation of lights and scheduling of night games, even though they knew he was not motivated by a good faith concern as to the best interests of defendant corporation, but solely by his personal views set forth above. It is charged that the directors are acting for a reason or reasons contrary and wholly unrelated to the business interests of the corporation; that such arbitrary and capricious acts constitute mismanagement and waste of corporate assets, and that the directors have been negligent in failing to exercise reasonable care and prudence in the management of the corporate affairs.

The question on appeal is whether plaintiff's amended complaint states a cause of action. It is plaintiff's position that fraud, illegality and conflict of interest are not the only bases for a stockholder's derivative action against the directors. Contrariwise, defendants argue that the courts will not step in and interfere with honest business judgment of the directors unless there is a showing of fraud, illegality or conflict of interest.

The cases in this area are numerous and each differs from the others on a factual basis. However, the courts have pronounced certain ground rules which appear in all cases and which are then applied to the given factual situation. The court in *Wheeler v. Pullman Iron and Steel Co.*, 143 Ill. 197, 207, 32 N.E. 420, 423 (1892), said:

> It is, however, fundamental in the law of corporations, that the majority of its stockholders shall control the policy of the corporation, and regulate and govern the lawful exercise of its franchise and business. Every one purchasing or subscribing for stock in a corporation impliedly agrees that he will be bound by the acts and proceedings done or sanctioned by a majority of the shareholders, or by the agents of the corporation duly

chosen by such majority, within the scope of the powers conferred by the charter, and courts of equity will not undertake to control the policy or business methods of a corporation, although it may be seen that a wiser policy might be adopted and the business more successful if other methods were pursued. The majority of shares of its stock, or the agents by the holders thereof lawfully chosen, must be permitted to control the business of the corporation in their discretion, when not in violation of its charter or some public law, or corruptly and fraudulently subversive of the rights and interests of the corporation or of a shareholder.

Plaintiff in the instant case argues that the directors are acting for reasons unrelated to the financial interest and welfare of the Cubs. However, we are not satisfied that the motives assigned to Philip K. Wrigley, and through him to the other directors, are contrary to the best interests of the corporation and the stockholders. For example, it appears to us that the effect on the surrounding neighborhood might well be considered by a director who was considering the patrons who would or would not attend the games if the park were in a poor neighborhood. Furthermore, the long run interest of the corporation in its property value at Wrigley Field might demand all efforts to keep the neighborhood from deteriorating. By these thoughts we do not mean to say that we have decided that the decision of the directors was a correct one. That is beyond our jurisdiction and ability. We are merely saying that the decision is one properly before directors and the motives alleged in the amended complaint showed no fraud, illegality or conflict of interest in their making of that decision.

Finally, we do not agree with plaintiff's contention that failure to follow the example of the other major league clubs in scheduling night games constituted negligence. Plaintiff made no allegation that these teams' night schedules were profitable or that the purpose for which night baseball had been undertaken was fulfilled. Furthermore, it cannot be said that directors, even those of corporations that are losing money, must follow the lead of the other corporations in the field. Directors are elected for their business capabilities and judgment and the courts cannot require them to forego their judgment because of the decisions of directors of other companies. Courts may not decide these questions in the absence of a clear showing of dereliction of duty on the part of the specific directors and mere failure to "follow the crowd" is not such a dereliction.

For the foregoing reasons the order of dismissal entered by the trial court is affirmed.

Points for Discussion

1. Would a statute help?

How helpful would the MBCA's language be to a claim like Shlensky's? Would the result be different under MBCA § 8.30 (Standards of Conduct for Directors)? Could you do any better in describing the scope of the BJR more precisely?

The Official Comment to MBCA § 8.31 (Standards of Liability for Directors) suggests an answer: "[The statutory] standard of judicial review for director conduct—deeply rooted in the case law—presumes that, absent self-dealing or other breach of the duty of loyalty, directors' decision making satisfies the applicable legal requirements." A plaintiff challenging the director's conduct in connection with a corporate decision thus has the burden of overcoming this presumption of regularity.

2. Negligence?

Should directors be subject to liability under a negligence standard? Consider three factors: voluntariness, judicial expertise, and risk. Does it matter that shareholders have voluntarily invested in the corporation, and therefore have taken the risk of bad board decisions? What are the pros and cons of after-the-fact litigation as a tool to evaluate board decisions? Finally, do shareholders—particularly diversified shareholders—worry about directors taking too much risk, or not enough risk? Given your answers to these questions, does it make sense that courts have not adopted a negligence standard?

3. Rationality vs. reasonableness.

A "rationality" standard focuses on whether a board decision can coherently be explained. A "reasonableness" standard focuses on directorial behavior and motivation. Is the standard in *Shlensky v. Wrigley* based on "rationality" or "reasonableness"? What are the advantages and disadvantages of each?

4. Waste.

One "residual" or "leftover" claim plaintiffs challenging a board decision can make is called "waste." Essentially, the claim is that a decision or transaction was a waste or spoliation of corporate assets. Waste claims rarely succeed because they face an extraordinarily high bar. As the Delaware Supreme Court has stated, there is waste only if "what the corporation has received is so inadequate in value that no person of ordinary, sound business judgment would deem it worth that which the corporation has paid." *Grobow v. Perot*, 539 A.2d 180, 189 (Del. 1988). Thus, the waste standard shields directors from liability and board decisions from review, even when the decision seems clearly unwise or imprudent.

Only if a corporate transaction results in no benefit to the corporation—such as issuing stock without consideration or using corporate funds to discharge personal obligations—have courts found corporate waste. As one court observed, "rarest of all—and indeed, like Nessie, possibly non-existent—would be the case of disinterested business people making non-fraudulent deals (non-negligently) that meet the legal standard of waste!" *Steiner v. Meyerson*, 1995 WL 441999 at *5 (Del. Ch. 1995). Why wasn't the board's refusal in *Wrigley* to adopt nighttime baseball an instance of corporate waste?

B. *Smith v. Van Gorkom*

Given this backdrop, one would expect judges to hold directors liable for poor decisions rarely, if at all. We now turn to one such rare case. We begin with some background about the case and then provide a lengthy excerpt from the case. You should know that Delaware judicial opinions tend to be long and fact intensive, especially in important corporate law cases. So you can think of this case as a training exercise for reading other Delaware cases in real life. (At least we summarized some of the facts, which cuts down the reading some.) Finally, we discuss the reaction to the court's decision and some of the policy issues it raised.

1. Background of the Case

The Trans Union Corporation was a publicly traded company in the

Take Note!

Under the waste standard and through the operation of the BJR, good-faith board decisions are protected from judicial second-guessing. As we have seen in *Shlensky v. Wrigley* and *Kamin v. American Express Co.* (Chapter 12, Capital Structure), courts are prepared to uphold business decisions on the flimsiest of reasons.

In only a handful of cases have courts found good-faith board action so imprudent as to fall outside the BJR, such as when there are suspicions of conflicts of interest or other malfeasance, though the evidence is lacking. For example, in one famous case involving high-risk bank transactions during the height of the Great Depression, the court imposed liability on bank directors for approving the transactions during the precarious period after the 1929 stock market crash. *Litwin v. Allen*, 25 N.Y.S.2d 667 (N.Y. Sup. Ct. 1940). The court faulted the bank directors for approving a transaction "so improvident, so risky, so unusual and unnecessary to be contrary to fundamental conceptions of prudent banking practice."

Although some commentators have explained *Litwin* as imposing higher duties on bank directors, who were often viewed as appropriate deep pockets before federal bank deposit insurance, the case had overtones of self dealing. The company benefited by the financing transactions was the holding company for a business group in which the bank's parent, J.P. Morgan & Company, was deeply committed. Although the court concluded the plaintiffs had failed to show a conflict of interest, the heightened court scrutiny of the transaction suggested doubts about the good faith of the bank directors.

rail leasing business. Its chairman and chief executive officer was Jerome W. Van Gorkom, who was nearing retirement age when the events in the case occurred. Its board of directors consisted of five company officers and five outside directors. Four of the latter were CEOs of large public corporations; the fifth was the former dean of the University of Chicago Business School.

Trans Union had been facing a major business problem relating to investment tax credits (ITCs). Its competitors generated sufficient taxable income to allow them to make use of all ITCs they generated and took these tax benefits into account in setting the terms of their railcar leases. Trans Union, however, did not have sufficient income to take advantage of all of its ITCs, but nevertheless had to match its competitors' prices. In July 1980, Trans Union management submitted its annual revision of the company's five-year forecast to the board. That report discussed alternative solutions to the ITC problem and concluded that the company had sufficient time to develop its course of action. The report did not mention the possible sale of the company.

On August 27, Van Gorkom met with senior management to consider the ITC problem. Among the ideas mentioned were selling Trans Union to a company with a large amount of taxable income and engaging in a leveraged buyout. This latter alternative was discussed again at a management meeting on September 5. At that meeting, the chief financial officer, Donald Romans, presented preliminary calculations for a leveraged buyout based on a price between $50 and $60 per share, but did not state that these calculations established a fair price for the company. They merely "ran the numbers" at $50 and $60 per share for a "rough" estimate of the cash flow needed for a leveraged buyout. While Van Gorkom rejected the leveraged buyout idea at the time, he stated that he would be willing to sell his own shares at $55 per share.

> **FYI**
>
> The named plaintiff in *Van Gorkom*, B. Alden Smith, was also motivated by tax concerns, but of a different kind. Smith's <u>main beef</u> with the deal was not the price, but the fact that it would trigger his obligation to pay capital gains taxes. Smith wanted the deal to be done as a tax-free reorganization in which he would receive stock instead of cash, but the board had decided differently. It would have been fruitless for Smith to challenge the board's decision about how to structure the deal—that would fall under the BJR—so he decided to institute a class action and challenge the way the board had decided on and disclosed the negotiations of the price instead.

Then, without consulting the board of directors or any officers, Van Gorkom decided to meet with Jay A. Pritzker, a corporate takeover specialist he knew socially. Prior to that meeting, Van Gorkom instructed Trans Union's controller, Carl Peterson, to prepare a confidential calculation of the feasibility of a leveraged buyout at $55 per share. On September 13, Van Gorkom proposed a sale of Trans Union to Pritzker at $55 per share. Two days later, Pritzker advised Van Gorkom that he was interested in a purchase at that price. By September 18, after two more meetings that included two Trans Union officers and an outside consultant, Van Gorkom knew that Pritzker was ready to propose a cash-out merger at $55 per share if Pritzker could also have the option to buy one million shares of Trans Union treasury stock at $38 per share (a price which was 75 cents above the current market price). Pritzker also insisted that the Trans Union board act on his proposal within three days, *i.e.*, by Sunday, September 21, and instructed his attorney to draft the merger documents.

On September 19, without consulting Trans Union's legal department, Van Gorkom engaged outside counsel as merger specialists. He called for meetings of senior management and the board of directors for the next day, but only those officers who had met with Pritzker knew the subject of the meetings.

Senior management's reaction to Pritzker's proposal was completely negative. Romans objected both to the price and to the sale of treasury shares (shares that Trans Union previously had repurchased in the market) to Pritzker as a "lock-up." Immediately after this meeting, Van Gorkom met with the board. He made a twenty-minute oral presentation outlining the Pritzker offer, but did not furnish copies of the proposed merger agreement. Nor did he tell the board that he was the one who had approached Pritzker and mentioned the $55 price. Van Gorkom stated that: Pritzker would purchase all outstanding Trans Union shares for $55 each and Trans Union would be merged into a wholly-owned entity Pritzker formed for this purpose; for 90 days Trans Union would be free to receive, but not to solicit competing offers; other bidders could be furnished only published, rather than proprietary, information; the Trans Union board had to act by Sunday evening, September 21; the offer was subject to Pritzker obtaining financing by October 10, 1980; and if Pritzker met or waived the financing contingency, Trans Union was obliged to sell him one million newly issued shares at $38 per share. According to Van Gorkom, the issue for the board was whether $55 was a fair price rather than the best price. He said that putting Trans Union "up for auction" through a 90-day "market test" would allow the free market an opportunity to judge whether $55 was fair. Outside counsel advised the board that they might be sued if they did not accept the offer, and that a fairness opinion from an investment banker was not legally required.

At the board meeting, Romans stated that his prior studies in connection with a possible leveraged buyout did not indicate a fair price for the stock or a valuation of the company. However, it was his opinion that $55 was "at the beginning of the range" of a fair price.

The board meeting lasted two hours, at the end of which the board approved the merger, with two conditions: (1) Trans Union reserved the right to accept any better offer during the 90-day market test period; and (2) Trans Union could share its proprietary information with other potential bidders. At that time, however, the board did not reserve the right actively to solicit other bids.

That evening Van Gorkom signed the as-yet-unamended merger agreement, still unread either by himself or the other board members, "in the midst of a formal party which he hosted for the opening of the Chicago Lyric Opera."

On September 22, Trans Union issued a press release announcing a "definitive" merger agreement with Marmon Group, Inc., an affiliate of a Pritzker holding company. Within ten days, rebellious key officers threatened to resign. Van Gorkom met with Pritzker, who agreed to modify the agreement to include the conditions imposed by the board, provided that the "dissident" officers agreed to stay with Trans Union for at least six months following the merger.

The board reconvened on October 8 and, without reading the text, approved the proposed amendments regarding the 90-day market test and solicitation of other bids. The board also authorized the company to employ its investment banker to solicit other offers.

Although the amendments had not yet been prepared, Trans Union issued a press release on the following day stating that it could actively seek other offers and had retained an investment banker for that purpose. The release also said that Pritzker had obtained the necessary financing commitments and had acquired one million shares of Trans Union at $38 per share and that if Trans Union had not received a more favorable offer by February 1, 1981, its shareholders would meet to vote on the Pritzker bid. Van Gorkom executed the amendments to the merger agreement on October 10, without consulting the board and apparently without fully understanding that the amendments significantly constrained Trans Union's ability to negotiate a better deal.

Trans Union received only two serious offers during the market test period. One, from General Electric Credit Corporation, fell through when Trans Union would not rescind its agreement with Pritzker to give GE Credit extra time. The other offer, a leveraged buyout by management (except Van Gorkom) arranged through Kohlberg, Kravis, Roberts & Co. (KKR) was made in early December at $60 per share. It was contingent upon completing equity and bank financing, which KKR said was 80% complete, with terms and conditions substantially the same as the Pritzker deal. Van Gorkom, however, did not view the KKR deal as "firm" because of the financing contingency (even though the Pritzker offer had been similarly conditioned) and he refused to issue a press release about it. KKR planned to present its offer to the Trans Union board, but withdrew shortly before the scheduled meeting, noting that a senior Trans Union officer had withdrawn from the KKR purchasing group after Van Gorkom spoke to him. Van Gorkom denied influencing the officer's decision, and he made no mention of it to the board at the meeting later that day.

The shareholder lawsuit was brought on December 19, 1980. Management's proxy statement was mailed on January 21 for a meeting scheduled for February 10, 1981. The Trans Union board met on January 26 and gave final approval to the Pritzker merger, as well as a supplement to its proxy statement that was mailed the next day. On February 10, 1981, the shareholders approved the Pritzker merger by a large majority.

Smith v. Van Gorkom

488 A.2d 858 (Del. 1985)

HORSEY, JUSTICE (for the majority).

We turn to the issue of the application of the business judgment rule to the September 20 meeting of the Board.

The Court of Chancery concluded from the evidence that the Board of Directors' approval of the Pritzker merger proposal fell within the protection of the business judgment rule. The Court found that the Board had given sufficient time and attention to the transaction, since the directors had considered the Pritzker proposal on three different occasions, on September 20, and on October 8, 1980 and finally on January 26, 1981. On that basis, the Court reasoned that the Board had acquired, over the four-month period, sufficient information to reach an informed business judgment on the cash-out merger proposal. The Court ruled:

> that given the market value of Trans Union's stock, the business acumen of the members of the board of Trans Union, the substantial premium over market offered by the Pritzkers and the ultimate effect on the merger price provided by the prospect of other bids for the stock in question, that the board of directors of Trans Union did not act recklessly or improvidently in determining on a course of action which they believed to be in the best interest of the stockholders of Trans Union.

The Court of Chancery made but one finding; *i.e.*, that the Board's conduct over the entire period from September 20 through January 26, 1981 was not reckless or improvident, but informed. This ultimate conclusion was premised upon three subordinate findings, one explicit and two implied. The Court's explicit finding was that Trans Union's Board was "free to turn down the Pritzker proposal" not only on September 20 but also on October 8, 1980 and on January 26, 1981. The Court's implied, subordinate findings were: (1) that no legally binding agreement was reached by the parties until January 26; and (2) that if a higher offer were to be forthcoming, the market test would have produced it, and Trans Union would have been contractually free to accept such higher offer. However, the Court offered no factual basis or legal support for any of these findings; and the record compels contrary conclusions.

Under Delaware law, the business judgment rule is the offspring of the fundamental principle, codified in 8 Del.C. § 141(a), that the business and affairs of a Delaware corporation are managed by or under its board of directors. In carrying out their managerial roles, directors are charged with an unyielding fiduciary duty to the corporation and its shareholders. The business judgment rule exists to protect and promote the full and free exercise of the managerial power granted to Delaware directors. The rule itself "is a presumption that in making a business decision, the directors of a corporation acted on an informed basis, in good faith and in the honest belief that the action taken was in the best interests of the company." *Aronson v. Lewis*, 473 A.2d 805, 812 (Del.1984). Thus, the party attacking a board decision as uninformed must rebut the presumption that its business judgment was an informed one.

The determination of whether a business judgment is an informed one turns on whether the directors have informed themselves "prior to making a business decision, of all material information reasonably available to them." *Id.*

Under the business judgment rule there is no protection for directors who have made "an unintelligent or unadvised judgment." *Mitchell v. Highland-Western Glass*, 167 A. 831, 833 (Del.Ch.1933). A director's duty to inform himself in preparation for a decision derives from the fiduciary capacity in which he serves the corporation and its stockholders. Since a director is vested with the responsibility for the management of the affairs of the corporation, he must execute that duty with the recognition that he acts on behalf of others. Such obligation does not tolerate faithlessness or self-dealing. But fulfillment of the fiduciary function requires more than the mere absence of bad faith or fraud. Representation of the financial interests of others imposes on a director an affirmative duty to protect those interests and to proceed with a critical eye in assessing information of the type and under the circumstances present here.

Thus, a director's duty to exercise an informed business judgment is in the nature of a duty of care, as distinguished from a duty of loyalty. Here, there were no allegations of fraud, bad faith, or self-dealing, or proof thereof. Hence, it is presumed that the directors reached their business judgment in good faith, and considerations of motive are irrelevant to the issue before us.

The standard of care applicable to a director's duty of care has also been recently restated by this Court. In *Aronson*, we stated:

> While the Delaware cases use a variety of terms to describe the applicable standard of care, our analysis satisfies us that under the business judgment rule director liability is predicated upon concepts of gross negligence. (footnote omitted)

We again confirm that view. We think the concept of gross negligence is also the proper standard for determining whether a business judgment reached by a board of directors was an informed one.

In the specific context of a proposed merger of domestic corporations, a director has a duty under 8 Del.C. § 251(b), along with his fellow directors, to act in an informed and deliberate manner in determining whether to approve an agreement of merger before submitting the proposal to the stockholders. Certainly in the merger context, a director may not abdicate that duty by leaving to the shareholders alone the decision to approve or disapprove the agreement. Only an agreement of merger satisfying the requirements of 8 Del.C. § 251(b) may be submitted to the shareholders under § 251(c).

It is against those standards that the conduct of the directors of Trans Union must be tested, as a matter of law and as a matter of fact, regarding their exercise of an informed business judgment in voting to approve the Pritzker merger proposal.

III.

The issue of whether the directors reached an informed decision to "sell" the Company on September 20, 1980 must be determined only upon the basis of the information then reasonably available to the directors and relevant to their decision to accept the Pritzker merger proposal. This is not to say that the directors were precluded from altering their original plan of action, had they done so in an informed manner. What we do say is that the question of whether the directors reached an informed business judgment in agreeing to sell the Company, pursuant to the terms of the September 20 Agreement presents, in reality, two questions: (A) whether the directors reached an informed business judgment on September 20, 1980; and (B) if they did not, whether the directors' actions taken subsequent to September 20 were adequate to cure any infirmity in their action taken on September 20. We first consider the directors' September 20 action in terms of their reaching an informed business judgment.

–A–

On the record before us, we must conclude that the Board of Directors did not reach an informed business judgment on September 20, 1980 in voting to "sell" the Company for $55 per share pursuant to the Pritzker cash-out merger proposal. Our reasons, in summary, are as follows:

The directors (1) did not adequately inform themselves as to Van Gorkom's role in forcing the "sale" of the Company and in establishing the per share purchase price; (2) were uninformed as to the intrinsic value of the Company; and (3) given these circumstances, at a minimum, were grossly negligent in approving the "sale" of the Company upon two hours' consideration, without prior notice, and without the exigency of a crisis or emergency.

As has been noted, the Board based its September 20 decision to approve the cash-out merger primarily on Van Gorkom's representations. None of the directors, other than Van Gorkom and Chelberg, had any prior knowledge that the purpose of the meeting was to propose a cash-out merger of Trans Union. No members of Senior Management were present, other than Chelberg, Romans and Peterson; and the latter two had only learned of the proposed sale an hour earlier. Both general counsel Moore and former general counsel Browder attended the meeting, but were equally uninformed as to the purpose of the meeting and the documents to be acted upon.

Without any documents before them concerning the proposed transaction, the members of the Board were required to rely entirely upon Van Gorkom's 20-minute oral presentation of the proposal. No written summary of the terms of the merger was presented; the directors were given no documentation to support the adequacy of $55 price per share for sale of the Company; and the Board had before it nothing more than Van Gorkom's statement of his understanding of the substance of an agreement which he admittedly had never read, nor which any member of the Board had ever seen.

Under 8 Del.C. § 141(e) "directors are fully protected in relying in good faith on reports made by officers." The term "report" has been liberally construed to include reports of informal personal investigations by corporate officers. However, there is no evidence that any "report," as defined under § 141(e), concerning the Pritzker proposal, was presented to the Board on September 20. Van Gorkom's oral presentation of his understanding of the terms of the proposed Merger Agreement, which he had not seen, and Romans' brief oral statement of his preliminary study regarding the feasibility of a leveraged buy-out of Trans Union do not qualify as § 141(e) "reports" for these reasons: The former lacked substance because Van Gorkom was basically uninformed as to the essential provisions of the very document about which he was talking. Romans' statement was irrelevant to the issues before the Board since it did not purport to be a valuation study. At a minimum for a report to enjoy the status conferred by § 141(e), it must be pertinent to the subject matter upon which a board is called to act, and otherwise be entitled to good faith, not blind, reliance. Considering all of the surrounding circumstances—hastily calling the meeting without prior notice of its subject matter, the proposed sale of the Company without any prior consideration of the issue or necessity therefore, the urgent time constraints imposed by Pritzker, and the total absence of any documentation whatsoever—the directors were duty bound to make reasonable inquiry of Van Gorkom and Romans, and if they had done so, the inadequacy of that upon which they now claim to have relied would have been apparent.

The defendants rely on the following factors to sustain the Trial Court's finding that the Board's decision was an informed one: (1) the magnitude of the premium or spread between the $55 Pritzker offering price and Trans Union's current market price of $38 per share; (2) the amendment of the Agreement as submitted on September 20 to permit the Board to accept any better offer during the "market test" period; (3) the collective experience and expertise of the Board's "inside" and "outside" directors; and (4) their reliance on Brennan's legal advice that the directors might be sued if they rejected the Pritzker proposal. We discuss each of these grounds *seriatim:*

(1)

A substantial premium may provide one reason to recommend a merger, but in the absence of other sound valuation information, the fact of a premium alone does not provide an adequate basis upon which to assess the fairness of an offering price. Here, the judgment reached as to the adequacy of the premium was based on a comparison between the historically depressed Trans Union market price and the amount of the Pritzker offer. Using market price as a basis for concluding that the premium adequately reflected the true value of the Company was a clearly faulty, indeed fallacious, premise, as the defendants' own evidence demonstrates.

The record is clear that before September 20, Van Gorkom and other members of Trans Union's Board knew that the market had consistently undervalued the worth of Trans Union's stock, despite steady increases in the Company's operating income in the seven years preceding the merger. The Board related this occurrence in large part to Trans Union's inability to use its ITCs as previously noted. Van Gorkom testified that he did not believe the market price accurately reflected Trans Union's true worth; and several of the directors testified that, as a general rule, most chief executives think that the market undervalues their companies' stock. Yet, on September 20, Trans Union's Board apparently believed that the market stock price accurately reflected the value of the Company for the purpose of determining the adequacy of the premium for its sale.

The parties do not dispute that a publicly-traded stock price is solely a measure of the value of a minority position and, thus, market price represents only the value of a single share. Nevertheless, on September 20, the Board assessed the adequacy of the premium over market, offered by Pritzker, solely by comparing it with Trans Union's current and historical stock price.

Indeed, as of September 20, the Board had no other information on which to base a determination of the intrinsic value of Trans Union as a going concern. As of September 20, the Board had made no evaluation of the Company designed to value the entire enterprise, nor had the Board ever previously considered selling the Company or consenting to a buy-out merger. Thus, the adequacy of a premium is indeterminate unless it is assessed in terms of other competent and sound valuation information that reflects the value of the particular business.

Despite the foregoing facts and circumstances, there was no call by the Board, either on September 20 or thereafter, for any valuation study or documentation of the $55 price per share as a measure of the fair value of the Company in a cash-out context. It is undisputed that the major asset of Trans Union was its cash flow. Yet, at no time did the Board call for a valuation study taking into account that highly significant element of the Company's assets.

We do not imply that an outside valuation study is essential to support an informed business judgment; nor do we state that fairness opinions by independent investment bankers are required as a matter of law. Often insiders familiar with the business of a going concern are in a better position than are outsiders to gather relevant information; and under appropriate circumstances, such directors may be fully protected in relying in good faith upon the valuation reports of their management.

Here, the record establishes that the Board did not request its Chief Financial Officer, Romans, to make any valuation study or review of the proposal to determine the adequacy of $55 per share for sale of the Company. The Board rested on Romans' elicited response that the $55 figure was within a "fair price range" within the context of a leveraged buy-out. No director sought any further information from Romans. No director asked him why he put $55 at the bottom of his range. No director asked Romans for any details as to his study, the reason why it had been undertaken or its depth. No director asked to see the study; and no director asked Romans whether Trans Union's finance department could do a fairness study within the remaining 36-hour period available under the Pritzker offer.

Had the Board, or any member, made an inquiry of Romans, he presumably would have responded as he testified: that his calculations were rough and preliminary; and, that the study was not designed to determine the fair value of the Company, but rather to assess the feasibility of a leveraged buy-out financed by the Company's projected cash flow, making certain assumptions as to the purchaser's borrowing needs. Romans would have presumably also informed the Board of his view, and the widespread view of Senior Management, that the timing of the offer was wrong and the offer inadequate.

The record also establishes that the Board accepted without scrutiny Van Gorkom's representation as to the fairness of the $55 price per share for sale of the Company—a subject that the Board had never previously considered. The Board thereby failed to discover that Van Gorkom had suggested the $55 price to Pritzker and, most crucially, that Van Gorkom had arrived at the $55 figure based on calculations designed solely to determine the feasibility of a leveraged buy-out.[19] No questions were raised either as to the tax implications of a cash-out merger or how the price for the one million share option granted Pritzker was calculated.

We do not say that the Board of Directors was not entitled to give some credence to Van Gorkom's representation that $55 was an adequate or fair price. Under § 141(e), the directors were entitled to rely upon their chairman's opinion of value and adequacy, provided that such opinion was reached on a sound basis. Here, the issue is whether the directors informed themselves as to all information that was reasonably available to them. Had they done so, they would have learned of the source and derivation of the $55 price and could not reasonably have relied thereupon in good faith.

None of the directors, Management or outside, were investment bankers or financial analysts. Yet the Board did not consider recessing the meeting until a later hour that day (or requesting an extension of Pritzker's Sunday evening deadline) to give it time to elicit more information as to the sufficiency of the offer, either from inside Management (in particular Romans) or from Trans Union's own investment banker, Salomon Brothers, whose Chicago specialist in merger and acquisitions was known to the Board and familiar with Trans Union's affairs.

---

[19] As of September 20 the directors did not know: that Van Gorkom had arrived at the $55 figure alone, and subjectively, as the figure to be used by Controller Peterson in creating a feasible structure for a leveraged buy-out by a prospective purchaser; that Van Gorkom had not sought advice, information or assistance from either inside or outside Trans Union directors as to the value of the Company as an entity or the fair price per share for 100% of its stock; that Van Gorkom had not consulted with the Company's investment bankers or other financial analysts; that Van Gorkom had not consulted with or confided in any officer or director of the Company except Chelberg; and that Van Gorkom had deliberately chosen to ignore the advice and opinion of the members of his Senior Management group regarding the adequacy of the $55 price.

Thus, the record compels the conclusion that on September 20 the Board lacked valuation information adequate to reach an informed business judgment as to the fairness of $55 per share for sale of the Company.

(2)

This brings us to the post-September 20 "market test" upon which the defendants ultimately rely to confirm the reasonableness of their September 20 decision to accept the Pritzker proposal. In this connection, the directors present a two-part argument: (a) that by making a "market test" of Pritzker's $55 per share offer a condition of their September 20 decision to accept his offer, they cannot be found to have acted impulsively or in an uninformed manner on September 20; and (b) that the adequacy of the $17 premium for sale of the Company was conclusively established over the following 90 to 120 days by the most reliable evidence available—the marketplace. Thus, the defendants impliedly contend that the "market test" eliminated the need for the Board to perform any other form of fairness test either on September 20, or thereafter.

Again, the facts of record do not support the defendants' argument. There is no evidence: (a) that the Merger Agreement was effectively amended to give the Board freedom to put Trans Union up for auction sale to the highest bidder; or (b) that a public auction was in fact permitted to occur.

(3)

The directors' unfounded reliance on both the premium and the market test as the basis for accepting the Pritzker proposal undermines the defendants' remaining contention that the Board's collective experience and sophistication was a sufficient basis for finding that it reached its September 20 decision with informed, reasonable deliberation.[21] Compare *Gimbel v. Signal Companies, Inc.*, 316 A.2d 599 (Del.Ch.1974), *aff'd per curiam*, 316 A.2d 619 (Del.1974). There, the Court of Chancery preliminarily enjoined a board's sale of stock of its wholly-owned subsidiary for an alleged grossly inadequate price. It did so based on a finding that the business judgment rule had been pierced for failure of management to give its board "the opportunity to make a reasonable and reasoned decision." The Court there reached this result notwithstanding the board's sophistication

---

[21] Trans Union's five "inside" directors had backgrounds in law and accounting, 116 years of collective employment by the Company and 68 years of combined experience on its Board. Trans Union's five "outside" directors included four chief executives of major corporations and an economist who was a former dean of a major school of business and chancellor of a university. The "outside" directors had 78 years of combined experience as chief executive officers of major corporations and 50 years of cumulative experience as directors of Trans Union. Thus, defendants argue that the Board was eminently qualified to reach an informed judgment on the proposed "sale" of Trans Union notwithstanding their lack of any advance notice of the proposal, the shortness of their deliberation, and their determination not to consult with their investment banker or to obtain a fairness opinion.

and experience; the company's need of immediate cash; and the board's need to act promptly due to the impact of an energy crisis on the value of the underlying assets being sold—all of its subsidiary's oil and gas interests. The Court found those factors denoting competence to be outweighed by evidence of gross negligence; that management in effect sprang the deal on the board by negotiating the asset sale without informing the board; that the buyer intended to "force a quick decision" by the board; that the board meeting was called on only one-and-a-half days' notice; that its outside directors were not notified of the meeting's purpose; that during a meeting spanning "a couple of hours" a sale of assets worth $480 million was approved; and that the Board failed to obtain a *current* appraisal of its oil and gas interests. The analogy of *Signal* to the case at bar is significant.

(4)

Part of the defense is based on a claim that the directors relied on legal advice rendered at the September 20 meeting by James Brennan, Esquire, who was present at Van Gorkom's request. Unfortunately, Brennan did not appear and testify at trial even though his firm participated in the defense of this action.

Several defendants testified that Brennan advised them that Delaware law did not require a fairness opinion or an outside valuation of the Company before the Board could act on the Pritzker proposal. If given, the advice was correct. However, that did not end the matter. Unless the directors had before them adequate information regarding the intrinsic value of the Company, upon which a proper exercise of business judgment could be made, mere advice of this type is meaningless; and, given this record of the defendants' failures, it constitutes no defense here.[22]

A second claim is that counsel advised the Board it would be subject to lawsuits if it rejected the $55 per share offer. It is, of course, a fact of corporate life that today when faced with difficult or sensitive issues, directors often are subject to suit, irrespective of the decisions they make. However, counsel's mere acknowledgement of this circumstance cannot be rationally translated into a justification for a board permitting itself to be stampeded into a patently unadvised act. While suit might result from the rejection of a merger or tender offer, Delaware law makes clear that a board acting within the ambit of the business judgment rule faces no ultimate liability. Thus, we cannot conclude that the mere threat of litigation, acknowledged by counsel, constitutes either legal advice or any valid basis upon which to pursue an uninformed course.

---

[22] Nonetheless, we are satisfied that in an appropriate factual context a proper exercise of business judgment may include, as one of its aspects, reasonable reliance upon the advice of counsel. This is wholly outside the statutory protections of 8 Del.C. § 141(e) involving reliance upon reports of officers, certain experts and books and records of the company.

–B–

[The court examined the board's post-September 20 conduct and determined this conduct did not cure the deficiencies in its September 20 actions.]

IV.

As to questions which were not originally addressed by the parties in their briefing of this case the parties' response, including reargument, has led the majority of the Court to conclude: (1) that since all of the defendant directors, outside as well as inside, take a unified position, we are required to treat all of the directors as one as to whether they are entitled to the protection of the business judgment rule; and (2) that considerations of good faith, including the presumption that the directors acted in good faith, are irrelevant in determining the threshold issue of whether the directors as a Board exercised an informed business judgment. For the same reason, we must reject defense counsel's *ad hominem* argument for affirmance: that reversal may result in a multi-million dollar class award against the defendants for having made an allegedly uninformed business judgment in a transaction not involving any personal gain, self-dealing or claim of bad faith.

Plaintiffs have not claimed, nor did the Trial Court decide, that $55 was a grossly inadequate price per share for sale of the Company. That being so, the presumption that a board's judgment as to adequacy of price represents an honest exercise of business judgment (absent proof that the sale price was grossly inadequate) is irrelevant to the threshold question of whether an informed judgment was reached.

V.

The defendants ultimately rely on the stockholder vote of February 10 for exoneration. The defendants contend that the stockholders' "overwhelming" vote approving the Pritzker Merger Agreement had the legal effect of curing any failure of the Board to reach an informed business judgment in its approval of the merger.

The parties tacitly agree that a discovered failure of the Board to reach an informed business judgment in approving the merger constitutes a voidable, rather than a void, act. Hence, the merger can be sustained, notwithstanding the infirmity of the Board's action, if its approval by majority vote of the shareholders is found to have been based on an informed electorate. *Cf. Michelson v. Duncan*, 407 A.2d 211 (Del.1979), *aff'g in part and rev'g in part*, 386 A.2d 1144 (Del. Ch.1978). The disagreement between the parties arises over: (1) the Board's burden of disclosing to the shareholders all relevant and material information; and (2) the sufficiency of the evidence as to whether the Board satisfied that burden.

In *Lynch v. Vickers Energy Corp.*, this Court held that corporate directors owe to their stockholders a fiduciary duty to disclose all facts germane to the transaction at issue in an atmosphere of complete candor. Applying this standard to the record before us, we find that Trans Union's stockholders were not fully informed of all facts material to their vote on the Pritzker Merger and that the Trial Court's ruling to the contrary is clearly erroneous. We list the material deficiencies in the proxy materials: (1) The fact that the Board had no reasonably adequate information indicative of the intrinsic value of the Company, other than a concededly depressed market price, was without question material to the shareholders voting on the merger. (2) We find false and misleading the Board's characterization of the Romans report in the Supplemental Proxy Statement. Nowhere does the Board disclose that Romans stated to the Board that his calculations were made in a "search for ways to justify a price in connection with" a leveraged buy-out transaction, "rather than to say what the shares are worth." (3) We find misleading the Board's references to the "substantial" premium offered. The Board gave as their primary reason in support of the merger the "substantial premium" shareholders would receive. But the Board did not disclose its failure to assess the premium offered in terms of other relevant valuation techniques, thereby rendering questionable its determination as to the substantiality of the premium over an admittedly depressed stock market price.

The burden must fall on defendants who claim ratification based on shareholder vote to establish that the shareholder approval resulted from a fully informed electorate. On the record before us, it is clear that the Board failed to meet that burden.

VI.

To summarize: we hold that the directors of Trans Union breached their fiduciary duty to their stockholders (1) by their failure to inform themselves of all information reasonably available to them and relevant to their decision to recommend the Pritzker merger; and (2) by their failure to disclose all material information such as a reasonable stockholder would consider important in deciding whether to approve the Pritzker offer.

We hold, therefore, that the Trial Court committed reversible error in applying the business judgment rule in favor of the director defendants in this case.

On remand, the Court of Chancery shall conduct an evidentiary hearing to determine the fair value of the shares represented by the plaintiffs' class, based on the intrinsic value of Trans Union on September 20, 1980. Thereafter, an award of damages may be entered to the extent that the fair value of Trans Union exceeds $55 per share.

Reversed and Remanded for proceedings consistent herewith.

McNEILLY, JUSTICE, dissenting:

The majority opinion reads like an advocate's closing address to a hostile jury. And I say that not lightly. Throughout the opinion great emphasis is directed only to the negative, with nothing more than lip service granted the positive aspects of this case. In my opinion Chancellor Marvel (retired) should have been affirmed. The Chancellor's opinion was the product of well reasoned conclusions, based upon a sound deductive process, clearly supported by the evidence and entitled to deference in this appeal. Because of my diametrical opposition to all evidentiary conclusions of the majority, I respectfully dissent.

It would serve no useful purpose, particularly at this late date, for me to dissent at great length. I restrain myself from doing so, but feel compelled to at least point out what I consider to be the most glaring deficiencies in the majority opinion. The majority has spoken and has effectively said that Trans Union's Directors have been the victims of a "fast shuffle" by Van Gorkom and Pritzker. That is the beginning of the majority's comedy of errors. The first and most important error made is the majority's assessment of the directors' knowledge of the affairs of Trans Union and their combined ability to act in this situation under the protection of the business judgment rule.

Trans Union's Board of Directors consisted of ten men, five of whom were "inside" directors and five of whom were "outside" directors. The "inside" directors were Van Gorkom, Chelberg, Bonser, William B. Browder, Senior Vice–President–Law, and Thomas P. O'Boyle, Senior Vice–President–Administration. At the time the merger was proposed the inside five directors had collectively been employed by the Company for 116 years and had 68 years of combined experience as directors. The "outside" directors were A.W. Wallis, William B. Johnson, Joseph B. Lanterman, Graham J. Morgan and Robert W. Reneker. With the exception of Wallis, these were all chief executive officers of Chicago based corporations that were at least as large as Trans Union. The five "outside" directors had 78 years of combined experience as chief executive officers, and 53 years cumulative service as Trans Union directors.

The inside directors wear their badge of expertise in the corporate affairs of Trans Union on their sleeves. But what about the outsiders? Dr. Wallis is or was an economist and math statistician, a professor of economics at Yale University, dean of the graduate school of business at the University of Chicago, and Chancellor of the University of Rochester. Dr. Wallis had been on the Board of Trans Union since 1962. He also was on the Board of Bausch & Lomb, Kodak, Metropolitan Life Insurance Company, Standard Oil and others.

William B. Johnson is a University of Pennsylvania law graduate, President of Railway Express until 1966, Chairman and Chief Executive of I.C. Industries Holding Company, and member of Trans Union's Board since 1968.

Joseph Lanterman, a Certified Public Accountant, is or was President and Chief Executive of American Steel, on the Board of International Harvester, Peoples Energy, Illinois Bell Telephone, Harris Bank and Trust Company, Kemper Insurance Company and a director of Trans Union for four years.

Graham Morgan is a chemist, was Chairman and Chief Executive Officer of U.S. Gypsum, and in the 17 and 18 years prior to the Trans Union transaction had been involved in 31 or 32 corporate takeovers.

Robert Reneker attended University of Chicago and Harvard Business Schools. He was President and Chief Executive of Swift and Company, director of Trans Union since 1971, and member of the Boards of seven other corporations including U.S. Gypsum and the Chicago Tribune.

Directors of this caliber are not ordinarily taken in by a "fast shuffle." I submit they were not taken into this multi-million dollar corporate transaction without being fully informed and aware of the state of the art as it pertained to the entire corporate panorama of Trans Union. True, even directors such as these, with their business acumen, interest and expertise, can go astray. I do not believe that to be the case here. These men knew Trans Union like the back of their hands and were more than well qualified to make on the spot informed business judgments concerning the affairs of Trans Union including a 100% sale of the corporation. Lest we forget, the corporate world of then and now operates on what is so aptly referred to as "the fast track." These men were at the time an integral part of that world, all professional business men, not intellectual figureheads.

The majority of this Court holds that the Board's decision, reached on September 20, 1980, to approve the merger was not the product of an *informed* business judgment, that the Board's subsequent efforts to amend the Merger Agreement and take other curative action were *legally and factually* ineffectual, and that the Board did *not deal with complete candor* with the stockholders by failing to disclose all material facts, which they knew or should have known, before securing the stockholders' approval of the merger. I disagree.

At the time of the September 20, 1980 meeting the Board was acutely aware of Trans Union and its prospects. The problems created by accumulated investment tax credits and accelerated depreciation were discussed repeatedly at Board meetings, and all of the directors understood the problem thoroughly. Moreover, at the July 1980 Board meeting the directors had reviewed Trans Union's newly prepared five-year forecast, and at the August 1980 meeting Van Gorkom presented the results of a comprehensive study of Trans Union made by The Boston Consulting Group. This study was prepared over an 18 month period and consisted of a detailed analysis of all Trans Union subsidiaries, including competitiveness, profitability, cash throw-off, cash consumption, technical competence and future prospects for contribution to Trans Union's combined net income.

At the September 20 meeting Van Gorkom reviewed all aspects of the proposed transaction and repeated the explanation of the Pritzker offer he had earlier given to senior management. Having heard Van Gorkom's explanation of the Pritzker's offer, and Brennan's explanation of the merger documents the directors discussed the matter. Out of this discussion arose an insistence on the part of the directors that two modifications to the offer be made. First, they required that any potential competing bidder be given access to the same information concerning Trans Union that had been provided to the Pritzkers. Second, the merger documents were to be modified to reflect the fact that the directors could accept a better offer and would not be required to recommend the Pritzker offer if a better offer was made.

I have no quarrel with the majority's analysis of the business judgment rule. It is the application of that rule to these facts which is wrong. An overview of the entire record, rather than the limited view of bits and pieces which the majority has exploded like popcorn, convinces me that the directors made an informed business judgment which was buttressed by their test of the market.

———

2. Aftermath of the Case

The defendant directors of Trans Union settled *Van Gorkom* by agreeing to pay $23.5 million to the plaintiff class. The payments were made to approximately 12,000 former shareholders of Trans Union who held stock between September 19, 1980 and February 10, 1981. Of that amount, the directors' liability insurance carrier paid about $10 million. The $13.5 million balance was paid by the Pritzker group on behalf of the Trans Union directors, even though the Pritzker group was not a defendant. The Pritzker group made the payment on the condition the individual directors would each contribute 10% of their uninsured liability to a charity of Pritzker's choice, although Van Gorkom actually ended up making charitable contributions on behalf of some of the directors.

Van Gorkom created a firestorm in much of the corporate community and among academics, judges, and commentators. Few had believed that the Delaware Supreme Court would hold experienced directors personally liable in a case in which the shareholders received a 50% premium over the existing market price for their stock. Some criticized *Van Gorkom* as a fundamentally misguided decision, one of the worst in corporate law. Others praised the case for its focus on corporate governance and fiduciary duty.

Lawyers and corporate directors continue to discuss the decision, and its role in the history of corporate law. As you can see from the roundtable discussion below, the embers of the firestorm still glowed fifteen years after the decision:

Ira Millstein: This case sent shock waves through the boardrooms of the United States because I guarantee you 99% of boards didn't think that anything wrong had happened. Most everybody wrote about the decision as "the Delaware courts are going nuts." Most academics thought it was crazy. Most directors were horrified.

Boris Yavitz: What Ira is describing as a typical board is pretty much what I saw in the very early years of my service, which goes back to about 1975. Most boards were not much more than rubber stamps. The CEO said "Jump" and directors were allowed just one question: How high? It wasn't a matter of not arguing with the boss—you typically didn't even question him.

Steven Friedman: Everybody seems to imply that the process was wrong but the end result was right. You see in the published accounts that KKR was willing to pay $60, and also that GE Capital was willing to pay more. Both of them were turned off by the fact that there was a signed merger agreement and a clear message of "Don't mess with my deal." So I think that we should criticize this board not just for the process but for their decision.

Boris Yavitz: What happened is that all directors got the message: It is *procedure, procedure, procedure* that counts. Everything else doesn't mean very much. We were clearly panicked about what could happen if we didn't do what the lawyers said. We went through a tightly scripted process, which we hoped would end up with us not being sued but, even more hopefully, end up with the right decision. It was of great concern to me that we directors seemed to abandon much of our judgment to the security guards.

Ira Millstein: On behalf of the legal community, I will say that this was happening for a good reason, which was that you *hadn't* been doing your job. What happened with *Smith v. Van Gorkom* is it gave the lawyers an opportunity to act like lawyers for change. Most lawyers knew generally what was required—that the board had to make a good faith judgment. But if you went into a boardroom before *Smith v. Van Gorkom* and tried to talk about legal obligations, they'd say, "We have more important things to do than listen to you tell us about what we ought to be doing." When *Smith* came down, you were able to walk into a boardroom for the first time in my experience and really be heard. That was a good thing to have happen. Up until then it was more missionary work— talking about good and evil and how you really "ought" to do your jobs.

Roundtable: The Legacy of "Smith v. Van Gorkom," 24 Directors and Boards 28, 32–37 (Spring 2000).

Points for Discussion

1. Becoming informed.

Van Gorkom focused attention on the board decision-making process. Spurred in part by the case, a certain board meeting decorum has come to be understood as standard. The Official Comment to MBCA § 8.30(b) describes the standard of conduct for how directors should become informed:

> The phrase "becoming informed," in the context of the decision-making function, refers to the process of gaining sufficient familiarity with the background facts and circumstances in order to make an informed judgment. Unless the circumstances would permit a reasonable director to conclude that he or she is already sufficiently informed, the standard of care requires every director to take steps to become informed about the background facts and circumstances before taking action on the matter at hand. The process typically involves review of written materials provided before or at the meeting and attention to/participation in the deliberations leading up to a vote. It can involve consideration of information and data generated by persons other than legal counsel, public accountants, etc., retained by the corporation, as contemplated by subsection (e)(2); for example, review of industry studies or research articles prepared by unrelated parties could be very useful. It can also involve direct communications, outside of the boardroom, with members of management or other directors. There is no one way for "becoming informed," and both the method and measure—"how to" and "how much"—are matters of reasonable judgment for the director to exercise.

Does this description suggest that board decision making must adhere to standards of boardroom "due process," as some commentators reading the case have suggested?

2. Individual vs. collective decision making.

Is every director individually required to perform duties in good faith and in a manner they believe is in the best interests of the corporation? Or is the standard of conduct applied to the board as a whole? Boards generally are collegial bodies that make collective decisions. So what should the court do if a particular director plays a more prominent role? Conversely, what if one director is a slacker? Can deficient performance of one director be overcome? Or does every director need to be sufficiently informed? Suppose that the Trans Union defendants had accepted the court's invitation to invoke individual defenses. What legal theory would the court have used to exonerate individual directors, even though the court found the directors collectively to have been grossly negligent in not being fully informed about the fair value of Trans Union? Are there varying degrees of gross negligence for different directors? These questions remain difficult, and open.

3. Reliance.

Directors frequently rely on opinions provided by attorneys, accountants, engineers, financial specialists, and other expert professional advisors. In general, such reliance is justified and protects directors who rely on such advice in good faith, even if the advice turns out to be poor. In *Van Gorkom*, the court rejected the directors' argument that they were protected from liability because they relied on the information that Van Gorkom presented to them. Was that decision sound policy? Or should the directors have been entitled to rely on the information? Reliance might not be justified if a report contains on its face sufficient warning of its own inadequacy to put a reasonable director on notice that better information should be demanded. And reports prepared by or under the supervision of corporate employees who have a personal interest in the outcome of the decision on which they bear may require closer scrutiny than usual. How much homework do you think a director should do before relying on others?

4. Causation.

In decision-making cases, the plaintiffs charge that if directors had been sufficiently informed they would not have approved the deal that caused losses to the corporation or its shareholders. In other words, plaintiffs allege that the defendant directors' breach of duty, and not other factors, caused the loss. For example, in *Van Gorkom* the plaintiffs established that Trans Union's directors had been grossly negligent in agreeing to sell the company for $55 per share. However, that did not necessarily mean the directors were liable, because their gross negligence might not have caused any damages. Indeed, the Delaware Supreme Court remanded the case with instructions that the Court of Chancery "conduct an evidentiary hearing to determine the fair value of Trans Union's stock as of the date of the board's decision. Thereafter, an award of damages may be entered to the extent that the fair value of Trans Union exceeds $55 per share." The implication of the Supreme Court's use of "may" appeared to be that if the Court of Chancery determined Trans Union had not been worth more than $55 per share, no damages would be awarded.

Should the court in *Van Gorkom* have addressed causation earlier in its decision, before conducting a detailed inquiry into the board's conduct?

5. Fairness opinions.

One significant issue in *Van Gorkom* was whether the board was required to seek a "fairness opinion" from an investment bank. Although the court did not hold that such an opinion is really required, many commentators and lawyers have assumed that a fairness opinion is a necessity in every corporate acquisition. In fact, the

Trans Union board may actually have been presented with a valuation study of the company before the first September meeting. According to Robert Pritzker (brother of Jay Pritzker and later CEO of the Marmon Group), the Boston Consulting Group had prepared an 18-month study of Trans Union, which apparently concluded the company had a value of $55/share. The Delaware Supreme Court was aware of the Boston Consulting Group study, and Justice McNeilly's dissent refers to it as "a comprehensive study" supporting his conclusion that the board was "acutely aware of Trans Union and its prospects." The majority opinion in a footnote, however, states "no one even referred to [the Boston Consulting Group study] at the September 20 meeting; and it is conceded that these materials do not represent valuation studies." What role should a fairness opinion have played in the merger decision, and in the case? What are the pros and cons of fairness opinions?

FYI

The value of Pritzker's option to buy Trans Union shares can be calculated with some precision using the Black-Scholes option pricing model. Only a handful of data points is required, and it is not necessary to understand the intricacies of the model in order to intuit and use its results. Versions of the model are available online for free—just search for "Black-Scholes option pricing model."

Some of the data required are given in the case; the other data are available elsewhere. The six required variables are: (1) the stock price at the time the option was granted, (2) the exercise price of the option, (3) the time remaining before expiration, (4) the risk-free interest rate, (5) the stock's dividend yield, and (6) the stock's volatility.

We can look at data from the case and other sources: (1) the stock price at the relevant time is given in the opinion as $37.25; (2) the exercise price of the option also is given, $38; (3) the time remaining before expiration is 134 days, the number of days from September 20, 1980, until February 1, 1981; (4) the risk-free interest rate in effect until the date of maturity of the option, based on available data for the yields on comparable maturity United States treasury bills, was 10.17%; (5) given that Trans Union paid an annual dividend of $2.36 per share during 1980, its dividend yield was approximately 6.3%.

The remaining variable, volatility, is more difficult to estimate. The most accurate method of estimating volatility would be to calculate the volatility implied by the prices of Trans Union options being traded in September 1980; however, there were no such options traded at the time. The next most accurate method is to calculate volatility using historical prices of Trans Union stock. This method suggests a volatility measure of approximately 25.4%. Given these data, the Black-Scholes estimate of the value of Pritzker's option on September 20 is approximately $2.48 million. The table below summarizes these results.

Stock Price	$37.25
Exercise Price	$38.00
Days to Expiration	134
Risk-free Rate	10.17%
Dividend Yield	6.30%
Volatility	29.30%
Option Value	$2.48 per share

The bottom line is that the grant of one million options to Pritzker on September 20, 1980, was extremely valuable ($2.48 million). Suppose that instead of granting Pritzker an option, the board had given him a suitcase filled with that much cash. Would that have changed the board's approach? Or the court's? Likewise, Van Gorkom's negotiation of the option down to one million from 1.75 million shares saved Trans Union a considerable sum of money—about $1.8 million.

Today, one would expect both the prospective purchaser of a company and its board to attempt to evaluate such an option using the above methodology. In such instances, lawyers advising participants in mergers need to understand the basics of option valuation. Trans Union's directors, and its counsel, might have fared better if they had.

C. Avoiding Director Liability

In this final section, we address three ways directors can avoid personal liability: exculpation, indemnification, and insurance. First, in large part as a reaction to *Van Gorkom*, many states enacted legislation during the 1980s to reduce the risk of directors' personal liability for monetary damages. These statutes permitted corporations to include in their charters "exculpation" provisions, which eliminated or reduced the personal liability of directors for monetary damages. Although this legislative reaction was focused on the decision-making context, the statutes apply more generally to exculpate director actions in other settings. (In other words, although we introduce exculpation in this chapter, you should keep in mind that exculpation provisions also can apply to director liability in other contexts, including setting executive compensation (Chapter 22, Executive Compensation) and board oversight of corporate legal compliance (Chapter 23, Board Oversight).

In addition, corporate statutes permit corporations to "indemnify" directors, not only for liability, but for the expenses of defending against lawsuits. The details of indemnification statutes can be complicated, but they generally permit corporations to protect directors in even broader contexts than those covered by exculpation.

Finally, corporations may "insure" directors against liability, sometimes in ways that go beyond indemnification. Such director and officer, or D&O, insurance is common, and serves as yet another protection for directors.

1. Exculpation

Our discussion of exculpation begins with DGCL § 102(b)(7), which was adopted by the Delaware legislature in response to *Van Gorkom*. Section 102(b)

(7) permits Delaware corporations to adopt charter provisions limiting directors' personal liability for certain breaches of duty. The statute is not self-executing. The board must propose and the shareholders must adopt any exculpatory provision in the articles of incorporation.

DGCL § 102
Contents of Certificate of Incorporation

(b) the certificate of incorporation may also contain any or all of the following matters:

(7) A provision eliminating or limiting the personal liability of a director to the corporation or its stockholders for monetary damages for breach of fiduciary duty as a director, provided that such provision shall not eliminate or limit the liability of a director:

(i) For any breach of the director's duty of loyalty to the corporation or its stockholders;

(ii) for acts or omissions not in good faith or which involve intentional misconduct or a knowing violation of law;

(iii) under § 174 of this title [which covers unlawful payment of dividends]; or

(iv) for any transaction from which the director derived an improper personal benefit.

---

a. Exculpation Exclusions

Section 102(b)(7) does not permit corporations to limit directors' personal liability for all breaches of duty. Instead, there are four exceptions. Looking at subsections (i) and (iv), you'll notice they cover situations involving violations of the duty of loyalty and improper personal benefits to directors. In interpreting these "loyalty"-focused exclusions, the Delaware courts initially assumed that there was a clear dividing line between cases involving breaches of the duty of care compared to breaches of the duty of loyalty. As we have discussed, that care-loyalty dividing line is no longer clear, and as you will see in the chapters on executive compensation and board oversight, it is becoming increasingly blurred. It doesn't help that the terms "duty of loyalty" and "not in good faith" are not defined in the statute.

The result is that plaintiffs' attorneys will often try to characterize conduct as implicating the duty of loyalty and thus excluded from exculpation under subsection (i) of Section 102(b)(7). Indeed, some cases can be reframed as involving self interest rather than gross negligence. For example, the plaintiff in *Van Gorkom* might have argued that Van Gorkom acted out of a desire to maximize his personal gain before his impending retirement and the other directors acceded to his "fast shuffle." The contours of the duty of loyalty are covered in greater detail in Chapter 21, Director Conflicts.

As for subsection (iii) of Section 102(b)(7), recall from the discussion of capital structure in Chapter 12 that directors can be personally liable for declaring dividends or approving other distributions that violate the legal capital requirements. Whatever you might think of the wisdom of legal capital restrictions on corporate distributions, corporations cannot exculpate directors from liability for violating those restrictions. In other words, even after Section 102(b)(7), directors are always potentially on the hook for declaring an improper dividend.

The remaining subsection (ii) of Section 102(b)(7) has proved to be the most important. It has three parts, which we can label "not in good faith," "intentional misconduct," and "knowing violations." The second two parts are relatively straightforward. If a director engages in intentional or knowing wrongdoing, the director remains potentially liable. That is, we can think of directors as having a duty of obedience to corporate norms and non-corporate law that cannot be exculpated.

The key remaining phrase—"not in good faith"—has been an important focus of the courts for more than a decade. Whether a director's actions are "not in good faith"—which the Delaware courts have understood to mean the director "consciously disregarded" his or her duties—often will be the determining factor in deciding if he or she can be personally liable. Good faith will be the critical issue in several of the cases we look at in this module on corporate fiduciary duties, particularly in Chapter 22, Executive Compensation, and Chapter 23, Board Oversight.

As with the "duty of loyalty" exclusion, there is ambiguity about whether a director's conduct can be described as in good faith or not in good faith. Can a director act in good faith and yet be grossly negligent? To avoid director exculpation, plaintiffs' attorneys will plead that particular director action was "not in good faith," and courts will have to determine whether that action is exculpated. For example, *Van Gorkom* found that the directors' failure to inform themselves constituted gross negligence. But what if the plaintiff had alleged that the directors actions were "not in good faith." As we will see, a lot rides on the judicial determination of what "not in good faith" means.

b. Compare Delaware and MBCA

Other state statutes resemble Delaware's in some ways, but differ in others. For example, MBCA § 2.02(b)(4) permits corporations to adopt a charter provision to reduce or exculpate directors' personal liability for certain fiduciary duty breaches. The MBCA excludes from its coverage liability for improperly received financial benefits, intentional infliction of harm on the corporation or the shareholders, intentional violations of criminal law, and unlawful distributions, including dividends. Thus, the MBCA avoids the Delaware terms of "duty of loyalty" and "not in good faith," but introduces questions about what is an "improper financial benefit" or "intentional infliction of harm."

One thing you should notice is that both the Delaware and MBCA exculpation provisions apply only to liability for monetary damages; they do not permit corporations to exculpate directors from equitable relief for breaching their fiduciary duties. In addition, both provisions require that the exculpation provision be placed in the articles, thus requiring shareholder approval.

c. Policy Questions

Exculpating directors raises serious public policy questions. Why shouldn't directors be liable for grossly negligent actions? Why should a one-time vote by shareholders insulate directors from personal liability forever? On the other hand, if corporations can exculpate directors from liability for gross negligence, why not permit them to go further? If shareholders want to exculpate their directors from violations of the duty of loyalty, why shouldn't they be permitted to do so? And should claims against directors for breaching their fiduciary duties hinge on how plaintiffs' lawyers frame the claims and how judges interpret them?

Take Note!

Note that the exculpation statutes allow for exculpation of directors, but not officers or other corporate agents. The reasons for exculpating directors—to encourage risk-taking in making decisions on the board and to allow detachment in overseeing corporate activities—do not apply as strongly for officers and others involved in the day-to-day management of the corporation. As a result, plaintiffs will sometimes point to actions taken by corporate officials in their non-directorial capacities. But as we will see below, the policy reasons for permitting exculpation of directors, but not officers, do not apply to indemnification and insurance when officers face personal liability for acting in their corporate capacity.

2. Indemnification

Exculpation is not the only way corporations can help directors avoid the threat of personal liability. Corporations also can directly pay for, or reimburse, the damages and costs of directors and officers, as well as other corporate officials. Corporate statutes provide for both permissive and mandatory indemnification. In analyzing indemnification issues, you can think of three categories.

First are the payments that corporations may indemnify (permissive). Second are the payments that corporations must indemnify (mandatory). Third are the payments that corporations may not indemnify (prohibited). The statutes attempt to draw the lines among these three categories.

Historically, courts addressed indemnification issues case by case, with unclear and often unsatisfactory results. In 1941, New York enacted the first indemnification statute. Today, every state has adopted such a statute, and many are comprehensive.

a. Permissive Indemnification

We now consider Delaware's approach to indemnification in greater detail. The provisions are contained in DGCL § 145. Sections 145(a) and (b) provide for permissive indemnification. Section 145(a) covers lawsuits brought by third parties, including class actions. Section 145(b) applies to derivative actions brought on behalf of the corporation. Thus, you'll notice the direct-derivative distinction that we discussed in the previous chapter also matters to indemnification.

The Delaware statutory provisions are a bit of a slog, but worth the effort. As you read them, notice (1) who is covered, (2) what is indemnified, (3) the standards of conduct required for indemnification, and (4) the effect of an action being concluded against the covered person.

DGCL § 145

Indemnification of Officers, Directors, Employees and Agents

(a) A corporation shall have power to indemnify any person who was or is a party or is threatened to be made a party to any threatened, pending or completed action, suit or proceeding, whether civil, criminal, administrative or investigative (other than an action by or in the right of the corporation) by reason of the fact that the person is or was a director, officer, employee or agent of the corporation, or is or was serving at the request of the corporation as a director, officer, employee or agent of another corporation, partnership, joint venture, trust or other enterprise, against expenses (including attorneys' fees), judgments, fines and amounts paid in settlement actually and reasonably incurred by the person in connection with such action, suit or proceeding if the person acted in good faith and in a manner the person reasonably believed to be in or not opposed to the best interests of the corporation, and, with respect to any criminal action or proceeding, had no reasonable cause to believe the person's conduct was unlawful. The termination of any action, suit or proceeding by judgment, order, settlement, conviction, or upon a plea of nolo contendere or its equivalent, shall not, of itself, create a presumption that the person did not act in good faith and in a manner which the person reasonably believed to be in or not opposed to the best interests of the corporation, and, with respect to any criminal action or proceeding, had reasonable cause to believe that the person's conduct was unlawful.

(b) A corporation shall have power to indemnify any person who was or is a party or is threatened to be made a party to any threatened, pending or completed action or suit by or in the right of the corporation to procure a judgment in its favor by reason of the fact that the person is or was a director, officer, employee or agent of the corporation, or is or was serving at the request of the corporation as a director, officer, employee or agent of another corporation, partnership, joint venture, trust or other enterprise against expenses (including attorneys' fees) actually and reasonably incurred by the person in connection with the defense or settlement of such action or suit if the person acted in good faith and in a manner the person reasonably believed to be in or not opposed to the best interests of the corporation and except that no indemnification shall be made in respect of any claim, issue or matter as to which such person shall have been adjudged to be liable to the corporation unless and only to the extent that the Court of Chancery or the court in which such action or suit was brought shall determine upon application that, despite the adjudication of liability but in view of all the circumstances of the case, such person is fairly and reasonably entitled to indemnity for such expenses which the Court of Chancery or such other court shall deem proper.

Notice that both Section 145(a) and 145(b) cover a broad range of corporate actors—directors, officers, employees, and agents (even when from another entity serving at the request of the corporation). Notice also the standard of conduct required for indemnification, which requires "good faith" and a specified "reasonable belief."

The primary difference between Section 145(a) and 145(b) is coverage. Section 145(a) permits broad indemnification of both expenses and amounts paid in damages or settlement of non-corporate claims. Section 145(b) permits narrower indemnification only of expenses in a corporate (derivative) suit, and only if the person to be indemnified was not adjudged liable to the corporation. In other words, Section 145(b)—on its own—does not permit corporations to indemnify directors for judgments or amounts paid in settlement of derivative suits. The rationale for this distinction is that because the ultimate plaintiff in a derivative suit is the corporation, the corporation should keep any judgment or settlement amount. If the corporation reimbursed a director for that amount, the corporation would essentially be paying from one pocket what it had just received in another pocket—a circularity problem.

Before you conclude that Section 145(b) prohibits indemnification of amounts paid in derivative suits, consider Section 145(f).

DGCL § 145

Indemnification of Officers, Directors, Employees and Agents

(f) The indemnification and advancement of expenses provided by, or granted pursuant to, the other subsections of this section shall not be deemed exclusive of any other rights to which those seeking indemnification or advancement of expenses may be entitled under any bylaw, agreement, vote of stockholders or disinterested directors or otherwise, both as to action in such person's official capacity and as to action in another capacity while holding such office.

Does Section 145(f) permit a corporation to indemnify a director for settlement or judgment amounts in derivative actions? Put another way, if there is a conflict, which provision prevails, Section 145(b) or Section 145(f)?

Read Sections 145(a) and 145(b) again, carefully. What is the function of the "good faith" language in both sections? How does this language fit with the "not in good faith" language in Section 102(b)(7), which was adopted at the same time? What kind of director conduct is in the "prohibited" category, and may not be subject to indemnification?

b. Mandatory Indemnification

The Delaware indemnification provisions then change gears. Section 145(c) provides for *mandatory indemnification* when the director or officer has prevailed. Even if there has been a falling out with a particular corporate actor, indemnification is as of right when the covered person has successfully defended an action or proceeding arising from his or her corporate role. Notice, though, that this mandatory indemnification covers only expenses.

> ## DGCL § 145
> ### Indemnification of Officers, Directors, Employees and Agents
>
> (c) To the extent that a present or former director or officer of a corporation has been successful on the merits or otherwise in defense of any action, suit or proceeding referred to in subsections (a) and (b) of this section, or in defense of any claim, issue or matter therein, such person shall be indemnified against expenses (including attorneys' fees) actually and reasonably incurred by such person in connection therewith.

What constitutes "success on the merits or otherwise"? The phrase "on the merits" is clear enough. If a director actually prevails, even on a technical defense, the corporation must indemnify him or her for expenses. The meaning of "or otherwise" is less clear. For example, indemnification of expenses would be required for a settlement in which a director pays no money and assumes no liability, and the case is dismissed with prejudice. But if a suit is dismissed without prejudice, indemnification would not be required.

c. Advancement of Expenses

Notice that thus far the focus has been after-the-fact indemnification—that is, payment by the corporation to the covered person after the litigation or proceeding has concluded. For many corporate actors, this may present a serious financial burden if they must undertake their own defense and pay the ongoing costs of litigation, hoping for corporate indemnification (mandatory or permissive) later on. Can the corporation advance payments for litigation expenses? Should a director or officer who later will be indemnified have to pay for the ongoing costs of litigation, or can the corporation make advance payments for litigation expenses? Section 145(e) permits such advances, but it also raises difficult policy issues.

> ## DGCL § 145
> ### Indemnification of Officers, Directors, Employees and Agents
>
> (e) Expenses (including attorneys' fees) incurred by an officer or director in defending any civil, criminal, administrative or investigative action, suit or proceeding may be paid by the corporation in advance of the final disposition of such action, suit or proceeding upon receipt of an undertaking by or on behalf of such director or officer to repay such amount if it shall ultimately be determined that such person is not entitled to be indemnified by the corporation as authorized in this section. Such expenses (including attorneys' fees) incurred by former directors and officers or other employees and agents may be so paid upon such terms and conditions, if any, as the corporation deems appropriate.

Requiring directors to fund their own litigation expenses or post a bond up front would create a divide between rich and poorer directors. Moreover, as a practical matter, shareholder litigation can be expensive, and directors and officers without sufficient resources to pay for ongoing litigation expenses might be forced to settle on terms unfavorable to the corporation. The advancement-of-expenses provision essentially allows corporations to "lend" money to their directors or officers for these expenses. Advancement of expenses remains controversial. Agreements for the advancement of expenses are frequently litigated, especially when there are reasons to doubt that the director or officer had been acting in the corporation's best interests.

Take Note!

Recall from our discussion of corporate federalism (Chapter 5, Corporate Federalism) that federal law increasingly is intruding on areas traditionally reserved for state law. Indemnification is no exception. Section 402 of the Sarbanes-Oxley Act added a new Section 13(k) to the Securities and Exchange Act of 1934, making it unlawful for a public company "to extend or maintain credit, to arrange for the extension of credit, or to renew an extension of credit, in the form of a personal loan to or for any director or executive officer." It appears that this provision does not prohibit companies from advancing litigation expenses to *former* directors and officers, although the application to *current* directors and officers is less clear.

Section 402 was adopted in response to the publicity generated by the large loans that some companies had been giving their executives during the period before the accounting scandals of the early 2000s. Most notoriously, WorldCom, a company that collapsed because of accounting irregularities just prior to the enactment of Sarbanes-Oxley in 2002, advanced a $400 million loan to Bernard Ebbers, its later-convicted chief executive officer. Although Congress clearly intended to prohibit such loans, it is less clear whether the statute applies to other advances that corporate directors and officers frequently receive. At least one court has taken the view that a corporation's advancement of the litigation costs of directors or officers, as those costs are incurred and subject to repayment if indemnification is ultimately disallowed, is not a prohibited "personal loan" under Sarbanes-Oxley.

d. Policy Questions

In general, corporate indemnification of corporate officials raise difficult policy questions. Will responsible people be willing to serve as directors if they are forced to bear the upfront cost of defending their conduct whenever it is challenged? On the other hand, why help directors or officers who intentionally harm their corporations? Civil and criminal laws exist to deter wrongful conduct—doesn't indemnification frustrate the purpose of those laws? Indemnification policy requires a balancing act between encouraging good director behavior and deterring bad.

3. D&O Insurance

Finally, corporations are permitted to purchase insurance policies that cover their directors and officers. Unlike the statutory provisions for exculpation and indemnification, the statutes authorizing the purchase of D&O insurance are typically straightforward. DGCL § 145(g) is representative.

> ### DGCL § 145
> ### Indemnification of Officers, Directors, Employees and Agents: Insurance
>
> (g) A corporation shall have power to purchase and maintain insurance on behalf of any person who is or was a director, officer, employee or agent of the corporation, or is or was serving at the request of the corporation as a director, officer, employee or agent of another corporation, partnership, joint venture, trust or other enterprise against any liability asserted against such person and incurred by such person in any such capacity, or arising out of such person's status as such, whether or not the corporation would have the power to indemnify such person against such liability under this section.

Insurance companies began to offer D&O insurance policies during the 1960s, when an increasing number of lawsuits began to generate fears of personal liability for corporate officials. During the corporate litigation explosion of the 1980s, which coincided with a rise in merger and acquisition activity, some insurance companies cut back on their D&O coverage and significantly increased premiums. In the 1990s, coverage returned and premiums stabilized. Following the spate of corporate scandals that came to light in the early 2000s, D&O premiums and deductibles rose, fewer items were covered, and the number of insurance companies offering D&O coverage dwindled to a handful. During the 2010s, the market for D&O insurance remained concentrated, and premiums diverged based on industry and size. Most corporate directors will insist on significant D&O insurance coverage.

a. Two Parts of D&O Policies

D&O policies consist of two separate but integral parts. The first part reimburses the corporation for its lawful expenses in connection with indemnifying its directors and officers, thus encouraging indemnification by the corporation. The second part of the D&O policy covers claims against individual directors or officers acting in their corporate capacity, thus reducing their exposure when the corporation is unable or unwilling to indemnify. This coverage often extends to claims (including judgments, settlements, and attorneys' fees) arising in court litigation, as well as administrative, regulatory, and investigative proceedings.

D&O insurance protects beyond corporate indemnification. First, the standard D&O policy may cover amounts paid in judgment or settlement in a derivative suit. Second, D&O insurance may cover conduct that does not satisfy the statutory standards for indemnification. For example, in *Van Gorkom*, because the directors were adjudged to have been grossly negligent in not informing themselves sufficiently prior to approving the merger, statutory indemnification might not have been available. Nonetheless, since the directors had not been "dishonest or fraudulent," the corporation's insurance carrier paid $10 million—the full policy limit—as part of the $23.5 million settlement of the case. Finally, D&O coverage is available even if the corporation becomes insolvent or refuses to pay indemnification, assuming the policy requirements are satisfied.

> **Practice Pointer**
>
> D&O coverage is subject to significant limitations. Many policies have a deductible amount for each director and officer and for the corporation. Sometimes there are co-pays, which means the insured bears a certain percentage (such as 5%) of the loss above the deductible amount. In addition, D&O exclusions are many and significant, and they vary from policy to policy:
>
> - Dishonest, fraudulent, or criminal acts. Sometimes these exclusions are triggered merely if there are *allegations* of such conduct, while others require an actual *adjudication*.
>
> - Claims alleging conduct by directors or officers detrimental to the corporation for their own personal gain or profit. A common example is insider trading.
>
> - Claims involving libel and slander, bodily harm or property damages, and pollution.
>
> - Claims against a director or officer brought directly by the corporation, though not necessarily derivative suits (most insurers seek to stay clear of internal disputes).

b. D&O Exclusions and Coverage Denial

The D&O insurance exclusion of "dishonest, fraudulent or criminal conduct" has potentially important ramifications for executives in corporations that have experienced "accounting irregularities" and have had to restate their financial statements. Some policy exclusions only apply if there is a *judgment* finding such conduct, creating incentives for executives to settle the charges without admitting liability. When a corporation restates its financials, coverage may also turn on whether the financial misstatements were dishonest or intentional, or merely the result of an honest error in accounting or business judgment. To ensure access to D&O coverage, plaintiffs in securities fraud class actions will often couch their claims in terms of both fraud and negligence. Nonetheless, under some policies, mere *allegations* of dishonest or intentional conduct are enough to exclude coverage.

D&O policies, like other insurance policies, can allow the insurance company to deny coverage and rescind the policies if if there were "material misrepresentations" in the policy application. As you would expect, D&O policy applications include extensive descriptions of the corporation and its finances, including the latest annual report, and financial statements. In addition, the insured must disclose knowledge of "any act, error or omission that might give rise to a claim under the policy."

Rescission gained much importance after recent financial scandals in the 2000s. For example, several insurance companies that underwrote D&O policies for Enron sought to rescind coverage on the ground that Enron misled insurers when it renewed its D&O policies based on earnings that were subsequently significantly restated. One issue was whether the misrepresentations must have been knowing or intentional, or whether merely showing a material misrepresentation could be grounds for rescission. Some states permit rescission if the misrepresentation is material *or* fraudulent. If materiality is at issue, the insurance company will have to show that the financial statements were important in writing the policy or evaluating the risk.

Food for Thought

Ralph Nader, a long-time critic of corporate power, has questioned why corporations are permitted to indemnify or insure wrongful conduct by directors and officers. Nader asks: why should an executive who is convicted of allowing a harmful drug to injure several thousand people avoid the costs of a criminal fine, when the same act as a private individual would send him to jail? He says, "An untenable double standard has been created. The more powerful an executive becomes, the less likely he is to pay for an abuse of power."

c. Policy Questions

To some, it is troubling that corporate law permits a corporation to insure its executives for conduct sufficiently egregious to be outside the scope of indemnification. Moreover, these critics point out, D&O insurance can be expensive and is paid for almost entirely by the corporation.

Defenders of D&O insurance respond with a simple argument: the scope of insurance coverage is a question of insurance law rather than corporate law. The statute only authorizes the purchase of insurance and leaves the determination of coverage limits to insurance companies and state insurance commissioners. In addition, if corporations did not purchase D&O insurance for their executives, one would expect that the executives would demand additional compensation to purchase it for themselves.

Who should bear the risks of executive malfeasance? Supporters of the present system argue that insurance companies, and their regulators, should decide this through exclusions and pricing decisions. They say the markets will police any problems, because if D&O insurance is harmful to a corporation, shareholders can choose to invest in corporations that do not insure. However, this argument assumes that shareholders have information about the D&O coverage and payments, that they act on this information, and that their actions influence executive behavior. Are any of these assumptions true?

The bottom line policy question is simple: law or markets? The phenomenon of D&O insurance presents this question in stark form. How much should society entrust to insurance markets the setting of limits on corporate governance? But the question is not limited to D&O insurance. Indeed, it is a question fundamental to director decision making, which—as we have seen—is limited somewhat by law, but is more generally an area where society entrusts to directors—subject to market pressures—the oversight of corporate behavior, for better or for worse.

CHAPTER 21

Director Conflicts

This chapter addresses the "traditional" duty of loyalty, the duty a director owes when he or she enters into a transaction with the corporation. Such transactions raise the possibility that the director's personal interests may be contrary to those of the corporation. The duty of loyalty requires a director to place the corporation's best interests above his or her own, and opens the door for a reviewing court to be sure this is true.

In some ways, director conflicts are easier to analyze than director breaches of duty in the decision-making context covered in the previous chapter. But in other ways they are more difficult. Self-dealing cases are more straightforward analytically, because they typically involve relatively straightforward legal questions about whether conflicts existed and whether the conflicted dealings were fair to the corporation. Moreover, these questions often arise under statutes that frame the issues. However, duty of loyalty cases can be difficult to resolve because they depend so extensively on the particular facts.

Keep in mind that director self dealing is not necessarily bad. Indeed, for many corporations self-dealing transactions may be a fact of life. Suppose a corporate director proposes to sell land to his or her corporation. Obviously, there is a conflict, because a high price will benefit the director personally, while a low price will benefit the corporation whose interest the director is supposed to serve. This is a classic "self-dealing" transaction. But it is not necessarily unfair to the corporation. Indeed it might be beneficial, or even crucial, to the corporation. Directors are often uniquely positioned to help their corporations, even if they personally benefit from the dealings as well.

Food for Thought

The Introductory Comment to the 1989 version of MBCA Subchapter F took great care not to disparage director conflicts.

"It is important to keep firmly in mind that it is a contingent risk we are dealing with—that an interest conflict is not in itself a crime or a tort or necessarily injurious to others. Contrary to much popular usage, having a 'conflict of interest' is not something one is 'guilty of'; it is simply a state of affairs. Indeed, in many situations, the corporation and the shareholders may secure major benefits from a transaction despite the presence of a director's conflicting interest. Further, while history is replete with selfish acts, it is also oddly counterpointed by numberless acts taken contrary to self interest."

The duty of loyalty arises in numerous contexts, some of which we will consider in later chapters, including executive compensation (Chapter 22), transactions involving corporate groups (Chapter 24), insider trading (Chapter 29), and various kinds of corporate deals (Chapters 30–32). The nature of judicial review may differ with each context, but the basic question remains the same: how should a court evaluate business transactions when a corporate fiduciary has a personal interest in the transaction that conflicts with corporate interests?

This chapter begins with an overview of the issues presented in director self-dealing transactions and the historical evolution of the duty of loyalty, including the traditional approach to director self-dealing transactions and the newer approach under the MBCA. Next, we consider the elements that courts examine in determining the fairness of a transaction—namely, fair price and fair process (approval by informed, disinterested decision makers). Finally, we discuss the ability of corporate directors and executives to take business opportunities that properly belong to the corporation, a problem that has generated a separate director conflicts doctrine known as the "corporate opportunity doctrine."

A. Statutory Approaches to Director Conflicts

We begin by describing the common law background of modern duty of loyalty statutes. Then we consider three statutory examples: California, Delaware, and the MBCA. You will notice a steady relaxation of the standards that courts use to judge the fairness of self-dealing transactions, starting with a flat prohibition on such transactions and ending with the forgiving business judgment rule.

1. Evolution of Duty of Loyalty in Director Self-Dealing Cases

The law applicable to director conflicts evolved significantly during the previous century. As of the late nineteenth century, the general common law rule was that a corporation or its shareholders could void a conflicted transaction between a director and the corporation. At the time, judges doubted that the conflicted director or the remaining directors could put the corporation's interests ahead of the conflicted director's personal interests. It didn't matter if conflicted directors removed themselves from the decision-making process on the transaction. A director, like a trustee, simply wasn't supposed to engage in self dealing. Period.

Second, by the early twentieth century, the courts recognized the need for some flexibility in approaching conflicted transactions, and the general rule changed to focus on a two-pronged approach that permitted certain forms of director self dealing. A conflicted deal was valid if it was both (1) approved by a disinterested majority of the other directors and (2) was not unfair or fraudulent. This meant that even if the process of approval was fair, the transaction was voidable if its substance was unfair to the corporation.

Third, during the next fifty years, the courts relaxed the level of scrutiny of self-dealing transactions and adopted a more permissive approach. By 1960, self-dealing transactions were no longer automatically voidable. Instead, the courts reviewed such transactions to assess whether the transaction was substantively fair, taking into account the transaction's terms and price.

Take Note!

Director conflicts are not necessarily limited to board members who benefit directly from a transaction. Even directors who do not have a direct financial interest in a transaction may have corporate or other positions that are linked to the transacting director.

For example, an outside director may be a member of a law firm that depends on receiving work from an inside director (such as the company's general counsel) who assigns legal work for the corporation. Can such an outside director exercise truly independent judgment on a transaction involving the general counsel, even if the director will not directly benefit financially from the transaction? And even if there were no financial interest, there may be personal dimensions if the interested director is a family member or life-long friend.

Today, corporate statutes dealing with director conflicts of interest are generally narrow in scope. They define conflicts that trigger heightened judicial review as those in which a director has a "financial" interest, although sometimes commentary to the statutes and judicial interpretations take into account the structural bias among directors to accommodate fellow directors. What are the advantages and disadvantages of such an approach?

Contemporary statutes, such as DGCL § 144 and former MBCA § 8.31, codify the common law development that director's conflicted transactions are not automatically invalid. Although they mention both disinterested approval (by shareholders or the board) and a judicial finding of fairness, these statutes do not specify when a transaction is valid. Over time, courts have had to resolve whether approval by directors or shareholders should be dispositive, or whether the court should engage in its own review of director self dealing.

Subchapter F of the MBCA, adopted in 1989 and revised in 2005, sought to overcome the interpretive problems these statutes pose. As discussed below, Subchapter F follows a safe harbor approach. By providing bright-line definitions of who is an "interested" director, what constitutes a "conflicting interest transaction," and who are "qualified directors," Subchapter F attempts to provide greater prospective certainty and reduce judicial intervention.

2. Traditional Approach (California): Judicial Intrusion

The following case involved a transaction approved by interested directors, who also owned a majority of the corporation's voting stock. The defendants argued that the transaction had been approved in their capacity as shareholders and therefore the court could not inquire into its fairness.

Stanley and Sturgis controlled a majority of the shares of Remillard-Dandini Company, which owned all the shares of San Jose Brick & Tile, Ltd. Stanley and Sturgis controlled the boards of directors of Remillard-Dandini and San Jose Brick & Tile, and were executive officers of both corporations and drew salaries from them. Remillard-Dandini and San Jose Brick & Tile (the "manufacturing companies") sold bricks to Remillard-Dandini Sales Corporation (the "sales corporation"), which was wholly owned, controlled, and operated by Stanley and Sturgis.

Plaintiff, a minority shareholder of Remillard-Dandini, alleged that Stanley and Sturgis had used their controlling position to have the manufacturing companies enter into contracts with the sales corporation, so that the manufacturing companies were stripped of their sales function. The plaintiff further alleged that under these contracts Stanley and Sturgis, through their ownership of the sales corporation, realized profits that should have gone to the manufacturing companies.

Remillard Brick Co. v. Remillard-Dandini Co.

241 P.2d 66 (Cal. Dist. Ct. App. 1952)

PETERS, PRESIDING JUSTICE.

It is argued that, since the fact of common directorship was fully known to the boards of the contracting corporations, and because the majority stockholders consented to the transaction, the minority stockholder and directors of the manufacturing companies have no legal cause to complain. In other words, it is argued that if the majority directors and stockholders inform the minority that they are going to mulct the corporation, section 820 of the Corporations Code* constitutes an impervious armor against any attack on the transaction short of actual fraud. If this interpretation of the section were sound, it would be a shocking reflection on the law of California. It would completely disregard the first sentence of section 820 setting forth the elementary rule that "Directors and officers shall exercise their powers in good faith, and with a view to the interests of the corporation," and would mean that if conniving directors simply disclose their dereliction to the powerless minority, any transaction by which the majority desire to mulct the minority is immune from attack. That is not and cannot be the law.

Section 820 of the Corporations Code is based on former section 311 of the Civil Code, first added to our law in 1931. Before the adoption of that section it was the law that the mere existence of a common directorate, at least where the vote of the common director was essential to consummate the transaction, invalidated the contract. That rule was changed in 1931 when section 311 was added to the Civil Code, and limited to a greater extent by the adoption of section 820 of the Corporations Code. If the conditions provided for in the section appear, the transaction cannot be set aside simply because there is a common directorate. Here, undoubtedly, there was a literal compliance with subdivision b of the section. The fact of the common directorship was disclosed to the stockholders, and the majority stockholders, did approve the contracts.

But neither section 820 of the Corporations Code nor any other provision of the law automatically validates such transactions simply because there has been a disclosure and approval by the majority of the stockholders. That section does

---

*Section 820 of the Corporations Code, enacted in 1947, provided:

Directors and officers shall exercise their powers in good faith, and with a view to the interests of the corporation. No contract or other transaction between a corporation and one or more of its directors, or between a corporation and any corporation, firm, or association in which one or more of its directors are directors or are financially interested, is either void or voidable because such director or directors are present at the meeting of the board of directors or a committee thereof which authorizes or approves the contract or transaction, or because his or their votes are counted for such purpose, if the circumstances specified in any of the following subdivisions exist:

(a) The fact of the common directorship or financial interest is disclosed or known to the board of directors or committee and noted in the minutes, and the board or committee authorizes, approves, or ratifies the contract or transaction in good faith by a vote sufficient for the purpose without counting the vote or votes of such director or directors.

(b) The fact of the common directorship or financial interest is disclosed or known to the shareholders, and they approve or ratify the contract or transaction in good faith by a majority vote or written consent of shareholders entitled to vote.

(c) The contract or transaction is just and reasonable as to the corporation at the time it is authorized or approved.

Common or interested directors may be counted in determining the presence of a quorum at a meeting of the board of directors or a committee thereof which authorizes, approves, or ratifies a contract or transaction.

not operate to limit the fiduciary duties owed by a director to all the stockholders, nor does it operate to condone acts which, without the existence of a common directorate, would not be countenanced. That section does not permit an officer or director, by an abuse of his power, to obtain an unfair advantage or profit for himself at the expense of the corporation. The director cannot, by reason of his position, drive a harsh and unfair bargain with the corporation he is supposed to represent. If he does so, he may be compelled to account for unfair profits made in disregard of his duty. Even though the requirements of section 820 are technically met, transactions that are unfair and unreasonable to the corporation may be avoided. California Corporation Laws by Ballantine and Sterling (1949 ed.), p. 102, § 84. It would be a shocking concept of corporate morality to hold that because the majority directors or stockholders disclose their purpose and interest, they may strip a corporation of its assets to their own financial advantage, and that the minority is without legal redress.

Here the unchallenged findings demonstrate that Stanley and Sturgis used their majority power for their own personal advantage and to the detriment of the minority stockholder. They used it to strip the manufacturing companies of their sales functions—functions which it was their duty to carry out as officers and directors of those companies. There was not one thing done by them acting as the sales corporation that they could not and should not have done as officers and directors and in control of the stock of the manufacturing companies. It is no answer to say that the manufacturing companies made a profit on the deal, or that Stanley and Sturgis did a good job. The point is that those large profits that should have gone to the manufacturing companies were diverted to the sales corporation. The good job done by Stanley and Sturgis should and could have been done for the manufacturing companies. If Stanley and Sturgis, with control of the board of directors and the majority stock of the manufacturing companies, could thus lawfully, to their own advantage, strip the manufacturing companies of their sales functions, they could just as well strip them of their other functions. If the sales functions could be stripped from the companies in this fashion to the personal advantage of Stanley and Sturgis, there would be nothing to prevent them from next organizing a manufacturing company, and transferring to it the manufacturing functions of these companies, thus leaving the manufacturing companies but hollow shells. This should not, is not, and cannot be the law.

It is hornbook law that directors, while not strictly trustees, are fiduciaries, and bear a fiduciary relationship to the corporation, and to all the stockholders. They owe a duty to all stockholders, including the minority stockholders, and must administer their duties for the common benefit. The concept that a corporation is an entity cannot operate so as to lessen the duties owed to all of the stockholders. Directors owe a duty of highest good faith to the corporation and its stockholders. It is a cardinal principle of corporate law that a director cannot, at the expense of the corporation, make an unfair profit from his position. He is precluded from receiving any personal advantage without fullest disclosure to and consent of *all* those affected. The law zealously regards contracts between corporations with interlocking directorates, will carefully scrutinize all such transactions, and in case of unfair dealing to the detriment of minority stockholders, will grant appropriate relief. Where the transaction greatly benefits one corporation at the expense of another, and especially if it personally benefits the majority directors, it will and should be set aside. In other words, while the transaction is not voidable simply because an interested director participated, it will not be upheld if it is unfair to the minority stockholders. These principles are the law in practically all jurisdictions.

Points for Discussion

1. How much does formality matter?

Notice that the California statute plainly validates director self dealing that is "disclosed or known to the shareholders, and they approve or ratify the contract or transaction in good faith by a majority vote or written consent of shareholders entitled to vote." Was the problem in the case that there was no formal shareholder action? Why should such formality matter? If the problem was not a lack of formalities, why does the court not accept the action by a shareholder majority?

2. Fairness.

The court in *Remillard* interpreted the California statute to include considerations of fairness. What factors would be relevant in a fairness review of the contract between the manufacturing companies and the sales corporation? Could the manufacturing companies deal with the related sales corporation, or were they required to sell directly or only through unaffiliated firms?

3. Aftermath.

After the *Remillard* decision, the California legislature amended its statutory code to disqualify shares voted by interested directors in a shareholder vote. Would the case have come out differently under the amended statute? Suppose the contract between the manufacturing companies and the sales corporation had been submitted to only disinterested shareholders. Would the court have undertaken a review of its fairness?

---

3. Evolving Approach (Delaware): Deference to Process

Delaware has a typical director self-dealing statute, which like the modern California statute provides that an interested-director transaction will not automatically be void or voidable if *either* there has been informed, disinterested board approval *or* informed shareholder approval *or* the transaction is fair to the corporation.

DGCL § 144
Interested Directors; Quorum

(a) No contract or transaction between a corporation and 1 or more of its directors or officers, or between a corporation and any other corporation, partnership, association, or other organization in which 1 or more of its directors or officers, are directors or officers, or have a financial interest, shall be void or voidable solely for this reason, or solely because the director or officer is present at or participates in the meeting of the board or committee which authorizes the contract or transaction, or solely because any such director's or officer's votes are counted for such purpose, if:

(1) The material facts as to the director's or officer's relationship or interest and as to the contract or transaction are disclosed or are known to the board of directors or the committee, and the board or committee in good faith authorizes the contract or transaction by the affirmative votes of a majority of the disinterested directors, even though the disinterested directors be less than a quorum; or

(2) The material facts as to the director's or officer's relationship or interest and as to the contract or transaction are disclosed or are known to the shareholders entitled to vote thereon, and the contract or transaction is specifically approved in good faith by vote of the shareholders; or

(3) The contract or transaction is fair as to the corporation as of the time it is authorized, approved or ratified, by the board of directors, a committee or the shareholders.

(b) Common or interested directors may be counted in determining the presence of a quorum at a meeting of the board of directors or of a committee which authorizes the contract or transaction.

a. Meaning of DGCL § 144

Under this statute, what role does a court have in reviewing the transaction's fairness to the corporation? Because the statute is written in the disjunctive, one possible answer is that there should be judicial review for fairness only if there had been no prior approval by an informed, disinterested decision maker. If this interpretation were correct, it would reduce judicial scrutiny (and, hence, potentially be less protective for minority shareholders), particularly when compared to the early days of the common law. This approach, however, could be viewed as efficient because it would give prospective certainty to a transaction in which the decisional process is fair, presumably on the theory that good process identifies substantive fairness in most instances.

Alternatively, the statute might be read as simply removing the absolute prohibition against interested-director transactions without specifying when such transactions are valid. Support for this reading comes from the statutory language that a transaction that satisfies one or more of the tests is not void or voidable solely because of the director's interest. Under this construction, the statute can be seen as relating primarily to the burden of proof in litigation challenging a conflict of interest transaction rather than establishing standards for the validity of the transaction itself. Thus, under this interpretation the burden of establishing validity initially would be on the interested director, but would shift to the shareholder challenging the transaction if there had been full disclosure and approval by disinterested decision makers. This interpretation leaves to the court the question of the transaction's fairness, with approval by informed, disinterested decision makers only shifting the burden on the question of fairness.

b. Evolving Court Interpretations of DGCL § 144

Delaware court decisions illustrate the difficulties in interpreting DGCL § 144. Some earlier decisions stated that the court retains a role in determining fairness, even if the self-dealing transaction is approved by informed, disinterested decision makers. Other decisions suggest that the review by appropriate corporate decision makers displaces judicial review.

In *Fliegler v. Lawrence,* 361 A.2d 218 (Del. 1976), a shareholder brought a derivative suit on behalf of Agau Mines against its officers and directors (including the named defendant Lawrence) and another corporation, United States Antimony Corp. (USAC), which was owned primarily by Lawrence and the other defendants. Lawrence had acquired, in his individual capacity, certain mining properties which he transferred to USAC. Agau later acquired USAC in exchange for 800,000 shares of Agau stock. Fliegler, a minority shareholder of Agau, challenged Agau's acquisition of USAC, claiming it was unfair. The defendants contended that they had been relieved of the burden of proving fairness because Agau's shareholders had ratified the transaction pursuant to § 144(a)(2).

The court held that the purported ratification did not affect the burden of proof because the majority of shares voted in favor of the acquisition were cast by the defendants in their capacity as Agau stockholders. Only one-third of the disinterested shareholders cast votes. Thus, the *Fliegler* court determined that despite the absence of any provision in § 144(a)(2) requiring *disinterested* shareholder approval of an interested-director transaction, it would impose such a requirement before shifting the burden of proof from the interested director to the challenging shareholder.

The court then addressed the proper interpretation of the disjunctive language of § 144. The court rejected the argument that compliance with § 144(a)(2) automatically validated the transaction and concluded that the statute "merely removes an 'interested director' cloud when its terms are met and provides against invalidation of an agreement 'solely' because such a director or officer is involved. Nothing in the statute sanctions unfairness to Agau or removes the transaction from judicial scrutiny."

In *Marciano v. Nakash*, 535 A.2d 400 (Del. 1987), the court found to be fair a director self-dealing transaction that, because of a deadlock at both the shareholder and director level, had not been approved by either disinterested shareholders or directors. The court characterized *Fliegler* as having "refused to view § 144 as either completely preemptive of the common law duty of director fidelity or as constituting a grant of broad immunity" and cited with approval *Fliegler's* "merely removes an 'interested director' cloud" language. In a footnote, however, the court observed:

> Although in this case none of the curative steps afforded under section 144(a) were available because of the director-shareholder deadlock, a non-disclosing director seeking to remove the cloud of interestedness would appear to have the same burden under section 144(a)(3), as under prior case law, of proving the intrinsic fairness of a questioned transaction which had been approved or ratified by the directors or shareholders. On the other hand, approval by fully-informed disinterested directors under section 144(a)(1), or disinterested stockholders under section 144(a)(2), permits invocation of the business judgment rule and limits judicial review to issues of gift or waste with the burden of proof upon the party attacking the transaction.

Without explicitly addressing the tension between *Fliegler* and *Marciano*, the following decision by the Delaware Supreme Court embraces the view that § 144 creates a safe harbor for director self-dealing transactions.

Benihana of Tokyo, Inc. v. Benihana, Inc.

906 A.2d 114 (Del. 2006)

BERGER, JUSTICE.

In this appeal, we consider whether Benihana, Inc. was authorized to issue $20 million in preferred stock and whether Benihana's board of directors acted properly in approving the transaction. We conclude that the Court of Chancery's factual findings are supported by the record and that it correctly applied settled law in holding that the stock issuance was lawful and that the directors did not breach their fiduciary duties. Accordingly, we affirm.

Factual and Procedural Background

Rocky Aoki founded Benihana of Tokyo, Inc. (BOT), and its subsidiary, Benihana, which own and operate Benihana restaurants in the United States and other countries. Aoki owned 100% of BOT until 1998, when he pled guilty to insider trading charges. In order to avoid licensing problems created by his status as a convicted felon, Aoki transferred his stock to the Benihana Protective Trust. The trustees of the Trust were Aoki's three children and the family's attorney.

Benihana, a Delaware corporation, has two classes of common stock. There are approximately 6 million shares of Class A common stock outstanding. Each share has 1/10 vote and the holders of Class A common are entitled to elect 25% of the directors. There are approximately 3 million shares of Common stock outstanding. Each share of Common has one vote and the holders of Common stock are entitled to elect the remaining 75% of Benihana's directors. Before the transaction at issue, BOT owned 50.9% of the Common stock and 2% of the Class A stock. The nine member board of directors is classified and the directors serve three-year terms.

In 2003, conflicts arose between Aoki and his children. In August, the children were upset to learn that Aoki had changed his will to give his new wife Keiko control over BOT.

The Aoki family's turmoil came at a time when Benihana also was facing challenges. Many of its restaurants were old and outmoded. Benihana hired WD Partners to evaluate its facilities and to plan and design appropriate renovations. The resulting Construction and Renovation Plan anticipated that the project would take at least five years and cost $56 million or more. Wachovia offered to provide Benihana a $60 million line of credit for the Construction and Renovation Plan, but the restrictions Wachovia imposed made it unlikely that Benihana would be able to borrow the full amount. Because the Wachovia line of credit did not assure that Benihana would have the capital it needed, the company retained Morgan Joseph & Co. to develop other financing options.

On January 9, 2004, after evaluating Benihana's financial situation and needs, Fred Joseph, of Morgan Joseph, met with Joel Schwartz (Benihana's CEO), Darwin Dornbush (Benihana's general counsel) and John E. Abdo (a member of the board's executive committee). Joseph expressed concern that Benihana would not have sufficient available capital to complete the Construction and Renovation Plan and pursue appropriate acquisitions. Benihana was conservatively leveraged, and Joseph discussed various financing alternatives, including bank debt, high yield debt, convertible debt or preferred stock, equity and sale/leaseback options.

The full board met with Joseph on January 29, 2004. He reviewed all the financing alternatives that he had discussed with the executive committee, and recommended that Benihana issue convertible preferred stock. Joseph explained that the preferred stock would provide the funds needed for the Construction and Renovation Plan and also put the company in a better negotiating position if it sought additional financing from its bank.

Joseph gave the directors a board book, marked "Confidential," containing an analysis of the proposed stock issuance (the Transaction). The book included, among others, the following anticipated terms: (i) issuance of $20,000,000 of preferred stock, convertible into Common stock; (ii) dividend of 6% +/- 0.5%; (iii) conversion premium of 20% +/- 2.5%; (iv) buyer's approval required for material corporate transactions; and (v) one to two board seats to the buyer. At trial, Joseph testified that the terms had been chosen by looking at comparable stock issuances and analyzing the Morgan Joseph proposal under a theoretical model.

The board met again on February 17, 2004, to review the terms of the Transaction. The directors discussed Benihana's preferences and Joseph predicted what a buyer likely would expect or require. For example, Schwartz asked Joseph to try to negotiate a minimum on the dollar value for transactions that would be deemed "material corporation transactions" and subject to the buyer's approval. Schwartz wanted to give the buyer only one board seat, but Joseph said that Benihana might have to give up two. Joseph told the board that he was not sure that a buyer would agree to an issuance in two tranches, and that it would be difficult to make the second tranche non-mandatory. As the Court of Chancery found, the board understood that the preferred terms were akin to a "wish list."

Shortly after the February meeting, Abdo contacted Joseph and told him that BFC Financial Corporation was interested in buying the new convertible stock. In April 2004, Joseph sent BFC a private placement memorandum. Abdo negotiated with Joseph for several weeks.[5] They agreed to the Transaction on the following basic terms: (i) $20 million issuance in two tranches of $10 million each, with the second tranche to be issued one to three years after the first; (ii) BFC obtained one seat on the board, and one additional seat if Benihana failed to pay dividends for two consecutive quarters; (iii) BFC obtained preemptive rights on any new voting securities; (iv) 5% dividend; (v) 15% conversion premium; (vi) BFC had the right to force Benihana to redeem the preferred stock in full after ten years; and (vii) the stock would have immediate "as if converted" voting rights. Joseph testified that he was satisfied with the negotiations, as he had obtained what he wanted with respect to the most important points.

On April 22, 2004, Abdo sent a memorandum to Dornbush, Schwartz and Joseph, listing the agreed terms of the Transaction. He did not send the memorandum to any other members of the Benihana board. Schwartz did tell four directors that BFC was the potential buyer. At its next meeting, held on May 6, 2004, the entire board was officially informed of BFC's involvement in the Transaction. Abdo made a presentation on behalf of BFC and then left the meeting. Joseph distributed an updated board book, which explained that Abdo had approached Morgan Joseph on behalf of BFC, and included the negotiated terms. The trial court found that the board was not informed that Abdo had negotiated the deal on behalf of BFC. But the board did know that Abdo was a principal of BFC. After discussion, the board reviewed and approved the Transaction, subject to the receipt of a fairness opinion.

On May 18, 2004, after he learned that Morgan Joseph was providing a fairness opinion, Schwartz publicly announced the stock issuance. Two days later, Aoki's counsel sent a letter asking the board to abandon the Transaction and pursue other, more favorable, financing alternatives. The letter expressed concern about the directors' conflicts, the dilutive effect of the stock issuance, and its "questionable legality." Schwartz gave copies of the letter to the directors at the May 20 board meeting, and Dornbush advised that he did not believe that Aoki's concerns had merit. Joseph and another Morgan Joseph representative then joined the meeting by telephone and opined that the Transaction was fair from a financial point of view. The board then approved the Transaction.

During the following two weeks, Benihana received three alternative financing proposals. Schwartz asked three outside directors to act as an independent committee and review the first offer. The committee decided that the offer was inferior and not worth pursuing. Morgan Joseph agreed with that assessment. Schwartz referred the next two proposals to Morgan Joseph, with the same result.

---

[5] BFC, a publicly traded Florida corporation, is a holding company for several investments. Abdo is a director and vice chairman. He owns 30% of BFC's stock.

On June 8, 2004, Benihana and BFC executed the Stock Purchase Agreement. On June 11, 2004, the board met and approved resolutions ratifying the execution of the Stock Purchase Agreement and authorizing the stock issuance. Schwartz then reported on the three alternative proposals that had been rejected by the ad hoc committee and Morgan Joseph. On July 2, 2004, BOT filed this action against all of Benihana's directors, except Kevin Aoki, alleging breaches of fiduciary duties; and against BFC, alleging that it aided and abetted the fiduciary violations.

The Court of Chancery held that Benihana was authorized to issue the preferred stock with preemptive rights, and that the board's approval of the Transaction was a valid exercise of business judgment. This appeal followed.

Discussion

[The court first decided that Benihana's certificate of incorporation authorized the board to issue preferred stock with preemptive rights.]

A. Section 144(a)(1) Approval

<u>Section 144</u> of the Delaware General Corporation Law provides a safe harbor for interested transactions, like this one, if "the material facts as to the director's relationship or interest and as to the contract or transaction are disclosed or are known to the board of directors . . . and the board . . . in good faith authorizes the contract or transaction by the affirmative votes of a majority of the disinterested directors."

After approval by disinterested directors, courts review the interested transaction under the business judgment rule, which "is a presumption that in making a business decision, the directors of a corporation acted on an informed basis, in good faith and in the honest belief that the action taken was in the best interest of the company."

BOT argues that § 144(a)(1) is inapplicable because, when they approved the Transaction, the disinterested directors did not know that Abdo had negotiated the terms for BFC.[14] Abdo's role as negotiator is material, according to BOT, because Abdo had been given the confidential term sheet prepared by Joseph and knew which of those terms Benihana was prepared to give up during negotiations. We agree that the board needed to know about Abdo's involvement in order to make an informed decision. The record clearly establishes, however, that the board possessed that material information when it approved the Transaction on May 6, 2004 and May 20, 2004.

---

[14] BOT argued to the trial court that the directors who voted on the Transaction were not disinterested or independent. BOT is not pressing that claim on appeal.

Shortly before the May 6 meeting, Schwartz told three of the outside directors that BFC was the proposed buyer. Then, at the meeting, Abdo made the presentation on behalf of BFC. Joseph's board book also explained that Abdo had made the initial contact that precipitated the negotiations. The board members knew that Abdo is a director, vice-chairman, and one of two people who control BFC. Thus, although no one ever said, "Abdo negotiated this deal for BFC," the directors understood that he was BFC's representative in the Transaction. As one of the outside directors testified, "whoever actually did the negotiating, [Abdo] as a principal would have to agree to it. So whether he sat in the room and negotiated it or he sat somewhere else and was brought the results of someone else's negotiation, he was the ultimate decision-maker." Accordingly, we conclude that the disinterested directors possessed all the material information on Abdo's interest in the Transaction, and their approval at the May 6 and May 20 board meetings satisfies § 144(a)(1).

B. Abdo's alleged fiduciary violation

BOT next argues that the Court of Chancery should have reviewed the Transaction under an entire fairness standard because Abdo breached his duty of loyalty when he used Benihana's confidential information to negotiate on behalf of BFC. This argument starts with a flawed premise. The record does not support BOT's contention that Abdo used any confidential information against Benihana. Even without Joseph's comments at the February 17 board meeting, Abdo knew the terms a buyer could expect to obtain in a deal like this. Moreover, as the trial court found, "the negotiations involved give and take on a number of points" and Benihana "ended up where it wanted to be" for the most important terms. Abdo did not set the terms of the deal; he did not deceive the board; and he did not dominate or control the other directors' approval of the Transaction. In short, the record does not support the claim that Abdo breached his duty of loyalty.

C. Dilution of BOT's voting power

Finally, BOT argues that the board's primary purpose in approving the Transaction was to dilute BOT's voting control. BOT points out that Schwartz was concerned about BOT's control in 2003 and even discussed with Dornbush the possibility of issuing a huge number of Class A shares. Then, despite the availability of other financing options, the board decided on a stock issuance, and agreed to give BFC "as if converted" voting rights. According to BOT, the trial court overlooked this powerful evidence of the board's improper purpose.

Here, however, the trial court found that "the primary purpose of the . . . Transaction was to provide what the directors subjectively believed to be the best financing vehicle available for securing the necessary funds to pursue the agreed upon Construction and Renovation Plan for the Benihana restaurants." That factual determination has ample record support, especially in light of the trial court's credibility determinations. Accordingly, we defer to the Court of Chancery's conclusion that the board's approval of the Transaction was a valid exercise of its business judgment, for a proper corporate purpose.

Points for Discussion

1. Process.

Notice how the Delaware Supreme Court in *Benihana* details the board deliberations in the case. Does this suggest that the focus on board process, which began in *Smith v. Van Gorkom*, has now reached its zenith in Delaware? That is, even when director loyalty is questioned, will Delaware courts refuse to inquire into the substance of the transaction if it was approved by informed, disinterested, independent directors?

2. Burden shifting.

Generally, as we have seen, the challenger of a director self-dealing transaction bears the initial burden to show that a director had a conflicting interest in a corporate transaction, and then the burden shifts to the director (and those who seek to uphold the transaction) to show the transaction was fair to the corporation. How does the court in *Benihana* deal with the question of burden shifting in director self-dealing transactions?

---

4. Modern Statutes (MBCA): Procedural Safe Harbor

As noted above, in 1989, the Committee on Corporate Laws of the American Bar Association adopted Subchapter F to replace the then existing MBCA § 8.31—whose language was similar to that of DGCL § 144. (Former MBCA § 8.31 should not be confused with the present MBCA § 8.31, which deals with the standards for director liability.) In 2005, Subchapter F was revised to clarify its coverage and specify the procedures necessary to validate a director self-dealing transaction—a safe harbor.

Subchapter F attempts to provide clarity about what constitutes director self dealing and when self-dealing transactions are valid. Specifically, it defines a "director's conflicting interest transaction" (or "DCIT") and states that a DCIT is immune from attack if it is authorized by "qualified" directors, disinterested shareholders, or a court under a fairness standard. Any of these three forms of authorization insulates the transaction from judicial review on the basis of the director conflict.

Subchapter F thus raises two key questions: what is a DCIT? who is a "qualified" director? MBCA § 8.60 defines a DCIT as a transaction by the corporation in which the director (1) is a party, (2) has a "material financial interest," or (3) knows that a "related person" is a party or had a material financial interest. Each of the terms in quotes is further defined. A "material financial interest" is one that would reasonably be expected to impair the director's judgment when authorizing the transaction. A "related person" is someone on a precisely enumerated family tree (from spouse to half sibling), someone who lives in the director's house, an entity controlled by the director or someone on the family tree, an entity in which the director serves as director, partner or trustee, or an entity controlled by the director's employer.

Who is a qualified director? MBCA § 1.43 (added in 2005) defines a "qualified director" as someone who does not have a conflicting interest in the transaction or one who has no "material relationship" with a conflicted director (that is, there is no "actual or potential benefit or detriment that would reasonably be expected to impair the director's judgment" when considering the DCIT). The MBCA clarifies that directors do not become unqualified just because he was nominated or elected to the board by a conflicted director, or serve with the conflicted director on the board of another corporation.

In order for a DCIT to be insulated from judicial review, a majority of "qualified directors" (at least two) must authorize it. They must deliberate and vote on their own, without the presence or participation of the conflicted director. Normal quorum requirements are relaxed, and a quorum exists if a majority of the board's qualified directors (again, at least two) is present.

As you can see, the MBCA seeks to provide clear yes-or-no answers to directors and lawyers who shepherd director self-dealing transactions through the corporate board. For example, a conflicted director who fails to disclose to the board his interest in a transaction (where the other directors do not know) or fails to reveal material information (such as that the land he is selling is sinking into an abandoned coal mine) cannot claim the MBCA safe harbor for board approval. On the other hand, if the DCIT is approved by informed directors who have neither a conflicting interest in the transaction nor financial ties to the conflicted director, the transaction falls within the safe harbor even if the directors are all close personal friends.

Points for Discussion

1. What's the difference?

How do the California, Delaware, and MBCA approaches differ? For example, how would *Remillard* and *Benihana* have been decided in a jurisdiction that had adopted Subchapter F? In what ways is the Delaware approach different from that of Subchapter F?

2. How bright?

What are the advantages and disadvantages of Subchapter F and its bright-line definition of a "director's conflicting interest transaction"? For example, what if the corporation enters into a transaction with a director's young cousin, who was orphaned and raised by the director like an only child? Are you satisfied by the explanation that the narrowly circumscribed definition of "related person" under Subchapter F was intended to leave some questionable situations immune from judicial scrutiny on the ground (as explained in the Official Comment) that "the legislative draftsman who chooses to suppress marginal anomalies by resorting to generalized statements of principle will pay a cost in terms of predictability"?

3. Can a court dodge Subchapter F?

What is the standard of review if the requisite number of qualified directors approve a DCIT, following the procedures laid out in Subchapter F? What are the alternatives for a court convinced that the terms of the DCIT are manifestly unfair to the corporation?

B. Board Approval, Shareholder Approval, and Fairness

Although the statutory tests vary for determining the validity of a director self-dealing transaction, they tend to focus on three factors: board approval, shareholder approval, and fairness. We now consider these factors in greater detail.

1. Court-Determined Fairness

As we've seen, judicial review of director self-dealing transactions has changed over time and various statutory safe harbors remove such transactions from exacting judicial scrutiny, That is, the statutes take the view that that approval by informed, disinterested, independent directors or shareholders may be a better gauge of "fairness" to the corporation than a judicial inquiry. But absent such approval, courts are still called on to review the "fairness" of director self-dealing transactions. So we begin with the question: what is "fairness"?

The judicial inquiry into fairness looks at both procedure and substance. The procedural inquiry typically focuses on the internal corporate process followed in obtaining approval by directors or shareholders. This part of the fairness inquiry dovetails with what we already have covered regarding director and shareholder approval. The courts focus on how the transaction was approved, the disclosure given decision makers, the ability of directors to be objective, and the effect of shareholder ratification.

Whereas procedural fairness overlaps with the other "approval" categories, substantive fairness typically is a separate inquiry. Substantive fairness focuses on a comparison of the fair market value of the transaction to the price the corporation actually paid, as well as the corporation's need for and ability to consummate the transaction. The test often has been articulated as "whether the proposition submitted would have commended itself to an independent corporation."

To the extent that this formulation contemplates independent arms-length negotiation as providing the basis for fair market value, a range of prices can satisfy the test of substantive fairness. Consider the Official Comment to Subchapter F, MBCA § 8.60:

Terms of the transaction. If the issue in a transaction is the "fairness" of a price, "fair" is not to be taken to imply that there is one single "fair" price, all others being "unfair." It is settled law that a "fair" price is any price within a range that an unrelated party might have been willing to pay or willing to accept, as the case may be, for the relevant property, asset, service or commitment, following a normal arm's-length business negotiation. The same approach applies not only to gauging the fairness of price, but also to the fairness evaluation of any other key term of the deal.

Benefit to the corporation. In considering the "fairness" of the transaction, the court will be required to consider not only the market fairness of the terms of the deal—whether it is comparable to what might have been obtainable in an arm's length transaction—but also whether the transaction was one that was reasonably likely to yield favorable results. Thus, if a manufacturing company that lacks sufficient working capital allocates some of its scarce funds to purchase a sailing yacht owned by one of its directors, it will not be easy to persuade the court that the transaction was "fair" in the sense that it was reasonably made to further the business interests of the corporation. The facts that the price paid for the yacht was a "fair" market price, and that the full measure of disclosures made by the director is beyond challenge, may still not be enough to defend and uphold the transaction.

Although a director self-dealing transaction that is substantively "fair" generally should be upheld, the process of decision making often becomes an important factor in the substantive inquiry. In other words, process seems to matter to all aspects of director conflicts, and unfair process may be viewed as evidence of unfair substance. Why would a director hide details or pressure other parties if the deal was substantively fair?

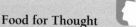

Food for Thought

Consider the following description of the factors relevant to a fairness inquiry. Do you agree with this list? Are there any factors you think are missing?

"While the concept of 'fairness' is incapable of precise definition, courts have stressed such factors as whether the corporation received in the transaction full value in all the commodities purchased; the corporation's need for the property; its ability to finance the purchase; whether the transaction was at the market price, or below, or constituted a better bargain than the corporation could have otherwise obtained in dealings with others; whether there was a detriment to the corporation as a result of the transaction; whether there was a possibility of corporate gain siphoned off by the directors directly or through corporations they controlled; and whether there was full disclosure—although neither disclosure nor shareholder assent can convert a dishonest transaction into a fair one."

Shlensky v. South Parkway Building Corp., 166 N.E.2d 793, 801–02 (Ill. 1960).

Points for Discussion

1. Which fairness factor(s)?

Fairness thus turns on (1) the terms of the transaction, (2) the benefit to the corporation, and (3) the process of decision making. Which of these three factors should matter most in an analysis of a director self-dealing transaction? Why?

2. Pleading/proving a case.

What facts would be most helpful to a plaintiff attacking a self-dealing transaction that was approved by the corporation's board of directors? What about a transaction that was approved by shareholders?

3. Advising.

Assume you are advising a startup company's board of directors. What guidance can you give the board about director conflicts, given the relevant statutes and judicial approaches?

---

2. Approval by Informed, Disinterested, Independent Directors

As modern courts (and corporate statutes) have come to accept that disinterested and independent directors can determine fairness in transactions involving director conflicts, one of the most litigated questions has been whether the directors who approved the deal were informed, disinterested, and independent.

Take Note!

Judicial deference to process, whether the self-dealing transaction was approved by directors or shareholders, depends on all material facts as to the transaction and the director's interest being properly disclosed. A useful illustration is the *Benihana* case. Remember that the court's conclusion that the business judgment rule applied turned on the court's finding that the directors who approved the financing package at issue in the case were sufficiently informed, including about the conflicted director's role in negotiating the terms of the package.

a. Distinction Between Interest and Independence

To help you understand the limits to board approval, we first consider the distinction between "interest" and "independence." Chancellor Chandler explained this distinction, which frequently arises when the plaintiff alleges demand futility in a derivative suit:

Although interest and independence are two separate and distinct issues, these two attributes are sometimes confused by parties.

A disabling "interest," as defined by Delaware common law, exists in two instances. The first is when (1) a director personally receives a benefit (or suffers a detriment), (2) as a result of, or from, the challenged transaction, (3) which is not generally shared with (or suffered by) the other shareholders of his corporation, and (4) that benefit (or detriment) is of such subjective material significance to that particular director that it is reasonable to question whether that director objectively considered the advisability of the challenged transaction to the corporation and its shareholders. The second instance is when a director stands on both sides of the challenged transaction. This latter situation frequently involves the first three elements listed above. As for the fourth element, whenever a director stands on both sides of the challenged transaction he is deemed interested and allegations of materiality have not been required.

"Independence" does not involve a question of whether the challenged director derives a benefit *from the transaction* that is not generally shared with the other shareholders. Rather, it involves an inquiry into whether the director's decision resulted from that director being *controlled* by another. A director can be controlled by another if in fact he is *dominated* by that other party, whether through close personal or familial relationship or through force of will. A director can also be controlled by another if the challenged director is *beholden* to the allegedly controlling entity. A director may be considered beholden to (and thus controlled by) another when the allegedly controlling entity has the unilateral power (whether direct or indirect through control over other decision makers), to decide whether the challenged director continues to receive a benefit, financial or otherwise, upon which the challenged director is so dependent or is of such subjective material importance to him that the threatened loss of that benefit might create a reason to question whether the controlled director is able to consider the corporate merits of the challenged transaction objectively.

Confusion over whether specific facts raise a question of interest or independence arises from the reality that similar factual circumstances may implicate *both* interest and independence, one but not the other, or neither. By way of example, consider the following: Director *A* is both a director and officer of company *X*. Company *X* is to be merged into company *Z*. Director *A*'s vote in favor of recommending shareholder approval of the merger is challenged by a plaintiff shareholder.

Scenario One. Assume that one of the terms of the merger agreement is that director *A* was to be an officer in surviving company *Z*, *and* that maintaining his position as a corporate officer in the surviving company was material to director A. That fact might, when considered in light of *all* of the facts alleged, lead the Court to conclude that director A had a disabling interest.

Scenario Two. Assume that director C is both a director and the majority shareholder of company X. Director C had the power plausibly to threaten director A's position as officer of corporation X should director A vote against the merger. Assume further that director A's position as a corporate officer is material to director A. Those circumstances, when considered in light of *all* of the facts alleged, might lead the Court to question director A's independence from director C, because it could reasonably be assumed that director A was controlled by director C, since director A was beholden to director C for his position as officer of the corporation. Confusion over whether to label this disability as a disqualifying "interest" or as a "lack of independence" may stem from the fact that, colloquially, director A was "interested" in keeping his job as a corporate officer. Scenario Two, however, raises only a question as to director A's independence since there is nothing that suggests that director A would receive something *from the transaction* that might implicate a disabling interest.

If a plaintiff's allegations combined all facts described in both Scenario One *and* Scenario Two, it might be reasonable to question *both* director A's interest and independence. Conversely, if all the facts in both scenarios were alleged *except* for the materiality of Director A's position as a corporate officer (perhaps because director A is a billionaire and his officer's position pays $20,000 per year and is not even of prestige value to him) then *neither* director A's interest nor his independence would be reasonably questioned. The key issue is not simply whether a particular director receives a benefit from a challenged transaction not shared with the other shareholders, or solely whether another person or entity has the ability to take some benefit away from a particular director, but whether the possibility of gaining some benefit or the fear of losing a benefit is likely to be of such importance to that director that it is reasonable for the Court to question whether valid business judgment or selfish considerations animated that director's vote on the challenged transaction.

Orman v. Cullman, 794 A.2d 5, 25–26 n.50 (Del. Ch. 2002)

Corporate statutes make clear that directors with a direct or indirect financial interest are deemed "interested." But the statutes usually do not address what kind of *non-financial relationship* with an interested director will call into question the approval by a director who otherwise would be considered disinterested. We now turn to this question.

As we have seen, federal law, including stock exchange rules, requires a certain degree of director independence. But state law goes further with respect to the approval of conflicted transactions. For example, Official Comment 5 to former MBCA § 8.31 suggests such a director with such a non-financial interest would be considered "interested" (though perhaps the statute should have used the term "non-independent") if the director had "a relationship with the other parties to the transaction such that the relationship might reasonably be expected to affect his judgment in the particular matter in a manner adverse to the corporation."

b. Discerning Director Independence

We next look at two cases that illustrate how courts have sought to discern director "independence"—the first involving the dismissal of a derivative suit by a board-appointed "special litigation committee" and the second involving board approval of a director self-dealing transaction. As you consider these cases, you should ask whether the same standards of "independence" should be applied in both contexts.

The first case involved Oracle Corporation, a leading computer company. In response to a derivative suit that alleged insider trading by the company's CEO and other prominent directors, the board of directors formed a special litigation committee (SLC) of two newly-elected directors to investigate and act on the allegations. *In re Oracle Corp. Derivative Litigation*, 824 A.2d 917 (Del. Ch. 2003). In a detailed (and somewhat unusual) judicial critique of director independence, then-Vice Chancellor Strine determined that the two SLC members were not sufficiently independent of the defendants to decide to terminate the derivative suit. Strine reached this conclusion even though both SLC members were academics of great stature with impeccable credentials, who had undertaken a thorough review of the allegations and, assisted by outside counsel, had interviewed 70 witnesses, reviewed volumes of internal company communications, and prepared a 1110-page report that detailed their investigation and the reasons to terminate the litigation.

> The question of independence "turns on whether a director is, *for any substantial reason,* incapable of making a decision with only the best interests of the corporation in mind." That is, the independence test ultimately "focuses on impartiality and objectivity." In this case, the SLC has failed to demonstrate that no material factual question exists regarding its independence.

During discovery, it emerged that the two SLC members—both of whom are professors at Stanford University—are being asked to investigate fellow Oracle directors who have important ties to Stanford, too. One of the directors, another Stanford professor, had taught one of the SLC members as a Ph.D. student and now serves with him at a Stanford research institute; another director is a Stanford alumnus who has contributed millions of dollars to Stanford, including to Stanford units with which one of the SLC members is closely affiliated; and another director (Oracle's CEO) has donated large sums to Stanford through a personal foundation and through Oracle, and was considering making additional multi-million dollar donations when the SLC members joined the Oracle board. Taken together, these and other facts cause me to harbor a reasonable doubt about the impartiality of the SLC.

It is no easy task to decide whether to accuse a fellow director of insider trading. For Oracle to compound that difficulty by requiring SLC members to consider accusing a fellow professor and two large benefactors of their university of conduct that is rightly considered a violation of criminal law was unnecessary and inconsistent with the concept of independence recognized by our law. The possibility that these extraneous considerations biased the inquiry of the SLC is too substantial for this court to ignore. I therefore deny the SLC's motion to terminate.

The second case involved Martha Stewart, a business and media personality so influential and ubiquitous that she is known simply as "Martha." *Beam ex. rel. Martha Stewart Living Omnimedia, Inc. v. Stewart*, 845 A.2d 1040 (Del. 2004). In a derivative suit, the plaintiff had alleged that Martha Stewart breached her duties of loyalty and care by selling stock of another company (ImClone) and then making misleading statements to the media. The defendants sought dismissal on the grounds that the plaintiff was first required to make a demand on the board.

The plaintiff contended that demand was futile because social and business connections on the board created a reasonable doubt as to the independence of a majority of the directors. The Court of Chancery concluded, however, that demand was required because the plaintiff had not alleged specific facts to demonstrate a lack of independence, and the Delaware Supreme Court affirmed. Here is a key excerpt:

> A variety of motivations, including friendship, may influence the demand futility inquiry. But, to render a director unable to consider demand, a relationship must be of a bias-producing nature. Allegations of mere personal friendship or a mere outside business relationship, standing alone, are insufficient to raise a reasonable doubt about a director's

independence. In this connection, we adopt as our own Vice Chancellor Strine's analysis in *Oracle*:

> Some professional or personal friendships, which may border on or even exceed familial loyalty and closeness, may raise a reasonable doubt whether a director can appropriately consider demand. This is particularly true when the allegations raise serious questions of either civil or criminal liability of such a close friend. Not all friendships, or even most of them, rise to this level and the Court cannot make a *reasonable* inference that a particular friendship does so without specific factual allegations to support such a conclusion.

The facts alleged by Beam regarding the relationships between Stewart and these other members of MSO's board of directors largely boil down to a "structural bias" argument, which presupposes that the professional and social relationships that naturally develop among members of a board impede independent decisionmaking.

Critics will charge that by requiring the independence of only a majority of the board we are ignoring the structural bias common to corporate boards throughout America, as well as the other unseen socialization processes cutting against independent discussion and decisionmaking in the boardroom. The difficulty with structural bias in a demand futile case is simply one of establishing it in the complaint for purposes of Rule 23.1.

In the present case, the plaintiff attempted to plead affinity beyond mere friendship between Stewart and the other directors, but her attempt is not sufficient to demonstrate demand futility. Even if the alleged friendships may have preceded the directors' membership on MSO's board and did not necessarily arise out of that membership, these relationships are of the same nature as those giving rise to the structural bias argument.

Allegations that Stewart and the other directors moved in the same social circles, attended the same weddings, developed business relationships before joining the board, and described each other as "friends," even when coupled with Stewart's 94% voting power, are insufficient, without more, to rebut the presumption of independence. They do not provide a sufficient basis from which reasonably to infer that Martinez, Moore and Seligman may have been beholden to Stewart. Whether they arise before board membership or later as a result of collegial relationships among the board of directors, such affinities—standing alone—will not render presuit demand futile.

That is not to say that personal friendship is always irrelevant to the independence calculus. But, for presuit demand purposes, friendship must be accompanied by substantially more in the nature of serious allegations that would lead to a reasonable doubt as to a director's independence. To create a reasonable doubt about an outside director's independence, a plaintiff must plead facts that would support the inference that because of the nature of a relationship or additional circumstances other than the interested director's stock ownership or voting power, the non-interested director would be more willing to risk his or her reputation than risk the relationship with the interested director.

In short, the Delaware Supreme Court seemed amenable to a broader concept of director independence in the context of demand futility than when an SLC requests dismissal of a derivative suit. Note that the *Martha Stewart* court presumed that outside directors are independent even if they move in the same social circles as the conflicted director. To show bias in a demand futility case, there must be real evidence.

Food for Thought

Can directors be truly independent? Professor Charles Elson, one of the leading experts on Delaware corporate law and a director himself on a number of public corporation boards, questions whether most directors can truly be independent.

There are three problems with a management-appointed board that leads to ineffective oversight. First, personal and psychic ties to the individuals who are responsible for one's appointment to a board make it difficult to engage in necessary confrontation. It is always tough to challenge a friend, particularly when the challenging party may one day, as an officer of another enterprise, end up in the same position. Second, conflicts with a manager who is also a member of one's own board may lead to future retribution on one's own turf, thus reducing the incentive to act. Third, and most important, when one owes one's own board position to the largesse of management, any action taken that is inimical to management may result in a failure to be renominated to the board, which—given the large fees paid to directors and the great reputational advantage of board membership—malfunction as an effective club to stifle dissension. This is why the development of substantial director compensation, a consequence of management control, has acted to stifle board oversight of management, and has, in fact, enhanced management domination.

3. Disinterested Shareholder Approval

A director self-dealing transaction can be insulated from judicial review if it is approved or subsequently ratified by shareholders, provided that the material facts as to the transaction and the director's interest were disclosed to the shareholders. At common law, informed shareholder ratification created a presumption that the transaction was fair. Thus, many courts indicated that shareholder ratification shifts the burden of proof to the party challenging the transaction to show that the terms were so unequal as to amount to waste. However, when interested directors owned a majority of the shares, shareholder ratification generally did not shift the burden.

The shareholder-approval provisions of the interested-director statutes seem to codify the common law. Thus, an interested-director transaction is not void or voidable if the director's interest is disclosed to the shareholders and the shareholders approve the transaction. Technical compliance with the statutory procedures, however, will not immunize a transaction from scrutiny for fairness where the interested directors hold a majority of the shares voted in favor of the transaction.

To avoid the uncertainty of whether shareholder approval is valid if the interested directors vote their shares, it is now common to obtain "majority of the minority" shareholder approval as a condition of the transaction. In fact, some statutes do not permit the voting of shares owned by interested directors when shareholders are asked to approve a director self-dealing transaction. *See* Cal. Corp. Code § 310(a)(1).

Approval by shareholders, compared to that by directors, has the disadvantage that shareholders are not in a position to negotiate the terms of the transaction. Their approval or ratification is "take it or leave it." Should approval by a majority of disinterested shareholders be given conclusive weight? Or is there still a role for the court to ensure fairness? And what is the role of a "waste" claim, an allegation that shareholder approval should not—or cannot—insulate the transaction from review because it was a waste of corporate assets?

The following cases discuss these questions. The first involves a director stock option plan that was ratified by shareholders of a public company. The second involves an acquisition of a public company by another company in which directors of the acquired company had a substantial financial interest.

Lewis v. Vogelstein

699 A.2d 327 (Del. Ch. 1997)

ALLEN, CHANCELLOR.

This shareholders' suit challenges a stock option compensation plan for the directors of Mattel, Inc., which was approved or ratified by the shareholders of the company at its 1996 Annual Meeting of Shareholders ["1996 Plan" or "Plan"].

I.

The facts as they appear in the pleading are as follows. The Plan was adopted in 1996 and ratified by the company's shareholders at the 1996 annual meeting. It contemplates two forms of stock option grants to the company's directors: a one-time grant of options on a block of stock and subsequent, smaller annual grants of further options.

With respect to the one-time grant, the Plan provides that each outside director will qualify for a grant of options on 15,000 shares of Mattel common stock at the market price on the day such options are granted (the "one-time options"). The one-time options are alleged to be exercisable immediately upon being granted although they will achieve economic value, if ever, only with the passage of time. It is alleged that if not exercised, they remain valid for ten years.

With respect to the second type of option grant, the Plan qualifies each director for a grant of options upon his or her re-election to the board each year (the "Annual Options"). The maximum number of options grantable to a director pursuant to the annual options provision depends on the number of years the director has served on the Mattel board. Those outside directors with five or fewer years of service will qualify to receive options on no more than 5,000 shares, while those with more than five years service will qualify for options to purchase up to 10,000 shares. Once granted, these options vest over a four year period, at a rate of 25% per year. When exercisable, they entitle the holder to buy stock at the market price on the day of the grant. According to the complaint, options granted pursuant to the annual options provision also expire ten years from their grant date, whether or not the holder has remained on the board.

When the shareholders were asked to ratify the adoption of the Plan, as is typically true, no estimated present value of options that were authorized to be granted under the Plan was stated in the proxy solicitation materials.

II.

As the presence of valid shareholder ratification of executive or director compensation plans importantly affects the form of judicial review of such grants, it is logical to begin an analysis of the legal sufficiency of the complaint by analyzing the sufficiency of the attack on the disclosures made in connection with the ratification vote.

A. Disclosure Obligation:

[The court rejected plaintiff's claim that defendants had a duty to disclose the estimated present value of the stock option grants to which directors might become entitled under the 1996 Plan.]

III.

I turn to the motion to dismiss the complaint's allegation to the effect that the Plan, or grants under it, constitute a breach of the directors' fiduciary duty of loyalty. As the Plan contemplates grants to the directors that approved the Plan and who recommended it to the shareholders, we start by observing that it constitutes self-dealing that would ordinarily require that the directors prove that the grants involved were, in the circumstances, entirely fair to the corporation. However, it is the case that the shareholders have ratified the directors' action. That ratification is attacked only on the ground just treated. Thus, for these purposes I assume that the ratification was effective. The question then becomes what is the effect of informed shareholder ratification on a transaction of this type (i.e., officer or director pay).

A. Shareholder Ratification Under Delaware Law:

What is the effect under Delaware corporation law of shareholder ratification of an interested transaction? The answer to this apparently simple question appears less clear than one would hope or indeed expect. Four possible effects of shareholder ratification appear logically available: First, one might conclude that an effective shareholder ratification acts as a complete defense to any charge of breach of duty. Second, one might conclude that the effect of such ratification is to shift the substantive test on judicial review of the act from one of fairness that would otherwise be obtained (because the transaction is an interested one) to one of waste. Third, one might conclude that the ratification shifts the burden of proof of unfairness to plaintiff, but leaves that shareholder-protective test in place. Fourth, one might conclude (perhaps because of great respect for the collective action disabilities that attend shareholder action in public corporations) that shareholder ratification offers no assurance of assent of a character that deserves judicial recognition. Thus, under this approach, ratification on full information would be afforded no effect. Excepting the fourth of these effects, there are cases in this jurisdiction that reflect each of these approaches to the effect of shareholder voting to approve a transaction.

In order to state my own understanding I first note that by shareholder ratification I do not refer to every instance in which shareholders vote affirmatively with respect to a question placed before them. I exclude from the question those instances in which shareholder votes are a necessary step in authorizing a transaction. Thus the law of ratification as here discussed has no direct bearing on shareholder action to amend a certificate of incorporation or bylaws. Nor does that law bear on shareholder votes necessary to authorize a merger, a sale of substantially all the corporation's assets, or to dissolve the enterprise. For analytical purposes one can set such cases aside.

1. *Ratification generally*: I start with principles broader than those of corporation law. Ratification is a concept deriving from the law of agency which contemplates the ex post conferring upon or confirming of the legal authority of an agent in circumstances in which the agent had no authority or arguably had no authority. To be effective, of course, the agent must fully disclose all relevant circumstances with respect to the transaction to the principal prior to the ratification. Beyond that, since the relationship between a principal and agent is fiduciary in character, the agent in seeking ratification must act not only with candor, but with loyalty. Thus an attempt to coerce the principal's consent improperly will invalidate the effectiveness of the ratification.

Assuming that a ratification by an agent is validly obtained, what is its effect? One way of conceptualizing that effect is that it provides, after the fact, the grant of authority that may have been wanting at the time of the agent's act. Another might be to view the ratification as consent or as an estoppel by the principal to deny a lack of authority. In either event the effect of informed ratification is to validate or affirm the act of the agent as the act of the principal.

Application of these general ratification principles to shareholder ratification is complicated by three other factors. First, most generally, in the case of shareholder ratification there is of course no single individual acting as principal, but rather a class or group of divergent individuals—the class of shareholders. This aggregate quality of the principal means that decisions to affirm or ratify an act will be subject to collective action disabilities; that some portion of the body doing the ratifying may in fact have conflicting interests in the transaction; and some dissenting members of the class may be able to assert more or less convincingly that the "will" of the principal is wrong, or even corrupt and ought not to be binding on the class. In the case of individual ratification these issues won't arise, assuming that the principal does not suffer from multiple personality disorder. Thus the collective nature of shareholder ratification makes it more likely that following a claimed shareholder ratification, nevertheless, there is a litigated claim on behalf of the principal that the agent lacked authority or breached its duty. The second, mildly complicating factor present in shareholder ratification is the fact that in corporation law the "ratification" that shareholders provide will often not be directed to lack of legal authority of an agent but will relate to the consistency of some authorized director action with the equitable duty of loyalty. Thus shareholder ratification sometimes acts not to confer legal authority—but as in this case—to affirm that action taken is consistent with shareholder interests. Third, when what is "ratified" is a director conflict transaction, the statutory law—in Delaware Section 144 of the Delaware General Corporation Law—may bear on the effect.

2. *Shareholder ratification:* These differences between shareholder ratification of director action and classic ratification by a single principal, do lead to a difference in the effect of a valid ratification in the shareholder context. The principal novelty added to ratification law generally by the shareholder context, is the idea—no doubt analogously present in other contexts in which common interests are held—that, in addition to a claim that ratification was defective because of incomplete information or coercion, shareholder ratification is subject to a claim by a member of the class that the ratification is ineffectual (1) because a majority of those affirming the transaction had a conflicting interest with respect to it or (2) because the transaction that is ratified constituted a corporate waste. As to the second of these, it has long been held that shareholders may not ratify a waste except by a unanimous vote. The idea behind this rule is apparently that a transaction that satisfies the high standard of waste constitutes a gift of corporate property and no one should be forced against their will to make a gift of their property. In all events, informed, uncoerced, disinterested shareholder ratification of a transaction in which corporate directors have a material conflict of interest has the effect of protecting the transaction from judicial review except on the basis of waste.

B. The Waste Standard:

The judicial standard for determination of corporate waste is well developed. Roughly, a waste entails an exchange of corporate assets for consideration so disproportionately small as to lie beyond the range at which any reasonable person might be willing to trade. Most often the claim is associated with a transfer of corporate assets that serves no corporate purpose; or for which no consideration at all is received. Such a transfer is in effect a gift. If, however, there is *any substantial* consideration received by the corporation, and if there is a *good faith judgment* that in the circumstances the transaction is worthwhile, there should be no finding of waste, even if the fact finder would conclude *ex post* that the transaction was unreasonably risky. Any other rule would deter corporate boards from the optimal rational acceptance of risk. Courts are ill-fitted to attempt to weigh the "adequacy" of consideration under the waste standard or, ex post, to judge appropriate degrees of business risk.

[The court concluded that plaintiff's complaint should not be dismissed because the one time option grants to the directors were sufficiently unusual as to require further inquiry into whether they constituted waste. This portion of the court's opinion is set forth in Chapter 22, Executive Compensation.]

Harbor Finance Partners v. Huizenga

751 A.2d 879 (Del. Ch. 1999)

STRINE, VICE CHANCELLOR.

This matter involves a challenge to the acquisition of AutoNation, Incorporated by Republic Industries, Inc. A shareholder plaintiff contends that this acquisition (the "Merger") was a self-interested transaction effected for the benefit of Republic directors who owned a substantial block of AutoNation shares, that the terms of the transaction were unfair to Republic and its public stockholders, and that stockholder approval of the transaction was procured through a materially misleading proxy statement (the "Proxy Statement").

The Rule 12(b)(6) motion: The complaint fails to state a claim that the disclosures in connection with the Merger were misleading or incomplete. The affirmative stockholder vote on the Merger was informed and uncoerced, and disinterested shares constituted the overwhelming proportion of the Republic electorate. As a result, the business judgment rule standard of review is invoked and the Merger may only be attacked as wasteful. As a matter of logic and sound policy, one might think that a fair vote of disinterested stockholders in support of the transaction would dispose of the case altogether because a waste claim must be supported by facts demonstrating that "no person of ordinary sound business judgment" could consider the merger fair to Republic and because many disinterested and presumably rational Republic stockholders voted for the Merger. But under an unbroken line of authority dating from early in this century, a non-unanimous, although overwhelming, free and fair vote of disinterested stockholders does not extinguish a claim for waste. The waste vestige does not aid the plaintiff here, however, because the complaint at best alleges that the Merger was unfair and does not plead facts demonstrating that no reasonable person of ordinary business judgment could believe the transaction advisable for Republic. Thus I grant the defendants' motion to dismiss under Chancery Court Rule 12(b)(6).

II. Legal Analysis

4. Why Doesn't A Fully Informed, Uncoerced Vote Of Disinterested Stockholders Foreclose A Waste Claim?

Although I recognize that our law has long afforded plaintiffs the vestigial right to prove that a transaction that a majority of fully informed, uncoerced independent stockholders approved by a non-unanimous vote was wasteful, I question the continued utility of this "equitable safety valve."

The origin of this rule is rooted in the distinction between voidable and void acts, a distinction that appears to have grown out of the now largely abolished *ultra vires* doctrine. Voidable acts are traditionally held to be ratifiable because the corporation can lawfully accomplish them if it does so in the appropriate manner. Thus if directors who could not lawfully effect a transaction without stockholder approval did so anyway, and the requisite approval of the stockholders was later attained, the transaction is deemed fully ratified because the subsequent approval of the stockholders cured the defect.

In contrast, void acts are said to be non-ratifiable because the corporation cannot, in any case, lawfully accomplish them. Such void acts are often described in conclusory terms such as "ultra vires" or "fraudulent" or as "gifts or waste of corporate assets." Because at first blush it seems it would be a shocking, if not theoretically impossible, thing for stockholders to be able to sanction the directors in committing illegal acts or acts beyond the authority of the corporation, it is unsurprising that it has been held that stockholders cannot validate such action by the directors, even on an informed basis.

One of the many practical problems with this seemingly sensible doctrine is that its actual application has no apparent modern day utility insofar as the doctrine covers claims of waste or gift, except as an opportunity for Delaware courts to second-guess stockholders. There are several reasons I believe this to be so.

First, the types of "void" acts susceptible to being styled as waste claims have little of the flavor of patent illegality about them, nor are they categorically *ultra vires*. Put another way, the oft-stated proposition that "waste cannot be ratified" is a tautology that, upon close examination, has little substantive meaning. I mean, what rational person would ratify "waste"? Stating the question that way, the answer is, of course, no one. But in the real world stockholders are not asked to ratify obviously wasteful transactions. Rather than lacking any plausible business rationale or being clearly prohibited by statutory or common law, the transactions attacked as waste in Delaware courts are ones that are quite ordinary in the modern business world. Thus a review of the Delaware cases reveals that our courts have reexamined the merits of stockholder votes approving such transactions as: stock option plans; the fee agreement between a mutual fund and its investment advisor; corporate mergers; the purchase of a business in the same industry as the acquiring corporation; and the repurchase of a corporate insider's shares in the company. These are all garden variety transactions that may be validly accomplished by a Delaware corporation if supported by sufficient consideration, and what is sufficient consideration is a question that fully informed stockholders seem as well positioned as courts to answer. That is, these transactions are neither per se *ultra vires* or illegal; they only become "void" upon a determination that the corporation received no fair consideration for entering upon them.

Second, the waste vestige is not necessary to protect stockholders and it has no other apparent purpose. While I would hesitate to permit stockholders to ratify a blatantly illegal act—such as a board's decision to indemnify itself against personal liability for intentionally violating applicable environmental laws or bribing government officials to benefit the corporation—the vestigial exception for waste has little to do with corporate integrity in the sense of the corporation's responsibility to society as a whole. Rather, if there is any benefit in the waste vestige, it must consist in protecting stockholders. And where disinterested stockholders are given the information necessary to decide whether a transaction is beneficial to the corporation or wasteful to it, I see little reason to leave the door open for a judicial reconsideration of the matter.

The fact that a plaintiff can challenge the adequacy of the disclosure is in itself a substantial safeguard against stockholder approval of waste. If the corporate board failed to provide the voters with material information undermining the integrity or financial fairness of the transaction subject to the vote, no ratification effect will be accorded to the vote and the plaintiffs may press all of their claims. As a result, it is difficult to imagine how elimination of the waste vestige will permit the accomplishment of unconscionable corporate transactions, unless one presumes that stockholders are, as a class, irrational and that they will rubber stamp outrageous transactions contrary to their own economic interests.

In this regard, it is noteworthy that Delaware law does not make it easy for a board of directors to obtain "ratification effect" from a stockholder vote. The burden to prove that the vote was fair, uncoerced, and fully informed falls squarely on the board. Given the fact that Delaware law imposes no heightened pleading standards on plaintiffs alleging material nondisclosures or voting coercion and given the pro-plaintiff bias inherent in Rule 12(b)(6), it is difficult for a board to prove ratification at the pleading stage. If the board cannot prevail on a motion to dismiss, the defendant directors will be required to submit to discovery and possibly to a trial.

Nor is the waste vestige necessary to protect minority stockholders from oppression by majority or controlling stockholders. Chancellor Allen recently noted that the justification for the waste vestige is "apparently that a transaction that satisfies the high standard of waste constitutes a gift of corporate property and no one should be forced against their will to make a gift of their property." This justification is inadequate to support continued application of the exception. As an initial matter, I note that property of the corporation is not typically thought of as personal property of the stockholders, and that it is common for corporations to undertake important value-affecting transactions over the objection of some of the voters or without a vote at all.

In any event, my larger point is that this solicitude for dissenters' property rights is already adequately accounted for elsewhere in our corporation law. Delaware fiduciary law ensures that a majority or controlling stockholder cannot use a stockholder vote to insulate a transaction benefiting that stockholder from judicial examination. Only votes controlled by stockholders who are not "interested" in the transaction at issue are eligible for ratification effect in the sense of invoking the business judgment rule rather than the entire fairness form of review. That is, only the votes of those stockholders with no economic incentive to approve a wasteful transaction count.

Third, I find it logically difficult to conceptualize how a plaintiff can ultimately prove a waste or gift claim in the face of a decision by fully informed, uncoerced, independent stockholders to ratify the transaction. The test for waste is whether any person of ordinary sound business judgment could view the transaction as fair.

If fully informed, uncoerced, independent stockholders have approved the transaction, they have, it seems to me, made the decision that the transaction is "a fair exchange." As such, it is difficult to see the utility of allowing litigation to proceed in which the plaintiffs are permitted discovery and a possible trial, at great expense to the corporate defendants, in order to prove to the court that the transaction was so devoid of merit that each and every one of the voters comprising the majority must be disregarded as too hopelessly misguided to be considered a "person of ordinary sound business judgment." In this day and age in which investors also have access to an abundance of information about corporate transactions from sources other than boards of directors, it seems presumptuous and paternalistic to assume that the court knows better in a particular instance than a fully informed corporate electorate with real money riding on the corporation's performance.

Finally, it is unclear why it is in the best interests of disinterested stockholders to subject their corporation to the substantial costs of litigation in a situation where they have approved the transaction under attack. Enabling a dissident who failed to get her way at the ballot box in a fair election to divert the corporation's resources to defending her claim on the battlefield of litigation seems, if anything, contrary to the economic well-being of the disinterested stockholders as a class. Why should the law give the dissenters the right to command the corporate treasury over the contrary will of a majority of the disinterested stockholders? The costs to corporations of litigating waste claims are not trifling.

For all these reasons, a reexamination of the waste vestige would seem to be in order. Although there may be valid reasons for its continuation, those reasons should be articulated and weighed against the costs the vestige imposes on stockholders and the judicial system.

Points for Discussion

1. A place for "waste" review?

Note that Chancellor Allen and Vice Chancellor Strine expressed different views on whether a court should review a corporate transaction ratified by a majority of disinterested shareholders. Allen concluded that under Delaware law the transaction is still subject to judicial review under a "waste" standard. Strine applied this approach, but called for a reexamination of the "waste vestige" and noted in dicta that it is unnecessary, paternalistic, and costly. Who is more persuasive? And, by the way, what is the law in Delaware when judges on the Court of Chancery take different stances on the same question?

2. Review under "waste" standard and the business judgment rule.

As you may have also noticed, judicial review of corporate transactions for "waste" inquires into whether corporate decision makers approved a transaction in which no rational businessperson could conclude the corporation received fair value in the transaction. Is review under the "waste" standard consistent with the premises of the business judgment rule? How can it be said that directors are presumed to be informed, to act in good faith, and to not have conflicting interests when a court can determine that they approved an irrational business deal? Or is it that sometimes lack of information, bad faith, and conflicts of interest may not be provable—but something smells wrong—and the "waste" standard provides judges a safety valve?

C. Corporate Opportunity Doctrine

The corporate opportunity doctrine is a subset of director conflicts and the duty of loyalty. It forbids a director, officer, or managerial employee from diverting to himself any business opportunity that "belongs" to the corporation. In a 1939 decision laying out the doctrine, the Delaware Supreme Court held that a corporate fiduciary cannot take a business opportunity if (1) it is one that the corporation can financially undertake, (2) it is within the line of the corporation's business and advantageous to the corporation, and (3) it is one in which the corporation has an interest or a reasonable expectancy. *Guth v. Loft*, 5 A.2d 503 (Del. 1939). *Guth v. Loft* significantly expanded the corporate opportunity doctrine and represents the transformative case in this area.

As with many loyalty concepts, the corporate opportunity doctrine is simple to state but difficult to apply. Which "opportunities" should be turned over to the corporation and which can properly be exploited by the individual? When a business opportunity is presented to a corporate insider (usually a director or officer), can he accept it for himself or must he first offer it to the corporation? And are there opportunities that belong to the corporation so that the insider cannot take them even if the corporation, for some reason, is unable to do so?

To answer these questions, one must balance competing interests. On one hand, corporate managers are expected to further the corporation's expansion potential, and should not be allowed to advance their own economic interests at the expense of their corporation. On the other hand, corporate managers have their own entrepreneurial interests, and society benefits when persons are permitted to develop and exploit new business possibilities.

Guth v. Loft <u>involved a dispute</u> between Charles G. Guth and a company he once ran, known as Loft, Inc. But it really is a story about Pepsi-Cola, the soft drink. Pepsi-Cola was invented in the late nineteenth century, and quickly became a popular drink. However, the Pepsi-Cola company rode a roller coaster of spiraling costs and declining profits and by 1931 it was declared bankrupt for a second time.

Guth, a colorful businessman who had made a fortune in candy and bottling businesses, took over Pepsi-Cola when Coca-Cola Company, a supplier to his businesses, rejected his demands for a volume discount. Guth vowed he would "show them" by purchasing Pepsi-Cola. Guth tweaked Pepsi-Cola's formula and reduced prices, and within a few years the company was thriving. Guth owned 91% of Pepsi-Cola's shares.

Meanwhile, Guth's other company, Loft, Inc., was crumbling, and Guth agreed to sell back his Loft shares. The remaining shareholders of Loft were furious about how Guth had treated them, pointing out that Loft had paid Pepsi-Cola's startup expenses and that it was Loft's soda fountains, capital, and employees that had made Pepsi-Cola a success. The shareholders brought a suit on behalf of Loft against Guth, alleging that Guth's investment in Pepsi-Cola had been the taking of a corporate opportunity of Loft. The complaint alleged Guth could not have undertaken the Pepsi-Cola venture on his own: he lacked the funds; and it was his position at Loft that made the deal possible. Guth responded that the Pepsi-Cola opportunity was not an opportunity meant for Loft, which was primarily in the retail candy business.

After a 46-day trial, Loft won and the Delaware Supreme Court affirmed, expanding the corporate opportunity doctrine to include a broader "line of business" test in addition to a narrower "interest or expectancy" test (both are described below).

Notice that the corporate opportunity doctrine, compared to other types of fiduciary duties, focuses on *potential* harm to the corporation, not actual harm. The unlawful usurpation of a corporate opportunity happens when the corporate manager takes the opportunity, without presenting it to the corporation. The corporation might have rejected the opportunity, and even if the corporation had accepted it, the opportunity might not have been profitable. For this reason, the usual remedy for the unlawful taking of a corporate opportunity is for the corporation to receive the profits the manager derived from the opportunity, if any—that is, the corporate manager must hold the opportunity in "constructive trust" for the corporation.

We cover the corporate opportunity doctrine by presenting a well-known Delaware case and then examining several categories of tests. Our goal is to give you a sense of where the lines are drawn between those opportunities that belong to the corporation and those that do not.

1. Delaware's Approach to Corporate Opportunities

Broz v. Cellular Information Systems, Inc.

673 A.2d 148 (Del. 1996)

Veasey, Chief Justice.

Robert F. Broz ("Broz") is the President and sole stockholder of RFB Cellular, Inc. ("RFBC"), a Delaware corporation engaged in the business of providing cellular telephone service in the Midwestern United States. At the time of the conduct at issue in this appeal, Broz was also a member of the board of directors of plaintiff below-appellee, Cellular Information Systems, Inc. ("CIS"). CIS is a publicly held Delaware corporation and a competitor of RFBC.

Broz has been the President and sole stockholder of RFBC since 1992. RFBC owns and operates an FCC license area, known as the Michigan-4 Rural Service Area Cellular License ("Michigan-4"). The license entitles RFBC to provide cellular telephone service to a portion of rural Michigan. Although Broz' efforts have been devoted primarily to the business operations of RFBC, he also served as an outside director of CIS at the time of the events at issue in this case. CIS was at all times fully aware of Broz' relationship with RFBC and the obligations incumbent upon him by virtue of that relationship.

In April of 1994, Mackinac Cellular Corp. ("Mackinac") sought to divest itself of Michigan-2, the license area immediately adjacent to Michigan-4. To this end, Mackinac contacted Daniels & Associates ("Daniels") and arranged for the brokerage firm to seek potential purchasers for Michigan-2. In compiling a list of prospects, Daniels included RFBC as a likely candidate. In May of 1994, David Rhodes, a representative of Daniels, contacted Broz and broached the subject of RFBC's possible acquisition of Michigan-2. Broz later signed a confidentiality agreement at the request of Mackinac, and received the offering materials pertaining to Michigan-2.

Michigan-2 was not, however, offered to CIS. Apparently, Daniels did not consider CIS to be a viable purchaser for Michigan-2 in light of CIS' recent financial difficulties. The record shows that, at the time Michigan-2 was offered to Broz, CIS had recently emerged from lengthy and contentious Chapter 11 proceedings. Pursuant to the Chapter 11 Plan of Reorganization, CIS entered into a loan agreement that substantially impaired the company's ability to undertake new acquisitions or to incur new debt. In fact, CIS would have been unable to purchase Michigan-2 without the approval of its creditors.

During the period from early 1992 until the time of CIS' emergence from bankruptcy in 1994, CIS divested itself of some fifteen separate cellular license systems. CIS contracted to sell four additional license areas on May 27, 1994, leaving CIS with only five remaining license areas, all of which were outside of the Midwest.

On June 13, 1994, following a meeting of the CIS board, Broz spoke with CIS' Chief Executive Officer, Richard Treibick ("Treibick"), concerning his interest in acquiring Michigan-2. Treibick communicated to Broz that CIS was not interested in Michigan-2. Treibick further stated that he had been made aware of the Michigan-2 opportunity prior to the conversation with Broz, and that any offer to acquire Michigan-2 was rejected. After the commencement of the PriCellular tender offer, in August of 1994, Broz contacted another CIS director, Peter Schiff ("Schiff"), to discuss the possible acquisition of Michigan-2 by RFBC. Schiff, like Treibick, indicated that CIS had neither the wherewithal nor the inclination to purchase Michigan-2. In late September of 1994, Broz also contacted Stanley Bloch ("Bloch"), a director and counsel for CIS, to request that Bloch represent RFBC in its dealings with Mackinac. Bloch agreed to represent RFBC, and, like Schiff and Treibick, expressed his belief that CIS was not at all interested in the transaction. Ultimately, all the CIS directors testified at trial that, had Broz inquired at that time, they each would have expressed the opinion that CIS was not interested in Michigan-2.

On June 28, 1994, following various overtures from PriCellular concerning an acquisition of CIS, six CIS directors entered into agreements with PriCellular to sell their shares in CIS at a price of $2.00 per share. These agreements were contingent upon, *inter alia*, the consummation of a PriCellular tender offer for all CIS shares at the same price. Financing difficulties ultimately caused PriCellular to delay the closing date of the tender offer from September 16, 1994 until October 14, 1994 and then again until November 9, 1994.

On August 6, September 6 and September 21, 1994, Broz submitted written offers to Mackinac for the purchase of Michigan-2. During this time period, PriCellular also began negotiations with Mackinac to arrange an option for the purchase of Michigan-2. PriCellular's interest in Michigan-2 was fully disclosed to CIS' chief executive, Treibick, who did not express any interest in Michigan-2, and was actually incredulous that PriCellular would want to acquire the license. Nevertheless, CIS was fully aware that PriCellular and Broz were bidding for Michigan-2 and did not interpose CIS in this bidding war.

In late September of 1994, PriCellular reached agreement with Mackinac on an option to purchase Michigan-2. The exercise price of the option agreement was set at $6.7 million, with the option remaining in force until December 15, 1994. Pursuant to the agreement, the right to exercise the option was not transferrable to any party other than a subsidiary of PriCellular. Therefore, it could not have been transferred to CIS. The agreement further provided that Mackinac was free to sell Michigan-2 to any party who was willing to exceed the exercise price of the Mackinac-PriCellular option contract by at least $500,000. On November 14, 1994, Broz agreed to pay Mackinac $7.2 million for the Michigan-2 license, thereby meeting the terms of the option agreement. An asset purchase agreement was thereafter executed by Mackinac and RFBC.

Nine days later, on November 23, 1994, PriCellular completed its financing and closed its tender offer for CIS. Prior to that point, PriCellular owned no equity interest in CIS.

APPLICATION OF THE CORPORATE OPPORTUNITY DOCTRINE

The doctrine of corporate opportunity represents but one species of the broad fiduciary duties assumed by a corporate director or officer. A corporate fiduciary agrees to place the interests of the corporation before his or her own in appropriate circumstances. The classic statement of the doctrine is derived from the venerable case of *Guth v. Loft, Inc.*

The corporate opportunity doctrine, as delineated by *Guth* and its progeny, holds that a corporate officer or director may not take a business opportunity for his own if: (1) the corporation is financially able to exploit the opportunity; (2) the opportunity is within the corporation's line of business; (3) the corporation has an interest or expectancy in the opportunity; and (4) by taking the opportunity for his own, the corporate fiduciary will thereby be placed in a position inimicable to his duties to the corporation. The Court in *Guth* also derived a corollary which states that a director or officer *may* take a corporate opportunity if: (1) the opportunity is presented to the director or officer in his individual and not his corporate capacity; (2) the opportunity is not essential to the corporation; (3) the corporation holds no interest or expectancy in the opportunity; and (4) the director or officer has not wrongfully employed the resources of the corporation in pursuing or exploiting the opportunity. *Guth*, 5 A.2d at 509.

Thus, the contours of this doctrine are well established. It is important to note, however, that the tests enunciated in *Guth* and subsequent cases provide guidelines to be considered by a reviewing court in balancing the equities of an individual case. No one factor is dispositive and all factors must be taken into account insofar as they are applicable. Cases involving a claim of usurpation of a corporate opportunity range over a multitude of factual settings. Hard and fast rules are not easily crafted to deal with such an array of complex situations. In the instant case, we find that the facts do not support the conclusion that Broz misappropriated a corporate opportunity.

We note at the outset that Broz became aware of the Michigan-2 opportunity in his individual and not his corporate capacity. As the Court of Chancery found, "Broz did not misuse proprietary information that came to him in a corporate capacity nor did he otherwise use any power he might have over the governance of the corporation to advance his own interests." 663 A.2d at 1185. In fact, it is clear from the record that Mackinac did not consider CIS a viable candidate for the acquisition of Michigan-2. Accordingly, Mackinac did not offer the property to CIS. In this factual posture, many of the fundamental concerns undergirding the law of corporate opportunity are not present (*e.g.*, misappropriation of the corporation's proprietary information). The burden imposed upon Broz to show adherence to his fiduciary duties to CIS is thus lessened to some extent. Nevertheless, this fact is not dispositive.

We turn now to an analysis of the factors relied on by the trial court. First, we find that CIS was not financially capable of exploiting the Michigan-2 opportunity. The record shows that CIS was in a precarious financial position at the time Mackinac presented the Michigan-2 opportunity to Broz. Having recently emerged from lengthy and contentious bankruptcy proceedings, CIS was not in a position to commit capital to the acquisition of new assets. Further, the loan agreement entered into by CIS and its creditors severely limited the discretion of CIS as to the acquisition of new assets and substantially restricted the ability of CIS to incur new debt.

Second, while it may be said with some certainty that the Michigan-2 opportunity was within CIS' line of business, it is not equally clear that CIS had a cognizable interest or expectancy in the license. Under the third factor laid down by this Court in *Guth*, for an opportunity to be deemed to belong to the fiduciary's corporation, the corporation must have an interest or expectancy in that opportunity. As this Court stated in *Johnston*, 121 A.2d at 924, "[f]or the corporation to have an actual or expectant interest in any specific property, there must be some tie between that property and the nature of the corporate business." Despite the fact that the nature of the Michigan-2 opportunity was historically close to the core operations of CIS, changes were in process. At the time the opportunity was presented, CIS was actively engaged in the process of divesting its cellular license holdings. CIS' articulated business plan did not involve any new acquisitions. Further, as indicated by the testimony of the entire CIS board, the Michigan-2 license would not have been of interest to CIS even absent CIS' financial difficulties and CIS' then current desire to liquidate its cellular license holdings. Thus, CIS had no interest or expectancy in the Michigan-2 opportunity.

Finally, the corporate opportunity doctrine is implicated only in cases where the fiduciary's seizure of an opportunity results in a conflict between the fiduciary's duties to the corporation and the self-interest of the director as actualized by the exploitation of the opportunity. In the instant case, Broz' interest in acquiring and profiting from Michigan-2 created no duties that were inimicable to his obligations to CIS. Broz, at all times relevant to the instant appeal, was the sole party in interest in RFBC, a competitor of CIS. CIS was fully aware of Broz' potentially conflicting duties. Broz, however, comported himself in a manner that was wholly in accord with his obligations to CIS. Broz took care not to usurp any opportunity which CIS was willing and able to pursue. Broz sought only to compete with an outside entity, PriCellular, for acquisition of an opportunity which both sought to possess. Broz was not obligated to refrain from competition with PriCellular. Therefore, the totality of the circumstances indicates that Broz did not usurp an opportunity that properly belonged to CIS.

In concluding that Broz had usurped a corporate opportunity, the Court of Chancery placed great emphasis on the fact that Broz had not formally presented the matter to the CIS board. In so holding, the trial court erroneously grafted a new requirement onto the law of corporate opportunity, *viz.*, the requirement of formal presentation under circumstances where the corporation does not have an interest, expectancy or financial ability.

The teaching of *Guth* and its progeny is that the director or officer must analyze the situation *ex ante* to determine whether the opportunity is one rightfully belonging to the corporation. If the director or officer believes, based on one of the factors articulated above, that the corporation is not entitled to the opportunity, then he may take it for himself. Of course, presenting the opportunity to the board creates a kind of "safe harbor" for the director, which removes the specter of a *post hoc* judicial determination that the director or officer has improperly usurped a corporate opportunity. Thus, presentation avoids the possibility that an error in the fiduciary's assessment of the situation will create future liability for breach of fiduciary duty. It is not the law of Delaware that presentation to the board is a necessary prerequisite to a finding that a corporate opportunity has not been usurped.

In concluding that Broz usurped an opportunity properly belonging to CIS, the Court of Chancery held that "[f]or practical business reasons CIS' interests with respect to the Mackinac transaction came to merge with those of PriCellular, even before the closing of its tender offer for CIS stock." Based on this fact, the trial court concluded that Broz was required to consider PriCellular's prospective, post-acquisition plans for CIS in determining whether to forego the opportunity or seize it for himself. Had Broz done this, the Court of Chancery determined that he would have concluded that CIS was entitled to the opportunity by virtue of the alignment of its interests with those of PriCellular.

We disagree. Broz was under no duty to consider the interests of PriCellular when he chose to purchase Michigan-2. At the time Broz purchased Michigan-2, PriCellular had not yet acquired CIS. Any plans to do so would still have been wholly speculative. Accordingly, Broz was not required to consider the contingent and uncertain plans of PriCellular in reaching his determination of how to proceed.

In reaching our conclusion on this point, we note that certainty and predictability are values to be promoted in our corporation law. Broz, as an active participant in the cellular telephone industry, was entitled to proceed in his own economic interest in the absence of any countervailing duty. The right of a director or officer to engage in business affairs outside of his or her fiduciary capacity would be illusory if these individuals were required to consider every potential, future occurrence in determining whether a particular business strategy would implicate fiduciary duty concerns.

We hold that Broz did not breach his fiduciary duties to CIS.

———————

2. Corporate Opportunity Tests

We now consider several categories of corporate opportunity tests applied by the courts. It is important to note upfront that these tests are often characterized as default rules, which corporate participants can waive. Indeed, Delaware has a statutory provision, DGCL § 122(17), which explicitly permits corporations to waive the protections of the corporate opportunity doctrine.

> ### DGCL § 122
> ### Specific Powers
>
> Every corporation created under this chapter shall have power to—
>
> (17) Renounce, in its certificate of incorporation or by action of its board of directors, any interest or expectancy of the corporation in, or in being offered an opportunity to participate in, specified business opportunities or specified classes or categories of business opportunities that are presented to the corporation or one or more of its officers, directors or stockholders.

A corporation or board of directors can choose to identify "classes or categories of business opportunities" by line or type of business, identity of originator, identity of the party or parties to or having an interest in the business opportunity, identity of the recipient of the business opportunity, periods of time, or geographical location. Many investors find waiver attractive, particularly for close or early-stage corporations. For example, venture capitalists often invest in numerous companies and are presented with numerous corporate opportunities. They might not invest in a corporation if they thought the investment would restrict their other opportunities.

However, the application of DGCL § 122(17) is not as clear as many would like. The comment to the subsection says it "does not change the level of judicial scrutiny that will apply to the renunciation of an interest or expectancy of the corporation in a business opportunity, which will be determined by the common law of fiduciary duty, including the duty of loyalty." Does that mean DGCL § 122(17) really is not much of a default rule, and the courts will analyze corporate opportunity disputes even when corporations have opted out of the doctrine? What should be the standard of review if the board renounces a business opportunity (business judgment rule or fairness)? Does it matter how the corporation renounces (in its articles or by board resolution)? Does the absence of a renunciation suggest that the corporation has an interest or expectancy in an opportunity?

Given these uncertainties, even corporations that opt out of the corporate opportunity doctrine may be subject to one or more of the categories of judicial tests. Below are a few of these categories. There are no clear lines here, and cases depend greatly on the facts, so we have included a few excerpts from some of the classic cases in the area.

Interest or expectancy. The interest or expectancy analysis is the earliest judicial test, and it is difficult to apply. The key point is that corporate opportunities are not limited to actual ownership. They include "interests" or "expectancies" that are less than an enforceable legal right. In *Litwin v. Allen*, 25 N.Y.S.2d 667, 686 (Sup. Ct. 1940), the court suggested how to discern whether the corporation has an interest or expectancy:

> This corporate right or expectancy, this mandate upon directors to act for the corporation, may arise from various circumstances, such as, for example, the fact that directors had undertaken to negotiate in the field on behalf of the corporation, or that the corporation was in need of the particular business opportunity to the knowledge of the directors, or that the business opportunity was seized and developed at the expense, and with the facilities of the corporation. It is noteworthy that in cases which have imposed this type of liability upon fiduciaries, the thing determined by the court to be the subject of the trust was a thing of special and unique value to the beneficiary; for example, real estate, a proprietary formula valuable to the corporation's business, patents indispensable or valuable to its business, a competing enterprise or one required for the growth and expansion of the corporation's business or the like.

Line of business. Under the line of business test, a corporation has a prior claim to a business opportunity presented to an officer or director that falls within the firm's particular line of business. The test is closely related to the "interest or expectancy" standard, but includes a practicality assessment of the corporation's ability to take on the business opportunity. In *Guth v. Loft*, 5 A.2d 503, 514 (Del. 1939), the court explained the concept as follows:

> The phrase is not within the field of precise definition, nor is it one that can be bounded by a set formula. It has a flexible meaning, which is to be applied reasonably and sensibly to the facts and circumstances of the particular case. Where a corporation is engaged in a certain business, and an opportunity is presented to it embracing an activity as to which it has fundamental knowledge, practical experience and ability to pursue, which, logically and naturally is adaptable to its business having regard for its financial position, and is one that is consonant with its reasonable needs and aspirations for expansion, it may be properly said that the opportunity is in the line of the corporation's business.

Thus, if a business proposition would require a corporation to modify its operating infrastructure beyond a certain threshold, the business opportunity would be found to be outside the corporation's line of business. Courts will typically apply the test to extend beyond a corporation's existing operations. The rationale for such an application is simple. Courts recognize that corporations are dynamic entities. Furthermore, shareholders reasonably expect that a corporation will go beyond the status quo and take advantage of highly profitable, but safe, opportunities.

Food for Thought

The line of business test becomes even more difficult to apply when a director or officer wears more than one hat. In *Johnston v. Greene*, 121 A.2d 919 (Del. 1956), Odlum, a financier, who was an officer and director of numerous corporations, was offered in his individual capacity the chance to acquire all the stock of Nutt-Shel, as well as some related patents. Although the business of Nutt-Shel had no close relation to the business of Airfleets, Inc., of which Odlum was president, Odlum turned over to Airfleets the opportunity to buy the stock of Nutt-Shel. But he purchased the patents for his friends and associates and, to a limited extent, for himself. Airfleets, which had a large amount of cash, had the financial capability to buy the patents. The board of Airfleets, dominated by Odlum, voted to buy only the stock. In a shareholders' derivative action against Odlum and the directors, the Delaware Supreme Court found that Odlum had not breached his duty in the purchase of the patents. In discussing the problem of multiple conflicting loyalties, the court stated:

> At the time when the Nutt-Shel business was offered to Odlum, his position was this: He was the part-time president of Airfleets. He was also president of Atlas—an investment company. He was a director of other corporations and a trustee of foundations interested in making investments. If it was his fiduciary duty, upon being offered any investment opportunity, to submit it to a corporation of which he was a director, the question arises, Which corporation? Why Airfleets instead of Atlas? Why Airfleets instead of one of the foundations? So far as appears, there was no specific tie between the Nutt-Shel business and any of these corporations or foundations. Odlum testified that many of his companies had money to invest, and this appears entirely reasonable. How, then, can it be said that Odlum was under any obligation to offer the opportunity to one particular corporation? And if he was not under such an obligation, why could he not keep it for himself?

> Plaintiff suggests that if Odlum elects to assume fiduciary relationships to competing corporations he must assume the obligations that are entailed by such relationships. So he must, but what are the obligations? The mere fact of having funds to invest does not ordinarily put the corporations "in competition" with each other, as that phrase is used in the law of corporate opportunity. There is nothing inherently wrong in a man of large business and financial interests serving as a director of two or more investment companies, and both Airfleets and Atlas (to mention only two companies) must reasonably have expected that Odlum would be free either to offer to any of his companies any business opportunity that came to him personally, or to retain it for himself—provided always that there was no tie between any of such companies and the new venture or any specific duty resting upon him with respect to it.

In short, which corporation does a director serve when on multiple boards?

Economic capacity. Another important factor in deciding whether there has been a usurpation of a corporate opportunity is whether the corporation has the economic capacity to take the opportunity. The importance of the corporation's ability to pay for the opportunity varies case by case. Some courts treat incapacity as an indication the opportunity was not of interest to the corporation, others that the corporation would have rejected it. Further, some courts focus on whether the corporation had liquid assets available, while others look to the corporation's financial solvency more generally and ask whether it could raise enough money to pay for the opportunity.

Corporate rejection. Courts broadly accept the notion that a manager can take a corporate opportunity if the corporation has rejected it. The important question is whether the opportunity was presented to, and rejected after full disclosure by, disinterested, independent corporate decision makers. By accepting the opportunity, the corporation precludes the manager from developing it individually. Proper rejection, however, precludes the corporation from later claiming the corporate opportunity.

Remedies. In general, the remedy for a breach of fiduciary duty is the award of damages in the amount of the harm the corporation suffered from the breach. When dealing with the taking of a corporate opportunity, however, the problem of the appropriate remedy is more complex. Recall that the harm when a corporate manager takes a corporate opportunity occurs before it is known how the corporation might have developed it and whether it will be profitable. The harm to the corporation is not actual, but instead the deprivation of the right to take the opportunity for itself.

One possible remedy for usurpation of a corporate opportunity is to assess damages according to the potential profits lost by the corporation, based on a calculation of the estimated value of the opportunity at the time of the taking given its likely returns and their risk. Another possible remedy is to assess the actual profits realized by the usurping manager on the theory of unjust enrichment. Such profits would be easy to measure if the manager had already sold the opportunity, although valuation problems may arise.

Courts have chosen the latter approach. The traditional remedy is the imposition of a constructive trust on the manager's new business. This approach eliminates messy valuation problems and assumes that the manager's actual profits approximate the corporation's potential lost profits. However, the offending manager is entitled to expenditures made in pursuing and developing the opportunity, including reasonable compensation.

———————

Points for Discussion

1. Corporate expansion vs. entrepreneurship.

Notice that the corporate-opportunity cases seem to go in two directions. Sometimes the courts focus on the corporation's expectancies and line of business—that is, the corporation's expansion potential. Sometimes the courts focus on the insider's interests in developing an outside business—that is, individual entrepreneurial motivations. Why not consider business opportunities only from the perspective of the corporation?

2. Waiver of fiduciary duties.

Delaware's statutory provision that allows the corporation to renounce an interest in specified business opportunities effectively means that the corporation is permitted to waive fiduciary duties. Notice that this provision applies only to the waiver of the corporate opportunity doctrine, but not to the waiver of director self-dealing duties. Why should the corporation be able to waive its interests in business opportunities, but not director loyalty in self-dealing transactions? And does the statutory provision allow directors on the board to approve such a renunciation when they have an interest in the outside business opportunity? Are we back at *Remillard* asking whether a statute seeming to define the scope of fiduciary duties should be read on its face?

CHAPTER 22

Executive Compensation

Executive compensation, the payment of directors and officers, presents a classic conflict of interest. But it also presents an opportunity. On one hand is the concern that managers will pay themselves too much money to the detriment of shareholders. On the other hand is the potential to use compensation to incentivize managers to act in the interests of shareholders and create value for the corporation. Executive compensation is a double-edged sword, with the possibility of self dealing and excessive cost yet also the opportunity for alignment of interests and overall gain.

How should corporations achieve the right balance? Answers pour in from all directions. State corporate statutes empower the board of directors to set executive compensation; state courts generally defer to board-set executive compensation, particularly if approved by shareholders; federal securities law requires public companies to disclose the details of their top executives' compensation and prohibits public companies from giving personal loans to their executives; federal tax law historically limited the deductibility of compensation above $1 million per year paid to an employee; and the stock exchanges specify the tasks and composition of the board's compensation committee of listed companies.

In recent years, no area of corporate governance has provoked as much public debate, outrage, and publicity as executive compensation. Starting with Plato's dictum that nobody in a community, including its leaders, should earn more than five times that of the average worker, critics have pointed to the spiraling compensation of CEOs in large U.S. companies. While average CEO compensation was 42 times average worker pay in 1980, it has climbed to 250 or more times average pay in the 2010s. The median annual income of CEOs of large corporations recently has been about $15 million, whereas median full-time annual worker wages have been around $40,000.

We begin this chapter with an example. Next we turn to the policy and process of executive compensation and the debate surrounding whether current pay levels in public companies are defensible. Then we summarize how federal law has increasingly regulated the form, disclosure, and liability surrounding executive pay (a significant federalization of this area of corporate governance), while state courts have continued to resolve important disputes case-by-case. Finally we describe the pay litigation involving The Disney Company, the most notable Delaware case involving judicial scrutiny of executive pay.

A. Real-World Example

Compensation of corporate executives takes many forms. A typical package includes some combination of salary, bonuses, stock options, stock-based plans, deferred compensation (pension) plans, and fringe benefits (or "perks"). We begin our discussion by looking at the packages paid to the named executive officers of Alphabet Inc., the parent company of Google. We chose Alphabet in part because its approach raises some fundamental questions about executive compensation. The details were described in the company's 2018 proxy statement filed with the SEC.

Notably, the co-founders of Google (and parent Alphabet), Larry Page and Sergey Brin, take only a $1 salary and do not participate in the company's cash bonus or equity programs. Through a dual-class structure, Page and Brin hold about 10% of Alphabet's overall equity and control 51% of the voting power. The Executive Summary to the compensation disclosure explains: "Larry and Sergey have voluntarily elected to only receive nominal cash compensation for their services as CEO and President, respectively, of Alphabet. As significant stockholders, a large portion of their personal wealth is tied directly to Alphabet's stock price performance, which provides direct alignment with stockholder interests."

Although the total value of the pay package for the other Alphabet and Google executives was higher than average, the components are typical of the pay packages of most U.S. public companies—particularly in the emphasis on stock-based compensation. The company explains: "We believe in pay for performance. A portion of compensation is tied to performance for all employees. The proportion of overall pay tied to performance is higher for employees at more senior levels in the organization, reflecting their opportunity for higher impact on company performance." Take a look at Alphabet's Summary Compensation Table:

Name and Principal Position	Year	Salary ($)	Bonus ($)	Stock Awards ($)	Option Awards ($)	Non-Equity Incentive Plan Compensation ($)	Non-Qualified Deferred Compensation Earnings ($)	All Other Compensation ($)	Total ($)
Larry Page CEO, Co-Founder	2017	1	-	-	-	-	-	-	1
	2016	1	-	-	-	-	-	-	1
	2015	1	-	-	-	-	-	-	1
Sergey Brin President, Co-Founder	2017	1	-	-	-	-	-	-	1
	2016	1	-	-	-	-	-	-	1
	2015	1	-	-	-	-	-	-	1
Eric E. Schmidt, Former Executive, Chairman	2017	1,250,000	-	-	-	-	2,798,606	677,986	4,726,592
	2016	1,250,000	-	-	-	-	2,430,685	629,106	4,309,791
	2015	1,254,808	6,000,000	-	-	-	-	783,370	8,038,178
Sundar Pichai CEO, Google	2017	650,000	-	-	-	-	-	683,557	1,333,557
	2016	650,000	-	198,695,790	-	-	-	372,410	199,718,200
	2015	652,500	-	99,829,142	-	-	-	150,460	100,632,102
Ruth M. Porat CFO, Alphabet and Google	2017	650,000	-	-	-	-	-	38,638	688,638
	2016	650,000	-	38,313,173	-	-	-	110,956	39,074,129
	2015	395,000	5,000,000	25,052,554	-	-	-	603,932	31,051,486
David C. Drummond Chief Legal Officer, Alphabet	2017	650,000	-	-	-	-	-	14,252	664,252
	2016	650,000	-	-	-	-	-	14,387	664,387
	2015	652,500	-	-	-	-	-	20,323	672,823

The notes to the table explained that "all other compensation" includes "401(k) company match of up to $9,000, life insurance premiums paid by the company for the benefit of the named executive officer, personal use of company aircraft, and the market value of a holiday gift given to each employee, net of tax withholding, unless otherwise noted." Sundar Pichai's listing under that column in 2017, for example, included "$637,538 for personal security and $33,599 for personal use of aircraft chartered by the company."

The board articulated its philosophy as follows:

We designed our employee and executive compensation programs to support three goals:

- Attract and retain the world's best talent

- Support our culture of innovation and performance

- Align employee and stockholder interests

Points for Discussion

1. How much, for what?

Sundar Pichai was named as CEO of Google during the company's re-organization in 2015 to a structure with Alphabet as the parent holding company. In 2016, Google's sales rose 22.5%, net income rose 19%, and the company maintained its top position in the internet advertising industry. Shares of Alphabet rose 5% in 2016, while the broader NASDAQ Composite Index did even better, increasing 10%. What was Pichai's total pay package in 2016, his first full calendar year at the helm of Google? How much of it was based on actual performance? How much was meant as inducement for future performance? What do you make of Larry Page and Sergey Brin's $1 salaries? What are the advantages and disadvantages to the above compensation packages, compared to more typical compensation, which would include larger annual cash bonuses?

2. Stock vs. options.

What is the difference between paying a CEO with stock grants, compared to stock options? How is each accounted for in the company's financial statements? What does it mean that stock options, if exercised, can "dilute" other shares? What are the differences in executive incentives between being paid with stock compared to stock options?

B. Policy and Process

Before we get to the law governing executive compensation, we are going to highlight a few issues of policy and process. Policy questions about executive pay are inevitably intertwined with how pay is actually set.

1. Policy Debate on What Is "Fair Pay"

Are corporate executives in U.S. corporations worth the pay they receive? Those who defend the pay levels of top executives point out that executive talent is in short supply. It is not unusual for a CEO terminated by one corporation to find a number of job offers from others. To identify and motivate the few executives able to lead large public businesses, corporations must offer a large enough prize for potential CEOs—a "tournament" award. In addition, once CEOs are identified, corporations and their pay committees must compete to keep the scarce talent. Pay packages may sometimes be more about executive retention than pay for performance.

Those who criticize the high levels of executive pay in U.S. corporations doubt that there is a shortage of executive talent. They question the proportion and size of executive pay packages. Can an employee-manager, as opposed to the entrepreneur who creates a business, ever be worth $1 billion over his career? These critics find it hard to believe that CEOs as a group are so scarce or so talented that their managerial services could be worth so much. They point out that successful companies in Europe and Japan are able to hire executives for a fraction of the cost of U.S. executives, without heavy reliance on stock options or "reward for failure" termination fees.

For other critics, the question is one of incentives. Even if CEOs are in short supply, corporations have not designed executive pay to motivate optimal results. Before the 1990s, the prevalent compensation model linked executive pay to company size, which prompted executives to focus on revenues and acquisitions, not profits or stock price. Then, in response to academic arguments that stock-based compensation "ties managers to the mast," executive pay in the 1990s increasingly tended toward stock option grants. Compensation committees viewed stock options as essentially free and awarded them widely.

Do stock options, whose value depends on rising stock prices, actually align CEO incentives with shareholders interests? Critics of stock options have made several arguments that options are a poor form of payment:

Expensive. The cost to the company is generally greater than the value to the executives. Why? A rational CEO would rather have $1 million in a diversified portfolio (or in cash) than $1 million of his company's stock options—given that the CEO's business reputation, salary, bonus, retirement, and other compensation is tied to the company. Thus to pay $1 million of value (to the CEO), studies show the company must grant $2 million of options. CEOs prize diversification, like anyone else.

Poor alignment. Stock options align incentives in only one direction since managers (unlike shareholders) suffer no downside losses if stock prices fall. This makes managers with options more willing to gamble. And if prices fall, managers will often seek additional compensation to make up for the decline, which means they win either way.

Poor design. Stock options can become valuable if an executive merely stays in office during a rising market. "Outperformance" options, whose value depends on the company's stock beating a selected index, never caught on.

Distorted incentives. Because dividends are not paid on options, CEOs who receive option grants have an incentive to have the company retain cash and reduce dividends. In fact, the dividends paid by public companies have decreased dramatically.

Encourages fraud. Executives with options have an incentive to increase their company's stock price—sometimes no matter the cost. Options become an "inducement for greed" as CEOs manipulate reported earnings to push the share price up, then sell before the price falls.

In response to these criticisms, many companies have redesigned their stock-based compensation plans. Grants of stock options are down, while grants of restricted stock that vest in the future (sometimes based on company performance) are up significantly. In addition, rather than focus on stock price appreciation, these incentive plans increasingly are pegged to other performance measures, such as net income, cash flow, even customer satisfaction. Newer stock options are granted at a premium (above the current market price) and are not subject to adjustment, so if performance is poor, executives receive no payouts. Further, Congress enacted changes to the tax code in 2017 that eliminated an exception for performance-based compensation from the tax deductibility limit of $1 million per employee each year. The exception had previously encouraged the use of performance-based compensation such as stock options.

Despite these changes, the criticism continues. Some have argued that there is a disconnect between executive pay levels and company performance and that current pay levels for U.S. executives are best explained by greed and cronyism, not arm's-length bargaining. Even early advocates of stock options as a way of aligning manager and shareholder interests concluded that stock options tempt managers to choose business strategies, make investments, and juggle accounting numbers so the company looks good when stock options become exercisable. Some commentators have expressed concern about the overall amount of pay from a social perspective, particularly in light of rising economic inequality.

What should be done? Some say, nothing. They point out that there is no evidence of what optimal pay levels should be or that the compensation system is broken. In fact, there is some indication this system is self-correcting and functional. Although pay has risen at the top-performing companies, it has fallen at the bottom-performing companies. Pay is becoming better linked to performance. Moreover, studies show that companies managed by skilled CEOs who are highly paid—where "skill" is measured by a track record of maintaining good performance and reversing bad performance—significantly outperform companies managed by skilled, but poorly-paid CEOs. High pay may create better incentives. And finally, executive compensation overall is not a significant percentage of most company's revenues or profits. For many companies, CEO pay is just a rounding error.

Others argue that the compensation system just needs find-tuning. For example, they urge more transparency on the impact of pay packages in a forward-looking "Compensation Discussion & Analysis" that would be subject to shareholder approval, as in Britain. In the process, the compensation committee would be forced to confront whether pay really is creating the right incentives and to stake their reputation on it working. Not surprisingly, compensation consultants have urged better design in pay packages. Some would de-emphasize stock options and focus on stock grants that vest upon meeting particular targets. Some would have compensation committees focus on "strategic value" created by managers, rather than short-term earnings figures. And, instead of repricing out-of-the-money options, some have suggested that poorly-performing companies sell their executives new lower-priced options, thus creating some downside discomfort.

Others assert that the compensation system is broken. Some with this view argue that three mechanisms are absent from the system: (1) truly independent directors, acting at arm's length, who design pay packages that maximize shareholder value; (2) market and social forces that constrain executives from negotiating for nonoptimal pay packages; and (3) shareholders that exercise their voting and litigation rights to block nonoptimal pay arrangements. They urge that boards become more answerable to shareholders, including by permitting shareholders to nominate directors to the board. By contrast, others who view the compensation system as broken highlight the perils of performance-based pay and argue it is overrated as a tool for improving long-term corporate value. They urge a return to moderately-sized pay packages that focus on salary.

2. Process for Setting Executive Pay

Executive pay, like other business decisions, is ultimately determined by the board of directors. In public corporations, setting executive pay is usually delegated to a compensation committee of the board. Codifying a "best practice" adopted by many public companies over the last two decades, the NYSE and NASDAQ listing standards generally require that the compensation committee of listed companies be composed *solely* of three or more "independent directors," as defined in the listing standards. The scope of authority and duties of the compensation committee must be specified in a written charter.

Decision-making processes vary by corporation and evolve over time. A leading pay consultant, writing in the early 1990s, described the process for setting executive compensation:

> Imagine yourself as the CEO of a large company. Being a red-blooded American who has fought his way to the top of the organization, you're always ready to earn more money. After talking to your CEO buddies and getting a pay consultant, you have to decide on the line of attack you will be pursuing with your board. If yours is a great-performing company, then, you only have to mention your performance, followed by the mantra "We want to pay for performance," and your compensation consultant will be on his way.
>
> If yours is a poor-performing company, you have a bit more of an uphill struggle to get a raise. But nothing is impossible if you have the right attitude and the right consultant. First, you should admit the company is having some hard times, and you promptly and predictably blame the hard times on external events. If you are the head of a major automobile company, for example, you point to the fact that every one of the Big Three automakers is in trouble, not just your company, and you excoriate the Japanese for not playing the international trade game fairly. Once you finish laying the blame off onto others, you note that you are starting to lose key people. Performance has been so bad that you haven't been able to pay bonuses, and even salary increases have slowed to a crawl. What's more, all those options that were awarded to you three years ago are underwater; that is, the strike prices of the options—what you have to pay to exercise them— are now a lot higher than the current market price.

That wasn't the way things were supposed to work out. The market price was supposed to rise above the strike price so as to give you a good profit. But all those external, and uncontrollable, events intervened to produce an unintended result. During this part of the discussion, you note to the consultant that an executive in your company can quit, cross the street, and go to work for a competitor whose stock has also fallen. But in so doing, he will be exchanging underwater stock options for new options where the strike price is equal to the current market price, and not higher. He'll recommend to the board that they simply erase the old strike price on each executive's option agreement and substitute a new, lower strike price.

The consultant will never stop to ponder a difficult problem of logic. If it makes sense to reward a CEO in good times, because that is only just, and if it makes sense to reward a CEO in bad times, because you need to keep him with the company, and if there are only two types of times—good times and bad times—then just when, pray tell, is the CEO ever going to get his pay cut? The answer, distressingly, is never.

No matter how the consulting assignment starts, it will almost always end in the meeting room of the compensation committee of the board. It is here that the consultant will make his recommendations. The CEO, with his company-paid consultant, will have the advantage. The CEO is an informed seller of his talents, and the compensation committee is an uninformed buyer. It meets only a few times a year, and then only for an hour or so each time. Its members are not pay experts, and they are not given any independent counsel of their own. So they must of necessity rely heavily on what the company's compensation consultant is telling them.

While you're pondering this process, think also about the fact that many of the compensation committee members may be the personal friends of the CEO. And think about the fact that it is the CEO who suggests to the board members how much they should pay themselves. In saying this, I don't mean to suggest that compensation committee members and board members are dishonest people who are willing to sell themselves for a few bucks. Rather, I am only observing that there is a climate of friendship and trust operating here, rather than the more cautious attitude that one usually presents toward someone who is trying to sell you something that will cost you quite a bit of money.

So that's how they do it. A lot of rationalization goes on, and a lot of high-priced talent is retained to prove a conclusion that the CEO has already made. And everybody wins. The CEO gets a raise, the compensation consultant gets his bills paid, and the compensation committee goes home feeling good that it is paying for performance or keeping good people or both. Or almost everybody wins. Everybody but the shareholders.

Graef S. Crystal, In Search of Excess: The Overcompensation of American Executives 42–50 (1991).

Many boards of directors use outside experts to assist in the evaluation of executives and the development of a compensation program. The independence of compensation consultants and the board decision-making process have come under increasing scrutiny in recent decades.

In determining whether to engage a particular consultant, a compensation committee typically considers various factors that could affect independence, such as the other services performed by the consultant for the corporation, the amount of fees paid, and any existing personal and business relationships between the consultant and the corporation, including executives. Further, stock exchange listing standards give authority to compensation committees to approve consultant fees in order to make clear that the consultant works for the committee rather than the executives.

In addition, companies have designed practices to increase independent oversight, and the appearance of such, for example using executive sessions of the board or compensation committee to have discussions without members of management present. At the committee's discretion, independent compensation consultants or counsel are often present for committee meetings, including during executive sessions.

Documentation and disclosure are also important. Corporate governance experts encourage corporations to maintain records of the decision-making process and approval of executive compensation, including minutes of compensation committee and board meetings, and to put in place written procedures for granting and issuing equity awards. The SEC rules on disclosure of executive compensation—besides requiring tabular presentation of the pay of the company's CEO and for other highest paid executives—also require disclosure of the process by which compensation is set in the company.

––––––––––

C. Legal Landscape on Executive Pay

We next consider some federal and state legal issues related to executive compensation. Although executive compensation, like the duty of loyalty generally, had been the focus of state law, more recently federal regulation has come to occupy the area as federal regulators focused on the increase in the level of executive compensation. We begin with an overview of federal law, which traditionally has focused on disclosure of executive pay in public companies, but lately has sought to create substantive rights for shareholders—a notable federal intrusion into corporate governance. We then look at state law, which has come to emphasize boardroom process.

1. Federal Law: Shift from Disclosure to Corporate Governance

Over the past two decades federal law has taken a good deal of interest in executive pay—no doubt a reaction to the public attention that the subject has gotten in the headlines. Although no federal law directly regulates pay levels, certain tax and disclosure rules adopted in the early 1990s have played a role in the setting of executive compensation. In 1993, Congress responded to an outcry about high executive compensation by revising the tax laws to disallow corporate deductions for executive compensation paid to the CEO and the four highest-paid executives in excess of $1 million per year. An exception was made for compensation based on performance goals (1) determined by a compensation committee composed solely of outside directors, (2) approved by shareholders after disclosure of material terms, and (3) certified by the compensation committee to have been met. *See* Internal Revenue Code § 162(m) (Congress removed this exception in 2017).

Many critics argued that the upward spiral in executive pay could be traced back to this tax law exception. Because stock options satisfied the performance-based requirements of the new tax statute, corporations had an incentive to grant stock options instead of paying salaries. The tax revisions weren't meant to deter excessive pay, but they actually encouraged one form of pay, options, by making them cheaper from a tax perspective.

SEC disclosure rules. At about the same time as the changes to the tax code, the SEC responded in 1992 to the public outcry against overpaid executives and significantly revised its rules on disclosure of executive compensation in public companies. Moving away from a narrative approach, the rules required the use of numerical tables to permit comparisons of executive pay over time and across companies. Then, in 2006, the disclosure rules were again revised to provide a clearer and more complete picture of executive pay, including a single figure for total compensation and present valuation of option grants.

Today the SEC rules require the company's annual proxy statement to disclose the compensation of the CEO, the CFO, and the three highest-paid executives for the current and two preceding fiscal years. Such information as salary, bonus, stock awards, option grants, incentive plan payments, increases in pension value, and perquisites must be disclosed in tabular form, sometimes with detailed footnotes. In addition, current information about stock-based compensation awarded in the past, such as stock grants and stock options, must be presented in tabular form. Finally, the SEC rules require information on post-employment retirement benefits and deferred compensation, as well as any change-of-control termination fees.

Company disclosures of executive pay have been carefully followed by the business press, which uses them to report annually on the highest paid executives and "grade" their relative worth. Although there had originally been some hope that SEC-mandated disclosure would shame board compensation committees into reining in compensation excesses, the greater information fueled an upward spiral in pay levels as companies sought to out-compensate each other. During the 1990s institutional shareholders seemed indifferent. But in the 2000s and 2010s, shareholder proposals on the structuring and approval of executive pay regularly received significant support.

The 2006 amendments to the SEC disclosure rules responded to criticisms that the true picture of executive pay was often obfuscated, particularly with respect to the terms and real value of option grants and retirement plans. The SEC rules thus require tabular presentations (for easier comparisons across companies) and improved narratives of how executive pay is set and earned. Under the rules, disclosure begins with a Compensation Discussion and Analysis that identifies the underlying compensation policies and decisions reflected in the tables. The CD&A must identify the objectives and design of the company's pay plans, the elements of pay and why they were chosen, and how pay levels were determined. The CD&A must also address particular topics, such as whether the company engages in benchmarking of executive pay, the role that company executives played in the setting of pay, and the company's policies for the recovery of performance-based pay if financial results are ever restated.

Sarbanes-Oxley: a substantive volley. While the SEC has focused on disclosure of executive pay in public companies, Congress has taken aim at specific pay practices. In the Sarbanes-Oxley Act in 2002—the congressional response to the spate of corporate and accounting scandals of the early 2000s—Congress introduced some corporate governance reforms related to executive pay.

Prohibition of loans to insiders. In response to stories of profligate (often undisclosed) lending by public companies to corporate insiders, Congress prohibited public companies from giving "personal loans" to directors and executive officers. Securities Exchange Act § 13(k),

Sarbanes-Oxley § 402. The provision contains a limited exception for loans to insiders made in the normal course of the company's business, such as a credit card offered by a bank to its executives on the same terms as offered to other customers.

The federal prohibition, which displaces state law, changes "business as usual." For example, companies have to assess whether they can give executives such perks as travel advances, personal use of a company credit card (subject to reimbursement), retention bonuses (again subject to reimbursement), indemnification advances by the company (where the executive must reimburse the company if ultimately not entitled to indemnification), loans from 401(k) plans, and cashless exercise of stock options (where the company or a broker gives the executive a short-term loan so the executive can exercise the options and then repay the loan once he sells the underlying shares).

Disgorgement of incentive pay. Responding to stories of corporate executives profiting from misstated financial information, Sarbanes-Oxley also requires the disgorgement of incentive pay made when company financials had been misstated. If a public company is forced to restate its financial statements as a result of misconduct, the company's CEO and CFO must reimburse the company for any incentive pay (such as bonuses or equity-based compensation) received from the company during the 12-month period after the misstated financials were issued or filed. Sarbanes-Oxley § 304, 15 U.S.C. § 7243.

The provision, however, raised a variety of uncertainties—not the least of which was whether the reimbursement action could be brought directly by shareholders, by the company (or shareholders in a derivative suit), or only through an enforcement action by the SEC. Also unclear was what constituted "misconduct" and whether the CEO or CFO subject to reimbursement must have been personally engaged in the misconduct.

Lower courts have concluded that § 304 does not create a private cause of action, but can only be enforced by the SEC. Although the SEC came under fire in the years following the adoption of § 304 for failing to seek clawbacks, since 2009 the agency has been using the section to reach corporate executives, even in cases where they were not personally involved in the misconduct that led to financial restatements.

Dodd-Frank: more federal pressure on executive pay. The Dodd-Frank Act of 2010 responded to the Financial Crisis of 2008. Although primarily instituting sweeping reforms of the financial sector, the Act also focused on some aspects of corporate governance in public companies—particularly executive pay. One of the most important changes introduced by Dodd-Frank has been the advisory vote the law gives to shareholders in public companies on the pay packages of the company's top executives. But before describing this "say on pay," you may find interesting the other forays of Dodd-Frank into corporate governance on executive pay.

Shareholder vote on golden parachutes. Dodd-Frank gives shareholders an advisory vote on executive pay packages that arise in mergers or other corporate acquisitions. When a company seeks shareholder approval for an acquisition, the company must now disclose any special pay arrangements for company executives, such as "golden parachutes." And shareholders can voice their displeasure if company executives seem to be getting a windfall in the deal.

Clawbacks of incentive pay. In an effort to strengthen and expand the clawback remedy adopted in Sarbanes-Oxley, Dodd-Frank mandates that the stock exchanges require their listed companies to adopt procedures to recover up to three years of incentive pay from current and former company executives whenever the company must restate its financials. This mandate expands on the Sarbanes-Oxley clawback remedy by (1) covering more executives than just the CEO and CFO, (2) expanding the clawback period from one year to three years, and (3) applying to all restatements, not just those due to misconduct. Companies are only required to claw back incentive-based pay that exceeds what would have been paid under the restated financials. Additionally, if the company fails to seek a clawback, the SEC can bring an action to enforce the recovery—but, as with Sarbanes-Oxley, there is no express private cause of action. Most public companies have adopted clawback policies.

Compensation disclosure. Dodd-Frank requires public companies to include new disclosures in their annual proxy statements. First, the company must show the relationship between executive pay actually paid and the company's financial performance. This "pay versus performance" disclosure responds to the growing view of shareholders that executives should not be able to reap excessive salaries while the company is failing. Second, companies must disclose a "pay ratio": the CEO's total compensation divided by the median compensation of the company's other employees. For example, if the CEO makes $15 million and the median employee makes $50,000, the company's pay ratio would be 300. This pay ratio disclosure has been controversial: the ratios are high, it is difficult to determine median pay, and disclosure creates tension (especially among workers who are paid below the median).

"Say on pay." Perhaps the most important corporate governance reform instituted by Dodd-Frank has been the requirement for all public companies of an advisory (nonbinding) shareholder vote on executive pay. Following the lead of Britain and a crescendo of successful shareholder proposals seeking "say on pay" votes, the Act gave shareholders the right to vote for or against the pay packages of the company CEO and the four other top-paid executives. The "say on pay" vote must take place at least every three years, though most companies have opted to conduct the vote annually.

Prior to its inclusion in Dodd-Frank at the behest of the institutional shareholder lobby, "say on pay" had generated a heated debate. Proponents said that an advisory shareholder vote would help constrain excessive and poorly-designed executive pay. Opponents said it would create an unnecessary and costly distraction for management; others argued that "say on pay" should be resolved on a company-by-company basis, not as a federal mandate.

Ultimately, Congress sought to allay the concerns in both camps. While shareholders must be given an advisory vote on the pay of the company's top executives, the frequency of the vote is left to companies to decide. And the Act specifically states that the vote should not be construed to have substantive effects: it can neither overrule any pay decisions by the board nor imply additional fiduciary duties for directors.

Since 2011, the first year that companies were required to include "say on pay" proposals on the company proxy card, the results have been mixed. As anticipated, shareholders have generally given broad support for management pay packages—generally above 90 percent support. Failed "say on pay" votes have been few, representing less than 1.5 percent of the total. At these companies, there was typically a volatile mix of poor company performance and high executive pay. Also relevant were negative "say on pay" recommendations from the proxy advisory firm Institutional Shareholder Services (ISS). Only companies that received a negative ISS recommendation ended up having a negative "say on pay" vote.

The effect of a negative "say on pay" vote—or even a vote with less than 70 percent support—has been interesting. Many companies receiving low shareholder support (or even negative ISS recommendations) have undertaken additional communication with shareholders about the company's pay practices or have sometimes changed those practices entirely—even retroactively. Although "say on pay" has not unleashed a revolution in executive pay practices, as some proponents had hoped, it has resulted in a new dynamic in shareholder-management relationships.

In addition, some companies that have received negative "say on pay" votes have been sued. Shareholders have claimed that the directors failed in their fiduciary duties or engaged in corporate waste. Most of the suits were dismissed, but some withstood motions to dismiss. What would you advise a board that fails to receive shareholder support for its pay practices? The next section suggests an answer: focus on the board's deliberative process.

2. State Law: Mostly Process

Under state corporate law, directors must act with care and in good faith in informing themselves and making decisions about executive compensation, but courts generally defer to their business judgment in the absence of conflicts of interest. Judicial review usually focuses on the decision-making process rather than the amount or structure of compensation. So long as the compensation committee consulted with pay experts, considered the pay scales at comparable companies, and deliberated in good faith, courts have accepted board process over judicial second-guessing. The waste standard represents the outer limit of this deference—it inquires into whether the directors irrationally squandered corporate assets.

By contrast, when interested or dominated directors set their own or others' compensation, the duty of loyalty is implicated and courts will then use the more rigorous standard of entire fairness, which considers whether both the process and substance were fair to the corporation.

Food for Thought

The judicial attitude is perhaps best exemplified by former Chancellor Allen's holding that a grant of immediately exercisable stock options is not corporate waste if "there is some rational basis for directors to conclude that the amount and form of compensation is appropriate." *Steiner v. Meyerson,* 1995 WL 441999 (Del. Ch. 1995). Chancellor Allen observed:

> Absent an allegation of fraud or conflict of interest courts will not review the substance of corporate contracts; the waste theory represents a theoretical exception to the statement very rarely encountered in the world of real transactions. There surely are cases of fraud; of unfair self dealing and, much more rarely negligence. But rarest of all—and indeed, like Nessie, possibly non-existent—would be the case of disinterested business people making non-fraudulent deals (non-negligently) that meet the legal standard of waste!

Shareholder approval of executive compensation plans can be an important part of the process and affect judicial review if there is shareholder litigation. The classic case involved an American Tobacco shareholder-approved bylaw from the 1920s stating that officers would receive bonuses based on the corporation's net profits. American Tobacco's profits soared during the 1930s, and so did its officers' bonuses—so much so that shareholders brought derivative suits to recover those bonuses as excessive and wasteful payments. The courts rejected these claims, noting that the payments were large, but emphasizing that shareholders had agreed to the payment plan.

Over time, shareholder approval has become a crucial aspect of executive compensation plans. Corporations typically seek to secure approval to reduce the likelihood of shareholder suits concerning compensation and to receive a favorable standard of review if there is litigation: "waste"—an almost insuperable burden for plaintiffs to show.

Points for Discussion

1. Federal vs. state.

Should executive compensation be governed by federal or state law? What are the advantages and disadvantages of each?

2. Regulation vs. litigation.

The federal approach has been focused on establishing regulations to govern conduct in advance, whereas the state approach has been focused on adjudicating conduct after the fact as presented in litigation. Which approach—*ex ante* regulation or *ex post* litigation—is more likely to be effective in the area of executive compensation?

3. Director compensation.

Historically, executive compensation has attracted far greater attention than the compensation that directors receive for their board service. However, director compensation can also present issues of excessive pay and give rise to claims of breach of fiduciary duties and waste.

Directors have the responsibility to determine their own compensation. Although boards and committees often seek the advice of an independent compensation consultant, they cannot eliminate the inherent conflict of interest by having management or a consultant make the determination. In setting their own pay, directors unavoidably enter into an interested transaction, which may be subject to entire fairness review if challenged. Shareholder approval of specific awards or a self-executing compensation plan, which does not give the board any further discretion to determine award levels, may provide a defense to a shareholder challenge and result in the application of the business judgment rule.

Some see director compensation as an opportunity to align directors' interests with those of shareholders. Many corporations use restricted stock grants or stock options as a component of director compensation. Some corporations even have stock ownership guidelines that require directors to hold a minimum amount of the corporation's stock while serving as a director.

If you were advising directors about setting their compensation, what practices would you recommend? What should directors be mindful about in this context?

D. The Landmark Delaware Case: *Disney*

Perhaps the most famous case involving executive compensation arose from a $130 million severance package of cash and stock options paid by The Walt Disney Company to Michael Ovitz, a Hollywood talent agent who had been hired as the number-two executive at Disney and was terminated after just 14 months.

The case had a number of twists and turns. In 1997, after Disney agreed to pay Ovitz the severance of approximately $130 million, shareholder-plaintiffs filed a derivative suit in Delaware challenging the payment. In 1998, the Delaware Court of Chancery dismissed the complaint, stating that a large severance package alone is not enough to show a lack of due care or to constitute waste. On appeal, the Delaware Supreme Court (*Brehm v. Eisner*) concluded the complaint was weak, but suggested the plaintiffs seek an inspection of Disney's "books and records" and permitted the filing of an amended complaint. In 2002, after obtaining documents and e-mails from Disney, the plaintiffs filed an amended complaint that painted a picture of board indifference and abdication of responsibility. In 2003, the Chancery Court accepted the amended complaint, concluding that it adequately alleged the Disney directors breached their "duty of good faith."

After extensive discovery, the Chancery Court conducted a 37-day trial with 24 witnesses and 1,033 trial exhibits that filled more than 22 binders. In its 2005 decision, the court found for the defendants on all counts, concluding that the directors' conduct was less than ideal, but not in bad faith or grossly negligent. The plaintiffs appealed again to the Delaware Supreme Court.

The facts were as follows. In 1994, Disney President and Chief Operating Officer, Frank Wells, died in a tragic helicopter crash. Only three months later, Michael Eisner, Disney's Chairman and Chief Executive Officer, had quadruple bypass heart surgery. The two events crystallized that successor planning had to become a priority at the company.

For nearly 25 years, Eisner had a social and professional relationship with Hollywood power-player Michael Ovitz, the leading partner and co-founder of Creative Artists Agency ("CAA"), a premier talent agency. At that time, CAA had 550 employees and a roster of about 1,400 of Hollywood's top actors, directors, writers, and musicians, generating about $150 million in annual revenues and an annual income of over $20 million for Ovitz. In 1995, when Ovitz began negotiations to leave CAA and join Music Corporation of America ("MCA"), Eisner became interested in recruiting Ovitz to join Disney.

Eisner and Irwin Russell, who was a Disney director and chairman of the compensation committee, first approached Ovitz about joining Disney. Both Russell and Eisner negotiated with Ovitz. Eisner had talks with Ovitz about the skills and experience needed at Disney. At some point in these talks, Ovitz came to believe that he and Eisner would run Disney together as co-CEOs. Russell led negotiations on the financial terms of the Ovitz employment contract. From the beginning Ovitz made it clear he was making $20 to $25 million a year at CAA and he would not give up his 55% interest in the firm without "downside protection." During the summer of 1995, the parties agreed to a draft version of Ovitz's employment agreement (the "OEA") modeled after Eisner's and the late Mr. Wells' employment contracts.

Under the draft OEA, Ovitz would receive a five-year contract with two tranches of options—first, a tranche with three million options vesting in equal parts in the third, fourth, and fifth years of employment, and if the value of those options at the end of the five years had not appreciated to $50 million, Disney would make up the difference; second, a tranche of two million options that would vest immediately if Disney and Ovitz opted to renew the contract. The proposed OEA also provided that absent defined causes, neither party could terminate the agreement without penalty. If Ovitz walked away for any reason other than those permitted under the OEA, he would forfeit any benefits remaining under the OEA and could be enjoined from working for a competitor. If Disney fired Ovitz for any reason other than gross negligence or malfeasance, Ovitz would be entitled to a non-fault payment (Non-Fault Termination or "NFT"), which consisted of his remaining salary, $7.5 million a year for unaccrued bonuses, the immediate vesting of his first tranche of options, and a $10 million cashout payment for the second tranche of options.

Russell prepared and gave Ovitz and Eisner a "case study" to explain the terms of the draft OEA. Russell expressed concern that the negotiated terms represented an extraordinary level of executive compensation, but he acknowledged that Ovitz was an "exceptional corporate executive" and "highly successful and unique entrepreneur" who merited "downside protection and upside opportunity." Coming from being a leading partner in a private firm, Ovitz would have to adjust to a smaller amount of cash compensation, but Russell noted that the negotiated salary for Ovitz would still be very large for Disney as it was higher than any other corporate officer's salary, even the CEO's. Moreover, the stock options granted under the OEA would exceed the standards applied within Disney and would "raise very strong criticism." Russell recommended additional study of this issue.

To assist in evaluating the financial terms of the OEA, Russell recruited Graef Crystal, an executive compensation consultant, and Raymond Watson, a member of Disney's compensation committee and a past Disney board chairman who had helped structure Wells' and Eisner's compensation packages. On August 10, Russell, Watson, and Crystal met and discussed a set of values using different and various inputs and assumptions, accounting for different numbers of options, vesting periods, and potential proceeds of option exercises at various times and prices.

Two days later, Crystal faxed to Russell a memo concluding that the OEA would provide Ovitz with approximately $23.6 million per year for the first five years, or $23.9 million a year over seven years if Ovitz exercised the two-year renewal option. Crystal opined those amounts would approximate Ovitz's current annual compensation at CAA. Additional discussion, however, lead to Crystal's concern that the draft OEA gave Ovitz a situation of low risk and high return: Ovitz could hold the first tranche of options, wait out the five-year term, collect the $50 million guarantee, and then exercise the in-the-money options and receive an additional windfall. Russell responded that the guarantee wouldn't function as Crystal believed. Crystal then revised his original memo, adjusting the value of the OEA to $24.1 million per year. Up to that point, only three Disney directors—Eisner, Russell, and Watson—had been involved in the negotiations and knew the status of the draft OEA.

While Russell, Watson, and Crystal were finalizing their analysis of the OEA, Eisner told Ovitz about the options being structured in the two tranches rather than a single grant, and that Ovitz would join Disney only as President, not as a co-CEO with Eisner. After deliberating, Ovitz said he would accept those terms, and that evening Ovitz, Eisner, and their families celebrated together.

On August 14, Eisner and Ovitz signed a letter agreement, which outlined the basic terms of Ovitz's employment, and stated that the agreement (which would ultimately be drafted as a formal contract) was subject to approval by Disney's compensation committee and board of directors. Russell, Watson, and Eisner contacted each of the board members and informed them of the impending new hire. At that time, Disney also issued a public press release announcing the hiring of Ovitz and the reaction was extremely positive: Disney's stock price rose 4.4% in a single day, thereby increasing Disney's market capitalization by over $1 billion.

On September 26, 1995, the compensation committee (Russell, Watson, Poitier, and Lozano) met for one hour to consider the proposed terms of the OEA, among other agenda items. A term sheet was distributed at the meeting, although a draft of the OEA was not. The committee discussed historical comparables, such as Eisner's and Wells' option grants, and the factors that Russell, Watson, and Crystal had considered in setting the size of the option grants and the termination provisions of the contract. Watson shared the spreadsheet analysis that he had performed in August and discussed his findings with the committee. Crystal did not attend the meeting, although he was available by telephone to respond to questions if needed, but no one from the committee called. After Russell's and Watson's presentations, the General Counsel Sandy Litvack also responded to substantive questions. The committee voted unanimously to approve the OEA terms, subject to "reasonable further negotiations within the framework of the terms and conditions" described in the OEA.

Immediately after, the Disney board met in executive session. Eisner led the discussion relating to Ovitz, and Watson then explained his analysis, and both Watson and Russell responded to questions from the board. After further deliberation, the board voted unanimously to elect Ovitz as President.

Ovitz's tenure as President began on October 1, 1995, the date that the OEA was executed. When Ovitz took office, the initial reaction was optimistic. By the fall of 1996, however, it had become clear that Ovitz was "a poor fit with his fellow executives." By then the Disney directors were discussing that the disconnect with Ovitz was likely irreparable and that he would have to be terminated. Multiple theories arose as to why Ovitz did not succeed: he failed to follow Eisner's directives and generally did very little; Eisner's micromanaging prevented Ovitz from having the authority necessary to make the changes that Ovitz thought were appropriate; Ovitz was not given enough time for his efforts to bear fruit; Ovitz simply did not adapt to the Disney culture or fit in with other executives. General Counsel Litvack, with Eisner's approval, told Ovitz that he was not working out at Disney and that he should start looking for a graceful exit from Disney and a new job. Eisner also met several times with Ovitz and tried to persuade him to leave Disney. On September 30, 1996, the Disney board met. During an executive session of that meeting, and in small group discussions where Ovitz was not present, Eisner told the other board members of the continuing problems with Ovitz's performance.

During this period, Eisner was also working with Litvack to explore whether Disney could terminate Ovitz for cause so that it would not owe Ovitz the NFT payment. Litvack reviewed the OEA, refreshed himself on the meaning of "gross negligence" and "malfeasance," reviewed all the facts concerning Ovitz's performance, and consulted the co-head of Disney's litigation department and another in-house attorney. Litvack advised Eisner that he did not believe there was cause to terminate Ovitz under the OEA, and that it would be inappropriate, unethical, and a bad idea to attempt to coerce Ovitz (by threatening a for-cause termination) into negotiating for a smaller NFT package than the OEA provided. If pressed by Ovitz's attorneys, Disney would have to admit that in fact there was no cause, which could subject Disney to a wrongful termination lawsuit. Litvack also believed that attempting to avoid legitimate contractual obligations would harm Disney's reputation as an honest business partner and would affect its future business dealings.

In December 1996, Disney terminated Ovitz. Although the board did not meet to vote on the termination, most, if not all, of the Disney directors trusted Eisner's and Litvack's conclusion that there was no cause to terminate Ovitz, and that Ovitz should be terminated without cause even though that involved making the costly NFT payment.

In re The Walt Disney Company Derivative Litigation

906 A.2d 27 (Del. 2006)

JACOBS, JUSTICE.

II. SUMMARY OF APPELLANTS' CLAIMS OF ERROR

The appellants claim that the Disney defendants breached their fiduciary duties to act with due care and in good faith by (1) approving the OEA, and specifically, its NFT provisions; and (2) approving the NFT severance payment to Ovitz upon his termination—a payment that is also claimed to constitute corporate waste. [The appellants also asserted claims against Ovitz, which the Court rejected in Part III.]

IV. THE CLAIMS AGAINST THE DISNEY DEFENDANTS

1. The Due Care Determinations

Our law presumes that "in making a business decision the directors of a corporation acted on an informed basis, in good faith, and in the honest belief that the action taken was in the best interests of the company." Those presumptions can be rebutted if the plaintiff shows that the directors breached their fiduciary duty of care or of loyalty or acted in bad faith. If that is shown, the burden then shifts to the director defendants to demonstrate that the challenged act or transaction was entirely fair to the corporation and its shareholders.

Because no duty of loyalty claim was asserted against the Disney defendants, the only way to rebut the business judgment rule presumptions would be to show that the Disney defendants had either breached their duty of care or had not acted in good faith. At trial, the plaintiff-appellants attempted to establish both grounds, but the Chancellor determined that the plaintiffs had failed to prove either.

The appellants challenge the Court of Chancery's determination that the full Disney board was not required to consider and approve the OEA, because the Company's governing instruments allocated that decision to the compensation committee. This challenge also cannot survive scrutiny.

As the Chancellor found, under the Company's governing documents the board of directors was responsible for selecting the corporation's officers, but under the compensation committee charter, the committee was responsible for establishing and approving the salaries, together with benefits and stock options, of the Company's CEO and President. The compensation committee also had the charter-imposed duty to "approve employment contracts, or contracts at will" for "all corporate officers who are members of the Board of Directors regardless of salary." That is exactly what occurred here. The full board ultimately selected Ovitz as President, and the compensation committee considered and ultimately approved the OEA, which embodied the terms of Ovitz's employment, including his compensation.

The Delaware General Corporation Law (DGCL) expressly empowers a board of directors to appoint committees and to delegate to them a broad range of responsibilities, which may include setting executive compensation. Nothing in the DGCL mandates that the entire board must make those decisions. At Disney, the responsibility to consider and approve executive compensation was allocated to the compensation committee, as distinguished from the full board. The Chancellor's ruling—that executive compensation was to be fixed by the compensation committee—is legally correct.

The appellants next challenge the Chancellor's determination that although the compensation committee's decision-making process fell far short of corporate governance "best practices," the committee members breached no duty of care in considering and approving the NFT terms of the OEA. That conclusion is reversible error, the appellants claim, because the record establishes that the compensation committee members did not properly inform themselves of the material facts and, hence, were grossly negligent in approving the NFT provisions of the OEA.

In our view, a helpful approach is to compare what actually happened here to what would have occurred had the committee followed a "best practices" (or "best case") scenario, from a process standpoint. In a "best case" scenario, all committee members would have received, before or at the committee's first meeting on September 26, 1995, a spreadsheet or similar document prepared by (or with the assistance of) a compensation expert (in this case, Graef Crystal). Making different, alternative assumptions, the spreadsheet would disclose the amounts that Ovitz could receive under the OEA in each circumstance that might foreseeably arise. One variable in that matrix of possibilities would be the cost to Disney of a non-fault termination for each of the five years of the initial term of the OEA. The contents of the spreadsheet would be explained to the committee members, either by the expert who prepared it or by a fellow committee member similarly knowledgeable about the subject. That spreadsheet, which ultimately would become an exhibit to the minutes of the compensation committee meeting, would form the basis of the committee's deliberations and decision.

Had that scenario been followed, there would be no dispute (and no basis for litigation) over what information was furnished to the committee members or when it was furnished. Regrettably, the committee's informational and decision-making process used here was not so tidy. That is one reason why the Chancellor found that although the committee's process did not fall below the level required for a proper exercise of due care, it did fall short of what best practices would have counseled.

The Disney compensation committee met twice: on September 26 and October 16, 1995. The minutes of the September 26 meeting reflect that the committee approved the terms of the OEA (at that time embodied in the form of a letter agreement), except for the option grants, which were not approved until October 16—after the Disney stock incentive plan had been amended to provide for those options. At the September 26 meeting, the compensation committee considered a "term sheet" which, in summarizing the material terms of the OEA, relevantly disclosed that in the event of a non-fault termination, Ovitz would receive: (i) the present value of his salary ($1 million per year) for the balance of the contract term, (ii) the present value of his annual bonus payments (computed at $7.5 million) for the balance of the contract term, (iii) a $10 million termination fee, and (iv) the acceleration of his options for 3 million shares, which would become immediately exercisable at market price.

Thus, the compensation committee knew that in the event of an NFT, Ovitz's severance payment alone could be in the range of $40 million cash, plus the value of the accelerated options. Because the actual payout to Ovitz was approximately $130 million, of which roughly $38.5 million was cash, the value of the options at the time of the NFT payout would have been about $91.5 million. Thus, the issue may be framed as whether the compensation committee members knew, at the time they approved the OEA, that the value of the option component of the severance package could reach the $92 million order of magnitude if they terminated Ovitz without cause after one year. The evidentiary record shows that the committee members were so informed.

On this question the documentation is far less than what best practices would have dictated. There is no exhibit to the minutes that discloses, in a single document, the estimated value of the accelerated options in the event of an NFT termination after one year. The information imparted to the committee members on that subject is, however, supported by other evidence, most notably the trial testimony of various witnesses about spreadsheets that were prepared for the compensation committee meetings.

The compensation committee members derived their information about the potential magnitude of an NFT payout from two sources. The first was the value of the "benchmark" options previously granted to Eisner and Wells and the valuations by Watson of the proposed Ovitz options. The committee's second source of information was the amount of "downside protection" that Ovitz was demanding. The committee members knew that by leaving CAA and coming to Disney, Ovitz would be sacrificing "booked" CAA commissions of $150 to $200 million—an amount that Ovitz demanded as protection against the risk that his employment relationship with Disney might not work out. Ovitz wanted at least $50 million of that compensation to take the form of an "up-front" signing bonus. Had the $50 million bonus been paid, the size of the option grant would have been lower. Because it was contrary to Disney policy, the compensation committee rejected the up-front signing bonus demand, and elected instead to compensate Ovitz at the "back end," by awarding him options that would be phased in over the five-year term of the OEA.

Despite its imperfections, the evidentiary record was sufficient to support the conclusion that the compensation committee had adequately informed itself of the potential magnitude of the entire severance package, including the options, that Ovitz would receive in the event of an early NFT.

The appellants' final claim in this category is that the Court of Chancery erroneously held that the remaining members of the old Disney board had not breached their duty of care in electing Ovitz as President of Disney. The only properly reviewable action of the entire board was its decision to elect Ovitz as Disney's President. The Chancellor determined that in electing Ovitz, the directors were informed of all information reasonably available and, thus, were not grossly negligent. We agree.

Well in advance of the September 26, 1995 board meeting the directors were fully aware that the Company needed—especially in light of Wells' death and Eisner's medical problems—to hire a "number two" executive and potential successor to Eisner. There had been many discussions about that need and about potential candidates who could fill that role even before Eisner decided to try to recruit Ovitz. Before the September 26 board meeting Eisner had individually discussed with each director the possibility of hiring Ovitz, and Ovitz's background and qualifications. The directors thus knew of Ovitz's skills, reputation and experience, all of which they believed would be highly valuable to the Company. The directors also knew that to accept a position at Disney, Ovitz would have to walk away from a very successful business—a reality that would lead a reasonable person to believe that Ovitz would likely succeed in similar pursuits elsewhere in the industry. The directors also knew of the public's highly positive reaction to the Ovitz announcement, and that Eisner and senior management had supported the Ovitz hiring. Indeed, Eisner, who had long desired to bring Ovitz within the Disney fold, consistently vouched for Ovitz's qualifications and told the directors that he could work well with Ovitz.

The board was also informed of the key terms of the OEA (including Ovitz's salary, bonus and options). Russell reported this information to them at the September 26, 1995 executive session, which was attended by Eisner and all non-executive directors. Russell also reported on the compensation committee meeting that had immediately preceded the executive session. And, both Russell and Watson responded to questions from the board. Relying upon the compensation committee's approval of the OEA and the other information furnished to them, the Disney directors, after further deliberating, unanimously elected Ovitz as President.

Based upon this record, we uphold the Chancellor's conclusion that, when electing Ovitz to the Disney presidency the remaining Disney directors were fully informed of all material facts, and that the appellants failed to establish any lack of due care on the directors' part.

2. The Good Faith Determinations

The Court of Chancery held that the business judgment rule presumptions protected the decisions of the compensation committee and the remaining Disney directors, not only because they had acted with due care but also because they had not acted in bad faith. In its Opinion the Court of Chancery defined bad faith as follows:

Upon long and careful consideration, I am of the opinion that the concept of intentional dereliction of duty, a conscious disregard for one's responsibilities, is an appropriate (although not the only) standard for determining whether fiduciaries have acted in good faith. Deliberate indifference and inaction in the face of a duty to act is, in my mind, conduct that is clearly disloyal to the corporation. It is the epitome of faithless conduct.

Because of the increased recognition of the importance of good faith, some conceptual guidance to the corporate community may be helpful. The precise question is whether the Chancellor's articulated standard for bad faith corporate fiduciary conduct—intentional dereliction of duty, a conscious disregard for one's responsibilities—is legally correct. In approaching that question, we note that the Chancellor characterized that definition as "an appropriate (although not the only) standard for determining whether fiduciaries have acted in good faith." That observation is accurate and helpful, because as a matter of simple logic, at least three different categories of fiduciary behavior are candidates for the "bad faith" pejorative label.

The first category involves so-called "subjective bad faith," that is, fiduciary conduct motivated by an actual intent to do harm. That such conduct constitutes classic, quintessential bad faith is a proposition so well accepted in the liturgy of fiduciary law that it borders on axiomatic. We need not dwell further on this category, because no such conduct is claimed to have occurred, or did occur, in this case.

The second category of conduct, which is at the opposite end of the spectrum, involves lack of due care—that is, fiduciary action taken solely by reason of gross negligence and without any malevolent intent. In this case, appellants assert claims of gross negligence to establish breaches not only of director due care but also of the directors' duty to act in good faith. Although the Chancellor found, and we agree, that the appellants failed to establish gross negligence, to afford guidance we address the issue of whether gross negligence (including a failure to inform one's self of available material facts), without more, can also constitute bad faith. The answer is clearly no.

Both our legislative history and our common law jurisprudence distinguish sharply between the duties to exercise due care and to act in good faith, and highly significant consequences flow from that distinction. The Delaware General Assembly has addressed the distinction between bad faith and a failure to exercise due care (i.e., gross negligence) in two separate contexts [director exculpation and indemnification pursuant to sections 102(b)(7) and 145 of the DGCL].

That leaves the third category of fiduciary conduct, which falls in between the first two categories of (1) conduct motivated by subjective bad intent and (2) conduct resulting from gross negligence. This third category is what the Chancellor's definition of bad faith—intentional dereliction of duty, a conscious disregard for one's responsibilities—is intended to capture. The question is whether such misconduct is properly treated as a non-exculpable, nonindemnifiable violation of the fiduciary duty to act in good faith. In our view it must be, for at least two reasons.

First, the universe of fiduciary misconduct is not limited to either disloyalty in the classic sense (i.e., preferring the adverse self-interest of the fiduciary or of a related person to the interest of the corporation) or gross negligence. Cases have arisen where corporate directors have no conflicting self-interest in a decision, yet engage in misconduct that is more culpable than simple inattention or failure to be informed of all facts material to the decision. To protect the interests of the corporation and its shareholders, fiduciary conduct of this kind, which does not involve disloyalty (as traditionally defined) but is qualitatively more culpable than gross negligence, should be proscribed. A vehicle is needed to address such violations doctrinally, and that doctrinal vehicle is the duty to act in good faith. The Chancellor implicitly so recognized in his Opinion, where he identified different examples of bad faith as follows:

> A failure to act in good faith may be shown, for instance, where the fiduciary intentionally acts with a purpose other than that of advancing the best interests of the corporation, where the fiduciary acts with the intent to violate applicable positive law, or where the fiduciary intentionally fails to act in the face of a known duty to act, demonstrating a conscious disregard for his duties. There may be other examples of bad faith yet to be proven or alleged, but these three are the most salient.

Those articulated examples of bad faith are not new to our jurisprudence. Indeed, they echo pronouncements our courts have made throughout the decades.

Second, the legislature has also recognized this intermediate category of fiduciary misconduct, which ranks between conduct involving subjective bad faith and gross negligence. Section 102(b)(7)(ii) of the DGCL expressly denies money damage exculpation for "acts or omissions not in good faith or which involve intentional misconduct or a knowing violation of law." By its very terms that provision distinguishes between "intentional misconduct" and a "knowing violation of law" (both examples of subjective bad faith) on the one hand, and "acts . . . not in good faith," on the other. Because the statute exculpates directors only for conduct amounting to gross negligence, the statutory denial of exculpation for "acts . . . not in good faith" must encompass the intermediate category of misconduct captured by the Chancellor's definition of bad faith.

For these reasons, we uphold the Court of Chancery's definition as a legally appropriate, although not the exclusive, definition of fiduciary bad faith. We need go no further. [The Court then concluded that payment of the severance payout to Ovitz was in good faith on the facts presented.]

V. THE WASTE CLAIM

The appellants' final claim is that even if the approval of the OEA was protected by the business judgment rule presumptions, the payment of the severance amount to Ovitz constituted waste. This claim is rooted in the doctrine that a plaintiff who fails to rebut the business judgment rule presumptions is not entitled to any remedy unless the transaction constitutes waste. The Court of Chancery rejected the appellants' waste claim, and the appellants claim that in so doing the Court committed error.

To recover on a claim of corporate waste, the plaintiffs must shoulder the burden of proving that the exchange was "so one sided that no business person of ordinary, sound judgment could conclude that the corporation has received adequate consideration." A claim of waste will arise only in the rare, "unconscionable case where directors irrationally squander or give away corporate assets." This onerous standard for waste is a corollary of the proposition that where business judgment presumptions are applicable, the board's decision will be upheld unless it cannot be "attributed to any rational business purpose."

The claim that the payment of the NFT amount to Ovitz, without more, constituted waste is meritless on its face, because at the time the NFT amounts were paid, Disney was contractually obligated to pay them. The payment of a contractually obligated amount cannot constitute waste, unless the contractual obligation is itself wasteful. Accordingly, the proper focus of a waste analysis must be whether the amounts required to be paid in the event of an NFT were wasteful ex ante.

[The appellants'] claim does not come close to satisfying the high hurdle required to establish waste. The approval of the NFT provisions in the OEA had a rational business purpose: to induce Ovitz to leave CAA, at what would otherwise be a considerable cost to him, in order to join Disney.

VI. CONCLUSION

For the reasons stated above, the judgment of the Court of Chancery is affirmed.

Points for Discussion

1. *Disney vs. Van Gorkom.*

In *Van Gorkom*, thirteen directors of Trans Union were held personally liable for approving a merger in a two-hour meeting without receiving documents summarizing the deal or relevant valuation information. By contrast, in *Disney*, the directors were exonerated after approving Ovitz's pay package in a one-hour meeting of the compensation committee without discussing or receiving documentation on the financial impact of a "no-fault termination." What explains the different conclusions in these two major cases? Do you think the members of the Disney compensation committee really understood that if Ovitz were terminated after one year without cause he would be entitled to receive $130 million—basically for not having worked out?

2. Advise.

What advice can you give directors about how to meet their burden of showing their actions were in good faith to claim protection under a § 102(b)(7) exculpation clause? When, according to the Supreme Court, might an executive compensation committee lack good faith? For example, after the *Disney* decision, would the committee members lack good faith if they failed to obtain a pay consultant's report on the financial implications of a pay package under various assumptions? That is, are *pro forma* reports by pay consultants (showing different "what if" scenarios) now required by Delaware law? Should the directors be required to obtain a valuation of option grants?

3. Who cares?

Ovitz's $130 million would seem like a lot of money, but it was nothing to Disney, a fraction of one percent of the value of the corporation's shares. Why the fuss?

4. Options backdating.

A pay practice that was widespread in the 2000s presented a challenge to the courts. What happens when a company backdates options by issuing (and pricing) executive stock options on one date, but "back-dating" them (and pricing them with a lower exercise price) as of an earlier date. For example, suppose a corporation's share price is $80 on September 1 and $100 on October 1. Now suppose the board's compensation committee meets on October 1 and awards stock options to various officers—but instead of setting an exercise price of $100, as specified in the company's employee stock option plan, the committee gives the officers a nice bonus and backdates the options to September 1, thus setting the exercise price at $80? Suddenly the options are "in the money" and immediately worth at least $20, the difference between the current share price and the option exercise price.

Is this a violation of the fiduciary duties of the directors on the compensation committee? Is it corporate waste? Is it fraudulent if the committee says it granted the option as of September 1? Is it illegal?

Backdating was a common practice until 2006, and it led to dozens of lawsuits. In those suits, some brought as class actions and some as derivative suits, shareholders claimed that backdating options to coincide with market lows was illegal and unprotected by the business judgment rule. In a prominent derivative case, *Ryan v. Gifford*, 918 A.2d 341 (Del. Ch. 2007), Chancellor Chandler held that demand on the board was excused and allowed the case to go forward because the directors had acted in bad faith.

Based on the allegations of the complaint, I am convinced that the intentional violation of a shareholder approved stock option plan, coupled with fraudulent disclosures regarding the directors' purported compliance with that plan, constitute conduct that is disloyal to the corporation and is therefore an act in bad faith.

I am unable to fathom a situation where the deliberate violation of a shareholder approved stock option plan and intentional false disclosures is anything but an act of bad faith. It certainly cannot be said to amount to faithful and devoted conduct of a loyal fiduciary. Well-pleaded allegations of such conduct are sufficient to rebut the business judgment rule and to survive a motion to dismiss.

CHAPTER 23

Board Oversight

In addition to making decisions, directors also oversee the corporation's affairs. This "oversight" function is increasingly important, particularly with respect to managing the financial and regulatory risks that corporations face.

Recall that a corporation's shareholders delegate the power to manage and direct the corporation's affairs to the board of directors. The board then delegates some of that power to the corporation's officers and employees. Directors are not expected to directly oversee every aspect of a corporation's business. Therefore, one of the difficult questions with respect to oversight is: how do directors fulfill their oversight responsibilities? How much should they do? How much must they do? Are the duties of care and loyalty both implicated?

We begin our discussion of board oversight duties with a "classic" case of director oversight failure. Next, we consider the oversight duties of directors of modern corporations. Then, we examine the Delaware courts' treatment of oversight claims and the concept of "good faith." Finally, we look more closely at the board's oversight of risk management, with a particular focus on the Financial Crisis of 2008.

A. "Classic" Case of Oversight Failure

Francis v. United Jersey Bank is a "classic" case in the area of director oversight. It is an unusual case in some ways: the corporation was a family business, and the family was not very well functioning. Moreover, the corporation was in the reinsurance industry, which has some peculiar features not common to other businesses. Nevertheless, this case remains a starting point for the analysis of board oversight.

The corporation at issue, Pritchard & Baird, Intermediaries Corp., was a reinsurance broker, a firm that arranged contracts between insurance companies by means of which companies that wrote large policies sold participations in those policies to other companies in order to share the risks. According to the custom in the industry, the selling company paid the applicable portion of the premium to the broker, which deducted its commission and forwarded the balance to the reinsuring company. Thus, the broker handled large amounts of money as a fiduciary for its clients.

As of 1964, all the stock of Pritchard & Baird was owned by Charles Pritchard, Sr., one of the firm's founders, and his wife and two sons, Charles, Jr. and William. They were also the four directors. Charles, Sr. dominated the corporation until 1971, when he became ill and the two sons took over management of the business. Charles, Sr. died in 1973, leaving Mrs. Pritchard and the sons as the only remaining directors.

Contrary to the industry practice, Pritchard & Baird did not segregate its operating funds from those of its clients; instead, it deposited all funds in the same account. From this account Charles, Sr. had drawn "loans" that correlated with corporate profits and were repaid at the end of each year. After his death, Charles, Jr. and William began to draw ever larger amounts that greatly exceeded profits (they continued to characterize these payments as "loans"). The sons drew these payments from something known as the "float," the extra money available to them after Pritchard & Baird had received an insurance premium and before it had to forward the premium to the reinsurer.

By 1975 the corporation was bankrupt. This action was brought by the trustees in bankruptcy against Mrs. Pritchard and the bank as administrator of her husband's estate. Mrs. Pritchard died during the pendency of the proceedings, and her executrix was substituted as defendant. As to Mrs. Pritchard, the principal claim was that she had been negligent in the conduct of her duties as a director of the corporation.

Francis v. United Jersey Bank

432 A.2d 814 (N.J. 1981)

POLLOCK, J.

The "loans" were reflected on financial statements that were prepared annually as of January 31, the end of the corporate fiscal year. Although an outside certified public accountant prepared the 1970 financial statement, the corporation prepared only internal financial statements from 1971–1975. In all instances, the statements were simple documents, consisting of three or four 8 x11 inch sheets.

The statements of financial condition from 1970 forward demonstrated:

	Working Capital Deficit	**Shareholders' Loans**	**Net Brokerage Income**
1970	$389,022	$509,941	$807,229
1971	Not available	Not available	Not available
1972	$1,684,289	$1,825,911	$1,546,263
1973	$3,506,460	$3,700,542	$1,736,349
1974	$6,939,007	$7,080,629	$876,182
1975	$10,176,419	$10,298,039	$551,598

Mrs. Pritchard was not active in the business of Pritchard & Baird and knew virtually nothing of its corporate affairs. She briefly visited the corporate offices in Morristown on only one occasion, and she never read or obtained the annual financial statements. She was unfamiliar with the rudiments of reinsurance and made no effort to assure that the policies and practices of the corporation, particularly pertaining to the withdrawal of funds, complied with industry custom or relevant law. Although her husband had warned her that Charles, Jr. would "take the shirt off my back," Mrs. Pritchard did not pay any attention to her duties as a director or to the affairs of the corporation.

After her husband died in December 1973, Mrs. Pritchard became incapacitated and was bedridden for a six-month period. She became listless at this time and started to drink rather heavily. Her physical condition deteriorated, and in 1978 she died. The trial court rejected testimony seeking to exonerate her because she "was old, was grief-stricken at the loss of her husband, sometimes consumed too much alcohol and was psychologically overborne by her sons." That court found that she was competent to act and that the reason Mrs. Pritchard never knew what her sons "were doing was because she never made the slightest effort to discharge any of her responsibilities as a director of Pritchard & Baird."

Individual liability of a corporate director for acts of the corporation is a prickly problem. Generally directors are accorded broad immunity and are not insurers of corporate activities. The problem is particularly nettlesome when a third party asserts that a director, because of nonfeasance, is liable for losses caused by acts of insiders, who in this case were officers, directors and shareholders. Determination of the liability of Mrs. Pritchard requires findings that she had a duty to the clients of Pritchard & Baird, that she breached that duty and that her breach was a proximate cause of their losses.

As a general rule, a director should acquire at least a rudimentary understanding of the business of the corporation. Accordingly, a director should become familiar with the fundamentals of the business in which the corporation is engaged. Because directors are bound to exercise ordinary care, they cannot set up as a defense lack of the knowledge needed to exercise the requisite degree of care. If one feels that he has not had sufficient business experience to qualify him to perform the duties of a director, he should either acquire the knowledge by inquiry, or refuse to act.

Directors are under a continuing obligation to keep informed about the activities of the corporation. Otherwise, they may not be able to participate in the overall management of corporate affairs. Directors may not shut their eyes to corporate misconduct and then claim that because they did not see the misconduct, they did not have a duty to look. The sentinel asleep at his post contributes nothing to the enterprise he is charged to protect.

Directorial management does not require a detailed inspection of day-to-day activities, but rather a general monitoring of corporate affairs and policies. Accordingly, a director is well advised to attend board meetings regularly. Regular attendance does not mean that directors must attend every meeting, but that directors should attend meetings as a matter of practice. A director of a publicly held corporation might be expected to attend regular monthly meetings, but a director of a small, family corporation might be asked to attend only an annual meeting. The point is that one of the responsibilities of a director is to attend meetings of the board of which he or she is a member.

While directors are not required to audit corporate books, they should maintain familiarity with the financial status of the corporation by a regular review of financial statements. In some circumstances, directors may be charged with assuring that bookkeeping methods conform to industry custom and usage. The extent of review, as well as the nature and frequency of financial statements, depends not only on the customs of the industry, but also on the nature of the corporation and the business in which it is engaged. Financial statements of some small corporations may be prepared internally and only on an annual basis; in a large publicly held corporation, the statements may be produced monthly or at some other regular interval. Adequate financial review normally would be more informal in a private corporation than in a publicly held corporation.

The review of financial statements, however, may give rise to a duty to inquire further into matters revealed by those statements. Upon discovery of an illegal course of action, a director has a duty to object and, if the corporation does not correct the conduct, to resign.

In certain circumstances, the fulfillment of the duty of a director may call for more than mere objection and resignation. Sometimes a director may be required to seek the advice of counsel concerning the propriety of his or her own conduct, the conduct of other officers and directors or the conduct of the corporation. Sometimes the duty of a director may require more than consulting with outside counsel. A director may have a duty to take reasonable means to prevent illegal conduct by co-directors; in any appropriate case, this may include threat of suit.

A director is not an ornament, but an essential component of corporate governance. Consequently, a director cannot protect himself behind a paper shield bearing the motto, "dummy director." The New Jersey Business Corporation Act, in imposing a standard of ordinary care on all directors, confirms that dummy, figurehead and accommodation directors are anachronisms with no place in New Jersey law.

The factors that impel expanded responsibility in the large, publicly held corporation may not be present in a small, close corporation. Nonetheless, a close corporation may, because of the nature of its business, be affected with a public interest. For example, the stock of a bank may be closely held, but because of the nature of banking the directors would be subject to greater liability than those of another close corporation. Even in a small corporation, a director is held to the standard of that degree of care that an ordinarily prudent director would use under the circumstances.

A director's duty of care does not exist in the abstract, but must be considered in relation to specific obligees. In general, the relationship of a corporate director to the corporation and its stockholders is that of a fiduciary. Shareholders have a right to expect that directors will exercise reasonable supervision and control over the policies and practices of a corporation. The institutional integrity of a corporation depends upon the proper discharge by directors of those duties.

While directors may owe a fiduciary duty to creditors also, that obligation generally has not been recognized in the absence of insolvency. With certain corporations, however, directors are deemed to owe a duty to creditors and other third parties even when the corporation is solvent. Although depositors of a bank are considered in some respects to be creditors, courts have recognized that directors may owe them a fiduciary duty. Directors of nonbanking corporations may owe a similar duty when the corporation holds funds of others in trust.

As a reinsurance broker, Pritchard & Baird received annually as a fiduciary millions of dollars of clients' money which it was under a duty to segregate. To this extent, it resembled a bank rather than a small family business. Accordingly, Mrs. Pritchard's relationship to the clientele of Pritchard & Baird was akin to that of a director of a bank to its depositors.

As a director of a substantial reinsurance brokerage corporation, she should have known that it received annually millions of dollars of loss and premium funds which it held in trust for ceding and reinsurance companies. Mrs. Pritchard should have obtained and read the annual statements of financial condition of Pritchard & Baird. Although she had a right to rely upon financial statements prepared in accordance with [New Jersey law], such reliance would not excuse her conduct.

From those statements, she should have realized that, as of January 31, 1970, her sons were withdrawing substantial trust funds under the guise of "Shareholders' Loans." The financial statements for each fiscal year commencing with that of January 31, 1970, disclosed that the working capital deficits and the "loans" were escalating in tandem. Detecting a misappropriation of funds would not have required special expertise or extraordinary diligence; a cursory reading of the financial statements would have revealed the pillage. Thus, if Mrs. Pritchard had read the financial statements, she would have known that her sons were converting trust funds. When financial statements demonstrate that insiders are bleeding a corporation to death, a director should notice and try to stanch the flow of blood.

In summary, Mrs. Pritchard was charged with the obligation of basic knowledge and supervision of the business of Pritchard & Baird. Under the circumstances, this obligation included reading and understanding financial statements, and making reasonable attempts at detection and prevention of the illegal conduct of other officers and directors. She had a duty to protect the clients of Pritchard & Baird against the policies and practices that would result in the misappropriation of money they had entrusted to the corporation. She breached that duty.

The judgment of the Appellate Division is affirmed.

———————

Points for Discussion

1. When does the BJR apply?

The court stated, "a director is held to the standard of that degree of care that an ordinarily prudent director would use under the circumstances." Did the court give Mrs. Pritchard business judgment rule protection? Why or why not?

2. How much more?

Clearly, directors must do more than Mrs. Pritchard did to fulfill their oversight duties. But how much more? Consider the guidance to directors offered in the official comment to MBCA § 8.30 (as revised in 2008).

> ### MBCA § 8.30
> ### Standards of Conduct for Directors
>
> **Official Comment:**
>
> In discharging the Section 8.01 duties associated with the board's over-sight function, the standard of care entails primarily a duty of attention. In contrast with the board's decision-making function, which generally involves informed action at a point in time, the oversight function is concerned with a continuum and the duty of attention accordingly involves participatory performance over a period of time.

3. Real or aspirational?

For corporate lawyers, it is important to differentiate between the real versus the aspirational aspects of the duty of care. Often corporate lawyers are asked to counsel directors on proper behavior, in a preventive mode to avoid any risk of liability, rather than to identify specific litigation and liability consequences of particular conduct. Other times, the issue is whether particular conduct or decisions create director liability. One type of advice might involve merely avoiding liability, whereas another type of advice might involve something more, and a higher standard.

How does the "standard of conduct" described in the comments to MBCA § 8.30 differ from the "standard of liability" laid out in MBCA § 8.31?

Professor Melvin Eisenberg has drawn a distinction between standards of conduct and standards of liability:

> A standard of conduct states how an actor should conduct a given activity or play a given role. A standard of review states the test a court should apply when it reviews an actor's conduct to determine whether to impose liability or grant injunctive relief.

> In many or most areas of law, these two kinds of standards tend to be conflated. For example, the standard of conduct that governs automobile drivers is that they should drive carefully, and the standard of review in a liability claim against a driver is whether he drove carefully.

> The conflation of standards of conduct and standards of review is so common that it is easy to overlook the fact that whether the two kinds of standards are

or should be identical in any given area is a matter of prudential judgment. Perhaps standards of conduct and standards of review in corporate law would always be identical in a world in which information was perfect, the risk of liability for assuming a given corporate role was always commensurate with the incentives for assuming the role, and institutional considerations never required deference to a corporate organ. In the real world, however, these conditions seldom hold, and the standards of review in corporate law pervasively diverge from the standards of conduct.

How would this distinction assist you in advising a corporation's directors?

MBCA § 8.31
Standards of Liability for Directors

(a) [A director may liable to the corporation or its shareholders for any failure to take any action as a director, if]

(2) the challenged conduct consisted or was the result of:

(iv) a sustained failure of the director to devote attention to ongoing oversight of the business and affairs of the corporation, or a failure to devote timely attention, by making (or causing to be made) appropriate inquiry when particular facts and circumstances of significant concern materialize that would alert a reasonably attentive director to the need for such inquiry.

Official Comment:

In contrast with the decision-making function, which generally involves action taken at a point in time, the oversight function under section 8.01(b) involves ongoing monitoring of the corporation's business and affairs over a period of time. Although the facts will be outcome-determinative, deficient conduct involving a sustained failure to exercise oversight—where found actionable—has typically been characterized by the courts in terms of abdication and continued neglect by a director to devote attention, not a brief distraction or temporary interruption. Also embedded in the oversight function is the need to inquire when suspicions are aroused. This need to inquire is not a component of ongoing oversight, and does not entail proactive vigilance, but arises when, and only when, particular facts and circumstances of material concern (e.g., evidence of embezzlement at a high level or the discovery of significant inventory shortages) surface.

4. A "simple housewife"?

The trial court's opinion in *Francis v. United Jersey Bank*, 392 A.2d 1233 (Law Div. 1978), contains the following passage:

> It has been urged in this case that Mrs. Pritchard should not be held responsible for what happened while she was a director of Pritchard & Baird because she was a simple housewife who served as a director as an accommodation to her husband and sons. Let me start by saying that I reject the sexism which is unintended but which is implicit in such an argument. There is no reason why the average housewife could not adequately discharge the functions of a director of a corporation such as Pritchard & Baird, despite a lack of business career experience, if she gave some reasonable attention to what she was supposed to be doing. The problem is not that Mrs. Pritchard was a simple housewife. The problem is that she was a person who took a job which necessarily entailed certain responsibilities and she then failed to make any effort whatever to discharge those responsibilities. The ultimate insult to the fundamental dignity and equality of women would be to treat a grown woman as though she were a child not responsible for her acts and omissions.

Should courts take into account the background of directors in determining whether they satisfied their oversight responsibilities? If so, what factors are most appropriate and relevant? Some statutes refer to "the care a person in a like position" would reasonably believe appropriate; others refer to the care "an ordinarily prudent person in a like position would exercise." Do these statutes mean there is a single, unitary standard of care, or are the director's expertise and experience relevant in determining the appropriate standard of care?

For example, would a director with an accounting background have greater responsibilities to uncover management fraud? Would a labor union representative elected to the board under a collective bargaining agreement be more responsible for overseeing employee relations? Are lawyers serving on a board supposed to be sensitive to legal compliance? What are the responsibilities of an investment banker whose only contribution at board meetings is in connection with proposed financings?

B. Developments in Oversight Duties

In a large corporation, directors delegate the ongoing operation of the business to management. How much oversight of management is required? To what extent must the directors inquire into the details of the corporation's financial statements, which have been reviewed and certified by the corporation's independent public accountants? Can directors rely on management to bring problems to their attention? Must directors establish monitoring systems to ensure management and other employees are complying with their legal responsibilities?

Historically, the debate about monitoring compliance centered on whether directors *should* institute legal compliance programs (an aspirational standard) or whether directors face *liability* for failure to do so (a legal duty). Questions also arose whether a monitoring duty arose only after a "triggering event" that put directors on notice that the corporation was not in compliance or whether such programs were part of a legal duty of care.

1. *Graham v. Allis-Chalmers*: Respond to Red Flags

One much-cited statement of a director's duty to create legal compliance programs comes from *Graham v. Allis-Chalmers Manufacturing Co.*, 188 A.2d 125 (Del. 1963). The case involved a derivative action against the directors of Allis-Chalmers, a multi-division manufacturing firm with over 31,000 employees. Suit was brought after the company and four non-director employees were indicted for price-fixing violations of the federal antitrust laws.

The derivative action alleged that the director defendants had either actual knowledge of the illegal price-fixing or knowledge of facts that should have put them on notice. In discovery, however, there was no evidence that any director actually knew of the price-fixing or of facts suggesting that lower-level employees were violating the antitrust laws. So the plaintiffs shifted their theory to claim the directors were liable for failing to institute a monitoring system that would have allowed directors to learn of and prevent the antitrust violations.

The Delaware Supreme Court pointed out that the company's operating policy was to delegate price-setting authority "to the lowest possible management level capable of fulfilling the delegated responsibility." The board, although it annually reviewed departmental profit goals, did not participate in decisions setting specific product prices. The Court stated, "By reason of the extent and complexity of the company's operations, it is not practicable for the Board to consider in detail specific problems of the various divisions."

The plaintiffs pointed to two 1937 FTC decrees against Allis-Chalmers that had enjoined the company from fixing prices on certain electrical equipment. The plaintiffs argued that the decrees, which should have alerted the directors to past antitrust activity, put them on notice to identify and prevent such activity in the future. The Court was not impressed:

The difficulty the argument has is that only three of the present directors knew of the decrees, and all three of them satisfied themselves that Allis-Chalmers had not engaged in the practice enjoined and had consented to the decrees merely to avoid expense and the necessity of defending the company's position. Under the circumstances, we think knowledge by three of the directors that in 1937 the company had consented to the entry of decrees enjoining it from doing something they had satisfied themselves it had never done, did not put the Board on notice of the possibility of future illegal price fixing.

Plaintiffs have wholly failed to establish either actual notice or imputed notice to the Board of Directors of facts which should have put them on guard, and have caused them to take steps to prevent the future possibility of illegal price fixing and bid rigging. Plaintiffs say that as a minimum in this respect the Board should have taken the steps it took in 1960 when knowledge of the facts first actually came to their attention as a result of the Grand Jury investigation. Whatever duty, however, there was upon the Board to take such steps, the fact of the 1937 decrees has no bearing upon the question, for under the circumstances they were [put on] notice of nothing.

Plaintiffs are thus forced to rely solely upon the legal proposition advanced by them that directors of a corporation, as a matter of law, are liable for losses suffered by their corporations by reason of their gross inattention to the common law duty of actively supervising and managing the corporate affairs.

The precise charge made against these director defendants is that, even though they had no knowledge of any suspicion of wrongdoing on the part of the company's employees, they still should have put into effect a system of watchfulness which would have brought such misconduct to their attention in ample time to have brought it to an end. On the contrary, it appears that directors are entitled to rely on the honesty and integrity of their subordinates until something occurs to put them on suspicion that something is wrong. If such occurs and goes unheeded, then liability of the directors might well follow, but absent cause for suspicion there is no duty upon the directors to install and operate a corporate system of espionage to ferret out wrongdoing which they have no reason to suspect exists.

In the last analysis, the question of whether a corporate director has become liable for losses to the corporation through neglect of duty is determined by the circumstances. If he has recklessly reposed confidence in an obviously untrustworthy employee, has refused or neglected cavalierly to perform his duty as a director, or has ignored either willfully or through inattention obvious danger signs of employee wrongdoing, the law will cast the burden of liability upon him. This is not the case at bar, however, for as soon as it became evident that there were grounds for suspicion, the Board acted promptly to end it and prevent its recurrence.

Graham grew out of the heavy electrical equipment price-fixing conspiracy, one of the first instances in which executives of major corporations received jail terms for antitrust violations. Despite evidence in the criminal cases and similar evidence in *Graham* that subordinate employees had concealed their illegal behavior from their supervisors, there was skepticism in the press and Congress that senior executives were, in fact, unaware of what was going on.

Instead, under Allis-Chalmers' decentralized structure, there were indications that the heads of the various organizational units faced significant pressure to show steadily increasing profits for their segments. Profits were expected regardless of the conditions in the particular markets in which the organizational units operated. If true, was the court too quick to say that when a board creates such a mode of management it need not establish "a corporate system of espionage"?

2. *Caremark:* Institute Monitoring Systems

Three decades after *Graham v. Allis-Chalmers*, the Delaware Court of Chancery set a new direction for the board's oversight duties by stating (in dicta) that a board's oversight duties required more than simply responding to red flags. *In re Caremark International Inc.*, 698 A.2d 959 (Del. Ch. 1996). The company involved, Caremark, had been the subject of an extensive four-year investigation by the United States Department of Health and Human Services and the Department of Justice regarding its compliance with health care provider regulations. In 1994, Caremark pleaded guilty to mail fraud and agreed to pay civil and criminal fines to various private and public parties, totaling approximately $250 million.

A shareholder derivative suit followed, alleging the Caremark directors breached their duty of care. As the court explained:

> The claim is that the directors allowed a situation to develop and continue which exposed the corporation to enormous legal liability and that in so doing they violated a duty to be active monitors of corporate performance. The complaint thus does not charge either director self-dealing or the more difficult loyalty-type problems arising from cases

of suspect director motivation, such as entrenchment or sale of control contexts. The theory here advanced is possibly the most difficult theory in corporation law upon which a plaintiff might hope to win a judgment.

The Court of Chancery's opinion ruled on a proposed settlement as to which there were no objectors. Although appeal was unlikely, the court took the opportunity to explain its view of the law in this area, more than thirty years after the Delaware Supreme Court's opinion in *Graham v. Allis-Chalmers*:

> Director liability for a breach of the duty to exercise appropriate attention may, in theory, arise in two distinct contexts. First, such liability may be said to follow from a board decision that results in a loss because that decision was ill advised or "negligent." [This] class of cases will typically be subject to review under the director-protective business judgment rule, assuming the decision made was the product of a process that was either deliberately considered in good faith or was otherwise rational.

> The second class of cases in which director liability for inattention is theoretically possible entail circumstances in which a loss eventuates not from a decision but, from unconsidered inaction. Most of the decisions that a corporation, acting through its human agents, makes are, of course, not the subject of director attention. Legally, the board itself will be required only to authorize the most significant corporate acts or transactions: mergers, changes in capital structure, fundamental changes in business, appointment and compensation of the CEO, etc. As the facts of this case graphically demonstrate, ordinary business decisions that are made by officers and employees deeper in the interior of the organization can, however, vitally affect the welfare of the corporation and its ability to achieve its various strategic and financial goals. In the face of financial and organizational disasters, what is the board's responsibility with respect to the organization and monitoring of the enterprise to assure that the corporation functions within the law to achieve its purposes?

In 1963, the Delaware Supreme Court in *Graham v. Allis-Chalmers Mfg. Co.* addressed the question of potential liability of board members for losses experienced by the corporation as a result of the corporation having violated the antitrust laws of the United States. The claim asserted was that the directors ought to have known of it and if they had known they would have been under a duty to bring the corporation into compliance with the law and thus save the corporation from the loss. The Delaware Supreme Court concluded that, under the facts as they appeared, there was no basis to find that the directors had breached a duty to be informed of the ongoing operations of the firm. In notably colorful terms, the court stated that "absent cause for suspicion there is no duty upon the directors to install and operate a corporate system of espionage to ferret out wrongdoing which they have no reason to suspect exists." The Court found that there were no grounds for suspicion in that case and, thus, concluded that the directors were blamelessly unaware of the conduct leading to the corporate liability.

How does one generalize this holding today? Can it be said today that, absent some ground giving rise to suspicion of violation of law, that corporate directors have no duty to assure that a corporate information gathering and reporting systems exists which represents a good faith attempt to provide senior management and the Board with information respecting material acts, events or conditions within the corporation, including compliance with applicable statutes and regulations? I certainly do not believe so.

A broad interpretation of *Graham v. Allis-Chalmers*—that it means that a corporate board has no responsibility to assure that appropriate information and reporting systems are established by management— would not, in any event, be accepted by the Delaware Supreme Court in 1996, in my opinion. In stating the basis for this view, I start with the recognition that in recent years the Delaware Supreme Court has made it clear—especially in its jurisprudence concerning takeovers, from *Smith v. Van Gorkom* through *QVC v. Paramount Communications*—the seriousness with which the corporation law views the role of the corporate board. Secondly, I note the elementary fact that relevant and timely information is an essential predicate for satisfaction of the board's supervisory and monitoring role under Section 141 of the Delaware General Corporation Law. Thirdly, I note the potential impact of the federal organizational sentencing guidelines on any business organization. Any rational person attempting in good faith to meet an organizational governance responsibility would be bound to take into account this development and the enhanced penalties and the opportunities for reduced sanctions that it offers.

In light of these developments, it would, in my opinion, be a mistake to conclude that our Supreme Court's statement in Graham concerning "espionage" means that corporate boards may satisfy their obligation to be reasonably informed concerning the corporation, without assuring themselves that information and reporting systems exist in the organization that are reasonably designed to provide to senior management and to the board itself timely, accurate information sufficient to allow management and the board, each within its scope, to reach informed judgments concerning both the corporation's compliance with law and its business performance.

Obviously the level of detail that is appropriate for such an information system is a question of business judgment. And obviously too, no rationally designed information and reporting system will remove the possibility that the corporation will violate laws or regulations, or that senior officers or directors may nevertheless sometimes be misled or otherwise fail reasonably to detect acts material to the corporation's compliance with the law. But it is important that the board exercise a good faith judgment that the corporation's information and reporting system is in concept and design adequate to assure the board that appropriate information will come to its attention in a timely manner as a matter of ordinary operations, so that it may satisfy its responsibility.

Thus, I am of the view that a director's obligation includes a duty to attempt in good faith to assure that a corporate information and reporting system, which the board concludes is adequate, exists, and that failure to do so under some circumstances may, in theory at least, render a director liable for losses caused by non-compliance with applicable legal standards.

Generally where a claim of directorial liability for corporate loss is predicated upon ignorance of liability creating activities within the corporation, as in *Graham* or in this case, in my opinion only a sustained or systematic failure of the board to exercise oversight—such as an utter failure to attempt to assure a reasonable information and reporting system exits—will establish the lack of good faith that is a necessary condition to liability. Such a test of liability—lack of good faith as evidenced by sustained or systematic failure of a director to exercise reasonable oversight—is quite high.

The court concluded, based on the facts in the case at hand, that the directors had not breached a duty:

I conclude, in light of the discovery record, that there is a very low probability that it would be determined that the directors of Caremark breached any duty to appropriately monitor and supervise the enterprise. Indeed the record tends to show an active consideration by Caremark management and its Board of the Caremark structures and programs that ultimately led to the company's indictment and to the large financial losses incurred in the settlement of those claims. It does not tend to show knowing or intentional violation of law. Neither the fact that the Board, although advised by lawyers and accountants, did not accurately predict the severe consequences to the company that would ultimately follow from the deployment by the company of the strategies and practices that ultimately led to this liability, nor the scale of the liability, gives rise to an inference of breach of any duty imposed by corporation law upon the directors of Caremark.

Although Chancellor Allen's description of the updated oversight duty of directors was only dicta (there was no need for him to reject the *Graham* "red flags" test in approving the *Caremark* settlement), the claim laid out by Allen became known as a "*Caremark* claim." After the case, plaintiff-shareholders began to sue directors for breaching their fiduciary duty by failing to assure that an adequate corporate information and reporting system existed to help prevent corporate malfeasance (e.g., employee misconduct or violations of law) and was monitored with proper oversight. As we will see below, a decade after *Caremark*, the Delaware Supreme Court clarified the board of directors' oversight duty and the role of good faith.

3. Federal Overlay

Although state law has traditionally been the source of oversight responsibility, increasingly federal law plays a role. After the corporate and accounting scandals that came to light in the early 2000s, Congress federalized a number of areas of corporate governance, including internal controls over financial accounting and disclosure systems in public companies. The Public Company Accounting Reform and Investor Protection Act of 2002 (known as the Sarbanes-Oxley Act), besides creating a new self-regulatory body called the Public Company Accounting Oversight Board to regulate the accounting profession, mandates oversight by corporate boards, senior management, and even company lawyers of company financial reporting. One of the most onerous provisions of Sarbanes-Oxley is Section 404, which requires that managers of public corporations establish and maintain an adequate internal control structure and procedures for financial reporting, and include an assessment of these controls in the corporation's annual report.

C. Modern Approach to Oversight and "Good Faith"

In 2006, about forty years after *Graham v. Allis-Chalmers*, the issue of oversight responsibility squarely came before the Delaware Supreme Court again. By this time, a decade had also passed since the Court of Chancery's opinion in *Caremark*, and the Delaware Supreme Court had begun giving more attention to "good faith."

The concept of "good faith" arises in several aspects of director fiduciary duties. Recall that the BJR presumes that directors act in good faith. When directors rely on experts, courts ask whether the reliance was made in good faith. When judges analyze the independence of directors, they often inquire into whether decisions by the directors were made in good faith.

In addition, Delaware's § 102(b)(7) specifically permits companies to limit the personal liability of directors for monetary damages for breaches of fiduciary duties, with an important exception for actions "not in good faith." In other words, even if a company adopts an exculpation clause to the full extent permitted by § 102(b)(7), directors still can be personally liable if they do not act in "good faith." This is important because it means that when a corporation has a § 102(b)(7) provision in its certificate of incorporation, plaintiffs are deterred from bringing breach of the duty of care claims against directors, but could potentially still go forward with a suit if they instead characterized the conduct as "not in good faith."

For many years, it was unclear whether directors owed an independent duty of good faith, in addition to the duties of care and loyalty. Some courts and commentators referred to a "triad" of duties, including good faith. Others assumed that there was no free-standing duty of good faith; instead, good faith was a component of the of the duty of care or the duty of loyalty. The Delaware courts used the term "good faith" in analyzing the board's action, although ultimately the Delaware Supreme Court stopped short of establishing an independent duty of good faith.

In *Disney*, as we saw in Chapter 22, the Delaware Supreme Court stated that a failure to act in good faith amounted to something more than a violation of the duty of care. It did not delineate the precise differences between good faith and care, but it gave some examples:

> A failure to act in good faith may be shown, for instance, where the fiduciary intentionally acts with a purpose other than that of advancing the best interests of the corporation, where the fiduciary acts with the intent to violate applicable positive law, or where the fiduciary intentionally fails to act in the face of a known duty to act, demonstrating a conscious disregard for his duties. There may be other examples of bad faith yet to be proven or alleged, but these three are the most salient.

When the concept of "good faith" arose in a monitoring or oversight case, the claims generally were characterized as *Caremark* claims that fell under the duty of care. Then, in *Stone v. Ritter*, the Delaware Supreme Court finally clarified some of the questions surrounding the application of good faith, and applied a new good faith approach in the context of a *Caremark* claim. That case is next, along with an excerpt from a Delaware decision applying some of the new good faith and *Caremark* concepts.

Stone v. Ritter

911 A.2d 362 (Del. 2006)

HOLLAND, JUSTICE.

This is an appeal from a final judgment of the Court of Chancery dismissing a derivative complaint against fifteen present and former directors of AmSouth Bancorporation ("AmSouth"), a Delaware corporation. The plaintiffs-appellants, William and Sandra Stone, are AmSouth shareholders and filed their derivative complaint without making a pre-suit demand on AmSouth's board of directors (the "Board"). The Court of Chancery held that the plaintiffs had failed to adequately plead that such a demand would have been futile.

The Court of Chancery characterized the allegations in the derivative complaint as a "classic Caremark claim," and recognized that: "generally where a claim of directorial liability for corporate loss is predicated upon ignorance of liability creating activities within the corporation . . . only a sustained or systematic failure of the board to exercise oversight—such as an utter failure to attempt to assure a reasonable information and reporting system exists-will establish the lack of good faith that is a necessary condition to liability."

In this appeal, the plaintiffs acknowledge that the directors neither "knew nor should have known that violations of law were occurring," i.e., that there were no "red flags" before the directors. Nevertheless, the plaintiffs argue that the Court of Chancery erred by dismissing the derivative complaint which alleged that "the defendants had utterly failed to implement any sort of statutorily required monitoring, reporting or information controls that would have enabled them to learn of problems requiring their attention." The defendants argue that the plaintiffs' assertions are contradicted by the derivative complaint itself and by the documents incorporated therein by reference.

During the relevant period, AmSouth's wholly-owned subsidiary, AmSouth Bank, operated about 600 commercial banking branches in six states throughout the southeastern United States and employed more than 11,600 people. In 2004, AmSouth and AmSouth Bank paid $40 million in fines and $10 million in civil penalties to resolve government and regulatory investigations pertaining principally to the failure by bank employees to file "Suspicious Activity Reports" ("SARs"), as required by the federal Bank Secrecy Act ("BSA") and various anti-money-laundering ("AML") regulations. No fines or penalties were imposed on AmSouth's directors, and no other regulatory action was taken against them.

The government investigations arose originally from an unlawful "Ponzi" scheme operated by Louis D. Hamric, II and Victor G. Nance. In August 2000, Hamric, then a licensed attorney, and Nance, then a registered investment advisor with Mutual of New York, contacted an AmSouth branch bank in Tennessee to arrange for custodial trust accounts to be created for "investors" in a "business venture." That venture (Hamric and Nance represented) involved the construction of medical clinics overseas. In reality, Nance had convinced more than forty of his clients to invest in promissory notes bearing high rates of return, by misrepresenting the nature and the risk of that investment. Relying on similar misrepresentations by Hamric and Nance, the AmSouth branch employees in Tennessee agreed to provide custodial accounts for the investors and to distribute monthly interest payments to each account upon receipt of a check from Hamric and instructions from Nance.

The Hamric-Nance scheme was discovered in March 2002, when the investors did not receive their monthly interest payments. Thereafter, Hamric and Nance became the subject of several civil actions brought by the defrauded investors in Tennessee and Mississippi (and in which AmSouth also was named as a defendant), and also the subject of a federal grand jury investigation in the Southern District of Mississippi. Hamric and Nance were indicted on federal money-laundering charges, and both pled guilty.

The government authorities found that since April 24, 2002, AmSouth has been in violation of the anti-money-laundering program requirements of the Bank Secrecy Act, that "AmSouth's compliance program lacked adequate board and management oversight," and that "reporting to management for the purposes of monitoring and oversight of compliance activities was materially deficient."

It is a fundamental principle of the Delaware General Corporation Law that "the business and affairs of every corporation organized under this chapter shall be managed by or under the direction of a board of directors." Thus, "by its very nature a derivative action impinges on the managerial freedom of directors." Court of Chancery Rule 23.1, accordingly, requires that the complaint in a derivative action "allege with particularity the efforts, if any, made by the plaintiff to obtain the action the plaintiff desires from the directors or the reasons for the plaintiff's failure to obtain the action or for not making the effort."

To excuse demand "a court must determine whether or not the particularized factual allegations of a derivative stockholder complaint create a reasonable doubt that, as of the time the complaint is filed, the board of directors could have properly exercised its independent and disinterested business judgment in responding to a demand." The plaintiffs assert that the incumbent defendant directors "face a substantial likelihood of liability" that renders them "personally interested in the outcome of the decision on whether to pursue the claims asserted in the complaint," and are therefore not disinterested or independent.[12]

Critical to this demand excused argument is the fact that the directors' potential personal liability depends upon whether or not their conduct can be exculpated by the section 102(b)(7) provision contained in the AmSouth certificate of incorporation. Such a provision can exculpate directors from monetary liability for a breach of the duty of care, but not for conduct that is not in good faith or a breach of the duty of loyalty. The standard for assessing a director's potential personal liability for failing to act in good faith in discharging his or her oversight responsibilities has evolved beginning with our decision in _Graham v. Allis-Chalmers Manufacturing Company_, through the Court of Chancery's _Caremark_ decision to our most recent decision in _Disney_.

[The Court then summarized the _Graham_ and _Caremark_ decisions, quoting extensively from each decision.]

The _Caremark_ Court recognized that "the duty to act in good faith to be informed cannot be thought to require directors to possess detailed information about all aspects of the operation of the enterprise." The Court of Chancery formulated the following standard for assessing the liability of directors where the directors are unaware of employee misconduct that results in the corporation being held liable:

> Generally where a claim of directorial liability for corporate loss is predicated upon ignorance of liability creating activities within the corporation, as in _Graham_ or in this case, only a sustained or systematic failure of the board to exercise oversight—such as an utter failure to attempt to assure a reasonable information and reporting system exists—will establish the lack of good faith that is a necessary condition to liability.

As evidenced by the language quoted above, the _Caremark_ standard for so-called "oversight" liability draws heavily upon the concept of director failure to act in good faith. That is consistent with the definition(s) of bad faith recently approved by this Court in its recent _Disney_ decision, where we held that a failure to act in good faith requires conduct that is qualitatively different from, and more culpable than, the conduct giving rise to a violation of the fiduciary duty of care (i.e., gross negligence). In _Disney_, we identified the following examples of conduct that would establish a failure to act in good faith:

---

[12] The fifteen defendants include eight current and seven former directors. The complaint concedes that seven of the eight current directors are outside directors who have never been employed by AmSouth. One board member, C. Dowd Ritter, the Chairman, is an officer or employee of AmSouth.

A failure to act in good faith may be shown, for instance, where the fiduciary intentionally acts with a purpose other than that of advancing the best interests of the corporation, where the fiduciary acts with the intent to violate applicable positive law, or where the fiduciary intentionally fails to act in the face of a known duty to act, demonstrating a conscious disregard for his duties. There may be other examples of bad faith yet to be proven or alleged, but these three are the most salient.

The third of these examples describes, and is fully consistent with, the lack of good faith conduct that the *Caremark* court held was a "necessary condition" for director oversight liability, i.e., "a sustained or systematic failure of the board to exercise oversight—such as an utter failure to attempt to assure a reasonable information and reporting system exists." Indeed, our opinion in *Disney* cited *Caremark* with approval for that proposition. Accordingly, the Court of Chancery applied the correct standard in assessing whether demand was excused in this case where failure to exercise oversight was the basis or theory of the plaintiffs' claim for relief.

It is important, in this context, to clarify a doctrinal issue that is critical to understanding fiduciary liability under *Caremark* as we construe that case. The phraseology used in Caremark and that we employ here—describing the lack of good faith as a "necessary condition to liability"—is deliberate. The purpose of that formulation is to communicate that a failure to act in good faith is not conduct that results, ipso facto, in the direct imposition of fiduciary liability. The failure to act in good faith may result in liability because the requirement to act in good faith "is a subsidiary element," i.e., a condition, "of the fundamental duty of loyalty." It follows that because a showing of bad faith conduct, in the sense described in *Disney* and *Caremark*, is essential to establish director oversight liability, the fiduciary duty violated by that conduct is the duty of loyalty.

This view of a failure to act in good faith results in two additional doctrinal consequences. First, although good faith may be described colloquially as part of a "triad" of fiduciary duties that includes the duties of care and loyalty, the obligation to act in good faith does not establish an independent fiduciary duty that stands on the same footing as the duties of care and loyalty. Only the latter two duties, where violated, may directly result in liability, whereas a failure to act in good faith may do so, but indirectly. The second doctrinal consequence is that the fiduciary duty of loyalty is not limited to cases involving a financial or other cognizable fiduciary conflict of interest. It also encompasses cases where the fiduciary fails to act in good faith. As the Court of Chancery aptly put it in *Guttman*, "a director cannot act loyally towards the corporation unless she acts in the good faith belief that her actions are in the corporation's best interest."

We hold that *Caremark* articulates the necessary conditions predicate for director oversight liability: (a) the directors utterly failed to implement any reporting or information system or controls; or (b) having implemented such a system or controls, consciously failed to monitor or oversee its operations thus disabling themselves from being informed of risks or problems requiring their attention. In either case, imposition of liability requires a showing that the directors knew that they were not discharging their fiduciary obligations. Where directors fail to act in the face of a known duty to act, thereby demonstrating a conscious disregard for their responsibilities, they breach their duty of loyalty by failing to discharge that fiduciary obligation in good faith.

The plaintiffs contend that demand is excused under Rule 23.1 because AmSouth's directors breached their oversight duty and, as a result, face a "substantial likelihood of liability" as a result of their "utter failure" to act in good faith to put into place policies and procedures to ensure compliance with BSA and AML obligations. The Court of Chancery found that the plaintiffs did not plead the existence of "red flags"—facts showing that the board ever was aware that AmSouth's internal controls were inadequate, that these inadequacies would result in illegal activity, and that the board chose to do nothing about problems it allegedly knew existed." In dismissing the derivative complaint in this action, the Court of Chancery concluded:

> This case is not about a board's failure to carefully consider a material corporate decision that was presented to the board. This is a case where information was not reaching the board because of ineffective internal controls. . . . With the benefit of hindsight, it is beyond question that AmSouth's internal controls with respect to the Bank Secrecy Act and anti-money laundering regulations compliance were inadequate. Neither party disputes that the lack of internal controls resulted in a huge fine—$50 million, alleged to be the largest ever of its kind. The fact of those losses, however, is not alone enough for a court to conclude that a majority of the corporation's board of directors is disqualified from considering demand that AmSouth bring suit against those responsible.

The KPMG Report evaluated the various components of AmSouth's longstanding BSA/AML compliance program. The KPMG Report reflects that AmSouth's Board dedicated considerable resources to the BSA/AML compliance program and put into place numerous procedures and systems to attempt to ensure compliance. According to KPMG, the program's various components exhibited between a low and high degree of compliance with applicable laws and regulations.

The KPMG Report describes the numerous AmSouth employees, departments and committees established by the Board to oversee AmSouth's compliance with the BSA and to report violations to management and the Board:

BSA Officer. Since 1998, AmSouth has had a "BSA Officer" "responsible for all BSA/AML-related matters including employee training, general communications, CTR reporting and SAR reporting," and "presenting AML policy and program changes to the Board of Directors, the managers at the various lines of business, and participants in the annual training of security and audit personnel;"

BSA/AML Compliance Department. AmSouth has had for years a BSA/ AML Compliance Department, headed by the BSA Officer and comprised of nineteen professionals, including a BSA/AML Compliance Manager and a Compliance Reporting Manager;

Corporate Security Department. AmSouth's Corporate Security Department has been at all relevant times responsible for the detection and reporting of suspicious activity as it relates to fraudulent activity, and William Burch, the head of Corporate Security, has been with AmSouth since 1998 and served in the U.S. Secret Service from 1969 to 1998; and

Suspicious Activity Oversight Committee. Since 2001, the "Suspicious Activity Oversight Committee" and its predecessor, the "AML Committee," have actively overseen AmSouth's BSA/AML compliance program. The Suspicious Activity Oversight Committee's mission has for years been to "oversee the policy, procedure, and process issues affecting the Corporate Security and BSA/AML Compliance Programs, to ensure that an effective program exists at AmSouth to deter, detect, and report money laundering, suspicious activity and other fraudulent activity."

The KPMG Report reflects that the directors not only discharged their oversight responsibility to establish an information and reporting system, but also proved that the system was designed to permit the directors to periodically monitor AmSouth's compliance with BSA and AML regulations. For example, as KPMG noted in 2004, AmSouth's designated BSA Officer "has made annual high-level presentations to the Board of Directors in each of the last five years." Further, the Board's Audit and Community Responsibility Committee (the "Audit Committee") oversaw AmSouth's BSA/AML compliance program on a quarterly basis. The KPMG Report states that "the BSA Officer presents BSA/AML training to the Board of Directors annually," and the "Corporate Security training is also presented to the Board of Directors."

The KPMG Report shows that AmSouth's Board at various times enacted written policies and procedures designed to ensure compliance with the BSA and AML regulations. For example, the Board adopted an amended bank-wide "BSA/AML Policy" on July 17, 2003—four months before AmSouth became aware that it was the target of a government investigation. That policy was produced to plaintiffs in response to their demand to inspect AmSouth's books and records pursuant to section 220 and is included in plaintiffs' appendix. Among other things, the July 17, 2003, BSA/AML Policy directs all AmSouth employees to immediately report suspicious transactions or activity to the BSA/AML Compliance Department or Corporate Security.

In this case, the adequacy of the plaintiffs' assertion that demand is excused depends on whether the complaint alleges facts sufficient to show that the defendant directors are potentially personally liable for the failure of non-director bank employees to file SARs. Delaware courts have recognized that "most of the decisions that a corporation, acting through its human agents, makes are, of course, not the subject of director attention." Consequently, a claim that directors are subject to personal liability for employee failures is "possibly the most difficult theory in corporation law upon which a plaintiff might hope to win a judgment."

For the plaintiffs' derivative complaint to withstand a motion to dismiss, "only a sustained or systematic failure of the board to exercise oversight—such as an utter failure to attempt to assure a reasonable information and reporting system exists—will establish the lack of good faith that is a necessary condition to liability." As the *Caremark* decision noted:

> Such a test of liability—lack of good faith as evidenced by sustained or systematic failure of a director to exercise reasonable oversight—is quite high. But, a demanding test of liability in the oversight context is probably beneficial to corporate shareholders as a class, as it is in the board decision context, since it makes board service by qualified persons more likely, while continuing to act as a stimulus to good faith performance of duty by such directors.

Food for Thought

The standard for establishing a *Caremark* claim is very high. One notable case illustrating the difficulty for plaintiffs to win on a *Caremark* claim involved improprieties relating to the Mexican subsidiary of Wal-Mart. In 2012, the *New York Times* published an exposé describing an alleged bribery scheme and cover-up perpetrated by executives at this subsidiary. Derivative suits followed. After years of lengthy litigation, in 2018, the Delaware Supreme Court ruled that the suit was precluded by an Arkansas court that had already granted a motion to dismiss for failure to adequately plead demand futility.

It is indeed rare for *Caremark* claim cases to get past the motion to dismiss stage of litigation. One recent case that has managed to do so involved a claim that Wells Fargo directors knew or consciously disregarded that bank employees were fraudulently creating millions of accounts without customer consent. The bank paid a $185 million fine, which turned out to be just the beginning as additional investigations commenced that brought to light even more extensive wrongdoing. In the derivative suit in the Northern District of California concerning the fraudulent customer accounts, plaintiffs pointed to a lengthy list of events that allegedly put the directors on notice of the fraudulent practices, including complaints through the company's ethics hotline, an employee whistleblower lawsuit, several wrongful termination lawsuits that included allegations of unethical practices, and government investigations and inquiries. In March 2019, the parties settled their dispute and Wells Fargo agreed to a cash payment of $240 million plus other concessions.

More broadly, these cases raise the question of what it means for the law to establish the possibility of oversight liability but to have little case law actually holding directors accountable.

The KPMG Report—which the plaintiffs explicitly incorporated by reference into their derivative complaint—refutes the assertion that the directors "never took the necessary steps to ensure that a reasonable BSA compliance and reporting system existed." KPMG's findings reflect that the Board received and approved relevant policies and procedures, delegated to certain employees and departments the responsibility for filing SARs and monitoring compliance, and exercised oversight by relying on periodic reports from them. Although there ultimately may have been failures by employees to report deficiencies to the Board, there is no basis for an oversight claim seeking to hold the directors personally liable for such failures by the employees.

With the benefit of hindsight, the plaintiffs' complaint seeks to equate a bad outcome with bad faith. The lacuna in the plaintiffs' argument is a failure to recognize that the directors' good faith exercise of oversight responsibility may not invariably prevent employees from violating criminal laws, or from causing the corporation to incur significant financial liability, or both, as occurred in *Graham*, *Caremark* and this very case. In the absence of red flags, good faith in the context of oversight must be measured by the directors' actions "to assure a reasonable information and reporting system exists" and not by second-guessing after the occurrence of employee conduct that results in an unintended adverse outcome. Accordingly, we hold that the Court of Chancery properly applied *Caremark* and dismissed the plaintiffs' derivative complaint for failure to excuse demand by alleging particularized facts that created reason to doubt whether the directors had acted in good faith in exercising their oversight responsibilities.

The judgment of the Court of Chancery is affirmed.

Points for Discussion

1. Decisions vs. oversight.

Should the Delaware courts treat claims involving decision making (as in the *Van Gorkom* and *Disney* cases) similarly to those involving oversight (as in *Caremark* and *Stone v. Ritter*)? Why might the courts distinguish between these two categories of cases?

2. Good faith and monitoring.

What must a plaintiff allege to establish that a defendant director violated the good faith prong of the duty of loyalty? After *Stone v. Ritter*, how would you advise directors regarding their monitoring duties?

3. Duties of loyalty and care.

After *Stone v. Ritter*, is a *Caremark* claim categorized as a breach of the duty of care or the duty of loyalty? If it is a duty of loyalty claim, what is left for the duty of care?

4. Red flags.

Graham v. Allis-Chalmers imposed a duty of inquiry only when there were "obvious signs" of employee wrongdoing. In contrast, *Caremark* required some sort of monitoring system even absent a red flag. How would you advise a board implementing a system of monitoring legal compliance? Is it enough just to set up a monitoring system? Or do the directors also bear some independent responsibility for detecting or responding to red flags? In other words, what should be the board's approach to red flags?

5. Duty of obedience.

By the way, are the duties of care and loyalty enough to describe the corporate legal landscape? Consider a board decision to have the corporation engage in conduct that violates the law. If after careful deliberations and a well-informed cost-benefit analysis, a board composed entirely of directors without any personal financial stake in the decision arrived at the conclusion it would be in the best (financial) interests of the corporation to violate a particular legal norm, what duty is violated?

First, there would seem to be no care breach: the directors were informed and deliberative. Second, there would seem to be no loyalty breach: none had a conflicting personal financial interest, and they were all genuinely seeking only to promote the best interests of the corporation. Yet, from *Allis-Chalmers* to *Caremark* to *Stone v. Ritter*, there is a clear judicial consensus that decisions to knowingly violate the law are beyond the pale.

It would seem there is another duty at work: a duty of obedience. Do directors have a duty to respect legal norms, both internal and external? And should failure to respect such norms trigger personal liability? How can such a duty of obedience be rationalized as part of the duty of loyalty?

6. Private Sources of Guidance.

How do directors learn about what they need to do to fulfill their fiduciary duties? There are some private sources of guidance for directors. The American Bar Association's Business Law Section publishes The Corporate Director's Guidebook, a book that outlines the director's responsibilities. Directors are often advised to read this Guidebook, or a similar book. In addition, there are many specialized courses for directors, and new directors are well advised to take one.

In general, these materials and courses advise that directors be aware of the company's major plans and objectives, evaluate the performance of managers, implement senior executive succession plans, adopt corporate governance policies, review financial and operating information, and ensure that a system of periodic and timely reporting of important matters to the board is in place. Directors generally are required to serve on one or more committees, including audit, compensation, and nominating and governance, and should be prepared to make and evaluate decisions in these areas. Obviously, directors also should become familiar with the specifics of the corporation's business.

D. Oversight of Risk Management

During 2008, numerous corporations—and the markets themselves—were brought to the brink of collapse during an epic financial crisis. The crisis led many directors to reevaluate their approach to risk management. It also led plaintiffs' attorneys to sue several financial institutions. Some of those cases alleged that the directors had violated their oversight responsibilities.

1. Early Financial Risk Cases

Historically, some courts have held directors to heightened duties in their role overseeing financial risks. We consider two such cases below.

In *Brane v. Roth*, 590 N.E.2d 587 (Ind. Ct. App. 1992), the directors of a rural grain elevator cooperative authorized the co-op's manager to engage in hedging transactions for the co-op to protect against losses from changes in grain prices. The manager did not hedge sufficiently and the co-op suffered substantial losses. In a derivative suit by the stockholders against the directors, the trial court found that "the directors breached their duties by retaining a manager inexperienced in hedging; failing to maintain reasonable supervision over him; and failing to attain knowledge of the basic fundamentals of hedging to be able to direct the hedging activities and supervise the manager properly."

The Indiana Court of Appeals affirmed the trial court's judgment for the plaintiffs. On appeal the directors argued that they should have been protected by the BJR because they had relied appropriately on the manager. In rejecting this argument, the court noted that the BJR does not protect directors who "failed to inform themselves of all material information reasonably available to make their decision." That conclusion seems consistent with the BJR since "judgment" implies an informed judgment.

But then the court switched analytic gears, finding that the directors' "failure to provide adequate supervision of the manager's actions was a *breach of their duty of care* to protect Co-op's interests in a reasonable manner." Finding that the BJR did not shield the directors from liability, the court rejected a gross negligence standard for the directors' monitoring and held, instead, that ordinary negligence (the standard under the then-existing Indiana statute) was all that was required. The effect was to impose liability for violating a *standard of conduct*, not the higher *standard of liability* arguably mandated by the BJR.

Hoye v. Meek, 795 F.2d 893 (10th Cir. 1986), another case in which a court looked to statutory *standards of conduct* and disregarded the teachings of the BJR illustrates the same point. In *Hoye*, the Guaranty Trust Company, of which Meek was a director and president, suffered large losses from some of its investments. In a suit by the trustee in bankruptcy, the trial court held that Meek had breached his duty of care by failing to curb the extent of the investment and to monitor the company's investment decisions and results, and by delegating excessive authority to his son. On appeal, the Tenth Circuit rejected Meek's argument that he was entitled to the protection of the BJR and stated:

> We are not persuaded by appellant's argument that, because Maxwell had operated the company at a profit for seven years, the directors' and

president's duty to monitor activities was dissipated. Directors and officers are charged with knowledge of those things which it is their duty to know and ignorance is not a basis for escaping liability. Where suspicions are aroused, or should be aroused, it is the directors' duty to make necessary inquiries. We hold that appellant failed to make the necessary inquiries. He had a duty to keep abreast of Guaranty's investments, particularly investments that posed a double risk of decrease in market price and an increase in transactional costs.

Appellant of course would not be required to have the ability to predict increasing interest rates during the two-year period here involved. A decision made in good faith, based on sound business judgment, would not alone subject appellant to liability. But in order to come within the ambit of the business judgment rule, a director must be diligent and careful in performing the duties he has undertaken. In the instant case, appellant's breach of duty resulted from both his delegation of authority to Maxwell without adequate supervision and his failure to avert Guaranty's continued exposure to increasing indebtedness.

2. *Citigroup*: Oversight of Subprime Risk

One might have concluded from these earlier cases that boards of financial institutions would be held to higher standards with respect to oversight of financial risk. The Delaware courts have confronted this question in disputes arising out of the Financial Crisis of 2008 and have rejected much of the analysis of the earlier cases. Instead, as the case below illustrates, the Delaware courts have applied a BJR analysis to claims that the board did not properly oversee financial risks. It is an important and useful case, not only as an application of *Caremark* and *Stone v. Ritter*, but also because it gives you a window into some of the details of the financial crisis.

In re Citigroup Inc. Shareholder Derivative Litigation

964 A.2d 106 (Del. Ch. 2009)

CHANDLER, CHANCELLOR.

This is a shareholder derivative action brought on behalf of Citigroup Inc., seeking to recover for its losses arising from exposure to the subprime lending market. Plaintiffs, shareholders of Citigroup, brought this action against current and former directors and officers of Citigroup, alleging, in essence, that the defendants breached their fiduciary duties by failing to properly monitor and manage the risks the Company faced from problems in the subprime lending market and for failing to properly disclose Citigroup's exposure to subprime assets. Plaintiffs allege that there were extensive "red flags" that should have given defendants notice of the problems that were brewing in the real estate and credit markets and that defendants ignored these warnings in the pursuit of short term profits and at the expense of the Company's long term viability.

Plaintiffs allege that since as early as 2006, defendants have caused and allowed Citigroup to engage in subprime lending that ultimately left the Company exposed to massive losses by late 2007. Beginning in late 2005, house prices, which many believe were artificially inflated by speculation and easily available credit, began to plateau, and then deflate. Adjustable rate mortgages issued earlier in the decade began to reset, leaving many homeowners with significantly increased monthly payments. Defaults and foreclosures increased, and assets backed by income from residential mortgages began to decrease in value. By February 2007, subprime mortgage lenders began filing for bankruptcy and subprime mortgages packaged into securities began experiencing increasing levels of delinquency. In mid-2007, rating agencies downgraded bonds backed by subprime mortgages.

Business Lingo

"Subprime" generally refers to borrowers who do not qualify for favorable "prime" interest rates, typically because they have weak credit histories, low credit scores, high debt burdens relative to the amount they are borrowing, or high loan-to-value ratios. A "loan-to-value" ratio represents the amount of a loan relative to the value of a property. For example, a borrower who made a downpayment of $20,000 on a $200,000 home and then borrowed the remaining $180,000 would have a loan-to-value ratio of 90% ($180,000 divided by $200,000). During 2006 and 2007, many subprime borrowers obtained loans with no downpayment, or a loan-to-value ratio of 100%.

Much of Citigroup's exposure to the subprime lending market arose from its involvement with collateralized debt obligations ("CDOs")—repackaged pools of lower rated securities that Citigroup created by acquiring asset-backed securities, including residential mortgage backed securities ("RMBSs"), and then selling rights to the cash flows from the securities in classes, or tranches, with different levels of risk and return.

According to plaintiffs, Citigroup's alleged $55 billion subprime exposure was in two areas of the Company's Securities & Banking Unit. The first portion totaled $11.7 billion and included securities tied to subprime loans that were being held until they could be added to debt pools for investors. The second portion included $43 billion of super-senior securities, which are portions of CDOs backed in part by RMBS collateral.

By late 2007, it was apparent that Citigroup faced significant losses on its subprime-related assets. Plaintiffs allege that defendants are liable to the Company for breach of fiduciary duty for failing to adequately oversee and manage Citigroup's exposure to the problems in the subprime mortgage market, even in the face of alleged "red flags." As will be more fully explained below, the "red flags" alleged in the eighty-six page Complaint are generally statements from public documents that reflect worsening conditions in the financial markets, including the subprime and credit markets, and the effects those worsening conditions had on market participants, including Citigroup's peers. By way of example only, plaintiffs' "red flags" include the following:

May 27, 2005: Economist Paul Krugman of the *New York Times* said he saw "signs that America's housing market, like the stock market at the end of the last decade, is approaching the final, feverish stages of a speculative bubble."

May 2006: Ameriquest Mortgage, one of the United States' leading wholesale subprime lenders, announced the closing of each of its 229 retail offices and reduction of 3,800 employees.

February 12, 2007: ResMae Mortgage, a subprime lender, filed for bankruptcy. According to *Bloomberg,* in its Chapter 11 filing, ResMae stated that "the subprime mortgage market has recently been crippled and a number of companies stopped originating loans and United States housing sales have slowed and defaults by borrowers have risen."

Business Lingo

RMBSs are securities whose cash flows come from residential debt such as mortgages. When people borrow money to buy a home, their mortgage loans typically are bundled together and then sold as RMBSs. RMBSs then can be combined in various ways, including in CDOs. Just imagine that everyone in your class has a loan, and think of the bundle of all of those loans as an RMBS. Then a CDO might represent an investment in some of the RMBSs from various classes around the country. For example, a CDO might collect loans from students whose last names begin with A. Or students who have the worst history of repaying their credit cards. Just about any financial claim can be bundled—or "securitized"—using a CDO or some similar technique. The investments in CDO tranches typically vary by seniority, just like the capital structure of a corporation: the safest tranches are called "super senior" and are supposed to be like senior debt, the middle tranches can be like debentures or preferred stock, and the riskiest tranches are like equity. Indeed, CDOs typically are formed as corporations, often in tax or regulatory havens such as Bermuda or the Cayman Islands.

April 18, 2007: Freddie Mac announced plans to refinance up to $20 billion of loans held by subprime borrowers who would be unable to afford their adjustable-rate mortgages at the reset rate.

July 10, 2007: Standard and Poor's and Moody's downgraded bonds backed by subprime mortgages.

August 1, 2007: Two hedge funds managed by Bear Stearns that invested heavily in subprime mortgages declared bankruptcy.

August 9, 2007: American International Group, one of the largest United States mortgage lenders, warned that mortgage defaults were spreading beyond the subprime sector, with delinquencies becoming more common among borrowers in the category just above subprime.

October 18, 2007: Standard & Poor's cut the credit ratings on $23.35 billion of securities backed by pools of home loans that were offered to borrowers during the first half of the year. The downgrades even hit securities rated AAA, which was the highest of the ten investment-grade ratings and the rating of government debt.

Plaintiffs' argument is based on a theory of director liability famously articulated by former-Chancellor Allen in *In re Caremark*. When directors are alleged to be liable for a failure to monitor liability creating activities, the *Caremark* Court stated that while directors could be liable for a failure to monitor, "only a sustained or systematic failure of the board to exercise oversight—such as an utter failure to attempt to assure a reasonable information and reporting system exists—will establish the lack of good faith that is a necessary condition to liability."

In *Stone v. Ritter,* the Delaware Supreme Court approved the *Caremark* standard for director oversight liability and made clear that liability was based on the concept of good faith, which the *Stone* Court held was embedded in the fiduciary duty of loyalty and did not constitute a freestanding fiduciary duty that could independently give rise to liability. Thus, to establish oversight liability a plaintiff must show that the directors *knew* they were not discharging their fiduciary obligations or that the directors demonstrated a *conscious* disregard for their responsibilities such as by failing to act in the face of a known duty to act. The test is rooted in concepts of bad faith; indeed, a showing of bad faith is a *necessary condition* to director oversight liability.

Plaintiffs' Caremark *Allegations*

Plaintiffs' theory of how the director defendants will face personal liability is a bit of a twist on the traditional *Caremark* claim. In a typical *Caremark* case, plaintiffs argue that the defendants are liable for damages that arise from a failure to properly monitor or oversee employee misconduct or violations of law. For example, in *Caremark* the board allegedly failed to monitor employee actions in violation of the federal Anti-Referral Payments Law; in *Stone,* the directors were charged with a failure of oversight that resulted in liability for the company because of employee violations of the federal Bank Secrecy Act.

In contrast, plaintiffs' *Caremark* claims are based on defendants' alleged failure to properly monitor Citigroup's *business risk,* specifically its exposure to the subprime mortgage market. In their answering brief, plaintiffs allege that the director defendants are personally liable under *Caremark* for failing to "make a good faith attempt to follow the procedures put in place or failing to assure that adequate and proper corporate information and reporting systems existed that would enable them to be fully informed regarding Citigroup's risk to the subprime mortgage market." Plaintiffs point to so-called "red flags" that should have put defendants on notice of the problems in the subprime mortgage market and further allege that the board should have been especially conscious of these red flags because a majority of the directors (1) served on the Citigroup board during its previous Enron related conduct and (2) were members of the ARM [Audit and Risk Management] Committee and considered financial experts.

Although these claims are framed by plaintiffs as *Caremark* claims, plaintiffs' theory essentially amounts to a claim that the director defendants should be personally liable to the Company because they failed to fully recognize the risk posed by subprime securities. When one looks past the lofty allegations of duties of oversight and red flags used to dress up these claims, what is left appears to be plaintiff shareholders attempting to hold the director defendants personally liable for making (or allowing to be made) business decisions that, in hindsight, turned out poorly for the Company. Delaware Courts have faced these types of claims many times and have developed doctrines to deal with them—the fiduciary duty of care and the business judgment rule. These doctrines properly focus on the decision-making process rather than on a substantive evaluation of the merits of the decision. This follows from the inadequacy of the Court, due in part to a concept known as hindsight bias, to properly evaluate whether corporate decision-makers made a "right" or "wrong" decision.

Additionally, Citigroup has adopted a provision in its certificate of incorporation pursuant to 8 Del. C. § 102(b)(7) that exculpates directors from personal liability for violations of fiduciary duty, except for, among other things, breaches of the duty of loyalty or actions or omissions not in good faith or that involve intentional misconduct or a knowing violation of law. Because the director defendants are "exculpated from liability for certain conduct, 'then a serious threat of liability may only be found to exist if the plaintiff pleads a *non-exculpated* claim against the directors based on particularized facts.'" Here, plaintiffs have not alleged that the directors were interested in the transaction and instead root their theory of director personal liability in bad faith.

Turning now specifically to plaintiffs' *Caremark* claims, one can see a similarity between the standard for assessing oversight liability and the standard for assessing a disinterested director's decision under the duty of care when the company has adopted an exculpatory provision pursuant to Section 102(b)(7). In either case, a plaintiff can show that the director defendants will be liable if their acts or omissions constitute bad faith. A plaintiff can show bad faith conduct by, for example, properly alleging particularized facts that show that a director *consciously* disregarded an obligation to be reasonably informed about the business and its risks or *consciously* disregarded the duty to monitor and oversee the business.

The Delaware Supreme Court made clear in *Stone* that directors of Delaware corporations have certain responsibilities to implement and monitor a system of oversight; however, this obligation does not eviscerate the core protections of the business judgment rule—protections designed to allow corporate managers and directors to pursue risky transactions without the specter of being held personally liable if those decisions turn out poorly. Accordingly, the burden required for a plaintiff to rebut the presumption of the business judgment rule by showing gross negligence is a difficult one, and the burden to show bad faith is even higher. Additionally, as former-Chancellor Allen noted in *Caremark*, director liability based on the duty of oversight "is possibly the most difficult theory in corporation law upon which a plaintiff might hope to win a judgment."

Business decision-makers must operate in the real world, with imperfect information, limited resources, and an uncertain future. To impose liability on directors for making a "wrong" business decision would cripple their ability to earn returns for investors by taking business risks. Indeed, this kind of judicial second guessing is what the business judgment rule was designed to prevent, and even if a complaint is framed under a *Caremark* theory, this Court will not abandon such bedrock principles of Delaware fiduciary duty law.

In this case, plaintiffs allege that the defendants are liable for failing to properly monitor the risk that Citigroup faced from subprime securities. While it may be possible for a plaintiff to meet the burden under some set of facts, plaintiffs in this case have failed to state a *Caremark* claim sufficient to excuse demand based on a theory that the directors did not fulfill their oversight obligations by failing to monitor the business risk of the company.

The allegations in the Complaint amount essentially to a claim that Citigroup suffered large losses and that there were certain warning signs that could or should have put defendants on notice of the business risks related to Citigroup's investments in subprime assets. Plaintiffs then conclude that because defendants failed to prevent the Company's losses associated with certain business risks, they must have consciously ignored these warning signs or knowingly failed to monitor the Company's risk in accordance with their fiduciary duties. Such conclusory allegations, however, are not sufficient to state a claim for failure of oversight that would give rise to a substantial likelihood of personal liability, which would require particularized factual allegations demonstrating bad faith by the director defendants.

Plaintiffs do not contest that Citigroup had procedures and controls in place that were designed to monitor risk. Plaintiffs admit that Citigroup established the ARM Committee and in 2004 amended the ARM Committee charter to include the fact that one of the purposes of the ARM Committee was to assist the board in fulfilling its oversight responsibility relating to policy standards and guidelines for risk assessment and risk management. The ARM Committee was also charged with, among other things, (1) discussing with management and independent auditors the annual audited financial statements, (2) reviewing with management an evaluation of Citigroup's internal control structure, and (3) discussing with management Citigroup's major credit, market, liquidity, and operational risk exposures and the steps taken by management to monitor and control such exposures, including Citigroup's risk assessment and risk management policies. According to plaintiffs' own allegations, the ARM Committee met eleven times in 2006 and twelve times in 2007.

Plaintiffs argue that demand is excused because a majority of the director defendants face a substantial likelihood of personal liability because they were charged with management of Citigroup's risk as members of the ARM Committee and as audit committee financial experts and failed to properly oversee and monitor such risk.[63] As explained above, however, to establish director oversight liability plaintiffs would ultimately have to prove bad faith conduct by the director defendants. Plaintiffs fail to plead any particularized factual allegations that raise a reasonable doubt that the director defendants acted in good faith.

---

[63] Directors with special expertise are not held to a higher standard of care in the oversight context simply because of their status as an expert. Directors of a committee charged with oversight of a company's risk have additional responsibilities to monitor such risk; however, such responsibility does not change the standard of director liability under *Caremark* and its progeny, which requires a showing of bad faith. However, plaintiffs have not alleged facts showing that they demonstrated a conscious disregard for duty, or any other conduct or omission that would constitute bad faith. Even directors who are experts are shielded from judicial second guessing of their business decisions by the business judgment rule.

The warning signs alleged by plaintiffs are not evidence that the directors consciously disregarded their duties or otherwise acted in bad faith; at most they evidence that the directors made bad business decisions. The "red flags" in the Complaint amount to little more than portions of public documents that reflected the worsening conditions in the subprime mortgage market and in the economy generally. Plaintiffs fail to plead "particularized facts suggesting that the Board was presented with 'red flags' alerting it to potential misconduct" at the Company. That the director defendants knew of signs of a deterioration in the subprime mortgage market, or even signs suggesting that conditions could decline further, is not sufficient to show that the directors were or should have been aware of any wrongdoing at the Company or were consciously disregarding a duty somehow to prevent Citigroup from suffering losses. Nothing about plaintiffs' "red flags" supports plaintiffs' conclusory allegation that "defendants have not made a good faith attempt to assure that adequate and proper corporate information and reporting systems existed that would enable them to be fully informed regarding Citigroup's risk to the subprime mortgage market." Indeed, plaintiffs' allegations do not even specify how the board's oversight mechanisms were inadequate or how the director defendants knew of these inadequacies and consciously ignored them. Rather, plaintiffs seem to hope the Court will accept the conclusion that since the Company suffered large losses, and since a properly functioning risk management system would have avoided such losses, the directors must have breached their fiduciary duties in allowing such losses.

It is well established that the mere fact that a company takes on business risk and suffers losses—even catastrophic losses—does not evidence misconduct, and without more, is not a basis for personal director liability. That there were signs in the market that reflected worsening conditions and suggested that conditions may deteriorate even further is not an invitation for this Court to disregard the presumptions of the business judgment rule and conclude that the directors are liable because they did not properly evaluate business risk. What plaintiffs are asking the Court to conclude from the presence of these "red flags" is that the directors failed to see the extent of Citigroup's business risk and therefore made a "wrong" business decision by allowing Citigroup to be exposed to the subprime mortgage market.

Director oversight duties are designed to ensure reasonable reporting and information systems exist that would allow directors to know about and prevent wrongdoing that could cause losses for the Company. There are significant differences between failing to oversee employee fraudulent or criminal conduct and failing to recognize the extent of a Company's business risk. Directors should, indeed must under Delaware law, ensure that reasonable information and reporting systems exist that would put them on notice of fraudulent or criminal conduct within the company. Such oversight programs allow directors to intervene and prevent frauds or other wrongdoing that could expose the company to risk of loss as a result of such conduct. While it may be tempting to say that directors have the same duties to monitor and oversee business risk, imposing *Caremark*-type duties on directors to monitor business risk is fundamentally different. Citigroup was in the business of taking on and managing investment and other business risks. To impose oversight liability on directors for failure to monitor "excessive" risk would involve courts in conducting hindsight evaluations of decisions at the heart of the business judgment of directors. Oversight duties under Delaware law are not designed to subject directors, even expert directors, to *personal liability* for failure to predict the future and to properly evaluate business risk.[78]

Conclusion

Citigroup has suffered staggering losses, in part, as a result of the recent problems in the United States economy, particularly those in the subprime mortgage market. It is understandable that investors, and others, want to find someone to hold responsible for these losses, and it is often difficult to distinguish between a desire to blame someone and a desire to force those responsible to account for their wrongdoing. Our law, fortunately, provides guidance for precisely these situations in the form of doctrines governing the duties owed by officers and directors of Delaware corporations. This law has been refined over hundreds of years, which no doubt included many crises, and we must not let our desire to blame someone for our losses make us lose sight of the purpose of our law. Ultimately, the discretion granted directors and managers allows them to maximize shareholder value in the long term by taking risks without the debilitating fear that they will be held personally liable if the company experiences losses. This doctrine also means, however, that when the company suffers losses, shareholders may not be able to hold the directors personally liable.

---

[78] If defendants had been able to predict the extent of the problems in the subprime mortgage market, then they would not only have been able to avoid losses, but presumably would have been able to make significant gains for Citigroup by taking positions that would have produced a return when the value of subprime securities dropped. Query: if the Court were to adopt plaintiffs' theory of the case, then why not hold them liable for failing to profit for the Company by predicting market events that, in hindsight, the director should have seen because of certain red (or green?) flags? If one expects director prescience in one direction, why not the other?

Points for Discussion

1. Is overseeing risk different?

The early cases involving financial risk implicitly recognized that the board might be able to play a more helpful role in risk management than in other areas. Why wouldn't that rationale apply to Citigroup? Should directors of financial institutions be more responsible than directors of non-financial institutions for overseeing risk management? Does the high compensation of directors of financial institutions affect your analysis?

2. Are red flags ever red enough?

The court rejected the plaintiffs' argument that the directors should have been especially sensitive to Citigroup's risks. What were the flaws in plaintiffs' red flags argument? What kinds of red flags might enable a plaintiff to prevail? For example, what if the directors had known that a significant downturn in housing prices would cause Citigroup to lose so much money that it would become insolvent? If that knowledge would have triggered some heightened oversight duty, should directors have an obligation to obtain that knowledge, or confirm that such risks do not exist? For

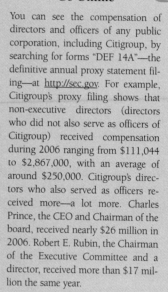

Go Online

You can see the compensation of directors and officers of any public corporation, including Citigroup, by searching for forms "DEF 14A"—the definitive annual proxy statement filing—at http://sec.gov. For example, Citigroup's proxy filing shows that non-executive directors (directors who did not also serve as officers of Citigroup) received compensation during 2006 ranging from $111,044 to $2,867,000, with an average of around $250,000. Citigroup's directors who also served as officers received more—a lot more. Charles Prince, the CEO and Chairman of the board, received nearly $26 million in 2006. Robert E. Rubin, the Chairman of the Executive Committee and a director, received more than $17 million the same year.

example, should Citigroup's directors have been obligated to ask how a significant downturn in housing prices (or changes in other financial variables) would affect the corporation's financial condition?

CHAPTER 24

Duties Within Corporate Groups

With power comes responsibility. Thus, directors and officers have fiduciary duties to the corporation and its shareholders. Fiduciary duties also extend to controlling shareholders, creating a glue that binds together corporate groups.

It may seem curious to you that controlling shareholders have duties to minority shareholders. After all, corporate law is clear that shareholders may vote their shares as they please, without obligation to fellow shareholders. Compared to directors and officers, who voluntarily assume the role of fiduciary inherent in their corporate office, controlling shareholders never formally assent to fiduciary responsibilities. Yet courts impose special duties when shareholders have control—duties analogous to those of directors and officers, though as you will see they are different in subtle and important ways.

This chapter looks at fiduciary duties in corporate groups in three settings, each of which presents a conflict of interest for the controlling shareholder. First, we consider intra-group transactions, such as parent-subsidiary dealings and dealings between a subsidiary and other corporations controlled by the parent, sometimes called affiliates. Second, we discuss "freeze-out" transactions, usually accomplished through a merger in which the parent acquires the subsidiary and the minority shareholders receive cash for their shares. We also consider alternatives to cash-out mergers and examine how courts review these transactions. These topics—cash-out mergers and their alternatives—arise in an area of practice known as "M&A" that we examine in further detail in Chapters 31 and 32.

> **Business Lingo**
>
> A "subsidiary" is a corporation controlled by another corporation, usually called the "parent corporation." The parent can hold all of the subsidiary's voting shares, making it a "wholly-owned subsidiary," or less than all voting shares, but enough to give it effective control, making it a "partially-owned subsidiary."
>
> If the parent has multiple subsidiaries, each corporation subject to the parent's common control is an "affiliate." These affiliates and subsidiaries may have further subsidiaries, which are then considered part of the same "corporate group."

The basic issues. Corporate statutes generally do not address intra-group transactions. Although courts look to director duties for guidance in reviewing the actions of controlling shareholders, there is no provision analogous to DGCL § 144. The standard of review for transactions with the controlling shareholder has been fairness. Unlike director self-dealing transactions, transactions with controlling shareholders (even when approved by disinterested directors or a majority of the minority stockholders) have not received the presumptions of the business judgment rule.

The fiduciary duties of controlling shareholders, and the standard of review, frequently are not as onerous as those of directors and officers. One reason for a lower standard is that controlling shareholders, unlike corporate managers, usually have paid for their control. Minority shareholders know this, or should, and courts recognize the prerogatives of the controlling shareholder. In other words, with power comes not only responsibility, but certain privileges as well.

A. Transactions Within Corporate Groups

Controlling shareholders often use their control to engage in transactions with their controlled corporations—what else would you expect? Parent-subsidiary transactions occur regularly and rarely give rise to litigation. But fairness always is, or should be, on the mind of the parent. The following case, foundational in the U.S. law of corporate groups, illustrates the judicial approach to intra-group dealings, both between the parent and its partially-owned subsidiaries and between group affiliates.

What's That?

When does a shareholder have "control" of a corporation and thus become subject to these various duties? Generally, control means the power to determine the policies of a corporation's business and affairs, and it can exist in several ways.

First, there can be *de jure* control. Absent special rules for board elections or shareholder voting, the owner of more than 50% of a corporation's shares effectively controls that corporation because he can elect a majority of the board and decide any matters submitted to a shareholder vote.

Second, there can be *de facto* control. The owner of a significant block of shares, less than 50%, can often mobilize sufficient votes to elect a board majority. For example, in a public corporation with dispersed shareholders, the SEC takes the position that holding more than 20% of the company's shares (without any other large block owners) generally constitutes effective control. The question is whether the block owner actually controls corporate conduct. The presumption is non-majority shareholders are not dominant, and the plaintiff bears the burden to prove domination. Courts have examined the block owner's relationship with board members, and whether the block owner can dictate the terms of the transaction.

Sinclair Oil Corp. v. Levien

<u>280 A.2d 717 (Del. 1971)</u>

WOLCOTT, CHIEF JUSTICE.

This is an appeal by the defendant, Sinclair Oil Corporation (hereafter Sinclair), from an order of the Court of Chancery, in a derivative action requiring Sinclair to account for damages sustained by its subsidiary, Sinclair Venezuelan Oil Company (hereafter Sinven), organized by Sinclair for the purpose of operating in Venezuela, as a result of dividends paid by Sinven, the denial to Sinven of industrial development, and a breach of contract between Sinclair's wholly-owned subsidiary, Sinclair International Oil Company, and Sinven.

Sinclair, operating primarily as a holding company, is in the business of exploring for oil and of producing and marketing crude oil and oil products. At all times relevant to this litigation, it owned about 97% of Sinven's stock. The plaintiff owns about 3000 of 120,000 publicly held shares of Sinven. Sinven, incorporated in 1922, has been engaged in petroleum operations primarily in Venezuela and since 1959 has operated exclusively in Venezuela.

Sinclair Oil Corporation was founded by Harry Sinclair in 1916 and competed with Standard Oil, which had been founded by John D. Rockefeller. By the 1920s, Sinclair had expanded to Venezuela, where it acquired a majority interest in the company that would become Sinven. Sinclair established absolute control over Sinven by the late 1950s, with 97% of its stock and total domination of its board.

Sinclair's logo was a brontosaurus, which came from a dinosaur exhibit that the company sponsored at the Chicago World's Fair of 1933–34 that told the story of how petroleum deposits were formed during the Age of Dinosaurs. Sinclair used rubber brontosauruses as promotional items, and some company locations included life-size models of the mascot.

Sinclair nominates all members of Sinven's board of directors. The Chancellor found as a fact that the directors were not independent of Sinclair. Almost without exception, they were officers, directors, or employees of corporations in the Sinclair complex. By reason of Sinclair's domination, it is clear that Sinclair owed Sinven a fiduciary duty. Sinclair concedes this.

The Chancellor held that because of Sinclair's fiduciary duty and its control over Sinven, its relationship with Sinven must meet the test of intrinsic fairness. The standard of intrinsic fairness involves both a high degree of fairness and a shift in the burden of proof. Under this standard the burden is on Sinclair to prove, subject to careful judicial scrutiny, that its transactions with Sinven were objectively fair.

Sinclair argues that the transactions between it and Sinven should be tested, not by the test of intrinsic fairness with the accompanying shift of the burden of proof, but by the business judgment rule under which a court will not interfere with the judgment of a board of directors unless there is a showing of gross and palpable overreaching. A board of directors enjoys a presumption of sound business judgment, and its decisions will not be disturbed if they can be attributed to any rational business purpose. A court under such circumstances will not substitute its own notions of what is or is not sound business judgment.

We think, however, that Sinclair's argument in this respect is misconceived. When the situation involves a parent and a subsidiary, with the parent controlling the transaction and fixing the terms, the test of intrinsic fairness, with its resulting shifting of the burden of proof, is applied. The basic situation for the application of the rule is the one in which the parent has received a benefit to the exclusion and at the expense of the subsidiary.

A parent does indeed owe a fiduciary duty to its subsidiary when there are parent-subsidiary dealings. However, this alone will not evoke the intrinsic fairness standard. This standard will be applied only when the fiduciary duty is accompanied by self-dealing—the situation when a parent is on both sides of a transaction with its subsidiary. Self-dealing occurs when the parent, by virtue of its domination of the subsidiary, causes the subsidiary to act in such a way that the parent receives something from the subsidiary to the exclusion of, and detriment to, the minority stockholders of the subsidiary.

We turn now to the facts. The plaintiff argues that, from 1960 through 1966, Sinclair caused Sinven to pay out such excessive dividends that the industrial development of Sinven was effectively prevented, and it became in reality a corporation in dissolution.

From 1960 through 1966, Sinven paid out $108,000,000 in dividends ($38,000,000 in excess of Sinven's earnings during the same period). The Chancellor held that Sinclair caused these dividends to be paid during a period when it had a need for large amounts of cash. Although the dividends paid exceeded earnings, the plaintiff concedes that the payments were made in compliance with 8 Del.C. § 170, authorizing payment of dividends out of surplus or net profits. However, the plaintiff attacks these dividends on the ground that they resulted from an improper motive—Sinclair's need for cash. The Chancellor, applying the intrinsic fairness standard, held that Sinclair did not sustain its burden of proving that these dividends were intrinsically fair to the minority stockholders of Sinven.

Since it is admitted that the dividends were paid in strict compliance with 8 Del.C. § 170, the alleged excessiveness of the payments alone would not state a cause of action. Nevertheless, compliance with the applicable statute may not, under all circumstances, justify all dividend payments. If a plaintiff can meet his burden of proving that a dividend cannot be grounded on any reasonable business objective, then the courts can and will interfere with the board's decision to pay the dividend.

A dividend declaration by a dominated board will not inevitably demand the application of the intrinsic fairness standard. But if such a dividend is in essence self-dealing by the parent, then the intrinsic fairness standard is the proper standard. For example, suppose a parent dominates a subsidiary and its board of directors. The subsidiary has outstanding two classes of stock, X and Y. Class X is owned by the parent and Class Y is owned by minority stockholders of the subsidiary. If the subsidiary, at the direction of the parent, declares a dividend on its Class X stock only, this might well be self-dealing by the parent. It would be receiving something from the subsidiary to the exclusion of and detrimental to its minority stockholders. This self-dealing, coupled with the parent's fiduciary duty, would make intrinsic fairness the proper standard by which to evaluate the dividend payments.

Consequently it must be determined whether the dividend payments by Sinven were, in essence, self-dealing by Sinclair. The dividends resulted in great sums of money being transferred from Sinven to Sinclair. However, a proportionate share of this money was received by the minority shareholders of Sinven. Sinclair received nothing from Sinven to the exclusion of its minority stockholders. As such, these dividends were not self-dealing. We hold therefore that the Chancellor erred in applying the intrinsic fairness test as to these dividend payments. The business judgment standard should have been applied.

We conclude that the facts demonstrate that the dividend payments complied with the business judgment standard and with 8 Del.C. § 170. The motives for causing the declaration of dividends are immaterial unless the plaintiff can show that the dividend payments resulted from improper motives and amounted to waste. The

Make the Connection

Dividend payments are subject to "legal capital" rules that are meant to protect corporate creditors from shareholders who withdraw cash and leave the corporation unable to fulfill its credit obligations. *See* Chapter 12, Capital Structure.

Dividend policy in *close corporations* is also subject to exacting judicial review under the "oppression" doctrine. *See* Chapter 26. If a minority shareholder can show that dividend policy (typically, the refusal of the majority to pay dividends) frustrates the minority's "reasonable expectations," the court may order dissolution of the corporation or the buyout of the minority's interest at a "fair value."

plaintiff contends only that the dividend payments drained Sinven of cash to such an extent that it was prevented from expanding.

The plaintiff proved no business opportunities which came to Sinven independently and which Sinclair either took to itself or denied to Sinven. As a matter of fact, with two minor exceptions which resulted in losses, all of Sinven's operations have been conducted in Venezuela, and Sinclair had a policy of exploiting its oil properties located in different countries by subsidiaries located in the particular countries.

From 1960 to 1966 Sinclair purchased or developed oil fields in Alaska, Canada, Paraguay, and other places around the world. The plaintiff contends that these were all opportunities which could have been taken by Sinven. The Chancellor concluded that Sinclair had not proved that its denial of expansion opportunities to Sinven was intrinsically fair. He based this conclusion on the following findings of fact. Sinclair made no real effort to expand Sinven. The excessive dividends paid by Sinven resulted in so great a cash drain as to effectively deny to Sinven any ability to expand. During this same period Sinclair actively pursued a company-wide policy of developing through its subsidiaries new sources of revenue, but Sinven was not permitted to participate and was confined in its activities to Venezuela.

However, the plaintiff could point to no opportunities which came to Sinven. Therefore, Sinclair usurped no business opportunity belonging to Sinven. Since Sinclair received nothing from Sinven to the exclusion of and detriment to Sinven's minority stockholders, there was no self-dealing. Therefore, business judgment is the proper standard by which to evaluate Sinclair's expansion policies.

Since there is no proof of self-dealing on the part of Sinclair, it follows that the expansion policy of Sinclair and the methods used to achieve the desired result must, as far as Sinclair's treatment of Sinven is concerned, be tested by the standards of the business judgment rule. Accordingly, Sinclair's decision, absent fraud or gross overreaching, to achieve expansion through the medium of its subsidiaries, other than Sinven, must be upheld.

Even if Sinclair was wrong in developing these opportunities as it did, the question arises, with which subsidiaries should these opportunities have been shared? No evidence indicates a unique need or ability of Sinven to develop these opportunities. The decision of which subsidiaries would be used to implement Sinclair's expansion policy was one of business judgment with which a court will not interfere absent a showing of gross and palpable overreaching. No such showing has been made here.

Next, Sinclair argues that the Chancellor committed error when he held it liable to Sinven for breach of contract.

In 1961 Sinclair created Sinclair International Oil Company (hereafter International), a wholly owned subsidiary used for the purpose of coordinating all of Sinclair's foreign operations. All crude purchases by Sinclair were made thereafter through International.

On September 28, 1961, Sinclair caused Sinven to contract with International whereby Sinven agreed to sell all of its crude oil and refined products to International at specified prices. The contract provided for minimum and maximum quantities and prices. The

> **Make the Connection**
>
> Directors are also prevented from usurping corporate opportunities. *See* Chapter 21, Director Conflicts. But compare the way in which courts define corporate opportunities for directors under the "expectancy" and "line of business" tests, and the "unique need or ability" test that the court articulates here. That is, directors may be subject to greater limitations when business opportunities come their way, compared to business opportunities within corporate groups.

plaintiff contends that Sinclair caused this contract to be breached in two respects. Although the contract called for payment on receipt, International's payments lagged as much as 30 days after receipt. Also, the contract required International to purchase at least a fixed minimum amount of crude and refined products from Sinven. International did not comply with this requirement.

Clearly, Sinclair's act of contracting with its dominated subsidiary was self-dealing. Under the contract Sinclair received the products produced by Sinven, and of course the minority shareholders of Sinven were not able to share in the receipt of these products. If the contract was breached, then Sinclair received these products to the detriment of Sinven's minority shareholders. We agree with the Chancellor's finding that the contract was breached by Sinclair, both as to the time of payments and the amounts purchased.

Although a parent need not bind itself by a contract with its dominated subsidiary, Sinclair chose to operate in this manner. As Sinclair has received the benefits of this contract, so must it comply with the contractual duties.

Under the intrinsic fairness standard, Sinclair must prove that its causing Sinven not to enforce the contract was intrinsically fair to the minority shareholders of Sinven. Sinclair has failed to meet this burden. Late payments were clearly breaches for which Sinven should have sought and received adequate damages. As to the quantities purchased, Sinclair argues that it purchased all the products produced by Sinven. This, however, does not satisfy the standard of intrinsic fairness. Sinclair has failed to prove that Sinven could not possibly have produced or someway have obtained the contract minimums. As such, Sinclair must account on this claim.

Take Note!

Notice that intra-group dealings receive "intrinsic fairness" review. This means that the *substance* of the dealings are compared to the terms and price one would expect in an arm's-length, third-party transaction.

Under the "entire fairness" test that Delaware courts use for "cash-out mergers" (see below), judicial review encompasses both the *substance* of the transaction and the *process* by which the transaction was initiated, timed, negotiated, decided and disclosed. Thus, for business dealings between subsidiaries in a corporate group, it is worth noticing that the "intrinsic fairness" test does not mandate procedural hoops.

Finally, Sinclair argues that the Chancellor committed error in refusing to allow it a credit or setoff of all benefits provided by it to Sinven with respect to all the alleged damages. The Chancellor held that setoff should be allowed on specific transactions, e.g., benefits to Sinven under the contract with International, but denied an over all setoff against all damages claimed. We agree with the Chancellor, although the point may well be moot in view of our holding that Sinclair is not required to account for the alleged excessiveness of the dividend payments.

We will therefore reverse that part of the Chancellor's order that requires Sinclair to account to Sinven for damages sustained as a result of dividends paid between 1960 and 1966, and by reason of the denial to Sinven of expansion during that period. We will affirm the remaining portion of that order and remand the cause for further proceedings.

Points for Discussion

1. Shareholder consent?

Although not discussed in the opinion, Levien acquired his stock *after* Sinclair already owned 97% of Sinven. When he bought his stock, how did Levien expect Sinclair to conduct its business? Wasn't he on notice that Sinclair was likely to cause Sinven to pay large dividends at the end of each year? Should that affect the nature of the fiduciary duties that Sinclair owes to the minority shareholders of Sinven?

2. Intra-group cash flows.

The *Sinclair Oil* court decided not to interfere with Sinclair's decision to extract cash from Sinven. Do you agree with the court's holding on the dividend issue? It appears that Levien was unable to show that the payment of dividends caused Sinven to forego otherwise profitable investments. Would the result have changed if he had been able to demonstrate such a loss?

Compare the court's decision on the prerogatives of a *parent corporation* to manage intra-group cash flow with the discretion of *directors* to set the corporation's dividend policy. *See American Express v. Kamin* (Chapter 12, Capital Structure). Which standard of review is more deferential?

3. Intra-group business allocations.

The *Sinclair Oil* court also decided to steer clear of how Sinclair allocated business within the corporate group. Would the result have been different if Sinven had issued press statements or filed disclosure documents indicating that it was "constantly looking for oil exploration opportunities throughout the Americas"?

Compare the court's analysis of the corporate opportunity issue (the Alaskan and Paraguayan oil fields) to the responsibilities of directors in taking business opportunities in which the corporation has an expectancy. If a Sinven director had decided to pursue the oil field opportunities, wouldn't the director (at least) have been obligated to present the opportunity to Sinven for its consideration? *See Broz* (Chapter 21, Director Conflicts).

4. Intra-group contracting.

The *Sinclair Oil* court intervened with respect to the contract dealings between Sinven and other affiliates in the corporate group. What burdens does the court's holding place on such contract dealings? Is this burden greater or lesser than the burden a director faces in his dealing with the corporation?

Also, consider that Sinven won a judgment for $5.6 million on the contract claim, providing an (indirect) benefit for the public shareholders of approximately $168,000. Plaintiff's attorneys were awarded fees in excess of $1 million for recovering the $5.6 million.

5. Cost-benefit analysis of intra-group dealings.

Notice that the *Sinclair Oil* court, in reviewing intra-group costs, refused to offset the benefits of being in a group. For example, there may be advantages in being able to enter into intra-group transactions or to share group services, such as accounting, access to capital, personnel, and so on. Why should these benefits not be factored in? Will they be quantifiable—and by whom? Interestingly, some countries have laws that specifically permit controlling shareholders to claim offsetting benefits to group members. Would you feel comfortable investing in such corporate groups?

B. "Freeze-out" Transactions

As the litigation in *Sinclair Oil* makes clear, parent corporations often have good reasons to eliminate minority shareholders, which is often referred to generally as a "freeze out." For example, a shareholder of a public corporation might want to "go private" by acquiring a controlling stake and then paying cash to the remaining shareholders. How can this be done? Normally, private parties cannot force others to sell to them—the power of eminent domain is generally reserved to the state.

But in a corporation, "majority rule" allows controlling shareholders to structure transactions that force minority shareholders to accept cash for their shares. This can be accomplished in different ways. Each of these involve a deal structure that would "cash out" or "freeze out" the minority shareholders such that they would no longer own stock in the subsidiary or the ownership structure of the subsidiary would change through a sale to an outside buyer. This discussion will introduce you to some new vocabulary relevant to M&A deals. Here are possible structures:

Cash-out merger. The parent corporation uses its control of the subsidiary's board and its voting majority to arrange a merger between the partially-owned subsidiary and a wholly-owned corporation of the parent (or the parent itself). In the process, the minority shareholders receive cash in the merger or, if they are dissatisfied with the merger terms, in a proceeding known as a judicial appraisal.

Tender offer followed by merger. A bidder corporation makes a tender offer conditioned on acquiring at least a specified percentage of a corporation's stock. (Historically, this specified percentage was 90%, though many modern statutes permit a merger once the bidder owns a majority of the target corporation's stock.) If successful, the bidder then merges with the corporation under a streamlined procedure that requires only approval of the parent corporation's board of directors.

Sale to outside buyer. The parent corporation, rather than acquiring 100% ownership of the subsidiary, arranges for the subsidiary to be merged with an outside buyer. In the merger, the parent corporation and minority shareholders receive consideration as specified in the merger plan.

What are the fiduciary duties of the parent corporation when it cashes out minority shareholders? The answer to that question has changed over time, in ways that are often confusing—and remain in flux. Our purpose here is not to cover all of the details of the jurisprudence of cash-out mergers and their alternatives, but instead to give you a sense of what the key issues have been, are, and are likely to be.

1. Cash-out Mergers: Controlling Shareholders and the Fairness Standard

Mechanics of a cash-out merger. A cash-out merger is relatively straightforward. Typically, the parent corporation (P) organizes a new shell corporation (Newco) to which it transfers all its stock in the partially-owned subsidiary (S). Next, P has the boards of S and Newco enter into a merger agreement providing that, upon the merger of Newco into S, all the shareholders of S will receive cash for their S stock. P then votes all the stock of Newco in favor of the merger. P also votes its S stock for the merger and, if necessary, uses its control over the S proxy machinery to obtain the support of any additional shares needed to approve the merger. Under most corporate statutes, S shareholders who are dissatisfied with the merger terms can dissent and seek a judicial appraisal of the "fair value" of their stock, payable in cash.

Conflicts of interest. Cash-out mergers are fraught with conflicts. If P owns a majority of S stock, it can use its control of S's board and its ability to vote for approval of the merger to dictate the terms on which S's minority shareholders will be cashed out. Unless S's non-controlling shareholders can induce a court to intervene on equitable grounds, they are powerless to retain their equity interest in S or to alter the terms of the merger.

Take Note!

Over the last two decades the cash-out merger has been widely used as the second step in corporate takeovers. When a corporate bidder acquires majority (but less than 100%) control of a target company, the cash-out merger provides the means to consolidate control.

Once the target becomes a wholly-owned subsidiary, the parent is freed of nettlesome minority shareholders and thus any self-dealing duties to them. The parent can use the cash flow and assets of the target as it chooses, including to repay any debt it assumed in the acquisition.

Even if P has only de facto control of S and needs the support of other S shareholders to accomplish the cash-out, S's non-controlling shareholders may have trouble blocking an unfair cash-out merger. In a public corporation, the shareholders face collective action problems and lack a mechanism for bargaining with P. These problems are exacerbated by P's better understanding of S's business and assets—and therefore its value. P also will be in a position to time a cash-out merger so as to take advantage of shifts in interest rates, fluctuations in S's stock price, or drops in the value of S's assets (some of which P may have induced).

The availability of appraisal only partially mitigates the potential for P's abuse. Dissenting shareholders (at least in Delaware) must bear the significant out-of-pocket costs of appraisal. Thus, even if they obtain an award higher than the merger price, the effort may not be economically worthwhile. And even if most of the non-controlling shareholders of S believe their stock is worth more than the merger price, collective action problems will impede them from coordinating their joint efforts to pursue appraisal. Recognizing this, P may try to set the merger price just high enough to make appraisal cost-ineffective.

Despite the potential for abuse, a cash-out merger is not inevitably exploitative. P may have bona fide reasons for the transaction. P may anticipate operating efficiencies by combining P and S. And P may wish to engage in concededly fair transactions with S without the threat of litigation. P may wish to eliminate the expense of having public shareholders, thus avoiding reporting requirements and regulatory burdens. Or if P has acquired a controlling interest in S through a cash tender offer, a subsequent cash-out merger will give P access to the cash flows and assets of S that can be used to repay the acquisition debt P incurred in the tender offer. Of course, whatever the business reasons for the cash-out, P may actually offer the minority shareholders a fair price for their stock.

Practice Pointer

A number of factors almost guarantee that litigation follows a cash-out merger: the conflicts of interest and inherent potential for abuse; the large stakes involved; and the likelihood that any attorney who successfully challenges the merger (usually in a class action) will receive a substantial fee.

As you will see, the Delaware courts have sought to provide guidance to corporate lawyers on structuring cash-out mergers. Notice, especially, the role that independent directors are supposed to play. In the end, the Delaware courts seem to prefer that well-informed and properly-motivated business people, not judges, set the price in corporate transactions.

Delaware's approach prior to Weinberger. In 1977, the Delaware Supreme Court had held that a merger "made for the sole purpose of freezing-out minority stockholders is an abuse of the corporate process." *Singer v. Magnavox Co.*, 380 A.2d 969 (Del. 1977) (overruling earlier cases). In addition, the court reiterated the long-standing rule that the controlling shareholder bears the burden of demonstrating the "entire fairness" of the proposed merger. *See Sterling v. Mayflower Hotel Corp.*, 93 A.2d 107 (Del. 1952).

Singer (and two other contemporaneous decisions) established that a shareholder dissatisfied with the terms of a cash-out merger could avoid appraisal by challenging the merger's purpose. The *Singer* trilogy, which provided little guidance as to what constitutes a proper purpose or when a merger is "entirely fair," opened cash-out mergers to extended litigation. An aggrieved shareholder could simply allege that the merger had been effectuated "solely to cash-out minority shareholders at an inadequate price"—thus creating a factual issue as to whether the merger had a proper purpose and shifting the burden to the controlling shareholder to prove the merger was "entirely fair."

Weinberger v. UOP, 457 A.2d 701 (Del. 1983). *Weinberger* held in a "one-step" cash-out merger, where the board of a company with a controlling shareholder voted to approve a merger, the merger was subject to an "entire fairness" test. The court held that fairness has two basic aspects: fair dealing and fair price: "The former embraces questions of when the transaction was timed, how it was initiated, structured, negotiated, disclosed to the directors, and how the approvals of the directors and the stockholders were obtained. The latter aspect of fairness relates to the economic and financial considerations of the proposed merger, including all relevant factors: assets, market value, earnings, future prospects, and any other elements that affect the intrinsic or inherent value of a company's stock. However, the test for fairness is not a bifurcated one as between fair dealing and price. All aspects of the issue must be examined as a whole since the question is one of entire fairness. However, in a non-fraudulent transaction we recognize that price may be the preponderant consideration outweighing other features of the merger."

The court criticized whether the vote by minority stockholders was fully informed. The court noted that the determination of fair value should include a variety of factors, including the factors relevant to a discount cash flow analysis (which we covered in Chapter 11). Accordingly, the court found that basic aspects of both fair dealing and fair price were violated.

The court noted in footnote 7 of the opinion that "the result here could have been entirely different if UOP had appointed an independent negotiating committee of its outside directors to deal with Signal at arm's length."

Weinberger gave minority shareholders a potent tool in a cash-out merger—namely, a class action in which rescissory damages were a potential remedy. But it did not give minority shareholders a chance to exercise "hold up" power by claiming the transaction was primarily to benefit the controlling shareholder. That is, minority shareholders got a "big club," but not a "wrecking ball."

What constitutes fair dealing? The *Weinberger* approach reflects the judicial preference, particularly in Delaware, to review corporate process rather than to determine financial value—especially when there is no ready market, as in a cash-out merger. Determining a fair price calls for financial skills and acumen that judges may lack. Gauging decision-making processes is easier for judges, who assume that fair price follows fair dealing.

Accordingly, it became common after *Weinberger* for the boards of subsidiary corporations involved in cash-out mergers to create independent negotiating committees of outside directors to negotiate with the controlling shareholder and to condition such mergers on the approval of a majority of the minority shareholders. This led to a number of questions. For example, what is the standard of review if an independent committee negotiates on behalf of minority shareholders—entire fairness or BJR? And if the processes of the negotiating committee are inadequate, does the transaction automatically fail the "entire fairness" test?

Since *Weinberger*, the Delaware Supreme Court has attempted to answer the question posted in footnote 7, in various contexts. In *Kahn v. Lynch Communication Sys., Inc. (Lynch I)*, 638 A.2d 1110 (Del. 1994), the Delaware Supreme Court refused to accept, as a general matter, that the outside directors on a special negotiating committee can ever be sufficiently "independent" to warrant BJR review. The court also made clear that the negotiating committee cannot be "forced" to accept the merger by threats of a lower-priced tender offer or other means.

The case was celebrated as a "high water" mark in the protection of minority shareholders.

On remand the Chancery Court concluded that the controlling shareholder had borne its burden to show the cash-out merger satisfied the "entire fairness" test, despite the coercive pressure it had placed on the negotiating committee. Ultimately, the court accepted that the minority had done as well as they were going to do. The court found: (1) the cash-out was a viable financial alternative for the minority; (2) its initiation by the controlling shareholder did not financially disadvantage the minority; (3) any coercion was not "material" in the decision of the minority shareholders who approved the transaction; and (4) valuation reports and other information available to the negotiating committee indicated the price was fair.

The Delaware Supreme Court affirmed, pointing out that the *Weinberger* test "is not bifurcated or compartmentalized but one requiring an examination of all aspects of the transaction to gain a sense of whether the deal in its entirety is fair." *Kahn v. Lynch Communication Sys., Inc. (Lynch II)*, 669 A.2d 79 (Del. 1995).

Can outside directors be independent?

Is it realistic to think outside directors on a special negotiating committee can ensure a fair price for minority shareholders in a transaction with a dominant party? Despite claims that outside directors are at best "ornamental," corporate law over the past three decades has given greater prominence to outside directors, whether on the board or on board committees comprised of outside directors. One reason may be the role played by the investment bankers and lawyers who guide outside directors in their deliberations and negotiations.

Chancellor Allen considered the adequacy of outside directors in the context of a management buyout:

Consider the outside director who is asked to serve on a special committee to preside over a sale of the company. While he may receive some modest special remuneration for this service, he and his fellow committee members are likely to be the only persons intensely involved in the process who do not entertain the fervent hope of either making a killing or earning a princely fee. Couple that with the pressure that the seriousness and urgency of the assignment generate; the unpleasantness that may be required if the job is done right; and, the fact that no matter what the director does he will probably be sued for it, and you have, I think, a fairly unappetizing assignment.

Combine these factors with those that create feelings of solidarity with management directors, particularly the corporation's CEO, and it becomes, I would think, quite easy to understand how some special committees appear as no more than, in T.S. Eliot's phrase, "an easy tool, deferential, glad to be of use."

Only one factor stands against these pressures towards accommodation of the CEO: that is a sense of duty. When special committees have appeared to push and resist their colleagues, it has been, I submit, because the men and women who comprised the committee have understood that as a result of accepting this special assignment, they have a new duty and stand in a new and different relationship to the firm's management or its controlling shareholder.

Thus, I come to the role of the committee's advisors—the lawyers and investment bankers who guide the committee through the process of the sale of a public company. I regard the role of the advisors in establishing the integrity of this process as absolutely crucial. Indeed, the motives and performance of the lawyers and bankers who specialize in the field of mergers and acquisitions is to my mind the great, largely unexamined variable in the process. In all events, it is plain that quite often the special committee relies upon the advisors almost totally. It is understandable why. Frequently, the outside directors who find themselves in control of a corporate sale process have had little or no experience in the sale of a public company. They are in terra incognito. Naturally, they turn for guidance to their specialist advisors who will typically have had a great deal of relevant experience.

Thus, in my opinion, if the special committee process is to have integrity, it falls in the first instance to the lawyers to unwrap the bindings that have joined the directors into a single board; to instill in the committee a clear understanding of the radically altered state in which it finds itself and to lead the committee to a full understanding of its new duty.

William T. Allen, *Independent Directors in MBO Transactions: Are They Fact or Fantasy?* 45 BUS. LAW. 2055–58, 2060–63 (1990).

---

2. Alternatives to Cash-out Mergers

After *Lynch* controlling shareholders and their lawyers began to look for ways to avoid the demanding "entire fairness" review that the case lays out. There are other techniques, besides a cash-out merger, for a controlling shareholder to cash out minority shareholders. What standard of review applies to them?

We next consider the approaches taken by the Delaware courts when a parent corporation cashes out minority shareholders in a partially-owned subsidiary (1) under the expedited process for "short form" and "medium form" mergers permitted when the parent owns a specified percentage or more of the subsidiary's voting shares, and (2) by engaging first in a tender offer to reach a specified percentage threshold and then engaging in a short-form or medium-form merger.

As you will see, form seems to trump substance. By structuring a cash-out transaction other than as a cash-out merger subject to *Weinberger*, corporate planners avoid the heavy procedural requirements and judicial review that the "entire fairness" standard imposes. Once again "independent legal significance" rears its head.

Make the Connection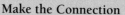

"Independent legal significance" is a corporate law doctrine that accepts that where a corporate transaction may be accomplished in more than one way—such as a statutory merger or a sale of assets—the form chosen frames the substantive rights of the parties.

a. Short-Form and Medium-Form Mergers

For many years, the "short-form" merger was the favored alternative. DGCL § 253 (like many state statutes) authorizes a "short form merger" between a parent corporation and its subsidiary, if the parent owns at least 90% of the subsidiary's stock. To effectuate the merger, the parent simply files a certificate setting forth its stock ownership and the terms of the merger, as set by the parent corporation's board of directors. No action is required of either the board or shareholders of the subsidiary. The parent corporation, however, must inform the subsidiary's minority shareholders of the terms of the merger and advise them of their appraisal rights if they are dissatisfied with the consideration offered by the parent. DGCL § 262(d)(2).

A short form merger, by definition, involves self dealing by the parent corporation. After *Weinberger,* it was generally assumed that the parent corporation also bears the burden of proving that the terms of the merger are entirely fair. But in 2001, the Delaware Supreme Court held that the entire fairness standard does not apply to short-form mergers, concluding instead that appraisal is the exclusive remedy for minority shareholders:

> Under settled principles, a parent corporation and its directors undertaking a short-form merger are self-dealing fiduciaries who should be required to establish entire fairness, including fair dealing and fair price. The problem is that § 253 authorizes a summary procedure that is inconsistent with any reasonable notion of fair dealing. In a short-form merger, there is no agreement of merger negotiated by two companies; there is only a unilateral act—a decision by the parent company that its 90% owned subsidiary shall no longer exist as a separate entity. The minority stockholders receive no advance notice of the merger; their directors do not consider or approve it; and there is no vote. Those who object are given the right to obtain fair value for their shares through appraisal.

> The equitable claim plainly conflicts with the statute. If a corporate fiduciary follows the truncated process authorized by § 253, it will not be able to establish the fair dealing prong of entire fairness. If, instead, the corporate fiduciary sets up negotiating committees, hires independent financial and legal experts, etc., then it will have lost the very benefit provided by the statute—a simple, fast and inexpensive process for accomplishing a merger. We resolve this conflict by giving effect the intent of the General Assembly. In order to serve its purpose, § 253 must be construed to obviate the requirement to establish entire fairness.

> Thus, we hold that, absent fraud or illegality, appraisal is the exclusive remedy available to a minority stockholder who objects to a short-form merger. In doing so, we also reaffirm *Weinberger's* statements about the scope of appraisal. The determination of fair value must be based on *all* relevant factors, including damages and elements of future value, where appropriate. So, for example, if the merger was timed to take advantage of a depressed market, or a low point in the company's cyclical earnings, or to precede an anticipated positive development, the appraised value may be adjusted to account for those factors.

> Although fiduciaries are not required to establish entire fairness in a short-form merger, the duty of full disclosure remains, in the context of this request for stockholder action. Where the only choice for the

minority stockholders is whether to accept the merger consideration or seek appraisal, they must be given all the factual information that is material to that decision.

Glassman v. Unocal Exploration Corp., 777 A.2d 242 (Del. 2001).

In 2013, the Delaware legislature adopted Section 251(h), now known as the "medium-form" merger provision. Section 251(h) eliminates the need for shareholder approval under certain conditions, among them: the target must be listed on a national securities exchange and the bidder must own at least the specified percentage of shares that would be entitled to vote on the merger. This specified number is often a majority, so that a "medium-form" merger typically requires that the bidder own just a majority, not 90%, of the target's shares in order to avoid a shareholder vote and complete the merger.

b. Tender Offer Followed by Merger

A two-step deal structure is also possible, in which a shareholder/bidder first makes a tender offer directly to minority shareholders to reach a specified percentage of ownership, followed by a second-step or "back-end" merger (e.g., pursuant to DGCL § 251(h)). In such a case, the directors of the controlled corporation have no direct decisional role. Whether the offer succeeds depends on whether the minority shareholders choose to accept it. Should the controlling shareholder have a duty to offer the minority a fair price?

The Delaware Supreme Court has held that "in the case of totally voluntary tender offers, courts do not impose any right of the shareholders to receive a particular price. Delaware law recognizes that, as to allegedly voluntary tender offers (in contrast to cash-out mergers), the determinative factor as to voluntariness is whether coercion is present, or whether full disclosure has been made." *Solomon v. Pathe Communications Corp.*, 672 A.2d 35 (Del. 1996).

Since the economic substance of (1) a cash-out merger and (2) a tender offer followed by a merger is much the same, shouldn't judicial review be the same? The Delaware courts have said no. Instead, judges focus on the structure of the tender offer and the disclosure to shareholders, but not on the offer's entire fairness.

For example, in *In re Pure Resources, Inc. Shareholders Litigation*, 808 A.2d 421 (Del. Ch. 2002), Vice Chancellor Strine weighed the policy differences between cash-out mergers and tender offers:

It is important to remember that the overriding concern of *Lynch* is the controlling shareholders have the ability to take retributive action in the wake of rejection by an independent board, a special committee, or the minority shareholders. That ability is so influential that the usual cleansing devices that obviate fairness review of interested transactions cannot be trusted.

The problem is that nothing about the tender offer method of corporate acquisition makes the 800-pound gorilla's retributive capabilities less daunting to minority stockholders. Indeed, many commentators would argue that the tender offer form is more coercive than a merger vote. In a merger vote, stockholders can vote no and still receive the transactional consideration if the merger prevails. In a tender offer, however, a non-tendering shareholder individually faces an uncertain fate. That stockholder could be one of the few who holds out, leaving herself in an even more thinly traded stock with little hope of liquidity. But whether or not one views tender offers as more coercive of shareholder choice than negotiated mergers with controlling stockholders, it is difficult to argue that tender offers are materially freer and more reliable measures of stockholder sentiment.

Business Lingo

"Time value of money" refers to the three-dimensional nature of money. Not only does money have a nominal dimension—let's say, $100—it also has time and risk dimensions. Thus, $100 to be received in three years is less valuable than $100 today—that's because present dollars can be consumed immediately. And a promise of $100 in three years carries uncertainty (or risk), further diminishing its present value. If your law professor promised to pay you $100 in three years, rather than $50 now, which is a better offer? Remember, it's your law professor.

For these and other reasons that time constraints preclude me from explicating, I remain less than satisfied that there is a justifiable basis for the distinction between the *Lynch* and *Solomon* lines of cases. Instead, their disparate teachings reflect a difference in policy emphasis that is far greater than can be explained by the technical differences between tender offers and negotiated mergers, especially given Delaware's director-centered approach to tender offers made by third-parties, which emphasizes the vulnerability of disaggregated stockholders absent important help and protection from their directors.

In the end, then-Vice Chancellor Strine compromised: tender offers were subject to greater scrutiny under the *Solomon* approach that focuses on the disclosure and structure of the tender offer—moving judicial review toward *Lynch*. Cash-out mergers were subject to greater deference under the *Lynch* approach that focuses on internal decision making by independent negotiating committees and approval by a majority of the minority. After *Pure Resources*, it remained unclear which method for cashing out minority shareholders would be less burdensome for controlling shareholders: cash-out-merger or tender offer.

3. Recent Developments: Evolving Standards in Litigation

Courts have continued to address the question of what standard of review applies in a controlled merger. In 2014, in the context of a controlling shareholder "going private" merger, the Delaware Supreme Court addressed the effect of conditioning the deal from the outset on having two layers of shareholder protection. *Kahn v. M&F Worldwide Corp.*, 88 A.3d 635 (Del. 2014) ("*MFW*"). The two protections were: (1) approval by an independent special committee, and (2) a vote by a majority of the shareholders unaffiliated with the controlling shareholder. In *Kahn v. Lynch*, the Delaware Supreme Court had held that the effect of using one or the other protections would shift the burden of proof under the entire fairness standard from the defendant to the plaintiff. The new question presented was, not the effect of either protection, but the combined effect of both of them.

Then-Chancellor Strine held that the effect of using both procedural protections was dramatic—the business judgment rule would apply:

> This conclusion is consistent with the central tradition of Delaware law, which defers to the informed decisions of impartial directors, especially when those decisions have been approved by the disinterested stockholders on full information and without coercion. Not only that, the adoption of this rule will be of benefit to minority stockholders because it will provide a strong incentive for controlling stockholders to accord minority investors the transactional structure that respected scholars believe will provide them the best protection, a structure where stockholders get the benefits of independent, empowered negotiating agents to bargain for the best price and say no if the agents believe the deal is not advisable for any proper reason, plus the critical ability to determine for themselves whether to accept any deal that their negotiating agents recommend to them. A transactional structure with both these protections is fundamentally different from one with only one protection. A special committee alone ensures only that there is a bargaining agent who can negotiate price and address the collective action problem facing stockholders, but it does not provide stockholders any chance to protect themselves. A majority-of-the-minority vote provides stockholders a chance to vote on a merger proposed by a controller-dominated board, but with no chance to have an independent bargaining agent work on their behalf to negotiate the merger price, and determine whether it is

a favorable one that the bargaining agent commends to the minority stockholders for acceptance at a vote. These protections are therefore incomplete and not substitutes, but are complementary and effective in tandem.

Subsequent courts have upheld this approach. As a result, parties can structure a transaction that satisfies the *MFW* conditions, and thereby hope to survive a challenge to the merger on a motion to dismiss. Of course, there remain questions about whether the independent special committee was truly independent and satisfied its duties, and whether the minority shareholder vote was informed and uncoerced.

It remains unclear how far the lower standard of review applied in *MFW* will extend. In *Corwin v. KKR Financial Holdings LLC*, 125 A.3d 304 (Del. 2015), the Delaware Supreme Court held that a transaction involving a *non-controlling* shareholder that is approved by a fully informed and uncoerced vote of the disinterested shareholders will be reviewed under the deferential business judgment standard. *Corwin* effectively ended the possibility of a successful challenge to board conduct in such a circumstance. Challenges to mergers after *Corwin* have often emphasized conflicts of interest, which can remove the protection of the BJR and invite judicial scrutiny of the transaction. Notably, the Delaware Supreme Court extended *Corwin*'s holding to cases involving a tender offer. *In re Volcano Corp. Stockholder Litig.*, *156 A.3d 697* (Del. 2017). We will return to the topic of M&A transactions in the final module of the book.

Test Your Knowledge

To assess your understanding of the Chapter 19, 20, 21, 22, 23, and 24 material in this module, click here to take a quiz.

MODULE VIII – CLOSE CORPORATIONS

CHAPTER 25

Planning in the Close Corporation

This module looks at the special problems in close corporations, where no ready market is available for shareholders to exercise their "exit" rights. This chapter introduces you to the main strategies used by shareholders in close corporations to protect their interests when the usual shareholder rights to vote and sell are not available. The next chapter describes how courts and corporate statutes have fashioned special remedies when shareholders are "oppressed" in the close corporation.

Corporate statutes try to fit corporations closely held by a few shareholders into the same legal clothes worn by publicly-held corporations. But it's a poor fit. The shareholders of a close corporation are likely to think of themselves as *partners* who incorporated their business to obtain limited liability or sometimes for tax reasons. They often find that the corporate rules of centralized management and majority control are at odds with their expectations of decentralized equality. They may wonder why they can't simply manage the business as they agree.

Given that starting a corporation is relatively easy, the participants in a close corporation often assume that exiting from their venture will be just as simple. They may assume that they will be able to withdraw and be paid their share, much as partnership law permits partners to withdraw from a partnership. However, the traditional rules of corporate law create a permanent structure under which shareholders cannot liquidate their investment, except by selling to others or when a majority agrees to a buyback or to dissolve the corporation. In a close corporation the absence of a public trading market for the corporation's shares means that the shareholders face illiquidity unless they can find a buyer for their shares and are not subject to trading restrictions, or unless they control the corporation's governance mechanisms.

This chapter addresses the issues of contracting in the close corporation. First, we explore what is meant by "close corporation" and point out the important planning role of lawyers play in the close corporation. Then we look at *shareholder* arrangements, usually related to share voting and liquidity (transfer) options, meant to accommodate the special needs in close corporations. Next, we consider *management* arrangements, usually involving limitations on board discretion over such matters as corporate offices, salaries, and dividends. These special arrangements deviate from the traditional corporate model and raise the issue whether corporate statutes (including modern ones) permit such deviations. Finally, we turn to the problem that even though the parties may agree to special arrangements that are valid and clear, their arrangements may arguably be *unfair* to one of the parties.

A. Preliminary Considerations

Before we turn to the various methods by which the corporate structure can be modified to allocate risks, authority, and duties in the close corporation, we thought you might find useful a more precise definition of "close corporation." And as you consider the special problems in the close corporation, you should be aware of the important role that lawyers have in helping the parties avoid disputes.

1. Close Corporation as Incorporated Partnership

At the outset, we must say that there is no generally agreed-upon definition of a "close" or "closely held" corporation. But there is a general sense in both case law and modern statutes that a close corporation is one with a relatively small number of shareholders and for whom there is no public market for the corporation's shares.

Make the Connection

This chapter looks at *ex ante* planning in the close corporation—that is, techniques to avoid disputes among the corporate participants. As we pointed out at the beginning of this book in Chapter 1, Introduction to the Firm, planning in business firms entails costs and inevitable gaps in predicting the future. The next chapter in this module looks at *ex post* dispute resolution in the close corporation—which usually arises when minority shareholders go to court and claim that the majority has been oppressive or otherwise unfair. Sometimes courts impose rules of fair conduct (fiduciary duties) and sometimes they fill in what they perceive to have been the parties' expectations. Is there a difference between the two approaches? We'll take up this question in the next chapter.

Here's some analysis of the question from <u>*Donahue v. Rodd Electrotype*</u> (an important case from Massachusetts that we will see again in the next chapter when we look at fiduciary duties in the close corporation):

There is no single, generally accepted definition. Some commentators emphasize an "integration of ownership and management," in which the stockholders occupy most management positions. Others focus on the number of stockholders and the nature of the market for the stock. In this view, close corporations have few stockholders; there is little market for corporate stock. The Supreme Court of Illinois adopted this latter view: "For our purposes, a close corporation is one in which the stock is held in a few hands, or in a few families, and wherein it is not at all, or only rarely, dealt in by buying or selling." We accept aspects of both definitions. We deem a close corporation to be typified by: (1) a small number of stockholders; (2) no ready market for the corporate stock; and (3) substantial majority stockholder participation in the management, direction and operations of the corporation.

As thus defined, the close corporation bears striking resemblance to a partnership. Commentators and courts have noted that the close corporation is often little more than an "incorporated" or "chartered" partnership. The stockholders "clothe" their partnership "with the benefits peculiar to a corporation, limited liability, perpetuity and the like." In essence, though, the enterprise remains one in which ownership is limited to the original parties or transferees of their stock to whom the other stockholders have agreed, in which ownership and management are in the same hands, and in which the owners are quite dependent on one another for the success of the enterprise. Many close corporations are "really partnerships, between two or three people who contribute their capital, skills, experience and labor."

But not all corporate participants may think of themselves as being in an incorporated partnership. Some academics have questioned the analogy and suggest that sometimes participants in a close corporation may not want to be governed by partnership principles. Corporate "default" rules differ from partnership "default" rules in many respects. Further, the tax consequences of operating as a corporation rather than a partnership also are strikingly different.

If participants in closely-held corporations know enough to incorporate, so they obtain limited liability or tax benefits, isn't it reasonable to assume they also know about other differences between corporations and partnerships? After all, they chose a corporation as their form of business, not a partner-

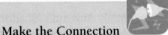

Make the Connection

Recall some of the differences between corporations and partnerships, which we described in Chapter 8, Organizational Choices. Only the board of directors has the power to act for the corporation, while each partner can act for the partnership in its ordinary business. Fundamental changes in the corporation can happen by majority rule, while a partnership requires unanimous agreement. Withdrawal from the corporation happens by selling one's shares to a new investor, while a withdrawing partner can force the dissolution of the partnership and then demand a cash payment for their interest.

ship. Moreover, participants in a close corporation can enter into contracts to adopt partnership-type rules. If they don't adopt partnership-like rules, isn't it appropriate to apply corporate rules?

2. Lawyer's Role in Close Corporation Planning

In the close corporation, the focus is on the bargaining and contracting by which the parties structure their own venture. The lawyer's job is to use the flexibility the law allows to anticipate potential problems and to create solutions from the outset, thus reducing the likelihood of problems or providing dispute resolution mechanisms should they arise. Thus, effective planning requires that the lawyer help the parties identify their true *interests* rather than their bargaining *positions*. In studying close corporations, you will want to pay attention as much to planning and dispute resolution as to legal doctrine.

Formal planning has many advantages. From a practical point of view, discussing the details of financial, control, and liquidity arrangements allows the parties to define their understandings and resolve any disagreements. Moreover, often parties in a close corporation will negotiate their agreements under a veil of ignorance, not knowing who in the future will want protection from majority over-reaching or who will later want to withdraw. Acting from self-interest, but ignorant of their eventual standing in the corporation, the parties will predictably allocate rights and burdens in their agreement to maximize their joint enterprise while protecting their mutual positions. In some close corporations, this might involve an egalitarian system in which all participants hold equal management, financial, and liquidity rights. In other close corporations the optimal allocation might entail specialized roles and responsibilities, with differentiated rights. In theory, the parties' agreement will embody a system of "private justice."

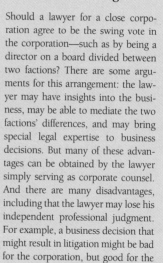

Food for Thought

Should a lawyer for a close corporation agree to be the swing vote in the corporation—such as by being a director on a board divided between two factions? There are some arguments for this arrangement: the lawyer may have insights into the business, may be able to mediate the two factions' differences, and may bring special legal expertise to business decisions. But many of these advantages can be obtained by the lawyer simply serving as corporate counsel. And there are many disadvantages, including that the lawyer may lose his independent professional judgment. For example, a business decision that might result in litigation might be bad for the corporation, but good for the lawyer and his law firm.

One influential Wall Street attorney once remarked, "most of us would be greatly relieved if ethics rules forbade lawyers from becoming their own client by acting as a director." Does this seem right? Or are the pressures to satisfy a client just too great?

The parties can define their understandings in a "promoters' contract" before proceeding to organize the corporation. Or, as happens more frequently, they can enter into a "shareholders' agreement," which binds them once the corporation has been organized. Some control devices must be set forth in the articles, while others may be included in a separate agreement, which should be signed before money changes hands.

Contracting to avoid disputes and specify rights has its limits. It can be expensive and time consuming. Even when shareholders are prepared to incur the expense, anticipating problems is difficult. There is also a danger of dissension if the parties discuss hypothetical problems that may never arise. Some planning usually is better than none, but a lawyer must exercise considerable judgment in advising the parties on how detailed their contractual arrangements should be.

For many years, planners of the close corporation confronted judicial antagonism to special arrangements—whether embodied in the articles, bylaws, or a separate agreement—if they departed too far from the traditional statutory model. Two parallel developments, starting mostly in the 1960s, substantially loosened this judicial attitude. First, courts have become more realistic about the special demands of close corporations and became far more tolerant of departures from the norm. Second, legislatures recognized the unnecessary rigidity of the traditional structure and created special rules for the close corporation.

Many corporation statutes now permit flexibility in planning the close corporation. The most common statutory approach, which is the one taken by the MBCA, is to presume all corporations are alike but expressly to authorize close corporations to adopt governance structures that vary from the traditional model. A second approach is the "comprehensive" close corporation statute, which allows the corporation to elect treatment under a special statutory regime. DGCL §§ 341–356 provides a good example of such a statute. Only a corporation that meets certain tests and elects close corporation status can use the special provisions of the Delaware statute. A small percentage of eligible corporations have elected to use these statutory close corporation provisions.

Close corporations, and good planning for their efficient operation, are important to U.S. capital formation and business activity. In fact, close corporations account for most of U.S. business activity, and family-owned businesses alone represent 95% of all U.S. businesses and are responsible for nearly 50% of U.S. employment.

Despite these modern trends, you still need to understand the older rules, not only because they may remain operative, but because they illuminate the evolving, modern approach. For this reason, we describe some cases that reflect traditional judicial thinking, even though some of their rules are obsolete. The policy questions these cases raise, however, retain much of their importance.

B. Realignments of Shareholder Control

Close corporation participants can realign the traditional corporate structure either at the shareholder level (by creating special voting or liquidity rights) or at the management level (by prescribing special board prerogatives or manager duties). The most basic control devices are those designed to assure that all or certain shareholders are represented on the corporation's board. Three non-mutual choices are available: (1) arrangements that ensure board representation; (2) arrangements that give some or all shareholders the ability to veto board decisions with which they disagree; or (3) arrangements that provide for dispute resolution.

Hypo 25.1

Assume that Justin, Kathy, and Lorenzo—the three business people we encountered in Chapter 12, Capital Structure—come to your law offices and explain their plan to buy a business they would own and operate in corporate form. Lorenzo, who will put in much of the capital, explains that he wants "some voice" in the business and expects to choose half of the board. The three have tentatively agreed on a four-member board of directors, consisting of the three of them and an additional director chosen by Lorenzo.

Without any special arrangements, how will the board be chosen under the default rules of the corporate statutes? Any advice about having a four-person board?

---

1. Cumulative Voting

There are two principal methods for conducting an election of directors. In straight voting (the default rule under <u>most corporate statutes</u>) each share is entitled to one vote for each open directorship, but a shareholder is limited in the number of votes she may cast for any given director to the number of shares she owns. Directors are elected by a plurality of the votes cast, so those who receive the most votes are elected, even if they receive less than a majority. This means that any shareholder or group of shareholders controlling 51% of the shares can elect all of the members of the board.

Cumulative voting, an alternative method, allows shareholder groups to elect directors in rough proportion to the shares held by each group and thus creates the possibility of minority representation on the board. Under cumulative voting, each share again by default carries one vote, but a shareholder may "cumulate" her votes across all of the directorships up for election and choose how to allocate her votes between them. Cumulating simply means multiplying the number of votes a shareholder is entitled to cast by the number of directors for whom she is entitled to vote. If there is cumulative voting, the shareholder may cast all her votes for one candidate or allocate them in any manner among a number of candidates.

The number of shares required to elect a given number of directors under a cumulative voting regime may be calculated by the following formula:

$$X = \frac{s \times d}{D + 1} + 1$$

Where

X = number of shares required to elect directors

s = number of shares represented at the meeting

d = number of directors it is desired to elect

D = total number of directors to be elected

Example 25.1

To understand this formula, let's work through a simple example. Suppose that four directors are to be elected at a meeting at which 1000 shares are represented and will vote. To elect one director, a minority group would have to control 201 shares. With that number, the minority would have 804 votes (201 × 4), which would all be cast for one candidate. The majority would have 3196 votes (799 × 4). Now if the majority distributed these equally among four candidates, each would receive 799 votes, and the one candidate receiving the minority's 804 votes would be guaranteed a seat. In other words, holding just over 20% of the shares guarantees the election of one of four directors.

Note that the reason for the "+ 1" at the end of the formula is to avoid the tie that would occur if, in this example, the minority controlled only 200 votes. Then it would be possible for five candidates each to receive 800 votes.

Under this formula, if only three directors were to be elected, the minority would need just over 25% to elect one director. What percentage is necessary to elect one member to a nine-member board? The answer: one vote more than 10%. The formula also can be used to calculate the number of votes needed to elect multiple directors to the board. Thus, to elect 5 members to the nine-member board would require one vote more than 50% (makes sense).

The availability of cumulative voting has varied significantly over time. During the early 20th century, many states made cumulative voting mandatory by statute or even state constitution. As corporate law became more permissive, many states came to treat cumulative voting as a matter of choice. In some states, cumulative voting arises unless the parties "opt out" in the articles of incorporation or sometimes the bylaws. Today, <u>in most states</u>, cumulative voting is available only if the parties "opt in" in the articles.

Hypo 25.2

Remember Justin, Kathy, and Lorenzo. Recall that Lorenzo received non-voting preferred stock, and voting common was allocated 20–40–40 among Lorenzo–Kathy–Justin.

What would happen if they used cumulative voting to elect directors? Assuming a four-member board of directors and 1000 shares of voting stock issued and outstanding, how many shares would Lorenzo need to elect himself to the board, to elect two directors, and to have majority control on the board?

One question that might have occurred to you is the value of board representation to a minority shareholder, if the shareholder will remain in the minority on the board. If the factions are badly split, minority representation may exacerbate tensions and drive critical decision making by the controlling shareholders outside the boardroom. Critics of cumulative voting argue that injecting factionalism into the boardroom undermines the board's functioning as a team. On the other hand, cumulative voting gives larger minority shareholders a voice and promotes divergent points of view, which may result in better decision making. And minority representation may discourage self dealing and other improper conduct by the majority because of more information to the minority's board representative.

The majority may seek to undermine the effectiveness of cumulative voting. One method is to classify the board of directors and stagger the election of directors so each class will be elected in different years. By staggering the elections, there will be fewer vacancies to be filled each year, thereby making it more difficult for a minority group to place a representative on the board. With fewer directors to be elected each year, the majority has the advantage even under cumulative voting.

Another method to dilute the effect of cumulative voting is to decrease the board size. This increases the percentage of shares necessary for a minority shareholder to elect one director. The courts have generally upheld this technique, even though it undermines cumulative voting. A planner may guard against the implementation of these techniques by inserting anti-circumvention provisions in the articles, such as requiring a supermajority vote to stagger the board or reduce the number of directors.

2. Class Voting

A simple technique for ensuring shareholder representation on the board, which is somewhat more flexible than cumulative voting, is class voting for directors. Class voting is permitted <u>by statute</u> and entails dividing the voting stock into two or more classes, each of which is entitled to elect one or more directors.

In the simple case of a corporation with three shareholders, each wishing to elect one director, three classes of shares would be created (usually denominated, somewhat prosaically, classes "A," "B," and "C"). Each class would have the right to elect one director. Since it is not necessary to issue (or authorize) the same number of shares for each class, class voting can be used to guarantee board representation to a shareholder who owns too few shares to elect a director through cumulative voting or even to add a "tie breaker" to a board. For example, a corporation <u>can issue</u> to its attorney one share of stock without financial rights, but that entitles him to elect one of the corporation's five directors.

The rights of the different classes may be adjusted in other ways as well. For example, each class might be required to approve all or certain actions that require shareholder approval. In fact, the number and variety of changes that can be built on this basic device are limited only by the imagination of the drafter. Classes can be created with different numbers of shares, different rights in the event of liquidation, or different dividend or preemptive rights.

FYI

Some companies have gone public with "dual-class" stock structures in which one share class is offered to the general public while the other is held by founders, executives, or a family. For example, when Google went public in 2004, the co-founders and CEO held Class B shares with ten times the voting power of the ordinary Class A shares that were sold to the public. In a letter to the public, one of the founders explained: "New investors will fully share in Google's long term economic future but will have little ability to influence its strategic decisions through their voting rights." Similarly, Facebook went public in 2012, offering Class A shares with a single vote per share, in contrast to Class B shares owned by corporate insiders that had ten votes per share. This structure allowed Facebook's founder-CEO, Mark Zuckerberg, to hold a majority of the voting power despite holding less than 10% of the economic value. When Lyft went public in 2019, the founders kept control because their Class B shares had twenty votes each, compared to one vote per share for Class A.

Multi-class stock structures can stir controversy. Supporters point out that they can allow visionary leaders to retain control and manage for the long-term interests of the corporation without having to bear excessive economic risk. Critics argue that these structures insulate corporate insiders from accountability and result in sub-optimal decision making. Some structures may even allow insiders to maintain control into perpetuity.

Class voting has its pitfalls. The principal problem is who fills the vacancy in a class when the director dies and is the sole holder of the stock. There are a number of possible answers to that question, but they all affect the future political balance within the company and introduce the possibility of an unwanted person being introduced into the corporate structure. The planner therefore must focus on the future implications of what appears to be a simple present solution.

Hypo 25.3

Return to Justin, Kathy, and Lorenzo. What capital structure might achieve their objective that Lorenzo will choose two directors, and Kathy and Justin one each?

Does this structure truly protect Lorenzo's interest to control half the board? What if Kathy and Justin enlist the director selected by Lorenzo so that he cooperates with them? What could be done to protect Lorenzo against this?

---

3. Shareholder Voting Arrangements

Shareholders typically use one of three types of devices to limit or control the manner in which shares will be voted: (a) voting trusts, (b) irrevocable proxies, and (c) vote pooling agreements. Sometimes an arrangement may have attributes of each.

Voting trust. Shareholders create a *voting trust* by conveying legal title to their stock to a voting trustee or a group of trustees pursuant to the terms of a trust agreement. This transfer is normally registered on the corporation's stock transfer ledger, which shows the trustees as legal owners of the shares. The transferring shareholders—now beneficiaries of the trust—receive voting trust certificates in exchange for their shares; these evidence their equitable ownership of their stock. Voting trust certificates usually are transferable and entitle the owner to receive whatever dividends are paid on the underlying stock. They are, in effect, shares of stock shorn of their voting power. Most corporate statutes, however, permit holders of voting trust certificates to exercise non-voting shareholder rights, including the right to inspect corporate books and to institute a derivative suit on behalf of the corporation. Since the terms of the trust agreement are a matter of contract, the trustees may be given full discretion to vote the shares in the trust for the election of directors and for any other matter to come before the shareholders, or may be limited to voting on only certain matters.

Earlier courts tended to view voting trusts with suspicion, in many cases holding them void as against public policy because they separated shareholders' voting power and economic ownership. State legislatures responded by passing statutes permitting voting trusts but subjecting them to certain regulations, usually a <u>duration limit</u> (such as 10 years) and a requirement that their terms be made a matter of public record so that other shareholders would know, or could learn, that a voting trust exists. Today virtually all jurisdictions have legislation dealing with voting trusts.

Some of the judicial disdain for the voting trust has survived, however, in the doctrine that a shareholder arrangement that amounts to a voting trust in operation but does not comply with the terms of a voting trust statute is invalid. Although an interesting line of cases from the 1950s and 1960s in Delaware grappled with this issue, the Delaware courts ultimately concluded that the separation of voting power and economic ownership in a close corporation was <u>not against public policy</u> if the parties had agreed to the arrangement. Again, "independent legal significance" rears its head.

Irrevocable proxy. As we saw in the chapter on corporate voting, it is common for a shareholder to give a proxy to someone else to vote her shares, and even to give that person entire discretion in voting the shares. But the ordinary proxy, like any agency power, <u>may be revoked</u> at the will of the principal, and the proxy holder remains subject to the control of the principal.

Sometimes, however, the parties want to make the grant of the proxy *irrevocable*, perhaps subject to some contingency or for a specified time. In such a case, the shareholder loses control of her vote for the period of the proxy, and "the vote is separated from ownership," the very problem that lay at the heart of courts' objections to voting trusts. Thus, many of the concerns that led courts to invalidate voting trusts are equally applicable to the *irrevocable proxy*. Earlier courts were reluctant to enforce irrevocable proxies, finding them to violate basic principles of agency law or to be against public policy.

<u>Agency law</u> has come to recognize the validity of an irrevocable grant of agency power "coupled with an interest." Likewise, the modern trend in <u>corporate law</u> is to recognize this principle and to uphold irrevocable proxies that are "coupled with an interest." What sort of interest supports an irrevocable proxy? The more conservative view is that the interest must be in (or pertain to) the stock itself, such as when a shareholder pledges her stock and grants the pledgee an irrevocable proxy to vote the stock. Other courts, rejecting a formalistic application of agency principles, have recognized the value of close corporation arrangements. Irrevocable proxies have been upheld, for example, where proxies have been promised as an inducement to new investors in the corporation.

Over time courts became less insistent on an interest linked to the stock. For example, when two or more shareholders agree to grant each other irrevocable proxies, the consideration being merely the mutual promises of the parties, it is hard to find a traditional "interest" sufficient to support the proxy. Nonetheless, courts came to enforce such proxies given the business realities of the close corporation. As one court put it, "The power to vote the stock was necessary in order to make control of the corporation secure."

Recognizing that the artificial requirement that a proxy must be coupled with an interest to be irrevocable makes little sense in the close corporation context, most state statutes have significantly relaxed the "with interest" requirement. For example, the <u>MBCA</u> permits irrevocable proxies when given to (1) a pledgee; (2) a person who purchased or agreed to purchase the shares; (3) a creditor of the corporation who extended it credit under terms requiring the appointment; (4) an employee of the corporation whose employment contract requires the appointment; or (5) a party to a valid voting agreement.

Vote pooling agreements. A common close corporation control device is the *vote pooling agreement.* As with voting trusts and irrevocable proxies, its basic purpose is to bind some (or all) of the shareholders to vote together—either in a particular way or pursuant to some specified procedure—on designated questions or all questions that come before the shareholders.

Consistent with the general voting freedom of corporate shareholders, many <u>corporate statutes</u> recognize the validity of such agreements. Often the difficulty is enforcement. The Official Comment to MBCA § 7.31 states:

> Section 7.31(b) provides that voting agreements may be specifically enforceable. A voting agreement may provide its own enforcement mechanism, as by the appointment of a proxy to vote all shares subject to the agreement; the appointment may be made irrevocable under section 7.22. If no enforcement mechanism is provided, a court may order specific enforcement of the agreement and order the votes cast as the agreement contemplates. This section recognizes that damages are not likely to be an appropriate remedy for breach of a voting agreement, and also avoids the result reached in *Ringling Bros.—Barnum & Bailey Combined Shows v. Ringling,* 53 A.2d 441 (Del. 1947).

The *Ringling Bros.* case, famous in Delaware law, raised the question whether a vote pooling agreement constituted an invalid voting trust or irrevocable proxy. Although deciding that the agreement was valid, the Delaware Supreme Court refused to infer any enforcement mechanism—thus rendering empty the parties' promises to pool their votes.

Ringling involved a pooling agreement between two minority shareholders who together held a majority voting bloc and agreed to act jointly in exercising their voting rights. In case of disagreement, the parties agreed to submit the disagreement to a named arbitrator designated by them. The case arose when, after a voting disagreement, one of the parties failed to follow the arbitrator's instructions about whom to elect as director.

In response to the argument that the agreement impermissibly separated ownership from control, the Delaware Supreme Court validated it. Finding that it simply gave the arbitrator the power to tell a party to vote, but without any power to compel the vote, the court found nothing to strike down and allowed the agreement to stand. But with nothing to enforce, the court disqualified the shares at issue. The effect was disastrous for the minority shareholder seeking to enforce the agreement, since she could not pool her votes with those of the other minority shareholder. As a result, she lost control to a third shareholder (not party to the agreement) and eventually was forced to sell.

Hypo 25.4

Suppose Justin, Kathy, and Lorenzo decide against cumulative voting and class shares to achieve their goals of board representation. What other alternatives do they have? Would a voting agreement accomplish their purposes? What basic provisions should it include? Are there legal restrictions that affect its validity?

And what if one of them does not comply his obligations under the agreement? What enforcement mechanisms, if any, should the agreement contain? You might be interested in looking at the relevant MBCA provisions and Delaware's close corporation statute.

C. Restrictions on Board Discretion

1. Shareholder Agreements: Common Law

A line of four cases from the New York Court of Appeals—the "big four"—explores the validity of shareholder agreements that limit board discretion. The cases were decided before the enactment of the New York statute that authorizes deviations from the traditional model of corporate governance in close corporations. Although some of the judicial analysis has been superseded by statute, the common-law principles continue to have vitality in the drafting and interpretation of shareholder agreements under modern corporate statutes.

The first case, *Manson v. Curtis*, 119 N.E. 559 (N.Y. 1918), involved an agreement between Manson and Curtis, two shareholders who held a majority (but not all) of the shares of a corporation. Under the agreement each party was to name three directors, with a seventh director to be elected as mutually agreed. In addition, they agreed that Manson would continue as general manager for a year. When Curtis refused to abide by the agreement and used his voting control to install his own directors, who named a different general manager, Manson sued. Even though the new manager had allegedly caused the business to go bankrupt, the court determined the agreement as a whole was invalid as its "fundamental and dominant intent and purpose" was to transfer management authority from the board to Manson. This deprived the directors of their statutory duty to manage the corporation. Even though the provision concerning election of directors was found to be "standing alone innocent and legal," the agreement was not capable of "severability."

The *Manson* court explained why the management aspects of the agreement were "illegal and void":

> The affairs of every corporation shall be managed by its board of directors. In corporate bodies, the powers of the board of directors are, in a very important sense, original and undelegated. The stockholders do not confer, nor can they revoke those powers. The directors convened as a board are the primary possessors of all the powers which the charter confers, and like private principals they may delegate to agents of their own appointment the performance of any acts which they themselves can perform. All powers directly conferred by statute, or impliedly granted, of necessity, must be exercised by the directors who are constituted by the law as the agency for the doing of corporate acts. In the management of the affairs of the corporation, they are dependent solely upon their own knowledge of its business and their own judgment as to what its interests require. Clearly the law does not permit the stockholders to create a sterilized board of directors.

The court in dictum, however, outlined the permissible scope of a shareholders' agreement. It pointed out that an agreement among shareholders, who together constitute a majority, "for the purpose of obtaining control of the corporation by the election of particular persons as directors is not illegal. Shareholders have the right to combine their interests and voting powers to secure such control of the corporation and the adoption of an adhesion by it to a specific policy and course of business." So long as the agreement is not inconsistent with the specific provisions in the articles or statute, and does not "contemplate any fraud, oppression or wrong against other stockholders," it is valid and binding.

The second case, <u>McQuade v. Stoneham</u>, 189 N.E. 234 (N.Y. 1934), involved a matter of sports ethics. The majority shareholder of the New York Giants baseball team brought in two new shareholders to bolster the organization after the baseball scandals of the World Series of 1919. The three agreed to use their best efforts to elect each other as directors and officers. The agreement specified their positions and salaries, and required that any change to the capital structure or the bylaws be approved only by unanimous consent. After a falling out, one of the minority shareholders sought to enforce the agreement. The court held the agreement to be invalid:

> Stockholders may, of course, combine to elect directors. That rule is well settled. "If stockholders want to make their power felt, they must unite. There is no reason why a majority should not agree to keep together." The power to unite is, however, limited to the election of directors and is not extended to contracts whereby limitations are placed on the power of directors to manage the business of the corporation by the selection of agents at defined salaries.

The anomaly that the court invalidated an agreement at a time when "freedom of contract" dominated judicial thinking was not lost on the court: "Public policy is a dangerous guide in determining the validity of a contract and courts should not interfere lightly with the freedom of competent parties to make their own contracts. Nor are we unmindful that McQuade has, so the court has found, been shabbily treated as a purchaser of stock from Stoneham. But Stoneham and McGraw were not trustees for McQuade as an individual. Their duty was to the corporation and its stockholders, to be exercised according to their unrestricted lawful judgment." Again the court invalidated the entire agreement, unable to separate the offending restrictions on board discretion and the permissible provisions on shareholder voting.

The third case, *Clark v. Dodge*, 199 N.E. 641 (N.Y. 1936), marked a shift in the thinking of the court. Here, the agreement was signed by all shareholders. Dodge was to vote for Clark as director and general manager, so long as Clark proved "faithful, efficient and competent." The court sustained Clark's claim for specific enforcement of the agreement. In distinguishing *McQuade*, the court held that the impairment of the directors' powers was slight:

> There was no attempt to sterilize the board of directors, as in the *Manson* and *McQuade* cases. The only restrictions on Dodge were (a) that as a stockholder he should vote for Clark as a director—a perfectly legal contract; (b) that as a director he should continue Clark as general manager, so long as he proved faithful, efficient and competent—an agreement which could harm nobody; (c) that Clark should always receive as salary or dividends one-fourth of the "net income." For the purposes of this motion, it is only just to construe that phrase as meaning whatever was left for distribution after the directors had in good faith set

aside whatever they deemed wise; (d) that no salaries to other officers should be paid, unreasonable in amount or incommensurate with services rendered—a beneficial and not a harmful agreement.

Significant in *Clark* was that all the shareholders had signed the agreement. As the court explained, "As the parties to the action are the complete owners of the corporation, there is no reason why the exercise of the power and discretion of the directors cannot be controlled by valid agreement between themselves, provided that the interest of creditors is not affected." Following *Clark*, the state of the law was (and remains) that all shareholders can agree to infringe "slightly" upon the statutory authority of the board of directors. So, too, a majority (even if less than all the stockholders) can agree to vote for certain persons as directors.

The last case of the "big four," <u>Long Park, Inc. v. Trenton-New Brunswick Theatres Co.</u>, 77 N.E.2d 633 (N.Y. 1948), made clear that the public policy against interfering with the traditional corporate structure continues to have force. As in *Clark*, the agreement was among all the shareholders and called for one of them to be "manager" with full authority to supervise the operation of the corporation, which ran a chain of movie theaters. The court invalidated the agreement:

> The directors may neither select nor discharge the manager, to whom the supervision and direction of the management and operation of the theatres is delegated with full authority and power. Thus the powers of the directors over the management of its theatres, the principal business of the corporation, were completely sterilized. We think these restrictions and limitations went far beyond the agreement in *Clark v. Dodge*. We are not confronted with a slight impingement or innocuous variance from the statutory norm, but rather with the deprivation of all the powers of the board insofar as the selection and supervision of the management of the corporation's theatres.

In the next case, the New York court moved significantly beyond its "sterilization" doctrine. The case involved Triggs Color Printing Corporation, a small firm founded by Frederick Triggs, Sr. in 1925. Over the decades, the business prospered and Frederick, Sr. involved his three sons. As of 1963, the corporation had issued 254 shares of voting stock: Triggs owned 149 shares and each of his three sons owned 35 shares.

In planning his estate, Frederick, Sr. decided that one of his three sons should control the business after he died. He picked Ransford, and transferred 36 additional shares to him, so that Ransford had 71 total shares, and the other two sons had 35 shares each. Frederick, Sr. and Ransford also entered into a written agreement in which they agreed to vote their shares together to elect both of them as directors and to guarantee each of them an annual salary, with Frederick, Sr. as chairman of the board and Ransford as president.

The agreement also stated: "It is the present contemplation of Frederick Triggs, Sr. to execute an agreement with the Corporation for the Corporation to repurchase his stock in the event of his death. In the event for any reason that such agreement has not been executed between the said Frederick Triggs, Sr. and the Corporation, then, in that event, the remaining Stockholder, to wit: Ransford D. Triggs, shall have the right and option to purchase the said stock of Frederick Triggs, Sr. for a period of sixty (60) days following the death of Frederick Triggs, Sr."

During the next few years, Ransford gradually assumed a bigger role in the business, and the corporation experienced financial difficulties. Ransford cut Frederick, Sr.'s salary, at first with Frederick, Sr.'s consent and later over his objection. As Frederick, Sr.'s influence waned, he began to regret favoring Ransford, and they had a falling out. In February 1970, Frederick, Sr. amended his will to give his 113 shares to his other two sons and to declare his 1963 agreement with Ransford null and void. Two months later, Frederick, Sr. died.

Ransford then sought to exercise his option to purchase his father's 113 shares from the estate, but the estate refused to transfer the shares. Four years later, Ransford sued to compel the estate to exercise the option. In response, the estate claimed that the 1963 agreement between Ransford and Frederick, Sr. was illegal.

Triggs v. Triggs

385 N.E.2d 1254 (N.Y. 1978)

JONES, JUDGE opinion of the court.

After a trial without a jury the court granted respondent specific performance of the stock purchase option. A majority at the Appellate Division agreed, and we now affirm.

Appellant contends that because the March 19, 1963 agreement was not executed or approved by all of the corporate shareholders, its provisions requiring the election of respondent and his father as officers and fixing their compensation constituted an impermissible restriction of the rights and obligations of the board of directors to manage the business of the corporation under the doctrine of *Manson v. Curtis*. No argument is made that the stock purchase option, standing alone would be invalid; the assertion is that the agreement must be read as a whole and that it must be invalidated in its entirety. The critical issue is whether, because of the initial inclusion of provisions which could have been said to fetter the authority of the board to select corporate officers and to fix their compensation, the stock purchase provision is now unenforceable.

The uncontroverted evidence is that in the years following the signing of the agreement, the assertedly illegal provisions of the agreement were ignored; no attempt was made to observe or enforce them and the management of corporate affairs was in no way restricted in consequence of the 1963 agreement. The evil to which the cited rule of law is addressed was never sought to be achieved nor was it realized. Although Triggs, Sr., and Ransford continued to serve as directors, the record discloses there were also three or four other, independent directors. That Triggs, Sr., continued to be elected chairman of the board (he was also elected corporate treasurer) and Ransford, corporate president and that for several years their salaries were fixed by the board at the figures stated in the March 19, 1963 agreement was in consequence of action freely taken by the entire board of directors and cannot be attributed to the sanction of the March 19, 1963 agreement of which the other directors, constituting a majority of the board, were wholly unaware. Indeed Triggs, Sr., took no exception when, on May 11, 1965, the board reduced his salary from $20,000 (the agreement figure) to $10,800, and when the board later entirely eliminated his salary his complaint in April of 1969 was predicated on the departure from the board's action of May 11, 1965 rather than on any asserted violation of the provisions of the March 19, 1963 agreement.

The legal issue here, too, depends on what is now an affirmed factual determination. The claim of illegality, raised for the first time some 13 years after the agreement had been signed, must fail because, as the trial court concluded, the March 19, 1963 agreement "did not in any way sufficiently stultify the Board of Directors in the operations of this business" within the doctrine on which appellant would rely.

Analytically we are presented with an agreement which in a single document deals with two different sets of obligations. On the one hand, the agreement contains the stock purchase option exercisable on the death of the father as to which, standing alone, there is no claim of illegality. On the other, there are the provisions with respect to the election of corporate officers and the fixation of their salaries, which are of questionable legality. Any illegality exists, however, only to the extent that the agreement operated to restrict the freedom of the board of directors to manage corporate affairs. The fact is that the courts below have enforced only the stock option provisions of the March 19, 1963 agreement.

Accordingly, the order of the Appellate Division should be affirmed, with costs.

GABRIELLI, JUDGE dissenting:

I respectfully dissent.

It has long been the law in this State that a corporation must be managed by the board of directors who serve as trustees for the benefit of the corporation and all its shareholders. To prevent control of the corporation from being diverted into the hands of individuals or groups who in some cases might not be subject to quite the same fiduciary obligations as are imposed upon directors as a matter of course, the courts have always looked unfavorably towards attempts to circumvent the discretionary authority given the board of directors by law. Such matters normally arise in the context of an agreement between shareholders to utilize their shares so as to force the board of directors to take certain actions. Unless in accord with some statutorily approved mechanism for shifting power from the board of directors to other parties, such agreements have been found valid only where the proponent of the agreement can prove that the violation of the statutory mandate is minimal and, more importantly that there is no danger of harm either to the general public or to other shareholders (*see Clark v. Dodge*).

The dispositive consideration must always be the possibility of harm to either the other shareholders or to the general public either prospectively at the time the agreement was entered into or at the time it is sought to be enforced. In those cases in which the agreement is made by less than all the shareholders, almost any attempt to reduce the authority granted to the board by law will create a significant potential for harm to other shareholders even if the potential for harm to the general public is minimal. This is so because the effect of such an agreement is to deprive the other shareholders of the benefits and protections which the law perceives to exist when the corporation is managed by an independent board of directors, free to use its own business judgment in the best interest of the corporation.

It has been suggested that the option should be severed from the other provisions of the agreement and separately enforced since it alone would not be illegal. The flaw in this argument is that it improperly assumes that decedent would have given plaintiff this option by itself, without the other parts of their agreement. This assumption is one in which we may not indulge. Indeed, it appears that the illegal parts of the agreement were an intrinsic part of the covenant between these parties.

FUCHSBERG, JUDGE dissenting:

My vote too is for reversal. However, the decisional path that I would take differs appreciably not only from that of the majority but from that of my fellow dissenters as well.

Specifically, unlike the other dissenters, I am of the opinion that the parties entered into an enforceable agreement. But I conclude that the agreement was not ambiguous and that, as a matter of law, it terminated in accordance with its terms during the father's lifetime.

I also take issue with the majority's reasoning that the option was enforceable only because it was separable from an otherwise illegal contract. In my view, the entire agreement is lawful qua agreement, and since it is one entered into between the controlling stockholders of a small, nonpublic corporation, it is not to be scrutinized by a rigid, hypertechnical reading of the Business Corporation Law.

Small, closely held corporations whose operation is dominated, as its stockholders and creditors usually are aware, by a particular individual or small group of individuals, must be distinguished, legally and pragmatically, from large corporations whose stock is traded on a public securities exchange and where the normal stockholders' relationship to those managing the corporation is bound to be impersonal and remote. Obviously, the latter's operations are rarely, if ever, covered by stockholders' agreements, and the Business Corporation Law itself is the sole restriction on their management.

In the close corporation, investors who themselves are not part of the dominant group commonly rely on the identities of the individuals who run the business and on the likelihood of their continuance in power. As a practical matter, these individuals will be expected to exercise a broad discretion and considerable informality in carrying out their management functions; this flexibility may be regarded as one of the strengths of a smaller organization. Indeed, faith in the integrity and ability of the managers is what usually motivates the investment. Looked at realistically, such corporations are frequently "little more than charter partnerships." Control of such matters as choice of officers and directors, amounts of executive salaries, and options to buy or sell each other's stock—exactly the sort of things with which the agreement before us dealt—is usually mapped out by agreements among stockholders.

In short, so long as an agreement between stockholders relating to the management of the corporation bears no evidence of an intent to defraud other stockholders or creditors, deviations from precise formalities should not automatically call for a slavish enforcement of the statute. This would not leave without remedy those minority stockholders in close corporations whose interests may be abused. Available to them and at least equally effective are the equitable remedies by which officers and directors can be made to respond for violations of their trust obligations (*Meinhard v. Salmon*).

———————

Points for Discussion

1. Share voting vs. management agreements.

What is the difference between an agreement among shareholders (1) to elect each other to the board and (2) to appoint each other to an office at a specified salary?

2. Sterilizing the board.

Why are agreements that limit the discretion of the board of directors against public policy—at least according to the common law?

3. Theoretical vs. actual harm.

What distinguishes the agreement in *McQuade v. Stoneham*, which no creditors or non-party shareholders objected to, and the agreement in *Clark v. Dodge*, which the court concluded could harm nobody? What approach does the court in *Triggs v. Triggs* take to a shareholder agreement that theoretically could harm non-party shareholders and creditors? What explains the shift in the analysis?

Hypo 25.5

Justin, Kathy, and Lorenzo agree to have a corporation with a three-person board, composed of each of them (or their representatives). In addition, Justin and Kathy separately agree in writing that as shareholders holding a majority of the company's voting shares and as directors they will vote to dissolve the corporation if it is not profitable after two years. (In a dissolution, the corporation's assets are sold for cash and the proceeds distributed to the shareholders.)

Two years later, the corporation is bleeding red ink, but Kathy has a change in heart and joins Lorenzo to vote against dissolution. Can Justin enforce their agreement?

---

2. Statutory Authorization of Restraints on Board Discretion

In 1963 the New York legislature amended its corporate statute to recognize the special contracting needs in the close corporation. N.Y.B.C.L. § 620 validates corporate articles that restrict the board in its management of the business or transfer management to a non-director, provided all the shareholders (voting and nonvoting) have authorized the provision and any person acquiring shares knows or consents to the provision. As the official note to the statute explains:

The provision authorized by paragraph (b) can be contained only in the certificate of incorporation. Because of the limitations that it must have unanimous consent of all shareholders, whether or not entitled to vote, and that the shares of the corporation must not be publicly traded either at the time of the agreement or thereafter, this provision can be practicably used only in close corporations. Paragraph (b) expands the ruling in *Clark v. Dodge* and, to the extent therein provided, overrules *Long Park, Inc. v. Trenton-New Brunswick Theatres Co.*, *Manson v. Curtis*, and *McQuade v. Stoneham*.

Other states have followed suit. In 1991 the MBCA was amended to validate shareholder agreements that modify the traditional corporate structure. Under MBCA § 7.32(a), an agreement among the shareholders is effective among the shareholders and the corporation even if it eliminates the board of directors or restricts board discretion, such as by mandating distributions, specifying who will be directors or officers, allocating voting power on the board, regulating employment by the participants, transferring management to a particular person, or requiring corporate dissolution on specified contingencies.

MBCA § 7.32
Shareholder Agreements

(b) An agreement authorized by this section shall be:

(1) set forth (i) in the articles of incorporation or bylaws and approved by all persons who are shareholders at the time of the agreement, or (ii) in a written agreement that is signed by all persons who are shareholders at the time of the agreement and is made known to the corporation; and

(2) subject to amendment only by all persons who are shareholders at the time of the amendment, unless the agreement provides otherwise.

(c) The existence of an agreement authorized by this section shall be noted conspicuously on the front or back of each certificate for outstanding shares or on the information statement required by section 6.26(b).

What happens if a close corporation agreement dealing with management prerogatives does not comply with the relevant authorizing statute? In *Zion v. Kurtz*, 405 N.E.2d 681 (N.Y. 1980), the New York Court of Appeals considered an agreement between the two shareholders of a Delaware corporation that specified that no "business or activities" could be conducted without the consent of the minority shareholder—a veto right. The agreement was not incorporated in the articles and thus did not comply with Delaware's special close corporation statute. The court nevertheless held that the agreement was enforceable.

The court observed that it was "clear from those provisions of the close corporation statute that the public policy of Delaware does not proscribe a provision such as that contained in the shareholders' agreement here in issue even though it takes all management functions away from the directors." Moreover, referring to N.Y.B.C.L. § 620(b), the court stated that it was also "clear that no New York public policy stands in the way of our application of the Delaware statute and decisional law above referred to." As to the failure to file the articles as a close corporation, as required by Delaware's statute, the majority observed that since "there are no intervening rights of third persons, the agreement requires nothing that is not permitted by statute, and all of the stockholders of the corporation assented to it, the certificate of incorporation may be ordered reformed, by requiring Kurtz to file the appropriate amendments, or more directly he may be held estopped to rely upon the absence of those amendments from the corporate charter."

Judge Gabrielli dissented, arguing that the effect of the agreement was to "sterilize" the board of directors. He contended that neither Delaware nor New York courts had shown tolerance for such extreme deviations from the traditional statutory norms. Although he admitted that the agreement might have been enforced in Delaware, had it been in the articles of incorporation, he viewed its inclusion there as mandatory under the statute. He pointed out that both the Delaware and New York statutes require that the close corporation "give notice of its unorthodox management structure through its filed certificate of incorporation. The obvious purpose of such a requirement is to prevent harm to the public before it occurs. If, as the majority's holding suggests, this requirement of notice to the public through the certificate of incorporation is without legal effect unless and until a third party's interests have actually been impaired, then the prophylactic purposes of the statutes governing 'close corporations' would effectively be defeated."

Points for Discussion

1. Statutory reform?

In what ways do the modern statutes on management agreements change the common law? In what ways do they restate the common law principle that limits on the discretion of the board of directors are against public policy?

2. Failure to comply with statute.

Why does the court in *Zion v. Kurtz* validate an agreement limiting the discretion of the board, even though the agreement did not comply with the statute? Would the agreement, which gave veto powers to the minority shareholder, have passed muster under the common law?

Hypo 25.6

Recall the agreement between Justin and Kathy, but not including Lorenzo, to dissolve the corporation if it is not profitable after two years.

Is the agreement enforceable under the New York statute (N.Y.B.C.L. § 620) or the MBCA? If it fails under the statute, is that the end of the inquiry?

---

3. Fiduciary Duties in Exercising Minority Rights

What are the duties of shareholders who assume management functions or acquire control prerogatives under a shareholders' agreement? The question arises most clearly when minority shareholders condition their investment in a close corporation on veto rights over some or all decisions of the majority.

Some statutes address the question by imposing duties on those who acquire board prerogatives. MBCA § 7.32(e) provides:

> An agreement authorized by this section that limits the discretion or powers of the board of directors shall relieve the directors of, and impose upon the person or persons in whom such discretion or powers are vested, liability for acts or omissions imposed by law on directors to the extent that the discretion or powers of the directors are limited by the agreement.

This shifting of duty raises the question whether a minority shareholder, who acquires a veto power by agreement, violates her fiduciary duties by exercising the power. The question sometimes is one of degree. A minority shareholder can use veto powers either selectively or to create a deadlock. Voting against a particular action, as when directors are evenly split on an issue or they divide 3–1 when an 80% vote is required, does not create a "deadlock"—the action simply is not approved, and the business continues to function. A "deadlock" arises when relations among the shareholders or directors have deteriorated to the point that virtually no action is possible—one faction says yes, the other says no.

The following case involves Atlantic Properties, a real estate company that four investors incorporated in 1951 to purchase and manage real estate. Each investor acquired 25 shares in the corporation, whose articles and bylaws provided: "No election, appointment or resolution by the Stockholders and no election, appointment, resolution, purchase, sale, lease, contract, contribution, compensation, proceeding or act by the Board of Directors or by any officer or officers shall be valid or binding upon the corporation until effected, passed, approved or ratified by an affirmative vote of eighty (80%) per cent of the capital stock issued outstanding and entitled to vote." The 80% provision, included at the request of Dr. Louis Wolfson, the corporation's founder, gave each shareholder a veto in corporate decisions.

Atlantic's sole holding was a parcel of land that included old mill structures that required extensive repairs. Nonetheless, from the beginning the company was profitable and showed a regular profit. The mortgage on the land was paid off, and Atlantic had no long-term debt. Although salaries and dividends were paid sporadically, Atlantic in 1961 had about $172,000 in retained earnings, more than half in cash.

Then disagreements and ill will arose between the shareholders. Dr. Wolfson wanted Atlantic to devote its earnings to repairs and improvements. The other shareholders wanted the corporation to declare dividends, but Dr. Wolfson voted against dividends. Although a no-dividend policy risked tax penalties under the Internal Revenue Code provisions relating to unreasonable accumulation of corporate earnings, Dr. Wolfson persisted in his refusal.

The IRS eventually imposed substantial penalty taxes on Atlantic. According to the Tax Court and on appeal, Dr. Wolfson's refusal to vote for the declaration of sufficient dividends was based in part on his purpose to avoid personal taxes.

The other shareholders then sued seeking a court determination of dividends to be paid by Atlantic, the removal of Dr. Wolfson as a director, and an order that Dr. Wolfson reimburse the corporation for the penalty taxes and related expenses. The trial judge concluded that Dr. "Wolfson's obstinate refusal to vote in favor of dividends was caused more by his dislike for other stockholders and his desire to avoid additional tax payments than by any genuine desire to undertake a program for improving Atlantic property." She also determined that Dr. Wolfson was liable to Atlantic for reimbursing the penalty taxes with interest, as well as attorneys' fees. She ordered the directors of Atlantic to declare "a reasonable dividend at the earliest practical date and reasonable dividends annually thereafter consistent with good business practice." In addition, the trial court retained jurisdiction of the case "for a period of five years to ensure compliance." Dr. Wolfson appealed.

Smith v. Atlantic Properties, Inc.

422 N.E.2d 798 (Mass. App. 1981)

Cutter, Justice.

1. The trial judge, in deciding that Dr. Wolfson had committed a breach of his fiduciary duty to other stockholders, relied greatly on broad language in *Donahue v. Rodd Electrotype Co.*, 367 Mass. 578, 586–597, 328 N.E.2d 505 (1975), in which the Supreme Judicial Court afforded to a minority stockholder in a close corporation equality of treatment (with members of a controlling group of shareholders) in the matter of the redemption of shares. The court relied on the resemblance of a close corporation to a partnership and held that "stockholders in the close corporation owe one another substantially the same fiduciary duty in the operation of the enterprise that partners owe to one another". That standard of duty, the court said, was the "utmost good faith and loyalty." The court went on to say that such stockholders "may not act out of avarice, expediency or self-interest in derogation of their duty of loyalty to the other stockholders and to the corporation."

In the *Donahue* case, the court recognized that cases may arise in which, in a close corporation, majority stockholders may ask protection from a minority stockholder. Such an instance arises in the present case because Dr. Wolfson has been able to exercise a veto concerning corporate action on dividends by the 80% provision which may have substantially the effect of reversing the usual roles of the majority and the minority shareholders. The minority, under that provision, becomes an ad hoc controlling interest.

2. With respect to the past damage to Atlantic caused by Dr. Wolfson's refusal to vote in favor of any dividends, the trial judge was justified in finding that his conduct went beyond what was reasonable. The other stockholders shared to some extent responsibility for what occurred by failing to accept Dr. Wolfson's proposals with much sympathy, but the inaction on dividends seems the principal cause of the tax penalties. Dr. Wolfson had been warned of the dangers of an assessment under the Internal Revenue Code, I.R.C. § 531 et seq. He had refused to vote dividends in any amount adequate to minimize that danger and had failed to bring forward, within the relevant taxable years, a convincing, definitive program of appropriate improvements which could withstand scrutiny by the Internal Revenue Service. Whatever may have been the reason for Dr. Wolfson's refusal to declare dividends (and even if in any particular year he may have gained slight, if any, tax advantage from withholding dividends) we think that he recklessly ran serious and unjustified risks of precisely the penalty taxes eventually assessed, risks which were inconsistent with any reasonable interpretation of a duty of "utmost good faith and loyalty."

3. The trial judge's order to the directors of Atlantic, "to declare a reasonable dividend at the earliest practical date and reasonable dividends annually thereafter," presents difficulties. It may well not be a precise, clear, and unequivocal command which (without further explanation) would justify enforcement by civil contempt proceedings. It also fails to order the directors to exercise similar business judgment with respect to Dr. Wolfson's desire to make all appropriate repairs and improvements to Atlantic's factory properties.

The somewhat ambiguous injunctive relief is made less significant by the trial judge's reservation of jurisdiction in the Superior Court, a provision which contemplates later judicial supervision. We think that such supervision should be provided now upon an expanded record. The present record does not disclose Atlantic's present financial condition or what, if anything, it has done (since the judgment under review) by way of expenditures for repairs and improvements of its properties and in respect of dividends and salaries. The judgment, of course, necessarily disregards the general judicial reluctance to interfere with a corporation's dividend policy ordinarily based upon the business judgment of its directors.

Although the reservation of jurisdiction is appropriate in this case, its purpose should be stated more affirmatively. Paragraph 2 of the judgment should be revised to provide: (a) a direction that Atlantic's directors prepare promptly financial statements and copies of State and Federal income and excise tax returns for the five most recent calendar or fiscal years, and a balance sheet as of as current a date as is possible; (b) an instruction that they confer with one another with a view to stipulating a general dividend and capital improvements policy for the next ensuing three fiscal years; (c) an order that, if such a stipulation is not filed with the clerk of the Superior Court within sixty days after the receipt of the rescript in the Superior Court, a further hearing shall be held promptly (either before the court or before a special master with substantial experience in business affairs), at which there shall be received in evidence at least the financial statements and tax returns above mentioned, as well as other relevant evidence. Thereafter, the court, after due consideration of the circumstances then existing, may direct the adoption (and carrying out), if it be then deemed appropriate, of a specific dividend and capital improvements policy adequate to minimize the risk of further penalty tax assessments for the then current fiscal year of Atlantic. The court also may reserve jurisdiction to take essentially the same action for each subsequent fiscal year until the parties are able to reach for themselves an agreed program.

Points for Discussion

1. Duty of utmost good faith and loyalty.

Remember the soaring rhetoric of Judge Cardozo in *Meinhard v. Salmon*? Does it make sense that co-shareholders should have the duties to each other of co-partners? Don't shareholders, in the corporate model, have prerogatives to act (or not act) as they choose, with fiduciary duties reserved to those who manage the corporation?

2. Minority duties to majority.

What justifies making Dr. Wolfson into a fiduciary? He testified that he asked for a veto right to protect him from the others "ganging" up on him. Has he "ganged" up on them?

3. The remedy!

Notice how the Massachusetts court takes over the financial decision making and capital improvements in the corporation. What about the business judgment rule? What about judges not being business experts?

Hypo 25.7

Suppose Justin and Kathy agreed that Lorenzo could veto any decision about payment of dividends or undertaking capital improvements. If Lorenzo refuses to permit payment of dividends, resulting in tax penalties assessed against the corporation, would the result be any different under the MBCA § 7.32 (laid out below) and *Smith v. Atlantic Properties*?

(e) An agreement authorized by this section that limits the discretion or powers of the board of directors shall relieve the directors of, and impose upon the person or persons in whom such discretion or powers are vested, liability for acts or omissions imposed by law on directors to the extent that the discretion or powers of the directors are limited by the agreement.

D. Contractual Transfer Provisions

1. Purposes and Legality of Transfer Provisions

When a closely-held business is organized as a partnership, each partner <u>has the power</u> to veto the admission into the partnership of a new member—a right of *delectus personae*. In the corporation, however, free transferability of shares is the default rule. In close corporations, where the participants may want to decide who are their co-shareholders, special arrangements are necessary to restrict share transferability.

Transfer provisions accomplish two purposes. They ensure the desired balance of control that might be undone if shares are transferred to another. They can also create a market for otherwise illiquid shares.

Historically, the validity and enforceability of transfer restrictions was somewhat controversial, given the general American legal principle that unreasonable restraints on alienation of personal property are void. As a result, a number of older decisions questioned the validity of corporate transfer restrictions. Over time, courts came to recognize the importance of such restrictions and became more tolerant in their approach.

Today <u>most corporate statutes</u> expressly authorize transfer restrictions. <u>Some statutes</u> even require them for close corporations.

2. Types of Transfer Provisions

Transfer restrictions preserve the ownership and control structure of the close corporation. They can take various forms:

Right of first refusal. Before a shareholder can sell her shares to a third person, they first must be offered to the corporation or to the remaining shareholders (or both) at the same price and on the same terms and conditions offered by the outsider. Typically, the right, if extended to the other shareholders, is given in proportion to their respective holdings. If any shareholder is unable to purchase or declines to do so, her allocation may be taken up proportionately by the remaining shareholders.

Practice Pointer

Liquidity is important in estate planning. A mechanism for the estate of a close corporation shareholder to sell the decedent's shares, for which there is no ready market, facilitates payment of the decedent's personal debts, estate administration, and federal and state estate taxes. The mechanism, such as a buy-sell agreement, must address who must buy the shares (the corporation or other shareholders), how the price is set, and how the purchase is funded. A buyout provision also allows the estate to diversify the assets passed to the heirs.

First option provision. Unlike a right of first refusal, the offer to <u>the corporation or the remaining shareholders</u> is made at a price and on terms fixed by agreement rather than by the outside offer. Even if the agreement calls for a right of first refusal, including a first option provision is useful to deal with non-sale transfers such as gifts or devises.

Consent. Transfers can be conditioned on the consent of the board of directors or the other shareholders. Modern statutes allow the parties to provide for a consent restriction if such "prohibition is not manifestly unreasonable."

In creating these restrictions, the planner must bear in mind that there are many ways for a shareholder to dispose of her shares. The most common are by sale or bequest. But the planner should also consider the possibility of inter vivos transfers by way of gifts, creation of trusts, pledges, or other means by which the right to vote the shares and receive dividends might pass to someone other than the original owner.

In addition, transfer provisions often specify the liquidity rights of shareholders who withdraw from the business.

Sale option. The withdrawing shareholder can receive an option to sell her shares (typically all) to the corporation or the remaining shareholders upon the occurrence of specified events, such as the death of the shareholder or the termination of his or her employment with the corporation.

Practice Pointer

Does a merger in which the majority agrees to sell to another company trigger an agreement that restricts the "disposition" of company shares, unless first offered to other shareholders? At least one court has held that a merger is a corporate act, not a shareholder act governed by an agreement on shareholder "dispositions." The court pointed out, "This is an area of law where formalities are important, as they are the method by which sophisticated businessmen make their contractual rights definite and limit the authority of the courts to redo their deal."

Buy-sell agreement. More commonly, the obligation to buy is combined with a reciprocal obligation to sell. A "buy-sell agreement" compels the corporation or the remaining shareholders to purchase the shares of another shareholder upon the occurrence of specified events, such as the death of a shareholder. If the designated purchaser is the corporation, the agreement is known as an "entity purchase" agreement or "redemption agreement." If the purchase obligation falls on the other shareholders, the agreement is known as a "cross-purchase" arrangement. Frequently the two approaches are combined.

Transfer provisions are most commonly negotiated and adopted when the close corporation is formed. What is the status of a shareholder who purchases shares (from the corporation or a shareholder) after the transfer provisions became effective? Whether the newcomer is bound may depend on how the transfer provisions are documented—in the articles of incorporation, a bylaw provision, or a separate contract among the shareholders. The newcomer may not be bound if the restriction is in a shareholders' agreement to which she is not a party. It is customary, therefore, to make transfer restrictions a part of the bylaws or the articles.

To be valid against a purchaser of shares without notice, the MBCA requires that the transfer restriction be noted "conspicuously" on the stock certificate itself. Even if not conspicuous, a transfer restriction is enforceable against a transferee with knowledge.

3. Valuation of Restricted Shares

The valuation of shares subject to a transfer agreement is of critical importance. There are a variety of techniques available:

Book value. This is a popular method but one that may lead to inequitable results. As we saw in Chapter 11, the book value of a company may bear little relationship to its value as an ongoing concern. Moreover, despite its apparent simplicity, book value turns out to be remarkably ambiguous. Does it, for example, include intangible assets, especially "goodwill"? What about income taxes that are accrued but unpaid, and may not appear on the books? If the corporation carries insurance on the life of the shareholder whose death triggers a buy-sell provision, are the insurance proceeds included? Should assets that have appreciated substantially be written up? If book value is used, these and other questions should be anticipated and resolved in the agreement.

Capitalized earnings. An agreement may establish a formula for capitalizing the earnings of the business. Like book value, however, this technique presents certain difficulties of drafting. It is especially critical that the earnings of the business be carefully defined. Moreover, a capitalization rate that captures the nature of the business when formed may not be appropriate as the business matures and diversifies.

Right of first refusal. When a principal concern is that one of the shareholders may sell his interest to an outsider, a provision that requires the shareholder, before selling, to offer his shares to the corporation (or the other shareholders) with the same price and terms offered by the outsider has great appeal. This approach may, however, substantially increase illiquidity, since a prospective buyer may well be put off by the risk of negotiating a sale only to have the shares bought by the corporation or other shareholders. Moreover, this approach is useful only for prospective sales to third parties and not for the transfer of shares by gift, devise, or inheritance.

Appraisal. Some of these pitfalls can be avoided by leaving the valuation to a later appraisal by a neutral third party according to a predetermined procedure. For example, a convenient technique is to provide for arbitration according to the rules of the American Arbitration Association or some other recognized arbitral organization. The disadvantage is that a professional appraisal of an ongoing business is expensive, often starting at $50,000 to $100,000.

Mutual agreement. Another relatively popular technique is for the parties to the agreement to set a value for the shares and to revise it at stated intervals, usually annually. While this may lead to a fairer price, it is subject to a number of drawbacks. The parties may forget to re-value the shares. They may not have enough comparative information or skill to value the company's business. And for psychological reasons, they may avoid contemplating the possibility of a falling out or of one of them departing.

A valuation method is of little use if the person obligated to purchase lacks the financial ability to do so. Unless some means of funding is provided, both the shareholders and the corporation may find themselves without the ready ability to purchase the shares. A corporate repurchase might require selling parts of the business, and the corporation might even be prevented by statutory restrictions from making the purchase under applicable legal capital rules.

If the putative purchaser is the corporation, one means of funding the purchase is the establishment of a sinking fund in which the corporation regularly sets aside money to be saved for that purpose. A second, and more common, technique is for the corporation to purchase and maintain life insurance on the lives of the shareholders in an amount adequate to fund all or a substantial part of any repurchase for which the corporation may become obligated on their death. Planners will often link the agreement's valuation of the shares to the level of insurance coverage. A third method of funding is to defer payment by the use of promissory notes or installment obligations.

4. Judicial Interpretation of Transfer Provisions

The following case addresses whether transfer restrictions should be enforced on their face, even when the result seems terribly unfair.

Concord Auto Auction, Inc. v. Rustin

627 F. Supp. 1526 (D. Mass. 1986)

YOUNG, DISTRICT JUDGE.

Close corporations, Concord Auto Auction, Inc. ("Concord") and E.L. Cox Associates, Inc. ("Associates") brought this action for the specific performance of a stock purchase and restriction agreement (the "Agreement"). Concord and Associates allege that Lawrence H. Rustin ("Rustin") as the administrator of E.L. Cox's estate ("Cox") failed to effect the repurchase of Cox's stock holdings as provided by the Agreement.

Both Concord and Associates are Massachusetts Corporations. Concord operates a used car auction for car dealers, fleet operators, and manufacturers. Associates operates as an adjunct to Concord's auction business by guaranteeing checks and automobile titles. Both are close corporations with the same shareholders, all siblings: Cox (now his estate), Powell, and Thomas. At all times relevant to this action, each sibling owned one-third of the issued and outstanding stock in both Concord and Associates.

To protect "their best interests" and the best interests of the two corporations, the three shareholders entered into a stock purchase and restriction agreement on February 1, 1983. The Agreement provides that all shares owned by a shareholder at the time of his or her death be acquired by the two corporations, respectively, through life insurance policies specifically established to fund this transaction. This procedure contemplates the "orderly transfer of the stock owned by each deceased Shareholder." At issue in the instant action are the prerequisites for and effect of the repurchase requirements as set forth in the Agreement.

This dispute arises because Rustin failed to tender Cox's shares as required by Paragraph 2, *Death of Shareholder*. Rustin admits this but alleges a condition precedent: that Powell, specifically, and Thomas failed to effect both the annual meeting and the annual review of the stock price set in the Agreement as required by Paragraph 6, *Purchase Price*: "Each price shall be reviewed at least annually no later than the annual meeting of the stockholders (commencing with the annual meetings for the year 1984)," here February 21, 1984. Rustin implies that, had the required meeting been held, revaluation would or should have occurred and that, after Cox's accidental death in a fire on March 14, 1984, Powell in particular as well as Thomas were obligated to revalue the stock prior to tendering the repurchase price.

There is no dispute that the bylaws call for an annual meeting on the third Tuesday of February, here February 21, 1984. There is no dispute that none took place or that, when Cox died, the stocks of each corporation had not been formally revalued. No one disputes that Paragraph 6 of the Agreement provides for a price of $672.00 per share of Concord and a price of $744.00 per share for Associates. This totals $374,976 which is covered by insurance on Cox's life of $375,000. There is no substantial dispute that the stock is worth a great deal more, perhaps even twice as much. No one seriously disputes that Paragraph 6 further provides that:

> all parties may, as a result of such review, agree to a new price by a written instrument executed by all the parties and appended to an original of this instrument, and that any such new price shall thereupon become the basis for determining the purchase price for all purposes hereof unless subsequently superceded pursuant to the same procedure. The purchase price shall remain in full force and effect and until so changed.

Rustin asserts that the explicit requirement of a yearly price review "clashes" with the provision that the price shall remain in effect until changed. He argues a trial is required to determine the intent of the parties:

> The question then arises, presenting this Court with a material issue of fact not susceptible to determination on a motion for summary judgment: Did the parties intend, either to reset, or at least to monitor, yearly, the correspondence between the Paragraph 6 price and the current value of the companies? If so, who, if anyone, was principally responsible for effecting the yearly review required by the Agreement, and for insuring an informed review?

In answering these questions the Court first outlines its proper role in the interpretation of this contract.

A Court sitting in diversity will apply the substantive law of the forum state, here Massachusetts. In Massachusetts as elsewhere, absent ambiguity, contracts must be interpreted and enforced exactly as written. Where the language is unambiguous, the interpretation of a contract is a question of law for the court. Further, contracts must be construed in accordance with their ordinary and usual sense.

Contrary to Rustin's assertion, the Court in applying these standards holds that there is no ambiguity and certainly no "clash" between the dual requirements of Paragraph 6 that there be an annual review of share price and that, absent such review, the existing price prevails. When, as here, the Court searches for the meaning of a document containing two unconditional provisions, one immediately following the other, the Court favors a reading that reconciles them. The Court rules that the Agreement covers precisely the situation before it: no revaluation occurred, therefore the price remains as set forth in the Agreement. This conclusion is reasonable, for the Agreement is not a casual memorialization but a formal contract carefully drafted by attorneys and signed by all parties.

Moreover, the Court interprets Paragraph 2 to provide, in unambiguous terms:

> "In the event of the death of any Shareholder subject to this agreement, his respective administrator *shall*, within sixty (60) days after the date of death give written notice thereof to each Company which notice *shall* specify a purchase date not later than sixty (60) days thereafter, *offering to each Company for purchase* as hereinafter provided, and *at the purchase price set forth in Paragraph 6*, all of the Shares owned on said date by said deceased Shareholder."

Rustin, therefore, was unambiguously obligated as administrator of Cox's estate to tender Cox's shares for repurchase by Concord and Associates. His failure to do so is inexcusable unless he raises cognizable defenses.

All of Rustin's defenses turn on two allegations: that his performance is excused because the surviving parties failed to review and to adjust upward the $374,976 purchase price. Rustin contends that the parties meant to review the price per share on an annual basis. No affidavit supports this assertion, nor does any exhibit. In fact, absent any evidence for this proposition, Rustin's assertion is no more than speculation and conjecture. While Rustin contends that the failure to review and revalue constitutes "unclean hands" and a breach of fiduciary duty which excuses his nonperformance, he places before the Court only argument not facts.

It simply does not follow that because a meeting was not held and the prices were not reviewed that a trial of the parties' intentions is required. The Agreement is the best evidence of the parties' intent. Although the text of the Agreement provides that share price "shall" be reviewed "at least annually," the Agreement also states that "The purchase price shall remain in full force and effect unless and until so changed."

Even if competent evidence adduced at trial would support Rustin's allegations, his proposition would of necessity require judicial intervention, a course this Court does not favor. Rustin produces not a shred of evidence that the parties intended that a court should intercede to set the share price in the event the parties failed to do so themselves. Every first year law student learns that although the courts can lead an opera singer to the concert hall, they cannot make her sing. *Lumley v. Gye*, 118 Eng.Rep. 749 (1853). While this Court will specifically enforce a consensual bargain, memorialized in an unambiguous written document, it will not order the revision of the share price. Such intrusion into the private ordering of commercial affairs offends both good judgment and good jurisprudence. Moreover, the record before the Court indicates that the parties fully intended what their competent counsel drafted and they signed.

Moreover, the nucleus of Rustin's premise is that somehow Powell should have guaranteed the review and revision of the share prices. On the contrary, nothing in the record indicates that a reasonable trier of fact could find that Powell's duties and responsibilities included such omnipotence. More to the point, the bylaws suggest that several individuals shared the responsibility for calling the required annual meeting: "In case the annual meeting for any year shall not be duly called or held, the Board of Directors or the President shall cause a special meeting to be held." Pursuant to the bylaws, Cox himself had the power, right, and authority to call a meeting of the stockholders of both companies, in order to review the price per share—or for any other purpose for that matter.

Furthermore, nothing in the record indicates that somehow Powell, Thomas, Concord, or Associates was charged with the duty of raising the share price. In fact, this is discretionary and consensual: "all parties *may*, as a result of such review, *agree* to a new price by a written instrument *executed by all parties*." Nowhere can the Court find any affirmative duty to guarantee either an annual meeting or a share price revision. To fault Powell for not doing by fiat what must be done by consensus credits Powell with powers she simply does not have. The mere fact that, as a shareholder of Concord and Associates, Powell benefits from the enforcement of the Agreement at the $374,976 purchase price does not, as matter of law, create an obligation on her part to effect a review or revision of the purchase price. One cannot breach a duty where no duty exists, and Rustin cannot manufacture by allegation a duty where neither the Agreement nor the bylaws lends any support.

Applying the above analysis, the Court discounts three of Rustin's defenses as meritless: that specific performance is not warranted because Concord and Associates breached the Agreement they seek to enforce; that they have unclean hands because they failed to effect a review and revaluation of the shares; and that specific performance is conditional upon an annual review of share value to be held no later than the third Tuesday of February. The record demonstrates no evidence that share transfer is conditional, rather it appears absolute and automatic. Absent a duty to "guarantee" the occurrence of the annual meeting or the "review," the Court cannot find that Powell's failure, if any, to upgrade the share price constitutes a fiduciary breach.

Of Rustin's fourth defense, that the value of the stock increased so substantially that specific enforcement would be unfair and unjust to Cox's estate, little need be said. This defense as well as Rustin's counterclaims rest on the allegation that Powell, in particular, and Thomas "knew" that a revaluation would result in a higher price and "failed to effect an annual review." Of Powell, Rustin argues that she had a "special responsibility" to effect a review of the purchase price because her siblings looked to her for financial expertise and to call a meeting. Nowhere is this "special responsibility" supported by the Agreement or the bylaws. Rustin also implies that the sisters "knew" that failure to revalue would inure to their benefit. This presumes they knew that Cox would die in an accidental fire three weeks after the deadline for the annual meeting. To call this preposterous understates it, for nothing immunized the sisters from an equally unforeseeable accident. Rustin's argument withers in the light of objectivity to a heap of conclusory straws.

Rustin goes on to argue that the sisters had a fiduciary duty to revalue the shares *after Cox's death* and *before tender*. Nowhere in the Agreement is there the slightest indication they were so obligated. Nowhere is there evidence of willfulness, intent to deceive, or knowing manipulation.

Agreements, such as those before the Court, "among shareholders of closely held corporations are common and the purpose of such contracts are clear."

Moreover, specific performance of an agreement to convey will not be refused merely because the price is inadequate or excessive. *Allen v. Biltmore Tissue Corp.*, 141 N.E.2d 812 (N.Y. 1957) ("The validity of the restriction on transfer does not rest on any abstract notion of intrinsic fairness of price. To be invalid, more than mere disparity between option price and current value of the stock must be shown"); *Renberg v. Zarrow*, 667 P.2d 465, 470 (Okla. 1983) ("In the absence of fraud, overreaching, or bad faith, an agreement between the stockholders that upon the death of any of them, the stock may be acquired by the corporation is binding. Even great disparity between the price specified in a buy-sell agreement and the actual value of the stock is not sufficient to invalidate the agreement.") The fact that surviving shareholders were allowed to purchase Cox' shares on stated terms and conditions which resulted in the purchase for less than actual value of the stock does not subject the agreement to attack as a breach of the relation of trust and confidence, there being no breach of fiduciary duty.

Rather than evidence of any impropriety, the Court rules that the purchase prices were carefully set, fair when established, evidenced by an Agreement binding all parties equally to the same terms without any indication that any one sibling would reap a windfall. The courts may not rewrite a shareholder's agreement under the guise of relieving one of the parties from the hardship of an improvident bargain. *Id.* at 471 (citations omitted). The Court cannot protect the parties from a bad bargain and it will not protect them from bad luck. Cox, the party whose estate is aggrieved, had while alive every opportunity to call the annual meeting and persuade his sisters to revalue their stock. Sad though the situation be, sadness is not the touchstone of contract interpretation.

The Agreement shall be specifically enforced. Rustin's counterclaims are dismissed and, for the reasons set forth above, the Court ALLOWS Concord's and Associates' motions for summary judgment on all matters. Rustin must sell the Cox shares for the $374,976 purchase price to which all parties agreed. Rustin is hereby ORDERED to:

(1) Deliver the certificates for the Cox shares fully endorsed for purchases pursuant to paragraphs 2 and 6 of the February 1, 1983 Agreement no later than thirty days after the date of this order.

(2) Accept a purchase price of $672.00 per share of Auction and $744.00 per share of Associates as set forth in paragraph 6 of the Agreement.

Points for Discussion

1. Strict construction.

Courts generally construe transfer provisions strictly, sometimes even ignoring the apparent intent of the parties. Isn't a rule of strict construction, as in the *Rustin* case, at odds with the general presumption of free alienability for corporate shares? Why would the courts place on the parties the burden of a weak or incomplete drafter?

2. Incomplete drafting.

Consider a two-shareholder agreement that states: "If either party desires to sell, transfer, assign or convey or otherwise dispose of any shares, an offer must be transmitted to the other party who then has the right to accept such offer in full or in part in the manner set forth in the agreement." How would you construe the agreement if one of the parties dies—a contingency not specifically mentioned in their agreement? *See Vogel v. Melish*, 196 N.E.2d 402 (Ill. App. 1964) (strictly construing the agreement to terminate "on alienation at the death of one of the parties").

3. Intent of parties?

Consider a bylaw provision that states: "No stockholder shall sell or give away his stock in the corporation without first offering to sell the same to the remaining stockholders substantially in proportion to the stock already owned by them." What seems to have been the intent? How would you construe the provision if one of the shareholders decided to sell her shares and offered them to the other shareholders on the condition they purchase all her shares in cash at the same time? If only one shareholder sought to accept the offer and the selling shareholder refused to sell to him alone, is the bylaw enforceable? *See Helmly v. Schultz*, 131 S.E.2d 924 (Ga. 1963) (refusing to enforce the provision since the bylaws contemplated a purchase by all the shareholders "each in his proportionate share").

CHAPTER 26

Oppression in the Close Corporation

All too frequently in a closely-held corporation, a day comes when the owners no longer get along with each other. Often, the minority shareholders will chafe under the traditional corporate law norm that gives majority shareholders control of the corporation. The majority will see their control as a prerogative of ownership.

As we saw in the last chapter, control mechanisms are available to protect minority shareholders, but they are not always used. The majority may refuse to concede control powers to the minority, and developing appropriate control mechanisms can be expensive. And even if mechanisms are created, they may be ill-suited to disputes when they actually arise.

This chapter addresses whether and how courts should fill the gaps left by the parties' incomplete arrangements. First, we look at the nature of dissension in close corporations. Next, we consider special fiduciary duties in close corporations and the nature of those duties. Then we consider how courts have sought to protect "reasonable expectations" in close corporations using the statutory remedy of involuntary dissolution for "oppression." We look at the remedies available to minority shareholders under the "oppression" statutes, including a buyout of their shares at a fair value set by the court. Finally, we consider how courts have responded to oppression in the limited liability company and the relevance of the corporate analogy.

Food for Thought

Close corporation conflicts can manifest themselves in many ways. There are reported cases in which shareholders stop talking to each other, while continuing their business for years. In one case, the dispute ended with "a violent attack with a heavy stick, inflicting wounds, which made it necessary to go to a hospital."

A. Dissension in the Close Corporation

Dissension in the close corporation takes two recurring forms. First are cases in which the majority cuts off minority shareholders from any financial return, thus leaving them holding illiquid stock that generates no current income. Second are cases in which the majority exercises control to frustrate the preferences of the minority.

Differences over matters of business policy or practice frequently arise from personal or family conflicts. As Professor Eric Chiappinelli has commented, the factual context of the dispute affects the judicial response:

A student who has taken the course in corporations and whose professor taught from any of the standard casebooks will understand that a number of the cases have very strong story lines, strong enough that some resemble books or plays in their richness. And many, like the great works of fiction, are set in families. *Francis v. United Jersey Bank* features a family business in which the father dies and the mother does not—perhaps cannot—stop her sons from looting $10 million from the business. *Theodora Holding Co. v. Henderson* involves a wife who tries but fails to obtain complete economic separation from her husband. Siblings also play a large role in corporate law cases. In *Triggs v. Triggs*, brothers gain and lose their father's favor. *Concord Auto Auction, Inc. v. Rustin* finds siblings torn between helping themselves and helping another sibling's heirs.

Perhaps most salient are the repetitive interpersonal processes that occur between family members. We expect both more and less of our relatives. On the one hand, we hold ourselves and other family members to higher duties and obligations than we would hold strangers or friends. Family members are not to engage in sharp financial practices with one another. There is no need for caveat emptor. In fact, to go further, we often expect a family member to provide for us financially if he or she is able.

Another aspect of family process dynamics is bad blood. Over the course of years and generations, some family members will have animosity toward others. This bad blood has two consequences. First, it means that reactions and retaliations toward a family member's actions may seem to outsiders to be disproportionate. Second, given the history of the relationship between the family members, seemingly small slights and injuries accrete that make possible very subtle and very effective oppression.

In addition to these patterns of interpersonal dynamics between family members, there are legal consequences of conceiving of a corporate setting as one involving "family." I believe that judges in deciding corporate law disputes among family members tend to be cognizant of the family dynamics and to take them into account when resolving cases. First, they tend to impose fiduciary-like duties on family members toward one another. In effect, courts sanction the abnorms of family relationships. The effect of judges' recognition of these family aspects is often masked in that the family member may already have fiduciary duties imposed by virtue of being directors or controlling shareholders.

I believe judges in these disputes use family law constructs to help them come to appropriate resolutions. The family law construct most analogous to many corporate law disputes is the issue of property distribution in marital dissolutions [governed] by statutes that typically direct the court to divide the property "equitably" or "in such proportions as the Court deems just after considering all relevant factors."

How courts respond to dissension in close corporations has turned on two factors. One is how the courts view close corporations. As we will see, courts in some states (such as Massachusetts) have analogized the relationship among close corporation participants to that of partners, holding shareholders to high standards of fairness. Courts in other states (particularly Delaware) have rejected the partnership analogy and held that when business participants adopt the corporate form, they also agree to the traditional norms of corporation law, including centralized management and majority rule.

The second factor is whether the state legislature has included in its corporate statute (as does the MBCA) provisions aimed at protecting shareholders in close corporations. Many state laws now authorize courts to order dissolution or to take other remedial actions to protect shareholders who show that the majority has oppressed the minority.

B. Judicial Protection of Minority Owners

1. Fiduciary Duties: Rights to Equal Treatment

In the following case, the Massachusetts court wrestles with the appropriate standard for resolving a dispute in a close corporation, attempting to reconcile partnership-type rules of equal treatment and corporate rules of majority prerogative. How well does the court do?

Wilkes v. Springside Nursing Home, Inc.

353 N.E.2d 657 (Mass. 1976)

HENNESSEY, CHIEF JUSTICE.

On August 5, 1971, the plaintiff (Wilkes) filed a bill in equity for declaratory judgment in the Probate Court for Berkshire County, naming as defendants T. Edward Quinn (Quinn), Leon L. Riche (Riche), the First Agricultural National Bank of Berkshire County and Frank Sutherland MacShane as executors under the will of Lawrence R. Connor (Connor), and the Springside Nursing Home, Inc. (Springside or the corporation). Wilkes alleged that he, Quinn, Riche and Dr. Hubert A. Pipkin (Pipkin) entered into a partnership agreement in 1951, prior to the incorporation of Springside, which agreement was breached in 1967 when Wilkes's salary was terminated and he was voted out as an officer and director of the corporation. Wilkes sought, among other forms of relief, damages in the amount of the salary he would have received had he continued as a director and officer of Springside subsequent to March, 1967.

A judgment was entered dismissing Wilkes's action on the merits. We granted direct appellate review. On appeal, Wilkes argued in the alternative that (1) he should recover damages for breach of the alleged partnership agreement; and (2) he should recover damages because the defendants, as majority stockholders in Springside, breached their fiduciary duty to him as a minority stockholder by their action in February and March, 1967.

We reverse so much of the judgment as dismisses Wilkes's complaint and order the entry of a judgment substantially granting the relief sought by Wilkes under the second alternative set forth above.

In 1951, Wilkes, Riche, Quinn, and Pipkin purchased a building to use as a nursing home. Ownership of the property was vested in Springside, a corporation organized under Massachusetts law.

Each of the four men invested $1,000 and subscribed to ten shares of $100 par value stock in Springside.[2] At the time of incorporation, it was understood by all of the parties that each would be a director of Springside and each would participate actively in the management and decision making involved in operating

---

[2] On May 2, 1955, and again on December 23, 1958, each of the four original investors paid for and was issued additional shares of $100 par value stock, eventually bringing the total number of shares owned by each to 115.

the corporation.[3] It was, further, the understanding and intention of all the parties that, corporate resources permitting, each would receive money from the corporation in equal amounts as long as each assumed an active and ongoing responsibility for carrying a portion of the burdens necessary to operate the business.

The work involved in establishing and operating a nursing home was roughly apportioned, and each of the four men undertook his respective tasks.

At some time in 1952, it became apparent that the operational income and cash flow from the business were sufficient to permit the four stockholders to draw money from the corporation on a regular basis. Each of the four original parties initially received $35 a week from the corporation. As time went on the weekly return to each was increased until, in 1955, it totalled $100.

In 1959, after a long illness, Pipkin sold his shares in the corporation to Connor, who was known to Wilkes, Riche and Quinn through past transactions with Springside in his capacity as president of the First Agricultural National Bank of Berkshire County. Connor received a weekly stipend from the corporation equal to that received by Wilkes, Riche and Quinn. He was elected a director of the corporation but never held any other office. He was assigned no specific area of responsibility in the operation of the nursing home but did participate in business discussions and decisions as a director and served additionally as financial adviser to the corporation.

In 1965 the stockholders decided to sell a portion of the corporate property to Quinn, who in addition to being a stockholder in Springside possessed an interest in another corporation that desired to operate a rest home on the property. Wilkes was successful in prevailing on the other stockholders of Springside to procure a higher sale price for the property than Quinn apparently wanted to pay. After the sale was consummated, the relationship between Quinn and Wilkes begain to deteriorate.

The bad blood between Quinn and Wilkes affected the attitudes of both Riche and Connor. As a consequence of the strained relations among the parties, Wilkes, in January of 1967, gave notice of his intention to sell his shares for an amount based on an appraisal of their value. In February of 1967 a directors' meeting was held and the board exercised its right to establish the salaries of its officers

---

[3] Wilkes testified before the master that, when the corporate officers were elected, all four men "were guaranteed directorships." Riche's understanding of the parties' intentions was that they all wanted to play a part in the management of the corporation and wanted to have some "say" in the risks involved; that, to this end, they all would be directors; and that "unless you [were] a director and officer you could not participate in the decisions of [the] enterprise."

and employees.[4] A schedule of payments was established whereby Quinn was to receive a substantial weekly increase and Riche and Connor were to continue receiving $100 a week. Wilkes, however, was left off the list of those to whom a salary was to be paid. The directors also set the annual meeting of the stockholders for March, 1967.

At the annual meeting in March, Wilkes was not reelected as a director, nor was he reelected as an officer of the corporation. He was further informed that neither his services nor his presence at the nursing home was wanted by his associates.

The meetings of the directors and stockholders in early 1967, the master found, were used as a vehicle to force Wilkes out of active participation in the management and operation of the corporation and to cut off all corporate payments to him. Though the board of directors had the power to dismiss any officers or employees for misconduct or neglect of duties, there was no indication in the minutes of the board of directors' meeting of February, 1967, that the failure to establish a salary for Wilkes was based on either ground. The severance of Wilkes from the payroll resulted not from misconduct or neglect of duties, but because of the personal desire of Quinn, Riche, and Connor to prevent him from continuing to receive money from the corporation. Despite a continuing deterioration in his personal relationship with his associates, Wilkes had consistently endeavored to carry on his responsibilities to the corporation in the same satisfactory manner and with the same degree of competence he had previously shown. Wilkes was at all times willing to carry on his responsibilities and participation if permitted so to do and provided that he receive his weekly stipend.

1. We turn to Wilkes's claim for damages based on a breach of the fiduciary duty owed to him by the other participants in this venture. In light of the theory underlying this claim, we do not consider it vital to our approach to this case whether the claim is governed by partnership law or the law applicable to business corporations. This is so because, as all the parties agree, Springside was at all times relevant to this action, a close corporation as we have recently defined such an entity in *Donahue v. Rodd Electrotype Co. of New England, Inc.*, 367 Mass. 578, 328 N.E.2d 505 (1975).

In *Donahue,* we held that "stockholders in the close corporation owe one another substantially the same fiduciary duty in the operation of the enterprise that partners owe to one another." As determined in previous decisions of this court, the standard of duty owed by partners to one another is one of "utmost good faith and loyalty."

---

[4] The bylaws of the corporation provided that the directors, subject to the approval of the stockholders, had the power to fix the salaries of all officers and employees. This power, however, up until February, 1967, had not been exercised formally; all payments made to the four participants in the venture had resulted from the informal but unanimous approval of all the parties concerned.

Thus, we concluded in *Donahue,* with regard to "their actions relative to the operations of the enterprise and the effects of that operation on the rights and investments of other stockholders," "stockholders in close corporations must discharge their management and stockholder responsibilities in conformity with this strict good faith standard. They may not act out of avarice, expediency or self-interest in derogation of their duty of loyalty to the other stockholders and to the corporation."

In the *Donahue* case we recognized that one peculiar aspect of close corporations was the opportunity afforded to majority stockholders to oppress, disadvantage or "freeze out" minority stockholders. In *Donahue* itself, for example, the majority refused the minority an equal opportunity to sell a ratable number of shares to the corporation at the same price available to the majority. The net result of this refusal, we said, was that the minority could be forced to "sell out at less than fair value," since there is by definition no ready market for minority stock in a close corporation.

"Freeze outs," however, may be accomplished by the use of other devices. One such device which has

Food for Thought

The *Wilkes* court distances itself from *Donahue,* decided just a year earlier, which set out an equal opportunity rule that may have been overbroad and ill-conceived. In *Donahue,* a minority shareholder complained of unequal treatment when the corporation repurchased the majority shareholder's interest, without making the same offer to the minority shareholder. Arguably the majority shareholder was differently situated as he had been involved in management of the corporation and a business reason existed for the repurchase, but the court nevertheless concluded that the majority shareholder had breached a duty owed to the minority.

proved to be particularly effective in accomplishing the purpose of the majority is to deprive minority stockholders of corporate offices and of employment with the corporation. F.H. O'Neal, "Squeeze-Outs" of Minority Shareholders 59, 78–79 (1975). This "freeze-out" technique has been successful because courts fairly consistently have been disinclined to interfere in those facets of internal corporate operations, such as the selection and retention or dismissal of officers, directors and employees, which essentially involve management decisions subject to the principle of majority control. As one authoritative source has said, "Many courts apparently feel that there is a legitimate sphere in which the controlling directors or shareholders can act in their own interest even if the minority suffers." F.H. O'Neal, *supra* at 59 (footnote omitted).

The denial of employment to the minority at the hands of the majority is especially pernicious in some instances. A guaranty of employment with the corporation may have been one of the "basic reasons why a minority owner has invested capital in the firm." The minority stockholder typically depends on his salary as the principal return on his investment, since the "earnings of a close corporation are distributed in major part in salaries, bonuses and retirement benefits." 1 F.H. O'Neal, CLOSE CORPORATIONS § 1.07 (1971).[5] Other noneconomic interests of the minority stockholder are likewise injuriously affected by barring him from corporate office. Such action severely restricts his participation in the management of the enterprise, and he is relegated to enjoying those benefits incident to his status as a stockholder. In sum, by terminating a minority stockholder's employment or by severing him from a position as an officer or director, the majority effectively frustrate the minority stockholder's purposes in entering on the corporate venture and also deny him an equal return on his investment.

The distinction between the majority action in *Donahue* and the majority action in this case is more one of form than of substance. Nevertheless, we are concerned that untempered application of the strict good faith standard enunciated in *Donahue* to cases such as the one before us will result in the imposition of limitations on legitimate action by the controlling group in a close corporation which will unduly hamper its effectiveness in managing the corporation in the best interests of all concerned. The majority, concededly, have certain rights to what has been termed "selfish ownership" in the corporation which should be balanced against the concept of their fiduciary obligation to the minority.

Therefore, when minority stockholders in a close corporation bring suit against the majority alleging a breach of the strict good faith duty owed to them by the majority, we must carefully analyze the action taken by the controlling stockholders in the individual case. It must be asked whether the controlling group can demonstrate a legitimate business purpose for its action. In asking this question, we acknowledge the fact that the controlling group in a close corporation must have some room to maneuver in establishing the business policy of the corporation. It must have a large measure of discretion, for example, in declaring or withholding dividends, deciding whether to merge or consolidate, establishing the salaries of corporate officers, dismissing directors with or without cause, and hiring and firing corporate employees.

When an asserted business purpose for their action is advanced by the majority, however, we think it is open to minority stockholders to demonstrate that the same legitimate objective could have been achieved through an alternative course of action less harmful to the minority's interest. If called on to settle a dispute, our

---

[5] We note here that the master found that Springside never declared or paid a dividend to its stockholders.

courts must weigh the legitimate business purpose, if any, against the practicability of a less harmful alternative.

Applying this approach to the instant case it is apparent that the majority stockholders in Springside have not shown a legitimate business purpose for severing Wilkes from the payroll of the corporation or for refusing to reelect him as a salaried officer and director. The master's subsidiary findings relating to the purpose of the meetings of the directors and stockholders in February and March, 1967, are supported by the evidence. There was no showing of misconduct on Wilkes's part as a director, officer or employee of the corporation which would lead us to approve the majority action as a legitimate response to the disruptive nature of an undesirable individual bent on injuring or destroying the corporation. On the contrary, it appears that Wilkes had always accomplished his assigned share of the duties competently, and that he had never indicated an unwillingness to continue to do so.

It is an inescapable conclusion from all the evidence that the action of the majority stockholders here was a designed "freeze out" for which no legitimate business purpose has been suggested. Furthermore, we may infer that a design to pressure Wilkes into selling his shares to the corporation at a price below their value well may have been at the heart of the majority's plan.[6]

In the context of this case, several factors bear directly on the duty owed to Wilkes by his associates. At a minimum, the duty of utmost good faith and loyalty would demand that the majority consider that their action was in disregard of a long-standing policy of the stockholders that each would be a director of the corporation and that employment with the corporation would go hand in hand with stock ownership; that Wilkes was one of the four originators of the nursing home venture; and that Wilkes, like the others, had invested his capital and time for more than fifteen years with the expectation that he would continue to participate in corporate decisions. Most important is the plain fact that the cutting off of Wilkes's salary, together with the fact that the corporation never declared a dividend, assured that Wilkes would receive no return at all from the corporation.

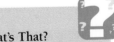

What's That?

"Dissolution" is the formal extinguishment of the corporation's legal life. "Liquidation" is the process of reducing the corporation's assets to cash or liquid assets, after which the corporation becomes a liquid shell. "Winding up" is the process of liquidating the assets, paying off creditors, and distributing what remains to shareholders.

---

[6] This inference arises from the fact that Connor, acting on behalf of the three controlling stockholders, offered to purchase Wilkes's shares for a price Connor admittedly would not have accepted for his own shares.

2. The question of Wilkes's damages at the hands of the majority has not been thoroughly explored on the record before us. Wilkes, in his original complaint, sought damages in the amount of the $100 a week he believed he was entitled to from the time his salary was terminated up until the time this action was commenced. However, the record shows that, after Wilkes was severed from the corporate payroll, the schedule of salaries and payments made to the other stockholders varied from time to time. In addition, the duties assumed by the other stockholders after Wilkes was deprived of his share of the corporate earnings appear to have changed in significant respects. Any resolution of this question must take into account whether the corporation was dissolved during the pendency of this litigation.

Therefore our order is as follows: So much of the judgment as dismisses Wilkes's complaint and awards costs to the defendants is reversed.

Points for Discussion

1. Freeze-out tactics.

Notice the ways in which the majority owners sought to "freeze out" the minority owner Wilkes. After the majority removed Wilkes from his corporate position and discontinued his salary, they continued their long-standing policy of not paying dividends; they distributed to themselves corporate profits in the form of salaries and bonuses; and they offered to buy out Wilkes at a price they would not have accepted for their own shares. Does this seem fair? How might Wilkes have protected himself?

2. Compare to partnership.

If Wilkes had been a partner, <u>partnership law</u> would have allowed him to withdraw and demand payment in cash for the fair value of his ownership interest. Why did the court not treat this as a case governed by partnership law?

3. Equal treatment vs. balancing of interests.

The *Wilkes* court was not writing on a blank slate. The court's earlier decision in *Donahue* had set out a rule of "equal treatment" when majority shareholders preferentially redeemed the shares of one of their own, while excluding the minority shareholders. The *Wilkes* court decided not to extend the "equal treatment" rule to operational decisions—here the employment and compensation of a co-owner. Instead, the court articulated a balancing test. Does this approach overly involve the court, contrary to the wisdom of the business judgment rule, in inquiring into how majority owners run their business?

4. Non-contractual remedy.

In the end, the *Wilkes* court decided that the majority breached its fiduciary duties to the minority owner. The effect was to recognize rights for Wilkes that he had not obtained by contract. Does it make sense to assume that the co-owners would have negotiated for financial compensation if one of them were removed from the business without "legitimate business purposes" or without considering "less harmful alternatives"? That is, does the court leave enough room for legitimate freeze outs?

5. Valuation of minority interests.

Notice that the court does not resolve how Wilkes is to be compensated for the majority's breach of its fiduciary duties. Does it make sense that Wilkes would have continued to receive $100/month, even though he was no longer working in the business? Or should the court attempt to ascertain what portion of the $100/month was a return on investment and what was compensation for services? Can a court make those distinctions?

2. Prerogatives of Majority Control

Courts have shown varying degrees of sensitivity to claims of unequal treatment raised by minority shareholders. Most, like *Wilkes*, have rejected *Donahue*'s "utmost good faith and loyalty" test in favor of approaches that allow majority shareholders flexibility to manage the corporation's business as they see fit.

One recurring issue is whether a minority shareholder who is dismissed as an employee has a claim for a fiduciary breach. In many close corporations, shareholders view employment as an intrinsic aspect of their investment. And if the corporation is subject to double taxation on dividends, amounts paid as salary and bonuses often represent implicit dividends. Separating employment and corporate financial claims in the close corporation has proved difficult.

For example, in *Merola v. Exergen Corp.*, 668 N.E.2d 351 (Mass. 1996), a minority shareholder brought a fiduciary claim after being terminated from employment for commenting critically about an extra-marital relationship by the company's president and majority shareholder. The minority shareholder, Merola, claimed that he had joined the company on the understanding he would be able to invest in company shares and become a major shareholder. And after being hired, Merola had purchased a significant number of shares. The trial judge ruled that the majority shareholder, Pompei, had terminated Merola for no legitimate business purpose, thus breaching a fiduciary duty to honor the reasonable expectations that Merola had concerning his investment of time and money in the company.

On appeal, the Massachusetts Supreme Judicial Court rejected the linkage between Merola's shareholding and employment rights:

> Even in close corporations, the majority interest "must have a large measure of discretion, for example, in declaring or withholding dividends, deciding whether to merge or consolidate, establishing the salaries of corporate officers, dismissing directors with or without cause, and hiring and firing corporate employees." *Wilkes v. Springside Nursing Home, Inc.*, 370 Mass. 842, 851, 353 N.E.2d 657 (1976).

> Principles of employment law permit the termination of employees at will, with or without cause excepting situations within a narrow public policy exception.

> Here, although the plaintiff invested in the stock of Exergen with the reasonable expectation of continued employment, there was no general policy regarding stock ownership and employment, and there was no evidence that any other stockholders had expectations of continuing employment because they purchased stock. The investment in the stock was an investment in the equity of the corporation which was not tied to employment in any formal way.

> Unlike the *Wilkes* case, there was no evidence that the corporation distributed all profits to shareholders in the form of salaries. On the contrary, the perceived value of the stock increased during the time that the plaintiff was employed. The plaintiff first purchased his stock at $2.25 per share and, one year later, he purchased more for $5 per share. This indicated that there was some increase in value to the investment independent of the employment expectation. Neither was the plaintiff a founder of the business, his stock purchases were made after the business was established, and there was no suggestion that he had to purchase stock to keep his job.

> The plaintiff testified that, when he sold his stock back to the corporation four years after being terminated, he was paid $17 per share. This was a price that had been paid to other shareholders who sold their shares to the corporation at a previous date, and it is a price which,

after consulting with his attorney, he concluded was a fair price. With this payment, the plaintiff realized a significant return on his capital investment independent of the salary he received as an employee.

We conclude that this is not a situation where the majority shareholder breached his fiduciary duty to a minority shareholder. Although there was no legitimate business purpose for the termination of the plaintiff, neither was the termination for the financial gain of Pompei or contrary to established public policy. Not every discharge of an at-will employee of a close corporation who happens to own stock in the corporation gives rise to a successful breach of fiduciary duty claim.

The following case provides insight into Delaware's approach to close corporations. Specifically, the case addresses the question whether the board in a close corporation breached its fiduciary duties by failing to provide liquidity rights to non-employee minority shareholders, while providing such rights to employee-shareholders.

The plaintiffs were descendants of E.C. Barton, the founder of a successful closely-held lumber business incorporated in Delaware. As shareholders of non-voting Class B stock, they complained that the company's board had denied them liquidity rights that had been extended to themselves and other employees holding company shares. In particular, employees who owned Class B stock were allowed under the company's employee stock ownership plan (ESOP) to take cash for their shares when they left the company; this liquidity was not available to non-employee Class B shareholders.

Before his death, Mr. Barton had owned all the company's stock. Under his will, he directed that the company's Class A stock go to company employees, and that most of the Class B stock go to his family. Even though Class B stock represented 75% of the company's total equity, it did not have voting rights. In effect, the company became employee-operated, but primarily for the financial benefit of the founder's family.

Business Lingo

An "employee stock ownership plan" (or ESOP) is a retirement plan in which the company contributes its stock to the plan for the benefit of the company's employees. With an ESOP, the employee never buys or holds the stock directly.

An ESOP should not be confused with an employee stock option plan, which is not a retirement plan. Instead, employee stock option plans give employees the right (or option) to buy their company's stock at a set price within a certain period of time.

Nixon v. Blackwell

626 A.2d 1366 (Del. 1993)

VEASEY, CHIEF JUSTICE.

V. Applicable Principles of Substantive Law

Defendants contend that the trial court erred in not applying the business judgment rule. Since the defendants benefited from the ESOP beyond that which benefited other stockholders generally, the defendants are on both sides of the transaction. For that reason, we agree with the trial court that the entire fairness test applies to this aspect of the case. Accordingly, defendants have the burden of showing the entire fairness of those transactions.

The trial court in this case, however, appears to have adopted the novel legal principle that Class B stockholders had a right to "liquidity" equal to that which the court found to be available to the defendants. It is well established in our jurisprudence that stockholders need not always be treated equally for all purposes. To hold that fairness necessarily requires precise equality is to beg the question:

> Many scholars, though few courts, conclude that one aspect of fiduciary duty is the equal treatment of investors. Their argument takes the following form: fiduciary principles require fair conduct; equal treatment is fair conduct; hence, fiduciary principles require equal treatment. The conclusion does not follow. The argument depends on an equivalence between *equal* and *fair* treatment. To say that fiduciary principles require equal treatment is to beg the question whether investors would contract for equal or even equivalent treatment.

Frank H. Easterbrook and Daniel R. Fischel, *The Economic Structure of Corporate Law* 110 (1991) (emphasis in original). This holding of the trial court overlooks the significant facts that the minority stockholders were not: (a) employees of the Corporation; (b) entitled to share in an ESOP; or (c) protected by specific provisions in the certificate of incorporation, bylaws, or a stockholders' agreement.

There is support in this record for the fact that the ESOP is a corporate benefit and was established, at least in part, to benefit the Corporation. Generally speaking, the creation of ESOPs is a normal corporate practice and is generally thought to benefit the corporation. If such corporate practices were necessarily to require equal treatment for non-employee stockholders, that would be a matter for legislative determination in Delaware. There is no such legislation to that effect. If we were to adopt such a rule, our decision would border on judicial legislation.

Accordingly, we hold that the Vice Chancellor erred as a matter of law in concluding that the liquidity afforded to the employee stockholders by the ESOP and the key man insurance required substantially equal treatment for the non-employee stockholders.

We hold on this record that defendants have met their burden of establishing the entire fairness of their dealings with the non-employee Class B stockholders, and are entitled to judgment. The record is sufficient to conclude that plaintiffs' claim that the defendant directors have maintained a discriminatory policy of favoring employee Class A stockholders over Class B non-employee stockholders is without merit.

The directors have followed a consistent policy originally established by Mr. Barton, the founder of the Corporation, whose intent from the formation of the Corporation was to use the Class A stock as the vehicle for the Corporation's continuity through employee management and ownership. The directors' actions following Mr. Barton's death are consistent with Mr. Barton's plan. An ESOP, for example, is normally established for employees. Accordingly, there is no inequity in limiting ESOP benefits to the employee stockholders. Indeed, it makes no sense to include non-employees in ESOP benefits. The fact that the Class B stock represented 75 percent of the Corporation's total equity is irrelevant to the issue of fair dealing. The Class B stock was given no voting rights because those stockholders were not intended to have a direct voice in the management and operation of the Corporation. They were simply passive investors—entitled to be treated fairly but not necessarily to be treated equally.

VI. No Special Rules for a "Closely-Held Corporation" Not Qualified as a "Close Corporation" Under DGCL Subchapter XIV

We wish to address one further matter which was raised at oral argument before this Court: Whether there should be any special, judicially-created rules to "protect" minority stockholders of closely-held Delaware corporations.

The case at bar points up the basic dilemma of minority stockholders in receiving fair value for their stock as to which there is no market and no market valuation. It is not difficult to be sympathetic, in the abstract, to a stockholder who finds himself or herself in that position. A stockholder who bargains for stock in a closely-held corporation and who pays for those shares can make a business judgment whether to buy into such a minority position, and if so on what terms. One could bargain for definitive provisions of self-ordering permitted to a Delaware corporation through the certificate of incorporation or bylaws by reason of the provisions in 8 Del.C. § 102, 109, and 141(a). Moreover, in addition to such mechanisms, a stockholder intending to buy into a minority position in a Delaware corporation may enter into definitive stockholder agreements, and such agreements may provide for elaborate earnings tests, buy-out provisions, voting trusts, or other voting agreements. *See, e.g.*, 8 Del.C. § 218.

The tools of good corporate practice are designed to give a purchasing minority stockholder the opportunity to bargain for protection before parting with consideration. It would do violence to normal corporate practice and our corporation law to fashion an ad hoc ruling which would result in a court-imposed stockholder buy-out for which the parties had not contracted.

In 1967, when the Delaware General Corporation Law was significantly revised, a new Subchapter XIV entitled "Close Corporations; Special Provisions," became a part of that law for the first time. Subchapter XIV is a narrowly constructed statute which applies only to a corporation which is designated as a "close corporation" in its certificate of incorporation, and which fulfills other requirements, including a limitation to 30 on the number of stockholders, that all classes of stock have to have at least one restriction on transfer, and that there be no "public offering." 8 Del.C. § 342. Accordingly, subchapter XIV applies only to "close corporations," as defined in section 342. "Unless a corporation elects to become a close corporation under this subchapter in the manner prescribed in this subchapter, it shall be subject in all respects to this chapter, except this subchapter." 8 Del.C. § 341. The corporation before the Court in this matter, is not a "close corporation." Therefore it is not governed by the provisions of Subchapter XIV.[7]

One cannot read into the situation presented in the case at bar any special relief for the minority stockholders in this closely-held, but not statutory "close corporation" because the provisions of Subchapter XIV relating to close corporations and other statutory schemes preempt the field in their respective areas. It would run counter to the spirit of the doctrine of independent legal significance, and would be inappropriate judicial legislation for this Court to fashion a special judicially-created rule for minority investors when the entity does not fall within those statutes, or when there are no negotiated special provisions in the certificate of incorporation, bylaws, or stockholder agreements.

---

[7] We do not intend to imply that, if the Corporation had been a close corporation under Subchapter XIV, the result in this case would have been different. "Statutory close corporations have not found particular favor with practitioners. Practitioners have for the most part viewed the complex statutory provisions underlying the purportedly simplified operational procedures for close corporations as legal quicksand of uncertain depth and have adopted the view that the objectives sought by the subchapter are achievable for their clients with considerably less uncertainty by cloaking a conventionally created corporation with the panoply of charter provisions, transfer restrictions, bylaws, stockholders' agreements, buy-sell arrangements, irrevocable proxies, voting trusts or other contractual mechanisms which were and remain the traditional method for accomplishing the goals sought by the close corporation provisions." David A. Drexler, Lewis S. Black, Jr., and A. Gilchrist Sparks, III, Delaware Corporation Law and Practice § 43.01 (1993).

Points for Discussion

1. Discriminatory structure.

Notice that the Delaware approach places significant weight on the capital structure implemented by the corporate planner. In *Nixon v. Blackwell*, the corporation's founder chose to have his family provided for financially with non-voting Class B shares, for which no redemption rights were provided. The founder then assigned control of the corporation to voting Class A shares, the majority of which were held by employees through an ESOP under which redemption rights were provided in the event of the employee-shareholders' withdrawal or death. Is this differential treatment a violation of the majority's duty of "utmost good faith and loyalty" to minority shareholders?

2. Reconcile the approaches.

Can the Massachusetts "equal opportunity" and the Delaware "traditional" approach be reconciled? In theory, the Massachusetts approach requires that the minority receive the same shareholder-level rights as the majority, while the Delaware approach does not require equal treatment unless the parties have negotiated for it.

In the end, both approaches seek to enforce what the court assumes to be the parties' expectations. The real difference may lie in the willingness of the two courts to look beyond the formal corporate documents—and to forgive a failure in lawyering. In Massachusetts, the *Wilkes* court found no formal documents and created fiduciary duties to fill the perceived gaps. In Delaware, the *Nixon* court found a clear capital structure and refused to conclude that there were any gaps. While Wilkes got the benefit of the doubt in Massachusetts, would he (and his lawyer) have been treated the same way in Delaware? Or would they have been chastised for not obtaining contractual protections in the corporate documents? Why did the *Nixon* court apply the entire fairness standard?

3. Harsh rules and drafting incentives.

The "traditional" Delaware approach avoids the line-drawing required under the Massachusetts approach that seeks *ex post* to approximate the parties' expectations, whether under the "equal opportunity" test or the "legitimate business purposes" analysis. Such *ex post* judicial relief creates disincentives for the parties themselves to identify and negotiate their own relationship. Perhaps such judicial involvement makes sense when the parties, particularly in older corporations before formal contracting in close corporations became commonplace, failed formally to establish their rights. Does it make sense in more recent corporations where special contracting is widely recognized and practiced?

4. Case-by-case duties?

If the role of courts in close corporation cases is to fill in the terms of the close corporation "contract," what aspects of the parties' relationship should the courts consider? For example, the *Wilkes* court looked at the long-standing informal practices and income expectations that the parties had developed; and the *Merola* court considered how the minority shareholder had actually acquired (and later sold) shares in the corporation. Should fiduciary duties vary according to the particular expectations and practices in the corporation?

5. Choosing a default rule.

On the assumption that the parties can negotiate for different levels of protection, what should be the default rule? Some commentators have argued for a default rule of strong fiduciary protections for minority shareholders, absent an agreement otherwise. How would such a rule affect investment in close corporations? Would strong fiduciary protections encourage or discourage investment? Arguably, if the rule overly favored minority investors, majority owners could negotiate (and pay) for limits on minority protections.

Another default rule might be to tailor fiduciary protections according to what the parties would likely have negotiated in their particular close corporation. To avoid the costs of *ex ante* bargaining, an *ex post* tailored default rule places the parties in the position they would have bargained for. Does such an approach give too much weight to the interests of minority shareholders, who are encouraged to obtain from a sympathetic judge what they could not get through negotiation with the majority? Or is this simply an efficient way to minimize bargaining costs?

---

3. Choice of Law in Close Corporation Disputes

As we saw in Chapter 5, the traditional choice of law for corporations is the internal affairs doctrine, which creates a system of incorporation-based private ordering. Under this approach, internal disputes in a corporation, such as among shareholders or between shareholders and managers, are resolved by the law of the state of incorporation. Should this approach govern disputes in close corporations, or should the courts look to the public policy of the state where the corporation and its owners are doing business?

Few courts have addressed the question, though a couple of cases in Massachusetts have taken different approaches. In a dispute between shareholders in a close corporation incorporated in Delaware but doing business in Massachusetts, the court considered whether the internal affairs doctrine applied or whether the shareholders should be treated as "incorporated partners" subject to Massachusetts' duty of good faith and fair dealing. *Harrison v. NetCentric Corp.*, 744 N.E.2d 622 (Mass. 2001). The court applied Delaware's less-protective norms and affirmed the dismissal of a minority shareholder's claim that the majority shareholders breached their duties of good faith and fair dealing when they fired him and sought to repurchase his stock. The court noted that Delaware has explicitly declined "to fashion a special judicially-created rule for minority investors" who can protect themselves by contract.

The Massachusetts court explained that the internal affairs doctrine avoids "conflicting demands" and protects party expectations by leaving to only one state the regulation of internal corporate disputes. The court stated this has been the long-standing approach in Massachusetts for both public and close corporations, even though analysis of "significant relationships" has become commonplace in choice of law cases involving other areas of Massachusetts law. Following the approach of most other states, the Massachusetts court reaffirmed its "policy that the State of incorporation dictates the choice of law regarding the internal affairs of a corporation." The court noted that the company's founders had chosen to incorporate in Delaware, apparently to attract venture capital financing. Their agreements, particularly the non-compete and stock repurchase provisions, anticipated that the majority should have significant flexibility in personnel decisions.

In another Massachusetts case, however, where a closely-held Delaware corporation had been merged into a Massachusetts corporation, the Massachusetts court adopted a functional approach that focused on the "significant relationships" of the parties to the state and applied Massachusetts law to both the pre-merger and post-merger company. *Demoulas v. Demoulas Super Mkts., Inc.*, 677 N.E.2d 159, 169 (Mass. 1997). The court reasoned that it would be a "cumbersome and unnecessarily formalistic exercise" to apply different rules to corporate conduct that spanned two periods. Although it was unclear whether Delaware and Massachusetts self-dealing standards would produce different outcomes, the case suggests that in close corporations the internal affairs doctrine may not be monolithic.

C. Statutory Remedies for Oppression

1. Statutory Oppression Doctrine

Over the last three decades, courts have used involuntary dissolution statutes similar to MBCA § 14.30(2) (which we lay out below) to craft broad protections for minority shareholders who complain of "oppression" by majority shareholders. The Official Comment to MBCA § 14.30 advises courts to be "cautious" when considering claims of oppression "so as to limit [such cases] to genuine abuse rather than instances of acceptable tactics in a power struggle for control of a corporation." MBCA § 14.34 (also below) specifies a procedure for defendants to buyout plaintiffs when a claim of oppression is made.

MBCA § 14.30
Grounds for Judicial Dissolution

The [court] may dissolve a [closely held] corporation:

(a)(2) in a proceeding by a shareholder if it is established that:

(i) the directors are deadlocked in the management of the corporate affairs, the shareholders are unable to break the deadlock, and irreparable injury to the corporation is threatened or being suffered, or the business and affairs of the corporation can no longer be conducted to the advantage of the shareholders generally, because of the deadlock;

(ii) the directors or those in control of the corporation have acted, are acting, or will act in a manner that is illegal, oppressive, or fraudulent;

(iii) the shareholders are deadlocked in voting power and have failed, for a period that includes at least two consecutive annual meeting dates, to elect successors to directors whose terms have expired; or

(iv) the corporate assets are being misapplied or wasted.

———————

MBCA § 14.34
Election to Purchase in lieu of Dissolution

(a) In a proceeding under section 14.30(a)(2) to dissolve a corporation, the corporation may elect or, if it fails to elect, one or more shareholders may elect to purchase all shares owned by the petitioning shareholder at the fair value of the shares.

(b) An election to purchase pursuant to this section may be filed with the court at any time within 90 days after the filing of the petition under section 14.30(a)(2) or at such later time as the court in its discretion may allow.

These statutes raise three important interpretive questions. First, when is majority conduct "oppressive?" Second, when a court finds oppression, what remedy is appropriate—dissolution or buy-out? Third, where a corporation or shareholder elects to exercise buy-out rights under MBCA § 14.34, how is the "fair value" of the complaining shareholder's stock to be determined?

Corporate statutes usually provide that a corporation can be dissolved with the approval of the board of directors and the shareholders. *See* MBCA §§ 14.02–14.07. In the case of both voluntary and court-ordered dissolutions, corporate existence is terminated in an orderly fashion: the corporation sells off its assets, pays off its creditors, and distributes whatever remains to its shareholders. But a dissident shareholder who brings suit seeking dissolution often will be less interested in terminating the corporation's legal existence than in using the threat of dissolution as leverage to bargain for a better price for her stock.

Whether a threat of dissolution is effective may depend on the nature of the corporation's business. If a business derives its value almost entirely from the corporation's tangible assets, shareholders who wish to continue to operate the business probably will have to pay fair market value for those assets, since other prospective purchasers could use them to equally good effect. But if a business derives most of its value from its economic goodwill supplied by the presence of the majority owners, dissolution may disserve the minority's interests, because the majority may be able to purchase the corporation's tangible assets for its fair market value and to capture the associated goodwill at no additional cost. In such a situation, a mandatory buyout of her shares at their "fair market value" will better serve the minority's interests. That is so because, in valuing the minority's shares, most courts take account of the value of the corporation's economic goodwill.

At first glance, dissolution or a mandatory buyout may appear a sensible solution to oppression. But on closer examination, the problem is more complex. First, how might the forced sale of business assets affect the corporation's viability and thus other corporate constituents, such as employees or creditors? Second, will dissolution (or even a buyout) enable one shareholder group to acquire the business at a price unfair to others? Third, is the petitioning shareholder merely seeking to liquidate an investment or is there another, darker agenda?

The following case is widely viewed as the ground-breaking event for the "oppression" doctrine. Under the doctrine, courts have used the involuntary dissolution statute to create liquidity and financial rights for minority shareholders whose "reasonable expectations" have been frustrated by majority opportunism. The case raises a fundamental question whether courts should intervene when minority owners have failed to protect their interests by contract.

Matter of Kemp & Beatley, Inc.

473 N.E.2d 1173 (N.Y. 1984)

COOKE, CHIEF JUDGE.

When the majority shareholders of a close corporation award *de facto* dividends to all shareholders except a class of minority shareholders, such a policy may constitute "oppressive actions" and serve as a basis for an order made pursuant to section 1104–a of the Business Corporation Law dissolving the corporation. In the instant matter, there is sufficient evidence to support the lower courts' conclusion that the majority shareholders had altered a long-standing policy to distribute corporate earnings on the basis of stock ownership, as against petitioners only. Moreover, the courts did not abuse their discretion by concluding that dissolution was the only means by which petitioners could gain a fair return on their investment.

I

The business concern of Kemp & Beatley, incorporated under the laws of New York, designs and manufactures table linens and sundry tabletop items. The company's stock consists of 1,500 outstanding shares held by eight shareholders. Petitioner Dissin had been employed by the company for 42 years when, in June 1979, he resigned. Prior to resignation, Dissin served as vice-president and a director of Kemp & Beatley. Over the course of his employment, Dissin had acquired stock in the company and currently owns 200 shares.

Petitioner Gardstein, like Dissin, had been a long-time employee of the company. Hired in 1944, Gardstein was for the next 35 years involved in various aspects of the business including material procurement, product design, and plant management. His employment was terminated by the company in December 1980. He currently owns 105 shares of Kemp & Beatley stock.

Apparent unhappiness surrounded petitioners' leaving the employ of the company. Of particular concern was that they no longer received any distribution of the company's earnings. Petitioners considered themselves to be "frozen out" of the company; whereas it had been their experience when with the company to receive a distribution of the company's earnings according to their stockholdings, in the form of either dividends or extra compensation, that distribution was no longer forthcoming.

Gardstein and Dissin, together holding 20.33% of the company's outstanding stock, commenced the instant proceeding in June 1981, seeking dissolution of Kemp & Beatley pursuant to section 1104–a of the Business Corporation Law.

Their petition alleged "fraudulent and oppressive" conduct by the company's board of directors such as to render petitioners' stock "a virtually worthless asset." Supreme Court referred the matter for a hearing, which was held in March 1982.

N.Y. Bus. Corp. Law § 1104–a
Petition for Judicial Dissolution under Special Circumstances

(a) The holders of shares representing twenty percent or more of the votes of all outstanding shares of a corporation . . . no shares of which are listed on a national securities exchange or regularly quoted in an over-the-counter market . . . entitled to vote in an election of directors may present a petition of dissolution on one or more of the following grounds:

> (1) The directors or those in control of the corporation have been guilty of illegal, fraudulent or oppressive actions toward the complaining shareholders;

> (2) The property or assets of the corporation are being looted, wasted, or diverted for non-corporate purposes by its directors, officers or those in control of the corporation.

(b) The court, in determining whether to proceed with involuntary dissolution pursuant to this section, shall take into account:

> (1) Whether liquidation of the corporation is the only feasible means whereby the petitioners may reasonably expect to obtain a fair return on their investment; and

> (2) Whether liquidation of the corporation is reasonably necessary for the protection of the rights and interests of any substantial number of shareholders or of the petitioners.

Upon considering the testimony of petitioners and the principals of Kemp & Beatley, the referee concluded that "the corporate management has by its policies effectively rendered petitioners' shares worthless, and the only way petitioners can expect any return is by dissolution". Petitioners were found to have invested capital in the company expecting, among other things, to receive dividends or "bonuses" based upon their stock holdings. Also found was the company's "established buyout policy" by which it would purchase the stock of employee shareholders upon their leaving its employ.

The involuntary-dissolution statute (Business Corporation Law, § 1104–a) permits dissolution when a corporation's controlling faction is found guilty of "oppressive action" toward the complaining shareholders. The referee considered oppression to arise when "those in control" of the corporation "have acted in such a manner as to defeat those expectations of the minority stockholders which formed the basis of [their] participation in the venture." The expectations of petitioners that they would not be arbitrarily excluded from gaining a return on their investment and that their stock would be purchased by the corporation upon termination of employment, were deemed defeated by prevailing corporate policies. Dissolution was recommended in the referee's report, subject to giving respondent corporation an opportunity to purchase petitioners' stock.

Supreme Court confirmed the referee's report. It, too, concluded that due to the corporation's new dividend policy petitioners had been prevented from receiving any return on their investments. Liquidation of the corporate assets was found the only means by which petitioners would receive a fair return. The court considered judicial dissolution of a corporation to be "a serious and severe remedy." Consequently, the order of dissolution was conditioned upon the corporation's being permitted to purchase petitioners' stock. The Appellate Division affirmed, without opinion.

At issue in this appeal is the scope of section 1104–a of the Business Corporation Law. Specifically, this court must determine whether the provision for involuntary dissolution when the "directors or those in control of the corporation have been guilty of oppressive actions toward the complaining shareholders" was properly applied in the circumstances of this case. We hold that it was, and therefore affirm.

II

Judicially ordered dissolution of a corporation at the behest of minority interests is a remedy of relatively recent vintage in New York.

Section 1104–a (subd. [a], par. [1]) describes three types of proscribed activity: "illegal", "fraudulent", and "oppressive" conduct. The first two terms are familiar words that are commonly understood at law. The last, however, does not enjoy the same certainty gained through long usage. As no definition is provided by the statute, it falls upon the courts to provide guidance.

The statutory concept of "oppressive actions" can, perhaps, best be understood by examining the characteristics of close corporations and the Legislature's general purpose in creating this involuntary-dissolution statute. It is widely understood that, in addition to supplying capital to a contemplated or ongoing enterprise and expecting a fair and equal return, parties comprising the ownership of a close corporation may expect to be actively involved in its management and operation. The small ownership cluster seeks to "contribute their capital, skills, experience and labor" toward the corporate.

As a leading commentator in the field has observed: "Unlike the typical shareholder in the publicly held corporation, who may be simply an investor or a speculator and cares nothing for the responsibilities of management, the shareholder in a close corporation is a co-owner of the business and wants the privileges and powers that go with ownership. His participation in that particular corporation is often his principal or sole source of income. As a matter of fact, providing employment for himself may have been the principal reason why he participated in organizing the corporation. He may or may not anticipate an ultimate profit from the sale of his interest, but he normally draws very little from the corporation as dividends. In his capacity as an officer or employee of the corporation, he looks to his salary for the principal return on his capital investment, because earnings of a close corporation, as is well known, are distributed in major part in salaries, bonuses and retirement benefits." (O'Neal, CLOSE CORPORATIONS [2d ed.], § 1.07, at pp. 21–22)

Shareholders enjoy flexibility in memorializing these expectations through agreements setting forth each party's rights and obligations in corporate governance. In the absence of such an agreement, however, ultimate decision-making power respecting corporate policy will be reposed in the holders of a majority interest in the corporation (*see, e.g.,* Business Corporation Law, § 614, 708). A wielding of this power by any group controlling a corporation may serve to destroy a stockholder's vital interests and expectations.

As the stock of closely held corporations generally is not readily salable, a minority shareholder at odds with management policies may be without either a voice in protecting his or her interests or any reasonable means of withdrawing his or her investment. This predicament may fairly be considered the legislative concern underlying the provision at issue in this case; inclusion of the criteria that the corporation's stock not be traded on securities markets and that the complaining shareholder be subject to oppressive actions supports this conclusion.

Defining oppressive conduct as distinct from illegality in the present context has been considered in other forums. The question has been resolved by considering oppressive actions to refer to conduct that substantially defeats the "reasonable expectations" held by minority shareholders in committing their capital to the particular enterprise (*see, e.g., Exadaktilos v. Cinnaminson Realty Co.,* 167 N.J.Super. 141, 153–156, 400 A.2d 554, *affd.* 173 N.J.Super. 559, 414 A.2d 994). This concept is consistent with the apparent purpose underlying the provision under review. A shareholder who reasonably expected that ownership in the corporation would entitle him or her to a job, a share of corporate earnings, a place in corporate management, or some other form of security, would be oppressed in a very real sense when others in the corporation seek to defeat those expectations and there exists no effective means of salvaging the investment.

Given the nature of close corporations and the remedial purpose of the statute, this court holds that utilizing a complaining shareholder's "reasonable expectations" as a means of identifying and measuring conduct alleged to be oppressive is appropriate. A court considering a petition alleging oppressive conduct must investigate what the majority shareholders knew, or should have known, to be the petitioner's expectations in entering the particular enterprise. Majority conduct should not be deemed oppressive simply because the petitioner's subjective hopes and desires in joining the venture are not fulfilled. Disappointment alone should not necessarily be equated with oppression.

Rather, oppression should be deemed to arise only when the majority conduct substantially defeats expectations that, objectively viewed, were both reasonable under the circumstances and were central to the petitioner's decision to join the venture. It would be inappropriate, however, for us in this case to delineate the contours of the courts' consideration in determining whether directors have been guilty of oppressive conduct. As in other areas of the law, much will depend on the circumstances in the individual case.

The appropriateness of an order of dissolution is in every case vested in the sound discretion of the court considering the application (*see* Business Corporation Law, § 1111, subd. [a]). Under the terms of this statute, courts are instructed to consider both whether "liquidation of the corporation is the only feasible means" to protect the complaining shareholder's expectation of a fair return on his or her investment and whether dissolution "is reasonably necessary" to protect "the rights or interests of any substantial number of shareholders" not limited to those complaining (Business Corporation Law, § 1104–a, subd. [b], pars. [1], [2]). Implicit in this direction is that once oppressive conduct is found, consideration must be given to the totality of circumstances surrounding the current state of corporate affairs and relations to determine whether some remedy short of or other than dissolution constitutes a feasible means of satisfying both the petitioner's expectations and the rights and interests of any other substantial group of shareholders (*see, also,* Business Corporation Law, § 1111, subd. [b], par. [1]).

N.Y. Bus. Corp. Law § 1111
Judgment or Final Order of Dissolution

(a) In an action or special proceeding under this article if, in the court's discretion, it shall appear that the corporation should be dissolved, it shall make a judgment or final order dissolving the corporation.

(b) In making its decision, the court shall take into consideration the following criteria:

(1) In an action brought by the attorney-general, the interest of the public is of paramount importance.

(2) In a special proceeding brought by directors or shareholders, the benefit to the shareholders of a dissolution is of paramount importance.

(3) In a special proceeding brought under section 1104–a (Petition for judicial dissolution under special circumstances) dissolution is not to be denied merely because it is found that the corporate business has been or could be conducted at a profit.

By invoking the statute, a petitioner has manifested his or her belief that dissolution may be the only appropriate remedy. Assuming the petitioner has set forth a *prima facie* case of oppressive conduct, it should be incumbent upon the parties seeking to forestall dissolution to demonstrate to the court the existence of an adequate, alternative remedy. A court has broad latitude in fashioning alternative relief, but when fulfillment of the oppressed petitioner's expectations by these means is doubtful, such as when there has been a complete deterioration of relations between the parties, a court should not hesitate to order dissolution. Every order of dissolution, however, must be conditioned upon permitting any shareholder of the corporation to elect to purchase the complaining shareholder's stock at fair value (*see* Business Corporation Law, § 1118).

> ## N.Y. Bus. Corp. Law § 1118
> ## Purchase of Petitioner's Shares; Valuation
>
> (a) In any proceeding brought pursuant to section [1104–a], any other shareholder or shareholders or the corporation may, at any time within ninety days after the filing of such petition or at such later time as the court in its discretion may allow, elect to purchase the shares owned by the petitioners at their fair value and upon such terms and conditions as may be approved by the court.
>
> (b) If one or more shareholders or the corporation elect to purchase the shares owned by the petitioner but are unable to agree with the petitioner upon the fair value of such shares, the court may stay the proceedings brought pursuant to section 1104–a and determine the fair value of the petitioner's shares as of the day prior to the date on which such petition was filed, exclusive of any element of value arising from such filing but giving effect to any adjustment or surcharge found to be appropriate in the proceeding under section 1104–a.

One further observation is in order. The purpose of this involuntary dissolution statute is to provide protection to the minority shareholder whose reasonable expectations in undertaking the venture have been frustrated and who has no adequate means of recovering his or her investment. It would be contrary to this remedial purpose to permit its use by minority shareholders as merely a coercive tool. Therefore, the minority shareholder whose own acts, made in bad faith and undertaken with a view toward forcing an involuntary dissolution, give rise to the complained of oppression should be given no quarter in the statutory protection.

III

There was sufficient evidence presented at the hearing to support the conclusion that Kemp & Beatley had a long-standing policy of awarding *de facto* dividends based on stock ownership in the form of "extra compensation bonuses." Petitioners, both of whom had extensive experience in the management of the company, testified to this effect. Moreover, both related that receipt of this compensation, whether as true dividends or disguised as "extra compensation", was a known incident to ownership of the company's stock understood by all of the company's principals. Finally, there was uncontroverted proof that this policy was changed either shortly before or shortly after petitioners' employment ended. Extra compensation was still awarded by the company. The only difference was that stock ownership was no longer a basis for the payments; it was asserted that the basis became services rendered to the corporation. It was not unreasonable for the fact finder to have determined that this change in policy amounted to nothing less than an attempt to exclude petitioners from gaining any return on their investment through the mere recharacterization of distributions of corporate income. Under the circumstances of this case, there was no error in determining that this conduct constituted oppressive action within the meaning of section 1104–a of the Business Corporation Law.

Nor may it be said that Supreme Court abused its discretion in ordering Kemp & Beatley's dissolution, subject to an opportunity for a buy-out of petitioners' shares. After the referee had found that the controlling faction of the company was, in effect, attempting to "squeeze-out" petitioners by offering them no return on their investment and increasing other executive compensation, respondents, in opposing the report's confirmation, attempted only to controvert the factual basis of the report. They suggested no feasible, alternative remedy to the forced dissolution. In light of an apparent deterioration in relations between petitioners and the governing shareholders of Kemp & Beatley, it was not unreasonable for the court to have determined that a forced buy-out of petitioners' shares or liquidation of the corporation's assets was the only means by which petitioners could be guaranteed a fair return on their investments.

Accordingly, the order of the Appellate Division should be modified, with costs to petitioners-respondents, by affirming the substantive determination of that court but extending the time for exercising the option to purchase petitioners-respondents' shares to 30 days following this court's determination.

Points for Discussion

1. Judicial sympathy.

The oppression doctrine is mostly quite favorable to minority shareholders. The courts have exercised significant discretion in inferring extra-contractual financial and liquidity rights on behalf of minority shareholders. More often than not, courts have found that minority shareholders have "reasonable expectations" in continued employment or an ongoing return on their investment. Hasn't the pendulum swung too far? Isn't the reasonable expectations standard too vague, thus inviting disgruntled minority shareholders to coerce majority shareholders by threatening in bad faith to initiate lawsuits seeking dissolution?

2. Court-created liquidity right.

Under the reasonable expectations standard, courts have moved away from searching for egregious conduct by majority shareholders (the approach in fiduciary duty cases) toward considering the illiquid position of the minority shareholder. Thus, when majority action harms minority interests, courts have found oppression, even though the majority's action may have been justified by legitimate business purposes. For example, courts have used the oppression doctrine to award relief from employment termination without any explanation why an employer's traditional discretion to terminate employment for any reason should be limited in the close corporation setting.

3. Which reasonable expectations?

One question that permeates the oppression cases is when should reasonable expectations be gauged. Should it be at the time of investment or over the course of the corporation's life? Most courts have focused on the minority shareholder's expectations at the time he invested in the business. A "time of investment" focus, however, fails to recognize changes in post-investment expectations. Viewing the oppression doctrine as enforcing the bargain struck between majority and minority shareholders, it may make sense to see such "investment bargains" as arising throughout the minority's participation in the close corporation.

———

2. Remedies in Oppression Cases

A common remedy in oppression cases is for the majority to be ordered to buyout the minority's shares—a sort of equitable distribution following the corporate divorce. Although this is often seen as a clean solution, and the buyout remedy of MBCA § 14.34 seems to encourage it, the remedy may not necessarily fit the "reasonable expectations" that the court is supposedly enforcing.

The following case raises the question whether a buyout is appropriate when the expectations were that the minority shareholder would have an ongoing role and financial return from the corporation, not necessarily a buyout option. The case is from Massachusetts. Notice how far the state's close corporation law has come since *Donahue* and *Wilkes* were decided in the 1970s.

Brodie v. Jordan

857 N.E.2d 1076 (Mass. 2006)

COWIN, J.

In this case we are asked to consider the appropriate remedy for a "freeze-out" of a minority shareholder by the majority shareholders in a close corporation. The plaintiff, Mary M. Brodie, is a shareholder in Malden Centerless Grinding Co., Inc. (Malden). The defendants, Robert J. Jordan and David J. Barbuto (collectively, defendants), are the corporation's two other shareholders.

1. *Background.* Malden is a Massachusetts corporation that operates a small machine shop and produces metal objects such as ball bearings. The plaintiff's now deceased husband, Walter S. Brodie (Walter), was one of the founding members of the company and served as its president from 1979 to 1992. Barbuto has been a shareholder, a director, and the treasurer of the company since its formation. Jordan has been an employee of the company since 1975 and a shareholder, director, and officer since 1984; he is the one responsible for the day-to-day operation of the business. Beginning in 1984, Walter, Barbuto, and Jordan each held one-third of the shares of the corporation and all three served as directors. By 1988, however, Walter was no longer involved in the company's day-to-day operation and only met with Barbuto and Jordan two to three times each year. After Walter and the defendants began to disagree over various management issues, Walter made a number of requests that the company purchase his shares, but those requests were rejected.

The corporation has not paid any dividends to shareholders since 1989. As an employee, Jordan receives a salary at a rate set by the board of directors (Barbuto and himself). Jordan participates in a profit-sharing plan made available by the corporation and has the use of a company vehicle. Barbuto received director's fees from the corporation until 1998. He owns the building that houses Malden's corporate offices and receives rent from the corporation. Barbuto also owns a separate corporation, Barco Engineering, Inc., which is a customer of Malden and for which Malden regularly performs services on an open credit account. Walter received compensation from the company prior to 1992, and was paid a consultant's fee in 1994 and 1995. However, neither Walter nor the plaintiff appears to have received any compensation or other money from the corporation since 1995.

In 1992, Walter was voted out as president and director of Malden, and Jordan was elected president. Walter died in 1997. The plaintiff was appointed Walter's executrix and inherited his one-third interest in Malden. She attended a Malden shareholders' meeting in July, 1997, at which she nominated herself, through counsel, as a director, but Barbuto and Jordan voted against her election.

At this same meeting, the plaintiff asked Jordan and Barbuto to perform a valuation of the company so that she could ascertain the value of her shares, but such a valuation was never performed.

In 1998, the plaintiff filed the instant suit. Prior to and since that time, the defendants failed to provide her with various financial and operational company information that she requested. At the time of trial, the defendants had failed to hold an annual shareholder's meeting for the previous five years, and the plaintiff had not participated in any company decision-making.

2. *Discussion.* The parties do not dispute that Malden is a close corporation. "Stockholders in a close corporation owe one another substantially the same fiduciary duty in the operation of the enterprise that partners owe to one another" (footnotes omitted). *Donhaue v. Rodd Electrotype Co. of New England, Inc.*, 328 N.E.2d 505 (Mass. 1975).

Majority shareholders in a close corporation violate this duty when they act to "freeze out" the minority. We have defined freeze-outs by way of example:

> The squeezers [those who employ the freeze-out techniques] may refuse to declare dividends; they may drain off the corporation's earnings in the form of exorbitant salaries and bonuses to the majority shareholder-officers and perhaps to their relatives, or in the form of high rent by the corporation for property leased from majority shareholders; they may deprive minority shareholders of corporate offices and of employment by the company; they may cause the corporation to sell its assets at an inadequate price to the majority shareholders.

What these examples have in common is that, in each, the majority frustrates the minority's reasonable expectations of benefit from their ownership of shares.

We have previously analyzed freeze-outs in terms of shareholders' "reasonable expectations" both explicitly and implicitly. A number of other jurisdictions, either by judicial decision or by statute, also look to shareholders' "reasonable expectations" in determining whether to grant relief to an aggrieved minority shareholder in a close corporation.

In the present case, the Superior Court judge properly analyzed the defendants' liability in terms of the plaintiff's reasonable expectations of benefit. The judge found that the defendants had interfered with the plaintiff's reasonable expectations by excluding her from corporate decision-making, denying her access to company information, and hindering her ability to sell her shares in the open market. In addition, the judge's findings reflect a state of affairs in which the defendants were the only ones receiving any financial benefit from the corporation. The Appeals Court determined that the findings were warranted, and the defendants have not sought further appellate review with respect to liability. Thus, the only question before us is whether, on this record, the plaintiff was entitled to the remedy of a forced buyout of her shares by the majority. We conclude that she was not so entitled.

a. *Remedies for freeze-out of minority shareholder.* The proper remedy for a freeze-out is "to restore [the minority shareholder] as nearly as possible to the position [s]he would have been in had there been no wrongdoing." Because the wrongdoing in a freeze-out is the denial by the majority of the minority's reasonable expectations of benefit, it follows that the remedy should, to the extent possible, restore to the minority shareholder those benefits which she reasonably expected, but has not received because of the fiduciary breach.

If, for example, a minority shareholder had a reasonable expectation of employment by the corporation and was terminated wrongfully, the remedy may be reinstatement, back pay, or both. *See Wilkes v. Springside Nursing Home, Inc.*, 353 N.E.2d 657 (Mass. 1976) (awarding minority shareholder damages for lost employment). Similarly, if a minority shareholder has a reasonable expectation of sharing in company profits and has been denied this opportunity, she may be "entitled to participate in the favorable results of operations to the extent that those results have been wrongly appropriated by the majority." The remedy should neither grant the minority a windfall nor excessively penalize the majority.

b. *The Superior Court judge's remedy.* Courts have broad equitable powers to fashion remedies for breaches of fiduciary duty in a close corporation, and their choice of a particular remedy is reviewed for abuse of discretion. Here, the Superior Court judge ordered the defendants to buy out the plaintiff at the price of an expert's estimate of her share of the corporation, a remedy that no Massachusetts appellate court has previously authorized. The problem with this remedy is that it placed the plaintiff in a significantly *better* position than she would have enjoyed absent the wrongdoing, and well exceeded her reasonable expectations of benefit from her shares.

In this case, it is undisputed that neither the articles of organization nor any corporate bylaw obligates Malden or the defendants to purchase the plaintiff's shares. Thus, there is nothing in the background law, the governing rules of this particular close corporation, or any other circumstance that could have given the plaintiff a reasonable expectation of having her shares bought out.

In ordering the defendants to purchase the plaintiff's stock at the price of her share of the company, the judge created an artificial market for the plaintiff's minority share of a close corporation—an asset that, by definition, has little or no market value. Thus, the remedy had the perverse effect of placing the plaintiff in a position superior to that which she would have enjoyed had there been no wrongdoing.

c. *Considerations on remand.*   As we have indicated, the remedy for the defendants' breach of fiduciary duty is one that protects the plaintiff's reasonable expectations of benefit from the corporation and that compensates her for their denial in the past. For breaches visited upon the plaintiff resulting in deprivations that can be quantified, money damages will be the appropriate remedy. Prospective injunctive relief may be granted to ensure that the plaintiff is allowed to participate in company governance, and to enjoy financial or other benefits from the business, to the extent that her ownership interest justifies.

In devising a remedy that grants the plaintiff her reasonable expectations of benefit from stock ownership in Malden, the judge may consider the fact that the plaintiff has received no economic benefit from her shares. If the defendants have denied the plaintiff any return on her investment while "draining off the corporation's earnings" for themselves, the judge may consider, among other possibilities the propriety, of compelling the declaration of dividends.

Points for Discussion

1. Corporate or partnership approach?

Is it not reasonable for shareholders in a close corporation to expect that the corporation (or the other shareholders) will buy out their shares when the shareholder withdraws or dies? Certainly, in a partnership (absent an agreement otherwise) the withdrawal or death of a partner has the effect of dissociation, which may lead to a dissolution or a buyout. Why did the Massachusetts court in *Brodie v. Jordan* not treat the parties' relationship as one of an incorporated partnership?

2. Buyout expectation.

According to the court, the minority shareholder Mary Brodie had sought to have her shares valued so she could sell them. That is, she had an expectation that when her husband died and was no longer working in the business that the shares would be sellable. The other shareholders frustrated her attempts to obtain information to value her shares, perhaps on the assumption that once the shares had been valued, they or the corporation would be obligated to buy them back. Without a buyback option, what is a non-employee minority shareholder to expect from her investment?

3. Effect of court order.

An order compelling dividends, like a dissolution order, is rarely the end of the story. Instead, the court's order typically frames the settlement negotiations over how and how much the majority will pay for the minority's shares. If you were Mary Brodie, which would be more desirable—a buyout order or an order for the payment of dividends (past and future)?

4. Evolving judicial approach.

Over time, courts have come to understand that a dissolution order does not terminate the business. Instead, a dissolution order has the effect of forcing one camp (usually the majority) to buy out the other camp (usually the minority). Perhaps for this reason, orders that require a buyout on specified terms have become more common.

5. Fair value proceeding.

In recognition that a buyout order is a common remedy in oppression cases, the MBCA § 14.34 (borrowing from the New York dissolution statute) permits majority shareholders in a close corporation to avoid dissolution by electing to buy out at "fair value" the shares of a shareholder who petitions for involuntary dissolution. As the Official Comment explains, this provision gives the majority a "call" option as to the minority's shares to prevent strategic abuse of the dissolution procedure. Under this procedure, the shareholders who elect to purchase must give notice to the court within 90 days of the petition and then negotiate with the petitioning shareholder. If after 60 days the negotiations fail, the court must stay the proceedings for involuntary dissolution and order a buyout and determine the "fair value" of the petitioner's shares. If the petitioner had "probable grounds" for relief under the misconduct provisions of the involuntary dissolution statute, the award may include the petitioner's litigation costs (attorneys' and expert fees).

---

3. Valuation of Minority Shares

A key issue in oppression cases is the valuation of the complaining shareholder's shares in a court-ordered buyout or when the corporation (or another shareholder) exercises buyout rights under MBCA § 14.34. The buyout statute, like the appraisal statutes that apply to valuing dissenters' shares in a merger or other fundamental corporate transactions, requires that the minority's shares be purchased at "fair value."

One important question is whether minority shares should be discounted to reflect their lack of control and non-marketability. A strict market-based approach (what a willing outside buyer would pay in a fully-disclosed arms-length transaction) would take account of the reality that minority shares are not proportionally as valuable as majority shares, since they lack meaningful control rights. Although minority shares have a right to the proportional payment of any dividends or other distributions, the discretion to make such payments lies with the majority. Moreover, minority shares in a close corporation, unlike minority shares in a publicly traded corporation or majority shares of a close corporation, lack a ready market—further diminishing their value.

Should a court's buyout order in an oppression case discount minority shares to reflect their lack of control and non-marketability? The question is significant since valuation experts often opine that the lack of control can diminish the value of minority shares by 30–40% compared to majority shares, and the lack of marketability by another 30–40%. In all, minority shares may have a market value less than half of what a full-control, fully marketable ownership interest in the same business would command.

Practice Pointer

What other relief is available in cases of oppression? Besides ordering dissolution or a buyout, courts have used their inherent equity authority to devise other remedies in deadlock or "freeze out" cases: (1) order dissolution at a specified future date, unless the shareholders resolve their differences; (2) appoint a receiver to operate the corporation, until the differences are resolved; (3) appoint a "special fiscal agent" to report to the court on ongoing business operations and treatment of the minority; (4) retain jurisdiction for the protection of the minority shareholders; (5) order an accounting by the majority for funds allegedly misappropriated; (6) enjoin continuing acts of "oppressive" conduct; (7) order the declaration of dividends; (8) award damages to minority shareholders for "oppressive" conduct by the majority.

See Baker v. Commercial Body Builders, Inc., 507 P.2d 387 (Or. 1973) (listing forms of relief).

> ### Example 26.1
>
> Suppose a closely-held corporation—based on its earnings potential—has a value of $1,000,000. The corporation has two shareholders, A with 60% of the shares and B with 40%. A controls the board, and thus can fix salaries and set dividends. This control over cash flow, along with the other emoluments of majority control, make A's interest worth more than 60%—typically, 70% or even 80%. Thus, B has an economic interest worth only 20–30% of the overall business. That is, B can expect that his shares will be discounted from their proportional value.
>
> Likewise, B has fewer possibilities of selling his "non-control" shares, compared to A. Any buyer of B's shares, already apprehensive about assuming a minority position, would further worry about re-selling the interest—particularly since (by definition) there is no ready market for closely-held minority shares. That is, in addition to discounting for lack of control, the buyer would also discount for lack of marketability.

Most courts have concluded that it would be inequitable to apply a discount for lack of control or non-marketability in a close corporation valuation proceeding. *See* Chapter 8, Organizational Choices. Courts have explained that to allow the majority to buy out the minority at a discount would penalize the minority for exercising their statutory rights and tempt the majority to engage in activities creating dissension. That is, if the majority values the business at 100% of its earnings power or asset value, any discount applied to the minority's shares would reward the majority oppressor and penalize the minority.

> ### Example 26.2
>
> Suppose a corporation has two shareholders with equal 50/50 shares in the equity, with one shareholder managing the corporation. At least one court has ordered the buy out of the passive shareholder in favor of the shareholder who managed the business. *Balsamides v. Protameen Chemicals, Inc.*, 734 A.2d 721 (N.J. 1999) (resolving "feud" between two 50% shareholders).

As you can see, valuation of shares in a close corporation buyout is not just a matter of financial methodology but, rather, depends on what courts consider to be fair and equitable.

Test Your Knowledge

To assess your understanding of the Chapter 25 and 26 material in this module, click here to take a quiz.

MODULE IX – STOCK TRADING

CHAPTER 27

Securities Markets

The next three chapters are part of a module on stock trading. This topic might especially pique your interest. Stock trading is the stuff of feature films, high-society gossip, and Internet chat. Which stocks should you buy? Which should you sell? And what are the basic legal rules?

This chapter briefly introduces you to securities markets, with a focus on how corporations issue shares in public stock trading markets. The next chapter amplifies our earlier discussion of shareholder litigation by identifying the key elements relevant to class actions brought by investors claiming securities fraud. In the final chapter of this module we discuss the "hot topic" of insider trading: when is it illegal to buy or sell shares using inside information about a corporation?

We start with an overview of securities markets, including a discussion of the theory of market efficiency and some historical background and context. Then we turn to the federal registration requirement for securities offerings, and some of its exceptions.

Of necessity, we will only scratch the surface of these issues. Securities regulation courses cover more details about these topics, in greater depth. That said, we offer this background about the securities markets and their regulation in the hope you will better understand the ways corporations are regulated and to put into context the chapters that follow on securities fraud and insider trading.

Business Lingo

"Going public" refers to a private corporation's decision to issue securities to the public and thereby be subject to the system of federal regulation of securities markets. In contrast, "going private" refers to the mirror opposite: the decision by a public corporation to go back to being a private corporation. Most of the world's largest corporations are public (their shares are publicly traded on stock exchanges), but there are some prominent examples of large private corporations. For example, Koch Industries, Cargill, and IKEA are privately owned and a number of startups have grown to significant size before being acquired by other companies or going public.

The central message of this chapter is that securities markets are governed primarily by federal law and involve primarily public corporations. Private corporations, sometimes referred to as close or closely held, issue securities, but those securities do not trade in public securities markets. The distinction between public and private corporations already has been important in this course, but now it comes to occupy center stage. Indeed, a private corporation's decision about whether to "go public" or a public corporation's decision about whether to "go private" is among the most important in the corporation's life. The decision is driven by the benefits and costs of accessing the public securities markets and operating as a public company.

A. Overview of Securities Markets

We begin by discussing two important background issues: market efficiency and the historical background of the securities markets. Market efficiency relates to how the securities markets generate prices. Understanding some history and context of securities markets also should help you understand some of the issues that follow in this module.

1. Market Efficiency

One important idea that permeates all three chapters in this module is the notion of "market efficiency." The idea is that information known to some participants in a market is impounded into the market price so it's as though all participants are aware of the information at the same time. Participants in securities markets absorb information from news sources, government reports, company disclosures, and stock trading patterns. They use this data to estimate future cash flows and the risk that such cash flows may not materialize and thus to establish the current price at which they are willing to buy or sell the stock. That is, they engage in a constant ongoing process of valuing corporate securities using the techniques we described in Chapter 11, Numeracy for Lawyers. When they decide a stock is undervalued, their demand to buy the stock leads to an increase in price (in general, greater demand in a market results in higher prices). Conversely, when participants sell stock that they believe is overvalued, their selling depresses the price. Thus, the information that market participants absorb from various sources is impounded into the price of the company's stock.

Of all the existing information about a company, how much actually is impounded into stock prices? If the stock market is completely "informationally efficient"—that is, it reflects *all* information, *both publicly available and privately held*, about risks and cash flows, we would expect that trading by insiders would not be profitable because whatever information an insider possessed would already be reflected in the stock price. We would also predict that dissemination of false or misleading information about a public company would cause no harm because the market price would reflect that the misinformation was false or misleading.

Although there is substantial evidence that stock markets in the United States respond to new information almost instantaneously (for example, company earnings announcements are sometimes read by computers and trading happens in less than a second) and with relative efficiency (new prices remain stable until new information changes them), they are not perfectly informationally efficient. Corporate insiders, who have access to information about anticipated changes in their companies' businesses, can earn abnormal returns (that is returns in excess of market averages, adjusted for risk) when they trade their companies' stock. Nevertheless, because of the relatively high degree of informational efficiency, non-insiders generally cannot expect to earn abnormal returns by trading on the basis of publicly available information. This is an important point: it means (and many studies confirm) that even sophisticated investors, such as mutual fund managers, generally cannot and do not outperform the market after expenses—except through luck. As a result, many pension plans and even individual investors have abandoned the hope of beating the market and have turned to low-cost index funds, which simply hold the stocks in a market segment, such as the S&P 500, at the lowest possible cost. In fact, the largest institutional investors today are Blackrock and Vanguard, both offering mostly low-cost index funds.

There is a good deal of evidence that U.S. public stock markets are relatively efficient at impounding publicly-available information. The securities laws are built on this assumption, requiring that companies disclose relevant information when they sell securities to investors and when their securities are traded in public stock markets. In this way, market intermediaries have enough company-specific information to ensure that market prices reflect relevant information—and thus that investors are trading at that price. Likewise, the securities antifraud rules assume that if investors buy or sell when the market price is skewed by materially false or misleading information, the investors will suffer losses because, when the truth is revealed, the market can be expected to re-price the security to reflect the true information.

How informationally efficient are U.S. securities markets? Opinions vary, although the market crisis of 2007–08 created some challenges for the proponents of market efficiency. For example, consider the chart below of the share price of Citigroup, one of the country's largest bank and one that nearly collapsed during the crisis.

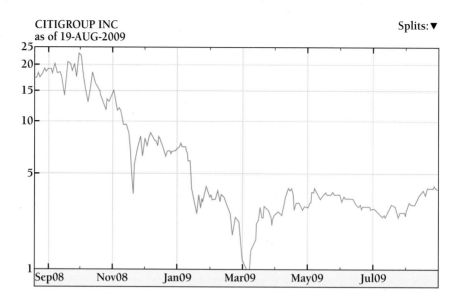

What story might support such wild fluctuations in Citigroup's stock price? Some critics of market efficiency argue that these swings did not reflect new information, but instead were the result of investor panic—that is, the markets sometimes don't just process information about future returns and risks, but instead are driven by pangs of human fear and greed. Some have argued that Citigroup was essentially insolvent as of fall 2008, if not earlier, so that its share price should have been near zero, but that the hope of a government rescue buoyed the share price. Then the decline of its stock price to near zero during early March 2009 may have reflected investors' views that a rescue package was unlikely or perhaps the fear that the country's banking system was in a free-fall, with Citibank leading the way. The subsequent increase in stock price may have been due to changing expectations about a government rescue or the hope that capitalism will always right itself. Pause for a second: how do you interpret the chart?

> ### Go Online
>
> We are not just picking on Citigroup here. Go to http://finance.yahoo.com and look at the stock price fluctuations of just about any company during this period. What accounts for the fall and subsequent rise?

2. Securities Markets Background

Depending on how you define a security, there have been securities markets for hundreds, or perhaps thousands, of years. In Europe, merchants traded financial interests in a range of business ventures. Over time, this trading became centrally located. For example, in the seventeenth century the Dutch traded shares of companies at the Amsterdam Stock Exchange.

In the United States, securities trading began in New York in 1792, when two dozen stock traders signed the "Buttonwood Agreement" (under a buttonwood tree on Wall Street). During the following century, some trading moved indoors, where a few brokers had rented space; other brokers continued to trade outdoors, on the curb of Wall Street. One of the indoor groups established the organization now known as the New York Stock Exchange, or the NYSE, and it became the premier location for trading securities of U.S. corporations.

After the stock market crash of 1929, investment in all kinds of securities plummeted. During the following three years, reports emerged about many massive corporate frauds. Congress convened a set of hearings on "Stock Exchange Practices" to investigate some of the most wide-ranging scandals, particularly the fraudulent sale of shares by corporations founded by Samuel Insull and Ivar Kreuger, two of the most notorious financiers of the era. By 1933, the American public was outraged about these frauds and was losing faith in securities markets.

Federal securities laws. In response, Congress enacted the Securities Act of 1933, a federal securities law aimed at restoring public confidence in corporate securities and the stock markets in general. To reassure investors of the soundness of corporate securities, Congress created a kind of "truth in securities" system for the issuance of securities to the public. Like today's requirement that food producers attach a label describing their product's ingredients, calorie count, and fat content, the Securities Act of 1933 requires issuers of securities to "register" their stock

Food for Thought

How can so many smart people, with so many tools and so much information, be so fundamentally mistaken? One answer is that investors are simply trying to anticipate what other investors believe particular securities are worth. Fundamental analysis of risk and return has become a game of out-guessing the crowd. As John Maynard Keynes observed after the stock market crash of 1929:

> Professional investment may be likened to those newspaper competitions in which the competitors have to pick the six prettiest faces from a hundred photographs, the prize being awarded to the competitor whose choice most nearly corresponds to the average preference of the competitors as a whole; so that each competitor has to pick, not those faces which he himself finds prettiest, but those which he thinks likeliest to catch the fancy of the other competitors, all of whom are looking at the problem from the same point of view.

John Maynard Keynes, THE GENERAL THEORY OF EMPLOYMENT, INTEREST AND MONEY 156 (1936).

issuance and provide investors with detailed information about the company, its management, its plans and finances, and the securities being offered. The theme of the 1933 Securities Act is disclosure, built on a philosophy that information will help protect investors and promote confidence in the integrity of the markets.

In 1934, Congress adopted a companion statute, the Securities Exchange Act of 1934, which created the Securities and Exchange Commission (SEC) to administer the 1933 Securities Act. The 1934 Act also creates periodic disclosure obligations, and regulates the buying and selling of securities by investors in securities trading markets. It contains the prohibitions against fraud that form the basis for the securities fraud class actions we describe in Chapter 28 and the insider trading cases we will read in Chapter 29.

These federal laws began a dramatic shift away from state regulation of securities markets. Originally, § 18

Today, trading of stocks in the United States is roughly split between the NYSE and NASDAQ (the National Association of Securities Dealers Automated Quotations). The primary difference between the NYSE and NASDAQ is the method of trading. On the NYSE, shares are traded in a "specialist" system, where buy and sell orders are routed through an individual, the "specialist," who stands on the floor of the exchange and acts as an intermediary for buyers and sellers. On the NASDAQ, shares are traded in an "over the counter" system, where dealer members post online the prices at which they will buy and sell securities, and other dealers then transact online at those prices. Older, more established firms tend to list their shares on the NYSE, while newer technology firms tend to prefer the NASDAQ.

of the 1933 Securities Act expressly preserved state securities laws, better known as "blue sky" laws after (some say) an early judicial opinion condemning "speculative schemes which have no more basis than so many feet of blue sky." Blue sky laws generally prohibited fraudulent statements in connection with the sales of securities and also required the registration of securities with a state regulator before they could be sold or traded. Because of the overlapping federal and state requirements, when large public offerings were sold in many states, someone (usually counsel for the underwriters) had to "blue sky" the issue to be sure it complied with the laws of every state in which securities were to be offered.

In 1996, Congress responded to claims that state "blue sky" laws imposed significant costs on U.S. capital formation with few benefits and amended § 18 of the 1933 Securities Act to preempt state regulation for many securities offerings. Specifically, § 18 now precludes state registration requirements for many offerings of securities, including securities that will be listed on the NYSE or NASDAQ and securities that will be exempt from registration under SEC rules as private placements (which we discuss below).

However, some powers are still available to the states. Section 18 still allows states to bring antifraud proceedings, and many state attorneys general do. States also may require that issuers of securities not listed on an exchange pay fees and file documents "substantially similar" to those filed with the SEC. In addition, states may require registration of offerings subject to the intrastate exemption and small-offering exemptions (which we also discuss below).

Example 27.1

XYZ, Inc. is a publicly-traded company that went public many years ago. Investor Group Ltd. has proposed to take XYZ private by merging XYZ into a subsidiary of Investor Group, with the shareholders of XYZ receiving cash for their shares. The XYZ board accepts the merger and, after full disclosure, the XYZ shareholders vote to approve it.

The result of this "going private" transaction is that XYZ (provided its debt is not listed on a stock exchange) is no longer publicly-traded and subject to the reporting requirements of the 1934 Act. Not only does this reduce the company's regulatory costs, but it also allows it to operate without having to reveal company information to the public, including competitors.

Broker agreements. In addition to federal and state law, securities trading also is governed by contract. Most of you will buy and sell securities at some point, and your likely entry point will be through a broker (whether at an office or online). When you open an account to trade securities, the broker will require that you sign an agreement. Few people read these agreements carefully, just as few people read the financial statements and filings of the companies whose shares they buy. The agreements are mostly boilerplate, but they include some important "private law" provisions that govern much securities trading. For example, brokerage agreements typically provide that disputes will be subject to arbitration, not litigation.

Another important, but often overlooked, provision in many brokerage agreements relates to the voting of corporate shares. In simple terms, private contracts in securities markets frequently remove the ability of shareholders to vote the shares they hold. This disenfranchisement would be a surprise to many shareholders, if they were aware of it.

Here's how it happens. When you open a brokerage account, you have several alternatives, some of which include a provision permitting brokers to lend out your shares. As a result, and often without your knowledge, your broker will take the shares in your account and lend them to someone else.

As long as your shares are loaned out, you technically do not hold the rights, including the voting rights, associated with those shares. In order to vote those shares, you would have to ask your broker to recall the loaned out shares and put them back in your account. Most people are not aware when their shares are loaned-out and do not understand the consequences. The shares that have been loaned out can be sold to another buyer, and that buyer—not the original holder of the shares—will hold the rights associated with those shares. Large institutional investors demand that brokers pay them for the right to lend out their shares, but individual investors frequently permit brokers to lend their shares for free. Individuals often do not read their brokerage agreements, which give this permission, or realize that their brokers can make significant profits by lending out their customer's shares.

This chapter, however, is not meant to be a deep dive into the complex, ever-changing securities markets. Instead, we return to our overview of how the securities markets are regulated. Since the 1930s, the linchpin of securities regulation in the United States has been the requirement that the offering of securities must be registered before they can be sold. We turn now to this important requirement.

B. Registration Requirement for Public Offerings

In general, the offering of securities in the United States must be registered. This "registration requirement" marks a key distinction between public and private corporations. The central provision is § 5 of the 1933 Securities Act.

Section 5 does three things. First, it prohibits any person from offering any security unless a registration statement for that security has been filed with the SEC. Second, it permits sales of the security only after the registration statement has become effective—where the SEC holds the "starting gun." Third, it requires that a "statutory prospectus" (which includes the most important information in the registration statement) be delivered to the buyer before or when the security is sold. Schedule A to the 1933 Securities Act, as amplified and interpreted by SEC regulations, sets forth the information an issuer selling securities to the public must include in the registration statement.

The penalty for violating § 5 is harsh. An unregistered offering that fails to satisfy an exemption creates strict liability. Under § 12(a)(1) of the 1933 Securities Act, every investor is allowed to rescind her purchase and receive a refund plus interest. In such an action, the burden of proof rests with the person seeking to establish the exemption. In other words, a corporation and its advisors issue unregistered securities at their peril.

The SEC provides corporations and their lawyers with guidance regarding registration. According to the SEC, the purpose of registration is to require enough disclosure to enable investors and their intermediaries to make informed judgments about whether to buy a corporation's securities. The SEC reviews registration statements in an effort to ensure that corporations issuing securities *ex ante* disclose required information. However, the SEC does not guarantee the accuracy of the information contained in a registration statement or a prospectus. Instead, the securities laws, particularly the system of securities litigation, give investors the right to recovery if a corporation made incomplete or inaccurate disclosures. This is why securities litigation *ex post* is such an important part of securities markets.

It is expensive for corporations to prepare and file registration statements, and a corporation's initial public offering, or IPO, is an especially costly and rigorous process. In addition to rules promulgated under the Securities Act of 1933, the SEC also includes information on its website, as well as registration forms that are designed to minimize the burden and expense of complying with registration requirements. In general, the registration forms require that corporations describe their properties and business, the securities offered for sale, their management, and also their financial statements, which must be certified by independent accountants.

Registration statements and prospectuses become available online on the SEC's massive website shortly after being filed with the SEC. The SEC staff then begins reviewing and examining the filings to determine whether they comply with federal disclosure requirements. Once the SEC declares the registration statement "effective," the securities may be sold.

Take Note!

It is worth reading one part of § 5 to see how important federal regulation has become to securities markets. The federal power to require the registration of securities is broad and stems from the impact of securities on interstate commerce and the use of the mails. Indeed, the title of § 5 is "Prohibitions Relating to Interstate Commerce and the Mails." How far does subpart (a) of § 5 reach?

a. Sale or delivery after sale of unregistered securities

Unless a registration statement is in effect as to a security, it shall be unlawful for any person, directly or indirectly—

1. to make use of any means or instruments of transportation or communication in interstate commerce or of the mails to sell such security through the use or medium of any prospectus or otherwise; or

2. to carry or cause to be carried through the mails or in interstate commerce, by any means or instruments of transportation, any such security for the purpose of sale or for delivery after sale.

As an example of the guidance provided by the SEC, we have included some excerpts from a "question and answer" document designed for small businesses contemplating "going public." In reality, most initial public offering involve large businesses, not small ones—think Facebook in 2012 or Lyft in 2019—but the SEC guidance is designed to reach a wide audience and to encourage small businesses to raise capital in the public markets.

Securities and Exchange Commission
Information for Small Businesses
<u>Going Public</u>

Should my company "go public"?

Companies go public for a number of reasons, and these reasons can be different for each company. Some of the reasons include:

- To raise capital and potentially broaden opportunities for future access to capital.

- To increase liquidity for a company's stock, which may allow owners and employees to more easily sell stock.

- To acquire other businesses with the public company's stock.

- To attract and compensate employees with public company stock and stock-option compensation.

- To create publicity, brand awareness, and prestige for a company.

Before deciding to become a public company, there are important factors to consider:

- Your company's public offering will take time and money to accomplish.

- Your company will take on significant new obligations, such as filing SEC reports and keeping shareholders and the market informed about the company's business operations, financial condition, and management, which will take a significant amount of time for your company's management and result in additional costs.

- Your company and you may be liable if these new legal obligations are not satisfied.

- You may lose some flexibility in managing your company's affairs, particularly when public shareholders must approve your company's actions.

- Information about your company, such as financial statements and disclosures about material contracts, customers and suppliers, will become available to the general public (including your competitors).

What is a registration statement?

Registration statements have two principal parts

- Part I is the prospectus, the legal offering or "selling" document. Your company—the "issuer" of the securities—must describe in the prospectus important facts about its business operations, financial condition, results of operations, risk factors, and management. It must also include audited financial statements. The prospectus must be delivered to everyone who buys the securities, as well as anyone who is made an offer to purchase the securities.

- Part II contains additional information that the company does not have to deliver to investors but must file with the SEC, such as copies of material contracts.

The SEC's guidance includes links to <u>Form S-1</u>, the standard form used to prepare a registration statement, along with information about how to prepare non-financial disclosures, in what is known as <u>Regulation S-K</u>, and information about required financial statements in <u>Regulation S-X</u>. The details of these disclosures are covered in specialized courses on securities regulation, but here are some examples of the kind of information that is required:

- a description of the company's business, properties, and competition;

- a description of the risks of investing in the company;

- a discussion and analysis of the company's financial results and financial condition as seen through the eyes of management;

- the identity of the company's officers and directors and their compensation;

- a description of material transactions between the company and its officers, directors, and significant shareholders;

- a description of material legal proceedings involving the company and its officers and directors;

- a description of the company's material contracts;

- a description of the securities being offered;

- the plan for distributing the securities;

- the intended use of the proceeds of the offering; and

- financial statements prepared in accordance with generally accepted accounting principles in the United States and audited by an independent certified public accountant registered with the Public Company Accounting Oversight Board or "PCAOB."

Points for Discussion

1. Why registration?

What is the purpose of the registration requirement? Do you think the information the SEC requires accomplishes this purpose? What would happen to the securities markets if corporations were permitted to sell securities without registration?

2. Federal vs. state.

Much of corporate law is about state law. Yet the securities markets are governed primarily by federal law. Why the difference? Is the federalization of securities market regulation good policy?

C. Exemptions from Registration

You might think of the federal securities registration requirement as a piece of Swiss cheese: the holes can be just as important as the solid. Federal securities laws requires registration, but also provides several exemptions from registration. We spend the rest of this chapter describing some of these exemptions.

From the beginning Congress recognized that a strict registration rule without exceptions would be overbroad and unworkable. There isn't an adequate federal interest to justify the time and expense of registration for offerings that are relatively small or local, and thus adequately regulated at the state level. Further, there was a recognition that sophisticated investors who "can fend for themselves" do not need (or deserve) the expensive protection provided by registration. The statute thus provides several important exemptions. Keep in mind, though, that even offerings that are exempt from registration remain subject to the anti-fraud provisions of the securities laws.

Sections 3 and 4 of the 1933 Securities Act effectively focus the registration requirement on primarily large issuances of securities to public investors. We first cover the exemption for stock market trading—that is, trading by persons other than the issuer, underwriter, or dealer. This is the most widely used exemption, although it remains the least discussed, even here. Then we turn to the private placement exemption, the most important exemption for companies (large and small) seeking to raise capital from sophisticated private investors. This gets a good bit more coverage here. Next are the exemptions for intrastate offerings and small offerings, including a new exemption created by Congress in 2012 for small online crowdfunding offerings. As we go through these exemptions, you'll notice that we highlight which ones are not subject to state "blue sky" registration under preemptions created by Congress.

1. Exemption for Stock Trading

Section 4(a)(1) contains the broadest registration exemption. Without it, securities trading markets would grind to a halt. Section 4(a)(1) exempts from registration "transactions by any person other than the issuer, underwriter, or dealer." This exemption permits trading in previously issued securities by most individuals, people like you and your classmates, who likely are not issuers, underwriters, or dealers. The § 4(a)(1) exemption is not complicated, but it warrants its own subpoint because it is used so frequently, even though few of the people using it recognize they are doing so. If nothing else, you can use your knowledge of the § 4(a)(1) exemption to stump your friends and relatives who trade securities without registering their sales.

> **FYI**
>
> The numbering of the registration exemptions under the 1933 Securities Act was changed by Congress in the JOBS Act of 2012. Although securities *aficionados* continue to refer to § 4(1) and § 4(2), these exemptions are technically now § 4(a)(1) and § 4(a)(2). We are going with the modern numbering, even though it still seems a bit strange to us—and most likely to your professor.

2. Statutory Private Placement Exemption

The private placement exemption in § 4(a)(2)—a total of nine words—is the most important for capital formation, and so we ask you to spend more time with it. Section 4(a)(2) exempts from registration "transactions by an issuer not involving any public offering." It is generally known as the "private placement exemption." Factors under which an offering is considered exempt under § 4(a)(2) include: whether investors in the offering are sufficiently sophisticated so that they do not need the protection of registration requirements; whether the investors have access to all material investment information.

Example 27.2

Suppose you represent JKL Corporation, a closely-held business that needs additional capital. You help prepare a private placement memo that lays out information about the company and an offering to sophisticated investors. You prepare a cover letter for the investors that describes the offering's exemption from registration.

Your participation in the marketing of the private placement makes you a "statutory seller" under § 12(a)(1) and thus liable to investors if the placement turns out not to be exempt from registration. A sales effort to just one unqualified investor could ruin the whole exemption. For this reason, lawyers and accountants (and other professionals) are reluctant to do anything that might be seen as selling a private placement.

Section 4(a)(2) is important to both small and large businesses. Without the exemption, small closely-held corporations would have to undertake an expensive registration process when issuing stock to corporate insiders, even though they are the ones who best know the business. And larger corporations that raise money from institutional investors would have to register the securities even when the investors have the means privately to obtain all the information they need from the issuer.

Because the statutory private placement exemption creates a number of uncertainties for issuers, the SEC promulgated a safe harbor rule (Rule 506, Regulation D) that defines when an investor is "accredited" and thus sufficiently sophisticated to qualify for the statutory exemption. Rule 506 offerings sold only to accredited investors can be broadly advertised, thus allowing the issuer to access national (and international) investors who meet the SEC accredited-investor standards. Offerings under Rule 506 are also exempt from state "blue sky" registration under a preemption provision added by Congress in 1996. For these reasons, most capital formation in this country now happens through Rule 506.

There are a number of other exemptions. For example, Section 3(a)(11), the "intrastate offering" exemption, exempts from registration any security that is part of an issue *offered and sold* exclusively to "persons resident within" one state by a corporation "incorporated by and doing business within" that state. One errant offer to an out-of-state investor subjects the whole offering to rescission liability under § 12(a)(1). As a result, the intrastate offering exemption is not frequently used.

There is also a series of SEC-designed small offering exemptions that create safe harbors from registration for securities offerings that might not satisfy the private placement exemption. Regulation A creates a kind of "mini-registration" process for offerings of up to $50 million in a 12-month period by nonpublic companies that are not disqualified because of criminal or regulatory misdeeds. The exemption, now known as Reg A+ to distinguish it from its anemic predecessor, has become popular for startup companies unwilling to pay for a full-blown IPO. Instead of filing a registration statement, the issuer prepares and files an "offering circular" with the SEC before commencing the offering. The offering circular is a simplified disclosure document that the issuer can prepare either in a registration-type or question-and-answer format. Financial information is required, but for Reg A+ offerings of less than $20 million it need not be audited. Importantly, Reg A+ offerings that are limited to sophisticated "accredited" investors (or to non-accredited investors subject to certain income and net worth caps) are exempt from state "blue sky" registration. And securities purchased in a Reg A+ offering can be re-sold—thus allowing for trading markets in securities issued under Reg A+—subject only to the condition that the issuer provides ongoing disclosures.

Another small offering exemption, meant to coordinate with state "blue sky" laws, can be found in Rule 504 of Reg D. The SEC promulgated Reg D in 1982, and revised it significantly in 2016, to facilitate smaller offerings (now up to $5 million) by nonpublic companies seeking to sell to a broad range of investors without the expense and delays of an initial public offering. General advertising and the ability of investors to re-sell their securities is permitted if the Rule 504 offering is registered under a state "blue sky" law that requires a state filing and a disclosure document for investors, or if the offering is limited to accredited investors.

Finally, the SEC—as authorized by Congress in the Jumpstart Our Business Startups Act of 2012, also known as the JOBS Act—created in 2016 an exemption for online securities offerings made to public investors. This exemption, aimed at giving small businesses direct access to capital from small investors, allows for financial "crowdfunding." Like popular websites, such as Kickstarter, that allow many contributors to fund social, literary, technological and artistic causes, the SEC's crowdfunding exemption is meant to allow small nonpublic companies to raise up to $1 million per year from small investors, subject to individual caps that vary depending on the annual income/net worth of the investor. The offering can only be made online, and only through a securities firm's website or a registered crowdfunding portal. The SEC exemption specifies the information about the issuer and the offering that investors must receive, with the requirement that for offerings above $500,000 the issuer's financials must be audited by a CPA. Importantly, securities purchased in a crowdfunding are not subject to resale restrictions, and states are preempted from requiring "blue sky" registration of the offering.

* * *

As you can tell, the SEC exemptions are a labyrinth of definitions, categories, and conditions. They're really a lot of fun to learn. This chapter provides a basic overview and prepares you for a deeper dive in more advanced courses.

Points for Discussion

1. Why exemptions?

What do you think of the blanket requirement of registration, with its many and encompassing exemptions? Would it have been better policy for Congress or the SEC to identify which categories of securities offerings must be registered and leave the others alone?

2. Sophistication and size.

Do the exemptions do a good job of excluding those offerings for which full-blown SEC registration might be overkill—that is, relatively small offerings and offerings targeted at sophisticated investors? Do you agree with the premise that sophistication and offering size should be important in determining whether securities offerings should be registered with the SEC? Why or why not?

3. Crowdfunding anyone?

Despite the opening provided by Congress and the SEC for small companies to directly access investors online, financial crowdfunding has not taken off. Since the SEC's crowdfunding rules were promulgated in 2016, relatively few companies have raised new capital using this exemption. What explains this? Perhaps the problem is a lack of market efficiency. Would you invest in a small company where no professional intermediaries are involved in setting the price of the offered securities? Remember our look at business valuation (Chapter 11, Numeracy for Corporate Lawyers) and ask yourself who in an exempt crowdfunding can be counted on to undertake a reliable valuation of the offered securities? Or perhaps the requirements on crowdfunding portals adds transaction costs that decreases the utility to companies that are crowdfunding for less than $1 million? How should investor protection and capital formation goals be balanced?

CHAPTER 28

Securities Fraud

> ### Securities Exchange Act of 1934
> ### § 10 – Manipulative and Deceptive Devices
>
> It shall be unlawful for any person . . .
>
> (b) to use or employ, in connection with the purchase or sale of any security, any manipulative or deceptive device or contrivance in contravention of such rules and regulations as the Commission may prescribe.

In the last chapter, we saw how federal regulation requires companies in public securities markets to provide investors with information in SEC-mandated disclosure documents. What happens when that disclosure is false or misleading? This chapter addresses that question, focusing on the ability of investors who have traded on the basis of company misinformation to bring an action to recover their trading losses from the company and insiders (or others) responsible for the deception.

These actions can be brought by the government or by private parties, typically as a class, and arise mostly under § 10(b) of the Securities Exchange Act of 1934 (set forth above). Rule 10b–5 promulgated under § 10(b) compels honest and full disclosure in all securities-related communications. It creates an important shareholder protection against management deception to securities markets. The possibility of liability for making false or misleading statements of material fact disciplines corporate management perhaps as much as state-based fiduciary duties. In fact, many corporate executives say they worry more about being sued for securities fraud under federal law than for breach of fiduciary duties under state law.

Rule 10b–5 has created a sprawling area of law. In fact, there are whole law courses devoted to the topic of securities fraud under Rule 10b–5. For our purposes we will look at how the Supreme Court has shaped the contours of securities fraud class actions (which we abbreviate here for ease of reference as SFCAs). These lawsuits not only are part of the regulatory infrastructure of U.S. stock markets, but they guide management of public companies (especially officers) in their communications to securities markets and thus their dealings with shareholders.

This chapter gives an overview of how federal SFCAs operate and their role in corporate governance. First, we look at the basic contours of private actions under Rule 10b–5—as crafted both by the Supreme Court and by important legislative reforms. Second, we consider three crucial elements of an SFCA: the materiality of the alleged misrepresentations, the scienter (or state of mind) of the defendant, and the reliance of shareholders in public markets on the misrepresentations. In particular, you will notice how the Supreme Court has created a separate, non-overlapping body of disclosure law that regulates corporate governance as a co-equal with state fiduciary law.

Practice Pointer

Securities fraud class actions (SFCAs) have been the principal tool used by plaintiffs' lawyers to vindicate shareholder interests in such scandals as Enron, WorldCom, and the subprime mortgage debacle. For example, settlements in Enron, against investment banks that sold the company's debt securities without fully investigating or disclosing the company's precarious finances, totaled more than $6 billion.

In addition, plaintiffs' lawyers have increasingly sought not only money damages as compensation on behalf of deceived investors, but also concessions from management to make internal reforms to corporate governance. In fact, other than state fiduciary review of corporate acquisitions and lapses in board oversight, management misdeeds in public companies are mostly regulated by federal disclosure law and securities fraud litigation.

A. Private Securities Fraud Actions Under Rule 10b–5

The federal courts, with the Supreme Court showing the way, have used Rule 10b–5 to create an impressive judge-made regime against securities fraud. Not only are press releases and disclosure documents filed by public companies subject to the rule's prohibition against false and misleading statements, but so are information in private securities transactions, proposed corporate mergers, and even activities by broker-dealers that harm their customers.

1. Judge-Made Elements

Over time, federal courts have articulated the elements of a private cause of action under Rule 10b–5. Basically, any purchaser or seller of a security can sue any person (including a corporation) that (1) makes materially false or misleading statements (2) with an intent to deceive (3) upon which the plaintiff relies (4) causing losses to the plaintiff. The action can be brought as a class action, thus consolidating many smaller claims into one large lawsuit. The action must be brought in federal court, subject to a statute of limitations that runs for 5 years after the fraud (though within two years after the plaintiff has notice of the fraud).

This all sounds straightforward, and the basics of a 10b–5 action are. But there are numerous subtleties and complexities. Here is a summary of the major Supreme Court decisions and their holdings:

Issue	Case	Holding
Who is a plaintiff?	Blue Chip Stamps v. Manor Drug Stores (1975)	Only actual "purchasers and sellers" have standing, even if the alleged fraud induced an investor not to trade
Who is a defendant?	Central Bank of Denver v. First Interstate Bank of Denver (1994)	Defendant must be a "primary violator" whose statements induced investors to trade (merely aiding and abetting does not create private liability)
	Stoneridge Investment Partners LLC v. Scientific-Atlanta, Inc. (2008)	There is no "scheme liability" for those who helped perpetuate a fraud, if they were invisible to investors
	Janus Capital Group, Inc. v. First Derivative Traders (2011)	Only those with "ultimate control" over false statements can be liable under 10b–5
	Lorenzo v. SEC (2019)	Person who "disseminates" false or misleading statement with intent to defraud (even though not "maker" of statement) can be liable under 10b-5
What constitutes a false or deceptive statement?	Santa Fe Industries, Inc. v. Green (1977)	Rule 10b–5 only regulates deception, not unfair corporate transactions or breaches of fiduciary duties; claims of an unfair merger price are not actionable
Elements of securities fraud		
(1) When is information material?	TSC Industries, Inc. v. Northway, Inc. (1976)	Information is material "if there is a substantial likelihood that a reasonable investor would consider it important in deciding whether to buy or sell securities"
	Basic, Inc. v. Levinson (1988)	Information about future (speculative) events is material by "balancing the probability the event will occur and the anticipated magnitude of the event" to the affected company
(2) What level of culpability must be shown?	Ernst & Ernst v. Hochfelder (1976)	Negligence is not actionable; the defendant must have had a "mental state embracing intent to deceive, manipulate, or defraud"
	Tellabs, Inc. v. Makor Issues & Rights (2008)	Pleading standard met when the alleged "inference of scienter is at least as strong as any opposing inference"
(3) How do plaintiffs show reliance?	Basic, Inc. v. Levinson (1988)	Reliance by investors in developed securities markets is presumed when publicly available information is reflected in market price

	<u>Halliburton Co. v. Erica P. John Fund, Inc.</u> (2014) (Halliburton II)	When plaintiff seeks class certification based on allegedly false statements in public stock market, defendants may before certification "defeat the presumption of reliance through evidence that alleged misrepresentation did not actually affect market price of stock"
(4) How do plaintiffs show causation?	<u>Dura Pharmaceuticals, Inc. v. Broudo</u> (2005)	Actual economic loss proximately caused by the fraud must be alleged and proved—such as by showing drop in market price when truth was revealed
What is the statute of limitations?	<u>Lampf, Pleva, Lipkind, Prupis & Petigrow v. Gilbertson</u> (1991)	Uniform federal limitations period applies to 10b–5 actions, rather than borrowed state limitations period
Must action be brought in federal court?	<u>Merrill Lynch, Pierce, Fenner & Smith, Inc. v. Dabit</u> (2006)	Shareholders who were induced by fraud *not to sell* cannot sue in state court; and such "holders" do not have 10b–5 standing in federal court

As you can see, the Supreme Court has had to balance competing concerns with Rule 10b–5. For example, in deciding that only actual purchasers and sellers have standing under the rule, the Court (in *Blue Chip Stamps*) voiced concerns about securities fraud actions being used as "vexatious litigation" brought merely for their settlement value. But in its decision presuming that investors rely on false information directed at public securities markets, the Court (in *Basic*, which was reaffirmed in *Halliburton II*) said that without a presumption that investors rely on the integrity of stock prices set in public markets there could be no private SFCA.

2. Statutory Requirements

Although the elements of a Rule 10b–5 action are judge-made, Congress has added a number of legislative glosses. The most important come from the Private Securities Litigation Reform Act of 1995 (PLSRA), which sought to

What's That?

Rule 10b–5 requires that the fraud be "in connection with" the purchase or sale of securities. What does "in connection with" mean? Courts have interpreted the term broadly. For one, there is no requirement of privity. Thus, public statements by a corporation are actionable even if the corporation does not engage in any securities trading itself.

In addition, there is no requirement that the fraud be related to the price of the securities that are traded. Thus, the Supreme Court has held that a stockbroker who falsely assures a customer that his securities account will be safe and then sells securities from the account and pockets the proceeds has committed a fraud "in connection with" securities trading.

tighten some of the procedures and pleading standards in securities fraud actions, especially SFCAs. The PSLRA, aimed mostly at abusive class actions alleging securities fraud, affects a number of the elements of a Rule 10b–5 action:

Issue	Statutory provision	Rule
Plaintiff	PSLRA - Exchange Act § 21D(a)(3)	Lead plaintiff in SFCA must be "most adequate plaintiff," defined as investor with largest financial stake in the action
Defendant	PSLRA - Exchange Act § 20(e)	SEC can bring enforcement actions that impose aiding and abetting liability (implicitly private plaintiffs cannot)
Elements of securities fraud		
(1) materiality	PSLRA - Exchange Act § 21E(c)(1)(A)(i)	Forward-looking statements that are identified as such and "accompanied by meaningful cautionary statements" are not actionable
(2) false and misleading statements	PSLRA - Exchange Act § 21D(b)(2)	Complaint that alleges statements that omit material information must specify which statements were misleading and why
(3) scienter	PSLRA - Exchange Act § 21D(b)(2)	Plaintiff must, for every false or misleading statement, "state with particularity facts giving rise to a strong inference that the defendant acted with the required state of mind"
	PSLRA - Exchange Act § 21D(g)(10)	"Knowing" defendants are subject to joint and several liability; "unknowing" defendants (presumably those who were only reckless) are subject to proportionate liability
(4) causation	PSLRA - Exchange Act § 21D(b)(4)	Plaintiff has burden to prove the false or misleading statement caused the plaintiff's loss
(5) damages	PSLRA - Exchange Act § 21D(e)	Damages are capped at the difference between trading price and the average daily price during the 90-day period after corrective disclosure.
Statute of limitations	Sarbanes-Oxley - 28 U.S.C. § 1658(b)	Private securities fraud actions must be brought within two years after the discovery of facts constituting the violation, but no later than five years after such violation.
Federal court	Securities Litigation Uniform Standards Act of 1998	All SFCAs alleging fraud "in connection with the purchase or sale" of securities must be brought in federal court

As you can see, Congress has also blown hot and cold about securities fraud litigation. For example, many of the PSLRA provisions add requirements or constraints on private enforcement that force Rule 10b–5 plaintiffs to "thread the eye of a needle." Yet Congress has also breathed life into securities fraud actions, for example, by leaving intact the judicial presumption of reliance in public markets and lengthening in Sarbanes-Oxley the statute of limitations.

How to proceed in our look at SFCAs? One approach might be to lay out in more detail all of the Supreme Court 10b–5 cases—each a fascinating set of facts and compelling legal analysis. But that would be too much. After all, this is meant to be an overview of securities fraud in a book mostly about corporate law, not securities regulation. Instead, we decided to give you a sense of the operation and thinking behind SFCAs and their role in corporate governance by exploring two of the most important 10b–5 cases. The first, *Basic, Inc. v Levinson*, reaches some critical conclusions about what misinformation can be the basis of a private 10b–5 action and whether securities fraud litigation can be maintained as class actions in federal court. The second, *Tellabs v. Makor Issues & Rights*, reflects how the Supreme Court has wrestled with the duality of Rule 10b–5 actions, which are seen as useful medicine for U.S. securities markets, with potentially dangerous side effects.

Points for Discussion

1. Ebb and flow.

Look at the dates of the Supreme Court's 10b–5 decisions. In the 1970s the Court pared back the reach of the private 10b–5 cause of action. The Court reversed lower court decisions that 10b–5 private liability could be based on negligent misstatements, could arise when an investor was induced not to trade, and could extend to unfair transactions argued to be tantamount to fraud. The Court was adamant that Rule 10b–5 referred to fraud, given the "manipulative or deceptive device or contrivance" language of § 10(b).

In the 1980s and 1990s, the Court clarified what constitutes material information in public stock markets and opened the federal courthouse doors to SFCAs, though carefully limiting who could be sued as defendants. In the 2000s, post-PSLRA, the Court adjusted how open the door is for private securities fraud litigation, particularly for SFCAs. It tightened even further who could be defendants, made it more difficult to prove losses arising from securities fraud, and limited the ability of plaintiffs to circumvent the federal procedural restrictions by going to state court. But the Court also clarified how plaintiffs could get past the pleading phase with well-pled inferences of intentional wrongdoing.

Finally, in the 2010s, the Court reaffirmed the "fraud on the market" theory on which SFCAs are based, while providing defendants additional tools to seek early dismissal of SFCA cases when the alleged misstatements had not affected market prices and the entity sued did not have ultimate control over the alleged misstatements.

2. Corporate federalism.

One of the most important decisions in the Supreme Court's extensive 10b–5 jurisprudence came in *Santa Fe Industries v. Green*, 430 U.S. 462 (1977). The case squarely presented the issue whether *unfair corporate practices* could be tantamount to fraud. The stakes were high. If Rule 10b–5 covered unfair practices, corporate governance disputes could easily migrate from state courts enforcing fiduciary duties to federal courts enforcing broad securities fraud standards.

The case arose from a squeezeout merger at an allegedly unfair price, the corporate defendant had disclosed all of the relevant facts in the merger, including that the minority shareholders were to be paid $150 per share, even though the company's net assets had a value of $640 per share. The Court stated:

> The "fundamental purpose" of the Act is to implement a "philosophy of full disclosure"; once full and fair disclosure has occurred, the fairness of the terms of the transaction is at most a tangential concern of the statute.

> There was no "omission" or "misstatement" in the information statement accompanying the notice of merger. On the basis of the information provided, minority shareholders could either accept the price offered or reject it and seek an appraisal in the Delaware Court of Chancery. Their choice was fairly presented, and they were furnished with all relevant information on which to base their decision.

The reasoning behind a holding that the complaint in this case alleged fraud under Rule 10b–5 could not be easily contained. The result would be to bring within the Rule a wide variety of corporate conduct traditionally left to state regulation. This extension of the federal securities laws would overlap and quite possibly interfere with state corporate law.

In short, claims of *unfair* treatment of shareholders are a matter for state corporate law—in particular, state court claims for breaches of fiduciary duty and state procedures for appraisal of fair value.

Take Note!

While Congress has whittled away at private 10b–5 liability, it has embraced the use of Rule 10b–5 in criminal cases charging securities fraud. For example, in response to Enron and other scandals, Congress increased criminal penalties for each offense from a maximum of 5 years to 10 years. Judges (and juries) have not been squeamish about imposing heavy criminal sanctions, for example, Enron CEO Jeff Skilling received a sentence of 24 years, which 57% of surveyed corporate executives believed was actually too lenient.

B. Selected Elements of a Securities Fraud Class Action

Recall that in a private securities fraud action the plaintiff must prove the defendant (1) made materially false or misleading statements (2) with an intent to deceive (3) upon which the plaintiff relied (4) causing losses to the plaintiff.

In a typical SFCA, the class representative identifies a group of investors who bought or sold securities during the period the market was deceived by the corporation's false or misleading statements. The main issues, typically, turn on whether the statements were "material" and whether the plaintiff has adequately alleged that the corporation (and its executives) acted with "scienter" (that is, intentionally or recklessly) in making the statements. Both issues are usually resolved on a motion to dismiss. Usually absent from this inquiry is whether individual investors actually knew about the statements and relied on them, given the 10b–5 presumption of reliance when the alleged deception operated as a "fraud on the market," which we will study in more detail below.

The following two cases explore the materiality, scienter, and reliance elements of an SFCA. We have broken the first case, *Basic Inc. v. Levinson*, into two parts—the first dealing with standards of materiality in public stock markets and the second dealing with whether investor reliance should be presumed in public markets. The second case, *Tellabs v. Makor Issues & Rights*, deals with the demanding "scienter" pleading standards of the PSLRA.

As the table above illustrated, the Supreme Court has addressed numerous other aspects of SFCAs, but the excerpts that follow are meant to give you a sense of the arguments surrounding the critical issues of materiality, scienter, and reliance. As you read these cases, notice the importance that the Court (and the parties) attach to resolving these issues at the pleading stage. Because SFCAs rarely go to trial, the effect of a case surviving a motion to dismiss is that it will almost always then be settled.

1. Materiality

Basic Inc. v. Levinson

485 U.S. 224 (1988)

JUSTICE BLACKMUN delivered the opinion of the Court.

This case requires us to apply the materiality requirement of § 10(b) of the Securities Exchange Act of 1934, and the Securities and Exchange Commission's Rule 10b–5, in the context of preliminary corporate merger discussions.

I

Prior to December 20, 1978, Basic Incorporated was a publicly traded company primarily engaged in the business of manufacturing chemical refractories for the steel industry. As early as 1965 or 1966, Combustion Engineering, Inc., a company producing mostly alumina-based refractories, expressed some interest in acquiring Basic, but was deterred from pursuing this inclination seriously because of antitrust concerns it then entertained. In 1976, however, regulatory action opened the way to a renewal of Combustion's interest.

Beginning in September 1976, Combustion representatives had meetings and telephone conversations with Basic officers and directors, including petitioners here, concerning the possibility of a merger. During 1977 and 1978, Basic made three public statements denying that it was engaged in merger negotiations.[4] On December 18, 1978, Basic asked the New York Stock Exchange to suspend trading in its shares and issued a release stating that it had been "approached" by another company concerning a merger. On December 19, Basic's board endorsed

---

[4] On October 21, 1977, after heavy trading and a new high in Basic stock, the following news item appeared in the Cleveland Plain Dealer:

> "Basic President Max Muller said the company knew no reason for the stock's activity and that no negotiations were under way with any company for a merger. He said Flintkote recently denied Wall Street rumors that it would make a tender offer of $25 a share for control of the Cleveland-based maker of refractories for the steel industry."

On September 25, 1978, in reply to an inquiry from the New York Stock Exchange, Basic issued a release concerning increased activity in its stock and stated that

> "management is unaware of any present or pending company development that would result in the abnormally heavy trading activity and price fluctuation in company shares that have been experienced in the past few days."

On November 6, 1978, Basic issued to its shareholders a "Nine Months Report 1978." This Report stated:

> "With regard to the stock market activity in the Company's shares we remain unaware of any present or pending developments which would account for the high volume of trading and price fluctuations in recent months."

Combustion's offer of $46 per share for its common stock, and on the following day publicly announced its approval of Combustion's tender offer for all outstanding shares.

Respondents are former Basic shareholders who sold their stock after Basic's first public statement of October 21, 1977, and before the suspension of trading in December 1978. Respondents brought a class action against Basic and its directors, asserting that the defendants issued three false or misleading public statements and thereby were in violation of § 10(b) of the 1934 Act and of Rule 10b–5. Respondents alleged that they were injured by selling Basic shares at artificially depressed prices in a market affected by petitioners' misleading statements and in reliance thereon.

The District Court held that, as a matter of law, any misstatements were immaterial: there were no negotiations ongoing at the time of the first statement, and although negotiations were taking place when the second and third statements were issued, those negotiations were not "destined, with reasonable certainty, to become a merger agreement in principle."

The United States Court of Appeals for the Sixth Circuit reversed the District Court's summary judgment, and remanded the case.

We granted certiorari to resolve the split among the Courts of Appeals as to the standard of materiality applicable to preliminary merger discussions.

II

The 1934 Act was designed to protect investors against manipulation of stock prices. Underlying the adoption of extensive disclosure requirements was a legislative philosophy: "There cannot be honest markets without honest publicity. Manipulation and dishonest practices of the market place thrive upon mystery and secrecy."

The Court previously has addressed various positive and common-law requirements for a violation of § 10(b) or of Rule 10b–5. The Court also explicitly has defined a standard of materiality under the securities laws, *see TSC Industries, Inc. v. Northway, Inc.*, 426 U.S. 438 (1976), concluding in the proxy-solicitation context that "an omitted fact is material if there is a substantial likelihood that a reasonable shareholder would consider it important in deciding how to vote." It further explained that to fulfill the materiality requirement "there must be a substantial likelihood that the disclosure of the omitted fact would have been viewed by the reasonable investor as having significantly altered the 'total mix' of information made available." We now expressly adopt the *TSC Industries* standard of materiality for the § 10(b) and Rule 10b–5 context.

III

The application of this materiality standard to preliminary merger discussions is not self-evident. Where the impact of the corporate development on the target's fortune is certain and clear, the *TSC Industries* materiality definition admits straightforward application. Where, on the other hand, the event is contingent or speculative in nature, it is difficult to ascertain whether the "reasonable investor" would have considered the omitted information significant at the time. Merger negotiations, because of the ever-present possibility that the contemplated transaction will not be effectuated, fall into the latter category.

A

Petitioners urge upon us a Third Circuit test for resolving this difficulty. Under this approach, preliminary merger discussions do not become material until "agreement-in-principle" as to the price and structure of the transaction has been reached between the would-be merger partners. By definition, then, information concerning any negotiations not yet at the agreement-in-principle stage could be withheld or even misrepresented without a violation of Rule 10b–5.

Three rationales have been offered in support of the "agreement-in-principle" test. The first derives from the concern that an investor not be overwhelmed by excessively detailed and trivial information, and focuses on the substantial risk that preliminary merger discussions may collapse: because such discussions are inherently tentative, disclosure of their existence itself could mislead investors and foster false optimism. The other two justifications for the agreement-in-principle standard are based on management concerns: because the requirement of "agreement-in-principle" limits the scope of disclosure obligations, it helps preserve the confidentiality of merger discussions where earlier disclosure might prejudice the negotiations; and the test also provides a usable, bright-line rule for determining when disclosure must be made.

The first rationale "assumes that investors are nitwits, unable to appreciate— even when told—that mergers are risky propositions up until the closing." Disclosure, and not paternalistic withholding of accurate information, is the policy chosen and expressed by Congress. We have recognized time and again, a "fundamental purpose" of the various Securities Acts, "was to substitute a philosophy of full disclosure for the philosophy of caveat emptor and thus to achieve a high standard of business ethics in the securities industry."

The second rationale, the importance of secrecy during the early stages of merger discussions, also seems irrelevant to an assessment whether their existence is significant to the trading decision of a reasonable investor. We need not ascertain whether secrecy necessarily maximizes shareholder wealth for this case does not concern the timing of a disclosure; it concerns only its accuracy and completeness. We face here the narrow question whether information concerning the existence and status of preliminary merger discussions is significant to the reasonable investor's trading decision. The "secrecy" rationale is simply inapposite to the definition of materiality.

The final justification offered in support of the agreement-in-principle test seems to be directed solely at the comfort of corporate managers. A bright-line rule indeed is easier to follow than a standard that requires the exercise of judgment in the light of all the circumstances. But ease of application alone is not an excuse for ignoring the purposes of the Securities Acts and Congress' policy decisions.

We therefore find no valid justification for artificially excluding from the definition of materiality information concerning merger discussions, which would otherwise be considered significant to the trading decision of a reasonable investor, merely because agreement-in-principle as to price and structure has not yet been reached by the parties or their representatives.

C

Even before this Court's decision in *TSC Industries*, the Second Circuit had explained the role of the materiality requirement of Rule 10b–5, with respect to contingent or speculative information or events. Under such circumstances, materiality "will depend at any given time upon a balancing of both the indicated probability that the event will occur and the anticipated magnitude of the event in light of the totality of the company activity."

In a subsequent decision, the late Judge Friendly, writing for a Second Circuit panel, applied the *Texas Gulf Sulphur* probability/magnitude approach in the specific context of preliminary merger negotiations. After acknowledging that materiality is something to be determined on the basis of the particular facts of each case, he stated:

> "Since a merger in which it is bought out is the most important event that can occur in a small corporation's life, to wit, its death, we think that inside information, as regards a merger of this sort, can become material at an earlier stage than would be the case as regards lesser transactions— and this even though the mortality rate of mergers in such formative stages is doubtless high."

We agree with that analysis.

Whether merger discussions in any particular case are material therefore depends on the facts. Generally, in order to assess the probability that the event will occur, a factfinder will need to look to indicia of interest in the transaction at the highest corporate levels. Without attempting to catalog all such possible factors, we note by way of example that board resolutions, instructions to investment bankers, and actual negotiations between principals or their intermediaries may serve as indicia of interest. To assess the magnitude of the transaction to the issuer of the securities allegedly manipulated, a factfinder will need to consider such facts as the size of the two corporate entities and of the potential premiums over market value. No particular event or factor short of closing the transaction need be either necessary or sufficient by itself to render merger discussions material.[17]

As we clarify today, materiality depends on the significance the reasonable investor would place on the withheld or misrepresented information. Because the standard of materiality we have adopted differs from that used by both courts below, we remand the case for reconsideration of the question whether a grant of summary judgment is appropriate on this record.

Points for Discussion

1. Securities fraud class action.

The case shows you the structure of an SFCA. Shareholders claimed they sold their shares because of false and misleading statements by the corporation, which corporate officials knew were false, and then sought damages from the corporation equal to the difference between the price at which they sold and the eventual merger price that they lost out on. The claims were brought as a class action in which one representative (Levinson) and class counsel (a specialized part of the corporate bar) sought to vindicate the principle of full and honest disclosure in securities markets.

2. Reasonable investor in public markets.

The *TSC Industries* materiality standard refers to what a "reasonable investor" would consider important in a securities transaction. Who is this investor?

---

[17] To be actionable, of course, a statement must also be misleading. Silence, absent a duty to disclose, is not misleading under Rule 10b–5. "No comment" statements are generally the functional equivalent of silence. *See* New York Stock Exchange Listed Company Manual § 202.01 (premature public announcement may properly be delayed for valid business purpose and where adequate security can be maintained).

It has been suggested that given current market practices, a "no comment" statement is tantamount to an admission that merger discussions are underway. That may well hold true to the extent that issuers adopt a policy of truthfully denying merger rumors when no discussions are underway, and of issuing "no comment" statements when they are in the midst of negotiations. There are, of course, other statement policies firms could adopt; we need not now advise issuers as to what kind of practice to follow, within the range permitted by law. Perhaps more importantly, we think that creating an exception to a regulatory scheme founded on a prodisclosure legislative philosophy, because complying with the regulation might be "bad for business," is a role for Congress, not this Court.

The Supreme Court's probability plus magnitude test in *Basic* essentially frames the question as one of expected value: what does particular information tell you about the likelihood of a corporate event taking place (like a merger or payment of dividends) and the financial significance of that event? This is precisely the calculation that stock analysts perform in evaluating information and its relevance to prices in public stock markets.

3. Duty to disclose?

What if the corporate officials in *Basic* had simply stayed quiet and said nothing about the merger negotiations? Is failure to disclose *material* information a violation of Rule 10b–5? The Supreme Court distinguishes a "duty to disclose" and the question of whether particular statements are material. Unless there is a duty to disclose in an SEC filing or to update or correct statements that are "still alive," a company need not disclose material information—no matter how important investors might find it. That is, there is no duty of continuous disclosure under the U.S. securities laws.

Make the Connection

Normally, silence is not actionable under Rule 10b–5. But as we will see when we study insider trading, there is a duty to speak when defendants have a relationship of trust and confidence with the plaintiff. *See Chiarella v. United States*, 445 U.S. 222 (1980). A duty to speak also arises when majority owners deal with minority shareholder-employees in a close corporation. *See Jordan v. Duff & Phelps, Inc.*, 815 F.2d 429 (7th Cir. 1987) (holding securities firm liable for remaining silent when the firm repurchased the shares of an employee who resigned on the eve of a lucrative merger offer).

Practice Pointer

The SEC has issued guidance permitting public companies to *not* disclose pending merger negotiations in their disclosure filings, in recognition of the value of confidential negotiations.

How would you advise the corporate executives in *Basic* to have responded to press inquiries about rumors that the company was engaged in merger negotiations?

4. Meaning of "no comment."

Often when we hear politicians say "no comment," we can infer they have something to hide. What about corporate "no comment" statements? The Supreme Court addressed this in *Basic v. Levison* in its important footnote 17. Is that clarification convincing?

2. Scienter

As we have seen, the Supreme Court has required plaintiffs in 10b–5 actions to prove the defendant's scienter, a "mental state embracing intent to deceive, manipulate, or defraud." Generally, this means plaintiffs must show that the defendant was aware of the truth and appreciated the propensity of his statement to mislead.

In addition, Congress has sought to make it hard for shareholders who claim they were misled in their stock trading by creating a heightened pleading standard in 10b–5 actions. Under the PSLRA a complaint alleging securities fraud must "state with particularity facts giving rise to a strong inference that the defendant acted with the required state of mind." Exchange Act § 21D(b)(2). Failure to adequately plead scienter is a frequent basis for dismissing SFCAs. What "facts" must be pled? What constitutes a "strong inference"? Those were the questions before the Supreme Court in the next case.

Tellabs, Inc. v. Makor Issues & Rights, Ltd.

551 U.S. 308 (2007)

JUSTICE GINSBURG delivered the opinion of the Court.

Exacting pleading requirements are among the control measures Congress included in the PSLRA. The PSLRA requires plaintiffs to state with particularity both the facts constituting the alleged violation, and the facts evidencing scienter, i.e., the defendant's intention "to deceive, manipulate, or defraud." *Ernst & Ernst v. Hochfelder*, 425 U.S. 185, 194, & n. 12 (1976); *see* 15 U.S.C. § 78u–4(b)(1), (2). This case concerns the latter requirement. As set out in § 21D(b)(2) of the PSLRA, plaintiffs must "state with particularity facts giving rise to a strong inference that the defendant acted with the required state of mind." 15 U.S.C. § 78u–4(b)(2).

I

Petitioner Tellabs, Inc., manufactures specialized equipment used in fiber optic networks. During the time period relevant to this case, petitioner Richard Notebaert was Tellabs' chief executive officer and president. Respondents (Shareholders) are persons who purchased Tellabs stock between December 11, 2000, and June 19, 2001. They accuse Tellabs and Notebaert (as well as several other Tellabs executives) of engaging in a scheme to deceive the investing public about the true value of Tellabs' stock.

Beginning on December 11, 2000, the Shareholders allege, Notebaert (and by imputation Tellabs) "falsely reassured public investors, in a series of statements that Tellabs was continuing to enjoy strong demand for its products and earning record revenues," when, in fact, Notebaert knew the opposite was true. From December 2000 until the spring of 2001, the Shareholders claim, Notebaert knowingly misled the public in four ways. First, he made statements indicating that demand for Tellabs' flagship networking device, the TITAN 5500, was continuing to grow, when in fact demand for that product was waning. Second, Notebaert made statements indicating that the TITAN 6500, Tellabs' next-generation networking device, was available for delivery, and that demand for that product was strong and growing, when in truth the product was not ready for delivery and demand was weak. Third, he falsely represented Tellabs' financial results for the fourth quarter of 2000 (and, in connection with those results, condoned the practice of "channel stuffing," under which Tellabs flooded its customers with unwanted products). Fourth, Notebaert made a series of overstated revenue projections, when demand for the TITAN 5500 was drying up and production of the TITAN 6500 was behind schedule. Based on Notebaert's sunny assessments, the Shareholders contend, market analysts recommended that investors buy Tellabs' stock.

The first public glimmer that business was not so healthy came in March 2001 when Tellabs modestly reduced its first quarter sales projections. In the next months, Tellabs made progressively more cautious statements about its projected sales. On June 19, 2001, the last day of the class period, Tellabs disclosed that demand for the TITAN 5500 had significantly dropped. Simultaneously, the company substantially lowered its revenue projections for the second quarter of 2001. The next day, the price of Tellabs stock, which had reached a high of $67 during the period, plunged to a low of $15.87.

On December 3, 2002, the Shareholders filed a class action in the District Court for the Northern District of Illinois. After the first complaint was dismissed for failing to plead their case with the particularity the PSLRA requires, the Shareholders amended their complaint, adding references to 27 confidential sources and making further, more specific, allegations concerning Notebaert's mental state. The District Court again dismissed, this time with prejudice, determining they had insufficiently alleged that he acted with scienter.

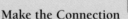

Make the Connection

Remember from Civil Procedure that a dismissal with prejudice bars the complaint from being amended.

The Court of Appeals for the Seventh Circuit reversed in relevant part. It concluded that the Shareholders had sufficiently alleged that Notebaert acted with the requisite state of mind.

We granted certiorari to resolve disagreement among the Circuits on whether, and to what extent, a court must consider competing inferences in determining whether a securities fraud complaint gives rise to a "strong inference" of scienter.

II

In an ordinary civil action, the Federal Rules of Civil Procedure require only "a short and plain statement of the claim showing that the pleader is entitled to relief." Fed. Rule Civ. Proc. 8(a)(2). Prior to the enactment of the PSLRA, the sufficiency of a complaint for securities fraud was governed not by Rule 8, but by the heightened pleading standard set forth in Rule 9(b). Rule 9(b) applies to "all averments of fraud or mistake"; it requires that "the circumstances constituting fraud . . . be stated with particularity" but provides that "malice, intent, knowledge, and other condition of mind of a person may be averred generally."

Setting a uniform pleading standard for § 10(b) actions was among Congress' objectives when it enacted the PSLRA. Designed to curb perceived abuses of the § 10(b) private action—"nuisance filings, targeting of deep-pocket defendants, vexatious discovery requests and manipulation by class action lawyers," the PSLRA installed both substantive and procedural controls. Notably, Congress prescribed new procedures for the appointment of lead plaintiffs and lead counsel. Congress also "limited recoverable damages and attorney's fees, provided a 'safe harbor' for forward-looking statements, . . . mandated imposition of sanctions for frivolous litigation, and authorized a stay of discovery pending resolution of any motion to dismiss." And in § 21D(b) of the PSLRA, Congress "imposed heightened pleading requirements in actions brought pursuant to § 10(b) and Rule 10b–5."

Under the PSLRA's heightened pleading instructions, any private securities complaint alleging that the defendant made a false or misleading statement must: "state with particularity facts giving rise to a strong inference that the defendant acted with the required state of mind." In the instant case the District Court and the Seventh Circuit disagreed on whether the Shareholders "stated with particularity facts giving rise to a strong inference that Notebaert acted with scienter."

Food for Thought

As you read the rest of the material on Rule 10b–5, think about why the Court refers to these suits as "lawyer-driven litigation." Who benefits the most from Rule 10b–5 actions?

With no clear guide from Congress other than its "intention to strengthen existing pleading requirements," Courts of Appeals have diverged in construing the term "strong inference." Among the uncertainties, should courts consider competing inferences in determining whether an inference of scienter is "strong"? Our task is to prescribe a workable construction of the "strong inference" standard, a reading geared to the PSLRA's twin goals: to curb frivolous, lawyer-driven litigation, while preserving investors' ability to recover on meritorious claims.

III

A

We establish the following prescriptions: *First*, faced with a Rule 12(b)(6) motion to dismiss a § 10(b) action, courts must, as with any motion to dismiss for failure to plead a claim on which relief can be granted, accept all factual allegations in the complaint as true.

Second, courts must consider the complaint in its entirety, as well as other sources courts ordinarily examine when ruling on Rule 12(b)(6) motions to dismiss, in particular, documents incorporated into the complaint by reference, and matters of which a court may take judicial notice. The inquiry is whether *all* of the facts alleged, taken collectively, give rise to a strong inference of scienter, not whether any individual allegation, scrutinized in isolation, meets that standard.

Third, in determining whether the pleaded facts give rise to a "strong" inference of scienter, the court must take into account plausible opposing inferences. The Seventh Circuit expressly declined to engage in such a comparative inquiry. A complaint could survive, that court said, as long as it "alleges facts from which, if true, a reasonable person could infer that the defendant acted with the required intent." But in § 21D(b)(2), Congress did not merely require plaintiffs to "provide a factual basis for their scienter allegations," *i.e.*, to allege facts from which an inference of scienter rationally *could* be drawn. Instead, Congress required plaintiffs to plead with particularity facts that give rise to a "strong"—*i.e.*, a powerful or cogent—inference.

The strength of an inference cannot be decided in a vacuum. The inquiry is inherently comparative: How likely is it that one conclusion, as compared to others, follows from the underlying facts? To determine whether the plaintiff has alleged facts that give rise to the requisite "strong inference" of scienter, a court must consider plausible, nonculpable explanations for the defendant's conduct, as well as inferences favoring the plaintiff. Yet the inference of scienter must be more than merely "reasonable" or "permissible"—it must be cogent and compelling, thus strong in light of other explanations. A complaint will survive, we hold, only if a reasonable person would deem the inference of scienter cogent and at least as compelling as any opposing inference one could draw from the facts alleged.[5]

Tellabs contends that when competing inferences are considered, Notebaert's evident lack of pecuniary motive will be dispositive. The Shareholders, Tellabs stresses, did not allege that Notebaert sold any shares during the class period. While it is true that motive can be a relevant consideration, and personal financial gain may weigh heavily in favor of a scienter inference, we agree with the Seventh Circuit that the absence of a motive allegation is not fatal.

Tellabs also maintains that several of the Shareholders' allegations are too vague or ambiguous to contribute to a strong inference of scienter. For example, the Shareholders alleged that Tellabs flooded its customers with unwanted products, a practice known as "channel stuffing." But they failed, Tellabs argues, to specify whether the channel stuffing allegedly known to Notebaert was the illegitimate kind (*e.g.*, writing orders for products customers had not requested) or the legitimate kind (*e.g.*, offering customers discounts as an incentive to buy). We agree that omissions and ambiguities count against inferring scienter. We reiterate, however, that the court's job is not to scrutinize each allegation in isolation but to assess all the allegations holistically. In sum, the reviewing court must ask: When the allegations are accepted as true and taken collectively, would a reasonable person deem the inference of scienter at least as strong as any opposing inference?

IV

We emphasize that under our construction of the "strong inference" standard, a plaintiff is not forced to plead more than she would be required to prove at trial. A plaintiff alleging fraud in a § 10(b) action, we hold today, must plead facts rendering an inference of scienter *at least as likely as* any plausible opposing inference. At trial, she must then prove her case by a "preponderance of the evidence." Stated otherwise, she must demonstrate that it is *more likely* than not that the defendant acted with scienter.

Neither the District Court nor the Court of Appeals had the opportunity to consider the matter in light of the prescriptions we announce today. We therefore vacate the Seventh Circuit's judgment and remand the case so it may be reexamined in accord with our construction of § 21D(b)(2).

---

[5] Justice Scalia objects to this standard on the ground that "if a jade falcon were stolen from a room to which only A and B had access," it could not "possibly be said there was a 'strong inference' that B was the thief." We suspect, however, that law enforcement officials as well as the owner of the precious falcon would find the inference of guilt as to B quite strong—certainly strong enough to warrant further investigation.

Justice Scalia, concurring in the judgment.

I fail to see how an inference that is merely "at least as compelling as any opposing inference," can conceivably be called what the statute here at issue requires: a "strong inference." If a jade falcon were stolen from a room to which only A and B had access, could it *possibly* be said there was a "strong inference" that B was the thief? I think not, and I therefore think that the Court's test must fail. In my view, the test should be whether the inference of scienter (if any) is *more plausible* than the inference of innocence.

————

Points for Discussion

1. True to the spirit of PLSRA?

Based on your understanding of the PSLRA, in which Congress sought to discourage frivolous 10b–5 lawsuits, whose position seems more consistent with the statute's purpose? Shouldn't allegations by shareholders (and their counsel) of intentional deceit be subjected to a higher threshold of proof? Or did *Tellabs* seek to encourage 10b–5 lawsuits when they seem meritorious?

2. What's the big deal?

Why does it matter whether the tie goes to the plaintiff? Isn't this a theoretical exercise? Won't a judge, looking at the allegations in a complaint, be able to determine which inferences (intent to mislead or innocent mistake) are more "cogent and compelling"?

3. Guidance from the Court?

Does *Tellabs* provide useful guidance to lower courts that must decide whether or not to allow securities fraud actions to proceed? For example, the Court says the inferences pointing to scienter must be "cogent and compelling," not simply "reasonable and permissible." What does this mean? The Court also says that for there to be scienter the corporate insider need not be motivated by personal gain, but would evidence that the insider had sold his stock after making a false statement provide a "cogent and compelling" inference of scienter?

Think about the allegations in the case. Given that the CEO Notebaert was aware of internal reports that the company's flagship product was experiencing difficulties, would it be reasonable to infer that he knew his optimistic statements were false? Why did the Supreme Court remand the case?

————

3. Reliance in Public Markets (and Shareholder Losses)

Reliance and causation, elements of traditional common-law deceit, are also elements of a private 10b–5 action. The reliance requirement tests whether the plaintiff's trading was linked to the alleged misrepresentations—it weeds out claims where the misrepresentation had little or no impact on the plaintiff's investment decision. The causation requirement, like proximate cause in tort law, tests

Take Note!

The SEC has the authority to bring enforcement actions under Rule 10b–5, seeking injunctive relief or civil penalties. The SEC need not prove reliance or causation, but simply that there were materially false or misleading statements made with scienter.

the link between the misrepresentation and the plaintiff's loss—it weeds out claims where the securities fraud was not "responsible" for the investor's loss.

Basic Inc. v. Levinson

485 U.S. 224 (1988)

[The part of the opinion laying out the facts and addressing addressing materiality appear earlier in this chapter.]

We must also determine whether a person who traded a corporation's shares on a securities exchange after the issuance of a materially misleading statement by the corporation may invoke a rebuttable presumption that, in trading, he relied on the integrity of the price set by the market.

IV

A

We turn to the question of reliance and the fraud-on-the-market theory. Succinctly put:

> The fraud on the market theory is based on the hypothesis that, in an open and developed securities market, the price of a company's stock is determined by the available material information regarding the company and its business. . . . Misleading statements will therefore defraud purchasers of stock even if the purchasers do not directly rely on the misstatements. . . . The causal connection between the defendants' fraud and the plaintiffs' purchase of stock in such a case is no less significant

than in a case of direct reliance on misrepresentations." Peil v. Speiser, 806 F. 2d 1154, 1160–1161 (3d Cir. 1986).

Our task, of course, is not to assess the general validity of the theory, but to consider whether it was proper for the courts below to apply a rebuttable presumption of reliance, supported in part by the fraud-on-the-market theory.

In their amended complaint, the named plaintiffs alleged that in reliance on Basic's statements they sold their shares of Basic stock in the depressed market created by petitioners. Requiring proof of individualized reliance from each member of the proposed plaintiff class effectively would have prevented respondents from proceeding with a class action, since individual issues then would have overwhelmed the common ones. The District Court found that the presumption of reliance created by the fraud-on-the-market theory provided "a practical resolution to the problem of balancing the substantive requirement of proof of reliance in securities cases against the procedural requisites of Fed. Rule Civ. Proc. 23." The District Court thus concluded that with reference to each public statement and its impact upon the open market for Basic shares, common questions predominated over individual questions, as required by Fed. Rule Civ. Proc. 23(a)(2) and (b)(3).

Petitioners and their amici complain that the fraud-on-the-market theory effectively eliminates the requirement that a plaintiff asserting a claim under Rule 10b–5 prove reliance. They note that reliance is and long has been an element of common-law fraud, and argue that because the analogous express right of action includes a reliance requirement, so too must an action implied under § 10(b).

We agree that reliance is an element of a Rule 10b–5 cause of action. Reliance provides the requisite causal connection between a defendant's misrepresentation and a plaintiff's injury. There is, however, more than one way to demonstrate the causal connection. Indeed, we previously have dispensed with a requirement of positive proof of reliance, where a duty to disclose material information had been breached, concluding that the necessary nexus between the plaintiffs' injury and the defendant's wrongful conduct had been established. *See Affiliated Ute Citizens v. United States*, 406 U.S. at 153–154.

The modern securities markets, literally involving millions of shares changing hands daily, differ from the face-to-face transactions contemplated by early fraud cases, and our understanding of Rule 10b–5's reliance requirement must encompass these differences.

"In face-to-face transactions, the inquiry into an investor's reliance upon information is into the subjective pricing of that information by that investor. With the presence of a market, the market is interposed between seller and buyer and, ideally, transmits information to the investor in the processed form of a market price. Thus the market is performing a substantial part of the valuation process performed by the investor in a face-to-face transaction. The market is acting as the unpaid agent of the investor, informing him that given all the information available to it, the value of the stock is worth the market price." *In re LTV Securities Litigation*, 88 F. R. D. 134, 143 (N.D. Tex. 1980).

The importance of the fraud-on-the market theory was recognized when the case went to the Supreme Court. Amicus briefs urging the Court not to create a presumption of reliance were filed for the American Corporate Counsel Association, various accounting firms, including Arthur Andersen & Co., and the American Institute of Certified Public Accountants. The United States Department of Justice, with the support of the SEC, filed an amicus brief favoring a presumption of reliance.

B

Presumptions typically serve to assist courts in managing circumstances in which direct proof, for one reason or another, is rendered difficult. Requiring a plaintiff to show a speculative state of facts, i.e., how he would have acted if omitted material information had been disclosed, or if the misrepresentation had not been made, would place an unnecessarily unrealistic evidentiary burden on the Rule 10b–5 plaintiff who has traded on an impersonal market.

Arising out of considerations of fairness, public policy, and probability, as well as judicial economy, presumptions are also useful devices for allocating the burdens of proof between parties. The presumption of reliance employed in this case is consistent with, and, by facilitating Rule 10b–5 litigation, supports, the congressional policy embodied in the 1934 Act.

The presumption is also supported by common sense and probability. Recent empirical studies have tended to confirm Congress' premise that the market price of shares traded on well-developed markets reflects all publicly available information, and, hence, any material misrepresentations. It has been noted that "it is hard to imagine that there ever is a buyer or seller who does not rely on market integrity. Who would knowingly roll the dice in a crooked crap game?" An investor who buys or sells stock at the price set by the market does so in reliance on the integrity of that price. Because most publicly available information is reflected in market price, an investor's reliance on any public material misrepresentations, therefore, may be presumed for purposes of a Rule 10b–5 action.

C

The Court of Appeals found that petitioners "made public material misrepresentations and plaintiffs sold Basic stock in an impersonal, efficient market. Thus the class, as defined by the district court, has established the threshold facts for proving their loss." The court acknowledged that petitioners may rebut proof of the elements giving rise to the presumption, or show that the misrepresentation in fact did not lead to a distortion of price or that an individual plaintiff traded or would have traded despite his knowing the statement was false.

Any showing that severs the link between the alleged misrepresentation and either the price received (or paid) by the plaintiff, or his decision to trade at a fair market price, will be sufficient to rebut the presumption of reliance. For example, if petitioners could show that the "market makers" were privy to the truth about the merger discussions here with Combustion, and thus that the market price would not have been affected by their misrepresentations, the causal connection could be broken. Similarly, if, despite petitioners' allegedly fraudulent attempt to manipulate market price, news of the merger discussions credibly entered the market and dissipated the effects of the misstatements, those who traded Basic shares after the corrective statements would have no direct or indirect connection with the fraud. Petitioners also could rebut the presumption of reliance as to plaintiffs who would have divested themselves of their Basic shares without relying on the integrity of the market.

────────────

Justice White, with whom Justice O'Connor joins, concurring in part and dissenting in part.

I

A

At the outset, I note that there are portions of the Court's fraud-on-the-market holding with which I am in agreement. Most importantly, I agree the fraud-on-the-market presumption must be capable of being rebutted by a showing that a plaintiff did not "rely" on the market price. For example, a plaintiff who decides, months in advance of an alleged misrepresentation, to purchase a stock; one who buys or sells a stock for reasons unrelated to its price; one who actually sells a stock "short" days before the misrepresentation is made—surely none of these people can state a valid claim under Rule 10b–5.

B

For while the economists' theories which underpin the fraud-on-the-market presumption may have the appeal of mathematical exactitude and scientific certainty, they are—in the end—nothing more than theories which may or may not prove accurate upon further consideration. Thus, while the majority states that, for purposes of reaching its result it need only make modest assumptions about the way in which "market professionals generally" do their jobs, and how the conduct of market professionals affects stock prices, I doubt that we are in much of a position to assess which theories aptly describe the functioning of the securities industry.

Food for Thought

Do you agree with Justice White— should the Court rely on economic theories to prove legal concepts, or adhere to historical precedents, such as requiring a specific showing of reliance?

Consequently, I cannot join the Court in its effort to reconfigure the securities laws, based on recent economic theories, to better fit what it perceives to be the new realities of financial markets. I would leave this task to others more equipped for the job than we.

C

At the bottom of the Court's conclusion that the fraud-on-the-market theory sustains a presumption of reliance is the assumption that individuals rely "on the integrity of the market price" when buying or selling stock in "impersonal, well-developed markets for securities." It is this aspect of the fraud-on-the-market hypothesis which most mystifies me.

The meaning of this phrase "integrity of the market price" eludes me, for it implicitly suggests that stocks have some "true value" that is measurable by a standard other than their market price. While the scholastics of medieval times professed a means to make such a valuation of a commodity's "worth," I doubt that the federal courts of our day are similarly equipped.

Even if securities had some "value"—knowable and distinct from the market price of a stock—investors do not always share the Court's presumption that a stock's price is a "reflection of [this] value." Indeed, "many investors purchase or sell stock because they believe the price *inaccurately* reflects the corporation's worth." If investors really believed that stock prices reflected a stock's "value," many sellers would never sell, and many buyers never buy.

I do not propose that the law retreat from the many protections that § 10(b) and Rule 10b–5, as interpreted in our prior cases, provide to investors. But any extension of these laws, to approach something closer to an investor insurance scheme, should come from Congress, and not from the courts.

———————

Points for Discussion

1. Effect of presumption.

According to the Court, what must a plaintiff in an SFCA show to avoid having to prove that each class member relied on the alleged misrepresentations? What is the effect of the Court's presumption of reliance in "well-developed stock markets"? What must the plaintiffs show to get the presumption? What must the defendant show to overcome the presumption? How likely is it that a defendant would be able to overcome the presumption?

Notice, as did the Court, that without a presumption of reliance private SFCAs would not be possible. Why does the Court seem to believe that private enforcement is necessary to combat securities fraud in stock markets? Wouldn't it be better if the SEC, using its public enforcement powers, were the one to decide what deceptions harmed investors and which ones undermined the integrity of the stock markets? Or, perhaps, the stock markets themselves (especially the NYSE and NASDAQ) should do the policing, given their strong interest in market integrity.

2. Should reliance be presumed?

In his dissent Justice White asserted that the courts are not institutionally well-suited to decide whether one economic theory is better than another one. Does the majority base its presumption of reliance on an economic theory? Or was the majority just making law?

Justice White also points out (in a part of the opinion we did not include) that nearly all of the plaintiffs made money from their sale of Basic stock, which during the class period rose from $20 to $30. Does it make sense to protect these shareholders, who sold in a rising market? Did they believe in the integrity of the market price?

In short, there is reason to question the presumption of reliance. Perhaps the Supreme Court was making law—though maybe for a good cause. For many years after *Basic*, corporate reformers urged that the case be overruled. In 2014, the

Supreme Court had its chance—and seriously considered overruling or modifying *Basic's* presumption of reliance—but ended up declining to do so. *Halliburton Co. v. Erica P. John Fund, Inc.*, 573 U.S. 258 (2014) (*Halliburton II*). The Court seemed to accept that too much water had already passed under the bridge. Congress, which over the years had tinkered with many of the elements of a 10b–5 action, seemed to agree with the Court's conclusion in *Basic* that a presumption of reliance in developed stock markets is good law.

Go Online

To get a sense for the types of SFCAs that have been filed over the years, along with current data on pending cases and recent settlements, you can go to the Stanford Securities Class Action Clearinghouse website (securities.stanford.edu). The site is a cornucopia of information, including all pleadings, court opinions, dismissals, and settlement data for all post-PSLRA securities fraud class actions. The site also includes charts and studies that summarize the results of this potent litigation tool.

3. Circularity of recovery from corporation.

Each year approximately 200 SFCAs are filed in the United States, most of them "classic" cases of corporate misrepresentations that, when disclosed, usually result in dramatic price drops. Eventually, many of these cases are settled, with class members recovering (some) of their trading losses.

Who pays when a corporation defrauds the market and is sued in an SFCA? In the typical case, when the corporation issues fraudulently optimistic news, those investors who bought at artificially-inflated prices recover from the corporation (and sometimes from D&O insurance maintained by the corporation). Payment by the corporation, assuming it is solvent, is thus ultimately borne by the shareholders, including the luckless shareholders who held during the period of false optimism. (The lucky shareholders who sold to the plaintiffs keep their windfall gains.) In short, 10b–5 recovery against the corporation essentially results in one shareholder group (the unlucky holders) subsidizing another shareholder group (the buying victims).

Given that most shareholders (particularly institutional shareholders) are diversified, corporate recovery essentially involves the flow of money from one pocket to another. The only "dead weight" losses come from the costs of litigation—especially the fees paid to lawyers for the plaintiffs and to lawyers for the defendants. Is there any way to justify such a circular system?

For some, the answer is deterrence. To the extent that corporate managers (specifically and generally) respond to SFCA litigation by improving disclosure and corporate governance might the system be seen as cost-effective. Although studies indicate that companies that settle SFCAs subsequently undertake corporate governance reforms and then financially out-perform their peers, many continue to question whether the benefits of SFCAs are worth their costs.

4. State liability for securities fraud?

So an obvious question is how state law, particularly in Delaware, handles fraudulent corporate statements in public markets. The simple answer: incompletely. Although Delaware courts recognize that corporate officials have a "duty of disclosure" that permits shareholders to sue for materially false or misleading statements, there is no state-law presumption of reliance for "fraud on the market." The result is that except in corporate acquisitions where shareholders must decide whether to sell their shares or seek appraisal, state disclosure law is mostly dead letter.

The leading Delaware case on the "duty of disclosure" that arises when directors make false statements in public markets offers a curious lesson in double-speak. *Malone v. Brincat*, 722 A.2d 5 (Del.1998). In the following excerpt, notice how the Delaware court speaks in grandiloquent terms about the duties of corporate directors to be completely honest in their communications to shareholders, but then backs away (without much explanation) from creating an effective remedy:

> Whenever directors communicate publicly or directly with shareholders about the corporation's affairs, with or without a request for shareholder action, directors have a fiduciary duty to shareholders to exercise due care, good faith and loyalty. It follows *a fortiori* that when directors communicate publicly or directly with shareholders about corporate matters the *sine qua non* of directors' fiduciary duty to shareholders is honesty.

> Shareholders are entitled to rely upon the truthfulness of all information disseminated to them by the directors: public statements made to the market, including shareholders; statements informing shareholders about the affairs of the corporation without a request for shareholder action; and, statements to shareholders in conjunction with a request for shareholder action.

> When corporate directors impart information they must comport with the obligations imposed by both the Delaware law and the federal statutes and regulations of the United States Securities and Exchange Commission. In deference to the panoply of federal protections that are available to

investors in connection with the purchase or sale of securities of Delaware corporations, this Court has decided not to recognize a state common law cause of action against the directors of Delaware corporations for "fraud on the market."

When the directors are not seeking shareholder action, but are deliberately misinforming shareholders about the business of the corporation, either directly or by a public statement, there is a violation of fiduciary duty. That violation may result in a derivative claim on behalf of the corporation or a cause of action for damages.

> **Make the Connection**
>
> As we have seen, the Delaware courts require disclosure by directors and controlling shareholders when shareholders are asked to sell their shares or seek appraisal—whether in a traditional merger, a tender offer by a controlling shareholder, or a tender offer by the corporation for its own shares (a self-tender). And we will soon see in Chapter 30 (Sale of Control) that the duty has also been applied in the context of mergers, including short-form mergers, even though no shareholder vote is required and appraisal rights are available.

Here the complaint alleges (if true) an egregious violation of fiduciary duty by the directors in knowingly disseminating materially false information. Then it alleges that the corporation lost about $2 billion in value as a result. Then it merely claims that the action is brought on behalf of the named plaintiffs and the putative class. It is a *non sequitur* rather than a syllogism.

The plaintiffs never expressly assert a derivative claim on behalf of the corporation or allege compliance with Court of Chancery Rule 23.1, which requires pre-suit demand or cognizable and particularized allegations that demand is excused. If the plaintiffs intend to assert a derivative claim, they should be permitted to replead to assert such a claim and any damage or equitable remedy sought on behalf of the corporation. Likewise, the plaintiffs should have the opportunity to replead to assert any individual cause of action and articulate a remedy that is appropriate on behalf of the named plaintiffs individually, or a properly recognizable class consistent with Court of Chancery Rule 23, and our decision in *Gaffin*.[47]

---

[47] *Gaffin v. Teledyne, Inc.*, 611 A.2d at 474 ("A class action may not be maintained in a purely common law or equitable fraud case since individual questions of law or fact, particularly as to the element of justifiable reliance, will inevitably predominate over common questions of law or fact.").

In the case, the plaintiffs had claimed that the directors had systematically and intentionally overstated corporate earnings over the course of four years. When the company finally corrected its financials, the stock price plummeted. While troubled by the fraud, the Court made clear that the only shareholder remedies would be in a derivative suit showing that the fraud affected *company value* or by individual shareholders showing they had individually relied to their detriment on the false financials.

Is it any wonder that shareholders (and plaintiffs' counsel) rarely bring "duty of disclosure" cases in Delaware?

———————

CHAPTER 29

Insider Trading

Suppose you have inside information about a company that, when revealed to the public, is sure to cause the price of the company's stock to skyrocket. Perhaps you have advance notice about a new blockbuster product. Or maybe you learned the company is about to disclose record earnings. When are you prohibited from using this information to buy company shares? That, in a nutshell, is the question we address in this chapter.

Trading based on insider information is rampant and has been for a long time. Yet so are insider-trading investigations and prosecutions. The SEC and Department of Justice are aggressive in targeting illegal insider trading, in the belief that it is crucial to deter such trading to maintain confidence in our financial markets. They bring dozens of high-profile cases every year.

Like the other securities markets issues addressed in this three-chapter module, the law of insider trading today is defined primarily by federal law. Yet its history is rooted in state law and the basic fiduciary duties that we addressed in earlier chapters. Accordingly, we begin this chapter with a discussion of the leading state approaches. We then describe the three main Supreme Court insider trading cases, which set forth the current law on insider trading. But before we discuss the law of insider trading, we first address the reasons for prohibiting insider trading and ask the most basic question: what is wrong with trading while in possession of inside information?

Take Note!

It's important to understand that most stock trading by corporate insiders is perfectly legal—and often desirable. For example, when an executive buys company stock because he believes in the company, this trading is not illegal if the executive has material nonpublic information. Or when a long-serving director leaves the board and sells her company stock, this trading is not illegal unless the director has material information not available to the market. As a general rule, stock trading by insiders is illegal only when they are aware of price-sensitive information not available to others—that is, when they have material nonpublic information.

A. Insider Trading Policy

Imagine two possible approaches to insider trading in financial markets. In the first, which we might label the "Wild West," anyone would be permitted to trade based on any information advantage. Even CEOs could buy and sell shares of their companies before they or the company disclosed important details to the public. In the second, which we might label the "level playing field," no one would be permitted to trade based on any information advantage. Even investors who had scrutinized a company's financial statements and determined that its shares were undervalued would be prohibited from buying shares unless they first disclosed their analysis to the market.

There are downsides to each of these polar approaches. In the "Wild West," insiders could take unfair advantage of other stock traders and cause investors to lose confidence in stock investing. In the "level playing field," those with an information advantage (even if fairly obtained) would not be able to profit from their insights and investors would have little incentive to participate in the stock markets. But what, precisely, would be the harm of a "Wild West"? And what exactly are the costs of a "level playing field"? To address these questions, we consider arguments for and against insider trading.

1. Arguments for Insider Trading

Some have made the provocative (and controversial) argument that insider trading is good and should not be prohibited. That is, investors and stock markets would be better off in the "Wild West."

Insider trading signals information to stock markets. Those who <u>argue</u> for insider trading point out that such trading transmits critical and difficult-to-communicate information to the stock markets, permitting smoother price movements before inside information is ultimately disclosed. Insiders who buy on undisclosed good news drive up the price, and insiders who sell on undisclosed bad news drive it down. Moreover,

Make the Connection

Recall our earlier discussion about the "informational efficiency" of stock markets from Chapter 27, Securities Markets. As information about a company enters the market—whether good news or bad news—the forces of supply and demand cause the market price to adjust. Buying on favorable inside information will put upward pressure on the price of the stock; and selling on unfavorable inside information will put downward pressure on the stock price. As the stock price moves, it will more accurately reflect the value of the stock. Insider trading will serve to direct capital to its highest-valued use.

competitively-sensitive information can be transmitted to stock markets, without disclosing its specific contents.

But the argument raises questions. Wouldn't stock markets and investors prefer full disclosure, as opposed to smoother prices? And isn't actual disclosure of good or bad news clearer and more effective than signaling through insider trading? And if widespread insider trading did signal information the company might not want to disclose, such as a top-secret new product or a disastrous earnings report, wouldn't the corporate preference for nondisclosure be compromised?

In addition, it's unclear whether stock prices respond to trading volume. Moreover, even when markets know that insiders are trading (as required by federal reporting requirements), price responses are skewed. Studies show that markets react quickly when insiders buy (presumably on the basis of good news), but only slightly when insiders sell (perhaps uncertain why the insider is selling).

Insider trading compensates management. Those who argue for insider trading point out that it can be seen as a form of executive compensation that creates incentives for managers to take risks that benefit investors. Because managers are inherently risk-averse, the possibility of profitable insider trading encourages managers to make business decisions with net positive value, even if the decisions are highly risky. If the risks pay off, everyone—insiders and outsiders—shares in a larger pie.

But again, there are questions. If managers can profit by selling company stock or stock options before bad news is disclosed, doesn't this create an incentive to produce bad results? And if insider trading on bad news is a reward for taking risks that sometimes don't pan out, why wouldn't managers simply aim for failure?

Perhaps insider trading could be limited to trading on good news. But this form of executive compensation raises additional questions. How can insider trading accurately measure the insider's contribution, if any, to particular good news in the firm? And, if all the insiders are given carte blanche to trade on good news, who will mind the store? Won't insiders become focused on maximizing their individual stock trading positions, instead of advancing the company's best interests?

2. Arguments Against Insider Trading

The arguments against insider trading and for its prohibition are varied—and suggest different legal approaches based on concerns ranging from fairness to economics.

Insider trading is unfair. The most fundamental argument against insider trading is that insiders should not be allowed to benefit from information generated for a corporate purpose. Accordingly, insiders who trade on inside information unfairly exploit shareholders in the company (or investors about to become shareholders) who trusted the insiders to be working for the company's best interest, not their own.

But is this intuitive argument valid? Trading in the securities of publicly-held companies occurs primarily on anonymous stock markets in which buyers and sellers are randomly matched with each other. It has been argued that insider trading does not harm investors who trade with insiders, but rather harms those whose trades are affected by the insider's trades. Under this analysis, if the insider's buying causes the price to rise, those investors induced to sell are harmed when they fail to profit from the subsequent good news. Similarly, if an insider's selling causes the price to fall, those investors induced to buy suffer a price decrease when bad news is ultimately disclosed.

But remember that it is unclear whether trading volume actually affects trading patterns and the stock price. In informationally efficient markets, additional buying or selling may not constitute "new information" that changes stock valuations. Therefore, concerns about the unfairness of insider trading could perhaps be better expressed in terms of a harm to perceptions of the integrity and fairness of the market more generally rather than specific harm to individuals trading with insiders.

Insider trading distorts company disclosures. Another argument is that insider trading, if permitted, would interfere with informational efficiency in stock markets. Insiders would be encouraged to manipulate corporate disclosures or time truthful disclosure to the markets so they could exploit their informational advantage. At the extreme, investors might regard markets as so distorted that they would be unwilling to trade.

According to this argument, informational flows in and out of the company would be distorted if insider trading were permitted. Disclosure delays would be predictable as information flowed up the corporate ladder and insiders at each rung took advantage of it before passing it along. Further, once particular insiders had traded, they would seek to release the information expeditiously to assure their trading profits—even when disclosure might be contrary to the company's best interests.

Make the Connection

The concern that insider trading would induce insiders to manipulate corporate disclosures may have been at the heart of the regulation of short-swing trading by designated insiders. As we will see at the end of this chapter, § 16 of the Securities Exchange Act of 1934 calls for the disgorgement of any insider-trading profits based on trades during a six-month window, thus reducing the incentives of corporate insiders to manipulate stock prices for their own trading benefit.

But, as some have asserted, why would insiders want to manipulate the content or timing of disclosures if doing so would undermine the credibility of the firm in its communications to investors? This rejoinder may be wishful thinking. It assumes that the incentives for insiders to bolster corporate credibility outweigh their personal incentives to trade profitably in their company's stock. As we have seen, many securities fraud class actions involve the release by corporate executives of false or misleading information aimed at making more profitable their personal trading in the company's stock.

Insider trading is theft of company information. Others argue that insider trading is essentially the use of private information owned by the company. As such, prohibitions against insider trading can be seen as protection of intellectual property.

Just as trade secrets, patents, and other informational property are protected to encourage the production of socially valuable information, inside information is protected to encourage companies to create it. For example, a mining company that strikes a rich ore deposit will want to use this information to obtain mining rights from adjacent property owners, without running the risk that insider trading will reveal the strike.

Insider trading prohibitions simply recognize that as between the company and the insider, valuable company information belongs to the company, not the insider. The prohibition against insider trading is a way of protecting company information. Not only does treating inside information as company property encourage its production (good news), but protecting adverse information from insider exploitation (bad news) also reduces the company's cost of capital and increases its reputation for integrity.

But if insider trading exploits company property, why don't we see private enforcement of insider trading rules? Certainly, companies enforce their rights in patents, trademarks, and other valuable proprietary information; but the norm in insider trading cases is *public enforcement* (often prosecutions of insiders). Perhaps lack of private enforcement reflects doubts about whether insider trading actually causes harm to the corporation. For example, it is unclear whether insider trading causes companies to lose opportunities, such as the acquisition of mineral rights, or injures the corporate reputation.

Nonetheless, viewing insider trading as theft of proprietary information—where detection is costly and difficult, and valuing the loss may be impossible—explains why public enforcement may be necessary. Since detection of insider trading requires systems of securities surveillance, private civil enforcement may be inadequate to create sufficient disincentives. Only through public systems of surveillance, such as stock markets and government regulators, and through public enforcement, including criminal sanctions, is inside information adequately protected from insider exploitation.

Insider trading increases firms' cost of capital. Many argue that insider trading undermines investor confidence in stock markets. According to this argument, if insider trading were permitted, investors would take precautions and discount the company's stock price, thereby raising the company's cost of capital (the price at which the company can borrow money or sell securities). When investors in a stock market can't figure out whether insiders are trading on material, nonpublic information, they will assume the worst. They will either not invest in the market or discount the stock of all companies by the risk of insider trading. In jurisdictions without insider trading regulation and enforcement, studies show that this investor self-insurance increases firms' cost of capital.

Why don't firms proactively respond to this possible problem by incurring bonding and monitoring costs to signal to investors their lower

Food for Thought

Countries without insider trading regulation or enforcement often experience wide spreads in bid-ask prices. What does this mean? Normally, the difference between the broker's buying price (bid) and selling price (ask) reflects the "commission" the broker charges for acting as intermediary between sellers and buyers. Thus, if the bid price is $19.90 and the ask price is $20.10, the broker is effectively charging $0.20 for buying stock from one investor and selling it to another investor. But if there is a risk of stock traders using undisclosed inside information, the broker will protect herself by charging a bigger spread—let's say, bid $19.50 and ask $20.50. In this way, if a trader with inside information knows more than the broker, the spread protects the broker. But the effect is a less liquid market. Who wants to pay a one dollar spread, buying stock for $20.50 and knowing that you could resell it for only $19.50?

likelihood of insider trading? The answer is that many do. For example, most U.S. public companies now limit when insiders can trade in their company's stock. Using "blackouts" and "trading windows," many companies permit insiders to trade only for a specified period (typically 7–30 days) after earnings announcements and other important corporate information is released. One study found that this self-regulation both suppresses trading by insiders and narrows the bid-ask spread for the company's stock. Not only do company-imposed policies affect insider trading but market intermediaries such as brokers price securities to reflect the reduced risk of insider trading once companies adopt such policies.

B. State Law on Insider Trading

We've observed that insider trading regulation is mostly federal. Why is this? The following typical state case offers an answer. State courts have decided that insider trading on public stock markets, provided there is no actual fraud, does not violate state corporate fiduciary law. Instead, state courts have decided that in most circumstances, all shareholders, including insiders, have the freedom to do with their shares as they please. Insiders might have duties to the corporation, but state courts have held that they generally do not have duties to individual shareholders.

You might wonder why we are studying state insider trading law, if it's mostly toothless. There are a couple of reasons. First, state law has some relevance in close corporations where, as you'll soon see, "special facts" can be the basis for fiduciary liability. Second, it's useful to understand that insider trading regulation is part of the corporate federalism dynamic. Building on state-based fiduciary concepts, federal law actually fills the gaps left by state law and creates new doctrine. In any event, the case is short, and we put most of the analysis in the points for discussion that follow.

By way of background, the case arose when a stockholder of the Cliff Mining Company, whose stock was listed on the Boston Stock Exchange, sought relief for losses suffered when he sold on the exchange 700 shares of the company's stock to the defendants, who were officers and directors of the corporation. The court accepted the trial judge's findings that Cliff had started exploration for copper on its land in 1925, acting on certain geological surveys. However, the exploration was not successful, and the company removed its equipment in May 1926.

Meanwhile, in March 1926, an experienced geologist wrote a report theorizing about the existence of copper deposits in the region of the company's holdings. The defendants, believing there was merit to the theory, secured options to land adjacent to the copper belt. Also, anticipating an increase in the value of the stock if the theory proved correct, the defendants purchased shares of the company's stock through an agent.

When the plaintiff learned of the termination of the original exploratory operations from a newspaper article—for which defendants were in no way responsible—he immediately sold his stock.

Goodwin v. Agassiz

<u>186 N.E. 659 (Mass. 1933)</u>

RUGG, CHIEF JUSTICE.

The contention of the plaintiff is that the purchase of his stock in the company by the defendants without disclosing to him as a stockholder their knowledge of the geologist's theory, their belief that the theory was true, the keeping secret the existence of the theory, discontinuance by the defendants of exploratory operations begun in 1925 on property of the Cliff Mining Company and their plan ultimately to test the value of the theory, constitute actionable wrong for which he as stockholder can recover.

The trial judge ruled that based on all the circumstances developed by the trial there was no fiduciary relation requiring such disclosure by the defendants to the plaintiff before buying his stock in the manner in which they did.

The directors of a commercial corporation stand in a relation of trust to the corporation and are bound to exercise the strictest good faith in respect to its property and business. The contention that directors also occupy the position of trustee toward individual stockholders in the corporation is plainly contrary to repeated decisions of this court and cannot be supported. "There is no legal privity, relation, or immediate connection, between the holders of shares in a bank, in their individual capacity, on the one side, and the directors of the bank on the other."

The principle thus established is supported by an imposing weight of authority in other jurisdictions.

Purchases and sales of stock dealt in on the stock exchange are commonly impersonal affairs. An honest director would be in a difficult situation if he could neither buy nor sell on the stock exchange shares of stock in his corporation without first seeking out the other actual ultimate party to the transaction and disclosing to him everything which a court or jury might later find that he then knew affecting the real or speculative value of such shares. Fiduciary obligations of directors ought not to be made so onerous that men of experience and ability will be deterred from accepting such office. Law in its sanctions is not coextensive with morality. It cannot undertake to put all parties to every contract on an equality as to knowledge, experience, skill and shrewdness. It cannot undertake to relieve against hard bargains made between competent parties without fraud.

On the other hand, directors cannot rightly be allowed to indulge with impunity in practices which do violence to prevailing standards of upright businessmen. Therefore, where a director personally seeks a stockholder for the purpose of buying his shares without making disclosure of material facts within his peculiar knowledge and not within reach of the stockholder, the transaction will be closely scrutinized and relief may be granted in appropriate instances. *Strong v. Repide*, 213 U.S. 419 (1909).

The precise question to be decided in the case at bar is whether the defendants as directors had a right to buy stock of the plaintiff, a stockholder. The facts found afford no ground for inferring fraud or conspiracy. The only knowledge possessed by the defendants not open to the plaintiff was the existence of a theory formulated in a thesis by a geologist as to the possible existence of copper deposits where certain geological conditions existed common to the property of the Cliff Mining Company and that of other mining companies in its neighborhood. Whether that theory was sound or fallacious, no one knew, and so far as appears has never been demonstrated. The defendants made no representations to anybody about the theory. No facts found placed upon them any obligation to disclose the theory.

The stock of the Cliff Mining Company was bought and sold on the stock exchange. The identity of buyers and sellers of the stock in question in fact was not known to the parties and perhaps could not readily have been ascertained. The plaintiff was no novice. He was a member of the Boston stock exchange and had kept a record of sales of Cliff Mining Company stock. He acted upon his own judgment in selling his stock. He made no inquiries of the defendants or of other officers of the company. The result is that the plaintiff cannot prevail.

Decree dismissing bill affirmed with costs.

Points for Discussion

1. Majority rule.

Goodwin sets out the "majority rule" that directors and officers have no state-based fiduciary duty to disclose material nonpublic information when trading company securities in an impersonal market. Is this consistent with the "duty of disclosure" that corporate managers have to be honest in their communications with shareholders? *See* Chapter 17, Shareholder Information Rights. Is this consistent with the other duties imposed on corporate fiduciaries that we have studied? *See* Chapter 20, Board Decision Making ("duty of care" of directors to fully inform shareholders in a merger); Chapter 24, Duties within Corporate Groups (duty of subsidiary's board to disclose material information to minority shareholders when structuring squeeze-out transaction with controlling shareholder).

2. Materiality.

Perhaps *Goodwin* did not actually involve insider trading because the information available to the insiders (the geologist's theory) was not material—that is, it was not information that reasonable investors would have considered important in valuing Cliff Mining's stock. Is that why the court rejected the plaintiff's claim? Would the outcome have been different if the insiders had traded after learning of a major mineral strike on the company's land?

3. Special rules.

Goodwin recognized that a different rule might apply when insiders purchase stock in face-to-face transactions—the "special facts doctrine" enunciated in *Strong v. Repide*, 213 U.S. 419 (1909). Under this doctrine, although an insider normally owes no fiduciary duty to individual shareholders, a plaintiff may have a remedy when, in particular circumstances, nondisclosure amounts to unconscionable behavior by the insider.

Other state courts (the first case was in Kansas) have gone further and have held that directors and officers have a fiduciary duty to disclose material non-public information in any face-to-face stock transaction with a shareholder, regardless of special circumstances. *See Hotchkiss v. Fischer*, 16 P.2d 531 (Kan. 1932).

Note some of the limits of these special rules. First, they do not apply to impersonal stock markets. Second, they apply only to transactions between insiders and existing shareholders; selling to a new investor is not covered.

4. Fraud.

Goodwin left open the possibility that shareholders may have recourse against insiders who commit fraud when they trade in their company's securities. The common law tort of deceit, which varies somewhat from state to state, basically requires the plaintiff to prove five elements: (1) The defendant misrepresented a material fact (2) with knowledge of its falsity or

Take Note!

The facts in the above two "special facts" cases reeked of wrongdoing. In *Strong* the defendant was a director, majority shareholder, and general manager of the corporation. He was in negotiations to sell otherwise worthless property owned by the corporation to the U.S. government at a substantial price. To hide his identity from the selling shareholder, he used an undisclosed agent to purchase the plaintiff's shares at a price that did not reflect the pending (and very lucrative) deal with the government.

In *Hotchkiss* the defendant was a director and president of the corporation. He refused to answer an inquiry from the plaintiff, a shareholder and "impoverished widow," about whether the corporation would declare a dividend, but offered to buy her stock at $1.25 per share. Three days after she sold, the board declared a dividend of $1.00 per share—an instant 80% return on the stock sold by the widow.

with reckless disregard for the truth and (3) with the intention that the plaintiff rely, and (4) the plaintiff justifiably relied on defendant's misrepresentation (5) to her detriment.

Traditional fraud law suffers from several serious drawbacks from a plaintiff's perspective. In a typical case of insider trading the defendant makes no statements, material or otherwise, when trading in company stock. Even if silence could be actionable—because of a special relationship between the parties—the plaintiff must prove her reliance on the silence, which may be nearly impossible.

5. Corporate recovery.

Isn't the corporation, given its interest in the faithfulness of its fiduciaries and the integrity of trading in its stock, harmed by insider trading? Shouldn't the corporation be able to recover the ill-gotten gains of corporate fiduciaries who misused inside information?

Before the development of federal insider trading law, which began in earnest in the 1980s, some state courts had held that the corporation could recover trading profits realized by insiders, even though it had suffered no loss. But the cases seem to have died on the vine.

In 1949 the Delaware Chancery Court said that a corporation engaged in an undisclosed stock repurchase program could recover from insiders who knew about the program and had competed against the corporation by purchasing stock for themselves. *Brophy v. Cities Service Co.*, 70 A.2d 5 (Del. Ch. 1949). According to the court, corporate recovery was possible even if the corporation did not suffer any actual financial loss.

In 1969 the New York Court of Appeals came to a similar conclusion, holding that a corporation could recover against insiders who traded on nonpublic corporate information, even though the corporation suffered no loss. *Diamond v. Oreamuno*, 248 N.E.2d 910 (N.Y. 1969).

But neither case has generated much of a progeny. *Brophy*, though widely cited, has never been used in Delaware to permit corporate recovery of insider trading profits. And *Diamond* has not been followed in New York and has specifically been rejected in two other jurisdictions. Some judges have stated concerns about *vertical* federalism difficulties if state law sought to regulate insider trading covered by federal law.

C. Federal Law on Insider Trading

Despite these forays of state law into insider trading, most regulation in this area is federal. Congress's earliest attempt to rein in insider trading was through the enactment of § 16 of the Securities Exchange Act of 1934. But § 16—which we describe more fully in the final section of this chapter—only applies to purchases and sales by specified insiders of their own company's stock within a six-month period. It creates a remedy that forces the insider to disgorge their trading profits, but has proved to be ineffective against the most common forms of insider trading. For example, it does not apply to trading by insiders who have held their stock more than six months; nor does it apply to trading by outsiders on the basis of material nonpublic information.

Instead, the SEC and the courts have relied primarily on the SEC's Rule 10b–5 to regulate the intentional misuse of inside information. Rule 10b–5—which was the subject of the previous chapter on securities fraud—frequently has been described as a "judicial oak" that grew from little more than a "legislative acorn." Authority for the rule—the legislative acorn—comes from § 10(b) of the Securities Exchange Act of 1934, which authorizes the SEC to promulgate rules forbidding the use of "any manipulative or deceptive device or contrivance" in connection with the purchase or sale of any security. Borrowing language from § 17(a) of the Securities Act of 1933, which applies to deception in the sale of securities, the SEC drafted Rule 10b–5 to cover deception "in connection with the *purchase* or *sale* of securities."

When it adopted Rule 10b–5, the SEC had little idea that courts would seize on the rule to make it the mainstay of U.S. securities fraud regulation. Significantly, the rule itself contains no express language prohibiting insider trading. Nevertheless, over the years the SEC and the Supreme Court have inventively interpreted Rule 10b–5 to contain a general prohibition against insider trading in open-market transactions, as well as in face-to-face dealings. Specifically, the Court has built a federal common law regime built on the notion that it is "deceptive" when a person trades in securities in breach of fiduciary duties to the source of that information.

We turn next to the triumvirate of landmark Supreme Court insider trading cases—the classical theory (*Chiarella*), the tipper-tippee corollary (*Dirks*), and the misappropriation theory (*O'Hagan*)—each an important branch of the 10b–5 "judicial oak." Here's a quick primer:

Many texts describing U.S. insider trading law begin with *In the Matter of Cady, Roberts & Co.*, 40 S.E.C. 907 (1961). The case, a colorful SEC enforcement action, provided the theoretical basis for early federal judicial cases on insider trading.

Curtiss-Wright Corporation, a major aircraft manufacturer, had announced that it was developing a new internal combustion engine. As you might guess, the company's stock price rose dramatically. A few weeks later, the company's board of directors met and decided, surprisingly, to cut the company's dividend rate by 40%. One of the directors, a member of a securities firm, left the board meeting during a recess and called from a payphone to tell his office about the dividend cut. On hearing this, a sales rep at the firm sold Curtiss-Wright stock held in various customer accounts. Later that day when news of the dividend cut was released to various financial wire services, the stock price fell 15%.

In a disciplinary case against the firm and the sales rep, the SEC began by intoning that Rule 10b–5 was meant to protect investors and had created "managerial duties and liabilities unknown to the common law." Then, citing the "special facts" cases we saw before, the SEC said that when corporate insiders have material nonpublic information they are under a duty to disclose the information before trading or to "forego the transaction." The SEC explained this disclose-or-abstain duty "rests on two principal elements; first, the existence of a relationship giving access to information intended to be available only for a corporate purpose and not for the personal benefit of anyone, and second, the inherent unfairness involved where a party takes advantage of such information knowing it is unavailable to those with whom he is dealing." The SEC acknowledged that it might have been a different case if the securities firm had surmised there would be a dividend cut based on "perceptive analysis of generally known facts." In the end, the SEC suspended the sales rep for 20 days—and the interpretation of Rule 10b–5 as an insider-trading prohibition had arrived. How does the Supreme Court treat this early SEC enforcement action in *Chiarella*?

- *Chiarella* establishes the "classical theory" of insider trading—a 10b–5 violation can occur when there is a duty to disclose arising from a relationship of trust and confidence (fiduciary duty) between the parties to the transaction, such as the relationship that the Court said corporate insiders have to corporate shareholders.

- *Dirks* extends the classical theory to "tippers" and "tippees." The Court holds that tipping by an insider can be a breach of fiduciary duty if "the insider will benefit, directly or indirectly, from his disclosure" and that a "tippee" violates Rule 10b–5 if she "knows or should know that there has been a breach." In its famous footnote 14, *Dirks* also indicates that an outsider (such as an underwriter, accountant, attorney, or consultant who receives nonpublic corporate information with the expectation that it will be kept confidential) is considered a "temporary insider" and cannot trade on the basis of that information.

- *O'Hagan* establishes the "misappropriation theory" of insider trading—trading on the basis of material nonpublic information in breach of a duty owed to the source of the information. This conduct violates Rule 10b–5, even though the misappropriator owes no duty to the person with whom she trades.

Note that all three cases, and subsequent district and appellate court cases, focus on fiduciary duty. As you read the cases, ask whether this focus on fiduciary duty is consistent with our earlier policy discussion of the pros and cons of insider trading.

1. *Chiarella* and the "Classical" Theory

Chiarella sets out the theory for regulating "classical" insider trading—that is, insider trading by company insiders in their own company's stock. The theory proceeds from the notion that insiders have a duty of "trust and confidence" to the company and its shareholders. But, as we have seen, state law imposes such a duty only in limited circumstances. As you read this case and those that follow, some important questions arise. Where does the duty not to trade on inside information come from? Where does the Supreme Court get the authority to define the contours of that duty? And what does any of this have to do with the reasons to prohibit insider trading?

Chiarella v. United States

445 U.S. 222 (1980)

JUSTICE POWELL delivered the opinion of the Court.

The question in this case is whether a person who learns from the confidential documents of one corporation that it is planning an attempt to secure control of a second corporation violates § 10(b) of the Securities Exchange Act of 1934 if he fails to disclose the impending takeover before trading in the target company's securities.

Petitioner is a printer by trade. In 1975 and 1976, he worked as a "markup man" in the New York composing room of Pandick Press, a financial printer. Among documents that petitioner handled were five announcements of corporate takeover bids. When these documents were delivered to the printer, the identities of the acquiring and target corporations were concealed by blank spaces or false names. The true names were sent to the printer on the night of the final printing.

The petitioner, however, was able to deduce the names of the target companies before the final printing from other information contained in the documents. Without disclosing his knowledge, petitioner purchased stock in the target companies and sold the shares immediately after the takeover attempts were made public. By this method, petitioner realized a gain of slightly more than $30,000 in the course of 14 months. Subsequently, the SEC began an investigation of his trading activities. In May 1977, petitioner entered into a consent decree with the SEC in which he agreed to return his profits to the sellers of the shares. On the same day, he was discharged by Pandick Press.

In January 1978, petitioner was indicted on 17 counts of violating § 10(b) of the Securities Exchange Act of 1934 and SEC Rule 10b–5. After petitioner unsuccessfully moved to dismiss the indictment, he was brought to trial and convicted on all counts.

The Court of Appeals for the Second Circuit affirmed petitioner's conviction. We granted certiorari, and we now reverse.

This case concerns the legal effect of the petitioner's silence. The District Court's charge permitted the jury to convict the petitioner if it found that he willfully failed to inform sellers of target company securities that he knew of a forthcoming takeover bid that would make their shares more valuable. In order to decide whether silence in such circumstances violates § 10(b), it is necessary to review the language and legislative history of that statute as well as its interpretation by the Commission and the federal courts.

Although the starting point of our inquiry is the language of the statute, § 10(b) does not state whether silence may constitute a manipulative or deceptive device. Section 10(b) was designed as a catchall clause to prevent fraudulent practices. But neither the legislative history nor the statute itself affords specific guidance for the resolution of this case. When Rule 10b–5 was promulgated in 1942, the SEC did not discuss the possibility that failure to provide information might run afoul of § 10(b).

The SEC took an important step in the development of § 10(b) when it held that a broker-dealer and his firm violated that section by selling securities on the basis of undisclosed information obtained from a director of the issuer corporation who was also a registered representative of the brokerage firm. In *Cady, Roberts & Co.*, the Commission decided that a corporate insider must abstain from trading in the shares of his corporation unless he has first disclosed all material inside information known to him. The obligation to disclose or abstain derives from an affirmative duty to disclose material information which has been traditionally imposed on corporate "insiders," particular officers, directors, or controlling stockholders. We, and the courts have consistently held that insiders must disclose material facts which are known to them by virtue of their position but which are not known to persons with whom they deal and which, if known, would affect their investment judgment.

The Commission emphasized that the duty arose from (i) the existence of a relationship affording access to inside information intended to be available only for a corporate purpose, and (ii) the unfairness of allowing a corporate insider to take advantage of that information by trading without disclosure.

That the relationship between a corporate insider and the stockholders of his corporation gives rise to a disclosure obligation is not a novel twist of the law. At common law, misrepresentation made for the purpose of inducing reliance upon the false statement is fraudulent. But one who fails to disclose material information prior to the consummation of a transaction commits fraud only when he is under a duty to do so. And the duty to disclose arises when one party has information "that the other party is entitled to know because of a fiduciary or similar relation of trust and confidence between them." In its *Cady, Roberts* decision, the Commission recognized a relationship of trust and confidence between the shareholders of a corporation and those insiders who have obtained confidential information by reason of their position with that corporation. This relationship gives rise to a duty to disclose because of the "necessity of preventing a corporate insider from taking unfair advantage of the uninformed minority stockholders."

Thus, silence in connection with the purchase or sale of securities may operate as a fraud actionable under § 10(b) despite the absence of statutory language or legislative history specifically addressing the legality of nondisclosure. But such liability is premised upon a duty to disclose arising from a relationship of trust and confidence between parties to a transaction. Application of a duty to disclose prior to trading guarantees that corporate insiders, who have an obligation to place the shareholder's welfare before their own, will not benefit personally through fraudulent use of material nonpublic information.

The petitioner was convicted of violating § 10(b) although he was not a corporate insider and he received no confidential information from the target company. Moreover, the "market information" upon which he relied did not concern the earning power or operations of the target company, but only the plans of the acquiring company. Petitioner's use of that information was not a fraud under § 10(b) unless he was subject to an affirmative duty to disclose it before trading. In this case, the jury instructions failed to specify any such duty. In effect, the trial court instructed the jury that petitioner owed a duty to everyone; to all sellers, indeed, to the market as a whole. The jury simply was told to decide whether petitioner used material, nonpublic information at a time when "he knew other people trading in the securities market did not have access to the same information."

The Court of Appeals affirmed the conviction by holding that "*anyone*—corporate insider or not—who regularly receives material nonpublic information may not use that information to trade in securities without incurring an affirmative duty to disclose." Although the court said that its test would include only persons who regularly receive material nonpublic information, its rationale for that limitation is unrelated to the existence of a duty to disclose. The Court of Appeals, like the trial court, failed to identify a relationship between petitioner and the sellers that could give rise to a duty. Its decision thus rested solely upon its belief that the federal securities laws have "created a system providing equal access to information necessary for reasoned and intelligent investment decisions."

The use by anyone of material information not generally available is fraudulent, this theory suggests, because such information gives certain buyers or sellers an unfair advantage over less informed buyers and sellers.

This reasoning suffers from two defects. First not every instance of financial unfairness constitutes fraudulent activity under § 10(b). Second, the element required to make silence fraudulent "a duty to disclose" is absent in this case. No duty could arise from petitioner's relationship with the sellers of the target company's securities, for petitioner had no prior dealings with them. He was not their agent, he was not a fiduciary, he was not a person in whom the sellers had placed their trust and confidence. He was, in fact, a complete stranger who dealt with the sellers only through impersonal market transactions.

We cannot affirm petitioner's conviction without recognizing a general duty between all participants in market transactions to forgo actions based on material, nonpublic information. Formulation of such a broad duty, which departs radically from the established doctrine that duty arises from a specific relationship between two parties, should not be undertaken absent some explicit evidence of congressional intent.

As we have seen, no such evidence emerges from the language or legislative history of § 10(b). Moreover, neither the Congress nor the Commission ever has adopted a parity-of-information rule. Instead the problems caused by misuse of market information have been addressed by detailed and sophisticated regulation that recognizes when use of market information may not harm operation of the securities markets. For example, the Williams Act limits but does not completely prohibit a tender offeror's purchases of target corporation stock before public announcement of the offer. Congress' careful action in this and other areas contrasts, and is in some tension, with the broad rule of liability we are asked to adopt in this case.

We see no basis for applying such a new and different theory of liability in this case. As we have emphasized before, the 1934 Act cannot be read "more broadly than its language and the statutory scheme reasonably permit." Section 10(b) is aptly described as a catch-all provision, but what it catches must be fraud. When an allegation of fraud is based upon nondisclosure, there can be no fraud absent a duty to speak. We hold that a duty to disclose under § 10(b) does not arise from the mere possession of nonpublic market information. The contrary result is without support in the legislative history of § 10(b) and would be inconsistent with the careful plan that Congress has enacted for regulation of the securities markets.

In its brief to this Court, the United States offers an alternative theory to support petitioner's conviction. It argues that petitioner breached a duty to the acquiring corporation when he acted upon information that he obtained by virtue of his position as an employee of a printer employed by the corporation. The breach of this duty is said to support a conviction under § 10(b) for fraud perpetrated upon both the acquiring corporation and the sellers.

We need not decide whether this theory has merit for it was not submitted to the jury.

The jury instructions demonstrate that petitioner was convicted merely because of his failure to disclose material, nonpublic information to sellers from whom he bought the stock of target corporations. The jury was not instructed on the nature or elements of a duty owed by petitioner to anyone other than the sellers. Because we cannot affirm a criminal conviction on the basis of a theory not presented to the jury, we will not speculate upon whether such a duty exists, whether it has been breached, or whether such a breach constitutes a violation of § 10(b).

The judgment of the Court of Appeals is reversed.

Chief Justice Burger, dissenting.

I believe that the jury instructions in this case properly charged a violation of § 10(b) and Rule 10b–5, and I would affirm the conviction.

As a general rule, neither party to an arm's-length business transaction has an obligation to disclose information to the other unless the parties stand in some confidential or fiduciary relation. This rule permits a businessman to capitalize on his experience and skill in securing and evaluating relevant information; it provides incentive for hard work, careful analysis, and astute forecasting. But the policies that underlie the rule also should limit its scope. In particular, the rule should give way when an informational advantage is obtained, not by superior experience, foresight, or industry, but by some unlawful means. I would read § 10(b) and Rule 10b–5 to encompass and build on this principle: to mean that a person who has misappropriated nonpublic information has an absolute duty to disclose that information or to refrain from trading.

The Court's opinion, as I read it, leaves open the question whether § 10(b) and Rule 10b–5 prohibit trading on misappropriated nonpublic information. Instead, the Court apparently concludes that this theory of the case was not submitted to the jury. In the Court's view, the instructions given the jury were premised on the erroneous notion that the mere failure to disclose nonpublic information, however acquired, is a deceptive practice. And because of this premise, the jury was not instructed that the means by which Chiarella acquired his informational advantage—by violating a duty owed to the acquiring companies—was an element of the offense.

The evidence shows beyond all doubt that Chiarella, working literally in the shadows of the warning signs in the printshop, misappropriated—stole to put it bluntly—valuable nonpublic information entrusted to him in the utmost confidence. He then exploited his ill-gotten informational advantage by purchasing securities in the market. In my view, such conduct plainly violates § 10(b) and Rule 10b–5. Accordingly, I would affirm the judgment of the Court of Appeals.

Points for Discussion

1. Type of trading.

What type of insider trading—"classical" or "misappropriation"—did Chiarella engage in? Who was hurt by his trading?

2. Nature of duty.

The Court decides that § 10(b) and Rule 10b–5 regulate trading on material nonpublic information when there is a relation of "trust and confidence" between the trading parties. Under state law, do corporate fiduciaries have

Even though Vincent Chiarella was not convicted of a criminal violation of the securities laws, he was held liable in a civil enforcement action by the SEC to pay back his trading profits. He was also fired from Pandick Press and blacklisted among Wall Street financial printers. After several years of unemployment, Chiarella got back his old job when his printers' union obtained his reinstatement.

such a duty to shareholders—or to investors who are buying company stock from them? Where does the duty inferred by the Supreme Court come from?

Food for Thought

Note that *Chiarella* frames the prohibition against insider trading as arising from an insider's duty to "disclose or abstain." Does this mean that if an insider discloses material nonpublic information and then trades on the basis of that information, there's no 10b–5 violation? Technically, the answer would seem to be yes—provided that the disclosure sufficiently alerts shareholders (or the market) of the material nonpublic information and gives the market time to absorb the information. Of course, once this had happened and the trading price reflects the information, there is no incentive for the insider to trade on it. And it is possible that the disclosure would violate some other duty under the law.

But the question remains. When is disclosure of material nonpublic information sufficient so an insider has satisfied his "disclose or abstain" duty—and need no longer abstain? For example, would posting the inside information on a social media site, such as Facebook, be enough to then trade on that information? Or what about a "tweet" by a CEO who had millions of followers on Twitter? Or is the answer that only disclosure that effectively eliminates any informational advantage will do? That is, the "disclose or abstain" duty is really a duty to abstain.

3. Chiarella's conviction.

Chiarella's criminal conviction was overturned. Why? If the jury had been instructed to find a violation of § 10(b) if Chiarella had used information that he was obligated to keep confidential, would this conviction have stood?

---

2. *Dirks* and the Tipper-Tippee Liability

Chiarella clarified that § 10(b) and Rule 10b–5 make it unlawful for a corporate insider to use material nonpublic information to trade in that corporation's stock. Does the same prohibition apply to a noninsider who has obtained material nonpublic information from an insider? In other words, how do the insider trading prohibitions apply to tippers and tippees?

First, some vocabulary. A *tipper* is a person who discloses material nonpublic information. A *tippee* is a person who receives material nonpublic information from a tipper. If the tippee then discloses the information, he becomes a tipper, and the person to whom he discloses becomes a *subtippee*.

Note that the tipper can hold different positions. The tipper might be an insider, such as a director, officer or employee of the corporation. Or the tipper might be a constructive insider, such as a corporate lawyer or accountant, who has a confidential relationship with the corporation.

Likewise, a tippee might hold a range of positions. The tippee's relationship with the tipper can vary, from husband-wife to more distant family members to friends to a range of professional and nonprofessional relationships (doctor-patient, priest-penitent, softball team captain-first baseman, and so on).

Finally, who actually trades on the information can vary. Both the tipper and the tippee might trade. Or just the tippee. Or only a subtippee (or remote sub-subtippees). All of these permutations affect the analysis, and the facts in tipper-tippee case can be quite complex. But we start with the basic tipper-tippee case, so you have a sense of the key factors courts look to in assessing tipper-tippee liability.

As you read the following case, keep in mind that the market's ability to accurately price securities depends on market participants having access to new information on a timely basis. What happens if there are unfair disparities in the information available to market participants? Does the Court's approach to tipper-tippee liability account for these policy questions?

Dirks v. Securities and Exchange Commission

463 U.S. 646 (1983)

JUSTICE POWELL delivered the opinion of the Court.

Petitioner Raymond Dirks received material nonpublic information from "insiders" of a corporation with which he had no connection. He disclosed this information to investors who relied on it in trading in the shares of the corporation. The question is whether Dirks violated the antifraud provisions of the federal securities laws by this disclosure.

In 1973, Dirks was an officer of a New York broker-dealer firm who specialized in providing investment analysis of insurance company securities to institutional investors. On March 6, Dirks received information from Ronald Secrist, a former officer of Equity Funding of America. Secrist

You'll notice that Justice Lewis Powell wrote both the *Chiarella* and the *Dirks* opinions. This is not surprising, given that he was the only corporate/securities lawyer on the Supreme Court. In fact, Powell (who served on the Court from 1972–1987) is responsible for writing most of the important securities and corporate law decisions of the Court. Recall that *CTS v. Dynamics* (Chapter 5, Corporate Federalism) and *Bank of Boston v. Bellotti* (Chapter 7, Corporation as Political Actor) were written by Powell. The other justices on the Court deferred to Powell's expertise on securities/corporate matters, and he influenced the other justices on the Court to narrow the reach of federal and state regulation into corporate affairs.

alleged that the assets of Equity Funding, a diversified corporation primarily engaged in selling life insurance and mutual funds, were vastly overstated as the result of fraudulent corporate practices. Secrist also stated that various regulatory agencies had failed to act on similar charges made by Equity Funding employees. He urged Dirks to verify the fraud and disclose it publicly.

Dirks decided to investigate the allegations. He visited Equity Funding's headquarters in Los Angeles and interviewed several officers and employees of the corporation. The senior management denied any wrongdoing, but certain corporation employees corroborated the charges of fraud. Neither Dirks nor his firm owned or traded any Equity Funding stock, but throughout his investigation he openly discussed the information he had obtained with a number of clients and investors. Some of these persons sold their holdings of Equity Funding securities, including five investment advisers who liquidated holdings of more than $16 million.[2]

While Dirks was in Los Angeles, he was in touch regularly with William Blundell, the *Wall Street Journal*'s Los Angeles bureau chief. Dirks urged Blundell to write a story on the fraud allegations. Blundell did not believe, however, that such a massive fraud could go undetected and declined to write the story. He feared that publishing such damaging hearsay might be libelous.

During the two-week period in which Dirks pursued his investigation and spread word of Secrist's charges, the price of Equity Funding stock fell from $26 per share to less than $15 per share. This led the New York Stock Exchange to halt trading on March 27. Shortly thereafter California insurance authorities impounded Equity Funding's records and uncovered evidence of the fraud. Only then did the SEC file a complaint against Equity Funding[3] and only then, on April 2, did the *Wall Street Journal* publish a front-page story based largely on information assembled by Dirks. Equity Funding immediately went into receivership.

The SEC began an investigation into Dirks' role in the exposure of the fraud. After a hearing by an administrative law judge, the SEC found that Dirks had aided and abetted violations of § 17(a) of the Securities Act of 1933, § 10(b) of the Securities Exchange Act of 1934, and SEC Rule 10b–5, by repeating the allegations of fraud to members of the investment community who later sold their Equity Funding stock. The SEC concluded: "Where 'tippees'—regardless of their motivation or occupation—come into possession of material 'information that

---

[2] Dirks received from his firm a salary plus a commission for securities transactions above a certain amount that his clients directed through his firm. But "it is not clear how many of those with whom Dirks spoke promised to direct some brokerage business through Dirks' firm to compensate Dirks, or how many actually did so."

[3] On March 9, 1973, an official of the California Insurance Department informed the SEC's regional office in Los Angeles of Secrist's charges of fraud. Dirks himself voluntarily presented his information at the SEC's regional office beginning on March 27.

they know is confidential and know or should know came from a corporate insider,' they must either publicly disclose that information or refrain from trading." Recognizing, however, that Dirks "played an important role in bringing Equity Funding's massive fraud to light," the SEC only censured him.

Dirks sought review in the Court of Appeals for the District of Columbia Circuit. The court entered judgment against Dirks "for the reasons stated by the Commission in its opinion." Judge Wright, a member of the panel, issued an opinion stating that "the obligations of corporate fiduciaries pass to all those to whom they disclose their information before it has been disseminated to the public at large."

In view of the importance to the SEC and to the securities industry of the question presented by this case, we granted a writ of certiorari. We now reverse.

We were explicit in *Chiarella* in saying that there can be no duty to disclose where the person who has traded on inside information "was not the corporation's agent, was not a fiduciary, or was not a person in whom the sellers of the securities had placed their trust and confidence." Not to require such a fiduciary relationship, we recognized, would "depart radically from the established doctrine that duty arises from a specific relationship between two parties" and would amount to "recognizing a general duty between all participants in market transactions to forego actions based on material, nonpublic information." This requirement of a specific relationship between the shareholders and the individual trading on inside information has created analytical difficulties for the SEC and courts in policing tippees who trade on inside information. Unlike insiders who have independent fiduciary duties to both the corporation and its shareholders, the typical tippee has no such relationships.[14] In view of this absence, it has been unclear how a tippee acquires the *Cady, Roberts* duty to refrain from trading on inside information.

The SEC's position in this case is that a tippee "inherits" the *Cady, Roberts* obligation to shareholders whenever he receives inside information from an insider. This view differs little from the view that we rejected as inconsistent with congressional intent in *Chiarella*. In that case, the Court of Appeals agreed with the SEC and affirmed Chiarella's conviction, holding that "*anyone*—corporate insider

---

[14] Under certain circumstances, such as where corporate information is revealed legitimately to an underwriter, accountant, lawyer, or consultant working for the corporation, these outsiders may become fiduciaries of the shareholders. The basis for recognizing this fiduciary duty is not simply that such persons acquired nonpublic corporate information, but rather that they have entered into a special confidential relationship in the conduct of the business of the enterprise and are given access to information solely for corporate purposes. When such a person breaches his fiduciary relationship, he may be treated more properly as a tipper than a tippee. For such a duty to be imposed, however, the corporation must expect the outsider to keep the disclosed nonpublic information confidential, and the relationship at least must imply such a duty.

or not—who regularly receives material nonpublic information may not use that information to trade in securities without incurring an affirmative duty to disclose." Here, the SEC maintains that anyone who knowingly receives nonpublic material information from an insider has a fiduciary duty to disclose before trading.

In effect, the SEC's theory of tippee liability appears rooted in the idea that the antifraud provisions require equal information among all traders. This conflicts with the principle set forth in *Chiarella* that only some persons, under some circumstances, will be barred from trading while in possession of material nonpublic information. We reaffirm today that "a duty to disclose arises from the relationship between parties and not merely from one's ability to acquire information because of his position in the market." Imposing a duty to disclose or abstain solely because a person knowingly receives material nonpublic information from an insider and trades on it could have an inhibiting influence on the role of market analysts, which the SEC itself recognizes is necessary to the preservation of a healthy market. It is commonplace for analysts to "ferret out and analyze information," and this often is done by meeting with and questioning corporate officers and others who are insiders. And information that the analysts obtain normally may be the basis for judgments as to the market worth of a corporation's securities. The analyst's judgment in this respect is made available in market letters or otherwise to clients of the firm. It is the nature of this type of information, and indeed of the markets themselves, that such information cannot be made simultaneously available to all of the corporation's stockholders or the public generally.

The conclusion that recipients of inside information do not invariably acquire a duty to disclose or abstain does not mean that such tippees always are free to trade on the information. The need for a ban on some tippee trading is clear. Not only are insiders forbidden by their fiduciary relationship from personally using undisclosed corporate information to their advantage, but they may not give such information to an outsider for the same improper purpose of exploiting the information for their personal gain. Similarly, the transactions of those who knowingly participate with the fiduciary in such a breach are "as forbidden" as transactions "on behalf of the trustee himself." Thus, the tippee's duty to disclose or abstain is derivative from that of the insider's duty.

Thus, some tippees must assume an insider's duty to the shareholders not because they receive inside information, but rather because it has been made available to them *improperly*. Thus, a tippee assumes a fiduciary duty to the shareholders of a corporation not to trade on material nonpublic information only when the insider has breached his fiduciary duty to the shareholders by disclosing the information to the tippee and the tippee knows or should know that there has been a breach.

In determining whether a tippee is under an obligation to disclose or abstain, it thus is necessary to determine whether the insider's "tip" constituted a breach of the insider's fiduciary duty. All disclosures of confidential corporate information are not inconsistent with the duty insiders owe to shareholders. In contrast to the extraordinary facts of this case, the more typical situation in which there will be a question whether disclosure violates the insider's *Cady, Roberts* duty is when insiders disclose information to analysts. Whether disclosure is a breach of duty depends in large part on the purpose of the disclosure. This standard was identified by the SEC itself in *Cady, Roberts*: a purpose of the securities laws was to eliminate "use of inside information for personal advantage." Thus, the test is whether the insider personally will benefit, directly or indirectly, from his disclosure. Absent some personal gain, there has been no breach of duty to stockholders. And absent a breach by the insider, there is no derivative breach.

To determine whether the disclosure itself "deceives, manipulates, or defrauds" shareholders, the initial inquiry is whether there has been a breach of duty by the insider. This requires courts to focus on objective criteria, *i.e.,* whether the insider receives a direct or indirect personal benefit from the disclosure, such as a pecuniary gain or a reputational benefit that will translate into future earnings. There are objective facts and circumstances that often justify such an inference. For example, there may be a relationship between the insider and the recipient that suggests a *quid pro quo* from the latter, or an intention to benefit the particular recipient. The elements of fiduciary duty and exploitation of nonpublic information also exist when an insider makes a gift of confidential information to a trading relative or friend. The tip and trade resemble trading by the insider himself followed by a gift of the profits to the recipient.

Determining whether an insider personally benefits from a particular disclosure, a question of fact, will not always be easy for courts. But it is essential, we think, to have a guiding principle for those whose daily activities must be limited and instructed by the SEC's inside-trading rules, and we believe that there must be a breach of the insider's fiduciary duty before the tippee inherits the duty to disclose or abstain. In contrast, the rule adopted by the SEC in this case would have no limiting principle.

Under the inside-trading and tipping rules set forth above, we find that there was no actionable violation by Dirks. It is undisputed that Dirks himself was a stranger to Equity Funding, with no pre-existing fiduciary duty to its shareholders. He took no action, directly or indirectly, that induced the shareholders or officers of Equity Funding to repose trust or confidence in him. There was no expectation by Dirks' sources that he would keep their information in confidence. Nor did Dirks misappropriate or illegally obtain the information about Equity Funding. Unless the insiders breached their *Cady, Roberts* duty to shareholders in disclosing the nonpublic information to Dirks, he breached no duty when he passed it on to investors as well as to the *Wall Street Journal.*

It is clear that neither Secrist nor the other Equity Funding employees violated their *Cady, Roberts* duty to the corporation's shareholders by providing information to Dirks. The tippers received no monetary or personal benefit for revealing Equity Funding's secrets, nor was their purpose to make a gift of valuable information to Dirks. As the facts of this case clearly indicate, the tippers were motivated by a desire to expose the fraud. In the absence of a breach of duty to shareholders by the insiders, there was no derivative breach by Dirks.

Points for Discussion

1. Basis for tipping liability.

Does the Court explain how § 10(b) and Rule 10b–5 extend beyond those who have a relation of "trust and confidence" to encompass those who obtain information from such a person?

2. Stock analysts.

What attitude does the majority opinion take toward stock analysts, whose job is to ascertain price-sensitive information and share it with clients?

3. Benefit to tipper.

After *Dirks,* lower courts wrestled with what constitutes a "personal benefit" sufficient to create tipping liability—coming to conflicting conclusions. Some courts narrowly interpreted *Dirks* and held that the personal benefit received by the tipper had to be tangible, a sort of kickback for passing confidential information, or otherwise part of a meaningfully close relationship. Other courts interpreted *Dirks* to cover situations in which the tipper was in a friend or family relationship with the tippee and had a personal reason for tipping inside information. The question thus came down to whether the tipper had to receive a "tangible" benefit or whether receiving a "psychic" benefit was enough and if so how close of a relationship would suffice.

In 2016, the Supreme Court resolved this circuit split. *United States v. Salman,* 137 S. Ct. 420 (2016). The Court reaffirmed the original language of *Dirks* and held that a family member is personally benefitted (and thus breaches a duty) by giving confidential information to a relative who trades on the tip. The Court viewed *Dirks* as "easily" resolving the question and concluded that "giving a gift of trading information [to a trading relative] is the same thing as trading by the tipper followed by a gift of the proceeds." In the case, which involved the trading by a sub-tippee, a Citigroup insider had given his brother confidential information about M&A clients of the bank with the expectation that his brother would trade on it. The Court held the insider's tip to his brother was a breach of his duty of trust and confidence to Citigroup and its clients. Then when his brother passed this information to their brother-in-law Salman, this duty was acquired and breached by Salman when he traded on the information with full knowledge that it had been improperly tipped originally. The Court made clear that the lower court's view that the tipper must receive something of a "pecuniary or similarly valuable nature" was "inconsistent" with *Dirks*.

---

3. *O'Hagan* and the "Misappropriation" Theory

Chiarella and *Dirks* resolved three major issues. First, they confirmed that § 10(b) and Rule 10b–5 made it unlawful for an insider or temporary insider of a corporation to trade that corporation's stock on the basis of material nonpublic information. Second, they confirmed that it was unlawful for an insider or temporary insider, acting in breach of a fiduciary duty owed to the corporation, to disclose to another (to "tip") material nonpublic information about that corporation for personal benefit. Third, they rejected the "level playing field" principle—in other words, they held

Practice Pointer

Here's a colorful case testing the "personal benefit" test of *Dirks*. In *SEC v. Switzer*, 590 F. Supp. 756 (W.D. Okla. 1984), Switzer, then the football coach of the University of Oklahoma, was sitting in the bleachers at a track meet. He overheard Platt, the CEO of Phoenix Resources Company, tell his wife that he might be out of town the following week because there was a chance that Phoenix would be liquidated. Platt's purpose in telling his wife about the trip, according to the court, was so she could make child care arrangements. The Platts did not know that Switzer was on a bench behind them during this conversation. Switzer, who knew of Platt's position with Phoenix, along with several of Switzer's friends, bought Phoenix stock in the expectation that its liquidation would lead to a price spike. The SEC argued that Switzer and his friends were liable under Rule 10b–5 as tippees. The court held, however, that Platt did not breach a fiduciary duty to Phoenix's shareholders by disclosing the information because he did not personally benefit, directly or indirectly, from the disclosure. Accordingly, under *Dirks*, Switzer and his friends were not liable as tippees.

Suppose the CEO had turned to Switzer, "Hey, coach, I know you like to play the stock market. You might be interested to know that my company might be liquidated." Would the result be different?

that § 10(b) and Rule 10b–5 did not bar outsiders and nontippees from trading simply because they possessed material nonpublic information not available to other traders.

However, *Chiarella* and *Dirks* left an important question open. What about traders who were neither insiders nor tippees? What about *outsiders* who obtained material nonpublic information and traded on the basis of that information? When did such outsiders violate § 10(b) and Rule 10b–5? After *Chiarella* and *Dirks*, the circuit courts were split on the question of whether such outsider trading was unlawful and the theory on which such liability might be based.

In their attempts to go after outsiders, prosecutors had developed the "misappropriation" theory, referenced in *Chiarella* but not ruled upon in that case. According to the theory, it was unlawful even for a person who had no connection to a corporation to trade in the corporation's securities on the basis of material nonpublic information if the person had misappropriated the information from some third party.

The misappropriation theory faced several potential challenges. Most prominently, the Supreme Court had made clear that § 10(b) addressed only deception, not trading that was financially unfair. Misappropriating inside information might be unfair, but how was it "deceptive"? Wasn't there something different about deceiving the source of information and deceiving a participant in the marketplace? And wasn't "theft" different from "deception"?

For example, if I broke into a corporation's headquarters, stole some valuable information and then sold that information to one of the corporation's competitors, I would be guilty of theft. But had I violated § 10(b)? That would seem a stretch; after all, such a theft did not even involve the trading of securities. Would it matter if I used the proceeds from the theft to buy the corporation's securities? Again, that seemed too attenuated; the securities purchase was only incidental to the theft of information.

However, what if the valuable information I stole was inside information that I could profit from *only* by trading the corporation's securities? Or if the *ordinary* way to profit from such information was by trading? Was there a way to distinguish the theft of material nonpublic information that typically was valuable in the securities markets (such as early information on a merger, an earnings release, or a new product launch)? Could § 10(b) be stretched to cover the theft of information and subsequent securities trading, even by an outsider?

In applying the "classical" theory, the courts had interpreted the "deception" component of § 10(b) as requiring a breach of fiduciary duty. But was a breach of duty to the source of the information (the "misappropriation" theory) deceptive in the same way as a breach of duty to the corporation and shareholders (the "classical" theory)? The identity of the source of the information, and that person's relationship to the corporation, was crucial to the analysis of whether the misappropriation theory prohibited trading under § 10(b). Did it make sense for liability to depend on these factors?

Moreover, why should liability depend on whether there was a breach of fiduciary duty? If § 10(b) was directed at ensuring the integrity of securities markets, why did it matter whether the "misappropriation" from the source of the information was wrongful? For example, what if the source of the information told the outsider it was permissible to trade on the information? In that case, the outsider would not breach a fiduciary duty because there would be no "deception" of the source. But does that conclusion make sense? Why should § 10(b) liability depend on whether the source of the information gave the outsider permission to use it to his or her advantage?

Finally, Rule 10b–5 required that the deception be "in connection with" the trading of securities. Did the misappropriation theory satisfy this "in connection with" requirement? What if the source of the information, presumably injured by the misappropriator's breach of fiduciary duty, was not a participant in any relevant securities transaction? Was there a way to connect (1) the misappropriator's breach of a fiduciary duty owed to the source of the information with (2) the misappropriator's trading in securities?

These questions were thorny, but without the misappropriation theory, the government would be unable to prosecute many instances of unfair trading that prosecutors believed to be wrongful. Interestingly, the trading by James O'Hagan in the case that you are about to read was *not* an example of wrongful trading that would have fallen through the cracks without the misappropriation theory. The government could, and did, prosecute and convict O'Hagan for other violations of law such as Rule 14e-3 concerning trading in connection with a tender offer. Nevertheless, *O'Hagan* became the vehicle for the Supreme Court to answer these fundamental questions and to set forth a roadmap for future cases.

FYI

In 1980, after *Chiarella*, and relying on its rulemaking authority under § 14(e) of the Exchange Act, the SEC adopted Rule 14e-3(a) which specifically prohibits trading on the basis of material, nonpublic information about tender offers.

The rule applies once "a substantial step or steps to commence" a tender offer has occurred. It prohibits any person who knows or has reason to know material nonpublic information about a pending tender offer, originating from a bidder or target company, from trading on the basis of this information. For the full text, see Rule 14e–3(a).

In *O'Hagan*, the Supreme Court validated the SEC's authority to promulgate Rule 14e-3. In addition, the case raised the bigger question of the viability of the misappropriation theory of insider trading liability under Rule 10b-5, which is not limited to the tender offer context.

United States v. O'Hagan

521 U.S. 642 (1997)

JUSTICE GINSBURG delivered the opinion of the Court.

Respondent James Herman O'Hagan was a partner in the law firm of Dorsey & Whitney in Minneapolis, Minnesota. In July 1988, Grand Metropolitan PLC (Grand Met), a company based in London, England, retained Dorsey & Whitney as local counsel to represent Grand Met regarding a potential tender offer for the common stock of the Pillsbury Company, headquartered in Minneapolis. Both Grand Met and Dorsey & Whitney took precautions to protect the confidentiality of Grand Met's tender offer plans. O'Hagan did no work on the Grand Met representation. Dorsey & Whitney withdrew from representing Grand Met on September 9, 1988. Less than a month later, on October 4, 1988, Grand Met publicly announced its tender offer for Pillsbury stock.

On August 18, 1988, while Dorsey & Whitney was still representing Grand Met, O'Hagan began purchasing call options for Pillsbury stock. Each option gave him the right to purchase 100 shares of Pillsbury stock. By the end of September, he owned 2,500 unexpired Pillsbury options, apparently more than any other individual investor. O'Hagan also purchased, in September 1988, some 5,000 shares of Pillsbury common stock, at a price just under $39 per share. When Grand Met announced its tender offer in October, the price of Pillsbury stock rose to nearly $60 per share. O'Hagan then sold his Pillsbury call options and common stock, making a profit of more than $4.3 million.

The Securities and Exchange Commission initiated an investigation into O'Hagan's transactions, culminating in a 57-count indictment. The indictment alleged that O'Hagan defrauded his law firm and its client, Grand Met, by using for his own trading purposes material, nonpublic information regarding Grand Met's planned tender offer. According to the indictment, O'Hagan used the profits he gained through this trading to conceal his previous embezzlement and conversion of unrelated client trust funds. A jury convicted O'Hagan on all counts, and he was sentenced to a 41-month term of imprisonment.

A divided panel of the Court of Appeals for the Eighth Circuit reversed all of O'Hagan's convictions. Liability under § 10(b) and Rule 10b–5, the Eighth Circuit held, may not be grounded on the "misappropriation theory" of securities fraud on which the prosecution relied.

Decisions of the Courts of Appeals are in conflict on the propriety of the misappropriation theory under § 10(b) and Rule 10(b)–5. We granted certiorari and now reverse the Eighth Circuit's judgment.

We address first the Court of Appeals' reversal of O'Hagan's convictions under § 10(b) and Rule 10b–5. Following the Fourth Circuit's lead, the Eighth Circuit rejected the misappropriation theory as a basis for § 10(b) liability. We hold, in accord with several other Courts of Appeals that criminal liability under § 10(b) may be predicated on the misappropriation theory.

Section 10(b) proscribes (1) using any deceptive device (2) in connection with the purchase or sale of securities, in contravention of rules prescribed by the Commission. The provision, as written, does not confine its coverage to deception of a purchaser or seller of securities; rather, the statute reaches any deceptive device used "in connection with the purchase or sale of any security."

Under the "traditional" or "classical theory" of insider trading liability, § 10(b) and Rule 10b–5 are violated when a corporate insider trades in the securities of his corporation on the basis of material, nonpublic information. Trading on such information qualifies as a "deceptive device" under § 10(b), we have affirmed, because "a relationship of trust and confidence exists between the shareholders of a corporation and those insiders who have obtained confidential information by reason of their position with that corporation." That relationship, we recognized, "gives rise to a duty to disclose or to abstain from trading because of the 'necessity of preventing a corporate insider from taking unfair advantage of uninformed stockholders.' " The classical theory applies not only to officers, directors, and other permanent insiders of a corporation, but also to attorneys, accountants, consultants, and others who temporarily become fiduciaries of a corporation.

The "misappropriation theory" holds that a person commits fraud "in connection with" a securities transaction, and thereby violates § 10(b) and Rule 10b–5, when he misappropriates confidential information for securities trading purposes, in breach of a duty owed to the source of the information. Under this theory, a fiduciary's undisclosed, self-serving use of a principal's information to purchase or sell securities, in breach of a duty of loyalty and confidentiality, defrauds the principal of the exclusive use of that information. In lieu of premising liability on a fiduciary relationship between company insider and purchaser or seller of the company's stock, the misappropriation theory premises liability on a fiduciary-turned-trader's deception of those who entrusted him with access to confidential information.

The two theories are complementary, each addressing efforts to capitalize on nonpublic information through the purchase or sale of securities. The classical theory targets a corporate insider's breach of duty to shareholders with whom the insider transacts; the misappropriation theory outlaws trading on the basis of nonpublic information by a corporate "outsider" in breach of a duty owed not to a trading party, but to the source of the information. The misappropriation theory is thus designed to "protect the integrity of the securities markets against abuses by 'outsiders' to a corporation who have access to confidential information that will affect the corporation's security price when revealed, but who owe no fiduciary or other duty to that corporation's shareholders."

In this case, the indictment alleged that O'Hagan, in breach of a duty of trust and confidence he owed to his law firm, Dorsey & Whitney, and to its client, Grand Met, traded on the basis of nonpublic information regarding Grand Met's planned tender offer for Pillsbury common stock. This conduct, the Government charged, constituted a fraudulent device in connection with the purchase and sale of securities.[5]

We agree with the Government that misappropriation, as just defined, satisfies § 10(b)'s requirement that chargeable conduct involve a "deceptive device or contrivance" used "in connection with" the purchase or sale of securities. We observe, first, that misappropriators, as the Government describes them, deal in deception. A fiduciary who "pretends loyalty to the principal while secretly converting the principal's information for personal gain," "dupes" or defrauds the principal.

Deception through nondisclosure is central to the theory of liability for which the Government seeks recognition. As counsel for the Government stated in explanation of the theory at oral argument: "To satisfy the common law rule that a trustee may not use the property that has been entrusted to him, there would have to be consent. To satisfy the requirement of the Securities Act that there be no deception, there would only have to be disclosure."[6]

The misappropriation theory advanced by the Government trains on conduct involving manipulation or deception. Because the deception essential to the misappropriation theory involves feigning fidelity to the source of information, if the fiduciary discloses to the source that he plans to trade on the nonpublic information, there is no "deceptive device" and thus no § 10(b) violation—although the fiduciary-turned-trader may remain liable under state law for breach of a duty of loyalty.[7]

---

[5] The Government could not have prosecuted O'Hagan under the classical theory, for O'Hagan was not an "insider" of Pillsbury, the corporation in whose stock he traded. Although an "outsider" with respect to Pillsbury, O'Hagan had an intimate association with, and was found to have traded on confidential information from, Dorsey & Whitney, counsel to tender offeror Grand Met. Under the misappropriation theory, O'Hagan's securities trading does not escape Exchange Act sanction, as it would under the dissent's reasoning, simply because he was associated with, and gained nonpublic information from, the bidder, rather than the target.

[6] Under the misappropriation theory urged in this case, the disclosure obligation runs to the source of the information, here, Dorsey & Whitney and Grand Met. Chief Justice Burger, dissenting in *Chiarella*, advanced a broader reading of § 10(b) and Rule 10b–5; the disclosure obligation, as he envisioned it, ran to those with whom the misappropriator trades. 445 U.S. at 240 ("a person who has misappropriated nonpublic information has an absolute duty to disclose that information or to refrain from trading"). The Government does not propose that we adopt a misappropriation theory of that breadth.

[7] Where, however, a person trading on the basis of material, nonpublic information owes a duty of loyalty and confidentiality to two entities or persons—for example, a law firm and its client—but makes disclosure to only one, the trader may still be liable under the misappropriation theory.

We turn next to the § 10(b) requirement that the misappropriator's deceptive use of information be "in connection with the purchase or sale of a security." This element is satisfied because the fiduciary's fraud is consummated, not when the fiduciary gains the confidential information, but when, without disclosure to his principal, he uses the information to purchase or sell securities. The securities transaction and the breach of duty thus coincide. This is so even though the person or entity defrauded is not the other party to the trade, but is, instead, the source of the nonpublic information. A misappropriator who trades on the basis of material, nonpublic information, in short, gains his advantageous market position through deception; he deceives the source of the information and simultaneously harms members of the investing public.

The misappropriation theory targets information of a sort that misappropriators ordinarily capitalize upon to gain no-risk profits through the purchase or sale of securities. Should a misappropriator put such information to other use, the statute's prohibition would not be implicated. The theory does not catch all conceivable forms of fraud involving confidential information; rather, it catches fraudulent means of capitalizing on such information through securities transactions.

The Government notes another limitation on the forms of fraud § 10(b) reaches: "The misappropriation theory would not apply to a case in which a person defrauded a bank into giving him a loan or embezzled cash from another, and then used the proceeds of the misdeed to purchase securities." In such a case, the Government states, "the proceeds would have value to the malefactor apart from their use in a securities transaction, and the fraud would be complete as soon as the money was obtained." In other words, money can buy, if not anything, then at least many things; its misappropriation may thus be viewed as sufficiently detached from a subsequent securities transaction that § 10(b)'s "in connection with" requirement would not be met.

The misappropriation theory comports with § 10(b)'s language, which requires deception "in connection with the purchase or sale of any security," not deception of an identifiable purchaser or seller. The theory is also well-tuned to an animating purpose of the Exchange Act: to insure honest securities markets and thereby promote investor confidence. Although informational disparity is inevitable in the securities markets, investors likely would hesitate to venture their capital in a market where trading based on misappropriated nonpublic information is unchecked by law. An investor's informational disadvantage vis-a-vis a misappropriator with material, nonpublic information stems from contrivance, not luck; it is a disadvantage that cannot be overcome with research or skill.

In sum, the misappropriation theory, as we have examined and explained it in this opinion, is both consistent with the statute and with our precedent. Vital to our decision that criminal liability may be sustained under the misappropriation theory, we emphasize, are two sturdy safeguards Congress has provided regarding scienter. To establish a criminal violation of Rule 10b–5, the Government must prove that a person "willfully" violated the provision. *See* 15 U.S.C. § 78ff(a). Furthermore, a defendant may not be imprisoned for violating Rule 10b–5 if he proves that he had no knowledge of the rule. O'Hagan's charge that the misappropriation theory is too indefinite to permit the imposition of criminal liability, thus fails not only because the theory is limited to those who breach a recognized duty. In addition, the statute's "requirement of the presence of culpable intent as a necessary element of the offense does much to destroy any force in the argument that application of the statute" in circumstances such as O'Hagan's is unjust.

The Eighth Circuit erred in holding that the misappropriation theory is inconsistent with § 10(b).

————————

Points for Discussion

1. You've come a long way, baby.

Would Justice Powell, who wrote the opinions in *Chiarella* and *Dirks*, have decided *O'Hagan* the same way that Justice Ginsburg did? Notice that in *Chiarella* Powell explained that liability under the antifraud provisions of § 10(b) and Rule 10b–5 arose because of a relationship of "trust and confidence *between the parties.*" Was there such a relationship in *O'Hagan*?

2. We are family.

The misappropriation theory hinges on a breach of duty to the source of the information. But does the theory apply only to established business relationships, such as lawyer-client or employer-employee? Or does it apply to more informal nonbusiness relationships, such as in a family? In one well-known case, *United States v. Chestman*, 947 F.2d 551 (2d Cir. 1991) *(en banc), cert. denied* 503 U.S. 1004 (1992), the court held that a son-in-law who learned of plans to sell a family-controlled corporation did not owe a duty to the family, despite being asked to keep the plans confidential, because "kinship alone does not create the necessary relationship." Other cases, however, held family members to a duty of trust and confidence.

In Rule 10b5–2, the SEC responded to ambiguities about when a person owes a duty to the source of information for purposes of misappropriation theory. The SEC's view was insider trading by family members harms the market just as much as other forms of insider trading. Moreover, the SEC wanted to establish a bright-line rule to avoid intrusive inquiries into family relationships. Subpart (b) of the rule enumerated three non-exclusive circumstances in which "duties of trust and confidence" would exist under the misappropriation theory. Existence of such a duty, in turn, would support a finding of liability under Rule 10b–5. Here are the key provisions of the SEC rule. Does this clear things up?

Rule 10b5–2
Securities and Exchange Act of 1934

(b) *Enumerated "duties of trust or confidence."* For purposes of [the "misappropriation" theory of insider trading under Section 10(b) of the Act and Rule 10b–5], a "duty of trust or confidence" exists in the following circumstances, among others:

1. Whenever a person agrees to maintain information in confidence;

2. Whenever the person communicating the material nonpublic information and the person to whom it is communicated have a history, pattern, or practice of sharing confidences, such that the recipient of the information knows or reasonably should know that the person communicating the material nonpublic information expects that the recipient will maintain its confidentiality; or

3. Whenever a person receives or obtains material nonpublic information from his or her spouse, parent, child, or sibling; provided, however, that the person receiving or obtaining the information may demonstrate that no duty of trust or confidence existed with respect to the information, by establishing that he or she neither knew nor reasonably should have known that the person who was the source of the information expected that the person would keep the information confidential, because of the parties' history, pattern, or practice of sharing and maintaining confidences, and because there was no agreement or understanding to maintain the confidentiality of the information.

---

3. State of mind.

What state of mind triggers liability in a case of insider trading? In *O'Hagan*, the Supreme Court said only that the trading must be "on the basis" of material nonpublic information. Lower courts have split on whether insider trading liability requires a showing that the trader was in "knowing possession" of inside information or a heightened requirement that the trader "used" the information in trading. The Second Circuit accepted the "knowing possession" standard when a young attorney tipped inside information about transactions involving clients of his law firm. The court justified the lower "knowledge" standard as simpler to apply and consistent with the expansive nature of Rule 10b–5 and its focus on the duty to disclose or abstain from insider trading. Other courts, however, have insisted on a showing the trader "used" the information, particularly when a defendant's state of mind is at issue in criminal cases.

In 2000, the SEC adopted Rule 10b5–1 to clarify this aspect of insider trading liability. Rule 10b5–1(b) provides that, for purposes of insider trading, a person trades "on the basis" of material nonpublic information if the trader is "aware" of the material nonpublic information when making the purchase or sale. In its release accompanying the rule, the SEC explained that "aware" is a commonly used English word, implying "conscious knowledge," with clearer meaning than "knowing possession." What level of knowledge or intent should be required before a trader (or tipper) will be liable for insider trading? And who has the authority to determine what state of mind is necessary, the SEC or the courts?

4. Tipping in misappropriation cases.

Courts have applied the same "benefit to tipper" analysis in cases involving misappropriated information as is used when insiders disclose company secrets. Does this make sense? In *United States v. Libera*, 989 F.2d 596 (2d Cir. 1993), employees of a publishing company with access to advance copies of *Business Week* magazine sent the copies to tippees. The publishing company had a policy prohibiting its employees from disclosing the magazine's contents before publication. The Second Circuit concluded that, as a matter of law, the employer-employee relationship was sufficient to establish a duty not to disclose, a duty the printer's employees breached by providing advance copies of the magazine to others. The court also held that a tipper could be liable even if the tipper did not know that the tippee would trade on the basis of the information. The tipper's knowledge she is breaching a duty to the owner of the information "suffices to establish the tipper's expectation that the breach will lead to some kind of misuse." The court reasoned, "This is so because it may be presumed that the tippee's interest in the information is, in contemporary jargon, not for nothing. To allow a tippee to escape liability because the government cannot prove to a jury's satisfaction that the tipper knew exactly what misuse would result from the tipper's wrongdoing would not fulfill the purpose of the misappropriation theory, which is to protect property rights in information."

Food for Thought

Consider the facts of *SEC v. Yun*, 327 F.3d 1263 (11th Cir. 2003). David Yun, the president of Scholastic Book Fairs, explained to his wife Donna that his Scholastic stock options had become less valuable because he believed the company's stock price would drop after an upcoming earnings announcement. David told Donna not to disclose this information to anyone, and Donna agreed to keep the information secret. The next evening, Donna attended an awards banquet and apparently talked to some of her co-workers about the pending Scholastic earnings announcement. One of her co-workers, Jerry Burch, called his broker the next day and, based on information he said he obtained at a cocktail party, purchased put options. When Scholastic announced its unexpectedly weak earnings and its share price dropped 40%, Burch realized a profit of $269,000.

Did Donna have a fiduciary duty to David (or Scholastic) that prevented her from tipping Burch? The Eleventh Circuit concluded that "a spouse who trades in breach of a reasonable and legitimate expectation of confidentiality held by the other spouse sufficiently subjects the former to insider trading liability." Based on evidence that David had granted Donna access to confidential information "in reasonable reliance on a promise that she would safeguard the information" and that "Donna had agreed in this instance to keep the information confidential," the court concluded a jury could find that a duty of confidentiality existed between them.

Must Donna have intended to gain a personal benefit when she tipped Burch? The Eleventh Circuit reasoned that the "personal benefit" requirement is the same whether the tip is from an insider (classical theory) or from an outsider (misappropriation theory). Thus, the court concluded "an outsider who tips (rather than trades) is liable if he intends to benefit from the disclosure." As *Dirks* held, a benefit can include a gift to a trading relative or friend. In the case, the court concluded there was enough evidence that Donna had expected to benefit from her tip to Burch by maintaining a good relationship between a friend and a frequent partner in real estate deals.

5. 10b5–1 plans.

SEC Rule 10b5–1, besides clarifying when trading is "on the basis" of inside information, also set forth affirmative defenses designed to allow corporate insiders and others to structure securities trading plans when they are not aware of inside information and cannot influence these trading plans even if they later become aware of inside information. Courts have recognized that individual trading plans executed pursuant to Rule 10b5–1 may provide a defense against insider trading charges.

Read through the relevant language of the rule, below. What are the key factors in setting up a 10b5–1 plan? How would you advise a client who wanted to set up fifty-two 10b5–1 plans, one for each week in the upcoming year, so that he could either sell securities pursuant to the plan during a particular week (when his inside information suggests the stock price is high) or cancel the plan for that week (when his inside information suggests the stock price is low)?

<u>Rule 10b5–1</u>
<u>Securities and Exchange Act of 1934</u>

(c)(1)(i) A person's purchase or sale is not "on the basis of" material nonpublic information if the person making the purchase or sale demonstrates that:

A. Before becoming aware of the information, the person had:

    1. Entered into a binding contract to purchase or sell the security,

    2. Instructed another person to purchase or sell the security for the instructing person's account, or

    3. Adopted a written plan for trading securities;

B. The contract, instruction, or plan described in paragraph (c)(1)(i)(A) of this Section:

    1. Specified the amount of securities to be purchased or sold and the price at which and the date on which the securities were to be purchased or sold;

    2. Included a written formula or algorithm, or computer program, for determining the amount of securities to be purchased or sold and the price at which and the date on which the securities were to be purchased or sold; or

    3. Did not permit the person to exercise any subsequent influence over how, when, or whether to effect purchases or sales; provided, in addition, that any other person who, pursuant to the contract, instruction, or plan, did exercise such influence must not have been aware of the material nonpublic information when doing so; and

C. The purchase or sale that occurred was pursuant to the contract, instruction, or plan. A purchase or sale is not "pursuant to a contract, instruction, or plan" if, among other things, the person who entered into the contract, instruction, or plan altered or deviated from the contract, instruction, or plan to purchase or sell securities (whether by changing the amount, price, or timing of the purchase or sale), or entered into or altered a corresponding or hedging transaction or position with respect to those securities.

> ii. Paragraph (c)(1)(i) of this section is applicable only when the contract, instruction, or plan to purchase or sell securities was given or entered into in good faith and not as part of a plan or scheme to evade the prohibitions of this section.

6. Trading by members of Congress.

So what happens when the source of material nonpublic information is Congress? Do members of Congress and congressional staffers have duties not to trade on information they learn in their official roles, where that information could affect stock prices of particular companies or industries? You would think that such a duty is well-established. But it was not until 2012 that Congress made clear that insider-trading restrictions also apply to members of Congress and legislative aides. In the Stop Trading on Congressional Knowledge (STOCK) Act, Congress specified that congressional persons owe duties to the United States, as well as to Congress and the U.S. citizens, with respect to material nonpublic information derived from their position or gained from performing their official responsibilities. Thus, members of Congress and their aides—as well as any recipients who trade on congressionally sourced information—can be liable for insider trading under a misappropriation theory.

In addition, just as corporate insiders must report their trading in their corporation's stock, members of Congress and their aides must report their stock trades above $1,000 within 30 to 45 days of the trade. Not only does such reporting allow the public (and the press) to compare congressional stock trading with congressional activities, it also can serve as the basis for public and private insider-trading actions. One tricky question raised by the STOCK Act, though, is how it will be enforced—especially given the evidentiary barriers created by the Constitution's "Speech or Debate" clause that immunizes lawmakers for their official legislative activities.

---

4. Remedies for Insider Trading

As we have seen, insider trading can be punished as a crime with the possibility of prison time and fines. But what about civil remedies? Section 20A of the Exchange Act creates a private right of action on behalf of contemporaneous traders against insiders, constructive insiders, tippers, and tippees (as well as their controlling persons) who trade while in possession of material, nonpublic information. Liability in such cases is limited to the actual profits realized or losses avoided reduced by the amount of any disgorgement obtained by the SEC under its broad authority to seek injunctive relief.

Pursuant to § 21A of the Exchange Act, which has been used significantly more than § 20A, the SEC is authorized to seek judicially imposed civil penalties against insiders, constructive insiders, tippers, and tippees of up to three times the profits gained or the losses avoided in unlawful insider trading. These civil penalties are *in addition* to other remedies. Thus, an insider, tipper, or tippee may be required to disgorge her profits, whether in an SEC or private action, and pay a treble damage penalty. The civil penalty can be imposed only at the insistence of the SEC.

Section 21A also permits the imposition of civil penalties on controlling persons, such as employers, of up to $1 million or three times the insider's profits (whichever is greater) if the controlling person knowingly or recklessly disregards the insider trading by persons under its control. It also encourages private watchdogs by providing for the payment of bounties to people who provide information concerning insider trading.

In other areas of corporate law that we have covered in this casebook, plaintiffs' securities lawyers have played a prominent role in enforcing violations of law. Should this approach also be followed for insider trading violations? Or should the SEC be the primary enforcer? More generally, should insider trading civil remedies be expanded to match those in other areas of corporate and securities law, or should the remedies in those other areas be restricted to match those of insider trading?

D. Section 16: Disgorgement of Short-Swing Trading Profits

Insider trading was one of the problems Congress attempted to address in the Securities Exchange Act of 1934. Responding to a public outcry against reports of insider trading and the perceived inadequacy of state common law, Congress created a novel regulatory scheme. Rather than prohibit trading on the basis of material nonpublic information, Congress attacked one narrow type of stock trading often associated with the misuse of inside information, namely "short-swing" trading—the purchase and resale by insiders of public company stock within a relatively short period of time.

Since the capital gains period of the tax laws at the time was six months, there was good reason to suspect that in most cases someone with access to inside information who bought and sold within six months (and therefore forewent the favorable tax treatment available for profits made on trades separated by a longer period) was doing so to take advantage of some special knowledge. It was only a step from this perception to the simple and readily enforceable, if crude, principle of § 16(b) of the 1934 Act, which provides:

> "For the purpose of preventing the unfair use of information which may have been obtained by such beneficial owner, director, or officer by reason of his relationship to the issuer, any profit realized by him from any purchase and sale, or any sale and purchase, of any equity security of such issuer . . . within any period of less than six months . . . shall inure to and be recoverable by the issuer, irrespective of any intention on the part of such beneficial owner, director or officer in entering into such transaction . . ."

Although the section explicitly states that its purpose is "preventing the unfair use of information," there is no need to show any such "unfair use." It is a rule of strict liability and all that needs to be shown are offsetting trades within six months by someone with the necessary relationship to the corporation.

Section 16 applies to the directors and officers, as well as any person who is the "beneficial owner" of more than 10% of a class of equity securities, of any public corporation (one registered under § 12 of the 1934 Act). For purposes of § 16, an "officer" includes executive officers, chief financial or accounting officers, as well as any person, regardless of title, who performs significant "policy-making functions" in the corporation. Further, courts have concluded that a corporation or partnership may be considered to be a "director" under § 16 if a member or officer of the entity is "deputized" to represent the partnership or corporation as a director of the corporation in whose shares it trades. Section 16(b) applies to officers and directors trading in their corporation's securities while they are in office and extends to purchases or sales they make after they leave office, so long as still within six months.

For purposes of determining a person's status as a more than 10% shareholder, it is necessary to count the beneficial ownership of all equity securities, including those securities that could be acquired through the exercise of conversion rights. Unlike officers and directors, a beneficial owner may be liable under § 16(b) only if he owned more than 10% of the stock at the time of *both* purchase and sale. Officers and directors are treated differently from beneficial owners because the former are deemed to have more ready access to confidential business information.

To ensure that potential plaintiffs can learn about short-swing trading, § 16(a) requires those covered by the statute to file reports with the SEC disclosing the ownership of their equity securities, as well as any changes in that ownership. Initial reports must be filed electronically 10 days after a person becomes an insider, and updated reports must be filed electronically 2 days after any changes in the insider's holdings.

The remedy for short-swing trading is a self-contained, hybrid derivative suit set forth in § 16(b). A security holder, who need not be a contemporaneous owner, must first make a demand on the directors unless demand would be futile. Thereafter, the corporation has 60 days to decide whether to institute suit. If it does not, the action may be maintained by the holder, who must hold shares at suit and through trial. Any "profit" that is recovered, which courts compute by matching purchases and sales by the insider within any six-month period, goes to the corporation. Courts interpret the statute to allow for matching a purchase and sale in any order (e.g., sale followed by purchase) that would theoretically give rise to profits within six months and will calculate § 16(b) liability so as to maximize the amount recovered by the company.

Why would a security holder bring a § 16(b) action if any recovery goes to the corporation, producing only the remotest benefit to him? As with conventional derivative suits, attorneys' fees are available for a successful § 16(b) plaintiff. The plaintiff's counsel thus becomes the moving force in § 16(b) litigation. Indeed, courts have held that it is no defense to a § 16(b) action that the suit was motivated primarily by the desire to obtain such fees.

Test Your Knowledge

To assess your understanding of the Chapter 27, 28, and 29 material in this module, click here to take a quiz.

Module X – M&A

CHAPTER 30

Control and Voting

The next three chapters are part of a module on "mergers and acquisitions," or "M&A." M&A is an advanced business law topic that typically is taught in a separate course. But if you were assigned to read this module, your professor has decided to give you some exposure to M&A in the introductory course, and that is what these three chapters will do. We will only cover the basics.

M&A involves the buying and selling of corporations, including both public and private corporations. Some see M&A as the sexiest topic of corporate law, filled with tales of high-powered takeover ploys and ingenious defensive gambits. Lurking behind every story are fundamental questions about the corporation in society and the role of corporate law: Are corporate takeovers good or bad? Who should share in the financial rewards of a takeover? Are shareholders (and others) better served by activist boards or passive boards? What should be the attitude of corporate law toward takeovers?

All of these chapters deal with the right of shareholders to sell their shares, part of the triumvirate of shareholder rights to vote, sue, and sell. Fundamentally, M&A involves the sale of control of a corporation. But there are limitations on controlling shareholders when they sell their shares. In addition, there are various rules regarding voting in M&A, because it is a fundamental transaction for shareholders; in addition, shareholders sometimes have the right to opt out of an M&A transaction by seeking an "appraisal" remedy. This chapter covers these topics. The next chapter describes devices used by incumbent boards to discourage takeovers and how courts review these antitakeover devices. The final chapter describes devices used by boards to protect negotiated deals and how courts view these deal protections.

A. Controlling

Corporate control is valuable. If you have control, you can choose the board and don't have to worry as much about agency costs. Shareholders with control can command a premium for their shares, and buyers who believe they can manage the corporation better will pay the premium.

Control also can be exploited. If you own control, you may find it easier to misappropriate corporate assets, to appoint yourself to corporate office and pay yourself lavishly, or to enter into self-dealing transactions on unfair terms. Although the duties of care and loyalty still apply, you know that breaches are difficult to detect, challenge, and remedy.

But control changes can also be good. They can put corporate assets in the hands of more efficient managers. Even shareholders who did not sell their shares and others who remain in the corporation may be better off after control is sold, if the new buyer is better at running the business.

This section deals with corporate law's attempt to distinguish between good and bad transfers of control. We consider the control premium and then look at the two aspects of the duties of shareholders who sell control, when control is sold to someone who loots the company and when selling control involves a corporate opportunity. Finally, we look at agreements to put others into board positions— and whether this constitutes the illegal sale of a corporate office.

As you read these cases, think about what constitutes "control." Obviously, majority ownership gives a shareholder the ability to make decisions that require a majority. But what about shareholders who own a smaller percentage, but nevertheless are influential? In one recent case, Delaware Vice Chancellor Slights found that it was reasonable to conceive that Elon Musk, the CEO and Chair of Tesla Motors, Inc., controlled the Tesla Board in connection with its takeover of Solar-City Corporation, even though Musk held just 22% of Tesla's shares at the time. *See In re Tesla Motors, Inc. Stockholder Litigation*, C.A. No. 12711–VCS (Del. Ch. Mar. 28, 2018). In general, the courts will consider a shareholder to have control if they either own more than 50% of the voting power of a corporation or if they own less than 50% of the voting power but exercise control such as through de facto influence of the board.

1. Sharing of Control Premium?

Control shares command a premium. For example, if you own 60% of a corporation's shares and the other shares trade in a market at $20 per share, you should expect someone to pay more than that for your shares. In fact, studies show that control shares usually sell for 30–50% more than non-control shares. That is, your shares may well fetch $30 per share! That's because you get to elect the board and decide such matters as business strategy, executive pay, and dividend policy.

Should controlling shareholders be allowed to realize this "control premium"? One potential answer is that control sales are unfair to minority shareholders so that any control sale to an outsider should be made only as part of an offer to purchase shares on the same terms from all shareholders. After all, corporate law says all shares are by default equal.

But another potential answer is that such egalitarianism would discourage control transfers, potentially keeping corporate assets out of the hands of those who value them most and are best able to use them efficiently. On this theory, owners of control should be able to keep their control premiums, so long as other corporate constituents are no worse off as a result.

Corporate law sides with the second view: that it should be easy to transfer control. Accordingly, corporate law provides that control can be sold at a premium, subject to exceptions only in special circumstances.

> Recognizing that those who invest the capital necessary to acquire a dominant position in the ownership of a corporation have the right of controlling that corporation, it has long been settled law that, absent looting of corporate assets, conversion of a corporate opportunity, fraud or other acts of bad faith, a controlling stockholder is free to sell, and a purchaser is free to buy, that controlling interest at a premium price.

Zetlin v. Hanson Holdings, Inc., 48 N.Y.2d 684, 685 (1979).

2. Selling to a Potential Looter

Return to our example of the corporation whose shares are trading for $20. Suppose you own 60% of the corporation's shares and someone has offered to buy your entire stake for $30 per share. Does it matter what that person plans to do with the corporation after gaining control? Does it matter if you suspect the buyer will loot the corporation? And, by the way, what is "looting"?

The following case addresses these questions.

Harris v. Carter

582 A.2d 222 (Del. Ch. 1990)

ALLEN, CHANCELLOR.

The litigation arises from the negotiation and sale by one group of defendants (the Carter group) of a control block of Atlas stock to Frederic Mascolo; the resignation of the Carter group as directors and the appointment of the Mascolo defendants as directors of Atlas, and, finally, the alleged looting of Atlas by Mascolo and persons associated with him.

Plaintiff is a minority shareholder of Atlas. He brought this action after the change in control from the Carter group to the Mascolo group had occurred. The amended complaint purported to assert claims derivatively on behalf of Atlas. It is alleged that the Carter group, *qua* shareholders, owed a duty of care to Atlas to take the steps that a reasonable person would take in the circumstances to investigate the *bona fides* of the person to whom they sold control. It is said that the duty was breached here, and that if it had been met the corporation would have been spared the losses that are alleged to have resulted from the transactions effected by the board under the domination of Mascolo. There is no allegation that the Carter group conspired with Mascolo. Indeed the Carter group did not sell for cash but for shares of common stock of a corporation that plaintiff claims was a worthless shell and which was later employed in the transactions that are said to constitute a looting of Atlas. Thus, accepting the allegations of the complaint, they suggest that the Carter group was misled to its own injury as well as the injury of Atlas and its other shareholders. This claim was set forth, albeit as a direct claim and perhaps less elaborately, in the original pleading.

The amended complaint seeks appointment of a receiver, rescission, and damages.

I.

The facts as alleged appear as follows.

The Company

Atlas Energy Corporation is a Delaware corporation which, before Mascolo acquired control of it, engaged in oil and gas exploration and production. It conducted its business primarily through the acquisition of oil and gas properties which were resold to drilling programs. It then acted as sponsor and general partner of the drilling programs.

The Stock Exchange Agreement

The Carter group, which collectively owned 52% of the stock of Atlas, and Mascolo entered into a Stock Exchange Agreement dated as of March 28, 1986. That agreement provided that the Carter group would exchange its Atlas stock for shares of stock held by Mascolo in a company called Insuranshares of America ("ISA") and contemplated a later merger between ISA and Atlas. ISA was described in the preamble to the Stock Exchange Agreement as "a company engaged in the insurance field by and through wholly-owned subsidiaries." The Stock Exchange

Agreement contained representations and warranties by Mascolo to the effect that ISA owned all of the issued and outstanding capital stock of Pioneer National Life Insurance Company and Western National Life Insurance Company. It is alleged that those representations were false. ISA did not own stock in either company and had no insurance subsidiaries.

In the course of negotiations, the Mascolo group furnished the Carter group with a draft financial statement of ISA that reflected an investment in Life Insurance Company of America, a Washington corporation ("LICA"). No representation concerning LICA was made in the Stock Exchange Agreement, however. The existence of a purported investment by ISA in LICA was fictitious. It is alleged that the draft ISA financial statement was sufficiently suspicious to put any reasonably prudent business person on notice that further investigation should be made. Indeed Atlas' chief financial officer analyzed the financial statement and raised several questions concerning its accuracy, none of which were pursued by the Carter group.

The Stock Exchange Agreement further provided that Mascolo would place in escrow 50,000 shares of Louisiana Bankshares Inc. 8% cumulative preferred stock, $10 par value. It was agreed that if Atlas consummated an exchange merger for all of the outstanding common stock of ISA on agreed upon terms within 365 days of the date of the Stock Exchange Agreement, the bank stock would be returned to Mascolo. If no merger took place within the specified time, then that stock was to be distributed *pro rata* to the Carter group members.

It was agreed, finally, that as part of the stock exchange transaction, the members of the Carter group would resign their positions as Atlas directors in a procedure that assured that Mascolo and his designees would be appointed as replacements.

The gist of plaintiff's claim against the Carter defendants is the allegation that those defendants had reason to suspect the integrity of the Mascolo group, but failed to conduct even a cursory investigation into any of several suspicious aspects of the transaction: the unaudited financial statement, the mention of LICA in negotiations but not in the representations concerning ISA's subsidiaries, and the ownership of the subsidiaries themselves. Such an investigation, argues plaintiff, would have revealed the structure of ISA to be fragile indeed, with minimal capitalization and no productive assets.

The charges against the Mascolo defendants are that the Mascolo defendants caused the effectuation of self-dealing transactions designed to benefit members of the Mascolo group, at the expense of Atlas.

Mascolo purchased the Carter group's stock on March 28, 1986. Also on that day the newly elected Atlas board (*i.e.,* the Mascolo defendants) adopted resolutions that, among other things:

(a) changed Atlas' name to Insuranshares of America, Inc.;

(b) effectuated a reverse stock split converting each existing Atlas share into .037245092 new shares, thus reducing the 26,849,175 Atlas shares to approximately 1,000,000 shares;

(c) reduced Atlas authorized capitalization to 10,000,000 shares, $.10 par value;

(d) approved the acquisition of all of the outstanding common stock of ISA in consideration for 3,000,000 post-reverse stock split Atlas shares;

(e) elected defendant Mascolo as chairman of the board, Johnson as president, Devaney as treasurer and Ager as vice president;

(f) approved the negotiation of the sale of Atlas' oil properties "with a series of potential buyers";

(g) approved the purchase of 200,000 shares of the common stock of Hughes Chemical Corporation at $3 per share with an option to acquire an additional 1,000,000 shares at $5 per share for a 12-month period and for $10 per share for a consecutive 12-month period;

(h) ratified the actions of the company's prior officers and directors and released them from any liability arising as a consequence of their relationship to the company.

It is alleged, essentially, that defendants approved the ISA and Hughes chemical transactions without any credible information about the business or assets of either of those companies.

The ISA Transaction

Plaintiff asserts that ISA is nothing more than a corporate shell. Pursuant to the Stock Exchange Agreement Mascolo acquired a controlling (52%) stock interest in Atlas in exchange for 518,335 ISA shares. Atlas then acquired all the outstanding ISA shares in exchange for 3,000,000 newly issued shares of Atlas common stock. As a result of that transaction, the Mascolo group as a whole came to own 75% of Atlas' shares. The minority shareholders of Atlas saw their proportionate ownership of Atlas reduced from 48% before the ISA transaction to 12% upon its consummation. For Atlas to exchange 3,000,000 of its shares for the stock of this "corporate shell" was, argues plaintiff, equivalent to issuing Atlas stock to the Mascolo group (the holders of the ISA stock) without consideration.

The Hughes Chemical Purchase

Hughes Chemical Corporation is a North Carolina corporation with its sole place of operations in Fletcher, North Carolina. Mr. Mascolo and two of his associates (who are referred to in the amended complaint as members of the Mascolo group but who are not named as defendants) were stockholders and directors of Hughes Chemical. Plaintiff asserts that in March, 1986, Mascolo caused Atlas to acquire shares of Hughes Chemical at a price unfair to Atlas and its stockholders.

The MPA Transactions

Defendant Devaney, elected by Mascolo to the Atlas board, was president and a principal stockholder of MPA Associates, Inc., a Utah corporation ("MPA"). On April 20, 1986, Atlas entered into an agreement with MPA for the sale to MPA of Atlas' oil and gas properties. In exchange for those properties, MPA issued to Atlas a $5,000,000 secured promissory note, and 2,000,000 shares of MPA common stock, representing 31.8% of the MPA shares issued and outstanding after such issuance. It was agreed that until the MPA Note was fully paid, Atlas would receive 40% of the net cash flow from the oil and gas properties attributable to sales of oil and gas in excess of certain specified prices. Plaintiff alleges that, as a result of the MPA transaction, the MPA Note and stock became Atlas' principal assets.

After MPA's acquisition of the oil and gas properties, Devaney discovered that certain Atlas creditors had claims on the cash flow from those properties. MPA did not make the payments to Atlas required by the MPA Note. On June 2, 1987, Devaney and Mascolo reached an agreement which essentially rescinded the MPA Agreement. Mascolo transferred his Atlas stock to Devaney in exchange for shares of an unrelated corporation. The MPA Note was canceled and Atlas transferred its 2,000,000 MPA shares to MPA, all in exchange for a return of the oil and gas properties originally sold to MPA. Devaney and/or his nominees assumed control of Atlas.

* * *

Finally, I turn to the Carter defendants motion to dismiss for failure to state a claim upon which relief may be granted. This motion raises novel questions of Delaware law. Stated generally the most basic of these questions is whether a controlling shareholder or group may under any circumstances owe a duty of care to the corporation in connection with the sale of a control block of stock. If such a duty may be said to exist under certain circumstances the questions in this case then become whether the facts alleged in the amended complaint would permit the finding that such a duty arose in connection with the sale to the Mascolo group and was breached.

While Delaware law has not addressed this specific question, one is not left without guidance from our decided cases. Several principles deducible from that law are pertinent. First, is the principle that a shareholder has a right to sell his or her stock and in the ordinary case owes no duty in that connection to other shareholders when acting in good faith.

Equally well established is the principle that when a shareholder presumes to exercise control over a corporation, to direct its actions, that shareholder assumes a fiduciary duty of the same kind as that owed by a director to the corporation. A sale of controlling interest in a corporation, at least where, as is alleged here, that sale is coupled with an agreement for the sellers to resign from the board of directors in such a way as to assure that the buyer's designees assume that corporate office, does, in my opinion, involve or implicate the corporate mechanisms so as to call this principle into operation.

More generally, it does not follow from the proposition that ordinarily a shareholder has a right to sell her stock to whom and on such terms as she deems expedient, that no duty may arise from the particular circumstances to take care in the exercise of that right. It is established American legal doctrine that, unless privileged, each person owes a duty to those who may foreseeably be harmed by her action to take such steps as a reasonably prudent person would take in similar circumstances to avoid such harm to others. While this principle arises from the law of torts and not the law of corporations or of fiduciary duties, that distinction is not, I think, significant unless the law of corporations or of fiduciary duties somehow privileges a selling shareholder by exempting her from the reach of this principle. The principle itself is one of great generality and, if not negated by privilege, would apply to a controlling shareholder who negligently places others foreseeably in the path of injury.

That a shareholder may sell her stock (or that a director may resign his office) is a right that, with respect to the principle involved, is no different, for example, than the right that a licensed driver has to operate a motor vehicle upon a highway. The right exists, but it is not without conditions and limitations, some established by positive regulation, some by common-law. Thus, to continue the parallel, the driver owes a duty of care to her passengers because it is foreseeable that they may be injured if, through inattention or otherwise, the driver involves the car she is operating in a collision. In the typical instance a seller of corporate stock can be expected to have no similar apprehension of risks to others from her own inattention. But, in some circumstances, the seller of a control block of stock may or should reasonably foresee danger to other shareholders; with her sale of stock will also go control over the corporation and with it the opportunity to misuse that power to the injury of such other shareholders. Thus, the reason that a duty of care is recognized in any situation is fully present in this situation. I can find no universal privilege arising from the corporate form that exempts a controlling shareholder who sells corporate control from the wholesome reach of this common-law duty.

Thus, I conclude that while a person who transfers corporate control to another is surely not a surety for his buyer, when the circumstances would alert a reasonably prudent person to a risk that his buyer is dishonest or in some material respect not truthful, a duty devolves upon the seller to make such inquiry as a reasonably prudent person would make, and generally to exercise care so that others who will be affected by his actions should not be injured by wrongful conduct.

The cases that have announced this principle have laid some stress on the fact that they involved not merely a sale of stock, but a sale of control over the corporation. Thus, the agreement that the sellers would resign from the board in a way that would facilitate the buyers immediately assuming office was given importance. That circumstance is pleaded here as well.

One cannot determine (and may not on this type of motion determine) whether Mr. Carter and those who acted with him were in fact negligent in a way that proximately caused injury to the corporation. Indeed one cannot determine now whether the circumstances that surrounded the negotiations with Mascolo were such as to have awakened suspicion in a person of ordinary prudence. The test of a Rule 12(b)(6) motion is, as noted above, permissive. It is sufficient to require denial of this motion to dismiss that I cannot now say as a matter of law that under no state of facts that might be proven could it be held that a duty arose, to the corporation and its other shareholders, to make further inquiry and was breached. In so concluding I assume without deciding that a duty of care of a controlling shareholder that may in special circumstances arise in connection with a sale of corporate control is breached only by grossly negligent conduct.

That Mr. Carter may well have been misled to his own detriment may be a factor affecting the question whether a duty to inquire arose, as Carter might be assumed to be a prudent man when dealing with his own property. But that assumption is essentially evidentiary and can be given no weight on this motion.

For the foregoing reasons the pending motions will be denied.

_____

Points for Discussion

1. Investigate what?

Chancellor Allen adopts a test that requires a corporate seller to investigate the buyer if put on notice that the buyer is deceptive or not truthful. What if the buyer has a reputation for running businesses into the ground, through sheer incompetence? Does the duty to investigate extend to investigating the business practices of feckless corporate managers?

2. Seller also victim.

Notice that the Carter group was not accused of conspiring with Mascolo and his crowd. In fact, they were apparently duped into accepting worthless securities for their interest in Atlas. Why should the Carter group be held to a standard of inquiry that is more demanding than the standard they used to protect their own interests? Doesn't the business judgment rule teach that absent a conflicting interest, fraud or illegality, courts should not second-guess the judgment of business people?

3. High price.

In many cases, the purchase price may seem abnormally high for a particular type of business. Must a seller look a gift horse in the mouth? For example, if the buyer is unknown to the seller, does the seller have a duty to investigate? What would this investigation involve? How much above current market prices must the offered price be before the duty is triggered?

---

3. Selling a Corporate Opportunity

Sometimes corporations have special business advantages—such as patents, market niches, customer relationships—that are particularly valuable to particular buyers. Should owners of control be able essentially to sell these business advantages without sharing the premium with other non-control shareholders? The following famous case gives a surprising answer.

Perlman v. Feldmann

219 F.2d 173 (2d Cir. 1955)

CLARK, CHIEF JUDGE.

This is a derivative action brought by minority stockholders of Newport Steel Corporation to compel accounting for, and restitution of, allegedly illegal gains which accrued to defendants as a result of the sale in August, 1950, of their controlling interest in the corporation. The principal defendant, C. Russell Feldmann, who represented and acted for the others, members of his family owning a total of 37%, was at that time not only the dominant stockholder, but also the chairman of the board of directors and the president of the corporation. Newport, an Indiana corporation, operated mills for the production of steel sheets for sale to manufacturers of steel products, first at Newport, Kentucky, and later also at other places in Kentucky and Ohio. The buyers, a syndicate organized as Wilport Company, a Delaware corporation, consisted of end-users of steel who were interested in securing a source of supply in a market becoming ever tighter in the Korean War. Plaintiffs contend that the consideration paid for the stock included compensation for the sale of a corporate asset, a power held in trust for the corporation by Feldmann as its fiduciary. This power was the ability to control the allocation of the corporate product in a time of short supply, through control of the board of directors; and it was effectively transferred in this sale by having Feldmann procure the resignation of his own board and the election of Wilport's nominees immediately upon consummation of the sale.

The essential facts found by the trial judge are not in dispute. Newport was a relative newcomer in the steel industry with predominantly old installations which were in the process of being supplemented by more modern facilities. Except in times of extreme shortage Newport was not in a position to compete profitably with other steel mills for customers not in its immediate geographical area. Wilport, the purchasing syndicate, consisted of geographically remote end-users of steel who were interested in buying more steel from Newport than they had been able to obtain during recent periods of tight supply. The price of $20 per share was found by Judge Hincks to be a fair one for a control block of stock, although the over-the-counter market price had not exceeded $12 and the book value per share was $17.03. But this finding was limited by Judge Hincks' statement that "what value the block would have had if shorn of its appurtenant power to control distribution of the corporate product, the evidence does not show." It was also conditioned by his earlier ruling that the burden was on plaintiffs to prove a lesser value for the stock.

Both as director and as dominant stockholder, Feldmann stood in a fiduciary relationship to the corporation and to the minority stockholders as beneficiaries thereof. Although there is no Indiana case directly in point, the most closely analogous one emphasizes the close scrutiny to which Indiana subjects the conduct of fiduciaries when personal benefit may stand in the way of fulfillment of trust obligations.

In Indiana, then, as elsewhere, the responsibility of the fiduciary is not limited to a proper regard for the tangible balance sheet assets of the corporation, but includes the dedication of his uncorrupted business judgment for the sole benefit of the corporation, in any dealings which may adversely affect it.

It is true, as defendants have been at pains to point out, that this is not the ordinary case of breach of fiduciary duty. We have here no fraud, no misuse of confidential information, no outright looting of a helpless corporation. But on the other hand, we do not find compliance with that high standard which we have just stated and which we and other courts have come to expect and demand of corporate fiduciaries. In the often-quoted words of Judge Cardozo: "Many forms of conduct permissible in a workaday world for those acting at arm's length, are forbidden to those bound by fiduciary ties. A trustee is held to something stricter than the morals of the market place. Not honesty alone, but the punctilio of an honor the most sensitive, is then the standard of behavior. As to this there has developed a tradition that is unbending and inveterate. Uncompromising rigidity has been the attitude of courts of equity when petitioned to undermine the rule of undivided loyalty by the 'disintegrating erosion' of particular exceptions." *Meinhard v. Salmon,* supra, 249 N.Y. 458, 464, 164 N.E. 545, 546, 62 A.L.R. 1. The actions of defendants in siphoning off for personal gain corporate advantages to be derived from a favorable market situation do not betoken the necessary undivided loyalty owed by the fiduciary to his principal.

The corporate opportunities of whose misappropriation the minority stockholders complain need not have been an absolute certainty in order to support this action against Feldmann. If there was possibility of corporate gain, they are entitled to recover.

This rationale is equally appropriate to a consideration of the benefits which Newport might have derived from the steel shortage. In the past Newport had used and profited by its market leverage by operation of what the industry had come to call the "Feldmann Plan." This consisted of securing interest-free advances from prospective purchasers of steel in return for firm commitments to them from future production. The funds thus acquired were used to finance improvements in existing plants and to acquire new installations. In the summer of 1950 Newport had been negotiating for cold-rolling facilities which it needed for a more fully integrated operation and a more marketable product, and Feldmann plan funds might well have been used toward this end.

Further, as plaintiffs alternatively suggest, Newport might have used the period of short supply to build up patronage in the geographical area in which it could compete profitably even when steel was more abundant. Either of these opportunities was Newport's, to be used to its advantage only. Only if defendants had been able to negate completely any possibility of gain by Newport could they have prevailed. It is true that a trial court finding states: "Whether or not, in August, 1950, Newport's position was such that it could have entered into 'Feldmann Plan' type transactions to procure funds and financing for the further expansion and integration of its steel facilities and whether such expansion would have been desirable for Newport, the evidence does not show." This, however, cannot avail the defendants, who—contrary to the ruling below—had the burden of proof on this issue, since fiduciaries always have the burden of proof in establishing the fairness of their dealings with trust property.

Defendants seek to categorize the corporate opportunities which might have accrued to Newport as too unethical to warrant further consideration. It is true that reputable steel producers were not participating in the gray market brought about by the Korean War and were refraining from advancing their prices, although to do so would not have been illegal. But Feldmann plan transactions were not considered within this self-imposed interdiction; the trial court found that around the time of the Feldmann sale Jones & Laughlin Steel Corporation, Republic Steel Company, and Pittsburgh Steel Corporation were all participating in such arrangements. In any event, it ill becomes the defendants to disparage as unethical the market advantages from which they themselves reaped rich benefits.

We do not mean to suggest that a majority stockholder cannot dispose of his controlling block of stock to outsiders without having to account to his corporation for profits or even never do this with impunity when the buyer is an interested customer, actual or potential for the corporation's product. But when the sale necessarily results in a sacrifice of this element of corporate good will and consequent unusual profit to the fiduciary who has caused the sacrifice, he should account for his gains. So in a time of market shortage, where a call on a corporation's product commands an unusually large premium, in one form or another, we think it sound law that a fiduciary may not appropriate to himself the value of this premium. Such personal gain at the expense of his coventurers seems particularly reprehensible when made by the trusted president and director of his company. In this case the violation of duty seems to be all the clearer because of this triple role in which Feldmann appears, though we are unwilling to say, and are not to be understood as saying, that we should accept a lesser obligation for any one of his roles alone.

Hence to the extent that the price received by Feldmann and his codefendants included such a bonus, he is accountable to the minority stockholders who sue here. And plaintiffs, as they contend, are entitled to a recovery in their own right, instead of in right of the corporation (as in the usual derivative actions), since neither Wilport nor their successors in interest should share in any judgment which may be rendered. Defendants cannot well object to this form of recovery, since the only alternative, recovery for the corporation as a whole, would subject them to a greater total liability.

The case will therefore be remanded to the district court for a determination of the question expressly left open below, namely, the value of defendants' stock without the appurtenant control over the corporation's output of steel. We reiterate that on this issue, as on all others, relating to a breach of fiduciary duty, the burden of proof must rest on the defendants. Judgment should go to these plaintiffs and those whom they represent for any premium value so shown to the extent of their respective stock interests.

The judgment is therefore reversed and the action remanded for further proceedings pursuant to this opinion.

SWAN, CIRCUIT JUDGE dissenting:

With the general principles enunciated in the majority opinion as to the duties of fiduciaries I am, of course, in thorough accord. But, as Mr. Justice Frankfurter, "to say that a man is a fiduciary only begins analysis; it gives direction to further inquiry. To whom is he a fiduciary? What obligations does he owe as a fiduciary? In what respect has he failed to discharge these obligations?" My brothers' opinion does not specify precisely what fiduciary duty Feldmann is held to have violated or whether it was a duty imposed upon him as the dominant stockholder or as a director of Newport. Without such specification I think that both the legal profession and the business world will find the decision confusing and will be unable to foretell the extent of its impact upon customary practices in the sale of stock.

The power to control the management of a corporation, that is, to elect directors to manage its affairs, is an inseparable incident to the ownership of a majority of its stock, or sometimes, as in the present instance, to the ownership of enough shares, less than a majority, to control an election. Concededly a majority or dominant shareholder is ordinarily privileged to sell his stock at the best price obtainable from the purchaser. In so doing he acts on his own behalf, not as an agent of the corporation. If he knows or has reason to believe that the purchaser intends to exercise to the detriment of the corporation the power of management acquired by the purchase, such knowledge or reasonable suspicion will terminate the dominant shareholder's privilege to sell and will create a duty not to transfer the power of management to such purchaser. The duty seems to me to resemble the obligation which everyone is under not to assist another to commit a tort rather than the obligation of a fiduciary. But whatever the nature of the duty, a violation of it will subject the violator to liability for damages sustained by the corporation. Judge Hincks found that Feldmann had no reason to think that Wilport would use the power of management it would acquire by the purchase to injure Newport, and that there was no proof that it ever was so used. Feldmann did know, it is true, that the reason Wilport wanted the stock was to put in a board of directors who would be likely to permit Wilport's members to purchase more of Newport's steel than they might otherwise be able to get. But there is nothing illegal in a dominant shareholder purchasing from his own corporation at the same prices it offers to other customers. That is what the members of Wilport did, and there is no proof that Newport suffered any detriment therefrom.

My brothers say that "the consideration paid for the stock included compensation for the sale of a corporate asset", which they describe as "the ability to control the allocation of the corporate product in a time of short supply, through control of the board of directors; and it was effectively transferred in this sale by having Feldmann procure the resignation of his own board and the election of Wilport's nominees immediately upon consummation of the sale." The implications of this are not clear to me. If it means that when market conditions are such as to induce users of a corporation's product to wish to buy a controlling block of stock in order to be able to purchase part of the corporation's output at the same mill list prices as are offered to other customers, the dominant stockholder is under a fiduciary duty not to sell his stock, I cannot agree. For reasons already stated, in my opinion Feldmann was not proved to be under any fiduciary duty as a stockholder not to sell the stock he controlled.

Points for Discussion

1. Minority not harmed.

The Second Circuit's opinion does not mention the following finding of fact from the District Court opinion:

> Since the Wilport nominees took over the management of Newport on August 31, 1950, substantial improvements have been made in Newport's property and the corporation has enjoyed continued prosperity. Although the Wilport stockholders have purchased substantial quantities of steel from Newport, no sales were made at less than Newport's quoted mill prices. There is no evidence of any sort that Newport has suffered from mismanagement or inefficient management since August 31, 1950, or that it has suffered or is likely hereafter to suffer any harm whatever at the hands of its new management, or that its new management has in any way failed to do anything which should have been done for the good of the corporation.

In light of this finding, why did the Second Circuit reverse the trial court's decision? What precisely did Feldmann do that was wrong?

Would it be relevant to you that Wilport apparently approached Feldmann originally with a proposal to acquire the whole company in a merger, which would have meant all shareholders would have shared in any control premium? Feldmann suggested that Wilport could acquire control less expensively by buying only his shares. Does that change your view of the case?

2. Meaning of case.

Perlman provoked a spirited debate. Some argued that the case involves the wrongful appropriation of a corporate opportunity, namely the right to buy price-controlled steel during wartime shortages. Others interpret it to establish a duty to share a control premium with all of a corporation's shareholders. Do you read the case as limited to its special facts or as a broader statement of the duty of controlling shareholders to share their control premium?

You should know that most courts have refused to follow *Perlman*, including courts in Indiana whose corporate law the Second Circuit was attempting to interpret. Instead, courts have generally accepted that a controlling shareholder can sell its controlling interest (even when the corporation has assets of particular value to the buyer) without sharing the control premium with noncontrolling shareholders or the corporation.

3. Damages (paid to minority shareholders).

On remand, the District Court computed damages based on the investment value of Newport's common stock using a capitalization of its earnings. It then ordered Feldmann to distribute to Newport's public shareholders their pro rata share of the amount by which the purchase price he received exceeded that figure. Does this suggest a sharing of the value of wartime steel or the sharing of a control premium?

Business Lingo

The "capitalization of earnings" method of valuation uses a company's current earnings and applies a multiplier based on the price-earnings ratios of similar companies (with comparable growth and risk profiles). This simple calculation gives an idea of what the company might fetch if sold as an on-going business.

For a description of other corporate valuation methods, you can look back at Chapter 11, Numeracy for Corporate Lawyers.

4. Sale of Office

Control of the corporation's business is vested in the board of directors. Just acquiring a majority of the corporation's shares does not give you immediate control of the business. For this reason, the usual practice when a buyer acquires a control block is for the existing directors to resign (one by one) and to have the vacancies filled (one by one) by new directors chosen by the buyer.

Is this legal? Remember that directors, elected by all the shareholders, cannot sell their corporate office.

The following case, arising in the unusual circumstance of a buyer wishing to rescind its purchase. The plaintiff had contracted to purchase defendant's 28.3% interest in Republic Pictures for $8 per share, approximately $2 above the price at which the stock sold on the New York Stock Exchange. The contract required the seller to deliver resignations of a majority of Republic's directors and to cause the election of persons designated by the buyer. The seller refused to go ahead with this condition and claimed as a defense in a suit for breach of contract that to do so would be illegal.

The court unanimously reversed a judgment for the defendant-seller.

Essex Universal Corp. v. Yates

305 F.2d 572 (2d Cir. 1962)

LUMBARD, CHIEF JUDGE.

Despite the disagreement evidenced by the diversity of our opinions, my brethren and I agree that such a provision does not on its face render the contract illegal and unenforceable, and thus that it was improper to grant summary judgment. Judge Friendly would reject the defense of illegality without further inquiry concerning the provision itself (as distinguished from any contention that control could not be safely transferred to the particular purchaser). Judge Clark and I are agreed that on remand, which must be had in any event to consider other defenses raised by the pleadings, further factual issues may be raised by the parties upon which the legality of the clause in question will depend; we disagree, however, on the nature of those factual issues, as our separate opinions reveal. Accordingly, the grant of summary judgment is reversed and the case is remanded for trial of the question of the legality of the contested provision and such further proceedings as may be proper on the other issues raised by the pleadings.

It is established beyond question under New York law that it is illegal to sell a corporate office or management control by itself (that is, accompanied by no stock or insufficient stock to carry voting control). The rationale of the rule is undisputable: persons enjoying management control hold it on behalf of the corporation's stockholders, and therefore may not regard it as their own personal property to dispose of as they wish. Any other rule would violate the most fundamental principle of corporate democracy, that management must represent and be chosen by, or at least with the consent of, those who own the corporation.

Essex was, however, contracting with Yates for the purchase of a very substantial percentage of Republic stock. If, by virtue of the voting power carried by this stock, it could have elected a majority of the board of directors, then the contract was not a simple agreement for the sale of office to one having no ownership interest in the corporation, and the question of its legality would require further analysis. Such stock voting control would incontestably belong to the owner of a majority of the voting stock, and it is commonly known that equivalent power usually accrues to the owner of 28.3% of the stock. For the purpose of this analysis, I shall assume that Essex was contracting to acquire a majority of the Republic stock, deferring consideration of the situation where, as here, only 28.3% is to be acquired.

Republic's board of directors at the time of the aborted closing had fourteen members divided into three classes, each class being "as nearly as may be" of the same size. Directors were elected for terms of three years, one class being elected at each annual shareholder meeting on the first Tuesday in April. Thus, absent the immediate replacement of directors provided for in this contract, Essex as the hypothetical new majority shareholder of the corporation could not have obtained managing control in the form of a majority of the board in the normal course of events until April 1959, some eighteen months after the sale of the stock. The first question before us then is whether an agreement to accelerate the transfer of management control, in a manner legal in form under the corporation's charter and bylaws, violates the public policy of New York.

There is no question of the right of a controlling shareholder under New York law normally to derive a premium from the sale of a controlling block of stock. In other words, there was no impropriety per se in the fact that Yates was to receive more per share than the generally prevailing market price for Republic stock.

The next question is whether it is legal to give and receive payment for the immediate transfer of management control to one who has achieved majority share control but would not otherwise be able to convert that share control into operating control for some time. I think that it is.

A fair generalization may be that a holder of corporate control will not, as a fiduciary, be permitted to profit from facilitating actions on the part of the purchasers of control which are detrimental to the interests of the corporation or the remaining shareholders. There is, however, no suggestion that the transfer of control over Republic to Essex carried any such threat to the interests of the corporation or its other shareholders.

Given this principle that it is permissible for a seller thus to choose to facilitate immediate transfer of management control, I can see no objection to a contractual provision requiring him to do so as a condition of the sale. Indeed, a New York court has upheld an analogous contractual term requiring the board of directors to elect the nominees of the purchasers of a majority stock interest to officerships. *San Remo Copper Mining Co. v. Moneuse*, 149 App.Div. 26, 133 N.Y.S. 509 (1st Dept.1912). The court said that since the purchaser was about to acquire "absolute control" of the corporation, "it certainly did not destroy the validity of the contract that by one of its terms defendant was to be invested with this power of control at once, upon acquiring the stock, instead of waiting for the next annual meeting."

The easy and immediate transfer of corporate control to new interests is ordinarily beneficial to the economy and it seems inevitable that such transactions would be discouraged if the purchaser of a majority stock interest were required to wait some period before his purchase of control could become effective. Conversely it would greatly hamper the efforts of any existing majority group to dispose of its interest if it could not assure the purchaser of immediate control over corporation operations. I can see no reason why a purchaser of majority control should not ordinarily be permitted to make his control effective from the moment of the transfer of stock.

Thus if Essex had been contracting to purchase a majority of the stock of Republic, it would have been entirely proper for the contract to contain the provision for immediate replacement of directors. Although in the case at bar only 28.3 per cent of the stock was involved, it is commonly known that a person or group owning so large a percentage of the voting stock of a corporation which, like Republic, has at least the 1,500 shareholders normally requisite to listing on the New York Stock Exchange, is almost certain to have share control as a practical matter. If Essex was contracting to acquire what in reality would be equivalent to ownership of a majority of stock, i.e., if it would as a practical certainty have been guaranteed of the stock voting power to choose a majority of the directors of Republic in due course, there is no reason why the contract should not similarly be legal. Whether Essex was thus to acquire the equivalent of majority stock control would, if the issue is properly raised by the defendants, be a factual issue to be determined by the district court on remand.

Because 28.3 per cent of the voting stock of a publicly owned corporation is usually tantamount to majority control, I would place the burden of proof on this issue on Yates as the party attacking the legality of the transaction. Thus, unless on remand Yates chooses to raise the question whether the block of stock in question carried the equivalent of majority control, it is my view that the trial court should regard the contract as legal and proceed to consider the other issues raised by the pleadings. If Yates chooses to raise the issue, it will, on my view, be necessary for him to prove the existence of circumstances which would have prevented Essex from electing a majority of the Republic board of directors in due course. It will not be enough for Yates to raise merely hypothetical possibilities of opposition by the other Republic shareholders to Essex' assumption of management control. Rather, it will be necessary for him to show that, assuming neutrality on the part of the retiring management, there was at the time some concretely foreseeable reason why Essex' wishes would not have prevailed in shareholder voting held in due course. In other words, I would require him to show that there was at the time of the contract some other organized block of stock of sufficient size to outvote the block Essex was buying, or else some circumstance making it likely that enough of the holders of the remaining Republic stock would band together to keep Essex from control.

Reversed and remanded for further proceedings not inconsistent with the judgment of this court.

FRIENDLY, CIRCUIT JUDGE concurring:

Chief Judge Lumbard's thoughtful opinion illustrates a difficulty, inherent in our dual judicial system, which has led at least one state to authorize its courts to answer questions about its law that a Federal court may ask. Here we are forced to decide a question of New York law, of enormous importance to all New York corporations and their stockholders, on which there is hardly enough New York authority for a really informed prediction what the New York Court of Appeals would decide on the facts here presented.

I have no doubt that many contracts, drawn by competent and responsible counsel, for the purchase of blocks of stock from interests thought to "control" a corporation although owning less than a majority, have contained provisions like paragraph 6 of the contract sub judice. However, developments over the past decades seem to me to show that such a clause violates basic principles of corporate democracy. To be sure, stockholders who have allowed a set of directors to be placed in office, whether by their vote or their failure to vote, must recognize that death, incapacity or other hazard may prevent a director from serving a full term, and that they will have no voice as to his immediate successor. But the stockholders are entitled to expect that, in that event, the remaining directors will fill the vacancy in the exercise of their fiduciary responsibility. A mass seriatim resignation directed by a selling stockholder, and the filling of vacancies by his henchmen at the dictation of a purchaser and without any consideration of the character of the latter's nominees, are beyond what the stockholders contemplated or should have been expected to contemplate. This seems to me a wrong to the corporation and the other stockholders which the law ought not countenance, whether the selling stockholder has received a premium or not. Right in this Court we have seen many cases where sudden shifts of corporate control have caused serious injury. To hold the seller for delinquencies of the new directors only if he knew the purchaser was an intending looter is not a sufficient sanction. The difficulties of proof are formidable even if receipt of too high a premium creates a presumption of such knowledge, and, all too often, the doors are locked only after the horses have been stolen. Stronger medicines are needed—refusal to enforce a contract with such a clause, even though this confers an unwarranted benefit on a defaulter, and continuing responsibility of the former directors for negligence of the new ones until an election has been held. Such prophylactics are not contraindicated, as Judge Lumbard suggests, by the conceded desirability of preventing the dead hand of a former "controlling" group from continuing to dominate the board after a sale, or of protecting a would-be purchaser from finding himself without a majority of the board after he has spent his money. A special meeting of stockholders to replace a board may always be called, and there could be no objection to making the closing of a purchase contingent on the results of such an election. I perceive some of the difficulties of mechanics such a procedure presents, but I have enough confidence in the ingenuity of the corporate bar to believe these would be surmounted.

Hence, I am inclined to think that if I were sitting on the New York Court of Appeals, I would hold a provision like Paragraph 6 violative of public policy save when it was entirely plain that a new election would be a mere formality—i.e., when the seller owned more than 50% of the stock. I put it thus tentatively because, before making such a decision, I would want the help of briefs, including those of amici curiae, dealing with the serious problems of corporate policy and practice more fully than did those here, which were primarily devoted to argument as to what the New York law has been rather than what it ought to be. Moreover, in view of the perhaps unexpected character of such a holding, I doubt that I would give it retrospective effect.

As a judge of this Court, my task is the more modest one of predicting how the judges of the New York Court of Appeals would rule, and I must make this prediction on the basis of legal materials rather than of personal acquaintance or hunch. Also, for obvious reasons, the prospective technique is unavailable when a Federal court is deciding an issue of state law. Although *Barnes v. Brown*, 80 N.Y. 527 (1880), dealt with the sale of a majority interest, I am unable to find any real indication that the doctrine there announced has been thus limited. True, there are New York cases saying that the sale of corporate offices is forbidden; but the New York decisions do not tell us what this means and I can find nothing, save perhaps one unexplained sentence in the opinion of a trial court in *Ballantine v. Ferretti*, 28 N.Y.S.2d 668, 682 (1941), to indicate that New York would not apply *Barnes v. Brown* to a case where a stockholder with much less than a majority conditioned a sale on his causing the resignation of a majority of the directors and the election of the purchaser's nominees.

Chief Judge Lumbard's proposal goes part of the way toward meeting the policy problem I have suggested. Doubtless proceeding from what, as it seems to me, is the only justification in principle for permitting even a majority stockholder to condition a sale on delivery of control of the board—namely that in such a case a vote of the stockholders would be a useless formality, he sets the allowable bounds at the line where there is "a practical certainty" that the buyer would be able to elect his nominees and, in this case, puts the burden of disproving that on the person claiming illegality.

Attractive as the proposal is in some respects, I find difficulties with it. One is that I discern no sufficient intimation of the distinction in the New York cases, or even in the writers, who either would go further in voiding such a clause. When an issue does arise, the "practical certainty" test is difficult to apply. Judge Lumbard correctly recognizes that, from a policy standpoint, the pertinent question must be the buyer's prospects of election, not the seller's—yet this inevitably requires the court to canvass the likely reaction of stockholders to a group of whom they know nothing and seems rather hard to reconcile with a position that it is "right" to insert such a condition if a seller has a larger proportion of the stock and "wrong" if he has a smaller. At the very least the problems and uncertainties arising from the proposed line of demarcation are great enough, and its advantages small enough, that in my view a Federal court would do better simply to overrule the defense here, thereby accomplishing what is obviously the "just" result in this particular case, and leave the development of doctrine in this area to the State, which has primary concern for it.

I would reverse the grant of summary judgment and remand for consideration of defenses other than a claim that the inclusion of paragraph 6 ex mero motu renders the contract void.

————————

Points for Discussion

1. Buyer of less than 51%.

When a buyer buys a minority interest in a corporation, aren't shareholders disenfranchised if their elected directors resign and replace themselves with nominees chosen by the buyer? Is it enough if the shareholders receive notice of the change and have a chance at the next board election to choose a different slate of directors?

2. Level of selling director's ownership.

Does analysis of the legality of the sale of shares by a shareholder-director who promises he will resign his board seat depend on the size of the holding? That is, would a director-shareholder who sells a 4% interest for an above-market premium and agrees to resign be more suspect than a director-shareholder who sells a 49% interest with the same promise?

3. Remedy.

What should be the remedy if a director-shareholder sells his shares in a way that violates the rule against selling an office? Should the sale be rescinded? Should the director-shareholder be forced to disgorge any control premium? Can the promised board resignation and replacement go forward once the control premium has been repaid?

———————

B. Voting in M&A

We next look at shareholder rights to vote and to cash out their shares through appraisal in M&A transactions. These rights are a cornerstone of corporate governance.

1. Shareholder Voting and Appraisal Rights

Certain fundamental corporate changes, after being initiated by the board, must be approved by a shareholder majority. When is shareholder approval required? Although statutes vary, shareholders generally have the right to vote on amendments to the articles of incorporation, significant mergers, the sale of all or substantially all of a corporation's assets, and corporate dissolution—that is, transactions that change the corporation's form, scope, or continuity.

You can think of these shareholder voting rights as a *veto power*, since shareholders can block fundamental changes, but cannot initiate them. But shareholders do not have the power to veto every change. Many transactions that fundamentally change the corporation's business, such as the acquisition of a new division for cash or a major change in product focus, do not trigger shareholder voting rights, even though those changes are important.

Historically at common law, fundamental corporate changes required unanimous shareholder approval. Consequently, one shareholder could block any fundamental change, even a change as simple as extending the life of a corporation beyond its original term. The idea was that the charter was a contract, both among the corporation's shareholders and between the corporation and the state, and every shareholder had vested rights.

State legislatures began to recognize that the unanimity requirement created the potential for tyranny by the minority. Enterprising investors could purchase stock in a company in anticipation of a proposed fundamental change and threaten to veto the change, thus forcing the majority to repurchase their shares at a premium. Legislatures responded by amending corporate statutes to allow fundamental changes crafted by the board of directors and approved by a majority or super-majority of its shareholders.

Legislatures also granted dissenting shareholders a right to "opt out" of certain fundamental changes. Today shareholders can dissent from certain transactions and demand that the corporation pay them in cash the "fair value" of their shares as determined by a court in an appraisal proceeding, even though the requisite majority approves the transaction. Corporate statutes provide detailed procedural requirements that a shareholder must fulfill to perfect and exercise their right to appraisal. Requirements may include, for example, delivering to the corporation a written demand for appraisal and not voting in favor of the proposed merger. *See* DGCL § 262.

Appraisal substitutes an exit right for the veto right. Appraisal also places a floor on the value of minority shares when the majority approves fundamental changes that affect the minority's interests. Whatever the rationale for appraisal statutes, three points are clear. First, every corporate statute authorizes shareholders to demand appraisal as to certain fundamental changes and to require the corporation to repurchase their stock in cash for its fair value. Second, corporation statutes vary from state to state on when shareholders have voting and appraisal rights. Third, sometimes shareholders have voting rights in a transaction, but not appraisal rights.

2. Shareholder Rights in Corporate Combinations

A corporate combination places the business operations of two or more corporations under the control of one management. The voting and appraisal rights that arise in corporate combinations provide a glimpse into how corporate statutes balance board prerogative, shareholder oversight, and minority protection.

Take Note!

Business and tax considerations often dominate the choice of corporate combination. For example, if selling assets (as opposed to a merger) would trigger significant financial or tax obligations, the combination can be structured so the corporation holding the assets survives the transaction—thus avoiding these obligations. Similarly, if the acquiring firm wants to operate the acquired firm as an internal division, to avoid the administrative burden of maintaining a subsidiary, the combination can be structured to create only one surviving entity.

Sometimes it is possible for the board to approve a corporate combination without shareholder voting or appraisal rights. Sometimes shareholders must vote to approve the combination, but do not get an appraisal remedy. And sometimes the combination triggers both full voting and appraisal rights.

To illustrate, we will consider four basic negotiated combination techniques: (1) statutory merger, (2) triangular merger, (3) sale of assets, and (4) tender offer. We designate the principal corporation surviving the combination (the parent corporation) as P, any subsidiary of P as S, and the corporation to be acquired (the target corporation) as T.

a. Statutory Merger

In a statutory merger, P and T begin as separate legal entities and end up as one entity. To do this, the boards of P and T must first adopt a *plan of merger* that—

- designates which corporation (here P) is to survive the merger

- describes the terms and conditions of the merger

- specifies how shares of T will be converted into shares of P (or other property, such as cash or bonds)

- sets forth any amendments to P's articles of incorporation necessary to effectuate the plan of merger.

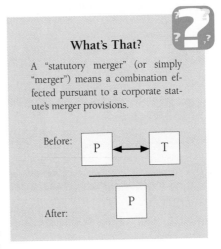

What's That?

A "statutory merger" (or simply "merger") means a combination effected pursuant to a corporate statute's merger provisions.

Before: P ⟷ T

After: P

The boards of each of the constituent corporations must approve the plan of merger. *See* DGCL § 251. The plan of merger then is submitted to the shareholders of T, as well as the shareholders of P if their approval is required. Once approved by shareholders, the plan of merger is filed with the secretary of state's office and the merger becomes effective.

What is the effect of a statutory merger? By operation of law, T immediately ceases to exist, the assets of T become the assets of P, and the liabilities of T become the liabilities of P. No formal conveyances or assignments need to be executed—it happens automatically. All shares of T are converted into shares of P, unless the plan of merger calls for consideration in the form of cash or other property. The shareholders of P retain their shares.

Make the Connection

Many state statutes also provide for "short-form" and "medium-form" mergers in which shareholders do not vote, but have the right to seek appraisal. See Chapter 24, Duties within Corporate Groups.

Voting rights. Voting rights vary from state to state. Many statutes, including in Delaware, require that statutory mergers be approved by an absolute majority of the shareholders of both P and T. But the vote of P shareholders is not required in a "whale-minnow merger" that does not increase by more than 20% the outstanding voting shares of P.

The MBCA requires that a statutory merger be approved only by a simple majority of the shareholders of T. The vote by P shareholders is required if the merger involves a *dilutive share issuance* where P is to issue new shares with voting power equal to at least 20% of the voting power that existed prior to the merger. In addition, the P shareholders must vote if the plan of merger would change the number of shares they hold after the merger or otherwise fundamentally affect their share rights.

Make the Connection

What if a merging corporation has more than one class of shareholders? Some statutes require class voting—that is, the separate approval by each class of shares to be converted (or substantially changed) in the merger. Delaware does not require class voting, unless required in the plan of merger or in the articles of incorporation. (You may remember this from Chapter 5, Corporate Federalism, where we looked at choice of law rules when different states imposed different corporate rules.)

Appraisal rights. Appraisal in a statutory merger also varies from state to state, with some statutes sometimes eliminating the appraisal remedy if shareholders have a market into which they can sell their shares.

Some statutes (including those based on the pre-1999 MBCA) link appraisal rights to voting rights. Thus, T shareholders entitled to vote on the merger can dissent and seek an appraisal, and P shareholders have appraisal rights if the merger is significant enough to require their approval. The current MBCA generally makes appraisal rights available only to T shareholders entitled to vote on the merger and not subject to a "market out" exception (described below). P shareholders do not have appraisal rights, unless they are entitled to vote on the merger and their shares do not remain outstanding afterward. Delaware's statute also generally limits appraisal rights to T shareholders, whether or not they were entitled to vote on the merger, unless Delaware's "market out" exception applies (described next). P shareholders have appraisal rights if they were entitled to vote on the merger and the

Take Note!

The MBCA, as revised in 1999, asks whether a business combination, whatever its form, will dilute substantially the voting power of the acquiring corporation's shareholders. If the combination involves a "dilutive share issuance"—that is, the issuance of shares with voting power of more than 20% of the voting power that existed prior to the combination—the acquiring corporation's shareholders must vote to approve. MBCA § 6.21(f).

The goal is substance over form. Voting rights in fundamental corporate changes are the same, regardless of how the transaction is structured. This approach follows a pattern adopted in some larger states, such as California and New Jersey. It also tracks rules of the New York Stock Exchange and NASDAQ, whose listing rules require a shareholder vote on any merger or other transaction that dilutes by more than 18.5% the voting power of existing shareholders (roughly the dilution when a corporation issues shares with voting power equal to more than 20% of existing voting power).

"market out" exception does not apply.

As noted, shareholders must follow the procedural requirements to perfect and exercise their right of appraisal. The use of appraisal rights in Delaware has become more common and controversial, as hedge funds have sought to profit by purchasing shares after a merger is announced. Note that the appraisal remedy is only valuable if a judge determines that the fair value of the shares is greater than the amount offered in the merger. If a judge says the merger price was fair, the appraisal remedy is zero.

> A "minority discount" reflects the lower price that minority shares command, compared to controlling shares. The discount arises both in public trading markets and in private transactions of closely-held stock. *See* Chapter 24, Duties within Corporate Groups.

The "market out" exception assumes shareholders dissatisfied with the terms of a merger do not need a judicial valuation remedy if there is a public market for their stock. The exception reflects the view that a stock's current market price is more likely to reflect accurately the stock's value than a later valuation by a judge or judicially appointed appraiser.

The MBCA "market out" exception prevents shareholders of T from seeking appraisal if their stock was publicly traded before the merger and they receive (or retain) cash or marketable stock in the merger. (Recall that P shareholders do not have appraisal rights if they retain their shares, whether publicly traded or not.) By contrast, Delaware's "market out" exception prevents shareholders of P or T from seeking appraisal if their stock was publicly traded before and will be publicly traded after the merger. Delaware law distinguishes between T shareholders who are "required" to take cash and T shareholders who have a choice among cash, shares, or other consideration. T shareholders who are "required" to take cash are entitled to appraisal rights, but T shareholders who have a choice of consideration are not. Thus, a stock-for-cash merger can trigger appraisal rights in Delaware, but not under the MBCA.

Many have expressed misgivings about the "market out" exception, and the pre-1999 MBCA did not include it. Why not? Some questioned whether a stock's market value always equals its "true" value, and whether the market might be "demoralized" or be too thin to absorb a large sale of shares. Moreover a "market out" exception might not make sense if shareholders hold "restricted" stock that they could not sell publicly.

The current MBCA also reflects some concern that public markets might not adequately protect shareholders, particularly when a merger involves a conflict of interest. For example, the current MBCA "market out" exception does not apply to a squeeze-out merger that involves a 20% or more shareholder. Nor does it apply to a management buyout, where an insider group has the power to elect one-fourth or more of the board.

b. Triangular Merger

It is easy to transfer assets through a statutory merger. But a statutory merger can expose P to unknown or contingent liabilities associated with T's business. P can use a "triangular merger" to address such exposure.

In a triangular merger, P creates a subsidiary corporation—we'll call it "S"—that merges with T. The merger between S and T can be done so that either is the surviving corporation. If S is the surviving corporation, we refer to the transaction as a "forward triangular merger." If T is the surviving corporation, it is a "reverse triangular merger." In either event, at the time of the merger, the consideration is transferred to the T shareholders and their T stock is cancelled. After the merger, P has a

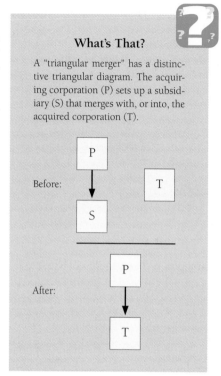

What's That?

A "triangular merger" has a distinctive triangular diagram. The acquiring corporation (P) sets up a subsidiary (S) that merges with, or into, the acquired corporation (T).

wholly-owned subsidiary that has the assets and liabilities of T.

Structuring the deal as a triangular merger can avoid exposing P to the liabilities associated with T's business, avoid disturbing the operations of T's business, and may be preferable from a tax perspective. For T's shareholders, it makes little difference whether the combination is structured as a statutory merger or a triangular merger. In either case, T's shareholders are entitled to vote on the merger and, if they dissent and do not have a market out, they can exercise appraisal rights.

Under many statutes, including Delaware's, structuring a combination as a triangular merger means only S

Take Note!

A *statutory share exchange* accomplishes the same result as a triangular merger. As with a statutory merger, the boards of P and T first must approve a plan of exchange that spells out the terms on which shares of T will be exchanged for P shares (or cash or other property). (Delaware law contains no provision for a statutory share exchange.) Under the MBCA, T shareholders then must approve the plan of exchange and may seek appraisal, subject to the market out exception. P shareholders have voting rights whenever the statutory share exchange involves a dilutive share issuance by P, but do not have appraisal rights, even if they are entitled to vote, since they retain their shares.

shareholders vote on the merger—not P shareholders. Who are S's shareholders? Remember that P obtains S's shares when it sets up S. That means P's board can direct the voting of S's shares, without input from P's shareholders. Thus, a triangular merger effectively denies to P shareholders the right to vote on the business combination or exercise appraisal rights. The form of the combination determines the availability of substantive shareholder rights.

The current MBCA is very different. It favors substance over form. If a triangular merger involves a dilutive share issuance by P—that is, if P will issue shares in the merger that will comprise more than 20% of P's outstanding shares *before* the merger—the approval of P shareholders is required. But even if P's shareholders are entitled to vote, they would not have appraisal rights, because they retain their shares in the transaction. This result is the same as in a statutory merger of T into P.

c. Sale of Assets

Alternatively, P can buy the assets of T, using as consideration some combination of its own stock, cash, or other securities. Structuring an acquisition as a purchase of assets can have relatively high transaction costs, but can avoid liabilities of the target. As with all the other combination techniques (except the tender offer), the first step in a sale of assets is agreement by the boards of P and T. Then the shareholders of T, the selling corporation, must approve the terms of the sales agreement. Under the MBCA, T shareholders also have appraisal rights, subject to the "market out" exception. But if T is a Delaware corporation, appraisal is not available in a sale of assets.

Example 30.1

Signal, a diversified conglomerate incorporated in Delaware, sells its wholly-owned subsidiary Oil & Gas to another oil company. Oil & Gas represents 26% of Signal's total assets, 41% of its net worth, and 15% of its revenues and earnings. Is approval of the sale by Signal's shareholders required? (DGCL § 271 requires shareholder approval for the sale of "all or substantially all" of the assets of a Delaware corporation.)

Shareholder approval is not required for every "major" corporate restructuring. Instead, the question is whether the "sale is in fact an unusual transaction that strikes at the heart of the corporate existence and purpose or one made in the regular course of business of the seller." The court further explained, "If the sale is of assets quantitatively vital to the operation of the corporation and is out of the ordinary and substantially affects the existence and purpose of the corporation," shareholder approval is required. Although Signal began as an oil and gas company, it expanded over time into other significant businesses, including snack foods, aircraft, aerospace, uranium enrichment, and truck manufacturing. Thus, the sale of Oil & Gas did not constitute a sale of "all or substantially all" of the conglomerate's assets.

See *Gimbel v. Signal Cos.*, 316 A.2d 599 (Del. Ch. 1974), *aff'd per curiam*, 316 A.2d 619 (Del. 1974); *see also Hollinger Inc. v. Hollinger, Intl., Inc.*, 858 A.2d 342 (Del. Ch. 2004) (applying the *Gimbel* test to a corporation's sale of a group of newspapers accounting for about 57% of the corporation's value and concluding that the sale did not constitute "substantially all" of the corporation's assets and no shareholder vote was required).

Under the current MBCA, which takes a unified approach to all dilutive share issuances, P shareholders have voting rights if P issues stock equal to more than 20% of its stock then outstanding as part of its purchase of T's assets. However, P shareholders do not have appraisal rights, because they retain their shares. Under most other statutes, including Delaware's, the issuance of stock to purchase assets (including all the assets of another corporation) is treated the same as any other transaction involving the issuance of previously authorized stock: it is a matter of board discretion. Thus, P shareholders have no voting or appraisal rights in an asset purchase.

Take Note!

In a sale of assets, the acquiring corporation (P) and acquired corporation (T) remain intact. Only after the sale does the acquired corporation dissolve, pay its debts and then distribute the net proceeds to its shareholders.

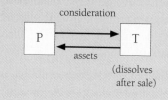

Most notably, in a sale of assets transaction, P may, but need not, also assume some or all of T's liabilities. Structuring a deal as an asset sale may be attractive for this reason. For example, professional services firms often structure their business combinations as asset sales so that they acquire desired assets such as client lists, but leave behind liabilities such as those that arise from issuing opinions. Alternatively, T may retain sufficient liquid assets to pay off its liabilities.

In some circumstances, a purchaser may become responsible for liability associated with the assets. One such circumstance occurs when the asset purchase violates the Fraudulent Conveyances Act (discussed in Chapter 13, Piercing the Corporate Veil). Also, in many states, statutory requirements or common law principles relating to "successor liability" may result in P being held responsible for certain of T's liabilities, even though they are not formally transferred in the deed or other sale documents. In response to this risk of successor liability, business lawyers sometimes use a separately incorporated subsidiary (the triangular form) for the asset purchase.

Example 30.2

This time assume Signal is incorporated in an MBCA jurisdiction when it sells its Oil & Gas subsidiary.

The MBCA jettisons the terms "all or substantially all" and instead requires shareholder approval "if the disposition would leave the corporation without a significant continuing business activity." MBCA § 12.02. Under a bright-line test, shareholder approval is not required if the selling corporation retains businesses that constitute at least 25% of its consolidated assets and 25% of either its consolidated revenues or pre-tax earnings from pre-transaction operations.

A stock-for-assets transaction can be functionally identical to a statutory merger if T is dissolved after the sale and P assumes T's liabilities. Then P will own all of T's assets and P will be owned by its shareholders and the former T shareholders.

Example 30.3

Loral buys for cash all of the assets of Arco, a Delaware corporation. Arco then dissolves and distributes its assets (the cash in the transaction) to its shareholders. The asset sale and dissolution are approved by a majority of Arco's shareholders, but some shareholders who voted against the transaction argue it's really a "de facto" merger—entitling them to appraisal rights. They assert that substance should trump form.

Delaware law does not provide for an appraisal in asset sales. Shareholders must abide by board decisions and majority rule. Any protection comes from the fiduciary duties of the directors who proposed the sale and the self-interest of fellow shareholders who approved it. *See Hariton v. Arco Electronics, Inc.*, 188 A.2d 123 (Del. 1963) (rejecting "de facto" merger doctrine in Delaware).

---

d. Tender Offers

P can also acquire control of T by offering to purchase T shares directly from T shareholders, either for P stock or for cash or other property. Through a *tender offer*, P can acquire control of T without the approval of T's board. Unlike the other combination techniques, T shareholders "approve" the transaction by individually accepting P's offer rather than through a formal vote. There are no appraisal rights. Instead, T shareholders who do not wish to accept P's offer can simply refuse to tender their shares.

Once P purchases and can vote a majority of T shares, P can control T by electing its nominees to T's board. P shareholders have no right to approve the purchase, unless P offers its shares as consideration and either lacks sufficient authorized shares to effectuate the exchange or the issuance would constitute a dilutive share issuance. And P shareholders do not have appraisal rights in the tender offer, since their shares are not reduced in the transaction.

What's That?

A "tender offer" is a contractual offer to buy shares from current shareholders, typically at a premium above prevailing market prices. The tender offer usually carries certain conditions, such as that shares be "tendered" (turned over to the offeror's agent) by a specified date and that a specified percentage of shares, such as 51%, be tendered.

Shareholders can be offered cash or other consideration for their shares. If the offeror offers its own stock, it is known as an "exchange offer." Tender offers are the subject of federal securities regulation.

After acquiring a controlling interest, P may seek to acquire the remaining T shares in a "second-step" transaction, such as a statutory or short-form merger, so P can operate T free of minority T shareholders. Whether either corporation's shareholders have voting or appraisal rights in the second-step transactions will depend on the form of the transaction and the applicable corporate statutes. Although "hostile" tender offers, undertaken without board approval, were common historically, the takeover defenses that companies began adopting during the 1980s takeover wave have effectively eliminated this use of tender offers. Instead, the more common use of tender offers today is as the mechanism for acquirers to obtain the target company's shares, after they have taken over control of the board.

e. Comparison Chart

In short, these basic techniques allow one management team to gain control of another business. In a stock-for-stock transaction where shares of P are the only consideration paid to the shareholders of T, each technique will generate the same result: T shareholders will become P shareholders, and P will own T's assets (either directly or through a wholly-owned subsidiary).

The following chart summarizes the voting and appraisal rights in a stock-for-stock business combination of equals in which P acquires T by issuing previously authorized shares constituting more than 20% of its outstanding shares as consideration—that is, a dilutive share issuance. The charts look at (1) the MBCA as revised in 1999, (2) the pre-1999 MBCA, which is still the law in some states, and (3) the DGCL.

You will notice a few things. First, shareholder rights vary according to the structure of the transaction under the pre-1999 MBCA and Delaware law. Second, shareholder rights do not vary under the revised MBCA, which seeks to have substance trump form. Third, T shareholders always get voting rights, but their appraisal rights vary from statute to statute.

Statutory Merger

	P (Surviving Corp)		T (Acquired Corp)	
	Vote	Appraisal	Vote	Appraisal
Revised MBCA	Y	N	Y	Y*
Pre-1999 MBCA	Y	Y	Y	Y
DGCL	Y	Y**	Y	Y**

Triangular Merger (or Statutory Share Exchange)

	P (Surviving Corp)		T (Acquired Corp)	
	Vote	Appraisal	Vote	Appraisal
Revised MBCA	Y	N	Y	Y*
Pre-1999 MBCA	N	N	Y	Y
DGCL	N	N	Y	Y**

Sale of Assets

	P (Surviving Corp)		T (Acquired Corp)	
	Vote	Appraisal	Vote	Appraisal
Revised MBCA	Y	N	Y	Y*
Pre-1999 MBCA	N	N	Y	Y
DGCL	N	N	Y	N

* No, if "market out exception" applies. The market out exception applies if shares of T are publicly traded before and after the transaction, unless there is a conflict of interest. MBCA § 13.02(b).

** No, if "market out" exception applies. Market out exception applies if shares are publicly traded before and after the transaction. DGCL § 262(b).

CHAPTER 31

Antitakeover Devices

The previous chapter addressed the sale of control. Frequently, a sale of control will be "friendly," in that the target corporation's board approves the transaction. In many cases, the target corporation's board welcomes the deal and does not see a need to protect the corporation against a takeover.

In contrast, potential purchasers can seek to acquire control of a corporation in a "hostile" manner. Such deals are called "hostile," because they are done without the consent of the target corporation's board.

Here is a basic preliminary question to consider in thinking about a hostile deal: which parties see the deal as hostile? Is a deal that directors and officers view as hostile also hostile to shareholders? Most hostile deals appear quite friendly to shareholders, at least in the short run, because the acquirer offers to buy shares at a high price. In addition, the hostile nature of a deal can change over time. Directors might initially oppose an offer, but then change their position if the terms become more favorable. Thus, directors can use takeover defenses to extract more favorable terms for shareholders.

This chapter is divided into three parts. First, we explore the ways directors can attempt to protect corporations from hostile takeovers by using antitakeover devices. These protections also can help directors negotiate superior terms in friendly deals. We begin by describing various forms of antitakeover devices. Some can be complex; others are straightforward. Corporate lawyers play a significant role in helping directors consider and adopt antitakeover devices.

Second, we turn to a discussion of the competing arguments for and against the use of these devices. Antitakeover defenses are at the heart of the debate about the role and purpose of corporations.

Finally, we will cover the judicial review of antitakeover devices. Judges classify antitakeover devices into several discrete categories, and the survival of a particular defense frequently will depend on which category it is deemed to fit.

A. Some Leading Defenses

Recall that potential acquirers can use two basic mechanisms in their quests for control of a targeted corporation. First, they can make a tender offer. In a tender offer, the bidder offers to buy shares directly from the target's shareholders at a substantial premium. Second, they can seek control through a proxy contest. In a proxy contest, the potential acquirer presents a competing slate of directors, and tries to persuade shareholders to oust the target's incumbent board in favor of the proposed replacement directors.

There are numerous ways for directors and officers to protect their corporations from such unwanted suitors. Some are designed to prevent unsolicited acquisitions; others merely delay a takeover or make it more costly. Some require shareholder approval; others can be implemented by boards alone, sometimes even after a hostile bidder has emerged.

Make the Connection

As discussed in the chapter on public shareholder activism, activist shareholders can employ both tender offers and proxy contests in their efforts to take control. Tender offers were common during the 1980s, but have become less frequent more recently. In contrast, proxy contests have become more common, particularly from activist hedge funds, which often hold substantial stakes in corporations and can afford the costly proxy process.

Takeover defenses are constantly in flux. Corporate lawyers adapt their takeover defense advice in response to new case law and changes in the markets. For now, the following basic list of antitakeover devices will give you a good overview of the leading tools boards use as defenses.

1. Classified Boards

If shareholders have the right to elect every director annually, the corporation is subject to the risk that an insurgent could replace every director in a single election, and thereby take over the company. One way to prevent—or at least delay—a takeover is to "classify" or "stagger" the terms of directors, so that only a portion are elected each year. For example, if one-third of the directors are up for reelection each year, it will take a potential bidder two election cycles to obtain control of the board. Corporations frequently have boards that are classified or staggered into three groups.

Many states, including Delaware, permit corporations to create a classified board either in the articles of incorporation or the bylaws. For example, consider DGCL § 141(d).

DGCL § 141
Board of Directors

(d) The directors of any corporation organized under this chapter may, by the certificate of incorporation or by an initial bylaw, or by a bylaw adopted by a vote of the stockholders, be divided into 1, 2 or 3 classes; the term of office of those of the first class to expire at the first annual meeting held after such classification becomes effective; of the second class 1 year thereafter; of the third class 2 years thereafter; and at each annual election held after such classification becomes effective, directors shall be chosen for a full term, as the case may be, to succeed those whose terms expire.

Other states, and the MBCA, require that a classified board be created through the articles. Because board approval is required to amend the articles, classified board provisions contained in the articles are difficult to attack. In contrast, it is possible for shareholders to amend the terms of classified board provisions contained in the bylaws.

Classified boards that potential bidders cannot circumvent can be a powerful antitakeover device. Essentially, classified boards force a hostile bidder to wait at least a year to obtain control of the board by replacing the directors. Moreover, they require an insurgent to win two elections, rather than just one. Empirical evidence suggests that classified boards are effective in reducing the likelihood of takeovers.

2. Poison Pills

Recall that "poison pills" are antitakeover devices that dilute the stake of a potential acquirer. The term comes from the poisonous pills spies sometimes would carry to commit suicide before they were captured and interrogated by the enemy. In the corporate world, the term's meaning is less lethal. A corporate poison pill is intended to dilute the interests of an acquirer, to make a takeover less attractive by making the acquisition prohibitively expensive. It is the corporate version of a pill a spy might take to make it more difficult for the enemy to capture him or her.

Although "poison pill" is the commonly used term—many corporate lawyers simply just call it a "pill"—the actual antitakeover device typically is labeled a "shareholder rights plan." In a shareholder rights plan, the corporation issues additional "rights" that attach to its outstanding shares. These new rights cannot be traded separately and initially have terms that make them have little value.

Take Note!

Normally, poison pills are not triggered. But in late 2008, a poison pill with a low 5% threshold adopted by Selectica, Inc., a software company incorporated in Delaware, was actually triggered. This pill differed from traditional poison pills because of its low ownership trigger of just 5% (most poison pills have higher triggers, in the range of 15%). The rationale for the lower 5% trigger was to protect Selectica's "net operating losses," which could generate tax advantages for Selectica by offsetting future income (thereby reducing future taxes). Selectica claimed this tax benefit could be lost in a takeover. Meanwhile, Versata, Inc., a competitor with similar technologies and customers, had made several offers to acquire Selectica, but Selectica had rejected all of them. When Selectica adopted its 5% threshold pill, Versata intentionally triggered the pill and sued, claiming the pill was invalid. Versata was willing to incur the share dilution consequence of the pill as one cost in its overall strategy to take over Selectica. (Ultimately, the Delaware courts held that this pill was valid.)

The rights plan specifies some "triggering" event, usually when a potential acquirer buys a specified percentage of the corporation's shares. For example, the trigger might occur when anyone purchases more than 15% of the outstanding shares.

Next, the rights plan provides that upon a triggering event, the holder has the option to buy additional shares at a low price. Importantly, the rights plan provides that the acquirer who triggered the change in the terms of the rights is not entitled to this benefit. In other words, after the triggering event, every shareholder *other than the potential acquirer* has the right to buy more shares of the corporation at a steep discount. When these shareholders exercise this option, the acquirer's position will be diluted.

Poison pills are almost never triggered. Nor do they prevent hostile takeovers entirely. Instead, they potentially strengthen a target board's powers in responding to a takeover attempt, and give it greater leverage in negotiations with a potential acquirer.

In practice, an acquirer typically will condition any deal on the redemption of the rights. Rights plans typically give the board the right to redeem the rights at a nominal price, such as $0.0001 per right, until a triggering event occurs. Rights holders do not have the rights of a shareholder, such as the right to vote or receive dividends, until the rights are exercised. The board retains the ability to amend the terms of the rights, other than the purchase price, as long as the rights are redeemable. After the rights are redeemed, the board may amend the rights as long as the amendments do not adversely affect the interests of the rights holders.

The key to a rights plan is that the board may unilaterally, without share-holder approval, authorize issuance of the rights. Likewise, the board may redeem the rights without shareholder approval. If shareholders want to strip the board of such powers, they can do so by amending the articles of incorporation. Absent an amendment prohibiting a board from adopting a rights plan, the board has the power to adopt a plan, even after a potential acquirer has emerged. Thus, even corporations without a poison pill can be said to have a "shadow pill," a takeover defense they can adopt if needed. Of course, courts might look skeptically on a board's decision to adopt a last-minute poison pill to thwart a takeover, but they have that power nonetheless.

DGCL § 157

Rights and options respecting stock

(a) Subject to any provisions in the certificate of incorporation, every corporation may create and issue, whether or not in connection with the issue and sale of any shares of stock or other securities of the corporation, rights or options entitling the holders thereof to acquire from the corporation any shares of its capital stock of any class or classes, such rights or options to be evidenced by or in such instrument or instruments as shall be approved by the board of directors.

Moran v. Household International, Inc., 500 A.2d 1346 (Del. 1985), held that DGCL § 157 gives the board of a Delaware corporation authority to adopt a share-holder rights plan. Poison pills proliferated after *Moran*, and became many companies' first line of defense against hostile bids. Takeover cases decided after *Moran* focus on when a target's directors are obliged to redeem a poison pill and, in particular, whether and when a target's directors can rely on a pill to "just say no" to a bidder who offers to purchase all of a company's stock for a premium that most shareholders would find attractive.

Take Note!

One key aspect of antitakeover devices is who controls them. If share-holders can create or eliminate an antitakeover device, the directors will not find it particularly useful in deterring acquirers. Thus, one key question to ask when analyzing a takeover defense is: who can create it and who can eliminate it? Classified boards are more effective defenses if they are in the articles, not merely in the bylaws. Conversely, poison pills are unlikely to be effective defenses if shareholders can remove them through changes in bylaws.

3. Share Repurchases

Another way for the board to defend against a takeover is by pur-chasing the corporation's own shares. Directors can authorize the repurchase of shares, either by the corporation directly or through an employee stock ownership plan or pension plan. Share repurchases can signal support of shareholder interests, and their effect can be to increase the price of the corporation's shares. To the extent share repurchases increase the share price, they make a takeover more expensive and thereby deter potential acquirers.

One form of share repurchase—known as "greenmail"—can be effective at deterring a particular unwanted acquirer. Greenmail is derived from the terms "blackmail" and "greenback," and involves the purchase of a potential acquirer's shares at a premium. Essentially, the acquirer agrees to give up a takeover in exchange for payment of a premium. The term "greenmail" has acquired a negative connotation, because some people see it as resembling a bribe to get the potential acquirer to go away. Like the adoption of a rights plan, the repurchase of shares is a decision the board can make unilaterally.

4. Lock-ups

Boards can make the corporation a less attractive target by agreeing to transactions with third parties that "lock up" some or all of the value sought by a bidder. Lock ups are antitakeover devices because they reduce or eliminate the financial incentives of a bidder to buy the corporation. If the bidder cannot "unlock" the value that has been transferred to a third party, it will have a reduced incentive to pursue a takeover.

For example, the board might agree to sell the corporation's "crown jewels," its most prized assets, to another corporation. Once those assets are off limits, the target corporation is no longer worth pursuing. Alternatively, the board might agree to give a third party an option to purchase unissued shares, thus diluting the bidder. These transactions also lock up value that a bidder might otherwise have obtained, and thus deter takeover attempts.

B. Should Boards Be Permitted to Adopt Antitakeover Devices?

Takeover defenses present fundamental policy questions. On one hand, directors are in a good position to evaluate the costs and benefits of agreeing to a takeover versus preserving the corporation. If one is skeptical about whether the corporation's share price reflects its long-term opportunities, one might believe that directors would have a better sense of a corporation's intrinsic value, and therefore would be in a position to thwart takeover threats that endanger the corporation's longer-term approach.

On the other hand, shareholders are investors who would like to maximize their gains, and understandably would be attracted by an opportunity to sell their shares for a substantial premium. Most shareholders are passive and have little direct involvement in the affairs of the corporation. Indeed, the directors are fiduciaries for those shareholders interests. Some shareholders would see a board's resistance to a takeover as an anti-shareholder approach that is meant to entrench the directors, and to benefit them and the corporation's officers, at the expense of shareholders.

Corporate law generally entrusts the management and affairs of the corporation to its board, and the directors then delegate responsibilities to the corporation's officers. Recall that DGCL § 141(a) provides as follows:

> The business and affairs of every corporation organized under this chapter shall be managed by or under the direction of a board of directors, except as may be otherwise provided in this chapter or in its certificate of incorporation.

Put simply, the fundamental question, with which we have been concerned throughout the book, is for whose benefit the corporation should be run. In the context of takeovers, the question is who should decide as to whether a corporation should continue its existence in its present form. More specifically, under what circumstances should the management of a target company be allowed to employ defensive tactics against a takeover that the target shareholders might want to accept?

What role do takeovers play in the economy? In a system of corporate governance? What role should the legal system play in regulating takeovers? What standard of review should a court employ in adjudicating control disputes that involve both business decisions and conflicts of interest? The discussion of antitakeover devices provides an opportunity to revisit some of the policy questions we addressed early in this book.

1. Property vs. Entity Revisited

A fundamental issue of corporate governance arises in takeover jurisprudence: How should power be allocated between a corporation's shareholders and its board of directors? The board of a target company employs powerful defenses to deter a tender offer, often undertaking major corporate transactions they would not have undertaken otherwise and incurring heavy debt in the process. Giving the board the authority to act on behalf of the corporation in response to a tender offer could further shareholders' interests because the board and the managers are arguably the most knowledgeable about the corporation. Though shareholders may find it tempting to sell their shares for a premium above the current market price, the board may be able to provide greater value in the long term. A board's resistance to an unwanted bid may also help the shareholders obtain a higher price for their shares. However, a target board's efforts to defeat a bid may weaken the shareholders' ability to hold directors and managers accountable. This is troublesome because part of the target managers' motivation in employing takeover defenses is self-serving. They want to preserve their positions at the corporation.

When courts first considered whether certain defensive tactics were proper, they had difficulty determining which of two standards of review to apply—the business judgment rule for claims that management violated its duty of care or the intrinsic fairness test for claims that management violated its duty of loyalty. Hostile takeover defense tactics seemed a cross between the two duties. Although the desirability of a target's acquisition is an issue of business judgment, the target management has conflicted interests because the transaction directly threatens their jobs. Should defensive tactics be reviewed under a lax standard or a strict one? Corporate law had left open this question.

This controversy reflects the debate about the purpose and nature of the corporation that we introduced early in this book. Those who view the corporation as the "property" of its owners argue that boards should only be able to adopt limited defensive measures, such as providing shareholders with the information they need to make informed decisions and helping shareholders overcome collective action problems. Because shareholders are the owners of the corporation, they should be permitted to sell their shares to a willing buyer for a premium price over the stock's current market value.

In contrast, those who embrace the "entity" concept of the corporation argue that managers should have more discretion to resist unwanted tender offers. When the corporation is seen as a social institution with a public purpose, the issue is not simply whether shareholders should have the unfettered discretion to accept a bidder's premium offer. Rather, a target's board of directors should have the ability to defend the corporation from a takeover that the board genuinely believes undervalues the long-term productivity of the company and threatens other legitimate corporate interests, such as the company's employees, consumers, or the local community.

Whether courts should give management broad freedom to resist an unwanted tender offer depends not only on whether one accepts Chancellor Allen's entity view of the corporation, but also on whether one believes that directors confronting a hostile takeover bid are more likely to be motivated by self-interest or by a concern for the corporation's long-term well being. Defensive tactics are entrenchment mechanisms. As such, those who believe managers' decisions are influenced or dominated by self-interested motives oppose giving management unfettered discretion to resist an unwanted takeover bid. Those who advocate for increasing shareholders' power in corporate takeovers argue that because shareholders have a common investment interest in maximizing firm value they can effectively discipline management overreaching.

In part, the case law adheres to the property model in stating that a corporation's purpose is to maximize shareholder wealth. But cases also reflect the entity model because they permit directors to consider both the corporation's long-term interests and constituents other than shareholders.

2. Role of Takeovers in Disciplining Management

The threat of hostile takeovers may prevent management misconduct. An active market for corporate control arguably encourages management to run the business profitably because, if the company's stock price falls, the company would be vulnerable to a takeover bid. Under this view of corporate governance, target company shareholders should be allowed to accept a tender offer for a premium over the current market price of their shares because it motivates entrenched managers to run the company in a way that maximizes shareholder value. Managers want to avoid losing their jobs in a hostile takeover. This perspective assumes an efficient market where stock prices accurately reflect a company's true value. In such a market, the bidder will look for a target company whose stock price is below the bidder's own assessment of value of the target's assets. A low stock-market valuation thus indicates that the company is underperforming, either because of bad management or because of underutilized assets.

The problem with this argument is that the stock price may not reflect a company's true value. Most economists now believe that financial markets are only relatively efficient. If stock prices provide an imprecise estimate of the value of the corporation, two results follow. First, if the hostile bid was made based on an incorrectly priced stock, then shareholder choice means both good and bad managers could lose their jobs. Thus, managers are no longer motivated to be faithful to the corporation or risk losing their jobs because they might lose their jobs regardless. Second, managers are often more knowledgeable than the market about the true value of their company.

Finally, hostile takeovers require a great deal of money. A bidder corporation that makes a premium, all-cash, all-shares offer to the shareholders of a large target corporation may need to borrow money to finance the takeover. With the availability of debt financing, the bidder can borrow large sums from groups of investors who participate in the financing of the target. Foreign lenders have increased the amount of available capital to make it possible for the bidder to acquire the target. But, there is always the issue of how much the target is really worth. The concept of "winner's curse" suggests that the amount of money it takes to win a competitive takeover bid might be just enough to make it a bad deal.

3. Do Takeovers Create Wealth?

In considering takeovers, and particularly tender offers, perhaps the most fundamental question is whether they create, or simply redistribute, wealth. Because shareholders of target companies often enjoy great gains and shareholders of bidder companies usually receive slight gains, some economists conclude that the higher stock prices are evidence that takeovers create wealth. Although the source is uncertain, some scholars believe that the gains do not result from monopoly profits. They suggest that the clear public policy implication is that no impediments to hostile takeover bids should be allowed.

However, others find the empirical studies of corporate takeovers less certain. In some situations, shareholders of target and bidder companies are hurt by takeovers. Although an unsuccessful tender offer followed by a successful second offer for a higher price results in better gains for target shareholders, when an initial offer is defeated and there is no second offer, the target corporation's share price eventually returns to its pre-bid level and the target shareholders have lost the opportunity to tender their shares for a premium. In addition, the shareholders of the acquiring corporation may only break even, at best, in merger transactions.

Even if corporate takeovers do increase shareholder wealth, the public policy directive is unclear. Shareholders are not the only group whose interests are implicated in a takeover. A takeover affects every corporate constituency—shareholders, managers, employees, customers, creditors, suppliers, and the local communities where the company operates. These constituents' interests often conflict. While the shareholders of a target company might sell their shares for a premium, thousands of employees of the target company might lose their jobs. Takeover activity can distract managers from the day-to-day operations of their corporations. Although the stock gains are objectively measurable, they do not reflect the gains and losses of the other constituents. The added wealth to shareholders may not justify the significant losses to the constituents of the target corporation.

Ultimately, society can be worse off from a takeover bid that benefits shareholders. For example, bidders may be willing to terminate implicit long-term contracts with other stakeholders (employees, suppliers and the community) that existing management would honor. Sometimes these terminations result in benefits to the community as well as to stockholders, when the stakeholders can replace their old relationships without cost. In that event, assets have been moved to more productive uses. The stock gains measure society's gains. But at times the stakeholder losses may exceed shareholder gains if the consequences of job and supplier losses produce a ripple effect of further community losses.

4. Federalism and Takeovers

Since the 1980s, states have adopted antitakeover statutes. The argument concerning the desirability of such statutes is a part of the larger debate over jurisdictional competition that we examined in our discussion of federalism, in which we saw that the basic argument in support of competition is that it promotes the development of more efficient corporation laws. In the setting of antitakeover statutes, the argument appears to break down. Numerous econometric studies demonstrate that when a state adopts a strong antitakeover law, the market value of corporations chartered in that state declines. Some see these studies as strong evidence that, at least in this respect, competition among the states reduces rather than maximizes shareholder wealth.

A further regulatory issue is the extent to which federal law should control tender offers. In *CTS Corp. v. Dynamics Corp. of America*, the Supreme Court suggested that states have considerable, but not unlimited, scope to regulate takeover bids. Of course, Congress has the constitutional power to preempt state law affecting tender offers and defenses against them. As a policy issue, it may not make sense to continue to allow state legislatures to make rules governing the affairs of national and multinational corporations. Because states' treatment of takeovers could be a "race for the bottom," some have argued that Congress should pass a federal law that lets the shareholders of every public corporation choose whether state or federal rules will govern managers' ability to resist hostile takeover bids.

C. Judicial Approaches to Antitakeover Devices

As noted above, antitakeover tactics create a potential conflict between the interests of shareholders and directors. The courts have recognized this potential conflict, but have struggled in deciding which standard of review to apply when evaluating a board's response to a perceived takeover threat. Essentially, the courts take three approaches.

First, the courts can apply the business judgment rule. As we have discussed at several points in this book, a transaction approved by a majority of independent, disinterested directors receives the protection of the business judgment rule, a judicial presumption protecting the decision from review. The courts have made it clear that they often will apply the business judgment rule when an M&A transaction involves adequate process. For example, the business judgment rule standard applies when a transaction has been approved by a fully-informed, uncoerced majority of the disinterested shareholders. This doctrine has become known as the *Corwin* doctrine, based on *Corwin v. KKR Financial Holdings LLC*, 125 A.3d 304 (Del. 2015). Historically, the courts applied the business judgment rule in other contexts as well, including selective repurchases of stock, as in the classic case of *Cheff v. Mathes*, 199 A.2d 548 (Del. Ch. 1964), which the Delaware courts continue to reference.

Second, the courts apply an intermediate level of scrutiny. As in the duty of loyalty context, the courts recognize that when directors make decisions that might be motivated more by self-interest than the interests of shareholders, this conflict generates a need to examine the facts more closely. In these cases, board decisions are not protected by the business judgment rule. Instead, the courts inquire into the board's response to a perceived takeover threat and the question of whether the directors acted based on self-interest (to preserve their positions and those of the officers) or based on what the directors believed was in the best interests of the shareholders. *Unocal vs. Mesa Petroleum* is the leading case representing this intermediate standard.

Third, the courts apply a strict level of scrutiny. When it is apparent that a takeover attempt or attempts have proceeded so far that the corporation can be deemed "for sale," the role of the board shifts. Whereas the board typically is entitled to preserve the long-term interests of the corporation, even in the presence of a potential conflict of interest, once the company is for sale the board must act to maximize the value of the corporation in a sale for the benefit of the shareholders. Judges view antitakeover measures with great skepticism once a company is for sale. *Revlon v. MacAndrews & Forbes Holdings* embodies this third, more rigorous approach. Companies that are for sale are often said to be in "*Revlon* mode."

Since the "classic" cases, the courts have filled in some of the gaps in the application of these tests. For example, one of the most significant cases during the 2010s involved the year-long battle for control of Airgas, Inc. The Airgas board defended against an offer by Air Products and Chemicals, Inc., rejecting the offer as "grossly inadequate," and refusing to redeem the company's poison pill, even when Air Products repeatedly raised its offer. Ultimately, the Delaware Chancery Court ruled in favor of Airgas, and Air Products withdrew its offer. *Air Prods. & Chem., Inc. v. Airgas, Inc.*, 16 A.3d 48, 128 (Del. Ch. 2011). Fortunately for the Airgas shareholders, the company eventually sold to another buyer for double the final bid that Air Products had offered. In contrast, the courts have been more likely to scrutinize directors' resistance to takeovers, including pressure from hedge fund activists, if the plaintiff shareholders allege that the directors faced a conflict of interest.

You will cover the details of these more recent cases in an M&A course. Our objective here is to familiarize you with the "classic" cases under each approach.

Although they represent distinct standards of judicial review you might ask whether the lines between the different approaches are really as crisp as they might appear. When might a board facing a threat similar to the one in *Unocal* be deemed to be in "*Revlon* mode"? And what if the outside bid in *Revlon* had been an offer of stock and not cash?

1. *Unocal* Proportionality Test: Intermediate Standard of Review

Most case law on corporation law issues develops at a snail's pace. Landmark decisions resolving major issues and changing the law's direction are separated by decades. However, beginning in 1985, the Delaware courts issued a series of decisions in rapid succession that almost completely reshaped the law governing corporate managers' responsibilities when they resist threats to control or agree to sell control. Many other jurisdictions have followed these cases.

Because these cases involved "real time" battles for corporate control, the Delaware courts faced serious logistical challenges, not only in keeping up with the cases at issue, but in anticipating the creativity of the lawyers and investment bankers who advised bidders and target companies. The Delaware judges knew these market actors would respond instantly to their decisions, so they wrote narrow opinions and avoided sweeping pronouncements. Many commentators have praised the flexibility of this approach, though others would have preferred greater certainty and precision.

Unocal Corporation v. Mesa Petroleum Co. marks the beginning of Delaware's contemporary approach to regulating transactions involving a change of control. Mesa had made a hostile takeover bid for 51% of Unocal stock. Unocal believed this bid was both coercive and inadequate. In response, Unocal offered to repurchase its own securities from its shareholders but excluded Mesa from the offer. In determining the validity of excluding Mesa, the court declined to apply a business judgment rule standard of review. Instead, the court created an intermediate standard and applied a two-pronged "proportionality" test to determine (1) whether the board had reasonable grounds for believing a threat to the corporation existed and (2) whether the defensive measures taken were reasonable in relation to the perceived threat.

Unocal Corp. v. Mesa Petroleum Co.

493 A.2d 946 (Del.1985)

MOORE, JUSTICE.

We confront an issue of first impression in Delaware—the validity of a corporation's self-tender for its own shares which excludes from participation a stockholder making a hostile tender offer for the company's stock.

The Court of Chancery granted a preliminary injunction to the plaintiffs, Mesa Petroleum Co., Mesa Asset Co., Mesa Partners II, and Mesa Eastern, Inc. (collectively "Mesa")[1] enjoining an exchange offer of the defendant, Unocal Corporation for its own stock. The trial court concluded that a selective exchange offer, excluding Mesa, was legally impermissible. We cannot agree with such a blanket rule. The factual findings of the Vice Chancellor, fully supported by the record, establish that Unocal's board, consisting of a majority of independent directors, acted in good faith, and after reasonable investigation found that Mesa's tender offer was both inadequate and coercive. Under the circumstances the board had both the power and duty to oppose a bid it perceived to be harmful to the corporate enterprise. On this record we are satisfied that the device Unocal adopted is reasonable in relation to the threat posed, and that the board acted in the proper exercise of sound business judgment. We will not substitute our views for those of the board if the latter's decision can be "attributed to any rational business purpose." Accordingly, we reverse the decision of the Court of Chancery and order the preliminary injunction vacated.

The factual background of this matter bears a significant relationship to its ultimate outcome.

> **FYI**
>
> T. Boone Pickens was one of the leading (and most colorful) takeover artists of the 1980s. He founded Mesa Petroleum in the 1950s, and by the 1980s it had become of the world's largest independent oil companies. Then, rather than drill for oil in the field, Mesa began to drill for oil on Wall Street by seeking to acquire other oil and gas companies. Some of the takeovers succeeded, but many failed—including bids for Unocal, Gulf Oil, and Philips Petroleum. In the 1990s, Pickens made acquisitions in other industries and later founded United Shareholders Association to influence corporate governance in large companies. He stayed in the limelight in the 2000s, first helping fund the Swift Boat Vets who questioned candidate John Kerry's military record and later espousing the "Pickens Plan" to promote energy alternatives to oil, including wind and solar power. His plan to build the world's largest wind farm, however, has not yet panned out.

---

[1] T. Boone Pickens, Jr., is President and Chairman of the Board of Mesa Petroleum and President of Mesa Asset and controls the related Mesa entities.

On April 8, 1985, Mesa, the owner of approximately 13% of Unocal's stock, commenced a two-tier "front loaded" cash tender offer for 64 million shares, or approximately 37%, of Unocal's outstanding stock at a price of $54 per share. The "back-end" was designed to eliminate the remaining publicly held shares by an exchange of securities purportedly worth $54 per share. However, pursuant to an order entered by the United States District Court for the Central District of California on April 26, 1985, Mesa issued a supplemental proxy statement to Unocal's stockholders disclosing that the securities offered in the second-step merger would be highly subordinated, and that Unocal's capitalization would differ significantly from its present structure. Unocal has rather aptly termed such securities "junk bonds."

Unocal's board consists of eight independent, outside directors and six insiders. It met on April 13, 1985, to consider the Mesa tender offer. Thirteen directors were present, and the meeting lasted nine and one-half hours. The directors were given no agenda or written materials prior to the session. However, detailed presentations were made by legal counsel regarding the board's obligations under both Delaware corporate law and the federal securities laws. The board then received a presentation from Peter Sachs on behalf of Goldman Sachs & Co. and Dillon, Read & Co. discussing the bases for their opinions that the Mesa proposal was wholly inadequate. Mr. Sachs opined that the minimum cash value that could be expected from a sale or orderly liquidation for 100% of Unocal's stock was in excess of $60 per share. In making his presentation, Mr. Sachs showed slides outlining the valuation techniques used by the financial advisors, and others, depicting recent business combinations in the oil and gas industry. The Court of Chancery found that the Sachs presentation was designed to apprise the directors of the scope of the analyses performed rather than the facts and numbers used in reaching the conclusion that Mesa's tender offer price was inadequate.

Mr. Sachs also presented various defensive strategies available to the board if it concluded that Mesa's two-step tender offer was inadequate and should be opposed. One of the devices outlined was a self-tender by Unocal for its own stock with a reasonable price range of $70 to $75 per share. The cost of such a proposal would cause the company to incur $6.1–6.5 billion of additional debt, and a presentation was made informing the board of Unocal's ability to handle it. The directors were told that the primary effect of this obligation would be to reduce exploratory drilling, but that the company would nonetheless remain a viable entity.

The eight outside directors, comprising a clear majority of the thirteen members present, then met separately with Unocal's financial advisors and attorneys. Thereafter, they unanimously agreed to advise the board that it should reject Mesa's tender offer as inadequate, and that Unocal should pursue a self-tender to provide the stockholders with a fairly priced alternative to the Mesa proposal. The board then reconvened and unanimously adopted a resolution rejecting as grossly inadequate Mesa's tender offer. Despite the nine and one-half hour length of the meeting, no formal decision was made on the proposed defensive self-tender.

On April 15, the board met again with one member still absent. This session lasted two hours. Unocal's Vice President of Finance and its Assistant General Counsel made a detailed presentation of the proposed terms of the exchange offer. A price range between $70 and $80 per share was considered, and ultimately the directors agreed upon $72. The board was also advised about the debt securities that would be issued, and the necessity of placing restrictive covenants upon certain corporate activities until the obligations were paid. The board's decisions were made in reliance on the advice of its investment bankers, including the terms and conditions upon which the securities were to be issued. Based upon this advice, and the board's own deliberations, the directors unanimously approved the exchange offer. Their resolution provided that if Mesa acquired 64 million shares of Unocal stock through its own offer (the Mesa Purchase Condition), Unocal would buy the remaining 49% outstanding for an exchange of debt securities having an aggregate par value of $72 per share. The board resolution also stated that the offer would be subject to other conditions that had been described to the board at the meeting, or which were deemed necessary by Unocal's officers, including the exclusion of Mesa from the proposal (the Mesa exclusion). Any such conditions were required to be in accordance with the "purport and intent" of the offer.

Unocal's exchange offer was commenced on April 17, 1985, and Mesa promptly challenged it by filing this suit in the Court of Chancery. On April 22, the Unocal board met again and was advised by Goldman Sachs and Dillon Read to waive the Mesa Purchase Condition as to 50 million shares. This recommendation was in response to a perceived concern of the shareholders that, if shares were tendered to Unocal, no shares would be purchased by either offeror. The directors were also advised that they should tender their own Unocal stock into the exchange offer as a mark of their confidence in it.

Another focus of the board was the Mesa exclusion. Legal counsel advised that under Delaware law Mesa could only be excluded for what the directors reasonably believed to be a valid corporate purpose. The directors' discussion centered on the objective of adequately compensating shareholders at the "back-end" of Mesa's proposal, which the latter would finance with "junk bonds". To include Mesa would defeat that goal, because under the proration aspect of the exchange offer (49%) every Mesa share accepted by Unocal would displace one held by another stockholder. Further, if Mesa were permitted to tender to Unocal, the latter would in effect be financing Mesa's own inadequate proposal.

On April 29, 1985, the Vice Chancellor temporarily restrained Unocal from proceeding with the exchange offer unless it included Mesa. The trial court recognized that directors could oppose, and attempt to defeat, a hostile takeover which they considered adverse to the best interests of the corporation. However, the Vice Chancellor decided that in a selective purchase of the company's stock, the corporation bears the burden of showing: (1) a valid corporate purpose, and (2) that the transaction was fair to all of the stockholders, including those excluded.

The issues we address involve these fundamental questions: Did the Unocal board have the power and duty to oppose a takeover threat it reasonably perceived to be harmful to the corporate enterprise, and if so, is its action here entitled to the protection of the business judgment rule?

Mesa contends that the discriminatory exchange offer violates the fiduciary duties Unocal owes it. Mesa argues that because of the Mesa exclusion the business judgment rule is inapplicable, because the directors by tendering their own shares will derive a financial benefit that is not available to all Unocal stockholders. Thus, it is Mesa's ultimate contention that Unocal cannot establish that the exchange offer is fair to all shareholders, and argues that the Court of Chancery was correct in concluding that Unocal was unable to meet this burden.

Unocal answers that it does not owe a duty of "fairness" to Mesa, given the facts here. Specifically, Unocal contends that its board of directors reasonably and in good faith concluded that Mesa's $54 two-tier tender offer was coercive and inadequate, and that Mesa sought selective treatment for itself. Furthermore, Unocal argues that the board's approval of the exchange offer was made in good faith, on an informed basis, and in the exercise of due care. Under these circumstances, Unocal contends that its directors properly employed this device to protect the company and its stockholders from Mesa's harmful tactics.

We begin with the basic issue of the power of a board of directors of a Delaware corporation to adopt a defensive measure of this type. Absent such authority, all other questions are moot. Neither issues of fairness nor business judgment are pertinent without the basic underpinning of a board's legal power to act.

The board has a large reservoir of authority upon which to draw. Its duties and responsibilities proceed from the inherent powers conferred by 8 Del.C. § 141(a), respecting management of the corporation's "business and affairs." Additionally, the powers here being exercised derive from 8 Del.C. § 160(a), conferring broad authority upon a corporation to deal in its own stock. From this it is now well established that in the acquisition of its shares a Delaware corporation may deal selectively with its stockholders, provided the directors have not acted out of a sole or primary purpose to entrench themselves in office.

Finally, the board's power to act derives from its fundamental duty and obligation to protect the corporate enterprise, which includes stockholders, from harm reasonably perceived, irrespective of its source. Thus, we are satisfied that in the broad context of corporate governance, including issues of fundamental corporate change, a board of directors is not a passive instrumentality.

Given the foregoing principles, we turn to the standards by which director action is to be measured. In *Pogostin v. Rice*, Del.Supr., 480 A.2d 619 (1984), we held that the business judgment rule, including the standards by which director conduct is judged, is applicable in the context of a takeover.

When a board addresses a pending takeover bid it has an obligation to determine whether the offer is in the best interests of the corporation and its shareholders. In that respect a board's duty is no different from any other responsibility it shoulders, and its decisions should be no less entitled to the respect they otherwise would be accorded in the realm of business judgment. There are, however, certain caveats to a proper exercise of this function. Because of the omnipresent specter that a board may be acting primarily in its own interests, rather than those of the corporation and its shareholders, there is an enhanced duty which calls for judicial examination at the threshold before the protections of the business judgment rule may be conferred.

This Court has long recognized that:

> We must bear in mind the inherent danger in the purchase of shares with corporate funds to remove a threat to corporate policy when a threat to control is involved. The directors are of necessity confronted with a conflict of interest, and an objective decision is difficult.

Bennett v. Propp, Del.Supr., 187 A.2d 405, 409 (1962). In the face of this inherent conflict, directors must show that they had reasonable grounds for believing that a danger to corporate policy and effectiveness existed because of another person's stock ownership. *Cheff v. Mathes*, 199 A.2d at 554–55. However, they satisfy that burden "by showing good faith and reasonable investigation." Furthermore, such proof is materially enhanced, as here, by the approval of a board comprised of a majority of outside, independent directors who have acted in accordance with the foregoing standards.

In the board's exercise of corporate power to forestall a takeover bid, our analysis begins with the basic principle that corporate directors have a fiduciary duty to act in the best interests of the corporation's stockholders. As we have noted, their duty of care extends to protecting the corporation and its owners from perceived harm whether a threat originates from third parties or other shareholders. But such powers are not absolute. A corporation does not have unbridled discretion to defeat any perceived threat by any Draconian means available.

The restriction placed upon a selective stock repurchase is that the directors may not have acted solely or primarily out of a desire to perpetuate themselves in office. Of course, to this is added the further caveat that inequitable action may not be taken under the guise of law. The standard of proof established in *Cheff v. Mathes* is designed to ensure that a defensive measure to thwart or impede a take-over is indeed motivated by a good faith concern for the welfare of the corporation and its stockholders, which in all circumstances must be free of any fraud or other misconduct. However, this does not end the inquiry.

B.

A further aspect is the element of balance. If a defensive measure is to come within the ambit of the business judgment rule, it must be reasonable in relation to the threat posed. This entails an analysis by the directors of the nature of the takeover bid and its effect on the corporate enterprise. Examples of such concerns may include: inadequacy of the price offered, nature and timing of the offer, questions of illegality, the impact on "constituencies" other than shareholders (i.e., creditors, customers, employees, and perhaps even the community generally), the risk of non-consummation, and the quality of securities being offered in the exchange. While not a controlling factor, it also seems to us that a board may reasonably consider the basic stockholder interests at stake, including those of short-term speculators, whose actions may have fueled the coercive aspect of the offer at the expense of the long-term investor. Here, the threat posed was viewed by the Unocal board as a grossly inadequate two-tier coercive tender offer coupled with the threat of greenmail.

Specifically, the Unocal directors had concluded that the value of Unocal was substantially above the $54 per share offered in cash at the front end. Furthermore, they determined that the subordinated securities to be exchanged in Mesa's announced squeeze-out of the remaining shareholders in the "back-end" merger were "junk bonds" worth far less than $54. It is now well recognized that such offers are a classic coercive measure designed to stampede shareholders into tendering at the first tier, even if the price is inadequate, out of fear of what they will receive at the back end of the transaction. Wholly beyond the coercive aspect of an inadequate two-tier tender offer, the threat was posed by a corporate raider with a national reputation as a "greenmailer."[13]

---

[13] The Chancery Court noted that "Mesa has made tremendous profits from its takeover activities although in the past few years it has not been successful in acquiring any of the target companies on an unfriendly basis." Moreover, the trial court specifically found that the actions of the Unocal board were taken in good faith to eliminate both the inadequacies of the tender offer and to forestall the payment of "greenmail."

In adopting the selective exchange offer, the board stated that its objective was either to defeat the inadequate Mesa offer or, should the offer still succeed, provide the 49% of its stockholders, who would otherwise be forced to accept "junk bonds," with $72 worth of senior debt. We find that both purposes are valid.

However, such efforts would have been thwarted by Mesa's participation in the exchange offer. First, if Mesa could tender its shares, Unocal would effectively be subsidizing Mesa's continuing effort to buy Unocal stock at $54 per share. Second, Mesa could not, by definition, fit within the class of shareholders being protected from its own coercive and inadequate tender offer.

Thus, we are satisfied that the selective exchange offer is reasonably related to the threats posed. The board's decision to offer what it determined to be the fair value of the corporation to the 49% of its shareholders, who would otherwise be forced to accept highly subordinated "junk bonds," is reasonable and consistent with the directors' duty to ensure that the minority stockholders receive equal value for their shares.

Mesa contends that it is unlawful, and the trial court agreed, for a corporation to discriminate in this fashion against one shareholder. It argues correctly that no case has ever sanctioned a device that precludes a raider from sharing in a benefit available to all other stockholders. However, as we have noted earlier, the principle of selective stock repurchases by a Delaware corporation is neither unknown nor unauthorized. The only difference is that heretofore the approved transaction was the payment of "greenmail" to a raider or dissident posing a threat to the corporate enterprise. All other stockholders were denied such favored treatment, and given Mesa's past history of greenmail, its claims here are rather ironic.

However, our corporate law is not static. It must grow and develop in response to, indeed in anticipation of, evolving concepts and needs. Merely because the General Corporation Law is silent as to a specific matter does not mean that it is prohibited. In the days when *Cheff, Bennett, Martin* and *Kors* were decided, the tender offer, while not an unknown device, was virtually unused, and little was known of such methods as two-tier "front-end" loaded offers with their coercive effects. Then, the favored attack of a raider was stock acquisition followed by a proxy contest. Various defensive tactics, which provided no benefit whatever to the raider, evolved. Thus, the use of corporate funds by management to counter a proxy battle was approved. Litigation, supported by corporate funds, aimed at the raider has long been a popular device.

More recently, as the sophistication of both raiders and targets has developed, a host of other defensive measures to counter such ever-mounting threats has evolved and received judicial sanction. These include defensive charter amendments and other devices bearing some rather exotic, but apt, names: Crown Jewel, White Knight, Pac Man, and Golden Parachute. Each has highly selective features, the object of which is to deter or defeat the raider.

Thus, while the exchange offer is a form of selective treatment, given the nature of the threat posed here the response is neither unlawful nor unreasonable. If the board of directors is disinterested, has acted in good faith and with due care, its decision in the absence of an abuse of discretion will be upheld as a proper exercise of business judgment.

To this Mesa responds that the board is not disinterested, because the directors are receiving a benefit from the tender of their own shares, which because of the Mesa exclusion, does not devolve upon all stockholders equally. However, Mesa concedes that if the exclusion is valid, then the directors and all other stockholders share the same benefit. The answer of course is that the exclusion is valid, and the directors' participation in the exchange offer does not rise to the level of a disqualifying interest.

Nor does this become an "interested-director transaction" merely because certain board members are large stockholders. As this Court has previously noted, that fact alone does not create a disqualifying "personal pecuniary interest" to defeat the operation of the business judgment rule.

Mesa also argues that the exclusion permits the directors to abdicate the fiduciary duties they owe it. However, that is not so. The board continues to owe Mesa the duties of due care and loyalty. But in the face of the destructive threat Mesa's tender offer was perceived to pose, the board had a supervening duty to protect the corporate enterprise, which includes the other shareholders, from threatened harm.

Mesa contends that the basis of this action is punitive, and solely in response to the exercise of its rights of corporate democracy. Nothing precludes Mesa, as a stockholder, from acting in its own self-interest. However, Mesa, while pursuing its own interests, has acted in a manner which a board consisting of a majority of independent directors has reasonably determined to be contrary to the best interests of Unocal and its other shareholders. In this situation, there is no support in Delaware law for the proposition that, when responding to a perceived harm, a corporation must guarantee a benefit to a stockholder who is deliberately provoking the danger being addressed. There is no obligation of self-sacrifice by a corporation and its shareholders in the face of such a challenge.

Here, the Court of Chancery specifically found that the "directors' decision [to oppose the Mesa tender offer] was made in the good faith belief that the Mesa tender offer is inadequate." Given our standard of review, we are satisfied that Unocal's board has met its burden of proof.

In conclusion, there was directorial power to oppose the Mesa tender offer, and to undertake a selective stock exchange made in good faith and upon a reasonable investigation pursuant to a clear duty to protect the corporate enterprise. Further, the selective stock repurchase plan chosen by Unocal is reasonable in relation to the threat that the board rationally and reasonably believed was posed by Mesa's inadequate and coercive two-tier tender offer. Under those circumstances the board's action is entitled to be measured by the standards of the business judgment rule. Thus, unless it is shown by a preponderance of the evidence that the directors' decisions were primarily based on perpetuating themselves in office, or some other breach of fiduciary duty such as fraud, overreaching, lack of good faith, or being uninformed, a Court will not substitute its judgment for that of the board.

In this case that protection is not lost merely because Unocal's directors have tendered their shares in the exchange offer. Given the validity of the Mesa exclusion, they are receiving a benefit shared generally by all other stockholders except Mesa. In this circumstance the test of *Aronson v. Lewis*, 473 A.2d at 812, is satisfied. If the stockholders are displeased with the action of their elected representatives, the powers of corporate democracy are at their disposal to turn the board out.

With the Court of Chancery's findings that the exchange offer was based on the board's good faith belief that the Mesa offer was inadequate, that the board's action was informed and taken with due care, that Mesa's prior activities justify a reasonable inference that its principle objective was greenmail, and implicitly, that the substance of the offer itself was reasonable and fair to the corporation and its stockholders if Mesa were included, we cannot say that the Unocal directors have acted in such a manner as to have passed an "unintelligent and unadvised judgment." The decision of the Court of Chancery is therefore Reversed, and the preliminary injunction is Vacated.

Points for Discussion

1. The rationale for excluding Mesa.

What do the following two sentences from the opinion mean? "To include Mesa would defeat that goal, because under the proration aspect of the exchange offer (49%) every Mesa share accepted by Unocal would displace one held by another stockholder. Further, if Mesa were permitted to tender to Unocal, the latter would in effect be financing Mesa's own inadequate proposal." Why was it necessary for Unocal to exclude Mesa from its exchange offer? (The Williams Act, a federal statute, regulates tenders offers and requires that if a tender offer is for less than all of the corporation's shares, the bidder must accept tendered shares on a pro-rata basis.) Why did Unocal waive the Mesa Purchase Condition?

2. Other constituencies.

The court says that in evaluating a threat, a target board may consider "the impact on 'constituencies' other than shareholders (i.e., creditors, customers, employees, and perhaps even the community generally)." Does this language dramatically expand the board's ability to resist an unwanted offer? If not, what limits are there on this concept?

3. Effect on future cases.

Unocal held that the "proportionality" requirement was satisfied because the Mesa exclusion, though discriminatory, was necessary to make Unocal's self-tender an effective response to Mesa's coercive and inadequate two-tier, front-end loaded takeover bid. Thus, the court effectively eliminated such bids. However, *Unocal* left unanswered several major questions. How would the court assess a similar response to a non-coercive bid? What defensive actions, if any, would the court consider proportionate if a bid threatened only the interests of non-shareholder constituencies?

---

3. *Revlon*: When the Corporation Is "For Sale"

In the events leading up to *Revlon, Inc. v. MacAndrews & Forbes Holdings, Inc.*, Ronald Perelman, a successful American businessman who was chairman of the board and CEO of Pantry Pride, met with Michel Bergerac, a Frenchman who was chairman of the board and CEO of Revlon, to discuss Pantry Pride's possible friendly acquisition of Revlon. The meeting, in August 1985, went badly, with Bergerac dismissing Perelman's offer of $40 to $50 a share as considerably below Revlon's intrinsic value. Perhaps in part because of Bergerac's strong personal antipathy for Perelman, Revlon rebuffed all of Pantry Pride's subsequent attempts to discuss a possible acquisition.

Perelman made another attempt. This time, Pantry Pride offered to acquire Revlon in a negotiated transaction at $42 to $43 per share or in a hostile tender offer at $45. Again, Bergerac rejected any possible Pantry Pride acquisition.

Faced with the possibility of a hostile takeover bid by Pantry Pride, Revlon's 14-member board took several defensive measures. (Six of the directors held senior management positions and two others owned significant blocks of Revlon stock. Four of the remaining six directors had been associated with entities that had business relationships with Revlon.) First, the Revlon board met with counsel and investment banker Lazard Freres to consider the impending hostile takeover bid. The board voted to repurchase up to 5 million shares of its common stock and to adopt a Note Purchase Rights plan. The plan permitted the rights holders to exchange their stock for a $65 one-year note unless someone acquired all the Revlon stock at $65 per share.

On August 23, Pantry Pride made an all-cash, all-shares tender offer at $47.50 per share, subject to obtaining financing and to the redemption of the rights. The Revlon board rejected the offer, then made its own offer to the Revlon shareholders to exchange notes for 10 million shares of common stock. The notes contained various covenants, the most important of which was a covenant against incurring future debt. Ultimately, Revlon accepted the full 10 million shares in the exchange offer.

On September 16, Pantry Pride announced a revised offer at $42 per share, conditioned on receiving 90% of the stock (or less, if Revlon removed the rights). Because of the exchange offer, the revised offer was the economic equivalent of Pantry Pride's earlier higher bid. Again the Revlon board rejected the offer. Pantry Pride increased its bid to $50 per share, then again to $53.

Meanwhile, the Revlon board agreed to a leveraged buyout in the form of a merger with Forstmann Little in which the Revlon shareholders would receive $56 per share, Forstmann would assume the debt incurred in the exchange offer, and Revlon would redeem the rights and waive the note covenants for Forstmann or any offer superior to Forstmann's. Immediately after the merger was announced, the market price of the notes fell substantially.

On October 7, Pantry Pride increased its bid to $56.25, subject to cancellation of the rights and the waiver of the note covenants. Two days later, it declared its intention to top any competing bid.

In response, Forstmann offered $57.25 per share and agreed to support the market price of the notes after the covenants were removed. The offer also required Revlon to grant Forstmann a lock-up option on two of its divisions at a price well below Lazard Freres' valuation if anyone else acquired 40% of the Revlon stock. Finally, Revlon was to pay a $25 million cancellation fee if the merger agreement was terminated or anyone else acquired more than 19.9% of Revlon's stock. The Revlon board accepted the offer because the price exceeded Pantry Pride's bid, the noteholders were protected against a decline in value of their notes, and Forstmann's financing was secure.

Pantry Pride promptly sued to invalidate the agreement and, on October 22, raised its bid to $58, conditioned upon the nullification of the rights, the waiver of the note covenants, and the granting of an injunction against the lock-up.

The *Revlon* court considered whether directors have unlimited powers to defend their corporation from threats to its policy and effectiveness or whether, at a certain point, their obligations to the corporation and shareholders change. As you read *Revlon*, consider at what point the board's duty changes from preserving the corporation to maximizing the corporation's value for the benefit of the shareholders and whether the board would have recognized that such a change had occurred.

Revlon, Inc. v. MacAndrews & Forbes Holdings, Inc.

506 A.2d 173 (Del. 1985)

MOORE, JUSTICE.

In this battle for corporate control of Revlon, Inc., the Court of Chancery enjoined certain transactions designed to thwart the efforts of Pantry Pride, Inc., to acquire Revlon.[1] The defendants are Revlon, its board of directors, and Forstmann Little & Co. and the latter's affiliated limited partnership (collectively, Forstmann). The injunction barred consummation of an option granted Forstmann to purchase certain Revlon assets (the lock-up option), a promise by Revlon to deal exclusively with Forstmann in the face of a takeover (the no-shop provision), and the payment of a $25 million cancellation fee to Forstmann if the transaction was aborted. The Court of Chancery found that the Revlon directors had breached their duty of care by entering into the foregoing transactions and effectively ending an active auction for the company. The trial court ruled that such arrangements are not illegal per se under Delaware law, but that their use under the circumstances here was impermissible. We agree. Thus, we granted this expedited interlocutory appeal to consider for the first time the validity of such defensive measures in the face of an active bidding contest for corporate control. Additionally, we address for the first time the extent to which a corporation may consider the impact of a takeover threat on constituencies other than shareholders. *See Unocal Corp. v. Mesa Petroleum Co.*, 493 A.2d 946, 955 (Del. 1985).

In our view, lock-ups and related agreements are permitted under Delaware law where their adoption is untainted by director interest or other breaches of fiduciary duty. The actions taken by the Revlon directors, however, did not meet

---

[1] The nominal plaintiff, MacAndrews & Forbes Holdings, Inc., is the controlling stockholder of Pantry Pride. For all practical purposes their interests in this litigation are virtually identical, and we hereafter will refer to Pantry Pride as the plaintiff.

this standard. Moreover, while concern for various corporate constituencies is proper when addressing a takeover threat, that principle is limited by the requirement that there be some rationally related benefit accruing to the stockholders. We find no such benefit here.

Thus, under all the circumstances we must agree with the Court of Chancery that the enjoined Revlon defensive measures were inconsistent with the directors' duties to the stockholders. Accordingly, we affirm.

We turn first to Pantry Pride's probability of success on the merits. The ultimate responsibility for managing the business and affairs of a corporation falls on its board of directors. In discharging this function the directors owe fiduciary duties of care and loyalty to the corporation and its shareholders. These principles apply with equal force when a board approves a corporate merger; and of course they are the bedrock of our law regarding corporate takeover issues. While the business judgment rule may be applicable to the actions of corporate directors responding to takeover threats, the principles upon which it is founded—care, loyalty and independence must first be satisfied.

If the business judgment rule applies, there is a "presumption that in making a business decision the directors of a corporation acted on an informed basis, in good faith and in the honest belief that the action taken was in the best interests of the company." However, when a board implements anti-takeover measures there arises "the omnipresent specter that a board may be acting primarily in its own interests, rather than those of the corporation and its shareholders." This potential for conflict places upon the directors the burden of proving that they had reasonable grounds for believing there was a danger to corporate policy and effectiveness, a burden satisfied by a showing of good faith and reasonable investigation. In addition, the directors must analyze the nature of the takeover and its effect on the corporation in order to ensure balance—that the responsive action taken is reasonable in relation to the threat posed.

The first relevant defensive measure adopted by the Revlon board was the Rights Plan, which would be considered a "poison pill" in the current language of corporate takeovers—a plan by which shareholders receive the right to be bought out by the corporation at a substantial premium on the occurrence of a stated triggering event. By 8 *Del.C.* §§ 141 and 122(13), the board clearly had the power to adopt the measure. Thus, the focus becomes one of reasonableness and purpose.

The Revlon board approved the Rights Plan in the face of an impending hostile takeover bid by Pantry Pride at $45 per share, a price which Revlon reasonably concluded was grossly inadequate. Lazard Freres had so advised the directors, and had also informed them that Pantry Pride was a small, highly leveraged company bent on a "bust-up" takeover by using "junk bond" financing to buy Revlon cheaply, sell the acquired assets to pay the debts incurred, and retain the profit for itself.[1] In adopting the Plan, the board protected the shareholders from a hostile takeover at a price below the company's intrinsic value, while retaining sufficient flexibility to address any proposal deemed to be in the stockholders' best interests.

To that extent the board acted in good faith and upon reasonable investigation. Under the circumstances it cannot be said that the Rights Plan as employed was unreasonable, considering the threat posed. Indeed, the Plan was a factor in causing Pantry Pride to raise its bids from a low of $42 to an eventual high of $58. At the time of its adoption, the Rights Plan afforded a measure of protection consistent with the directors' fiduciary duty in facing a takeover threat perceived as detrimental to corporate interests. Far from being a "show-stopper," as the plaintiffs had contended in *Moran*, the measure spurred the bidding to new heights, a proper result of its implementation.

Although we consider adoption of the Plan to have been valid under the circumstances, its continued usefulness was rendered moot by the directors' actions on October 3 and October 12. At the October 3 meeting the board redeemed the Rights conditioned upon consummation of a merger with Forstmann, but further acknowledged that they would also be redeemed to facilitate any more favorable offer. On October 12, the board unanimously passed a resolution redeeming the Rights in connection with any cash proposal of $57.25 or more per share. Because all the pertinent offers eventually equaled or surpassed that amount, the Rights clearly were no longer any impediment in the contest for Revlon. This mooted any question of their propriety under *Moran* or *Unocal*.

The second defensive measure adopted by Revlon to thwart a Pantry Pride takeover was the company's own exchange offer for 10 million of its shares. The directors' general broad powers to manage the business and affairs of the corporation are augmented by the specific authority conferred under 8 *Del.C.* § 160(a), permitting the company to deal in its own stock. However, when exercising that power in an effort to forestall a hostile takeover, the board's actions are strictly held to the fiduciary standards outlined in *Unocal*. These standards require the directors to determine the best interests of the corporation and its stockholders, and impose an enhanced duty to abjure any action that is motivated by considerations other than a good faith concern for such interests.

The Revlon directors concluded that Pantry Pride's $47.50 offer was grossly inadequate. In that regard the board acted in good faith, and on an informed basis, with reasonable grounds to believe that there existed a harmful threat to the

---

[1] A "bust-up" takeover generally refers to a situation in which one seeks to finance an acquisition by selling off pieces of the acquired company, presumably at a substantial profit.

corporate enterprise. The adoption of a defensive measure, reasonable in relation to the threat posed, was proper and fully accorded with the powers, duties, and responsibilities conferred upon directors under our law.

However, when Pantry Pride increased its offer to $50 per share, and then to $53, it became apparent to all that the break-up of the company was inevitable. The Revlon board's authorization permitting management to negotiate a merger or buyout with a third party was a recognition that the company was for sale. The duty of the board had thus changed from the preservation of Revlon as a corporate entity to the maximization of the company's value at a sale for the stockholders' benefit. This significantly altered the board's responsibilities under the *Unocal* standards. It no longer faced threats to corporate policy and effectiveness, or to the stockholders' interests, from a grossly inadequate bid. The whole question of defensive measures became moot. The directors' role changed from defenders of the corporate bastion to auctioneers charged with getting the best price for the stockholders at a sale of the company.

This brings us to the lock-up with Forstmann and its emphasis on shoring up the sagging market value of the Notes in the face of threatened litigation by their holders. Such a focus was inconsistent with the changed concept of the directors' responsibilities at this stage of the developments. The impending waiver of the Notes covenants had caused the value of the Notes to fall, and the board was aware of the noteholders' ire as well as their subsequent threats of suit. The directors thus made support of the Notes an integral part of the company's dealings with Forstmann, even though their primary responsibility at this stage was to the equity owners.

The original threat posed by Pantry Pride—the break-up of the company—had become a reality which even the directors embraced. Selective dealing to fend off a hostile-but-determined bidder was no longer a proper objective. Instead, obtaining the highest price for the benefit of the stockholders should have been the central theme guiding director action. Thus, the Revlon board could not make the requisite showing of good faith by preferring the noteholders and ignoring its duty of loyalty to the shareholders. The rights of the former already were fixed by contract. The noteholders required no further protection, and when the Revlon board entered into an auction-ending lock-up agreement with Forstmann on the basis of impermissible considerations at the expense of the shareholders, the directors breached their primary duty of loyalty.

The Revlon board argued that it acted in good faith in protecting the noteholders because Unocal permits consideration of other corporate constituencies. Although such considerations may be permissible, there are fundamental limitations upon that prerogative. A board may have regard for various constituencies in discharging its responsibilities, provided there are rationally related benefits accruing to the stockholders. However, such concern for non-stockholder interests is inappropriate when an auction among active bidders is in progress, and the object no longer is to protect or maintain the corporate enterprise but to sell it to the highest bidder.

Revlon also contended that it had contractual and good faith obligations to consider the noteholders. However, any such duties are limited to the principle that one may not interfere with contractual relationships by improper actions. Here, the rights of the noteholders were fixed by agreement, and there is nothing of substance to suggest that any of those terms were violated. The Notes covenants specifically contemplated a waiver to permit sale of the company at a fair price. The Notes were accepted by the holders on that basis, including the risk of an adverse market effect stemming from a waiver. Thus, nothing remained for Revlon to legitimately protect, and no rationally related benefit thereby accrued to the stockholders. Under such circumstances we must conclude that the merger agreement with Forstmann was unreasonable in relation to the threat posed.

A lock-up is not per se illegal under Delaware law. Its use has been approved in an earlier case. Such options can entice other bidders to enter a contest for control of the corporation, creating an auction for the company and maximizing shareholder profit. Current economic conditions in the takeover market are such that a "white knight" like Forstmann might only enter the bidding for the target company if it receives some form of compensation to cover the risks and costs involved. However, while those lock-ups which draw bidders into the battle benefit shareholders, similar measures which end an active auction and foreclose further bidding operate to the shareholders' detriment.

Recently, the United States Court of Appeals for the Second Circuit invalidated a lock-up on fiduciary duty grounds similar to those here. *Hanson Trust PLC v. ML SCM Acquisition Inc.*, 781 F.2d 264 (2d Cir. 1986).

The court stated:

> In this regard, we are especially mindful that some lock-up options may be beneficial to the shareholders, such as those that induce a bidder to compete for control of a corporation, while others may be harmful, such as those that effectively preclude bidders from competing with the optionee bidder.

In *Hanson Trust*, the bidder, Hanson, sought control of SCM by a hostile cash tender offer. SCM management joined with Merrill Lynch to propose a leveraged buy-out of the company at a higher price, and Hanson in turn increased its offer.

Then, despite very little improvement in its subsequent bid, the management group sought a lock-up option to purchase SCM's two main assets at a substantial discount. The SCM directors granted the lock-up without adequate information as to the size of the discount or the effect the transaction would have on the company. Their action effectively ended a competitive bidding situation. The *Hanson* court invalidated the lock-up because the directors failed to fully inform themselves about the value of a transaction in which management had a strong self-interest. "In short, the Board appears to have failed to ensure that negotiations for alternative bids were conducted by those whose only loyalty was to the shareholders."

The Forstmann option had a similar destructive effect on the auction process. Forstmann had already been drawn into the contest on a preferred basis, so the result of the lock-up was not to foster bidding, but to destroy it. The board's stated reasons for approving the transactions were: (1) better financing, (2) noteholder protection, and (3) higher price. As the Court of Chancery found, and we agree, any distinctions between the rival bidders' methods of financing the proposal were nominal at best, and such a consideration has little or no significance in a cash offer for any and all shares. The principal object, contrary to the board's duty of care, appears to have been protection of the noteholders over the shareholders' interests.

While Forstmann's $57.25 offer was objectively higher than Pantry Pride's $56.25 bid, the margin of superiority is less when the Forstmann price is adjusted for the time value of money. In reality, the Revlon board ended the auction in return for very little actual improvement in the final bid. The principal benefit went to the directors, who avoided personal liability to a class of creditors to whom the board owed no further duty under the circumstances. Thus, when a board ends an intense bidding contest on an insubstantial basis, and where a significant by-product of that action is to protect the directors against a perceived threat of personal liability for consequences stemming from the adoption of previous defensive measures, the action cannot withstand the enhanced scrutiny which *Unocal* requires of director conduct.

In addition to the lock-up option, the Court of Chancery enjoined the no-shop provision as part of the attempt to foreclose further bidding by Pantry Pride. The no-shop provision, like the lock-up option, while not per se illegal, is impermissible under the *Unocal* standards when a board's primary duty becomes that of an auctioneer responsible for selling the company to the highest bidder. The agreement to negotiate only with Forstmann ended rather than intensified the board's involvement in the bidding contest.

It is ironic that the parties even considered a no-shop agreement when Revlon had dealt preferentially, and almost exclusively, with Forstmann throughout the contest. After the directors authorized management to negotiate with other parties, Forstmann was given every negotiating advantage that Pantry Pride had been denied: cooperation from management, access to financial data, and the exclusive opportunity to present merger proposals directly to the board of directors. Favoritism for a white knight to the total exclusion of a hostile bidder might be justifiable when the latter's offer adversely affects shareholder interests, but when bidders make relatively similar offers, or dissolution of the company becomes inevitable, the directors cannot fulfill their enhanced Unocal duties by playing favorites with the contending factions. Market forces must be allowed to operate freely to bring the target's shareholders the best price available for their equity. Thus, as the trial court ruled, the shareholders' interests necessitated that the board remain free to negotiate in the fulfillment of that duty.

In conclusion, the Revlon board was confronted with a situation not uncommon in the current wave of corporate takeovers. A hostile and determined bidder sought the company at a price the board was convinced was inadequate. The initial defensive tactics worked to the benefit of the shareholders, and thus the board was able to sustain its *Unocal* burdens in justifying those measures. However, in granting an asset option lock-up to Forstmann, we must conclude that under all the circumstances the directors allowed considerations other than the maximization of shareholder profit to affect their judgment, and followed a course that ended the auction for Revlon, absent court intervention, to the ultimate detriment of its shareholders. No such defensive measure can be sustained when it represents a breach of the directors' fundamental duty of care. In that context the board's action is not entitled to the deference accorded it by the business judgment rule. The measures were properly enjoined. The decision of the Court of Chancery, therefore, is AFFIRMED.

Points for Discussion

1. *Revlon* mode.

What does it mean to say that a company is "for sale"? What factors would you point to in advising a target corporation's directors who have asked whether they are in "*Revlon* mode"? How would you decide when to advise a board that its duties are to conduct an auction to sell the company at the highest possible price?

2. When is a sale inevitable?

What is the basis for the court concluding that "when Pantry Pride increased its offer to $50 per share, and then to $53, it became apparent to all that the break-up of the company was inevitable"?

3. Focus on the lock-up and no shop.

What was the effect of the "lock-up option" and the "no shop provision" on Pantry Pride? Which "circumstances" made their use impermissible?

4. Advising corporations in takeovers.

What factors would you advise a board facing a takeover to focus on in determining both what their duties are and what they need to do to satisfy those duties? How should they determine what kind of scrutiny a court is likely to apply to their decisions?

CHAPTER 32

Deal Protection Devices

The previous chapter covered antitakeover devices, mechanisms that corporations use to deter unwanted suitors. Now, we switch to a different but related set of tactics known as deal protection devices. Corporations use these techniques to ensure any takeover that occurs will be with a *wanted* suitor, not an unwanted one. In other words, whereas antitakeover devices attempt to thwart takeover bids, deal protection devices embrace takeovers, but attempt to ensure that they are done with a preferred buyer.

Deal protection devices typically are contractual arrangements that "protect" a deal by motivating the parties to ensure that the deal goes through. For example, in the *Revlon* case discussed at the end of the previous chapter, the Revlon board entered into a "no shop" provision in which it agreed to deal exclusively with Forstmann Little (the wanted suitor), not with Pantry Pride (the unwanted suitor). Corporations often use one or more of these devices. We begin this chapter by describing several of the leading ones.

Once we have the key vocabulary in hand, we turn to some of the leading cases in the area: the outlier case of *Omnicare*, which illustrates an extreme version of deal protection; *Paramount v. Time* and the "just say no" approach of using deal protection devices; *Paramount v. QVC* and the analysis of how change of control in a deal affects the analysis of deal protection; and *Chesapeake v. Shore* and the tensions between protecting deals and infringing shareholder voting. Be warned: these cases present complex fact patterns and the legal analysis often can seem less than clear. Still, these cases should give you a sense of the most important parameters that matter to courts deciding challenges to deal protection devices. These judicial decisions are important not just for the legal principles they state, but to acclimate you to some complicated real-world aspects of deal making. As we have noted, you will read many more cases, and cover much more detail about deal protection in M&A, in an advanced course. Our goal here is to acquaint you with the basics.

At the outset, you might ask a straightforward question: why do parties use deal protection devices? Some of the cases express concerns about these devices harming shareholders, but there are good reasons for the parties to a deal to use them. Negotiating an acquisition is expensive, for both the target and the acquirer. In particular, the acquirer must invest resources to determine if paying a premium for the target shares is a good idea. The target knows its business; the acquirer does not. As a result, acquirers often want some assurance that the target will move forward with a deal before they will agree to incur substantial costs to investigate the target. If acquirers thought the target would walk away from a deal, or renege in favor of another bidder who offered a higher price, they might decide not to negotiate in the first place. Thus, deal protection devices facilitate dealmaking by committing targets to stay with a deal.

Much of the law of deal protection is driven by Delaware cases (remember that about half of all public corporations are incorporated in Delaware). Although these cases address specific deal protection devices, they also frame lawyers' understandings of how other new devices might survive judicial scrutiny in the future. Lawyers and their clients are constantly creating innovative tools to protect transactions, and they look to these cases for guidance about how a future Delaware judge might assess a novel device. As Oliver Wendell Holmes famously noted, the law is a prediction of what a judge will do.

Make the Connection

Judicial decisions in deal protection cases do not arise in a vacuum. As we saw in several other chapters, much of the law in this area is driven by plaintiffs' lawyers. Lawyers who advise corporate clients about dealmaking must take into account the fact that there is a good chance their deals will be negotiated in the heat of battle, as plaintiff "deal litigation" teams are waiting to pounce on any deal containing suspect deal protections. These deal litigation teams resemble small militias: they are armed with legal theories and skills at obtaining discovery, and they swoop in when they believe a deal is not delivering the maximum value for shareholders. Some see these litigation teams as heroes of shareholders; others view them as parasites who extract some of a deal's value in legal fees but add little value. Whatever your view, it is important to remember that most cases in this area are brought by plaintiffs' lawyers who specialize in challenging deal protection devices.

A. Some Deal Protection Devices

We start by describing some of the different tools corporations use to protect their deals. These devices are designed to ensure that a corporation's managers complete a deal with the terms they want. They can subsidize a deal with a wanted suitor, or they can impose costs on or obstacles to a deal with an unwanted suitor. These devices can be used on their own, or in tandem. Here are some key examples.

1. Termination Fees

Termination fees protect deals by requiring that the target corporation agree to pay a pre-agreed amount to the acquirer if the target terminates the deal. What triggers a termination fee can vary: examples include failing to close the deal by a specified date, failing to submit the deal to shareholders for approval, and doing a deal with another company. (This is why termination fees are sometimes called "break-up fees.") The size of termination fees also can vary: courts have approved termination fees ranging between 1–5% of the share price.

2. Lock-ups

Lock-ups give the acquirer the right to buy certain assets of the target company for a bargain price. These assets are then "locked up"—no other potential acquirer can buy them for a comparable price. Like termination fees, lock-ups impose costs that make targets less attractive to competing acquirers. Indeed, termination fees and lock-ups have similar effects on the incentives of the various actors in a deal drama, even though they impose costs in different ways. Lock-ups frequently target the most valuable assets of a target (the "crown jewels").

Food for Thought

Deal protection devices that impose costs, such as termination fees, potentially deter deals, because they make it more expensive for another corporation to outbid the acquirer. For example, suppose you are considering challenging an acquirer that has agreed to pay $100 per share for the target in a deal with a $3 per share termination fee. You believe the acquirer is paying too little; you think the target really is worth $102 per share. But if you bid $102 per share, you will trigger the termination fee, which will make the target worth $3 per share less to you—or just $99 per share (even assuming your $102 estimate is correct). Because of the termination fee, you would only bid at most $99 per share, and therefore would not be a threat to the deal at $100 per share. Thus, the $3 per share termination fee would deter you from bidding.

Deal protection devices, such as termination fees, that impose costs on outside bidders also incentivize the acquirer and target to do a deal. They provide comfort to an acquirer worried about incurring the expense of negotiating with a target who might abandon the deal, by assuring that at minimum the acquirer will get the termination fee. And they provide an incentive for a target to complete a deal with the acquirer to avoid incurring the additional cost of the termination fee.

In recent years, lawyers have invented and used increasingly complex lock-ups. For example, "matching rights" give bidders rights to match competing offers. "Information rights" can protect bidders by promising that they will receive all written and oral communications by others about competing offers.

3. No-Shops

No-shops prohibit the target from soliciting other acquirers. As with other deal protection devices, the specific terms can vary. For example, many no-shops permit targets to negotiate with a corporation that approaches the target and makes a sufficiently attractive unsolicited offer. Stronger provisions, known as "no-talks," prohibit companies from even speaking to third parties about a potential deal.

Like other devices, no-shops may include an exception for unsolicited offers that directors would be legally obligated to consider. Such limitations are a response to cases suggesting that target directors need to retain the ability to consider unsolicited offers in order to satisfy their fiduciary duties to shareholders. Such limitations are known as "fiduciary outs." Merger agreements can contain fiduciary outs that apply more generally to deal protection devices other than no-shops. Such fiduciary out clauses permit target directors to terminate a merger agreement if their fiduciary duties require them to do so.

A related deal protection device is a "go-shop" provision, which allows the target to seek other buyers for a specified period after an agreement with an acquirer is signed. As with a no-shop provision, the analysis of go-shops depends on specific terms, including the time period. Naturally, courts are more suspicious of go-shops that give a target only a few weeks than they are of go-shops that last for a few months.

4. Voting Agreements

Target directors can protect a deal by obtaining the agreement of shareholders to vote their shares to approve a merger. If enough shareholders agree to support a merger, the deal will be well protected; it would be a waste of time for another acquirer to approach a corporation whose shareholders already have agreed to a merger.

The protection of voting agreements can be made even stronger if the merger agreement also contains a provision *requiring* that the deal be submitted for shareholder approval. Such provisions are known as "Section 251(c) provisions," after DGCL Section 251(c), which permits target directors to submit a merger for shareholder approval even if they no longer recommend it. A Section 251(c) provision goes one step further than Delaware law, by making voluntary action mandatory. In other words, the parties agree upfront that the target directors will be required to submit their deal for shareholder approval. If the deal must be submitted for shareholder approval, and the shareholders already have agreed to approve it, it will be virtually impossible for another bidder to do a deal with the target, even if it offers a substantial premium.

B. Too Much Deal Protection: The Outlier Case of *Omnicare*

We begin our discussion of the law of deal protection with a brief description of one of the most controversial cases in the area. *Omnicare, Inc. v. NCS Healthcare, Inc.*, 818 A.2d 914 (Del. 2003), does not represent the majority view, and it does not reflect the dominant practice with respect to deal protection devices. But it does illustrate one of the two poles of the possible approaches to deal protection, and it is helpful to consider *Omnicare* upfront, before delving into the more detailed and nuanced approaches in other cases, many of which were decided earlier.

Here are the two poles.

No deal protection	Complete deal protection
Open to any competing bids	Closed to any competing bids

At one extreme, a target board might decide not to adopt any deal protection devices. It might instead elect to leave its deal open to any competing bids. Of course, an acquirer might never agree to such a deal, but it is at least a theoretical possibility: a deal with no protection at all.

At the other extreme, a target board might decide to adopt deal protection devices that are so restrictive as to make any competing bids impossible. Such a deal might be rare, but again it is possible: a deal with the ultimate protection.

Many of the deal protection devices you will encounter in the reported cases, and most of the devices you will see in practice, are somewhere in the middle of this spectrum. But *Omnicare* found that the protections at issue in that case were at the far right of the continuum above. Many commentators disagreed with this assessment, which is one reason the case is so controversial. Even so, *Omnicare* is at minimum a useful illustration of what can happen when deal protection is too strict, at least in the eyes of a few judges.

Omnicare involved a stock-for-stock merger agreement between NCS Healthcare and Genesis Health Ventures. NCS was on the brink of bankruptcy and had thoroughly shopped the company in hopes of finding a buyer. Unable to find another bidder, the NCS board agreed that it was in the company's best interest to merge with Genesis. However, Genesis made it clear that it had no interest in being a "stalking horse" for NCS. To ensure that the merger went through, Genesis insisted on several aggressive deal-protection measures that would prevent

NCS from accepting any competing proposals. First, Genesis obtained advance approval from two controlling NCS shareholders who agreed to vote all of their shares in favor of the merger. Second, the NCS board agreed to a "force the vote" provision that required the merger agreement to be submitted to a shareholder vote even if the NCS board later withdrew its recommendation for the merger. Finally, the NCS board agreed to omit any effective "fiduciary out" clause for these two provisions in the merger agreement.

When Omnicare subsequently launched a competing cash tender offer for all NCS stock, the defensive provisions in the merger agreement effectively prevented shareholders of NCS from accepting Omnicare's offer. Even though the NCS board recommended that its shareholders vote against the merger with Genesis, the deal protection measures operated to ensure that the NCS-Genesis merger would go through. Omnicare sued to enjoin the merger agreement between NCS and Genesis.

The Delaware Supreme Court, in a 3–2 decision, invalidated the combination of deal protection measures—the "force the vote" provision, the voting agreements, and the lack of a fiduciary out. The Supreme Court reasoned that Delaware law does not permit a target board to lock-up a transaction absolutely. Under these circumstances, the defensive measures "completely prevented the board from discharging its fiduciary responsibilities to the minority stockholders when Omnicare presented its superior transaction." As such, the majority held that this combination of deal protections was invalid and unenforceable under *Unocal*. The majority stated:

> Although the minority shareholders were not forced to vote for the Genesis merger, they were required to accept it because it was *a fait accompli*. The record reflects that the defensive devices employed by the NCS board were preclusive and coercive in the sense that they accomplished *a fait accompli*. In this case, despite the fact that the NCS board has withdrawn its recommendation for the Genesis transaction and recommended its rejection by the stockholders, the deal protection devices approved by the NCS board operated in concert to have a preclusive and coercive effect. Those tripartite defensive measures—the Section 251(c) provision, the voting agreements, and the absence of an effective fiduciary out clause—made it 'mathematically impossible' and 'realistically unattainable' for the Omnicare transaction or any other proposal to succeed, no matter how superior the proposal.

In a strongly worded dissent, Chief Justice Veasey argued that the majority failed to recognize the complex business reality in which the agreement was entered into. This was a situation where the NCS board and its controlling shareholders had "concluded a lengthy search and intense negotiation process in the context of insolvency and creditor pressure where no other viable bid had emerged." The Genesis deal was "the only game in town." In the dissent's view, the process by which the board agreed to the deal protection devices showed that the NCS board made an informed, good faith decision in a time of crisis. In these circumstances, the dissent argued, the NCS board had acted within the bounds of its fiduciary duties. The Court should not second guess the board's business judgment because in hindsight the Omnicare deal presented a superior offer for NCS's shareholders.

Omnicare was an unusual case in many ways, including the nature of the reported decision and dissent. Rarely are there dissenting opinions in Delaware Supreme Court decisions. More significantly, the sweeping language in the majority opinion seemed to change the rules surrounding the use of deal protection strategies in merger agreements. The decision was broadly worded and raised questions about the continued validity of deal protection devices that Delaware courts had previously upheld. Chief Justice Veasey expressed his hope that *Omnicare* would be interpreted narrowly.

Subsequent decisions by the Delaware courts suggest that deal protection provisions remain viable after *Omnicare*—just as they were before it—so long as they are used in the right combination and with the right limitations. The Delaware courts generally have limited *Omnicare* to its facts, and have considered carefully the risks and real-world factors that confront directors when they approve deal protection devices. Moreover, deal lawyers have been careful to include only devices that would be less onerous than those described in *Omnicare* (in other words, deal lawyers use only devices that would place their deal to the left of the devices used in *Omnicare* on the spectrum above). For example, some parties responded to *Omnicare* by structuring voting agreements so that the approval of a "majority of the minority" of public shareholders was required to complete the deal; that limitation meant there was no guarantee that a deal would be completed even though a majority of the other shareholders had agreed to vote in favor of the deal.

Nevertheless, you should keep *Omnicare* in mind, not only as an example of the kind deal protection devices a target board perhaps should not adopt, but also as a reminder that corporate lawyers and directors inevitably must adopt deal protection devices with a view to what a handful of judges ultimately might say. We now turn back to what judges actually have said in a few of the other leading deal protection cases. These cases continue to define the broad parameters governing the judicial assessment and corporate use of deal protection devices today.

C. Using Deal Protection Devices to "Just Say No": *Paramount v. Time*

Let's take a step back and remember that, in general, the board has the responsibility for managing the business and affairs of the corporation. The business judgment rule protects director decisions by presuming that the directors acted in the best interests of the corporation. Thus, one approach to assessing director decisions has been to apply the business judgment rule.

However, some courts have been concerned about applying the business judgment rule in assessing deal protection devices. Their concern is that, when control of the corporation is at stake, if target boards have too much freedom, then they will use these devices to further their own interests, not those of shareholders. A similar concern arose with takeover defenses and, as we saw in the previous chapter on antitakeover devices, the Delaware courts have established two other legal regimes—other than the business judgment rule—to govern disputes about sales of control and responses to threats to control.

In one approach, when a corporation is for sale, the strict standard of *Revlon* applies and the board must effectively conduct an auction to maximize shareholder value. Under *Revlon*, the board's duty shifts from preserving the corporate entity to getting the best price available for its stockholders. Long-term considerations disappear; the short-term selling price becomes supreme.

A second approach provides that, when a board takes defensive action in response to a hostile takeover bid, but does not seek to sell control, the intermediate standard of *Unocal* governs, and defensive actions can be permissible. The board can take into account long-term factors, and may consider corporate constituents other than shareholders. The important dividing line between *Revlon* and *Unocal* was—and is—whether a corporation is "for sale."

However, *Revlon* did not say when a corporation was "for sale." In *Revlon,* the court said the key moment arrived when "it became apparent to all that the break-up of the company was inevitable," and at that moment an auction was required. But that general statement didn't provide much guidance about the specific facts that would delineate when it was "apparent to all" that the break-up was "inevitable."

Nor did *Revlon* state precisely what a board was permitted to do when the corporation was "for sale." *Revlon* established that the board of a target company did not have unfettered discretion to counter a hostile bid. However, the court made it clear that, consistent with *Unocal*, a target company's board could use a poison pill and other takeover defenses to oppose a bid that it reasonably concluded was clearly inadequate. At the same time, the court said the board could not employ a takeover defense directed at protecting the interests of a non-shareholder constituency unless that defense also provided some significant financial benefit to the target company's shareholders.

1. Clarification of *Revlon* Duties

Paramount Communications, Inc. v. Time, Inc. attempted to clarify when the board's *Revlon* duties were triggered. The case stands, in contrast to *Revlon*, for the proposition that a corporation is not automatically "for sale" every time a board enters negotiations with a third party about a possible acquisition. Although the board has an obligation to secure the highest possible price for the corporation's shareholders, the board does not necessarily have to auction the corporation to the highest bidder. In other words, there are situations in which the board can "just say no."

The facts of the case are complicated, but are an interesting slice of entertainment industry history. Some members of the board of Time, Inc., a Delaware corporation, wanted to expand in the entertainment industry. Time's traditional business was book and magazine publishing, and it owned cable television franchises and provided pay television programming through its Home Box Office and Cinemax subsidiaries. However, several of Time's outside directors resisted the plan to expand. They viewed such a move as a threat to "Time Culture." They feared that a merger with an entertainment company would divert Time's focus from news journalism and threaten Time's editorial integrity.

In June 1988, management distributed a comprehensive long-range plan that examined strategies for the 1990s. Warner Communications was

Food for Thought

The late 1980s takeover cases presented the dominant question addressed in this casebook: for whose benefit should the corporation be run? The question was presented specifically in the context of whether boards should be permitted to rely on poison pills to reject uninvited, all-cash tender offers, or whether courts should require that boards abandon efforts to protect their deals and accept an offer of a premium to the shareholders. Before 1989, several Delaware cases had invalidated the board's reliance on poison pills to "just say no." As Chancellor Allen put it, in *City Capital Associates L.P. v. Interco, Inc.*, 551 A.2d 787, 799–800 (Del. Ch. 1988):

> To acknowledge that directors may employ the recent innovation of "poison pills" to deprive shareholders of the ability effectively to accept a noncoercive offer, after the board has had a reasonable opportunity to explore or create alternatives or attempt to negotiate on the shareholders' behalf, would, it seems to me, be so inconsistent with widely shared notions of corporate governance as to threaten to diminish the legitimacy and authority of our corporate law.

named as a potential acquisition candidate. Time's chairman and CEO J. Richard Munro and president and COO N.J. Nicholas then met with each outside director to discuss long-term strategies, specifically a combination with Warner, whose business they felt complemented Time better than other potential merger candidates. After these discussions, Time's board approved, in principle, a strategic plan for expansion and authorized continued merger discussions with Warner.

Talks between Time and Warner began in August 1988. Although Time had preferred an acquisition involving all cash or cash and securities, it agreed to a stock-for-stock exchange so that Warner's stockholders could retain an equity interest in the new corporation. Time also insisted on having control of the board in order to preserve "a management committed to Time's journalistic integrity." Negotiations failed when the parties could not agree on who would be the top executives of the new corporation. Time pursued other merger alternatives.

In January 1989, Time resumed talks with Warner. Time's board ultimately approved a stock-for-stock merger with Warner on March 3, 1989. The merger would give the Warner shareholders 62% of the combined company. The new company would have a 24-member board, with Time and Warner each initially represented by 12 directors. The board would have entertainment and editorial committees controlled respectively by Warner and Time directors. The rules of the New York Stock Exchange required Time's shareholders to approve the merger. However, because the transaction was cast as a triangular merger, Delaware law did not.

At the March 3 meeting, Time's board adopted several defensive tactics. It agreed to an automatic share exchange with Warner that gave Warner the right to receive 11.1% of Time's outstanding common stock. Time also sought and paid for "confidence letters" from its banks in which the banks agreed to not finance a hostile acquisition of Time. Time agreed to a no-shop clause preventing it from considering any other consolidation proposal regardless of the merits. After the announcement of the transaction, Time publicized the lack of debt in the transaction as being one of its chief benefits. Time scheduled the shareholder vote for June 23 and sent out its proxy materials for the merger on May 24.

On June 7, Paramount Communications announced a $175 per share, all-cash, all-shares "fully negotiable" offer for Time. Time's board found that Paramount's offer was subject to three conditions: (1) that Time terminate its merger agreement and share exchange agreement with Warner; (2) that Paramount obtain acceptable cable franchise transfers from Time; and (3) that DGCL § 203 (the antitakeover statute) not apply to any subsequent Time-Paramount merger. Time believed that it would take at least several months to satisfy these conditions.

Although Time's financial advisers informed the board that Time's per share value was materially higher than Paramount's $175 offer, the board was concerned that shareholders would not appreciate the long-term benefits of the Warner merger if given the opportunity to accept the Paramount offer. Therefore, Time sought the NYSE's approval to complete the merger without stockholder approval. The NYSE refused.

A day after Paramount announced its offer, Time formally rejected it. Because it continued to believe that the offer presented a threat to Time's control of its own destiny and the "Time Culture," the board chose to recast the form of the Warner transaction. Under the new proposal, Time would make an immediate all-cash offer for 51% of Warner's outstanding stock at $70 per share. The remaining 49% would be purchased at some later date for a mixture of cash and securities worth $70 per share. Time would fund the acquisition of Warner by incurring $7 billion to $10 billion of debt, despite its original assertion that the debt-free nature of the combination was one of its principal benefits. Time also agreed to pay $9 billion to Warner for its goodwill. As a condition of accepting the revised transaction, Warner received a control premium and guarantee that the corporate governance provisions in the original merger agreement would remain. Time agreed not to employ its poison pill against Warner, and unless enjoined, to complete the transaction.

On June 23, 1989, Paramount raised its offer to $200 per share while continuing to maintain that all aspects of the offer were negotiable. On June 26, Time's board rejected the second offer on the grounds that it was still inadequate and that Time's acquisition of Warner "offered a greater long-term value for the stockholders and, unlike Paramount, was not a threat to Time's survival or 'culture.'"

Two groups of Time shareholders (collectively referred to as "Shareholder Plaintiffs") and Paramount sought to enjoin Time's tender offer. The Court of Chancery denied the plaintiffs' motions. The plaintiffs appealed.

Paramount Communications, Inc. v. Time, Inc.

571 A.2d 1140 (Del. 1989)

HORSEY, JUSTICE.

The Shareholder Plaintiffs first assert a *Revlon* claim. They contend that the March 4 Time-Warner agreement effectively put Time up for sale, triggering *Revlon* duties, requiring Time's board to enhance short-term shareholder value and to treat all other interested acquirers on an equal basis. The Shareholder Plaintiffs base this argument on two facts: (i) the ultimate Time-Warner exchange ratio of .465 favoring Warner, resulting in Warner shareholders' receipt of 62% of the combined company; and (ii) the subjective intent of Time's directors as evidenced in their statements that the market might perceive the Time-Warner merger as putting Time up "for sale" and their adoption of various defensive measures.

The Shareholder Plaintiffs further contend that Time's directors, in structuring the original merger transaction to be "takeover-proof," triggered *Revlon* duties by foreclosing their shareholders from any prospect of obtaining a control premium. In short, plaintiffs argue that Time's board's decision to merge with Warner imposed a fiduciary duty to maximize immediate share value and not erect unreasonable barriers to further bids. Therefore, they argue, the Chancellor erred in finding: that Paramount's bid for Time did not place Time "for sale;" that Time's transaction with Warner did not result in any transfer of control; and that the combined Time-Warner was not so large as to preclude the possibility of the stockholders of Time-Warner receiving a future control premium.

Paramount asserts only a *Unocal* claim in which the shareholder plaintiffs join. Paramount contends that the Chancellor, in applying the first part of the *Unocal* test, erred in finding that Time's board had reasonable grounds to believe that Paramount posed both a legally cognizable threat to Time shareholders and a danger to Time's corporate policy and effectiveness. Paramount also contests the court's finding that Time's board made a reasonable and objective investigation of Paramount's offer so as to be informed before rejecting it. Paramount further claims that the court erred in applying *Unocal's* second part in finding Time's response to be "reasonable." Paramount points primarily to the preclusive effect of the revised agreement which denied Time shareholders the opportunity both to vote on the agreement and to respond to Paramount's tender offer. Paramount argues that the underlying motivation of Time's board in adopting these defensive measures was management's desire to perpetuate itself in office.

The Court of Chancery posed the pivotal question presented by this case to be: Under what circumstances must a board of directors abandon an in-place plan of corporate development in order to provide its shareholders with the option to elect and realize an immediate control premium? As applied to this case, the question becomes: Did Time's board, having developed a strategic plan of global expansion to be launched through a business combination with Warner, come under a fiduciary duty to jettison its plan and put the corporation's future in the hands of its shareholders?

While we affirm the result reached by the Chancellor, we think it unwise to place undue emphasis upon long-term versus short-term corporate strategy. Two key predicates underpin our analysis. First, Delaware law imposes on a board of directors the duty to manage the business and affairs of the corporation. This broad mandate includes a conferred authority to set a corporate course of action, including time frame, designed to enhance corporate profitability.[12] Thus, the question

---

[12] In endorsing this finding, we tacitly accept the Chancellor's conclusion that it is not a breach of faith for directors to determine that the present stock market price of shares is not representative of true value or that there may indeed be several market values for any corporation's stock. We have so held in another context.

of "long-term" versus "short-term" values is largely irrelevant because directors, generally, are obliged to chart a course for a corporation which is in its best interests without regard to a fixed investment horizon. Second, absent a limited set of circumstances as defined under *Revlon,* a board of directors, while always required to act in an informed manner, is not under any *per se* duty to maximize shareholder value in the short term, even in the context of a takeover. In our view, the pivotal question presented by this case is: "Did Time, by entering into the proposed merger with Warner, put itself up for sale?" A resolution of that issue through application of *Revlon* has a significant bearing upon the resolution of the derivative *Unocal* issue.

We first take up plaintiffs' principal *Revlon* argument, summarized above. In rejecting this argument, the Chancellor found the original Time-Warner merger agreement not to constitute a "change of control" and concluded that the transaction did not trigger *Revlon* duties. The Chancellor's conclusion is premised on a finding that "before the merger agreement was signed, control of the corporation existed in a fluid aggregation of unaffiliated shareholders representing a voting majority—in other words, in the market." The Chancellor's findings of fact are supported by the record and his conclusion is correct as a matter of law. However, we premise our rejection of plaintiffs' *Revlon* claim on different grounds, namely, the absence of any substantial evidence to conclude that Time's board, in negotiating with Warner, made the dissolution or break-up of the corporate entity inevitable, as was the case in *Revlon.*

Under Delaware law there are, generally speaking and without excluding other possibilities, two circumstances which may implicate *Revlon* duties. The first, and clearer one, is when a corporation initiates an active bidding process seeking to sell itself or to effect a business reorganization involving a clear break-up of the company. However, Revlon duties may also be triggered where, in response to a bidder's offer, a target abandons its long-term strategy and seeks an alternative transaction involving the breakup of the company. Thus, in *Revlon,* when the board responded to Pantry Pride's offer by contemplating a "bust-up" sale of assets in a leveraged acquisition, we imposed upon the board a duty to maximize immediate shareholder value and an obligation to auction the company fairly. If, however, the board's reaction to a hostile tender offer is found to constitute only a defensive response and not an abandonment of the corporation's continued existence, *Revlon* duties are not triggered, though *Unocal* duties attach.[14]

The plaintiffs insist that even though the original Time-Warner agreement may not have worked "an objective change of control," the transaction made a

---

[14] Within the auction process, any action taken by the board must be reasonably related to the threat posed or reasonable in relation to the advantage sought. Thus, a *Unocal* analysis may be appropriate when a corporation is in a *Revlon* situation and *Revlon* duties may be triggered by a defensive action taken in response to a hostile offer. Since *Revlon,* we have stated that differing treatment of various bidders is not actionable when such action reasonably relates to achieving the best price available for the stockholders.

"sale" of Time inevitable. Plaintiffs rely on the subjective intent of Time's board of directors and principally upon certain board members' expressions of concern that the Warner transaction *might* be viewed as effectively putting Time up for sale. Plaintiffs argue that the use of a lock-up agreement, a no-shop clause, and so-called "dry-up" agreements prevented shareholders from obtaining a control premium in the immediate future and thus violated *Revlon*.

We agree with the Chancellor that such evidence is entirely insufficient to invoke *Revlon* duties; and we decline to extend *Revlon's* application to corporate transactions simply because they might be construed as putting a corporation either "in play" or "up for sale." The adoption of structural safety devices alone does not trigger *Revlon*. Rather, as the Chancellor stated, such devices are properly subject to a *Unocal* analysis.

Finally, we do not find in Time's recasting of its merger agreement with Warner from a share exchange to a share purchase a basis to conclude that Time had either abandoned its strategic plan or made a sale of Time inevitable. The Chancellor found that although the merged Time-Warner company would be large (with a value approaching approximately $30 billion), recent takeover cases have proven that acquisition of the combined company might nonetheless be possible. The legal consequence is that *Unocal* alone applies to determine whether the business judgment rule attaches to the revised agreement.

We turn now to plaintiffs' *Unocal* claim. We begin by noting, as did the Chancellor, that our decision does not require us to pass on the wisdom of the board's decision to enter into the original Time-Warner agreement. That is not a court's task. Our task is simply to review the record to determine whether there is sufficient evidence to support the Chancellor's conclusion that the initial Time-Warner agreement was the product of a proper exercise of business judgment.

There is detailed the evidence of the Time board's deliberative approach to expand, beginning in 1983. Time's decision to combine with Warner was made only after what could be fairly characterized as an exhaustive appraisal of Time's future as a corporation. After concluding that the corporation must expand to survive, and beyond journalism into entertainment, the board combed the field of available entertainment companies. By 1987, Time had focused upon Warner; by late July 1988 Time's board was convinced that Warner would provide the best "fit" for Time to achieve its strategic objectives. The record attests to the zealousness of Time's executives, fully supported by their directors, in seeing to the preservation of Time's "culture," i.e., its perceived editorial integrity in journalism. We find ample evidence in the record to support the Chancellor's conclusion that the Time board's decision to expand the business of the company through its March 3 merger with Warner was entitled to the protection of the business judgment rule.

The Chancellor reached a different conclusion in addressing the Time-Warner transaction as revised three months later. He found that the revised agreement was defense-motivated and designed to avoid the potentially disruptive effect that Paramount's offer would have had on consummation of the proposed merger were it put to a shareholder vote. Thus, the court declined to apply the traditional business judgment rule to the revised transaction and instead analyzed the Time board's June 16 decision under *Unocal*. The court ruled that *Unocal* applied to all director actions taken, following receipt of Paramount's hostile tender offer, that were reasonably determined to be defensive. Clearly that was a correct ruling and no party disputes that ruling.

Unocal involved a two-tier, highly coercive tender offer. In such a case, the threat is obvious: shareholders may be compelled to tender to avoid being treated adversely in the second stage of the transaction. In subsequent cases, the Court of Chancery has suggested that an all-cash, all-shares offer, falling within a range of values that a shareholder might reasonably prefer, cannot constitute a legally recognized "threat" to shareholder interests sufficient to withstand a *Unocal* analysis. *AC Acquisitions Corp. v. Anderson, Clayton & Co.,* 519 A.2d 103 (Del. Ch. 1986); *Grand Metropolitan, PLC v. Pillsbury Co.,* 558 A.2d 1049 (Del. Ch. 1988); *City Capital Associates v. Interco, Inc.,* 551 A.2d 787 (Del. Ch. 1988). In those cases, the Court of Chancery determined that whatever threat existed related only to the shareholders and only to price and not to the corporation.

From those decisions, Paramount and the individual plaintiffs extrapolate a rule of law that an all-cash, all-shares offer with values reasonably in the range of acceptable price cannot pose any objective threat to a corporation or its shareholders. Thus, Paramount would have us hold that only if the value of Paramount's offer were determined to be clearly inferior to the value created by management's plan to merge with Warner could the offer be viewed—objectively—as a threat.

Implicit in the plaintiffs' argument is the view that a hostile tender offer can pose only two types of threats: the threat of coercion that results from a two-tier offer promising unequal treatment for non-tendering shareholders; and the threat of inadequate value from an all-shares, all-cash offer at a price below what a target board in good faith deems to be the present value of its shares. Since Paramount's offer was all-cash, the only conceivable "threat," plaintiffs argue, was inadequate value. We disapprove of such a narrow and rigid construction of *Unocal,* for the reasons which follow.

Plaintiffs' position represents a fundamental misconception of our standard of review under *Unocal* principally because it would involve the court in substituting its judgment as to what is a "better" deal for that of a corporation's board of directors. To the extent that the Court of Chancery has recently done so in certain of its opinions, we hereby reject such approach as not in keeping with a proper *Unocal* analysis.

The usefulness of *Unocal* as an analytical tool is precisely its flexibility in the face of a variety of fact scenarios. *Unocal* is not intended as an abstract standard; neither is it a structured and mechanistic procedure of appraisal. Thus, we have said that directors may consider, when evaluating the threat posed by a take-over bid, the "inadequacy of the price offered, nature and timing of the offer, questions of illegality, the impact on 'constituencies' other than shareholders, the risk of nonconsummation, and the quality of securities being offered in the exchange." The open-ended analysis mandated by *Unocal* is not intended to lead to a simple mathematical exercise: that is, of comparing the discounted value of Time-Warner's expected trading price at some future date with Paramount's offer and determining which is the higher. Indeed, in our view, precepts underlying the business judgment rule militate against a court's engaging in the process of attempting to appraise and evaluate the relative merits of a long-term versus a short-term investment goal for shareholders. To engage in such an exercise is a distortion of the *Unocal* process and, in particular, the application of the second part of *Unocal*'s test, discussed below.

In this case, the Time board reasonably determined that inadequate value was not the only legally cognizable threat that Paramount's all-cash, all-shares offer could present. Time's board concluded that Paramount's eleventh-hour offer posed other threats. One concern was that Time shareholders might elect to tender into Paramount's cash offer in ignorance or a mistaken belief of the strategic benefit which a business combination with Warner might produce. Moreover, Time viewed the conditions attached to Paramount's offer as introducing a degree of uncertainty that skewed a comparative analysis. Further, the timing of Paramount's offer to follow issuance of Time's proxy notice was viewed as arguably designed to upset, if not confuse, the Time stockholders' vote. Given this record evidence, we cannot conclude that the Time board's decision of June 6 that Paramount's offer posed a threat to corporate policy and effectiveness was lacking in good faith or dominated by motives of either entrenchment or self-interest.

Paramount also contends that the Time board had not duly investigated Paramount's offer. Therefore, Paramount argues, Time was unable to make an informed decision that the offer posed a threat to Time's corporate policy. Although the Chancellor did not address this issue directly, his findings of fact do detail Time's exploration of the available entertainment companies, including Paramount, before determining that Warner provided the best strategic "fit." In addition, the court found that Time's board rejected Paramount's offer because Paramount did not serve Time's objectives or meet Time's needs. Thus, the record does, in our judgment, demonstrate that Time's board was adequately informed of the potential benefits of a transaction with Paramount. We agree with the Chancellor that the Time board's lengthy pre-June investigation of potential merger candidates, including Paramount, mooted any obligation on Time's part to halt its merger process with Warner to reconsider Paramount. Time's board was under no obligation to negotiate with Paramount. Time's failure to negotiate cannot be fairly found to have been uninformed. The evidence supporting this finding is materially enhanced by the fact that twelve of Time's sixteen board members were outside, independent directors.

We turn to the second part of the *Unocal* analysis. The obvious requisite to determining the reasonableness of a defensive action is a clear identification of the nature of the threat. As the Chancellor correctly noted, this "requires an evaluation of the importance of the corporate objective threatened; alternative methods of protecting that objective; impacts of the 'defensive' action, and other relevant factors." It is not until both parts of the *Unocal* inquiry have been satisfied that the business judgment rule attaches to defensive actions of a board of directors. As applied to the facts of this case, the question is whether the record evidence supports the Court of Chancery's conclusion that the restructuring of the Time-Warner transaction, including the adoption of several preclusive defensive measures, was a *reasonable response* in relation to a perceived threat.

Paramount argues that, assuming its tender offer posed a threat, Time's response was unreasonable in precluding Time's shareholders from accepting the tender offer or receiving a control premium in the immediately foreseeable future. Once again, the contention stems, we believe, from a fundamental misunderstanding of where the power of corporate governance lies. Delaware law confers the management of the corporate enterprise to the stockholders' duly elected board representatives. The fiduciary duty to manage a corporate enterprise includes the selection of a time frame for achievement of corporate goals. That duty may not be delegated to the stockholders. Directors are not obliged to abandon a deliberately conceived corporate plan for a short-term shareholder profit unless there is clearly no basis to sustain the corporate strategy.

Although the Chancellor blurred somewhat the discrete analyses required under *Unocal,* he did conclude that Time's board reasonably perceived Paramount's offer to be a significant threat to the planned Time-Warner merger and that Time's response was not "overly broad." We have found that even in light of a valid threat, management actions that are coercive in nature or force upon shareholders a management-sponsored alternative to a hostile offer may be struck down as unreasonable and non-proportionate responses.

Here, on the record facts, the Chancellor found that Time's responsive action to Paramount's tender offer was not aimed at "cramming down" on its shareholders a management-sponsored alternative, but rather had as its goal the carrying forward of a pre-existing transaction in an altered form. Thus, the response was reasonably related to the threat. The Chancellor noted that the revised agreement and its accompanying safety devices did not preclude Paramount from making an offer for the combined Time-Warner company or from changing the conditions of its offer so as not to make the offer dependent upon the nullification of the Time-Warner agreement. Thus, the response was proportionate. We affirm the Chancellor's rulings as clearly supported by the record. Finally, we note that although Time was required, as a result of Paramount's hostile offer, to incur a heavy debt to finance its acquisition of Warner, that fact alone does not render the board's decision unreasonable so long as the directors could reasonably perceive the debt load not to be so injurious to the corporation as to jeopardize its well being.

Applying the test for grant or denial of preliminary injunctive relief, we find plaintiffs failed to establish a reasonable likelihood of ultimate success on the merits. Therefore, we affirm.

———————

2. Aftermath of *Paramount* and Importance of "Change of Control"

After the court sustained the strategic Time-Warner merger in *Paramount v. Time*, it appeared that *Revlon* duties might apply only when the company put itself up for sale or took steps as to make the break-up of the company inevitable. Paramount read that analysis as providing some hope, and perhaps a road map. Paramount's board was committed to acquiring or merging with other companies in the entertainment, media, or communications industry. The unsuccessful bid for Time had been part of Paramount's goal of strategic expansion. It decided to try again, this time with a different target.

In 1990, Paramount first considered a possible combination with Viacom, which had a range of entertainment operations. Viacom was controlled by its Chairman and CEO Sumner M. Redstone, who indirectly owned approximately 85.2% of Viacom's voting Class A stock and approximately 69.2% of Viacom's nonvoting Class B stock through National Amusements, Inc., an entity 91.7% owned by Redstone. In September 1993, after a few months of negotiations between the companies, the Paramount board unanimously approved an agreement to merge Paramount into Viacom. Under that agreement, the Paramount board agreed to amend its poison pill plan to exempt the proposed merger with Viacom. In addition, the agreement had several defensive provisions designed to make competing bids more difficult, including a no-shop provision, a termination fee, and a stock option agreement.

Under the no-shop provision, Paramount agreed not to solicit, encourage, discuss, negotiate, or endorse any competing transaction unless: (a) a third party made an unsolicited proposal not subject to any material financing contingencies and (b) the Paramount board determined that it must negotiate with the third party to comply with its fiduciary duties.

The termination fee provision provided that Viacom would receive $100 million if: (a) Paramount terminated the merger agreement because of a competing transaction; (b) Paramount's stockholders did not approve the merger; or (c) the Paramount Board recommended a competing transaction.

The most significant defensive measure, the stock option agreement, gave Viacom an option to purchase approximately 19.9% of Paramount's outstanding common stock at $69.14 per share if the termination fee was triggered. The agreement also had two unusual provisions that were highly beneficial to Viacom: (a) Viacom was to pay for the shares with a senior subordinated note of questionable marketability rather than cash, avoiding the need to raise the $1.6 billion purchase price; and (b) Viacom could require Paramount to pay a cash sum equal to the difference between the purchase price and the market price of Paramount's stock. The stock option agreement had no limit to its maximum dollar value.

Paramount and Viacom publicly announced their proposed merger and indicated that it was a virtual certainty. Redstone described it as a "marriage" that would "never be torn asunder" and stated that only a "nuclear attack" could break the deal. Further, aware that QVC was also interested in acquiring Paramount, Redstone called QVC Chairman and CEO Barry Diller to discourage him from making a competing bid.

QVC was not discouraged. Instead, it proposed a merger with Paramount in which QVC would acquire Paramount for approximately $80 per share (0.893 shares of QVC common stock and $30 in cash) and indicated its willingness to negotiate further with Paramount. The Paramount board ignored this proposal without investigating its value. Thereafter, QVC moved to enjoin the Paramount-Viacom merger and announced an $80 tender offer for 51% of Paramount's outstanding shares (the remaining shares to be converted into QVC common stock in a second-step merger). This bid was $10 more per share than the consideration the Paramount shareholders would receive in the proposed Viacom merger. Viacom realized that it needed to revise the terms of the merger agreement and thus, as the Delaware Supreme Court stated, "in effect, the opportunity for a 'new deal' with Viacom was at hand for the Paramount Board. With the QVC hostile bid offering greater value to the Paramount stockholders, the Paramount Board had considerable leverage with Viacom."

The amended merger agreement did not substantially change the terms of the transaction other than offering the Paramount shareholders more consideration and providing the Paramount board slightly more flexibility. The defensive measures were not removed. Paramount did not use its leverage to eliminate the no-shop provision, the termination fee or the stock option agreement.

A bidding war between Viacom and QVC ensued. Viacom's highest tender offer price was $85 a share. QVC's was $90. The Paramount board continued to reject QVC's bid, despite its higher price, because the board determined that QVC's offer was not in the best interests of the shareholders. Several directors believed the Viacom merger would be more advantageous to Paramount's future business prospects than a QVC merger would be.

The Court of Chancery preliminarily enjoined Paramount's defensive measures designed to facilitate the strategic alliance with Viacom and thwart QVC's unsolicited, more valuable tender offer. The Delaware Supreme Court affirmed, holding that Paramount's merger agreement with Viacom constituted a sale of control, triggering the board's *Revlon* duties to auction the corporation to the highest bidder. *Paramount Communications v. QVC Network*, 637 A.2d 34 (Del. 1994). The court determined that the board violated its fiduciary duties in favoring the less-valuable Viacom merger over the QVC offer without adequately informing itself as to the terms of the QVC offer.

First, the Delaware Supreme Court explained in the *QVC* case, public shareholders owned a majority of Paramount's voting stock, so control of the corporation was maintained in "the fluid aggregation of unaffiliated shareholders" and not by a single entity. In the Paramount-Viacom transaction, the Paramount shareholders would receive a minority voting position in the new company. The new controlling shareholder would have the voting power to effect various corporate changes, including materially altering the nature of the corporation. Even though the Paramount board intended the merger with Viacom to further Paramount's long-term strategy, upon sale of control, the new controlling stockholder would have the power to alter that vision. Further, after the sale of the control, the former Paramount shareholders would no longer have leverage to demand a control premium for their shares. "As a result, the Paramount stockholders are entitled to receive, and should receive, a control premium and/or protective devices of significant value. There being no such protective provisions in the Viacom-Paramount transaction, the Paramount directors had an obligation to take the maximum advantage of the current opportunity to realize for the stockholders the best value reasonably available."

The court then held that when *Revlon* applies, the target board has a primary obligation to act reasonably to realize the best value available for the shareholders. This obligation requires the board to be particularly diligent and adequately informed in its negotiations, including a consideration of the cash value, non-cash value, and future value of a strategic alliance in the context of the entire situation and the likelihood of each alternative.

Most important, the court rejected Paramount's argument that the proposed merger did not trigger *Revlon* duties because the transaction did not contemplate a break-up or dissolution of the corporation as *Paramount* had suggested. Rather, returning to Chancellor Allen's decision in *Time-Warner,* the court noted that there had been "no change of control in the original stock-for-stock merger between Time and Warner because Time would be owned by a fluid aggregation of stockholders both before and after the merger." By contrast, if the Paramount-Viacom merger took effect, because CEO Redstone had 89% voting control of Viacom, control of the surviving corporation would no longer exist in a fluid market and the minority shareholders (the former Paramount shareholders) could no longer demand a control premium for their stock.

The court emphasized that in *Paramount v. Time*, it had stated that there were "generally speaking and *without excluding other possibilities*, two circumstances which may implicate *Revlon* duties." Here, the Paramount board did in fact contemplate a change in control because it unintentionally initiated a bidding war by agreeing to sell control of the corporation to Viacom when there was another potential acquirer, QVC, equally interested in bidding on the corporation. Thus the court held that:

> When a corporation undertakes a transaction which will cause: (a) a change in corporate control; or (b) a break-up of the corporate entity, the directors' obligation is to seek the best value reasonably available to the stockholders. This obligation arises because the effect of the Viacom-Paramount transaction, if consummated, is to shift control of Paramount from the public stockholders to a controlling stockholder, Viacom. Neither *Paramount v. Time* nor any other decision of this Court holds that a "break-up" of the company is essential to give rise to this obligation where there is a sale of control.

The court held that the Paramount board had breached its fiduciary obligations by: (1) ignoring QVC's offer, failing to examine critically the competing transactions; (2) failing to obtain and act with due care on reasonably available information that was necessary to compare the two offers to determine which transaction, or an alternative course of action, would provide the best value reasonably available to the shareholders; and (3) by failing to negotiate with both Viacom and QVC to achieve that value.

Even though provisions in the Paramount-Viacom merger agreement precluded the board from negotiating with QVC, the court held that the board's fiduciary duties overrode the terms of the contract. The court noted that the QVC offer gave Paramount an opportunity to renegotiate its contract with Viacom and modify the favorable defensive measures, which impeded the board's ability to realize the best value available for the Paramount shareholders, and was harshly critical of Paramount's failure to make any such effort in an attempt to "cling to its vision of a strategic alliance with Viacom." While Paramount was not obligated to sell the corporation to QVC, it was obligated to carefully evaluate QVC's bid. Indeed, as the court found, at one point, QVC's offer exceeded Viacom's by $1 billion, yet the Paramount board never considered it.

After *Revlon* and *QVC*, Chancellor Allen described the duties of a target board in a sale of control as follows:

> Existing uncertainty respecting the meaning of "*Revlon* duties" was substantially dissipated by the Delaware Supreme Court's opinion in *QVC*. The case teaches a great deal, but it may be said to support these generalizations at least: (1) where a transaction constituted a "change in corporate control", such that the shareholders would thereafter lose a further opportunity to participate in a change of control premium, (2) the board's duty of loyalty requires it to try in good faith to get the best price reasonably available (which specifically means that the board must at least discuss an interest expressed by any financially capable buyer), and (3) in such context courts will employ an (objective) "reasonableness" standard of review (both to the process and the result!) to evaluate whether the directors have complied with their fundamental duties of care and good faith (loyalty). Thus, QVC in effect mediates between the "normalizing" tendency of some prior cases and the more highly regulatory approach of others. It adopts an intermediate level of judicial review which recognizes the broad power of the board to make decisions in the process of negotiating and recommending a "sale of control" transaction, so long as the board is informed, motivated by good faith desire to achieve the best available transaction, and proceeds "reasonably."
>
> With respect to the important question of when these duties are enhanced—specifically, the duty to try in good faith to maximize current share value and the duty to reasonably explore all options (i.e., to talk with all financially responsible parties)—the court's teaching ironically narrowed the range of corporate transactions to which the principle of *Revlon* applies. That is, it explicitly recognized that where a stock for stock merger is involved, the business judgment of the board, concerning the quality and prospects of the stock the shareholders would receive in the merger, would be reviewed deferentially, as in other settings. The holding of *QVC*, however, was that where the stock to be received in the merger was the stock of a corporation under the control of a single individual or a control group, then the transaction should be treated for "*Revlon* duty" purposes as a cash merger would be treated. How this "change in control" trigger works in instances of mixed cash and stock or other paper awaits future cases.

Equity-Linked Investors, L.P. v. Adams, 705 A.2d 1040 (Del. Ch. 1997).

D. What About the Shareholder Franchise?: *Unocal* vs. *Blasius*

Another challenge for courts assessing deal protection devices is determining whether they infringe upon the shareholder franchise. In other words, do the deal protection devices at issue harm the shareholders' ability to exercise one of their fundamental rights, the right to vote? The courts have struggled with determining whether protective measures disenfranchise shareholders.

Recall <u>*Blasius Industries, Inc. v. Atlas Corp.*</u>, the voting rights case holding that with respect to board elections, incumbent directors are not entitled to act as "Platonic masters" who "know better than do the shareholders what is in the corporation's best interest." *Blasius* requires that the board provide a "compelling justification" for any "acts done for the primary purpose of impeding the exercise of the stockholder voting power." Board actions that disenfranchise shareholders are subject to a kind of strict scrutiny.

The strict *Blasius* standard is a stark contrast to the proportionality standard of *Unocal*, which allows a board considerable scope to decide whether a takeover bid is in the shareholders' best interests. Which standard should govern the target board's adoption of deal protection devices? How should judges, lawyers, and directors decide whether a particular device affects shareholder electoral rights? These are fundamental questions about how power is allocated between shareholders and directors, and they have puzzled the courts.

Ultimately, the question of which interest trumps—the protection of shareholder voting or the facilitating of deals through protection devices—requires an analysis of some fundamental policy issues. In the case below, Vice Chancellor Strine tries to strike a balance between the importance of shareholder voting rights and the realities of the marketplace for deals and devices to protect them.

Chesapeake Corp. v. Shore

<u>771 A.2d 293 (Del. Ch. 2000)</u>

STRINE, VICE CHANCELLOR.

This case involves a contest for control between two corporations in the specialty packaging industry, the plaintiff Chesapeake Corporation and the defendant Shorewood Packaging Corporation, whose boards of directors both believe that the companies should be merged. The boards just disagree on which company should acquire the other and who should manage the resulting entity.

Shorewood started the dance by making a 41%, all-cash, all-shares premium offer for Chesapeake. The Chesapeake board rejected the offer as inadequate, citing the fact that the stock market was undervaluing its shares. Chesapeake countered with a 40%, all-cash, all-shares premium offer for Shorewood. The Shorewood board, all of whose members are defendants in this case, turned down this offer, claiming that the market was also undervaluing Shorewood.

Recognizing that Chesapeake, a takeover-proof Virginia corporation, might pursue Shorewood, a Delaware corporation, through a contested tender offer or proxy fight, the Shorewood board adopted a host of defensive bylaws to supplement Shorewood's poison pill. The bylaws were designed to make it more difficult for Chesapeake to amend the Shorewood bylaws to eliminate its classified board structure, unseat the director-defendants, and install a new board amenable to its offer. These bylaws, among other things, eliminated the ability of stockholders to call special meetings and gave the Shorewood board control over the record date for any consent solicitation.

Take Note!

The same tensions regarding the shareholder franchise arise in the context of defensive tactics. For example, in *Unitrin, Inc. v. American General Corp.*, 651 A.2d 1361 (Del. 1995), the target, Unitrin, rejected American General's bid and approved a stock repurchase plan that increased the board's stock ownership and thereby made a proxy contest more difficult. Did that tactic impermissibly impinge on the shareholder franchise? The Delaware Supreme Court said no. It reasoned that a target board's decision to fend off a hostile takeover bid—even an all-cash, all-shares bid at a substantial premium—should not be viewed as coercive so long as it does not preclude a successful proxy fight. However, *Unitrin* left open the possibility that the Delaware courts could invalidate a target board's response to an unsolicited offer that completely foreclosed a proxy contest or was unreasonably disproportionate to the threat. (Some commentators and courts group *Unocal* and *Unitrin* together as representing the intermediate approach to takeovers.)

Most important, the bylaws raised the votes required to amend the bylaws from a simple majority to 66 2/3% of the outstanding shares. Because Shorewood's management controls nearly 24% of the company's stock, the 66 2/3% Supermajority Bylaw made it mathematically impossible for Chesapeake to prevail in a consent solicitation without management's support, assuming a 90% turnout.

Chesapeake then increased its offer, went public with it in the form of a tender offer and a consent solicitation, and initiated this lawsuit challenging the 66 2/3% Supermajority Bylaw. Shortly before trial, the Shorewood board amended the Bylaw to reduce the required vote to 60%.

Chesapeake challenges the 60% Supermajority Bylaw's validity on several grounds. Principally, Chesapeake contends that the Shorewood board, which is dominated by inside directors, adopted the Bylaw so as to entrench itself and without informed deliberations. It argues that the Bylaw raises the required vote to unattainable levels and is grossly disproportionate to the modest threat posed by Chesapeake's fully negotiable premium offer. Moreover, it claims that the defendants' argument that the Bylaw is necessary to protect Shorewood's sophisticated stockholder base, which is comprised predominately of institutional investors and management holders, from the risk of confusion is wholly pre-textual and factually unsubstantiated.

Was the Supermajority Bylaw Validly Adopted?

What is the Relevant Standard of Review: Unocal or Blasius?

Chesapeake and the defendant-directors part company on the standard of review that should apply to examine the validity of the Supermajority Bylaw. For its part, Chesapeake contends that the defendant-directors' primary purpose in adopting the Supermajority Bylaw was to interfere with or impede the exercise of the shareholder franchise. As such, Chesapeake argues that the compelling justification standard set forth in *Blasius Industries, Inc. v. Atlas Corp.* applies.

The defendant directors counter that the Supermajority Bylaw is not preclusive of stockholder action to amend the Shorewood bylaws. Moreover, the Bylaw was adopted as a defensive measure against a hostile tender offer. Therefore, the defendant directors argue that the *Unocal* standard of review is singularly applicable. This clash of arguments forces me to address an issue that our courts have struggled with for over a decade: to what extent is the *Blasius* standard of review viable as a standard of review independent of *Unocal* in a case where *Unocal* would otherwise be the standard of review?

In the wake of *Blasius,* Delaware courts have struggled with how broadly that case should be applied. In retrospect, this difficulty might have been anticipated. Because the test is so exacting—akin to that used to determine whether racial classifications are constitutional—whether it applies comes close to being outcome-determinative in and of itself. Therefore, in a moment of rather remarkable candor, the Delaware Supreme Court stated: the *Blasius* "burden of demonstrating a 'compelling justification' is quite onerous, *and is therefore applied rarely.*"

Of course, the fact that a test is "onerous" is not a reason not to apply it if the circumstances warrant. But it is not easy in most cases to determine whether the *Blasius* standard should be invoked. It is important to remember that it was undisputed in *Blasius* that the board's actions precluded the election of a new board majority and that the board intended that effect.

In the more typical case involving board actions touching upon the electoral process, the question of whether the board's actions are preclusive is usually hotly contested. And the preclusion question and the issue of the board's "primary purpose" are not easily separable. The line between board actions that influence the electoral process in legitimate ways (e.g., delaying the election to provide more time for deliberations or to give the target board some reasonable breathing room to identify alternatives) and those that preclude effective stockholder action is not always luminous. Absent confessions of improper purpose, the most important evidence of what a board intended to do is often what effects its actions have.

In such a case, the court must be rather deep in its analysis before it can even determine if the *Blasius* standard properly applies. Put another way, rather than the standard of review determining how the court looks at the board's actions, how the court looks at the board's actions influences in an important way what standard of review is to apply.

In addition, the Delaware Supreme Court and this court have both recognized the high degree of overlap between the concerns animating the *Blasius* standard of review and those that animate *Unocal*. For example, in *Stroud v. Grace,* the Delaware Supreme Court held that a "board's unilateral decision to adopt a defensive measure touching upon issues of control that purposely disenfranchises its shareholders is strongly suspect under *Unocal,* and cannot be sustained without a compelling justification."

The Supreme Court's *Unitrin* opinion seems to go even further than *Stroud* in integrating *Blasius's* concern over manipulation of the electoral process into the *Unocal* standard of review. Because the Unitrin board's actions came in the face of a tender offer coupled with a proxy fight, the Court cited extensively to *Stroud's* discussion of the interrelationship of *Blasius* and *Unocal* in such circumstances.

But when it came time to assess whether the Chancery Court's determination that the repurchase program was invalid was correct, the Supreme Court appeared to eschew any application of the compelling justification test.

Stroud and *Unitrin* thus left unanswered the question most important to litigants: when will the compelling justification test be used, whether within the *Unocal* analysis or as a free-standing standard of review? After *Unitrin,* this question became even more consequential, because that opinion appeared to accord target boards of directors quite a bit of leeway to take defensive actions that made it more difficult for an insurgent slate to win a proxy fight.

In reality, invocation of the *Blasius* standard of review usually signals that the court will invalidate the board action under examination. Failure to invoke *Blasius,* conversely, typically indicates that the board action survived (or will survive) review under *Unocal.*

Given this interrelationship and the continued vitality of *Schnell v. Chris-Craft,* one might reasonably question to what extent the *Blasius* "compelling justification" standard of review is necessary as a lens independent of or to be used within the *Unocal* frame. If *Unocal* is applied by the court with a gimlet eye out for inequitably motivated electoral manipulations or for subjectively well-intentioned board action that has preclusive or coercive effects, the need for an additional standard of review is substantially lessened. Stated differently, it may be optimal simply for Delaware courts to infuse our *Unocal* analyses with the spirit animating *Blasius* and not hesitate to use our remedial powers where an inequitable distortion of corporate democracy has occurred. This is especially the case when a typical predicate to the invocation of *Blasius* is the court's consideration of *Unocal* factors, such as the board's purpose and whether the board's actions have preclusive or coercive effects on the electorate.

For purposes of this case, however, I must apply the law as it exists. That means that *Unocal* must be applied to the Supermajority Bylaw because of its defensive origin. To the extent that I further conclude that the Supermajority Bylaw was adopted for the primary purpose of interfering with or impeding the stockholder franchise, the Bylaw cannot survive a *Unocal* review unless it is supported by a compelling justification.

The Analytical Tension Between Acknowledgment of "Substantive Coercion" as a Threat and a Board's Insistence that a Proxy Fight is Winnable Because its Electorate is Highly Sophisticated and Incentivized to Vote

In some respects, this case unavoidably brings to the fore certain tensions in our corporation law. For example, several cases have stated that a corporate board may consider a fully-financed all-cash, all-shares, premium to market tender offer a threat to stockholders on the following premise: the board believes that the company's present strategic plan will deliver more value than the premium offer, the stock market has not yet bought that rationale, the board may be correct, and therefore there is a risk that "stockholders might tender in ignorance or based upon a mistaken belief." A rather interesting term has emerged to describe this threat: "substantive coercion."[63]

One might imagine that the response to this particular type of threat might be time-limited and confined to what is necessary to ensure that the board can tell its side of the story effectively. That is, because the threat is defined as one involving the possibility that stockholders might make an erroneous investment or voting decision, the appropriate response would seem to be one that would remedy that problem by providing the stockholders with adequate information.

---

[63] In other contexts, typically involving whether management has "coerced" stockholders, our law uses a more traditional and rigorous construction of the word coercion.

In addition, it may be that the corporate board acknowledges that an immediate value-maximizing transaction would be advisable but thinks that a better alternative than the tender offer might be achievable. A time period that permits the board to negotiate for a better offer or explore alternatives would also be logically proportionate to the threat of substantive coercion.

But our law has, at times, authorized defensive responses that arguably go far beyond these categories. Paradoxically, some of these defensive responses have caused our law to adopt a view of stockholder voting capabilities that is a bit hard to reconcile. In *Unitrin,* for example, three reasons seemed to underlie the Supreme Court's conclusion that the repurchase program might not be preclusive. First, Unitrin's stockholder base was heavily concentrated within a small number of institutional investors. This concentration "facilitated the bidder's ability to communicate the merits of its position." Second, the fact that the insurgent would have to receive majorities from the disinterested voters uncommon in hotly contested elections in republican democracies was of "*de minimis*" importance "because 42% of Unitrin's stock was owned by institutional investors." As such, the Supreme Court found that "it is hard to imagine a company more readily susceptible than Unitrin to a proxy contest concerning a pure issue of dollars." Finally, the Supreme Court was unwilling to presume that the directors' block—which was controlled almost entirely by non-management directors—would not sell for the right price or vote themselves out of office to facilitate such a sale.

The first two premises of the Court's rejection of the Chancery Court's finding of preclusion seem somewhat contradictory to its acceptance of substantive coercion as a rationale for sweeping defensive measures against the American General bid. On the one hand, a corporate electorate highly dominated by institutional investors has the motivation and wherewithal to understand and act upon a proxy solicitation from an insurgent, such that the necessity for the insurgent to convince over 64% of the non-aligned votes to support its position in order to prevail is not necessarily preclusive. On the other, the same electorate must be protected from substantive coercion because it (the target board thinks) is unable to digest management's position on the long-term value of the company, compare that position to the view advocated by the tender offeror, and make an intelligent (if not risk-free) judgment about whether to support the election of a board that will permit them to sell their shares of stock.

If the consistency in this approach is not in the view that stockholders will always respond in a lemming-like fashion whenever a premium offer is on the table, then a possible reading of *Unitrin* is that corporate boards are allowed to have it both ways in situations where important stockholder ownership and voting rights are at stake. In approaching the case at hand, I apply a different reading of *Unitrin,* however.

Without denying the analytical tension within that opinion, one must also remember that the opinion did not ultimately validate the Unitrin defensive repurchase program. Rather, the Supreme Court remanded the case to the Chancery Court to conduct a further examination of the repurchase program, using the refined *Unocal* analysis the Court set forth. That analysis emphasized the need for trial courts to defer to well-informed corporate boards that identify legitimate threats and implement proportionate defensive measures addressing those threats. It was open for the court on remand to conclude, after considering the relevant factors articulated by the Supreme Court, that the repurchase program was invalid.

I therefore believe it is open to and required of me to examine both the legitimacy of the Shorewood board's identification of "substantive coercion" or "stockholder confusion" as a threat and to determine whether the Supermajority Bylaw is a non-preclusive and proportionate response to that threat. Indeed, the importance to stockholders of a proper *Unocal* analysis can hardly be overstated in a case where a corporate board relies upon a threat of substantive coercion as its primary justification for defensive measures. Several reasons support this assertion.

As a starting point, it is important to recognize that substantive coercion can be invoked by a corporate board in almost every situation. There is virtually no CEO in America who does not believe that the market is not valuing her company properly. Moreover, one hopes that directors and officers can always say that they know more about the company than the company's stockholders—after all, they are paid to know more. Thus, the threat that stockholders will be confused or wrongly eschew management's advice is omnipresent.

Therefore, the use of this threat as a justification for aggressive defensive measures could easily be subject to abuse. The only way to protect stockholders is for courts to ensure that the threat is real and that the board asserting the threat is not imagining or exaggerating it. If management claims that its communication efforts have been unsuccessful, shouldn't it have to show that its efforts were adequate before using the risk of confusion as a reason to deny its stockholders access to a bid offering a substantial premium to the company's market price? Where a company has a high proportion of institutional investors among its stockholder ranks, this showing is even more important because a "relatively concentrated percentage of such stockholdings would facilitate management's ability to communicate the merits of its position."

Our law should also hesitate to ascribe rube-like qualities to stockholders. *If stockholders are presumed competent to buy stock in the first place, why are they not presumed competent to decide when to sell in a tender offer after an adequate time for deliberation has been afforded them?*

Another related concern is the fact that corporate boards that rely upon substantive coercion as a defense are unwilling to bear the risk of their own errors. Corporate America would rightfully find it shocking if directors were found liable because they erroneously blocked a premium tender offer, the company's shares went into the tank for two years thereafter, and a court held the directors liable for the investment losses suffered by stockholders the directors barred from selling. But, because directors are not anxious to bear *any* of the investment risk in these situations, courts should hesitate before enabling them to make such fundamental investment decisions for the company's owners. It is quite different for a corporate board to determine that the owners of the company should be barred from selling their shares than to determine what products the company should manufacture. Even less legitimate is a corporate board's decision to protect stockholders from erroneously turning the board out of office.

It is also interesting that the threat of substantive coercion seems to cause a ruckus in boardrooms most often in the context of tender offers at prices constituting substantial premiums to prior trading levels. In the case of Shorewood, for example, shareholders had been selling in the market at the pre-Chesapeake Tender Offer price, which was much lower. Did Shorewood management make any special efforts to encourage these shareholders to hold? While I recognize that the sale of an entire company is different from day-to-day sales of small blocks, one must remember that the substantive coercion rationale is not one advanced on behalf of employees or communities that might be adversely affected by a change of control. Rather, substantive coercion is a threat to stockholders who might sell at a depressed price. The stockholder who sells in a depressed market for the company's stock without a premium is obviously worse off than one who sells at premium to that depressed price in a tender offer. But it is only in the latter situation that corporate boards commonly swing into action with extraordinary measures. The fact that the premium situation usually involves a possible change in management may play more than a modest role in that difference.

This leads to a final point. As *Unocal* recognized, the possibility that management might be displaced if a premium-producing tender offer is successful creates an inherent conflict between the interests of stockholders and management. There is always the possibility that subjectively well-intentioned, but nevertheless interested directors, will subconsciously be motivated by the profoundly negative effect a takeover could have on their personal bottom lines and careers.

Allowing such directors to use a broad substantive coercion defense without a serious examination of the legitimacy of that defense would undercut the purpose the *Unocal* standard of review was established to serve. For many of these reasons, Professors Gilson and Kraakman—from whom our courts adopted the term substantive coercion—emphasized the need for close judicial scrutiny of defensive measures supposedly adopted to address that threat.

Nothing in *Unitrin* is intrinsically inconsistent with the approach articulated by Professors Gilson and Kraakman; however, one must acknowledge that *Unitrin* mandates that the court afford a reasonable degree of deference to a properly functioning board that identifies a threat and adopts proportionate defenses after a careful and good faith inquiry. With those preliminary thoughts in mind, I turn to an examination of the Supermajority Bylaw.

Application of the Unocal and Blasius Standards of Review: Does the Supermajority Bylaw Pass Muster?

The Shorewood board had reasonable grounds to believe that the Chesapeake bid was inadequate, but not that the threat posed by Chesapeake's all-shares, all-cash tender offer was particularly dangerous. Shorewood's board did not come close to demonstrating that the risk of stockholder confusion also was a threat. Also, Shorewood's board failed to demonstrate that the Supermajority Bylaw, which required Chesapeake to secure the support of 88.05% of the disinterested shareholders, assuming a 90% turnout, to amend Shorewood's bylaws, was not preclusive or, even if that Bylaw was not preclusive, that it represented a proportionate response to the threat posed by Chesapeake's bid. Rather, the Bylaw constituted "an extremely aggressive and overreaching response to a very mild threat," especially given that the board "already had a poison pill in place that gave it breathing room and precluded the Tender Offer." Finally, the Supermajority Bylaw clearly was designed to interfere with or impede the exercise of the franchise by Shorewood's shareholders and that Shorewood's board had presented no compelling justification for the Bylaw. Consequently, the Bylaw is invalid under *Blasius* as well as *Unocal*.

Food for Thought

Shortly after deciding *Chesapeake*, Vice Chancellor Strine joined with former Chancellor Allen and Vice Chancellor Jacobs to write a law review article suggesting that the Delaware Supreme Court address more directly the tensions between *Blasius*, on the one hand, and *Unocal* (and *Unitrin*), on the other.

To elaborate, before *Blasius*, there were two "intermediate" standards of review: *Unocal* and *Revlon*. *Blasius* and its progeny, building upon *Schnell v. Chris-Craft Industries, Inc.*, appeared to add a third, namely, that board action taken "for the primary purpose of thwarting the exercise of a shareholder vote," even if done in subjective good faith, will not be upheld unless the board can show a "compelling justification" for its action. . . . The *Blasius* "compelling justification" requirement was a ringing endorsement of the need to afford maximum protection to the shareholders' right to vote for directors, against any interference with their right by the directors themselves.

Post-*Blasius* case law experience, however, exposed analytical difficulties in determining the proper scope of the "compelling justification" test. . . .

Since the early 1990s, the Court of Chancery and the Delaware Supreme Court began gradually to "fold" the *Blasius* standard into *Unocal*, effectively making the former a subset of the latter. . . . Unfortunately, neither *Stroud* nor *Unitrin* answered the question of whether the *Blasius* compelling justification test must always be used within the *Unocal/Unitrin* analytical framework, or whether in some circumstances *Blasius* can or should be used as a free-standing standard of review.

The fine analytical distinctions required by having parallel, coexisting standards of review that are similar in operation and result strike us as functionally unhelpful and unnecessary. The post-*Blasius* experience has shown that the *Unocal/Unitrin* analytical framework is fully adequate to capture the voting franchise concerns that animated *Blasius*, so long as the court applies *Unocal* "with a gimlet eye out for inequitably motivated electoral manipulations or for subjectively well-intentioned board action that has preclusive or coercive effects." Accordingly, we submit that the Supreme Court should square the circle and complete the doctrinal unification of *Blasius* and *Unocal*, by declaring that henceforth the analysis required by *Unocal*, as elaborated by *Unitrin*, will be used to analyze cases involving a board's interference with the shareholder vote as part of its resistance to a hostile takeover or board election contest.

William T. Allen, Jack B. Jacobs and Leo E. Strine, Jr., *Function Over Form: A Reassessment of Standards of Review in Delaware Corporation Law*, 56 Bus. Law. 1287, 1311–1316 (2001).

———

Points for Discussion

1. Substance vs. process.

Should courts apply different substantive standards to the different kinds of deal protection devices, based on the facts of each case? For example, should courts assess termination fees based on estimates of the acquirer's bidding costs and the chances that a competing bid will emerge? Should courts look specifically at the effect of voting agreements on shareholders, or the effect of no-shops on bidders? Or should courts look more to the process of adopting deal protection devices, which would not necessarily vary by type of device, as the courts did in *QVC* (and, in a different context, earlier in *Van Gorkom*)? How important should substance vs. process be in the judicial assessment of deal protection devices?

2. Short-term value vs. long-term value.

In deal protection cases, the courts often assess how the board compared its own assessment of the value of the corporation's shares with the value of an acquirer's offer. What is the rationale for a board's assessment that the current share price does not reflect the long-run value of the corporation? For example, could the board implement deal protection devices, and effectively "just say no," to an offer of double the current price of the corporation's shares? What could support a board's conclusion that the current price accurately reflected the value of the corporation?

3. Is shareholder voting still special?

What is left of *Blasius* after *Chesapeake* (at least in the context of deal protection devices)? Does the *Unocal* framework adequately address the concerns expressed in *Blasius*? How does *Unocal* address concerns about protecting the shareholder franchise?

4. The spectrum.

Is it possible to assess whether particular deal protection devices will pass judicial muster based on the degree of protection they offer? Put another way, is the key to assessing deal protection devices how much less attractive they make the target to other bidders? If so, why don't the courts explicitly frame their analysis in terms of weighing the costs of making a target less attractive vs. the benefits of ensuring that a deal is completed? Can you describe where the deal protection devices in the cases in this chapter would fit on the spectrum of deal protection, from none to absolute?

Test Your Knowledge

To assess your understanding of the Chapter 30, 31, and 32 material in this module, click here to take a quiz.